The **Rough Guide** to

Germany

written and researched by

James Stewart, Neville Walker and Christian Williams

**ROUGH
GUIDES**

www.roughguides.com

Contents

Colour section 1

Introduction 6
Where to go 11
When to go 14
Things not to miss 15

Basics 25

Getting there............................ 27
Getting around........................ 32
Accommodation....................... 38
Food and drink 42
The media................................ 48
Festivals................................... 50
Sports and outdoor activities... 51
Culture and etiquette 54
Shopping 55
Travel essentials 56

Guide 63

① Berlin and Brandenburg 65
② Saxony............................... 157
③ Saxony-Anhalt and the
   Harz 207
④ Thuringia........................... 253
⑤ Northern Bavaria:
   Franconia.......................... 297
⑥ Munich and central
   Bavaria.............................. 347
⑦ The Alps and eastern
   Bavaria.............................. 389
⑧ Baden-Württemberg 429

⑨ The Black Forest............... 483
⑩ Rhineland-Palatinate and
   Saarland............................ 511
⑪ Hesse................................ 549
⑫ North Rhine-Westphalia 599
⑬ Lower Saxony and
   Bremen 675
⑭ Hamburg and Schleswig-
   Holstein............................. 741
⑮ Mecklenburg-Western
   Pomerania......................... 811

Contexts 855

History 857
Books 882

Language 887

Travel store 899

Small print & Index 907

The great outdoors
colour section
following p.312

Christmas markets
colour section
following p.472

◄◄ Strandkorb and seagull on Sylt island ◄ Cologne cathedral

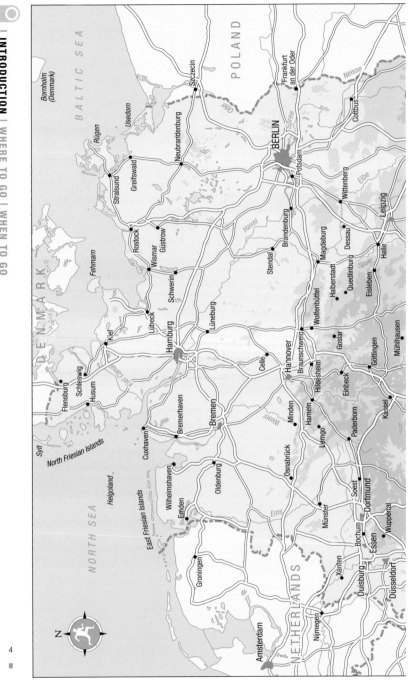

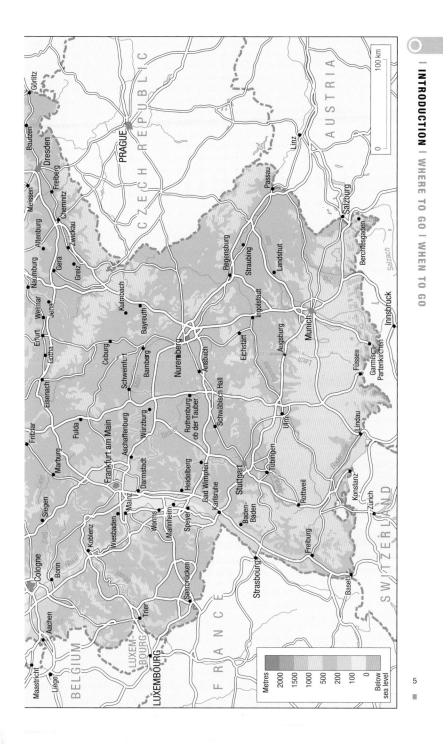

Metres	
2000	
1500	
1000	
500	
200	
100	
0	
Below sea level	

0   100 km

Introduction to

Germany

Though it remains far less well known or understood by outsiders than some of its neighbours, since reunification Germany has at last gained a higher profile as a travel destination, thanks in no small part to the remarkable resurgence of Berlin, one of the most fascinating and exciting cities in Europe. But the appeal of the reunified Germany is by no means limited to the capital. When legions of football fans descended on cities all over the country for the 2006 World Cup, they discovered a friendly, multi-ethnic and multicultural nation that was, for the most part, at ease with itself, finally happy to fly its own flag in a harmless display of national pride.

 It's now two decades since the events of 1989 swept away the Berlin Wall and brought to an uplifting end a turbulent and agonizing century for Germany, ill-served at crucial points in its brief history as a united nation state by erratic and adventurous rulers who twice led it into disaster – in 1918, as the vainglorious Kaiser Wihelm II's dream of empire ended in defeat, starvation and revolution; and at the end of World War II, as Hitler's vile race war rebounded in terrible fashion on the German people who had chosen him as their leader. There followed a period of forty-five years in which not one Germany but two faced each other across a tense international divide – the so-called Iron Curtain – throughout the years of the Cold War.

Yet political fragmentation is nothing new in German history. From the tenth century until the beginning of the nineteenth, the Holy Roman Empire provided no more than a loose semblance of sovereignty over a

vast collection of states big and small, secular and ecclesiastical, and it's this jumbled history, as much as the country's varied geography, that explains Germany's sheer diversity. According to an old German expression, city air makes you free, and for centuries many of Germany's greatest **cities** governed themselves without feudal overlords, a fact reflected in the fierceness of their civic pride and the splendour of their town halls. Among the proudest of all were the cities of the Hanseatic League, the proto-capitalist medieval trading bloc which spread not just wealth and commerce but the German language and architectural styles along the North Sea and Baltic coasts from the Netherlands to the gates of Russia.

In stark contrast to this urban freedom was the absolutist yoke of the innumerable feudal states, which ranged from substantial kingdoms such as Prussia, Saxony or Bavaria to tiny landgraviates and prince-bishoprics. Yet each made its contribution to Germany's heritage, in the architectural splendour and cultural life of many a former Residenzstadt, often with a full complement of palace, orchestra, picture gallery and opera house, once pleasures for the few, but now enjoyed by all. The Lutheran Reformation and its aftermath left their mark on Germany too: the north is predominantly Protestant while the south is more Catholic, yet the division is not clear cut. Staunchly Protestant towns alternate with devoutly Catholic ones, while in some places a civilized compromise was reached and the two traditions shared a single church.

Germany's contribution to the world of **classical music** is undeniable, and provides a powerful pretext for a visit, whether to experience at first hand the glories of the Berlin Philharmonic or of Wagner's *Ring* at Bayreuth, or simply to follow in the footsteps of great composers: Bach in Leipzig, Beethoven in Bonn. More modern tastes are catered for by the electronic dance rhythms of the annual **Love Parade**, relocated

Fact file

- Germany occupies 357,021 square kilometres of territory in Central Europe. It has land borders with nine countries totalling 3757km and a coastline of 2389km on the North and Baltic seas.

- Politically, Germany is a parliamentary democracy, with an upper house – the Bundesrat – and a lower house of parliament, the Bundestag, both of which are based in Berlin, though various ministries are based in Bonn and a few other constitutional functions are outside the capital, including the Bundesverfassungsgericht (constitutional court) in Karlsruhe. The administrative structure of Germany is decentralized, with the sixteen Länder having a high degree of autonomy from central government.

- Germany is the largest economy in the European Union, and it is the world's largest exporter. As the economic heart of the Eurozone it is also home to the headquarters of the European Central Bank.

- With a population of 82.3 million, Germany is the most populous nation in the European Union, and with 231 inhabitants per square kilometre it is also among its most densely populated and highly urbanized countries. The four largest cities are Berlin (3.4 million inhabitants), Hamburg (1.8 million), Munich (1.3 million) and Cologne (1 million).

to the Ruhr from its original home in Berlin but as massive as ever. Germany's reputation as the cradle of **modernism** is also well deserved, and a pilgrimage to the Bauhaus in Dessau or the Weissenhofsiedlung in Stuttgart is sure to please design fans. German modernism was preceded by the older traditions of the Romanesque, Gothic, Renaissance, Baroque and Rococo, each of which has left a rich legacy of artistic and architectural treasures, from soaring Gothic hall churches to the Baroque and Rococo pleasure palaces of the nation's eighteenth-century rulers. Germany's prowess in **fine art** is less well known, yet from the pioneering realism of Albrecht Dürer to the ethereal Romanticism of Caspar David Friedrich, the trenchant social observations of Georg Grosz and Otto Dix to the charismatic Joseph Beuys, it's a powerful tradition that is well worth discovering. Most German cities of any size have excellent galleries, with Berlin and Cologne hubs of the European contemporary art scene.

But the pleasures of a visit to Germany are not only intellectual. The excellence of its vastly diverse range of **beers** derives from the Reinheitsgebot, the world's oldest food purity law, which dates back to the sixteenth century; in recent years, Germany's **wine** industry has staged a comeback based on similar principles (see box opposite). Germany's **food** culture is traditionally characterized by wholesome but hearty dishes, a vast array of sausages and excellent but calorific cakes. Yet the impact of immigration, travel and increasing culinary ambition has been powerful, and it's a rare town in Germany nowadays that doesn't offer a wide selection of international options, usually including Balkan, Greek, Italian and Turkish at least. In the best restaurants, German tradition is wedded to a new emphasis on freshness, provenance and seasonality to stunning effect. And the prices won't break the bank.

A winemaking renaissance

Germany's wine growers did themselves no favours when, in the 1970s, they responded to growing demand for wine in countries that did not traditionally have a wine-drinking culture by exporting the cheapest and worst of what they produced. The result was to saddle German wine for decades with a reputation for poor quality.

All that is now changing. A new generation of young winemakers is eschewing high technology, chemicals and the temptations of the mass market in favour of organic production that reflects the *terroir*, or soil, and climate conditions of the region. In this they're greatly aided by the fact that Riesling, Germany's most widely grown grape variety, is not only reckoned by many to be the world's best white-wine grape variety, it also strongly reflects the conditions in which it has been grown. The result is a resurgence of light, drinkable dry wines that range in character from the elegantly crisp and fruity to the subtly mineral. German wines are increasingly common on wine lists in North America and highly successful in parts of Asia, where they match the cuisines well.

Germany's major wine regions are mostly in an arc that follows the country's balmy southwestern boundary and the course of the Rhine from the Mosel in the west to Baden in the south. To the east, wine is grown in more challenging climatic conditions in Franconia, Saale-Unstrut and along the Elbe near Dresden.

Though the dangers of over-indulgence are ever present, so too is the antidote. The tradition of the *Kur* or **spa** visit has endured to a far greater extent in Germany than in most other European countries, and if you want to unwind in saline or hot springs there's a vast choice of spa towns up and down

▼ Divers at Ammersee, Bavaria

the country, for the most part easily identified by the prefix Bad, meaning bath. In the summer, health-conscious Germans soak up the sun in city parks or head for the nation's endless forests and mountains, where provision for **hikers** and **cyclists** is excellent. In winter, the Alps tempt international visitors with the best array of downhill **ski runs**, while elsewhere, more low-key skiing for purely local enthusiasts is enjoyed almost anywhere there's a slope, a pommel lift and a supply of snow.

One unsung pleasure of a visit to Germany is the opportunity to meet its **people**. The officious neighbour who complains to the authorities if

▲ Berchtesgaden, Bavaria

you don't hang your socks out to dry in alphabetical order may not be entirely a creature of fiction, but as a visitor you're far more likely to be struck by warmth and open-mindedness of Germany's people – and particularly its young people – than by any mindless obsession with sticking to the rules. You can have fun testing how liberal a place is by observing how the locals react to the red Ampel-mann when crossing the street: the bigger and more laid-back the city, the more likely people are to ignore the no-jaywalking rule. In Berlin or Cologne it is mainly honoured in the breach. In contrast, the sight of upright citizens waiting patiently for the green light despite a total absence of traffic as far as the eye can see is still one of the more comic pleasures of travelling in small-town Germany.

Where to go

One of the delights of Germany is that – a few hotspots aside – the summer visitor crush is rarely oppressive. Though the country is highly urbanized, you're never far from a woodland footpath, a pristine lake or a challenging bike trail. That said, for many visitors one of Germany's cities will be their first taste of the country. The capital, **Berlin**, is a genuinely exciting place, a metropolis on fast-forward as it grows into its rediscovered role as the nation's capital while preserving evidence of its decisive – and not always happy – role in European history. Many of Germany's other major cities have proud histories as independent city states or as capitals of kingdoms in their own right, and thus there's nothing remotely "provincial" about the ancient yet liberal city of **Cologne**, the restored Baroque splendour of **Dresden** or the proud Bavarian metropolis of **Munich**, a sophisticated place with far more to offer than just beer and the Oktoberfest. The nation's financial capital, **Frankfurt**, impresses with its dynamic commercialism and international spirit, while placid **Bonn**, the former capital of West Germany, charms with its scenic setting and excellent museums. Elsewhere, designer-label **Düsseldorf** and laid-back **Stuttgart** embody different aspects of the German economic miracle, while the eastern city of **Leipzig** fizzes with new-found dynamism. Cool, mercantile

◄ Munich's Neues Rathaus

11

Re-inventing the urban scene

Germany has lately experienced a rush of high-budget, high-profile building projects – often by big-name international architects – that has added style and excitement to the urban landscape.

Berlin has led the way, at times seeming like a perpetual building site as one prestige project after another made the transition from drawing board to reality: Daniel Libeskind's Jewish Museum, the extensive new government quarter, including the Reichstag, and I.M. Pei's extension to the Deutsches Historisches Museum were all headline-grabbing projects, while Peter Eisenman's starkly powerful monument for the murdered Jews of Europe ensures that the Holocaust is remembered right at the heart of the capital.

But the action has not been limited to Berlin. In **Düsseldorf**, a bevy of star architects including Frank Gehry transformed a redundant dock into the Medienhafen, a funky new quarter where eye-catching architecture provides the setting for some of the city's best restaurants and bars. In **Munich**, Herzog & de Meuron's striking, seemingly weightless design for the Allianz-Arena has created a new symbol for the city, while a handsome new synagogue and museum has returned to it a highly visible Jewish presence. In the **Ruhr**, vast redundant industrial sites have been reworked in imaginative ways to create some of the most memorable cultural spaces in Europe.

And the stream of new projects shows little sign of abating. Herzog & de Meuron are working on plans to extend **Duisburg**'s Küppersmühle art gallery by building a translucent cube atop dockside silos. Equally audacious are the same architects' plans for the Elbphilharmonie, a **Hamburg** concert hall perched above a warehouse and the showpiece design for the ambitious redevelopment of the city's port area.

Hamburg looks askance at the antics of the rest of the country, maintaining a port city's familiarity with the wider world, while **Nuremberg** evokes the triumphs and tragedies of the nation's past. Germany's history as a fragmented collection of micro-states ensures that museums and cultural attractions of capital city quality are by no means limited to the bigger cities, and many of Germany's most rewarding towns and cities are quite modest in size: the cathedral cities of **Bamberg** and **Regensburg**; the brick-built Hanseatic ports of **Lübeck,**

▲ Berlin's Government Quarter

Stralsund and **Wismar**; the "Prussian Versailles" of **Potsdam**; and the micro-capitals like **Weimar, Schwerin** and **Eichstätt**. To add to this, Germany has university towns as evocative as any, and though **Heidelberg** may be the most famous, **Freiburg**, **Marburg** and **Tübingen** are just as charming. As for the nation's many spa towns, at their best – in **Baden-Baden, Bad Homburg** or **Wiesbaden**, for example – they combine health benefits with turn-of-the-century elegance and a lovely natural setting. For a potted version of Germany's cultural riches, Bavaria's **Romantic Road** is deservedly popular, a linear road journey that links Rococo churches with medieval cities and eccentric royal castles. Other tourist roads worth discovering include themed routes devoted to fairy tales, half-timbering or wine. Often, the most magical places – a fortress on a wooded crag, a placid village rising above vineyards, an ancient market square of improbable quaintness – await discovery on such routes. Nor should the country's undeniable natural beauty be overlooked. The **Bavarian Alps**, the **Black Forest** and the valleys of the **Rhine** and **Mosel** have long been celebrated internationally, but the talcum powder softness of **Rügen**'s beaches, the chic resorts of **Sylt** on the North Sea, the lonely splendour of the **Mecklenberg** lakes or the pristine vistas of the **Rhön Biosphere Reserve** have yet to make it onto the international travel agenda: the world's loss is, for the time being at least, the independent traveller's gain.

When to go

If you're intent on outdoor activities, you're most likely to be visiting Germany between **May** and **October**, when the weather is at its warmest. Much of the country receives its maximum rainfall in **midsummer**, so although the weather in June, July and August can be very warm, it can also be unpredictable. For more settled weather with sunshine and comfortable temperatures, **late spring** and **early autumn** – May, September and early October – are well worth considering: the Germans don't call the harvest season "goldener Oktober" for nothing. The **ski season** in the Alps runs between Christmas and the end of March. Germany's climate straddles the maritime climates of the western European seaboard and the more extreme conditions found further east. The prevailing wind is from the west, so that the mild climate of the Rhineland and North Sea coast quite closely resembles that of the UK or Ireland. Winters are more severe further east, while heading south the effects of steadily increasing altitude ensure Munich's summers are no warmer than those of Berlin. The balmiest climate in Germany is found in the wine-growing southwest, where it's not unusual to see lavender, Mediterranean pine, almond and even lemon trees.

Average daily temperatures

	Jan	Feb	Mar	Apr	May	June	July	Aug	Sept	Oct	Nov	Dec
Berlin												
Max °C	2	3	8	13	19	22	24	23	20	13	7	3
Min °C	-3	-3	0	4	8	12	14	13	10	6	2	-1
Max °F	36	37	46	55	66	72	75	73	68	55	45	37
Min °F	27	27	32	39	46	54	57	55	50	43	36	30
Frankfurt												
Max °C	3	5	11	16	20	23	25	24	21	14	8	4
Min °C	-2	-1	2	6	9	13	15	14	11	7	3	0
Max °F	37	41	52	61	68	73	77	75	70	57	46	39
Min °F	28	30	36	43	48	55	59	57	52	44	37	32
Hamburg												
Max °C	2	3	7	13	18	21	22	22	19	13	7	4
Min °C	-2	-2	-1	3	7	11	13	12	10	6	3	0
Max °F	36	37	45	55	64	70	72	72	66	55	45	39
Min °F	28	28	30	37	45	52	55	54	50	43	37	32
Munich												
Max °C	1	3	9	14	18	21	23	23	20	13	7	2
Min °C	-5	-5	-1	3	7	11	13	12	9	4	0	-4
Max °F	34	37	48	57	64	70	73	73	68	55	45	36
Min °F	23	23	30	37	45	52	55	54	48	39	32	25

things not to miss

It's not possible to see everything that Germany has to offer in one trip – and we don't suggest you try. What follows is a selective taste of the country's highlights, in no particular order – arranged in five colour-coded categories to help you find the very best things to see, do and experience. All entries have a page reference to take you straight into the Guide, where you can find out more.

01 Fairytale villages on the Romantic Road Page **344** • Take Bavaria's most famous road trip to discover a magic kingdom that's just as cute as Disney, but where the ancient towers, steep roofs and overflowing window boxes are all real.

02 **Schloss Neuschwanstein** Page **396** • Mad King Ludwig's maddest creation combines Wagnerian inspiration with a superbly dramatic alpine site to create a romantic fantasy from the age of chivalry.

04 **Ostalgie** Page **74** • Time-travel in a Trabant for a dose of Eastern Bloc nostalgia in Berlin.

03 **Stadtstrands** Page **770** • Grab a cold beer and kick back at the summertime city beaches that spring up in dozens of cities – some of the best are in Hamburg.

05 Dining in a Ratskeller

Page **44** • Defiantly old-fashioned, the restaurant in a town hall cellar is an essential venue for traditional German cooking, usually with a menu of local specialities.

06 The Ruhr's Industrial Heritage Trail Page **653** •

From scuba diving in a redundant gasometer to discovering contemporary design in a former coal mine, the Ruhr's re-invented industrial heritage offers some of Europe's most original travel experiences.

07 German wine Page **47** • High

local demand means that many German tipples barely leave the valleys where they are grown – justifying the rewarding quest to unearth them in situ, in charming little wine bars.

08 Hiking in the Allgäu, Bavaria Page **393** • Fabulous alpine scenery, clean

mountain air and a challenge for even the most serious hikers in Bavaria's beautiful south.

09 Frankfurt's Museum Embankment Page 560 •

With everything from old masters to old telephones to discover, there's a month's worth of rainy day fun on Frankfurt's cultural riverside.

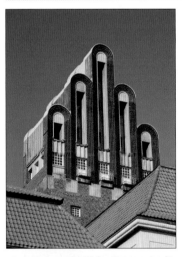

11 Jugendstil in Darmstadt

Page **567** • All the glitter and dash of the German version of Art Nouveau, in a bohemian artists' colony in leafy, laid-back Darmstadt.

10 Aachen's cathedral Page

630 • A magnificent architectural survivor from Charlemagne's time, Aachen's ancient cathedral is a taste of Byzantium in the heart of the city.

12 Getting afloat Page **756** •

Dip a paddle on Hamburg's canals, lose a week among the Mecklenburg lakes or simply go by riverboat not train – getting afloat in Germany is slow travel at its best.

13 Skiing, Garmisch-Partenkirchen Page **401** • Soak up the views from Garmisch's high-altitude pistes, or test your mettle on the fearsome Kandahar World Cup Run.

15 Beer gardens Page **46** • Dappled shade and cool, refreshing beer make a *Biergarten* the perfect place to laze your way through a hot summer's afternoon.

14 Christopher Street Day Page **129** • In both Berlin and Cologne, Germany's massive lesbian and gay communities certainly know how to throw a party.

16 North Sea islands Page **802** • To idle in *Strandkörbe* seats on an escapist rural idyll or skim across the sea on a kite-surf? Another tough decision to be made in western Germany's beach playground.

19

17 **Walpurgisnacht** Page **246** • Celebrate witchcraft among swirling mists in an age-old pagan festival in the Harz.

18 **Kaffee und Kuchen** Page **43** • Another national obsession: this elegant mid-afternoon sugar-rush is one to be lingered over, and should give you new legs for sightseeing afterwards.

19 **Pinakothek der Moderne, Munich** Page **363** • This iconic white building is a temple to modernism, from the classics of modern art to masterpieces of furniture and automotive design.

20 **Cologne** Page **603** • Two thousand years of art and history meet a thoroughly contemporary outlook on life in this liberal, cosmopolitan Rhineland metropolis.

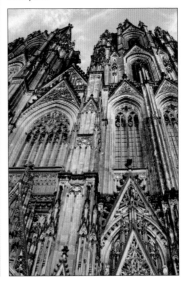

21 The Rathaus, Bamberg
Page **327** • *Trompe l'oeil* trickery meets a tricky, mid-river site in the impossibly picturesque town hall that launched a thousand flashbulbs.

23 Clubbing Page **124** • From the Love Parade to the big clubs electronic dance music rules in Germany, but there's plenty of room for quirkier sounds too.

22 Rügen's cliffs Page **828** •
The white cliffs in the Jasmund National Park have long lured holidaymakers, yet Germany's largest island remains a gentle pastoral place where it's easy to escape the crowds.

24 Long-distance cycling
Page **535** • Almost every major German river – including the Mosel, pictured – has a flat long-distance cyclepath alongside, offering a relaxing way to see the landscape and get off the beaten track.

25 **Wurst** Page **45** • From pale, lemony *Weisswurst* in the morning to post-clubbing *Currywurst* with ketchup and curry powder, there's a succulent German sausage for every occasion.

26 **Visiting a spa** Page **492** • Soak, sweat, rejuvenate – discover one of Germany's popular passions in one of its many saunas and spas.

27 **Cabaret, Berlin**
Page **128** • After years in the doldrums, the Berlin cabaret scene is begining to flourish once again.

28 The Zwinger, Dresden Page **168** • The most extravagant alfresco ballroom Germany ever built not only houses some blockbuster museums, it is also the finest monument of Saxony's reborn Baroque capital.

30 Bavarian Baroque Page **398** • From heavenly church interiors to the worldly comforts of its eighteenth-century palaces, Bavaria's Baroque mixes élan with excess to fabulous effect.

31 Carnival in Cologne Page **619** • Banish the winter blues, Rhineland style, with costumes and ritual silliness – but be sure not to wear a tie.

29 Christmas markets See *Christmas markets* colour section • Christmas cheer the way it's been for centuries.

Page **109** • Daniel Libeskind's stark but eloquent architectural play on the Jewish experience is but one of many extraordinary modern buildings in Berlin.

33 Oktoberfest, Munich

Page **373** • Munich's famous folk festival is the world's biggest excuse for a beer – and the beer comes in big measures, too.

34 The Romantic Rhine

Page **524** • Potter between Rhine-side castles and vineyards in the Germany of tourist brochures.

Basics

Basics

Getting there 27

Getting around 32

Accommodation.. 38

Food and drink.. 42

The media 48

Festivals 50

Sports and outdoor activities.................................... 51

Culture and etiquette 54

Shopping... 55

Travel essentials.. 56

Getting there

The quickest and easiest way to reach Germany is by air. While the national carrier is Lufthansa, over a hundred international airlines operating from nearly eight hundred destinations worldwide means you're unlikely to be stuck for a flight. A wide spread of airports throughout the country, many served by budget flight operators, means air is the cheapest method of arrival, too. However, a location at the heart of continental Europe opens up the possibility of road and rail travel, both not only more eco-friendly options but often cheaper than flying in then renting a car on extended trips.

The principle air-hub for long-haul international flights is Frankfurt, whose airport has its own major train station for onward connections, followed by Munich and Düsseldorf. Prices vary considerably by **season**, with the highest being around June to August. Fares drop during the "shoulder" seasons – September and October, and April and May – and you'll get the best prices during the low season, November to March, excluding Christmas and New Year when prices are hiked up. As ever, early bookers snatch the best deals. Note, too, that flying at **weekends** ordinarily raises the price of a round-trip fare; midweek prices are the cheapest.

Most points of arrival are well linked to the city centre via a cheap and efficient public transport system. If you plan to use public transport throughout a stay in the city, then multi-day tickets that cover your journey from the airport are available, the only exceptions being the backwater airports used by budget airlines, although even these are linked to a major destination by coordinated coach services.

Flights from the UK and Ireland

Over ten airlines fly daily to 25 destinations from airports throughout the UK and Ireland, from Inverness to Southampton. The two major players are British Airways and Lufthansa, though budget flights to small regional airports from the likes of Ryanair, easyJet, Air Berlin and Germanwings have significantly expanded the route network. Low-cost operators have also slashed the price of getting to the country. While a published single from the UK with the major carriers can be around £300, you can usually pick up similar flights with the budget carriers for around £50 including taxes, or from as little as £20 if you book a couple of months in advance. The downside is that the nitty-gritty of who flies where changes rapidly; the website of the UK's German Tourist Board (see p.61) or web-crawler flight search engines such as ⓦwww.skyscanner.net are a boon when making a booking direct with an airline.

Flights from the US and Canada

Thanks to competition as carriers scramble to provide routes, prices have reduced from the US and Canada in recent years. Lufthansa flies routes from most gateways at least daily and up to three times a day from major air hubs. It flies from: Atlanta, Boston, Charlotte, Chicago, Dallas, Denver, Houston, LA, Miami, New York, Orlando, Philadelphia, Portland, San Francisco, Seattle and Washington, DC. Other major carriers, including Continental, Delta, Singapore Airways or United, bolster the service, while Air Berlin and Air India flights go from smaller airports including Fort Myers or Cincinnati. In addition, Condor operates from Anchorage (summer only) and Fairbanks.

Most transatlantic flights are bound for **Frankfurt**, with a handful to **Munich** and **Düsseldorf**. Note that at the time of writing only Continental and Delta schedule routes **to Berlin**, both from New York. However, domestic connections are cheap and plentiful, by air or train.

East-coast flights are marginally cheaper than those from the west coast. As an idea of **prices**, the lowest discounted scheduled return flight to Frankfurt you're likely to find in low/high season, flying midweek, is US$500/1100 from New York, US$650/1300 from Chicago and US$650/1400 from Los Angeles.

There are fewer direct-flight options from Canada. The widest selection of flights, operated by Air Canada, Air Transat, LTU and Lufthansa, are out of Toronto, followed by Vancouver and a handful of flights from Ottawa and Calgary. Again, Frankfurt is the premier destination, then Munich. You are unlikely to make major savings by flying to the US first: low/high season fares to Frankfurt from Toronto are Can$780/1100; from Vancouver expect to pay from Can$980/1600.

Flights from Australia and New Zealand

Nearly all "direct" flights from Australia take around 22 hours to travel from Sydney, Melbourne or Perth to Frankfurt, via a few hours in Singapore. Qantas, British Airways and Singapore Airlines command the bulk of flights, with other carriers providing routes that require a transit and change of planes in the operators' hub city – usually in Asia or the Middle East – before continuing to Germany, though these cheaper fares can bump up journey times by a good ten hours – reputable agents such as STA come into their own here. Other stopover possibilities include the US and Canada, though North American flights tend to be more expensive.

The lowest **prices** from Sydney or Melbourne to Frankfurt in (European) high/low season are A$2200/1550, with those from Perth generally around A$200 cheaper, and those from Adelaide about the same more expensive. From New Zealand, low-season scheduled fares from Auckland start at around NZ$2400 and rise to NZ$2600 and upwards in the high season. Again Qantas, British Airways and Singapore Airlines are the big three, with most flights stopping at Singapore. Consequently **round-the-world tickets** often offer good-value fares compared with a standard return, not to mention a chance to break up the journey for some travel en route. For roughly the price of a long-haul return, you can buy multi-stopover or round-the-world tickets. A good agent such as STA is able to devise a travel plan pieced together from various airlines, with Germany just one destination on a ticket that is generally valid for a year. Prices for the basic Australia–Asia–Europe–US–Australia itinerary start from as little as A$1300. It's also possible to route overland segments into the journey. American agents offer similar deals, but the lower prices involved in a transatlantic trip mean round-the-world tickets are generally more expensive than a standard return ticket.

Trains

Three cheers for Eurostar (ⓦwww.eurostar .com). Its high-speed rail links – and the upgrade of the UK connecting line – has slashed travel times from St Pancras International, London, to Germany's rail gateway cities Aachen and Cologne to around five hours, or to six hours and thirty minutes for Frankfurt. Passengers must change at Brussels (1hr 50min from London) to join French-run Thalys or InterCity Express (ICE) express trains to Germany. Like air travel, prices vary according to the season, day and time, class of travel and also how far in advance tickets are booked. The caveat with train travel is that it is rarely cheaper than flying, especially if you start from outside London and hope to travel far beyond Cologne. However, the environmental benefits of train travel are huge, especially since Eurostar services are now carbon neutral. **Sleeper carriages** (Schlafwagen) also appeal for overnight journeys, permitting the romance of waking up at your destination and saving on a hotel overnight.

Single fares from London to Brussels start at £50 and can rise to £200; under-4s go free; promotions are published online and can provide bargains such as London–Cologne return for £80. Note that you cannot buy ongoing tickets via the Eurostar website. Long-distance train advice website ⓦwww.seat61.com is invaluable for planning. Arriving by train, the city **Hauptbahnhof** (main train station) is ubiquitously well-placed for the city's business

Six steps to a better kind of travel

At Rough Guides we are passionately committed to travel. We feel strongly that only through travelling do we truly come to understand the world we live in and the people we share it with – plus tourism has brought a great deal of benefit to developing economies around the world over the last few decades. But the extraordinary growth in tourism has also damaged some places irreparably, and of course climate change is exacerbated by most forms of transport, especially flying. This means that now more than ever it's important to travel thoughtfully and responsibly, with respect for the cultures you're visiting – not only to derive the most benefit from your trip but also in order to preserve the best bits of the planet for everyone to enjoy. At Rough Guides we feel there are six main areas in which you can make a difference:

- Consider what you're contributing to the local economy, and indeed how much the services you use do the same, whether it's through employing local workers and guides or sourcing locally grown produce and local services.
- Consider the environment on holiday as well as at home. Water is scarce in many developing destinations, and the biodiversity of local flora and fauna can be adversely affected by tourism. Patronise businesses that take account of this rather than those that trash the local environment for short-term gain.
- Give thought to how often you fly and what you can do to redress any harm that your trips create. Reduce the amount you travel by air; avoid short hops by air and more harmful night flights.
- Consider alternatives to flying, travelling instead by bus, train, boat and even by bike or on foot where possible. Take time to enjoy the journey itself as well as your final destination.
- Think about making all the trips you take "climate neutral" via a reputable carbon offset scheme. All Rough Guide flights are offset, and every year we donate money to a variety of charities devoted to combating the effects of climate change.
- Travel with a purpose, not just to tick off experiences. Consider spending longer in a place, and really getting to know it and its people – you'll find it much more rewarding than dashing from place to place.

centre, generally preceded by a string of outlying stations which may be more convenient for your accommodation.

Rail passes

If you plan to use the train extensively, look at rail passes. Since travel by train within Germany can prove good value with some canny planning, it's worth doing the sums via the website of national operator **Deutsche Bahn** to ensure a pass will prove cheaper than a flight and national rail pass (see p.32). Where other passes score is on a transcontinental trip. The **Eurail Pass** (aka Eurorail) comes in a variety of forms: the Global Pass (from US$519) permits unlimited travel within twenty countries from ten days to three months; the Select Pass (from US$329) allows three or fifteen days' travel within a two-month period; while the Regional Pass (from US$179) provides three to ten days' travel within two

countries. Under-25s are eligible for "Youth" passes, which are cheaper by about a third and only valid for second-class seats. Group passes are also available.

An alternative is the time-honoured **InterRail** pass, which is finally valid for travel within the UK. Again, the pass comes in formats that are either valid continuously or only for specified days within a set period. Prices start at €329 for five days' first-class travel within a ten-day period (€249 second-class or €159 youth card) and rise to €809 (€599/399) for a month's continuous travel. Note that passes require supplement payments for high-speed and couchettes of around €4 and €20 respectively.

Buses

In a nutshell, possible but neither fast nor particularly cheap compared with low-cost airlines; the journey will be long and uncomfortable, interrupted every three to four hours by stops at motorway service stations. The one advantage is that you can buy an open return at no extra cost. Services to all major cities in Germany are run by **Eurolines** from Victoria Coach Station in London, and are bookable through most travel agents and through any National Express agent. As an idea of times and advance prices, London–Cologne takes thirteen hours and costs around £60 one-way, London–Berlin twenty hours and £80. Prices include the cost of the ferry across the Channel; promotional "Funfares" provide discounts. Eurolines Passes, priced by season, cost £139–229 for 15 days' travel and £209–299 for 30 days. Under-26 passes are £20–50 cheaper. You may be able to pick up a faster ride – and often a cheaper one – via the German Mitfahrzent-ralen car-share system (see p.36).

Another option for a European tour is backpacker-friendly bus service **Busabout**, which operates a hop-on hop-off network of routes throughout the continent. Berlin, Dresden, Munich and Stuttgart are on the North Loop of its four designated circuits – it intersects with the South Loop into Italy and the French Riviera. A one-loop pass costs £299, a combined North–South Loop £509. The Flexitrip Pass, costing £259, allows more freedom, with six stops anywhere on the network and additional "flexistops" available for £29. All passes are valid for a season that lasts from May to October.

Ferries

At the time of writing, the only direct service from the UK to Germany – from Harwich to Cuxhaven, north Germany – had been out of action for several years. It was formerly operated by DFDS Seaways. Consequently all ferry-bound traffic from the UK is via France, Belgium or the Netherlands (see opposite). Year-round sea links to the German Baltic coast exist from Scandinavia, notably Sweden and Denmark, and Baltic nations such as Lithuania.

Car and motorbike

To enter Germany by car from the UK you have to slice through continental Europe via France, Belgium or the Netherlands;

which one depends largely upon your final destination. In terms of comfort, it is best to enter at France (Calais, Dunkerque or Le Havre) or Belgium (Zeebrugge) for the Ruhrgebiet and east and south Germany; and from the Netherlands (Amsterdam, Hoek van Holland or Rotterdam) for north Germany. However, because the ferry crossing to the latter is around six hours – longer when overnight, when reservation of a seat or cabin is mandatory – you may find it quicker from southern UK destinations to enter at Calais or Dunkerque, then zip northeast on the motorways. Wherever you enter, you'll be on toll-free motorway all the way into Germany. As a guide of driving times from Calais, allow eight hours to Hamburg (6hr from Hoek van Holland), six hours to Frankfurt, ten hours to Berlin and ten hours to Munich.

Departures across the Channel are roughly every hour by ferry from Dover to Calais and every two hours via the car-carrying Eurotunnel train from Folkestone. From the north or centre of England, longer routes across the North Sea are: Harwich to Hoek van Holland (Stena Line); Hull to Rotterdam and Zeebrugge (both P&O Ferries); Newcastle to Amsterdam (DFDS); and Rosyth to Zeebrugge (Norfolk Line). From Ireland, Cherbourg and Roscoff, in northwest France, are as close as it gets to Germany, both accessed from Dublin and Rosslare respectively and served by P&O Ferries. Fast it is not.

Airlines, agents and operators

Online booking

ⓦ www.ebookers.com (in UK), ⓦ www.ebookers.ie (in Ireland)
ⓦ www.expedia.co.uk (in UK), ⓦ www.expedia.com (in US), ⓦ www.expedia.ca (in Canada)
ⓦ www.lastminute.com (in UK)
ⓦ www.opodo.co.uk (in UK)
ⓦ www.orbitz.com (in US)
ⓦ www.travelocity.co.uk (in UK), ⓦ www.travelocity.com (in US), ⓦ www.travelocity.ca (in Canada), ⓦ www.travelocity.co.nz (in New Zealand)
ⓦ www.travelonline.co.za (in South Africa)
ⓦ www.zuji.com.au (in Australia)

Airlines

Aer Lingus ⓦ www.aerlingus.com
Air Berlin ⓦ www.airberlin.com
Air Canada ⓦ www.aircanada.com
Air France ⓦ www.airfrance.com
Air India ⓦ www.airindia.com
Air New Zealand ⓦ www.airnz.co.nz
Air Transat ⓦ www.airtransat.com
American Airlines ⓦ www.aa.com
bmi ⓦ www.flybmi.com
bmibaby ⓦ www.bmibaby.com
British Airways ⓦ www.ba.com
Cathay Pacific ⓦ www.cathaypacific.com
Condor ⓦ www.condor.com
Continental Airlines ⓦ www.continental.com
Delta ⓦ www.delta.com
easyJet ⓦ www.easyjet.com
Emirates ⓦ www.emirates.com
Etihad Airways ⓦ www.etihadairways.com
flyBE ⓦ www.flybe.com
Germanwings ⓦ www.germanwings.com
Gulf Air ⓦ www.gulfairco.com
Jet2 ⓦ www.jet2.com
KLM (Royal Dutch Airlines) ⓦ www.klm.com
Korean Air ⓦ www.koreanair.com
LOT ⓦ www.lot.com
Lufthansa ⓦ www.lufthansa.com
Malaysia Airlines ⓦ www.malaysiaairlines.com
Northwest ⓦ www.nwa.com
Qantas Airways ⓦ www.qantas.com
Ryanair ⓦ www.ryanair.com
Singapore Airlines ⓦ www.singaporeair.com
South African Airways ⓦ www.flysaa.com
Swiss ⓦ www.swiss.com
Thai Airways ⓦ www.thaiair.com
Thomas Cook Airlines ⓦ www.thomascook.com
Thomsonfly ⓦ www.thomsonfly.com
United Airlines ⓦ www.united.com
US Airways ⓦ www.usair.com

Agents and operators

North South Travel UK ☎ 01245/608 291,
ⓦ www.northsouthtravel.co.uk. Friendly,
competitive travel agency, offering discounted fares
worldwide. Profits are used to support projects in
the developing world, especially the promotion of
sustainable tourism.
STA Travel US ☎ 1-800/781-4040, UK
☎ 0871/2300 040, Australia ☎ 134 782,
New Zealand ☎ 0800/474 400, South Africa
☎ 0861/781 781; ⓦ www.statravel.com.
Worldwide specialists in independent travel;

also student IDs, travel insurance, car rental, rail
passes, and more. Good discounts for students and
under-26s.
Trailfinders UK ☎ 0845/058 5858, Ireland
☎ 01/677 7888, ⓦ www.trailfinders.com. One
of the best-informed and most efficient agents for
independent travellers.

Rail contacts

European Rail UK ☎ 020/7619 1083, ⓦ www
.europeanrail.com
Europrail International Canada ☎ 1-888/667-
9734, ⓦ www.europrail.net
Eurostar UK ☎ 0870 518 6186, outside UK
☎ (+44)12336 17575; ⓦ www.eurostar.com
Rail Europe US ☎ 1-888/382-7245, Canada
☎ 1-800/361-7245, UK ☎ 0844/848 4064,
Australia ☎ 03/9642 8644, South Africa ☎ 11/628
2319; ⓦ www.raileurope.com

Bus contacts

Busabout UK ☎ 020/7950 1661, ⓦ www
.busabout.com
Eurolines UK ☎ 0871/781 8181, ⓦ www
.eurolines.com

Ferry and Channel Tunnel contacts

Brittany Ferries UK ☎ 0870 907 6103,
Ireland ☎ 021/4277 801; ⓦ www.brittanyferries
.co.uk
DFDS Seaways UK ☎ 0871 522 9955, ⓦ www
.dfdsseaways.co.uk
Eurotunnel UK ☎ 0870 535 3535, ⓦ www
.eurotunnel.com
Irish Ferries UK ☎ 0870 517 1717, Ireland
☎ 0818/300 400; ⓦ www.irishferries.com
Norfolkline UK ☎ 0870 870 1020 (for Dover–
Dunkerque reservations) or ☎ 0844 499 0007 (for
Irish Sea reservations); ⓦ www.norfolkline.com
P&O Ferries UK ☎ 0871 664 5645, ⓦ www
.poferries.com
Sea France UK ☎ 0871 663 2546, ⓦ www
.seafrance.com
SpeedFerries UK ☎ 0871 222 7456, ⓦ www
.speedferries.com
Stena Line UK ☎ 0870 570 7070, Northern
Ireland ☎ 0870 520 4204, Ireland ☎ 01/204 7733;
ⓦ www.stenaline.co.uk
Superfast Ferries UK ☎ 0870 420 1267, ⓦ www
.superfast.ferries.org
Transmanche UK ☎ 0800 917 1201, ⓦ www
.transmancheferries.com

Getting around

Planes, trains and automobiles, not to mention buses, boats and bikes: Germany deals in the full deck of options for travel within the country, with one of the finest public transport systems in Europe. Unusually for a largely landlocked nation, it also affords considerable opportunities for travel on its arterial rivers – slow travel at its best in which the getting there is as much a reason to travel as the destination. Services operate on arterial rivers such as the Rhine, Mosel and Elbe, generally from April to October; details are provided in relevant destinations. Prices are more expensive than those for rail, but that's not really the point.

By air

Alongside national carrier Lufthansa, budget airlines such as Air Berlin and Hapag-Lloyd Express offer routes daily throughout the country, with single fares for as little as €30 including taxes. Business-centred Lufthansa flights are more expensive but still offer good value. It schedules the greatest number of routes and the most frequent departures, which can be hourly on popular destinations such as Hamburg–Munich. Advance bookings provide the usual discounts, although you can often pick up something surprisingly cheap for a fortnight's time. The real boon is the time-saving: Hamburg to Munich in an hour compared to six by train.

By train

The much-lauded national rail system operated by **Deutsche Bahn** (Ⓦ www.bahn .de, available in English) is not quite all it's hyped up to be. Even in Germany, trains are – shock, horror! – frequently a few minutes late and strikes are not unknown. Nevertheless, trains remain the workhorse of public transport and the nation has good reason to be proud of the efficient privatized system that emerged from the merged West and East networks in 1994. Its 43,900km of track is the most extensive in Europe, trains are frequent – generally hourly, with more services scheduled for rush hours – invariably clean, and prices, if not a bargain, are at least fair thanks to a fixed per-kilometre pricing system.

Kings of the rails are the flagship **Intercity-Express** (ICE) trains, which travel at speeds up to 300km/hr and offer the most comfort on board, including a bistro carriage and refreshments trolley-service. When making a reservation you can also request a seat in areas with boosted mobile-phone reception or none at all. Not as fast at 200km/hr nor as flash are **Intercity** (IC) and international **Eurocity** (EC) trains, though these still have electricity terminals in both classes and a buffet carriage. Local trains come as swift intercity **InterRegio-Express** (IRE), below which are **Regional-Express** (RE) trains then the local **Regionalbahn** (RB), which tend to stop at every station en route. Within the environs of a city, you're usually on **Stadt-Express** (SE) trains or the commuter S-Bahn trains.

The Deutsche Bahn website is a mine of information for planning, with an online timetable. On the ground, seek out the ServicePoint in city stations.

Tickets

Standard **tickets** (*Fahrkarten*), which are not restricted to any particular train and are refundable for a small administration charge, are priced according to the distance travelled, so a return costs twice as much as a single. Reservations (€2 per journey) are worthwhile for peak long-distance trains, especially the popular Friday late-afternoon getaway.

You can buy tickets over the counter at the Reisezentrum (travel centre) of larger stations or in all but the most backwoods rural stations from touchscreen vending machines that have instructions in English. You can also buy tickets on board for a nominal

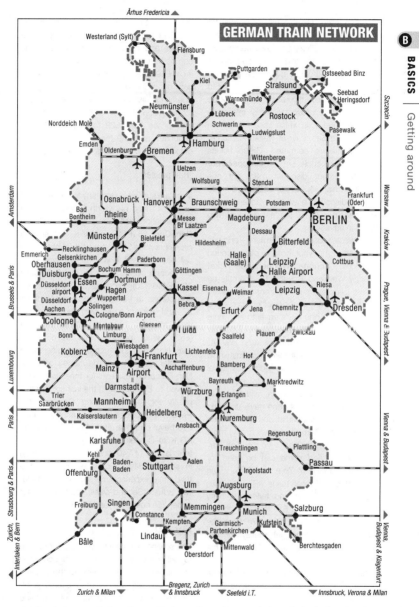

GERMAN TRAIN NETWORK

service charge, usually from the conductor or the driver on rural routes – in theory all trains now accept major credit cards. Telephone reservations are on ☎01805/99 66 33, online reservations via the website cost €3.50 for ticket postage, or for journeys over 50km, registered users can buy tickets online at no

surcharge up to ten minutes before departure – you'll require a print-out of the ticket as proof of purchase.

Because flexible standard tickets are far from cheap – in 2008 an ICE Hamburg–Berlin ticket costs €65, and an ICE Hamburg–Munich €122 – it's worth taking advantage of **discounted fares**. The **Sparpreis 25** and **Sparpreis 50** give 25 and 50 percent discounts respectively on return journeys for a specified day and train. The Sparpreis 25 tickets must be bought at least three days in advance and weekend restrictions apply to the Sparpreis 50 – the return trip cannot be sooner than the following Sunday unless you travel on Sunday, in which case you can on the following Saturday; at weekends same-day returns are permitted. Group tickets for up to six people are the **Gruppe&Spar 50** (50 percent discount if bought one day in advance), **Gruppe&Spar 60** (60 percent discount, a week in advance) and **Gruppe&Spar 70** (70 percent discount, two weeks in advance).

The greatest bargain in Germany – and one worth arranging your holiday plans around – is the **Schönes-Wochenende-Ticket** ("Happy Weekend Ticket"). This permits up to five people (or one parent/grandparent travelling with any number of children aged 14 or younger) one day's travel to anywhere in Germany between midnight Saturday or Sunday until 3am the following day. All yours for just €35 – it takes no Einstein to realize the savings on long-distance travel are astronomical. The weekday equivalent is the **Länder-Ticket**. Again valid for up to five people, this permits one day's unlimited second-class travel within one federal state from 9am until 3am the following day; most Länder-Tickets are also valid on Saturday and Sunday, and some can be used for overnight travel from 7pm until 6am. It can be used on all local trains (IRE, RE, RB, S-Bahn). Regulations and tariffs also vary by state, ranging from €19 to €29 if bought from ticket machines, €2 more from the Reisezentrum. Things get messy for city transport on both the Länder-Ticket and the Schönes-Wochenende-Ticket, with some states happy to accept it, others not. Check as you buy or consult the Deutsche Bahn website.

Finally a note about overnight trains. Private **CityNightLine** (CNL) trains to the Netherlands, Austria and Switzerland and Deutsche Bahn's **NachtZug** (NZ) to destinations throughout Germany as well as neighbouring countries offer travel in reclining seats, couchette or comfortable sleeper carriages, the latter all soothing curved corridors and soft lighting, with either a shower and toilet or a wash-basin inside compartments. Standard Globalpreis tickets (from €89 for a seat, from €129 for a sleeper) can be reduced by taking advantage of SparNight discounted fares. These reward a reservation at least three days in advance with prices from €29 for seat, €49 for a couchette and €69 for a sleeper. For more details see ⓦ www.nachtzugreise.de.

Rail passes

If you are staying in Germany for an extended period it may be worth investigating an annual national rail pass, the BahnCard. The **BahnCard 25** (€110 first class, €55 second class) provides 25 percent discounts, which will pay for itself if you spend over €200 on second-class rail travel; the **BahnCard 50** (€440/220) provides 50 percent off and comes at half-price to students under 27 and seniors over 60; and, if you're really travelling hard, the **BahnCard 100** (€5900/3500) provides free travel for a year. Note that these cards are different to the international rail cards named on p.29. Non-European residents (or those who have moved to Europe within the last six months) qualify for the month-long **German Rail Pass**. This provides free rail transport – plus free travel on Rhine and Mosel boats of the KD Köln–Düsseldorf line – for either five or ten days (£147.40 and £225 respectively) in second class. First class is around a third more expensive, as are twin tickets for two adults. Second-class Youth tickets for under-25s cost £117 and £155.

By bus

Bus services are very much the poor relation to rail travel. While efficient enough, they are slower and of little value to the average tourist bar the appeal of a scenic jaunt. Consequently, throughout we provide details of bus transport only where there is no train. You'll only need to fall back on a bus in remote rural destinations such as the Harz, the Thuringian Forest, the Black Forest or the Bavarian Alps – indeed, you may have no other choice. Regional companies operate local services that vary in frequency from every twenty minutes or so to daily or even fewer, with most routes scheduled to serve commuters from early morning to early evenings. Services can dry up entirely at weekends. In addition, buses need not adhere to strict schedules, so may leave earlier than times published – use the printed timetables as a guide only and arrive early. The exception to this is from the terminus, known in cities as a **Busbahnhof** or **Zentral Omnibus Bahnhof** (ZOB) and ubiquitously located near the train station. Tickets are bought either from kiosks or from the driver. If you intend to travel widely in a rural region ask about a day-card (Tageskarte) or week-card (Wochenkarte).

By car

Holders of any home national – or international driving licence – are permitted to drive in Germany and are required to have their full driving licence to hand. If driving your own car you will also require vehicle registration documents and a valid certificate of third-party insurance; note that in 2007 many UK insurers downgraded cover, so that UK comprehensive becomes continental third-party. If bringing your own car, be aware, too, that a growing number of cities – 32 as of 2010 – have implemented Low Emission Zones to reduce exhaust fumes. Vehicles in a central "Green Zone" must display an "Emission Badge" (*Umwelt Plakette*), which is bought for €5–10 from repair centres, dealers and MOT (Tüv) stations after assessment of the vehicle by a mechanic, or via the websites Ⓦwww .tuev-nord.de and www.tuev-sued.de. In practice this means pre-'93 petrol models and pre-'97 diesels will not pass unless retro-fitted with a catalytic converter. In theory, vehicles entering a Green Zone without a badge will be fined €40, though the rule is not widely enforced – yet.

The most celebrated of the two principal categories of road are the three- or four-lane **Autobahnen** (motorways), indicated with blue signs and an A rating. Famously, there are no speed limits. Forget the fantasies of bowling along at 200km/hr in your BMW, however. When futurist German synth-band Kraftwerk released their homage *Autobahn* in 1974, Germany had the most efficient and extensive road network in Europe. Now it is rather inadequate for a nation at the crossroads of European road transport. On pan-European routes like the east–west A8 it can seem a glorified lorry park for East European truckers. It can also seem as if a quarter of the network is subject to roadworks, which helps to explain the national obsession with traffic jams (*Staus*). In practice, you'll rarely get above the recommended speed limit of 130km/hr. Lorries are banned from driving on Autobahnen on Sunday and on Saturday during the summer holidays, making both good days to cover distance. Secondary B routes (Bundesstrassen) are usually dual carriageway, with three lanes on heavy sections, and have a speed limit of 100km/hr. Speed limits in urban areas are 50km/hr. All routes are toll free.

On-the-spot speeding fines are issued on a sliding scale: in excess of 10km per hour is €15, over 30km per hour is €60, etc up to a maximum of €425 for travelling in excess of 70km per hour over the limit. For serious offences, the police can confiscate vehicles. Traffic police are fair but determined – don't expect to weasel out of a fine with pleas of innocence. The maximum blood alcohol limit is 0.5mg/l. Penalties for those over the limit are severe – fines are steep, licences can be revoked – and even those involved in an accident but under the limit can have licences confiscated temporarily. The use of mobile phones while driving is forbidden except with a hands-free set.

On Autobahnen, emergency telephones are located every 1.5km for breakdown services; ask for Strassenwachthilfe. Phones connect to Germany's principal automobile organization Allegmeiner Deutscher Automobil Club (ADAC; Ⓦwww.adac.de), affiliated to the British AA and Canadian and American AAA, though check the extent of cover with your own breakdown service. Off the Autobahnen call ☎01802/22 22 22 for assistance.

On the road

Driving is on the right, overtaking on the left, and **seatbelts** are compulsory for drivers and passengers, including those in the back seats – whoever isn't wearing one will be fined, a law which extends to taxis though isn't rigorously enforced. Some states request (though do not demand) that headlights are on at all times. Carrying a reflective **hazard warning triangle** is mandatory and should be set up 100m behind the vehicle on the hard shoulder if required. In southern Germany snow chains are a good idea if you intend to venture onto Alpine backroads, but most routes are kept snow-free by frequent laying of grit and salt, and by snowploughs.

For first-time-foreign drivers, remember that anything approaching from the right commands respect and you will be safe – until **cities**. Here trams have the right of way regardless of their direction. Since tramstops are at the roadside, overtaking of stationary trams is forbidden. Pay special attention for pedestrians and cyclists in cities – you might receive a green light to pull away from a junction, but the road you turn into is often green for a pedestrian crossing. Treat every junction, therefore, as a potential accident and double-check before you turn. Signs for Stadt Mitte (city centre) or Altstadt (old town) lead you to a town's heart, orange signs announce an Umleitung (diversion), which can lead a merry dance but gets you there in the end.

Car parks (*Parkhaus*) are generally on the periphery of the pedestrianized centres; as ever, follow the blue P. While most car parks offer flat-rate overnight parking, some spring surprises – check to avoid a shock in the morning. Street parking is either pay-and-display or free for a specified time beneath a blue P, in which case cardboard "clocks" bought from motor stores are left on the dashboard to indicate the time of arrival.

Petrol – all Bleifrei (unleaded) and either Super Plus (98 octane) or Super (95 octane) – is available every 50km or so on Autobahnen, where major players are open 24 hours a day. All petrol stations are self-service.

Car rental

Car rental (*Autovermeitung*) is widely available, with multinational chains operating bureaux at all airports and often a desk at (or around) the Hauptbahnhof of most cities. Rack rates are steep – around €80–90 a day without a promotional deal – and if you're not fussed about cosmetics, smaller local outfits can offer better value. For the same reason fly-drive deals when booking a flight can pay off.

Auto Europe Ⓦ www.autoeurope.com
Avis Ⓦ www.avis.com
Budget Ⓦ www.budget.com
Dollar Ⓦ www.dollar.com
Europcar Ⓦ www.europcar.com
Europe by Car Ⓦ www.europebycar.com
Hertz Ⓦ www.hertz.com
Holiday Autos Ⓦ www.holidayautos.co.uk. Part of the LastMinute.com group.
National Ⓦ www.nationalcar.com
SIXT Ⓦ www.sixt.com
Thrifty Ⓦ www.thrifty.com

Taxis and car shares

Taxis – nearly always cream-coloured Mercedes-Benz – will only save money over well-priced public transport if you are in a group; even then the cost-saving will be minimal. Available cabs have rooftop lights lit, though it's rare to hail one on the street. Most gather at ranks in the city centres, most reliably outside the Hauptbahnhof or at ranks at the edges of the pedestrian centres. Fares are metered, priced per kilometre and rise slightly between 11pm and 6am and on Sunday. Some drivers may charge a nominal fee for large items of luggage.

Eco-aware Germany has a shared-car system called **Mitfahrzentralen** that operates as a form of organized hitchhiking (unorganized it's not recommended, by the way). Agencies in cities connect drivers with passengers, who pay towards fuel costs usually on the basis of an even split. Most agencies publish searchable online lists of journeys, many of them international, so you can see who's going your way – since all drivers are required to provide details of addresses and registration numbers, the ride should be safe. Prices vary according to passenger numbers, but you can expect to pay around €20 from Hamburg to Berlin, or €35 from Hamburg to Frankfurt. Website Ⓦ www.mitfahrzentralen.org publishes the offices of agencies, which exist in all large towns and cities throughout Germany, as well as operating a searchable database of rides. Other good online sources of journeys are Ⓦ www.mfz.de and www.drive2day.de.

Cycling

Cyclists have an easy ride in Germany: any small roads have dedicated cycle-paths, as do cities where you'll often be on the pavement. When you are forced onto the road in towns you will be treated with respect by drivers rather than rammed into a curb. A network of long-distance cycle-paths, often following rivers such as those along the Elbe or the Weser, make cycling between destinations an appealing prospect were it not for the distances involved – Germany is deceptively large by European standards. On all but ICE services, trains can accommodate bikes so long as you have purchased a Fahrrad-Karte (bicycle ticket) alongside a seat ticket – these cost €9 (€6.50 with a rail card) on IC and EC services, which generally have a dedicated carriage, and €4.50 or free on local services and the S-Bahn, depending on the state. You'll also find bike racks on the buses in popular touring areas such as Rügen or Sylt, and bikes are permitted on just about all ferry services. Cycle helmets are not required by law, but all cyclists must display front and back lights at night.

Bike rental is widely available in cities, usually from the Hauptbahnhof; the Deutsche Bahn website lists contact details for fifty Fahrrad-Vermietstationen. A highly convenient innovation introduced and run by DB is CallBikes. Silver-and-red, full-suspension bicycles can be rented at any time of day for €0.07 per minute (up to €15 per 24hr period), with no deposit or minimum charge. Users need to register a credit card (☏0700/05 22 55 22, ⓦwww.callabike.de). Registering your mobile will mean it will automatically debit your account when you call. Once you've registered, it's just a matter of calling the individual number on the side of a bike and receiving an electronic code to open the lock. To drop it off you can leave it on any street corner then ring up for a code to lock the bike and leave its location as a recorded message. Participating cities as of 2008 were Berlin, Frankfurt, Cologne, Munich, Stuttgart and Karlsruhe, though others seem sure to join. Otherwise, hostels are an excellent source of bike rental, or most cycle shops offer rental for around €10–15 a day; inquire at local tourist offices. If you're planning to stay for any length of time, it works out cheaper to buy a secondhand bike and sell it when you leave.

City transport

You have to salute municipal transport in Germany, which is ubiquitously efficient and fairly priced. The cornerstones of most systems in major cities are two rail systems, supplemented on the streets by buses and trams. Once on board all, illuminated signs and announcements ensure it's easy to find the right stop. Tickets are available from machines at stations, on trams or from bus drivers – but be sure to validate them by punching the ticket when you travel. An un-validated ticket is as good as no ticket at all and will result in a fine at spot-checks.

The mainstay of most city-centre systems is the **U-Bahn**, which is clean, punctual and rarely crowded. Running both under- and overground, these cover much of the centre: trains tend to run from 4am to around 12.30am, and all night on Friday and Saturday in the metropolises. After then, their routes are usually covered by night buses – denoted by a number with the prefix "N". The **S-Bahn** systems are a separate network of suburban trains that runs largely overground, is better for covering long distances fast, generally with larger distances between each stop. Within small and medium-sized towns, the tram or bus replaces the U-Bahn as the heart of city transport, operating a network of circuits. Otherwise, the modus operandi remains the same, the only exception being that you may have to buy tickets direct from the driver rather than from a vending machine at your stop.

Transport networks are usually divided into zones – A, B, C or 1, 2, 3, etc – and **ticket prices** vary according to their reach. Basic singles are called *Einzeltickets*, or you can usually buy a cheaper *Kurzstrecke*, a short-trip ticket that permits travel for a limited number of stops (no return journeys or transfers). Buying a day ticket (*Tageskarte*) will generally work out cheaper still – look out for group tickets (*Gruppenkarten*). Another possibility for short-term city visitors is the cards promoted by city tourist offices that provide 48 or 72 hours' unlimited travel alongside discounted entry to city sights. If not named after its city, it is often called a Welcome Card.

Accommodation

Sourcing a bed is rarely a problem in Germany and the range of accommodation – from half-timbered hostel to high-rise design hotel, pension to palace – means there's something to suit all budgets and tastes. There are two caveats: during high season in premier resorts and during major festivals, when you may struggle to find a room without a reservation, and when the expense accounts roll into town during city trade fairs known as Messe, when you may baulk at the prices demanded.

In the past decade the country's hoteliers have busied themselves updating what was a fairly frumpy hotel stock to at least a nod to contemporary decor, even if that does mean a preponderance of identikit, bland furnishings in cheaper places. Another trend is the emergence of an **independent hostel** sector. Though targeted at the backpacker market, these convivial hostels are open to all comers and often offer modern, funky doubles for around €20 less than you'd pay for a tired, cheap hotel. Even the latter are generally clean even if their decor saps the spirit.

While the strength of the euro means hotel accommodation is not quite the bargain it was a decade or so ago, Germany remains good value for money compared with the United Kingdom at least. Notwithstanding that **prices** vary hugely throughout the nation, you can expect to pay around €80–120 for a double in an average mid-range hotel. Many city hotels, especially those that target the executive market, offer cheaper weekend rates. Hostels charge about half that price for a double room, and under €30 for a dormitory. The other source of a cheap bed is rooms in **private houses** or **farms** – those in more remote regions such as the Black Forest and Bavarian Alps abound in country character and provide bargains to boot.

A peculiarly German quirk is the enduring love affair with the **sauna and spa** or "wellness" centre, which you'll find even in dated hotels – worth remembering before you thrill to the notion of a "spa hotel". Another national tradition is the *Kurtaxe*, which is charged in spa towns and "health" resorts, a definition extended to encompass most coastal resorts. This adds €2–4 to your hotel bill on the grounds that facilities are laid on for the resort's tourists.

For **reservations** most tourist offices will book all forms of accommodation either for free or for around €2–4 per person. Those in resorts are a good, first port-of-call if you arrive without a reservation in peak season. Many in destinations with a high visitor rate have touchscreen info-points outside, sometimes with a free telephone. And if you make a reservation be sure to notify staff about an expected arrival time after 6pm – or else your room may be given away.

Hotels

Many hotels in Germany have aligned themselves with a voluntary five-star Deutschen Hotelklassifizierung **rating system** based on the assessment of 280 criteria by an independent body. This ensures that participating one-star establishments have rooms of up to 12m squared, with en-suite toilet and shower; that three-star hotels offer larger rooms, a mini-bar and 24-hour call on reception even if they are not manned; and that in five-star places, you will enjoy rooms of at least 18m squared and luxuries such as 24-hour room service and reception, and laundry services. Most hotels have a restaurant – those named a "*Hotel garni*" serve breakfast only.

Whether aligned to the Deutschen Hotelklassifizierung system or not, German hotels are generally comfortable enough for you to have few complaints; they are clean, generally en suite except in the cheapest establishments, and rooms nearly always

Accommodation price codes

All the accommodation listed in this book is categorized by one of nine price codes. These represent the cost of a double room in high season, quoted at the official rack rate, although prices outside will fall dramatically. In hotels with a wide spread of accommodation, prices are listed as a range. Effectively, this means that anything in the ❶ category and most places in ❷ will be basic rooms without a bath. By category ❹ you can expect a simple lower-mid place, some with private amenities. At price ❺, you're moving into the upper end of the market; luxury is guaranteed at ❽; and at price code ❾ you're staying in some of the finest properties Europe can provide. Single rooms are sometimes half-price but more usually around two-thirds the price of a double. Alongside price codes for double rooms in hostels, we've also provided the price of beds in dormitories.

❶ €40 and under   ❹ €81–100   ❼ €151–200
❷ €41–60   ❺ €101–120   ❽ €201–250
❸ €61–80   ❻ €121–150   ❾ €251 and over

come with a TV. In the lower and mid-range, you can expect either a fairly anonymous business style or a dated Eighties throwback. Budget hotel chains Etap and Ibis provide functional modern rooms at rates comparable to a room in an independent hostel (see p.40). That said, a growing number of style hotels in the cities also offer interior style at affordable prices, and at the upper end you can have a pick of hotels with wow factor, with many luxury outfits installed in historic palaces or castles. All hotels provide **breakfast**, generally buffet-style and included in the price of your room, but double-check.

Pensions, inns, private rooms and farmstays

A shift away from the formality and anonymity of the blander hotel chains is the **pension**: by and large, smaller, cheaper establishments, often in large houses or in city apartment blocks. What they lack in mod-cons – you'll usually have to share bathroom amenities, for example – they make up in character in the form of personal service and homely decor. In Bavaria they are often called a **Gästehaus**; a similar style can be found in a **Gasthof** or a **Gaststätte**, which roughly translates into English as an inn. Accommodation is generally above a traditional restaurant – that it is often in a historic building is all part of the charm of a stay, although bear in mind that this means room dimensions are historic, too. For obvious reasons these

are especially prevalent in small towns and in the countryside. Both pensions and inns will provide breakfast.

A step down from the pension or inn is the **private room** in the house of locals. Priced from around €15, these are rarely more expensive than €30, making them a valuable alternative to the hostel for budget travellers. At their best, private rooms offer a chance to dip a toe into everyday life and to glean the insider information from a local host. Such intimacy may not be to all tastes, however. Tourist information offices can book rooms, or look for signs advertising *Zimmer frei* or *Fremdenzimmer*, or source rooms (and apartments) online at ⓦ www.bed-and-breakfast.de and www .bedandbreakfast.de.

One of the most notable developments in German accommodation in the past decade is the rise of **farmstays**. Beloved by city families as a rural escape, and often good bases for country pursuits such as walking or riding, these are classified either as Landurlaub (country holiday) – former farms or country houses with typical regional charm – or as Urlaub auf dem Bauernhof (farm holiday) which provide rooms on working farms and vintners. Many of the latter feature home-made produce for breakfast and, on occasion, evening meals – but you'll obviously need your own transport. Again, local tourist offices can recommend farmstays, or try farmstay organizations, all of which sell brochures or guidebooks.

Farmstay associations

Bauernhof & LandUrlaub Deutschland Haus der Land- und Ernährungswirtschaft, Claire-Waldoff-Str. 7, Berlin ☏030/31 90 42 20, ⊛www.bauernhofurlaub-deutschland.de.
DLG-Verlags Eschborner Landstr. 122, Frankfurt ☏06924/884 51, ⊛www.landtourismus.de.
Zentrale für den Landurlaub Maarstr. 96, Bonn ☏0228/96 30 20, ⊛www.bauernhofurlaub.com.

Youth hostels

Small wonder that the country which pioneered the youth hostel movement in 1912 retains a strong affinity to the concept. Over ninety years young, the German Youth Hostelling Association (Deutscher Jugendherbergswerk, or **DJH**) now has over 560 hostels throughout Germany to complement that first hostel, still going strong in Burg Altena in the Sauerland. This means you'll find a publicly funded DJH hostel in almost any town you roll into. The good news is that the majority have refurbished to provide modern accommodation and introduced contemporary facilities such as internet access. Most have also relaxed the institutional vibe, making them more welcoming for families – with en-suite rooms available and the lunchtime lock-out and 11pm curfew consigned to the past in city hostels. The bad news is that they can be insanely popular with school groups and are often located a bus ride from a town centre.

To stay at a hostel you must be a member of the Hostelling International association of your home country (see below). Non-members can buy a night's membership known as a Welcome Stamp for €3.10 – collect six stamps and you receive an International Guest Card for a year's reduced rates in hostels worldwide. The price of a dorm bed in Germany hovers around the €20 mark, with over-26s charged €3 extra; throughout the guide we have quoted the price for members under 26. The DJH website (⊛www.jugendherberge.de; available in English) acts as a portal for all hostels as well as regional websites. Around half of DJH hostels permit online booking.

Linen and breakfast are included in the price, and cheap half- or full-board is almost universally available; many hostels also provide packed lunches and a bistro. Creature comfort varies according to hostel category, which ranges from I (a functional bunk-down) to IV (comparative luxury). Opening hours also vary – while those in large cities are generally open 24/7, many close at 11pm. Reception times are generally morning and late afternoon only. Note, too, that unless otherwise confirmed reservations are held until 6pm; after that, a reserved room may be given to another guest. Guests are required to vacate rooms by 9am. Many hostels close for renovations between Christmas and New Year, sometimes even in January or February. A few remote members are only open for summer.

Youth hostel associations

Youth Hostel Association (YHA) England and Wales ☏0870 770 8868, ⊛www.yha.org.uk. Annual membership £15.95; 16–25s £9.95; family £22.95.
Scottish Youth Hostel Association ☏01786/891 400, ⊛www.syha.org.uk. Annual membership £8; under-16s free; over-60s £6; family £12.
Irish Youth Hostel Association Ireland ☏01/830 4555, ⊛www.irelandyha.org. Annual membership €20; under-18s free; family €40.
Hostelling International Northern Ireland ☏028/9032 4733, ⊛www.hini.org.uk.
Hostelling International–American Youth Hostels US ☏1-301/495-1240, ⊛www.hiusa .org. Annual membership $28; under-18s free; over 55 $18.
Hostelling International Canada ☏1-800/663-5777, ⊛www.hihostels.ca. Annual membership $35; under-18s free.
Australia Youth Hostels Association ☏02/9565 1699, ⊛www.yha.com.au. Annual membership $42; under-26s $32.
Youth Hostelling Association New Zealand ☏0800/278 299 or 03/379 9970, ⊛www.yha .co.nz. Annual membership $40; under-18s free.

Independent hostels

Few changes in German accommodation have benefited budget travellers as much as the rise of the independent hostel scene in the past decade. Unlike official DJH hostels, these backpacker-friendly hostels cater to independent travellers rather than groups – indeed, some refuse organized groups so as to preserve the communal vibe.

Independence also means generalizations are tricky. At a push, these hostels tend to be relaxed and friendly, with a young international clientele. Most are small in scale, often in converted houses or apartments in a city's nightlife district, and will typically provide a kitchen and laundry facilities, a communal TV lounge, internet access (or wi-fi) and perhaps a games room. Accommodation is in mixed dormitories, typically from four- to cheaper ten-bed, as well as in double or twin rooms, and a handful of singles. Some hostels operate single-sex dorms – washrooms are nearly always segregated. Bed linen is generally provided in the price of a bed – a few places charge a couple of euros – and a simple buffet breakfast is available for around €3–5.

Many hostels have noticeboards that advertise work and flyers of cheap activities – many also rent bikes. Staff are generally young, well-travelled and a wellspring of information on the local area. As appealing is that in the past few years some have morphed into outposts of quirky style at budget prices. The one negative to consider

is that city dorm rooms are not conducive to early nights, especially those in bar districts. Be aware, too, that the reception for smaller establishments tends to be open in the morning and late afternoon only.

At the last count, 44 independent hostels were listed under the **Backpacker Network** alliance (Ⓦwww.backpackernetwork.de). Its website provides links with Google maps, and sometimes photos and comments by former guests.

Camping

As a nation besotted with the outdoors, Germany will have erected a campsite fairly close to wherever you might like to pitch a tent. There are over 2500 sites nationwide, most sited beside lakes or in the bosom of some inspiring landscape. The good news is that most are above average by European standards: even the most basic will have a dedicated reception, often with a mini-shop, and offer full washing facilities, while high-end sites are more resorts than mere campsites, often with an outdoor pool, restaurants, a bar and a supermarket, and organized

---

Bin there, done that: recycling in Germany

Stay for a night in a hostel and the array of coloured bins in the kitchen reveals that Germany takes recycling seriously. The recycling industry turns over around €50 million annually and Germans, who have a long tradition of social consciousness, recycle more of their rubbish than most other European nations. Using the **Grüne Punkt** (Green Dot) icon that indicates material can be recycled, they now recycle up to seventy percent of some materials, including 41 percent of plastics, a figure only trumped by the Czech Republic according to a report in 2006. In Bavaria, only one percent of rubbish goes to landfill. Visitors are expected to do their bit – novices who place items in the wrong container will be quietly reprimanded.

Bins – of which there are up to five – are colour-coded. One, usually green or blue, is for **paper** (Papier) and cardboard, including waxed cartons; boxes should be flattened and emptied of any plastic wrappers. **Plastic** goes into the yellow bin, along with milk cartons, cans, polystyrene and **aluminium** (marked with the Green Dot icon of two interlocking arrows). Straightforward enough, so long as you don't stuff different materials inside each other; this stuff gets sorted by hand, so a plastic cup hidden inside a tin is strictly verboten. There's no need to rinse items but most Germans empty cans and plastics. **Glass** is usually collected in hostels to be taken to bottle banks, commonly in supermarket car parks. However, most bottles – glass and plastic – usually have a deposit (Pfand) on them of around €0.30–0.50 per item to be cashed at specified re-collection centres, most conveniently supermarkets. It's standard practice to return items in bulk rather than singly. **Biodegradables** – including coffee grounds and teabags – go in another bin, usually brown, after which there's hardly anything left over. What is goes in the one bin that takes genuine Müll (rubbish) – grey or black and usually empty.

activities for the kiddies. The bad news is that German campsites can be seriously uptight, often sterile places with row after tidy row of caravans and motorhomes sprouting a satellite TV antenna.

Most sites are open from April to October only, although some operate year-round, especially those in winter ski resorts. **Prices**, which vary according to the facilities, are by pitch and the number of people plus a car if you have one. Some charge a euro or two for showers – you may have to buy tokens from reception – and electricity, if required. The annual Camping Card (€18) of the European Federation of Campingsite Organizations (EFCO; www.campingeurope.com) provides 25 percent discounts.

The website of the Federal Association of German Campsites (BVCD; www.bvcd .de) has a searchable database of 1300 sites organized by region, and publishes a highly condensed guidebook of sites (€9.80) that can be ordered through its website. Online database Cris 24 (www.cris24.com), with a similar number, permits reservations or you'll find guidebooks in bookshops; that of national auto association the ADAC, *ADAC Camping-Caravaning-Führer*, is reliable. Free camping is illegal on environmental grounds.

Finally a note about **campervanning**, a mode of holiday-making dear to German hearts. As well as campsites, most towns and cities will provide a *Wohnmobil Parkplatz* (motorhome car park) for overnight stays; look for signs of a motorhome as you enter a town. These vary from free wasteground car parks at the town outskirts to reserved areas with drinking water and waste disposal. The latter charge around €10 a night – still cheaper than a hostel for a night and one which often puts you in the centre of a city.

Food and drink

Though neither as obsessive as the Italians nor as fussy as the French, Germans see eating as a serious business nevertheless. Consequently standards are high. You'll rarely find cause to criticize the quality in Germany even if you don't share a taste for its national cuisine. For most outsiders that means a taste of tradition – Bratwurst (grilled sausage), assorted cuts of pork and, of course, Sauerkraut. All present and munched daily, but to brand German cooking as its time-honoured dishes only is to overlook a foodie revolution that has rippled across the country over the last decade or so.

To complement the impressive range of regional cuisines from granny's cookbook, the nation's chefs have created a brand of light, modern cooking infused with international flavours. The Michelin guide reviewers now rave about the contemporary **Neue Deutsche Küche** (New German Cuisine) of the nation's superstar chefs as much as they do the gourmet *Bratwurst* produced in Bavaria's *Wurstküchen* (sausage kitchens). And menus throughout the country now show a taste for modern Mediterranean cooking as Germans look to reduce the calorie and cholesterol counts. Even the old oompah-and-*Schnitzel* joints have healthy salads these days. Indeed, even if not quite a gourmand's paradise, modern German cuisine is one of the great surprises of culinary Europe. Perhaps as importantly, the modern urban brasserie in Germany arguably represents better value than its French equivalent. On top of this, Germany keeps an excellent cellar of wine and spirits. And its beer should need no introduction.

Germany's share of **ethnic restaurants** tends to be those of its large immigrant groups – Italian, Greek and Turkish, with the ubiquitous Chinese thrown in and, in cities, the occasional Thai and sushi joint. Indian cuisine is less well represented, and often fairly mild.

Breakfast

It's rare for a hotel – or even a hostel come to that – not to provide **breakfast** (*Frühstuck*), generally in the price of your accommodation or for around €8–15 (around €5 in hostels). This usually proves excellent value for money, especially in the mid- and upper ends of the market. Most places allow you to browse at leisure from a Scandinavian-style *smorgasbørd* of mueslis and cereals, yoghurt, hard-boiled eggs, jams, marmalade and honey, as well as cheese and cold meats, usually ham and salami. Alongside this will be a regional assortment of the nation's three hundred varieties of bread – from simple crusty white rolls or brown rolls encrusted with sunflower or poppy seeds to damp, heavy *Schwarzbrot* (black bread), the gourmet's choice – the most famous is rye *Pumpernickel*. Watery orange juice aside, breakfast is usually washed down with coffee – always fresh and usually weaker than that of France and Italy – although you will also be offered tea, usually *Schwarz Tee* (black), or fruit teas.

Cafés also provide excellent breakfasts – for many younger Germans a café brunch is a weekend institution – though it's easy to spend €12–15 by the time you add in juice and coffee. A better budget option is to grab a coffee and sandwich at a bakery such as ubiquitous chain *Kamps* and use the stand-up counter (known as the *Stehcafé*) to eat it in the shop. These open from around 7am and you'll breakfast well for around €6.

Snacks and street food

Germany is a nation that invented fast food: Hamburg's meat rissoles became the hamburger, its sausages in bread were exported as the hot dog. The difference with German snacks is their high quality, which makes bites on the go a mini-meal rather than a guilty filler. Most quick snacks are served at **Imbiss** stands, invariably located at transport hubs and market squares, where you eat standing. The standard fare is a range of sausages plus hamburgers and occasionally meatballs or perhaps a greasy *Schnitzel*. Some *Imbiss* stalls specialize in spit-roast chicken, which typically comes as a half-bird (*Halbes Hähnchen*) at low prices. Mustard (*Senf*) comes free, ketchup and mayonnaise may cost a few euro extra. Larger towns and cities often have market stalls in a dedicated Markthalle, with a wide range of delicatessens under one roof, some rather upmarket and often with a few international cuisines. On the coast, fish replaces the traditional meat-fare in *Imbiss* stalls – often smoked and almost always served by the harbour, fresh fish comes in sandwiches (*Fischbrötchen*). Nationwide fish chain *Nordsee* prepares fast food alongside cheap meals.

In bakeries, there'll often be a corner to sit or else stand, known as a *Stehcafé*. Incidentally, German pretzels, known as *Brezeln* and covered in salt crystals, are a far superior snack to their American counterparts.

You'll find standard Italian and Asian takeaways everywhere, and also Turkish. It's no surprise that a country fond of fast food has embraced the kebabs of a large Turkish community; indeed, the idea of a kebab with salad in pitta bread is a German invention. Known as *Gyros* or *Döner*, these are generally of grilled lamb, sometimes chicken. British visitors will be pleasantly surprised.

Finally, a special word about *Kaffee und Kuchen* (coffee and cakes), a traditional Germanic treat equivalent to English tea. It is observed religiously by an older generation at late afternoon, and is best taken in an old-fashioned café. Most prepare fresh home-made gateaux piled with quantities of cream and chocolate to make dieters weep.

Traditional restaurants and meals

The tradition of lunch (*Mittagessen*) as the main meal of the day has been quashed by the pressure of modern work practices. Like most North Europeans, Germans are now as likely to grab a sandwich or snack and save the main meal until dinner (*Abendessen*). Nevertheless, cooked food (*warme Küche*) is served throughout the day except in more upmarket restaurants, which pause between meals, and on Ruhetag, when the establishment is closed; Sunday or Monday is a favourite.

The first choice for honest traditional food should be a **Gaststätte** or **Brauhaus**. Traditional and convivial, these are roughly equivalent to the British pub, so are relaxed venues in which to drink as well as eat, many providing a beer garden in summer. The latter (literally, "brew house") also means fresh beers brewed in-house. The cuisine is almost always **gutbürgerlich Küche** – unpretentious home-cooking that's filling, tasty and generally good value. Similar but slightly more upmarket is the **Ratskeller**, a German institution in the often-historic cellars of the town hall. These are reliable and strong on regional specialities if a little stuffy at times. Don't be surprised if you are asked to share a table in either, nor if your credit card is met with a dismissive shrug – most small *Gaststätten* only accept cash. German restaurants serve anything from posh traditional food, to a lighter take on German cuisine, often with a polyglot of Mediterranean accents, to sophisticated gourmet addresses serving exquisite *Neue Deutsche Küche*, a sort of German Nouvelle Cuisine. Wherever you go, the **menu** (*Speisekarte*) will be displayed outside.

Notwithstanding regional variations (see below), traditional starters (*Vorspeise*) are soups of the thin variety, or pâté. Things get more interesting for the main course (*Hauptgericht*), usually meat (*Fleisch* – no flinch from the truth in Germany) with one or two vegetable dishes and sometimes a side salad. As a rule of thumb, the meat in question will be some part of a pig. Every possible cut, plus knuckles and offal is served in a baffling variety of ways; ubiquitous German pork dishes are breaded fillet **Schnitzel**, **Schweinbraten** (roast pork), **Schweinhaxe**, a huge crispy knuckle which could have graced a medieval banqueting table, and **Eisbein**, salted knuckle or shin. And, of course, pork comes as sausages (**Würste**) – grilled, fried, boiled and baked, all are excellent (see box opposite). The standard beef dish tweaked with regional variations is **Sauerbraten** (roast and marinated in vinegar). **Game** (*Wild*), typically venison (*Hirsch*) or wild boar (*Wildschwein*), occasionally hare (*Hase*), and veal (*Kalb*), also provide respite from the pork-fest.

Lamb (*Lamm*) sometimes gets a look in, and chicken (*Hähnchen*) rarely. Except on the coast, **fish** is almost exclusively freshwater, typically salmon (*Lachs*), trout (*Forelle*) and *Zander* (a meaty pike-perch).

Vegetable side-dishes will nearly always feature some form of potato (*Kartoffel*), often the pub-favourite fry-up *Bratkartoffeln*, sometimes jacket potatoes (*Ofenkartoffeln*) or in traditional places stodgy potato dumplings (*Klösse* or *Knödel*). And, of course, there's **Sauerkraut**. The classic side-dish of green cabbage pickled in white-wine vinegar is an acquired taste – many outsiders find red-cabbage variety *Rotkohl* more palatable, especially as apple-spiced *Apfelrotkohl*. Worth a special mention is **asparagus** (*Spargel*), which is of the white variety and comes into season from April to late June to feature on dedicated menus throughout the land.

Desserts (*Nachspeise*) are usually light, often ice cream or fruit salad. The nation that brought the world Black Forest Gateau (*Schwarzwälder Kirschtorte*) tends to reserve cakes for late-afternoon *Kaffee und Kuchen* (see p.43).

Regional dishes

What comes as a surprise for most visitors resigned to a pork-and-spuds diet is the tremendous variety of regional cuisines.

Fresh seafood is always worth investigating on the **north coastal regions**: *Matjes* (herring) and white *Rotbarsch* like whiting are common. Hamburg vies with Berlin for the title of gourmet capital of Germany, and is arguably more cosmopolitan in its range of restaurants. Nevertheless, you'll still find traditional sailor's dish *Labskaus*, a filling mash of beef, pork, salted herring, potato, beetroot and gherkin, topped with a fried egg. *Aalsuppe*, a piquant eel and vegetable soup with fruits such as pear and prunes, is another one for adventurous diners. More conservative tastes will prefer *Rotes Gruz*, a dessert of red berries, and keep an eye open for *Pharisäer*, coffee with a swig of rum and topped with cream. You'll also find widespread use of *Nordseekrabben*, tiny North Sea shrimps.

Further south, lamb from the heather-clad plains of the **Lüneburg Heath** is excellent, while a traditional dish in **Lower Saxony** and

For better or Wurst: a primer on the German sausage

Few foods are as iconic of their home country as the German sausage (**Wurst**). Part of the national cuisine since the Middle Ages, sausages are taken seriously in their home nation. Yes, you'll find Germans guzzling them down with a dollop of mustard as fast food – a tradition exported by nineteenth-century émigrés to give the world the hot dog – but Michelin critics also list *Wurst* kitchens in Bavaria. All *Wurst* feature pork (and sometimes beef or veal), spices and peppercorns. What makes each distinctive are the herbs and spices. Aficionados say there are around a thousand regional varieties to sample. Good luck.

Blutwurst "Blood sausage" – black pudding. Eaten sliced and cold or fried.

Bockwurst A popular variety that is more fine veal than fine pork. Resembles a chubby frankfurter and is heated in liquid. Traditionally served with *Bock* beer in spring.

Bratwurst The common or garden sausage served countrywide. Varies by region – Bavaria's are finger-sized, Thuringia's are long and thin, for example – but usually made of finely minced pork and marjoram.

Braunschweiger Smoked liver sausage (*Leberwurst*) enriched with eggs and milk, so it is spreadable.

Currywurst A Berlin icon invented, they say, in 1949 by a bored *Imbiss* stall-holder. Basically a *Wiener* sliced, smothered in ketchup, then dusted with curry powder.

Frankfurter Not the same as the American variety, this contains fine, lean pork with a little salted bacon. Smoked then reheated in liquid.

Knockwurst (or **Knackwurst**). Short, plump, smoked sausage of finely minced lean pork, beef, spices and garlic. Typically poached or grilled then served with *Sauerkraut*.

Thüringer Rotwurst Speciality low-fat black sausage from Thuringia afforded protected geographical status under EU law.

Weisswurst Munich's "White sausage", so called for its being made of veal and fresh bacon. Flavoured with parsley, mace and cardamom, it is traditionally prepared before breakfast and eaten before lunch.

Wienerwurst Thought to be the source of the American Frankfurter. Pork and beef flavoured with coriander and garlic, grilled or fried.

Bremen is *Grünkohl mit Pinkel*, curly kale with spicy sausage.

North Rhine-Westphalia is known for smoked hams and dishes such as *Himmel und Erde* (literally "heaven and earth"), a gutsy casserole of puréed apple, onion and potato with black sausage, or winter-warmer *Dicke Bohnen*, a fava bean stew cooked with a splash of vinegar.

South of here, in the **Rhineland-Palatinate**, look for *Saumagen*, pig's stomach stuffed with cabbage like a German haggis. And around **Frankfurt** there's the marvellously named *Handkäse mit Musik*, cheese with onions in a spicy vinaigrette – the "music" in question refers to its effects on digestive systems. **Baden-Württemberg**, also known as **Swabia**, in southwest Germany boasts a

unique pasta-style cuisine – typically doughy *Spätzle* noodles coated in cheese or eaten pure as a side dish, and *Maultaschen*, like over-sized ravioli stuffed with meat, spinach, eggs or herbs. Beef, potato and *Spätzle* stew, *Gaisburger Marsch*, is another favourite. In the **Black Forest**, smoked hams are always worth tasting, trout is excellent and there is, of course, *Schwarzwälder Kirschtorte*, which bears no relation to the stodgy Black Forest Gateaux dolloped onto foreign plates in the 1970s.

Bavaria, the Land of beerhall-and-lederhosen cliché, comes good with a no-nonsense pig-fest, typically great hunks of *Schweinhaxe* (roast knuckle) and *Rippchen* (roast ribs). This is also the sausage capital of Germany: short and thin, those of Nürnberg and Regensburg are acclaimed by gourmets, though Munich acclaims its veal *Weisswurst* as far finer. Franconia in north Bavaria is renowned for carp. **Thruringians** will tell you the state's charcoal-grilled *Rostbratwurst* (grilled sausage) is better than anything produced in Bavaria, made to a recipe that dates from 1404.

Classics from **Saxony** include marinated braised beef (*Sauerbraten*), *Quarkkeulchen* (sweetened potato pancakes) and *Eierschecke* – similar to cheesecake. Dresden is renowned for *Christstollen*, a local Christmas cake.

And finally to **Berlin**, which has the full glut of modern restaurants of a capital city. By common consent, traditional Prussian cuisine is solid rather than exciting – perhaps the most iconic taste of Berlin is the *Currywurst* (see box, p.45).

Vegetarians

Not too long ago, Germany was almost a no-go zone for vegetarians. Innocuous-sounding tomato soups would come flecked with bacon, green salads would hide slivers of ham. No more. While still a nation fond of its meat, Germany has modern European attitudes to vegetarianism – indeed, many large towns will have a vegetarian restaurant. Even if not, salads are always meat-free unless stated, the ubiquity of Italian cuisine means vegetarian pasta dishes abound, and even traditional *Schnitzel* joints will list at least one vegetarian dish on the menu if they don't have a dedicated menu – short, admittedly, but there. Bear in mind, too, that even meat-obsessed Bavaria includes traditional German vegetarian options such as filling soups and potato dumplings as well as dedicated asparagus menus for much of the summer. Otherwise, modern bistros and cafés will always provide something tasty and wholesome, and more upmarket Turkish takeaways often provide cheap veggie dishes alongside the ubiquitous kebabs.

Drink

The standard beverage is **coffee**, always fresh and generally weaker than its counterparts from France or Italy unless you ask for an espresso. All the usual lattes and cappuccinos are on offer. **Tea** is most popular in the northern Länder of Lower Saxony, Bremen and Schleswig-Holstein where the Dutch influence is most pronounced. **Mineral water** (*Mineralwasser*) usually comes sparkling (*mit Gas*), although the muscle of corporates such as Evian and Volvic has pushed still water (*stilles*) onto the shelves.

Beer

And so to **beer**. Supped by all, *Bier* is not just the national drink but an integral part of German life, with distinct regional accents and seasonal quirks. Whether conglomerate or small **Hausbrauerei** (a brewery-cum-*Gaststätte*), 1200-plus brewers producing over 5000 brews adhere voluntarily to the 1516 **Reinheitsgebot**, a purity law that specifies that only barley, hops, water and yeast can be used for fermentation, perhaps why delicious chemical-free brews slip down dangerously easily – and won't give you a hangover, locals say. (Not true, incidentally, but the morning after is noticeably less brutal.) Beer comes in volumes of between 0.2 litres and 0.5 litres, either as draught (*vom Fass*) or in the bottle (*Flasche*).

Pils is the most familiar beer for visitors, golden in colour and with a hoppy, refreshing flavour. Many will also know **Export**, stronger than *Pils* and named because its high alcohol kept the beer fresh during travel. It is dry with a hint of sweetness, although not as sweet as **Helles**, a generic term for light brews. **Dunkel** is the generic name for dark beers, which are rich in malt and full-bodied, though not as heavy as catch-all name **Schwarzbier** (black beer). Its opposite is **Weissbier** (white beer, also *Weisse* or *Weissen*), a southern favourite now available country-wide. Brewed from wheat, it is pale, cloudy and tastes like fresh hay; *Hefeweissen* has a stronger kick of yeast and *Kristal-Weissen* is clearer with more fizz. In Berlin it comes with lactic acid as low-alcohol **Berliner Weisse**, often drunk *mit Grün* (with green woodruff syrup) and *mit Schuss* (raspberry syrup). Light or dark, **Bock** beers should be treated with respect because of a 6.5–7 percent alcohol content, which makes super-strength festival brew **Doppelbock** positively dangerous.

German wine regions

Ahr Small wine valley south of Bonn that specializes in reds – has a reputation for a light, sometimes elegant, *Spätburgunder*.

Baden Spread over a huge area from Heidelberg to the border and across to the Bodensee. Specializes in dry wines: *Spätburgunder*, Riesling and *Gewürztraminer*.

Franconia (Franken). Main valley and around. Grows dry wines as distinctive as the area's round-bellied *Bocksbeutel* bottles. Good *Silvaner*.

Hessiche Bergstrasse North of Heidelberg and west Germany's smallest area. Small producers, and reliable Riesling.

Mittelrehein More famous for scenery, the Middle Rhine grows a flinty underrated Riesling around the villages of Boppard and Bacharach.

Mosel–Saar–Ruwer Germany's most acclaimed – and exported – region, with a subtly elegant Riesling grown on the Mosel's sun-soaked slopes and a brilliant one in the Saar tributary. Also known for exciting new producers who keep the old hands sharp.

Nahe Rhine tributary whose fresh, well-balanced Riesling doesn't get the attention it deserves.

Palatinate (Pfalz). The growing region formerly known as Rheinpfalz south of Rheinhessen. A warm climate and fully ripe grapes produce classic, rich wines – the dry Riesling is increasingly well made.

Rheingau West of Wiesbaden, this is the best area of the Rhine valley, with a classic if rather old-fashioned Riesling and good reds.

Rheinhessen Riesling is the pick of this huge region between Mainz and Worms, its reputation on the up nationally.

Saale-Unstrut Riesling and *Gewürztraminer* whites, *Silvaner* and a Cistercian-rooted *Portugieser* red, plus sparkling *Sekt* wines at the river confluence by Naumberg, west of Leipzig.

Saxony (Sachsen). Small region centred on Meissen west of Dresden. Best known for a characterful Muscat-style *Müller-Thurgau*.

Württemberg Large and underrated area of small producers around Stuttgart. Go for reds – *Trollinger* and *Lemberger* – especially in the Neckar valley.

Lemonade shandy is known as **Radler** or **Alsterwasser** in Hamburg.

Local specialities abound. Dortmund, Germany's beer capital in terms of volume, is renowned for its Export; Düsseldorf brews a malty **Alt** beer, served with fruit in summer as *Altbierbowle*; and Cologne is proud of its light, refreshing **Kölsch** beer, routinely dismissed elsewhere as a glorified shandy, not helped by the small measures served in narrow *Stangen* glasses. Bavaria, the spiritual home of German beer and the beer garden, produces all the usuals plus sweet **Malzbier** (malt beer), like stout; Munich specials are *Märzenbier*, a powerful brew fermented in March for September knees-up, the Oktoberfest, and **Hofbräu**, formerly supped only by the royal court. Bamberg's smoky *Rauchbier* is another state special.

Wine

Such is the German love of beer it would possible to overlook its wines. The memory of sickly *Liebfraumilch* once exported to Britain may play its part. But in recent years Germany's better wines are being exported, prompting foreign wine-buffs to wax about a renaissance in German wine-making. Quite simply, German wines of the past decade have been superlatively good, aided by global warming and a return to Riesling rather than exotic crossbreeds. Of the thirteen areas in which wine is produced, most in the southwest, the most celebrated are those of the Rhine and Mosel valleys (see box above). Most areas produce wines that are *trocken* (dry) or *halbtrocken* (medium), though there are some *lieblich* (sweet) wines.

Another reason non-Germans may have steered away from German wine is that the classification system seems absurdly over-complicated alongside the classic French AOC standard. Basic plonk is sweetish **Tafelwein**, a better choice is **Landwein**, a dry, German *vin de pays*. By the **Qualitätswein** level you're in the good stuff, either *Qualitätswein bestimmter* Anbaugebiete (Qba) from defined regions or *Qualitätswein mit Prädiket* from specific vineyards. Of the latter, **Kabinett** wines are reserve wines – unsugared dry wines of natural personality and occasionally sublime – while **Spätlese** are produced from late-harvested grapes to produce fuller, usually dry flavours. **Auslese** wines are a step up in strength and sweetness, their intensity often prompting comparisons with honey. **Eiswein**, sharp with a concentrated often sweet flavour, is made from grapes harvested after being frozen. Sweeter still are rare **Beerenauslese**, produced from exceptionally ripe grapes.

Three-quarters of German wines are white (*Weisswein*), typically Rieslings, which comprise over a fifth of total wine output and at their best are sensational – light and elegant, often almost floral. *Silvaner* wines have more body, while *Gewürztraminers* are intense and highly aromatic in flavour. The German *Grauburgunder* is better known in English as Pinot Gris. Notable **reds** (*Rotwein*) are *Spätburgunder*, a German Pinot Noir, rich in colour, velvety in taste, and *Trollinger*, a light, fresh wine that's delicious in summer. **Rosé** (*Roséwein*) is less common. A notable addition to the cellar is Frankfurt's **Apfelwein** – cider – and at Christmas everywhere *Glühwein* (hot mulled wine, literally "glow wine"). More detail on German wines is published online at ⓦwww.germanwine.de.

Spirits

High-proof **Schnapps** spirits come in a range of regional flavours which rival that of beer: common varieties include *Kirschwasser* (cherry schnapps), served with ham in the Black Forest, and in Berlin a *Doppelkorn* (corn schnapps), traditionally tossed off with a knuckle of pork. Whether digestif, aperitif or simply a short, schnapps is served in 2cl measures and locals delight in claiming it is medicinal, an idea handed down over a millennium since monks began distillation of fruits and herbs.

The media

The foreigner's image of Germany is of a land of books, a serious country of deep thought and highbrow ideas. Certainly 95,000 new books are published each year in Germany and nothing else in the world comes close to the immense annual Frankfurt Book Fair. Yet Germany also has dynamic printed, television and radio sectors. It's also relatively easy to find British and US newspapers in large German towns, and in the cities larger newsagents carry many of the London-printed editions at lunchtime on the same day. The best place to look for foreign media is at newsagents in the main train station – those in cities also carry a small stock of international magazines.

Newspapers and magazines

The German press is characterized by the number of titles. At the national level, the daily newspaper market is dominated by a small number of publishers. Largest, with 24 percent of the market, is Axel Springer group, which prints both heavyweight newspapers and the "boulevard press" as Germany calls tabloids. The press is strongest at regional level, although many of the city-produced dailies are distributed nationwide. Germany's best-seller on the streets is sensationalist tabloid *BILD* (🌐www.bild.de), which shifts four million units daily. Of the dailies conservative *Frankfurter Allgemeine Zeitung* (🌐www.faz.net) enjoys considerable prestige, presumably thanks to its weighty opinions and business focus rather than dry content – an English-language version is included as a supplement in every issue of the *International Herald Tribune* – and Berlin-produced *Die Welt* (🌐www.welt.de) has a great influence on public opinion. At the other end of the political spectrum is the left-of-centre *Tageszeitung*, known as *"Taz"* (🌐www.taz.de) – not so hot on solid news, but with good in-depth articles on politics and ecology. It has the added advantage of being an easier read for non-native German speakers. Other nationwide papers include Munich's *Süddeutsche Zeitung* (🌐www.sueddeutsche.de) and *Frankfurter Rundschau* (🌐www.fr-online.de). The big name in financial reporting, alongside *Frankfurter Allgemeine Zeitung*, is Hamburg-based *Financial Times Deutschland* (🌐www.ftd.de) printed on the brand's trademark pink paper. Incidentally, Berlin-produced *The Local* (🌐www.thelocal.de) provides German news in English but is tricky to find even in its home Berlin – good online edition, though, with regional sections.

The German magazine sector is extremely buoyant, with some 870 magazines and 1100 specialized periodicals on the market, with weekly news magazines modelled on American *Time* magazine very popular. The sector is monopolized by the outstanding *Der Spiegel* (🌐www.spiegel.de), known for its investigative journalism and probably the most influential political publication in Germany. It also has an excellent English-language website. In a similar vein is Hamburg-based left-wing weekly *Die Zeit* (🌐www.zeit.de). Best seen as a weekly newspaper that focuses on analysis and background information, it appears every Thursday and, while left-wing in stance, includes a number of independently written reports on a variety of subjects.

Television and radio

While Länder are responsible for public broadcasting within each state, all contribute programmes for the nationwide principal TV channels "Das Erste" – run by ARD (Arbeitsgemeinschaft der Rundfunkanstalten Deutschlands; 🌐www.ard.de) – and ZDF (Zweites Deutsches Fernsehen; 🌐www.zdf.de) somewhat approximate BBC channels or a down market PBS. There is an ongoing digitization of terrestrial TV – both ARD and ZDF offer a range of free digital channels.

Otherwise major commercial channels dominate, foremost among them Sat, RTL and VOX. All channels seem to exist on a forced diet of US reruns clumsily dubbed into German. Germany has an above-average percentage of cable households – 53 percent. With cable TV, available in larger hotels, you'll be able to pick up the locally available cable channels, with over twenty to choose from, including MTV, BBC World, and the ubiquitous CNN.

Radio in Germany is very much a regional affair. According to the various broadcasting laws of the various states, some Länder prefer a variety of commercial radio stations, others opt for diverse programming within a limited number of stations. Spin a dial and you'll find some decent dance music, American rock and the occasional rap show (mainly late at night) alongside classical, cheese and soft rock. The only nationwide English-speaking radio station is the BBC World Service (90.2FM). British Forces station BFBS (🌐www.ssvc.com/bfbs) pumps out programming modelled on BBC radio in localized areas – principally western Lower Saxony and Westphalia. BFBS has chart hits and classics plus hourly news, BFBS 2 has more chat plus BBC news programmes from Radio 4 and sport from BBC Radio Five Live. Frequencies vary by area – check the website or scan from (roughly) 95FM to 106FM.

Festivals

Germans like their festivals. From city to village, wherever there are people there'll usually be a festival of some kind, whether a major event for thousands that programmes international artists or just a summer fair. The diversity is astounding – high-quality classical music and theatre events, wine festivals, unbridled parties and atmospheric Christmas markets. Notwithstanding the latter, most are staged from May to August, when you're almost sure to roll into a good-humoured town centre crammed with stalls and stages, with much food and beer being consumed by all. On top of local secular events, Germany observes a large number of pagan and religious festivals in its calendar.

National tourism website ⓦwww.germany -tourism.de has a searchable database of events. See individual town accounts in the Guide for more information of local events.

January and February

Karneval (also known as Fasching or Fastnet). Seven weeks before Easter. Pagan-rooted pre-Lent speciality of the Rhineland and Bavaria, where it's known as Fasching. Warm-up events throughout late January climax in late February (or early March) with costumed parades and considerable revelry. Cologne has the most celebrated Karneval, followed by Düsseldorf and Mainz, or Munich's more jolly Fasching. Black Forest events are more traditional, the unique event in Rottweil, Baden-Württemberg, almost pagan.

March and April

Easter Late March or early April. Sacred pomp throughout Catholic Germany – especially impressive in Bavaria.
Walpurgisnacht April 30, Harz. Celebration of the witches' sabbath with costumed parades and music throughout the Harz area.

May

Hafengeburtstag Hamburg, weekend closest to May 7. Tall ships and flotilla parades in world's largest harbour festival. ⓦwww .hafengeburtstag.de.
Passionsspiele Oberammergau, May–Sept. Once-a-decade passion play by locals of a Bavarian village, celebrated nationwide. Next is 2010. ⓦwww.passionsspiele2010.de.
Karneval der Kulturen Berlin, last weekend in May. Berlin celebrates its ethnic diversity in a

"Carnival of Cultures" – expect around 1.5 million people. ⓦwww.karneval-berlin.de.
Rhein im Flammen "Rhine in Flames". May–Sept, Rhineland. Start of the firework spectaculars along the Rhine from Bonn to Bingen; culminates in August in Koblenz. ⓦwww.rhein-in-flammen.de.
Leipziger Honky Tonk Saturday, usually mid-May, Leipzig. In theory a music festival in a hundred boozers, actually Europe's largest pub crawl.
Africa Festival End of May, Würzburg. Europe's largest celebration of African culture: dance, music and parades. ⓦwww.africafestival.org.

June

Christopher Street Day June–July, nationwide. Parades and parties for gay pride events, over thirty years young – largest events in Berlin, Munich and Cologne. ⓦwww.csd-deutschland.de.
Wave-Gotik-Treffen Whitsun (first weekend in June or last in May), Leipzig. Around 25,000 Goths muster for the world's largest doom-fest. ⓦwww .wave-gotik-treffen.de.
Bachfest Mid-June, Leipzig. Week-long celebration of the great composer in the city where he produced his finest works. ⓦwww.bach-leipzig.de.
Kieler Woche Last week in June, Kiel. Long-standing fixture on the international sailing circuit: races, parades and parties. ⓦwww.kieler-woche.de.

July

Schützenfeste Early July, Hannover. Biggest and best of the Marksmen festivals in Lower Saxony and the Rhineland area. ⓦwww.schuetzenfest -hannover.de.
Love Parade Saturday mid-July, North Rhine-Westphalia. Not quite the anarchic event it was of old and shifted from Berlin to the Ruhr – Essen in 2007, and Dortmund in 2008 – due to bureaucratic

reluctance. The next parties (2009–11) will be in Bochum, Gelsenkirchen and Duisburg, after which it may move back to Berlin. Ⓦ www.loveparade.de.

Kinderzeche Mid-July, Dinkelsbühl. Celebrated children's folklore pageant that re-enacts the town's capitulation to a Swedish siege in the Thirty Years' War. Ⓦ www.kinderzeche.de.

August

Bayreuth Festspiele late July–Aug, Bayreuth. Prestigious Wagnerian opera spectacular in the composer's Festspielhaus. Buy tickets as far in advance as possible. Ⓦ www.bayreuther -festspiele.de.

Weinfeste late Aug–Sept, Rhine–Mosel area. Traditionally a celebration of the annual grape harvest, in fact an excuse for a knees-up. Three of the best are in Rudesheim, Mainz and Dürkheimer, which cites its mid-Sept Wurstmarkt as the biggest wine bash in the world.

Gäubodenfest Mid-Aug, Straubing. Hugely popular Bavarian folk jamboree – folk displays, beer, music, funfairs and more beer. Ⓦ www.volksfest -straubing.de.

September and October

Canstatter Volksfest Late Sept–Oct, Stuttgart. Two weeks of oompah bands in traditional costume and fairground attractions in the world's second-largest beer festival; a less touristy alternative to the Oktoberfest.

Oktoberfest Mid-Sept to Oct, Munich. Perhaps the most epic beer-swill on the planet, its fame drawing legions of foreigners among the six million drinkers who descend on the city – six million litres of beer are drunk and over a hundred ox are grilled during it. Ⓦ www.oktoberfest.de.

November

Martinsfest Nov 10–11, north Baden and Rhineland. Festival to honour jovial fourth-century St Martin; marked by a goose lunch on the day and, in the Upper Rhine, preceded by evening children's lantern processions.

December

Christmas markets (Weihnachtsmarkt or Christkindelsmarkt), nationwide. Traditional homespun Germany at its most charming – superb crafts and food stalls, carols and gallons of *Glühwein*. Celebrated markets are in Lübeck, Nürnburg and Augsburg.

Sports and outdoor activities

From the soupy mud-flats of the North Sea to the Alps in southern Bavaria there's a lot to enjoy in Germany's great outdoors. And such is the variety of the country's landscapes you can participate in a huge array of activities – there's even a hardcore crew of dedicated German surfers. For more on these, and Germany's national parks, see the "Great outdoors" colour section. However, the most popular activity of all – even if only followed from a bar stool – is football. Matches of the Bundesliga are cheaper than for the UK's Premier League and attract a passionate following.

Football

Without question the number-one spectator sport in Germany, ever since *Fussball* was imported by an English expat to Dresden in 1874. The national team lifted the 1954 World Cup before Germany even had a professional national league. Fast-forward a few decades and the team cemented its reputation for invincibility with a style that emphasized hard work and commitment over individual flair. Not only has Germany won three World Cups and three European championships, it has not lost a penalty shoot-out since 1976, as millions of England fans rue.

Club matches of the **Bundesliga** (Ⓦwww .bundesliga.de, in English), the German premier league founded in 1963, can be something of a disappointment after such a build-up – many of the most talented homegrown players are lured abroad to leagues in England and Italy. Nevertheless, a match of the 18-strong league is a must for any football fan worth the name, not least because facilities in club stadiums are superb after they were renovated to host the Euro 2006 tournament. The most successful club is Bayern Munich, a regular fixture in the European Champions League with a record twenty league cups in its trophy cabinet. Other big names include Borussia Mönchengladbach, with five titles, Borussia Dortmund, whose 83,000 capacity crowd – the largest in Europe – put up with occasional moody performances, Werder Bremen, and Hamburger SV, the only team never to have been relegated.

The league runs from mid-August to the end of May, and tickets for games, most played on Saturday, can be bought at stadium gates on matchday or at ticket shops – often a dedicated fan shop – in the preceding week for all but the biggest games. The league website lists fixtures, that of the German Tourist Board in the UK, Ⓦwww.germany-tourism.co.uk, provides contacts for each ground. Expect to pay from €10–15 for the cheapest seats and up to €50 for the best. Some fans may be fairly lumpen – with much boozed-up bellowing of club anthems – but matches are generally non-threatening affairs.

Hiking and walking

Germany has an abundance of scenic walks and long-distance hikes, and no matter where you go there'll be a well-marked trail or pleasant short stroll. In the past decade Germany has developed a taste for so-called **Nordic Walking**, a fitness pursuit whose participants stride purposefully with ski poles.

Popular areas include the Saarland, the Harz, the Black Forest, the Bavarian Alps, Saxon Switzerland and the Thuringian Forest. The latter two are home respectively to arguably Germany's most scenic long-distance walk, the 112km **Malerweg**, and its most popular, the **Rennsteig** (168km). Details are in relevant chapters. A useful source of walking information is Wanderbares Deutschland (Ⓦwww.wanderbares -deutschland.de), a marketing body whose German-language website provides details of walks nationwide, including information of trail lengths and marks, plus links to their websites where relevant. The good news is that along many of these you'll find hotels and inns that provide specialized accommodation for hikers. The bad is that many paths are through thick pine forest, so that views can be limited. Kompass publishes hiking maps of popular walking areas (see p.59). Bookshops stock any number of walking guides (*Wanderführer*).

Cycling

Quite simply a joy. Over two hundred long-distance cycle routes across the country provide 42,000km of excellent touring. Dedicated cycle-paths off the main road typically follow river valleys – the classic for any saddle-junkie is the **Elberadweg** (Elbe Cycle Route; Ⓦwww.elberadweg.de), which follows the river for 860km as it slices northwest from Schöna in Saxon Switzerland to Cuxhaven on the North Sea. However, there is an abundance of marked cross-country routes to choose from – pootling through the little-known water-world of the Mecklenburg Lakes Cycle Route, for example, or bowling along the Baltic coast, even exploring the Ruhrgebiet's industrial heart. Mountain biking is also excellent thanks to legion of dedicated forest trails, such as the **Mountain Bike Rennsteig** trail, which tracks through the Thuringian Forest parallel to Germany's most popular footpath.

The national tourist board's *Discovering Germany by Bike* brochure is a model of good information on the majority of multi-day routes, with guide maps, tourist information contacts and sights en route, and details of tour operators. It is also available as a download from its website, where you'll find an abundance of information and interactive maps. Another good contact is Bremen-based **Allgemeiner**

Deutscher Fahrrad-Club (ADFC; ⓦwww
.adfc.de), the national cycling federation that
grades long-distance trails from the cyclists'
viewpoint with one to five stars. It also
publishes a handy brochure of five thousand
cyclist-friendly accommodation options, *Bett
& Bike* (ⓦwww.bettundbike.de), available at
bookshops. Cycle maps are widely available
through local tourist offices. For details of
taking a bike on the train, see p.37.

Winter sports

The German ski holiday is a happy one
characterized by first-class facilities, low
prices and a charmingly retro après-ski
scene of gutsy German food in a country
Gaststätte. The premier ski and snowboard
destinations lie in the **Bavarian Alps** south
of Munich, centred on Garmisch-Partenkirchen, a former Olympic Games town
with a lively après-ski whose facilities are
being upgraded for the 2011 Alpine World
Ski Championship. The pistes lie above on
Germany's highest mountain, Zugspitze
(2964m), which straddles the Austrian
border – on the plateau, there are 20km
of pistes ranging from 700m to 3km and
a snowboard park; on its slopes are 40km
of cross-country trails. Nearby ski village
Oberammergau has the finest cross-country
skiing in Germany – all 90km of it – as well
as steep pistes on the Laber hills (1683m).
Steeper still is the Dammkar-tunnel near
Mittenwald on the other side of Garmisch-
Partenkirchen, its forty percent incline hill
one of the most challenging in Germany.
The **Allgäu** area in southwest Bavaria
offers the largest continuous ski area in
Germany, with 500km of downhill slopes,
including some deep-snow off-piste skiing,
and 200 ski lifts. Outside of Bavaria, the
Black Forest offers good downhill skiing,
the low-lying **Harz** and the **Sauerland**
regions focus on cross-country skiing,
weather permitting, and there are lesser
scenes in the **Thuringian Forest** highlands
around Oberhof and on the Czech border
in south **Saxony**. The season begins in
mid-November in Bavaria (usually Dec
elsewhere) and runs to around February,
sometimes March in a good year.

Ski rental and lessons are widely available
at the resorts, either at ski shops or at

ski schools, often located on the pistes
themselves. As a rough guide of prices,
you'll pay €20 per day for a set of boots,
poles and skis or snowboard. Ski-lift passes
average €25–30 a day.

Watersports

Riddled by waterways, lapped by seas,
Germany provides a good range of watersports. The UK-based German Tourist Board
website (ⓦwww.germany-tourism.co.uk) is a
good portal for an overview, with an interactive
map and marketing brochure *The Fascination
of Water* available as a download.

Even in the major cities, boat rental is
available by the hour on most lakes and
waterways, generally from April to September,
sometimes to October. **Canoeing** and
kayaking is also popular on the country's
rivers: principally the Rhine and Danube –
both busy with traffic – the Elbe and their
tributaries as well as the Weser. The
overlooked River Oder on the border of
Poland appeals for its lack of development.
Arguably the most appealing multi-day
canoeing in Germany is in the **Müritz
National Park** in Mecklenburg-Western
Pomerania, where you can **canoe-and-camp**
through a mosaic of lakes. Similar experiences are available in the Spreewald south of
Berlin, and in the Schleswig-Holstein lakes
from Eutin to Kiel. Rental is best sourced
through local tourist-information centres – if
you are renting equipment for river trips, try to
find one that offers transport, thereby allowing
a one-way trip. If your German is up to it, the
Federal Association of Canoeing Tourism
(Bundesvereinigung Kanutouristik; ⓦwww
.kanutouristik.de) or Kajak Channel (ⓦwww
.kajak-channel.de) are good portals on tours,
the latter including whitewater trips.

Motor- or **houseboat** holidays are popular
on Lake Müritz, Germany's second-largest
lake, and in the waterways of Brandenburg,
north of Berlin. Rental of leisure craft, which
typically sleep up to eight people, is usually
by the week; no licences are required for
most waterways for craft under 13m. Again,
the UK's German Tourist Board website is
a good source of companies, as is motor
organization ADAC, which has a German-
only section on watersports at ⓦwww.adac
.de/ReiseService/Wassersport.

The coasts are playgrounds for **sailing**, **windsurfing** and **kite-surfing** – holiday resorts on Rügen and Sylt offer rental outfits, the latter a stop on the Windsurf World Cup tour. As a rule of thumb, you'll find flat water in the Baltic off Rügen and waves in the more challenging conditions of the North Sea off Sylt. Consequently, the latter is also home to Germany's **surfing** scene – generally wind-slop but which has its days when the weather allows. Again, rental is available locally.

Culture and etiquette

Germany is a modern, cosmopolitan country, its society shaped by a plurality of lifestyles and ethnic and cultural diversity. If you had images of a conservative, homespun people in Lederhosen and feathered hats, dispense with them now. In the cities Germans are traditionally quite a gruff lot who don't suffer fools gladly, though much of this attitude is laced with a sardonic wit. Another defining attribute is their sense of orderliness and respect for rules and authority. However, attitudes vary across the country – as a rule of thumb, southerners are more conservative than the liberals of the north.

Meanwhile, the country's metropolises, such as Berlin and Hamburg, are famous for their live-and-let-live attitude. This tolerance comes in part from the cities' appeal for unconventional Germans who relocate from elsewhere in the country, and partly from their large immigrant populations with their more laissez faire attitudes. This open-mindedness also extends to tolerating people smoking more or less everywhere – except in restaurants – and flouting the jaywalking rules.

Even here, however, foreigners should be aware of a few points of protocol. First is the use of **du** and **Sie** (you) to strangers, which, though not the cultural minefield of French, still requires careful negotiation. Du is used for friends – or young people of your own age – only, and the more formal Sie is expected from everyone else you speak to, whether waiters or shop assistants and especially the police and officialdom. In the same way, notwithstanding that Germany is far more relaxed than it was even a decade ago, it expects some degree of self-control in day-to-day life. Shouting is likely to be met with a dismissive shrug at best and barely concealed disdain at worst.

Whatever the stereotype would have you believe Germans don't take themselves all that seriously – and, yes, they enjoy a joke – nor are they as prudish as the popular image suggests. Indeed, *Frei Korper Kultur* ("free body culture", or nude sunbathing) is more likely to shock visitors. The country that introduced naturist flights to the world – from Erfurt to Usedom in January 2008 – also has dedicated nude areas on most beaches, and even in some public parks. Be aware, too, that nude spa-going is common.

Service is, as a rule, included in the bill. For **tipping**, rounding up a café, restaurant or taxi bill to the next euro or so is acceptable in most cases, though when you run up a particularly large tab you will probably want to add some more. If the service was appalling, however, there's absolutely no need to tip.

Germany has banned **smoking** in public places – sort of. At the time of writing just over half of the states forbid lighting up in restaurants, bars, cinemas and theatres, but in March 2008 some – stand up Saxony and Saarland – rescinded prohibition laws for some venues, a move which prompted the Federal Medical Society to suggest nicotine addiction be classified as an illness to help smokers quit. Until a national ruling resolves the hotchpotch of state law assume you can't – or ask first.

Shopping

Quality and precision – the watchwords of German produce – means most visitors to the country will already be familiar with many of its exports besides its beer. There are names like Adidas, Birkenstock or Boss, Nivea, Mont Blanc pens, Villeroy & Boch or Meissen china. Prices for these brands are not significantly cheaper than elsewhere in Europe, although the choice is wider. All cities have a local alternative quarter with a quota of independent boutiques and vintage outlets for local hipsters. Those in Berlin and to a lesser extent Hamburg also support superb record shops – a good place to browse for cutting-edge electronica.

And then, of course, there is the wonderland of German **crafts**. Wooden toys are excellent – ubiquitously beautifully crafted with superb attention to detail, and often with a regional flavour. **Christmas markets** are an excellent opportunity to pick these up – Nürnburg, a historical crafts centre, arguably offers the best choice, although many towns also have a Yule-themed shop which is open year-round. If you must buy one, **cuckoo clocks**, made in southern Germany since the eighteenth century, can be bought in touristy shops throughout the Black Forest region.

Clothing and shoe sizes

Women's clothing									
American	4	6	8	10	12	14	16	18	
British	8	10	12	14	16	18	20	22	
Continental	38	40	42	44	46	48	50	52	

Women's shoes									
American	5	6	7	8	9	10	11		
British	3	4	5	6	7	8	9		
Continental	36	37	38	39	40	41	42		

Men's shirts									
American	14	15	15.5	16	16.5	17	17.5	18	
British	14	15	15.5	16	16.5	17	17.5	18	
Continental	36	38	39	41	42	43	44	45	

Men's shoes									
American	7	7.5	8	8.5	9.5	10	10.5	11	11.5
British	6	7	7.5	8	9	9.5	10	11	12
Continental	39	40	41	42	43	44	44	45	46

Men's suits									
American	34	36	38	40	42	44	46	48	
British	34	36	38	40	42	44	46	48	
Continental	44	46	48	50	52	54	56	58	

Travel essentials

Costs

By the standards of Europe, prices in Germany are reasonable; Berlin, for example, is well short of the excesses of Paris and London and with quality to match. Nevertheless, the country has the potential to become expensive, especially if you're set on its flashy nightspots or swanky restaurants, and hotel accommodation can bleed the bank of the budget traveller. One point to note is that there can be large differences in prices between regions and cities – Cologne is noticeably cheaper than near-neighbour Düsseldorf, for example.

Assuming you intend to eat and drink in moderately priced places, use public transport sparingly and say at hostels, the bare minimum living-cost you could get by on is €45 (£36/US$58) a day, including a hostel bed (around €20), snacks and drinks, an evening meal (€10), and a little for museums and entertainment. A more realistic figure if you want to travel by rail and see as much of a destination as possible (not to mention party at night), would be €80 daily.

Crime and safety

Crime is low by Anglo-Saxon standards, but not nonexistent, and the standard modern tensions exist. Statistically, crime is more prevalent in eastern states of the former GDR, fuelled by bitterness about rising prices and depressed economies. Small-minded attitudes often exist in small towns, and xenophobic neo-Nazi thugs can target those who look "foreign" – non-white. A police crackdown in recent years has helped, but it does happen in depressed small towns. Paradoxically, east German city centres are safer. Indeed, crime in German cities remains modest in comparison with European cities of equal size. The type you're most likely to encounter is **petty crime** such as pickpocketing or bag-snatching in shopping precincts or busy U-Bahns.

As far as **personal safety** is concerned, obviously you should use common sense in cities. But even the rougher neighbourhoods feel more dangerous than they actually are. Those run-down U-Bahn stations or train stations with a crowd of drunks look alarming when compared to the rest of the country, but wouldn't stand out in most other European cities. The situation in city suburbs is a little trickier, in Berlin, for example. With caution it's fine, but muggings and casual violence do occur, particularly to those who stand out.

If you do have something **stolen** (or simply lost), or suffer an attack you'll need to register the details at the local police station: this is usually straightforward, but inevitably there'll be bureaucratic bumph to wade through. Make a note of the crime report number – or, better still, ask for a copy of the statement itself – for your insurance company.

The two offences you might unwittingly commit concern identity papers and jaywalking. By law you need to carry **proof of your identity** at all times. A driver's licence or ID card is fine, but a passport is best. It's essential that you carry all your documentation when driving – failure to do so may result in an on-the-spot fine. **Jaywalking** is also illegal and you can be fined if caught.

Emergencies

Police: ☎110
Fire and ambulance: ☎112

Electricity

Supply runs at 220–240V, 50Hz AC; sockets generally require a two-pin plug with rounded prongs. Visitors from the UK will need an adaptor, visitors from North America may need a transformer, though most of those supplied with electrical equipment – like cameras, laptops and mobile phones – are designed to accommodate a range of voltages.

Entry requirements

British and other EU nationals can enter Germany on a valid passport or national identity card for an indefinite period. US,

Canadian, Australian and New Zealand citizens do not need a visa to enter Germany, and are allowed a stay of ninety days within any six-month period. South Africans need to apply for a visa, from the German Embassy in Pretoria (see below), which will cost around R260 depending on the exchange rate. Visa requirements vary for nationals of other countries; contact your local German embassy or consulate for information.

In order to **extend a stay** once in the country all visitors should contact the **Ausländeramt** (Alien Authorities) in the nearest large town: addresses are in the phone books. For embassies in Berlin see p.133. Many countries have consulates in major cities elsewhere in Germany, typically Hamburg, Munich, Düsseldorf or Cologne.

German embassies abroad

UK 23 Belgrave Square, London SW1X 8PZ ☎020/7824 1300, ⌨www.london.diplo.de.
Ireland 31 Trimelston Ave, Booterstown, Blackrock, Oo Dublin ☎01/269 30 11, ⌨www.dublin.diplo.de.
US 4645 Reservoir Rd NW, Washington, DC 20007-1998 ☎202/298-4000, ⌨www.germany.info.
Canada 1 Waverley St, Ottawa, ON K2P 0T8 ☎613/232-1101, ⌨www.ottawa.diplo.de.
Australia 119 Empire Circuit, Yarralumla, Canberra 2600 ☎02/6270 1911, ⌨www.germanembassy.org.au.
New Zealand 90–92 Hobson St, Wellington ☎04/736 063, ⌨www.wellington.diplo.de.
South Africa 180 Blackwood St, Arcadia, Pretoria 0083 ☎012/427 8900, ⌨www.pretoria.diplo.de.

Gay and lesbian travellers

Germany has a legendary gay and lesbian culture in its major cities and gay pride event Christopher Street Day is celebrated throughout the nation. Along with the two metropolises of Berlin and Hamburg, Cologne is one of the world's great gay cities, with one in ten of the population either gay or lesbian. The scene in Berlin – home to the world's first gay organization in 1897 and ruled by openly gay mayor, Klaus Wowereit – centres around the districts of Schöneberg, Kreuzberg and Prenzlauer Berg. That of Hamburg is in St Georg, and in Cologne there are two

main gay districts – around Rudolfplatz and close to the river around Alter Markt and Heumarkt. Other thriving gay centres are in Munich and Frankfurt. Details of local scenes are provided in the sections on relevant destinations. Otherwise newsstand listings magazines have information on gay and lesbian clubnights and events.

In contrast, small-town Germany is inevitably more socially conservative – staunch Catholic towns of Bavaria can be hostile and physical assaults are not unknown in depressed towns of east Germany.

Health

The standards of healthcare in Germany are as good as anywhere in the world. For immediate medical attention, head for the 24-hour emergency room of a major **hospital**; details are provided in destination listings. In the event of an **emergency**, phone ☎112 for an ambulance (*Krankenwagen*). If you need a **doctor**, call ☎01804/22 55 23 62 (⌨www.calladoc.com; calls cost €0.24 per minute) for an English-language service that will discuss your symptoms and refer you or send an English-speaking doctor. Should you become ill, doctors are your first point of call – you should only visit a hospital for a genuine emergency (*Notfall*) or after referral by a doctor. Doctor surgery hours are 9am to midday and 3 to 6pm weekdays except on Wednesday afternoon.

As a member of the European Union, Germany has free reciprocal health agreements with other member states, whose citizens can apply for a free **European Health Insurance Card** (EHIC, ⌨www.ehic.org.uk), which will give you free, or cut-rate treatment, but will not pay for repatriation. The EHIC allows you to claim back costs and is available from post offices in the UK. Without this you'll have to pay in full for all medical treatment, which is expensive – currently €30 for a visit to the doctor. Non-EU residents will need to insure themselves against all eventualities, including medical costs, and are strongly advised to take out some form of travel insurance (see p.58).

Staff at **Apotheken** (pharmacies) provide over-the-counter advice, usually in English, and basic medicines for minor health upsets. Marked by a green cross, pharmacies are generally open on weekdays 8.30am to 6.30pm and on Saturday mornings. They also operate late opening hours (24hr in cities) by rota – a list of the current incumbent and its address is displayed in windows. For more involved medicines you must provide a *Rezept* (prescription) either obtained from your home doctor or a local one.

Since pre-Roman days, Germany has sworn by the curative powers of **spa waters**, a fixation which peaked in the mid-1800s. Towns which have Bad as a prefix or include Baden (baths) in their titles (spa doyenne Baden-Baden or Wiesbaden) offer a baffling array of restorative spa facilities – enjoyable if not always efficacious.

Insurance

Even though EU healthcare privileges apply in Germany, an insurance policy is a wise precaution to cover against theft, loss and illness or injury.

If buying a policy check the small print for waivers on "danger sports" – common activities such as mountain biking can sneak in among the usual skiing and rock climbing. A supplement payment provides cover. If you need to make a claim, you should keep receipts for medicines and medical treatment, and in the event you have anything stolen, you must obtain an official statement (*Anzeige*) from the police.

Internet

Germany has embraced the internet age with a passion. Most German towns operate a municipal website, generally with good tourism information; the best feature a searchable database of festivals and cultural events and allow you to book accommodation via tourist information. Addresses are generally

the name of the town – ⓦwww.hamburg .de, for example – and tourist destinations and larger cities provide an English-language version. Large museums, hotels and even some restaurants also have a web presence. Be aware when hunting addresses that letters with an umlaut are rendered with an e – ä becomes ae, ü becomes ue and so on – and Germans often prefer to hyphenate words rather than run them on.

Online access is good in medium-sized towns and cities, where **internet cafés** cost about €1–4 per half-hour. "Callshops" – discount international call centres – often in the streets around the main train station often have computers. Most backpacker hostels also provide a connection, often free. Larger hotels and a growing number of cafés have free wi-fi hotspots.

Laundry

Larger hotels generally provide a laundry service – but at a cost. Most hostels offer cheaper wash-and-dry for around €5 a load. Launderettes are a little cheaper, with an average load costing around €4 to wash and dry. Hours tend to be daily 7am–10pm; addresses can be found listed under "Waschsalon" in the *Yellow Pages* (*Gelbe-Seiten*). One popular nationwide chain is Schell und Sauber and some in cities come with a bar attached and free wi-fi.

Left luggage

Left-luggage lockers at the large main train stations allow storage for time periods of 24 to 72 hours. Charges for lockers range around €2 for 24 hours, then €2–5 thereafter. Many hostels provide free storage for a few days on the quid pro quo that you stay the night on your return.

Living in Germany

Berlin and to a lesser extent Hamburg are magnets for young people from Germany and all over Europe. The capital's reputation as a politicized, happening city with a dynamic arts scene and tolerant attitudes means there is a large English-speaking community: something that will work to your advantage for jobs and housing, and to your disadvantage in competition. **Work permits** (*Arbeitserlaubnis*) aren't required for EU nationals working in Germany, though everyone else will need one – and, theoretically, should not even look for a job without one. Long-term permits are a world of complicated and tedious bureaucracy. It's essential to seek advice from an experienced friend, especially when completing official forms. The best official place for advice is the **Auswärtiges Amt** (German Federal Foreign Office; ⓦwww .auswaertiges-amt.de), whose website has the latest information – in English – on entry into Germany and local contact details.

All those who want to stay in Germany for longer than three months – including EU citizens – must technically first **register** their residence (*Anmeldung*) at an Einwohner-meldeamt. For **non-EU nationals** – North Americans, Australasians and everybody else – finding legal work is extremely difficult, unless you've secured the job before arrival. Citizens of Australia, New Zealand and Canada between 18 and 30 can apply for a working holiday visa, enabling legal work in Germany for ninety days in a twelve-month period: contact German embassies for details.

For long-term **accommodation**, while newspapers advertise apartments and rooms, it's much quicker and less traumatic to sign on at one of the several **Mitwohnzentralen**, accommodation agencies that specialize in long-term sublets in apartments. When you find a place to live, you need to first **register** your **residence** (*Anmeldung*) at an Einwohner-meldeamt. The form for this requires a signature from your landlord.

Mail

Post offices of **Deutsche Post** (ⓦwww .deutschepost.de) and their unmissable bright yellow postboxes pep up the streetscape. Post offices are often located near (or with a branch inside) the main train station. Standard post office opening hours are Monday to Friday 8am to 6pm, Saturday and Sunday 8am to 1pm, although the main office will operate longer hours. These often have separate parcel offices (marked *Pakete*), usually a block or so away; and you can also buy stamps from the small yellow machines next to some postboxes and at some newsagents.

Mail to the UK usually takes three days; to North America one week; and to Australasia two weeks. A postcard costs €0.65 to send within Europe or €1 worldwide; letters under 50g cost €1 within Europe and €2 worldwide. When posting a letter, make sure you distinguish between the slots marked for various postal codes. Boxes marked with a red circle indicate collections late in the day and on Sunday.

Maps

Your best bet for a country map is the companion edition to this book: the *Rough Guides Map: Germany* (£5.99/US$9.99/ CAN$13.99) produced on rip- and waterproof paper. Rough Guides also produces a *Berlin* map (£4.99/US$8.99/CAN$11.99), published in 2008, to include the best the city can offer and that marks sights, restaurants and bars. Elsewhere town maps are available from tourist information offices, usually free of charge, otherwise for a nominal sum. Larger bureaux in cities or tourist regions – the Rhine valley, Harz mountains or Black Forest, for example – also provide free regional maps. Both are generally adequate for orientation, though don't rely on the latter for touring. Commercially produced maps available at larger bookshops are a joy. Falkplan and motor organization Allegmeiner Deutscher Automobil Club (ADAC) are consistently excellent, with distances indicated for the smallest lanes and clear town plans. Kompass (ⓦwww.kompass.at) publish a full range of walking and cycling maps.

Money and banks

Germany uses the **euro** as its currency, which divides into 100 cents. There are seven euro **notes** – in denominations of 500, 200, 100, 50, 20, 10 and 5 euros, each a different colour and size – and eight different **coin** denominations, including 2 and 1 euros, then 50, 20, 10, 5, 2 and 1 cents. Euro coins feature a common EU design on one face, but different country-specific designs on the other. All euro coins and notes can be used in twelve countries that share the currency (Austria, Belgium, Finland, France, Germany, Greece, Ireland, Italy, Luxembourg, Portugal, Spain and the Netherlands). At the time of writing, €1 was worth £0.80/$US1.3/AUS$1.9/ZAR13; for current rates go to ⓦwww.xe.com.

Banks are plentiful and their hours usually Monday to Friday 9am to 3pm, two days a week to 6pm. It may be worth shopping around several banks (including the savings banks or *Sparkasse*), as the rates of exchange offered can vary, as can the amount of commission deducted. The latter tends to be a flat rate, meaning that small-scale transactions should be avoided whenever possible. In any case, the several **Wechselstuben** (bureaux de change) at the main train stations in cities, offer better rates, as well as being open outside normal banking hours and weekends, usually daily 8am–8pm, a couple of hours longer on either side in the nation's principal travel hubs.

Debit and **credit cards**, once a foreign concept, are becoming a part of everyday life, though their use is not as widespread as in the UK or North America. Cash is still the currency of choice, particularly in bars and restaurants. Major credit and debit cards (such as American Express, MasterCard and Visa) are good in department stores, mid- to up-market restaurants, and an increasing number of shops and petrol stations. Should you want to get **cash** on your plastic, the best way is from any of the many **ATMs**. You can withdraw as little as €20; however they do charge a minimum fee, often around €2.50, and charge two to four percent of the withdrawal as commission. In addition to credit cards, most bank debit cards, part of either the Cirrus or Plus systems, can be used for withdrawing cash, and carry lower fees than credit cards; you home bank may levy a commission for use of the card abroad. Various banks will also give an advance against your credit card, subject to a minimum of the equivalent of £60/$100 – stickers in bank windows indicate which cards they're associated with. Make sure you have a personal identification number (PIN) that's designed to work overseas.

Opening hours and public holidays

Opening hours on **public holidays** generally follow Sunday hours: most shops will be closed and museums and other attractions will follow their Sunday schedules. **Public holidays** fall on January 1, Good Friday, Easter Monday, May 1, Ascension Day (40 days after Easter), Whitsun, October 3, November 3 and December 25 and 26.

Shops and markets: Business hours are generally Monday to Friday 9am to 6pm and Saturday 9am to 2pm, although some bakeries open on Sunday mornings, and department and brand-name stores will stay open till 8pm on weekdays and till 4pm on Saturday, both legal closing times. Conversely, many shops in smaller towns still close for lunch, generally from midday to 2pm. Outside of trading hours, small supermarkets in train and petrol stations supply the basics. Produce markets (usually weekdays in towns) operate between 9am to 1pm.

Banks and exchange: Depends upon the bank, but generally weekdays 8.30am to 5pm and no later than 6pm. Bureaux de change at airports and main train stations are normally open daily 8am to 8pm.

Tourist information: Generally Monday to Friday 9am to 6pm, Saturday 9am to 2pm, closed Sunday, but consult relevant chapters.

Museums and tourist attractions: The handful that open on Mondays are exceptions that prove the rule – with infuriating regularity, tourism in Germany is strictly a Tuesday-to-Sunday 9am to 6pm business. Some sights also close at lunchtime. Many museums close from November to March, which is also closed-season for tourist-orientated regions such as the Moselle and Rhine valleys.

Restaurants: Generally 10am to midnight, although smarter restaurants tend to take Sunday or Monday as Ruhetag (closing day).

Churches: Access is generally excellent, usually open all day and all week, though respect services. Churches in Catholic southern Germany tend to observe longer hours than their northern counterparts.

Phones

You can make local and **international calls** from most phone boxes in the city – marked

Calling home from abroad

Note that the initial zero is omitted from the area code when dialling the UK, Ireland, Australia and New Zealand from abroad.

Australia international access code + 61
New Zealand international access code + 64
UK international access code + 44
US & Canada international access code + 1
Ireland international access code + 353
South Africa international access code + 27

international – which are generally equipped with basic instructions in English. Virtually every pay phone you'll find takes coins and **cards**. The latter come in €5, €10 and €20 denominations and are available from all post offices and some shops. Phone boxes with a ringing bell symbol indicate that you can be called back on that phone. Another option is to use one of the many **phone shops** offering cheap international calls, usually alongside internet services, which can be found throughout the city. The cheapest time to call abroad is between 9pm and 8am.

Unless you have a tri-band phone, it is unlikely that a mobile bought for use in the US will work outside North America. You should be able to use your mobile phone in Berlin if it's been connected via the GSM system common to the rest of Europe, Australia, New Zealand and South Africa. If you haven't used your mobile phone abroad before, check with your phone provider whether it will work in Germany, and what the call charges are.

If you are in Germany for a while, consider getting a local SIM card for your phone. These are available through the phone shops and even corner stores and tend to cost around €15, often including some credit. To use a different SIM card in your phone, it will need to be unlocked, if it isn't already, to accept the cards of different providers. The phone shops will be able to advise where this is possible locally. Expect to pay around €10 for this instant service. Top-up cards can be bought in supermarkets, kiosks and phone shops.

Calling Germany from abroad the **international code** is ☏49. For **directory enquiries** in English call ☏118 37; the service costs an initial €0.20, then €1 per minute.

Time

Germany is in the Central European Time Zone, one hour ahead of Greenwich Mean Time: one hour ahead of British time, nine hours ahead of US Pacific Standard Time and six hours ahead of Eastern Standard Time. Daylight savings time (summer time) applies from the end of March to the end of October, when clocks are put forward one hour.

Tourist information

In a word, excellent. The national tourist board produces a stack of brochures on regions and holiday themes. Its website, @www.germany-tourism.de is a good resource for ideas and planning. Most regional tourist boards, cities and small towns also maintain an online presence, the majority with informative tourism pages in English. On the ground, you'll find a walk-in tourist office almost wherever you go, even in villages; information is provided in the Guide. These typically stock a good spread of pamphlets and brochures – usually in English in larger towns and cities, where one member of staff will be near-fluent. Tourist information offices will reserve accommodation, either for free or for a nominal charge of a few euros per person.

German tourist offices abroad

UK & Ireland PO Box 2695, London W1A 3TN ☏020/7317 0908, @www.germany-tourism.co.uk.
US 122 E 42nd St, Suite 200, New York, NY 10168-0072 @www.cometogermany.com.
Canada 480 University Ave, Suite 1410, Toronto, ON M5G 102 ☏416/968 1685, @www.cometogermany.com.
Australia PO Box 1461, Sydney NSW 2001 ☏02/8296 0488, @www.germany-tourism.de.

Travellers with disabilities

Access and facilities for the disabled (**Behinderte**) are fair to good in large towns and cities: most major museums, public buildings and a fair whack of the public-transport system are wheelchair-friendly, and an active disabled community is on hand for helpful advice. Nearly four hundred Deutsche Bahn train stations have lifting aides or ramps. It also offers assistance to travellers with disabilities upon reservation; call ☎01805/512 512, Monday to Friday 8am to midnight, Saturday 8am to 2pm. Under certain conditions, the disabled and their escorts travel by train free or at reduced rates. You can find more information in the brochure *Informationen für Behinderte Reisende* (Information for Disabled Travellers), available at all DB ticket counters or by ordering online.

The German Tourist Board website has links to dedicated state providers. NatKo (Nationale Koordiationsstelle Tourismus für Allee; National Tourism Coordination Agency for All People; Ⓦwww.natko.de) handles enquiries over "Tourism without barriers", supported by the main associations for the disabled in Germany. Its German-language website publishes information and addresses for state travel-advice centres for tourists with disabilities as well as a list of tour operators who offer suitable programmes. Website Ⓦwww.you-too.net publishes reliable information on the accessibility of public buildings, accommodation or leisure activities. For formal and in-depth information in Berlin, try **Mobidat** (Ⓦwww .mobidat.net), an activist group that campaigns for better access for people with disabilities. They have a great wealth of information on wheelchair-accessible hotels and restaurants, city tours for travellers with disabilities and local transport services. Finally if you speak German, you might like to browse the online version of the quarterly magazine *Handicap* (Ⓦwww.i-motio.de), for its hundreds of articles and active forums.

Travelling with children

Children and Germany are a good match. This is an orderly, safe country with an indulgent attitude towards youngsters. It is the land of familiar fairytales such as the Pied Piper of Hamlyn (Hameln) which revels in traditional folk festivals. Its hills are dotted with castles steeped in gory legends and there are plenty of activities – and theme parks – to entertain young thrill-seekers. Concession rates or free entry are standard practice, the main problem being that the definition of child for discounts varies enormously – you're safe to assume under-12s count, often under-16s, while under-18s qualify for "youth" fares on transport.

Public transport provides discounts for children under 16 and infants under 4 years old travel free of charge. Group rail tickets also provide good value (see p.34). All international car rental companies can provide child seats on request for around €5 a day. Service centres on the motorways have excellent baby-changing amenities.

All but luxury hotels are child-friendly. Most can rustle up a cot and have family rooms with a double bed and two singles, or else can provide an extra bed for a small charge. Larger hotels may allow children to go free, otherwise you're looking at the standard discount of thirty percent. More than three hundred hotels nationwide permit children under 15 to stay free in a scheme organized by national rail Deutsche Bahn to promote child-friendliness in Germany (search on Ⓦwww.bahn.de under "*Kinder kostenlos*" for participating hotels). One option definitely worth considering is **farmstays** (see p.40) – endless space to romp around and often including activities such as cycling and riding.

Cafés and standard restaurants are relaxed about kids in their premises and menus offer few real challenges, though high-end restaurants are a different matter, particularly in cities, and especially at dinner. High-end country places are more relaxed but it's worth double-checking. **Baby-changing facilities** are common in public toilets; breast-feeding is acceptable in public so long as you are discreet.

Concessions are standard practice for sights, tours and travel passes – again, expect around 30–50 percent discount. The best science museums offer interactive exhibits and most large cities have a zoo; see Ⓦwww .zoo.de for a full list.

Guide

Guide

1 Berlin and Brandenburg 65

2 Saxony 157

3 Saxony-Anhalt and the Harz 207

4 Thuringia 253

5 Northern Bavaria: Franconia 297

6 Munich and central Bavaria 347

7 The Alps and eastern Bavaria 389

8 Baden-Württemberg 429

9 The Black Forest 483

10 Rhineland-Palatinate and Saarland 511

11 Hesse 549

12 North Rhine-Westphalia 599

13 Lower Saxony and Bremen 675

14 Hamburg and Schleswig-Holstein 741

15 Mecklenburg-Western Pomerania 811

Berlin and Brandenburg

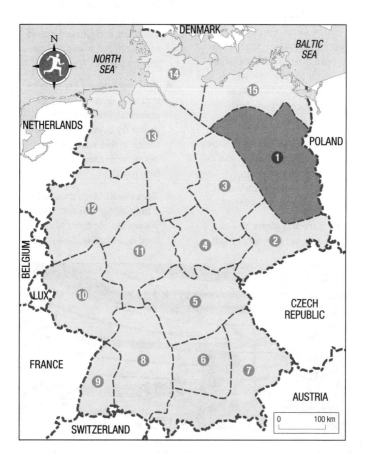

CHAPTER 1 # Highlights

✳ **The Reichstag and the Brandenburg Gate** Germany's two most famous landmarks are practically neighbours, and the view from the Reichstag's glass cupola provides a great handle on the city. See p.79

✳ **The Pergamonmuseum** The Greek Pergamon Altar and Babylon's Ishtar Gate are among the spectacular antiquities in this world-class museum, one of many great collections in Berlin. See p.94

✳ **Berlin Wall Memorial** See the Wall as it once was in the only remaining, completely preserved section. See p.101

✳ **Bars and clubs** You can party all night every night in Berlin's bewildering array of bars and clubs. See p.124

✳ **Potsdam** An easy day out from Berlin, Potsdam harbours several fine palaces, including the fabled park Sanssouci. See p.135

✳ **Sachsenhausen** The former concentration camp for both the Nazis and Soviets makes for a grim but rewarding day-trip from Berlin. See p.147

✳ **Tropical Islands** For a quick and easy getaway from the cheerless Brandenburg winter try overnighting on the beach in this vast tropical dome; unmissable for kids. See p.153

✳ **Spreewald** Mess around in a boat along lush and sleepy waterways, or cycle along their quiet banks. See p.153

▲ The Reichstag

Berlin and Brandenburg

As Germany's largest, most happening city, **Berlin's** lure is obvious. Its pace is frantic: new buildings sprout up; nightlife is frenetic, its trends whimsical; the air crackles with creativity and graffiti is ubiquitous; even brilliant exhibitions and installations are quickly replaced. The results are mesmerizing. Less dynamic are the sleepy, marshy lowlands of the surrounding state of **Brandenburg**, whose small regional towns, empty rambling churches, crumbling Gothic monasteries and faded palaces hint at a mighty Prussian past.

Violent settlement of the region by Germanic tribes in the Dark Ages led to the creation of the margravate of Brandenburg in 1157, a marshy frontier territory on the eastern edge of the Holy Roman Empire. Berlin slowly rose to become its capital and from 1415 Brandenburg became the possession of the Hohenzollern dynasty, who embraced the Reformation in 1538. Brandenburg merged with Prussia in 1618, then became entangled in the Thirty Years' War, as a result of which it was devastatingly plundered and then depopulated.

Rebirth was slow, but gathered increasing momentum as Prussia grew strong on the back of its relative social tolerance – towards Huguenots and Jews in particular – resulting in rapid industrialization throughout the eighteenth and nineteenth centuries. With increasing economic power came military might and expansionist ambitions, which sparked two centuries of military adventures and horse-trading diplomacy which culminated in the forging of German unity in 1871 and the creation of the second German Reich. Within two centuries Berlin had gone from also-ran provincial town to Germany's capital. But within the century both it and Brandenburg would be irrevocably changed by World War II demolition and Cold War division – which cut through Berlin's heart and robbed Brandenburg of all territory east of the Oder. With the fall of the Berlin Wall and reinstatement of Germany's federal government in Berlin, old bonds with its Brandenburg hinterland are being re-forged, while in its centre the almost endless number of building projects is entering the final phase of patching Berlin up, a process that is generating a lot of new, exciting modern architecture, monuments and spaces, though thankfully not without leaving many fascinating reminders of the city's history. All this is complemented by scores of museums that document every

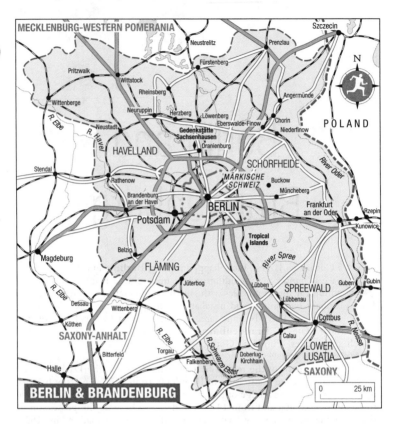

BERLIN & BRANDENBURG

aspect of Berlin and its past, not to mention its many artistic and archeological treasures. But it's not all stern history, heavyweight museums and high culture, Berlin is also endlessly vibrant: there always seems to be something new, challenging and quirky going on.

Though rubbing shoulders with Berlin, Brandenburg's capital **Potsdam** could barely be more staid and provincial, yet it's the state's most obvious destination thanks to generations of Hohenzollerns who favoured the city with fabulous palaces and gardens. Elsewhere in Brandenburg, water has been the most conspicuous force, leaving the landscape with a dense web of canals and rivers. The more attractive major towns such as **Brandenburg an der Havel** straddle them, spreading across several islands, but elsewhere the waterways produce vitally important **wetland landscapes**. This is best appreciated in the **Spreewald**, where the indigenous Sorbs, a Slavic people, keep their traditions alive, but the **Unteres Odertal National Park** is even better for observing primordial ecosystems at work. Thousands of lakes and ponds produce the pleasant backdrop of Brandenburg's most bucolic rural retreats: towns like **Buckow** and **Rheinsberg** brim with boating, cycling and hiking opportunities.

Berlin

As heart of the Prussian kingdom, cultural centre of the Weimar Republic, headquarters of Hitler's Third Reich and a key frontline flashpoint in the Cold War, **BERLIN** has long been a weather vane of European and even world history. But World War II left the city devastated, with bombs razing 92 percent of all its shops, houses and industry, to such an extent there was serious debate about leaving it in ruins and starting afresh nearby.

However, in the years that followed the city did a remarkable job rebuilding itself and some of its heritage. Reconstructions of its sixteenth-century core have been made in the **Nikolaiviertel**, while nearby stand many rebuilt grand nineteenth-century buildings with an unmistakable Neoclassical stamp that stem from the time when the city prospered as capital of the Second Reich. Pockets of traditional nineteenth-century tenements are found in inner-city residential quarters, but little from the Third Reich has survived, and no one has cared to rebuild it, with the notable exception of the 1936 Olympic Stadium.

So much for historic Berlin; the rest is the product of rebuilding after the war in a time of division by the Allied powers, first ideologically and then physically by the **Berlin Wall**. The two halves competed with the conflicting ambitions and philosophies of the Cold War. West Berlin became a capitalist showcase of experimental architecture fuelled by subsidies – buildings like the **Philharmonie** and the **Neue Nationalgalerie** stem from this time – while in the east vast projects such as the apartment blocks of **Karl-Marx-Allee** and radical design of the **TV tower** tried to demonstrate the people-power of socialism. But on both sides of the divide the era also produced vast unpleasant housing estates on the fringes, soulless prefabricated dwellings that still remain reality for thousands of Berliners.

During the Cold War, West Berlin's unorthodox character made it a magnet for those seeking alternative lifestyles – hippies and punks, gays and lesbians, artists and musicians all flocked here, attracted by a military service loophole and the huge subsidies from West Germany which funded a prodigious and cutting-edge **arts** scene. Non-Germans came too, lured to Germany by promises of work, and to Berlin by its tolerance. Large numbers of Turks, Greeks and Italians arrived in the 1960s making Berlin Germany's most cosmopolitan city – a fact reflected in the excellent variety of **cuisines** on offer in the city's restaurants, cafés and bars.

In November 1989 the world's media converged on the Brandenburg Gate to watch Berliners chipping away at the Berlin Wall and witness the extraordinary scenes of the border opening for good. Since then, there has inevitably been friction between those from the east, used to a slower pace of life, and those from the west who quickly moved into the best parts of the eastern city, along with the western companies which began to redevelop whole swathes of land. When the German government decided to move back to Berlin, it brought a whole host of new building projects: the result is a remarkable gathering of stimulating contemporary buildings. Yet you don't have to go far out of the centre to find areas untouched by federal funding, which are still in the grip of the city's ongoing economic woes. As the hipster mayor of Berlin, Klaus Wowereit, proudly proclaims, Berlin is certainly "poor but sexy". But it is not somewhere that wallows in self-pity, instead a vibrant place where cutting-edge designs and concepts have plenty of room to breathe, giving it more dynamism

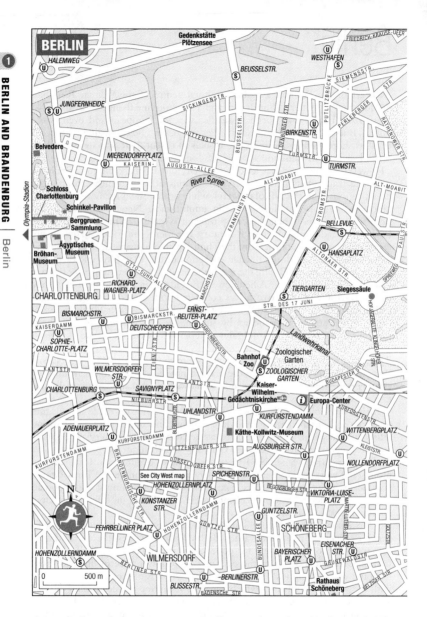

than anywhere else in Germany, especially in its legendary, nonstop **nightlife**, and energetic **contemporary arts** scene.

Unlike Paris, Amsterdam or London, Berlin isn't a city where you can simply stroll and absorb the atmosphere; it's a remarkably difficult place to get a handle on, with several main drags and no clear centre. Most visitors begin their exploration in the central and most historic **Mitte** district, along the city's premier boulevard, **Unter den Linden**, and at key sights such as the **Brandenburg**

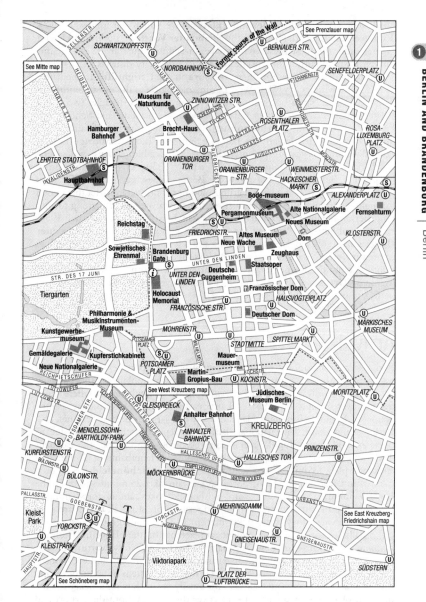

See Prenzlauer map
See Mitte map
See West Kreuzberg map
See East Kreuzberg-Friedrichshain map
See Schöneberg map

Gate and the **Reichstag**. This is an area where the Berlin Wall once stood and where modern buildings have long since sprouted, particularly around Potsdamer Platz, but it's also the fringes of Berlin's nineteenth-century imperial showpiece quarter, and its attendant **state museums** of the Museum Island still survive with extraordinary collections of art and archeology. Other areas of interest in Mitte include the reconstructed sixteenth-century enclave, the **Nikolaiviertel**, and almost adjacent to it the old centre of East Berlin with its windswept plazas around **Alexanderplatz** above which the imposing 1960s TV tower stands guard. Nearby is the **Spandauer Vorstadt**, Berlin's old Jewish quarter, and the best-preserved nineteenth-century quarter in the centre, though it's now fairly touristy. The residential inner-city districts that encircle Mitte particularly shine for their **restaurants** and **nightlife**. Immediately southwest of Mitte, **City West**, West Berlin's old centre, is the most commercial neighbourhood. Not a borough in its own right, the area straddles two rather sedate, middle-class districts of Charlottenburg-Wilmersdorf and Schöneberg. Further out of town, **Charlottenburg** has its own gathering of fairly high-profile attractions, particularly the Baroque **Schloss Charlottenburg** – Berlin's pocket Versailles with its opulent chambers, wanderable gardens, and several excellent museums – along with the iconic 1930s **Olympic Stadium**. Meanwhile, **Schöneberg** is famous for Berlin's oldest gay village. East from here, **Kreuzberg** has long been a grungy and nonconformist district that's good for nightlife, though these days it vies for the crown with its happening former East Berlin neighbour, **Friedrichshain**, which boasts some unusual 1950s architectural leftovers. Again in the former East and just as hip is **Prenzlauer Berg**, whose cobbled streets are among the few places where the atmosphere of prewar Berlin has been preserved. Berlin's suburbs also offer a few interesting sights, notably the former **Stasi** headquarters and prison in Lichtenberg, and the dense **Grunewald** forest on the city's southwestern fringe, which offers a perfect respite from the urban bustle.

Arrival

Berlin's two international **airports** (ⓌCwww.berlin-airport.de) both lie within easy reach of the city centre via its cheap and efficient public transport system; the furthest is only 25 minutes by train from the Hauptbahnhof where trains from all over Europe converge. Tegel airport is just northwest of the city centre, Schönefeld, south of the city. Plans to build one large airport at Schönefeld – Berlin Brandenburg International (BBI) – to replace both are afoot, due to open in 2011. From **Tegel**, several buses head into the city, but the frequent TXL bus (daily 5am–midnight; every 15–20min) to Hauptbahnhof (25min) and Alexanderplatz (35min) is generally the most useful. **Schönefeld** has its own train station, from where the Airport Express train takes 25 minutes to reach the Hauptbahnhof. The S-Bahn from Schönefeld takes about forty minutes (4.30am–11pm), but is more frequent and serves more stops; all tickets are valid on either service. Lines at the ticket machines in the underground passageway can usually be avoided by using identical machines on the platform. Given the frequency and efficiency of public transport, taxis are hardly worthwhile, but typical rates into the centre from Tegel and Schönefeld are €20 and €35 respectively. Public transport **tickets** are valid on the entire system of trams, buses and suburban and underground trains, so it's usually worth buying a ticket for the duration of your visit on arrival – to cover the journey from the airport and inner-city journeys.

Long-distance **trains** arrive at the swanky Hauptbahnhof, which has late-opening shops and all the other facilities you'd expect. Many services will also stop at other major stations such as Bahnhof Zoo, Alexanderplatz and the Ostbahnhof. A train ticket to Berlin may well include use of zones A and B of the city's public transport system (see opposite); check with the conductor or ticket office.

Most long-distance **buses** stop at the Zentraler Omnibusbahnhof or ZOB (central bus station), Masurenallee, Charlottenburg, west of the centre, near the Funkturm. Several local buses, including the frequent #X49 service, Kaiserdamm U–Bahn and Westkreuz S–Bahn stations link it to the city centre. If **arriving by car**, your likely approach from the west will be the A2 Autobahn, but from any direction you'll meet the Berliner Ring (A10), a circular motorway around the city which is well worth following round to the right side of town rather than deal with inner-city traffic.

Information

Berlin Tourismus Marketing (**BTM**; call centre Mon–Fri 8am–7pm, Sat & Sun 9am–6pm; ☎030/25 00 25, ⓦwww.berlin-tourist-information.de), provides the city with five tourist information offices which all have a wide selection of bumph – including a useful **what's on magazine**. They sell tickets to many upcoming events and offer a free accommodation booking service. Another good source of general tips and advice as well as travel information and bookings is the helpful EurAide office in Zoo Station (inside behind the Reisezentrum; daily: June–Oct 8am–noon & 1–6pm; Nov–May 8am–noon & 1–4.45pm; ⓦwww.euraide.de), which is specifically for English-speaking travellers.

Tourist information offices

Alexa Shopping Center Grunerstr. 20, U- & S-Bahn Alexanderplatz. Mon–Sat 10am–10pm, Sun 11am–4pm.

Brandenburg Gate Pariser Platz (south wing), S-Bahn Unter den Linden. Daily 10am–6pm.

Hauptbahnhof S-Bahn Hauptbahnhof. Daily 8am–10pm.

Neues Kranzler Eck Kurfürstendamm 23, U- & S-Bahn Zoologischer Garten. Mon–Sat 10am–8pm, Sun 10am–6pm.

Reichstag S-Bahn Unter den Linden. Daily: Nov–March 10am–6pm; April–Oct 8am–8pm.

City transport

Berlin's efficient and inexpensive **public transport** network is run by the BVG (☎030/194 49, ⓦwww.bvg.de) and looks complicated at first glance but quickly becomes easy to navigate. Fast suburban (**S-Bahn**) and underground trains (**U-Bahn**) form the backbone of the system and are supplemented on the streets by **buses** and **trams**. Trains run all night on Friday and Saturday but otherwise from 4am to around 1am when their routes are generally covered by **night buses** – whose numbers are prefixed by "N". Buses and trams called MetroBus or MetroTram run particularly frequently, often all night, and have numbers preceded by "M". On all services, onboard illuminated signs and announcements make finding the right stop easy.

All BVG services share the same **tickets**, valid for transfers between different modes of transport as well as all other services within the regional system, including buses and trams in Potsdam, Oranienburg and even Regional Express trains (marked RE) within the city limits. The network is divided into ticket zones A, B and C; a basic single ticket (Einzelticket) for Zone A and B costs €2.10, a ticket for all three zones costs €2.70. Tickets are valid for two hours and allow unlimited transfers, but not return journeys. A *Kurzstrecke*, or short-trip ticket, costs €1.20 and allows you to travel up to three train or six bus stops (no transfers). A day-ticket (*Tageskarte*; €6.30 for zones A, B and C) is valid until 3am the next morning. A seven-day ticket (*Sieben-Tage-Karte*) is €31.30 for all zones. Other money-saving possibilities include a **small group ticket** (Kleingruppenkarten) valid for a whole day's travel for up to five people (zones A, B & C €16.10), and a couple of cards that include concessionary rates at a host of attractions and discounts at participating tour companies, restaurants and theatres: the **Welcome Card** (€16 for 48hr, €21 for 72hr) allows one adult and three children unlimited travel, while the City Tour Card (ⓦwww.citytourcard.com) allows unlimited travel in the A and B zones for one adult and one child (€15.50 for 48hr, €20.50 for 72hr). The main difference between the two is who their partners are. All public transport tickets are available from machines – which have an English-language option – on station platforms and on trams, but be sure to validate them by punching the ticket at the red or yellow machines before you travel; failing to do so results in €40 fines at spot checks. Bus drivers can also sell tickets, though only single and day-tickets.

Berlin's cream-coloured **taxis** are plentiful and always metered but inexpensive enough that if you're travelling in a small group, the expense can be similar

Tours

Fierce competition between several English-language **walking tour** companies means that the quality of all is very high. A four-hour city tour should cost around €12. Companies include Original Berlin Walks (℡030/301 91 94, ⓦwww.berlinwalks.com), Insider Tours (℡030/692 31 49, ⓦwww.insiderberlintours.com) and New Berlin Tours (℡030/510 50 03 01, ⓦwww.newberlintours.com), who offer a city-centre tour that's technically free, though generous tips are expected. All companies also offer special interest tours such as the Third Reich, Jewish life, Potsdam and Sachsenhausen.

Insider and New Berlin also run **cycling tours**, as does specialist Fat Tire Bike Tours (℡030/24 04 79 91, ⓦwww.fattirebiketoursberlin.com), who charge €18 for a guided four-hour pedal around central Berlin astride a beach-cruiser bike. If it sounds too much like hard work consider **hiring** a rickshaw and driver with Velotaxi (℡030/44 31 94 28, ⓦwww.velotaxi.de), whose tours start at €15.

Bus tours also abound, though you may find that buying a day-ticket and hopping on and off the public #100 and #200 bus services between Bahnhof Zoo and Alexanderplatz, guidebook in hand, more flexible, cheaper and more informative. Most commercial tours depart from the Kurfürstendamm between Breitscheidplatz and Knesebeckstrasse. Companies include Severin + Kühn (℡030/880 41 90, ⓦwww.severin-kuehn-berlin.de) and Tempelhofer Reisen (℡030/752 40 57, ⓦwww.tempelhofer.de). A basic two-hour tour costs about €18.

Boats cruise Berlin's numerous city-centre canals and suburban lakes regularly in summer. Usually you can just turn up at quayside stops around the Spree Island and buy a ticket on the spot. Reederei Riedel (℡030/61 65 79 30, ⓦwww.reederei-riedel.de) offers an hour-long Stadtkernfahrt (€7.50); a three-hour Brückenfahrt (€15), which runs a loop around central Berlin; and day-trips (€17) out to the Pfaueninsel and the Wannsee in the west of the city, and to the Müggelsee in the east. Very similar tours are also offered by Reederei Winkler (℡030/349 95 95, ⓦwww.reederei-winkler.de) and Stern und Kreis Schiffahrt (℡030/536 36 00, ⓦwww.sternundkreis.de). Berlin Wassertaxi (℡030/65 88 02 03, ⓦwww.berliner-wassertaxi.de) concentrate on cheap city-centre jaunts.

If all the above seems too conventional, try exploring Berlin by **Trabant**, the cute 26-horse power GDR fibreglass car, with Trabi Safari (℡030/27 59 22 73, ⓦwww.trabi-safari.de; from €30 per person per hr), or by insanely fun **go-kart** with Kart 4 You (℡ 0800/750 75 10, ⓦwww.kart4u.de; 3hr €49).

to public transport. They cruise the city day and night and congregate at useful locations. Taxi firms include City Funk (☎030/21 02 02), Funk Taxi Berlin (☎030/26 10 26) and Spree Funk (☎030/44 33 22).

An extensive network of bike paths makes **cycling** a quick and convenient way of getting around the city. You can also take your bike on the U- and S-Bahn, with a Fahrrad ticket. One good company for bike rental with five branches in central Berlin is Fahrradstation, Auguststrasse 29a (Mon–Fri 10am–7pm, Sat 10am–3pm; ☎030/28 59 96 61; U-Bahn Weinmeisterstrasse), and Leipziger Strasse 56 (Mon–Fri 8am–8pm, Sat & Sun 10am–4pm; ☎030/66 64 91 80). Rates are €15 per day or €50 per week and can be booked online at ⓦwww.fahrradstation.com.

Accommodation

Berlin has plenty of **hotels, pensions, hostels** and **campsites**, as well as **private rooms** and **apartments** for short term rent, but it's best to book at least a couple of weeks in advance. For quick results, try the BTM **reservation service** (☎030/25 00 25, ⓦwww.berlin-tourist-information.de) who specialize in hotels and pensions. They do have private rooms on their books, but you'll find a better selection via local accommodation agencies where **private rooms** start at €20 per night. Try Bed & Breakfast in Berlin (☎030/44 05 05 82, ⓦwww.bed-and-breakfast-berlin.de), Citybed (☎030/23 62 36 10, ⓦwww.citybed.de) and Zimmervermittlung 24 (☎030/56 55 51 11, ⓦwww.zimmervermittlung24.com).

Hotels and pensions

There's considerable overlap between what pensions and hotels – and even hostels (see p.77) – in Berlin offer. Almost all are of a good standard, so deciding on which part of town to stay in is often the most important choice, despite the great public transport. **Mitte** is best for sightseeing but its main restaurant and nightlife district, around Oranienburger Strasse in the **Spandauer Vorstadt**, is a little touristy. To get under the skin of the city one of the surrounding boroughs can be a good choice: **Prenzlauer Berg** and **Schöneberg** are both happening neighbourhoods, but **Friedrichshain** and **Kreuzberg** are home to the most cutting-edge nightlife. **City West**, the staid old centre of West Berlin, has a concentration of accommodation, particularly moderately-priced guesthouses, though they are somewhat stranded from Berlin's brightest lights.

Mitte
See map, pp.80–81.

🏋 Adlon Unter den Linden 77 ☎030/226 10, ⓦwww.hotel-adlon.de. The jewel of Berlin's prewar luxury hotels now re-created in all its excessive splendour. Prices are fit for a Kaiser too, starting at €335. S-Bahn Unter den Linden. ➒

🏋 art'otel Berlin Mitte Wallstr. 70–73 ☎030/24 06 20, ⓦwww.artotel.de. Smart, lively hotel with quirky decor – lots of contemporary and modern art – in a quiet corner of Berlin, close to the U-Bahn. U-Bahn Märkisches Museum. ➐

Grosser Kurfürst Neue Rossstr. 11–12 ☎030/24 60 00, ⓦwww.deraghotels.de. Sleek hotel in a turn-of-the-twentieth-century building, with straightforward, spotless rooms and spacious suites. Facilities include laundry, wi-fi, sauna and steambath. U-Bahn Märkisches Museum. ➏

🏋 Hackescher Markt Grosse Präsidentenstr. 8 ☎030/28 00 30, ⓦwww.hotel-hackescher -markt.de. Quirky little hotel on a quiet side-street, but in the midst of the Hackescher Markt scene. Has an eclectic mix of furnishings and many nice touches, like under-floor heating in the en-suite bathrooms. The quieter rooms overlook the courtyard. S-Bahn Hackescher Markt. ❼

Honigmond Hotel Invalidenstr. 122 ☏ 030/28 44 55 77, ⓦ www.honigmond-berlin. de. Downtown bargain in a charming 1845 building. Rooms are sparsely furnished and the original wooden floors create an authentic elegance. Guests can relax in the back garden. U-Bahn Zinnowitzer Str. ❺

🏃 **Hotel Taunus** Monbijouplatz 1 ☏ 030/283 52 54, ⓦ www.hoteltaunus.com. No-frills budget hotel with perhaps the best-value rooms in central Berlin: clean and simple but tiny. En-suite rooms cost an extra €10. The reception is open 9am–7pm. S-Bahn Hackescher Markt. ❶

Intermezzo Gertrude-Kolmar-Str. 5 ☏ 030/22 48 90 96, ⓦ www.hotelintermezzo.de. Spartan women-only pension (children up to age 10 accepted) within walking distance of Potsdamer Platz and Unter den Linden. Not all rooms are en suite. U-Bahn Mohrenstr. ❹

Märkischer Hof Linienstr. 133 ☏ 030/282 71 55, ⓦ www.maerkischer-hof-berlin.de. On the doorstep of Oranienburger Strasse's restaurants and nightlife and within strolling distance of Unter den Linden. Rooms are comfortable but unexciting with TV and mini-bar. U-Bahn Oranienburger Tor. ❹

🏃 **Motel One** Alexanderplatz ☏ 030/20 05 40 80, ⓦ www.motel-one.com. The stylish lobby – flat-screen TVs and wacky, modular 1970s furniture – suggest far higher prices than the cheerfully straightforward en-suite rooms command. The country-wide chain has several locations in Berlin. Free wi-fi. U- & S-Bahn Alexanderplatz. ❸

Park Inn Alexanderplatz ☏ 030/238 90, ⓦ www .parkinn.de. Big, ugly GDR-vintage tower block bang in the middle of things, giving it unbeatable city views and unrivalled convenience – even if the nine hundred en-suite rooms are nothing special. U- & S-Bahn Alexanderplatz. ❺

Westin Grand Hotel Friedrichstr. 158–164 ☏ 030/202 70, ⓦ www.westin.com/berlin. GDR-era hotel originally serving party bigwigs but since overhauled to provide oodles of traditional upmarket luxury, making it more atmospheric than some of its rivals. U-Bahn Französische Str. ❾

City West
See map, p.104.

California Kurfürstendamm 35 ☏ 030/88 01 20, ⓦ www.hotel-california.de. Well-appointed hotel in the thick of the Ku'damm with huge chandeliers and elegant cornicing. The large en-suite rooms have becoming nineteenth-century touches, though

the cheaper rooms just seem dated and a little plain. Excellent buffet breakfast included. U-Bahn Uhlandstr. ❸

🏃 **Funk** Fasanenstr. 69 ☏ 030/882 71 93, ⓦ www.hotel-pensionfunk.de. Interesting re-creation of a prewar flat, with furniture and objects from the 1920s and 1930s, when this was the home of Danish silent-movie star Asta Nielsen. Given this and its location, it's a bargain. The cheapest rooms share bathrooms. U-Bahn Uhlandstr. ❹

Herberge Grosse Kantstr. 71 ☏ 030/324 81 38, ⓦ www.herbergegrosse.de. Friendly pension high above a busy street, with just three rooms and excellent facilities: internet access, cable TV and use of the communal kitchen and laundry are all included in the price, and bike rental is available. Free pick-up can be arranged from the train stations and the airport. S-Bahn Wilmersdorfer Str. ❷

🏃 **Kettler** Bleibtreustr. 19 ☏ 030/883 49 49. Tiny, charming 1920s-style pension on a lively, café-lined street. A multitude of knick-knacks, Berlin memorabilia and patterned wallpaper add character, and rooms are themed by artist or performer (choose between the likes of Callas or Toulouse-Lautrec) and have showers, but share toilets. S-Bahn Savignyplatz. ❷

Friedrichshain
See map, pp.110–111.

🏃 **East Side Hotel** Mühlenstr. 6 ☏ 030/29 38 33, ⓦ www.eastsidehotel.de. Small, laid-back modern hotel overlooking the East Side Gallery. Many rules are refreshingly absent: you can check in or out, order room service, or have breakfast in the café 24hr a day. Original artwork in the hotel includes quirky murals by Birgit Kinder, who painted the Trabant on the East Side Gallery. Under-15s stay free in their parents' rooms. U- & S-Bahn Warschauer Str. ❺

IntercityHotel Berlin Am Ostbahnhof 5 ☏ 030/29 36 80, ⓦ www.berlin.intercityhotel.de. Sleek but budget-conscious business hotel at the Ostbahnhof, so very convenient for the S-Bahn and the Friedrichshain scene. Rooms are the usual international standard, and a buffet breakfast and a free travel pass for the duration of your stay is included. Rates vary wildly depending on city events and demand. S-Bahn Ostbahnhof. ❹

Ostel Wriezener Karree 5 ☏ 030/25 76 86 60, ⓦ www.ostel.eu. Step back into the haze of browns and oranges of 1970s GDR at this themed budget hotel near the Ostbahnhof.

The rendition is so accurate it's creepy, but the whole thing is done with a sense of humour and is just the ticket for a fix of *Ostalgie*. Most rooms share bathrooms, although en-suite conversions are under way. Dorm beds (€9) and good-value singles are also available. S-Bahn Ostbahnhof. **❷**

Hostels

At the last count there were close to a hundred hostels in Berlin; the vast majority are independent and often smart, clean and quite sophisticated with their own bar, social areas, internet terminals, buffet breakfasts and universally absent curfews. Many also have private rooms.

Mitte
See map, pp.80–81.

Circus Hostel Weinbergsweg 1a ✆030/28 39 14 33, ⊛www.circus-berlin.de. Top-notch hostel in fantastic location, with helpful staff and good facilities. The high-ceilinged rooms are plain though bright, with large windows and no bunk-beds. The hostel has its own, decent bar. U-Bahn Rosenthaler Platz. Dorms €17–21; singles €33; doubles **❷**.

Citystay Hostel Rosenstr. 16 ✆030/23 62 40 31, ⊛www.citystay.de. Berlin's best-located hostel in easy walking distance of the S-Bahn, Fernsehturm and Museum Island. Large, clean and well-run with a good stock of private rooms, some en suite. Communal areas include a pleasant leafy courtyard. Facilities include an all-night bar, restaurant and internet. S-Bahn Hackescher Markt. Dorms €17–25; singles €40; doubles **❷**.

Downtown Baxpax Ziegelstr. 28 ✆30/27 87 48 80, ⊛www.baxpax.de. Great hostel with busy communal areas in a handy, yet relatively quiet location, with all the usual facilities – internet, bar, breakfast buffet, games room, bike rental – and a relaxed vibe. Avoid the fifty-bed dorm (€13) if you are a light sleeper in favour of an eight-bed (€15) or smaller (€19–21) dorm. S-Bahn Oranienburger Str. Dorms €13–21; singles €29; doubles **❷**.

St Christopher's Hostel Rosa-Luxemburg-Str. 39–41 ✆030/81 45 39 60, ⊛www .st-christophers.co.uk. Well-run branch of a British hostel chain, with big 24-hour bar, offering pub grub and occasional live events. The hostel layout means you should get a good night's sleep despite the bar noise. Rates include basic breakfast, linen and free wi-fi. U-Bahn Rosa-Luxemburg-Platz. Dorms (some single-sex) €20–26; singles €40; doubles **❸**.

Prenzlauer Berg
See map, p.114.

Acksel Haus Belforter Str. 21 ✆030/44 33 76 33, ⊛www.ackselhaus.de. Small, offbeat hotel on an attractive residential street in the midst of the lively Prenzlauer Berg scene. U-Bahn Senefelderplatz. **❻**

East Kreuzberg–Friedrichshain
See map, pp.110–111.

Eastern Comfort Mühlenstr. 73–77, Friedrichshain ✆030/66 76 38 06, ⊛www.eastern-comfort.com. Sleep bobbing on the river Spree in a range of accommodation – from spacious doubles (€76), through cabin bunks (€16) all the way to bedding down on the deck in a tent (€12). All cabins except dorms are en suite and the boat has internet and wi-fi. Highly unconventional and lots of fun, the social area and bar are lively into the small hours. U- & S-Bahn Warschauer Str.

Die Fabrik Schlesische Str. 18, Kreuzberg ✆030/611 71 16, ⊛www.diefabrik.com. Hip but quiet hostel in a converted factory. Unusually, the dorm beds aren't bunk beds. Bedding is included in the price, breakfasts aren't. U-Bahn Schlesisches Tor. Dorms €18; singles €38; doubles **❷**.

Hostel X Berger Schlesische Str. 22, Kreuzberg ✆030/69 53 18 63, ⊛www.hostelxberger.com. A friendly vibe reigns at this somewhat dowdy, but clean, hostel that's a hop, skip and a stagger from several of Kreuzberg's and Friedrichshain's best clubs and has good transport links into the city. Common areas include a basic kitchen but little else. Free wi-fi. U-Schlesisches Tor. Dorms €12–17; singles €28; doubles **❷**.

Odyssee Globetrotter Hostel Grünberger Str. 23, Friedrichshain ✆030/29 00 00 81, ⊛www .globetrotterhostel.de. Imaginatively decorated and sociable hostel hard by the Friedrichshain scene and with a happening bar of its own – making the hostel's late checkout times especially convenient. U-Bahn Frankfurter Tor. Dorms €13.50–19.50; single €36; doubles **❷**.

Zehlendorf

Jetpak Pücklerstr. 54 ☎030/83 25 011, ⓦwww.jetpak.de. One-of-a-kind hostel, family-run and with a laid-back international vibe, out in the woods on the southwestern edge of Berlin. The large communal spaces have plenty on offer, including movies, bikes, free internet, and lots of indoor and outdoor games. Bring

supplies as there are no stores in the vicinity. Recommended for those driving to Berlin since you can avoid negotiating and parking in the centre. U-Bahn Günzelstrasse or Fehrberliner Platz then bus #115 to Pücklerstrasse; frequent night buses from the centre stop a safe 10min walk away. Dorms €14–17; singles €25; doubles ❷.

Campsites

Camping in Berlin can be fun, since its most central campsite is an easy walk from the Hauptbahnhof and the suburban campsites quite rural and relaxing, though they are too far from the centre to conveniently take in much nightlife.

Campingplatz Am Krossinsee Wernsdorfer Str. 38 ☎030/675 86 87. Woodland campground just outside the southeastern suburb of Schmöckwitz, with easy access to local lakes. Bungalows available too (€32.25). From S-Bahn Grünar take tram #68 to Schmöckwitz, and from there catch bus #733 to the grounds.

Campingplatz Kladow Krampnitzer Weg 111–117, Spandau ☎030/365 27 97. Friendly campsite on the western side of the Havel lake, with excellent facilities, including a free crèche, bar, restaurant, shop and showers. U-Bahn Rathaus Spandau, then bus #X34 to Alt-Kladow stop, change to the #234 to "Selbitzer Strasse", walk west to the end of the road following "DCC" signs.

Tentstation Seydlitzstr. 6 ☎030/39 40 46 50, ⓦwww.tentstation.de. Bohemian campsite surrounding a defunct lido in the otherwise dreary residential district of Moabit – but an easy walk from the Hauptbahnhof. Facilities are basic, but made up for by the chance to play basketball, football, volleyball and table-tennis or party until 1am in the groovy campsite bar, whose programme of weekly events ranges from gigs to DJs to recitals and films. Rates are €11 per person in your own tent, or you can rent one for €4 per night (sleeping mats €1 extra). Reception daily 8am–11pm. S-Bahn Hauptbahnhof. Open May–Sept.

Mitte

The natural place to start exploring Berlin is at the city's most famous landmark, the **Brandenburg Gate**. The surrounding area is dense with heavyweight attractions: Germany's parliament, the **Reichstag**, is on one side, the giant **Holocaust Memorial** on the other, while opposite spreads the giant **Tiergarten** park. Stimulating contemporary architecture dots the park's fringes, the most eye-catching being the soaring buildings of **Potsdamer Platz**. Since the fall of the Wall this bustling entertainment quarter has slowly re-established itself as Berlin's Piccadilly Circus or Times Square, as it was in the 1930s. Neighbouring here is the **Kulturforum**, an agglomeration of cultural institutions that includes several high-profile art museums.

The grid of streets around Unter den Linden, which runs east from the Brandenburg Gate, includes **Friedrichstrasse**, a luxury shopping avenue once interrupted by **Checkpoint Charlie**, and the **Gendarmenmarkt**, a fine plaza with two elegant churches. A larger square, **Bebelplatz**, lies just northeast, alongside a stretch of Unter den Linden where stately Neoclassical buildings pave the way to **Museum Island**, housing Berlin's foremost collections of art and antiquities. Further east again is the area that formed the GDR's socialist showpiece quarter, centred around the broad concrete plaza of **Alexanderplatz** and the distinctive **Fernsehturm** television tower. The only real break from the area's modernity is the **Nikolaiviertel**, a rebuilt version of Berlin's historic core. Northwest of here is the **Spandauer Vorstadt**, once the heart of the city's Jewish community, with some fascinating reminders of those days, though today it's best known for the restaurants, bars and nightlife of **Oranienburger Strasse**.

The Brandenburg Gate, Pariser Platz and Unter den Linden

Heavily laden with historical association, the **Brandenburg Gate** (Brandenburger Tor), modelled after the entrance of Athens' Acropolis, was built as a city-gate-cum-triumphal-arch in 1791 and soon became a symbol of German solidarity. In 1806 Napoleon marched under the arch and took home the **Quadriga**, the horse-drawn chariot that tops the gate. It was returned a few years later, and the revolutionaries of 1848 and 1918 met under its form, as did the Nazis with their torch-lit marches. The Berlin Wall placed the Gate in the East in a heavily guarded death-strip, and the opening of the border here just before Christmas 1989 symbolically re-created the historic east–west axis of the city.

The Brandenburg Gate looms over the ornamental gardens of **Pariser Platz**. On its southeast corner stands the rebuilt, legendary **Hotel Adlon** (see p.75), once one of Europe's grandest hotels. The original was host to luminaries from Charlie Chaplin to Lawrence of Arabia and Kaiser Wilhelm II, and was regarded throughout the continent as the acme of luxury and style. Just across the square lies the **Berlin Kennedy Museum** (daily 10am–6pm; €7; ☎030/20 65 35 70, ⓦ www.thekennedys.de), an intriguing homage to John F. Kennedy, explored in three hundred photos and dozens of relics. The highlights are exhibits relating to JFK's eight-hour visit to Berlin on June 26, 1963, when the city's emotions ran high, as shown in wonderful footage of ecstatic crowds. Kennedy's city parade included a stop at a viewing platform in front of the Brandenburg Gate – draped for the occasion by the Russians in enormous red flags and communist placards – before he delivered his impassioned "Berliner" speech (see p.108).

The leafy grand boulevard that runs east of Pariser Platz is **Unter den Linden**, or "beneath the lime trees", for the trees that line its central island. The first saplings were planted by Friedrich Wilhelm, the Great Elector, during the seventeenth century, to line the route from his palace to the hunting grounds in the Tiergarten (see p.82). It gradually became the main thoroughfare of Imperial Berlin and site of many foreign embassies, yet after the war and until 1989 the western extremity of Unter den Linden led nowhere and, lined by infrequently visited embassies, the street had a strangely empty and decorative feel. Today the boulevard bustles with shops and cafés, though their presence is relatively muted.

The Reichstag

Directly behind the Brandenburg Gate a line of cobbles marks the course of the Berlin Wall where for 28 years it separated the Gate from the other great emblem of national unity, the **Reichstag** – now once again the seat of Germany's parliament. The imposing nineteenth-century Neoclassical Reichstag immediately impresses, its stolid, bombastic form wholly in keeping with its pivotal role in history. It was built to house a sham parliament answerable only to the Kaiser, but in November 1918, Philipp Scheidemann declared the founding of the German Republic from a window here, paving the way for the Weimar Republic, which lasted just fourteen years before the Nazis claimed power. Their coup came partly

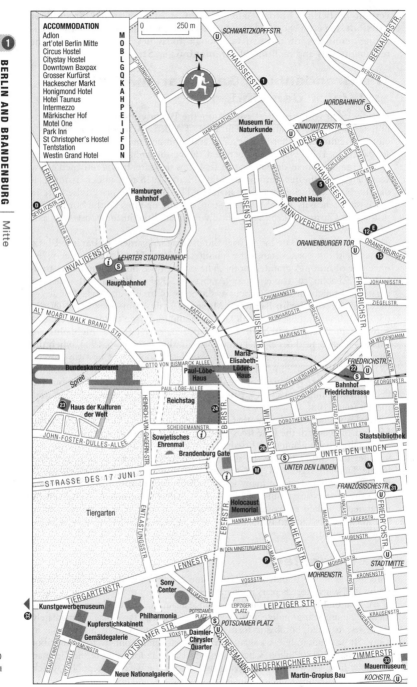

ACCOMMODATION

Adlon	M
art'otel Berlin Mitte	O
Circus Hostel	B
Citystay Hostel	L
Downtown Baxpax	G
Grosser Kurfürst	Q
Hackescher Markt	K
Honigmond Hotel	A
Hotel Taunus	H
Intermezzo	P
Märkischer Hof	E
Motel One	I
Park Inn	J
St Christopher's Hostel	F
Tentstation	D
Westin Grand Hotel	N

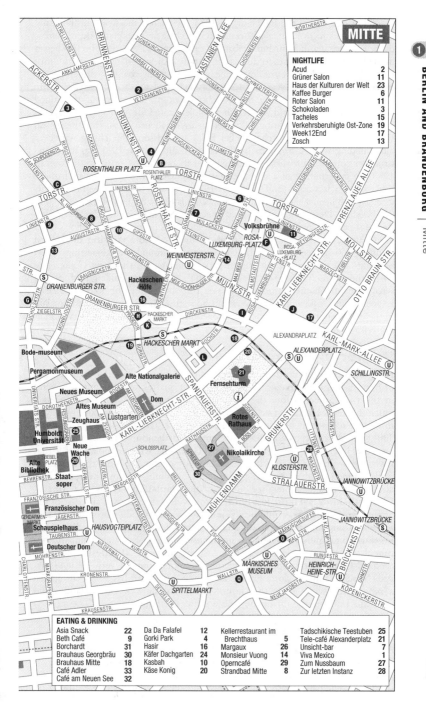

as a result of a fire in the Reichstag in 1933, seen across the world in flickering newsreels, which gave Hitler an excuse to introduce an emergency decree effectively instigating a dictatorship. Debate as to who actually started the fire began immediately and continues to this day. In a show trial, an itinerant ex-communist Dutch bricklayer, Marius van der Lubbe, was successfully charged with arson and executed the following year, but it's more likely that the Nazis started the fire themselves. Equally famously, the Reichstag became a symbol of the Allied victory at the end of World War II, when soldiers raised the Soviet flag on its roof – even though heavy fighting still raged below. Evidence of this fighting is still visible in the scores of patched bullet holes around some Reichstag windows. The building was left in tatters by the conflict, and only in 1971 was its reconstruction completed to house a museum of its own and Germany's history. In 1990 the government of a reunified Germany decided to move its parliament back, though it wasn't until April 19, 1999, that this happened – once all its interiors had been refashioned and a new cupola (daily 8am–10pm; free) set atop the building. Designed by British architect Sir Norman Foster, this giant glass **dome** supported by a soaring, mirrored column has become the building's main visitor attraction. A circular ramp spirals up the inside to a **viewing deck** with stunning 360-degree views of the city. In the foreground the Regierungsviertel buildings and the massive Tiergarten park dominate, but the Sony Center (see p.84), the Fernsehturm (see p.97) and the shimmering golden roof of the synagogue on Oranienburger Strasse (see p.100) are other obvious landmarks. Expect to queue for entry for at least an hour, though if you arrive early or late in the day it can be a bit quicker – or, for immediate entry, make a reservation at the *Käfer Dachgarten* restaurant (see p.121).

Regierungsviertel

Foreground views from the Reichstag are filled with the cutting-edge designs of Berlin's **Regierungsviertel**, or government quarter, which clings to a bend in the river Spree. Before the war, luxurious apartments here overlooked a much shorter Siegessäule (see opposite) in front of the Reichstag, until this was moved to its present position to make way for a "Great Hall of the People". This giant structure, based loosely on Rome's Parthenon, was to be the centrepiece of Hitler's and Speer's World Capital Germania, with a cupola so large that it was impossible to build with the technology of the day. Now the strikingly well-designed modern federal government buildings occupy the space. The elegant offices and conference rooms of the **Paul-Löbe-Haus** and **Maria-Elisabeth-Lüders-Haus**, just north of the Reichstag and west and east of the Spree respectively, are symbolically joined via a footbridge over the former East–West border, while an underground tunnel linking them to the Reichstag is meant to tangibly represent the interconnectedness of government. Another tunnel was planned to connect them to the imposing **Bundeskanzleramt** (Federal Chancellery), opposite, but the money ran out. Cleverly designed by Axel Schultes and Charlotte Frank, the Bundeskanzleramt has as its centrepiece a nine-storey white cube that houses the chancellor's accommodation, and earns the building the nickname "the washing machine".

The Tiergarten

A huge swathe of peaceful green parkland smack in the middle of Berlin, the **Tiergarten** was originally designed by Peter Lenné as a hunting ground for Elector Friedrich III, but now provides a great antidote to the bustle and noise of the city. The park is most easily accessed by bus #100 between Bahnhof Zoo and Alexanderplatz, but best appreciated on foot or by bike. At the least, wander along the Landwehrkanal, and the pretty little group of ponds that make up the grand-sounding **Neuer See**. In summer there's a popular beer garden here, the *Café am Neuen See*, where it's also possible to rent **boats** by the hour.

Approached by great boulevards at the centre of the Tiergarten, is the eye-catching **Siegessäule** (Victory Column; April–Oct Mon–Fri 9.30am–6.30pm, Sat & Sun 9.30am–7pm; Nov–March Mon–Fri 10am–5pm, Sat & Sun 10am–5.30pm; €2.20; bus #100). Topped with a gilded Winged Victory, the column celebrates Prussia's military victories (chiefly over France in 1871) and was moved here from in front of the Reichstag on Hitler's orders in 1938. The mosaics at the column's base show the unification of the German peoples and incidents from the Franco-Prussian War. The four bronze reliefs beside depict the main wars and the victorious marching of the troops into Berlin; these were removed after 1945 and taken to Paris, only to be returned when the lust for war spoils had subsided. The **Siegessäule**'s summit offers a good view of the surroundings, but climbing its 285 steps is no mean feat.

The Holocaust Memorial and prewar Regierungsviertel

Beside the Brandenburg Gate, the dignified and surreal **Holocaust Memorial** (℡030/26 39 43 36, Ⓦwww.holocaustmahnmal.de; S-Bahn Unter den Linden) – officially the "National Memorial to the Murdered Jews of Europe" – was unveiled in May 2006 after close to seventeen years of planning and heated debate over its scale, design, location and cost, then six years of design and building. It's the work of New York architect Peter Eisenman, who was inspired by the densely clustered gravestones in Prague's Jewish graveyard. The entire site – which is about the size of three football pitches – is covered with 2711 tightly spaced, oblong, dark grey pillars of varying heights. There is no single entrance, and visitors must find their own way through the maze to the centre where the blocks are well above head height, intending to convey a sense of gloom, isolation and solitude. At night, 180 lights create a stunning yet sombre space. The underground **information centre** (Tues–Sun 10am–8pm, last admission 7.15pm; free; tours in English Sun 4pm, €3), in the southeast corner of the monument, relates several carefully researched and expertly presented life stories of selected Jewish victims of the Holocaust. The exhibition **audio tour** (€5) is largely unnecessary.

The Holocaust Memorial lies at the northern end of Berlin's **prewar Regierungsviertel**, or government quarter. From 1871 onwards government buildings stood shoulder to shoulder here, including the Chancellery and, after the Republic was established in 1918, the Presidential Palace. Today little remains, but trying to figure out what was where can be a compelling activity, made easier by the presence of information boards with photographs and descriptions of former buildings, mostly along Wilhelmstrasse. One such board lies a couple of minutes' walk south of the Holocaust Memorial along Gertrude-Kolmar-Strasse at the site of Hitler's bunker, where the Führer spent his last days, issuing meaningless orders as the Battle of Berlin raged above. Here Hitler married Eva Braun and wrote his final testament. On April 30, 1945, he shot himself, and his body was hurriedly burned by loyal officers.

Potsdamer Platz and around

The skyscrapers of **Postdamer Platz**, at the Tiergarten's southeastern corner, are Berlin at its most thrustingly commercial and modern. Within the bold architectural forms lie the obligatory shopping malls with restaurants, cafés, a theatre, and a film multiplex with 3D cinema. Said to have been the busiest square in prewar Europe, **Potsdamer Platz** was once surrounded by stores, bars and clubs and pulsed with life day and night. The war left it severely battered, though it regained some of its vitality in the chaos immediately afterwards as a black market at the junction of the Soviet, American and British sectors. Later, the Cold War was played out here in words, with the western authorities relaying their version of the news to East Berliners by means of an electronic newsboard – countered by an eastern billboard exhorting West Berliners to shop in cheap East Berlin stores. This ended with the coming of the Wall, which finally put a physical seal on the ideological division of Potsdamer Platz. On the eastern side all the buildings were razed to give the GDR's border guards a clear field of fire, while in the West only a couple of battered survivors remained as a reminder of the way things used to be. For years western tourists could gaze at the East from a viewing platform here, and ponder the sight of prewar tramlines disappearing at the base of the Wall. The dismantling of the Wall then produced one of Europe's most valuable lots, quickly carved up by multinationals who built sprawling commercial complexes and an entire power, water and sewage, and subway infrastructure from scratch in two decades of frantic building work. This made Potsdamer Platz Berlin's most muscular display of commercial power – and not to everyone's taste – but though the main groups of buildings are all strikingly different somehow their approaches harmonize.

The Sony Center and Filmmuseum

The bravely twenty-first–century glass cylinder of the Helmut Jahn–designed **Sony Center** is the most eye-catching building on Potsdamer Platz. Several glass-sheathed buildings surround an airy, circular courtyard, sheltered by a conical glass rotunda, creating a huge atrium, open to the elements yet providing respite from the urban racket. Berliners have adopted the courtyard as a place to congregate for major sporting events – particularly football matches – when big screens are rolled out to a near-stadium atmosphere. Within the Sony Center, the **Filmmuseum Berlin** (Tues–Sun 10am–6pm, Thurs until 8pm; €6; Ⓦwww.filmmuseum-berlin.de) provides a superb introduction to the history of German cinema and television, with a useful free audio guide in English. Using a bevy of clips, reconstructions and artefacts it plots the course of German cinema through various technical innovations, stars and major releases. The museum is particularly strong on Marlene Dietrich, since it inherited much of her estate on her death in 1992 – and quite a haul it was too: over 3000 documents, 15,000 photos and some 3000 items of clothing stuffed into sixty valises.

DaimlerChrysler quarter and around

Looming over the Sony Center and offsetting it with its red-brick solidity the **DaimlerChrysler quarter** is a homage to Chicago's school of architecture. Its **Panorama Punkt** (Tues–Sun 11am–7.30pm; €3), at the top of the complex's tallest skyscraper, provides stellar city views, with the exposed nature of the outdoor viewing deck providing an immediacy you won't find in the Fernsehturm, its main rival. A two-minute walk beyond the **DaimlerChrysler quarter** along Stresemannstrasse on Niederkirchnerstrasse is the **Martin–Gropius-Bau** (Mon & Wed–Sun 10am–8pm; prices vary; ☎030/25 48 60, Ⓦwww.gropiusbau .de; S- & U-Bahn Potsdamer Platz), a magnificently restored building designed in 1877 by Martin Gropius, a pupil of Schinkel and the uncle of Bauhaus guru Walter, which houses changing exhibitions of art, photography and architecture.

Beside it, and a tatty remnant of the Berlin Wall, is the former headquarters of the Gestapo and SS. Little has been done with the plot since their destruction at the end of the war, although a museum of Nazi history is planned. Until then the outdoor exhibition, **The Topography of Terror** (daily: May–Sept 10am–8pm; Oct–April 10am–6pm; free; Ⓦwww.topographie.de; S- & U-Bahn Potsdamer Platz), is well worth investigating. A numbered series of noticeboards with photographs and German texts (audio guides in English are free but require ID as a deposit) indicate the sites of the most important buildings and reveal gruesome insights – the ground beneath the exhibition once held the cellars where prisoners were interrogated and tortured. On the opposite side of the street stands the best-preserved building of the former Third Reich government quarter: Hermann Göring's fortress-like **Luftfahrtministerium** (Air Ministry), a rare relic of the Nazi past that has survived very much intact. It now houses the Federal Finance Ministry.

The Kulturforum

The cluster of museums and cultural spaces that make up the Kulturforum, to the west of Potsdamer Platz, could easily fill a day of your time. Many of its buildings were designed in the 1960s by Hans Scharoun, including the honey-coloured **Philharmonie**, home of the Berlin Philharmonic. Equally world-class is the **Kunstgewerbemuseum** for applied art, the **Gemäldegalerie** for old masters and the **Neue Nationalgalerie** of twentieth-century and contemporary art.

The Philharmonie

Frequently considered the world's best, from the 1960s to the 1980s the Berlin Philharmonic orchestra became inextricably associated with genius conductor Herbert von Karajan until he retired in 1989. Looking at the gaudy building and bearing in mind von Karajan's famously short temper with artists, it's easy to see why Berliners nicknamed it "Karajan's circus". However, Scharoun's complicated floor-plan around the orchestra offers top-notch acoustics and views, regardless of your seat. Other than going to a performance (see p.127), you can also view the interior of the building on free tours (in German; daily 1pm). In the same building, and continuing the musical theme, the **Musik-instrumenten museum** (Tues–Fri 9am–5pm, Thurs 9am–10pm, Sat & Sun 10am–5pm; €4 or with a *Bereichskarte*, see p.92; Ⓦwww.sim.spk-berlin.de), is disappointing, despite its comprehensive collection of instruments from the fifteenth century to the present.

The Kunstgewerbemuseum

Over the road from the Philharmonie, the **Kunstgewerbemuseum** (Museum of Applied Arts; Tues–Fri 10am–6pm, Sat & Sun 11am–6pm; €8; see p.92) holds an encyclopedic but seldom dull collection of European arts and crafts from the Middle Ages on. Renaissance, Baroque and Rococo pieces (wonderful silver and ceramics), along with Jugendstil, Art Deco and Bauhaus objects are all present, as are some sumptuous pieces from the Middle Ages and Early Renaissance collections. Highlights are Lüneburg's municipal silver and an eighth-century purse-shaped **reliquary** that belonged to Duke Widikund, leader of the Saxon resistance to Charlemagne.

The Gemäldegalerie

A stupendous collection of early European paintings, the **Gemäldegalerie** (Picture Gallery; Mon–Wed & Fri–Sun 10am–6pm, Thurs 10am–10pm; €8; see p.92) is the real jewel of the Kulturforum. Highlights include **German work** from the Middle Ages and Renaissance such as the large *Wurzach Altar* of 1437, from the workshop of the great Ulm sculptor Hans Multscher, landscapes by Albrecht Altdorfer, and several superbly observed portraits by Albrecht Dürer and Hans Holbein the Younger. The gallery's **Netherlandish section** features fifteenth- and sixteenth-century art and includes works by Jan van Eyck, Jan Gossaert, Quentin Massys and Pieter Bruegel the Elder, whose *Netherlandish Proverbs* is an amusing, if opaque, illustration of over a hundred sixteenth-century proverbs. The later **Dutch and Flemish collections**, with their large portraits of Van Dyck and fleshy canvases of Rubens, are another strong point in the gallery. But the high points of this section are several paintings by **Rembrandt**: though *The Man in the Golden Helmet* has been proved to be the work of his studio rather than the artist himself, this does little to detract from the elegance and power of the portrait. Finally, the **Italian section** spanning the Renaissance to the eighteenth century, is particularly strong on works from the Florentine Renaissance, including important paintings by Botticelli, Caravaggio, Poussin, Claude and Canaletto.

Sharing its main entrance with the Gemäldegalerie, the **Kupferstichkabinett** (Engraving Cabinet; Tues–Fri 10am–6pm, Sat & Sun 11am–6pm; €8, see box, p.92; ☏030/266 20 02) holds an extensive collection of European medieval and Renaissance prints, drawings and engravings. The collection includes Botticelli's exquisite drawings for Dante's *Divine Comedy*.

The Neue Nationalgalerie

At the southeast corner of the Kulturforum, and by far its finest building is the **Neue Nationalgalerie** (Tues, Wed & Fri 10am–6pm, Thurs 10am–10pm, Sat & Sun 11am–6pm; €8; see box, p.92). Designed by Mies van der Rohe in 1965, the building comprises a severe glass box, its ceiling seemingly almost suspended above the ground, its clarity of line and detail oozing intelligent simplicity. The gallery divides between the permanent collection, featuring works from the beginning of the twentieth century onwards, including paintings of the "Brücke" group, work by **Braque**, **Gris** and **Picasso**, and temporary exhibits, often of contemporary art. Previous works include Mark Wallinger's performance piece during which he locked himself into the gallery for ten nights in a row dressed in a bear suit – a tribute to the city's symbol – pacing the floor in a daze and gazing at onlookers, a video of which won him the Turner Prize in 2007.

The diplomatic district

The area immediately west of the Kulturforum was once filled by the ostentatious residences of the well heeled – fine villas with long, narrow gardens overlooking the Tiergarten – before the Nazis forcibly acquired them to create a **diplomatic district**. The war saw the area comprehensively destroyed, and while the West German government was in Bonn, few countries made much of their plots. Once the government returned to Berlin many re-established their presence, producing a stimulating showcase of contemporary architecture. It's best admired by walking along Tiergartenstrasse, where you'll see the dignified **Egyptian Embassy**, the flamboyant **Austrian Embassy** by Viennese architect Hans Hollein, and the **Indian Embassy** hewn from rough-cut red sandstone. Further west you reach the two unmistakable Nazi-era edifices of Germany's closest prewar allies: the **Japanese**, **Italian** and **Spanish embassies**. Providing a sharp contrast are the bold, bright lines of the area's most exciting contemporary buildings around the corner on Klingelhöferstrasse where the stunning **Nordic Embassy** provides offices for Denmark, Sweden, Finland, Iceland and Norway, and playfully reflect changes in light or weather and is most dramatic at night. More simplicity and modernist beauty is next door at the avant-garde **Mexican Embassy**.

On the eastern edge of the diplomatic district is Stauffenbergstrasse, which takes its name from Count Claus Schenk von Stauffenberg, one of the instigators of the July Bomb Plot. At no. 13–14 stands the **Bendlerblock**, the German Defence Ministry and former Wehrmacht headquarters, where Stauffenberg was chief of staff; a memorial stands in the courtyard here where he was executed by firing squad. The floors where he worked are occupied by the absorbing **Gedenkstätte Deutscher Widerstand** (Memorial to German Resistance; Mon–Wed & Fri 9am–6pm, Thurs 9am–8pm, Sat & Sun 10am–6pm; free), a huge collection of photos and documents covering the many groups who actively opposed the Third Reich – an eclectic mix that included communists, Jews, Quakers and aristocrats. A free English audio tour (ID required) covers the highlights in around forty minutes.

Friedrichstrasse

Back at Potsdamer Platz a walk three blocks east brings you to **Friedrichstrasse**, a street of bland modern offices and malls that crosses Unter den Linden, where high-end boutiques rub shoulders with more everyday shops, including several good bookshops. Before the war Friedrichstrasse was busy with cafés, bars and restaurants and was a well-known prostitutes' haunt. Nazi puritanism dealt the first blow to this thriving Vergnügungsviertel (Pleasure Quarter), and the work was finished by Allied bombers, who razed the street. Rebuilt considerably wider, what had once been a narrow, slightly claustrophobic street became a broad, desolate road, its busiest corner **Bahnhof Friedrichstrasse**, formerly the heavily guarded main border crossing point for western visitors to East Berlin. Since reunification, Friedrichstrasse has been extensively redeveloped into a shopping arcade, while under the tracks just to the southeast a series of fascinating old antiques stores thrives.

Friedrichstrasse's southern end is its most interesting stretch, as the former site of **Checkpoint Charlie**, an Allied military post and gateway between the two Berlins. With its dramatic "YOU ARE NOW LEAVING THE AMERICAN SECTOR" signs and border guards, it became the best-known Iron Curtain crossing and scene of repeated border incidents, including a standoff between American and Soviet forces in October 1961, when tanks from both sides growled at each other for a few days. The original border post is in the Allied Museum (see p.117), though a **replica** marks the original site. One place to get a feel for the border and what it meant is at the adjacent and jumbled **Mauermuseum**, Friedrichstrasse 44 (Wall Museum; daily 9am–10pm; €9.50; Ⓦ www.mauermuseum.de; U-Bahn Kochstrasse), where photos and artefacts document all manner of ingenious escape plans – using tunnels, diving gear, glides and adapted cars – all more a tribute to tenacious creativity, rather than a true document of what the division really meant to the German people.

The Gendarmenmarkt

A five-minute walk north along Friedrichstrasse brings you within a block of the immaculately restored **Gendarmenmarkt**. It's now hard to imagine that all its buildings were almost obliterated during the war and that rebuilding lasted well into the 1980s. The square was originally home to Berlin's main market until the Gendarme regiment set up their stables here in 1736. With the departure of the military, Frederick the Great ordered an architectural revamp in an attempt to mimic the Piazza del Popolo in Rome.

The Berlin Wall

After the war, Berlin was split among Britain, France, the US and USSR. Each sector was administered by the relevant country, and was to exist peacefully with its neighbours under a unified city council. But, almost from the outset, antagonism between the Soviet and other sectors was high. Only three years after the war, Soviet forces closed the land-access corridors to the city from the western zones in what became known as the **Berlin Blockade**: it was successfully overcome by a massive **airlift** of food and supplies that lasted nearly a year. This, followed by the 1953 uprising, large-scale cross-border emigration (between 1949 and 1961, the year the Wall was built, over three million East Germans – almost a fifth of the population – fled to West Germany) and innumerable "incidents", led to the building of what the GDR called an "an antifascist protection barrier".

The Wall was erected overnight on **August 13, 1961** when, at 2am, forty thousand East German soldiers, policemen and workers' militia went into action closing U- and S-Bahn lines and stringing barbed wire across streets leading into West Berlin to cordon off the Soviet sector. The Wall followed its boundaries implacably, cutting through houses, across squares and rivers, with its own cool illogicality. Many Berliners were rudely evicted from their homes, while others had their doors and windows blocked by bales of barbed wire. Suddenly the British, American and French sectors of the city were corralled some 200km inside the GDR, and though they reinforced patrols, the Allies did nothing to prevent the sealing of the border.

Most people in West and East Berlin were taken by surprise. Crowds gathered and extra border guards were sent to prevent trouble. A tiny number – including a few border guards – managed to find holes in the new barrier and flee west. But within a few days, building workers were reinforcing the barbed wire and makeshift barricades with bricks and mortar. As an additional measure, West Berliners were no longer allowed to cross the border into East Berlin. From 1961 onwards the GDR strengthened the Wall making it almost impenetrable – in effect two walls separated by a *Sperrgebiet* (forbidden zone), dotted with watchtowers and patrolled by soldiers and dogs. It was also known as the *Todesstreifen* (death strip) as border troops were under instructions to shoot anyone attempting to scale the Wall: any guard suspected of deliberately missing was court-martialled, and his family could expect severe harassment from the authorities. Over the years, over two hundred people were **killed** endeavouring to cross the Wall.

An oddity of the Wall was that it was built a few metres inside GDR territory; the West Berlin authorities therefore had little control over the **graffiti** that covered it. The Wall was an ever-changing mixture of colours and slogans.

Late in 1989 the East German government, spurred by Gorbachev's glasnost and confronted by a tense domestic climate, realized it could stay stable no longer. To an initially disbelieving and then jubilant Europe, travel restrictions for GDR citizens were lifted on November 9, 1989 – effectively, the Wall had ceased to matter, and pictures of Berliners, East and West, hacking away at the detested symbol filled newspapers and TV bulletins around the world. Within days, enterprising characters were renting out hammers and chisels so that souvenir hunters could take home their own chip of the Wall.

Today, especially in the city centre, it's only possible to tell exactly where the Wall ran by the simple row of cobbles that has been placed along much of its former course. Few significant stretches remain, the sections devoted to the East Side Gallery (see p.113) and the Berlin Wall Memorial (see p.101) being the most notable.

At the southern end of the square, the **Deutscher Dom**, built in 1708 for the city's Lutheran community, hosts a dull exhibition (Wed–Sun 10am–7pm, Thurs open until 10pm; free) on Germany's democratic history. A wander up through the Dom with its labyrinth of galleries is the highlight. More impressive and eye-catching is the **Französischer Dom** at the northern end of the square. Built as a simple place of worship for Berlin's influential Huguenots at the beginning of the eighteenth century, the appealing Baroque **tower** added some eighty years later overwhelms the church itself. Once complete, renovation work on the tower will enable access via a spiral staircase (daily 9am–7pm; €3) to a balcony and will provide good views over the square. Another attraction is its fine tower bells – which ring daily at noon, 4pm and 7pm. At the base of the tower is the entrance to the **Hugenottenmuseum** (Tues–Sat noon–5pm, Sun 11am–5pm; €2), detailing the history of the Huguenots in France and their arrival in numbers in Prussia thanks to guarantees of rights and religious freedom.

Between the two churches stands Schinkel's Neoclassical **Konzerthaus Berlin** (formerly called the **Schauspielhaus**). Dating from 1817, it was built around the ruins of Langhans' burned-out National Theatre, retaining the latter's exterior walls and portico columns. A broad sweep of steps leads up to the main entrance and into an interior of incredible opulence, where chandeliers, marble, gilded plasterwork and pastel-hued wall paintings all compete for attention.

Bebelplatz and around

Two blocks northeast of the Gendarmenmarkt, the lime trees no longer define Unter den Linden as it opens out onto a string of imposing Neoclassical buildings around **Bebelplatz**. This was designed as eighteenth-century Berlin's showpiece quarter in its days as capital of Brandenburg-Prussia – when it suddenly competed with the likes of Paris, Vienna and Prague. Its buildings were intended to project an image of solidity, permanence and power, and after the heavy bombing and shelling of World War II they were extensively restored. Most were designed under, and even by, **Frederick the Great**, who still overlooks proceedings as Christian Rauch's nineteenth-century equestrian monument at the centre of Unter den Linden, with the help of architect **Georg Wenzeslaus von Knobelsdorff**. Intended as both a tribute to the grandeur of ancient Rome and to himself, the square never quite fulfilled such lofty ambitions. Bleak and unimpressive, its only feature is the **Empty Library** at its centre, a monument to the plaza's most infamous event. It was here, on May 10, 1933, that the **Büchverbrennung** took place, demonstratively in front of the university, in which twenty thousand books which conflicted with Nazi ideology went up in smoke. The ingenious monument, by Micha Ullmann, is simply a room of empty shelves set underground beneath a pane of glass; it's spectacular at night when a beam of light streams out.

Humboldt Universität and Alte Bibliothek

Humboldt Universität, on the north side of Bebelplatz, was built in 1748 as a palace for Frederick's brother. In 1809 the philologist, writer and diplomat Wilhelm Humboldt founded a school here that became the University of Berlin, later renamed in his honour. Flanking the entrance gate are statues of Wilhelm and his brother Alexander, famous for his exploration of Central and South America. Humboldt alumni include Karl Marx, Friedrich Engels and Karl Liebknecht, the socialist leader and proclaimer of the first German Republic, murdered in 1919. The philologists Jacob and Wilhelm Grimm, and Albert Einstein, are some of the best-known former members of staff. Crowding the western side of Bebelplatz with its curved Baroque facade is the **Alte Bibliothek**, a former royal library, built between 1775 and 1780, where Lenin spent time poring over dusty tomes while waiting for the Russian Revolution.

Staatsoper, Sankt-Hedwigs-Kathedrale and Opernpalais

Knobelsdorff's Neoclassical **Staatsoper**, on the western side of the square, is among its plainer buildings, and best viewed from Unter den Linden, where an imposing portico marks the main entrance. Now totally reconstructed after extensive war damage, it is one of Berlin's leading opera houses (see p.128). Just behind the Staatsoper another Knobelsdorff creation, the stylistically incongruous **Sankt-Hedwigs-Kathedrale** (Mon–Sat 10am–5pm, Sun 1–5pm; free), was inspired by the Pantheon in Rome and built as a place of worship for the city's Catholic minority in 1747 and is still in use. Reduced to a shell on March 2, 1943, the cathedral was not reconstructed until 1963, a restoration that left it with an oddly modern interior.

East of the Staatsoper and back in view of Unter den Linden lies a lawn dotted with dignified **statues of Prussian generals**. The Baroque building behind is the eighteenth-century **Opernpalais**. Known as the Prinzessinpalais (Princess's Palace) before the war, for being the swanky town house of Friedrich Wilhelm III's three daughters, it's now home to a couple of pricey restaurants and the genteel *Operncafé* (see p.119).

The Friedrichwerdersche Kirche and Bauakademie

By ducking under two sets of arches in Bebelplatz's southeast corner you'll come to the **Friedrichwerdersche Kirche** in which the **Schinkel Museum** (daily 10am–6pm; free; ⓦ www.smb.spk-berlin.de; S-Bahn Hausvogteiplatz) fittingly celebrates the work of the man, who was born around the time that Frederick died and who would add the next layer of architecture to the Prussian capital (see box below). The church itself is a rather plain neo-Gothic affair, a stylistic departure for Schinkel and inspired by churches he had seen in England in 1826. A detailed history of the church is provided in the upper gallery of the museum, which also details Schinkel's achievements. A jumble of nineteenth-century German Neoclassical statuary crowds the ground floor.

Before World War II the block to the east of here, on the banks of the Spree, was the site of the **Bauakademie**, Karl Friedrich Schinkel's architectural school.

Karl Friedrich Schinkel

The incredibly prolific architect **Karl Friedrich Schinkel** (1781–1841) was without doubt one of the most influential German architects of the nineteenth century. Nearly every town in Brandenburg has a building that Schinkel had, at the very least, some involvement in, and a lasting testimony to his importance is the fact that even today the very heart of Berlin, with its distinctive Neoclassical stamp, is essentially defined by his work. His first ever design, the **Pomonatempel** in Potsdam, was completed while he was still a 19-year-old student in Berlin. Despite this auspicious beginning, his architectural career did not take off immediately and for a while he worked as a landscape artist and theatre-set designer. Towards the end of the first decade of the nineteenth century he began submitting architectural designs for great public works, and, in 1810, he secured a job with the administration of Prussian buildings.

In 1815 he was given a position in the new Public Works Department, and between 1815 and 1830 he designed some of his most renowned buildings, including the Grecian-style **Neue Wache** (see opposite), the elegant **Schauspielhaus** (see p.89), and the **Altes Museum** (p.93) with its striking Doric columns. Later in his career Schinkel experimented with other architectural forms, a phase marked by the Romanesque **Charlottenhof** in Potsdam (see p.143).

This 1836 building is widely considered one of modern architecture's true ancestors with its rejection of classicism in favour of a brick exterior and terracotta ornamentation. The GDR demolished it in 1962 – despite its relatively light war damage – in favour of a prefab for its foreign ministry which became one of the first buildings to be demolished after the *Wende*. It was replaced by a grassy field with a statue of Schinkel in the middle, but there are proposals to rebuild the Bauakademie. As an advertisement and fundraising incentive, a corner section of the building has been reconstructed on its original site. The rest of the building has been re-created using scaffolding, wrapped in a canvas facade.

The Neue Wache

Schinkel's most celebrated surviving creation, the **Neue Wache**, is on Unter den Linden east of Humboldt Universität. Built between 1816 and 1818 as a guardhouse for the royal watch, it resembles a Roman temple and served as a police station until 1918. In 1930 it became a memorial to the military dead of World War I, and in 1957 the GDR extended this to include those killed by the Nazis. These days it serves as the "National Memorial to the Victims of War and Tyranny", and inside a granite slab covers the tombs of an unknown soldier and an unknown concentration camp victim. At the head of this memorial stone is a statue, depicting a mother clutching her dying son, an enlargement of a small sculpture by Käthe Kollwitz (see p.105).

The Deutsches Historisches Museum

One of Berlin's finest Baroque buildings, the old Prussian Arsenal or **Zeughaus**, lies just east of the Neue Wache. Many of its decorative elements are the work of Andreas Schlüter, notably the walls of the museum's inner courtyard, where vivid reliefs depict the contorted faces of dying warriors. In the late nineteenth century the Zeughaus was turned into a museum devoted to the exploits of the Prussian army and has been a museum of sorts ever since, though often at the mercy of extreme political ideologies. Today, as the **Deutsches Historisches Museum** (daily 10am–6pm; €4; ☎030/20 30 40, ⓦwww.dhm.de; S-Bahn Hackescher Markt), it presents a balanced and tempered historical narrative using the museum's immense collection to chart German history from the Dark Ages on. The **collection** of art and artefacts and narrative description is arranged so that it's easy to skip epochs or immerse yourself; pick up the audio guide if your German is minimal. Inevitably the museum focuses overwhelmingly on military escapades, though it does show how various periods affected the masses. However, the Prussian-centric narrative that results fails to break from fairly familiar ground or provide much social history.

The **I.M. Pei Bau**, an eye-catching, swirling, glass building behind the Zeughaus, is part of the museum, and the work of American-Chinese architect I.M. Pei – famous for his glass pyramid at Paris's Louvre. The building is given over to temporary exhibitions on German social history from the past couple of centuries, using first-class exhibition techniques to explore frequently difficult subjects.

The Spreeinsel

At its eastern end, Unter den Linden leads to the **Spreeinsel**, the island in the middle of the River Spree that formed the core of the medieval twin towns of Berlin-Cölln. From the fifteenth century onwards, by virtue of its defensive position, it became the site of the Hohenzollern Residenz – the fortress-cum-palace of the family who controlled Berlin and Brandenburg. Originally this was a martial, fortified affair, as much for protection from the perennially rebellious

Berliners as from outside enemies, but over the years domestic stability meant that the Residenz could be transformed into a Renaissance palace. Later it received a Baroque restyling, with virtually every local architect of note, including Schlüter, Schinkel and Schadow, contributing.

At the northern tip of the Spreeinsel – beyond a parade ground that has long since become an area of lawns known as the Lustgarden – lies a museum quarter known as **Museumsinsel** (**Museum Island**). This was added during the nineteenth century by the Hohenzollerns and really took off when German explorers and archeologists began returning with loot from sites in the Middle East so that, despite war losses and Soviet looting, some of the world's finest museums reside here. The building work here is part of a large-scale reorganization and remodelling due for completion in 2015; in the meantime, the closure of some sections and their reshuffling as collections move between buildings will make parts temporarily inaccessible.

Schlossplatz

At the centre of the Spreeinsel there once stood the royal palace that for centuries dominated the heart of Berlin, and until the 1930s no city-centre building was allowed to stand any higher. On November 9, 1918, the abdication of the Kaiser brought to an end the Hohenzollern era, and after World War II the Schloss, a symbol of the imperial past, became an embarrassment to the GDR. They dynamited its ruins in 1950, even though it was no more badly damaged than a number of other structures that were subsequently rebuilt. In its place came the **Palast der Republik**, a piece of brutal 1970s modernism with bronzed, reflective windows that housed the GDR's parliament. Following the *Wende* – and a decade and a half of debate – it has been dismantled in order to make way for transitional projects and ultimately a re-creation of the Schloss, a process that will take until at least 2018. Now the only real reminder of the GDR in the vicinity is the one-time **Staatsrat**, or State Council, an early 1960s building on the southern side of the platz, with some *Zuckerbäcker* architectural touches. Its facade incorporates a chunk of the Berliner Schloss, notably the balcony from which Karl Liebknecht proclaimed the German socialist republic in 1918.

Berliner Dom

Northeast of the Schlossplatz lies the Spreeinsel's most striking building, the **Berliner Dom** (daily: April–Sept 9am–8pm; Oct–March 9am–5pm; €5), a hulking symbol of Imperial Germany that managed to survive the GDR.

Visiting the state museums

Berlin's state museums (@ www.smb.museum) are not only gathered at the Museum Island but also in groups in the Kulturforum (see p.85) and Charlottenburg (see p.105). As well as the basic museum entrance ticket (€4–10) tickets for each group can be bought; called a **Bereichskarte** (literally "area ticket"; €6–14), this provides admission to all museums in a grouping on the same day. Even better value is the **three-day ticket** (€19), which covers all the state museums and some of Berlin's private museums too – a total of seventy museums. Entry to all state museums is **free** during the last four hours of opening on Thursdays, but these and other museum opening hours are notoriously changeable and seasonal so check the website first. In all cases **special exhibitions** cost extra. Most exhibits are only in German, but some collections provide explanations and information sheets in English and many have excellent, multilingual **audio tours** included in the entrance price – though these cost around €4 at times when admission is free.

Built at the turn of the twentieth century as a grand royal church for the Hohenzollern family, it was a fussily ornate affair. The huge dome, flanked by four smaller ones, was meant to resemble that of St Peter's in Rome, but it was heavily damaged in the war, and much simplified during reconstruction. Its vault houses ninety sarcophagi containing the remains of various members of the Hohenzollern dynasty and six opulent sarcophagi, including those of Great Elector Wilhelm I, and second wife, Dorothea, housed in galleries at the northern and southern ends of the Predigtkirche, the octagonal main body of the church. For an overhead view, head for the **Kaiserliches Treppenhaus** (Imperial Staircase), a grandiose marble staircase at the southwest corner of the building, which leads past pleasantly washed-out paintings of biblical scenes to a balcony.

The Altes Museum and the Neues Museum

Overlooking the lawns of the Lustgarten, the striking Neoclassical **Altes Museum** (daily 10am–6pm, Thurs until 10pm; U- & S-Bahn Friedrichstrasse) is perhaps Schinkel's most impressive surviving work and now houses the **Collection of Classical Antiquities**: small sculpture and pottery from the city's famed Greek and Roman collections. Captivating items include *The Praying Boy*, a lithe and delicate bronze sculpture from Rhodes dating back to 300 BC, and the vase of Euphronios, decorated with an intimate painting of athletes in preparation – one of the finest Greek vases in the world. The Altes Museum is also home to Berlin's famous **Egyptian collection**, whose prize exhibit is the 3300-year-old *Bust of Queen Nefertiti*. There's no questioning its beauty – the queen has a perfect bone structure and gracefully sculpted lips – and the history of the piece is equally interesting. Created around 1350 BC, the bust probably never left the studio in Akhetatenin in which it was created, acting as a model for other portraits of the queen (its use as a model explains why the left eye was never drawn in). When the studio was deserted, the bust was left, and only discovered some three thousand years later in 1912. In 2009 the entire Egyptian collection is due to move into the **Neues Museum**, the building sandwiched between the Altes Museum and Pergamonmuseum. Bombed out in the war and left in decay for decades, the reconstruction of this extraordinary Neoclassical edifice forms part of the Museum Island's facelift.

Alte Nationalgalerie

Tucked just behind the Neues Museum is the slightly exaggerated Neoclassical **Alte Nationalgalerie** (daily 10am–6pm, Thurs until 10pm; U- & S-Bahn Friedrichstrasse), whose main body is a grandiose interpretation of a Corinthian temple, a huge statue of its royal patron, Friedrich Wilhelm IV, gracing the top of a double flight of stairs at the entrance. The museum houses the **nineteenth-century section** of Berlin's state art collection, which includes several noteworthy works of mid-nineteenth-century artists such as Anselm Feuerbach and Arnold Böcklin. The broad canvases of Adolph von Menzel strike a rather different note: though known for his depictions of court life under Frederick the Great, it's his interpretations of Berlin on the verge of the industrial age, such as *The Iron Foundry*, that demand attention here. Other rooms contain important **Impressionist** works by van Gogh, Degas, Monet and native son Max Liebermann, plus statues by Rodin. But it's in the paintings of the German Romantic, Classical and Biedermeier movements that the collection excels. Look for work by **Karl Friedrich Schinkel** (see p.90) and **Caspar David Friedrich**. Schinkel's paintings are meticulously drawn Gothic fantasies, often with sea settings. *Gothic Church on a Rock by the Sea* is the most moodily dramatic and didactic in purpose: the medieval knights in the foreground ride next to a prayer tablet – Schinkel believed that a rekindling of medieval piety would bring about moral regeneration. More dramatic are the works of **Friedrich**, which express a powerful elemental and religious approach to landscape. Particularly evident of the brooding and drama of his Romantic sensibility is the *Abbey Among Oak Trees* of 1809.

The Pergamonmuseum

The massive **Pergamonmuseum** (daily 10am–6pm, Thurs until 10pm; U- & S-Bahn Friedrichstrasse) was built in the early twentieth century in the style of a Babylonian temple primarily to house the treasure-trove of the **Department of Antiquities**, particularly the **Pergamon Altar**, a huge structure dedicated to Zeus and Athena, dating from 180 to 160 BC. The **frieze** shows a battle between the gods and giants and is tremendously forceful, with powerfully depicted figures writhing in a mass of sinew and muscle. The **Middle Eastern Section** has items going back four thousand years, including the enormous **Ishtar Gate**, the **Processional Way** and the facade of the **Throne Room** from Babylon, all of which date from the sixth century BC. It's impossible not to be awed by its size and remarkable condition, but at the same time bear in mind that much is a mock-up, built around the original finds. Look out for the weird mythical creatures that adorn the gate, and check the small model of the whole structure to get some idea of its enormous scale. Pride of place in the museum's **Islamic Section** goes to the relief-decorated facade of a Jordanian **Prince's Palace** at Mshatta, from 743 AD. Also worth seeking out is the **Aleppo Room**, a reception chamber with carved wooden wall decorations, reassembled after being removed from a merchant's house in present-day Syria.

The Bode-Museum

The stocky, neo-Baroque **Bode-Museum** (daily 10am–6pm, Thurs until 10pm; U- & S-Bahn Friedrichstrasse) at the northern tip of Museum Island suffered such heavy damage during World War II that it was scheduled for demolition, until Berliners protested in the streets. Several waves of renovation have swept the

▲ The Bode-Museum

1904 building since, the latest finishing in 2007. The result is impressive, with opulent entrances and stairways forming a seamless backdrop for one of Europe's most impressive **sculpture collections**, which spans the third to the nineteenth centuries. A particular strength is the early **Italian Renaissance**, though the **German collection** is equally authoritative. Also in the building is a solid collection of **Byzantine art**, particularly early Christian religious items; ornamental Roman sarcophagi and several intricate mosaics and ivory carvings are testament to Byzantium's sophistication. The Bode-Museum also houses an extraordinary **Numismatic collection**, worth at least a quick look for its gigantic size – around half a million coins – including some prized seventh-century ones which are among the earliest minted.

The DDR Museum

Not technically part of Museum Island, but immediately adjacent on the opposite bank of the Spree from the Berliner Dom, is the hands-on **DDR Museum**, Karl-Liebknecht-Strasse 1 (Mon–Fri & Sun 10am–8pm, Sat 10am–10pm; €3; ☏030/847 12 37 31, ⓦwww.ddr-museum.de), with its upbeat look at daily life in the GDR – achieved partly by glossing over gloomy issues like censorship and repression. Here are mementos of the school system, pioneer camps and the razzmatazz with which the feats of model workers were celebrated. Less impressive are East Germany's awkward polyester rivals to western fashions. A section devoted to travel includes the chance to sit behind the wheel of a Trabi, where you'll quickly appreciate the "fewer parts mean less trouble" principles upon which the fibreglass car was built. But the museum's highlight is the chance to mooch around a tiny reconstructed GDR apartment, ablaze with retro browns and oranges, where you're invited to nose through cupboards and cosy up on a sofa to speeches by Honecker: "*Vorwärts immer, rückwärts nimmer*" ("Always forwards, never backwards").

Alexanderplatz and around

During East Berlin's forty-year existence, while Unter den Linden was allowed to represent the glories of Berlin past, the area east of the Spreeinsel and around the major transport hub **Alexanderplatz** – easily located thanks to the gigantic **Fernsehturm**, or TV tower beside it – was meant to represent the glories of a modern socialist capital city. There's almost no trace of what once stood here; whole streets and neighbourhoods have vanished in favour of vast dreary concrete plazas encircled by matching buildings that house missable shops and cafés. However, a few rewarding corners include the **Nikolaiviertel**, a reconstructed Old Berlin neighbourhood, and two large prewar buildings, the **Rotes Rathaus**, seat of Berlin's administration, and the **Marienkirche**, Berlin's oldest church. Of the district's GDR legacy, a trip up the Fernsehturm provides fantastic views of the city and the adjacent windswept plaza Alexanderplatz is worth at least a quick look for its sorry-looking, communist-era **Brunnen der Völkerfreundschaft** ("Friendship of the Peoples Fountain"), which used to be a hangout for prostitutes and is now a graffiti-covered gathering place for itinerant punks. More dignified is the **Weltzeituhr** ("World Clock") in the square's southwest corner, central Berlin's best-known rendezvous point, which tells the time in different cities throughout the world, and is a product of the same architectural school as the Fernsehturm.

The Nikolaiviertel

The **Nikolaiviertel** is the GDR's 1980s attempt to re-create some of the old heart of Berlin on the site of the city's **medieval** core in a district razed overnight on June 16, 1944. One or two original buildings aside, almost all the pastel four- or five-storey town houses in the compact network of streets are replicas. Sadly, the district has barely taken seed, having the sterile feel of a living history museum that attracts only tourists and locals who work in the restaurants and *Gaststätten* – many good for traditional German food. At the centre of it all, is the Gothic **Nikolaikirche** (Tues–Sun 10am–6pm, Wed noon–8pm; free; ⓦ www.stadtmuseum.de), a thirteenth-century church, restored to its twin-towered prewar glory. The Nikolaikirche is one of the city's oldest churches and it was from here on November 2, 1539, that news of the Reformation was proclaimed to the citizens of Berlin. The distinctive needle-like spires date from a nineteenth-century restoration, or rather their design does – the building was thoroughly wrecked during the war, and much of what you see today is largely a rebuild. The church is now a **museum** that traces the building's history, although it is often given over to temporary exhibitions. An unusual interior feature is the bright colouring of the vault ribbings, which may look like a Sixties Pop Art addition, but actually follow a medieval pattern discovered by a restorer. Running past Nikolaikirche to the River Spree is **Propststrasse** where there are a couple of places associated with Heinrich Zille – the Berlin artist who produced earthy satirical drawings of local life around the turn of the twentieth century. A favourite watering hole of his – and another Berlin artist Otto Nagel – was the sixteenth-century *Gaststätte* **Zum Nussbaum** (see p.119), in the days when it stood on Fischerinsel before it was destroyed by wartime bombing. The replica is a faithful copy, right down to the walnut tree in the tiny garden. Down the street the little **Zille Museum** (April–Oct daily 11am–7pm; Nov–March Tues–Sun 11am–6pm; €3; ☎030/24 63 25 00, ⓦ www .heinrich-zille-museum.de) provides a good insight into the artist's life and work, but makes no allowances for non-German-speakers. Further, far more glamorous, insights into prewar Berlin can be found at the **Ephraim-Palais**, Poststrasse 16 (Tues & Thurs–Sun 10am–6pm, Wed noon–8pm; free; ⓦ www .stadtmuseum.de), a rebuilt eighteenth-century merchant's mansion that houses a museum of Berlin-related pictures, prints and maps from the seventeenth to nineteenth centuries.

The Rotes Rathaus

The largest old landmark amid all the brutalist modernity is the solid, nineteenth-century red-brick **Rotes Rathaus**. An intricate terracotta bas-relief at first-floor level illustrates the history of Berlin. The reconstruction of the Rathaus and thousands of other Berlin buildings is largely thanks to *Trümmer-frauen* or "rubble women", who cleared a hundred million tons of rubble created by wartime bombing and shelling, and whose deeds are commemorated by the **statue** of a robust-looking woman facing the Rathaus's eastern entrance. Women of all ages carried out the bulk of the early rebuilding work, since most of Berlin's adult male population was dead, disabled or in Allied POW camps. Despite this, the male contribution to the work is also marked by a statue of a man looking wistfully from the western end of the Rathaus.

The Marienkirche

On the other side of the large open plaza from the Rotes Rathaus lies the appealing medieval **Marienkirche** (daily: April–Oct 10am–6pm; Nov–March 10am–4pm; free; U- & S-Bahn Alexanderplatz). Its Gothic stone-and-brick nave dates to about 1270, but the tower was added in 1466, with the verdigris-coated upper section tacked on towards the end of the eighteenth century by Carl Gotthard Langhans. A small cross near the main entrance of the church was erected by local citizens as penance, after a mob immolated a papal representative on a nearby marketplace. Just inside the entrance, look out for the fifteenth-century *Totentanz*, a 22-metre frieze showing the dance of death. It's very faded, but there's a reconstruction of how it once looked, with Death a shroud-clad mummy popping up between all levels of society. The vaulted nave is plain and white but enlivened by opulent decorative touches, including Andreas Schlüter's magnificent **pulpit**, its canopy dripping with cherubs and backed by a cloud from which gilded sunrays radiate.

The Fernsehturm

Looming over the Berlin skyline like a giant olive on a cocktail stick the **Fernsehturm** (Television Tower; daily: March–Oct 9am–midnight; Nov–Feb 10am–midnight; €7.50; Ⓦ www.berlinerfernsehturm.de), is the highest structure in western Europe. This 365-metre-high transmitter was built during the isolationist 1960s, when the east part of the city was largely inaccessible to West Germans, and was intended as a highly visible symbol of the permanence of the GDR. Having outlasted the regime that conceived it, the Fernsehturm has become part of the scenery, and though few would champion its architectural merit, it does have a certain retro appeal. The tower provides a tremendous **view** (40km on a rare clear day) from the observation platform and the *Tele-café* (see p.119). There are usually long queues to go up – early evening is your best bet.

The Spandauer Vorstadt

The crescent-shaped area north of the River Spree between Friedrichstrasse and Alexanderplatz and known as the **Spandauer Vorstadt** emerged after the *Wende* as one of the most intriguing parts of unified Berlin. A wave of artists' squats, workshops and galleries sprang up here in the early 1990s, and some still survive. But today the district's appeal is based on its history as Berlin's affluent prewar **Jewish quarter** – and home to the city's largest synagogue, the **Neue Synagoge**, now a Jewish cultural centre – and as a booming **shopping**, **restaurant** and **nightlife** quarter, with its fashionable boutiques, ethnic restaurants and stylish bars catering primarily to visitors but good fun all the same. The S-Bahn station and convivial square, **Hackescher Markt**, provides the main focus, along with the main drag **Oranienburger Strasse**. At its western end lies Berlin's nebulous theatre district, where **Bertolt Brecht** lived and worked, while just beyond the northern fringes of the Spandauer Vorstadt are a couple of Berlin's most important sights: the **Berlin Wall Memorial**, the only remaining, entirely preserved section of the **Berlin Wall**; and a **World War II bunker** within the Gesundbrunnen U-Bahn station.

Hackescher Markt

The small, jumbled and slightly chaotic crossroads at **Hackescher Markt** has become one of Berlin's major tourist hubs, particularly the restaurants and cafés in and around its pedestrian plaza. Nearby the **Hackeschen Höfe**, a series of beautifully restored early twentieth-century Art Deco courtyards, also bustle with cafés, stores, galleries, theatres and cinemas. Though thoroughly gentrified

Stolpersteine

Look at the ground around the entrances to some Hackeschen Höfe and you'll see brass-plated cobblestones known as **Stolpersteine** (see p.614), or "stumbling blocks". These are some of the nine thousand laid into footpaths around Germany as a memorial to the victims of Nazi persecution: each carries a name, birth date and fate.

today, these courtyards preserve a layout common to much of prewar Berlin, where daily life was played out in a labyrinth of *Hinterhöfe*, or backyards, out of view of the main road. Within this warren, small-scale workshops lay cheek-by-jowl with housing, with rich and poor, housing and commerce crammed together, creating the squalid turn-of-the-twentieth-century urban culture satirized by Heinrich Zille (see p.96).

A good place to picture Zille's world is in the decrepit little alley beside the main Hackeschen Höfe, at Rosenthaler Strasse 39, where the small but excellent **Museum Blindenwerkstatt Otto Weidt** (daily 10am–8pm; free; ☎030/28 59 94 07, ⓦ www.blindes-vertrauen.de; S-Bahn Hackescher Markt) occupies the former broom and brush workshop of one Otto Weidt, who did what he could to protect his mostly deaf and blind, Jewish employees from Nazi persecution. Luckily his workshop was considered important to the war effort, enabling Weidt to prevent the deportation of his workers to concentration camps. But in the 1940s, as pressure grew, he resorted to producing false papers, bribing the Gestapo, and providing food and even hiding places to keep them alive, all at considerable personal risk. One small room, whose doorway was hidden by a cupboard, was the refuge for a family of four until their secret was discovered and they were deported and murdered in Auschwitz. The exhibition has relics of the wartime factory: brushes, photos and letters from the workers. It is all in German but an English translation is available.

Sophienstrasse and Grosse Hamburger Strasse

One entrance to the Hackeschen Höfe is on **Sophienstrasse**, a road first settled at the end of the seventeenth century and once the Spandauer Vorstadt's main street. Though extensively restored in the 1980s, in places this is only skin-deep and the pastel frontages of the old apartment houses conceal run-down, crumbling courtyards.

At its northern end Sophienstrasse intersects with **Grosse Hamburger Strasse**. Follow the latter north and you end up on **Auguststrasse**, the centre

▲ Hackeschen Höfe

Contemporary art in Berlin

The Hamburger Bahnhof (see p.103) may be the flagship venue for contemporary art in Berlin, but investigating the local scene can be more astounding and rewarding. Many of Berlin's estimated five thousand artists-in-residence regularly open their studios or exhibit at the hundreds of galleries around town. Auguststrasse in the Spandauer Vorstadt became a breeding ground of experimental art in the first years after the Wall came down, but has since settled down and become more commercialized. A useful and comprehensive source of information about what's on in city galleries is the English/German monthly magazine *artery berlin* (ⓦwww.artery-berlin .de), found in most galleries.

Galleries

Art Center Berlin Friedrichstr. 134, Mitte ⓣ030/27 87 90 27, ⓦwww.art-center -berlin.de. Berlin's largest exhibition space with international art on several floors. The work usually covers the full range of modern art, painting, sculpture, photography and video art and there are exhibitions of local interest too. Entry €4.50. U-Bahn Oranienburger Tor. Daily 11am–9pm.

Atelier Brandner Helmholtzstr. 2–9, Entrance E, Charlottenburg ⓣ030/30 10 05 75, ⓦwww.atelier-brandner.de. Southern German Matthias Brandner is among the most successful of the many painters who have flocked to Berlin's energetic, liberal atmosphere and cheap studio space. Though famed for his murals on buildings, it's his powerful abstract watercolours and oils that are on show at his studio. U-Bahn Turmstr. Daily noon–8pm.

Carlier Gebauer Holzmarkstr. 15–18, Mitte ⓣ030/280 8110, ⓦwww.carliergebauer .com. Under the arches of the S-Bahn, and tucked behind a petrol station, are a series of superb art spaces where you never quite know if you'll find home-grown or international art, but it's sure to be cutting-edge. S-Bahn Jannowitzbrücke. Tues–Sat 11am–6pm.

Galerie Wohnmaschine Tucholskystr. 36, Mitte ⓣ030/87 20 15, ⓦwww .wohnmaschine.de. Young gallery owner Friedrich Loock opened his first gallery in his flat and he now specializes in promoting the works of young, predominantly local, artists. U-Bahn Oranienburger Tor. Tues–Sat 11am–6pm.

Kunst-Werke Berlin Auguststr. 69, Mitte ⓣ030/243 45 90, ⓦwww.kw-berlin.de. Large gallery in a former factory building. Varies from has-been American artists carpetbagging their way into the city arts scene to astute reflections on contemporary Berlin. Also the main organizer of the Berlin Biennale (ⓦwww.berlinbiennale.de). U-Bahn Oranienburger Tor. Tues–Sun 2–6pm, Thurs noon–9pm.

of the 1990s Berlin art scene that's still dotted with workspaces and commercial galleries. Head south along Grosse Hamburger Strasse instead, and you'll quickly come to the **Missing House**, a unique and effective monument to Berlin's wartime destruction. A gap in the tenements marks where house no. 15–16 stood until destroyed by a direct hit during an air raid. In 1990 the French artist Christian Boltanski put plaques on the walls of the surviving buildings on either side, recalling the names, dates and professions of the former inhabitants of the vanished house. Further down the road is Berlin's oldest **Jewish cemetery**, established in 1672, and Berlin's first **Jewish old people's home**. The Nazis used the building as a detention centre for Jews, and 55,000 people were held here awaiting deportation to camps. A memorial tablet and a sculpted group of haggard-looking figures, representing deportees, mark the spot where the home stood. The grassed-over open space behind is the site of the cemetery itself. In 1943 the Gestapo smashed most of the headstones and dug up the remains of those buried here, using gravestones to shore up a trench they had excavated through the site. A few cracked headstones with Hebrew inscriptions line the graveyard walls. The only freestanding monument, erected after the war, commemorates Moses Mendelssohn on the spot where he is thought to have been buried; the philosopher and German Enlightenment figure founded one of Berlin's first Jewish schools on this street in 1778.

Oranienburger Strasse

Now principally known for its touristy **restaurants** and watering holes, before the war **Oranienburger Strasse** was the heart of Berlin's main **Jewish quarter**. During the initial waves of Jewish immigration from the seventeenth century onwards the area was densely populated and desperately poor, but by the nineteenth century Berlin's Jews had achieved a high degree of prosperity and assimilation, which culminated in the building of the grand **Neue Synagoge**, halfway down Oranienburger Strasse. The synagogue was inaugurated in the presence of Bismarck in 1866, a gesture of official recognition that, coming at a time when Jews in Russia were still enduring officially sanctioned pogroms, must have made many feel that their position in German society was finally secure. The Neue Synagoge was built in a mock-Moorish style, particularly apparent in its bulbous gilt-and-turquoise dome, and was Berlin's central synagogue for over sixty years, serving also as a venue for concerts, including one in 1930 by Albert Einstein in his lesser-known role as a violinist. Though badly damaged on Kristallnacht, the synagogue escaped destruction and remained a place of worship until 1940 when it was handed to the Wehrmacht for use as a warehouse until it was gutted by bombs in 1943. After the war the synagogue remained a ruin, though the building's facade remained intact until 1988, when it was restored as **Centrum Judaicum** (March & Oct Mon & Sun 10am–8pm, Tues–Thurs 10am–6pm, Fri 10am–2pm; April–Sept Mon & Sun 10am–8pm, Tues–Thurs 10am–6pm, Fri 10am–5pm; Nov–Feb Mon–Thurs & Sun 10am–6pm, Fri 10am–2pm; €3 plus extra for special exhibitions; ⓦhttp://mysql.snafu.de/cjudaicum), a museum and cultural centre, its reconstructed gilded dome once again becoming a Berlin landmark. Inside are two permanent exhibitions, one on the history and restoration of the synagogue itself and another on the Jewish life and culture in the area.

The stretch of **Oranienburger Strasse** further west is its busiest with cafés, bars and restaurants cheek-by-jowl, which after dark are joined by prostitutes openly soliciting here, their presence alongside gawping visitors faintly reminiscent of Amsterdam's red-light district. Another local oddity is the giant and fairly anarchic **Tacheles** (ⓦwww.tacheles.de), a ruined 1907 department-store building on the southern side of the street that was taken over by a group of young international artists in early 1990. This spurred the revitalization of the area and has become home and workplace to an ever-changing band of painters, sculptors, kindred spirits and hangers-on. There's a beer garden out back, and inside are several bars, and even a cinema, all accessed by a madly graffitied staircase.

Almost beside Tacheles, Oranienburger Strasse ends at Friedrichstrasse in a bland residential area that once formed the hub of Berlin's industrial revolution. Later, as the nucleus of a scattered **theatre district**, it became the centre of Bertolt Brecht's world, which you can explore at **Brecht-Haus**, Chausseestrasse 125 (Tues, Wed & Fri 10–11.30am, Thurs 10am–noon & 5–6.30pm, Sat 9.30am–1.30pm, guided tours every 30min; Sun 11am–6pm, guided tours on the hour; €3, book afternoon tours in advance on ☎030/282 20 03; U-Bahn Oranienburger Tor), just beyond the northern end of Friedrichstrasse. This was the final home and workplace of Brecht and his wife and collaborator Helene

Bertolt Brecht (1898–1956) is widely regarded as one of the leading German drama-
tists of the twentieth century. Born in Augsburg, he studied medicine, mainly to avoid
full military service in World War I. Working as an army medical orderly in 1918, his
experiences helped shape his passionate anti-militarism. Soon he drifted away from
medicine onto the fringes of the theatrical world, eventually winding up as a playwright
in residence at the Munich Kammerspiele in 1921, and moving to Berlin a few years
later. It wasn't until the 1928 premiere of *Die Dreigroschenoper* ("The Threepenny
Opera"), co-written with the composer Kurt Weill, that Brecht's real breakthrough
came. This marked the beginning of a new phase in Brecht's work. A couple of years
earlier he had embraced Marxism, an ideological step that had a profound effect on
his literary output, leading him to espouse a didactic "epic" form of theatre. The aim
was to provoke the audience, perhaps even move them to revolutionary activity. To
this end he developed the technique of **Verfremdung** ("alienation") to create a sense
of distance between spectators and the action unfolding before them. By using effects
such as obviously fake scenery, monotone lighting and jarring music to expose the
sham sentimentality of love songs, he hoped constantly to remind the audience that
what they were doing was watching a play – in order to make them judge, rather than
be drawn into, the action on stage. The result was a series of works that were pretty
heavy going.

In 1933, unsurprisingly, Brecht went into self-imposed exile, eventually ending up in
the States. His years away from Germany were among his most productive. The
political message was still very much present in his work, but somehow the dynamic
and lyrical force of his writing meant that it was often largely lost on his audience – at
the Zürich premiere of *Mutter Courage* in 1941, Brecht was dismayed to learn that the
audience in fact identified with his heroine, whom he had intended to serve as an
unsympathetic symbol of the senselessness of wartime sacrifice. Returning to
Europe, he finally settled in East Berlin in 1949, after a brief period in Switzerland. His
decision to try his luck in the Soviet-dominated Eastern sector of Germany was influenced by the offer to take over at the Theater am Schiffbauerdamm, the theatre where
the *Dreigroschenoper* had been premiered more than twenty years earlier. However,
before heading east, Brecht first took the precaution of gaining Austrian citizenship
and lodging the copyright of his works with a West German publisher. The remainder
of Brecht's life was largely devoted to running what is now known as the Berliner
Ensemble and facing up to his own tensions with the fledgling GDR.

Weigel and guided tours of its seven simply furnished rooms are an absolute
must for Brecht fans.

Both Brecht and Weigel are buried beside the Brecht-Haus in the **Dorotheen-
städtische Friedhof** (daily: May–Aug 8am–8pm; Sept–April 8am–4pm;
U-Bahn Oranienburger Tor), eastern Berlin's VIP cemetery. The other place
particularly significant for its associations with Brecht is the **Berliner
Ensemble**, tucked away on Bertolt-Brecht-Platz, a ten-minute walk southwest.
Built in the early 1890s, its rather austere exterior hides a rewarding and opulent
neo-Baroque interior. This is where, on August 31, 1928, the world premiere of
his *Die Dreigroschenoper* ("The Threepenny Opera") was staged, the first of 250
consecutive performances.

The Berlin Wall Memorial and the Gesundbrunnen bunkers

S-Bahn Nordbahnhof, just north of the Spandauer Vorstadt, is a couple of
minutes' walk via Gartenstrasse and Bernauer Strasse from the **Berlin Wall**

Memorial (Gedenkstätte Berliner Mauer). Bernauer Strasse was a street literally bisected by the Wall. Before the Wall you could enter or exit the Soviet Zone just by going through the door of one of the buildings, which is why, on August 13, 1961, some citizens, who woke up to find themselves on the wrong side of the newly established "national border", leapt out of windows to get to the West. Over the years, the facades of these buildings were cemented up and incorporated into the partition itself, until they were knocked down and replaced by the Wall proper in 1979. A short but complete section of the Wall, the only complete section left, remains at the corner of Bernauerstrasse and Ackerstrasse. Across the street at Bernauerstrasse 111, the **Wall Documentation Centre** (Tues–Sun: April–Oct 10am–6pm; Nov–March 10am–5pm; free; ⓦwww.berliner-mauer -dokumentationszentrum.de; S-Bahn Nordbahnhof) houses photos, sound recordings and information terminals.

Half a dozen blocks north, or a short U- or S-Bahn ride to the Gesund-brunnen station, lie several bunkers and other fascinating underground remains which can be toured with the nonprofit **Berliner Unterwelten** (☎030/49 91 05 17, ⓦwww.berlinerunterwelten.de), whose ticket office is in the southern entrance hall of the Gesundbrunnen U-Bahn station. Tickets are available from 10.30am on the day; all tours are one hour thirty minutes long, cost €9 and start within easy walking distance of the office. The tour of the main **Gesundbrunnen bunker: Tour 1** (English tours Mon, Fri, Sat & Sun 11am; April–Oct also Thurs 11am), explores a large, well-preserved World War II bunker, one of hundreds of public bunkers used towards the end of the war by Berliners waiting out Allied bombing raids. Today its rooms and passages contain countless artefacts from the time, among them various items cleverly crafted from military waste immediately after the war: helmets became pots, gas masks became oil lamps and tyres were used to sole shoes. If Tour 1 has whetted your appetite, try **Tour 2** (English tours April–Oct Thurs 1pm) which goes into the park opposite the Gesundbrunnen station to explore two of the seven levels of the **Humboldthain** anti-aircraft gun tower; or **Tour 3** (English tours Sat, Sun & Mon 1pm) which explores another World War II bunker, along with some Cold War-era tunnels and bunkers.

The Hauptbahnhof and around

Just west of the Spandauer Vorstadt lies a sizeable area recently colonized by Berlin's space-age **Hauptbahnhof** (train station), Europe's largest, which opened in time for the 2006 football World Cup. The five-level glass-and-steel station stands at the crossing point of an old **east–west** track along an 1882 viaduct between Bahnhof Zoo to Alexanderplatz – which provides a superb vantage point for many Mitte sights and a new **north–south** line that runs four storeys further down and fifteen metres under the Spree. The building's shape mirrors the crossing point: the glass hall follows the east–west line, while the gap between the two huge administrative blocks indicates the direction of the underground north–south track. Within this architectural tour-de-force, cleanliness, sterility and peacefulness rule, escalators move noiselessly and the bins shine. The normal mix of late-night bars, gambling dens and sex shops common to most major European stations are absent, as is Berlin's usual endless graffiti, with slightly uneasy results. Outside, huge empty plazas compound this feeling. There's still a lot missing here on a human scale though hangouts are slowly emerging alongside the Spree, where in summer sightseeing boats cruise past the bars, cafés and deckchairs that have colonized its banks. On the other, northern, side of the **Hauptbahnhof** lie a couple of isolated museums with worthwhile collections:

the **Hamburger Bahnhof**, with its contemporary art, and the **Museum für Naturkunde** with its top-drawer natural history collections.

The Hamburger Bahnhof and Museum für Naturkunde

The **Hamburger Bahnhof** is home to Berlin's premier contemporary art museum: the **Museum für Gegenwart**, Invalidenstrasse 50–51 (Museum for Contemporary Art; Tues–Fri 10am–6pm, Sat & Sun 11am–6pm; €6, free Thurs 2–6pm and 1st Sun of each month; ⓦ www.hamburgerbahnhof.de; U-Bahn Zinnowitzer Strasse or S-Bahn Lehrter Stadtbahnhof). Housed in the buildings of the former railway station, it is a spacious, effective setting for an impressive survey of postwar art from Rauschenberg, Twombly, Warhol, Beuys and Lichtenstein right up to Keith Haring and Donald Judd. The Warhol collection is excellent.

A five-minute walk east along the Invalidenstrasse leads to the **Museum für Naturkunde** (Natural History Museum; Tues–Fri 9.30am–5pm, Sat & Sun 10am–6pm; €3.50; U-Bahn Zinnowitzer Strasse), one of the world's largest natural history museums. Its origins go back to 1716, though the present building and most of the collection date from the 1880s. The museum's high point is a reconstructed brachiosaurus skeleton but it's also home to the fossil remains of an archaeopteryx, the oldest known bird. Elsewhere, amid the endless glass cases of stuffed animals, fossils and insects pinned on card, the rooms devoted to the evolution of vertebrates and the ape family stand out.

City West

Immediately southwest of Mitte, **City West**, West Berlin's old centre, is the most commercial neighbourhood where shopping streets lined with showcase Cold War building projects radiate from the crumbling spire of the **Kaiser-Wilhelm-Gedächtniskirche** (Kaiser Wilhelm Memorial Church) between rows of **department stores**. Berlin's **zoo** populates the western fringes of the Tiergarten park and lends its name to Bahnhof Zoo opposite, the main transport hub for **City West**. Though it feels like a coherent entity, City West isn't a borough in its own right, instead straddling the districts of Charlottenburg-Wilmersdorf and Schöneberg (see p.105).

The Zoologischer Garten

Berlin's zoo, or **Zoologischer Garten** (daily: mid-March to mid-Oct 9am–6.30pm; mid-Oct to mid-March 9am–5pm; €12; ⓦ www.zoo-berlin.de), harks back to 1844, surviving World War II to become one of Europe's most important zoos. It's a pleasantly landscaped place with reasonably large animal compounds, some peaceful nooks for quietly observing animal behaviour, and lots of benches that make it ideal for picnicking. Unusual highlights are the nocturnal **Nachttierhaus**, whose principle attraction is the bat cave, and a large glass-sided hippo-pool. There's also the chance to see Knut, the young polar bear who rocketed to stardom in 2007 on the back of his cuddly looks and the heart-warming story of his rejection by his mother and upbringing by a zoo keeper. The zoo's **aquarium** (daily 9am–6pm; €12) is fantastic and an excellent rainy-day option. The large, humid crocodile hall is the most memorable part, though most tanks are appealingly done. Despite the attractive price of the **combined day-ticket** (€18), trying to get around both zoo and aquarium in a day can be a rush.

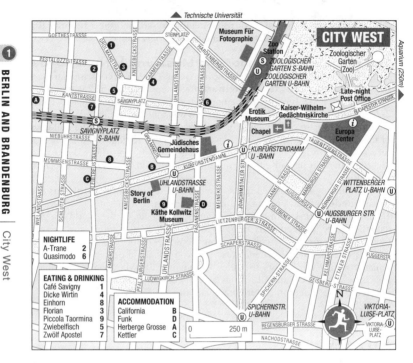

Museum für Fotographie

Behind Bahnhof Zoo, and reached through its back door, is the excellent **Museum für Fotographie**, Jebenesstrasse 2 (Tues, Wed & Fri–Sun 10am–6pm, Thurs 10am–10pm; €6 or see p.92, free Thurs 6–10pm; ☎030/31 86 48 25), which as home of the **Helmut Newton Foundation** focuses almost entirely on the work of this world-famous and locally born fashion and nude photographer. Artefacts include Newton's camera collection, a reconstruction of his quirky Monaco office, and his oversized made-to-measure beach-buggy – complete with monogrammed steering wheel. But the mainstay of the museum is Newton's extraordinary work: his heavily stylized portrait, glamour and nude photography, his celebrity portraiture and penchant for Amazonian women.

Kaiser-Wilhelm-Gedächtniskirche and around

A short two-block walk east of Bahnhof Zoo, the angular concrete **Breitscheidplatz** is a magnet for vendors, caricaturists and street musicians and often hosts fairs and festivals including a large Christmas market. It encircles the **Kaiser-Wilhelm-Gedächtniskirche** (Kaiser Wilhelm Memorial Church), a grand church built at the end of the nineteenth century and destroyed by British bombing in November 1943. Left as a reminder, it's a strangely effective memorial, the crumbling tower providing a hint of the old city. It's possible to go inside the remains of the nave (Mon–Sat 10am–4pm) where a small exhibit shows wartime destruction and a "before and after" model of the city centre. Adjacent, a modern **chapel** (daily 9am–7pm) contains a tender, sad charcoal sketch by Kurt Reubers, *Stalingrad Madonna*, dedicated to all those who died during the Battle of Stalingrad. The district's two main shopping streets radiate from Breitscheidplatz. **Tauentzienstrasse**, an otherwise rather bland chain-store drag, has at its eastern end Europe's largest department store, the venerable **KaDeWe**, whose excellent top-storey food court is an ideal stop after a hard shop. Meanwhile, **Kurfürstendamm** (universally called **Ku'damm**) blazes the trail **west**, its litany of shops and cafés dazzling with the neon of big labels.

Käthe-Kollwitz-Museum and The Story of Berlin

In among the consumer jungle of Ku'damm are two good museums. The **Käthe-Kollwitz-Museum**, 24 Fasanenstrasse (Mon & Wed–Sun 11am–6pm; €5; ⓦwww.kaethe-kollwitz.de; U-Bahn Uhlandstrasse), displays the moving early twentieth-century radical left-wing antiwar art of Käthe Kollwitz. Born in 1867, she lived almost all her life in Prenzlauer Berg and following the death of her son in World War I, her woodcuts, lithographs, prints and sculptures became explicitly pacifist, often dwelling on the theme of mother and child. With the death of her grandson in World War II her work became sadder yet and more poignant. She died in 1945, shortly before the end of the war. Back on the Ku'damm and just west of the Uhlandstrasse U-Bahn, **The Story of Berlin** at nos. 207–208 (daily 10am–8pm, last admission 6pm; €9.30; ⓦwww.story-of-berlin.de), contains an excellent and inventive multimedia exhibition – extensively labelled in English – that's an ideal first step in unravelling Berlin's history. On the way around you'll be confronted with life-size dioramas, film clips, noises, flashing lights, smoke and smells, which illustrate the trawl through the highs and lows of the city's turbulent past. Great for kids, though it takes at least two hours to do it justice, not including a bonus tour of a 1970s Allied-built Cold War nuclear bunker below – which can be done another day on the same ticket if you've run out of time or energy in the museum.

Charlottenburg-Wilmersdorf and Schöneberg

The rather sedate, white and middle-class districts of **Charlottenburg-Wilmersdorf** and **Schöneberg** are inner-city Berlin at its most affluent and restrained. However, Charlottenburg has its own gathering of fairly high-profile attractions, particularly the Baroque **Schloss Charlottenburg** – Berlin's pocket Versailles with its opulent chambers, wanderable gardens, and several excellent nearby **museums** – along with the iconic 1930s **Olympic Stadium**. Meanwhile, **Schöneberg** is famous for being Berlin's oldest **gay village**.

Schloss Charlottenburg

After the unrelieved modernity of most of Charlottenburg, the Baroque curves of **Schloss Charlottenburg** (ⓦwww.spsg.de; bus #M45 from Bahnhof Zoo) come as a surprise. Commissioned as a country house by the future Queen Sophie Charlotte in 1695, the Schloss expanded throughout the eighteenth and early nineteenth centuries to provide a summer residence for Prussian kings, with master builder Schinkel providing the final touches. Unsurprisingly much of the Schloss was levelled in the war, so many of the reconstructed buildings are now far too perfect for their supposed age. The various parts of the Schloss can be visited and paid for separately, but **combined day-tickets** are the best value (€7); these give access to all Schloss buildings, but not the tour of the royal apartments in the Altes Schloss, nor the Museum für Vor- und Frühgeschichte, one of Berlin's municipal museums.

The Altes Schloss

The entrance to the **Altes Schloss** (Old Palace; Tues–Fri 9am–5pm, Sat & Sun 10am–5pm, last tour 4pm; tour of lower-floor royal apartments and upper floors €8, upper floors only €2), the main building, lies immediately behind a grand statue of Friedrich Wilhelm. Its upper floors can be visited without joining a tour and include the apartment of Friedrich Wilhelm IV and a collection of silver and tableware, but to view the lower floor, with its sumptuous Baroque chambers and bedrooms of Friedrich I and Sophie Charlotte and ancestral portrait gallery, you're obliged to go on a German-only **tour** – free English pamphlets are offered. The Knobelsdorff-designed **Neuer Flügel** (New Wing; Tues–Fri 10am–6pm, Sat & Sun 11am–6pm; €5 including audio guide) includes an elegant Golden Gallery and adjacent White Hall, whose eighteenth-century ceiling was replaced at the end of the nineteenth century by a marble-and-gold confection with full electric illumination. Next door, the Concert Room contains a superb collection of works by **Watteau**, including the outstanding *The Embarcation for Cythera*, a delicate Rococo frippery tinged with sympathy and sadness. The western wing of the Schloss once contained an orangerie but now houses exhibitions and the **Museum für Vor- und Frühgeschichte** (Museum of Pre- and Early History; Tues–Fri 9am–5pm, Sat & Sun 10am–5pm; €3, see p.92 for combination ticket information, free Thurs 1–5pm; ⓦwww.smb.museum), an unexciting collection of archeological discoveries from the Berlin area, due to move to the Neues Museum (see p.93) in 2009.

The Schloss Gardens

Laid out in the French style in 1697, the bucolic **Schloss Gardens** (usually daily 9am–5pm, till 9pm in the summer; free) were transformed into an English-style landscaped park in the early nineteenth century; after severe war damage, they were mostly restored to their Baroque form. Just east of the Schloss and at the edge of the gardens proper, is the **Neuer Pavillon** (also called the Schinkel Pavillon), designed by Schinkel for Friedrich Wilhelm III, and where the king preferred to live, away from the excesses of the main building. Square and simple, it houses some of Schinkel's drawings and plans. Deeper into the gardens, on the north side of the lake, is the **Belvedere** (April–Oct Tues–Fri noon–5pm, Sat & Sun 10am–5pm; Nov–March Tues–Fri noon–4pm; €2), built as a teahouse in 1788 and today housing a missable Berlin porcelain collection. On the western side of the gardens a long, tree-lined avenue leads to the hushed and shadowy **Mausoleum** (April–Oct Tues–Sun 10am–5pm; €1), where Friedrich Wilhelm III lies: the carved image on his sarcophagus making him seem a good deal younger than seventy. He commissioned the mausoleum to be built thirty years earlier for his wife, Queen Luise, whose own delicate sarcophagus apparently depicts her not dead but sleeping, though it's hard to tell. Later burials here include Kaiser Wilhelm I, looking every inch a Prussian king.

Museum Berggruen

Though you could happily spend a whole day wandering the Schloss and its gardens, the wonderful **Museum Berggruen** (Tues–Sun 10am–6pm; €6, free Thurs 2–6pm; ⓦwww.smb.museum), opposite its gates, beckons with a collection that's unmissable for fans of twentieth-century art and specifically Picasso. Heinz Berggruen, a young Jew forced to flee Berlin in 1936, ended up as an art dealer in Paris, where he got to know Picasso and his circle and assembled a collection of personal favourites. In 1996 the city gave him this building to show off, in a comfortable, uncrowded setting, his revered collection, which includes a dozen or so Picassos. Most of these have rarely been seen and steal the show – highlights include the richly textured Cubist *The Yellow Sweater* and large-scale *Reclining Nude* – but there's also a handful of Cézannes and Giacomettis and a pair of van Goghs. The top floor is very strong on Paul Klee, with works spanning the entire interwar period and so offering a meaningful insight into the artist's development. Be sure to pick up the audio tour, in English and included in the price of entry.

The Funkturm and Olympic Stadium

Western Charlottenburg is best known for its **Olympic Stadium**, where the world watched the 1936 Games and then, after a big revamp, the 2006 football World Cup. Guiding the way to it from the centre, is the Eiffel-Tower-like **Funkturm** (Tues–Sat 10am–11pm; €3.60; U-Bahn Kaiserdamm), built in 1928 as a radio and later becoming a TV transmission mast for the world's first regular TV service in 1941. Today the Funkturm only serves police and taxi frequencies, but the mast remains popular for the toe-curling views of the city centre from its 126-metre-high **observation platform**. It's easily reached from Bahnhof Zoo using bus #49 which goes on to stop "Flatowallee" near the **Olympic Stadium** (daily: April–Oct 10am–7pm; Nov–March 10am–4pm; exhibition €4; ☎030/25 00 23 22, Ⓔtour@olympiastadion-berlin.de, Ⓦwww.olympiastadion-berlin.de; U- & S-Bahn Olympiastadion). Built for the 1936 Olympic Games, the Olympic Stadium is one of the few fascist-era buildings left intact in the city, but despite being tainted by this the building is hugely impressive, the huge Neoclassical space a deliberate rejection of the modernist architecture that began to be in vogue in the 1930s. Inside, the stadium's sheer size comes as a surprise, since the seating falls away below ground level to reveal a much deeper auditorium than you would imagine. As Berlin's best football team Hertha BSC's home ground, the stadium is sometimes closed for sporting events or team practice, so check before trudging out. Calling or emailing ahead may also get you onto a tour (1hr; €8) of the stadium that requires a five-person minimum; otherwise you can explore some of the stadium independently with an audio tour (€2.50).

Schöneberg

Once a separate entity, **Schöneberg** was swallowed up by Greater Berlin as the city expanded in the late eighteenth and nineteenth centuries. By the 1920s and early 1930s it had become the centre for Berlin's sizeable gay community: there were around forty gay bars on and near to the road and rail intersection **Nollendorfplatz** alone, and gay life in the city was open, fashionable and well organized, with its own newspapers and community associations. Local theatres were filled with plays exploring gay themes, homosexuality in the Prussian army was little short of institutionalized, and gay bars, nightclubs and brothels proudly advertised themselves – there were even gay working men's clubs. A block away, at Nollendorfstrasse 17, stands the building in which **Christopher Isherwood** lived during his years in prewar Berlin. Under the Third Reich, however, homosexuality was brutally outlawed: gays and lesbians were rounded up and taken to concentration camps and often murdered. A red-granite plaque in the shape of a triangle at Nollendorfplatz U-Bahn station commemorates this.

NIGHTLIFE

Connection	5
Hafen	9
Heile Welt	4
Kumpelnest 3000	2
Neues Ufer	16
Scheune	8
Tom's Bar	7

EATING & DRINKING

Aroma	15
Baharat Falafel	12
Café Einstein	3
Café M	14
Carib	10
Edd's Thailändisches	1
Maharadscha	6
Storch	18
Tim's Canadian Deli	11
Tori Katsu	13
Toronto	17

Though the neigbourhood was blown to pieces during the war, **Schöneberg**'s gay village has proved more robust, and its attendant nightlife (see p.129) is still first class even though there's competition elsewhere in the city now, particularly Prenzlauer Berg. Schöneberg's other main attraction is **Rathaus Schöneberg**, the town hall in front of which John F. Kennedy made his "Berliner" speech, his rousing address on the Cold War situation here in 1963. It's a short bus ride from Nollendorfplatz on the #106.

Kreuzberg-Friedrichshain and around

Directly south of Mitte, the district of **Kreuzberg-Friedrichshain** loosely divides into the more middle-class and white **West Kreuzberg**, unkempt and bohemian **East Kreuzberg**, and **Friedrichshain**, a part of former East Berlin, whose low rents and central location have given it Berlin's most happening bar and nightlife scene.

Western Kreuzberg is mostly of interest for its museums, which include the impressive **Jewish Museum**, while eastern Kreuzberg is more a place for wandering between café-bars, art galleries and clothes shops along its main drag **Oranienstrasse**, which cater to its countercultural inhabitants (a mix of punks, old hippies and students). It's also famed for its large immigrant community, and the area around U-Bahn **Kottbusser Tor** is typical: a scruffy, earthy shambles of Turkish street vendors and cafés, the air filled with the aromas of southeast European cooking. However, signs of gentrification have begun to appear, and much of its vibrant café and **nightlife** scene has migrated over the Spree to Friedrichshain. Overwhelmingly residential, Friedrichshain was comprehensively destroyed during the war, losing over two thirds of its buildings – as much as any Berlin district – making almost everything on view today GDR-vintage. Thankfully this includes remnants of arguably the best GDR architecture in the city along **Karl-Marx-Allee**.

Finally, the area is also a great stepping-stone to intriguing nearby attractions, particularly the **Soviet War Memorial** in Treptower Park, the final resting place of thousands of Russians who died in the Battle of Berlin, and Berlin's most important Jewish graveyard at **Weissensee**.

Jüdisches Museum Berlin

An architectural burst of light in bland residential northern Kreuzberg, the **Jüdisches Museum Berlin**, Lindenstrasse 14 (Jewish Museum Berlin; Mon 10am–10pm, Tues–Sun 10am–8pm, tour times vary; ☎030/25 99 33 00; €5,

EATING
Altes Zollhaus 1
Milagro 4
Osteria No. 1 3

NIGHTLIFE
SchwuZ 2
Serene Bar 5

WEST KREUZBERG

Tempelhof Airport

0   300 m

tours €3; ⓦ www.jmberlin.de; U-Bahn Hallesches Tor or bus #248 from Alexanderplatz), tackles the difficult topic of history and culture of German Jewry. The extraordinary building, designed by Daniel Libeskind, has a ground plan that resembles a compressed lightning bolt (intended as a deconstructed Star of David), while the structure itself is sheathed in polished metallic facing, with windows – or, rather, thin angular slits – that trace geometric patterns on the exterior. The building's uncomfortable angles and severe lines create a disturbed and uneasy space to mirror the painful history covered by the exhibits. Though expertly crafted, the exhibition suffers from being a bit convoluted – an irony of the deliberately disorienting building – and unnecessarily long.

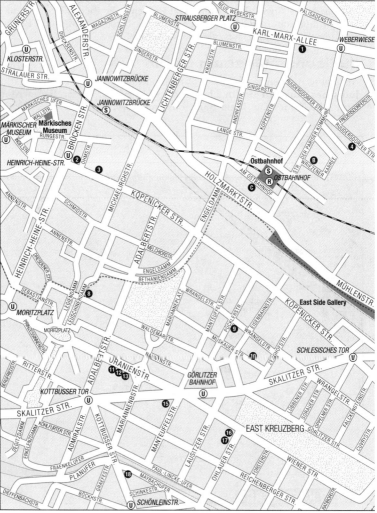

Berlinische Galerie and the Deutsche Technikmuseum Berlin

Just northeast of the Jewish Museum lies a vast former warehouse that's now the clinical home of the **Berlinische Galerie**, Alte Jakobstrasse 124–128 (Wed–Mon 10am–6pm; €8, €4 on 1st Mon of the month; ☎030/78 90 26 00, ⓦwww.berlinischegalerie.de; U-Bahn Hallesches Tor), where some of Berlin's darkest and most tortured pieces of art form the nucleus of the permanent collection. This includes pieces by Lesser Ury, George Grosz and Otto Dix, with almost all from the twentieth century when movements such as Secessionism, Dadaism and the New Objectivity called Berlin home. But the gallery

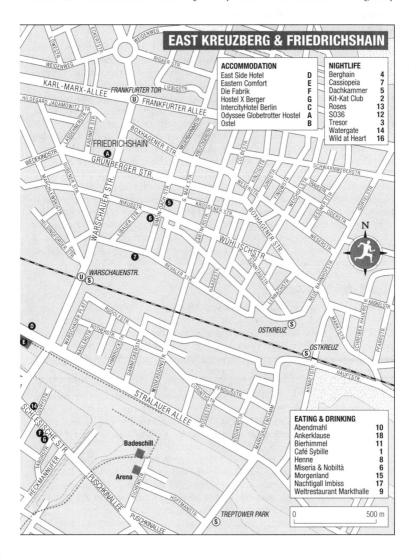

EAST KREUZBERG & FRIEDRICHSHAIN

ACCOMMODATION
East Side Hotel	D
Eastern Comfort	E
Die Fabrik	F
Hostel X Berger	G
IntercityHotel Berlin	C
Odyssee Globetrotter Hostel	A
Ostel	B

NIGHTLIFE
Berghain	4
Cassiopeia	7
Dachkammer	5
Kit-Kat Club	2
Roses	13
SO36	12
Tresor	3
Watergate	14
Wild at Heart	16

EATING & DRINKING
Abendmahl	10
Ankerklause	18
Bierhimmel	11
Café Sybille	1
Henne	8
Miseria & Nobiltà	6
Morgenland	15
Nachtigall Imbiss	17
Weltrestaurant Markthalle	9

0   500 m

really thrives on its expertly presented temporary exhibitions (extra charge). A brisk twenty-minute walk west of the **Berlinische Galerie** and **Jüdisches Museum**, through streets once levelled by wartime bombing, leads to the **Deutsche Technikmuseum Berlin**, Trebbiner Strasse 9 (German Technology Museum of Berlin; Tues–Fri 9am–5.30pm, Sat & Sun 10am–6pm; €4.50; Ⓦwww.dtmb.de; U-Bahn Möckernbrücke), a children's and button-pushers' delight. The technology section has plenty of experiments, antiquated machinery and computers to play with, alongside some elegant old cars and planes. The museum's collection of ancient steam trains and carriages is even more impressive.

Treptower Park and Sowjetisches Ehrenmal

Just south of East Kreuzberg, **Treptower Park** (S-Bahn Treptower Park) was designed as a place in which nineteenth-century tenement-dwellers could let off steam; by 1908 there were thirty-odd dance halls and restaurants here. A few beer gardens still exist, and boat rental is possible around the Insel der Jugend, the main hub of activity, but the park's main sight is the large and sobering **Sowjetisches Ehrenmal** (**Soviet Memorial**), where during the GDR era busloads of Soviet citizens came to pay their respects. It commemorates the Soviet Union's 305,000 troops killed in the Battle of Berlin in April and May 1945 and is the burial place of five thousand of them. It's best approached from the arched entrance on the south side of Puschkinallee which leads to a sculpture of a grieving woman representing the Motherland and a broad concourse sloping up between two vast triangles of red granite. From the viewing point between them, a long sunken park of mass graves – sculpted with frescoes of stylized scenes from the Great Patriotic War and quotes from Stalin with German translations – stretches out towards a vast symbolic statue of an idealized Russian soldier clutching a saved child and resting his sword on a shattered swastika: a typical piece of Soviet gigantism and built using marble from Hitler's Chancellery.

Karl-Marx-Allee

Friedrichshain's main road **Karl–Marx–Allee**, a vast boulevard lined with model 1950s and 1960s communist housing developments, was where the GDR Politbüro and Eastern Bloc dignitaries took the salute during the military parades. In September 1951, work began on turning this road into "Germany's first socialist street", by providing modern flats in the *Zuckerbäckerstil* (wedding-cake style), a mutated Classicism repeated across the Soviet bloc throughout the 1950s. Though the style was and is much derided in the West, the buildings were a well-thought-out and relatively soundly constructed attempt at housing that would live up to Berlin's great architectural tradition. The blocks begin south of U-Bahn Strausberger Platz, where the district of Friedrichshain begins, and where it's worth getting off to walk east for ten minutes to **Café Sybille**, Karl-Marx-Allee 72 (daily 10am–8pm; free; ☎030/29 35 22 03; U-Bahn Weberwiese), a stylish, minimalist café that's a pleasant stop in its own right but also has a worthwhile little exhibition on the history of the street. The buildings were to be "palaces for workers, not American eggboxes", and architectural plans were shipped direct from the USSR. From then on it was all about model workers putting in overtime and even donating a portion of their wages to see the project through. A lucky few even got to live in the apartments, but these were mostly for the well connected.

East Side Gallery

Friedrichshain's other main sight is the **East Side Gallery**, a 1.3-kilometre surviving stretch of Wall between U-Bahn Schlesisches Tor and the Ostbahnhof along the banks of the Spree, which has been daubed with various political and satirical murals, some imaginative, some trite, some impenetrable. One of the most telling shows Brezhnev and Honecker locked in a passionate kiss, with the inscription, "God, help me survive this deadly love". All the murals were done just after the Wall fell and resonate with the attitude and aesthetics of the day. It's also worth ducking through gaps in the wall to see the contemporary graffiti on the side that overlooks the Spree. Some of Berlin's best is here as the site attracts graffiti artists from around the world looking to make their mark on one of the artform's ultimate canvases. The Spree is also a popular summer hangout, with basic beach bars at various spots behind the East Side Gallery.

Volkspark Friedrichshain and the Jüdischer Friedhof Weissensee

Bus #200 heads northeast out of Mitte to run alongside **Volkspark Friedrichshain**, one of the city's best parks thanks to many sports facilities. It's also the final resting place for victims of the 1848 revolution where many of the 183 Berliners killed by the soldiers of King Friedrich Wilhelm IV were buried, their internment attended by 80,000 Berliners. Bus #200 continues on to its terminus on the fringes of the tidy middle-class **Weissensee** district and a block southwest of the **Jüdischer Friedhof Weissensee** (April–Oct Sun–Thurs 8am–5pm, Fri 8am–3pm; Nov–March Sun–Thurs 8am–4pm, Fri 8am–3pm; male visitors must cover their heads: borrow a skullcap from the cemetery office), Europe's largest Jewish graveyard, opened in 1880, when the Schönhauser Allee cemetery reached capacity. Immediately beyond the entrance is a Holocaust memorial, a circle of tablets bearing the names of all the large concentration camps. Beyond are cemetery administration buildings (where information is available), constructed in a similar mock-Moorish style to the Neue Synagoge (see p.100), and beyond them, row upon row of headstones stretch out, with the occasional extravagant family monument including some Art Nouveau graves and mausoleums designed by Ludwig Mies van der Rohe and Walter Gropius. More moving are the four hundred urns containing the ashes of concentration-camp victims. A handful of well-tended postwar graves are, paradoxically, symbols of survival – witness to the fact that the city still has a Jewish community.

Prenzlauer Berg

Fanning out immediately east of the city centre, the residential working-class district of **Prenzlauer Berg** fared relatively well in the war, being fought over street by street so that many of its turn-of-the-twentieth-century tenement blocks, though battle-scarred, survived, leaving the kind of leafy cobbled streets and intersections which typified prewar Berlin. This sense of history helped make Prenzlauer Berg a centre of bohemian culture even during the GDR days when large numbers of artists and young people seeking an alternative lifestyle chose to live here on the edge of established East German society – literally as well as figuratively, since the district's western boundary was marked by the Berlin Wall. After the *Wende* these pleasant corners with low rents were quickly

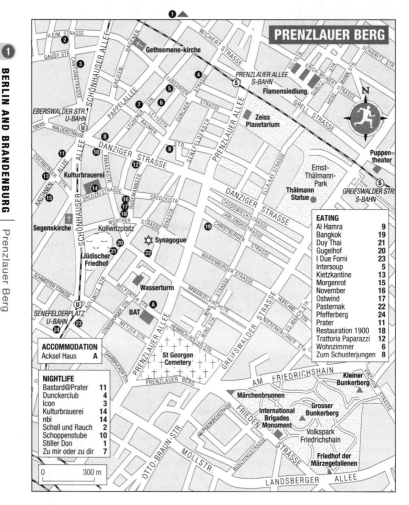

EATING

Al Hamra	9
Bangkok	19
Duy Thai	21
Gugelhof	20
I Due Forni	23
Intersoup	5
Kietzkantine	13
Morgenrot	15
November	16
Ostwind	17
Pasternak	22
Pfefferberg	24
Prater	11
Restauration 1900	18
Trattoria Paparazzi	12
Wohnzimmer	6
Zum Schusterjungen	8

ACCOMMODATION

Acksel Haus	A

NIGHTLIFE

Bastard@Prater	11
Dunckerclub	4
Icon	3
Kulturbrauerei	14
nbi	14
Schall und Rauch	2
Schoppenstube	10
Stiller Don	1
Zu mir oder zu dir	7

0   300 m

seized on as ripe for gentrification and settled by some of the best restaurants, cafés, bars and clubs in the city.

Schönhauser Allee, Kollwitzplatz and around

Schönhauser Allee, Prenzlauer Berg's main drag, is traced by the route of the U-Bahn from Alexanderplatz, but tram #M1 from Hackescher Markt provides a more interesting approach through some eastern Berlin backstreets en route to **U-Bahn Eberswalder Strasse**, the district's hub. Here, underneath the elevated railway tracks lies *Konnopke's*, Berlin's oldest and most famous sausage kiosk and as good a place as any for a quick *Currywurst*. North of the U-Bahn station, Schönhauser Allee becomes an old-fashioned shopping street that, thanks to cobbled streets and narrow shop facades, still retains a vaguely prewar feel.

Wandering the maze of Prenzlauer Berg's old streets, absorbing the atmosphere and looking out for Battle of Berlin bullet and shell marks on unrestored facades is an end unto itself, but for more structured sightseeing, start just southwest of U-Bahn Eberswalder Strasse at the **Kulturbrauerei** (see p.126), an agglomeration of cafés, bars, clubs, cinemas and venues in a former brewery built in the 1890s in the pseudo-Byzantine style then favoured by Berlin's architects. A block southeast of here lies the leafy green triangle of **Kollwitzplatz**, the focal point of Prenzlauer Berg's main sights. The street running north from the platz, **Husemannstrasse**, is a nineteenth-century tenement street restored to former glory in late GDR days in an attempt to recall the grandeur of old Berlin: raddled facades were covered with fresh stucco and new wrought-iron balconies installed, as has happened in neighbouring streets since. Meanwhile, a left turn from the southern corner of Kollwitzplatz leads to **Knaackstrasse**, where the huge red-brick **Wasserturm** (Water Tower) looms. Built in 1875 on the site of a pre-industrial windmill, its basement was briefly used by the SA as torture chamber when the Nazis came to power – the bodies of 28 victims were later found in the underground pipe network – but today the tower's been converted into quirky circular apartments. From Knaackstrasse, a left turn into **Rykestrasse** brings you to a still-functioning **synagogue**, an ornate edifice in the courtyard of no. 53 that was built in 1904–05 and survived both Kristallnacht and use as stables by the SA. Another main remnant of Jewish Berlin, on the opposite side of Kollwitzplatz, though its entrance is on Schönhauser Allee, is the **Jüdischer Friedhof** (Jewish Cemetery; Mon–Thurs 8am–4pm, Fri 8am–1pm), opened when space ran out at the Grosse Hamburger Strasse (see p.99), and with over twenty thousand people buried here. But for most, their last resting place is an anonymous one: in 1943 many of the gravestones were smashed.

The suburbs

Exploring Berlin's **suburbs** not only completes a picture of the city but also reveals a few surprises, many in quaint and bucolic spots but all well under an hour's journey by public transport from Mitte. Yet exploring Greater Berlin is not always attractive as this is where many of the city's blandest Cold War building projects have survived. Particularly in the east, old socialist silo-like apartment blocks and soulless shopping precincts appear more desperate-looking in comparison to flashy new post-*Wende* buildings – though the west has its high-rise ghettos too. The sprawling working-class district **Lichtenberg**, a mid-1970s model neighbourhood, and **Marzahn**, with its high-rises, high unemployment and reputation for mindless, often racially motivated, violence are two of the most notorious and least attractive eastern suburbs, and really only worth exploring for a sense of what constitutes everyday life for thousands of Berliners. However, Lichtenberg is also home to two sights of vital importance to anyone with an interest in oppression in the GDR, particularly by its secret police, the Stasi. Their headquarters at **Normannenstrasse** and prison at **Hohenschönhausen** are both preserved as haunting monuments.

All the other particularly worthwhile suburban destinations lie in attractive former small towns and villages that Berlin has gobbled up over time, but which retain something of their small-town feel, a sense heightened by the backdrop of lakes and woods that surround the city. The largest of these is the Grunewald forest and adjacent **Havel lake** in the southwestern corner of Berlin, where you will also find the **Allied Museum**, home to the original Checkpoint Charlie booth. The **Wannsee**, the largest bay in the Havel, is famed for its summertime bathing but also as the location of the **Wannsee villa**, where a Nazi conference sealed the fate of millions of Jews.

Gedenkstätte Hohenschönhausen

A potent antidote to *Ostalgie* – nostalgia for the GDR – is a visit to the grim former Stasi prison at **Gedenkstätte Hohenschönhausen**, Genslerstrasse 66 (Memorial Hohenschönhausen; daily 9am–4pm, tours in German Mon, Wed & Fri 11am & 1pm, Tues & Thurs 11am, 1pm & 3pm, Sat & Sun hourly until 4pm, tours in English by arrangement; €3, Mon free; ☏030/98 60 82 34, ⓦwww.stiftung-hsh.de), which offers an insight into the fear and oppression upon which the regime was founded. Hohenschönhausen began life in 1945 as a **Soviet Special Camp**, with 4200 inmates penned in together in horrendous living conditions. By 1946 around 3000 had died. Officially most had been interned because of suspected Nazi links, but in most cases there was no evidence. This made torture chambers vital for acquiring "confessions" that would usually lead to decades of forced labour – though ultimately almost all prisoners were declared innocent by the Russian authorities in the 1990s. In 1951 the Stasi (see box opposite) inherited the facility and turned it into a remand prison which was quickly blotted from city maps. The smallest sign of resistance or opposition to the state, including comments written in personal letters – which were all routinely steamed open – would earn you a spell inside. Typically, you'd be caught unawares on your way to work, bundled into a van and brought here. The former prisoners who lead tours deliver an absorbing insight into the psychological rather than physical abuse that followed in the solitary world of padded cells, tiny exercise yards, endless corridors and interrogation rooms.

To get here take tram #M5 from Hackescher Markt or, if you're already in Lichtenberg, bus #256 from U-Bahn Lichtenberg. Get off either tram or bus at Freienwalder Strasse at the end of which is the entrance to the former jail.

Gedenkstätte Normannenstrasse

One building in the huge former **Stasi headquarters** complex has become the **Forschungs- und Gedenkstätte Normannenstrasse** (Normannenstrasse Research and Memorial Centre; Mon–Fri 11am–6pm, Sat & Sun 2–6pm; €3.50; ⓦwww.stasimuseum.de; U-Bahn Magdalenenstrasse), a museum that uncovers the massive surveillance apparatus of the GDR's secret police. Walking along the bare, red-carpeted corridors and looking at the busts of Lenin and Felix Dzerzhinsky – founder of the Soviet Cheka, models for both the KGB and Stasi – it all seems part of a distant past, not an era which ended only in 1990. But then the obsessively neat office and apartment of **Erich Mielke**, the Stasi head from 1957 to October 1989, makes it all the more immediate. Everything is just as he left it: white and black telephones stand on the varnished wooden desk as though awaiting calls, and Mielke's white dress uniform hangs in a wardrobe. Other rooms have displays of Stasi surveillance apparatus described in German (English-language booklet €3), but which mostly speak for themselves. The many bugging devices and cameras – some concealed in watering cans and plant pots – reveal the absurd lengths the GDR went to in order to keep tabs on its citizens.

The Grunewald

Few people associate Berlin with hikes through dense woodland or swimming from crowded beaches, though that's just what the **Grunewald**

The Stasi

East Germany's infamous Staatssicherheitsdienst (State Security Service), or Stasi, kept tabs on everything in the GDR. It ensured the security of the country's borders, carried out surveillance on foreign diplomats, business people and journalists, and monitored domestic and foreign media. It was, however, in the surveillance of East Germany's own population that the organization truly excelled. Very little happened in the GDR without the Stasi knowing about it: files were kept on millions of innocent citizens and insidious operations were orchestrated against dissidents, real and imagined. By the *Wende* the Stasi had a budget of £1 billion and 91,000 full-time employees and 180,000 informers within the East German population, figures brought into context by the punier, albeit more ruthless, 7000-strong Nazi Gestapo.

At the beginning of 1991 former citizens of the GDR were given the right to see their Stasi files. Tens of thousands took the opportunity to find out what the organization had recorded about them, and, more importantly, who had provided the information; many a friendship and not a few marriages came to an end as a result. The process of unravelling truths from the archives also provided material for many a story, including Timothy Garton Ash's **book** *The File: A Personal History* and the **film** *Das Leben der Anderen* (Lives of Others). Not all documents survived though, many were briskly shredded as the GDR regime collapsed, resulting in an unenviable task for one government organization who spent literally years piecing them together to bring people to justice, thankfully with some success.

forests and the adjacent lakes offer. The **eastern edge** of the Grunewald is dotted with a series of modest but unusual **museums** that can be combined with time spent **hiking** in the forest to make a pleasant day out. All these museums are connected with the city centre by bus #115 from U-Bahn station Fehrberliner Platz and S-Bahn station Hohenzollern. The bus stops at Pücklerstrasse, just outside the **Brücke Museum**, Bussardsteig 9 (Wed–Mon 11am–5pm; €4; Ⓦ www.bruecke-museum.de), which has German Expressionist works by the group known as Die Brücke ("The Bridge"), who worked in Dresden and Berlin from 1905 to 1913, were banned by the Nazis and who painted cityscapes using rich colours and playful perspectives. A ten-minute walk west along Pücklerstrasse into the depths of the Grunewald, lies the royal hunting lodge **Jagdschloss Grunewald**, Hüttenweg 10 (mid-May to mid-Oct Tues–Sun 10am–5pm; mid-Oct to mid-May Sun tours at 11am, 1pm & 3pm; €2; Ⓣ 030/813 35 97), built in the sixteenth century and enlarged by Friedrichs I and II. Today it's a museum housing old furniture; Dutch and German paintings, including works by Cranach the Elder and Rubens; and a small hunting museum in the outbuildings. However, walking around the adjacent lake, the **Grunewaldsee**, may prove more stimulating than the collections. The Jagdschloss is also a good starting point for longer hikes into the Grunewald: a 45-minute ramble along the eastern side of the Grunewaldsee brings you to S-Bahn Grunewald; or you can walk south to U-Bahn Krumme Lanke in about an hour, crossing Hutten Weg and then Onkel-Tom-Strasse to then walk around the shores of Krumme Lanke lake. If you have an interest in Cold War Berlin, you should walk fifteen minutes southeast of the Jadgschloss Grunewald along Im Jagen to the **Allied Museum**, Clayallee 135 (Alliierten Museum; Thurs–Tues 10am–6pm; free; Ⓦ www.alliiertenmuseum.de; U-Bahn Oskar-Helena-Helm), whose well-presented exhibits include a segment of the Wall, a guard tower, and, most impressively, the original Checkpoint Charlie guard post. The rest of the museum is a bit dull, though the occasional spy story helps spice things up.

The Wannsee

Of the many lakes which dot, surround and generally enhance the Grunewald, the best known is the **Wannsee**. The main attraction here is Europe's largest inland beach, **Strandbad Wannsee**, a kilometre-long strip of pale sand that's packed as soon as the sun comes out. From here it's easy to wander into the forests and to smaller, less-populated beaches along the lakeside road **Havelchaussee**. Usefully, bus #218 from S-Bahn Wannsee and Nikolassee goes this way and runs along 6km of sandy coves where there are few facilities. This area is also a good one for a spot of hiking – both along the lakeshore and inland into the forest.

The **Wannsee villa**, Am Grossen Wannsee 56–58 (Haus der Wannsee Konferenze; daily 10am–6pm; free; ⓦwww.ghwk.de), is infamous as the location of the Wannsee Conference in which the Nazis elected to gas millions of Jews as a "final solution". The villa is now a memorial, with its exhibition explaining the conference and giving a deeply moving overview of the atrocities. Documents from the meeting are displayed and photographs of participants ranged around the walls, their biographies showing many lived to a comfortable old age. To get here, catch a #114 bus (about a 5min journey) from S-Bahn Wannsee and get off at "Haus der Wannsee-Konferenz".

After this, a useful nearby pick-me-up is the pleasant **Pfaueninsel** (Peacock Island; daily: March, April, Sept & Oct 9am–6pm; May–Aug 8am–9pm; Nov–Feb 10am–4pm; ferry €2; ⓦwww.spsg.de), an island that was once a royal fantasy getaway and now a bucolic landscaped park in which peacocks roam. No cars are allowed on the island (nor dogs), which is accessed by a regular passenger ferry from the terminus of bus #218 from S-Bahn Wannsee.

Eating and drinking

Berlin has all the restaurants, cafés and bars you'd expect from a major European capital, with virtually every imaginable type of food represented; indeed, the national cuisine generally takes a back seat to Greek, Turkish, Balkan, Indian and Italian specialities. In line with Berlin's rolling nightlife timetable, you can pretty much **eat and drink** around the clock. The majority of restaurants will happily serve until around 11pm, and even later it's not hard to find somewhere in most neighbourhoods. Eating at Berlin's restaurants is by international standards inexpensive: main courses start at around €6, and drinks aren't hiked up much more than in bars. For most of the restaurants listed below you can just walk in, though on weekend nights or at the most expensive places, booking is recommended.

In Berlin many places morph from one type of venue into another throughout the day. A good place to slurp a morning coffee and read a paper may well turn into a restaurant later on before rolling out the decks for a DJ until the small hours, when it closes to repeat the process all over again two or three hours later.

Cafés and cheap eats

Mitte

See map, pp.80–81.

Asia Snack Bahnhof Friedrichstr. For once dishes closely resemble the menu photos at this small place selling quick fixes of pan-Asian food; one of a number of joints under the S-Bahn tracks, and good for a quick lunch. U- & S-Bahn Friedrichstr. Daily 10am–late.

Beth Café Tucholskystr. 40 ☎030/281 31 35. Small and spartan, yet slightly snooty, vegetarian kosher café run by a small Orthodox Jewish congregation, with pretty courtyard seating outside and no smoking inside. The snacks and light meals are mostly Israeli and traditional Eastern European specialities, for about €2–9. S-Bahn Oranienburger Str. Sun–Thurs midday–8pm.

Café Adler Friedrichstr. 206 ☎030/251 89 65. Small café popular for its position by the site of Checkpoint Charlie, but which somehow avoids being too touristy. Serves breakfast and other meals: the soups are excellent, packed with fresh ingredients, and look out for the well-priced daily specials (€4–9). U-Bahn Kochstr. Mon–Sat 10am–midnight, Sun 10am–7pm.

Da Da Falafel Linienstr. 132 ☎030/27 59 69 27. Tiny, Middle Eastern *Imbiss* with sleek decor, some seating, and excellent falafel and shawarma sandwiches – the best of a clutch of cheap and cheerful options at this end of Oranienburger Strasse. U-Bahn Oranienburger Tor. Daily 10am–2am.

Gorki Park Weinbergsweg 25 ☎030/448 72 86. Tongue-in-cheek Soviet-themed café with 1970s Eastern Bloc-style furnishings and tasty and affordable Russian dishes like blinis and pelmeni (mains from €3.50). A large *Milchcafé* comes with a delicious molasses cookie, and the weekend brunch buffet (€8) is a treat. U-Bahn Rosenthaler Platz. Daily 9.30am until late.

Käse Konig Panoramastr. 1. Join local pensioners at this basic cafeteria serving decent, simple German and Central European food at low prices off a small daily menu – such as *Schnitzel* or goulash with boiled potatoes for around €6. Two branches share the same block. U- & S-Bahn Alexanderplatz. Mon–Sat 8am–7pm, Sun 10am–7pm.

Operncafé Opernpalais, Unter den Linden 5 ☎030/20 26 83. Elegant café in a former royal palace that evokes the atmosphere of Imperial Berlin. Amazing cakes! U-Bahn Französische Str. Daily 8am–midnight.

🏃 **Strandbad Mitte** Kleine Hamburger Str. 16 ☎030/24 62 89 63. At the end of a small street off the beaten tourist-track, this inviting café and bar, with some outdoor seating, makes a good retreat when it all gets too much. Excellent breakfasts served 9am–4pm. U-Bahn Rosenthaler Platz. Daily 9am–2am.

🏃 **Tele-café Alexanderplatz** Panorama Str. ☎030/242 33 33. This café, 207m above Berlin in the upper reaches of the TV tower, rotates so you can enjoy a wonderful panoramic view of the city while tucking into a pricey ice cream or an international menu (mains €9–14). The daily specials, particularly the soups, are the best options. Expensive as you have to pay to go up the tower too: make reservations or wait for a table. U- & S-Bahn Alexanderplatz. Daily 10am–11.30pm.

🏃 **Zum Nussbaum** Am Nussbaum 3 ☎030/242 30 95. In the heart of the Nikolaiviertel, this is a convincing copy of a prewar bar – destroyed in an air raid – that stood on the Fischerinsel and was favoured by the artists Heinrich Zille and Otto Nagel. Verges on the expensive, but it's a good place to soak up a bit of ersatz Old Berlin ambience. U-Bahn Klosterstr.

City West
See map, p.104.

Café Savigny Grolmanstr. 53 ☎030/31 51 96 12. Bright café serving superb coffee to an arty/media, mixed gay and straight crowd. Excellent for breakfast, served 9am–4pm. U-Bahn Ernst-Reuter Platz. Daily 9am–1am.

Dicke Wirtin Carmerstr. 9 ☎030/312 49 52. Traditional Berlin *Kneipe*, here since the 1920s and spruced up since. Pick from nine draught beers and basic snacks like *Schmalzbrot* (lard on bread). S-Bahn Savignyplatz. Daily noon–2am.

Einhorn Mommsenstr. 2 ☎030/881 42 41. Vegetarian wholefood at its best, with a fabulous lunch bar. Low prices (€3–6 per dish) mean it's often packed to standing, but the atmosphere remains friendly and relaxed. U-Bahn Uhlandstr. Mon–Fri 10am–5pm.

Piccola Taormina Uhlandstr. 29 ☎030/881 47 10. Enduringly popular wafer-thin pizza specialist with a strange setup: order what you want and pay at the bar, find a seat in the back room, listen up for a tannoy announcement when it's ready, then head back to the bar to collect. It's all a bit chaotic and very Italian, but well worth it for the food – slices from €1. U-Bahn Uhlandstr. Daily 10am–2am.

Zwiebelfisch Savignyplatz 7 ☎030/312 73 63. Corner bar that's a bit of a 1970s throwback for would-be arty and intellectual types. Jazz, earnest debate and good cheap grub, like goulash and Swabian *Maultaschen* (ravioli), served until 3am. S-Bahn Savignyplatz. Daily noon–6am.

Schöneberg
See map, p.108.

🏃 **Baharat Falafel** Winterfeldtstr. 37 ☎030/216 83 01. The best falafel in Berlin in a bare-bones vegetarian *Imbiss*, with some seating. U-Bahn Nollendorfplatz. Daily noon–2am.

Café Einstein Kurfürstenstr. 58 ☎030/261 50 96. Housed in a seemingly ancient German villa, this is about as close as you'll get to the ambience of the prewar Berlin *Kaffeehaus*, with international newspapers and breakfast served until 2pm. Occasional live music, and a good garden.

Expensive, though, and a little snooty. U-Bahn Nollendorfplatz. Daily 9am–midnight.

Café M Goltzstr. 34 ☏030/216 70 92. Though littered with tatty plastic chairs and precious little else, *M* is Berlin's favoured rendezvous for self-styled creative types – who usually drink Flensburger Pils. Usually packed, particularly for its famous breakfasts. U-Bahn Nollendorfplatz. Mon–Fri 8am until late, Sat & Sun 9am until late.

Tori Katsu Winterfeldtstr. 7 ☏030/216 34 66. Slightly chaotic Japanese *Imbiss* – here long before sushi became popular – specializing in breaded chicken dishes. U-Bahn Nollendorfplatz. Daily 11am–10pm.

Toronto Crellestr. 17 ☏030/781 92 30. A classy wood-panelled café that spills out onto a large leafy plaza – perfect on a fine summer day. It serves excellent home-made cake and a Sunday brunch buffet (10am–3pm; €8.70). U-Bahn Kleistpark. Mon–Sat 9am–12.30am, Sun 10am–midnight.

Kreuzberg-Friedrichshain
See maps, p.109 & pp.110–111.

Ankerklause Kottbusser Damm 104, Kreuzberg ☏030/693 56 49. Nautically themed pub overlooking a bucolic canal that's been transformed into a hip bar playing a mixture of techno and easy listening. Great breakfast choice (served until 4pm) with first-class French toast and a Mexican breakfast that will tide you over until dinner. Usually packed by 11pm. U-Bahn Kottbusser Tor. Tues–Sun 10am–4am, Mon 4pm–4am.

Bierhimmel Oranienstr. 183, Kreuzberg ☏030/615 31 22. Candlelit bar with a cosy 1950s cocktail lounge out back. Great atmosphere, and a second home to many locals; good for coffee and cakes in the afternoon and cocktails later on. U-Bahn Kottbusser Tor. Daily 1pm–3am.

Café Sybille Karl-Marx-Allee 72, Friedrichshain ☏030/29 35 22 03. Airy café with a *fin-de-siècle* feel – it's been here over a century – and a diverting exhibition about Karl-Marx-Allee in the back. Worth a visit for the cake and ice cream alone. U-Bahn Strausberger Platz. Daily 10am–8pm.

Milagro Bergmannstr. 12, Kreuzberg ☏030/692 23 03. Superb café-cum-restaurant; fiercely popular for its imaginative food and huge break-fasts (9am–4pm). Kloster beer on tap. U-Bahn Gneisenaustr. Daily 9am–1am.

Nachtigall Imbiss Ohlauerstr. 10, Kreuzberg ☏030/611 71 15. Arab specialities, including the delicious shawarma kebab – lamb and hummus in pitta bread. Good salads for vegetarians as well. U-Bahn Görlitzer Bahnhof. Daily 11.00am–1.00am.

Prenzlauer Berg
See map, p.114.

Al Hamra Raumerstr. 16 ☏030/42 85 00 95. Comfortable Arab café with shabby decor but decent Mediterranean food, beer, water pipes, backgammon and chess, plus internet terminals and wi-fi (€2 per hour). U-Bahn Eberswalder Str. Daily 10am–3am.

Duy Thai Kollwitzstr. 89 ☏030/44 04 74 44. Inexpensive and tasty Thai cuisine, including crispy duck with fruit, as well as many vegetarian and noodle dishes. U-Bahn Senefelderplatz. Mon–Fri noon–midnight, Sat & Sun 1pm–midnight.

I Due Forni Schönehauser Allee 10. Enormous paper-thin pizzas cooked and served with Italian panache in a vast restaurant with a huge multi-level patio. A full range of toppings is offered including a few unusual ones like horse meat (*Pferdefleisch*). The quality ensures the place packs out despite its size, so it's best to book between 8 and 10pm on Friday and Saturday. U-Bahn Senefelderplatz. Daily noon–midnight.

Intersoup Schliemannstr. 31 ☏030/23 27 30 45. Mellow den with an encyclopedic collection of excellent soups (€3.50–5) and a relaxing vibe. The place's trademark soup – Thai lemon grass, bean sprouts, noodle, coconut milk with chicken, tofu, fish or shrimp – is well worth a try. DJs play until late. S-Bahn Prenzlauer Allee. Daily noon–4am.

Kietzkantine Oderberger Str. 50, Prenzlauer Berg ☏030/448 44 84. Choose from just two or three excellent daily specials at rock-bottom prices in this hugely popular bistro. There's always something vegetarian, and students get a discount – order and pay at the till, the food will then be brought to your seat. U-Bahn Eberswalder Str. Mon–Fri 9am–4pm.

Morgenrot Kastanienallee 85 ☏030/44 31 78 44. Bohemian Berlin hits its stride in this collective café. Everything is organic and the vegetarian buffet breakfast (until 3pm) is excellent and costs between €4 and €8: pay according to how wealthy you consider yourself. U-Bahn Eberswalder Str. Tues–Fri 10am until late, Sat & Sun 11am–late.

November Husemannstr. 15 ☏030/442 84 25. Uncluttered, exposed-wood place, just north of Kollwitzplatz, with imaginative German daily specials (€7–13), a reasonable Sunday brunch (9am–4pm; €8) and outdoor seating in a pleasantly quiet residential street. U-Bahn Senefelderplatz. Mon–Fri 9am–2am, Sat & Sun 9am–3am.

Pasternak Knaackstr. 24 ☏030/441 33 99. Authentic upmarket Russian place that recalls the cafés and restaurants founded by Berlin's large

Russian émigré community during the 1920s. A nice spot for caviar and champagne, a *Milchcafé* or a more substantial meal from the good selection of Russian dishes, including borscht, pelmeni and blinis. The range of vodkas is suitably extensive. U-Bahn Senefelderplatz. Daily 10am until late.

Wohnzimmer Lettestr. 6 ☏ 030/445 54 58. The rumpled and ramshackle living-room atmosphere helps make this a relaxed and sociable hangout at any time of day – and the comfy sofas make leaving hard. Breakfast served until 4pm. U-Bahn Eberswalder Str. Daily 10am–4am.

Restaurants

Mitte

See map, pp.110–111.

Borchardt Französische Str. 47 ☏ 030/81 88 62 62. Re-creation of an elegant prewar French restaurant of the same name, with high ceilings and tiled floors, and one of the top restaurants in the city. Delectable beef dishes (mains €20–30) make regular appearances, though the menu changes daily. U-Bahn Französische Str. Daily noon–2am.

Hasir Oranienburger Str. 4 ☏ 030/28 04 16 16. Opulent Turkish restaurant with liveried waiters, in a courtyard near the Hackeschen Höfe. Look for the Grand Bazaar-style hawker at the entrance, but don't be put off: inside is one of Europe's finest Turkish restaurants. Predictably, the many lamb dishes are all great but there are plenty of veggie options too. Mains are mostly €12–15; very reasonable, given the quality. S-Bahn Hackescher Markt. Daily 11.30am–1am.

Käfer Dachgarten Platz der Republik 1 ☏ 030/22 62 99 33. Famous for its location on the Reichstag roof and its view of eastern Berlin, and specializing in gourmet renditions of regional German dishes (mains €7–26). Reservations allow you to skip the long lines at the front and nip in a side entrance. S-Bahn Unter den Linden. Daily 9.30am–midnight, with last orders taken at 9.30pm.

Kasbah Gipsstr. 2 ☏ 030/27 59 43 61. Fabulous little Moroccan restaurant with atmospheric dimness and Arabic charm. The unusual mix of starters include *zaalouk*, a fruity aubergine dip, and *pastilla*, a flaky pastry filled with chicken and onion and coated with cinnamon and icing sugar. Mains (€8–13) revolve around couscous, kofte (spicy meatballs) and a number of first-class tajines. Clubby music and cocktails encourage lingering after dinner. U-Bahn Weinmeisterstr. Tues–Sun 6pm–midnight.

Kellerrestaurant im Brechthaus Chausseestr. 125 ☏ 030/282 38 43. Atmospheric restaurant in the basement of Brecht's old house, decorated with Brecht memorabilia. The Viennese specialities (mains €9–15) are from recipes dreamt by Brecht's wife Helene Weigel, a busy actress with only East

German ingredients at her disposal, so don't expect anything elaborate or expensive. U-Bahn Oranienburger Tor. Daily 6pm–1am.

Margaux Unter den Linden 78, entrance on Wilhelmstr. ☏ 030/22 65 26 11. Upscale place with onyx walls, marble floors and burgundy upholstery. The daily menu is dictated by the best available ingredients which, washed down with a selection from the seven hundred wines, go down easier than the prices – mains €18–48 – though set three-course lunches (€35) and six-course dinners (€95) are good-value alternatives. S-Bahn Unter den Linden. Mon–Wed 7–10.30pm, Thurs–Sat noon–2pm & 7.30–10.30pm.

Monsieur Vuong Alte Schönhauser Str. 46 ☏ 030/30 87 26 43. Snazzy Vietnamese place with delicious soups and noodle dishes (€7–10) from a tiny menu – also look out for daily specials on the blackboard – all available without meat. Bench dining may squeeze you in with other diners. Don't miss the delicious jasmine and artichoke teas, and zesty fruit smoothies. U-Bahn Weinmeisterstr. Mon–Fri noon–midnight, Sat 4pm–midnight.

Tadschikische Teestuben Palais am Festungsgraben ☏ 030/204 11 12. This is the place to recline on fat cushions and sip exotic teas – such as the Pushkin with its tot of vodka, honey and raisins or the Chinese, which comes adorned with joss sticks and aniseed sweets (€6.50 each). But don't overlook the menu of tasty Russian and Tajik dishes (the latter mainly lamb), with most mains around the €10 mark. The intricately decorated interior is festooned with oriental carpets: 1974 gifts from the USSR to the GDR. U- & S-Bahn Friedrichstr. Mon–Fri 5pm–midnight, Sat & Sun 3pm–midnight.

Unsicht-bar Gormannstr. 14 ☏ 030/24 34 25 00. Novelty restaurant (run by an organization for the blind), where you eat in total darkness. First, pick a three- or four-course menu (€40–60), including a vegetarian option, then follow your blind or partially sighted waiter into the pitch-black for your meal. The idea is that without sight, other senses are heightened, but you'll likely discover, too, how hard it is to judge the amount of food on your plate, on your fork, or down your front. U-Bahn Weinmeisterstr. Wed–Sun 6pm–1am, occasionally Mon and Tues.

Viva Mexico Chausseestr. 36 ☏030/280 78 65. Authentic, family-owned Mexican restaurant with a vivacious vibe, fresh ingredients, moderate prices and salsa to die for. U-Bahn Zinnowitzer Str. Mon–Thurs noon–11pm, Fri noon–midnight, Sat & Sun 5pm–midnight.

Zur letzten Instanz Waisenstr. 14–16 ☏030/242 55 28. Berlin's oldest *Kneipe*, with a wonderfully old-fashioned interior and a great beer garden. Reasonably priced traditional dishes, all with legal-themed names like *Zeugen-Aussage* ("eyewitness account"), a reminder of the days when people used to drop in on the way to the nearby courthouse. Considered so authentically German that foreign heads of state are often brought here, including Mikhail Gorbachev in 1989. If all the meaty dishes (€8–13) look too heavy, try the simple *Boulette*, Berlin's home-made mince-and-herb burger, done here to perfection. U-Bahn Klosterstr. Mon–Sat noon–11pm, Sun noon–9pm.

City West
See map, p.104.

Florian Grolmanstr. 52 ☏030/313 91 84. Leading light of the local *Neue Deutsche Küche* movement, and as much a place for Berlin's beautiful people to be seen as it is a place to eat. The food, similar to French *nouvelle cuisine*, is light and flavourful and only moderately expensive: mains €13–22. S-Bahn Savignyplatz. Daily 6pm–3am.

Zwölf Apostel Bleibtreustr. 49 ☏030/312 14 33. Deluxe pizzeria that's been packing them in for years, with unusual toppings like smoked salmon and cream cheese and five types of calzone (mains: €8–24). The €5 weekday lunch (noon–4pm) is excellent. Booking recommended. S-Bahn Savignyplatz. Open 24hr.

Schöneberg
See map, p.108.

Aroma Hochkirchstr. 8 ☏030/782 58 21. Quality Italian restaurant and popular, so book ahead. Mains cost €7–15, the top-notch Sunday brunch buffet (until 4pm) €9.50. Also has a small photo gallery and shows Italian films on Tuesday nights. U- & S-Bahn Yorckstr. Mon–Fri 5.30pm–1am, Sat noon–1am, Sun 11am–1am.

Carib Motzstr. 31 ☏030/213 53 81. Classic Caribbean cuisine fused with European dishes (mains €11.50–15.50) and served by the friendly Jamaican owner. Reservations recommended. U-Bahn Nollendorfplatz. Daily 5pm–midnight.

Edd's Thailändisches Lutzowstr. 81 ☏030/215 52 94. Huge portions of superbly cooked, fresh Thai food make this a sumptuous place, popular all week. For the quality and authenticity – many recipes stem from Edd's gran, who cooked in Bangkok's Royal Palace – the prices are very reasonable (mains €8–15). Booking essential and credit cards not accepted. U-Bahn Kurfürstenstr. Tues–Fri 11.30am–4pm & 6pm–midnight, Sat 5pm until late, Sun 2pm–midnight.

Maharadscha Fuggerstr. 21 ☏030/213 88 26. The ambience may be German farmhouse, but the food is pure Indian, with dishes (€6–10) from every part of the subcontinent. It gets packed out for the Sunday buffet (noon–5pm; €6.90). U-Bahn Nollendorfplatz. Sun–Thurs 11.30am–midnight, Fri & Sat 11.30am–1am.

Storch Wartburgstr. 54 ☏030/784 20 59. Rustic eatery serving cuisine from the Alsace region. The excellent food, a mix of French and German, often including wild boar (mains €14–18), is served at long communal tables. Bookings advisable, though none are taken after 8pm. U-Bahn Eisenacher Str. Daily 6pm–1am (kitchen closes at 11.30pm).

Tim's Canadian Deli Maassenstr. 14 ☏030/21 75 69 60. One of the best North American restaurants in Berlin, its hearty menu including burgers, ribs, club sandwiches and buffalo meat, great fresh baked goods and generous breakfasts. U-Nollendorfplatz. Mon–Thurs 8am–1am, Fri & Sat 8am–3am, Sun 9am–1am.

Kreuzberg-Friedrichshain
See maps, p.109 & pp.110–111.

Abendmahl Muskauerstr. 9, Kreuzberg ☏030/612 51 70. Predominantly vegetarian restaurant (it also serves fish), magnificent in every respect: excellent food (especially the soups – try the *Kürbis* or pumpkin) and a busy but congenial atmosphere. Main courses (€10–17) have funky names and the Flaming Inferno, a spicy fish curry, is well worth trying, as are the so-called "deadly" ice creams. U-Bahn Görlitzer Bahnhof. Daily 6–11.30pm.

Altes Zollhaus Carl-Herz-Ufer 30, Kreuzberg ☏030/692 33 00. Very classy place in an old half-timbered building overlooking a canal, serving modern German food such as Brandenburg duck with *Kartoffelpuffer*, and *Zander*, a pike-like fish from the Havel. The three-course set menus cost €35. U-Bahn Prinzenstr. Tues–Sat 6pm–1am.

Henne Leuschnerdamm 25, Kreuzberg ☏030/614 77 30. Pub-style restaurant serving the best fried chicken (€6) in Berlin. The interior is original – it hasn't been changed, the owners claim, since 1905. U-Bahn Moritzplatz. Reservations essential. Daily 7pm–midnight.

🏃 **Miseria & Nobiltà** Kopernikusstr. 16,
Friedrichshain ☏030/29 04 92 49.
Lively and highly personable low-key Sardinian
restaurant, with flamboyant staff and phenomenal
home-made food. Booking recommended. U-
and S-Bahn Warschauer Str. Tues–Thurs
5pm–midnight, Fri & Sat 5pm until late.

🏃 **Morgenland** Skalitzer Str. 35, Kreuzberg
☏030/611 31 83. Relaxed café with a
welcoming vibe, which serves a mix of European
snacks. The amazing Sunday brunch buffet
(until 3pm; €7.50) seems to attract most of the
neighbourhood. U-Bahn Görlitzer Bahnhof. Daily
9.30am–2am.

Osteria No. 1 Kreuzbergstr. 71, Kreuzberg
☏030/786 91 62. Classy and popular Italian, run
by a collective, dishing up quality pizzas and oft-
changing pastas (€7–17) in a lush courtyard.
Particularly child-friendly (kids under 8 eat for free
on Sunday). Booking recommended. U-Bahn
Mehringdamm. Daily noon–midnight.

Weltrestaurant Markthalle Pücklerstr. 34,
Kreuzberg ☏030/617 55 02. Spacious restaurant
that attracts a young crowd to long communal
tables and hearty portions of German food. Look
out for the €7.50 daily special and leave space for
the phenomenal cakes. U-Bahn Görlitzer Bahnhof.
Daily 9am–midnight.

Prenzlauer Berg

See map, p.114.

Bangkok Prenzlauer Allee 46 ☏030/443 94 05.
Authentic and very good Thai and first choice in
Prenzlauer Berg for inexpensive dining (dishes
€3.30–9), so often a bit too busy for its own good.

U-Bahn Senefelderplatz. Daily 11am–11pm.

Gugelhof Knaackstr. 37 ☏030/442 92 29. Lively
Alsatian restaurant with inventive and beautifully
presented German, French and Alsatian food (mains
€7–17) – try the *Flammekuchen*, a thin-crust
Alsatian pizza. U-Bahn Senefelderplatz. Daily 6pm–
midnight, Sat & Sun 10am–midnight.

Ostwind Husemannstr. 13 ☏030/441 59 51.
Serene setting for superb modern and traditional
(and MSG-free) Chinese dining. Prices are a little
above average (mains €6.50–13.50), but justified
by the quality of the ingredients and preparation.
The Sunday brunch (all day; €8) is as good as
it is unusual. U-Bahn Eberswalder Str. Mon–Sat
6pm–1am, Sun 10am–1am.

🏃 **Restauration 1900** Husemannstr. 1
☏030/442 24 94. Traditional German
dishes that spring a few surprises, as well as some
pasta and vegetarian options (€9–15). Also
excellent for its Sunday buffet brunch (10am–4pm;
€8). Check out the photographs of the neighbourhood before and after reunification. U-Bahn
Eberswalder Str. Daily 10am–midnight.

Trattoria Paparazzi Husemannstr. 35 ☏030/
440 73 33. Top-rated place with outstanding
Italian food and a large wine list. Prices are
reasonable, given the quality, with mains €10–16.
U-Bahn Eberswalder Str. Daily 8pm–1am (kitchen
until 11.30pm).

Zum Schusterjungen Danziger Str. 9 ☏030/442
76 54. Large portions of no-nonsense German food
served in the back room of a locals' *Kneipe*. The
plastic and formica decor has echoes of the GDR and,
at around €8 per dish, the prices do too. U-Bahn
Eberswalder Str. Daily 11am–midnight.

Microbreweries and beer gardens

Mitte

See map, pp.80–81.

Brauhaus Georgbräu Spreeufer 4 ☏030/242 42
44. A merry touristy microbrewery, with excellent
beer and traditional German food. U-Bahn
Klosterstr. Daily 10am–midnight.

Brauhaus Mitte Karl-Liebknecht-Str. 13 ☏030/24
78 38 31 11. All the trappings of a Bavarian beer
hall including the excellent beers – try the delicious
Weissen, a cloudy Bavarian speciality – re-created
in the heart of Berlin. Good for basic pub-food with
well-priced lunch specials for €6. U- & S-Bahn
Alexanderplatz. Mon–Sat 10am–midnight, Sun
10am–11pm.

🏃 **Café am Neuen See** Lichtensteinallee 2
☏030/254 49 30. A little piece of Bavaria
smack in the middle of the Tiergarten; this beer

garden is next to a picturesque lake where you can
rent a rowing boat. Massive thin-crust pizzas are
served alongside frothing jugs. S- & U-Bahn
Zoologischer Garten. Daily 10am–11pm.

Prenzlauer Berg

See map, p.114.

Pfefferberg Schönhauser Allee 176, Prenzlauer
Berg ☏030/282 92 89. Popular outdoor beer
garden, in the courtyard of a former brewery, with
Czech and Bohemian tipples among its range of
draught beers. Food is limited to meaty items from
a couple of stalls. U-Bahn Senefelderplatz. Daily
11am until late.

Prater Kastanienallee 7–9, Prenzlauer Berg
☏030/44 48 56 88. In summer you can swig beer,
feast on *Bratwurst* and other native food, and listen

to Seventies German rock in this traditional beer garden; in winter the beer hall offers a similarly authentic experience. U-Bahn Eberswalder Str.

Beer hall Mon–Sat 6pm until late, Sun 10am until late; beer garden April–Sept daily noon till late.

Nightlife and entertainment

Since the days of the Weimar Republic, and even through the lean postwar years, Berlin has had some of the best – and steamiest – nightlife in Europe, an image fuelled by the drawings of George Grosz and films like *Cabaret*. Today's big draw is its world-class techno clubs, growing out of the local scene, and colonizing abandoned buildings around former no-go areas of the East–West border. Berlin also has a wide range of other **clubs**: from slick hangouts for the trendy to raucous dives, and incorporating **live music** of just about every sort. The city also has one of the world's finest **symphony orchestras**, and has a reputation as a leader of the avant-garde arising from its often experimental **theatre** and high-quality dance groups. There are scores of mainstream and art-house **cinemas**.

To find out what's on check the **listings magazines** *Tip* (ⓦ www.tip-berlin .de) and *Zitty* (ⓦ www.zitty.de), available at any newsstand, and the free magazine *030* (ⓦ www.berlin030.de), distributed in bars and cafés. The city's tourist information (see p.73) also produce a useful weekly guide (at ⓦ www .btm.de), and sell tickets in their offices and online. Otherwise the first place to try for tickets is *Hekticket*, which sells half-price tickets to same-day perform-ances from 4pm, with offices at Hardenberg Strasse, Charlottenburg (ⓣ 030/230 99 30, ⓦ www.hekticket.de; U- & S-Bahn Zoologischer Garten), and Karl-Liebknecht-Strasse, Mitte (ⓣ 030/24 31 24 31; U- & S-Bahn Alexanderplatz).

Bars and clubs

The distinction between cafés, bars, clubs and arts venues is notoriously fluid in Berlin, with considerable overlap between each, so check places listed on pp.118–123 too. **Opening times** are as relaxed and bars typically close between 1am and 5am, while clubs are even more open-ended – they rarely get going before midnight and some stay open beyond 6am. Berlin's clubs are smaller, cheaper and less exclusive than counterparts in London or New York. **Admission** is often free – though on weekends cover charges tend to run from €5 to €11. Don't worry too much about dress code as the prevalence of a shabby-chic aesthetic means you can get into most places without making much effort.

Several distinct nightlife areas have evolved in the city. The easiest place to bar-hop is Oranienburger Strasse in Mitte, though the Simon-Dach-Strasse in

---

Pub crawls

If the idea of venturing into Berlin's legendary nightlife seems overwhelming, or you fancy the company of young travellers, consider joining a **pub crawl tour**. For around €12 you'll be taken to around half a dozen watering holes and a club (cover charges included) at the end of it all. You'll be fed free shots on the street along the way, so it's not the most dignified way to spend an evening, but it can be good fun if the crowd's right. Try New Berlin Tours (ⓦ www.newberlintours.com), Insider Tours (ⓦ www.insiderberlintours.com), Insomniac Tours (ⓦ www.insomniactours.com) and My Berlin Tours (ⓦ www.berlinpubcrawl.eu). Between them there's at least one tour every night of the week.

Friedrichshain is also good, with far more locals around. More established places lie in **Prenzlauer Berg** and in **Schöneberg** and **western Kreuzberg**, where they tend to attract a slightly older crowd. With the **U- & S-Bahn** running nonstop on Friday and Saturday nights – and restarting from about 4am on other nights – jumping between areas of town could hardly be easier.

Mitte
See map, pp.80–81.

Acud Veteranenstr. 21 ☎030/44 35 94 97, ⓦwww.acud.de. Rock and blues are the mainstay of this ramshackle venue, with hip-hop and drum 'n' bass thrown in for good measure. There's also a gallery and movie theatre tucked inside. U-Bahn Rosenthaler Platz. Daily 9pm until late.

Grüner Salon Rosa-Luxemburg-Platz 2, Mitte ☎030/24 59 89 36, ⓦwww.gruener-salon.de. All-green club beside the *Roter Salon* that preserves something of the 1920s in its chandeliers and velvet. Renowned for its Thursday tango, Friday swing and Saturday cabaret (8–10pm) evenings. Entry €4–15. U-Bahn Rosa-Luxemburg-Platz. Thurs 9pm–4am, Fri & Sat 11pm–4am.

Kaffee Burger Torstr. 60 ☎030/28 04 64 95, ⓦwww.kaffeeburger.de. Russian-owned, smoky 1970s retro-bar legendary for its Russian-themed disco nights, but good any time, not least for the mad mix of genres – Balkan, surf rock, samba, rockabilly – that fills the small dancefloor. Readings and poetry often start evenings off, but it really fills up later on. Entry €3–5. U-Bahn Rosa-Luxemburg-Platz. Mon–Thurs until late, Fri & Sat 9/10pm until late, Sun 7pm until late.

Roter Salon Rosa-Luxemburg-Platz 2 ☎030/24 06 58 06. Tatty club within the Volksbühne theatre, with lurid red decor and chintzy furniture giving it the feel of a 1950s brothel. Readings, concerts and club nights are held here. Wed is soul and funk night, other nights a mix of electronica, ska and Brit-pop. Entry €5–6. U-Bahn Rosa-Luxemburg-Platz. Mon & Wed–Sat 11pm–4am.

Schokoladen Ackerstr. 169–170 ☎030/282 65 27, ⓦwww.schokoladen-mitte.de. The spartan, bare-brick interior of this former chocolate factory is a hangover from its time as a squatted building in the early post-*Wende* days. Now a venue for theatrical and art events, with live music on Saturday and decent contemporary cabaret on Sunday eve – particularly recommended if your German's up to it. U-Bahn Rosenthaler Platz. Mon–Thurs 8pm–4am, Fri & Sat 9pm–4am, Sun 7pm–4am.

Tacheles Oranienburger Str. 53–56 ☎030/282 61 85, ⓦwww.tacheles.de. This one-time department store became an artists' squat after the *Wende* and now has several very busy bars and clubs on its many levels. Among them is a beer garden, the

Café Zapata club, which has regular live music, a cinema, and several late-night art galleries. Don't be put off by the heavily graffitied stairwell, it leads up to the best spots. U-Bahn Oranienburger Tor. Daily 10am–late.

Verkehrsberuhigte Ost-Zone Monbijouplatz, S-Bahnbogen 153 ☎030/28 39 14 40. Great little bar for a dose of *Ostalgie* with your beer, since the decor is all GDR memorabilia. It's hidden away in the arches of the S-Bahn overlooking the Spree, which might be what keeps it from being touristy. S-Bahn Hackescher Markt. Daily 8pm–3am.

🏃 **Week12End** Alexanderplatz 5 ☎030/246 25 93 20, ⓦwww.week-end-berlin.de. Using the former premises of the GDR state travel agency, this is another of Berlin's creative transformations, and the twelfth-floor views over central Berlin are spectacular. All this makes up for the coolly offhand manner of most of its patrons as they groove to electronica. U- & S-Bahn Alexanderplatz. Fri & Sat 11pm until late.

Zosch Tucholskystr. 30 ☎030/280 76 64. Alternative place that started as a squat when the Wall came down, and has retained much of the feel. A good place for gigs and club nights in the cellar, where a fun-loving local Creole jazz band often plays amid the smoky ambience and constant chatter. U-Bahn Oranienburger Tor. Daily 4pm–5am.

Schöneberg
See map, p.108.

🏃 **Kumpelnest 3000** Lützowstr. 23 ☎030/261 69 18. Carpeted walls and a mock-Baroque effect attract a rough-and-ready crew of thirty-somethings to this erstwhile brothel, which gets going around 2am, when there's standing room only. The best place in the area, it's good fun and infamous as a hook-up bar for people of all sexual orientations. U-Bahn Kurfürstenstr. Daily 5pm–5am.

Kreuzberg-Friedrichshain
See map, pp.110–111.

Berghain Am Wriezener Bahnhof, Friedrichshain ⓦwww.berghain.de. Local clubbers will wait well over an hour to get into Berlin's king of clubs, where minimal techno and house cannonball around the gigantic concrete dancefloors of an old power plant. More laid-back bars and many relaxing back rooms (plus some infamous dark-rooms) offer alternatives for the evenly balanced gay and straight crowd. Photography strictly prohibited; you won't get in with a camera or if you look too conventional or like a foreign visitor. S-Bahn Ostbahnhof. Fri & Sat midnight until late.

Cassiopeia Reveler Str. 99, Friedrichshain ⓦ www.cassiopeia-berlin.de. Another former squat where the shambolic vibe has been preserved to produce a venue that's as odd, grungy and as hip and nebulous as any: on-site there's a skate-park, climbing wall, cinema, beer garden and four dancefloors. Always worth a look. S- & U-Bahn Warschauer Str. Mon–Fri 6pm until late, Sat & Sun 11am until late.

Dachkammer Simon-Dach-Str. 39, Friedrichshain ☏ 030/296 16 73. The largest and arguably most sociable place on the strip – the combination of a rustic bar downstairs and retro bar upstairs has made this a local classic. U- & S-Bahn Warschauer Str. Mon–Fri noon–1am, Sat & Sun 10pm–1am.

Kit-Kat Club Köpenicker Str. 76, entrance Brückenstr., Kreuzberg ⓦ www.kitkatclub.de. Famously debauched club, not for voyeurs but those looking for casual and public liaisons. The door policy is strict: wear something revealing or fetish-istic – check the website for guidelines, and for details of theme evenings. Gay parties are usually held during the week, at weekends it's a free-for-all. U-Bahn Heinrich-Heine-Str. Daily 11pm–6am.

SO36 Oranienstr. 190, Kreuzberg ☏ 030/61 40 13 06, ⓦ www.so36.de. Kreuzberg institution, whose heyday may have been the 1980s, but which is still going strong. It offers everything from gay-oriented house nights, Turkish and oriental pop to the odd punk concert – but avoids the mainstream like the plague. U-Bahn Kottbusser Tor. Daily 11pm–5am.

Tresor Köpenicker Str., Kreuzberg ☏ 030/229 06 11, ⓦ www.tresorberlin.de. A key player in Berlin's dance music scene with trouser-shaking techno booming in every nook of the convoluted bunker-style club. The volume, intensity and light show all have to be experienced to be believed. U-Bahn Heinrich-Heine-Str. Wed–Sat 11pm–6am.

Watergate Falckensteinstr. 49, Kreuzberg ☏ 030/61 28 03 95, ⓦ www.water-gate.de. Top Berlin club, with a glorious location by the Oberbaumbrücke overlooking the waters of the Spree. The club sprawls over two levels with a large main floor and a floor with a lounge, and the music is varied but mostly electronic. Entry €7–10. U- & S-Bahn Warschauer Str. Thurs–Sat 11pm until late.

Wild at Heart Wiener Str. 20, Kreuzberg ☏ 030/611 70 10, ⓦ www.wildatheartberlin.de.

Cornerstone live-music venue for rock 'n' roll, indie and punk, with something always going on well into the small hours. U-Bahn Görlitzer Bahnhof. Daily 8pm–4am.

Prenzlauer Berg

See map, p.114.

Bastard@Prater Kastanienallee 7–9 ☏ 030/44 04 96 69. Small club and live-music venue nestled in the *Prater* beer garden and theatre complex (see p.123). It caters to the intelligent electronica and post-rock crowd, with poetry slams and surreal, offbeat perform-ances – a good pot-luck choice. U-Bahn Eberwalder Str. Fri & Sat 11pm until late, occasional week-nights.

Dunckerclub Dunckerstr. 64 ☏ 030/445 95 09, ⓦ www.dunckerclub.de. Indie, industrial and unashamedly Goth refuge from the mainstream and techno. €2.50–3.50. S-Bahn Prenzlauer Allee. Mon–Thurs 10pm until late, Fri & Sat 11pm until late.

Icon Cantianstr. 15 ☏ 030/61 28 75 45, ⓦ www .iconberlin.de. Arguably the finest drum 'n' bass club in town, with local DJs being regularly joined by international bigwigs. The club divides into several bars, lounges and dance areas, making it easy to find your niche. Admission €3–6. U-Bahn Eberswalder Str. Mon & Sun 8pm until late, Fri 10.30pm until late, Sat 11.30pm until late.

Kulturbrauerei Knaackstr. 97 ☏ 030/48 49 44, ⓦ www.kulturbrauerei-berlin.de. Nineteenth-century brewery that's been turned into a multi-venue arts and cultural centre attracting frequent visits by local and mid-level bands. One club, *Soda* (ⓦ www.soda-berlin.de), thrives on soul, house and funk. U-Bahn Eberswalder Str. Mon from 8.30pm, Thurs & Sun from 8pm, Fri from 10.30pm, Sat from 11pm until late.

nbi Schönhauser Allee 36 ☏ 030/44 05 16 81, ⓦ www.neueeberlinerinitiative.de. The residential neighbourhood keeps the volume of the music here down, which the lounge-cum-club has used to its advantage, creating a comfortable environ-ment for the appreciation of cutting-edge electronica. DJs come here to hear each other experiment. U-Bahn Eberswalder Str. Daily 10pm until late.

Zu mir oder zu dir Lychener Str. 15 ☏ 0176/24 42 29 40. Groovy, very Seventies lounge-bar with a sociable vibe and lots of sofas. A good place to start an evening before heading down the road to the clubs of the *Kulturbrauerei* (see above), though its name translates as "your place or mine?" U-Bahn Eberswalder Str. Daily 8pm until late.

Live music

All but the most hardcore techno clubs frequently have **live music**; particularly good are *Acud*, *Schokoladen*, the *Kulturbrauerei*, *Prater* and *Wild at Heart* – see pp.124–126. For **large venues** you'll probably need to book in advance and get directions from a ticket office. Only **jazz**, blues and world music clubs tend to keep themselves separate from the rest of Berlin nightlife, so they're listed below; the city's biggest jazz festival is the late October or early November Jazz Fest Berlin (⑩ www.berlinerfestspiele.de).

Jazz, blues and world

A-Trane Bleibtreustr./Pestalozzistr., Charlottenburg. ☎ 030/313 25 50, ⑩ www.a-trane.de. Slick forum for the Berlin jazz scene and a good place to see both up-and-coming and well-known jazz artists in a comfortable, intimate setting. Best during Saturday night jams, when musicians arrive from other venues and join in at will throughout the evening. Entry €5–20, free on Mon and Sat. U-Bahn Savignyplatz. Daily 9pm until late.

Haus der Kulturen der Welt John-Foster-Dulles-Allee 10, Tiergarten ☎ 030/39 78 71 75, ⑩ www.hkw.de. The city's number one venue for world music is always worth checking out. S-Bahn Lehrter Bahnhof.

Quasimodo Kantstr. 12a, Charlottenburg ☎ 030/312 80 86, ⑩ www.quasimodo.de. Casual, smoky cellar bar that's one of Berlin's best jazz spots, with nightly programmes starting at 10pm. A high-quality mix of international, usually American, stars and up-and-coming names. Small, with a good atmosphere but a bit hard to find: go up to the terrace next to Theatre des Westens and follow the stairwell to the left of the café. Often free on weekdays, otherwise €5–25. U- & S-Bahn Zoologischer Garten. Daily 9pm–2am.

Classical music

For years classical music in Berlin meant one orchestra: the Berlin Philharmonic, but in the last decade or so it's had its supremacy questioned by the rise of the excellent **Deutsches Symphonie Orchester** and many smaller orchestras who often perform chamber concerts and recitals in the city's museums and historic buildings. A major annual music festival is the **Festtage** in the first half of April, organized by the Staatsoper, but staged at the Berlin Philharmonic. Also significant is the Musikfest Berlin (⑩ www.berlinerfestspiele.de), an acclaimed international music festival in the first half of September, when guest orchestras from around the world play innovative modern works.

Berliner Symphonie Orchester ⑩ www.berliner-symphoniker.de. Founded in 1952 and based in the Konzerthaus (see below), this maintains a fine reputation, conducted by Eliahu Inbal, though it does not compare to the Philharmonic. Tickets €7–30.

Deutsche Oper Bismarckstr. 35, Charlottenburg; box office ☎ 030/343 84 01 (Mon–Sat 11am–6pm), ⑩ www.deutscheoperberlin.de. Formerly West Berlin's premier opera house, built in 1961 after the Wall cut access to the Staatsoper. The place to hear Wagner and Strauss. Tickets €10–112. U-Bahn Deutsche Oper.

Deutsches Symphonie Orchester ⑩ www.dso-berlin.de. Currently under conductor Ingo Metzmacher and with no permanent base, though often at the Philharmonie and Konzerthaus. Tickets €10–55.

Komische Oper Behrenstr. 55–57, Mitte ☎ 030/47 99 74 00, ⑩ www.komische-oper-berlin.de. Less traditional than the Staatsoper, but reliable for well-staged operatic productions. The building doesn't look like much from the outside, but the interior is a wonderful 1890s frenzy of red plush, gilt and statuary and is a great place to enjoy cutting-edge interpretations of modern works alongside the usual fare – and at half the ticket prices of the Deutsche Oper. Tickets €8–62. S-Bahn Unter den Linden.

Konzerthaus Berlin (Schauspielhaus) Gendarmenmarkt, Mitte; box office ☎ 030/20 30 90, ⑩ www.konzerthaus.de. A super venue, with two concert spaces in the Schinkel-designed building: the Grosser Konzertsaal for orchestras and the Kammermusiksaal for smaller groups and chamber orchestras. Look out for performances on the Konzerthaus's famed organ. Tickets €5–40. U-Bahn Stadtmitte.

Philharmonie Herbert-von-Karajan-Str. 1, Mitte; box office ☎ 030/25 48 89 99, ⑩ www.berlin-philharmonic.de. You'll have to be minted to afford it but a visit to the Berlin Philharmonic, in the acoustically near-perfect Philharmonie, is a world-class experience. Directed since 2002 by Simon Rattle who has slowly created his own distinctive sound, moving the orchestra away from their traditional Germanic comfort zone of Brahms and Beethoven. The Philharmonie also contains the smaller Kammermusiksaal for more intimate performances, and your best chance of getting a ticket is when guest orchestras are playing. Tickets €8–61. U- & S-Bahn Potsdamer Platz.

Rundfunk Symphonieorchester Berlin ⓦwww .rsb-online.de. After the Philharmonic, the second-oldest orchestra in Berlin and a little more daring than its older sister. The orchestra appears at both the Philharmonie and the Konzerthaus.

Staatsoper Unter den Linden 5–7, Mitte; box office ☎030/20 35 45 55 (Mon–Sat 10am–8pm, Sun 2–8pm), ⓦ www.staatsoper-berlin.de. The city's oldest and grandest music venue, built for Frederick the Great in 1742 to a Knobelsdorff design. and at the forefront of the international opera scene. Tickets €8–120. U-Bahn Friedrichstr.

Theatre, cabaret and dance

Mainstream **civic and private theatres** in Berlin tend to be dull, unadventurous and expensive, yet the **fringe** scene is vibrant and brims with **experimental work**. Check under "Off-Theater" in *Tip* or *Zitty* for performances that are often held in various clubs – see p.124. Though 1920s and 1930s Berlin was famed for its rich and intense **cabaret scene**, when hundreds of small clubs presented often deeply satirical and political acts, the Nazis quickly suppressed them and the scene never recovered. Most of today's shows are either semi-clad titillation or drag shows, though a few places are increasingly worth trying. However, most cabaret venues make their money by charging high bar prices.

Admiralspalast Friedrichstr. 101, Mitte ☎030/31 98 90 00, ⓦ www.admiralspalast.de. Reopening in 2006 after extensive renovations, the Admiralspalast again provides the round-the-clock entertainment it did in its 1920s heyday – though without the brothel it incorporated then. The eclectic events programme includes comedy, live music, burlesque and opera, and there's a casino. Tickets €10–60. U- & S-Bahn Friedrichstr.

Bar Jeder Vernunft Scharperstr. 24, Wilmersdorf ☎030/883 15 82, ⓦ www.bar-jeder-vernunft.de. Hip young venue for the long-running *Cabaret* musical – based on stories by Christopher Isherwood – that does a fabulous job of standing in for his Kit Kat Club. The talented cast effectively capture the decadence of Weimar-era Berlin against the backdrop of the Nazi rise to power. Tickets €14–30. U-Bahn Spichernstr.

Berliner Ensemble Bertolt-Brecht-Platz 1, Mitte ☎030/28 40 81 55, ⓦwww.berliner-ensemble.de. Brecht's old theatre where he is still the staple fare; the rest of the programme is given over to reliable pieces by Henrik Ibsen, Friedrich Schiller and the like. There are also occasional experimental productions on the *Probebühne* (rehearsal stage). Tickets €4–32. U- & S-Bahn Friedrichstr.

Chamäleon Rosenthaler Str. 40–41, Mitte ☎030/400 05 90, ⓦwww.chamaeleonberlin.de. Lively, innovative cabaret and vaudeville shows with jugglers, acrobats and the like. Seating is around tables and there's a bar, so there's no harm

in turning up early. Tickets €25–37. S-Bahn Hackescher Markt.

Deutsches Theater Schumannstr. 13a, Mitte ☎030/28 44 12 21, ⓦ www.deutsches-theater.de. Good, solid productions taking in everything from Schiller to Mamet make this one of Berlin's best theatres and invariably sold out. Also includes a second theatre, the Kammerspiele des Deutschen Theaters, and Die Baracke, an experimental stage. Tickets €4–42. U-Bahn Oranienburger Tor.

Freunde der Italienischen Oper Fidicinstr. 40, Kreuzberg ☎030/691 12 11, ⓦwww.thefriends.de. Tiny courtyard theatre specializing in fringe productions performed in English. Tickets €8–14. U-Bahn Platz der Luftbrücke.

Kalkscheune Johannisstr. 2, Mitte ☎030/59 00 43 40, ⓦ www.kalkscheune.de. Creative cabaret shows – authentic but without the nostalgia. Tickets €8–18. U-Bahn Oranienburger Tor.

La Vie en Rose Flughafen Tempelhof, Kreuzberg ☎030/69 51 30 00, ⓦ www.lavieenrose-berlin.de. A drag variety revue with lots of glitter and lots of skin. There's also a piano bar. Tickets €10–15. U-Bahn Platz der Luftbrücke.

Maxim-Gorki-Theater Am Festungsgraben 2, Mitte ☎030/20 22 11 15, ⓦ www.gorki.de. Consistently good productions of modern works like Tabori's *Mein Kampf* and Schaffer's *Amadeus*. More experimental works are staged on the Studiobühne (studio stage). Tickets €12–26. U- & S-Bahn Friedrichstr.

Staatsballett ⓦ www.staatsballett-berlin.de. Berlin's premier ballet company performs at the Staatsoper and Deutsche Oper; see opposite.
Tanzfabrik Berlin Möckernstr. 68, Kreuzberg ☏ 030/786 58 61, ⓦ www.tanzfabrik-berlin.de. Experimental and contemporary works, usually fresh and exciting. Tickets €10. U- & S-Bahn Yorckstr.
Volksbühne Rosa-Luxemburg-Platz, Mitte ☏ 030/247 67 72, ⓦ www.volksbuehne-berlin.de. One of Berlin's most adventurous and interesting

theatres with highly provocative performances – nudity and throwing things at the audiences crop up fairly regularly and there's a high chance of witnessing a partial audience walkout. Tickets €10–21. U-Bahn Rosa-Luxemburg-Platz.
Wintergarten Potsdamer Str. 96, Tiergarten ☏ 030/25 00 88 88, ⓦ www.wintergarten-variete.de. A glitzy attempt to re-create the Berlin of the 1920s, with live acts from all over the world – cabaret, musicians, dance, mime, magicians. Tickets €18–35. U-Bahn Kurfürstenstr.

Cinemas

When the all-night drinking gets too much, it's always possible to wind down in front of the silver screen. Art-house cinemas are common and the rise of the multiplex theatres means there are more mainstream English-language screenings. **Ticket** prices range from €7 to €11, with significant reductions on *Kinotag* (KT in the listings magazines). In February, the **Berlinale** (ⓦ www .berlinale.de) film festival dominates the city's cultural life. Second only to Cannes among European festivals, it offers a staggering number of films from all around the world.

Cinestar Sony Center Potsdamer Str. 4, Tiergarten ☏ 030/26 06 62 60. Eight-screen cinema in the bowels of the Cony Center, with almost every screen in the original (usually English) language; most films are of the Hollywood blockbuster variety. U- & S-Bahn Potsdamer Platz.
Hackeschen Höfe Rosenthalerstr. 40–41, Mitte ☏ 030/283 46 03. Five-screen multiplex on the top

floor of the busy Hackeschen Höfe. Upscale independent foreign films and documentaries, sometimes in English. S-Bahn Hackescher Markt.
Zeughaus-Kino Unter den Linden 2, Mitte ☏ 030/20 30 44 21. Cinema in the Zeughaus which often unearths fascinating films from the pre- and postwar years. S-Bahn Hackescher Markt.

Gay and lesbian Berlin

Berlin's gay and lesbian scenes rival any in the world and make it a magnet for gay men and women from all over Germany and Europe. This has been the case since the 1920s, when Christopher Isherwood and W.H. Auden were both drawn to a city where, in sharp contrast to the homophobia and repression in the rest of Europe, the gay community did not live in fear of harassment and legal persecution. Weimar Berlin's gay scene in the 1920s and early 1930s was prodigious before it was brutally outlawed and persecuted in the Third Reich.

Happily, this persecution is a distant memory today and Berlin is as accepting of all stripes of the gay and lesbian community as anywhere. The charismatic city mayor, Klaus Wowereit, nicknamed "Wowi", is openly gay and it's not uncommon to see transvestites at their glitziest dancing atop tables at even conservative bashes. Unwelcoming places are hard to find, but all the same you might like to target a few gay hot-spots. The German/English-language **Berlin von Hinten** (€12) is the city's most useful gay **guidebook**; monthly gay **magazine Siegessäule** (ⓦ www.siegessaeule.de) has listings of events and is free from most gay bars and venues. As in many other large cities, **lesbians** in Berlin have a much lower profile than gay men. There's no real distinction between bars and cafés for lesbians and straight women, and many of Berlin's women-only bars have a strong lesbian following. Monthly publication

Blattgold (Ⓦ www.blattgold-berlin.de) lists all lesbian groups and events and is available from feminist meeting places and bookshops.

Finally, the best time to arrive and plunge yourself into the hurly-burly is during **Gay Pride Week**, centred around the **Christopher Street Day parade** (Ⓦ www.csd-berlin.de) on the last Saturday in June every year.

Bookshops, museums and venues

AHA–Lesben- und Schwulenzentrum
Mehringdamm 61, Kreuzberg ☎ 030/692 36 00, Ⓦ www.aha-berlin.de. Nonprofit organization that provides premises for gay and lesbian groups and organizes workshops and events. U-Bahn Mehringdamm.

Ana Koluth Karl-Liebknecht-Str. 13 ☎ 030/24 72 69 03, Ⓦ www.anakoluth.de. Exceptionally well-stocked lesbian bookstore, which also puts on regular exhibitions and readings; check the website. U-Bahn Alexanderplatz. Mon–Fri 10am–8pm, Sat 10am–4pm.

Begine Potsdamer Str. 139, Schöneberg ☎ 030/215 14 14, Ⓦ www.begine.de. Women's centre with a programme of earnest lectures and films (Sept–May), and excellent performances by women musicians and dancers. U-Bahn Bülowstr. Daily 6pm until late.

EWA Prenzlauer Allee 6, Prenzlauer Berg ☎ 030/442 55 42, Ⓦ www.ewa-frauenzentrum.de. EWA offers courses and various cultural events. It also has an airy women-only café-gallery with a children's play area. Good for what's-on information and flyers. U-Bahn Rosa-Luxemburg-Platz. Mon–Thurs 10am–11pm, Fri 10am–3pm.

Frauenzentrum Schokofabrik Mariannenstr. 6, Kreuzberg; ☎ 030/615 29 99, Ⓦ www.schokofabrik .de. One of Europe's largest women's centres, with a café/gallery, sports facilities (including hamam, a women-only Turkish bath) and diverse events. U-Bahn Kottbusser Tor. Mon–Thurs 10am–2pm, Fri noon–4pm.

Prinz Eisenherz Buchladen GmbH Bleibtreustr. 52, Charlottenburg ☎ 030/313 99 36, Ⓦ www .prinz-eisenherz.com. Friendly gay bookstore that's excellent for relaxed browsing, free magazines and what's-on posters and leaflets. U-Bahn Wittenberg-platz. Mon–Sat 10am–8pm.

Schwules Museum Mehringdamm 61, Kreuzberg Ⓦ 030/69 59 90 50, Ⓦ www.schwulesmuseum.de. Interesting, but low-profile gay museum with changing exhibitions (entrance €5) on local and international gay history, and library material to browse through. U-Bahn Mehringhamm. Mon, Wed–Fri & Sun 2–6pm, Sat 2–7pm.

Spinnboden Anklamer Str. 38, Mitte ☎ 030/448 58 48, Ⓦ www.spinnboden.de. A comprehensive archive of every aspect of lesbian experience, with a collection of books, videos, posters and magazines. U-Bahn Bernauer Str. Wed & Fri 2–7pm.

Bars and clubs

In addition to what's below, many largely straight clubs have gay nights – particularly *Berghain*, *Kit Kat Club* and *Kumpelnest 3000* (see pp.125–126). Nights not to miss are the stalwart **GMF** events (Ⓦ www.gmf-berlin.de), which pop up at different venues around town – think stripped-to-the-waist revellers dancing to pounding house-music.

Connection Fuggerstr. 33, Schöneberg ☎ 030/23 62 74 44. Gay entertainment complex including refined American sports bar – *Prinzknecht* – all bare brick and gleaming chrome, attracting a broad range of middle-aged gay men and some women. Very popular house and techno club at weekends. U-Bahn Wittenbergplatz. Daily 3pm–late.

Hafen Motzstr. 19, Schöneberg ☎ 030/211 41 18. Adjacent to *Tom's Bar* (see opposite), this mixed place is a long-established, cruisey bar for thirty- and forty-somethings, and always packed – a great place to start a night out. U-Bahn Nollendorfplatz. Daily 8pm until late.

Heile Welt Motzstr. 5, Schöneberg ☎ 030/21 91 75 07. The youngest and trendiest bar in Schöneberg provides a second living room for many locals; great cocktails and convivial atmosphere. U-Bahn Nollendorfplatz. Daily 6pm–late.

Neues Ufer Hauptstr. 157, Schöneberg ☎ 030/78 95 97 00. Lovely neighbourhood gay bar, where Bowie used to drink in the 1970s when it was *Anderes Ufer*. U-Bahn Kleistpark. Daily 11am–2am.

Roses Oranienstr. 187, Kreuzberg ☎ 030/615 65 70. Kitsch gay club with a strong lesbian presence. One of the venues of choice for a solo night out for either sex. U-Bahn Kottbusser Tor. Daily 9.30pm–5am.

Schall und Rauch Gleimstr. 23, Prenzlauer Berg ℡030/443 39 70. Tasteful, designer elegance in this hip, young, mixed bar. A place to see and be seen – and eat, thanks to an imaginative and ever-changing menu. U-Bahn Schönhauser Allee. Daily 9am–2am.

Scheune Motzstr. 25, Schöneberg ℡030/213 85 80. Very popular leather club with regular theme parties for devotees of rubber, uniforms or sheer nakedness. Darkroom, baths and other accoutrements. U-Bahn Nollendorfplatz. Mon–Thurs 9pm–7am, nonstop Fri 9pm–Mon 7am.

Schoppenstube Schönhauser Allee 44, Prenzlauer Berg ℡030/442 82 04. The best-known gay place in eastern Berlin, this is really two very different bars: a pleasant wine-bar upstairs, and a steamy cruisers' haven downstairs. Knock for entry, and if the doorman likes the look of you you're in. U-Bahn Eberswalder Str. Daily 10pm until late.

🏃 SchwuZ Mehringdamm 61, Kreuzberg ℡030/69 50 78 89, ⓦwww.schwuz.de. Dance club well loved by all stripes of the gay community, and always crowded and convivial. One floor has the usual Eighties and disco mixes, the other more experimental tunes. Highly recommended. U-Bahn Mehringdamm. Fri & Sat 11pm–late.

Serene Bar Schwiebusser Str. 2, Kreuzberg ℡030/69 04 15 80, ⓦwww.serenebar.de. Great lesbian hangout, particularly on Saturdays when the big dancefloor packs out; the bar is also used by many special interest groups as a meeting point: table tennis, amateur photography and so on. The entrance is a little tucked away down an alley. U-Bahn Platz-der-Luftbrücke. Tues 6pm until late, Wed & Thurs 8pm until late, Sat 9pm until late.

Stiller Don Erich-Weinert-Str. 67, Prenzlauer Berg ℡0172/18 20 168. Slightly intellectual neighbourhood bar with a gay clientele running right across the age spectrum. U-Bahn Schönhauser Allee. Daily 8pm until late.

🏃 Tom's Bar Motzstr. 19, Schöneberg ℡030/213 45 70, ⓦwww.tomsbar.de. Dark, sweaty and debauched cruising establishment with a large darkroom. Possibly Berlin's most popular gay bar, and a great place to finish off an evening. Drinks are two for the price of one on Monday night. Men only. U-Bahn Nollendorfplatz. Daily 10pm–late.

Shopping

Multistorey **department stores** tend to rule Berlin, but a remarkable number of small and quirky specialist shops have survived the onslaught. Below is a selection of some of the more interesting, but the list is far from exhaustive. If you like browsing and foraging you'll find a second home in the city's many **flea markets** – good places to find relics of the Eastern Bloc – and **secondhand clothes shops**.

Glitz and dazzle are the prerogatives of **Wittenbergplatz** and the **Kurfürstendamm**, with its two miles of large chain stores, while **Friedrichstrasse** in the east, though more modest in size, is as opulent. Many of the city's funkiest speciality shops and expensive boutiques are concentrated in **Charlottenburg** and **Prenzlauer Berg**. Ethnic foods and "alternative" businesses are mostly in **Kreuzberg**, along Oranienstrasse and Bergmannstrasse.

Books, newspapers and magazines

Artificium Rosenthaler Str. 40–41, in the Hackeschen Höfe, Mitte ℡030/30 87 22 80, ⓦwww.artificium.com. Nineteenth- and twentieth-century art, architecture, photography and the like. S-Bahn Hackescher Markt. Mon–Thurs 10am–9pm, Fri & Sat 10am–10pm.

Berlin Story Unter den Linden 40, Mitte ℡030/20 45 38 42, ⓦwww.berlinstory.de. The city's most extensive bookshop on itself, with everything from travel guides to specialist histories, and offered in a range of languages. U- & S-Bahn Friedrichstr. Daily 10am–7pm.

Dussmann Friedrichstr. 90, Mitte ℡030/20 25 24 00, ⓦwww.kulturkaufhaus.de. A huge emporium of books, CDs, videos and software. U- & S-Bahn Friedrichstr. Mon–Sat 10am–10pm.

Hugendubel Branches at Friedrichstr. 83, Mitte (U- & S-Bahn Friedrichstr.), Potsdamer Platz shopping mall, Mitte (U- & S-Bahn Potsdamer Platz), and Tauentzienstr. 13, Charlottenburg

(U-Bahn Kurfürstendamm) ☎ 0181/48 44 84, ⓦ www.hugendubel.de. Huge general bookstore with a section devoted to English-language paperback fiction. Mon–Sat 9.30am–8pm.

Museum für Fotografie Jebensstr. 2 ☎ 030/20 90 55 66. Small bookshop in the foyer of the museum – you can browse without paying admission – with a glut of books on photography, art and design – many at reduced prices. U- & S-Bahn Zoologischer Garten. Wed & Fri–Sun 10am–6pm, Thurs 10am–10pm.

Music

DaCapo Kastanienallee 96, Prenzlauer Berg ☎ 030/448 17 71, ⓦ www.da-capo-vinyl.de. Vinyl-only new and used record shop with a wide selection of jazz, 1960s–80s rock and releases on East German label Amiga. U-Bahn Eberswalderstr. Mon–Fri 11am–7pm, Sat 11am–4pm.

DNS Records Alte Schönhauser Str. 39, Mitte ☎ 030/247 98 35, ⓦ www.dns-music.com. Listening stations and a large selection of the newest of club dance music on CD and vinyl. U-Bahn Weinmeisterstr. Mon–Fri 11am–8pm, Sat 11am–4pm.

Hard Wax Paul-Lincke-Ufer 44a, Kreuzberg ☎ 030/61 13 01 11, ⓦ www.hardwax.com. Premier dance-music specialist. Techno, trance: you name it, they should have it. And if they haven't, they'll get it for you. U-Bahn Görlitzer Bahnhof. Mon–Sat noon–8pm.

L&P Classics Knesebeckstr. 33–34, Charlottenburg ☎ 030/88 04 30 43, ⓦ www.lpclassics.de. Store devoted entirely to classical music. U-Bahn Uhlandstr. Mon–Sat 10am–8pm.

Mr Dead & Mrs Free Bülowstr. 5, Schöneberg ☎ 030/215 14 49, ⓦ www.deadandfree.com. Primarily pop, folk, indie and country records on independent labels, mostly on vinyl. U-Bahn Nollendorfplatz. Mon–Fri 11am–7pm, Sat 11am–4pm.

Soultrade Sanderstr. 29, Kreuzberg ☎ 030/694 52 57. Specialists in black music including soul, hip-hop, funk, house and jazz. U-Bahn Schönleinstr. Mon–Fri 11am–8pm, Sat noon–6pm.

Clothes

Berlinomat Frankfurter Allee 89, Friedrichshain ☎ 030/42 08 14 45, ⓦ www.berlinomat.com. The showcase for more than thirty Berlin designers, Berlinomat stocks a large and varied assortment of clothing, accessories and unique souvenirs. The prices, considering they're designer, are reasonable. U- & S-Bahn Frankfurter Allee. Mon–Fri 11am–8pm, Sat 10am–6pm.

Claudia Skoda Alte Schönhauser Str. 35, Mitte ☎ 030/280 72 11, ⓦ www.claudiaskoda.com. Berlin's knit-master and most famous designer. U-Bahn Weinmeisterstr. Mon–Fri noon–8pm, Sat noon–7pm.

Garage Ahornstr. 2, Schöneberg ☎ 030/211 27 60. Largest secondhand clothes store in Europe – good for jackets, coats and jeans. Prices are according to weight. U-Bahn Nollendorfplatz. Mon–Wed 11am–7pm, Thurs & Fri 11am–8pm, Sat 10am–4pm.

Humana Frankfurter Tor 3, Friedrichshain ☎ 030/422 20 18, ⓦ www.humana-de.org. Gigantic branch of a local secondhand chain, offering great bargains on items that are (again) in style. One of a dozen stores in Berlin, with another under the S-Bahn tracks at Alexanderplatz. U-Bahn Frankfurter Tor. Mon–Fri 10am–7pm, Sat 10am–4pm.

Lisa D. Rosenthaler Str. 40–41 (in the Hackeschen Höfe), Mitte ☎ 030/282 90 61, ⓦ www.lisad.com. One of Berlin's very few local designers to have made a name for herself, Lisa D. favours fitted dresses in muted colours. S-Bahn Hackescher Markt. Mon–Sat 11am–7.30pm, Sun noon–4pm.

Respectmen Neue Schönhauser Str. 14, Mitte ☎ 030/283 50 10, ⓦ www .respectmen.de. Good tailoring and nice design mark out this men's store featuring suits and casual wear. S-Bahn Hackescher Markt. Mon–Fri noon–8pm, Sat noon–6pm.

Secondo Mommsenstr. 61, Charlottenburg ☎ 030/881 22 91. Exclusively designer clothes at massively knock-down prices: most items are in top condition, though of course many designs are a bit dated. A number of similar shops lie up and down the street. S-Bahn Savignyplatz. Mon–Fri 11am–7pm, Sat 11am–3pm.

Sgt. Peppers Kastanienallee 91, Prenzlauer Berg ☎ 030/448 11 21. Mixed bag of vintage 1960s and 1970s, and the store also has its own label of retro-wear. U-Bahn Eberswalder Str. Mon–Fri 11am–7pm, Sat 11am–4pm.

Soma Alte Schönhauser Str. 27, Mitte ☎ 030/281 93 80, ⓦ www.soma-berlin.de. Young Berlin designers and club-wear in the front of the shop, secondhand in the rear. S-Bahn Hackescher Markt. Mon–Fri noon–8pm, Sat 11am–6pm.

Souvenirs

Ampelmann Galerie Shop Hackeschen Höfe V, Mitte ☎ 030/44 04 88 01, ⓦ www.ampelmann.de. Celebration of the traffic-light man (Ampelmann) that reigns supreme on the eastern side of the city. He was threatened with replacement with the svelte West Berlin counterpart and has since become a cult object. Pick up T-shirts, mugs, lights and so on here. S-Bahn Hackescher Markt. Mon–Fri noon–6pm, Sat noon–4pm.

Mondos Arts Schreinerstr. 6, Friedrichshain ☎030/42 01 07 78, ⊛www.ost-shop.de. GDR-kitsch heaven devoted to cult of the Ampelmann, Sandmann (a cult character from children's TV) and the Trabi, and stockist of virtually every other imaginable piece of *Ostalgie*. Lots of fun, even if you can't reminisce. U-Bahn Samariterstr. Mon–Fri 10am–7pm, Sat 11am–4pm.

Department stores

KaDeWe Tauentzienstr. 21, Schöneberg ☎030/212 10, ⊛www.kadewe-berlin.de. From designer labels to the extraordinary international delicatessen there's everything the consumer's heart desires at this, the largest department store on the continent. U-Bahn Wittenbergplatz. Mon–Fri 10am–8pm, Sat 9.30–8pm.

Flea markets and junk shops

Flohmarkt am Boxhagener Platz Boxhagener Platz, Friedrichshain. Small flea market catering to the needs of the student quarter and good for old Eastern Bloc memorabilia. U- & S-Bahn Warschauer Str. Sun 9am–4pm.

Flohmarkt am Tiergarten Strasse des 17 Juni, north side of road near Ernst-Reuter-Platz, Charlottenburg. Pleasant enough for a Sunday-morning stroll, but the most expensive of the flea markets, and with horribly tourist-oriented wares. Good for embroidery and lace, though. S-Bahn Tiergarten. Sat & Sun 10am–5pm.

Hallentrödelmarkt Treptow Eichenstr. 4, Treptow. Ideal rainy-day option: there's something of everything in this huge indoor flea market. The stalls are all permanent fixtures and thoroughly chaotic. S-Bahn Treptower Park – head north along Hoffmannstr. parallel to the Spree River. Sat & Sun 10am–4pm.

Zille-Hof Fasanenstr. 14, Charlottenburg. Not so much a flea market as an overgrown junk-shop with reproduction curios, old street signs and a miscellany of interesting junk. Not especially cheap, but the pleasure is in rummaging as much as in buying. U-Bahn Uhlandstr. Mon–Fri 8am–5pm, Sat 8am–1pm.

Listings

Car rental All the major car rental agencies are represented, although the best deals are often found through local operators, in the *Yellow Pages* under "Autovermietung"; you should be able to get something for under €30 a day. Hertz ☎01808/93 88 14, ⊛www.hertz.com; Robben & Wientjes, Prinzenstr. 90–91, Kreuzberg ☎030/61 67 70 (U-Bahn Moritzplatz) and Prenzlauer Allee 96 ☎030/42 10 36 (U-Bahn Prenzlauer Allee); SIXT ☎030/212 98 80.

Embassies Australia, Wallstr. 76–79 ☎030/8 80 08 80, ⊛www.australian-embassy.de; Canada, Friedrichstr. 95 ☎030/20 31 20, ⊛www.dfait-maeci .gc.ca; Ireland, Friedrichstr. 200 ☎030/22 07 20, ⊛www.botschaft-irland.de, New Zealand, Friedrichstr. 60 ☎030/20 62 10, ⊛www.nzembassy .com; South Africa, Tiergartenstr. 18 ☎030/22 07 30, ⊛www.suedafrika.org; UK, Wilhelmstr. 70–71 ☎030/20 45 70, ⊛www.britischebotschaft.de; US, Clayallee 170 ☎030/832 92 33, ⊛www.germany .usembassy.gov.

Health There's a 24hr pharmacy in the Hauptbahnhof. If you need a doctor, call English-language service ☎01804/22 55 23 62, ⊛www.calladoc .com; calls cost €0.24 per min. Charité Campus Mitte, Schumann Strasse 20–21, Mitte (☎030/450 50; S-Bahn Hauptbahnhof), is a hospital with a 24hr emergency room.

Internet Online access in Berlin is excellent. Larger hotels, a growing number of cafés, and all the main train stations have wi-fi hot spots – and there's a free one in the Sony Center (see p.84). Access in internet cafés costs about €1–4 per 30min.

Laundry Listed as "Waschsalon" in the *Yellow Pages*, and dotted throughout the city, one popular chain is Schell und Sauber, with a branch at Torstrasse 115 (daily 7am–10pm; U-Bahn Rosenthaler Platz), which has free wi-fi and a small café.

Police The emergency phone number for the police is ☎110; for all non urgent matters such as reporting a crime after the event or having your car impounded – call the 24-hour hotline ☎030/46 64 46 64. They will pass you on to the relevant district station.

Post office The post office (Postämt) with the longest hours is at Bahnhof Friedrichstrasse (under the arches at Georgenstrasse 12; Mon–Fri 6am–10pm, Sat & Sun 8am–10pm; ⊛www .deutschepost.de).

Sport and saunas Ars Vitalis, Hauptstr. 19, Schöneberg ☎030/788 35 63, ⊛www.ars-vitalis .de. Excellent private gym, where a day-pass (€25) gives you access to all the usual equipment as well as a good range of classes, and three different saunas. Masseurs are on standby. U-Bahn Kleistpark. Thermen am Europa-Center, Nürnberger Str. 7, Charlottenburg ☎030/257 57 60, ⓦwww .thermen-berlin.de. Big sauna complex with no less than nine saunas, as well as indoor and outdoor saltwater pools, fitness rooms and beauty treatments. A three-hour visit costs €16.50; towels available for rent. U-Bahn Wittembergplatz. Mon–Sat 10am–11pm, Sun 10am–9pm.

Brandenburg

When Berlin's city fringes don't seem like breather enough from its bustle, an expedition into its sleepy **Brandenburg** hinterland might be just the thing. Escaping the Land's major roads to cruise the flat tree-lined avenues that typify Brandenburg's minor roads is a pleasure, particularly by bike; you'll discover a state replete with gentle scenery, a patchwork of beech forests, fields of dazzling rapeseed and sunflower and heathland sewn together by a multitude of rivers, lakes and waterways. Brandenburg's unsung attractions were explored by Theodor Fontane (see box opposite), who divided the region into four geographical entities that still hold: the **Havelland**, immediately west of Berlin; the area around the town of **Rheinsberg** on the border of Mecklenburg-Western Pomerania to the north; the **Oderland**, or those lands in the catchment of the Oder, which now mostly straddle the Polish border east of Berlin; and, most popular of all, the **Spreewald**, a short drive southeast.

Almost all the state's headline attractions are in **Potsdam**, a town whose size is effectively doubled by landscaped gardens dotted with royal piles and follies. Part of the **Havelland**, Potsdam is also surrounded by lakes and rivers, and the area's other main town, **Brandenburg an der Havel**, spreads over several islands. The town of **Oranienburg** is less attractive and of interest primarily as the site of former concentration camp **Sachsenhausen**. The **Rheinsberg region** is also known for its many lakes, though the town's palace is an attraction in its own right and a popular classical music venue, and the thick surrounding forest has many pleasant hiking trails. The **Oderland** contains more of the same, particularly in and around the spa town Buckow in the **Märkische Schweiz**, Brandenburg's self-proclaimed Switzerland. Other points of interest are closer to the Oder itself, particularly the **Unteres Odertal Nationalpark** on the Polish border, an ecologically important wetland environment, flooded for much of the year and so providing an ideal and peaceful habitat for various birds. It lies beside the giant **Schorfheide**, a heathland reserve, whose low-key attractions include a dignified ruined monastery at Chorin and an impressive ship hoist at Niederfinow. Finally, Brandenburg's most popular and heavily touristed area is the **Spreewald**, centred on **Lübbenau**. The web of gentle waterways here is particularly popular for punting and canoeing, and the region made all the more enjoyable and intriguing by the presence of a **Sorb** minority, Germany's largest indigenous non-German community, and an astounding array of local **gherkins**, sold as snacks on the streets.

Worth a look before you travel, the website of Tourismus Marketing Brandenburg (☎0331/200 47 47, ⓦwww.brandenburg-tourism.com) includes an accommodation booking facility. Also worth investigating is the Brandenburg-Berlin Ticket, which allows up to five people to travel anywhere within

Theodor Fontane and his Brandenburg wanderings

Regarded by many as Germany's most important nineteenth-century Realist writer, Huguenot novelist and poet **Theodor Fontane** (1819–98) pioneered the German social novel, most famously *Effi Briest* (1894), which was turned into a film by Rainer Werner Fassbinder in 1974. Fontane's work offered insights into the lives of people across different social classes in an original style later dubbed Poetic Realism and often compared to the work of Thomas Hardy. But he's far less well known for his contribution to travel writing, which was well ahead of its time for its fusion of literary style, historical insight and narrative adventure. It also challenged the notion that exploring the exotic reaps the greatest rewards, suggesting instead that with the right approach your immediate surroundings can prove as bountiful. This notion came to him during a stint in Britain, which, as an Anglophile in the service of the Prussian intelligence agency, he knew well. While rowing on a Scottish loch it occurred to him that corners of his native Prussia were every bit as beautiful – he came from near Rheinsberg – yet uncelebrated and generally considered among Germany's least appealing regions. So between 1862 and 1889 he set out to champion his homeland, compiling the five-tome *Wanderungen durch die Mark Brandenburg* (Wanderings through the Mark of Brandenburg), based on his whimsical walks around the state: "I travelled through the Mark and found it richer than I dared to hope. The earth beneath every footfall was alive and produced ghosts ... wherever the eye rested, everything bore a broad historic stamp." His project would marry Prussian national identity with Romanticism in ways that often mirrored the writings of Sir Walter Scott, whose style was in vogue at the time. Fontane's wanderings are certainly worth dipping into, despite their off-putting length – at least they didn't end up as the twenty tomes he once planned – and as you travel around the region you'll certainly find enough quotes from his work on tourist office literature. Last respects can be paid at Fontane's grave in Berlin's Französischer Friedhof.

Brandenburg for one day (9am–3am) on all regional trains (RE, IRE, RB) as well as the entire Berlin BVG network. The ticket costs €24 online at ⓦ www .bahn.de, or €26 from train stations; for timetables see ⓦ www.vbb-online.de.

Potsdam

For most visitors **POTSDAM** means **Sanssouci**, Frederick the Great's splendid landscaped park of architectural treasures which once completed Berlin as the grand Prussian capital. However, Potsdam's origins date back to the tenth-century Slavonic settlement Poztupimi, and predate Berlin by a couple of hundred years. The castle built here in 1160 marked the first step in the town's gradual transformation from sleepy fishing backwater to **royal residence** and **garrison town**, a role it enjoyed under the Hohenzollerns until the abdication of Kaiser Wilhelm II in 1918. World War II left Potsdam badly damaged: on April 14, 1945, a bombing raid killed four thousand people, destroyed many fine Baroque buildings and reduced its centre to ruins. Less than four months later – on August 2 – the victorious Allies converged on Potsdam's **Schloss Cecilienhof** to hammer out the details of a division of Germany and Europe. Potsdam itself ended up in the Soviet zone, where modern "socialist" building programmes steadily erased many architectural memories of the town's uncomfortably prosperous imperial past. Yet it's this past that has given us its most popular sights. Apart from those of Park Sanssouci, there are more across the Havel in **Babelsberg**, which is best known as the site of the most important studio in German film history.

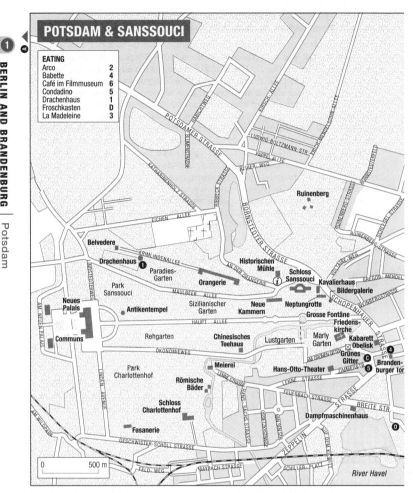

POTSDAM & SANSSOUCI

EATING

Arco	2
Babette	4
Café im Filmmuseum	6
Condadino	5
Drachenhaus	1
Froschkasten	D
La Madeleine	3

Arrival, information and town transport

All trains, including the S-Bahn from Berlin (around 30min) arrive in Potsdam's **Hauptbahnhof**, which incorporates a small shopping mall. The southern entrance delivers you to the city's main **bus station**, where you should pick up **bus** #695 or #X15 run by the Verkehrsbetrieb Potsdam (ViP; @ www.vip-potsdam.de) if you wish to hightail it straight to Schloss Sanssouci. Alternatively take #695, #X5, #650 or #606 to stop "Neues Palais" if you'd like to wander through the entire Sanssouci Park and back to the train station via the Altstadt. If you're bound for the town centre, you could take **tram** #92 from the Hauptbahnhof's west entrance, though it might be quicker and more interesting to simply head north for ten minutes' **walk** across the Lange Brücke into the centre. Use of Potsdam's local bus and tram services is covered by a zone C BVG ticket, so if you're coming from Berlin, buying an ABC day-ticket is the most economical way to get here and around.

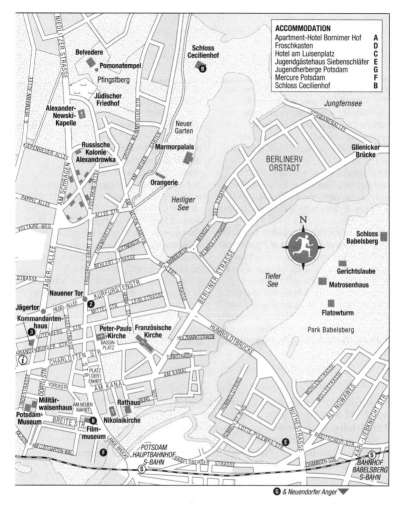

ACCOMMODATION
Apartment-Hotel Bornimer Hof	A
Froschkasten	D
Hotel am Luisenplatz	C
Jugendgästehaus Siebenschläfer	E
Jugendherberge Potsdam	G
Mercure Potsdam	F
Schloss Cecilienhof	B

Ⓖ & Neuendorfer Anger ▼

However, the most rewarding and practical way to explore Potsdam is to **rent a bike**, particularly for reaching the northern part of town as well as the area around **Babelsberg**. Rebhah Rent-a-Bike (daily Mon–Fri 9am–7pm, Sat & Sun 9am–8pm; €11 per day; ☏0331/270 62 10) operates out of a container in a park outside the Hauptbahnhof's northern entrance. They provide a free map of a seventeen-kilometre route that takes in all the main sites in a day.

Potsdam's well-equipped **tourist office** is at Brandenburger Strasse 3 (April–Oct Mon–Fri 9.30am–6pm, Sat & Sun 9.30am–4pm; Nov–March Mon–Fri 10am–6pm, Sat & Sun 9.30am–2pm; ☏0331/27 55 80, ⓦwww .potsdam-tourism.com), by the Brandenburg Gate.

Accommodation

In summer, accommodation in Potsdam can be hard to find, though the tourist office runs a **bookings hotline** (☏0331/27 55 80) and offers online booking at ⓦwww.potsdam-tourism.com (under heading "Hosts"). If you're on a budget try to get a private room (❸). The closest **campsite** is *Campingpark Sanssouci Gaisberg*, An der Pirschheide 1 (☎0331/9 51 09 88, ⓦwww.campingpark -sanssouci-potsdam.com; April–Nov), just south of Potsdam and connected to the city centre by tram #94.

Apartment-Hotel Bornimer Hof Rückerstr. 31 ☎0331/54 96 60, ⓦwww.apartmenthotel-bornimerhof.de. A hotel complex offering two-room suites and bungalows, some quite spacious, in a very quiet wooded setting north of town. Wide range of prices depending on size of apartment and its facilities. ❸

Froschkasten Kiezstr. 4 ☎0331/29 13 15. No-nonsense pine-furnished en-suite doubles above an inn, with a decent restaurant (see p.145), on the edge of the town centre. Breakfast included. ❹

Hotel am Luisenplatz Luisenplatz 5 ☎0331/97 19 00, ⓦwww.hotel-luisenplatz.de. Pleasant well-run hotel in an early eighteenth-century town house overlooking the quiet Luisenplatz, yet in the thick of things at the end of Brandenburger Strasse and just a couple of minutes' stroll from Park Sanssouci. Furnishings are vaguely in keep with the building, giving the compact guest-rooms an historic feel; the suites are much roomier, but twice the price. Prices include a superb breakfast and internet. ❻

Jugendgästehaus Siebenschläfer Lotte-Puewka-Str. 43 ☎0331/74 11 25, ⓦwww.jgh-potsdam.de. Basic but friendly hostel a 15min walk from the Hauptbahnhof in Babelsberg: take bus #695 along Babelsberger Strasse to Lotte-Puewka-Strasse. Dorms start at €12 per night in high season.

Jugendherberge Potsdam Schulstr. 9 ☎0331/581 31 00, ⓦwww.jh-potsdam.de. Slick modern hostel around the corner from S-Bahn Babelsberg with twelve-bed dorm rooms (€21.50) and smaller en-suite rooms (❷).

Mercure Potsdam Lange Brücke ☎0331/27 22, ⓦwww.mercure.com. A typical GDR-era high-rise in a central location with good views over town and standard hotel rooms. It's often possible to slash the rack rate by half by booking online. ❹

Schloss Cecilienhof Im neuen Garten ☎0331/29 24 98, ⓦwww.relexa-hotels.de. Housed in a wing of Schloss Cecilienhof (see p.144), this is the place to head for if you want a little luxury. Rooms have touches of old-fashioned class and pleasant views over the surrounding park and garden. Rates include an excellent buffet breakfast. ❺

The Town

North from the train station beyond Lange Brücke is the **Alter Markt**, the fringe of Potsdam's town centre. From here the northbound and arterial **Friedrich-Ebert-Strasse** leads to its pedestrianized main shopping street **Brandenburger Strasse**. Part of a Baroque quarter, it's best appreciated off the main drag, but in truth the town's attractions are minor in comparison with what awaits in Park Sanssouci.

The Alter Markt

The arresting outlines of the unmistakably GDR-era *Hotel Mercure* and the stately, domed **Nikolaikirche** frame the **Alter Markt**, the triangular plaza between. Its surging traffic and extensive building work make it an unprepossessing city gateway, but for most of its life it harboured bustling squares and streets. It was here that the town's earliest fortifications were built and where the medieval town flourished, a past that the highly visible excavations here continually unravel, as remnants of various crafts and the occasional buried treasure are found. But the Alter Markt is best known as the former site of the **Stadtschloss**, a Baroque residence built by the Great Elector between 1662 and 1669. World War II – specifically April 14 and 15, 1945 – reduced it to a bare, roofless shell, and the GDR demolished what remained in 1960 – around eighty percent of the building – to remove the last vestiges of Potsdam's grandest imperial buildings.

A parliament building (**Landtag**) for Brandenburg is planned on the site copying the footprint of the old Schloss; though it may end up a modern building, the gate to the palace forecourt, the domed **Fortunaportal**, has been reconstructed, completing the re-creation of three domed structures that traditionally dominated the Alter Markt. The most significant of these is the elegant, Schinkel-designed Neoclassical **Nikolaikirche** (Mon 2–5pm, Tues–Sat 10am–5pm, Sun 11.30am–5pm), while the third dome belongs to Potsdam's former **Rathaus** (daily Tues–Sun 10am–6pm; free), built during the mid-eighteenth century in Palladian Classical style. Under the GDR the building became an arts centre, a role it retains to this day. The **obelisk** in front of the Rathaus was designed by Knobelsdorff and originally bore four reliefs depicting the Great Elector and his successors. When re-erected during the 1970s these were replaced with reliefs of the architects who shaped much of Potsdam: Schinkel, Knobelsdorff, Gontard and Persius.

The Marstall, Filmmuseum and Am Neuen Markt

Across the main road, Friedrich-Ebert-Strasse, from the Nikolaikirche, lies the squat but elegant **Marstall**, the oldest town-centre survivor. Built as an orangerie towards the end of the eighteenth century and converted into stables by that scourge of frivolity, Friedrich Wilhelm I, the building owes its current appearance to Knobelsdorff, who extended and prettified it during the eighteenth century. Today it houses Potsdam's **Filmmuseum**, Breite Strasse 1a (daily 10am–6pm; €3.50; ☎0331/271 81 12, ⓦwww.filmmuseum-potsdam .de), which draws on material from Babelsberg's UFA studios nearby (see p.144) to present both a technical and artistic history of German film from 1895 to 1980, with some particularly fascinating material concerning the immediate postwar period. There's a vaguely hands-on feel, with a few visitor-operated bioscopes and numerous screens playing clips. The museum **cinema** is the best in Potsdam and there's also a good **café**. Just behind the Marstall, **Am Neuen Markt** leads to a few handsome vestiges of old Potsdam, including some improbably grand eighteenth-century coaching stables with an entrance in the form of a triumphal arch.

The Baroque quarter and around

North beyond Alter Markt you pass through an area once occupied by Potsdam's **Altstadt** before this was comprehensively destroyed in the war. Luckily, the **Baroque quarter** to the north survived the war substantially intact and slowly emerges along the north end of Friedrich-Ebert-Strasse. **Bassinplatz**, though disfigured by a huge modern bus station, offers a good introduction thanks to the nineteenth-century **Peter-Pauls-Kirche**, a replica of the campanile of San Zeno Maggiore in Verona. At the southeastern corner of the square lies the **Französische Kirche**, completed according to plans by Knobelsdorff in 1753, in imitation of the Pantheon in Rome, a recurring theme in German architecture of the period. Just north of Bassinplatz, lies the appealing **Holländisches Viertel** or "Dutch quarter", where 134 gabled, red-brick houses were put up by Dutch builders for immigrants from Holland who were invited to work in Potsdam by Friedrich Wilhelm I. The quarter has seen periods of dereliction since, but recent restoration and gentrification has produced a small colony of trendy shops and cafés.

From the Holländisches Viertel the **Baroque quarter** – built between 1732 and 1742 on the orders of Friedrich Wilhelm I – continues west around **Brandenburger Strasse**. The area – some 584 houses – was intended for tradespeople as the town rapidly expanded. On cross-street Lindenstrasse, the Dutch-style former **Kommandantenhaus**, nos. 54–55, is a building with uncomfortable associations: until the *Wende* it served as a Stasi detention centre known as the "Lindenhotel". It now houses **Gedenkstätte Lindenstrasse** (Tues–Thurs 10am–6pm; €3 with tour, €1.50 without): you can view the chilling cells and an exhibition details the building's use, which included a spell as a Nazi prison and "hereditary-health court", where decisions about compulsory sterilization were made. Further north up Lindenstrasse is the **Jägertor** or "Hunter's Gate", one of Potsdam's three surviving town gates, surmounted by a sculpture of a stag succumbing to a pack of baying hounds. Meanwhile, the triumphal **Brandenburger Tor** marks the western end of Brandenburger Strasse – built by Gontard in 1733 with a playfulness lacking in its Berlin namesake. The **Grünes Gitter** park entrance (see below) lies just beyond the northwestern corner of the adjacent **Luisenplatz**.

Park Sanssouci

Stretching west out of Potsdam's town centre, **Park Sanssouci** was built for Frederick the Great as a retreat after he decided in 1744 that he needed a residence where he could live "without cares" – "sans souci" in the French spoken in court. The task was entrusted to architect Georg von Knobelsdorff, who had already proved himself on other projects in Potsdam and Berlin. **Schloss Sanssouci**, on a hill overlooking the town, took three years to complete, while the extensive parklands were laid out over the following five years. As a finishing touch Frederick ordered the construction of the **Neues Palais** at the western end of the park, to mark the end of the Seven Years' War. Numerous additions over the following hundred and fifty years or so included the **Orangerie**. The park is most beautiful in spring, when the trees are in leaf and the flowers in bloom, and least crowded on weekdays. The main **visitors' centre** (daily: March–Oct 8.30am–5pm; Nov–Feb 9am–4pm; ☏331/969 42 02, ⓦwww.spsg.de) is by the historic windmill (see p.142).

The Grünes Gitter and around

The **Grünes Gitter** provides a southeastern entrance to Park Sanssouci and has an information kiosk. Immediately north of here is the 1850 Italianate **Friedenskirche** (mid-May to Oct daily 10am–6pm; free), designed by Persius for Friedrich Wilhelm IV. With its 39-metre-high campanile and lakeside setting, it conjures up the southern European atmosphere that Friedrich Wilhelm strove for by using the St Clemente Basilica in Rome as a model, and with the design centred on the magnificent Byzantine apse mosaic from Murano. Adjoining the church, the domed Hohenzollern mausoleum contains the tombs of Friedrich Wilhelm IV and his wife Elizabeth, and Friedrich III and his wife Victoria. The garden to the west is the **Marly-Garten**, once the kitchen garden of Friedrich I, who named it, with intentional irony, after Louis XIV's luxurious Marly park.

Combination tickets for Park Sanssouci buildings

Entrance to Park Sanssouci is free, although a €2 donation is suggested. If you plan to visit several buildings in the park, consider getting a **combination ticket**. A **Premium-Tageskarte** (€15) allows entry to all park buildings and is available only at Schloss Sanssouci. The regular **Tageskarte** (€12) is sold at all palaces, and the visitors' centre, and gives access to all buildings in Park Sanssouci except Schloss Sanssouci itself. Despite calling themselves *Tageskarten* (day-tickets), both the above are valid for two consecutive days.

Schloss Sanssouci

To approach **Schloss Sanssouci** as Frederick the Great might have done, make for the eighteenth-century **obelisk** on Schopenhauerstrasse. Beyond, Hauptallee runs through the ornate Knobelsdorff-designed **Obelisk-Portal** – two clusters of pillars flanked by the goddesses Flora and Pomona – to the **Grosse Fontäne**, the biggest of the park's many fountains, around which stand a host of Classical statues, notably Venus and Mercury. The approach to the Schloss itself leads up through terraced ranks of vines that are among the northernmost in Germany.

Frederick had definite ideas about what he wanted and worked closely with Knobelsdorff on the palace design, which was to be a place where the king, who had no great love for his capital, Berlin, or his wife, Elizabeth Christine, could escape both. It's a surprisingly modest one-storey Baroque affair, topped by an oxidized green dome and ornamental statues, looking out over the vine terraces towards the high-rises of central Potsdam.

The **interior** of Schloss Sanssouci (April–Oct Tues–Sun 9am–5pm; €8; Nov–March Tues–Sun 9am–4pm; €12) can only be visited by **guided tour**. These take place every twenty minutes and tickets for the whole day go on sale at 9am – arrive early as demand is high. Once inside, you'll find a frenzy of Rococo in the twelve rooms where Frederick lived and entertained his guests – a process that usually entailed quarrelling with them. The most eye-catching rooms are the opulent **Marmorsaal** (Marble Hall) and the **Konzertzimmer** (Concert Room), where the flute-playing king forced eminent musicians to play his own works on concert evenings. Frederick's favourite haunt was his library where, surrounded by two thousand volumes – mainly French translations of classics and a sprinkling of contemporary French writings – he could oversee work on his tomb. One of Frederick's most celebrated house guests was Voltaire, who lived here from 1750 to 1753, acting as a kind of private tutor to the king, finally leaving when he'd had enough of Frederick's behaviour, damning the king's intellect with faint praise and accusing him of treating "the whole world as slaves". In revenge Frederick had Voltaire's former room decorated with carvings of apes and parrots. The **Damenflügel**, the west wing of the Schloss

▲ Schloss Sanssouci

(mid-May to mid-Oct Sat & Sun 10am–5pm; €2), was added in 1840, and its thirteen rooms housed ladies and gentlemen of the court. Nearby on the terrace is a wrought-iron summerhouse protecting a weather-beaten copy of a Classical statue, while just to the south an eighteenth-century sculpture of Cleopatra looks over the graves of Frederick's horses.

Around Schloss Sanssouci

East of Schloss Sanssouci, overlooking the ornamental **Holländischer Garten**, or Dutch Garden, is the restrained Baroque **Bildergalerie** (mid-May to mid-Oct Tues–Sun 10am–5pm; included in price of guided tour), which, it's claimed, was the first building in Europe built specifically as a museum. Unfortunately, wartime destruction and looting scattered the contents, but the new collection includes Caravaggio's wonderful *Incredulity of St Thomas* and several works by Rubens and Van Dyck.

On the opposite side of the Schloss, from a point near the Cleopatra statue, steps lead down to the **Neue Kammern** (March Sat & Sun 10am–5pm; April–Oct Tues–Sun 10am–5pm; €4 with tour, €3 without), the architectural twin of the Bildergalerie, originally an orangerie and later a guesthouse. Immediately west is the prim **Sizilianischer Garten** or Sicilian Garden, crammed with coniferous trees and subtropical plants, complementing the **Nordischer Garten**, another ornamental garden just to the north, whose most interesting feature is the strange-looking **Felsentor** or Rock Gate, a gateway fashioned out of uncut stones and topped by a lumpen-looking eagle with outstretched wings.

Frederick was prepared to go to some lengths to achieve the desired carefree rural ambience for Sanssouci and retained an old wooden windmill as an ornament just north of the Neue Kammern. Four years after his death, this was replaced by a rustic-looking stone construction, the **Historische Mühle**, now a restaurant.

The Orangerie and around

From the western corner of the Sizilianischer Garten, **Maulbeerallee**, a road open to traffic, cuts through the park past the **Orangerie** (mid-May to mid-Oct Tues–Sun 10am–5pm; €3). This Italianate Renaissance-style structure with its belvedere towers is one of the most visually impressive buildings in the park. A series of terraces with curved retaining walls sporting waterspouts in the shape of lions' heads leads up to the sandy-coloured building, whose slightly down-at-heel appearance adds character.

It was built at the behest of Friedrich IV and, like the Friedenskirche (see p.140), inspired by architecture seen on his Italian travels. The facade is lined with allegorical statues set in niches, such as "Industry" who holds a cog wheel. The western wing of the building is still used as a refuge for tropical plants in winter, and during the summer it's possible to ascend the western tower for views of the Neues Palais and vistas of Potsdam's high-rises. The Orangerie also houses a gallery, the **Raphaelsaal**, with copies of paintings looted by Napoleon.

The Belvedere, Drachenhaus and Antikentempel

From the western wing of the Orangerie, the arrow-straight Krimlindenallee, lined with lime trees, leads towards a Rococo **Belvedere**, the last building to be built under Frederick the Great. It was the only building in the whole park to suffer serious war damage, but has now been restored to its former glory. A couple of hundred metres short of the Belvedere, a path off to the left leads to the **Drachenhaus**, a one-time vintner's house built in the style of a Chinese pagoda for the small vineyard nearby. Today the café inside (see p.145) is an ideal place to interrupt wanderings. Southwest of the Drachenhaus, a pathway leads to the **Antikentempel**, built in 1768 to house part of Frederick the Great's art collection. This domed rotunda is now the last resting place of a number of Hohenzollerns, including the Empress Auguste Victoria, and Hermine, the woman Wilhelm II married in exile, and who became known as the "last Empress".

The Neues Palais

Rising through the trees at the western end of Park Sanssouci, the **Neues Palais** (April–Oct Mon–Thurs, Sat & Sun 9am–5pm, €6 with tour, €5 without; Nov–March Mon–Thurs, Sat & Sun 9am–4pm, €5 with tour), is another massive Rococo extravaganza from Frederick the Great's time, built between 1763 and 1769 to reaffirm Prussian might after the Seven Years' War. At the centre of the palace is a huge green-weathered dome, topped by a crown, while the edges of the roof around the entire building are adorned by lines of Classical figures, mass-produced by a team of sculptors. The main entrance is in the western facade, and once inside, you'll find the interior predictably opulent, particularly as you enter the vast and startling **Grottensaal** on the ground floor which is decorated entirely with shells and semi-precious stones to form images of lizards and dragons. The equally huge **Marmorsaal** is the other highlight, with its beautiful floor of patterned marble slabs. The southern wing contains Frederick's apartments and theatre where he enjoyed Italian opera and French plays. The last imperial resident of the Neues Palais was Kaiser Wilhelm II, who packed sixty train carriages with the palace contents before fleeing with his family in November 1918, following the revolution and abdication. Facing the Neues Palais entrance are the **Communs**, a couple of Rococo fantasies joined by a curved colonnade. They look grandiose, but their purpose was mundane: they housed the palace serving and maintenance staff.

The Rehgarten and Park Charlottenhof

From the Neues Palais, Ökonomieweg leads east between the **Rehgarten** or Deer Garden, the former court hunting ground (and still home to a few deer) and **Park Charlottenhof**, created by Friedrich Wilhelm III as a Christmas present for his son, and today one of Sanssouci's quieter corners. A path leads over a bridge past a small farm building to the **Römische Bäder** (May–Oct Tues–Sun 10am–5pm; €3), built by Schinkel and Persius in convincing imitation of a Roman villa.

Across the lawns to the south is **Schloss Charlottenhof** (May–Oct Tues–Sun 10am–5pm; €4), another Roman-style building, again designed by Schinkel and Persius for Friedrich IV. Though designated a palace, it is, in reality, little more than a glorified villa, but its interior, unlike most Sanssouci buildings, is original. The effect is impressive: the hallway is bathed in blue light filtered through coloured glass decorated with stars, a prelude to the **Kupferstichzimmer**, or print room, whose walls are now covered in copies of Italian Renaissance paintings. Immediately east of Schloss Charlottenhof is the **Dichterhain** (Poets' Grove), an open space dotted with busts of Goethe, Schiller and Herder, among others. West of here through the woods and across a racetrack-shaped clearing called the **Hippodrom** is the **Fasanerie**, another Italian-style edifice built between 1842 and 1844.

On the Ökonomieweg – en route back to the Grünes Gitter entrance – you'll pass the slightly kitsch **Chinesisches Teehaus** (May–Oct Tues–Sun 10am–5pm;

€2), a kind of Rococo pagoda housing a small museum of Chinese and Meissen porcelain and surrounded by eerily lifelike statues of oriental figures.

The Neuer Garten and Schloss Cecilienhof

Immediately northeast of Potsdam's centre lies another large park complex, the **Neuer Garten,** where the **Marmorpalais** (Marble Palace; March Tues–Fri tours only; April–Oct Tues–Sun 10am–5pm; Nov–March Sat & Sun 10am–4pm; €5 with tour, €4 without; ☎0331/969 42 46) was built for Friedrich Wilhelm II, who died a premature death here in 1797, allegedly a consequence of his dissolute lifestyle. It has now been restored to an approximation of its original royal condition and the sumptuous rooms can be seen once again.

Also in the grounds of the Neuer Garten, but looking like a mock Elizabethan mansion, is **Schloss Cecilienhof** (April–Oct Tues–Sun 9am–5pm; Nov–March Tues–Sun 9am–4pm; €6 with tour, €5 without; ⓦwww.spsg.de; tram #92 or #96 to stop "Reiterweg/Alleestrasse" then change to bus #692). The last palace to be commissioned by the Hohenzollerns, it was begun in 1913 and completed in 1917, the war evidently doing nothing to change the architectural style. Cecilienhof would only rate a passing mention, were it not for the fact that the **Potsdam conference** – confirming earlier decisions made at Yalta about the postwar European order – was held here from July 17 to August 2, 1945. The conference was heavily symbolic, providing a chance for Truman, Stalin and Churchill (replaced mid-conference by Clement Attlee) to show the world that they had truly won the war by meeting in the heart of the ruined Reich. As a result, the main attraction inside is the **Konferenzsaal**, or conference chamber, which resembles an assembly hall of a minor British public school, where the Allies worked out details of the division of Europe. Everything has been left pretty much as it was in 1945, with the huge round table specially made in Moscow for the conference still in place. It's also possible to visit the delegates' workrooms, furnished in varying degrees of chintziness. Cecilienhof has been used as an expensive hotel and restaurant since 1960, both for the deep of pocket (see p.138).

Babelsberg

On the eastern bank of the Havel is **Babelsberg**, once a town but now officially part of Potsdam. Lining the banks of the Tiefer See is **Park Babelsberg**, Potsdam's third great park complex, designed by Lenné, and the least visited of the three. Tracks lead through the hilly, roughly wooded park to **Schloss Babelsberg** (closed for renovation; ⓦwww.spsg.de), a neo-Gothic architectural extravaganza, built by Schinkel at the behest of Prince Wilhelm, brother of Friedrich Wilhelm IV, and inspired by England's Windsor Castle.

But Babelsberg's real claim to fame is as the one-time heart of the German film industry. Founded in 1917, it was here that the UFA film studios rivalled Hollywood during the 1920s. Today the huge old studio complex is given over to **Filmpark Babelsberg** (April–Oct daily 10am–6pm; €17; ☎0331/721 27 55, ⓦwww.filmpark.de), and served by buses #690 from Babelsberg's S-Bahn station and #601 and #602 from Potsdam's Hauptbahnhof. It's mainly of interest to those with a good knowledge of the German film industry, with films produced here during its heyday including *Das Kabinett des Dr Caligari*, *Metropolis* and *Der Blaue Engel*. It's now reinvented itself as a theme park and visitors can wander through costume and props departments and watch technicians going through the motions of shooting film scenes. It's also possible to visit the hangar-like studio where Fritz Lang may have filmed *Metropolis* (no one is quite sure of the exact location) and admire a reproduction of his futuristic set. Aside from the film-related attractions are fairground rides and animal shows.

Eating, drinking and nightlife

Potsdam has an array of pleasant **cafés** and **restaurants**, with most along Brandenburger Strasse. For **nightlife** the best bet is the Lindenpark, Stahnsdorfer Strasse 76–78 (℡0331/74 79 70, Ⓦwww.lindenpark.de), over in Babelsberg, with regular "alternative" discos and live bands. Also recommended is the Waschhaus, Schiffbauergasse 1 (℡0331/271 56 26, Ⓦwww.waschhaus.de), just off Berliner Strasse on the way into town from the Glienicker Brücke, a large venue with galleries, open-air cinema and frequent live music. At the same address is Fabrik (℡0331/280 03 14, Ⓦwww.fabrikpotsdam.de), a theatre for contemporary dance and music.

Restaurants

Arco Friedrich-Ebert-Str. ℡0331/270 16 90. Small, fancy Italian restaurant occupying the east wing of the Nauener Tor, with some outdoor seating in summer. Serves excellent pan-continental food (mains around €9) and a sumptuous Sunday brunch buffet (€9). Daily 10am–3pm.

Café im Filmmuseum Breite Str. 1a ℡0331/201 99 96. Atmospheric Lebanese restaurant that's good for Lebanese tea or coffee. The small menu of tasty specialities (starters €6, mains €10) is best explored with several smaller dishes. Tues–Sun noon–midnight.

Condamo Luisenplatz 8 ℡0331/951 09 23. The casual surroundings overlooking a plaza and the Brandenburger Tor make this mid-priced Italian restaurant a perfect place to eat before or after tackling Sanssouci, just up the road. If you don't fancy the pasta and pizza, there's a wealth of perfectly good alternatives: chops, steaks and some pan-fried Iberian and South American food. Daily noon–late.

Cafés and bars

Babette Brandenburger Str. 71 ℡0331/29 16 48. Pleasant café with outdoor seating, in the shadow of the Brandenburger Tor, that's a good place to rest weary feet and have an indulgent *Torte* after trekking around Sanssouci Park. The large menu is also available in English and has a range of simple snacks (€7) and main meals (€9). Mon–Sat 9am–late, Sun 10am–late.

Drachenhaus Maulbeerallee 4a ℡0331/505 38 08. Genteel little café in the grounds of Schloss Sanssouci itself, housed in a pagoda-style building once used by royal vintners. You can also eat well here, with a choice of sturdy Brandenburg specialities or just a piece of florid *Torte*. March–Oct daily 11am–7pm, Nov–Feb Tues–Sun 11am–6pm.

Froschkasten Kiezstr. 4 ℡0331/29 13 15. One of the oldest and most authentic bars in Potsdam, this *Kneipe* also serves good, traditional German food, and does a good line in fish dishes too, particularly the grilled salmon fillet (€19). Mon–Sat noon–midnight, Sun noon–10pm.

La Madeleine Lindenstr. 9 ℡0331/270 54 00. A small *crêperie* featuring over thirty variations – some decidedly odd (chicken curry) – of the French variety. Prices range from €2.50 to €7.50. Daily noon–10pm.

Brandenburg an der Havel

A quintessential northern German red-brick city, **BRANDENBURG AN DER HAVEL**, 30km west of Potsdam, has roots that go back to a sixth-century Slavic settlement. From the tenth century onwards it rapidly expanded as a bishopric and then as margraval capital to become one of the region's leading towns. Wartime bombing and GDR industrialization both had considerable impact, yet its centre still boasts a network of old streets with many aged buildings. Their condition is often decrepit, but at least in many places the mood is lightened by the presence of the water: the heavily braided Havel River and a series of local lakes and canals split the town centre onto three islands – the **Neustadt**, the **Altstadt** and the **Dominsel**.

Arrival, information and accommodation

Long-distance trains pull into the **Hauptbahnhof**, a ten-minute walk from the town centre via Geschwister-Scholl-Strasse (or trams #6 and #9). The **tourist office**, Steinstrasse 66–67 (May–Sept Mon–Fri 10am–7pm, Sat & Sun 10am–3pm; Oct–April Mon–Fri 10am–7pm, Sat & Sun 10am–2pm; ℡03381/58 58 58, ⓦwww.stadt-brandenburg.de) lies just southwest of Neustädischer Markt and provides walking-tour audio guides (free with deposit) in English. They will also book private rooms (❷). Otherwise the cheapest **accommodation** is *Caasi*, Caasmannstrasse 7 (℡03381/32 90, ⓦwww.caasi.de; dorms €18, rooms ❷), a tower block that's part hostel, part hotel and has various handy facilities like kitchen and rental bikes. It tends to attract more longer-term guests than travellers. Among the pensions, *Zum Birnbaum*, Mittlestrasse 1 (℡03381/52 75 00, ⓦwww.pension-zum-birnbaum.de; ❷), is a good choice, with its clean if tiny rooms and cheerful host and a good location between the Hauptbahnhof and Neustadt. For a good standard business hotel, try *Sorat Hotel Brandenburg*, Altstädtische Markt 1 (℡03381/5970, ⓦwww.sorat-hotels.com; ❼), whose facilities include bike rental and free wi-fi, and whose rates are drastically reduced at the weekend.

The Town

The town's commercial centre is the **Neustadt**, new only in a relative sense since it was founded in the twelfth century, from when its fortifications also date. These include several preserved city gates, including the **Steintorturm** (Tues–Fri 9am–5pm, Sat & Sun 10am–5pm; €3) in the southwest, which now houses a small exhibition on local shipping and has good views over the city. From the Steintorturm, **Steinstrasse**, one of the town's main streets, runs northeast to **Neustädischer Markt**, a large central marketplace, where it meets the town's other main drag, **Hauptstrasse**. At their intersection stands the vast and lavishly detailed, Gothic **Katharinenkirche** (Mon–Sat 10am–5pm), its walls studded with decorative brickwork and gargoyles. The interior is worth a look for the elaborate *Meadow of Heaven* ceiling, dotted with Biblical characters.

Trundling trams and bland highstreet shopping define the rest of the Hauptstrasse, which leads northwest to the arched **Jahrtausendbrücke** and into the **Altstadt**. Beside the bridge are the moorings of several companies that rent kayaks and canoes and offer cruises, including Nordstern (℡03381/22 69 60, ⓦwww.nordstern-reederei.de) and Reederei Röding (℡03381/52 23 31, ⓦwww.fgs-havelfee.de). Hauptstrasse becomes Ritterstrasse, location of the **Stadtmuseum im Frey-Haus**, at no. 96 (Tues–Fri 9am–5pm, Sat & Sun 10am–5pm; €3; ℡03381/522048), a civic history museum that champions the local Lehmann factory – known for its mechanical toys and pottery. Beyond the museum, Ritterstrasse quickly leaves the commercial district, ending in a junction with Plauer Strasse: turn right and head a hundred metres northeast along it to arrive at the red-brick **Altstädtisches Rathaus**, complete with lanky *Roland* statue (see p.214); alternatively a left turn at the Plauer Strasse junction soon brings you to the start of Bergstrasse, a road that winds up **Marienberg**, a rather forlorn hill scarred by socialist building projects but blessed with good city views.

Back at the Neustädischer Markt, the **Mühlendamm** heads north out of the Neustadt, past the **Mühlentorturm**, another medieval fortification (that largely survived by serving as a grim jail) and over to the **Dominsel**, easily the town's prettiest neighbourhood since it escaped the worst of the bombing, which is named after the predominantly Gothic **Dom St Peter und Paul** (Mon–Fri 10am–4pm, Sat 10am–5pm, Sun 11am–5pm), with its gloomy atmospheric crypt and its colourful vaulted ceiling in the Bunte Kapelle, a side chapel. Note too the splendid fourteenth-century Bohemian altar in the south transept, with its unusually upbeat saints, and the resplendent Baroque organ (1723). Among the other ecclesiastical treasures in its **Dommuseum** (€3; same times) is a collection of medieval textiles, including the 1290 *Hungertuch*, a "hunger cloth" made to cover the altar during Lent, whose elegant embroideries depict scenes from Jesus' life.

Suffering of a far greater kind is the subject of the **Landesklinik Branden-burg**, Anton-Saefkow-Allee 2 (Tues & Thurs 10am–5pm; free), 9km northwest of the town centre (tram #B1 to "Plauer Landstrasse"), where the Nazis pioneered their murderous policies with a "euthanasia plan" for people with mental illnesses, which claimed ten thousand lives. Many were first subjected to sick psychiatric practices and experiments and the exhibition here spares no ghoulish detail.

Eating and drinking

During the day, the best places to head for a quick **snack** are the floating pontoons set up by local fishermen along the Mühlendamm, where fishy bites only cost a couple of euros.

Bismarck Terrassen Bergstr. 20 ☎ 03381/30 09 39. For that really earthy local feel, don't miss this pub festooned with kitsch Iron Chancellor memorabilia, offering huge helpings of regional food, including Bismarck's alleged favourite: half a duck with red cabbage and dumplings (€12). Daily specials cost around €7.
Cafébar Ritterstr. 76 ☎ 03381/22 90 48. By the Jahrtausendbrücke, and little bigger than a kiosk,

but enjoyable when the weather is good for its good home-made cakes and riverside seating.
Herzschlag Grosse Münzenstr. 17 ☎ 03381/41 04 14. Urbane lounge bar, with a good line in tapas and fajitas (€7–13).
Prawda Steinstr. 16 ☎ 03381/21 13 73. Hip place with a Russian theme and good breakfasts, burgers later on and then drinking until the early hours.

Gedenkstätte Sachsenhausen

A beastly vehicle for two of the twentieth century's most powerful and oppressive regimes, the former concentration camp of Sachsenhausen has been preserved as the unremittingly miserable **Gedenkstätte Sachsenhausen** (Sachsenhausen Memorial; daily: mid-March to mid-Oct 8.30am–6pm; mid-Oct to mid-March 8.30am–4.30pm; many exhibits close on Mon; free; Ⓦ www.gedenkstaette-sachsenhausen.de). This was one of the Nazis' main camps and a prototype upon which others were based. It was never designed for mass extermination, but all the same around half of the 220,000 prisoners who passed through its gates would never leave, as at the end of the war the camp was systematically used to kill thousands of Soviet POWs and Jewish prisoners on death marches. After the war the Soviets used the infrastructure for similar purposes.

To enter the camp, visitors pass through an **information centre** packed with books, where you can pick up the long-winded audio tour (€3) and a handy little leaflet (€0.50), with a plan of the camp on it, which is all that's really needed since there's plenty in English. At the entrance to the camp, its largest structure, the **New Museum**, charts the camp's origins and though impossibly detailed, is worth skimming. The camp was converted from a defunct brewery to political prison by the SA, who then rounded up locals – often classmates, colleagues or neighbours. The **camp** proper begins under the main **watchtower** and beyond a **gate** adorned with the ominous sign *Arbeit macht frei* ("Work frees"). Either side of the **watchtower** is the **death strip**, a piece of land around the entire camp perimeter where prisoners would be shot without warning. The perimeter fence itself was a high-voltage electric one, typical of all the Nazi camps, and site of frequent inmate suicides. Among the few **prison blocks** that remain – though all are largely reconstructions – one on the eastern side houses a thoughtful **museum** that details the fortunes of selected camp prisoners. Beside it, the **camp prison**, from which internees seldom returned, has rudimentary cells used mostly for solitary confinement, where prisoners were fed just enough to keep them alive. One cell, marked with a British flag, housed two captured British officers who were held manacled to a concrete block at the centre of their cell in near darkness for six months before being taken around the back of the prison and summarily shot. The prison yard is also the site of several tall wooden poles to which prisoners would be tied by their hands until their arms separated from their shoulder joints – a routine punishment for minor misdemeanours. Around the main **parade ground**, the two blocks at the heart of the complex were the prison **kitchen** and **laundry**. Inside the latter several films play, one particularly harrowing, one showing the camp on liberation. The gap between the two blocks, at the head of the parade, was formerly a public execution site where prisoners would be hung in front of assembled inmates as an example. At Christmas the SS put a decorated tree here.

Until recently, it was thought that the camp was not used for **systematic executions** until the end of the war, but evidence now shows that it was, if not on the scale elsewhere. This is the subject of various information boards close to a large memorial obelisk and at the western perimeter of the camp. These bring the relationship between victim and perpetrator to a more personal level by relating something of the lives of those killed and their murderers. Behind the boards and beyond the camp perimeter lie the pits in which summary executions took place – outfitted so that used bullets could be retrieved and recycled – and a building in which selected prison inmates were sent for what they thought were medicals only to be shot in the nape of the neck while their height was being measured, then incinerated. Finally at the northern tip of the camp an exhibition in a guard tower investigates the question of what the **local populace** knew and thought about the camp, using video interviews. Next door a large modern and visually impressive but rather too jumbled hall examines the **Soviet Special Camp** (1945–50) that existed here after the war. The Russians imprisoned 60,000 people with suspected Nazi links – though it's thought the majority were innocent – of which at least 12,000 died.

Practicalities

Tucked away in a northeastern suburb of the small town of Oranienburg, 35km north of Berlin, the former camp can be **reached** by S-Bahn (S1 from Berlin; around 1hr) or regional express train (25min from Hauptbahnhof). From the train station hourly buses (#M804 or #M821; BVG day-tickets valid) ply the route to the Gedenkstätte, but the signposted twenty-minute walk may prove quicker: start just north of the square beside the S-Bahn. Near the camp you'll pass a small plaque devoted to the six thousand who died on the *Todesmarch* – the march away from the front line on which the Nazis forced prisoners as the Russians approached. After visiting the camp, there is little else to keep you in Oranienburg, but if you've worked up an appetite, you might try the *Vietnam*

Bistro, Stralsunder Strasse 1 (Mon–Fri 10am–10pm, Sat & Sun 11am–10pm), just north of the train station, which serves up tasty Thai and pan-Asian dishes at extraordinarily low prices (mostly around €5 a dish).

Rheinsberg

Some 50km northwest of Berlin, venerable tree-lined avenues home in on the rolling forests that cradle lakes on Brandenburg's border with Mecklenburg-Western Pomerania – where this landscape is protected as Müritz National Park (see p.852). But just south, on the languid shores of Grieerickseee, lies the pretty little town of **RHEINSBERG**, where Frederick the Great claimed to have spent his happiest years as a young crown prince living in a modest Schloss, studying for the throne and giving occasional concerts.

Though royal musicians have long gone, **concerts** continue to be one of the town's big draws, with the Musikakademie Rheinsberg (☎033931/72 10, ⓦwww.musikakademie-rheinsberg.de) putting on concerts, ballet and musicals in the Schloss year-round, but particularly during the Rheinsberger Musiktage (May or June), which encompasses quite a range of genres, particularly jazz and chamber music, and the Kammeroper Schloss Rheinsberg (ⓦwww.kammeroper -rheinsberg.de), an opera festival of international standing that promotes young talent, in late June or mid-August.

Even outside concert times **Schloss Rheinsberg** (Tues–Sun: April–Oct 10am–5pm; Nov–March 10am–4pm; €6; ☎033931/72 60, ⓦwww.spsg.de) remains a popular attraction, its gardens free to wander around, and the price of entry to the buildings including an English-language audio guide. The Schloss was used as a sanatorium in GDR days, when much of its frivolity disappeared, but elegant highlights that survive include the Spiegelsaal (Mirror Hall), with its ceiling fresco by Antoine Pesne, and the Muschelsaal (Shell Hall) with its intricate Baroque detailing. Tickets to the Schloss are also valid in the **Tucholsky Literaturmuseum** (same hours; €3; ☎033931/390 07) in its north wing, whose subject is the life of Kurt Tucholsky (1890–1935). A pacifist and left-wing journalist, Tucholsky also wrote as Kaspar Hauser and was one of the foremost champions of the Weimar Republic. He left Germany in the early 1930s, preferring self-imposed exile in Sweden – and died there before the world war he predicted broke out. Rheinsberg provided Tucholsky with inspiration for his novel *Rheinsberg: Ein Bilderbuch für Verliebte* – a cheerful love story laced with criticism of bourgeois thought and nationalism. Theodor Fontane (see p.135) also waxed lyrical about the town.

Rheinsberg's tiny centre is worth a quick exploration, and though there are few real landmarks, it features genteel, leafy, cobbled streets and several **pottery** workshops on the south side of town, which carry on century-old local traditions. Digs south of the Schloss have traced the origins of the local industry to the early thirteenth century, and Rheinsberg continues to be known for ceramics and faïence (tin-glazed pottery), though today's most popular pieces are sturdy rustic ones with cream and dark blue glazes.

But much of Rheinsberg's real charm lies beyond the city limits and can be explored with **Reederei Halbeck** (☎033931/386 19, ⓦwww.schiffahrt -rheinsberg.de), at the lakeshore, whose half-day cruises of five local lakes cost €9.50; they also rent out rowing boats and kayaks from €5 per hr or €20 per day. If you'd rather stay on land, consider **renting bikes** from Fahrradhaus

Thäns, Schlossstrasse 16 (☏033931/26 22, ⓦwww.rhintour.de), from €6 per day; they and the tourist information staff can suggest good local rides.

Practicalities

Getting to Rheinsberg by **public transport** can be a headache and require a train and bus combination, but the easiest route from Berlin is by train via Löwenberg. Rheinsberg's **train station** is on the southeast edge of town, a five-minute walk from the **tourist office**, Kavalierhaus am Markt (Mon–Sat 10am–5pm, Sun 10am–4pm), beside the Schloss, who'll direct you to private rooms (❶–❷), for which vacancy signs hang throughout town. Of the **pensions** try *Pension Holländermühle*, Holländer Mühle 01 (☏033931/23 32, ⓦrheinsberg.de/hollaender -muehle; ❸), a ten-minute walk due south of the Schloss along Schanower Strasse, which has the novelty of being in an old windmill. If you'd rather stay in the centre, try *Zum Jungen Fritz*, Schlossstrasse 8 (☏033931/40 90, ⓦwww.junger-fritz.de; ❸), a small inn with tidy little rooms, cheery hosts and a free pass to the local gym. Also central is the more upscale *Der Seehof*, Seestrasse 18 (☏033931/40 30, ⓦwww.seehof-rheinsberg.de; ❺), a former mid-eighteenth-century farmhouse just north of the Schloss. All three options above have good regional **restaurants**; look out for delicious local fish dishes like zander. But the really unmissable local gastronomic quirk is *Eisfabrik*, Kurt-Tucholsky-Strasse 36, a great local ice-cream maker renowned for unusual flavours – including garlic, parsley or radish – that taste far better than they sound.

The Märkische Schweiz and Buckow

Rolling hills, crisp, clean air, trickling streams and languid lakes: the **Märkische Schweiz** has long been a popular middle-class getaway from Berlin's hubbub. Predictably, Theodor Fontane heaped praise on the region (see p.135) – though he conceded the Switzerland epithet was a hyperbole too far – and Bertolt Brecht and Helena Weigel, too, voted with their feet, spending several of their last summers together here in a pleasant lakeside cottage in the delightful little spa town of **BUCKOW**.

Buckow's disjointed geography comes from being wedged between three sizeable lakes, and its tiny **centre**, with a smattering of shops, huddles on the shores of one of them: the **Buckowsee**. However, much of the action, at least in summer, happens 1km north on the shores of the **Schermützelsee**, by far the largest lake. Here Strandbad Buckow provides an organized bathing beach where you can rent rowing boats or cruise the lake with Seetours (April–Oct; 1hr tour €6; ☏033433/232). Overlooking the beach from the south, a steep but narrow strip of land with grand lake views boasts Buckow's ritziest homes, mostly proud, prewar villas. Just southeast of all this bourgeois luxury and back on the lakefront lies the **Brecht-Weigel-Haus**, Bertolt-Brecht-Strasse 30 (April–Oct Wed–Fri 1–5pm, Sat & Sun 1–6pm; Nov–March Wed–Fri 10am– noon & 1–4pm, Sat & Sun 11am–4pm; €2; ☏033433/467), where the couple summered in the mid-1950s. The home is a memorial to their time here, complete with furnishings, photos, various documents and pretty gardens all preserved much as they were then.

Many **hiking** and **cycling paths** fan out around the town, with lakeside paths that are easy to find, even without the free map from the tourist office. For more adventurous sorties through thick woodland and up steep hills, either on foot or by **mountain bike**, head to the northeastern part of town where routes begin from the Schweizer Haus, a former visitors' centre which may reopen once funding is restablished. Some information boards about the local ecology and hiking routes remain – all that's needed given the good signposting throughout the network.

Practicalities

Buckow's gateway is the larger town of Müncheberg, 10km southeast, where regional trains arrive. The two are connected by bus #928 or #930 or, on weekends between Easter and October, by a small tourist train on the Buckower Kleinbahn (ⓦwww.buckower-kleinbahn.de). The **tourist office**, Wrezener Strasse 1a (April–Oct Mon–Fri 9am–noon & 1–5pm, Sat & Sun 10am–5pm; Nov–March Mon–Fri 9am–noon & 1–5pm, Sat & Sun 10am–2pm; ⓣ033433/575 00, ⓦwww.kurstadt-buckow.de), lies at the centre of things by Buckow's tiny main square, and can arrange **private rooms** around town (❷). More economical still is the spick-and-span DJH hostel, Berliner Strasse 36 (ⓣ033433/286, ⓦwww.jh-buckow.de; dorm beds €19), on the southern outskirts of town 1km from the centre, which has twins and eight-bed dorms. Central and reasonably priced *Zur Märkische Schweiz*, Hauptstrasse 73 (ⓣ033433/464; ❸), is a small, old-fashioned inn that's been providing simple rooms and square meals since 1860. A clear notch up is the *Bergschlösschen*, Königstrasse 12 (ⓣ033433/573, ⓦwww.bergschloesschen.com; ❹), a late nineteenth-century villa with a terrace, restaurant and sauna, whose rates are keen considering its style. Both the pension and hotel have decent **restaurants**; otherwise try *Castello Angelo*, Wriezener Strasse 1 (ⓣ033433/575 13; closed Tues), whose excellent and well-priced Italian dishes make its disturbing faux castle theme forgivable. Pizzas and pasta dishes are around €5–8. There's fish on the menu too, but if that's what you're after, make a bee-line for *Fischerkehle*, Fischerberg 7 (ⓣ033433/374), just south of the Schermützelsee and signposted off Berliner Strasse near the youth hostel, where you'll find fish and game dishes par excellence (mains €9–18).

Schorfheide and Unteres Odertal Nationalpark

Large tracts of heathland increasingly assert themselves as you travel northeast from Berlin and into a region known as the **Schorfheide**. Its gentle charms may fail to draw the crowds, but as a UNESCO Biosphere Reserve it's certainly ecologically important and within it a couple of sights are worth a detour, particularly the romantic Gothic ruins of **Kloster Chorin**, a monastery 61km from Berlin, and an impressive industrial monument in the form of a giant 1930s barge hoist at **Niederfinow**. Then, on Schorfheide's northeastern edge and hard on the Polish border, the **Unteres Odertal Nationalpark** offers great birdwatching and peaceful, traffic-free cycling.

Kloster Chorin

The product of sixty years' hard graft by a group of thirteenth-century Cistercian monks, **Kloster Chorin** (daily: April–Oct 9am–6pm; Nov–March 9am–4pm; €3, parking €2.50; ⓣ033366/703 77, ⓦwww.kloster-chorin.de) is one of Germany's grandest red-brick structures. Bristling with patterned brickwork, its impact in an age where such enormous buildings were rare must have been staggering, but after the monastery's dissolution in 1542, it gradually crumbled until its early nineteenth-century renovation in which Schinkel (see p.90) had a hand. A wander around it reveals sleek portals, gracefully elongated windows and a beautiful step gable on its western side, but its parkland setting – beside a pretty lake – is equally enchanting, particularly during the **Choriner Musiksommer** (℡03334/65 73 10, Ⓦwww.musiksommer-chorin.de; €6–22), a series of classical concerts held on summer weekends that showcase the building's fine acoustics.

To get to Kloster Chorin, take a **train** to the village of Chorin and follow signposted paths 1km south through the woods. To stay and eat inexpensively try *Gaststätte und Pension Fischerhof*, Dorfstrasse 39 (℡033364/508 78; ❷), in the village centre, or the more atmospheric and beautifully situated, if a touch chintzy, and with a more upmarket restaurant, *Waldsee Hotel* (℡033366/53 10, Ⓦwww.waldseehotel-frenz.de; ❹), in the woods just north of the monastery grounds.

Niederfinow and the Schiffshebewerk

For a rare remnant of Prussia's mighty industrial legacy, travel some 20km southeast of Chorin to the small community of **Niederfinow** – change trains at the workaday town of Eberswalde-Finow – whose **Schiffshebewerk** (ship hoist) is visible for miles around. A pleasant 2km walk along the main road from the train station, this gigantic steel trough within a lattice of enormous girders raises and lowers boats the 36m between the Oder River and the Oder-Havel Canal, providing a vital link for the regional shipping network. On completion in 1934 this engineering feat was the largest of its kind – the trough is almost 100m long and can handle thousand-tonne barges – and cut a process that took several painstaking hours to twenty minutes. You can watch the procedure from the street-level base of the structure for free, but the view is better from the upper canal platform (daily 9am–6pm; €1). Better still is to be part of it by being lifted in a boat, such as those belonging to Fahrgastschiffahrt Neumann (℡03334/244 05, Ⓦwww.finowkanalschiffahrt.de; €6), whose timetable and ticket office is in an information kiosk in one of a small group of buildings beside the adjacent car park, where there are also several *Imbiss* stands and a **visitors' centre** (daily: April–Oct 9am–6pm; Nov–March 9am–4pm; €1, parking €2.50; ℡033362/215, Ⓦwww.schiffshebewerk-niederfinow.info), which details the intricacies of the hoist's construction and operation and has information about a new structure, half the size again, that's planned for 2012. To stay the night or eat in the vicinity, try *Am Schiffshebewerk*, Hebewerkstrasse 43 (℡033362/700 99, Ⓦwww.hotel-schiffshebewerk; ❸), which has clean and spacious en-suite rooms, and solid traditional meals – as well as nice cakes – in its restaurant.

The Unteres Odertal Nationalpark

Don't expect expansive untrammelled wilds in the **Unteres Odertal National-park** (Lower Oder Valley National Park; Ⓦwww.nationalpark-unteres-odertal.eu) on the Polish border in Brandenburg's northeastern corner. The long, thin park – 60km long and as little as 2km wide in places – centres on a huge island in the centre of the Oder whose meadows, marsh and clusters of mixed woodland provide a peaceful habitat and an exceptional breeding ground for 100,000 geese and ducks as well as rare birds like sea eagle and black stork. October is the most spectacular month to visit, when 13,000 migratory cranes pass through on their way south. Binoculars are extremely useful, as is a bike since the park is crisscrossed by around 100km of flat and generally smooth bike paths.

Tropical islands in the Spreewald

Once home to zeppelins, an old airship hanger 60km south of Berlin has since 2004 housed **Tropical Islands** (☎035477/60 50 50, ⓦwww.tropical-islands.de), an indoor landscaped park the size of four football fields and containing all sorts of watery attractions – pools, lagoons, water slides, waterfalls, whirlpools, saunas among them – as well as a clutch of bars, restaurants and shops. The quality of the landscaping is first class, and its tropical shrubbery and tropical birds that flit around its undergrowth get to luxuriate in the constant 27°C temperature. A Disney-esque quality is added by various interior buildings and monuments – like the Bali, Borneo, Thai and Samoan pavilions – and regular evening dance shows, but what really sets the place apart is its laid-back vibe and convenience. A wristband received on entry handles all purchases electronically – to be paid off on exit – but best of all, the place is open all day, every day, allowing you to stay overnight. Tents can be rented, but most people just crash on the beach with a mat and blanket – allowing for stays for days, even, weeks or months for the same one-off complex entry charge of €25. Other one-off additional charges valid for your entire stay include use of waterslides (€3) and the immense, nudist sauna area (€6.50). Tropical Islands lies off the A13 motorway from Berlin (exit Staakow), and near Brand (Niederlausitz) train station where free shuttle buses wait for visitors. For an alternative, much-scaled down experience, visit the **Spreewaldtherme** (2hr €11; day ticket €23; ☎035603/188 50, ⓦwww.spreewald -therme.de), a top-notch spa and sauna complex in Burg, 18km east of Lübbenau.

The largest town in the area, and best public transport hub, is lacklustre **Schwedt**, 100km northeast of Berlin and location of the regional **tourist office**, Berliner Strasse 47 (May–Sept Mon–Fri 9am–12.30pm & 2–6pm, Sat 10am–12.30pm; Oct–April Mon–Fri 9am–12.30pm & 2–5pm; ☎03332/255 90, ⓦwww.unteres-odertal.de), who can help with **accommodation**. The best first move on arrival into town is probably to rent a **bike** or **canoe** from Fahrrad- und Touristikcenter Butzke, Kietz 11 (☎03332/83 95 00, ⓦwww .kanufahrradverleihbutzke.de), and explore the park from there. The obvious destination is the **Nationalparkhaus** (☎03332/267 72 44; €2; bus #468 from Schwedt), the National Park information centre in **Criewen**, 8km southwest along the riverbank path. The centre has plenty of lively displays on local wildlife, including a large aquarium. South from the information centre, and back towards the Oder, *Gasthaus Zur Linde*, Bernd-von-Arnim-Strasse 21 (☎03332/52 14 98; ❷), is a homey, traditional place with flowery pine-furnished rooms and reasonable local food, particularly fish and steaks, with most mains around €10.

The Spreewald and Lübbenau

The **Spreewald** is Brandenburg at its most attractive and touristy. Designated a UNESCO Biosphere Reserve, this gentle landscape of meadows and meandering waters 80km southeast of Berlin is home to Germany's Sorbic community (see box, p.155), but every bit as well known for its market gardening: famously it produces 40,000 tons of pickled gherkins every year, in a staggering number of varieties.

Gateway towns in the region include Lübben and Cottbus, but easily the most attractive hub is **LÜBBENAU**. Its unassuming Altstadt is crowded with hotels, restaurants and services, and with a million visitors a year strolling through its centre, it's a fairly touristy place worth avoiding on weekends and in the peak summer season. The most popular activity is taking a trip on *Kahn* – **punts** that cruise a network of mellow waterways – and these are offered by a clutch of similar operators (2hr trips €8), based at either the Kleiner Hafen, 100m northeast of the tourist office, or the Grosser Hafen 300m southeast. Though pleasant, these activities can be a little oversubscribed, so you might prefer to rent a **canoe or kayak** from the same operators (around €4 per hr), or from Bootsverleih Francke, Dammstrasse 72 (☏03542/27 22). Another way to escape crowds is to **cycle** the area's many flat and largely traffic-free paths; the signed **Gurken Radweg** follows the Spree to Berlin and is ideal for more adventurous overnight tours. Bikes can be rented from Fahrradverlieh Enrico Arndt, Dammstrasse 10–12 (☏03542/87 29 10).

The most popular trip by punt, canoe or bike is to **Lehde**, a protected village oft touted as the Venice of the Spreewald for its many waterways, which lies 3km east via signposted paths from Lübbenau's Grosser Hafen. Lehde's prime attraction is the excellent **Freilandmuseum** (daily: April to mid-Sept 10am–6pm; mid-Sept to Oct 10am–5pm; €3; ☏03542/24 72), an intriguing open-air museum with a Sorbian village, whose houses and farmhouses have been brought here from other parts of the region and furnished with traditional Sorbic household objects. Unusual are the buildings' large foundation stones that rest on top of timber poles driven deep into the marshy ground, and inside, beds designed for a whole family.

Back in Lübbenau, the **Spreewald-Museum**, Am Topfmarkt (Tues–Sun: April to mid-Oct 10am–6pm; mid-Oct to March 10am–5pm; €3; ☏03542/24/72), in the brick former courthouse, jail and town hall, offers more local cultural history. Meanwhile, the **Haus für Mensch und Natur**,

▲ Punts in Lehde, the Spreewald

Sorbs

Numbering just 60,000 people, **Sorbs** are Germany's only indigenous ethnic minority and they trace their ancestry back to the Slavic Wends who settled the swampy lands between the Oder and Elbe rivers in the fifth century. Conquered by Germanic tribes in the tenth century they found themselves forcibly, often brutally, Germanized throughout the Middle Ages, until their homeland – known as Lusatia (Łužica or Łužyca in Sorbian) – became divided between Prussia and Saxony in 1815. Their language takes two distinct dialects: **lower Sorbian**, with similarities to Polish, was spoken in Prussian areas and was generally suppressed; and **upper Sorbian**, a little like Czech, which is mostly spoken in Saxony and enjoyed a certain prestige. But emigration from both areas was widespread throughout the nineteenth century with many emigrating to Texas (to a town called Serbin) and Australia.

Persecution heightened under the Nazis – around 20,000 Sorbs are estimated to have been killed – but things rapidly improved in the GDR even though Lusatia was overrun by resettling Germans expelled from Poland at the end of the war, and then heavily industrialized, hastening the erosion of old ways. But at least the Sorbs were allowed some cultural autonomy, with their language granted equal status with German and their folk traditions encouraged, albeit for tourist purposes. Since the *Wende* cultural interest has been stepped up and colourful Sorbian festivals like the *Vogelhochzeit* on January 25, the Karnival, and their variant of *Walpurgisnacht* on April 30 have become well attended. However, despite all this, and bilingual street signs throughout the region, Sorbian is rarely heard and the minority still feels underrepresented and under-financed by the German state. They are petitioning the EU for greater recognition and the election of a Sorbian as Minister President in Saxony in 2000 should help their cause.

Schulstrasse 9 (April–Oct daily 10am–5pm; Nov–March Mon–Fri 10am–4pm; free; ☎03542/892 10), on the street behind the tourist office, has displays that explain, in German, why the area is a Biosphere Reserve.

Practicalities

Lübbenau's **train** and **bus station** lies on Poststrasse, about 500m south of the Altstadt; the **tourist office** at Ehm-Welk-Strasse 15 (April–Oct Mon–Fri 9am–6pm, Sat 9am–4pm; Nov–March Mon–Fri 9am–4pm; ☎03542/36 68, ⓦwww.spreewald-online.de), is well signposted. They will arrange **private rooms** (❶–❷), which are easily spotted in town by their *Gästezimmer* signs. The best budget alternative is *Naturcamping Am Schlosspark*, Schlossbezirk (☎03542/35 33, ⓦww.spreewaldcamping.de), where **campsites** cost €10, basic cabins €19, and facilities include bike and canoe rental. For more comfort in large riverside rooms, try the family-run **pension** *Am Alten Bauernhafen*, Stottoff 5 (☎03542/29 30, ⓦwww.am-alten-bauernhafen.de; ❷), or the classy *Hotel Schloss Lübbenau*, Schlossbezirk 6 (☎03542/87 30, ⓦwww.schloss-luebbenau.de; ❺), which, in the face of weak competition, has the town's best **restaurant**. Mains are €13–26, though the three-course set meal (€24) is better value. Of the less expensive places, *Strubel's*, Dammstrasse 3 (☎03542/27 98), is good for fishy local options; its fish platter of perch, eel and pike is a good choice.

Travel details

Trains

Berlin Hauptbahnhof to: Brand (Niederlausitz) (17 daily; 1 hr); Brandenburg an der Havel (every 15min; 50min); Chorin (every 30min; 45min); Dessau (15 daily; 2hr); Dresden (12 daily; 2hr 10min); Frankfurt Oder (every 30min; 1hr 10min); Hamburg (every 30min; 2hr 40min); Hannover (every 30min; 2hr 50min); Leipzig (every 30min; 2hr 20min); Lübbenau (every 30min; 1hr 30min); Munich (15 daily; 7hr 20min); Müncheberg (every 30min; 1hr); Niederfinow (7 daily; 1hr via Eberswalde); Potsdam (every 15min – including S-Bahn; 30min); Rheinsberg (5 daily; 1hr 20min); Schwedt (17 daily; 1hr 20min).

Bus

Müncheberg to Buckow (9 daily; 20min).
Schwedt to Criewen (10 daily; 20min).

Saxony

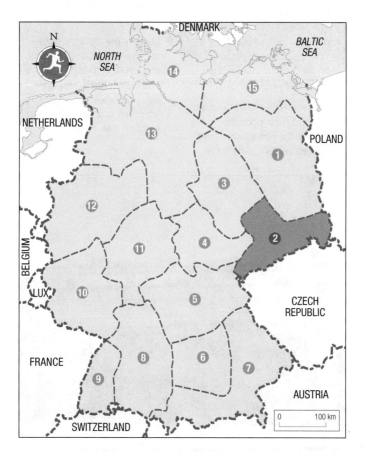

CHAPTER 2 # Highlights

* **Dresden** Baroque 'n' roll in the former Florence of the Elbe – after the glorious architecture and dazzling artistry, go bar-hopping in one of the most enjoyable *Szene* neighbourhoods in Germany. **See p.161**

* **Palaces around Dresden** The getting there is part of the package when Augustus the Strong's Baroque palaces can be reached by vintage train and steamship. **See p.174**

* **Meissen** Never mind Europe's first and finest porcelain factory, the picture-book-pretty Altstadt is idyllic. **See p.176**

* **Saxon Switzerland** Spectacular views and sandstone massifs in the most scenic corner of Saxony, best savoured on a week-long walk that has been voted the most beautiful in Germany, but which can be sampled on a day-trip from Dresden. **See p.179**

* **Leipzig** The dynamic trade-fair city that led the peaceful overthrow of the GDR regime has channelled its energy into a vigorous contemporary art scene and boisterous nightlife. **See p.190**

▲ The Zwinger courtyard, Dresden

Saxony

You'd expect **Saxony** (Sachsen), the state of the Saxons, to be a more robustly Germanic place. Yet if the concept is nebulous in history – the title was only coined for the state after a dynastic shuffle in the fifteenth century, leaving the heartland of the "tribe" northwest in Lower Saxony – it is elusive in character, too. Much of Saxony feels a mish-mash where the German cultural fabric is interwoven with that of Middle Europe. Geography is part to blame – this is, after all, a territory that nudges into Central Europe, and whose first settlers around 500 AD were the Slavic Sorbs. But there's also the scenery that, in places such as Saxon Switzerland, owes more to neighbouring Central Europe than anything else in the nation. Communism stirred some Soviet spice into the mix. Under GDR rule, the three largest cities of the regime outside the capital – Dresden, Leipzig and Chemnitz – found their ambitions stifled, or, worse, were simply allowed to moulder. Of the East German states outside Berlin, it may be Saxony that has benefited most from reunification, even if it remains little explored by foreigners away from the poster places.

Nowadays Saxony likes to promote itself as the "state of the arts": the Land where Johann Sebastian Bach spent nearly half his life, that nurtured Robert Schumann and whose distinctive landscapes inspired some of the finest work from Romantic painter Caspar David Friedrich. It is also the state that pioneered porcelain outside Asia and created some of the most ebullient Baroque architecture in Europe, both the products of Augustus the Strong, an absolutist Sun King under whose eighteenth-century rule Saxony blossomed into an artistic powerhouse. His legacy is evident wherever you go.

Erudite stuff. However, the state capital **Dresden** is evidence that Saxony doesn't only live in its past. Since reunification it has re-created the Baroque city that was shattered by the bombing raids of World War II, but it also fizzes with life in a bar and club scene that's as good a reason to visit as some of the biggest art blockbusters in Germany. **Leipzig** is similarly sized but entirely different in character: a dynamic mercantile city that has refound its rhythm after off-beat decades. The Land's communist legacy is most evident in erstwhile "Karl-Marx-Stadt" **Chemnitz**, worth visiting for its art and a nearby castle. Of the small towns, the most appealing is cobbled charmer **Meissen**, closely followed by **Görlitz**, hard against the Polish border, and **Bautzen**, capital of the indigenous Sorbs. Yet Saxony also provides more visceral pleasures: wines in **Radebeul** and the weird sculpted cliffs of **Saxon Switzerland**, the most scenic corner of the state, a paradise for walkers and rock-huggers alike.

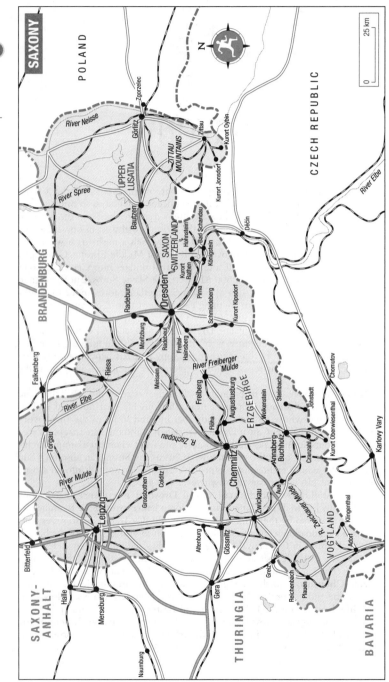

Dresden

DRESDEN is synonymous with devastation; in fact, it's all about regeneration. Only Berlin or Hamburg suffered such total obliteration in the war, and Dresden had far more to lose. For two centuries before its Altstadt was reduced to a smouldering heap in February 1945, it was acclaimed the most beautiful city in Germany. Italian master Canaletto immortalized it as a "Florence on the Elbe". Visitors on the Grand Tour gawped at a Baroque streetscape unparalleled in Europe. Dresden's coming of age was thanks to Elector Augustus the Strong (Augustus Der Stark; 1696–1763). No matter that the regent had an ugly absolutist streak, nor that the city's rejuvenation was all about personal vanity – a transformation to reflect the glory of a self-styled Saxony Sun King. Augustus gathered to his court a brilliant group of architects and artists. Between them they created a city of extraordinary grace in which nobles rode through perfect squares, were serenaded by church bells in elegant spires, or drifted up the Grand Canal of the Elbe to alfresco balls in the astonishing Zwinger.

Then came the bombs (see box below). After reunification Dresdeners – a notoriously bloody-minded bunch – began to rebuild the iconic buildings that had been left as ruins by the communists. Begun in 1990, the reconstruction became a metaphor for reconciliation, not just for East and West Germany but among wartime enemies. And when the wraps came off the Frauenkirche in 2005, the last icon of Europe's most striking Baroque city was resurrected.

Part of the attraction of the Altstadt is that it remains in the act of creation as the GDR past is airbrushed and the Baroque streetscape of its glory days

The bombing of Dresden

Historians continue to debate the bombing of Dresden. Some now describe it as immoral or a war crime, and no other Allied raid has attracted more condemnation than that launched on the night of February 13, 1945. Records show that RAF and USAF Command carried out an incendiary raid on a city that had hitherto escaped destruction. Thereafter the issue is contentious. Without doubt it was an annihilation: if the obliteration of the architectural gem of Germany does not put the raid in a different class, the casualty figures do. Around 25,000–35,000 people were killed in a city swollen by refugees; always sketchy at the time, the number of dead was exaggerated first by Nazi propagandists, who stated that 200,000 had died, then by the communists, who put the figure at 135,000.

The tragedy of Dresden is that the raid seems pointless. The stated military aim was to restrict movement of troops and armaments, and aid the Russian advance west. As leaflets dropped on the city explained: "To the people of Dresden: we were forced to bomb your city because of the heavy military traffic your railroad facilities have been carrying. Destruction of anything other than military objectives was unintentional." (As it turned out, those key railroads were knocked out for barely two days.) Allied bombing of civilian targets was nothing new. Yet Dresden, a city whose tradition of arts and humanism was so anathema to the Third Reich that Hitler had only visited twice, was no military lynchpin, and passing comments by High Command about shattering German morale at the end game of the war did not help the military's case. Contemporary Allied journalists and intelligentsia sniffed something rotten, something punitive, and the raid provoked the first public dissent over High Command bombing policy. Churchill, who must have approved the plan, distanced himself from it, leaving Air Chief Marshall Arthur "Bomber" Harris to carry the can. Few historians now concur that the attack shortened the war. As depressing is that "Dresden's Holocaust" is a cause célèbre of neo-Nazi parties.

reappears – regime apparatchiks would be disgusted. Consequently the city fabric is patchy in places except around the showpieces that extend behind the Elbe between the two axes of the Altstadt: civic space **Neumarkt**, home to the **Frauenkirche**; and the **Residenzschloss** and splendid **Zwinger** pleasure palace – the former with some of its finest museums, the latter not just the great glory of Baroque Dresden but a prize of Germany. The **Neustadt** on the north bank emerged from the war with barely a scratch. Originally the Baroque "new town" of its name, it splits between the Innere Neustadt south of Albertplatz and Äussere Neustadt, where most culture is of the bar variety.

Dresden today is as rooted in its past as ever. Yet the two districts are effectively strangers. In one you have historic buildings and museums, tour groups and cafés. In the other, the north-bank Neustadt, is the best bar district south of Berlin and an arty multicultural population for whom the historical city is just that – history. That they coexist happily accounts for much of Dresden's appeal as two cities in one.

Arrival and information

Dresden has two main **train stations**: the revamped Hauptbahnhof south of the Altstadt and Dresden-Neustadt in the north. Dresden-Mitte is en route to the latter at the far west edge of the Altstadt but not especially convenient. The **airport** (Ⓦwww.dresden-airport.de) lies 9km northwest of Dresden, linked to the Hauptbahnhof by S-Bahn line S2; double-decker trains run every thirty minutes and go via Dresden-Neustadt. Expect to pay €16–18 for a taxi; ranks in central Dresden are outside the Hauptbahnhof. To pre-book cabs call Alita (Ⓣ0351/857 11 11).

Helpful if beleaguered **tourist offices** are located near the Hauptbahnhof in a shopping mall at Prager Strasse 2 (Mon–Sat 10am–7pm; Ⓣ0351/49 19 21 00, Ⓦwww.dresden-tourist.de) and in the Schinkelwache on Theaterplatz by the Zwinger (Mon–Thurs 10am–6pm, Fri 10am–7pm, Sat & Sun 10am–5pm; same contacts). Both sell the 48-hour **Dresden-City-Card** (single €21, family €42) which takes care of all public transport and entry to most municipal museums except the Historisches Grünes Gewölbe. A 72-hour Dresden-Regio-Card extends coverage out to the region and provides free transport on all Elbe River ferries. The online portal for all **city museums** is Ⓦwww.skd-dresden.de.

City transport and tours

Municipal provider BVG (Ⓦwww.dvbag.de) operates a good **public transport** system to get between the north and south banks of the city and outlying sights; a single costs €1.80 or a four-card strip (*Kurzstrecke*) for single journeys of up to 2km is €4.50. Single day-tickets (*Tageskarte*) cost €4.50; those for a family (two adults, two children under 14) are €6 and for a group of up to five people €22. Useful transport centres are: the Hauptbahnhof; Postplatz, just south of the Zwinger; and Albertplatz in the Neustadt. Trams #3 and #7 go from the Hauptbahnhof to the Neustadt. Maps are available at DVB infopoints in the Hauptbahnhof, at the top of Prager Strasse on Waisenhausstrasse, and on Scheffelgasse west of Altmarkt. Cycle rickshaws tout for custom at tourist hotspots; try the Hauptbahnhof and beside the Frauenkirche.

Bicycles are a fast way to zip around even if things get interesting when cycle lanes disappear: try Engel Reisen at Ostra-Allee 29 (Mon–Sat 9am–1pm & 2–6pm; Ⓣ0351/281 92 06, Ⓦwww.engel-fahrradreisen.de) for rental.

The tourist offices are your best source of information on myriad **bus** and **walking tours** of the city; among the latter are night-walk tours and Baroque

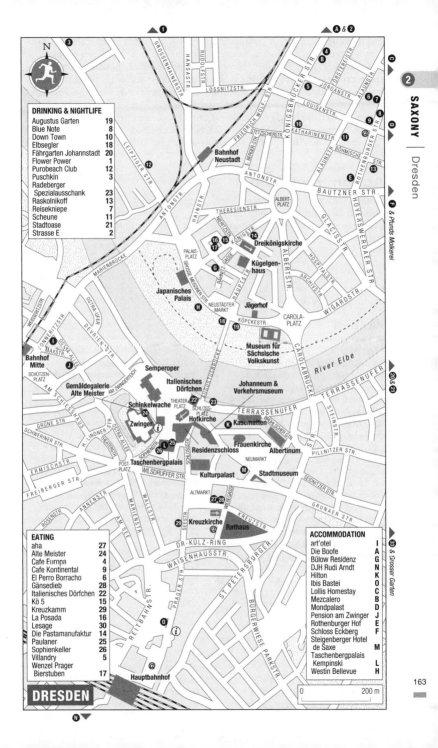

N

DRINKING & NIGHTLIFE

Augustus Garten	19
Blue Note	8
Down Town	10
Elbsegler	18
Fährgarten Johannstadt	20
Flower Power	1
Purobeach Club	12
Puschkin	3
Radeberger Spezialausschank	23
Raskolnikoff	13
Reisekniepe	7
Scheune	11
Stadtoase	21
Strasse E	2

EATING

aha	27
Alte Meister	24
Cafe Europa	4
Cafe Kontinental	9
El Perro Borracho	6
Gänsedieb	28
Italienisches Dörfchen	22
Kö 5	15
Kreuzkamm	29
La Posada	16
Lesage	30
Die Pastamanufaktur	14
Paulaner	25
Sophienkeller	26
Villandry	5
Wenzel Prager Bierstuben	17

ACCOMMODATION

art'otel	I
Die Boofe	A
Bülow Residenz	G
DJH Rudi Arndt	N
Hilton	K
Ibis Bastei	O
Lollis Homestay	C
Mezcalero	B
Mondpalast	D
Pension am Zwinger	J
Rothenburger Hof	E
Schloss Eckberg	F
Steigenberger Hotel de Saxe	M
Taschenbergpalais Kempinski	L
Westin Bellevue	H

Bahnhof Neustadt

Bahnhof Mitte

Dreikönigskirche

Kügelgen-haus

Japanisches Palais

Jägerhof

Museum für Sächsische Volkskunst

Semperoper

Italienisches Dörfchen

Gemäldegalerie Alte Meister

Johanneum & Verkehrsmuseum

Schinkelwache

Zwinger

Hofkirche

Kasematten

Frauenkirche

Residenzschloss

Albertinum

Taschenbergpalais

Kulturpalast

Stadtmuseum

Kreuzkirche

Rathaus

Hauptbahnhof

River Elbe

ALBERT-PLATZ

CAROLA-PLATZ

DRESDEN

0 — 200 m

strolls in the company of costumed actors. Ask at hostels about Neustadt pub-crawls should you need an incentive to explore the area's bar scene (unlikely).

Sächsische Dampfschiffahrt (Ⓦ www.saechsische-dampfschiffahrt.de) runs Elbe **river cruises** on what it claims is the world's oldest and largest fleet of paddle-steamers – trips depart from Dresdener Terrassenufer beside the Augustusbrücke and ply to up- and downriver destinations such as Meissen (single €11.40) and Saxon Switzerland (single to Bad Schandau €20.50) respectively. ConferenceBikes (Förstereistrasse 18a; ☎ 0351/206 09 23, Ⓦ www.cbikes.de) rents wacky six-seater "conference bikes" that position riders around a central circular handlebar – think fun not fast.

Accommodation

With Dresden's revival, international hotel names have moved in, allowing Dresden to stand toe to toe with anything in other major cities, with some swish options aspiring to Baroque splendour if your budget extends to it. A few excellent independent hostels take care of the budget scene, most in the thick of the Neustadt's nightlife. As ever, tourist offices book accommodation in advance at a cost of €3 per person. *Campingplatz Mockritz* (Boderitzer Strasse 30; ☎ 0351/471 52 50, Ⓦ www.camping-dresden.de), in suburbs 4km south, a fifteen-minute walk from Mockritz reached on bus #76 from the Hauptbahnhof, has simple units (❶) alongside tent pitches.

Altstadt

Hotels

art' otel Ostra-Allee 33 ☎ 0351/492 20, Ⓦ www.artotels.de. About 300m behind the Zwinger, this is an arty design hotel that has far more neutral decor in the rooms than the giant golden egg in the foyer suggests. ❺–❻

Hilton An der Frauenkirche 5 ☎ 0351/864 20, Ⓦ www.hilton.de/dresden. A Hilton with all the requisite international-quality service plus a dozen bars and restaurants, a spa and pool, and a location just off Neumarkt. ❻–❽

Ibis Bastei Prager Str. 5 ☎ 0351/48 56 20 00, Ⓦ www.ibis-dresden.de. One of three hotels in GDR towerblocks whose functional accommodation barely offers room to swing a suitcase. On the plus side all are affordable, decently sited for the sights and train station, and are hardly ever full. ❸–❹

Pension am Zwinger Ostra-Allee 27 (reception Maxstr. 3) ☎ 0351/89 90 01 00, Ⓦ www .pension-zwinger.de. 5min walk from the Zwinger and excellent value for its contemporary neutral rooms and apartments that make a virtue of simplicity. ❹

Steigenberger Hotel de Saxe Neumarkt 9 ☎ 0351/48 60, Ⓦ www.desaxe-dresden .steigenberger.de. Stylish understated modern decor from the Steigenberger chain in a Baroque-styled hotel rebuilt in 2006. ❻–❽

Taschenbergpalais Kempinski Taschenberg 3 ☎ 0351/491 20, Ⓦ www.kempinski-dresden.de. Dresden's premier address provides five-star superior luxury in the Baroque manor where Augustus the Strong installed his mistress. Restored post-*Wende* into an effortlessly classy number whose public areas showcase features by Zwinger architect Pöppelmann. "Kurfuersten" rooms have the best views and prices to match. Doubles from €240. ❽–❾

Hostels

DJH Rudi Arndt Hübnerstr. 11 ☎ 0351/471 06 67, Ⓦ www.jugendherberge.de. The official youth hostel is in an old house on a residential street three blocks behind the Hauptbahnhof. Dorms from €17.30.

Neustadt

Hotels

Bülow Residenz Rähnitzgasse 19 ☎ 0351/800 30, Ⓦ www.buelow-residenz.de. Still the "fine corner house with a huge entrance portal"

described in 1731 when it was the residence of Augustus the Strong's master builder. Now, however, a class act of Relais & Châteaux, with immaculate service and classic elegant style. Its

Michelin-starred *Caroussel* restaurant is superb. Doubles from €250. **❾**

Rothenburger Hof Rothenburger Str. 15–17 ☏0351/812 60, ⓦwww.dresden-hotel.de. Comfy family four-star that's well sited for forays into the Neustadt bar scene, rather old-fashioned but none the worse for it, and with a mini-spa. **❻**

Schloss Eckberg Bautzner Str. 134, Dresden-Loschwitz ☏0351/809 90, ⓦwww.schloss-eckberg.de. The fairytale romance of staying in this luxury neo-Gothic castle set in its own landscaped estate compensates for a location 3km east of Albertplatz (tram #11). Cheaper accommodation is in the modernized Kavalierhaus (ⓞ) in the grounds. **❽**

Westin Bellevue Grosse Meissner Str. 15 ☏0351/80 50, ⓦwww.westin.com/dresden. Guests in riverside rooms wake up to Canaletto's view of Baroque Dresden in this glamorous modern hotel in a refurbished courtyard palace. **❼–❽**

Hostels

Die Boofe Hechtstr. 10 ☏0351/801 33 61, ⓦwww.boofe.de. Friendly large hostel in a residential street close – but not too close – to the Neustadt bars.

Some en-suite accommodation, kitchens and common rooms on most floors, free wi-fi and table football in a ground-floor living area, and a courtyard beer garden. Love that sauna, too. Dorms €17–20, rooms **❷**, apartment **❸**.

Lollis Homestay Görlitzer Str. 34 ☏0351/810 84 58, ⓦwww.lollishome.de. Welcoming small place with a homely vibe and idiosyncratic themed decor: many rooms have platform beds or giant furnishings, one has a bed in a Trabant estate. Small but quirky and never swamped by large groups. Dorms €13–16, rooms **❶–❷**.

Mezcalero Königsbrücker Str. 64 ☏0351/81 07 70, ⓦwww.mezcalero.de. Mexican-styled guesthouse with bags of character for the post-backpacker market: expect bright colour-washes, wood floors and oddities such as a basin in a moulded tree-stump. Multi-bed rooms, one dorm, cheaper rooms share facilities. Dorm €17, rooms **❸**.

Mondpalast Louisenstr. 77 ☏0351/563 40 50, ⓦwww.mondpalast.de. Zodiac-themed hostel in the thick of the action in the Neustadt, with pleasant, modestly cool rooms in a nineteenth-century building. Check in at the café at the front. Dorms €13.50–19.50, rooms **❷**.

Neumarkt and the Frauenkirche

No monument is so potent a metaphor of reborn Dresden as the **Frauenkirche**. The church on Neumarkt was designed both as Germany's largest Protestant church and a piece of one-upmanship over the nearby Catholic Hofkirche by a town architect, Georg Bähr, and paid for almost entirely by public donation. Canaletto set up his easel wherever he could conspire to feature its landmark bell-like cupola, and the church was considered the pinnacle achievement of Protestant Baroque. Shattered by the 1945 raid, it lay in a heap of rubble piled against two fire-blackened towers as a communist memorial – a salute to the city's dead and an accusatory statement of the destruction wrought by the perfidious West. Small wonder it became a focus of silent peaceful protest during the *Wende*, when candles were placed amid the rubble. Following heated debate, the council voted on a rebuild in 1991, and a year ahead of schedule, at 10am on October 30, 2005, with some of the €180 million cost funded by British and American associations, the bells rang over a crowd of thousands to celebrate the re-consecration.

As locals are keen to point out, this is less a new church than a return of the old – its beautifully balanced structure is faithful to the original plans and its café-au-lait sandstone is freckled with original fire-blackened blocks. Within what is probably the busiest church in Saxony, delicately marbled galleries crammed Escher-esque into the lantern cupola fight a losing battle for attention with the explosion of gilt that is the high altar depicting Jesus in the olive grove, jigsawed together from two thousand original pieces. The original twisted crucifix dug out from the rubble is displayed by the exit door. Poignantly, the cross of the new church was produced by a silversmith from Coventry whose father was a bomber pilot in the 1945 raid. A separate entrance at the rear provides access to the tower (daily 10am–1pm & 2–6pm, till 4pm Nov–March; €8) whose windy balcony provides unrivalled views over the city and river.

▲ The Frauenkirche's interior, Dresden

With the church rebuilt, work has begun on the revival of **Neumarkt** itself. Pictured by Canaletto as the handsome heart of the Altstadt, the square is returning to its role as a civic centre-stage as town houses serve as cafés, hotels and luxury shopping.

Along Brühlsche Terrasse

When Augustus the Strong created a Baroque city to mirror his power and glory, he permitted a cabinet minister, the Earl of Brühl, a private garden on top of the city's ramparts. **Brühlsche Terrasse** was acclaimed the "balcony of Europe", a riverside belvedere that elbows behind the Frauenkirche as a grand terrace of steps, balustrades and busts of German cultural heroes, providing views from 15m above river level – all in all the best promenade in town. Access is via steps at either end of the belvedere. Beneath those northeast of the Frauenkirche you'll find the entrance to the **Museum Festung Dresden** (daily: April–Oct 10am–5pm; Nov–March 10am–4pm; €4; ⓦ www.schloesser-dresden.de), an atmospheric rummage through floodlit cannon rooms of what were advanced Renaissance fortifications. Above and to the left, the **Albertinum** pile is scheduled to reopen in mid-2009 after renovation as a palatial home for two city collections: the Galerie Neu Meister with nineteenth- and twentieth-century artwork – Caspar David Friedrich, French and German Impressionists, the Die Brücke movement and classic Modernists such as Otto Dix; and sculpture of the Skulpturensammlung which includes masterpieces by Balthasar Permoser, the sculptor behind the playful ornamentation of the Zwinger. (Times before renovation were Tues–Sun 10am–6pm.) The **Staatliche Kunstsammlungen** (Tues–Sun 10am–6pm) on the other side of the steps, meanwhile, remains raw from the damage of 1945 and serves as a foil for art and photography exhibitions.

From the Frauenkirche to Theaterplatz

Along Augustusstrasse, which leads northwest from Neumarkt, runs the 102-metre-long *Fürstenzug* frieze, mounted on the walls of the Schloss's stables, **Johanneum**. The 24,000 Meissen-china tiles depict Saxony's rulers from 1123 to 1904 – the state's very own Sun King, Augustus the Strong, is one of the few who gazes directly out from the medieval-styled pageant. The stables are worth a look for a colonnaded Italianate Renaissance courtyard – access is via an arch at the alley's east end. The front half of the ritziest stables ever built contains the **Verkehrsmuseum** (Transport Museum; Tues–Sun 10am–5pm; €4.50), with a wide range of land-, sea- and aircraft; the entrance is on Neumarkt.

    Schlossplatz, where Augustusstrasse terminates, has been a seat of power throughout Dresden's history: today it's the site of Saxony's parliament building, the Landtag, which boxes in the east side; previously it was the swaggering Renaissance gateway to the Residenzschloss, flanked by muscled warriors to reflect the might of the incumbent House of Wettin. The **Hofkirche** (also known as the Kathedrale) closes the square with a handsome dollop of Baroque. Augustus the Strong's son, Augustus III, erected the largest church in the state. His father had converted to Catholicism as a ruse to claim the Polish Crown, and so he commissioned a church to keep up appearances before the pope as the Protestant Frauenkirche inched into the sky. He also kept the plans secret. A wise move as it turned out because the Protestant council refused to acknowledge the church after it was completed in 1755 nor allow its bells to peal. A collaboration of an Italian and a German architect – adjacent square Italienischesdorf recalls the "Italian village" of masons – results in a quirky hybrid of Italianate exterior (the decidedly un-Germanic two balconies crowded with posturing saints and a lantern-like spire) and a solid Germanic interior which is a bit of a letdown: impressive in scale but plainly whitewashed. Furniture includes a Rococo pulpit held aloft on boiling clouds of putti thanks to Zwinger sculptor Balthasar Permoser and a prize organ by Gottfried Silbermann (concerts Wed & Sat 11.30am–noon). In the crypt lie assorted members of the House of Wettin along with Augustus the Strong's heart in a casket.

    Boxed in by Baroque, **Theaterplatz** is the most handsome square in Dresden. Its name derives from the **Semperoper** opera house (four or five tours a day; €7) at its back. The original building in which Wagner premiered *Tannhäuser, Rienzi* and *The Flying Dutchman* also did wonders for the career of its creator, Gottfried Semper, who went on to become a superstar architect of Europe and also a close friend of Wagner. The busts of playwrights and sculpture of Dionysus in a chariot pulled by panthers were rescued from an earlier venue destroyed by fire. Tickets for performances are sold at a desk in the Schinkelwache, a Neoclassical Schloss guardhouse turned tourist office.

The Residenzschloss

For much of the route you have been circling the **Residenzschloss** that occupies the central Altstadt west of Neumarkt. The neo-Renaissance residence of electors and kings of Saxony until 1918, the palace has a Renaissance core at its colossal bulk, though most of what you see is a post-reunification rebuild. For forty years the GDR regime paid lip service to the idea of restoration of the bomb-damaged derelict site but twiddled its thumbs. Work began in 1985 and was completed to coincide with the eight-hundredth anniversary of the city's founding in 1206. The latest project is to canopy the Italianate inner courtyard with a glass roof similar to that of London's British Museum. Restoration has returned the Grünes Gewölbe (Green Vault) collections to the palace they were intended for. One of the most sumptuous treasuries on the planet, these fancies are a legacy of Augustus the Strong – a real-life Ali Baba's cave of gold, silver, diamonds, ivory and mother of pearl craftsmanship designed to express the Elector's wealth and authority. The most fantastical objects are the work of Johann Melchior Dinglinger, Augustus's chief court jeweller who turned to Asian art in his later years to concoct ever more decadent fripperies to please his employer's jaded eye. Such is the scale of the collection – there are four thousand or so objects – they are split into two sections.

The first part, the **Historisches Grünes Gewölbe** (Wed–Mon 10am–7pm; €10), is displayed as Augustus the Strong knew it, in ever glitzier palace rooms of the west wing. Note that a dust-lock restricts admission to timed slots and the number of tickets on sale daily – buy in advance or come early. While the objects displayed on shelves and free-standing tables are less head-spinning than those in the Neues Grünes Gewölbe, seen in their mirrored, gilt-trimmed rooms they are intended as a Gesamtkunstwerk (total work of art). Highlights are the intimate Eck-Kabinet crammed with the tiny curios that so tickled Augustus, and the Juwelen-zimmer, intended to suggest the inside of a treasure chest, whose statuette of an African king bearing a tray of uncut crystal has become an icon of the collection's decadence.

The stand-alone dazzlers are in the **Neues Grünes Gewölbe** (Wed–Mon 10am–6pm; €6), a glut of objects that express better than words the grandiose and, ultimately, grotesque posturing of Augustus's Baroque. A cherry stone carved with 185 human faces or a jewelled miner's axe are typical. There's no faulting the workmanship, however. Highlights by Dinglinger include a Chinoiserie coffee set that was four years in the making; and in the same room a representation of the Court of Delhi on the birthday of the Grand Mogul Aureng-Zab, consisting of 137 gold and enamel figurines encrusted with over five thousand jewels. This thinly disguised homage to absolutism cost Augustus more than the Moritzburg hunting lodge north of Dresden (see p.175). More expensive still was a 400,000-thaler green diamond hat-clasp commissioned by Augustus III, who inherited his father's extravagant tastes. Dinglinger's personal favourite was the *Bath of Diana* that he crafted with Balthasar Permoser.

Alongside excellent views over the Zwinger, the palace tower **Hausmannsturm** (late March–Oct Wed–Mon 10am–6pm; €2.50) contains the ducal coin collection, the Münzkabinett (same times; €3).

The Zwinger

The **Zwinger** complex of buildings owes its name to an early "outer bailey" that guarded the Residenzschloss; thereafter the similarity ends. The great glory of Baroque Dresden, it was conceived as an alfresco ballroom for court high jinks by Augustus the Strong, who entrusted the commission to architect Matthäus Daniel Pöppelmann and sculptor Balthasar Permoser. The duo came up with one of the prize buildings of Germany. While the symmetrical layout of lawns and fountains is a paean to the order of the Age of Reason, the Zwinger courtyard is Baroque at its most playful. A balustraded one-storey wing broken by a gateway capped by the Polish Crown runs to dumpy corner pavilions, while at either end are lozenge-shaped ceremonial gateways – the eastern **Glockenspielpavillon** with a peal of forty Meissen china bells, and the **Wallpavillon** opposite, exuberant with heraldic froth and topped by a statue of Augustus carrying the world on his shoulders as Hercules. To the structure Permoser adds a sculptural carnival: festive putti, bare-breasted nymphs and satyrs who leer as caryatids. The only grouch in the party is a workmanlike north wing added in the mid-1800s to finally close the courtyard after work had stalled through lack of funds. It's worth circling the complex on the terrace to see it at its best, accessed via a stairway that zigzags within the Wallpavillon, behind which is the Nymphenbad fountain, an enchanting sunken nook whose nymphs are modelled on Tuscan Roman originals.

The Zwinger museums

The big draw of the Zwinger's four collections is the Saxon Electors' exquisite collection of Italian Old Masters in the **Gemäldegalerie Alte Meister** (Tues–Sun 10am–6pm; €7) in the north wing, though until mid-2009 it's also home to the sculpture-fest and the Galerie Neue Meister of the Albertinum (see p.166). Rather shunted into a corridor as you enter are seven Dresden scenes by Canaletto that helped spread Dresden's fame as a Florence of the North. The most celebrated work is Raphael's touching *Sistine Madonna*, its radiant Virgin and Child, already haunted by a knowledge of the child's fate, are probably less well known than the two bored cherubs who lounge at its base, stars of numerous postcards. All the other big guns of Italian art are here – Titian, Tintoretto, Correggio, Botticelli and Veronese to name a few – plus an outstanding Flemish and Dutch oeuvre that includes muscular works by Rubens, a room of Jan Bruegel the Elder, Van Dyke, and an intriguing Rembrandt self-portrait that depicts him carousing as the Prodigal Son with his surly new wife on his knee. Cranach and Dürer star for the Germans, but keep an eye out for a room of works by Dresden court painter Anton Raffael Mengs, which includes a fleshy image of Augustus III.

The **Rüstkammer** (same times; €3) opposite contains a hall of armour, its highlights the ceremonial swords of Saxony Electors and a suit of ornamental gold armour for Swedish king Erik XIV and his horse embossed with the labours of Hercules. Plans were afoot to shift the collection to the Residenzschloss at the time of writing. The Glockenspielpavillon, meanwhile, serves as a historic backdrop for the **Porzellansammlung** (same times; €6) with the world's largest hoard of porcelain. Thanks to Augustus the Strong, Dresden produced the first porcelain in Europe in 1707 before manufacture shifted to the town of Meissen a year later (see p.176). Early works on display show how Meissen artists stuck faithfully to the Ming-Dynasty Chinese and Japanese role models. Things get more interesting when Baroque forms develop – look, too, for a tubby Augustus in Roman-emperor mode – in a collection that benefits from a recent revamp to display items on gilded consoles against rich silks. A collection of early clocks and scientific instruments, the Mathematisch-Physikalischer Salon, is scheduled to reopen in 2010.

Around Altmarkt

While Baroque rules in the central Altstadt, communism characterizes the area south. If you arrive at the Hauptbahnhof, your first impression of Dresden is Prager Strasse, a broad boulevard whose newly acquired sheen of capitalism cannot quite cover the Soviet style, complete with Seventies atom fountains. The **Kulturpalast**, a late-Sixties cultural centre, skulks on the north side of Altmarkt – fans of GDR kitsch will enjoy the propaganda mosaic at its west end which traces the doctrine from Marx to proletariat brothers-in-arms. The regime bulldozed away rubble from the oldest city square to extend Altmarkt into a grand civic space of megalomaniac dimensions. The only concession is the blackened Protestant **Kreuzkirche** (tower: April–Oct Mon–Fri 10am–5.30pm, Sat 10am–4.30pm, Sun noon–5.30pm; Nov–March Mon–Sat 10am–3.30pm, Sun noon–4.30pm; €2) that dithers between late Baroque and early Neoclassicism. A postwar rebuild, depicted in photos at the rear, rethought the vaulted interior in rough concrete, an exercise in austerity that feels more cutting-edge gallery than church. It's especially dramatic during concerts of its acclaimed boys' choir, the Kreuzchoir; it gathers for vespers on Saturday at 6.30pm and Sunday service at 9am plus concerts advertised in the foyer. Behind the church, past a modern restaurant strip, lies a Rathaus that's overweight even by German standards, worth a visit for the views 100m up from its tower (daily April–Oct 10am–6pm; €2.50) and a foyer exhibition of ongoing beautification projects. A block north at Wilsdruffer Strasse 2 is a mildly diverting tale of town history in the **Stadtmusem** (Tues–Thurs, Sat & Sun 10am–6pm, Fri noon–8pm; €4).

The Grosser Garten and Panometer

Dresden's largest park, the **Grosser Garten**, rolls out a carpet of greenery southeast from the Altstadt. Its origins are as a pleasure garden of the ruling House of Wettin – a place for such idle pursuits as games, theatre or hunting – and was laid out accordingly in formal Baroque style until the switch to the current naturalistic parkland in vogue in the late eighteenth century. The 40m glass-skinned tower on Lennéstrasse on its northwestern fringes is Volkswagen's **Gläserne Manufaktur** (daily 8am–8pm; free), a "transparent factory" unveiled by the motor giant in 2001 as a miniature of its celebrated centre in Wolfsburg, Lower Saxony. At full tilt, 150 luxury-class motors roll out daily from a factory that is visible through the glass facade. Multimedia information terminals in the foyer – no small piece of architecture itself – guide you through the production process, or you can tour the assembly line (€4; reservation required ☏ 01805/89 62 68, ⓦ www.glaesernemanufaktur.de).

Ruler-straight avenues of trees channel you directly east to the **Palais** (April–Oct Wed–Sat 10am–6pm, Sun 11am–6pm; Nov–March Sat & Sun 11am–6pm; €3) at the park's centre, a residence that pioneered Baroque in Dresden and led to an entire cityscape. It houses a display of tatty sculpture, including fifty original Zwinger works by Balthasar Permoser. South of here lies a boating lake – rental is available at its west end. A student-run miniature steam train, the Dresdener Parkeisenbahn, runs a circuit of the park (every 20min; March & Oct Mon–Fri 1–5pm, Sat & Sun 10am–5pm; April–Sept daily 10am–6pm; €1.50–4). You can embark at any of five stations – there's one by the VW factory, another behind the palace (Palaisteich) and another at the east end of the lake. One stop is at the above-average **zoo** (daily 8.30am–6.30pm, till 4.30pm winter; €7) in the south of the park.

A good fifteen-minute walk behind the Grosser Garten via Winterbergstrasse – or tram #1 or #2 to "Liebstädter Strasse" – leads to the **Panometer** (Tues–Fri 9am–7pm, Sat & Sun 10am–8pm; €9; ⓦ www.asisi-factory.de) on Gasanstaltstrasse. One of Dresden's most intriguing sights, this 105m-by-12m painting wraps around the inside of a former gasworks to re-create a panorama of Dresden in 1756.

The Neustadt

The north-bank Neustadt is only on nodding terms with the historic Altstadt even though its origins were as Augustus the Strong's Baroque "new town", planned after a fire obliterated an earlier settlement in 1685. Incidentally, the mosque-like building that brings an unexpected exoticism to the vista west as you cross the river is actually the Yenidze, a cigarette factory built in 1909 which today contains offices and a restaurant – it's most impressive when the coloured glass dome is illuminated at night.

Augustus was a vain ruler. With great ceremony, three years after his death in 1733, his new district – first christened "New King's Town" – was inaugurated with a larger-than-life statue of the ruler as a Roman emperor – the *Goldener Reiter* statue on the north end of Augustusbrücke. A short way east, the city's oldest Renaissance building, the **Jägerhof**, houses regional folkcrafts and puppet displays of the Museum für Sächsische Volkskunst (Tues–Sun 10am–6pm; €3). Go west, however – take the riverside Elbe Meadows for views of the glorious Baroque city opposite – and you reach the **Japanisches Palais**. Augustus commissioned the quirky palace for his prize Meissen and Chinese porcelain, which explains the Chinoiserie flair to the roofline and courtyard. Shame, then, that it is given over to a plodding archeological museum, the **Landesmuseum für Vorgeschichte** (Tues–Sun 10am–6pm; €3) and a more entertaining ethnology collection, the **Museum für Völkerkunde** (same times; €4). Broad boulevard Königstrasse spears northeast from here as an unbroken row of Baroque town houses, many with the original courtyards – perhaps the finest picture of handsome old Dresden in the city. It's more successful than Hauptstrasse north of the gilded equestrian statue after GDR urban planners tinkered with it to create a pedestrianized precinct. Kügelgenhaus at no. 13 offers a snapshot of the original residences in the second-floor quarters of Dresden Romantic painter Gerhard von Kügelgen, preserved as the **Museum für Dresdener Romantik** (Wed–Sun 10am–6pm; €3). A little further is the Dreikönigskirche (tower March–Oct Tues–Sun 11am–4.30pm; €1.50), a rebuild of a church by Zwinger mastermind Pöppelmann. The high altar, shattered in the war, catches the eye, as does a walloping Renaissance *Danse Macabre* frieze.

The mood changes in the Äussere Neustadt north of Albertplatz. Its intimate nineteenth-century streetscape has emerged in recent decades as the beating heart of the city's alternative arts and nightlife scenes. The cappuccino classes are creeping in at the edges, but most of the multicultural area is defiantly unpolished – a place of funky galleries and independent boutiques, and the best bar scene south of Berlin. The unofficial icon at the heart of the area is the **Kunsthofpassage** (enter at Alaunstrasse 70 or Görlitzer Strasse 21), a web of interconnecting themed courtyards designed by local artists. Fortunately the tour groups don't seem to have caught on yet. Most are lured east to **Pfunds Molkerei** (Mon–Sat 10am–6pm, Sun till 3pm; free; tram #11) at Bautzerstrasse 79 by its *Guinness Book of Records* entry as "the most beautiful dairy in the world". Crowds in the late nineteenth-century cheesery are especially heavy at lunchtimes, though there's no faulting the charm factor, with its walls and ceiling a blur of hand-painted tiles.

Eating

Concurrent with Dresden's post-*Wende* revival has been the resurgence of its restaurant scene. In broad terms, the Altstadt is traditional, while restaurants in the Neustadt are more contemporary and international in flavour. However, Weisse Gasse in the Altstadt is a globe-trotting precinct of modern restaurants and style cafés, though fairly anonymous. Neumarkt café-culture is particularly atmospheric on summer evenings around the floodlit Frauenkirche.

Restaurants

Altstadt

Alte Meister Theaterplatz 1a ☎0351/481 04 26. Tuna and bak choi in a sweet chilli sauce or grilled *Wolfsbarsch* with potato-and-saffron risotto are typical of international dishes served in this sophisticated café-restaurant tucked away behind the Zwinger. A good terrace make this one for sunny days and warm evenings.

Gänsedieb Weisse Gasse 1 ☎0351/485 09 05. Laid-back and well-priced café-restaurant named after the "Goose Thief" fountain opposite – jellied goose and goose dripping on fresh bread available on an otherwise light menu of German and regional food.

Italienisches Dörfchen Theaterplatz 2–3 ℡0351/49 81 60. Three historic rooms make this Baroque house worth braving the tour groups for: there's German cuisine in the *Biersaal* and *Kurfürstenzimmer*, a handsome café, and upstairs top-notch Italian in *Bellotto*. All have a terrace overlooking the Elbe.

Lesage Lennéstr. 1 ℡0351/420 42 50. Slick restaurant serving international fusion food in the glass-skinned VW Gläserne Manufaktur – also has a stylish terrace bar. Closed Sun & Mon eve.

Sophienkeller Taschenberg 3 ℡0351 49 72 60. Touristy but fun medieval-themed cellar restaurant whose menu of dishes like roast suckling pig changes every century or so.

Neustadt

Kö 5 Königstr. 5a ℡0351/802 40 88. Rather formal traditional dining in an upmarket restaurant in a restored Baroque courtyard house. Dishes such as Saxony *Sauerbraten* (marinated beef) and *Tafelspitz* (boiled beef) feature on the good-value German menu.

La Posada Königstr. 3 ℡0351/801 57 91. Not just the most charming Spanish restaurant in Dresden, but one whose cuisine lives up to the looks – a beamed restaurant on one side of a cobbled courtyard, a rustic, tiled tapas place on the other. Eve only, closed Sun & Mon.

Villandry Jordanstr. 8 ℡0351/899 67 24. The finest dining in Äussere Neustadt is in this laid-back locals' bistro with a menu of superb seasonal Mediterranean cuisine. The vibe is cool without being forced, the courtyard idyllic in summer. Eve only, closed Sun.

Wenzel Prager Bierstuben Königstr. 1 ℡0351/804 20 10. Waitresses in traditional dress serve up sturdy stuff such as roast pork and dumplings in this Czech-styled traditional beerhall.

Cafés and cheap eats

Altstadt

aha Kreuzstr 7. Sweet café above a handicrafts shop that rustles up organic light dishes, many vegetarian, to mellow bossa-nova sounds – a pleasant spot for breakfast.

Kreuzkamm Seestr 6. Just off Altmarkt, this local institution for cake and luxury chocolates has been going strong for nearly two centuries.

Paulaner Taschenberg 3. Cheap, traditional dishes in an old-fashioned-styled *Gaststätte* from the reliable Bavarian brewery.

Neustadt

Cafe Europa Königsbrücker Str. 68. Open 24/7, this lowlit café-bar caters to locals taking a lazy breakfast as well as a late-night drinking den of the Neustadt club scene.

Cafe Kontinental Görlitzer Str 1. Good breakfasts, baked spuds, ciabatta sandwiches and a short daily Mediterranean menu in a quietly cool Neustadt café that morphs into a laid-back bar in the evenings.

El Perro Borracho Alaunstr. 70. "The Drunken Dog" serves tapas to an older crowd in the Kunsthof's arty courtyard – lovely for a drink when candle-lit in summer. Closed Mon lunch.

Die Pastamanufaktur An der Dreikönigskirche 9. Minimalist pasta place beloved by Dresden's style-conscious yuppies; well-priced for its contemporary flavours. Closed Sat eve & all Sun.

Drinking and nightlife

No city south of Berlin compares to Dresden for **bar-hopping**. Indeed, the Neustadt scene holds its own against anything in Germany if only because Äussere Neustadt packs such variety into so small an area; within a twenty-minute radius is everything from chic cocktail bars to retro modernist places in former squats, jazz bars to grungy rock dens via eclectic themed bars. Start north of Louisenstrasse on Alaunstrasse or Görlitzstrasse, then explore by instinct – most places close around 4am at weekends, but some operate 24/7, making for messy nights. Your best bet in the Altstadt is Weisse Gasse. Alongside riverside **beer gardens** listed (all summer only generally May–Sept) are two in the Grosser Garten – one at the west entrance, another on the north bank of the Carolasee lake.

For the latest on Dresden's feisty **club scene**, check locally produced *SAX* (€1.30; ⓦ www.cybersax.de), though freesheets such as *Blitz!* and *Dresdener* are fine; free booklet *Dresdener In* is nightlife only. Also try ⓦ www.dresden -nightlife.de for clubbing. The nightclubs listed here are all regulars, but live music venues also host clubnights – *Katy's Garage* and *Scheune* bar are always worth a look.

Bars

Blue Note Görlitzer Str. 2b, Neustadt. Sultry jazz club that hosts live gigs several times a week then segues into a (very) late-night bar.

Radeberger Spezialausschank Terrassenufer 1, Altstadt. Cosy panelled bar with a handsome beer garden on the Brühlsche Terrasse: the Radeberger refers to the beer, the Spezial to the fact some brews are produced under licence on-site.

Raskolnikoff Böhmischer Str. 34, Neustadt. Coolest of a quartet of bars away from the main drag, this is a former squat restored to a hip retro place with an artistic edge. Good food and one of the best courtyards in the area behind.

Reisekniepe Görlitzer Str. 15, Neustadt. Quirky little bar whose themed areas allow drinkers to globetrot within a single building.

Scheune Alaunstr. 36–40, Neustadt. A bastion of the alternative scene that has been going strong since it emerged as a GDR youth club. Ticks all boxes – eclectic, studenty bar and beer garden in summer, tasty Indian food in huge portions, a cinema and occasional gigs.

Beer gardens

Augustus Garten Wiesentorstr. 12. There's always space at this vast beer garden above the Elbe Meadows with a superb view of the illuminated Altstadt opposite.

Elbsegler Grosse Meissner Str. 15. Laid-back chill-out bar with house beats and Latin to soundtrack the view of the historic beauties opposite.

Fährgarten Johannstadt Käthe-Kollwitz-Ufer 23b. A 30min walk east of the Altstadt, this lazy-paced beer garden spread alongside the Elbe and canopied by birch trees, has a mellow family atmosphere and has been a local favourite since 1925.

Purobeach Club Leipziger Str. 15b ⓦ www .purobeach.com. Ibiza comes to Dresden in the form of a hip chill-out-bar-cum-club on the north bank – ideal for loafing on canopied beds by the pool. Eve only, except all day Sun.

Stadtoase Terrassenufer by the Albertbrücke. Dresden's best *Stadtstrand* (city beach) has imported 150 tonnes of fine sand to a riverside location a 10min walk east of the Altstadt: think lazy drinks in deckchairs and mellow beats.

Clubs

Down Town Katharinenstr. 11–13 ⓦ www.downtown-dresden.de. DJs spin a mixed box of party tunes – depending on the night, electro, house, big beat, indie or hip-hop. Keep an eye out for Thursday's legendary neo-rave Nasty Love Club, playground for fetishists and freaks.

Flower Power Erfurter Str. 11 ⓦ www .flowerpower.eu. Sweaty student favourite with unpretentious nights daily, mostly rock and oldies – beware the rock karaoke midweek.

Puschkin Leipzigerstr. 12 ⓦ www.puschkin-club .info. Hip nights coming from the left-field side of clubbing; jungle and drum 'n' bass, electro and disco. Always interesting. The club is located off Alexander-Puschkin-Platz.

Strasse E Werner-Hartmann-Str. 2 ⓦ www.strasse-e.de. A cultural centre in an industrial area 1km north of the Neustadt, whose eight or so club nights cover all bases: from disco and house to the dark side of Goth. If none of those appeal hip-hop and house club *Fahrenheit 100* (ⓦ www.fahrenheit100.com) at no. 3 is worth a look. Take tram #7 to "Industriegelände".

Live music and entertainment

Classical music buffs are well served thanks to two world-class symphony orchestras, the Dresdener Philharmonie and Staatskapelle – city churches also host concerts alongside the concert halls. A ticket desk in the Schinkelwache tourist office covers most events.

Theatre, variety and classical music

Carte Blanche Priessnitzstr. 10 ☏ 0351/20 47 20, ⓦ www.carte-blanche-dresden.de. Sequins and ostrich feathers in shamelessly glitzy *Travestie* shows.

Kulturpalast Altmarkt ☏ 0351/486 68 66, ⓦ www .kulturpalast-dresden.de. Home to the renowned Dresdener Philharmonie plus itinerant musicals.

Sächsische Staatsoper Theaterplatz 2 ☏ 0351/491 17 05, ⓦ www.semperoper.de. Dresden maintains its international reputation for opera in the spectacular Semperoper building. Music from the city's finest orchestras and brilliant staging in a sumptuous concert hall – a world-class act. Also stages some ballet.

Schauspielhaus Ostra-Allee 3 ⓣ0351/491 35 55, ⓦwww.staatsschauspiel-dresden.de. The city's premier stage hosts classic modern dramas.

Live music

Alter Schlachthof Gothaer Str. 11 ⓣ0351/43 13 10, ⓦwww.alter-schlachthof.de. A renovated industrial slaughterhouse schedules a broad programme of jazz and rock acts: from Calexico to MIA, Mogwai to Sigur Ros, via Kajagoogoo – you have been warned.

Beatpol Altbriesnitz 2a ⓣ0351/421 03 97, ⓦwww.beatpol.de. Small venue 1km east of the Altstadt, always worth checking out for indie-rock and alt-folk acts, and regularly featuring major-name touring international acts. Take tram #12 from Postplatz or bus #94 and alight on Meissner Landstr. just past the Aral garage.

Jazzclub Neue Tonne Königstr. 15 ⓣ0351/802 60 17, ⓦwww.jazzclubtonne.de. The city's leading jazz venue hosts gigs every Thursday and Friday and features many international acts. Look to *Blue Note* at other times (see p.173).

Katy's Garage Alaunstr. 48 ⓦwww.katysgarage.de. A good, gritty place of live rock bands and club nights, usually indie, drum n bass or dub.

Listings

Books and media Das Internationale Buch, Altmarkt 24, stocks international press and foreign-language titles, many at high discounts.

Car rental All operators maintain a desk at the airport. Hertz, Hauptbahnhof ⓣ0351/45 26 30; Avis, Friedrichstr. 24 ⓣ0351/496 96 13; Europcar, Strehlener Str. 5 (behind Hauptbahnhof) ⓣ0351/87 73 20.

Cinema Mainstream multi-screen Cinema XX (ⓦwww.cinemaxx.de) is at Hüblerstr. 8.

Hospital Krankenhaus Dresden-Friedrichstadt, Friedrichstr. 41 ⓣ0351/48 00.

Internet In the Altstadt: K&E Callshop, Wiener-Platz-Passagen outside the Hauptbahnhof (Mon–Fri 9am–10pm, Sat & Sun 10am–10pm); Easy, Pfarrfasse 1 beside Kreuzkirche (daily 8am–midnight). In the Neustadt: Mondial, cnr Louisenstr.

and Rothenburger Str. (Mon–Fri 10am–1am, Sat & Sun 11am–1am).

Laundry Waschsalon Crazy, Louisenstr. 6 (Mon–Sat 7am–11pm); Eco-Express Sb-Waschsalon, Königbrücker Str. 2 (daily 6am–10pm).

Post office Annenstr. 10 (Mon–Fri 9am–12.30pm & 1.30–6pm, Sat 9.30am–noon); Altmarktgalerie, enter from Wallstr. (Mon–Fri 8am–6pm, Sat 9am–noon).

Swimming Georg-Arnhold-Bad (Mon–Fri 9am–10pm, Sat & Sun 8am–11pm) has in- and outdoor pools at the western edge of the Grosser Garten at Hauptallee 2; Schwimmhalle Freiberger Platz (Mon 10am–1pm, Wed 6am–1pm, Tues, Thurs & Fri 6am–10pm, Sat 6am–7pm, Sun 1–6pm) is 10min south of the Zwinger on Freiberger Platz.

Around Dresden

Three destinations within 15km of Dresden have been day-trips at least since Augustus the Strong's day: two summer palaces of the absolutist Saxon Elector, **Schloss Pillnitz** and **Schloss Moritzburg**, and wine-suburb **Radebeul**. Although all are accessible by public transport, other options make the getting there as enjoyable as the destination: to Schloss Pillnitz a river cruise along the UNESCO-listed Elbe Valley; from Radeburg to Moritzburg a vintage steam train. The Elberadweg (ⓦwww.elberadweg.de) cycle trail is another option for Schloss Pillnitz and Radeburg.

Schloss Pillnitz

Augustus the Strong conceived **Schloss Pillnitz** as a love nest in which to dally with his mistress, the Countess of Cosel, an easy 10km southeast of court. But when their affair soured, Anna Constantia got the boot and in the early 1720s Augustus turned to his favourite architect, the Zwinger's Pöppelmann, to create a Versailles-inspired retreat spiced with a pinch of Oriental mystery; this was, remember, a ruler who admired the autocratic rule (and porcelain) of Chinese emperors. The complex's first two palaces – the Wasserburg and Bergpalais – either side of a courtyard garden appear unexpectedly exotic in such a Middle European landscape; Baroque rooflines swoop to pagoda points and beneath the lintels are fanciful (and none too accurate) Oriental scenes. Erected on the river bank in an allusion to Venice, the **Wasserburg** (May–Oct Wed–Mon 10am–6pm; €3) struggles to conjure much majesty in spartan rooms that are bare except for the odd piece of Augustus's china and furnishings such as his gilded thrones. More successful are the restored quarters in the **Bergpalais** opposite (May–Oct Tues–Sun 10am–6pm; €4). Following a fire in 1818 the closing wing of the U-shaped palace was rebuilt to create the Neoclassical **Neues Schloss** (April–Oct Tues–Sun 10am–5pm; Nov–March Sat & Sun tours 11am, noon, 1pm & 2pm; €6; ⓦ www.schloesser-dresden.de). Fairly shabby due to ongoing restoration, it has displays on palace history as a prelude to a court kitchen, a domed Neoclassical Festsaal and the palace chapel, whose rich decoration by a Nazarene court painter alludes to Italian Old Masters but without any of their insight.

As much of an attraction is the **park** (daily: May–Oct 9am–6pm; Nov–April 10am–4pm; free), mostly landscaped in naturalistic style except for a labyrinth of trimmed hornbeams opposite the Neues Schloss, designed by the ill-fated countess herself. Within you'll find the Venetian-style "Triton gondola" in which Augustus's son, Augustus III, processed upriver on Dresden's Grand Canal, the Elbe.

Bus #83 goes close to the palace from Comeniusplatz, north of the Grosser Garten. More conveniently, tram #1 goes from the city centre to its terminus, Kleinzschachwitz, from where it's a short walk to a river ferry (single €0.90, return €1.50) across to the Schloss. In the summer season four **steam ferries** of Sächsische Dampfschiffahrt (see p.164; single €9.60, return €14.80) stop on their route east.

Schloss Moritzburg

The village of Moritzburg 15km north of Dresden is another pleasure-park of Augustus the Strong, who was never going to be content with the hunting lodge he inherited from the House of Wettin. He ordered his beleaguered architect Pöppelmann to model it into a luxury Baroque palace along the lines of a French chateau. The product is pure theatre. **Schloss Moritzburg** (tours hourly: April–Oct daily 10am–5.30pm; Nov, Dec, Feb & March Tues–Sun 10am–4pm; Jan Sat & Sun 10am–4pm; €6.50, combination ticket €9; ⓦ www.schloss-moritzburg .de) rises like a wedding-cake decoration above an artificial lake spanned by a grand walkway on which stone trumpeters announce visitors. While the interior fails to live up to the promise outside, it impresses in places: the largest original decorated leather wall-hangings in the world; the Speisesaal (Dining Hall), bristling with plaster hunting trophies; and the Federzimmer, where the regent slept in a bed canopied by multicoloured feathers like a fairytale prince. The surrounding naturalistic Schlosspark is tailor-made for lazy summer days. Drift to its west end and you stumble upon the pink **Fasanenschlössen** (tours daily: May–Sept 10am–5.30pm; April & Oct 10am–4.30pm; €5), a dumpy Rococo lodge whose roofline nods to the fashion for chinoiserie. Surprising are the lighthouse and breakwater follies in the lake behind, where miniature frigates sailed in mock sea-battles while the princes ordered canon volleys of fireworks.

Although stripped of royal status in the constitutional reforms post-1918, the House of Wettin continued to own the palace. Prince Ernst Heinrich von Sachsen sheltered graphic artist and sculptor Käthe Kollwitz in 1944 after her house in Münster was destroyed, and the great Expressionist remained for what transpired to be her final year in lakeside **Käthe Kollwitz Haus** (April–Oct

Mon–Fri 11am–5pm, Sat & Sun 10am–5pm; Nov–March Tues–Fri noon–4pm, Sat & Sun 11am–4pm; €3) at Meissner Strasse 7. It has displays of her ever-compelling works.

Bus #326 (towards Radeburg/Grossenhain) to Moritzburg departs from Dresden-Neustadt. More enjoyable is the journey by vintage **steam train**, the Lössnitzgrundbahn (Ⓦwww.loessnitzgrundbahn.de). At least three departures a day go from S-Bahn station Radebeul-Ost.

Radebeul

Officially **RADEBEUL** is a separate town on the Elbe's west bank. Unofficially, Dresden's urban sprawl has whittled away its individuality to its present incarnation as a dormitory suburb. The big sight is the **Zeitreise DDR Museum** (Tues–Sun 10am–6pm; €7; Ⓦwww.ddr-museum-dresden.de) in the Wasapark at the junction of Meissner Strasse and Wasastrasse, with four floors of GDR memorabilia and kitsch. The surprise is that Radebeul is also a wine centre. On sun-soaked south-facing slopes above – go up Hoflösnitzstrasse by an Audi garage east of the tourist office – is **Höflossnitz** (Tues–Fri 10am–1pm & 2–6pm, Sat & Sun 10am–6pm; €2.30), a one-time wine estate of the House of Wettin with a museum of wine making, a *Weinstube* and restaurant. Weinbergstrasse opposite is home to other local wine producers: Weinhaus Aust (Sat & Sun from 10am; ☎0351/89 39 01 00, Ⓦwww.weingut-aust.de) produces highly rated whites; nearby charming producer *Alter Weinkeller* at no. 16 (Wed, Thurs & Sat from 4pm, Fri & Sun from 11am; ☎0351/836 48 21, Ⓦwww.alter-weinkeller-radebeul.de; rooms ❷) has a restaurant; and at no. 34 is sophisticated white-specialist Drei Herren (Thurs–Sat 2–6pm, Sun 11am–6pm; ☎0351/795 60 99, Ⓦwww.weingutdreiherren.de).

The international wine gongs go to **Schloss Wackerbarth** (☎0351/895 50, Ⓦwww.schloss-wackerbarth.de), 3km west, a wine estate founded around a Baroque palace where Augustus the Strong threw glittering court parties. A retail outlet offers tastings of modern wines (daily 9.30am–8pm; €1 per wine), but it's more enjoyable to try them on daily estate tours: those for wine are daily at 2pm, those of Saxony's oldest sparkling wine cellar are daily at 5pm (both €9). A *Gasthaus* provides top-notch international cuisine (circa €20 a main). Check the website, too, for summer concerts staged in front of the palace's terraces – as idyllic as it gets.

S-Bahn line S1 to Radebeul-Ost or Radebeul-Weintraube leaves you a ten-minute walk from the museum. The **tourist office** (March–Oct Mon–Fri 9am–6pm, Sat 9am–1pm; Nov–Feb Mon–Fri 10am–4pm, Sat 9am–1pm; ☎0351/194 33, Ⓦwww.radebeul.de) is at Meissner Strasse 152. S-Bahn station Radebeul-West is a ten-minute walk east of Schloss Wackerbarth. Alternatively tram #4 from central Dresden goes (eventually) to the Schloss via Meissner Strasse.

Meissen

MEISSEN's fate is to be synonymous with porcelain. All its coach-tour day-trippers make a beeline for the prestigious china factory founded by Augustus the Strong in 1710. Even if you don't visit that outlet, it's hard to escape porcelain in the town that pioneered its large-scale production outside of East Asia. Yet Meissen, 25km northwest of Dresden, is better visited for a picture-postcard medieval **Altstadt** that emerged from the war without a scratch, complete with charming cobbled streets and rainbow-coloured houses, the power base of the

Albrechtsburg castle and cathedral standing aloof on a rocky outcrop to the north above the River Elbe. Though hailed as the birthplace of Saxony because this is the earliest castle in the state, Meissen never developed into a major city. The famous porcelain factory is a twenty-minute walk southwest of the Altstadt. That you can reach the town by steam river-cruiser as well as S-Bahn only adds to the appeal as a day-trip from Dresden.

Arrival, information and accommodation

The **Bahnhof**, served by regional trains and frequent S-Bahn S1 from Dresden, is on the east bank of the Elbe; second Bahnhof Meissen-Triebischtal is on the west bank near the porcelain factory. Steamers of the Dresden **ferry line** Sächsische Dampfschiffahrt (see p.164; single €11.40, return €16.80) make two trips a day in summer. A footbridge from the Bahnhof and road bridge Altstadtbrücke link the modern east-bank city to the Altstadt opposite, both with a good view of the medieval town. The latter funnels you directly towards the Markt and the **tourist office** at no. 3 (April–Oct Mon–Fri 10am–6pm, Sat & Sun 10am–4pm; Nov–March Mon–Fri 10am–5pm, Sat 10am–3pm; ☎03521/419 40, ⓦ www .touristinfo-meissen.de). Meissen is an easy day-trip from Dresden – it looks its best on summer evenings and the S-Bahn permits late-night returns until long after the town has gone to bed. However, there's some appealing **accommodation** to choose from should you want to stay; the tourist office books budget **private rooms** (❶–❷).

Burgkeller Domplatz 11 ☎03521/414 00, ⓦ www.meissen-hotels.com. The smartest address in the old town is all about old-world elegance and a location overlooking the Altstadt from above; balcony rooms are worth the extra €10. The café/beer garden and restaurant boast the same views of the Altstadt's roofscape. ❺–❻

Fuschshöhl Hohlweg 7 ☎03521/45 94 81, ⓦ www.fuchshoehl.de. A 500-year-old town house at the top of Burgstrasse renovated into a small pension above a charming *Weinstube* furnished with bags of personality by its artist owner. Tasteful rooms – four with kitchenettes – are individually styled, with a dash of artistic flair and furnished with the occasional antique. A bargain. ❷–❸

Goldener Löwe Heinrichsplatz 6 ☎03521/411 10, ⓦ www.meissen-hotels.com. Pleasant, small hotel just off the Markt with a calm old-world ambience and antiques in some rooms. ❻

Herberge Orange Siebeneichener Str. 34 ☎03521/45 43 34, ⓦ www.herberge-orange.de. Small private hostel right on the river – it rents sit-on kayaks to guests – with ten rooms. It's located a 20min walk south of Altstadt. Dorms €11.50–13, rooms ❶

Welcome Parkhotel Meissen Hafenstr. 27–31 ☎03521/722 50, ⓦ www.welcome-hotels.com. Meissen's premier address, a four-star member of the Mercure chain, is in its own park on the north bank. Its Jugendstil villa seems to have rubbed off on the decor, which has more character than the usual business chain. ❻

The lower Altstadt

After over eight centuries of pulling at the threads, Meissen has knotted its **Altstadt** into a tight bundle of cobbled lanes. With no true sights, this is more a place to explore by instinct, though your starting point is likely to be the pretty centrepiece of the **Markt**, bordered on one side by a late-Gothic **Rathaus** with a three-piece suite of step-gabled facades. Massive carved portals on surrounding houses that jostle for space are worth a look: the Markt Apotheke at no. 9 has a Renaissance tympanum of Icarus above a walled medieval Meissen on the Elbe. The back of the square is framed by the **Frauenkirche** with the world's earliest carillon of what else but Meissen china bells (played at 6.30am, 8.30am, 11.30am, 2.30pm, 5.30pm & 8.30pm). Within, beneath Gothic vaults is a gilded altar (c.1500), and you can ascend the tower (daily 1–4pm, Mon–Sat 10am–noon; €2).

East of the Markt is **Heinrichsplatz** with a statue of Heinrich I who founded the first castle on the Albrechtsburg in 929 AD; they say he earned his nickname "der Vogler" ("the fowler") because he was bird-catching when confirmed as Germany's first king. A **Stadtmuseum** (daily 11am–5pm; €3) behind sets its displays in a Gothic Franciscan monastery; a colossal red wine press (1788), said to be the largest of its type in Germany, catches the eye. Bergstrasse, the former prestige street between the Markt's civic power-base and episcopal powers above, leads off the side of the Markt towards the Albrechtsburg, past a Meissen china retail outlet at no. 6.

The Albrechtsburg and the Dom

Several steep staircases from the end of Burgstrasse later, you enter a secluded courtyard atop Burgberg where Meissen made its debut a thousand years ago as Heinrich I's "Misni" castle on a defensive perch above the Elbe. As good a reason to ascend is for a river view from a terrace beside the Dom, or over the Altstadt from several cafés. Current castle, the **Albrechtsburg** (daily: March–Oct 10am–6pm; Nov–Feb 10am–5pm; €5, combination ticket with Dom €6), Germany's first residential palace, is a late fifteenth-century replacement that dithers between stronghold and palace – slab sides that rise sheer from the rock outcrop seem at odds with prestige windows like drawn theatrical curtains. It was commissioned as a symbol of Saxon power by two prince electors of the House of Wettin, Ernst and Albrecht. Unfortunately, the duo squabbled, work halted and by the time the palace was finished in 1520, the court had decamped to Dresden. Indeed, it was largely abandoned for two centuries until the ubiquitous Augustus the Strong installed within it Europe's first porcelain manufacturer in 1710. And what a factory: at the front architect Arnold von Westfalen added a French-styled octagonal Renaissance tower embedded with Old Testament imagery. The staircase within is a highlight of an interior also notable for eccentric stellar vaulting like a Cubist's take on Gothic. Decor in the hall-like rooms is a product of a nineteenth-century revamp after the china factory moved to its current premises (see below) in 1864. It's a typically over enthusiastic interpretation of medieval roots, with murals of the Wettin rulers seemingly lifted from a *Boy's Own* adventure – all good fun. A ground floor of sculpture is due to return to Dresden's Albertinum in 2009 (see p.166).

Arnold von Westfalen also tinkered with the **Dom** (daily: April–Oct 9am–6pm; Nov–March 10am–4pm; €2.50), which merges into the Albrechtsburg to update an early medieval structure into High Gothic – the landmark lattice spires were added in the early 1900s. The finest artwork is in the Fürstenkapelle, tacked onto the end of the nave as a mausoleum for the Wettin household, so protecting the original carved portal. German Renaissance heroes Cranach and especially Dürer are the influences for the ducal bronzes set into the floor, the latter especially evident in that of Duke George the Bearded, who gets a side chapel to himself. Italian artists added the enchanting Renaissance stucco in the 1670s. Other artwork of note is the rood screen and astonishingly advanced statues of Emperor Otto I and his wife Adelheid in the nave, both sculpted by Naumberg masters (c.1260). Inevitably, the Baroque crucifix is of local porcelain, created by court master-artist Johann Joachim Kaendler.

The Porzellan-Museum and Nikolaikirche

The number-one destination of every tour group to Meissen is the **Porzellan-Museum** (daily: May–Oct 9am–6pm; Nov–April till 5pm), 1.5km southwest of the centre on Talstrasse, whose modern glass-skinned hall envelops an original villa; arrive early or at lunchtime to escape the worst of the crush. Augustus the

Strong's china obsession is a tale of its own, the result of incarcerating alchemist Johann Friedrich Böttger in his mightiest stronghold, the Königstein (see p.183). While Dresden china – the first manufactured west of Asia – reflected the regent's aspirations to the omnipotence of oriental emperors, it was also intended to fill coffers: "my golden pheasant", as Augustus put it. The formula of Meissen china, branded by blue crossed swords, remains secret. Thirty-minute tours (English audio guides available; €8.50) take in a demonstration workshop of the four stages of hand-produced manufacture and the Schauhalle, which can be visited independently (€6). Its three thousand items span three centuries of manufacture in Meissen. Court artist Johann Joachim Kaendler stars, not least for the display's highlight, a 3.5m-high table decoration that graced the dining table of Augustus III. An on-site factory outlet stocks more china than a bull could smash – from the usual coquettish dolls and tea sets, to contemporary streamlined pieces influenced by Japan.

A short walk back up Talstrasse, then right on Kerstingstrasse, the **Nikolaikirche** (May–Sept Tues–Thurs & Sun 2–4pm) takes Meissen's porcelain obsession to new heights. The largest Meissen china figures ever cast, 2.5m-high, flank the altar of an intimate church completely clad in china as a memorial to the dead of World War I.

Eating and drinking

There are two must-dos of eating and drinking in Meissen. First is **Meissner Fummel**, a light cake that looks like a puff-pastry ostrich egg. It is notoriously fragile – the challenge, say locals, is to get it home in one piece. Second is to sample local **wines**. Whites tend to be sprightly and often fruity – Riesling, Muscat-style cross *Müller-Thurgau*, and, if you can find it, *Elbling*, a vine cultivated in the area since the Middle Ages. Reds – *Traminer* and *Blau Spätburgunder* – are aromatic and rich. Several *Weinstuben* are at the top of Burgstrasse beneath the Albrechtsburg.

Am Hundewinkel Görnische Gasse 4. Solid pub-grub lightened by fish dishes in what claims to be the oldest *Hausbrauerei* in Saxony, also serving local brew Meissner Schwerter. Closed Mon.

Café Zieger Rote Stufen 2. Traditional *Konditorei* at the top of Burgstrasse that has been a fixture for over 150 years – the best place to sample *Meissner Fummel*.

Domteller Domplatz 9 ☎03521/45 76 76. The oldest restaurant in Meissen prepares a good-value traditional menu – old favourites such as home-made beef roulade with potato dumplings or goulash steeped in beer – and views over the Altstadt from two terraces.

Ratskeller Markt 1 ☎03521/45 93 93. Ever-reliable choice for a good-value feed, with tables on the Markt in summer and a good list of local plonk available by the glass.

Vincenz Richler An den Frauenkirche 12 ☎03521/45 32 85. Beside the Frauenkirche, this *Weinhaus* from 1523 is as romantic as it is charming, with a choice between snug rooms and a lovely terrace. Local produce features on the traditional menu and wine list alike. Closed Mon.

zenSuR Heinrichsplatz 6 ☎03521/411 10. Gourmet cuisine in the highly rated restaurant of the *Goldener Löwe* hotel – the menu provides beautifully presented international dishes, from modern French and Mediterranean choices to surprises such as red snapper in coconut milk with shiitake mushrooms. Closed Tues & Wed, and Thurs lunch.

Saxon Switzerland

The area from Pirna, 18km east of Dresden, to the Czech border is commonly known as **Saxon Switzerland** (Sächsische Schweiz), but that was always a conceit of the Romantics. This is classic Middle Europe – 275 square kilometres of rolling fields through which the Elbe River carves a broad

steep valley, much of it protected as a national park (Ⓦ www.nationalpark
-saechsische-schweiz.de). What comes closer to the nub of some of the most
distinctive scenery in Germany is the area's second title, Elbsandsteingebirge
(Elbe Sandstone Mountains): table-topped outcrops cone suddenly above
the fields like miniature mesas, their summits sculpted over the aeons into
fantastical pinnacles.

With a maze of gorges to explore and iron ladders that ascend sheer faces,
this is superb hiking country, notably on the superb long-distance **Malerweg**
(Painters' Way) track if you have a week to spare. Indeed, the story goes that
the area's name stuck after eighteenth-century Swiss artists Adrian Zingg and
Anton Graff wrote postcards home from their walking holiday saying,
"Greetings from Saxon Switzerland". Later hikers included Caspar David
Friedrich, who added the picture to the postcard with works such as *Rambler
Above a Sea of Fog*. Rock climbing is also excellent. At a push you could tick
off the main sights on a long, rushed day-trip from Dresden – the **Bastei** area,
then a brisk walk that skirts around the Lilienstein outcrop to **Königstein**, for
example. However, these are landscapes to savour and which are at their best
away from the premier sights; set aside a couple of days at least.

Transport and activities in Saxon Switzerland

Transport
The **S1** from Dresden (and Meissen) tracks along the south bank of the river to
Rathen, Königstein, Bad Schandau and Schmilka approximately every half-hour;
frequent passenger (and bike) **ferries** from each village ply to north-bank destinations. Be aware if driving that the only **traffic bridges** are at Pirna, at the west end
of the area, and 2km west of Bad Schandau. An appealing way to access the area
is on **steam-cruisers** of Dresden ferry line Sächsische Dampfschiffahrt (3 daily; 5hr
30min; Ⓦ www.saechsische-dampfschiffahrt.de) from Dresden to Bad Schandau
via all destinations en route. From late April to October, a **bus service**, Sächsisch-
Böhmischer Nationalpark-Express, operated by Frank Nuhn Freizeit und Tourismus
(4 daily 9.50am–3.15pm; ☎035021/676 14, Ⓦ www.frank-nuhn-freizeit-und-tourismus
.de), shuttles from the Bastei to Königstein via Hohnstein and Bad Schandau, easing
the logistics of a whistle-stop day-trip.

Information and maps
Local **tourist offices** stock a full rack of brochures for walking. Other information
sources are national park centres at Bad Schandau and Königstein, official and
unofficial respectively, as well as area marketing board website Ⓦ www.saechsische
-schweiz-touristik.de.
   For **maps**, there's a general 1:25,000 *Topographische Wanderkarte der National-
parkregionen in der Sächsische-Böhmische Schweiz* (€9.60) or smaller area maps
(€4.90). In the region, they are best sourced from the Nationalpark Zentrum in Bad
Schandau, or from Bergsport Arnold, at Marktstrasse 5, Bad Schandau.

Hiking and rock-climbing
Day-hikes are numerous throughout the area: routes with sketch maps are printed
in the free promotional booklet *Erlebnis-Kompass*, a useful area overview of basic
walks around villages, available from tourist offices. From Königstein you can ascend
to two plateaux or embark on a four- to five-hour hike up to the Bastei. The best
base for day-walks, however, is Bad Schandau, with the Schrammsteine's fissured
labyrinth in its backyard. Long-distance route the **Malerweg** (Ⓦ www.malerweg.de)

The Bastei, Kurort Rathen and Hohnstein

Without question, the premier tourist destination in the area is the **BASTEI**. Out of a pleasant pastoral landscape of rape fields springs a fortress of fantastical sandstone pillars that tower over 300m-high above the pine forests. Almost as impressive as this natural double-take – one of Germany's most distinctive landscapes – is a panorama that sweeps over a meander in the mighty Elbe and south to the table-top slabs of Lilienstein and Pfaffenstein, and the walls of the mighty Königstein (see p.183). The name Bastei refers to the thirteenth-century Felsenburg fortress (daily 9am–6pm; €1.50, though access not restricted at other times) whose remnants are wedged among outcrops linked by wooden gangways. Signs point out carved stairways or the massive cistern at the core, but you'll need imagination or a peruse of a model of the castle (c.1400) displayed at the centre, where a massive cistern is hewed out of the rock, to make sense of what was a medieval city in the sky. The staggering views make the spot insanely popular – visit early to appreciate the grandeur of the site. As much of an attraction is the **Basteibrücke** that leapfrogs to the fortress on sheer outcrops – the picture-postcard view is from a lookout point reached via a path left before the bridge. Graffiti midway across reveals that tourists have visited since at least 1706.

was voted the most beautiful walk in Germany by hikers' bible *Wander* magazine in 2007. Regardless of whether the 112km trail, marked with a brush-stroke "M", truly tracks the route taken by Romantic painters, the wild circuit from Pirna offers a loop around major sights and remote landscapes on both sides of the Elbe – all in all highly recommended. Most walkers average 15km a day (approx 5hr) on an eight-day circuit, but you could cut out two by starting at Wehlen, the start of the best scenery. Area tourist offices stock a booklet of the trail with lists of accommodation en route.

Sandstone pinnacles make Saxon Switzerland hallowed ground among German **rock-climbers**. There are 745 official climbing rocks, and over 11,000 routes, most in the Schrammsteine. Bergsport Arnold (see above) has a respectable stock of climbing gear and guidebooks – staff are a good source of advice, too.

Cycling

The **cycle** route Elberadweg (ⓦwww.elberadweg.de), mainly along the south bank, but criss-crossing the river to avoid busy roads, is a superb option for touring. The tourist office in Bad Schandau rents bikes.

Activity tours

Among the many operators offering activity tours or rental in the area are:

Elbsandstein Reisen Through Bad Schandau tourist office ☏035022/900 31, ⓦwww .bad-schandau.de. Climbing and walking tours in the superb Schrammsteine area above Bad Schandau; from one-day excursions (from €40 per person) to five-day walking and multi-activity weeks (from €220, includes accommodation).

Hobbit Hikes ☏0351/323 58 57, ⓦwww.hobbit-hikes.de. Backpacker-friendly Dresden outfit that provides bespoke tours priced by group size, including short 4hr fixed-rope trips on exposed ridges and sections of the Malerweg.

Kanu Aktiv Tours Schandauerstr. 17–19, Königstein ☏035021/59 99 60, ⓦwww .kanu-aktiv-tours.de. One of the area's leading rental outfits for canoes, kayaks and rubber dinghies. Transfers are possible for a modest fee should you only want to paddle one way.

▲ Saxon Switzerland scenery near the Bastei

The natural glory of the site is marred somewhat by the *Berghotel* (☏035024/77 90, ⓦ www.bastei-berghotel.de; ❺–❻) and its *Panorama* restaurant, though a refurbishment has pepped up its GDR-era decor and added a spa. If you arrive by car, note that an inner **car park** is usually full by mid-morning, so you have to park by the turn-off 2.5km from the site, then catch the Bastei-Panorama-Express bus (€1.50 return).

Notwithstanding the tourist buses (see p.180) or bus #247 from Pirna, access by public transport is from pretty spa-resort **KURORT RATHEN**; a ferry links the Bahnhof to the north bank, from where it's a stiff thirty-minute ascent to the Bastei, passing the Flesenbühne open-air theatre en route, which stages crowd-pleasers in summer. The **tourist office** (Easter–Oct Mon–Fri 10am– noon & 1–6pm, Sat & Sun 9am–1pm; Nov–Easter Mon–Thurs 10am–noon & 1–6pm, Fri 10am–2pm; ☏035024/704 22, ⓦ www.kurort-rathen.de) in the *Haus des Gastes*, Fühllhölzelweg 1, books pensions and **private rooms** (❷). The premier **hotel** is riverside four-star *Elbschlösschen* (☏035024/750, ⓦ www .hotelelbschloesschen.de; ❺–❻). Another good choice is *Burg Altrathen*, Am Grünbach 10–11 (☏035024/76 00, ⓦ www.rathen-urlaub.de; ❸), with simple rooms in a hotel and pension among the ruins of a medieval hillside castle.

An alternative overnighter is **HOHNSTEIN** 5km north, a photogenic village whose layers of half-timbering and crumbling houses fold down a hillside. It has its own castle, too, albeit fairly tatty after heavy-handed restoration following its use as a POW camp, then one of the largest youth hostels in Germany, but with good views. The village is accessed on the Knotenweg path (marked by a green stripe) from the Bastei. The castle has above-average independent hostel accommodation (☏035975/812 02, ⓦ www.nfhw.de; ❶–❷) divided into family and youth sections, or *Weisser Hirsch* (☏035975/86 30, ⓦ www.ran-an-die-bastei .de; ❸), opposite, is a good choice for both a bed and for eating.

Königstein

Around an S-bend meander of the Elbe, **KÖNIGSTEIN** is the next stop east from Rathen. An anonymous oversized village, it vies with the Bastei in popularity because of **Festung Königstein** (daily: April–Sept 9am–8pm; Oct 9am–6pm; Nov–March 9am–5pm; €6), one of the largest hilltop fortifications in Europe, perched 360m up on a sandstone plateau; it's a tough thirty-minute walk west from the village on a short trip on the Festung-Express **bus** (April–Oct daily every hour; €4 return) from the village centre. What began as a thirteenth-century fortress was beefed up by successive rulers into a mighty citadel. Potential enemies took one look at its eyrie and massive walls that grew from the rock up to 42m high and dismissed it as impregnable. No raid was even attempted. The result is an architectural encyclopedia of military thinking up to the Napoleonic era scattered across the plateau. A highlight of the thirty buildings, many with displays of weaponry, is a 152m-deep well ordered by Augustus the Strong. Without an offensive role, the citadel served as a refuge for Saxony rulers and, from 1591 as the most secure prison in the state, the Georgenburg. An ambitious 19-year-old apothecary apprentice, Johann Friedrich Böttger, found himself inside after he promised Augustus he could alchemize gold. He failed, of course, but, nudged towards achievable goals by court scholar Ehrenfried Walter von Tschirnhaus, magicked instead "white gold" – the first porcelain in Europe. Other names behind the Georgenburg's bars include nineteenth-century social democrat August Bebel. In World War II it served as a POW camp and storehouse for Dresden's art. More than exhibits, however, it's the views that impress, especially of the Lilienstein (415m) and Pfaffenstein (434m) plateaux north and south respectively.

You can ascend to both via trails from Königstein village: they say Augustus the Strong hacked out that to the Lilienstein (5km; 2hr) in 1708, while the fissured plateau of the Pfaffenstein (8km; 3hr), the highest in the region, is beloved by rock-climbers for the landmark 43m Barbarine column on its south side. Pick up sketch maps from the tourist office.

Practicalities

Königstein's municipal **tourist office** (all year Mon–Fri 9am–6pm; May–Oct also Sat 9am–1pm & Sun 10am–1pm; Nov–April also Sat 9am–10.30pm; ☎03521/682 61, ⊛www.koenigstein.de) is by the church at Schreiberberg 2. The central Tourismus Elbsandsteingebirge (daily: April–Sept 9am–5pm, Oct–March till 3pm; ☎035021/671 71, ⊛www.tourismusverein-elbsandsteingebirge.de) at Bahnhofstrasse 1 is an excellent source of information on the region. The campsite *Camping Königstein* (☎035021/882 24, ⊛www.camping-koenigstein.de) occupies a spot by the river 500m south of the centre; turn left from the Bahnhof.

Accommodation options in the town include *Lindenhof* at Gohrischer Str. 10 (☎035021/682 43, ⊛www.lindenhof-koenigstein.de; ❸–❹), something of an early-Eighties timewarp, yet a passable option on a hillside above the village, and *Schräger's Gasthaus* in the centre at Kirchgasse 1 (☎035021/683 52, ⊛www.scharegers-gasthaus.de; ❷) with pleasant enough if small en-suites. On the north bank of the Elbe between Königstein and Halbestadt, hikers' hostel *Ferdinand's Homestay* (☎035022/547 75, ⊛www.ferdinandshomestay.de; closed Nov–March; dorms €12.50–17.50, rooms ❶–❷) is well sited for explorations of the Lilienstein above, or as a stop en route to the Bastei. It's tricky to find, so call first – at the time of writing the managers operate a free shuttle bus from the north-bank ferry jetty at noon and 6pm.

All the hotels have decent **restaurants** – the terrace of *Schrägers* is an appealing spot for country cooking in summer. *Amtshof* (closed Tues) at the corner of Piraner Strasse and the main road serves a daily menu of traditional dishes.

Bad Schandau and around

A comprehensive tourism infrastructure makes pocket-sized **BAD SCHANDAU**, 5km east of Königstein, the best base in Saxon Switzerland. An injection of capital after GDR doldrums has helped revive this late nineteenth-century spa resort, and there's also good walking in its backyard. A useful first stop is the national park information centre on the main road west of the centre, **Nationalpark Zentrum Sächsische Schweiz**, Dresdner Strasse 2 (April–Oct daily 9am–6pm; Nov–March Tues–Sun 9am–5pm; €4), with enlightening displays on the area's geology and fauna, plus enthusiastic staff and a good stock of maps in its shop. Notwithstanding the time-honoured pastime of a stroll in the central **Kurpark** – a museum (Tues–Sun 2–5pm; €2) at Badallee 10 on its east side documents the resort's history and Elbe shipping – the main attraction was traditionally the **Personenaufzug** lift which whisked spa-goers up to a viewing platform at 50m. Restoration of the 1904-vintage tower is due to be complete by summer 2009 (previously summer daily 9am–9pm; €1.50).

The obvious walk is one an hour east to a viewpoint ("**Schrammstein-aussicht**") of the Schrammsteine area that lies northeast. It forms the bulk of the national park area and has the largest fissured upland of the region – its labyrinth of columns attracts rock-climbers (see box, p.180). A good half-day circuit here goes via Ostrau, Lattengrund and the Grosses Schrammtor – ask in the tourist office. For longer hikes take historic tram, the Kirnitzschtalbahn (summer every 30min; winter every 70min), which departs from a terminus at the west side of the Kurpark, and rumbles up through a wooded canyon to Lichtenhainer Wasserfall 7km northeast, from where it's an easy walk to the eponymous waterfall and the Kuhstall (Cow Stall) rock arch. For tougher hikes, you could alight one stop before at Beuthenfall to access the Schrammsteine: up to viewpoints at Carolafelsen (459m) or Frienstein (455m), both around two hours thirty minutes each way; or for a serious day-hike over the Alfensteine plateau, then down the Heilige Stiege (Holy Steps) – rungs hammered into the rock – to riverside village Schmilka on the Czech border, from where you can either catch the S-Bahn or a ferry back to Bad Schandau (last boat in summer 5pm). Maps are essential – seek up-to-date advice from the Nationalpark Zentrum.

The end of the road 10km beyond Lichtenhainer Wasserfall is **HINTER-HERMSDORF**, a farming village and base for walking trails among rolling hills. Also here is an enchanting twenty-minute river trip in the Kirnitzsch Valley (Kirnitzschtal; tours daily Easter–Oct 9.30–4.30pm; €3 single, €5 return). You are paddled in a shallow-draft canoe through a wild fern-clad river gorge – an idyllic trip that feels another world to the tourist mills elsewhere. The embarkation point is at Obere Schleuse signposted 800m from a car park. Bus #241 links Bad Schandau and Hinterhermsdorf (six daily; 50min).

Practicalities

Bad Schandau's **Bahnhof** is on the opposite side of the Elbe; frequent ferries cross to the town centre. The main **tourist office** (April & Oct daily 9am–6pm; May–Sept daily 9am–9pm; Nov–March Mon–Fri 9am–6pm, Sat & Sun 9am–1pm; ☎035022/900 30, ⓦ www.bad-schandau.de) on the Markt is supported by a desk in the Bahnhof (April Mon–Fri 8am–5pm; May–Oct Mon–Sat 8am–6pm; Nov–March Mon, Tues, Thurs & Fri 8am–5pm; ☎035022/412 47). The main office has **bike rental**. Camping is at *Campingplatz Ostrauer Mühle* (☎035022/727 42, ⓦ www.ostrauer-muehle.de), 3km northwest on the Hinterhermsdorf road; it also has budget rooms in a guesthouse (❷). The premier hotel is luxury *Elbresidenz* on the Markt (☎0350/91 90, ⓦ www .elbresidenz-bad-schandau.de; ❼) with stylish contemporary decor in rooms that overlook the Markt or the river, and a beauty spa. Other options are *Lindenhof*, Rudolf-Sendig-Strasse 11 (☎035022/48 90, ⓦwww.lindenhof-bad-schandau .de; ❹), a rather elegant old pile set in a garden, most of whose rooms benefit from the high ceilings of its period building, or *Zum Rotes Haus*, Marktstrasse 10 (☎035022/423 43, ⓦwww.hotel-zum-roten-haus.de; ❹), a traditional *Gaststätte* just off the Markt with simple rooms and good-value half-pension deals in its traditional restaurant. *Elberesidenz* has the swishest **restaurants** in town, gourmet's choice *Sendig* (eve only, closed Sun & Mon), with contemporary international cuisine, and cheaper *Vital*, while cheerful, modern Italian restaurant *Gambrinus* beside the tourist office gets the nod from locals. The massage and **saunas** of Viva Vital spa in *Elbresidenz* are available to non-guests if pre-booked.

Bautzen

BAUTZEN, 60km east of Dresden, is the capital of the Sorbs, Germany's only indigenous minority who are derived from the Slavic Wends who migrated west around fifteen hundred years ago. Apart from the thrill of exotic street-names and the occasional institute and museum, or unless a visit coincides with a Sorb weekend market five weeks before Easter or an Easter Sunday festival, you'd be hard pushed to know, however. Only five percent of the local population are native Sorb – the Czech-influenced dialect is heard more commonly in villages north, linked by a cycle route. What defines a settlement that is a thousand years old is its historic Altstadt – a maze-like kernel guarded by seventeen medieval bastions that march above a river valley – the Spree River flows north to second Sorb stronghold Spreewald (see p.153).

Arrival, information and accommodation

Bautzen's **Bahnhof** is south of the Altstadt: go straight up Bahnhofstrasse, then right at the junction with Lauengraben to reach the Reichenturm. A helpful **tourist office** (March–Oct Mon–Fri 9am–6pm, Sat & Sun 9am–3pm; Nov–March Mon–Fri 9am–5pm; ☎03591/420 16, ⓦwww.bautzen.de) is at Hauptmarkt 1. Its **internet** terminal is free for short intervals, otherwise Internet Café Bautzen (Mon–Sat 11am–11pm, Sun 2–11pm) is on the second floor at Steinstrasse 11. Fahrradverleih Schlenkrich at Aussere Lauenstrasse 7 (☎03591/35 10 81) rents **bikes**. Lausitzer Töpferwaren, An der Fleischbänken 4, behind the Dom sells Sorb folkcrafts, including traditional blue-and-white pottery and painted Easter eggs.

The nearest **campsite** is *Camping Stausee Bautzen* (☎035828/764 30, ⓦwww .camping-bautzen.de), 2km north of Bautzen, beyond Burk village. Bus #3 goes at weekends only.

Alte Gerberi Uferweg 1 ☎03591/27 23 90, ⓦwww.hotel-alte-gerberei.de. There's charm by the pail-load in this pretty pension on the Spree – pleasingly unfussy old-fashioned rooms, the best with a view across to the Alte Wasserkunst, and a verdant courtyard for its rear restaurant (eve only, closed Sun). ❸

DJH Bautzen Am Zwinger 1 ☎03591/403 47, ⓦwww.jugendherberge-sachsen.de. The town youth hostel is in the former armoury tower of the medieval fortifications, 100m from the Nikolaiturm and near the bars of Schlossstrasse. Dorms from €17.30.

Dom Eck Breitengasse 2 ☎03591/50 13 30, ⓦwww.wjelbik.de. Sorb-owned hotel from the family behind the *Wjelbik* restaurant, with works by Sorb and German artists on the walls of modern en suites. Great price for the location just behind the Dom. ❸

Goldener Adler Hauptmarkt 4 ☎03591/486 60, ⓦwww.goldeneradler.de. Smart four-star in a handsome Baroque town house on Hauptmarkt; facilities in the cellars include a restaurant, bar, and the most romantic wine-bar in Bautzen. ❺

Schloss-Schänke Burgplatz 5 ℗ 03591/30 49 90, Ⓦ www.schloss-schaenke.net. Pleasant old-world place created from a Franciscan monastery, some rooms with original thirteenth-century stone walls. Furnishings are both more modern and more comfy than public areas suggest. ❸–❹

The Town

As good a place to start as any is the viewing platform of the cylindrical **Reichenturm** (daily April–Oct 10am–5pm; €1), which watches over the eastern Altstadt like a Baroque lighthouse. Built for town defence, it received its cap ten years after being built. A bad move, it transpired, as within four decades the tower assumed its 1.44m lean off-vertical – operations to shore up the tower in the 1950s revealed that the foundations were only 80cm deep. Pedestrian high-street Reichenstrasse channels from the tower to **Hauptmarkt**, enclosed by colourful Baroque town houses and a walloping two-tiered Rathaus crowned by a tower. Its most handsome facade is that on Fleischmarkt behind, which faces up to the **Dom St Petri**. An otherwise plain cathedral is notable for two quirks: the nave of the hall bends away to the right, presumably a ruse to squeeze extra length onto the plot, and as East Germany's only dual-denomination church. Because Catholics and Protestants agreed to share the cathedral when the Reformation rolled east from Thuringia, the nave divides halfway: at the back, the restrained church of Protestantism; in front Catholics celebrate the divine through decorative excess. The tower (July–Dec Sat & Sun 1–6pm; €1) offers roofscape views.

A Baroque gateway on which God and Jesus pose casually on a globe fronts the **Domstift**, a U-shaped residence of the cathedral dean. The building houses cathedral treasures in the **Domschatzkammer** (Mon–Fri 10am–noon & 1–4pm; free). West of here (left from the gate) are cobbled lanes that are Bautzen at its most charming. The area's thoroughfare is Schlossstrasse, main street of the medieval Altstadt in a district that was known as "On the hill of the mad"; why is unclear. Off its top is defence tower, the **Nikolaiturm** – they say the bust depicts a town clerk who attempted to betray the city to Hussites – and the entrance to the shell of the **Nikolaikirche**. A romantic ruin since it was shattered by cannonballs in the Thirty Years' War, it has a cemetery and an idyllic setting above the river; for the photo-album shot ascend to a viewpoint opposite via a path beyond the Nikolaiturm.

Bar street Schlossstrasse ends at **Schloss Ortenburg**, at the northeast tip of the Altstadt where Bautzen made its debut as a border-fortress c.600 AD. While the current Renaissance-styled model dates from the 1640s, it retains the gateway of a fifteenth-century predecessor ordered by Matthias Corvinus, King of Hungary and Bohemia – that's him on the tower's sandstone plaque. A sober Baroque salt cellar within the courtyard houses the **Sorbisches Museum** (April–Oct Mon–Fri 10am–5pm, Sat & Sun 10am–6pm; closes 1hr earlier Nov–March; €2.50; Ⓦ www.museum.sorben.com), with a homespun world of Sorb folk costume and crafts, including the traditional painted Easter eggs rolled downhill on Easter Sunday.

It's worth cutting right from the courtyard's far gateway to track the river en route to the **Alte Wasserkunst** tower (April–Oct daily 10am–5pm; Nov, Dec, Feb & March daily 10am–4pm; Jan Sat & Sun 10am–4pm; €2), a one-time defence tower with a half-timbered cap. You can ascend to the summit for an idyllic view of the fortifications marching along the riverbank and peruse waterworks that pumped river water to 86 troughs throughout the town. Adjacent to here is **Michaelskirche**; the story goes the Sorb church was erected because Archangel Michael came to Bautzen's aid against the Hussites in 1492. The picture-postcard view of the church and water tower above the Spree is from the Friedrichsbrücke south. Incidentally, they say the single-roofed former fisherman's cottage beneath, the oldest in Bautzen, has survived fire and wars due to the spell of a gypsy, hence its nickname as the **Hexenhäuschen** (Witch's House).

The antithesis to the Altstadt's charm is **Gedenkstätte Bautzen** (Tues–Sun 10am–5pm; free) east of the centre on Weigangstrasse (one block south of main road Löbauer Strasse). Hard to believe but Bautzen is synonymous in Germany with GDR-era paranoia. Critics of the party, renegade agents, even aspirant defectors, were incarcerated in Bautzen II, a prison under unofficial control of the Stasi secret police. Of the 2700 people imprisoned during its operation from 1956 to 1989, many in solitary confinement, eighty percent were jailed as political "enemies of the state". Officially, however, it never existed. Indeed, East German citizens remained ignorant of the oppression until prisoners were released during the peaceful revolution of 1989.

Eating and drinking

All the hotels have good **restaurants**; **drinking** is on restaurant-and-bar strip Schlossstrasse.

La Bodega Schlossstr. 11 ☎03591/409 21, Ⓦwww.labodega-bautzen.de. A short menu of quality Spanish cuisine is prepared in this small, rather classy place, worth a visit for tapas and wines in a rear garden. Also has simple and bright Mediterranean-styled rooms upstairs (❸).

L'Ambiente Cnr Innere Lauenerstr. and Kesselstr. ☎03591/442 63. A café by day with a large terrace on Hauptmarkt, this segues from 5.30pm into an upmarket restaurant with quality Italian and Mediterranean cooking; mains average €17. Closed Sun.

Monchshof Burglehn 1 ☎03591/49 01 41. "A table in the Middle Ages" is the catchphrase of this jolly, themed restaurant: think recipes that date back to 1560, earthenware jugs, waiters in sackcloth and a barely legible menu of Gothic script. All good fun.

Wjelbik Kornstr. 7 ☎03591/420 60. Sorbish speciality restaurant behind the Dom, whose dishes include a "Sorbish Suite" of *Schweinebraten* with Bautzen mustard and horseradish from the Spreewald. A little touristy, but quality is consistently good and prices are reasonable.

Görlitz

"For many simply the most beautiful city in Germany" proclaims the marketing board, thanks to an accolade bestowed by the chairman of the German Foundation for the Protection of Historic Monuments. It's only just in Germany, though. The postwar redraw of the map shifted the German–Polish border onto the Neisse River, thereby cleaving **GÖRLITZ** in two. Perhaps that's apt for an Altstadt that is pure central Europe – it flourished on the east–west Via Regia route that linked Kiev to Santiago de Compostela, and in 1815 was amalgamated into Silesia, a definitively Central European province along the Oder River that took in slices of modern Poland and the Czech Republic. The GDR regime surveyed the town and slapped a preservation order on the entire Altstadt, though they seemed less fussed that the four thousand listed buildings were allowed to moulder. Post-reunification investment has re-energized the Altstadt, and Untermarkt is arguably the finest town square in East Germany: less a collection of buildings than a living Old Master, gorgeous at dusk. "At nightfall I long to be in Görlitz," Goethe once sighed. Now film directors have taken notice: Görlitz was Paris in Jackie Chan's *Eighty Days Around the World* (2004) and its historic streets featured in Kate Winslet flick *The Reader* (2009).

Arrival, information and accommodation

The **Hauptbahnhof** is a fair way southwest of the centre: to reach the historic core north take Berliner Strasse, then cross An der Frauenkirche and Marienplatz, to reach Steinstrasse then Obermarkt. The **tourist office** is at Obermarkt 32 (April–Oct Mon–Fri 9am–7pm, Sat & Sun 9am–6pm; Nov–March Mon–Fri 9am–6pm, Sat 9am–4pm; ☎03581/475 70, ⓦwww.goerlitz.de & ⓦwww .europastadt-goerlitz.de). Der Fahrrad Laden at Fischmarkt 4 **rents bikes** (Mon–Fri 9am–6pm, Sat 9am–2pm; ☎03581/41 07 27). **Internet** access is at I-Point Görlitz (Mon–Sat 2–10pm, Sun 3–10pm) one block north of the Bahnhof at Schulstrasse 7.

A good spread of **accommodation** provides a lot of bed for your bucks. An information point on Untermarkt at the top of Peterstrasse provides free telephone calls to hotels and pensions – invaluable if you arrive out of tourist office hours.

Börse Untermarkt 16 ☎03581/764 20, ⓦwww .boerse-goerlitz.de. Four-posters and restored parquet floors in a smart but unstuffy hotel created from the Baroque merchant's hall and with an unbeatable location on Untermarkt. For a splurge, "Luxury" class is worth the extra €20. As glam is its *Gästehaus im Flüsterbogen* (same contacts), beautifully furnished with antiques and modern flair in bathrooms; check-in is at *Börse*. ❹–❻

Herberge Zum Sechsten Gebot Untermarkt 22 ☎03581/41 12 45, ⓦwww.boerse-goerlitz.de. A tasteful contemporary cheapie from the hotel *Börse* crew, in a courtyard off Untermarkt. Check-in is at the reception of hotel *Börse* opposite. ❸

Picobello Pension Uferstr. 32 ☎03581/42 00 10, ⓦwww.picobello-pension.de. Large hostel-style pension on the riverbank 10min walk from Untermarkt – turn right at the bottom of Neissstrasse. Simple, but a bargain for the location and with facilities such as bike rental and a sauna. ❷

Silesia Biesnitzer Str. 11 ☎03581/421 40, ⓦwww .hotel-silesia.net. Hugely spacious mid-range accommodation – many rooms with balconies – in a grand old nineteenth-century place on a corner by the train station. Friendly staff, too. ❸–❹

Tuchmacher Peterstr. 8 ☎03581/473 10, ⓦwww.tuchmacher.de. Kate Winslet is in the guestbook of this prestigious address in a patrician's Renaissance town house; some rooms feature restored painted ceilings. Tasteful decor is classic modern, with warm tones of saffron and ruby to complement old wood. ❻

Zum Hothertor Grosse Wallstr. 1 ☎03581/66 11 00, ⓦwww.zum-hothertor.de. Simple en-suite rooms lifted by colourful linen in a great-value hotel created from a renovated Baroque house. Located by the river in the atmospheric Nikolaivorstadt area. ❷

The southern Altstadt and Obermarkt

Görlitz has its iconic buildings and museums, but more than most towns in east Germany, its Altstadt rewards those who stray down whichever lane looks interesting. While the town emerged unscathed from the war, the urban fabric is patchy outside of the centre and there's little to detain you on the route north from the Hauptbahnhof through a district created by rapid nineteenth-century expansion. On **An der Frauenkirche**, an Art Nouveau department store now of the Karstadt chain is worth a look for its hall with pillars clad in marble and Venetian-styled stairways that arch beneath a patterned glass dome. Beyond on Marienplatz, the **Dicke Turm** ("fat tower") is not the lighthouse it appears to be but a remnant of the town's medieval defences named for walls 5.5m thick. It stands guard before elongated square Obermarkt, whose Baroque looks are only marginally spoiled by the square's role as a glorified car park. The murky green **Dreifaltigkeitskirche** at its corner has expanded erratically over seven centuries to create an idiosyncratic musty interior, with a prize Gothic altar in the St Barbara Chapel that backs an elongated nave. Have a look diagonally opposite the street in Verrätergasse ("traitors' alley") for a plaque bearing the legend DVRT, an acronym for *Der verräterischen Rotte Tor* ("the treacherous gang's gate") that records the house in which cloth merchants plotted to topple the town council in 1527. The west end of Obermarkt is guarded by the **Reichenbacher Turm** (Tue, Wed & Sun 10am–5pm, Thurs–Sat 10am–6pm; €1.50), former gateway to the Altstadt and a crammer in architectural style: a squat fourteenth-century square tower sprouts into a round tower from a century later, onto which is added a Baroque cap. The highest defence in the medieval city, it has history displays that are the epitome of tedium and, from within the former garret of a watchkeeper at its summit, views over Obermarkt. Tickets are bought from the Kaisertrutz opposite (Tues–Sun 10am–5pm; €3.50, includes Reichenbacher Turm and Barockhaus; Ⓦwww.museum-goerlitz.de), a one-time cannon bastion that now holds cultural exhibitions of the Kulturhistorisches Museum Görlitz.

Untermarkt and Neissstrasse

All of Görlitz is, in essence, a prelude to **Untermarkt**. There can be few more handsome squares in Germany than that off the east end of Obermarkt, ringed by the residences of patrician merchants and divided by an "island" of solid Baroque body and Renaissance fizz. At the corner of link-street Brüderstrasse – no mean patricians' parade itself – is the **Rathaus**, expanded through the centuries so it boxes in the west side. The best block is the original, with a carved early Renaissance staircase and balcony from which the mayor addressed the populace. They say the knight that opens his mouth to mark the minutes on a Baroque clock was a marvel of its day. Untermarkt 22 around the corner is celebrated for its Flüsterbogen ("whisper arch") that transmits sounds around its Gothic span, and the Renaissance **Ratsapotheke** at no. 24 is unmissable for its spidery astrological charts. Both face former Baroque merchants' hall **Alte Börse**, now a hotel, at the back of the island and the sixteenth-century corner **Waage** (weigh house), its corbels carved into portraits of town dignitaries. The south flank beside the Rathaus, fronted by a Gothic colonnade, was the prestigious address of cloth merchants – so-called **Görlizter Hallhausen** because of their bright hall-like atriums in which to inspect cloth. The Schönhof at no.1, Germany's oldest private Renaissance house (1526), has been restored to house the **Schlesische Museum zu Görlitz** (Tues–Sun 10am–5pm; €4), a brisk spin through Silesian history and craftsmanship that rambles over several floors and two buildings – start at the top to follow displays chronologically. Pick up English-language notes from the reception.

Barockhaus at Neissstrasse 30 (Tues–Sun 10am–5pm; €2, combination ticket €3.50) is, perhaps, more instantly gratifying as no explanation is required for its re-creation of a Baroque courtyard mansion; a little shabby in places and some rooms marred by lino, but a passable collection of furnishings with a cabinet of Old Masters such as Dürer, Hans Holbein the Younger and Martin Schöngauer. Rear rooms pay homage to Jakob Böhme, a local-born sixteenth-century polymath and alchemist who straddled medieval mysticism and philosophy. Adjacent **Biblisches Haus** impresses for Bible scenes on its facade. Downhill is the river and Poland – take your passport if you cross a footbridge to former Görlitz suburb Zgorzelec.

The northern Altstadt and Heiliges Grab

Peterstrasse, punctuated intermittently by swaggering carved portals, tracks north off Untermarkt from the Ratsapotheke. Town houses hem in the **Peterskirche** at the street's end – it is only inside the five-nave church that you appreciate a scale that testifies to the town's wealth in the Middle Ages. Its pride and joy is the so-called Sun Organ that fills most of a rear wall with rosettes of pipes like sun beams. The early eighteenth-century instrument is the work of an Italian master, its 57 registers trump in concerts at noon and at weekends. West via Nikolaistrasse, the late-Gothic church **Nikolaikirche** (March Thurs–Sun noon–4pm; April–Oct Mon–Sat 11am–5pm; €1), refurbished in 1925 as an Expressionist war memorial, lies at the heart of the **Nikolaivorstadt**, an atmospheric former craftsmen's quarter outside the Altstadt's boundary. The hillside cemetery above is a Gothic horror fantasy – full of crumbling mausoleums – while Steinweg, which continues west from Nikolaistrasse, preserves a medieval streetscape.

A ten-minute walk further west via Steinweg takes you to the **Heiliges Grab** (April–Sept Mon–Sat 10am–6pm, Sun 11am–6pm; €1.50; English notes available). This intriguing site, commissioned by a fifteenth-century citizen Georg Emmerich, is the only complete medieval reproduction of the Holy Sepulchre of Jerusalem. The future mayor returned home from a pilgrimage to the Holy Land to build a replica from measurements he had taken on site; hearsay has it that the pilgrimage was either in thanks for the marriage to his sweetheart, the mayor's daughter, or in penance at having made her pregnant out of wedlock while a student in Leipzig. At the front is a simple two-storeyed chapel whose "crack" represents a legend that the Crucifixion took place on the grave of Adam – as graffiti from 1543 shows, it was a tourist attraction almost as soon as it opened. The Romanesque box topped with a Moorish pavilion behind is the tomb itself.

Eating and drinking

Dining in Görlitz divides neatly around **Untermarkt** – upmarket restaurants on it and offshoot Peterstrasse lean towards international cuisine, while pubs on **Neissstrasse** prepare cheaper traditional fodder. Keep an eye open for Silesian dishes such as *Schlesisches Himmelreich*, a "Silesian heaven" of pork loin with dried plums and apricots, usually with potato dumplings and a butter sauce.

Acanthus Untermarkt 22 ☏ 03581/66 18 10. Popular unpretentious place that's all about its location in a rambling complex of cellars and a rear garden that overlooks the river. Closed lunch Mon–Fri.

Bürgerstübl Neissstr. 27 ☏ 03581/87 95 79. Silesian specials such as *Schlesisches Himmelreich* and smoked ribs in a sweet and sour sauce in one of Görlitz's oldest inns, its decor a timewarp back a century or two.

Filetto Peterstr. 1 ☏ 03581/42 11 31. Romantic and rather classy little Italian with a small garden for summer; tasty steaks and modern pastas are good value at around €8. Closed lunch Mon–Fri.

Lucie Schulte Untermarkt 22 ☏ 03581/41 02 60. Modern glass-skinned place in a courtyard off the square that's smart but nicely laid-back in style. Its seasonal menus of light international dishes offer the finest cuisine in town. Eve only.

Verrandenmühle Hotherstr. 20 ☏ 03581/40 66 61. "The easternmost gastronomy in Germany" is one selling point. The other is a veranda that juts into the river, making this a popular choice for a booze-up in summer. Service can be a misnomer when busy.

Leipzig

"Leipzig is the place for me! 'Tis quite a little Paris; people there acquire a certain easy finish'd air." So mused Goethe in his epic *Faust*. The second city of Saxony is no French *grande dame* – indeed, it's not much of a looker despite efforts to patch up the damage of war. But nor is it as languid. After decades stuck in a socialist rut, **LEIPZIG** is back in the groove. The architectural prizes that remain have been scrubbed up, and glass-and-steel offices are appearing at lightning pace. No city in the former East Germany exudes such unbridled ambition, but then none has so firm a bedrock for its self-confidence. In autumn 1989, tens of thousands of Leipzigers took to the streets in the first peaceful protest against the communist regime. Their candles ignited the peaceful revolution that drew back the Iron Curtain and achieved what two decades of Ostpolitik wrangling had failed to deliver. Not bad for a city of just half-a-million people. It's seductive to believe that this was inspired by the humanist call-to-arms *Ode To Joy* that Schiller had penned here two centuries earlier. In fact, the demonstrations were simply another expression of Leipzig's get-up-and-go. Granted market privileges in 1165, it emerged as a rampantly commercial city, a dynamic free-thinking place that blossomed as a cultural centre to attract names such as Bach, Mendelssohn, Schumann, Wagner and, of course, Goethe as a law student. Even the GDR rulers cultivated the trade fairs, allowing the city to maintain its dialogue with the West when other cities were isolated. In recent decades the same energy has found an outlet through a contemporary arts scene that can hold its own against those in the larger metropolises, and a nightlife that is refined and riotous by turns.

Arrival, information and city transport

Leipzig's **Hauptbahnhof** lies at the northern edge of a ring road that encircles the Altstadt. A sight in its own right, the grand 1880s building from the golden age of rail is among the largest rail termini in Europe, whose hall doubles as a large shopping centre where DJs and bands get the weekend going on Friday evening. The **airport**, Leipzig-Halle (ⓦwww .leipzig-halle-airport.de) 18km north, is linked by the Flughafen Express and slower Regional Express trains. A taxi will cost around €30. If you arrive **by car**, the cheapest central parking is in open-air car parks on Querstrasse, one block east of Georgiring. The most reliable **taxi** rank is outside the Hauptbahnhof; to pre-book a cab try Funktaxi (ⓣ0341/48 84) or Löwentaxi (ⓣ0341/98 22 22). The **tourist information** centre (Mon–Fri: March–Oct 9.30am–6pm; Nov–Feb 10am–6pm; all year Sat 9.30am–4pm, Sun 9.30am–3pm; general ⓣ0341/710 42 55, accommodation ⓣ0341/710 42 75, ⓦwww.leipzig.de) is diagonally opposite the train station at Richard-Wagner-Strasse 1. Its **Leipzig Card** (1 day €8.90, 3 days €18.50) provides free travel on all city public transport and discounts on museum entry.

At present, all routes of the **public transport** system operated by LVB (single €2, day-card €5.20; ⓦwww.lvb.de) circuit the Altstadt, bar bus #89 through the centre. By 2010, an extended project to put an S-Bahn stop beneath the Markt should come to fruition. Most routes pass outside the Hauptbahnhof; other transport hubs are Augustusplatz east of the Altstadt and Wilhelm-Leuschner-Platz south. **Bike rental** is available from Zweirad Eckhardt (ⓣ0341/961 72 74) at Kurt-Schumacher-Strasse 4 on the west side of the Hauptbahnhof.

Accommodation

No surprise that a city which prides itself on trade fairs is geared towards expense accounts. Leipzig's stock of budget accommodation is limited. As always, the tourist office books accommodation, including **private rooms** (❷). One worth a special mention is *Meisterzimmer* (ⓣ0178/374 44 65, ⓦwww .meisterzimmer.de; ❷), an über-cool loft apartment among the art ateliers of the Spinnerei complex in Leipzig-Plagwitz, 5km west of the centre. The nearest **campsite**, lakeside *Camping Auensee* (ⓣ0341/465 16 00, ⓦwww.camping -auensee.de; cabins ❷), is in woods at Gustav-Esche-Strasse 51, 5km northwest of the centre; take tram #10 or #11 towards Wahren/Schkeuditz and alight at "Annaberger Strasse".

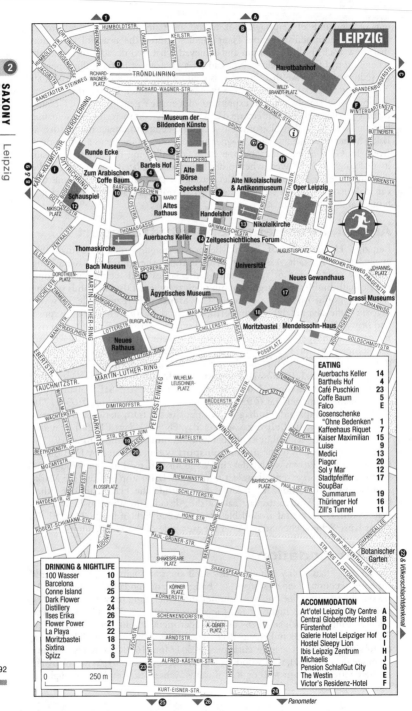

LEIPZIG

Hauptbahnhof

Museum der Bildenden Künste

Runde Ecke

Bartels Hof

Alte Börse

Zum Arabischen Coffe Baum

Speckshof

Alte Nikolaischule & Antikenmuseum

Oper Leipzig

Schauspiel

Altes Rathaus

Handelshof

Nikolaikirche

Thomaskirche

Auerbachs Keller

Zeitgeschichtliches Forum

Bach Museum

Universität

Ägyptisches Museum

Neues Gewandhaus

Grassi Museums

Neues Rathaus

Moritzbastei

Mendelssohn-Haus

Botanischer Garten

Panometer

EATING

Auerbachs Keller	14
Barthels Hof	4
Café Puschkin	23
Coffe Baum	5
Falco	E
Gosenschenke "Ohne Bedenken"	1
Kaffeehaus Riquet	7
Kaiser Maximilian	15
Luise	9
Medici	13
Piagor	20
Sol y Mar	12
Stadtpfeiffer	17
SoupBar Summarum	19
Thüringer Hof	16
Zill's Tunnel	11

DRINKING & NIGHTLIFE

100 Wasser	10
Barcelona	8
Conne Island	25
Dark Flower	2
Distillery	24
Ilses Erika	26
Flower Power	21
La Playa	22
Moritzbastei	18
Sixtina	3
Spizz	6

ACCOMMODATION

Art'otel Leipzig City Centre	A
Central Globetrotter Hostel	B
Fürstenhof	D
Galerie Hotel Leipziger Hof	C
Hostel Sleepy Lion	I
Ibis Leipzig Zentrum	H
Michaelis	J
Pension SchlafGut City	G
The Westin	E
Victor's Residenz-Hotel	F

0   250 m

& Völkerschlachtdenkmal

Hotels

Art'otel Leipzig City Centre Eutritzscher Str. 15
☏ 0341/30 38 40, ⓦ www.artotel-leipzig.com.
Leipzig's latest design hotel features a warmed-up
take on minimalism and artwork by local artists. A
10min walk north of the train station. ❺
Fürstenhof Tröndlinring 8 ☏ 0341/14 00,
ⓦ www.luxurycollection.com/fuerstenhof. Elegant
hotel in a patrician's mansion with a 200-year
tradition of seamless service. Decor in rooms
is surprisingly colourful, the grotto spa in the
basement is enjoyably kitsch, and there's a good
restaurant, *Villers* (eve only, closed Sun). ❼–❾
Galerie Hotel Leipziger Hof Hedwigstr. 1–3
☏ 0341/697 40, ⓦ www.leipziger-hof.de. One
of the city's more individual addresses thanks to
a gallery of artwork scattered throughout, some
paintings by major names of the Leipzig school.
En-suite rooms are comfy and there's a pleasant
restaurant and beer garden. ❹–❻
Ibis Leipzig Zentrum Brühl 69 ☏ 0341/218 60,
ⓦ www.ibishotel.com. The usual functional en-suite
rooms from the budget chain, worth considering for
its location in the north Altstadt. ❸
Michaelis Paul-Gruner-Str. 44 ☏ 0341/267 80,
ⓦ www.hotel-michaelis.de. The most appealing
address for the nightlife scene is this friendly small
hotel, which brings a designer eye to its spotless
modern en-suites. Good restaurant, too. ❺–❼
Pension SchlafGut City Brühl 64–66 ☏ 0341/211
09 02, ⓦ www.schlafgut-leipzig.de. Simple modern
one- to three-bed rooms in a central place that's
somewhere between hostel and budget hotel.
The cheapest accommodation shares amenities;
you can save more by forsaking extras such as
cleaning, a TV or breakfast. ❷
The Westin Gerberstr. 15 ☏ 0341/98 80,
ⓦ www.westin-leipzig.de. What looks like a dreary
GDR apartment block west of the train station is
actually a super-slick design hotel. Some rooms
boast astounding city views, and there is a
selection of very glam bars and restaurants that
optimize the building's space. ❺–❽
Victor's Residenz-Hotel Georgiring 13
☏ 0341/686 60, ⓦ www.victors-leipzig
.bestwestern.de. Reliable mid-range option of the
Best Western chain whose decor nods to the Art
Nouveau building. ❺–❼

Hostels

Central Globetrotter Hostel Kurt-Schumacher-Str.
41 ☏ 0341/149 89 60, ⓦ www.globetrotter-leipzig
.de. From the same owners as *Hostel Sleepy Lion*
and as colourful, with a useful location behind
the train station. Dorms up to eight beds, all with
shared bathrooms, some en-suite rooms. Dorms
€12.50–17, rooms ❷.
Hostel Sleepy Lion Käthe Kollwitz-Str. 3
☏ 0341/993 94 80, ⓦ www.hostel-leipzig.
de. Colourful, friendly place, well placed for the
nightlife on Gottschedstrasse. There's a good
common-room, and en-suite dorms that come
in three- to eight-bed varieties. Dorms €14–18,
rooms ❷.

The Nikolaikirche and around

The touchstone of modern history in Leipzig is the **Nikolaikirche** on Nikolaistrasse, whose sober early Gothic belies a theatrical interior, candy-coloured
Rococo, barely tempered by emergent Neoclassicism, with shaggy palm leaves
in place of Corinthian capitals. Its place in national history is as the wellspring of
the *Wende*. Monday services for peace held since 1982 (still going strong at 5pm)
assumed new significance in 1989 as refugees fled the GDR states. Party stooges
ordered to disrupt services paused instead to listen to sermons, then joined the
protests. Things came to a head after a brutal suppression of demonstrations
on October 7. A two-thousand-strong congregation filed out into the arms
of ten thousand sympathizers holding candles – the police were powerless, the
momentum unstoppable. A month later, the Berlin Wall fell; as one Stasi official
recalled later "We had been prepared for anything, but not prayers and candles."
On the church's north side, within the Alte Nikolaischule, a former church
school whose alumni include eighteenth-century philosopher Gottfried Leibniz
and Wagner, is the **Antikenmuseum** (Tues–Thurs, Sat & Sun noon–5pm; €2)
with a collection of first-rate antiquities. Highlights are a sculpted bronze mirror
circa 450 BC and its collection of Athenian vases.

You can cut a corner west through Specks Hof opposite. It is one of many
covered arcades that burrow through blocks in the central Altstadt, created to host
the city's trade fairs before they shifted out of town. This series of interconnecting

▲ The Nikolaikirche, Leipzig

courtyards has an embossed Art Nouveau bronze roof and fine tiles. The idea of its "fountain" is to rub the brass handles to set up resonance patterns in the bowl of water. You emerge diagonally opposite the **Zeitgeschichtliches Forum Leipzig** (Tues–Fri 9am–6pm, Sat & Sun 10am–6pm; free), on Grimmaische Strasse off Nikolaistrasse, a well-presented display that chronicles the rise and fall of the GDR from its response to the horror of the Nazi regime via communist kitsch and into contemporary politics. While you'll need English-language notes from the entrance desk to glean much about the exhibits, archive footage of GDR suppression of protest and the construction and destruction of the Berlin Wall packs a punch. Adjacent is Mädler-Passage, the Jugendstil doyenne of Leipzig's shopping arcades whose expensive boutiques would have been unthinkable in communist days. It also boasts literary connections – Goethe had Mephistopheles and Faust bamboozle a trio of ruffians with magic in its *Auerbachs Keller* (see p.198) before they rode away on a barrel, a scene commemorated in bronzes outside.

The Markt and around

The heart of the historic city is the **Markt**. Goethe, who knew Leipzig as a law student in the 1760s, strides from a plinth on Naschmarkt in front of the **Altes Börse**, a pleasingly tubby Baroque stock-exchange that doubles as a cultural centre. The adjacent Altes Rathaus is more bombastic – a walloping Renaissance structure that testifies to Leipzig's commercial clout and whose elongated length is said to have the longest inscription of any building anywhere. Long passed over as the town hall, it now contains the **Stadtgeschichtliches Museum Leipzig** (Tues–Sun 10am–6pm; €4, free first Tues of month), a potted run through early city history, and owns the only portrait of Johann Sebastian Bach painted in his lifetime. It's worth a visit for a magnificent 50m Festsaal lined with oils of assorted mayors. Temporary exhibitions are displayed in the Neubau cube on its north side (same times; €3, free first Tues of month). The Markt itself is on the west side of the Altes Rathaus, the venue of the trade fairs that shored up Leipzig's prosperity as early as 1190.

Off its west side, via bar-and-restaurant strip Barfussgässchen, a Baroque portal of a cherub who proffers a cup to an Ottoman Turk under a coffee tree announces Europe's oldest coffee shop, **Zum Arabischen Coffe Baum** (1711). The carving is said to have been donated by Augustus the Strong in thanks for the hospitality he had received from the landlady. That the Saxony Elector himself visited testifies to the coffee craze that swept Saxony from the late seventeenth century, even knocking beer off its pedestal as the favourite beverage. A top-floor museum (daily 11am–7pm; free) spins through European coffee culture, and you can sup in historic rooms like former visitors Bach, Goethe, Wagner and Schumann. The two leaders of a divided Germany, Helmut Kohl and Lothar de Maizière, met here to discuss reunification.

Ten minutes' walk beyond, at the fringe of the Altstadt at Dittrichring 24, is the **Runde Ecke**, former Leipzig headquarters of GDR secret police, the Stasi. Captured by citizens on December 4, 1989, the building was made famous by news footage of peaceful protesters placing candles on its steps. Out of respect for a too-recent past, it is preserved as a museum (daily 10am–6pm; free; English notes available), where surveillance equipment remains in drab rooms and exhibits document the regime's oppression and paranoia – citizens rescued over six miles of documents from the shredder despite the pulping of files throughout November.

Museum der bildenden Künste and around

Sachsenplatz north of the Markt epitomes modern Leipzig's go-ahead ambitions: communist eyesores have been replaced by a concrete-and-steel cube sheathed in glass to house the excellent **Museum der bildenden Künste** (Museum of Fine Arts; Tues, Thurs–Sun 10am–6pm, Wed noon–8pm; €5, free second Wed in month; ⓦ www.mdbk.de). Pure minimalism within – all white walls, pale wood and concrete – it makes an excellent gallery for Old Masters to shine in. If you're pressed for time seek out the big guns from the German late Middle Ages – Hamburg's Meister Francke, Cranach, whose sexual nymphs titillate under the pretence of Renaissance style, and Hans Baldung – and enjoyable works by Rubens and Hals, notably the latter's louche *Mulatto*, as well as a luminous seascape by Romantic Caspar David Friedrich. You're unlikely to miss Max Klinger's colossal marble sculpture of Beethoven, a swaggering work that sees the composer enthroned like a god, nor a soul-searing sculpture of *The Damned* by Dresden's Baroque master-sculptor, Balthasar Permoser. Max Beckmann gets a room to himself among a good oeuvre of Expressionist works, as does Neo Rauch, a figurehead of the New Leipzig School whose large-format works are inspired by the communist socialist–realist aesthetic.

The tangerine-and-cream **Romanus Haus** opposite on Katharinenstrasse is the finest of the city's Baroque mansions. It was named after its mayor owner, Franz Conrad Romanus, a favourite of Elector Augustus the Strong, who modernized the city and dug its western canals. Unfortunately he also had light fingers – arrested for embezzlement, he ended his days incarcerated in the Königstein.

South of the Markt

Off the southwest corner of the Markt rises the Gothic **Thomaskirche** (tower €2). Its place in the classical music canon is as the church where Johann Sebastian Bach served as cantor for his last 27 years, nearly half the life of a composer who had previously flitted around courts of Thuringia. He was interred in the graveyard in 1750. Major renovation of the church in the 1880s provided an excuse to exhume his remains and bring some scientific discipline to a long-standing debate about Bach's appearance. Measurements of the skeleton were used to create the bronze (1894) outside the church – the out-turned pocket is said to be a reference to his poor finances. The sculpture was paid for by Mendelssohn, then director of Leipzig's acclaimed Gewandhaus Orchester and who did much to rehabilitate a then underrated composer. He lies interred beneath a plaque in the chancel, and the celebrated boys' choir, the Thomanererchor, sings works from his vast canon in services (Fri 6pm, Sat 3pm), and in weekend concerts, often with the Gewandhaus Orchester. The **Bachmuseum** opposite (daily 11am–6pm; €4) is due to reopen following renovation at the end of 2009, with visual mementoes of the composer's Leipzig years – manuscripts, portraits and instruments of his time – soundtracked by snatches of contemporary works. A small display (same times; free) is in the foyer in the interim.

South of the church, at Burgstrasse 21, the **Ägyptisches Museum** (Tues–Sat 1–5pm, Sun 10am–3pm; €2) displays the university's collection of Egyptian antiquities which spans four millennia up to 600 AD, its highlight a carved cedarwood coffin with some unfinished reliefs. Nearby is the behemoth **Neues Rathaus**, an enjoyably overblown piece of imperial architecture of the late 1800s. Subtle it is not – monstrous in scale and absurd in revivalist architecture that even alludes to Venice's Bridge of Sighs. The foyer's staircase (Mon–Fri 8am–4.30pm; free) is just as preposterous.

The New Leipzig School: the Galerie für Zeitgenössische Kunst, Spinnerei and Tapetenwerk

Ten minutes' walk southwest from the Neues Rathaus across the ring road, near the university arts departments, a gutted villa at Karl-Tauchnitz-Strasse 11 serves as the **Galerie für Zeitgenössische Kunst** (Gallery of Contemporary Arts; Tues–Sun noon–7pm; €5, free Wed; ⓦwww.gfzk.de), with temporary exhibitions of post-1945, largely avant-garde abstract artwork that didn't square with the GDR aesthetic. The gallery's second space is adjacent glass-walled pavilion GfZK-2 (same times; prices vary); home, too, to a hip café redesigned by a local artist every couple of years. The gallery is one showcase of contemporary arts of the New Leipzig School whose pinnacle is arguably at the excellent **Spinnerei** art-factory (Tues–Sat 11am–6pm; free; ⓦwww.spinnerei.de). The one-time cotton-yarn manufacturing centre provides workshop space for over a hundred artists (including Neo Rauch) whose work is displayed in its thirteen galleries; the first, Eigen + Art (ⓦwww.eigen-art.com) in the former steam hall, remains one of the best. If you want to tap into the energy of Leipzig's artistic dynamo this is your place. The centre is in a rapidly gentrifying former industrial area 4km west of the GfZK complex at Spinnereistrasse 7, near Leipzig-Plagwitz S-Bahn station. While you're in the area, you could head three streets north to Lützner Strasse 91 (Leipzig-Lindenau S-Bahn) for the **Tapetenwerk** (Tues–Fri 2–6pm, Sat noon–5pm; free; ⓦwww.tapetenwerk.de), a five-gallery space created in a former wallpaper factory. Full listings of the exhibitions in over forty modern art galleries are in booklet *Kunstindex.Leipzig* and leaflet *Kunst in Leipzig* (also at ⓦwww.kunstinleipzig.de), available at the tourist office and galleries.

Augustusplatz and around

Nowhere in central Leipzig is so redolent of the GDR aesthetic as Augustusplatz at the eastern edge of the Altstadt. On either side is the regime's severe **Oper Leipzig** opera house to the north and the glass-walled **Neues Gewandhaus** concert hall, inaugurated in 1981 to the south. The enormous socialist-realist painting in its foyer was by a regime-approved Leipzig university artist, Sighard Gille. After reunification there was considerable debate about whether to keep GDR skyscraper the **Panorama Tower** that powers up at its side; that the silver-grey tricorn tower eradicated historic university edifices when it was built in 1970 did little to endear it to locals. Today you can zip up to the 29th floor for a viewing platform (9am–11pm; €2) and a bar and restaurant. The latest addition to the square by 2010 will be a striking glass university building adjacent, which will retain a 33-tonne relief of Marx from an unloved Soviet-style building.

The Grassi museums

The doyenne of city museums is the three collections of **Museen im Grassi**, presented in their entirety since 2008 following a six-year renovation of the complex wedged into the corner of Täubchenweg and Prager Strasse, 400m east of Augustusplatz. By far the finest museum is the two-millennia display of decorative arts in the **Museum für Angewandte Kunst** (Museum of Applied Arts; Tues–Sun 10am–6pm; €5, combination ticket €12; ⓦ www.grassimuseum .de). Refurbishment has brought innovative presentation to one of the richest collections of its type in Europe, ordered within permanent exhibitions themed as "Antiques to Historicism", "Asian Art" and "Art Nouveau to the present". You could lose several hours among over two thousand objects on display: starting at early Roman items, browsing through the treasures of the Leipzig council, and lingering in highlights such as a cabinet room of Italian Renaissance majolica ceramics or the so called Roman Hall, whose panels of painted ruins – the Romantic concept of beauty through decay – were rescued from a now-demolished palace near Leipzig, Schloss Eythla. Modern objects include works by the big guns of twentieth-century design such as Mies van der Rohe. The opposite wing of the complex houses the **Museum für Völkerkunde** (Musem of Ethnology; same times; €4), whose displays roam across Asia, Africa, America, Australia and Oceania – if you're pushed for time, make a beeline for Northeast Asia with one of only nine Kurile-Ainu feather dresses in the world, an eye-catching village complex built by craftsmen from the Gujarat region of India, or a North African Bedouin tent. The five thousand instruments on show in the **Museum für Musikinstrumente** (same times; €4), among them what is said to be the world's oldest piano (1726), is small beer by comparison even if a "sound laboratory" entertains.

South of the centre

A couple of sights warrant a trip outside the city centre. The closest, around 4km due south of Augustusplatz at Richard-Lehmann-Strasse 114, is the **Panometer** (Tues–Fri 9am–7pm, Sat & Sun 10am–8pm; €9; ⓦ www.panometer.de). It seems apt that artist and architect Yadegar Asisi has brought a city with a modern artistic bent what is claimed to be the world's largest panoramic painting, which wraps around the inside of a brick gasworks. The 360-degree panorama – over 100m long and 30m high – changes every fifteen months: past works have transported visitors to Everest and ancient Rome; the destination from April 2009 will be the Amazon rainforest. Take trams #9 or #16 to Richard-Lehmann-Strasse.

Hard to believe from the surrounding suburbs, but in 1813, the area witnessed the Battle of Nations, the defining clash of European superpowers that pitted the combined might of the Prussian, Austrian and Russian forces against the all-conquering army of Napoleon. The centenary of victory over the French army, which had hitherto romped unopposed all the way south to Croatia, was commemorated by the **Völkerschlachtdenkmal** (daily: April–Oct 10am–6pm; Nov–March 10am–4pm; €5, combination ticket €7; ⓦwww .voelkerschlachtdenkmal.de), a twenty-minute walk east of the Panometer on Richard-Lehmann-Strasse (or tram #15 to "Völkerschlachtdenkmal"), not far from where the diminutive French emperor issued the orders that lost the battle and, ultimately, saw him exiled on Elba. It's a colossus of a war memorial to the 54,000 allied dead, a concrete-and-granite construction 91m high, unyielding in style and with muscular 10m knights as guards of honour in the crypt. A lookout platform offers views, and at its base, the **Forum 1813** museum (same times; €3) provides context to the battle.

Eating

Leipzig's eating areas split neatly into three districts. Smartest and most central is **Drallewatsch**, centred on Barfüssgässchen and Kleine Fleischergasse west of the Markt. Chock-a-block with restaurants and bars, it takes on a Mediterranean buzz in summer. Less touristy are the **Schauspielviertel** along the Gottschedstrasse west of the Thomaskirche, a laid-back strip that woos a style-conscious crowd of late-twenty- and thirty-somethings. More local still is the attitude-free **Südmeile** district, around 2km south of the centre on Karl-Liebknecht-Strasse (tram #10 or #11), with a strip of alternative bars and multiethnic restaurants.

Restaurants

Auerbachs Keller Grimmaische Str. 2 (Mädler-Passage) ☏0341/21 61 00. A sixteenth-century tavern immortalized in Goethe's *Faust* – turn-of-the-twentieth-century murals celebrate the claim to fame. Touristy, of course, but the menu of traditional and regional food is upmarket.

Barthels Hof Hainstr. 1 ☏0341/14 13 10. Traditional Saxony dishes prepared in this perennially popular courtyard restaurant off the Markt. There are three traditional dining rooms to choose from in the sixteenth-century building.

Falco At *The Westin*, Gerberstr. 15 ☏0341/988 27 27. Gourmets acclaim the international cooking here – one German gourmet guide named it restaurant of the year in 2007. The hotel also has a first-class Japanese restaurant, *Yamoto*, while its sophisticated *Panorama* bar is worth a visit for both views and metropolitan glamour. *Falco* eve only Tues–Sat.

Gosenschenke "Ohne Bedenken" Menckerstr. 5, Leipzig-Gohlis ☏0341/566 23 60. A nineteenth-century *Gaststätte* 1km north of the centre that's worth the effort for the best beer garden in Leipzig as much as for its historic rooms and rich Gose beer, a local brew produced to a 1750s recipe. Take tram #12 to Gohliser Str. Closed Mon–Fri lunch.

Kaiser Maximilian Neumarkt 9–19 ☏0341/35 53 33 33. Sophisticated cellar restaurant with modern art on the walls and an older expense-account clientele. The menu is modern Italian and French-Mediterranean; mains average €20. Closed Sun Nov–April.

Medici Nikolaikirchhof 5 ☏0341/211 38 78. Sophisticated central Italian restaurant with a touch of industrial chic to its stylish modern dining room. Mains such as pike-perch on a bed of fennel with chilli-saffron broth are around €20, menus cost around €44. Closed Sun.

Piagor Münzgasse 3 ☏0341/149 47 78. Funky, modern bistro-style place 5min south of the Neues Rathaus whose laid-back vibe belies excellent modern German cuisine. Closed lunch Sat & Sun.

Stadtpfeiffer Augustusplatz 8 (in Gewandhaus) ☏0341/217 89 20. First-class modern cuisine that changes with the seasons and with faultless service in Leipzig's one-starred gourmet address; à la carte mains average €30–35, menus cost €88–108. Dinner only, closed Sun & Mon and all July & Aug.

Thüringer Hof Burgstr. 19 ☏0341/994 49 99. Good-value solid stuff such as Saxonian *Sauerbraten* with red cabbage and apple or lamb shoulder in rosemary-cream sauce, in a large beer hall.

Zill's Tunnel Barfüssgässchen 9 ☏0341/960 20 78. Today's restaurant, the current incarnation of a popular restaurant from 1841, now spreads over several levels between a tunnel-like cellar and a formal top-floor wine restaurant. The traditional regional cuisine is the same on each.

Cafés and cheap eats

Café Puschkin Karl-Liebknecht-Str. 74. A funky café-bar at the heart of the Südmeile scene: breakfasts till 4pm Mon–Sat, spuds and pasta in vast portions. Student heaven.

Coffe Baum Kleine Fleischergasse 4. A Leipzig institution frequented by Bach, Goethe and now almost every tourist to Leipzig. The various floors cover most bases: there are fine flavours such as pheasant with a nut crust in pricey first-floor restaurant *Lusatia* (closed Sun); light meals are served in *Wiener Café* and bistro-style *Café Français*.

Kaffeehaus Riquet Schuhmachergässchen 1. Smart Vienna-style coffee house that's worth a visit for an Art Nouveau exterior as much as its cakes and light lunches of salmon and chicken.

Luise Cnr Gottschedstr. and Bosestr. Always-busy airy café-bar whose laid-back cool is beloved by a savvy thirty-something crowd, especially in summer. The bistro-style menu prepares gourmet burgers and pastas.

Sol y Mar Gottschedstr. 4. Ibiza-esque chill-out lounge bar–restaurant with illuminated chiffon drapes, bed seats and a soundtrack of mellow house beats. The global menu ranges from dim sum to beef carpaccio.

SoupBar Summarum Münzgasse 5. Eight flavours of home-made soup – from the usuals to exotic flavours such as vanilla with forest berries – prepared fresh each day at bargain prices. Mon–Fri from 11am, Sat from 5pm.

Drinking and nightlife

Leipzig has long had a decent **bar scene**. After three years of student living, Goethe came to the conclusion that "in Leipzig one burns out as quickly as a bad torch". The **Schauspielviertel** west of the Thomaskirche is the hangout of choice for a stylish thirty-something crew. The city's alternative scene is the student-friendly **Südmeile**, around 2km south of the centre on Karl-Liebknecht-Strasse (tram #10 or #11) and home to more grungy boozing and the city's best nightclubs. That said, central student bar *Moritzbastei* is always worth checking out for gigs and weekend clubs.

Bars

100 Wasser Barfussgässchen 15. A bright explosion of colour like being inside a Kandinsky painting in a futuristic bar for older style-slaves – think Armani and sunglasses.

Barcelona Gottschedstr. 12. Intimate metropolitan-style bar with sensual ruby-red walls and a hip late-twenties crowd. There's a superb Spanish wine list and tapas, and a buzzy rear garden that rocks in summer.

Flower Power Riemannstr. 9. Psychedelic little bar-club in the Südmeile with booze-fuelled parties of super-solid sounds from the Sixties to the Eighties – best at weekends in the wee hours.

La Playa Altes Messegelände ⓦ www.beach-club-leipzig.de. With the help of potted palms, loungers, a pool, cocktails and a lot of imported sand, beach cool comes to the old trade-fair site southeast of the centre near the Völkerschlachtdenkmal: take tram #15 or #2 to "Altes Messegelände". Closed Oct–April.

Moritzbastei Universitätsstr. 9 ⓦ www.moritzbastei.de. A multipurpose bastion of student nightlife ever since students dug out the former city bastion in the 1970s. Bars and gig- and club-venues are within a warren of cellars. *Café Barbakane* in a well-like cocoon is a good central spot for Sunday brunch. Keep an eye open for outdoor cinema and arts in summer.

Sixtina Katharinenstr. 13. Absinthe and Goths in a dark bolthole opposite the Museum der bildenden Künste; a focus of doom-laden fun for the Wave-Gotik-Treffen goth-fest (see p.200).

Spizz Markt 9 ⓦ www.spizz.org. Terraces that straddle the Markt and Barfüssgässchen are prime position to people-watch and be watched in a rather posey central café-bar favoured by a stylish middle-aged set.

Clubs

Conne Island Koburger Str. 3 ⓦ www.conne-island.de. Hardcore, punk, drum n bass and hip-hop several times a week in a grungy (sub)cultural centre in the Leipzig-Connewitz district at the far end of alternative strip Karl-Liebknecht-Strasse. Also hosts gigs – watch out for kamikaze stage-divers.

Dark Flower Hainstr. 12–14 ⓦ www.darkflower.de. The goth and darkcore sister of retro club *Flower Power* (see above), which occasionally strays into doom-pop such as Depeche Mode and alt-rock.

Distillery Kurt-Eisner-Str. 108, cnr Lösinger Str. ⓦ www.distillery.de. Though house and techno are the mainstays, this place off the Südmeile provides a mash-up of electro, reggae, dancehall and old-skool funk and whatever else its DJs fancy.

Ilses Erika Haus der Demokratie, Bernhard-Göring-Str. 152 ⓦ www.ilseserika.de. One block east of the Südmeile scene, this attitude-free mainstay of student life hosts a regular programme of alternative clubs in its cellar venue, including midweekers, plus sweaty gigs.

Entertainment and live music

Local publication *kreuzer* (€2) is the pick of the newsstand listings magazines; freesheets *Blitz* and *Fritz* stocked in bars and the tourist office provide a brief rundown of what's on. The tourist office operates a ticket desk, and a commercial outlet is in bookshop Hugendubel at Peterstrasse 12–14 (Mon–Sat 9.30am–8pm; ☎0341/980 00 98). The city's **classical music** tradition is second to none thanks to Bach's boys' choir the Thomanenerchor and the world-class Gewandhaus Orchester. The pair often combine for concerts in the Thomaskirche. Other venues for classical music include the Bach-Museum's Bosehaus, and the Völkerschlachtdenkmal, whose crypt is renowned for superb acoustics.

Live music

naTo Karl-Liebknecht-Str. 48 ⓦwww.nato-leipzig .de. A focus of the city's alternative scene whose manifesto of "Art + communication" translates into gigs of indie, alt-folk and jazz, including international touring acts. It also hosts theatre, cabaret and regular art-house cinema.

Spizz Markt 9 ⓦwww.spizz.org. Jazz and boogie plus weekend jazz-funk clubbing for an older crowd in the heart of the Altstadt.

Werk II Kochstr. 132 ⓦwww.werk-2.de. Another Südmeile alternative cultural centre, this at the bottom of Karl-Liebknecht–Strasse in a renovated factory that hosts major German indie and punk acts, plus occasional touring international names several times a week.

Theatre and classical music

Krystallpalast Varieté Magazingasse 4 ☎0341/140 66 10, ⓦwww.krystallpalast.de.

"New vaudeville" in Leipzig's premier variety venue whose tradition of acrobats and jugglers, chanson and comedy dates back to the 1880s. Located in the Altstadt in a passage off Universitätsstr.

Neues Gewandhaus Augustusplatz 8 ☎0341/127 02 80, ⓦwww.gewandhaus.de. The home of the acclaimed Gewandhaus Orchester, also with a more intimate chamber music venue, the Mendelssohn-Saal.

Oper Leipzig Augustusplatz 12 ☎0341/126 11 15, ⓦwww.oper-leipzig.de. Alongside classic opera of the classical-music canon are contemporary works, plus a highly regarded ballet company and a crowd-pleaser showbiz musical a few times a month.

Schauspiel Bosestr. 1 ☎0341/126 81 68, ⓦwww.schauspiel-leipzig.de. The city's leading dramatic stage also serves as a front-of-house for associated contemporary venue Skala (☎0341/126 84 75) at Gottschedstr. 16.

Listings

Books and media Bookshop Hugendubel at Peterstr. 12–14 stocks foreign-language titles and some international press. Newsagent Ludwig on the upper floor of the Hauptbahnhof shopping arcade has up-to-date international media.

Car rental Unless stated, all the major companies maintain bureaux in the Hauptbahnhof and at the airport: Hertz ☎0341/477 37 12; Europcar, Wintergartenstr 2 (beside Hauptbahnhof) ☎0341/14 11 60; SIXT ☎1805/25 25 25; Avis ☎0341/961 14 00.

Cinema Commercial multi-screen CineStar (ⓦwww.cinestar.de) is on Burgplatz. Rep' cinema is at Kinobar Prager Frühling (ⓦwww.kinobar -leipzig.de) in the Haus der Demokratie, Bernhard-Göring-Str. 152.

Festivals All about the music: Europe's largest pub crawl, music festival Leipziger Honky Tonk, does the rounds of 100 boozers one Saturday in May; over Whitsun (first weekend in June or last in May),

25,000 Goths gather for the Wave-Gotik-Treffen (ⓦwww.wave-gotik-treffen.de), the world's largest Goth doom-fest; and week-long Bachfest (ⓦwww .bach-leipzig.de) is in the middle of June.

Internet Free access for up to 20min is available on the top floor of bookshop Lehmanns (Mon–Sat 9.30am–8pm), at the corner of Grimmaische Str. and Nikolaistr. Otherwise try: Internet & Call Shop, Nikolaistr. 40 (Mon–Sat 10am–11pm, Sun 11am–10pm), or Intertel Café, Brühl 64–66 (Dussmann Passage; daily 10am–10pm).

Laundry Schnell & Sauber, Dresdner Str. 19 (daily 6am–midnight); *Maga Pon* laundry and hip café-bar, Gottschedstr. 11 (from 9am).

Markets On the first Sat of the month, platform 24 of the Hauptbahnhof disappears beneath the stalls of an antique and flea market.

Post office Augustusplatz 2 (Mon–Fri 9am–8pm, Sat 9am–3pm); Hauptbahnhof (Mon–Sat 8am–10pm, Sun 11am–7pm).

Watersports The Weisse Elster and Karl-Heine-Kanal canals in parkland west of the city are a pleasant spot to lose a sunny afternoon. Bootshaus Klingerweg (April–Oct; ☎0341/480 65 45, ⓦwww.kanu-leipzig.de) at Klingerweg 2 (tram #11 or #12 to 'Clara-Zatkin-Park') has rental, or gondola excursions are available through *Da Vito* restaurant (Nonnenstr. 1b ☎0341/480 26 26, ⓦwww.da-vito-leipzig.de; €60 per hr for up to 5 people). For more high-octane stuff there's Kanu Wildwasser-Terrasse (11 May–Oct Wed 4–8pm, Fri 3–8pm, Sat noon–6pm, Sun 10am–6pm; ☎034297/14 33 80, ⓦwww.kanupark-markkleeberg.com), Germany's premier whitewater canoeing and rafting facility. One shot around a 270m section of artificial rapids by kayak costs €15, two rafting trips are €37; reservations required. It's in the Kanupark am Markkleeberger See, just beyond the city's south limits; take the Leipzig-Südost exit off the A38. A taxi will cost around €25.

Colditz

No matter that the pretty provincial town provided prized white clay for the Baroque china of Saxony Elector Augustus the Strong. Never mind the Schloss's origins as a Renaissance palace of the state's ruling House of Wettin. **COLDITZ**, 50km southeast of Leipzig, is inextricably linked in British minds with high-security POW camp Oflag IVC in Schloss Colditz (daily: April–Oct 10am–5pm, 1hr 30min tours in English 10.30am, 1pm & 3pm; Nov–March 10am–4pm, tours 11am & 2.30pm; €6; ⓦwww.schloss-colditz.com). Mention it to most Germans and you'll be met with a blank look. The most famous of all German POW camps, popularized first in a book by former inmate Major Pat Reid, *The Colditz Story*, then a film of the same name, looks the part. It stands on a high bluff above the town and probably would have been as secure as the Nazis believed were it not for the ingenuity of its inmates, most of them incarcerated here following their recapture after escapes from other camps. Wooden sewing machines manufactured fake German uniforms, forgers produced identification papers and banknotes. More astonishing were those plans that were never used: a glider built of wood and bedsheets, or a 44m tunnel dug by French prisoners over eight months in 1941–42 – they were just 14m short when it was discovered beneath the Schlosskapelle. Of the three hundred escape attempts, over a third were made by the British, who scored eleven home-runs. French escapees boasted an impressive hundred-percent record for their twelve attempts. Castle tours focus on the war history and permit a look at the French tunnel alongside documents and photographs in a **Fluchtmuseum** (Escape Museum).

One wing has been renovated as a **youth hostel** (☎0351/494 22 11, ⓦwww.djh-sachsen.de; dorms €18.90/21.90) – as managers joke, "We let you out in the morning." **Bus** #690 goes direct to Colditz from Leipzig Hauptbahnhof (4–5 daily; 1hr 30min) or you can catch a more frequent **train** to Grossbothen and change on to bus #619 for Colditz. The Schloss is unmissable above the town. The **tourist office** (April–Oct daily 10am–5pm; Nov–March Mon–Fri 10am–4pm; ☎034381/435 19, ⓦwww.colditz.de) is in the Rathaus on the Markt. It can advise on some pleasant country walks and boat rental to make a day of it.

Chemnitz and around

CHEMNITZ (pronounced "kemnitz") is a curio after Leipzig. When the GDR regime wanted to create its own outpost of Stalinist Russia to celebrate Karl Marx's seventieth birthday in 1953, it turned to Saxony's third-largest city, probably inspired by an industrial heritage that had earned it the nickname of a

"Saxon Manchester". In places, a city known for four decades as Karl-Marx-Stadt is a Soviet-style throwback that's as bizarre as it is controversial. Even reunification brought its own problems in the form of depopulation, although award-winning recent investment has reversed the trend and revived the city centre. From a tourist's point of view this makes Chemnitz a glimpse at a Soviet past that's all but absent from Leipzig, to add to the appeal of its three galleries and a day-trip east to **Schloss Augustusburg**.

Arrival, information and accommodation

Chemnitz's **Hauptbahnhof**, on the Dresden and Leipzig lines, is a few hundred metres northeast of the centre. The **tourist office** (Mon–Fri 9am–7pm, Sat 9am–4pm, Sun 10am–4pm; ☎0371/69 06 80, ⓦwww.chemnitz-tourismus.de) in the centre at Markt 1 is your best source of budget private accommodation (❶–❷), though most is in the suburbs.

Chemnitzer Hof Theaterplatz 4 ☎0371/68 40, ⓦwww.guennewig.de. The most appealing address in the centre is this upmarket Bauhaus-styled hotel beside the Kunstsammlungen with restored Thirties public areas and comfortable modern rooms. ❺–❻
DJH Chemnitz Augustusburger Str. 369 ☎0371/713 31, ⓦwww.jugendherberge-sachsen .de. The youth hostel is in a large house set in fields 2.5km east of the centre; buses to Augustusburg stop outside. Dorms from €17.40.
Mercure Kongress Brückenstr. 19 ☎0371/68 30, ⓦwww.mercure.com. Large, central three-star

business hotel in a refurbished tower opposite the Karl-Marx-Monument – nothing fancy, but a good, solid central option. ❸–❺
Seaside Residenz Bernsdorfer Str. 2 ☎0371/355 10, ⓦwww.residenzhotelchemnitz .de. Chemnitz's only four-star is in a GDR-era tower block 1km south of the centre opposite Bahnhof Chemnitz-Süd. Notwithstanding a refurb, there's an unintentionally retro vibe to room decor; free internet and DVD players for business class. ❸–❺

The Town

There's no escaping the communist past if you arrive by train. You emerge from the Hauptbahnhof onto north–south axis Strasse der Nationen, a processional boulevard down which grim socialist tenement blocks march. It leads to the centre past Theaterplatz on the right-hand side, where the **Kunstsammlungen Chemnitz** (Tues–Fri noon–7pm, Sat & Sun 11am–7pm; €7 or €12 combination ticket with Museum Gunzenhauser) displays art that spans from German Romantics such as Caspar David Friedrich to Expressionists of the Die Brücke group, notably a large collection of local son Karl Schmidt-Rottluff. The town's iconic relic of communism is the **Karl-Marx-Monument** at the junction of Brückenstrasse, a 7m statue cast by a Russian sculptor, Lew Kerbel. The god-sized bust fixes an unswerving glare at the city centre above the *Communist Manifesto* exhortation for "Working men of all countries, unite!" After reunification the town council mooted removing it, after over three-quarters of the population voted to revert from the city's communist moniker, Karl-Marx-Stadt, to the original Chemnitz. Instead, it was retained as a testament to the past, to the chagrin of some locals. Actually, it fits more easily into the streetscape than the medieval Rote Turm defence tower opposite.

Beyond lies the Markt, pedestrianized heart of the Altstadt whose restoration won Chemnitz a 2006 European award for urban renewal – its Galerie Kaufhof is a cathedral to capitalism unthinkable in the 1970s. The glass-skinned department store faces the Gothic **Altes Rathaus**, fronted by a carved Renaissance portal and conjoined on its right-hand side to the Art Nouveau **Neues Rathaus**. The Gothic Jakobikirche behind has also been refurbished. Across Bahnhofstrasse, behind the Galerie Kaufhof, courtyard department store DAStietz has enjoyed a new lease of life as a cultural centre with two museums: the **Neue Sächsische Galerie** (daily 10am–6pm, Wed till 8pm; €2, free Sun; www.neue-saechsische-galerie.de), with rotating displays of 12,000 postwar artworks from Saxony; and child-friendly natural history centre the **Museum für Naturkunde** (Mon, Tues, Thurs & Fri 10am–8pm, Sat & Sun 10am–6pm; €4). Arguably the most intriguing exhibit is free – a copse of tree trunks in the foyer that is estimated to have been fossilized in a volcanic eruption in the area 290 million years ago.

Newest and finest of the quota of galleries is **Museum Gunzenhauser** (same times & prices as Kunstsammlungen Chemnitz) on Zwickauer Strasse southeast. Its classic Modernist collection picks up the baton from its sister museum with more Expressionism – neo-primitive works of Die Brücke and Der Blaue Reiter artists such as Kirchner and Russian-born Alexej von Jawlensky, who edges from the colour blocks of Gaugin towards the boundary of abstraction – and with its first floor showing abstract works. All is a prelude to the world's largest collection of Otto Dix, leading light of the anti-Expressionist New Objectivity movement, who was seared by his experiences in the trenches of World War I and whose cynical and often comically grotesque images of 1920s Germany fell foul of the Nazis. He never lost that bite – outwardly tamer, later works are bitter allegories of suffering.

Two kilometres north of the centre, across the river in an old-world pocket that the communists overlooked, is a Renaissance **Schloss** of Saxony Electors, with a so-so local history museum (Tues–Fri 1–7pm, Sat noon–9pm, Sun 10am–6pm; €3) and a weighty Schlosskirche with a medieval scourging pillar. The same distance south from the centre, at Parkstrasse 58, **Villa Esche** (Wed & Fri–Sun 10am–6pm, free), is an immaculately restored industrialist's residence created – and furnished – by Art Nouveau pioneer Henry van de Velde.

Eating and nightlife

Restaurants are gathered around the Markt and in the charming historic Schlossviertel at the north tip of the Schlossteich lake. *Brauclub* (www.brauclub .de) at Neumarkt 2 spins house and r'n'b on Wednesday, Friday and Saturday – don't get too excited.

Kellerhaus Schlossberg 2 ☎0371/335 16 77. Not just the city's oldest restaurant, but its most charming, where traditional plates are served in a rustic seventeenth-century dining room – nice beer garden in summer, too. It's in the Schlossviertel north of the centre.

Ratskeller Markt 1 ☎0371/694 98 75. The venerable town-hall restaurant in the Neues Rathaus comes up trumps, with good regional cuisine and painted cellar-vaults that are an Art Nouveau take on medieval.

Turm-Brauhaus Neumarkt 2 ☎0371/909 50 95. Opposite the *Ratskeller*, this popular microbrewery prepares chunky pub-grub favourites such as *Schweinhaxe* (roast pork knuckle), *Schnitzel* and spare ribs. Fresh beers produced on-site slip down dangerously easily.

Villa Esche Parkstr. 58 ☎0371/236 13 63. Refined but relaxed restaurant in the former coach-house of Henry van de Velde's Art Nouveau villa, with a seasonal menu of gourmet Italian and modern German cuisine – the finest dining in the city. Closed Mon.

Augustusburg

Just under 15km east of Chemnitz, the tiny town of **AUGUSTUSBURG** drapes itself picturesquely over rock knuckle, the Schellenberg. The colossal white-and-pink wedding-cake decoration at the summit is **Schloss Augustusburg** (daily: April–Oct 9.30am–6pm; Nov–March 10am–5pm; individual prices below, combination ticket for Jagdtier- und Vogelkundemuseum, Kutschen-museum & Schlosskerker €6.60; www.die-sehenswerten-drei.de), whose stack of cubes and rectangles was created as a hunting lodge by Saxony Elector Augustus in 1572.

Guided tours (daily: April–Oct 10.30am, 12.30pm, 2pm & 4pm; Nov–March 11.30am, 1.30pm & 3.30pm; 50min; €3) explore historic apartments of the **Lindenhaus**; a sweet **Schlosskirche**, the high-water mark of Renaissance ecclesiastical architecture in Saxony, with an altarpiece by Cranach the Younger of the Elector and family beneath a Crucifixion set before his castle; and the **Brunnenhaus** wellhouse, whose original wooden machinery is still able to draw water from a 130m shaft, albeit without the two oxen originally required.

Other areas can be visited individually. For historical character there's former banqueting quarter **Hasenhaus** (€2.80), which gets its name from the amusing murals of anthropomorphized hares that gambol over the doorways, more appealing than the so-so hunting and regional nature displays of its **Jagdtier- und Vogelkundmuseum**. The former kitchen opposite houses the **Motorrad-museum** (€3.20), a rev-head's paradise of shiny motorbikes – from Gottfried Daimler's 1885 boneshaker, capable of a giddy 12km/hr with stabilisers, to sports and classic roadsters of international marques, including a section on Saxony brand DKW, the world's largest bike producer in the 1920s and 1930s. The **Marstall stables** (€1.60) behind contain a gilded Cinderella carriage (1790), which was pulled by six white chargers for the imperial coronation, among displays of coaches in the **Kutschenmuseum**; while the **Schlosskerker** (€1.60) dungeon is an orgy of torture instruments and grisly illustrations. There's also a **tower** (€1) for an elevated view over the quilt of fields and forest laid over hills that roll back to the Erzgebirge uplands south. By the castle gateway the **Sächsischer Adler-und Jagdfalkenhof** (April–Oct Tues–Sun approx every 2hr; €6) stages free-flight falconry displays in homage to the castle's hunting roots.

Practicalities

Access to Augustusburg by **public transport** from Chemnitz is either on bus #704 from the Hauptbahnhof (40min; 5 daily), or by more regular train connec-tions to Bahnhof Erdmannsdorf-Augustusburg, from where you can catch the 1911-vintage Drahtseilbahn funicular (€3.50 single, €4.50 return). The **tourist office** (Mon–Fri 9am–noon & 1–5pm, foyer open Sat & Sun 9am–5pm; ☎037291/395 50) is in the Rathaus on the main road beneath the Schloss at Marienberger Strasse 24. Brochures in the foyer provide accommodation options, among which is a **youth hostel** (☎037291/202 56, ✆www.jugendherberge -sachsen.de; dorms from €17.30) in the rear wings of the Schloss.

Zwickau

It seems rather unfair that a medium-sized city which gave Romantic composer Robert Schumann and the prestige Audi marque to the world is known instead for the Trabant. Yet such is the ironic nostalgia for GDR kitsch – *Ostalgie* as it is known – that the underpowered, plastic "people's car" used throughout the communist bloc is the most famous export of **ZWICKAU**, which lies in the foothills of the eastern Erzgebirge range. Such is the price of being the regime's Motor City for four decades. The tradition of motor manufacturing in Zwickau, ongoing in Volkswagen plants in southern suburbs, was initiated in 1909 by August Horsch, an entrepreneurial engineer who caught the wave of industrial success in the late 1800s. His legacy is an excellent motor museum north of the centre, the premier reason to visit – the centre is a pleasant enough but unremarkable assortment of historic islands, nineteenth-century grandeur and modern commercial shopping.

Arrival, information and accommodation

The **Hauptbahnhof** lies due west of the Altstadt and south of the August Horch Museum. The **tourist office** (Mon–Fri 9am–6.30pm, Sat 10am–4pm; ☎0375/271 32 49, ⓦwww.zwickau.de) is at the city's bull's-eye at Hauptstrasse 6, just off Hauptmarkt.

2

Achat Leipziger Str. 180 ☎0375/87 20, ⓦwww .achat-hotel.de. Modern business hotel of the Achat chain 2km north of the centre (tram #4 to "Neue Welt") with creature comforts such as a sauna, and there can be bargains at weekends. ❸–❺

Brauhaus Zwickau Peter-Breuer-Str. 12–20 ☎0375/303 20 32, ⓦwww.brauhaus-zwickau.de. An acceptable cheapie in a half-timbered wing above a restaurant that's on the doorstep of Zwickau's bar strip. ❸

Holiday Inn Kornmarkt 9 ☎0374/279 20, ⓦwww .holiday-inn.com. Zwickau's finest address, centrally located one block southwest of Hauptmarkt and all you'd expect from the international chain. ❹–❺

Jagdhaus Wald Idyll Talstr. 1, Hartenstein, 13km southeast of Zwickau ☎037605/840, ⓦwww.waldidyll.he-webpack.de. An elegant country retreat of the Romantik Hotels group created from a nineteenth-century hunting lodge among the pine woods south of Hartenstein. Decor style is grown-up modern-country, four-star facilities include a good spa centre and restaurant. ❺–❻

Merkur Bahnhofstr. 58 ☎0375/211 95 60, ⓦwww.merkur-hotel-zwickau.de. Acceptable rather than exciting old-fashioned hotel garni near the station – a decent fallback. ❸

The City

Unless time is tight the obvious place to commence a tour is in what's left of the historic Altstadt, arranged around two squares. The first you come to en route from the Hauptbahnhof is Marienplatz, named for the **Dom St Marien**, whose two-tiered Baroque tower (Wed & Thurs 3pm; €1) serves as a homing beacon. Within the Gothic church is a blockbuster display of art. The focus is the largest altar in the area, a riot of fiddly gilt from the workshop of Nürnberg master Michael Wolgemut, Dürer's tutor. Other eye-catchers are rare Protestant confessionals that place the priest and sinner face to face at eye level – their carved panels are to prevent lip-reading by the congregation – and, at the side of the chancel a Renaissance tower up which twists a staircase double-helix. Look, too, for a masterful pietà (1502) by Zwickau son Peter Breuer, a grief-stricken work infused with the emergent spirit of Renaissance humanism. The stack of fourteenth- and fifteenth-century houses occupied by medieval artisans opposite the Dom's portal is the oldest terrace in the state. Church employees were housed in the three restored **Priesterhäuser** (Priest Houses; Tues–Sun 1–6pm; €4) at the end. Some roughly plastered rooms furnished in medieval style, none more atmospheric than the soot-stained "black kitchens", have themed displays on contemporary crafts. A modern wing holds exhibitions.

Hauptmarkt, a block east of Marienplatz, is the commercial heart of Zwickau. The back of its elongated "L" is claimed by a walloping, castellated **Rathaus** and, adjacent, the **Gewandhaus**, a cloth-merchants' hall whose half-timbered upper experiments with Renaissance style. At the southwest corner of Hauptmarkt, **Robert-Schumann-Haus** (Tues–Fri 10am–5pm, Sat & Sun 1–5pm; €4; ⓦwww.robert-schumann-haus.de) documents the career of the Romantic composer who was born within on June 8, 1810. Schumann was always a passionate figure, as tumultuous in his words to concert pianist and later wife Clara Wieck as he was in the wild hallucinations during an 1854 concert tour that induced his mental breakdown and subsequent death. No surprise, then, that Clara, a premier-division pianist of her day, is a recurring theme, nor that her Bösendorfer grand is on display.

The mood changes outside of the ringed Altstadt among a grid of streets from the town's rapid nineteenth-century expansion. In the northwest on Johannis-strasse – up Alter Steinweg opposite the Rathaus across Dr-Friedrichs-Ring, then up Max-Pechsteinstrasse – the **Johannisbad** (Mon & Wed 10am–10pm, Tues & Thurs 8am–10pm, Fri 10am–11pm, Sat & Sun 9am–10pm; €1.50–4.50; Ⓦwww .johannisbad.de) is a gorgeous Art Nouveau swimming pool with a tiled gallery picked out in bottle green beneath windows like Arabic domes. No excuses: it sells swimming costumes and rents towels. About twenty minutes' walk west is a broad park that flanks main road Crimmitschauer Strasse. The Art Nouveau pavilion at its back houses the **Kunst Sammlungen** (Tues–Sun 1–6pm; €4) with the city's art collection, including a late-Gothic altar of morose saints by Breuer. A further twenty minutes up Crimmitschauer Strasse in what was the city outskirts, the **August Horch Museum** (Tues–Sun 9.30am–5pm; €5; Ⓦwww.horch-museum .de) occupies the former Audi factory that began operation in 1909. While eighty or so landmark motors from the Horch stable – its marques Audi, Horch, Wanderer and DKW merged as Auto-Union in the 1930s to give modern Audi its inter-locking four-rings logo – are a petrolhead's paradise, it is the presentational flair that sets many in period streetscapes that makes this such an enjoyable collection for all. Rather tatty after the vintage glories are assorted Trabants, a marque that origi-nated as the 1950s Zwickau P70 before it became the rattling 500cc workhorse of communism. Three million were exported in the 34 years until production ceased in 1991. The GDR army even commissioned an all-terrain Trabi. Small wonder Zwickau has a concrete Trabant memorial on Georgeplatz northwest of the Altstadt. The museum is located 2.5km from the Hauptbahnhof on Audistrasse: take tram #4 or buses #133, #111 and #158 from the station.

Eating and drinking

The best **restaurants** are in the hotels; worth a mention is historic *Hausbrauerei*, *Brauhaus Zwickau*, adjacent to the Priesterhäuser. Other options include nearby *Zur Grünhainer Kapelle* at Peter-Brauer-Strasse 3 and *Drei Schwäne*, 2km south of the centre at Tonstrasse 1, with modern Provencal and Tuscan cooking. The **beer garden** of *Brauhaus Zwickau* is a fine place for a summertime knees-up, otherwise Peter-Brauer-Strasse one block west is "Kneipenstrasse" (Pub Street), and surprisingly good for bar-hopping it is, too, at weekends. *Skylounge* at no. 19 is your spot if you crave metropolitan-style cocktail culture.

Travel details

Trains

Bautzen to: Görlitz (hourly; 30–40min).
Chemnitz to: Erdmannsdorf-Augustusburg (hourly; 15min).
Dresden to: Bad Schandau (every 30min; 25–45min); Bautzen (hourly; 1hr); Chemnitz (hourly; 1hr–1hr 20min); Görlitz (hourly; 1hr 15–1hr 40min); Leipzig (every 30min; 1hr 15min–1hr 40min); Meissen (every 30min; 35min); Zwickau (hourly; 1hr 35min–2hr 20min).
Leipzig to: Chemnitz (hourly; 55min); Grossbothen (hourly; 40min); Dresden (hourly; 1hr 10min–1hr 40min); Zwickau (hourly; 1hr 20min–1hr 40min).

Saxony-Anhalt and the Harz

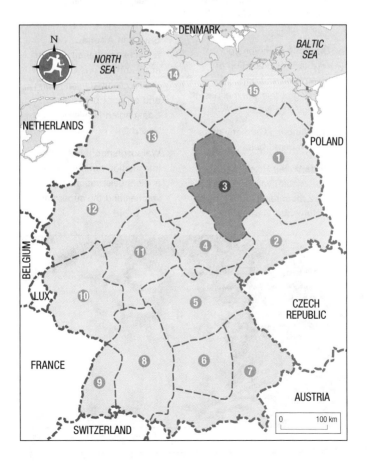

CHAPTER 3 # Highlights

✳ **Händel Festival** Spoil your ears with the melodious work of George Frideric Handel in his home town, Halle. See p.212

✳ **Lutherhaus Wittenberg** Discover the origins of the Protestant Reformation and the people who triggered it. See p.223

✳ **Bauhaus** Heighten your aesthetic appreciation of clean lines and creative thinking at this seminal design school. See p.227

✳ **Quedlinburg** Germany at its half-timbered best. See p.238

✳ **Bode Valley** Hike a deep and verdant valley to see the Harz mountains at their most picturesque. See p.243

✳ **Rübeland** Atmospheric limestone caverns that can be explored without the need for risky speleology. See p.243

✳ **Skiing** The varied terrain of Braunlage is the Harz's largest resort, with its most dependable conditions. See p.244

✳ **Sauna in Altenau** With facilities to rival any of the spas and saunas that dot the Harz, Altenau's saunas and outdoor pools also boast splendid views. See p.245

✳ **Walpurgisnacht** Let your imagination run riot during ancient celebrations of witches and the supernatural. See p.246

▲ Statue of Luther on Marktplatz, Wittenberg

Saxony-Anhalt and the Harz

axony-Anhalt (Sachsen-Anhalt) divides into two distinct landscapes: to the east sandy plains are scattered with farms, pastures, pine forests and bogs, and a series of gritty, post-industrial cities; while to the west the land suddenly rises into the gentle **Harz** mountains where sleepy villages nestle in dark forests. Though the range straddles the old border between East and West Germany and is today divided between Saxony-Anhalt and Lower Saxony, for convenience the entire range is covered in this chapter.

Extractive industries and large navigable rivers – particularly the Elbe and Saale – were of foremost importance in settling this region. Forestry, salt, copper, coal and lignite all played their part in shaping it over the centuries. And as a rich industrious area, it has regularly been a battleground, with the Thirty Years' War badly battering the region and World War II similarly levelling the largest cities. The state of Saxony-Anhalt was first formed after World War II when the occupying Russians cobbled together the former Duchy of Anhalt with the old Prussian province of Saxony. The union only lasted a few years before being divided in other ways, but was resurrected in the wake of German reunification in 1990 to produce a federal state, with **Magdeburg** its capital. In the decade that followed, heavy industrial production – which the GDR had feverishly built up – dropped by more than three-quarters and employment by more than nine-tenths, with high levels of unemployment particularly blighting the south of the state, where mining and chemical works had prevailed. Though the situation has stabilized today, the state remains one of Germany's poorest.

In the eastern portion of Saxony-Anhalt, the large university towns of **Halle** and **Magdeburg** offer the full range of urban distractions and some reasonable nightlife while the lands between them are of interest as the birthplace of the sixteenth-century Protestant Reformation – centred on **Lutherstadt Wittenberg** – and as the cradle of the Modernist movement at the **Bauhaus** school at **Dessau**.

As northern Germany's premier mountain playground, the main attractions in the **Harz** are outdoorsy: **hiking** and **cycling** in summer and **tobogganing** and **skiing** – particularly cross-country – in winter. The villages and regional towns are well equipped for all this, and noteworthy for some excellent spas to help you unwind at the end of the day, while the half-timbered town of **Quedlinburg** is pretty enough to deserve a place on anyone's German itinerary.

Road and **rail** links are good throughout Saxony-Anhalt, even putting its entire eastern half within reasonable day-trip territory of Berlin. The Harz needs and rewards more relaxed exploration, ideally on foot, by bike, or on its network of charming old **narrow-gauge railways**.

Eastern Saxony-Anhalt

The Elbe and its tributaries have sculpted the landscape of eastern **Saxony-Anhalt** and provided an infrastructure for trade and growth. In the south the large Saale tributary dominates and provides for the state's largest town **Halle**, the focus for a heavily industrialized, urbanized region that peters out in the east around **Lutherstadt Eisleben**, the town where Martin Luther was born, died, and is now relentlessly celebrated. In the south the town of **Naumburg** is famous for its grand cathedral but is also a gateway to Germany's most northerly wine region. Further north, the Elbe snakes its way across the landscape through all the most interesting towns including a couple in which two important intellectual movements emerged. In the sixteenth century **Lutherstadt Wittenberg** became the seat of the Protestant Reformation that changed Christianity forever, and today the town is an excellent place to get to grips with the earliest days of the movement and its most important players. Another very different but also radical movement emerged four hundred years later a short way upstream in **Dessau**, where the **Bauhaus design school** operated between 1925 and 1932, having a profound influence on architecture and design. Further downstream and to the north the Elbe broadens into the substantial river that enabled **Magdeburg** to become an important inland port and industrial conurbation, roles for which it severely suffered in World War II. Nevertheless, the town has rebuilt itself and become adventurous and energetic, qualities most evident in its modern architecture and nightlife. The exact opposite is true of the **Altmark**, the thinly populated heathland north along the Elbe, where a clutch of low-key towns – particularly **Tangermünde** – preserve a very traditional feel.

Cycling in eastern Saxony-Anhalt

The easy gradients of the fine riverside cycle-paths that join all its most rewarding towns have made Saxony-Anhalt popular for exploration by bike. The 980km **Elberadweg** (Elbe cycle path; ⓦwww.elberadweg.de) is excellent for a long-distance tour of the state, while the 65km **Gartenreichtour Fürst-Franz** and the **Unstrut radweg** between Freyburg and Naumburg are both ideal for a leisurely, long weekend. The government run website ⓦwww.radtouren-sachsen-anhalt.de, the best place for information and tips – though all in German.

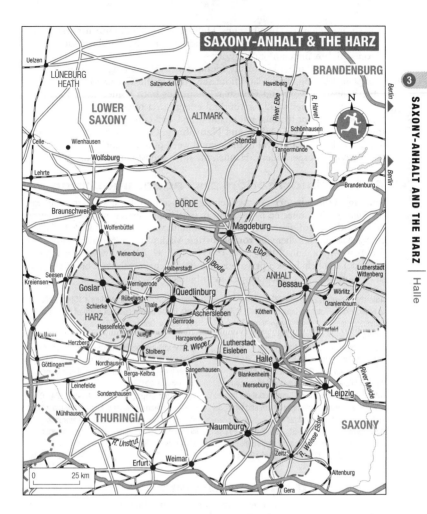

Halle

Sprawling across a sandy plain on the right bank of the Saale River, 37km northwest of Leipzig, **HALLE** got its name from the pre-Germanic word for salt, the presence of which encouraged settlement and extraction during the Bronze Age. The city continues to be an important industrial and commercial centre, and forms a large part of a regional concentration of industrial plants and cities called the *Chemiedreieck* (Chemical Triangle), even if its industrial heyday is long gone and its population – some 235,000 – is waning by around two thousand each year. Nevertheless, Halle remains the state's largest city in its most urbanized region.

The Altstadt centres around the Marktplatz, where sights include the city's main church and the **Händel-Haus**, the mansion where the composer was born. The **Moritzburg** to the northwest now houses an important art collection, while a few attractions outside the Altstadt together provide a picture of Halle's historical context, including the **Technisches Halloren- und Salinenmuseum**, which explores the town's origins and its salt industry, and the **Landesmuseum für Vorgeschichte**, museum of prehistory.

Halle's Martin Luther University, founded in 1694 and long a principal seat of Protestant learning, particularly flourished during the German Enlightenment when Christian Wolff and Christian Thomasius both resided here. Today, the university continues to add a youthful energy to a town that's thin on sights but is an important national rail junction, and well connected to other regional towns – particularly **Eisleben** and **Naumburg**. Otherwise the best reason to visit is the **Händel Festival** in the second week of June, which devotes itself to the work of George Frideric Handel, the town's most famous son.

Arrival, information and accommodation

Leipzig-Halle airport (ⓦwww.leipzig-halle-airport.de) lies 20km southeast of Halle and is connected by frequent trains for the thirteen-minute journey to its **Hauptbahnhof**. From here a fifteen-minute walk northwest leads to Halle's central Marktplatz, where the **tourist office**, Marktplatz 13 (Mon–Fri 9am–7pm, Sat 10am–4pm, Sun 10am–2pm; ☏0345/122 99 84, ⓦwww.stadtmarketing -halle.de), can help book a **private room** (❷) – generally the best budget option, since most of Halle's hotels are geared to business travellers.

Ankerhof Ankerstr. 2a ☏0345/232 32 00, ⓦwww.ankerhofhotel.de. Smart hotel in a stylishly converted nineteenth-century warehouse. The general ambience as well as the sauna and fitness facilities make it a bit of a bargain. ❹

Apart-Hotel Halle Kohlschütter Str. 5–6 ☏0345/525 90, ⓦwww.apart-halle.de. Jugendstil place, around 2km north of the centre, with rooms themed around German cultural figures. Included are use of a sauna, solarium and whirlpool and a very good breakfast buffet. ❹

DJH Halle August-Bebel-Str. 48a ☏0345/202 47 16, ⓦwww.jugendherberge.de/jh/halle. Jugendstil villa outside, institutional 1970s

within, Halle's youth hostel lies a 15min walk north of the centre and just north of the University quarter. Dorms €16.50.

Marthahaus Adam-Kuckhoff-Str. 5 ☏0345/510 80, ⓦwww.stiftung-marthahaus.de. Quiet, sparklingly clean and highly recommended Altstadt hotel, simply furnished and run by a Christian mission. Has a sauna. ❸

Rotes Ross Leipziger Str. 76 ☏0345/23 34 30, ⓦwww.kempinski-halle.de. Elegant top-flight hotel with all the usual trappings of a five-star place, including a sizeable fitness centre and 24-hour room service. ❼

The Marktplatz and around

Halle's focal point is its large **Marktplatz** from which many Altstadt streets radiate, including Leipziger Strasse, the main shopping street. Casting broad shadows across the **Marktplatz** from its southern edge, the **Roter Turm** has become the city's symbol. Started in 1418, the 84m tower took a staggering 88 years to complete and it wasn't until 1999 that its final touch was added: one of the world's largest Glockenspiels, involving 76 bells. The tower is also notable for a **Roland statue** (see p.214) on its eastern side, an eighteenth-century version of the twelfth-century original. The Roter Turm is actually the freestanding belfry of the late-Gothic market church behind, the **Unser Lieben Frauen** or **St Marien** (Jan & Feb Mon–Sat noon–5pm, Sun 3–5pm; March–Dec Mon–Sat 10am–5pm, Sun 3–5pm), another curious construction, since it's the result of a conversion job that levelled the body of two existent churches in 1529, then incorporated their two pairs of towers into a large, flamboyant Catholic church designed to spearhead a local Counter Reformation; eventually the church became Protestant. Martin Luther himself preached here on three occasions and his body was briefly stored here on its way from Eisleben to Wittenberg; a death mask is considered one of its great treasures. The **Hausmannstürme** (€2.50), the pair of rounded towers connected by a bridge, can be climbed for good town views.

Also gracing Halle's Marktplatz is a bronze of composer **George Frideric Handel** (born Georg Friedrich Händel), looking thoughtful. Halle's most celebrated son, his life is documented in some detail at the Baroque mansion where he was born: the **Händel-Haus**, Grosse Nikolaistrasse 5 (Mon–Wed & Fri–Sun 9.30am–5.30pm, Thurs 9.30am–7pm; €2.60; ☎0345/50 09 02 21, ⓌWwww.haendel-in-halle.de). The best touch in the rather dry exhibition is the opportunity to listen to some of his work, including the famous *Messiah*. Also rewarding is the collection of around seven hundred musical instruments, many from Handel's time, though not the most unusual ones, which include several glass instruments such as a Bohemian harmonica.

Far more offbeat is Halle's other main Altstadt museum, the **Beatles Museum**, Alter Markt 12 (Wed–Sun 10am–8pm; €5; ☎0345/290 39 00, ⓌWwww.beatlesmuseum.net), where a huge volume of memorabilia awaits to delight Fab Four fans or anyone in the mood for some 1960s nostalgia. The museum lies a short walk south of the Marktplatz, in the vicinity of the late-Gothic, late fourteenth-century **Moritzkirche** (Tues–Fri 11am–noon & 3–5pm) with its respectable little collection of wood carvings and sculptures.

The Knight Roland

Immortalized in the twelfth-century *Song of Roland* epic French poem, Roland was a knight in Charlemagne's forces, possibly even the king's nephew, who conquered much of Europe in the eighth century. His most famous hour came at the end of a rare military failure against the Moors in Spain in 778, when Charlemagne's forces retreated over the Pyrenees and their rearguard, which Roland commanded, was ambushed and Roland killed – largely, it seems, because he was too proud to blow his horn for reinforcements until it was too late, when the effort caused "blood to flow from his mouth and burst from his forehead".

The knight came to symbolize bravery, determination and steadfastness and by the late Middle Ages around fifty independent-minded German towns had erected giant statues of him in their marketplaces – equipped with his horn and an unbreakable sword of justice – as a defiant symbol of their rights, prosperity and above all their self-determination and independence from local nobility. Around twenty Rolands survive or have been rebuilt today – including in Halle, Magdeburg and Quedlinburg – though the most famous stands in Bremen.

The Moritzburg

A couple of minutes' walk northwest of the **Händel-Haus**, the stocky **Moritzburg** citadel dates back to the fifteenth century, though since it was pretty comprehensively destroyed by the Swedes and fire during the Thirty Years' War, most of it is a late nineteenth-century rebuild. Now it's home to **Kunstmuseum Moritzburg**, Friedemann-Bach-Platz 5 (Tues 11am–8.30pm, Wed–Sun 10am–6pm; €5; ☏0345/21 25 90, ⓦ www.kunstmuseum-moritzburg .de), a gigantic, three-thousand-item art collection. Various movements from late-Gothic up to GDR art are well represented in both painting and sculpture, but one strong-point is art from the turn of the twentieth century: Expressionism and the socially critical art of Max Leibermann and his contemporaries. Worth a particular look are two paintings actually painted in one of the castle's towers by Bauhaus-member **Lyonel Feininger** between 1929 and 1931. Known as the *Halle-Bilder* they are displayed alongside several pieces by other Bauhaus artists including Paul Klee, Hans Reichel and Fritz Winter.

Beyond the Altstadt

Just south of the Altstadt, and the roaring through-traffic along the Mortizzwinger, lies the **Franckesche Stiftung**, Franckeplatz 1 (☏0345/212 74 00, ⓦ www .francke-halle.de), an early eighteenth-century complex that was almost a town in itself, with its own school, orphanage, workshops, impressive public library, and three-thousand-strong population. Set up by theologian and scholar August Hermann Francke as an educational institution, it then developed under its own steam. The life of Francke and the complex's history are explored in the museum at its hub, the **Historisches Waisenhaus** (Historic Orphanage; Tues–Sun 10am–5pm; €3). More entertaining is the **Kunst- und Naturalienkammer** (Art and Natural History chamber; same times & ticket), a treasure-trove of all things that occupied the eighteenth-century scholastic mind, with a mock-up of the cosmic system and a pharmacists' workshop among a miscellany of curios from every corner of the globe.

A similar distance west of the Altstadt, a tall brick chimney poking from a gathering of half-timbered buildings announces the **Technisches Halloren- und Salinenmuseum**, Mansfelder Strasse 52 (Tues–Sun 10am–5pm; €2.10, free Thurs; ☏0345/209 32 30). On Sundays when the machinery is fired up you can view the salt-making process that effectively made Halle – the salt produced is sold in the shop – but on other days it's a case of appreciating the equipment's complexity and age.

There's much more to the **Landesmuseum für Vorgeschichte**, Richard-Wagner-Strasse 9 (Museum of Prehistory; Tues 9am–7.30pm, Wed–Fri 9am–5pm, Sat & Sun 10am–6pm; €4; ☏0345/524 73 63, ⓦwww.archlsa.de), which is often most rewarding for its temporary exhibitions. Otherwise its strong points are its Prehistoric, Stone and Bronze Age collections, together a staggering million items, many of which are carefully accompanied by diagrams and illustrations to help portray life in ancient times. Most memorable among them are some 125,000-year-old bull elephant skeletons, but the museum's greatest treasure is probably the *Himmelsscheibe von Nebra*, a 3600-year-old Bronze Age metal plate made of bronze on which gold reliefs represent astronomical phenomena and mysterious religious symbols.

The Landesmuseum can be reached on tram #7 (direction Kröllwitz), which goes on to the edge of town and **Burg Giebichenstein** (Tues–Fri 9am–6pm, Sat & Sun 9am–6.30pm; €2.10, Thurs free; ☏0345/292 62 60), the former residence of the bishop of Magdeburg. In fact the complex constitutes two castles, both destroyed in the Thirty Years' War. The overgrown and ruined twelfth-century Oberburg offers sweeping views of the meandering Saale, while the fifteenth-century Unterburg, built on the site of a tenth-century fort, was extensively rebuilt in the Baroque period, and survived thanks to its use as a prison; today it is partly occupied by an art college.

Eating, drinking and nightlife

Halle has the best culinary scene in the state, making it a good place to swap traditional German food for more cosmopolitan choices. The tourist office publishes a good and critical culinary brochure (free), but in German only. First choice for a night on the tiles is the lively **Kleine Ulrichstrasse** after which you can drift to nearby local clubs like *Flower Power*, Moritzburgring 1 (☏0345/688 88 88), which stays open until at least 5am, and *Turm*, Friedemann-Bach-Platz 5 (ⓦwww.turm-halle.de), in the atmospheric Moritzburg where there's usually something going on.

Bella Donna Grosse Ulrichstr. 47 ☏0345/682 53 50. Tiny Italian joint with open kitchen, cheerful vibe and large portions of all the usual Italian favourites, most around €7.

Café Nöö Grosse Klausstr. 11 ☏0345/202 16 51. Grungy but cheerful Bohemian place with good menu, mains for around €5 and a small terrace; open until 3am with regular live music.

Hallesches Brauhaus Grosse Nikolaistr. 2 ☏0345/21 25 70. The only microbrewery in the old town, with a good line in its own *Hallsch* beers and various hearty traditional favourites – the goulash with dumplings and dark-beer sauce (€8.90) is excellent.

Halloren Café Marktplatz 13 ☏0345/299 76 79. Excellent café, which shares its entrance with the tourist office, and has two hundred years of tradition behind its splendid cakes and handmade pralines.

Kaffeeschuppen Kleine Ulrichstr. 11 ☏0345/208 08 03. Hip café with excellent breakfasts (€4–8), and a good selection of inexpensive soups, salads and mains like noodles and curries. There's often live jazz in the evenings, making it also a good place to start a bar crawl down Kleine Ulrichstrasse.

Ökoase Kleine Ulrichstr. 27 ☏0345/290 16 04. Veggie place with moderately priced canteen lunches – soups €3, mains around €5 – turns into a fancier table-service restaurant in the evenings with rather more expensive and complex dishes like the good pumpkin-seed *Rösti* with pears and Roquefort (€8.50) or fried tofu with lemongrass in lime basmati rice (€9.50).

Wok-Bar Grosse Ulrichstr. 41 ☏0345/470 45 88. Stylish pan-Asian place that does stir-fries which you design yourself, or choose from a menu from around €9. There's even some quite good sushi. Various events, DJs and cocktail evenings keep the place ticking over until late.

Lutherstadt Eisleben

"Mein Vaterland war Eisleben" – "My fatherland was Eisleben" – is, like many things Luther said of his own life, not quite true. The reformer was certainly born and also died here, but in between spent precious little time in the place. Nevertheless the small, otherwise unprepossessing and sprawling little town is absolutely focused on him, having invented itself as a place of pilgrimage as early as 1689 when it started preserving its Luther-related landmarks and finally renaming itself **LUTHERSTADT EISLEBEN** in 1946. Today, the town's main attraction is **Luthers Geburtshaus**, the house where the reformer was born – now an excellent museum about him, his roots and the town. In fact Luther moved away from Eisleben aged one to the nearby settlement of **Mansfeld**, where he spent his formative years and which, for his most die-hard fans, is also worth a look.

The **Eisleber Wiesenmarkt** (Ⓦwww.wiesenmarkt.de), a giant Volksfest, takes place at the start of September and is the liveliest event on the annual calendar.

Arrival, information and accommodation

Eisleben's **train station** lies about 1km south of the town's market square and centre. The **tourist office**, Bahnhofstrasse 36 (Mon–Fri 10am–5pm, Tues 10am–6pm, Sat 9am–noon; ☏03475/60 21 24, Ⓦwww.eisleben-tourist.de), lies between the two at the junction of Hallesche Strasse, the main through-road. Also en route is *Parkhotel*, Bahnhofstrasse 12 (☏03475/540; ❷), the town's best budget **accommodation** in a family-run place with 1970s decor. More luxurious, and at the centre of the action, is the ⚐ *Graf von Mansfeld*, Markt 56 (☏03475/25 07 22, Ⓦwww.hotel-eisleben.de; ❹), which exudes elegance and history – four-poster beds and the like – for less money than usual. Another good option, though a five-minute walk east of the Markt along Lindenallee, is the *Hotel an der Klosterpforte*, Lindenstrasse 34 (☏03475/714 40, Ⓦwww.klosterpforte.com; ❹), with airy, pine-furnished rooms and its own microbrewery and restaurant which does an excellent Sunday brunch (noon–2.30pm; €14.50).

Luthers Geburtshaus and the St Petri-Pauli Kirche

Though easily the town's most worthwhile attraction, **Luthers Geburtshaus**, Lutherstrasse 15 (April–Oct daily 10am–6pm; Nov–March Tues–Sun 10am–5pm; €4; ☏03475/714 78 14), is not what it claims. Yes, the reformer was born here, but the house in which he first came to light actually burned down in 1689. What's now here stems from 1693 and has served as an almshouse and housed parts of the town administration. Nevertheless the museum has plenty of interesting content on the era and region into which Luther was born, and on the Reformation. This is done not only with displays of valuable old bibles and retables, but also by reconstructing a medieval kitchen thought to have been similar to the original. The museum also puts high-tech gadgets to good use, for example using Cranach the Elder's portraits of Luther's elderly parents to reconstruct how they might have looked at the time of his birth.

Modern audiovisual technology is also used well in an off-topic, but engrossing collection of **epitaph paintings** hauled from the Eisleben crypts of local worthies. At great expense they had themselves painted into biblical scenes, the significance and symbolism of which is expertly explained by touch-screen databases – in English as well as German. One area of the museum focuses on baptism, a topic of great importance to Luther. Luther himself was baptized at the fourteenth-century **St Petri-Pauli Kirche** (May–Oct Mon–Fri 1–3pm), practically next door.

The Markt and around

At the centre of Eisleben's compact **Altstadt**, which has tenth-century roots, lies the **Marktplatz**, where, predictably, a large bronze of Luther stands on a plinth decorated with scenes from his life. Part of the backdrop are the towers of the austere, Gothic **St Andreaskirche** (May–Oct Mon–Sat 10am–noon & 2–4pm, Sat & Sun 11am–1pm) where Luther delivered his last four sermons, from a pulpit that's been well preserved. Also in the church are the elaborate epitaphs to the Mansfeld family and an elegant high altar from the Nürnberg workshop. Opposite the southern side of the church lies **Luthers Sterbehaus**, Andreaskirchplatz (April–Oct daily 9am–5pm; Nov–March Tues–Fri 10am–4pm, Sat & Sun noon–4pm; €2; ☎03475/60 22 85), where Luther was long thought to have died. It's now known that he actually passed away down the road in what's now the *Graf von Mansfeld* hotel (see opposite), where he was temporarily living while he settled a legal dispute regarding the family copper works. Even so, the Sterbehaus has a reconstruction of Luther's last quarters, and a copy of his death mask and last testimony. The admission ticket also gets you into the **Regionalgeschichtliches Museum**, Münzgasse 7 (same hours), a local history museum a few metres down the road, whose exhibits include a Bronze Age boat.

Eating and drinking

Some of Eisleben's best places to eat are attached to hotels, with the **restaurant** at *Graf von Mansfeld*, Markt 56, one of the best in town, serving modern international food (mains €9–19) that includes dishes based around steaks octopus or herring. It has also cornered the local café market with its delicious home-made cakes. Elsewhere the dining scene is unusual for its attempts to provide meals to complement the sights, producing dishes that might have been served in medieval times. *Lutherschenke Eisleben*, Lutherstrasse 19 (☎03475/61 47 75), near the Geburtshaus, makes particular efforts with a hearty and meaty menu that includes deer, turkey (a new exotic food then) and pork-liver mains – priced around €11, though lunch specials cost €7. *Brauhaus Zum Reformator*, Friedensstrasse 12, also tries its hand at medieval dishes with the added benefit of some of its own microbrew beers to wash it all down. For a quick, filling and very inexpensive bite try *Schäfers*, Markt 12, a basic canteen at the back of a bakery on the marketplace, where a meal costs around €3.

Mansfeld-Lutherstadt

Though only 14km from Eisleben, the attractive little town of **MANSFELD-LUTHERSTADT** is a forty-minute journey away by bus (#372), so only really worth visiting with your own transport. Those who do make the journey will find a number of tight streets gathered below a largely sixteenth-century castle. The **tourist office**, Junghuhnstrasse 2 (☎034782/903 42, ⓦwww .mansfeld.eu), is in the centre of town by the church and just uphill from the **Luthers Elternhaus**, Lutherstrasse 26, where Luther spent his childhood, before departing for Magdeburg in 1497. The actual house was in fact torn down in 1805, but the neighbouring building has a small **museum** (mid-April to late Oct Tues–Fri 11am–4pm, 1st & 3rd Sat & Sun in month 11am–4pm; Nov–April Tues–Fri 11am–3pm) and as it's of a similar age it gives a good impression of life at the time.

Back up the hill by the tourist office is *Pension Schlossblick,* Junghuhnstrasse 4 (℡0162/415 16 34, Ⓦwww.mansfeld-pension.de; ❸), a great little bed-and-breakfast in a sixteenth-century building with fine views of the town's castle.

Naumburg and around

With lanes of tidy half-timbered houses fanning out from a central Marktplatz, **NAUMBURG** is a modest and attractive market-town that would certainly be worth a visit even without the spectacle of the four-spired **Naumburger Dom**, which rears up on the town's eastern side, and is what makes a trip here really worthwhile. The other reason to visit is the **Kirschfest**, a big shindig that breaks Naumburg's usual sleepy peace on the last weekend of June. A parade, fireworks and a fair celebrate the town's history, in particular an incident when the town's children confronted a Czech army that was laying siege to the town, and politely requested that the army depart so that the townsfolk could eat again, which, to everyone's delight, they duly did. With Naumburg's attractions quickly enjoyed, the close presence of the wine-growing town of **Freyburg** makes for a welcome side-trip (see p.220).

Arrival, information and accommodation

Naumburg's **Hauptbahnhof** lies 1.5km northwest of the Altstadt and is connected by both bus #2 and a more enjoyable 1892-era tourist tram (every 30min; 6am–8pm). The town **tourist office**, Markt 12 (April–Oct Mon–Fri 9am–6pm, Sat 9am–4pm, Sun 10am–1pm; Nov–March Mon–Fri 9am–6pm, Sat 9am–2pm; ℡03445/23 71 12, Ⓦwww.naumburg-tourismus.de), lies on the Markt and can help with booking **private rooms** (❷). *Camping Blütengrund* (℡03445/20 27 11, Ⓦwww.camping-naumburg.de) is a large and spacious riverside place 1.5km northeast of town, located conveniently beside a lido, and offering canoe rental.

DJH Naumburg Am Tennisplatz 9 ℡03445/70 34 22, Ⓦwww.jugendherberge.de/jh/naumburg. Large, well-organized but institutional youth hostel, a fairly stiff 1.5km walk uphill south of town. Dorms €12, but breakfast costs extra.
Hotel Stadt Aachen Markt 11 ℡03445/24 70, Ⓦwww.hotel-stadt-aachen.de. Vine-covered place on the Markt with a venerable feel born out of dark-wood antique furniture and floral touches. ❹

Hotel Toscana Topfmarkt 16 ℡03445/289 20, Ⓦwww.hotel-toscana-naumburg.de. Central place tucked just behind the market square with comfortable, fairly standard rooms, though some of those on the upper floors boast attractive exposed beams. Good breakfast buffet. ❸
Pension Hentschel Lindenhof 16 ℡03445/20 12 30. Small, inexpensive and very friendly, if dated, pension in an excellent location just south of the Dom. ❷

The Naumburger Dom

With its sturdy, pale-green towers rising high above the Altstadt to the northwest, the giant **Naumburger Dom** (March–Oct Mon–Sat 9am–6pm, Sun noon–6pm; Nov–Feb Mon–Sat 10am–4pm; €4) is doubtless one of Germany's finest Gothic structures. It dates back to 1213, when work on its oldest parts – including the east choir, transept and main body – began in the late Romanesque style. These, and substantial sections of the rest, were thrown up in an impressively short fifty years, though the northeast towers date from the fifteenth century, and the southwest towers were added in 1894 during the Romantic movement's celebration of Gothic.

▲ Statues of Margrave Ekkehard II and his wife Uta, Naumburger Dom

The sheer size of the place alone is overwhelming and engrossing enough, but the leaflet and audio tour (in German or English; included in the price) are useful in drawing your attention to many examples of extraordinary workmanship. The most impressive reside in the cathedral's **two choirs** of which the **western** – completed in 1260 – is the more rewarding, thanks to the extraordinary work of the **Master of Naumburg**, a sculptor about whom little is known. His **rood screen** of the Passion bursts with character and gesture and even includes some of the earliest botanically accurate depictions of plants and flowers. But it's the **Founders' Statues** for which the Master is justifiably most famous. These benefactors for the cathedral's construction may have been long dead by the time their statues were begun, yet the tender characterization of each is thoroughly captivating and they feature many Renaissance touches – putting the work a good century ahead of his time. Two statues in particular have captured the German imagination: that of **Margrave Ekkehard II** and his serenely beautiful wife **Uta**, who've become an idealized medieval couple that belong to the same chivalrous past as the *Nibelungen* saga (see p.520). The **eastern choir** is of less interest but don't miss one of its most contemporary touches: the banisters leading up to its main body were carved with all sorts of fantastical creatures in the 1980s by Magdeburg artist Heinrich Apel.

The Altstadt

Naumburg's **Altstadt**, though pretty, takes little longer than the Dom itself to explore. The five-minute walk southeast along Steinweg brings you to the Markt encircled by Gothic town houses, a town hall and a parish church. The Gothic **Rathaus** with its many Renaissance touches is the most striking building. A sculpture on the capital of its northeastern corner shows two dogs fighting over a bone: a metaphor for tensions between the town and its ruling prince-bishops.

Also on the square, at no. 18, is the **Hohe Lilie** (daily 10am–5pm: €2; ⓦwww
.museumnaumburg.de), a house that contains the town history museum whose
odds-and-ends include an unusual fourteenth-century drinking horn and a
Prunkstube, an elegant living room from 1526. Towering over the Markt from
the south is the **Wenzelskirche** (May–Oct Mon–Fri 10am–noon & 2–5pm;
Nov–April Mon–Fri 1–3pm) which boasts two paintings by Lucas Cranach
the Elder and an eighteenth-century organ once played and much praised by
Johann Sebastian Bach. The church tower can be climbed for superb views of
the Dom and its surroundings (April–Oct 10am–5pm; €1.50).

Other attractions in town include the **Marientor** (1455–56), a gate from
what were clearly formidable town fortifications, a five-minute walk northeast
of the Markt. In summer a puppet theatre regularly occupies its courtyard.
A similar distance from the Markt, but southeast, lies the **Nietzsche-Haus**,
Weingarten 18 (Tues–Fri 2–5pm, Sat & Sun 10am–4pm; €2; ☎03445/21 06
38), where philosopher Friedrich Nietzsche spent a good deal of his childhood.
Though packed with biographical information, the museum is a bit dry and
rather cowardly in avoiding some of the more interesting issues, particularly his
appeal to the Nazis.

Eating and drinking

Most places to eat and drink in Naumburg are either around the Markt or along
Steinweg en route to the Dom.

Mohrencafé am Dom Steinweg 16. Little
café close to the Dom entrance with a small
but delicious lunch menu: most dishes (around
€9 each) are served with red cabbage and
dumplings – but since they include rabbit and
duck selections – are by no means everyday.
Open 11am–4pm.

Pancha Domplatz 12a. Mexican place with a
pleasant terrace on which to sip a margarita and
enjoy the setting sun on the nearby Dom. Dishes go
well beyond the usual Tex-Mex taco-and-burrito
fare; mains average €8.

Pizzeria Firenze Markt 4. Standard Italian on the
marketplace, with very good pizzas and pastas for
around €7. Serves food until 11pm, and open
longer than elsewhere.

Toscana Topfmarkt 16. Though the name suggests
Italian, German standards are served here, including a
good local variation, the *Naumburger Rahmtöpfchen*
(€10.50), a pork chop smothered in creamy onion
sauce and served with potatoes and salad.

Verona Markt 8. First-rate café and ice-cream
parlour on the main square with plenty of outdoor
seating, which serves fine cakes.

Freyburg

At the centre of Europe's most northerly wine-district the tiny town of
FREYBURG, 11km north of Naumburg and best reached via pleasant cycling
trails or by boat along the Unstrut, is known for its sparkling wine and fine
castle. The second week in September, during its wine festival, is the best time
to be in town.

Above all Freyburg is known as the home of **Rotkäppchen**, Sektkellerei-
strasse 5 (tours Mon–Fri 11am & 2pm, Sat & Sun 11am, 12.30pm & 2pm; €5;
☎034464/340, ⓦwww.rotkaeppchen.de), a leading brand of German *Sekt*. Their
hour-long tours provide a good insight into the process and company, which
flourished throughout the GDR era and is now enjoying an *Ostalgie*-inspired
revival, and includes a glass of their sparkling wine, which might tempt you into
purchases in their well-priced shop. However, an even better place to sample
and buy is the **Winzervereinigung**, or Vintners' Union, who run a shop on
Querfurter Strasse on the northern edge of town (Mon–Fri 7am–6pm, Sat
10am–6pm, Sun 10am–4pm), and are happy to open any bottle in stock for you
to try for free. Wine, in the form of a wine museum, is also a big part of the

town's other attraction **Schloss Neuenburg** (Tues–Sun: April–Oct 10am–6pm; Nov–March 10am–5pm; €6; ☎034464/355 30, ⓦwww.schloss-neuenburg.de), a brooding eleventh-century castle that looks down upon the riverside town from the southeast.

Practicalities

Hourly **buses** and **trains** link Freyburg to Naumburg, but it's more fun to take the seventy-minute boat trip up the Unstrut on the MS *Fröhliche Dörte* (May–Sept 11am, 1.30pm & 4pm; €10 return; ☎034520/28 30) from the *Blütengrund Campsite* in Naumburg. Following the quiet marked cycle-routes between the two is also enjoyable; **bikes** can be rented from Fiedelak, Bahnhofstrasse 4, in Naumburg (☎03445/70 80; €6 per day).

Freyburg's **tourist office** (Mon–Fri 8am–6pm, Sat 8am–noon; ☎034464/272 60, ⓦwww.freyburg-info.de) is on its small Marktplatz, where *Café Merle*, Markt 12, serves good cakes and sundaes. For a full, traditional German meal try *Gaststätte Zur Haldecke*, Brückenstrasse 6 (closes 3pm Mon), which lies just south of the town centre close to Unstrut and offers a good selection of local wines.

Lutherstadt Wittenberg

Clinging to a scenic stretch of the Elbe, 80km northeast of Halle, the neat little town of Wittenberg is so inextricably associated with the actions of Martin Luther that it renamed itself **LUTHERSTADT WITTENBERG**. It was here that in 1508 the Augustinian monk arrived to study at the university of a relatively obscure three-thousand-strong town and ended up sparking off one of the most important philosophical debates in world history, catapulting the town to prominence and triggering the Protestant Reformation. Now Wittenberg basks in the glory of its golden era by celebrating the homes, workplaces and graves of the cast of characters who together created the Protestant Rome. Among them were professor and theologian **Philipp Melanchthon**, who added intellectual clout, and painter and printmaker **Lucas Cranach the Elder**, who, with his son, created a tangible image for the whole movement, which could be widely disseminated thanks to the recently invented printing press. Elector of Saxony **Frederick the Wise**, who shielded them all from the Papacy, lies buried in the town's Schlosskirche.

Fittingly all the main **festivals** in Lutherstadt Wittenberg revolve around Luther: the big events are the celebration of Luther's marriage in early June and **Reformation Tag** on October 31, which celebrates the publication of his 95 theses.

Collegienstrasse, Wittenberg's high street, becomes **Schlossstrasse** at its western end. Together they join virtually every sight in town.

Arrival, information and tours

Lutherstadt Wittenberg's **Hauptbahnhof** is an easy ten-minute walk northeast of Collegienstrasse where most points of interest lie, although the **tourist office**, Schlossstrasse 16 (Jan & Feb Mon–Fri 10am–4pm; April–Oct Mon–Fri 9am–6.30pm, Sat & Sun 10am–4pm; Nov, Dec & March Mon–Fri 10am–4pm, Sat 10am–2pm, Sun 11am–3pm; ☎03491/49 86 10, ⓦwww.wittenberg.de), is another ten minutes' walk away to just beyond the western end of Collegienstrasse. With this walk crossing the entire town centre, Wittenberg is clearly easy to explore on foot, but to explore more widely, there's the option of a ninety-minute **boat trip** on the Elbe aboard the MS *Lutherstadt Wittenberg* (€7.50;

Martin Luther

As the founder of Protestantism and modern written German – a side effect of translating the Bible into German – Martin Luther's (1483–1546) impact on German society has been as great as anyone's. Yet Luther's personality remains one of history's more elusive, in part because both he and generations of historians ever since have sought to manipulate his image.

Though born Martin Luder into the well-to-do family of Magarete and Hans Luder in Eisleben in 1483, Luther liked to talk of humble origins. He would talk of his father's hard mining life, and how his mother carried wood home on her back. In fact his father was a mine and smelting business owner and so his mother would rarely have needed to collect wood herself. Certainly, though, his upbringing was a hard one: "My parents always punished me severely and in a frightening way. My mother beat me for the sake of a single nut until blood flowed." His early life was governed by his father's ambition that he should become a lawyer. Luther began to study at the University of Erfurt until 1505 when during a thunderstorm, after a near miss from a lightning bolt, he swore he would become a **monk** if he survived. He followed this up and became a model Augustinian monk in Erfurt, following the order's rules so strictly that he became a priest in a little over eighteen months. He left to study theology in Wittenberg in 1508 and by 1512 had become a **Doctor of Theology**; by all accounts he was an excellent teacher and charismatic preacher.

In 1517 he wrote his famous **95 theses**, a document in which he attacked the issue of **indulgences** by the Church. These certificates could be bought from the papacy to give the purchaser less time in Purgatory, while the funds were used to raise revenues, to fund Vatican building projects, great cathedrals and, ironically, Wittenberg's university. Martin Luther blew the whistle on all this and found widespread support, in part because the latest round of indulgence selling was part of a high-profile campaign to raise funds for rebuilding St Peter's in Rome, which struck a nationalist chord against foreigners bleeding Germanic states of their wealth. This principled stand against authority and injustice has later been celebrated with vigorous embellishments: Luther probably didn't nail his 95 theses on the door of the Schlosskirche but rather circulated them like a memorandum. Nor is there historical evidence that he boldly stated at the Diet of Worms *"Hier stehe ich. Ich kann nicht anders."* (Here I stand. I can't do anything else), a slogan now on souvenir socks and T-shirts. He did, however, change his name to Luther, inspired by a Greek word for liberated.

Luther was clearly pious and principled and courageously ventured into territory that had cost other would-be reformers, notably Jan Huss a century earlier, their lives. Yet his defiant and stubborn actions – openly burning the papal bull that called for his excommunication for example – were born out of a sort of academic pedantry, that the Bible and not the papacy was the only source of truth, rather than a desire for rebellion, as he showed in his opposition to the Peasants' War (1524–25), which made him a hard figure for the GDR to swallow. Certainly Luther should be seen more as a conservative whose aim was to return to the original values of the Church, rather than someone who wanted to create a revolutionary new order. However the same can not always be said of those who adopted the Reformation, who often had self-interest in change: his protector Frederick the Wise, Elector of Saxony, for one must have been tired of emptying his coffers to the Catholic Church – he'd personally hoarded around five thousand indulgences to shorten his time in Purgatory by a reputed 1443 years.

℡03491/769 04 33), bookable at the tourist office, which also has information on the ample **canoeing** in the region. On land the choice is more unusual: the company Event & Touring (℡03491/66 01 95, ⓦwww.event-touring.com) offers guided tours in **Trabants**, which they also rent out (3hr €40).

Accommodation

The tourist office runs an accommodation hotline on ☎03491/41 48 48, which makes it easy to access the considerable stock of inexpensive **private rooms** (❷) in town. Otherwise there are plenty of choices and it's rarely hard to find a bed.

Hotels and pensions

Acron Hotel Am Hauptbahnhof 3 ☎03491/433 20, 🌐www.wittenberg-acron.de. Pleasant and modest hotel, if a little out of town, but close to the Hauptbahnhof offering nondescript rooms and bike rental. ❸

Alte Canzley Schlossstr. 3 ☎03491/42 91 90, 🌐www.alte-canzley .de. The noble old Chancellery building overlooking Schlosskirche, where kings and emperors have stayed, has now been revamped with spotless upmarket dark-wood furniture and beige furnishings. With sauna and superb organic restaurant (see p.225). ❹

Best Western Stadtpalais Wittenberg Collegienstr. 56–57 ☎03491/42 50, 🌐www .stadtpalais.bestwestern.de. Large hotel with some sixteenth-century touches – headboards and lithographs on walls – but mostly devoted to providing modern luxury. Look out for well-priced "Luther" packages which include a sixteenth century–style meal in its restaurant, a ticket to the Lutherhaus next door and entry into its sauna. Stays of more than one night attract big discounts. Breakfast not included. ❺

Pension am Schwanenteich Töpferstr. 1 ☎03491/40 28 07, 🌐www.wittenberg -schwanenteich.de. Small pension, 1min walk from the Marktplatz, with bright, airy and fairly minimalist en-suite rooms and wi-fi. ❸

Stadthotel Wittenberg Schwarzer Baer Schlossstr. 2 ☎03491/420 43 44, 🌐www .stadthotel-wittenberg.de. Central hotel in a venerable five-hundred-year-old building, with standard three-star modern hotel rooms, free parking and wi-fi. ❸

Hostels and camping

Brückenkopf Marina-Camp Elbe Brückenkopf 1 ☎03491/45 40, 🌐www.marina-camp-elbe.de. Well-run holiday village with hotel, cabins and campsites 1.5km from the city centre on a scenic spot on the banks of the Elbe and near Wittenberg-Elbtor train station. Facilities include a sauna. ❷

DJH hostel Schloss Schlossstr. 14/15 ☎03491/40 32 55, 🌐www.jugendherberge.de/jh /wittenberg. Good, clean and central lodgings, with the added attraction of occupying a castle, though interiors are institutional and 1970s. All rooms en suite but breakfast costs extra. Dorms €14; private two-bed rooms ❷.

The Lutherhaus

At the eastern end of Collegienstrasse, beside a small park, lies the **Lutherhaus**, at no. 54 (April–Oct daily 9am–6pm; Nov–March Tues–Sun 10am–5pm; €5; ☎03491/420 30, 🌐www.martinluther.de), the Augustinian monastery into which Luther entered, which was then dissolved during the Reformation with one wing becoming the Luther family residence. Today the reformer's quarters contain an extraordinary collection of items relating to him in a well-executed multimedia museum that's easily the most rewarding in town, particularly thanks to excellent signage in both German and English.

The museum is entered via the **Katharinenportal**, a gift to Luther from his wife in 1540. Among the collection's treasures are Luther's desk, pulpit and first editions of many of his books, along with some priceless oils by Cranach the Elder, particularly his much-celebrated painting of the commandments.

Viewing a room apparently left bare as Luther had it in 1535 is another attraction, and one visited by Tsar Peter the Great in 1702, as a bit of his graffiti on the doorframe attests. Others have left their mark on Luther's legacy too: one quirky section of the museum looks at the various biopic films of Luther's life and how they dramatized its key events through the looking glass of their own times.

The Luthereiche and Melanchthonhaus

Outside the Lutherhaus, and diagonally opposite the adjacent park, on the corner of Lutherstrasse and Am Hauptbahnhof, grows an old oak – the **Luthereiche** – which was planted in 1830 on the spot where in 1520 Luther publicly burned the papal bull threatening his excommunication. This was perhaps his best-documented display of courage and conviction – qualities that were probably his most important contribution to the Reformation. Certainly his eloquent close friend Philipp Schwarzerd, a lecturer and humanist expert in Greek and Hebrew, known as Philipp Melanchthon, was arguably more the brains of the movement. His house, the **Melanchthonhaus** at Collegienstrasse 60 (April–Oct Tues–Sun 10am–6pm; Nov–March Tues–Sun 10am–5pm; €5 or €6 combined with Lutherhaus; ☎03491/40 32 79), one of the finest remaining Renaissance houses in Wittenberg, lies a short walk from Luther's. His assistance in translating original texts can't be overestimated. The museum – in which his quarters have been extensively re-created – gives an impression of this calmer and less-outspoken man whose greatest contribution was to draft the Augsburg Confession, which later served as the constitution for the Lutheran faith.

The Kirchplatz and Marktplatz

Further west, Collegienstrasse broadens and bustles with shops and eventually empties into Wittenberg's large **Marktplatz** where two powerful nineteenth-century statues of Luther and Melanchthon stand: Luther's is the work of Berlin's Neoclassical designers Schadow and Schinkel. The Rathaus lies behind, while on the eastern side of the Marktplatz an alley cuts through a row of town houses to the **Stadtkirche St Marien** (April–Oct Mon–Sat 10am–5pm, Sun 11.30am–5pm; Nov–March Mon–Sat 10am–4pm, Sun 11.30am–4pm; ☎03491/40 32 01), in which many landmark Protestant events took place. It was here that the first Protestant services took place in 1521, where Luther preached his Lectern Sermons in 1522. It was also here that he married Katharina von Bora and all six of their children were baptized in the imposing and well-preserved Gothic font.

Architecturally, the church isn't particularly distinctive. It does date back to 1300, even if it wasn't completed until 1470, and its striking octagonal turrets weren't added until after the Reformation. Inside the main attraction is the fabulous **altar** (1547) by Lucas Cranach the Elder and his son, which depicts several Reformation figures, including the artist, Frederick the Wise and Philipp Melanchthon, in biblical contexts. In the central Last Supper, Luther is the disciple receiving the cup. At the back of the Altar the painting of Heaven and Hell was subject to an irreverent local medieval tradition in which students etched their initials on one part of the painting depending on their exam results. Also worth seeking out is the fine epitaph to Lucas Cranach the Younger, whose work was as accomplished as his father's.

Cranach the Elder's residence – and birthplace of his son – **Cranachhaus**, lies on the southern side of the Markt at no. 4. His studio now houses the

---

Wittenberg English Ministry

Between April and October the **Wittenberg English Ministry**, Schlossplatz 2 (☎03491/ 49 86 10, ⓦwww.wittenberg-english-ministry.com), offers the chance to worship in some of the same spaces as the first Protestants, but with services in English. These are generally scheduled for Wednesday 4pm, Friday 11.30pm and Saturday 6.30pm, but check notices at the tourist office.

Galerie im Cranachhaus, Schlossstrasse 1 (April–Oct Mon–Sat 10am–5pm, Sun 1–5pm; Nov–March also closed Mon; €4; ☎03491/420 19 11), which displays much of the work he produced to publicize and popularize the Reformation, along with exhibits on the life of this artist, local businessman and politician, who served as mayor of Wittenberg for several years. The importance of the printing press in disseminating the Reformation can't be overstated, so it's fitting that the yard behind the Cranachhaus is home to the **Historische Druckerstube**, Cranach-Hof (☎03491/43 28 17), where you can see printing presses rattle out various lithographs and leaflets, and have staff explain the processes and sell you the results.

The Haus der Geschichte and Schlosskirche

Beyond the Marktplatz, Collegienstrasse becomes **Schlossstrasse**, and a short way down it, at no. 6, lies the **Haus der Geschichte** (Tues–Fri 10am–5pm, Sat & Sun 11am–6pm; €4; ☎03491/40 90 04), an intriguing museum of life in the GDR and almost the only sight in town not concerned with the Reformation: a reminder that other things have happened in Wittenberg in the past five hundred years. Among these events was a huge influx of refugees from Poland at the end of the war – since the town had largely been spared bomb damage – and, of course, the impact of a new order in the form of the GDR regime. The commercial evolution of the GDR is documented in the museum through displays of various consumer durables from the time. One room shows basic refugee quarters, another the living room of a party bigwig, another a kitchen from the 1950s, another a kindergarten from the 1980s. The throwback to the late twentieth-century decor is enlivened by humorous and insightful tour guides – the museum can only be visited on tours in German, although English speakers are provided with a printed accompaniment.

Schlossstrasse then terminates in front of the old Schloss and the tourist office, where the most imposing building is the Gothic **Schlosskirche** (April–Oct Mon–Sat 10am–5pm, Sun 11.30am–5pm; Nov–March Mon–Sat 10am–4pm, Sun 11.30am–4pm). Repeatedly ravaged by fires and wars over the years, it is largely the product of the nineteenth century. Even the door on which church notices were pinned – where Luther allegedly nailed his 95 theses on October 31, 1517 – has long since gone, although a bronze door has since been added with Luther's theses inscribed in Latin. Inside the church and beneath the pulpit lies Luther's tombstone, opposite that of Philipp Melanchthon. Most other tombs are devoted to powerful locals and include the bronze epitaph and statue of Frederick the Wise. All this is regularly graced by choir and organ music (May–Oct Tues 2.30pm; free), while the rickety stairs up the **Schlossturm** next door (Mon–Fri noon–4pm, Sat & Sun 10am–4pm; €2) provide views over town.

Eating, drinking and nightlife

Wittenberg has a small range of **restaurants** and a sedate **nightlife**, though you might find inspiration in the local listings magazine *Ingo*. On Fridays (May–Oct) you might start the evening with a church concert in the Stadtkirche. Worth investigating is the local so-called *Lutherbrot*, a gingerbread with chocolate and sugar icing which has no real links to the reformer but is tasty all the same.

🏃 **Alte Canzley** Schlossstr. 3
☎03491/42 91 90. First-rate organic restaurant under fourteenth-century arches with an experimental and oft-changing menu that

includes the likes of orange-ginger soup, beef in a black-beer crust (€10) and the thoroughly refreshing but seriously oddball, asparagus ice cream.

Brauhaus Wittenberg Markt 6 ☎03491/43 31 30. Bustling brewpub, whose courtyard lies just off the marketplace where dark, light, wheat and seasonal beers wash down basic hearty dishes.
Independent Collegienstr. 44. Relaxed and cosmopolitan bar, popular with foreign students, that's a good place to start a night out in Wittenberg.
Marc de Café Pfaffengasse 5 ☎03491/45 91 14. Excellent café tucked in a quiet courtyard in the lane behind the tourist office. The fabulous cakes, excellent coffee and relaxed vibe encourage lingering.

Tante Emmas Markt 9 ☎03491/41 97 57. Traditional German food (mains €13) served in a ramshackle place just off the marketplace that bursts with curios (closed Mon).

Zum Schwarzen Baer/Wittenberger Kartoffelhaus Schlossstr. 2 ☎03491/41 12 00. Old-fashioned, dark-wood pub serving potatoes just about any way you could want them: fried, grilled, as salad, gratin and even potato cakes for dessert. Naturally there are various meat and fish accompaniments, and they're good too; mains average €8.

Dessau and around

DESSAU, the one-time capital of Anhalt-Dessau, 35km west of Wittenberg, was once an attractive town at the centre of a patchwork of palaces, parks and gardens. The latter have survived, but war damage, Stalinist rebuilding programmes and years of GDR neglect have made the town rather workaday. But what does justify the journey here are remnants of the Bauhaus movement. The **Bauhaus design school** was built here in 1925, making it a hub of Modernism and also the first place where many modern designs were implemented – these include the **Meisterhäuser**, the villas of the most influential thinkers, and the **Törten**, the first modern housing-estate. All this makes it a place of pilgrimage for architecture students the world over, but it is interesting enough to appeal to anyone inquisitive about the roots of modern design.

The belt of landscaped parks in and around Dessau have been collectively dubbed the **Gartenreich** (Garden Realm; ⓦwww.gartenreich.com) and offer days of unhurried exploration and picnicking. Their attendant Baroque and Neoclassical mansions are an additional draw. The most extensive and impressive of all the complexes is **Wörlitz** (see p.230), but the most convenient is **Park Georgium** (see p.228), a short walk from the Meisterhäuser in central Dessau.

Arrival, information and accommodation

All the most significant Bauhaus sights are within easy walking distance west of the **Hauptbahnhof** – the Bauhausgebäude lies a five-minute walk west via Schwabestrasse and Bauhausstrasse – while the town centre lies a similar distance to the east; to reach the outermost points of interest you'll need to catch buses or trams from in front of the Hauptbahnhof.

Dessau's **tourist office**, Zerbster Strasse 2c (April–Oct Mon–Fri 9am–6pm, Sat 9am–1pm; Nov–March Mon–Fri 9am–5pm, Sat 10am–1pm; ☎0340/204 14 42, ⓦwww.dessau-tourismus.de), lies in the town centre a signposted five-minute walk southeast of the Hauptbahnhof, and can help with **accommodation** (hotline ☎0340/220 30 03). The best budget places in town are run by the Bauhaus Foundation: the *Bauhaus Ateliergebäude*, Gropiusallee 38 (☎0340/650 83 18, ⓦwww.bauhaus-dessau.de), which offers a small number of rooms in the simple Bauhaus student accommodation (❷) and in the *Platte*, Heidestrasse 33 (❶), a 1970s GDR eleven-storey Plattenbau, a prefabricated high-rise with good views over the city and its many parks. More upmarket is *An den 7 Säulen*, Ebertallee 66 (☎0340/61 96 20, ⓦwww.pension7saeulen .de; ❸), a friendly family-run, bed-and-breakfast opposite the Meisterhäuser, with its own sauna.

Bauhausgebäude

Hub of the Bauhaus movement, not only in Dessau but worldwide, was the Bauhausgebäude, part of which now houses the **Stiftung Bauhaus Dessau**, Gropiusallee 38 (Bauhaus Foundation; Mon–Fri 10am–6pm; ☎0340/650 82 51, ⓦwww.bauhaus-dessau.de). The work of Walter Gropius, this white concrete building with its huge plate-glass windows was refurbished on its eightieth anniversary in 2006, making it look tremendously new. The famous Bauhaus logo graces the southern side, the photogenic "swimming pool" balconies its eastern wall.

At the time of its construction the building was an architectural sensation and prototype for several industrial construction techniques. The reinforced concrete skeleton allowed for curtain walling – outer walls designed to carry nothing but their own weight – and introduced wide-span building techniques that opened up more useable floor space by removing the need for supporting columns. These building techniques flourished around thirty years later during the 1950s and 1960s and dominated thereafter – a familiarity that takes away from the spectacle for the modern viewer.

Though still in use as Bauhaus Kolleg, a design school, the public can wander round much of the building, with the audio tour (€4 and in English) a useful accompaniment, particularly if you can't make the hour-long tours (Mon–Fri 11am & 2pm, Sat & Sun also 4pm; €4) in German which allow you into some areas that are otherwise locked. Both can be organized at the front desk on the first floor, which also sells tickets to Dessau's other Bauhaus attractions and is the entrance to the **Ausstellung im Bauhaus** (Exhibition in the Bauhaus; Mon–Fri 10am–6pm; €4), which explores the experimental applications of Bauhaus theory, with just about every sphere of art and design represented, including ceramics, furniture, theatre and visual art. Finally the well-stocked basement **book and gift shop** is also worth a look.

▲ The Bauhausgebäude, Dessau

24 hours of Bauhaus

If you're in Dessau on a Bauhaus pilgrimage, be sure to pick up a 24-hour ticket (€12) at the **Bauhausgebäude**. It gets you into all Bauhaus buildings open to the public and on all tours of them within a 24-hour period. To complete the experience dine at the *Bauhaus Mensa* or the *Kornhaus* restaurant (see p.230) and sleep in the *Ateliergebäude*, the school's former student accommodation (see p.226).

The Meisterhäuser

The series of four white cubist villas a five-minute walk from the Bauhausgebäude along Ebertallee is the **Meisterhäuser** (April–Oct Tues–Sun 10am–6pm; Nov–March 10am–5pm; €5; ⓦ www.meisterhaeuser.de) – turn right up Gropiusallee then left onto Ebertallee – which served as accommodation for the Bauhaus professors. Gropius's director's house and half of one of the others were lost in the war, but those that remain have been restored to their original condition and are open to the public. These quarters were supposed to espouse a philosophy of new industrial living, yet contained features and designs – such as large windows and complicated lighting systems – that put them well outside the pockets of the masses, so arguably contravened Bauhaus ideals. Sadly the original Bauhaus furnishings are lacking, because they are simply too expensive to buy, as the prices in the antique shop along Gropiusallee en route from the Bauhausgebäude attest. However, in their absence, photos of original setups help give an impression, as do the informative German-language **tours** (Tues–Fri 12.30pm, Sat & Sun also 1.30pm; €9).

The houses include that of German-American artist Lyonel Feininger – now home to the **Kurt-Weill-Zentrum**, which celebrates the work of the versatile musician from Dessau who's best known for cabaret pieces such as "Mack the Knife" in Brecht's *Threepenny Opera*. The other two duplexes are known as the **Muche/Schlemmer Haus** and the **Kandinsky/Klee Haus**, the latter notable for pastel walls chosen by the two designers and faithfully reproduced today.

Park Georgium and the Kornhaus

The large road junction just east of the Meisterhäuser – where Ebertallee, Gropiusallee and Kornhausstrasse meet – is presided over by some Neoclassical columns that announce the gateway to the **Park Georgium**, part of a series of parks or Gartenreich in and around Dessau. This and other buildings in the park – which include a number of faux ruins – come across as strange frippery after the austere Modernism of all the Bauhaus designs, particularly the ornate **Schloss Georgium** from 1780. It now houses the **Anhalt Art Gallery**, Puschkinallee 100 (Tues–Sun 10am–5pm; €3; ⓣ0340/61 38 74), a collection of old masters that includes Rubens, Hals and Cranach. The rest of the park extends north to the banks of the Elbe, a little over 1km away, and includes a **Lehrnpark**, a low-key zoo and botanic garden with various small native animals and over a hundred different kinds of tree.

From the northern edge of the **Park Georgium** it's a five-minute walk west along the Elbe to the **Kornhaus**, Bauhaus architect Carl Fieger's wonderfully curved 1930 restaurant (see p.230), beer and dance hall overlooking the Elbe, also reached via a 1.5km walk along Kornhausstrasse, or bus #10 or #11 from the Hauptbahnhof.

The Törten

A leafy 1920s prototype housing-estate, the **Törten** lies 7km southeast of central Dessau: take tram #1 from the Hauptbahnhof to Dessau Süd to stop "Damaschkestrasse", then follow signs to Bauhaus Architektur. This low-rise estate was created as a model housing development that tried to combine the economy of prefabricated components with airy designs, sizeable gardens and ultimately decent living conditions for the working classes. Sadly the building standards were nowhere near as good as Gropius's designs, and many of the houses have since been altered – often in twee non-Bauhaus ways – by the owners.

The **information** centre for the estate is in the cheerless **Stahlhaus**, Südstrasse 5 (Feb–Oct daily 10am–6pm; Nov–Jan Tues–Sun 10am–5pm; free; ☎0340/858 14 20), also the starting point for tours (Mon 2pm; Tues–Sun 2pm & 3pm; €4) of the estate in German which also explore the outside of the **Laubenganghäuser**, a red-brick apartment block by Hannes Meyer, the second Bauhaus director; **Haus Fieger**, Carl Fieger's futuristic home; and the **Konsumgebäude**, Gropius's corner-shop design.

The only dwelling to have been restored to its original design – and the only one open to the public – is the **Moses–Mendelssohn–Zentrum**, Mittelring 38

Bauhaus

Bauhaus, whose literal meaning in German is "building-house", has become a generic term for the aesthetically functional designs that emerged from the art and design school at Dessau. The Bauhaus movement began with the Novembergruppe, founded in 1918 by Expressionist painter Max Pechstein to utilize art for revolutionary purposes. Members included Bertolt Brecht and Kurt Weill, Emil Nolde, Eric Mendelssohn and architect Walter Gropius. In 1919 Gropius was invited by Germany's new republican government to oversee the amalgamation of the School of Arts and Crafts and the Academy of Fine Arts in Weimar into the Staatliche Bauhaus Weimar. The new institution was to break down barriers between art and craft, creating a new form of applied art. It attracted over two hundred students who studied typography, furniture design, ceramics, wood-, glass- and metalworking under exponents like Paul Klee, Wassily Kandinsky and László Moholy-Nagy.

Financial problems and opposition from the conservative administration in Weimar eventually forced a relocation to Dessau, chosen because, as home to a number of modern industrial concerns, notably an aeroplane factory and a chemical works, it could provide financial and material support. Dessau's **Bauhausgebäude**, designed by Gropius and inaugurated on December 4, 1926, is one of the classic buildings of modern times. Towards the end of the 1920s, the staff and students of the Bauhaus school became increasingly embroiled in the political battles of the time. As a result, Gropius was pressurized into resigning by the authorities and replaced by Swiss architect Hannes Meyer. He, in turn, was dismissed in 1930 because of the increasingly left-wing orientation of the school. His successor Ludwig Mies van der Rohe tried to establish an apolitical atmosphere, but throughout the early 1930s Nazi members of Dessau's town council called for an end to subsidies for the Bauhaus. Their efforts finally succeeded in the summer of 1932, forcing the school to close. Bauhaus then relocated to more liberal **Berlin**, setting up in a disused telephone factory. However, after the Nazis came to power, police harassment reached such a pitch that on July 20, 1933, Mies van der Rohe took the decision to shut up shop for good. He and many of his staff and students subsequently went into exile in the United States, where they helped found a successor movement known as the **International Style.**

(March–Oct daily 10am–7pm; Jan & Feb Sat & Sun 1–4pm; €2; ☎0340/850 11 99), where the life of this humanist, philosopher and Dessau native is explored. An English-language guide to the architecture is available at the front desk.

Eating and drinking

To fully immerse yourself in Bauhaus **eat** in the school's *Mensa*, Gropiusallee 38, a canteen in the same wing of the school as the exhibitions and shop. Mains here cost no more than €6, and are enjoyed on unforgiving benches in austere Bauhaus surroundings; there's always a veggie option. In the basement of the same building, the *Bauhaus Klub* offers light dishes and drinks until midnight. But for a full meal in Bauhaus surroundings try the 🎄 *Kornhaus*, Kornhausstrasse 146 (☎0340/640 41 41), which has a balcony overlooking the Elbe and serves contemporary cuisine, with fish dishes such as marinated Alaskan shellfish and organic vegetables often part of its very reasonable €16.50 three-course menu.

Elsewhere in Dessau, try browsing its main drag Zerbster Strasse for other options which include standard traditional German restaurants and pizzerias.

Wörlitz

With its Gothic follies and mock Classical statues dotting the manicured lawns, and swans and rowing boats bobbing on its tranquil lakes, **Wörlitz** mentally transports you to England. And it's the English country park that inspired Prince Leopold III and Anhalt's favourite court architect, Friedrich Wilhelm von Erdmannsdorff, who created this attractive stately home and country garden midway between Lutherstadt Wittenberg and Dessau at the end of the eighteenth century.

The park grows fairly seamlessly out of the village and all its main buildings cluster at the boundary of the two. These include the engaging Neoclassical **Schloss Wörlitz** (May–Sept Tues–Sun 10am–6pm; April, Oct & Nov Tues–Sun 10am–6pm; €4.50; ☎034905/409 20) whose Baroque decoration is rather muted and which can only be visited on an hour-long tour. **Day tickets** (€10) for sale at the Schloss include a tour as well as access to a number of other buildings in the park, including the **Gotisches Haus** (€4.50), the Prince's neo-Gothic residence, and that of his wife, the **Haus der Fürstin** (€4.50), which is mostly of interest for its temporary exhibitions about the park. You can also visit **Insel Stein** (€3), a mock Italian landscape, and a **synagogue** (€1), built for the local population at the Prince's expense. His opinion that "faith is, like love, unchangeable", is inscribed on the interior.

One good way to orientate yourself in the landscaped park is to take a popular gondola tour of its central lake (45min; €6). They depart according to demand from the dock behind the Schloss. Note the interesting array of bridges over the park waterways, each built in a different style and including a midget **Iron Bridge** – a quarter of the size of the original over the Severn in Britain. Wörlitz gets rather too busy on summer weekends, though this is also when classical concerts are held.

Practicalities

Wörlitz lies 19km west of Lutherstadt Wittenberg and 17km east of Dessau and is reachable from both by **bus** #334 every two hours for a journey time of around 45 minutes from either. A **train** also runs from Dessau (March–Nov Wed, Sat & Sun) though generally only making five round-trips per day, leaving from a separate station on the north side of Dessau's Hauptbahnhof. Buses and trains drop travellers off a short walk from the Wörlitz **tourist office**,

Förstergasse 26 (Feb Mon–Fri 9am–4pm, Sat & Sun 11am–3pm; March–Oct daily 9am–6pm; Nov–Jan Mon–Fri 9am–4pm; ☎034905/202 16, ⓦwww .woerlitz.de), which has useful maps and can help out with **accommodation** (hotline ☎034905/194 33). Otherwise try *Pension Zum Hauenden Schwein*, Erdmannsdorffstrasse 69 (☎034905/301 90, ⓦwww.pension-zum-hauenden -schwein.de; ❸), a traditional place with bright rooms, a good wine-bar, traditional **restaurant** and terrace. Inside the park grounds the only real option is the *Gastwirtschaft im Küchengebäude* (☎03495/02 23 38), a beer garden and restaurant in the old Schloss kitchens.

Magdeburg

MAGDEBURG is sometimes described as Berlin in miniature and there's some truth in this, even if it's not much larger than one of the capital's neighbourhoods. Certainly Magdeburg was destroyed to a similar extent, with World War II bombs levelling four-fifths of the city. Then postwar rebuilding projects blighted it with large socialist buildings, soulless boulevards, loveless plazas and windswept parks. However, tiny pockets of cobbled streets with nineteenth-century tenements survive, notably at the southern end of the city around **Hasselbachplatz**, where a buoyant **bar** and **club** scene has taken hold. Magdeburg has also struggled economically and is propped up by generous federal funding – in this case thanks to the town's role as capital of Saxony-Anhalt. With this economic boost has come a major makeover of many parts of town: bold new architecture has been welcomed around town and a large building by Friedensreich Hundertwasser has become a major landmark, offsetting the angular bleakness elsewhere.

All this modernity aside, Magdeburg is not without reminders of its lengthy history. Established as a trading post by Charlemagne in the tenth century, it became great under Emperor Otto I who chose it as his main residence, making it a significant political and cultural centre in medieval times and giving it Germany's oldest cathedral. It was badly hammered by siege and fires in the Thirty Years' War when two-thirds of the population – around 20,000 people – lost their lives; some heavyweight city defences still stem from this time. In the seventeenth century Magdeburg slowly resurfaced thanks in part to the work of **Otto von Guericke**, who was famous for his physics experiments, and though with the abolition of the city's bishopric in 1680 it lost most of its political importance, it continued to be a major port on the Elbe.

Ernst-Reuter-Allee, the town's major east–west thoroughfare, runs from the Hauptbahnhof to the Elbe. Partway along it – and beside the tourist office and giant Allee Center shopping mall – it intersects with **Breiter Weg**, the main north–south artery. Just northeast of the intersection lies the **Alter Markt**, the city's old marketplace, but most sights – including the **Dom** and Hasselbachplatz – are on or around Breiter Weg to the south.

Arrival, information and tours

From the **Hauptbahnhof** it's a short walk east along Ernst-Reuter-Allee, to the **tourist office**, at no. 12 (May–Sept Mon–Fri 10am–7pm, Sat 10am–4pm; Oct–April Mon–Fri 10am–6.30pm & Sat 10am–3pm; ☎0391/194 33, ⓦwww .magdeburg-tourist.de). Generally the city is easily walkable, but a good bus and tram network can speed things up (singles €1.50, day tickets €4). Boat company Weisse Flotte (☎0391/532 88 91, ⓦwww.weisseflotte-magdeburg.de) offers short cruises on the Elbe, with those that explore the **Wasserstrassenkreuz**,

an unusual 918m aqueduct across the Elbe, the most interesting (May–Sept daily 1pm; €20). For longer jaunts on the river, including trips to the Altmark (see p.236), try Reederei Kaiser (ⓦwww.reederei-kaiser.de) whose eight-hour day-trips (€22) stop at Tangermünde and Havelberg.

Accommodation

Accommodation in Magdeburg tends to be business-orientated, though the tourist office has plenty of private rooms on its books.

DJH Magdeburg Leiterstr. 10 ☎0391/532 10 10, ⓦwww.jugendherberge.de/jh/magdeburg. Large, modern and central, the youth hostel is well equipped, offering bike rental, wi-fi and en-suite dorm rooms for €20 per bed. Some double rooms too (❷).

Grüne Zitadelle Breiter Weg 9 ☎0391/62 07 80, ⓦwww.hotel-zitadelle.de. Stay in the wobbly world of Hundertwasser (see below). The decor in most rooms is curvaceous but restrained, but the bathroom mosaics are pure mayhem. Wi-fi available and there's a sauna too. ⑤

Herrenkrug Parkhotel Herrenkrug 3 ☎0391/850 80, ⓦwww.herrenkrug.de. Four-star pile set in a quiet bucolic park around 5km northeast of town, with good spa and a well-respected and funky Art Deco restaurant, and extensive pool and sauna facilities. ⑦

Hotel Ratswaage Ratswaageplatz 1 ☎0391/592 60, ⓦwww.ratswaage.de. Dependable and central four-star hotel a short walk north of the centre, with pool and sauna and fabulous breakfast buffet. Weekday rates are around a third cheaper. ⑥

Residenz Joop Jean-Burger-Str. 16 ☎0391/626 60, ⓦwww.residenzjoop.de. Elegant B&B in a small villa an easy walk from nightlife district Hasselbachplatz. The decor's a bit floral and chintzy, but the breakfast buffet excellent. Free wi-fi. ⑥

The Alter Markt and around

A block north of the main road Ernst-Reuter-Allee and behind the tourist office lies the **Alter Markt**, Magdeburg's traditional centre and location of the **Magdeburger Reiter**, Magdeburg's most famous artwork, which has the distinction of being the earliest (1240) equestrian statue north of the Alps. The gilded statue is a copy of the sandstone original, now in the **Kulturhistorisches Museum** (see p.234). The rider is generally thought to be Otto I, with two wives alongside; he looks on at a *Roland* statue and the late seventeenth-century Baroque **Rathaus** behind. The lady on the facade of the Rathaus is the Magdeburger Jungfrau, symbol of the city, and one of its main doors is of interest for scenes from Magdeburg's history carved by local artist Heinrich Apel. One scene is devoted to the experiments of **Otto von Guericke** (see box below) whose statue also commands attention on the square. His life and work, and a reconstruction of his study, are the subject of the interesting little **Otto-von-Guericke Museum**, Schleinufer 1 (Tues–Sun 10am–5pm; free; ☎0391/541 06 16), five minutes' walk north along the Elbe in the **Lukasklause**, a fifteenth-century brick tower that was once part of the town's defences.

Breiter Weg and around

As you walk south beside the clanking trams that rattle along the arterial Breiter Weg, the most eye-catching building is the **Grüne Zitadelle** (information office 10am–6pm; tours Mon–Fri 11am, 3pm & 5pm, Sat & Sun hourly 10am–5pm; ☎0391/400 96 50, ⓦwww.gruene-zitadelle.de), whose curvy, zany form

---

Otto von Guericke (1602–86)

So extraordinary was the life's work of Magdeburg-born Otto Guericke that he almost single-handedly wrote Magdeburg not only into the history books but also physics textbooks, accomplishments that earned him a knighthood and the surname von Guericke. His most important discovery came as the result of his **Magdeburg Hemispheres** experiments which demonstrated the principle of a vacuum. Using a home-made pump, he sucked the air from two copper hemispheres which had been joined together, creating a vacuum so powerful that even two teams of sixteen horses couldn't pull them apart – to the amazement of the 1654 Reichstag of Regensburg. Guericke also pioneered the use of a barometer to predict weather and conducted early electrical experiments. All this activity was vital in promoting Magdeburg as the city rebuilt itself after its destruction in the Thirty Years' War. As if that wasn't enough, Guericke juggled his scientific investigations with his other job, as a diplomatic representative and later city mayor – though he was better known locally as a vet and brewer.

is the unmistakable work of Viennese architect Friedensreich Hundertwasser. The building – a mix of apartments, shops and offices – was his last, and only completed in 2005, five years after his death, and can be visited on interesting fifty-minute tours.

Behind the Hundertwasser building, along Erhard-Hübener-Platz, lies **Kloster Unser Lieben Frauen**, Regierungsstrasse 4–6 (Tues–Sun 10am–5pm), an austere, late eleventh-century Romanesque church and Magdeburg's oldest building. Inside it has been stripped of all ornamentation to serve as a concert hall, but the door is worth a look for Heinrich Apel's unusual bronze door-handles: knock with the woman's necklace, then push down the man's cap to enter. Inside a modest **sculpture museum** (same times; €2) features works by Barlach and Rodin.

South of the Kloster lies a large square surrounded by Baroque mansions that lead up to Magdeburg's impressive cathedral with its distinctive octagonal turrets and spires. The **Dom St Mauritius und St Katharina** (Mon–Sat 10am–4pm, Sun 11.30am–4pm), one of Germany's most important Gothic structures, was begun in 1209 on the site of an earlier monastery church that was founded by Emperor Otto the Great in 926; there's some lopsided evidence of the original building on the south side. But the church was largely built in the fourteenth century and completed in 1520. Inside the vastness of the structure and its lofty ceilings immediately impress and serve to exaggerate its bleak emptiness. An English-language booklet available from the entrance desk explains all the main features and artworks which span eight centuries. Don't miss the tomb of Otto I, Ernst Barlach's contemplative memorial to the dead of World War I and the sculpture of the Magdeburger Virgins. **Church tours** are offered in German (Mon–Sat 2pm, Sun 11.30am; €3).

An atmospheric district of turn-of-twentieth-century tenements begins south of the Dom whose vague focus is **Hasselbachplatz**, the hub of the nightlife quarter. A five-minute walk west of the Dom, across Breiter Weg, lies the **Kulturhistorisches Museum** (Tues–Sun 10am–5pm; free but €2 donation requested; ☏0391/540 35 01, ⊛www.khm-magdeburg.de), Magdeburg's modest town history museum, whose most valuable treasure is the **Magdeburger Reiter** (see p.233).

The Marieninsel and Herrenkrugpark

What looks to be the eastern bank of the Elbe from Magdeburg's city centre is actually the Marieninsel, a large river island, that's almost entirely given over to the **Rotehornpark**, a large public park with playgrounds, picnic areas, beer gardens and rowing boats for rent, and the sort of place where there's often a travelling fair and weekend flea markets. It's an easy walk from the centre, but tram #6 also stops here, on its way to its terminus at **Herrenkrugpark**, another popular strolling and cycling spot on the north-eastern edge of town. Alight at stop Messegelände/Elbauenpark between the two parks and you'll be in front of the **Jahrtausendturm**, Tessenowstrasse 5a (April–Oct Tues–Sun 10am–6pm; €2.50 including Elbauenpark; ☏01805/25 19 99, ⊛www.elbauenpark.de), a funky piece of architecture and conical tower with an external walkway that spirals around it. Inside a very hands-on museum celebrates scientific achievement, including of course that of local hero Otto von Guericke (see p.233). It's great for kids, but a bit of a struggle if you can't read German. Surrounding it is the **Elbauenpark** (May–Sept 9am–8pm; Oct–April hours vary; €3), a collection of gardens whose most interesting feature is the **Schmetterlingshaus** (butterfly house; April–Oct Tues–Sun 10am–6pm; free).

Eating, drinking and nightlife

Though no gastronome's delight, it's easy enough to get a good meal in Magdeburg though many of the best places are a little way outside the centre. In contrast the busy and fairly studenty **nightlife** couldn't be more central, being concentrated within a couple of blocks of Hasselbachplatz at the southern end of the town centre. For event listings check the magazine *DATEs*, available at the tourist office – venues to check on include the **Stadthalle** (℡0391/59 34 50) in Stadtpark Rotehorn, which is a major venue for every kind of music. For high culture the main address is the **Theatre Magdeburg Opernhaus**, Universitätsplatz 9 (℡0391/540 64 44), home to opera and ballet companies and the Magdeburg Philharmonic. The **Johanniskirche** is also a popular venue for classical concerts.

Restaurants

Avalon Breiter Weg 227 ℡0179/123 93 03. Basement restaurant with several cosy corners and a "Celtic" theme that tends to just look traditionally German. Reasonable prices (mains from €6) attract a young crowd and the small menu has a variety of meats and some interesting sauces – such as the apple-and-horseradish sauce over a pork chop. A few basic dishes try to keep vegetarians happy.

Le Frog Heinrich-Heine-Platz 1 ℡0391/531 35 56. Brasserie in the Stadtpark, whose large beer garden regularly hosts live music. Good for breakfast and even better for Saturday and Sunday brunch, which tends to really draw the crowds. Otherwise the broad menu includes some local game and wild mushrooms along with a few good salads and veggie options. Mains average €11.

Liebig Liebigstr. 3 ℡0391/555 67 54. Trendy spot that's as much a bar and café as restaurant, though the international menu – which ranges from curries to steaks to Mediterranean dishes (all around €11) – is worth trying.

Petriförder Petriförder 1 ℡0391/5 97 96 00. Large restaurant with rather pleasant riverside location and a rambling menu that includes numerous Italian options (most pizzas are a very reasonable €6) but also a good line in *Schnitzel* (€11) and Argentinian steaks (€14).

Wenzel Prager Bierstuben Leiterstr. 3 ℡0391/544 66 16. Branch of a dependable, regional chain of rustic Czech places that specialize in good beers and various, moderately priced, heavy meat meals – all of which should apparently be chased by a *Becherovka*, an aniseed and cinnamon herbal liquor.

Cafés, bars and clubs

Café Central Leibnizstr. 34 ⓦwww .cafecentral.cc. Opulent, but relaxed *fin de siècle*-style hang out and a great place to play the board games that are supplied or appreciate the varied programme of cabaret, readings, films and lectures.

Café Lüder Allee Center. On the top level of Magdeburg's biggest mall, it may lack ambience, but the quality of the cakes at this *Konditorei* is hard to argue with.

Coco Otto-von-Guericke-Str. 56. Serving what are hands-down Magdeburg's best cocktails, and so very busy and sociable, particularly on Wednesdays when there's live music. Open until 5am.

Grüne Zitadelle Café Breiter Weg 9. Good café, ideal for a quick bite with various snacks, cakes and pasta dishes served amid funky Hundertwasser designs.

Magdeburger Zwickmühle Leiterstr. 2a ℡0391/541 44 26, ⓦwww.magdeburger -zwickmuehle.de. Popular satirical-cabaret bar, worth a visit if your German's up to it.

Prinzzclub Halberstädter Str. 113 ⓦwww .prinzzclub.de. Magdeburg's leading club and certainly where most visiting celebrities and bands end up on a night out. It has two bars and a lounge and often as not hip-hop thundering across its dance floor. Located 1km southwest of town along Halberstädter Strasse. Open Fri & Sat 11pm until late.

Strandbar Magdeburg Petriförder 1 ℡0175/594 00 59. Get bright white sands between your toes while you lounge on a deckchair and sip a cocktail. This small, urban beach beside the Elbe has a number of food stalls, and various sociable and well-attended events – including films, DJs and beach-volleyball contests. Daily 11am–1am.

The Altmark

North of Magdeburg, the Elbe flows into the secluded and gently rolling **Altmark** region where little disturbs the peace and seemingly hasn't for centuries, with all its most significant towns beautifully preserved medieval gems. **Stendal** is the regional and transport hub but more atmospheric and captivating are the small fortified towns of **Tangermünde** on the banks of the Elbe and, some 40km downstream at its confluence with the Havel, **Havelberg**.

The region is only lightly visited, and outside Stendal there are few services and little going on. The exception to this is Havelberg's **Pferdemarkt** on the first weekend in September when thousands of visitors descend on the town for the one-time horse market that's since become a flea market and giant fair with beer tents, fairground rides and handicrafts and one of eastern Germany's largest festivals.

Stendal is well connected to Magdeburg by train and linked to the other towns by several easy, flat **cycle paths**, all marked on a free map available from Stendal's tourist office, which also rents out bikes. The 24km round trip to Tangermünde is an easy option for most, while the 100km round trip between the three makes for a long day or a pleasant weekend. Another way of visiting is to sail up the Elbe from Magdeburg (see p.231).

Stendal

The Altmark's largest town by far, **STENDAL**, 60km from Magdeburg, has a fine medieval heritage that abruptly announces itself with several oversized city gates, including the **Tangermünder Tor** a short way up from the Bahnhof on the southwestern edge of a compact Altstadt. Its main pedestrian shopping street, Breite Strasse, bustles pleasantly and leads to the **Kornmarkt** central square around which gather a Renaissance **Rathaus**, a copy of the town's sixteenth-century *Roland* statue and the late Gothic, red-brick **Marienkirche**, whose astronomical clock is its main treasure. Further exploration of the town, a five-minute walk northwest, reveals **Winckelmann-Museum**, Winckelmannstrasse 37 (Tues–Sun 10am–noon & 1–5pm; €2.50), which celebrates the work of Johann Joachim Winckelmann, the father of German archeology who was born here in 1717. Just north lies the **Uenglinger Tor** (May–Sept Sat & Sun 10am–noon & 12.30pm–4pm; €2), which can be climbed for city views, while the mid-fifteenth-century **St Nikolai** church in the southwest corner of the Altstadt is arguably its most magnificent church thanks to some beautiful stained-glass in both its presbytery and transept.

The Kornmarkt is also the seat of the town's helpful **tourist office** (April–Oct Mon–Fri 9am–5pm, Sat & Sun 10am–1pm; Nov–March Mon–Fri 9am–5pm, Sat 10am–1pm; ☏03931/65 11 90, ⓦwww.stendal.de) who will book **accommodation**, though the *Schwarzer Adler*, Kornmarkt 5–7 (☏03931/41840, ⓦwww.altmarkhotel-schwarzer-adler.de; ❹), next door, is as good a choice as any and has a reasonable **restaurant**, cocktail bar and club. However, the cheap-and-cheerful two-hundred-year-old *Zur Grünen Laterne*, Hallstrasse 73, just off the square, is better for traditional inexpensive lunches; while a more adventurous choice for an evening meal is the *Jadran*, Winckelmannstrasse 32, whose inexpensive and spicy dishes hail from the Balkans (closed Mon & lunch Tues–Fri).

Tangermünde

A faded charm easily makes **TANGERMÜNDE**, 10km east of Stendal, the most delightful Altmark town with its cobblestone streets lined almost exclusively by half-timbered houses. Most of these hail from the seventeenth century, built after the town was destroyed by a fire in 1617, an event blamed on one Grete Minde, who was subsequently burned as a witch, and celebrated for her suffering two centuries later in the eponymous Theodor Fontane novel.

But the town's roots go back far further, and it was in medieval times that it grew rapidly and became a blossoming trade centre as a member of the Hanseatic League. For centuries it was also the seat of the Brandenburg margraves and then in the late fourteenth century, second royal residence of Charles IV, king of Bohemia, after Prague. Some of his **Burg** remains a part of the town's foreboding riverside defences though much of these date from after their destruction by the Swedes during the Thirty Years' War in 1640. Today it's given over to a small public park and the town's finest hotel (see below). Almost beside the Burg, lies the town's other grand building, the **St Stephanskirche**, a church built for the Augustinian monks brought into town by Charles IV in 1377. The magnificent late-Gothic structure was finally completed at the end of the fifteenth century, though many of its most interesting features came later, including a 1624 organ from the Hamburg workshop of Hans Scherer the Younger, a 1619 pulpit by Christopher Dehne and a font from 1508 by Heinrich Mente.

Southeast from here, reached via **Kirchstrasse**, one of the two main streets that run parallel through town and featuring many of the finest half-timbered houses with richly painted doorways, lies the Markt. Its timber-framed **Rathaus** is one of Tangermünde's oldest buildings, built during its commercial zenith of the 1430s, and is studded with a forest of gables and pinnacles. Further along, Kirchstrasse terminates beside the magnificent **Neustädter Tor**, another impressive remnant of the city walls from around 1300.

Practicalities

Tangermünde's **Bahnhof** lies a short walk north of the Altstadt and **tourist office**, which is at Kirchstrasse 59 (April–Oct daily 10am–6pm; Nov–March Mon–Fri 10am–6pm, Sat & Sun 1–4pm; ☏039322/223 93, ⓦwww.tourismus -tangermuende.de). A solid mid-range **accommodation** choice is the *Alte Brauerei*, Lange Strasse 34 (☏039322/441 45, ⓦwww.hotel-alte-brauerei.de; ❸), while *Schloss Tangermünde* (☏039322/73 73, ⓦwww.schloss-tangermuende.de; ❹) is the town's most prestigious address, with attentive service, dark-beamed rooms, and a reasonable value sauna. It also has the town's most upmarket **restaurant**, though the food at *Alte Brauerei* is decent: its range of salads, steaks and fish dishes cost around €8, the excellent Sunday brunch €15. Other traditional German choices are clustered around the church and include the intriguing ⚔ *Exempel*, Kirchstrasse 40, a former schoolhouse with original furnishings and various cheerful bits of clutter, which serves old-fashioned dishes such as pea soup as well as the local *Kuhschwanz* beer.

Havelberg

HAVELBERG centres on a compact Altstadt, a dense cluster of crooked houses that cheerfully squeeze together on a small island in the Havel River. The town was founded by Otto I in 948 as a Christian missionary outpost and its **Dom St Marien** (Mon–Fri 10am–5pm, Sat & Sun 10am–6pm), built between 1150 and 1170, dominates the town skyline. A cheerless and foreboding structure, its many Romanesque and Gothic features are the result of several rebuilds following a huge fire in the thirteenth century and several later redesigns. The chief treasure among many in its impressive interior is a fourteenth-century stone choir-screen into which is carved the Passion of Christ. An excellent English-language guide can be borrowed from the front desk to explain this and many other church features in detail.

Buses arriving in Havelberg stop on Uferstrasse, by the river and the town's **tourist office** (April–Sept Mon–Fri 9am–6pm, Sat & Sun 1–5pm; Oct–March Mon–Fri 9am–5pm, Sat 1–5pm; ☎039387/790 91, ⊛www.havelberg.de), which can help with **accommodation**; the **restaurant** *Belle Vista*, Domplatz 2, has superb town views from its terrace and does a good range of pizzas for around €6 and many pork and fish dishes for a little more.

The Harz

Unknown to much of the outside world but well loved as a mini-Black Forest to northern Germans, the **Harz** mountains lie where Saxony-Anhalt, Thuringia and Lower Saxony meet. Soaring peaks may be absent, but the region is blessed with thickly wooded low mountains and high hills between which nestle small villages and modest resort towns that form a pleasant backdrop for a variety of outdoor activities. The Harz also has two spectacular gateway towns packed with beautifully restored medieval architecture: **Quedlinburg** in the southeast and **Goslar** in the northeast. With their timber-framed buildings and Romanesque churches, both have made UNESCO's list of World Heritage sites, and also make fine bases for forays into the hills, though if you're reliant on public transport you'll need to rise early, as bus connections around the Harz take time. Trains are little faster, but several of the lines are narrow gauge and serviced by **steam trains**, making the journeys a delight in themselves.

Quedlinburg

If Disney were to mock up a small, medieval German town, it would probably resemble **QUEDLINBURG**, which lines the Bode River on the gently rolling foothills of the Harz, 59km southwest of Magdeburg. With well over a thousand crooked half-timbered houses crowding cobblestoned streets, and much of its medieval fortifications and churches well preserved, the town is deservedly popular and often bustles with visitors, but it's still large enough to escape the strolling masses at even the busiest times.

Quedlinburg's foundation dates back to a fortress built by Henry I (the Fowler) in 922, after which it quickly became a favourite residence for Saxon emperors; in 968 Otto I founded an imperial abbey there. The town flourished in the Middle Ages and as a Hanseatic League member and centre for dyes, paper production and engineering. Even today, plastic production and agricultural research are important, giving the town a purpose beyond simply being a living museum.

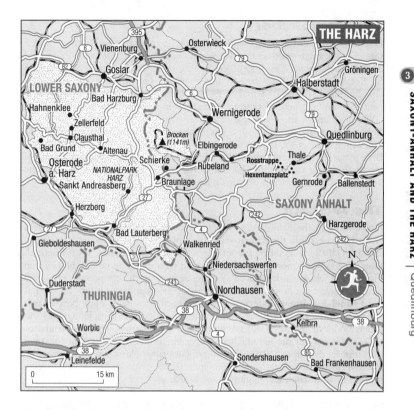

Arrival, information and accommodation

The **bus and train station** lie adjacent to one another a ten-minute walk southeast of the Markt, where the **tourist office** is at no. 2 (May–Oct Mon–Fri 9am–6.30pm, Sat 9.30am–4pm, Sun 9.30–3pm; Nov–April Mon–Fri 9am–6pm, Sat 9.30am–2pm; ☎03946/90 56 25, ⓦwww.quedlinburg.de).The town is easiest to explore on foot.

There's a good stock of city-centre **hotels** in historic buildings and at very similar prices; accommodation at the top end is noticeably absent, while for those on a budget there's a good, popular hostel. Private rooms can be the best option for many and are best booked through the tourist office (☎03946/90 56 34).

Am Brühl Billungstr. 11 ☎03946/961 80, ⓦwww .hotelambruehl.de. Family hotel with bright country-house-style rooms – scattered with antiques and frippery – a 10min walk from the Markt. ❺
DJH hostel Neuendorf 28 ☎03946/81 17 03, ⓦwww.jugendherberge.de/jh/quedlinburg/. Quiet, central but often full hostel. Dorm beds €15.50.
Schlossmühle Kaiser-Otto-Str. 28 ☎03946 /78 70, ⓦwww.schlossmuehle.de. Smart hotel with superb castle-views from many of its rooms, which have exposed beams, but are otherwise pretty standard. Also home to Quedlinburg's finest restaurant. ❸

Theophano Markt 13–14 ☎03946/963 00, ⓦwww.hoteltheophano.de. Traditional place in a heavyweight half-timbered building with rustic charm and an unbeatable central location; many rooms have canopied beds and there's an atmospheric cellar bar too. ❹
Zum Bär Markt 8–9 ☎03946/77 70, ⓦwww.hotelzumbaer.de. There's been a hotel here in the thick of things on the Markt for 250 years, so a sense of being part of a time-honoured tradition hangs in the air of the airy, pastel-furnished rooms. ❹

The Schlossberg

Perched on the **Schlossberg** (daily 6am–10pm), a knuckle of rock at the southern side of town, a sixteenth-century Renaissance castle on the site of an old fortress dominates the town. The hub of the Schloss is the Romanesque **Stiftskirche St Servatius** (Tues–Sat 10am–6pm, Sun noon–4pm; €4), the former abbey church. Built between 1070 and 1129, incorporating parts of the original tenth-century church, it hoards some aged treasures in its **Schatzkammer**.

West, just below the Schloss, and with superb views of the palace, stands the **Schlossmuseum**, Schlossberg 1 (Sat–Thurs 10am–4pm; €2.50; ☎03946/27 30), which displays a glut of local treasures that hark back as far as the Stone and Bronze ages, but also includes fine tenth-century treasures and a grisly array of torture instruments. As chilling, is an intriguing multimedia exhibition on the Nazi use of the site for propaganda purposes.

The Altstadt

Downhill from the Schlossberg on a street of half-timbered houses that curves around its base, stands the **Klopstockhaus**, Schlossberg 12 (Wed–Sun 10am–4pm; €3; ☎03946/26 10), birthplace of the of eighteenth-century poet Friedrich Gottlieb Klopstock, now devoted to the man who styled himself as the German Homer and whose work received some recognition in the symphonies of Gustav Mahler. Behind the house, in a robust turn-of-the-twentieth-century building, is the **Lyonel-Feininger-Galerie** (Tues–Sun: April–Oct 10am–6pm; Nov–March 10am–5pm; €6; ☎03946/22 38), with some drawings, woodcuts, lithographs and watercolours of the key Bauhaus protagonist on display. A couple of minutes' walk northwest lies the grandfather of Quedlinburg buildings at **Wordgasse 3** – its timbers date from 1310 making them Germany's oldest – which houses the **Fachwerkmuseum** (Fri–Mon 11am–4pm; €2.50; ☎03946/38 28) where half-timbered construction techniques are explained.

▲ Quedlinburg

Quedlinburg's colourful Markt is overlooked by a mix of buildings and styles, including several sixteenth-century guildhouses and a Renaissance **Rathaus**, which dates back to 1320 and is fronted by a *Roland* statue (1426; see p.214). Look out too, for the cobbles in the Markt laid out to represent the city's coat of arms and its protectorate dog Quedel. The cobbled lanes around the Markt are best explored at random, but try seeking out the **Gildehaus zur Rose** (Breite Strasse 39), a textbook of Renaissance carving, and the courtyard **Schuhhof**, Breite Strasse 51–2, where cobblers displayed wares in ground-floor workshops above which they lived.

Eating and drinking

Most of Quedlinburg's hotels (see p.239) also have good restaurants.

Brauhaus Lüdde Blasiistr. 14 ☏03946/70 52 06. Barn-sized microbrewery with a range of beers – *Pils, Alt* and seasonal beers – to wash down a range of heavy traditional meals.

Café Kaiser Finkenherd 8 ☏03946/51 55 52. Rustic café, with a terrace and a penchant for chicken dishes, plus inexpensive omelettes and salads and home-made cakes.

Café Romanik Mühlenstr. 21 ☏03946/90 14 31. Inexpensive sandwiches, snacks and delicious home-made cakes are offered in this charming galleried hall just behind the Schlossberg.

Ratskeller Markt 1 ☏03946/27 68. Consistently high-quality German cuisine,

a banquet of pork, veal or game in rich sauces; mains range €11–50. The wine list is a connoisseur's delight. Closed Wed & Jan.

Schlosskrug Am Dom Schlossberg 1 ☏03946/28 38. Well-priced regional cuisine in three historic houses within the Schloss walls. Closed Mon; open until 8pm on other days.

Theopano Markt 13–14 ☏03946/963 00. Modern cuisine – tapas-style Harz dishes, quiche and fresh soups (mains average €15) – and understated style with black-and-white photos, clean lines and dark-wood benches. There's a great Gothic wine-cellar at the same address.

The mountains

The Harz range of **mountains** covers a well-defined area about 100km long and 30km wide, though almost all the top-flight attractions are concentrated around **Thale**, almost a suburb of Quedlinburg, and the **Brocken**, the Harz's highest peak, with its captivating associations with the pagan festival Walpurgisnacht. Various low-key resort towns, including **Schierke** and **Braunlage** are dotted around it, offering peaceful, outdoorsy bases.

Though **transport** around the mountains is well organized, it's best to have your own wheels. Bus journeys often require several changes and can become cumbersome and lengthy, but are nevertheless useful shuttles for hikers – and even cyclists when there's space. The Harz's quaint narrow-gauge system of **railways** (see box, p.242) is a fun way of soaking up the atmosphere, and shouldn't be missed.

Thale

Upstream along the Bode River, 10km southeast of Quedlinburg, the Harz mountains suddenly rear up beside the modest steel-making town of **THALE** in scenery which awed Goethe and Heine alike. In particular two rugged outcrops – the **Hexentanzplatz** and the **Rosstrappe** – capture the imagination, partly for their mythical associations. Both are easily accessible by cable car while the lush **Bode Valley** which separates them is home to the **Hexenstieg** (see p.243), one of the Harz's most idyllic **hiking** routes and an easy day-hike. With a further 100km of marked trails in the vicinity, Thale makes for a superb base for a longer rambling holiday too.

The Harzer Schmalspurbahn

Among railway buffs the Harz is famous for having the largest narrow-gauge railway network in Europe: the **Harzer Schmalspurbahn** (℡ 03943/55 80, ⓦ www.hsb-wr.de). The 140km of track is plied largely by steam trains, and seeing the antique technology in action is as much part of the pleasure as the extraordinary terrain that's navigated in steep gradients and tight corners. It all adds up to an attractive way to appreciate the scenery and see some out-of-the-way places without doing the legwork yourself. **Tickets** can be bought for single journeys, or as a pass to the entire network (available at the main stations): €40 for three days and €45 for five days; children travel half-price, while a €60 family card gives two adults and two children access to the entire network for a day. The network divides into three lines:

The Harzquerbahn The 60km route twists all the way across the Harz in seventy bends between Wernigerode in the north and Nordhausen in the south. At its highest point, Drei Annen Hohne, you can transfer onto the Brockenbahn.

The Brockenbahn Climbs steeply from the Schierke up the Brocken up to a height of 1125m; scenically at its best in winter when the peaceful heights are blanketed in snow.

The Skeletbahn Beginning in Quedlinburg, this runs to the Eisfelder Tal where you can change onto the Harzquerbahn. The steam trains along this route are real antiques – the oldest from 1887.

The **Hexentanzplatz** ("witches' dance place"), once the site of a Celtic fortress, is full of supernatural and pagan associations and easily reached by car and cable car (daily: May–Sept 9.30am–6pm; Oct–April 10am–4.30pm; return €4.50). This is where the crones are said to have limbered up for Walpurgisnacht on the Brocken (see p.246), and these days it's a major magnet for modern-day would-be pagans on the same night. Otherwise there's little mystical atmosphere here at what has become a crowded coach-park lined with souvenir shops. But you can feed your imagination at the **Walpurgishalle** (May–Oct 10am–6pm; €1.50), a museum devoted to explaining pagan worship with many vivid drawings, but most ghoulish is the ancient Germanic sacrificial stone used here; exhibits are in German only.

The **Rosstrappe** opposite and to the north can also be reached by chairlift (daily: May–Sept 9.30am–6pm; Oct–April 10am–4.30pm; return €3.50) and was named for a legend in which Princess Brunhilde fled her unappealing husband-to-be Prince Bodo through the Harz on a mighty steed (or *Ross*), leaping the gorge from the Hexentanzplatz to leave a huge hoof imprint on the stone of the Rosstrappe. Meanwhile, in pursuit with more mortal skills, Bodo plunged into the valley creating an indentation in the river and becoming a hell-hound that guarded the valley.

Practicalities

Trains finishing the short trip from Quedlinburg pull into the **train and bus station** at the base of the Rosstrappe. The **tourist office** is in the park opposite at Bahnhofstrasse 2 (Mon–Fri 7am–5pm, Sat & Sun 9am–3pm; ℡ 03947/25 97, ⓦ www.thale.de); they can help with **accommodation**, which is only a problem around Walpurgisnacht. Along with a stock of **private rooms** the cheapest option is the DJH hostel, Bodetal-Waldkater (℡ 03947/28 81, ⓦ www .jugendherberge.de/jh/thale; dorms €15.50), close by and beautifully situated in the Bode Valley. The *Kleiner Waldkater*, Kleiner Waldkater 1 (℡ 03947/28 26, ⓦ www.kleiner-waldkater.de; ❷), next door, has basic wood-clad rooms, while one of the finest local options is the *Ferienpark Bodetal*, Hubertusstrasse 9–11

(☎03947/776 60, ⓦwww.ferienpark-bodetal.de; ➍), an apartment complex with pool, sauna and bike rental. It also has a beer garden and a reasonable **restaurant** with contemporary German food (mains around €12). The *Kleiner Waldkater* also does food, though of a more basic variety with *Schnitzels* around €8. The *Berghotel Hexentanzplatz*, up the mountain beside the Hexentanzplatz, serves traditional food with mains around €9–14 and good views to boot.

The Bode Valley

Arguably the finest local walk is the **Hexenstieg** along the Bode Valley (marked with blue triangles), which takes in spectacular scenery and rich flora, including gnarled trees hundreds of years old. It is best done by either taking a bus from Thale (#264 or #18) to the resort village of **TRESEBURG**, then walking the 10km back downstream, or for a longer walk take the chairlift up to Hexentanzplatz, walk the 10km trail (marked by red dots) to Treseburg, stop for lunch, then return to Thale via the Hexenstieg. Lunch options in Treseburg include *Fischerstube*, *Ferienhotel Forelle*, Oststrasse 28 (☎039456/56 40), which specializes in a bewildering array of local trout served on a terrace outside; and *Bergcafé*, Oststrasse 27 (☎039456/275), with its inexpensive selection of salads, soups and sandwiches.

Rübeland

The severe little town of **RÜBELAND** strung out along the Bode River, 15km from Thale, has been on the tourist map ever since the 600,000-year-old **Baumannshöhle** cave (daily: July & Aug 9am–5.30pm; Feb–June, Sept & Oct 9am–4.30pm; Nov–Jan 9am–3.30pm; €5; ☎039454/491 32, ⓦwww.harzer -hoehlen.de) was discovered by a fifteenth-century miner. Goethe toured the cave three times, as did Heine, treading in the footsteps of Stone Age inhabitants and Ice Age bears, some of whose skeletons are on display. Neighbouring **Hermannshöhle** is more modest, but its stalagmites and stalactites more impressive. It operates the same times and prices as Baumannshöle, though between November and April, the two sets of caves open on alternate days; call in advance to find out which is open when. Rübeland is reachable from Thale and Quedlinburg by bus via Blankenburg.

Schierke and the Brocken

The pretty village of **SCHIERKE** gathers at the foot of the **Brocken** (1142m), the Harz's highest peak, 15km west of Rübeland, and is the last stop for the narrow-gauge Brockenbahn. It's also a major outdoors centre. Hiking up the **Brocken** is the obvious attraction, but there are many other good **hiking**, **rock climbing** and **biking** routes in the area, and in winter first-class **snowshoeing** and **cross-country skiing** on a network of 70km of trails (see box, pp.244–245).

The best place for information on all these activities is the national-park visitor centre, **Nationalparkhaus Schierke**, Brockenstrasse 10 (☎039455/814 44), which has free brochures on hiking routes, including ones detailing two enjoyable shorter walks to two sets of jagged rock formations: the **Feuersteinklippen** are just thirty minutes' walk away, the **Scharcherklippen** ninety minutes. Another good source of information is DAV Basislager Brocken, Mühlenweg 1 (☎039455/515 46, ⓦwww.dav-basislager-brocken.de), who rent equipment for all activities.

The Brocken

Given its mystical reputation with respect to Walpurgisnacht, and as the highest peak in the Harz, the ascent of the **Brocken** is a vital part of a Harz itinerary

Healthy holidays in the Harz

As northern Germany's green lung and only range of proper hills, the Harz has a well-developed infrastructure for all the most common outdoor activities. And in typically German fashion, the perfect counter balance to all this exercise has been provided for with some first-class spa and sauna complexes.

Hiking

The rolling hills, low peaks and dark valleys of the Harz offer easy terrain for a huge network of well-signposted trails. Maps are readily available, particularly the inexpensive, user-friendly, waterproof and tear-proof ones published by Publicpress – easily recognizable by a logo of a sun wearing sunglasses – which cover a number of areas of the Harz at different scales, with 1:50,000 ones with hiking routes marked the most useful. With navigation very straightforward and with relatively easy terrain, it's easy to forget that the Harz is a highly changeable mountain environment, so be prepared for storms and sharp temperature changes.

With good trails everywhere there's no single **best base** for hiking the Harz, though Thale by the Bode Valley, and Schierke on the slopes of the Brocken are particularly good.

Cycling and mountain biking

Cycling the Harz is a pleasure if you're reasonably fit, though many of the roads have tight corners and fast traffic, so it's worth planning routes that take in as many of the even and fairly smooth forestry trails that criss cross the range as possible. Again, these are well marked on maps by Publicpress (see above), who have a range of cycling maps at a more useful smaller scale. **Mountain-bikers** are well served by the same network, and all the marked trails expertly documented in the book *Der Harz für Mountainbiker* (€13.60), which focuses on the Lower-Saxony end of the Harz and is available from all bookshops and tourist offices. These routes all tend to be a bit tame, so adventurous riders should try visiting Hahnenklee (Ⓦ www.bike-park-hahnenklee .de), 16km southeast of Goslar, where a range of single-track, north-shore and downhill routes can be accessed using a ski lift.

Winter sports

When snowfall cooperates, **skiing and snowboarding** are possible throughout the Harz and most of its towns are geared up for winter sports, making it easy and inexpensive to rent equipment. **Tobogganing** is very popular, with special runs in many places and the **cross-country skiing** trail network well developed.

for many. So if you are after peace then look elsewhere. Options to ascend it include by rail on the **Brockenbahn** (see p.242), by **horse–drawn wagon** – or **sleigh** in winter (both around €20; contact tourist information in Schierke) – or on foot. From Schierke, the sealed but traffic-free **Brockenstrasse** makes for a straightforward 12km hike, but is probably a better descent, taking the more interesting and scenic 7km route via Eckerloch up. The **Brockenmuseum** (daily 9.30am–5.30pm; €4; Ⓦ www.brockenmuseum.de) by the railway terminus near the summit has exhibits about geology and the mountain's mythology, but says little about the GDR era, when the Brocken was a military no-go area for Germans. An easy 2.5km path passes around the summit offering good views in all directions.

Practicalities

Schierke is connected by direct **bus** to Braunlage, and reachable from Quedlinburg with a couple of easy changes. **Tourist information** is available

The main **downhill centres** are at Braunlage and St Andreasberg in the central Harz and Hahnenklee in the north, but there are half a dozen smaller spots too. Braunlage often has the best conditions and offers a good selection of runs to keep most skiers and boarders happy for a long weekend. Check Ⓦwww.harz-ski.de for the latest conditions throughout the range.

Braunlage is also home to the **ice hockey** team Harzer Wölfe (Ⓦhttp://woelfe .hcmedia.de), a reasonably talented and fairly rabidly supported outfit who play in the stadium in the centre of town. Catching a game can be good fun for the atmosphere and chants alone.

Spas

The finest spas and saunas in the Harz are in some of its smallest towns. Good signposting means all are easy to find once you're there; enquire at a local tourist office for bus routes to the towns if you don't have your own transport. Three of the best are:

Heisser Brocken Karl-Reinecke-Weg 35, Altenau Ⓣ05328/91 15 70, Ⓦwww .kristalltherme-altenau.de. The newest and among the finest sauna complexes, 20km northwest of Braunlage, with excellent views over wooded hills from several outdoor pools (one with a waterfall). Three hours cost €10.80, massages are extra. Daily: April–Sept 9am–10pm; Oct–March 9am–11pm.

Vitamar Masttal 1, Bad Lauterberg Ⓣ05524/85 06 65, Ⓦwww.vitamar.de. Large family-friendly pool and sauna complex in the southwestern corner of the Harz, 46km east of Göttingen and 18km southwest of Braunlage. The pool has all sorts of gimmicks like wave machine, water slide, and various currents and jets. The sauna area is pure relaxation, in several different saunas with the option of taking part in free hourly therapies, some involving rubbing scented ice or honey into your body, others ending with fresh fruit in the garden. Three hours cost €9, fifteen percent discount after 6pm. Mon–Fri 10am–10pm, Sat 10am–9pm.

Sole-Therme Nordhäuser Str. 2a, Bad Harzburg Ⓣ05322/753 60, Ⓦwww.bad -harzburg.de/sole_therme.html. Rambling pool and sauna with many different heated outdoor pools, saunas and steam room, including one in which you rub salt into your body. At certain times the sauna area is single-sex, but these are coordinated with another sauna nearby to ensure there's always somewhere for everyone to sweat. A swim costs €7.50 for 2hr 30min; a day-ticket that includes the sauna area €12 or €7.50 after 7.30pm. Mon–Sat 8am–9pm, Sun 8am–7pm.

at the Kurverwaltung, Brockenstrasse 10 (Mon–Fri 9am–noon & 1–4pm, Sat 10am–noon & 2–4pm, Sun 10am–noon; Ⓣ039455/86 80), and, at the same address, the Nationalparkhaus in Schierke's upper town along the main road to the Brocken. Accommodation here and in the lower town is plentiful, particularly in **private rooms**, but often in short supply, so making advance reservations is worthwhile. The **youth hostel**, Brockenstrasse 48 (Ⓣ039455/510 66, Ⓦwww.jugendherberge.de/jh/braunlage; dorms from €19.50), is in the upper town. Other good options include the sparklingly clean *Hotel König*, Kirchberg 15 (Ⓣ039455/383, Ⓦwww.harz-hotel-koenig.de; ❸), where some rooms have a veranda, though not all are en suite. Fancier is the *Waldschlösschen*, Herman-Löns-Weg 1 (Ⓣ039455/86 70, Ⓦwww.waldschloesschen-schierke .de; ❹), which has particularly impressive views over to Braunlage from its good German restaurant – for maximum authenticity finish with the local schnapps, *Schierker Feuerstein*.

Braunlage

BRAUNLAGE sits at the foot of the Wurmberg (971m), the Harz's second-highest peak, where the regular snow has made the town a small **ski centre**. The Wurmberg is a reasonable ski hill – and boasts the longest cable-car in Germany – though its base can get slushy and off-puttingly busy at peak time, when a better option is to repair to the excellent network of cross-country skiing trails on the rolling hills about town, or to mess around on a toboggan – and there are good runs both on the Wurmberg and in town for this – look for signs to the Rodelbahn. Gear for all these winter activities is readily available in town: expect to pay around €20 for a ski or snowboard setup.

Braunlage is also a popular summer base for **hikers** and **bikers**, and the tourist office publishes useful free brochures on the local trail network.

Practicalities

Braunlage is connected by direct **bus** from Bad Harzburg, with passengers dropped on Herzog-Wilhelm-Strasse, the main road, from which it's a five-minute walk over the stream and up the hill along the other main road Elbingröder Strasse to the **tourist office** at no. 17 (Mon–Fri 9am–12.30pm & 2–5pm, Sat 9.30am–12.30pm; ☎05520/930 70, ⓦwww.braunlage.de). They will make **accommodation** bookings for you, including at a good stock of inexpensive **private rooms**. However the cheapest beds are in sparklingly clean DJH hostel, Von-Langen-Strasse 28 (☎05520/22 38; dorms from €18.30), at the edge of town in an attractive wooded area on a network of hiking and skiing trails. In town, another budget option is the cluttered but friendly *Pension Parkblick*, Elbingeröde Strasse 13 (☎05520/12 37; ❷), while *Hotel Harz-Wald*, Karl-Röhrig-Strasse 5a (☎05520/80 70, ⓦwww.relexa-hotel .de; ❹), has extensive fitness facilities, including swimming pool, sauna, steam room and mountain-bike rental – the latter available to non guests too. Best for an afternoon slice of cake is the old-fashioned *Omas Kaffeestube*, Elbingröder

---

Walpurgisnacht

According to legend, every year on April 30, witches and warlocks descend on the Harz to fly up the Brocken on broomsticks and goats for the **Walpurgisnacht** gathering. Here they exchange tall tales of the past year's evil deeds as foreplay to a Bacchanalian frenzy of fornication, including with the devil himself. The event was so vividly embellished that for centuries local peasants lived in fear of meetings with stray witches. By hanging crosses and herbs on house and barn doors they tried to protect themselves and their animals; church bells would toll and the most superstitious would crack whips to deter evil forces.

At some point this night became combined with age-old local festivals: the Celts celebrated this as the devil's final fling before spring triumphs over winter in celebrations similar to those in other Celtic areas, including Scotland's Beltane, while Germanic tribes celebrated the wedding of the gods Wodan and Freyen. The name Walpurgisnacht probably comes from Waldborg, the pagan goddess of fertility. Over the centuries as Christianity frowned on these celebrations they became a highlight of the black-magic calendar: Goethe's Faust joined a "whirling mob" of witches on the summit of the Brocken.

Today gatherings by New Age pagans and revellers occur all over the Harz on Walpurgisnacht, but the most popular places are at the Hexentanzplatz in Thale (see p.241) where 35,000 arrive for an organized celebration; and the trek up the Brocken from Schierke in which similar numbers come together for a more rough-and-ready experience that lasts until dawn.

▲ Snow-covered trees in the Harz

Strasse 2, whose specialities are various fortified coffees that go down a treat in winter. For a quick sandwich try *Puppe Brotzeit*, Am Brunnen 2, which uses local ingredients and will pack things up for your hiking trip or picnic, as well as having space to eat in. For a fuller sit-down meal try *Rialto*, Herzog-Wilhelm-Strasse 27, for good Italian standards.

Goslar and around

With an imperial past, a palatial prize of European Romanesque architecture and an Altstadt of medieval timber-framed beauties, **GOSLAR** is one of Germany's treats. A small town of just 48,000 people in the Harz foothills, perhaps, but a rich one figuratively and at one time literally. In the tenth century the discovery of silver transformed this daydreaming hamlet into one of northern Europe's leading medieval towns, whose deep coffers were loved by emperors and coveted by popes.

By the mid-eleventh century, less than a century after the first miners shouldered their picks, an imperial Diet (conference) of the Holy Roman Empire was held in the **Kaiserpfalz**, Goslar's new Romanesque palace. For over three hundred years the "treasury of German Emperors" ruled Germany's loose confederation of states as the seat of the Holy Roman Emperor and the city spent its wealth on home improvements – a building spree to give it the finery it deserved as a free imperial city (from 1342). Even a collective tightening of belts when the duke of Braunschweig-Wolfenbüttel snatched the mine in 1532 had its virtues: as funds dried up, so too did new building schemes, preserving the Altstadt as it was. As a POW camp in World War II it was also spared from bombing.

The area around the **Markt** is a cluster of showpiece buildings, from where one of the main streets, **Hoher Weg**, drives south to the **Kaiserpfalz**. Also south of town is the **Rammelsberg** mine, which until relatively recently still produced ores, and now offers tours. But the set pieces are only part of the attraction of Goslar: simply rambling around its huddled streets is pleasure enough, and there are many small but diverting museums dotted throughout the Altstadt.

Arrival, information and accommodation

Goslar **Bahnhof** lies at the northern edge of town, an easy ten-minute walk to the town centre: aim for the Neuwerkkirche's spires, continue down Rosentorstrasse and then Hokenstrasse to emerge at the Markt, home of the **tourist office** at no. 7 (May–Oct Mon–Fri 9.15am–6pm, Sat 9.30am–4pm, Sun 9.30am–2pm; Nov–April Mon–Fri 9.15am–4pm, Sat 9.30am–2pm; ☏05321/780 60, ⓦwww .goslarinfo.de). It sells a €9 **Museumpass**, which includes entry to the Rathaus, Kaiserpfalz, Goslarer Museum and Mönchehaus.

Goslar has plenty of **accommodation**, much of it in old timber-framed houses in the centre of town, most in the same price bracket. For less-expensive double rooms, get a list of **private rooms** from the tourist office.

The Markt

Goslar's showpiece **Markt**, a gorgeous huddle of buildings in sombre slate, zingy tangerine and clotted cream, is best admired crowd-free, so steer clear of 9am, noon, 3pm and 6pm when crowds gather for a parade of mining history which spins from a **Glockenspiel** at the top of its old treasury building. Atop a 1230 fountain is Goslar's icon – an imperial eagle which looks more like a hybrid pigeon caught mid-lay; behind here the fifteenth-century **Rathaus** (guided tours daily: May–Sept 9am–5pm; Oct–April 10am–4pm; €2) adds rhythm in gables, arches and Gothic windows that look spectacular when illuminated at night. The Rathaus's treasure is inside: on the wall and ceiling panels of its Huldigungssaal council chamber is a spectacular display of Renaissance fireworks by a mystery painter.

Beside the Rathaus, the **Kaiserworth Hotel** is in the old fifteenth-century guildhall of cloth merchants and cutters. Its emperors were dismissed by Romantic poet Heinrich Heine as "university janitors", but the satirical wit surely approved of its lively corbels and sculpture of the naked **Dukaten-männchen** who strains to excrete a ducat in a bizarre parable about the fate of debtors. The backdrop to this ensemble piece is the Romanesque **Marktkirche**; look for a baptismal font (1573) of Rammelsberg copper which a local craftsman cast as a pictorial bible, and a thirteenth-century

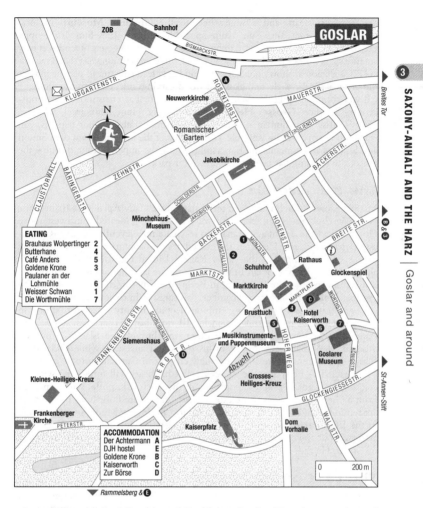

glass of patron saints Cosmas and Damian stained with ochre, azurite and verdigris dug from the mine.

Hoher Weg

Behind the Marktkirche, cherubs cavort, medieval ladies joust on cockerels and a saucy dairymaid hoiks her dress as she churns butter on the 1526 **Brusttuch house**, Hoher Weg 1; it's now a hotel, so nip in for a look at a spectacular dining room. Its wealthy owner is said to have gone into debt during the building, explaining the two monkeys who squabble over coins on the gable end. The bakers, opposite, were far more prosaic with their 1557 **guildhouse**: look for a gold pretzel and gingerbread on its facade.

Just past the cluttered **Musikinstrumente- und Puppen-Museum** (daily 11am–5pm; €3; ℡05321/269 45) on Hoher Weg, which features a medieval hurdy-gurdy it claims is Germany's oldest instrument, a path threads alongside the Abzucht stream and a waterwheel to the **Goslarer Museum** of local history (April–Oct Tues–Sun 10am–5pm; Nov–March Tues–Sun 10am–4pm; €3; ☎05321/433 94), whose exhibits include a charming seventeenth-century chemist's lab; a 1240 jewel-encrusted Gospel, the *Goslarer Evangeliar*; the *Bergkanne* (1477), a gloriously showy goblet of silver and gold featuring music-playing miners; the original Goslar eagle; and glass and wood-carvings rescued from the Dom.

If you continue up Hoher Weg past the architectural asceticism of a thirteenth-century hospice, **Grosses-Heiliges-Kreuz** (daily 11am–5pm; free), where a 1500s Christ with human hair now watches over craftsmen not patients, you reach the **Domvorhalle** vestibule. This is a relic of the imperial Dom of St Simon and St Judas and contains the Kaiserstuhl (1060), the imperial stone throne – the rest of the building has been covered by a car park.

The Kaiserpfalz

In 1868 Kaiser Wilhelm I rescued the **Kaiserpfalz** (daily: April–Oct 10am–5pm; Nov–March 10am–4pm; €4.50; ☎05321/311 96 93), located southwest of Hoher Weg, from a stint as a granary to re-create the eleventh-century Romanesque masterpiece of Heinrich III; indeed, it's probably more immaculate now than ever. In doing this, the canny Kaiser claimed the cachet of Germany's almost mythic Holy Roman Emperors; five years later he sat enthroned on the Kaiserstuhl to open the Reichstag in Berlin and usher in the Second Reich. In the vast **Reichsaal** debating chamber, paintings of historical triumphs (1897) celebrate a bombastic, emerging empire: Sleeping Beauty wakes for "spring in the new German Fatherland"; Heinrich III rides home after stern words with Pope Gregory VI; a crusading Barbarossa rips through the Islamic army; and a dignified Wilhelm acknowledges his peers and ancestors while Old Father Rhine and Legend write a glorious new chapter in German history.

Heinrich III's body may be in Speyer, but his heart will forever be with his creation, in a gilt box in a sarcophagus in the **Ulrichskapelle**, which morphs from a Greek cross to Romanesque octagon and where floor bolts by the door are reminders of its days as a prison. Look, too, for Henry Moore's *Goslar Warrior* in the **Pfalzgarten** behind the Kaiserpfalz; it won Moore the first Kaiserring art prize, but the sculptor refused to accept it until he had seen and approved of Goslar. He did.

The rest of the Altstadt

Back at the Markt, there's plenty more of Goslar's Altstadt to explore, much of it atmospheric residential backwaters off the tourist trail. Northwest of the Markt the **Mönchehaus Museum**, Mönchestrasse 1 (Tues–Sat 10am–5pm, Sun 10am–1pm; €3), holds a high-octane dose of modern painting and sculpture, including de Kooning, Ernst and Beuys, which works surprisingly well among its old beams. North on Rosentorstrasse, the former Romanesque collegiate church **Neuwerkkirche** (April–Oct Mon–Fri 10am–noon & 2.30–4.30pm, Sat 10am–noon) is uncharacteristic for its frippery: strikingly lavish outside, with polygonal towers punctuated by windows and an artistic apse, and with a contemporary rood screen and rich frescoes inside.

Towards the western edge of the Altstadt you enter into the **Frankenberger-viertel** miners' parish. The Baroque **Siemenshaus**, Schreiberstrasse 12 (Tues & Thurs 9am–noon; free), the family home of the Siemens family, is en route to and a world away from the humble houses of the miners on **Peterstrasse** at the southwestern edge of the district. Their parish church, the **Frankenberger Kirche**, has a fantastical Baroque altar.

Rammelsberg

From the **Frankenbergerviertel** follow in the footsteps of Golsar's miners by leaving the Altstadt to the south along Bergstrasse, crossing Clausthaler Strasse, and then tramping along Rammelsberg Strasse to the **Bergbaumuseum** (daily 9am–6pm; €10; ☎05321/75 00, ⓦwww.rammelsberg.de) at the former Rammelsberg silver mine, some 1.5km south of the Markt (bus #808). For a millennium this was the backbone of Goslar's economic clout, and it only ceased production in 1998. Now a museum, it chronicles this mining history, explaining the processes and, best of all, allowing you to don overalls and a miner's helmet and access to eighteenth- and nineteenth-century underground shafts.

Eating

Goslar has no shortage of **cafés** to while away an hour or so while soaking up its Altstadt atmosphere, and the **restaurants** are good too – though largely limited to German food. Many hotels (see p.248) have good restaurants as well.

Brauhaus Wolpertinger Marstallstr. 1 ☎05321/221 55. Microbrewery with several good beers, good pub food (mains €8.50–15) and a courtyard that's very lively until around midnight.

Butterhane Marktkirchhof 3 ☎05321/228 86. The food is pretty standard German favourites, but the outdoor seating a boon and on weekend nights it's the place to be after about 10pm.

Café Anders Hoher Weg 4 ☎05321/238 14. The smells alone make this a great address for that afternoon coffee and cake. The room upstairs is dizzy with Baroque decor, while the terrace has great Harz views.

Goldene Krone Breite Str. 46 ☎05321/344 90. Cosy rustic restaurant with standard North-German food (mains €8–18) and more international dishes on a seasonal menu. Also has a great old *Weinstube*. Reservations recommended.

Paulaner an der Lohmühle Gemeindehof 3–5 ☎05321/260 70. Bavarian chain with some added authenticity from Harz specials and a setting in a cosy inn next to the Abzucht stream. Prices are keen, with many mains around the €8 mark.

Weisser Schwan Münzstr.11 ☎05321/257 37. Steaks in all guises are the chef's speciality in this seventeenth-century coaching inn with a courtyard beer garden for summer eating. Mains cost around €13.

Die Worthmühle Worthstr. 4 ☎05321/434 02. Regional accents abound in the rustic-styled nooks of this moderately priced Harz speciality restaurant: in decor, in the good-value dishes such as wild boar and trout, and in the fruity local draught brew *Goslarer Gosebier*.

Bad Harzburg

Attractive and sleepy **BAD HARZBURG**, the smartest spa resort in the Harz, lies only 9km southeast of Goslar, and offers excellent access to hikes in the Harz. This is largely thanks to the presence of the **Burgberg Seilbahn** (daily May–Oct 9am–5pm; Nov–April 9am–4pm; €3 return; ☎05322/753 71), a cable car that climbs the Grosser Burgberg where Heinrich IV's eleventh-century castle has crumbled to its foundations. Excellent views remain though and a network of hiking trails fans out from here. The most straightforward return to town, but there are others to several mountain huts with restaurants: a board at the cable-car terminus shows which are open. Bad Harzburg's other great attractions are its **spas**. The Sole-Therme (see p.245) is the best and lies conveniently at the base of the cable car.

Practicalities

Frequent buses from Goslar drop passengers at the **Hauptbahnhof**, a five-minute walk north of town and a twenty-minute walk through the centre to the Seilbahn (or bus #871 or #873 to "Burgbergbahn" stop), beside which lies the **tourist office**, Nordhäuser Strasse 4 (Mon–Fri 8am–8pm, Sat 9am–4pm;

May–Oct also Sun 10am–1pm; ℡05322/75 330, ⓦwww.bad-harzburg.de). They can provide full **accommodation** listings, but one of the nicest places to stay is the central *Braunschweiger Hof*, Herzog-Wilhelm-Strasse 54 (℡05322/78 80, ⓦwww.hotel-braunschweiger-hof.de; ⑥), a comfortable hotel with four-star mod cons, but an easy-going rural feel. It also has one of the best **restaurants** in town. Atmospheric and inexpensive *Palmen-Café*, in the Trinkhalle, Im Badepark (℡05322/48 05), serves dishes like salmon in wine sauce or beef roulade with apple and red cabbage, in a Neoclassical building where spa-goers took the waters a century ago.

Travel details

Trains

Goslar to: Hannover (hourly; 1hr 20min).
Halle to: Dessau (frequent; 45min); Eisleben (hourly; 40min); Leipzig (frequent; 1hr 15min); Naumburg (12 daily; 30min); Wittenberg (frequent; 45min).
Lutherstadt Wittenberg to: Berlin (hourly; 45min).
Magdeburg to: Berlin (frequent; 95min); Dessau (frequent; 1hr 45min); Goslar (hourly; 2hr); Halle (frequent; 1hr 30min); Quedlinburg (hourly; 1hr 20min); Stendal (frequent; 1hr).
Quedlinburg to: Rübeland (frequent; 1hr 15min); Thale (frequent; 11min).

Buses

Braunlage to: Bad Harzburg (frequent; 40min); Schierke (9 daily; 15min).
Wörlitz to: Dessau (8 daily; 35min); Lutherstadt Wittenberg (6 daily; 45min).

Thuringia

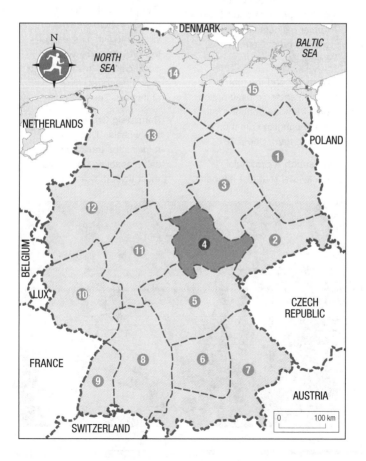

CHAPTER 4 # Highlights

* **Erfurt** The underrated state capital is as cultured as it is charming, its head count of students bringing energy – and bars – to a historic streetscape. **See p.256**

* **Weimar** An erudite town steeped in three centuries of cultural prowess and whose former residents read like a who's who of German arts. **See p.265**

* **Gotha** Spend the morning in a multifaceted museum, and the afternoon pottering into the Thuringian Forest on a historic tram. **See p.281**

* **Eisenach** A provincial backwater that just happens to be home to the Wartburg, as potent an icon of German identity as you could wish for where Luther hid and whose gloriously over-the-top halls inspired Wagner. **See p.283**

* **Touring small-town Thuringia** With your own transport there are cosy villages to find, castles to explore and pocket-sized ducal capitals to stroll in, in a region that offers slow travel at its best. **See p.288**

* **Rennsteig** On two legs or two wheels, "Der Runst" remains the track that any self-respecting trail-junkie must tick off. **See p.289**

▲ Erfurt's Dom

Thuringia

Culturally as much as geographically **Thuringia** (Thüringen) is the heartland of Germany. When the *Wende* pulled back the Iron Curtain in 1990, West Germans were relieved to find that the nation's "green heart" was spared the social realism (or concrete) of which the GDR regime was so fond. It remains the sort of place Germans have in mind when they talk of *Früher*, a time past when things were less complicated – a bucolic state where slow travel rules and no city is over 200,000 people. The surprise, then, is that if a competition were held to decide the nation's cultural big-hitter, flyweight Thuringia would be there in the finals. This is the legendary resting-place of Emperor Friedrich Barbarossa, Germany's real-life King Arthur, the font of Martin Luther's Reformation, the former stomping-ground of Bach and Lucas Cranach, and the state that inspired Schiller and Wagner. More than anyone else it is the state of Goethe, Germany's cultural colossus whose tread is seen everywhere. (Regarding another national icon, all Thuringians agree their *Bratwurst* is Germany's best – the squabble is over whether the finest are produced north or south of the Rennsteig footpath, Germany's favourite long-distance trail.)

As ever, the reason Thuringia punches far above its weight is historical. As the ruling Saxon House of Wettin bequeathed land equally between male heirs, an area that was far from large to begin with fragmented into a mosaic of small duchies – Saxe-Weimar and Saxe-Gotha, for example, or Saxe-Coburg, better known in Britain as the House of Windsor. An upshot of these tin-pot fiefdoms was an arts race that saw the area's dukes woo the finest musicians, painters, poets and philosophers to their courts as testament to their learning and magnificence.

Nowhere expresses this better than **Weimar**, a Thuringia-in-microcosm that lobbed the intellectual atom-bomb of the German Enlightenment, whose shockwaves were felt throughout Europe. Most cities would struggle to make such an impact, let alone a small, courtly town. Adjacent **Jena** has maintained its academic tradition and the student nightlife that goes with it, while **Gotha** and especially **Eisenach** have a cultural weight far above their modest size. The state capital is **Erfurt**, Luther's university city and perhaps the most underrated capital in Germany thanks to its marriage of historic looks and university dynamism.

The **Thuringian Forest** south could not be more different. This is the state's rural core, whose sleepy villages are tucked into the folds of an upland blessed by good walking and cycling trails. You can lose a happy week crisscrossing the area by bike on labelled routes or journey through its heart on the well-marked 168km **Rennsteig**, which traverses it. The state's many green landscapes also include the **Saale Valley** at the eastern fringe of the forest region, and the **Kyffhäuser** uplands to the north, site of the sixteenth-century Peasants' War sparked in the overlooked historic town of **Mülhausen**.

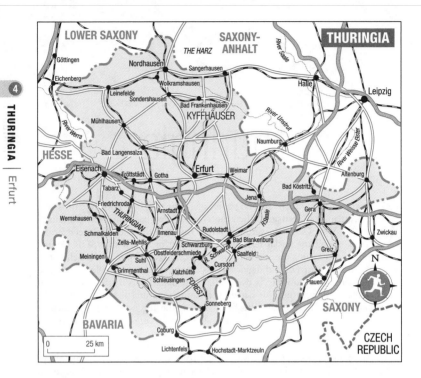

Two wheels aside, a car is a bonus for touring the Thuringian Forest region, where bus transport is sketchy. Elsewhere two Deutsche Bahn tickets simplify travelling **by train**. The Thüringen-Ticket provides up to five people one-day's unlimited weekday travel for €29; and the Hopper-Ticket (€6) covers return journeys within a fifty-mile radius from any destination in Thuringia or Saxony. The latter is included when you buy the longer versions of regional discount card the Thüringen Card (one day €13, three days €33, six days €53) from tourist offices state-wide.

Erfurt

Erfurt is a honeypot. A town would have to stand here even if the city had just been razed to the ground.

Martin Luther

So mused the most famous resident of Thuringia's state capital. While the father of the Reformation could also have acclaimed it as a fine little city bursting with character, ever the pragmatist, he got to the nub, as it is its location at the heart of Germany – and Europe – that was the making of **ERFURT**. While profits from woad helped fill coffers, its drip-feeds of finance were trade routes east–west from Paris to Russian city Novgorod, and north–south from the Baltic to Italy. Such was its wealth that the medieval city was hailed as "Efurtia turrita" because of its ninety spires.

With the merchants came progressive ideas and liberal attitudes. Luther's free thinking was nurtured at Erfurt's prestigious university, renowned as a cradle of humanism. Centuries later, in 1970, open-minded Erfurt hosted ice-breaker Ostpolitik talks between West and East Germany. Though the largest city in Thuringia Erfurt is pocket-sized, its easygoing Altstadt a traditional German townscape of the sort largely obliterated elsewhere by bombs and developers, and with a dynamo university that adds a sheen of modern style and passable nightlife. Put the two together and what's not to like? Few honeypots taste sweeter.

Erfurt has few set pieces; it's as an ensemble that the city impresses, with any street in the centre worth exploring, especially as you can walk from one side to the other in about twenty minutes. The axes of Erfurt's central Altstadt are the Episcopal powerbase **Domplatz**, **Fischmarkt**, the civic heart, and **Anger**, a broad plaza at the head of the shopping streets. North of the centre in the studenty **Andreasviertel** and around the **Augustinerkloster** are especially photogenic quarters. Drop the map and explore by instinct.

Arrival, information and city transport

The **Hauptbahnhof** lies at the southeast edge of the Altstadt, a ten-minute walk from the centre. The **airport** (Ⓦ www.flughafen-erfurt.de) is 3km west. Tram #4 travels direct from the terminus to Domplatz and Anger, the two hubs around which the **public transport** network revolves; a single costs €1.70, a day-ticket €4.20. Alternatively, a taxi from the airport will cost around €15. The main **tourist office** (April–Dec Mon–Fri 10am–7pm, Sat 10am–6pm, Sun 10am–4pm; Jan–March Mon–Sat 10am–6pm, Sun 10am–4pm; general Ⓣ 0361/664 00, accommodation Ⓣ 0361/66 40 110, Ⓦ www.erfurt-tourist-info .de) is behind the Rathaus at Benediktsplatz 1. A secondary information point (daily: April–Oct 11am–6.30pm; Nov & Dec 11am–4pm; Ⓣ 0361/601 53 84) in the Zitadelle Petersburg above Domplatz specializes in its locale but provides some general information. The main office can advise on a bewildering array of themed tours of the city. Both sell the **ErfurtCard** (48hr; €9) for free public transport, free entry to the municipal museums and a city tour, plus the usual discounts on scattered sights.

Accommodation

As well as a good range of **hotels**, Erfurt has a respectable quota of **budget accommodation**, with two excellent backpackers' hostels to go alongside a good youth hostel. The nearest **campsite**, *Freizeitpark Stausee Hohenfelden* (Ⓣ 036450/420 81, Ⓦ www.stausee-hohenfelden.de), the state's largest, compensates for a location 16km southeast with a lakeside setting. Bus #155 gets there – eventually.

Hotels

Am Kaisersaal Futterstr. 8 Ⓣ 0361/65 85 60, Ⓦ www.hotel-am-kaisersaal.de. Well-appointed, modern three-star set amid the café culture at the end of the Krämerbrücke. ❹

Augustinerkloster Augustinerstr. 10 Ⓣ 0361/664 01 10, Ⓦ www.erfurt-tourist-info.de. Guest rooms in the monastery where Luther studied (now a convent) are atmospheric cells that open on to a historic, tranquil courtyard – an antidote to the blander chains. Bookings are through tourist office. ❹

IBB Gotthardtstr. 27 Ⓣ 0361/674 00, Ⓦ www .ibbhotels.com. A partner of the Sorat chain with arguably the best location in Erfurt, at the end of the Krämerbrücke. Decor ranges from designer minimalism to modern country, some rooms with architectural features of the incorporated medieval inn. ❺

Mercure Grand Hotel am Dom Am Theaterplatz 2 Ⓣ 0361/644 50, Ⓦ www.grandhotelamdom.de. The only five-star address in town is a swish designer-modern chain-fare number with a tasteful palette of coffee and cream. ❺–❻

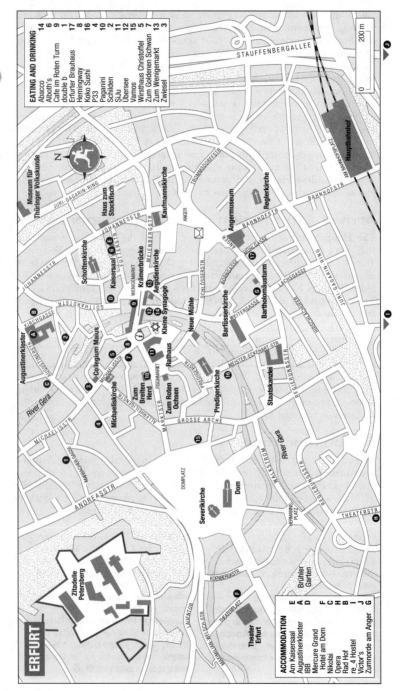

ERFURT

EATING AND DRINKING

Abacco	14
Alboth's	6
Cafe im Roten Turm	9
double b	1
Erfurter Brauhaus	17
Hemingway	8
Koko Sushi	16
P33	4
Paganini	10
Schilden	2
SiJu	11
Übersee	12
Vamos	15
Wirtshaus Christoffel	5
Zum Goldenen Schwan	7
Zum Wenigemarkt	13
Zwiesel	3

ACCOMMODATION

Am Kaisersaal	E
Augustinerkloster	A
IBB	D
Mercure Grand	F
Hotel am Dom	C
Nikolai	H
Opera	B
Rad Hof	I
re. 4 Hostel	J
Victor's	G
Zumnorde am Anger	G
Brühler Garten	

Museum für Thüringer Volkskunde

Haus zum Stockfisch

Augustinerkloster

Schottenkirche

Kaisersaal

Collegium Maius

Krämerbrücke

Kaufmannskirche

Aegidienkirche

Kleine Synagoge

Michaeliskirche

Zum Breiten Herd

Zum Roten Ochsen

Rathaus

Neue Mühle

Barfüßerkirche

Bartholomäusturm

Reglerkirche

Angermuseum

Predigerkirche

Staatskanzlei

Severikirche

Dom

Zitadelle Petersberg

Theater Erfurt

River Gera

0   200 m

Nikolai Augustinerstr. 30 ℡0361/59 81 70, Ⓦwww.hotel-nikolai-erfurt.com. Nothing flashy, just reproduction antiques and homely touches to a pleasant small hotel in a quiet photogenic corner of the Altstadt. ❹

Rad Hof Kirchgasse 1b ℡0361/602 77 61, Ⓦwww.rad-hof.de. Interesting little place directly behind the Augustinerkloster whose splashes of colour enliven five simple, individually styled rooms. ❷

Victor's Hässlerstr. 17 ℡0361/653 30, Ⓦwww.victors.de. A bland exterior hides a classy number of timeless Italianesque taste and comfortably elegant furnishings. South of the Hauptbahnhof, about 15min walk from the centre. ❻–❼

Zumnorde am Anger Anger 50–51 (enter on Weitergasse) ℡0361/568 00, Ⓦwww.hotel-zumnorde.de. Bedrooms are clean and spacious and, if not big on character, at least free of dated clutter. The restored town house is lifted by splashes of Art Deco and has a modern extension. ❻

Hostels

Opera Walkmühlstr. 13 ℡0361/60 13 13 60, Ⓦwww.opera-hostel.de. A cut above the usual hostel in its funky design leanings. Friendly and spacious throughout, with en-suite rooms as well as three- to seven-bed dorms, and well located about a 15min walk south of Domplatz (tram #1 or #2 to "Brühler Garten"). Dorms €13–22, rooms ❷

re_4 Hostel Puschkinstr. 21 ℡0361/600 01 10, Ⓦwww.re4hostel.com. Great hostel created from a former police station, hence the GDR memorabilia – ask for a look in room 13. Four-bed dorms are bright and cheerful, all bunk bed-free and with lockers. It's located south of the centre, about 1km west of the Hauptbahnhof via tram #5. Dorms €13–20, rooms ❷

Domplatz, the Dom and the Severikirche

The open space of **Domplatz** seems too handsome to be a child of war. French and Prussian forces met here in 1813 and the residential strip along its north fringe went up in smoke, leaving just the narrow half-timbered buildings that jostle for space on its east and south. The ashes were swept away, Domplatz expanded into the vacuum and now only its stones recall the travesty – cobbles demarcate the original Domplatz, flagstones indicate the rest. The High Gothic choir of the **Dom** looms over the platz like the bows of a cruise-liner, perched atop a massive medieval substructure that expands the hilltop of a previous Romanesque cathedral. A monumental staircase – a superb stage for evening spectaculars during summer's Domstufenfestspiele – sweeps up to a triangular porch tacked on the north side, while a large tracery arrow at its portal follows to the letter Gothic's guiding dictum to direct eyes up to heaven. Behind statues of the five wise virgins of St Matthew cradle goblets of oil beside foolish colleagues. The lofty cathedral within exudes the mysticism of the early church. Some of Germany's finest medieval stained glass fills the slender lancet windows that stretch full-length in the choir, while in the south transept are a number of artworks from the original Dom, noticeably the twelfth-century "Wolfram" candelabrum – with a bearded figure sprouting from dragons as a symbol of the light of Christianity. Nearby are the tombstone of Count von Gleichen, a thirteenth-century bigamist pictured with his two wives, and a Romanesque stucco altar of an enthroned Madonna ablaze with stars. Medieval altarpieces wrapped around the columns catch the eye – as does east Germany's largest mural of St John the Baptist, Gothic sea-monsters swimming around his legs – but the finest artwork is a sumptuous Cranach altarpiece in a north-aisle chapel that depicts the Madonna and saints Catherine and Barbara with the intimacy of a family snapshot. Tours twice daily (April–Oct Thurs–Sun; €2.50) ascend the tower to view the world's largest free-swinging medieval bell, the 2.5m-high *Gloriosa* whose deep toll sounds far beyond the town centre on religious high days, though there are no views.

Smaller than the Dom, the adjacent **Severikirche**, with a crown of three spires, refuses to be overshadowed. Near the entrance of a surprisingly spacious five-aisled hall church lies the fourteenth-century sarcophagus of St Severi, its sheer bulk softened through the use of pink sandstone and a beautifully rendered life-story of the saint whose remains arrived in Erfurt in 836 AD. Other eye-catchers are the St Michael who spears one of the most vivid medieval devils you'll ever see, and a font covered by an extravagant fifteen-metre Gothic trellis.

④ Zitadelle Petersberg

Why the **Zitadelle Petersberg** above Domplatz is not a major attraction nor even a festival venue is a mystery. The only complete Baroque town fortress in central Europe is protected in statute but overlooked by the city and visitors alike despite an illustrious history. Emperor Frederick Barbarossa, Germany's real-life King Arthur, summoned nobles for five imperial Diets in the Peterskirche during the twelfth century, one of which saw Saxon duke Henry the Lion, the founder of Munich and ruler of most of present-day Lower Saxony and Schleswig-Holstein, humbled for refusing to back a disastrous escapade in Italy. Mainz archbishops took a similarly tough stance after city riots in 1664 – they consulted the latest French military ideas to create the massive Baroque citadel that recycles stone from the city's churches, one reason why Erfurt is no longer the "city of spires" medieval visitors acclaimed. The fortress's barn-like Peterskirche houses modern international concrete sculpture as the **Forum Konkrete Kunst** (Wed–Sun: May–Oct 10am–6pm; Nov–April 10am–4pm; free; ⑩www.forum-konkrete -kunst-erfurt.de) and the tourist office in a glass-box at the centre organizes several tours (Fri–Sun, times vary; from €4), including a trip into the labyrinth beneath the fortifications by flame-torches. As good a reason to go as any is the panorama from its massive bastions.

Fischmarkt and around

Running from Domplatz to Fischmarkt, **Marktstrasse** tracks the trade route that linked Russia to the Rhine. A couple of diversions en route are south on Grosse Arche to a fine Renaissance portal of **Haus zum Sonneborn** (now the registry office), and north up Allerheiligenstrasse, where portholes at former Renaissance breweries at nos. 6 and 7 were stuffed with straw to announce a fresh beer had matured.

A hundred metres in distance from the Domplatz, a world away in atmosphere, **Fischmarkt** is the centre-stage of Erfurt's civic life, crowded by colourful Baroque and Renaissance town houses. A woad merchant treated himself to Renaissance mansion **Zum Breiten Herd** (1584), decorated with a frieze of the five senses that is answered on an adjacent 1893 guild house with the cardinal virtues of justice, fortitude, prudence and temperance. Another fine facade graces **Zum Roten Ochsen** (1562) on the west flank; a frieze depicts the days of the week and Greek muses along with the beaming Red Ox of its name. Today it contains the **Kunsthalle Erfurt** (Tues–Sun 11am–6pm, Thurs till 10pm; €3; ⑩www .kunsthalle-erfurt.de), which stages exhibitions, usually of modern art. The identity of the pot-bellied Roman soldier in front of it is something of a mystery; one theory suggests the Renaissance figure is a symbolic assertion of civic independence similar to the statues of Roland erected by Germany's Free Imperial cities. Another theory is that he is Erfurt's patron, St Martin. Either way, he gazes towards a tubby neo-Gothic **Rathaus** (Mon, Tues & Thurs 8am–6pm, Wed 8am–4pm, Fri 8am–2pm, Sat & Sun 10am–5pm; free) with murals inside of Romantic images of Tannhäuser and Faust legends alongside images of local hero Martin Luther. Behind, the **Kleine Synagoge** (Tues–Sun 11am–6pm; free) contains a small museum on Erfurt's Jewish community in a house consecrated for worship from 1840 to 1884. Its nearby predecessor at Waagegasse 8, the medieval

Alte Synagoge (⊛ www.alte-synagoge.erfurt.de), one of Europe's earliest Jewish synagogues, dating from the eleventh century, is due to open with a display of medieval treasure after renovation in summer 2009 – ask at the tourist office.

South of Fischmarkt, the **Neue Mühle** (tours Tues–Sun 10am–6pm; €1.50) is the last working watermill of fifty that once lined the Gera; you'll need good German to glean the nitty-gritty of its mechanism. Nearby is the **Predigerkirche** (May–Sept Tues–Sat 11am–4pm, Sun noon–4pm; free), medieval church of the Dominican "preacher" order; Germany's most famous mystic, Master Eckhart, a thirteenth-century friar cited by Schopenhauer, was around for its construction. Highlight of its understated interior is the carved-stone choir screen.

North of Fischmarkt and the Augustinerkloster

Former university quarter, the **Andreasviertel**, north of Fischmarkt is one of the Altstadt's backwaters, its main street the Michaelisstrasse, a student centre during the heyday of Erfurt's old university. Opened in 1392, the fifth native-language university in Germany blossomed into the largest centre of learning in central Europe. Its **Collegium Maius** midway along is undergoing protracted restoration from war damage. Opposite, Gothic university church **Michaeliskirche** is wedged into a corner with Allerheiligenstrasse. Within the nave where a congregation heard the radical ideas of a former philosophy student named Martin Luther in 1522 is a Baroque high altar – wood for all its marble looks – and a sonorous contemporary organ. From a lovely courtyard you can also ascend to the Dreifaltigkeitskapelle with an unusual oriel window.

Quieter still than Michaelisstrasse is the nest of streets of half-timbered buildings on the River Gera's eastern banks – don't miss postcard-pretty Kirchgasse, located at the back of the fourteenth-century **Augustinerkloster** (tours Mon–Sat hourly 10am–noon & 2–4/5pm, Sun 11am, 2pm & 3pm; €5), where Luther was a monk from 1505 to 1511. The story goes he signed up in gratitude for the monastery's hospitality when he was caught out by a storm. "One difficult sentence was sufficient to occupy my thoughts for the whole day," he wrote of his time here. Battered by the war, the Augustinian monastery has re-created a half-timbered nook similar to that in which the father of the Reformation studied as a novice – monastic rules of poverty forbid monks from owning their own cell – and there is a small ecclesiastical museum, not to mention charming cloisters. Having adopted his doctrines in 1525, Luther's church is suitably spartan in response to his condemnation of visual distractions, pepped up only with medieval stained glass in the choir.

Krämerbrücke and east

If the Dom has the majesty, Erfurt's second landmark has all the charm. It doesn't stretch the imagination too far to visualize medieval traders in floppy hats trundling carts across the **Krämerbrücke** (Merchants' Bridge) east of Fischmarkt. The longest inhabited bridge in Europe and the only one north of the Alps – Erfurt is quick to point out that its bridge existed before that of its southern counterpart, Florence's Ponte Vecchio – thrived almost as soon as burghers tired of rebuilding wooden footbridges over the River Gera and erected this stone span in 1325. Merchants hawked luxury spices, medicines, dyes, silk and paper in 64 toy-town houses. The number has halved, but the trade remains quality stuff, including antiques, art and jewellery. The house at no. 31 is open as the **Stiftung Krämerbrücke** (Nov–April Tues–Sun 10am–6pm; May–Oct daily 10am–6pm; free) where you can nose into medieval cellars and

▲ The Krämerbrücke, Erfurt

peruse displays about the bridge. The picture-postcard view is from the tower of the **Aegidienkirche** (Tues–Sun 11am–5pm; €1.50).

All trace of the travelling merchants who stabled horses in **Futterstrasse** (Fodder Street) east of Krämerbrücke has gone. So lucrative was this that stablers were the only Erfurt tradesmen able to afford Baroque town houses after the Thirty Years' War. Halfway along Kaisersaal is a former university ballroom in which Tsar Alexander I and Napoleon shook hands at the 1808 Erfurt Congress to renew the Franco-Prussian alliance. Johannesstrasse, at the end of Futterstrasse, is lined by Renaissance mansions erected by flush woad merchants, none more eye-catching than **Haus zum Stockfisch** (1607); its "dried cod" mark is depicted absurdly as a *Jaws* look-alike. It now contains the **Stadtmuseum** (Tues–Sun 10am–6pm; €1.50), a missable plod through the city's history. More enjoyable is the homespun world of traditional Thuringian lifestyles in the **Museum für Thüringer Volkskunde** (same times & price). Mask makers, glassblowers and woad printers are represented in its re-created workshops, and there are rooms of folk costume, tools and furnishings. The museum lies a block east at Juri-Gagarin-Ring 140a.

Around Anger

Johann Sebastian Bach's parents tied the knot in 1668 in the **Kaufmannskirche** (Merchants' Church) which caps the south end of Johannesstrasse and announces the spacious square Anger, which was the central market for wool, wheat, woad and wine. At its corner with Bahnhofstrasse, cultural doyenne the **Angermuseum** (ⓦ www.angermuseum.de) is scheduled to reopen by mid-2009 as a decorative and fine art collection after a protracted nine-year restoration.

A few hundred metres west, on Anger past the Bartholomäusturm, a surviving spire of a medieval church, is the **Staatskanzlei** (State Chancellery). Though nothing much to look at, the Baroque palace hosted one of German history's most celebrated meetings in 1808, between Emperor Napoleon and Johann

Wolfgang von Goethe. The breakfasting emperor saluted Goethe, "*Vous êtes un homme!*" and confessed he had read *The Sorrows of Young Werther* seven times. Come to Paris, Napoleon promised, and the German polymath would find a subject worthy of his skill, most likely the emperor's achievements, which he believed ranked alongside those of Roman rulers. Goethe never took up the offer, but found space in his study for a bust of the emperor thereafter.

Any street north from Anger past the Bartholomäusturm will take you to Franciscan monastery church **Barfüsserkirche** (Easter–Oct Tues–Sun 10am–1pm & 2–6pm; €1) left a shell after war damage except for a choir that provides an appropriate setting for a small display of medieval ecclesiastical art and scraps of stained glass (1235) of St Francis.

Ega-Cyriaksburg

Redressing the lack of green spaces in the centre is the **Ega** garden (daily: May–Sept 14 9am–8pm; March, April & Sept 15–Oct 9am–6pm; Nov–Feb 10am–4pm; €5), southwest of the centre in the grounds of the **Cyriaksburg** castle (tram #2 to "Egapark" from Anger). Visit in spring for the largest ornamental flowerbed in Europe (6000 square metres), plus rose, water and Japanese gardens to explore along with a tropical butterfly house and cafés. The slab-sided fortification itself has been handed over as gardening museum, the **Gartenbaumuseum** (March–Oct Tues–Sun 10am–6pm, July–Sept also Mon; same ticket; Ⓦwww .gartenbaumuseum.de).

Eating and drinking

Erfurt brings the zip of a federal capital and style sense of a university city to its historic buildings to good effect with its **restaurant** scene. There's also an abundance of **café** and **bar** culture: the former is strong at Wenigemarkt at the east end of the Krämerbrücke, the latter is focused in the former student quarter Michaelisstrasse.

Restaurants

Alboth's Futterstr. 15–16 ☎0361/568 82 07. Erfurt's finest international cuisine is prepared by Claus Alboth, a rising star among Thuringia's gourmet chefs with a taste for creative Mediterranean-fusion flavours. There's a 300-strong wine list. Eve only, closed Sun & Mon.

Erfurter Brauhaus Anger 21 ☎0361/562 58 27. Home-produced brews – a *Pils*, *Weizen*, *Dunkel* and a seasonal special – to go with *Schnitzels* and steaks in a cookbook of styles served in a no-nonsense beer hall.

Paganini Fischmarkt 13–16 ☎0361/653 06 92. In Erfurt's ritziest Renaissance mansion, a relaxed restaurant that serves Italian cuisine and commands the largest terrace space on the square. Freshwater fish is a speciality of the house.

Schildchen Schildgasse 3–4 ☎0361/5 40 22 90. A laid-back locals' *Gaststätte* they'd probably prefer to keep secret. Tasty dishes such as beef roulade with red cabbage or sole with cheese gratin on a bed of spinach come at embar-rassingly low prices. Closed Sun.

Wirsthaus Christoffel Michaelisstr. 41 ☎0361/2 62 69 43. Thuringian sausages served by the panful alongside robust basics that are priced in taler in an idiosyncratic Middle Ages–themed restaurant – all good fun.

Zum Goldenen Schwan Michaelisstr. 9 ☎0361/2 62 37 42. A room to suit every mood – a tavern downstairs, a bistro behind and a courtyard space – and sturdy regional dishes such as pork chops with a dollop of mustard washed down with unfiltered beers brewed on site.

Zum Wenigemarkt Wenigemarkt 13 ☎0361/6 42 23 79. Traditional eating at its best in a cosy restau-rant with dark-panelled walls. *Schlachtfestplatte* – a meat-feast of black and liver sausage and bacon served with *Sauerkraut* – is typical of a Thuringian menu which changes every century or so.

Cafés and bars

Abacco Kürschnergasse 7. Hip bar with a maximalist style that's as glamorous as it gets in Erfurt – think crystal chandeliers and cattle-hide bar stools within a half-timbered house. Expensive and very glossy.

Café im Roten Turm Krämerbrücke 17. Tasty soups and salads are served in this understated boutique-style café beneath the vaults of the Aegidienkirche.

double b Marbacher Gasse 10. Slow-paced bar with an older student clientele who enjoy the six beers on tap, all-day breakfasts and cheap steaks.

Hemingway Michaelisstr. 45. A more than usually atmospheric member of the cigar, whisky and cocktail chain, thanks to a low-lit backroom that features a chunk of the building's medieval fabric.

Koko Sushi Meister-Eckhart-Str. 8. Stylish, modern sushi joint and bar loved by students near the Predigerstrasse. The cheap food plates idle past on a conveyor belt to a soundtrack of chilled beats.

P33 Pergamenterstr. 33. Lofty modern lounge-bar hidden away off Michaelisstrasse. Regional DJs at weekends and a menu of fusion food. Closed Mon.

SiJu Fischmarkt 1. Ignore the self-conscious punning name ("see you") and this is a good choice within the glass-walled arcades of the Rathaus, that segues from daytime café to evening bar. The terrace is perfect for people-watching and light lunches. Closed Sun eve.

Übersee Kürschnergasse 8. More relaxed than neighbour *Abacco*, this club-styled bar is quietly hip without ever trying too hard. Its terrace overlooking the Krämerbrücke is one of the best in town.

Vamos Domplatz 15. As Spanish a tapas bar as you'll find in Erfurt, decorated with tiles and with *jamón* hanging from the ceiling. Guitar music on Friday evenings.

Zwiesel Michaelisstr. 31. No-frills student *Kneipe* on the drinking strip that also serves cheap eats.

Nightlife and entertainment

Tourist-office *Erfurtmagazin* is the best source of monthly cultural listings; free sister magazines *Blitz!* and *Fritz* cover gigs, clubs and cinemas. Summer classical **concerts** in the leafy Michaeliskirche courtyard are particularly romantic – the tourist office sells tickets for all events. Highlight of Erfurt's calendar is the **Krämerbrückenfest** towards the end of June, when food and beer stalls and performers in medieval costume engulf Erfurt's favourite bridge. The cathedral steps double as a stage for music and theatre during the **Domstufenfestspiele** in July and August.

Clubs and live music

Centrum Am Anger 7 ⓦwww.centrum-club.de. Popular with a younger crowd, a venue for rock gigs and club nights along the techno and drum 'n' bass line.

Clubeins Steigerstr. 18 ⓦwww.clubeins.de. Dressy place for deep house and r'n'b with some midweekers alongside the weekend regulars. Located 1km southwest of the centre; take tram #6.

Jazzkeller Fischmarkt 13–16 ⓦwww.jazzclub -erfurt.de. The only dedicated jazz venue in town. Concerts Fri & Sat.

Presseklub Dalbergsweg 1 ⓦwww.presseklub .net. Regular midweek salsa and Sunday sessions of jazzy funk sounds alongside house and classics in a lofty bar-club that hosts occasional gigs. It's located bang on Karl-Marx-Platz.

Studentenzentrum Engelsburg Allerheiligenstr. 20–21 ⓦwww.eburg.de. Grungy student all-rounder in the Altstadt that rocks to indie-electro clubnights and hosts live rock and metal bands in a warren of underground cellars. Also screens repertory cinema.

Theatre and classical music

Alte Oper Erfurt Theaterstr. 1 ☎0361/55 11 66, ⓦwww.alteopererfurt.de. *Travestie* and cabaret shows at weekends.

Kaisersaal Futterstr. 15–16 ☎0361/568 81 23. Cultural centre that hosts occasional concerts and recitals.

Theater Erfurt Theaterplatz ☎0361/223 30, ⓦwww.theater-erfurt.de. Modern multi-stage theatre with an eclectic ear for opera, operettas and concerts; also the leading dance and theatre stage. Tickets from Schlösserstrasse 4 (EVAG-Center, Anger).

Listings

Bike rental Radhaus am Dom, Kettenstr. 13 ☎0361/602 06 40.

Car rental All three have desks at the airport. Avis ☎0361/656 24 25; Europcar, Weimarische Str. 32a ☎0361/77 81 30; Hertz, Reisezentrum, Hauptbahnhof ☎0361/34 08 50.

Cinema Multi-screen venue Cinestar (ⓦwww .cinestar.de) is at Hirschlachufer 7.

Internet Internet Treff, Fischmarkt 5 (in Ratskellerpassage) Mon–Fri 10am–8pm, Sat 11am–7pm, Sun 3–8pm.
Post The main post office commands the west Anger (no. 66–73).

Taxis Ranks are at the Hauptbahnhof and main square Domplatz among other places. To book a cab call Taxigenossenschaft Erfurt ☎0361/ 66 66 66.

Weimar

Though modest in size, **WEIMAR** is the spiritual capital of German culture. A young Robert Schumann noted in his diary, "Germans are powerfully drawn to Weimar", and like those to Stratford in England they are not idle tourists so much as aesthete pilgrims come to revere a pantheon of intellectual and artistic saints. Saxe-Weimar dukes were patrons of Lucas Cranach and Johann Sebastian Bach as an overture to the town's finest hour in the late eighteenth century. During the rule of aesthete duke Carl August (1757–1828), the court capital was an intellectual hothouse of rare talents such as dramatist Friedrich Schiller, poet Christoph-Martin Wieland, theologian Johann Gottfried Herder and, more than anyone else, Johann Wolfgang von Goethe. The city flowered as the home of the German Enlightenment whose beauty and ideas astounded Europe. Later names in the roll call of honour include Franz Liszt, Richard Strauss, Friedrich Nietzsche and Bauhaus founders Walter Gropius, Paul Klee and Wassily Kandinsky. The town's name is also synonymous with the ill-fated Weimar Republic of post-imperial Germany.

Weimar is the museum city par excellence whose every street is steeped in a revered past. Thankfully it is charming, too, thanks to frantic efforts to buff up its looks as European City of Culture in 1999. Definitively small-scale, notwithstanding the handsome **Park an der Ilm** south and the odd gallery, almost everything worth seeing lies within a ten-minute radius of the **Markt** in the lattice of streets bound to the north by **Graben**, track of a medieval moat, and to the south by **Steubenstrasse**. Here you'll find the first-rate art in the ducal Schloss, a gorgeous Rococo library, the **Herzogin-Anna-Amalia-Bibliothek**, and **Goethe's house**. Erudite stuff and proof that Weimar most rewards those who apply their minds – others may find it rather provincial.

Arrival and information

The **Hauptbahnhof** is a twenty-minute walk north of the centre; several buses run to Goetheplatz at the western edge of the Altstadt. The hub of advice is the municipal **tourist office** at Markt 10 (April–Oct Mon–Sat 9.30am–7pm, Sun 9.30am–3pm; Nov–March Mon–Fri 9.30am–6pm, Sat & Sun 9.30am–2pm; general ☎03643/74 50, accommodation ☎03643/74 54 34, ⓦwww.weimar.de). Within are separate desks for the Buchenwald concentration camp site (ⓦwww.buchenwald.de) and an information point of Weimar cultural administrator Klassic Stiftung Weimar, which sells museum tickets and books and provides the usual flyers; the latter's visitor information office (Mon–Fri 10am–4pm; ☎03643/54 54 01, ⓦwww.klassik-stiftung .de) is at Frauenstrasse 4, and its website is the portal for all sights in Weimar. The **Weimar Card** (72hr, €10; 72hr extension €5) provides twenty percent discounts on the major museums and free entry to lesser attractions, plus free public transport. The most convenient **internet** access is at *Café Roxanne* (Mon–Sat from 10am, Sun from 1pm) at Markt 21.

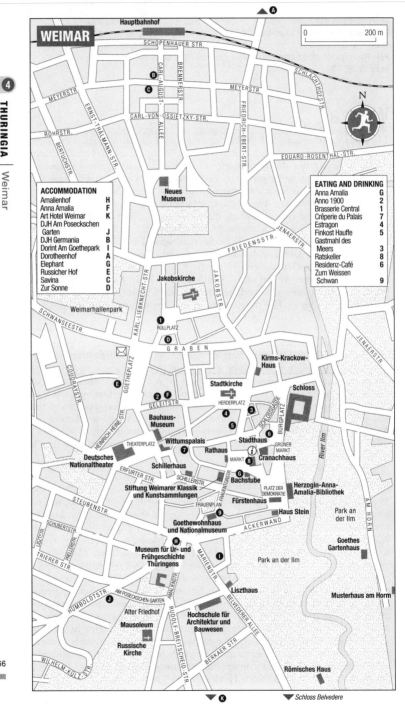

WEIMAR

Hauptbahnhof

SCHOPENHAUER STR.

0   200 m

N

SCHLACHTHOFSTR.

MEYERSTR.

CARL-AUGUST-ALLEE

BRENNERSTR.

MEYERSTR.

CARL-VON-OSSIETZKY-STR.

FRIEDRICH-EBERT-STR.

EDUARD-ROSENTHAL-STR.

ERNST-THÄLMANN-STR.

ROHRSTR.

BERTUCHSTR.

Neues
Museum

JENAERSTR.

FRIEDENSSTR.

JAKOBSTR.

ACCOMMODATION
Amalienhof   H
Anna Amalia   F
Art Hotel Weimar   K
DJH Am Poseckschen
 Garten   J
DJH Germania   B
Dorint Am Goethepark I
Dorotheenhof   A
Elephant   G
Russicher Hof   E
Savina   C
Zur Sonne   D

EATING AND DRINKING
Anna Amalia   G
Anno 1900   2
Brasserie Central   1
Crêperie du Palais   7
Estragon   4
Finkost Hauffe   5
Gastmahl des
 Meers   3
Ratskeller   8
Residenz-Café   6
Zum Weissen
 Schwan   9

Jakobskirche

KARL-LIEBKNECHT-STR.

SCHWANSEESTR.

Weimarhallenpark

COUDRAYSTR.

ROLLPLATZ

G R A B E N

GOETHEPLATZ

Kirms-Krackow-
Haus

JENAERSTR.

HEINRICH-HEINE-STR.

GELEITSTR.

Stadtkirche

HERDERPLATZ

Schloss

SCHLOSSGASSE

BURGPLATZ

River Ilm

Bauhaus-
Museum

THEATERPLATZ

Wittumspalais

Stadthaus

GRÜNER
MARKT

Deutsches
Nationaltheater

ERFURTER STR.

Schillerhaus

SCHILLERSTR.

Rathaus

MARKT

Cranachhaus

Stiftung Weimarer Klassik
und Kunstsammlungen

FRAUENTORSTR.

Bachstube

PLATZ DER
DEMOKRATIE

Herzogin-Anna-
Amalia-Bibliothek

STEUBENSTR.

FRAUENPLAN

Fürstenhaus

SCHUBERTSTR.

Goethewohnhaus
und Nationalmuseum

ACKERWAND

Haus Stein

Park an
der Ilm

AM HORN

LISZTSTR.

PRELLERSTR.

Museum für Ur- und
Frühgeschichte
Thüringens

MARIENSTR.

Park an der Ilm

Goethes
Gartenhaus

TRIERER STR.

AM POSECKSCHEN GARTEN

Liszthaus

Musterhaus am Horn

HUMBOLDTSTR.

Alter Friedhof

Mausoleum

Russische
Kirche

RUDOLF-BREITSCHEID-STR.

Hochschule für
Architektur und
Bauwesen

BELVEDERER ALLEE

BERKAER STR.

Römisches Haus

WILHELM-KULZ-STR.

Schloss Belvedere

Accommodation

Weimar's accommodation tends towards the more upmarket end, with budget options not its forte, which makes **private rooms** (❶–❷) booked through the tourist office worth considering. The good news is that there are four **youth hostels** – but brace yourself for school groups. A DJH service centre at Carl-August-Allee 13 (Mon 1–4pm, Tues 9am–noon & 1–5pm, Thurs 9am–noon & 1–4pm, Fri 9am–noon; ☎03643/85 00 00, ⊛www.djh-thueringen.de) helps with bookings.

Hotels and pensions

Amalienhof Amalienstr. 2 ☎03643/54 90, ⊛www
.amalienhof-weimar.de. Slice of Neoclassical Weimar
in a small church-affiliated hotel – well priced,
central and spacious. Big breakfast buffets. ❹–❺
Anna Amalia Geleitstr. 8–12 ☎03643/495 60,
⊛www.hotel-anna-amalia.de. Popular mid-range
place with modern spacious quarters spread across
three buildings in the town centre. ❹
Art Hotel Weimar Freiherr-vom-Stein-Allee 3a/b
☎03643/540 60, ⊛www.art-hotel-weimar.de.
Spotless design hotel in a villa south of the centre
that's stylish without ever showing off. Friendly
staff, too. ❺
Dorint Am Goethepark Beethovenplatz 1–2
☎03643/87 20, ⊛www.dorint.com. Classic
business-style accommodation that's more relaxed
than some in this upmarket chain. Also has good
spa facilities. ❻
Dorotheenhof Dorotheenhof 1, Schöndorf, 4km
north ☎03643/45 90, ⊛www.dorotheenhof.com.
Charming hotel of the Romantik group, sympathetically created from the manor estate of a cavalry
captain. Bus #7 from the Hauptbahnhof. ❻
Elephant Markt 19 ☎03643/80 20, ⊛www
.luxurycollection.com/elephant. Weimar's finest and
most historic address has hosted the great, the
good and the less laudable throughout the town's
history. Superbly located on the Markt, it nods to Art
Deco in style and has a first-class restaurant. ❼

Russicher Hof Goetheplatz 2 ☎03643/77 48
36, ⊛www.russischerhof.com. Sumptuous
traditional five-star that preserves much of
the grand-hotel ambience of its early 1800s
origins. ❼–❽
Savina Meyerstr. 60 ☎03643/866 90,
⊛www.pension-savina.de. Largest of the town's
pensions, this is an acceptable cheapie two streets
from the train station. ❸
Zur Sonne Rollplatz 2 ☎03643/862 90,
℮hotelzursonne@web.de. Fairly bland, simple
rooms but good value for a central location on a
quiet square. ❸

DJH youth hostels

Am Ettersberg Ettersberg-Siedlung ☎03643/42
11 11. Rustic place in a nature reserve just north of
the town; bookings through DJH *Maxim Gorki* (see
below). Bus #6 to "Obelisk" then 500m walk.
Dorms from €25.
Am Poseckschen Garten Humboldtstr. 17
☎03643/85 07 92. Near the Historiches Friedhof,
this is the most central of the quartet. Dorms
from €24.
Germania Carl-August-Allee 13 ☎03643/85 04
90. North of the centre near the Hauptbahnhof.
Dorms from €24.
Maxim Gorki Zum Wilden Graben 12 ☎03643/85
07 50. In the suburbs a fair schlep 5km south; bus
#5 or #8 to "Friedhof". Dorms from €25.

The Markt and Platz der Demokratie

Site of a weekday market and the tourist office, the **Markt** is as good an introduction to Weimar as any, ringed by a pleasing jumble of buildings. If the monuments
of the ducal town's Baroque flowering lie elsewhere, this is the wellspring of its
early roots, as evidenced by a pair of handsome Renaissance mansions on the
east side – the **Stadthaus**, a trade-turned-festivities centre picked out in green
tracery, and adjacent **Cranachhaus** where Lucas Cranach the Elder worked as
court painter for his final year in 1552; he followed erstwhile Elector Johann
Friedrich of Saxony to Weimar having stuck with him through five years of
captivity by his vanquisher, Emperor Karl V, and the Cranach winged-snake coat
of arms is above one window arch. The "anteroom for Weimar's living Valhalla",
Austrian poet Franz Grillparzer decided, was hotel *Elephant* on the south side of
the Markt. Acclaimed even in Goethe's day, author Thomas Mann set his novel

Lotte in Weimar, which imagines Goethe's painfully polite reunion with an old flame, in the hotel. Johann Sebastian Bach composed cantatas in an adjacent house while court organist then concert master from 1708. In 1718 the son of the orchestra leader stepped into his father's shoes and the ambitious Bach, furious at being passed over, stomped off to Köthen, although not before the duke imprisoned him for four weeks to prevent his departure.

Off the Markt's southeast corner aristocratic **Platz der Demokratie** is boxed in by Baroque palaces, finest being the Fürstenhaus (prince's house), a butterscotch ducal mansion that holds the **Hochschule für Musik Franz Liszt**. Its origins were as an early residence for then-prince Carl August, whose equestrian statue stands at the square's centre – that it is modelled on the memorial to Emperor Marcus Aurelius in Rome's Capitol speaks volumes about the swagger of the miniature state in the late 1700s. The misnamed Grünes Schloss encloses the east side of the elongated square. Here Goethe managed the library of Duchess Anna Amalia, the **Herzogin-Anna-Amalia-Bibliothek** (Tues–Sun 9.30am–2.30pm; €6.50), the mother of Carl August who piloted Weimar's ascent into the intellectual stratosphere. Restored after a severe fire in 2004 that destroyed fifty thousand tomes, the Rococo library is once more an exquisitely sensuous *Gesamtkuntswerk* (complete work of art) where busts of scholars stand on a gilt-trimmed gallery which houses one of the world's finest collection of German Enlightenment manuscripts. Entrance is limited to 250 people per day, so it's worth buying tickets early. Goethe pilgrims may want to go around the corner on Ackerwand to **Haus Stein**, the former ducal stables and home to Goethe's first great love, Charlotte Stein. That she was already married to the head stableman did not prevent his 1700 adoring letters.

The Schloss and Herderplatz

The ducal **Schloss** (Tues–Sun: April–Oct 10am–6pm; Nov–March 10am–4pm; €5) lies discreetly away from the east edge of the Altstadt at the head of Park an der Ilm. An absurdly ostentatious pile for what was a town of only six thousand people, the U-shaped palace was erected after a 1774 fire all but erased its predecessor – only the Renaissance gateway of the original remains. Goethe proffered advice for the new plans and is honoured for his trouble in a corridor of sumptuous first-floor chambers that also salute the town's other cultural heroes, Schiller, Wieland and Herder. The Festsaal in the other wing is a paean to sober Neoclassicism. Impressive though the architecture is, the reason to visit is the gallery of Old Masters. It kicks off on the ground floor with the heavy hitters of the German Renaissance, notably works by **Lucas Cranach the Elder** (1472–1553). Among the highlights are wedding portraits of sylph-eyed beauty Princess Sybille von Cleve and Johannn Friedrich and two images of his friend Martin Luther, bearded when in hiding in the Wartburg, Eisenach, as Jünker Jorg (Squire George) and shaved twenty years later. A couple of works by his contemporary Dürer introduce a cabinet of Renaissance curios next-door whose fripperies are an evocative testament to ducal decadence. Westphalian master Konrad von Soest stands out among the medieval artwork and Russian icons in the other wing, while works hung in the period rooms above fast-forward through the Enlightenment into Impressionism: star for the French is Monet's *Rouen Cathedral* caught in early morning; Max Beckmann and pre-Raphaelite-inspired Christian Rohlfs for the Germans.

The heart of the medieval town was **Herderplatz**, west of the Schloss. Its name and that of the much-remodelled Stadtkirche St Peter und Paul, usually known simply as the **Herderkirche**, are a homage to town pastor Johann Gottfried Herder (1776–1803), a poet-theologian remembered with such affection that flowers remain on his tomb in the nave. Complementing the artworks in the Schloss is the church's Crucifixion triptych, Cranach's swan song, completed by his son Lucas Cranach the Younger in 1555. A spurt of holy blood rains divine mercy onto the head of the snowy-bearded artist who stands beside Luther pointing to his doctrine. On the left wing are Johann Friedrich and his wife Sybille, now thirty years older than the young suitors Cranach pictured earlier. They died shortly afterwards – their flamboyant double-height tomb in the choir upstages the painter's tomb, shifted from the churchyard to the left of his creation, and which depicts the artist as a portly gent holding, presumably, an easel.

Just up from the church on Jakobstrasse is **Kirms-Krackow-Haus** (April–Oct Tues–Sun 10am–2pm; €2.50), a galleried courtyard residence that preserves intact a bourgeois residence of eighteenth-century Weimar. Notwithstanding the richly patterned wallpaper, its joy is as an ensemble piece that retains the personal effects of its owners.

Neues Museum

When Weimar's erudite aspic cloys, head to the Neues Museum (April–Oct daily 11am–6pm; Nov–March Tues–Sun 11am–4pm; €3.50) on Weimarplatz fifteen minutes' walk north of Herderplatz. The melted bronze figure outside is a taster of its refreshingly irreverent international art from the last four centuries, collated by a Cologne gallery owner, Paul Maenz, who clearly had a soft spot for minimal and conceptual work. Its building is no mean piece of architecture itself. Erected in 1869 as a ducal museum, it was rethought by the Nazis as the Halle der Volksgemeinschaft (People's Community Hall) – in a characteristic piece of posturing, they obliterated surrounding streets, so it would stand at the head of a monumental space named Adolf-Hitler-Platz. An adjunct to the museum is Rebecca Horn's *Konzert für Buchenwald* installation in tram-depot-turned-cultural-centre e-werk, east of the museum at Am Kirschberg 7 (May–Oct Sat & Sun noon–6pm; €1.50). Created as a memorial to victims of the Nazi concentration camp north of the city for Weimar's year as European Capital of Culture in 1999, it consists of a forty-metre-long wall of ashes behind glass.

Schillerstrasse and Theaterplatz

Schillerstrasse arcs away off Frauenplan southwest of the Markt as a leafy esplanade named for Friedrich Schiller (1759–1805). One of the founding fathers of Weimar Classicism, the itinerant poet and dramatist spent the last three years of his life at no. 12, **Schillerhaus** (April–Oct Wed–Mon 9am–6pm, Sat till 7pm except Oct; Nov–March Wed–Mon 9am–4pm; €4), and penned *The Bride from Messina* and *William Tell* in its attic study. That the eighteenth-century playwright had to find 4200 taler for his house helps explain its humble looks compared to Goethe's residence (see p.270). A modern museum tacked behind guides visitors around his life and works.

Weimar's awesome twosome share a plinth at the end of the street on **Theaterplatz** in a sculpture by Dresden-based Ernst Rietschel (1857). One of the great cultural icons of Germany (and Weimar's landmark), the bronze of the pair with the laurel wreath of destiny is known to every schoolchild, and copies stand in Cleveland, San Francisco and, bizarrely, Shanghai. The square is named after the rebuilt court theatre in which the 1919 National Assembly ratified the ill-fated Weimar Republic that fumbled with democracy and raging inflation until Hitler wrested power with low politicking in 1933. Opposite is the **Wittumspalais** (Tues–Sun 10am–6pm, Nov–March till 4pm; €4) where widowed Duchess Anna Amalia hosted intellectual gatherings in classical Weimar. At a symbolic round table, the arts patron surrounded herself with noble and bourgeois aesthetes – indeed, Weimar's intellectual flowering was largely due to this unique dialogue between nobility and the middle classes. The Neoclassical interiors are Weimar's most graceful.

The town followed up the German Enlightenment by pioneering **Jugendstil** and its successor **Bauhaus** a century later. Jugendstil was nurtured in the city by Belgian architect and painter Henry van de Velde after he was encouraged to set up an Arts and Crafts school here in 1902. The **Bauhaus-Museum** on Theaterplatz (daily 10am–6pm; €4.50) features a room of his organic shapes as context for the streamlined exponents of the Bauhaus design school of Walter Gropius, which flourished in Weimar until its move to Dessau in 1925.

Van de Velde also declared his stylistic manifesto on Weimar's streets: his **Hohe Pappeln** house (April–Oct Tues–Sun 1–6pm; €2.50) at Belvederer Allee 58 in south suburb Ehringsdorf (bus #1 or #12 to Papiergraben), was a key meeting point for the "New Weimar" school, and houses at Cranachstrasse 15 and 47. The first Bauhaus edifice constructed – and the only one erected in its birthplace – is **Haus am Horn**, a minimalist UNESCO-listed box created as a show home in 1923 by the movement's youngest designer, Georg Muche. A university exhibition space, it lies at Am Horn 61 in Park an der Ilm (see opposite).

Goethes Wohnhaus

If Weimar is the temple of German culture, **Goethes Wohnhaus** (Tues–Sun: April–Oct 9am–6pm, Sat till 7pm; Nov–March 9am–4pm; house €6.50, combined ticket €8.50) is its holy of holies. Within the town house on Frauenplan, southwest of the Markt, given to him by Duke Carl August in 1792, the nation's cultural colossus created masterpieces for fifty years until his death in 1832, including his crowning achievement *Faust*. He wrote to his benefactor in 1806 that he hoped he had "proven worthy of your gift, not having used it for a frivolous existence but to disseminate the knowledge of art and science". The garden was a botanical experiment for "pleasant and educational entertainment". Yet the house is as homely as it is erudite, best seen as an insight into the polymath's mind. The paintings,

▲ Statue of Goethe and Schiller, Weimar

Johann Wolfgang von Goethe

No figure commands German culture like **Johann Wolfgang von Goethe** (1748–1832). A lazy comparison is often made to Shakespeare, which underplays the achievements of the last great Renaissance man of European culture. Not content with producing some of the most insightful drama in the German language, Goethe penned poetry, novels, travelogues and short stories, as well as philosophical essays and treatises on theology, humanism and science. His influence on German philosophy is incalculable. Indeed, he didn't see himself as a writer and proposed near his death that he would be remembered for his quirky *Theory of Colours* treatise. "As to what I have done as a poet ... I take no pride in it," he said, "but that in my century I am the only person who knows the truth in the difficult science of colours – of that I am not a little proud." Misguidedly so as it turned out: the quirky hypothesis dismissed by Newton suggested that darkness is not an absence of light but a polar opposite that interacts with it, with colour arising where the two flow together. Science has rebuffed his theory, but the idea was popular with artists such as Turner and Kandinsky.

The Frankfurt-born son of a wealthy family, he trained as a lawyer but found fame in 1774 as the 26-year-old novelist of **The Sorrows of Young Werther**. Its semi-autobiographical tale of obsessive love not only became the best seller of the proto-Romantic Sturm und Drang movement, it so wowed 18-year-old Carl August that the Grand Duke of Saxe-Weimar-Eisenach took on Goethe as a court adviser in 1775. Goethe would remain there until his death, though paradoxically he was so wrapped up in official duties and science that literature went onto the back burner for that first decade. It was an Italian holiday from 1786 that rekindled his creative spark (and also sent countless young Germans who read his *Italian Journey* mooning around Italy). On his return two years later he teamed up with Schiller to continue his major prose achievement, **Wilhelm Meister**, a six-novel cycle. He also began the work on the two-part lyric drama **Faust**, which he would tinker with until his death. Ostensibly a narrative of the classic legend, his dramatic masterpiece strives to lay bare the soul of Western society. Small wonder that when Berlin erected its "Walk of Ideas", a 12m-high stack of books on Bebelplatz in 2006, all the illustrious names of German literature rested on a single giant tome of Goethe's.

Italian busts and *objets d'art* Goethe picked up as holiday souvenirs are in situ in rooms whose colours he chose for their mood-altering "sensual-moral effects" – an upshot of his colour studies. The staircase is modelled on those of Renaissance villas he had admired on Italian travels, and in the Juno room where his guests retired after dinner is the piano on which Mendelssohn showcased works in progress. Look, too, in the study where he dictated his works – Goethe only lifted a pen for poetry – for a bust of Napoleon that was placed there after the pair met in Erfurt to mutual declarations of admiration. The attached **Goethe-National-museum** (same times; €3.50) is a rather didactic catalogue of his achievements and those of his peers.

The southern Altstadt and Park an der Ilm

South of Frauenplatz on Humboldtstrasse is the **Museum für Ur- und Frühgeschichte Thüringens** (Museum of Pre- and Early Thuringian History; Tues 9am–6pm, Wed–Fri 9am–5pm, Sat & Sun 10am–5pm; €3.50), with excellent though overlooked displays of regional archeology from the dawn of man to the Romans and early medieval Frankish tribes. In the **Historischer Friedhof** cemetery one block behind, the Fürstengruft (daily: April–Oct 10am–6pm; Nov–March 10am–4pm; €2.50) was created as the ducal mausoleum for the House of Saxony-Weimar but also serves as the resting place for Goethe and Schiller after Carl August announced that he wanted to lie in state alongside the two brightest stars in Weimar's cultural firmament. Beside its severe Neoclassicism an Orthodox Russian church behind (same times; free) appears unexpectedly exotic. It was built in the 1860s for a daughter of the Tsar, Grand Duchess Maria Pavlovna.

South of Frauenplatz (via Marienstrasse) stands **Liszthaus** (April–Oct Wed–Mon 10am–6pm; €4), the cottage of the court gardener where the composer spent summers surrounded by adoring students from 1869–86, inadvertently laying the ground for the music college that bears his name. Only its upper four rooms are in the modest style Liszt favoured. Almost opposite on Geschwister-Scholl-Strasse is the Henry van der Velde–designed wing of the Bauhaus-Universität, wellspring of Walter Gropius's stylistic movement and still a university.

The prize of southern Weimar is **Park an der Ilm**. So expansive is the greenery that extends away from the Altstadt that Romantic author Adolf Stahr quipped, "Weimar is a park with a town inside." Goethe had a hand in its landscaping in English style, conceived as "a series of aesthetic pictures" in the manner of a Romantic landscape. In a canny bid to keep the writer in Weimar, Duke Carl August rewarded his garden plans in 1776 with the riverside **Goethes Gartenhaus** (daily: April–Oct 10am–6pm; Nov–March 10am–4pm; €4), his residence for six years before he moved to Frauenplan, and thereafter his favourite escape. Presumably it was more enchanting before most of the furnishings were stripped to preserve them from the happy hordes who visit. Within view – glinting white among the leaves south – is **Römisches Haus** (Tues–Sun; €2.50). Duke Carl August lived out summers in its mock-Classical temple, its muralled period rooms restored to their full lustre to serve as a backdrop for a so-so exhibit on the park.

Outside the centre: Schloss Belvedere and Buchenwald

Lack of space in the town centre limited the ambitions of Weimar's early eighteenth-century duke, Ernst August. In **Schloss Belvedere** (April–Oct Tues–Sun 10am–6pm; €2.50; bus #12) at the far edge of Weimar he found room for an airy summer palace suitable for a ruler who nurtured self-delusions about being a Saxon "Sun King", even if its Rococo style and canary-yellow paintjob seem a touch jolly for an absolutist. Duke Carl August used it as a summertime pleasure house and hunting lodge, and it's his porcelain that's displayed inside alongside weapons. Again Goethe supervised the garden's change from strict symmetrical landscape into today's naturalistic park for botany studies.

In the wooded heights of the Ettersburg, 10km northwest of central Weimar, is the **Gedenkstätte Buchenwald** (Tues–Sun: April–Oct 10am–6pm; Nov–March 10am–4pm; free; ⓦ www.buchenwald.de), reached by bus #6 from Goetheplatz or the Hauptbahnhof; take one to "Buchenwald" not "Ettersburg". Over the eight years from its opening in 1937 to hold "undesirables" and opponents of the Nazi regime to its liberation through a prisoner uprising in April 1945 after the SS guards fled as the Allies approached, more than 250,000 people were held captive in the concentration camp. Over 55,000 died, most of the daily two hundred death toll due to disease or exhaustion from forced labour in the armaments factories, but some killed through the torture and medical experiments of the SS; the inscription wrought into the gate and visible from the muster ground, "*Jedem das Seine*" (roughly "to each his own"), betrays the Nazi mentality that inmates were to blame for their incarceration. That a large quota of leading

Communist and Social Democrat political inmates were executed here made the camp a propaganda tool for the GDR authorities. It was only after the *Wende* in 1990 that mass graves were discovered with the remains of seven thousand pro-fascist sympathizers and regime opponents who had been worked to death here when it was the communists' Special Camp No. 2 after the war. While most of the buildings were razed to create a memorial to anti-fascist resistance in 1951, the large depot in which inmates' effects were sorted holds an exhibition centre that screens a thirty-minute documentary film (English subtitles) several times a day. An outlying building tackles the later camp. The prisoners' canteen, detention cells in the gatehouse, crematorium and pathology department can also be visited.

Eating and drinking

Weimar has traditional tastes in its central restaurants, with only hotels and smaller cafés featuring more international menus.

Anna Amalia *Hotel Elephant*, Markt 19 ☎03643/80 26 39. Under the tenure of Italian master chef Marcello Fabbri, this is easily the finest gourmet address in town, with a repertoire of fine modern European dishes served in an atmosphere of understated luxury. Lovely garden for summer, too. Eve only, closed Sun & Mon.

Anno 1900 Geleitstr. 12a ☎03643/90 35 71. Quietly swish café-restaurant that prepares light Italianesque cuisine in an Art Nouveau-styled conservatory – its terrace is a lovely spot for breakfasts (until 2pm), and there's live piano on Thursday to Saturday eve.

Brasserie Central Rollplatz 8. Laid-back locals' place on a quiet square – a pleasant spot to kick back with a drink before you sample a menu of French and German dishes.

Crêperie du Palais Am Palais 1. Cheap home-made quiche and couscous alongside the crêpes of its name in a sweet French-run backstreet café.

Estragon Herderplatz 3. The soup bar of organic market Rosmarin is a great spot for a central pit-stop: recipes change daily but expect fine home-made options such as chorizo and *Knockwurst*, lemon and salmon. Mon–Fri 10am–7pm, Sat till 4pm.

Feinkost Hauffe Kaufstr. 9–11. Attached to a superb delicatessen famed for its wines you'll find this tiny courtyard café that prepares the likes of pasta with salmon and truffles, among these Mediterranean dishes fresh each day. Lunch only, closed Sun.

Gastmahl des Meers Herderplatz 16 ☎03643/90 12 00. A lovely terrace garden is one reason to visit. Another is the good menu at this fish speci-ality restaurant. Closed Sun & Mon eve.

Ratskeller Markt 10 ☎03643/85 05 73. Located in the wine cellar of the town's former festivities centre, this has a good, solid, traditional menu that features regional dishes.

Residenz-Café Grüner Markt 4. Weimar's favourite cheap café, as adept at breakfasts and afternoon coffee as at Italian-influenced light bites on a terrace adjacent to the Schloss. And vegetarians rejoice – there is a dedicated meat-free menu.

Zum Weissen Schwan Frauentorstr. 23 ☎03643/90 87 51. Goethe raved about this historic inn with rustic decor. Some of Weimar's finest Thuringian traditional cooking is bolstered by a small clutch of international dishes. Closed Mon & Tues.

Entertainment

Don't come to Weimar for nightlife. Your best hopes for a grungy night out to counterbalance the cultural overdose is *Studentenklub Kasseturm* (Ⓦ www.kasseturm .de) at Goetheplatz 1, then *Studentenenclub Schützengasse* (Ⓦ www.schuetzengasse .de) at Schützengasse 2, where the booze is cheap, the rock and house club nights unashamedly gritty. Alternative cultural centre **e-werk**, north of the centre at Am Kirschberg 4 (Ⓦ www.strassenbahndepot.info), hosts occasional live gigs alongside cutting-edge art exhibitions and cinema in its venues created from a former tram depot. The mainstay of high culture is the **Deutsches National Theater** (☎03643/75 50, Ⓦ www.nationaltheater-weimar.de), on Theaterplatz, along with the mixed bag of mainstream crowd-pleasers staged at the **Congress Centrum Neue Weimarhalle** (☎03643/74 51 00, Ⓦ www.weimarhalle.de) – its gleaming glass box lies north of the centre on UNESCO-Platz.

Jena

JENA, the next stop east from Weimar, is another university centre that was an intellectual hothouse for the flowering of Classicism under Goethe and Schiller. Thereafter the similarities end. Compared to its somewhat languid neighbour, Jena positively hums with the energy of its 23,000 students – one in four of the population is connected with the university. The university's history of research also gives the city a scientific bent – it was accredited as the National City of Science 2008 and its dominance in precision optics through names such as Carl Zeiss and Schott Jenaer Glasswerk inspired the moniker "Lichtstadt" (Light Town). Jena is also less precious about its looks – the Altstadt was pounded by the Allies, then GDR urban-planners embarked on some architectural vandalism of their own. Restoration has returned pockets of charm and the setting in a bowl of wooded hills appeals, but neither is the point. Anyone of a scientific mindset will enjoy its museums while the nightlife is only bettered in Thuringia by Erfurt. All Jena's sights are within easy walking distance from the centre. To attempt the lot in a day, however, you're best off renting bikes.

Arrival, information and city transport

The most useful of Jena's three **train stations** is Jena-Paradies south of the centre ("paradise" refers to a surrounding park). Most trains on the Berlin–Munich line stop here en route to larger Jena-Saalbahnhof north of the town centre. Those from Erfurt and Weimar stop at Jena-West southwest of the centre and two blocks west of Paradies. By 2009 the **tourist office** (Mon–Fri 9.30am–7pm, Sat 9.30am–3/4pm; April–Oct also Sun 11am–3pm; ☏03641/49 80 50, ⓦwww .jena.de) should have shifted across from its current location at Johannisstrasse 23 to Markt 16. Its **JenaCard** (€8.90) provides 48 hours' free travel on public transport and entry to all municipal museums. **Bike rental** is on Löbdergraben, abutting the Markt, at Fahrradhaus Kemter (no. 24; ☏03641/44 15 33) and Fahrrad Kirscht (no. 8; ☏03641/44 15 39).

Accommodation

As ever the tourist office books **private rooms** (❶–❷). *Camping Jena* (☏03641/66 66 88, ⓦwww.camping-jena.com) is a great **campsite** 2km east of the centre at Am Erikönig off Karl-Liebknecht-Strasse (A7), which makes up in laid-back vibe what it lacks in mod cons – take tram #2 or #4; reception is in the old tram carriage.

Ibis Hotel City am Holzmarkt Teichgraben 1 ☏03641/81 30, ⓦwww.ibishotel.com. The usual identikit modern rooms from the chain, and on the snug side to boot, but keenly priced for the location. ❸

IJH Jena Am Herrenberge 3 ☏03641/68 72 30, ⓦwww.jena.jugendherberge.de. The town's "international youth hostel" is in a far-flung GDR-era apartment block in the southwest suburbs, best treated as a last resort after private rooms; take buses #10, #13 or #14 towards Beutenberg and alight at "Zeiss-Werk". Dorms from €24.

Schwarzer Bär Lutherplatz 2 ☏03641/40 60, ⓦwww.schwarzer-baer-jena.de. Good-value accommodation in a traditional, enjoyably old-fashioned four-star created from a central inn – former guests include Martin Luther in his Jünker Jorg disguise. ❹

Steigenberger Esplanade Carl-Zeiss-Platz 4 ☏03641/80 00, ⓦwww.jena.steigenberger.de. Large, central hotel of the prestige Steigenberger chain that's canopied by a spectacular glass roof to bring a light, airy feel. The modern business style is more welcoming than usual, too. ❺–❼

Zur Noll Oberlauengasse 20 ☏03641 597 70, ⓦwww.zur-noll.de. Pleasant rooms above a restaurant with an unrivalled location in the heart of the Altstadt. ❹

Zur Schweiz Quergasse 15 ☎ 03641/520 50,
ⓦ www.zur-schweiz.de. Comfy, old-fashioned

family-run place, well located off Jena's bar-strip
Wagnergasse. ❸

Around Eichplatz and the Markt

The best navigation mark in Jena is the **Intershop Tower** (also known as JenTower), which defines the central skyline with a landmark cylindrical tube of GDR vintage. The regime ignored protests in 1972 to construct a bold skyscraper for a bold communist future, and never mind that that meant bulldozing one of the city's medieval squares, **Eichplatz**. The 120m tower proved spectacularly unsuitable for its intended use as research institute for the Zeiss Foundation, so it was given to the university, then in the 1990s it was given its current mirrored sheen as a corporate headquarters. Far from lovable, it has become a city icon nevertheless, helped in part by its restaurant (see p.277) and viewing platform (daily 11am–midnight; €3).

What did survive GDR pipe-dreams is the square **Johannistor** beside the Intershop Tower, a medieval city gateway linked by a section of fourteenth-century town wall to the **Pulverturm**. On the other side of the Intershop Tower the southwest defence of Altstadt is demarcated by the octagonal **Anatomieturm**, so-called because anatomy lectures were held there – where Goethe discovered the human central jawbone. His five years in Jena were spent at the **Collegium Jenense**, the original university building housed in a Dominican abbey since 1548 – it was slated for demolition until the GDR succumbed to protests. Unpromising from its outside on Kollegienstrasse, the building's cobbled courtyard features a swaggering portal bearing the coat of arms of Saxe-Ernestine in honour of founder patron Prince Johann Friedrich "the Magnanimous". The foyer is usually open and houses displays of university memorabilia, such as Renaissance beer tankards and a desiccated human foot and arm studied by anatomy classes.

East of the glorified car park that is modern Eichplatz, the picturesque **Markt** retains some of the atmosphere of medieval Jena. The twin-peaked **Rathaus** at its southern corner straddles both squares, mounted on the Markt side with a Baroque tower that houses an astronomical clock. On the hour, devil-figure *Schnapphans* ("Snatching Hans") attempts to grab a golden sphere dangled by a pilgrim – acclaimed one of the "seven wonders of Jena" in years past, but don't get too excited. A portly statue of magnanimous Johann Friedrich I, or "Hanfried", stands in regal pomp at the centre of the square. Behind it rises one of the few historic houses in Jena, a late-Gothic construction with windows like theatre curtains beneath a half-timbered upper. It spins through town history as the **Stadtmuseum Göhre** (Tues, Wed & Fri 10am–5pm, Thurs 2–10pm, Sat & Sun 11am–6pm; €4), pinpointing the "seven wonders of Jena", and stages art exhibitions. There's also a café at the top (same times; free access). At Unterm Markt 12 on the south side of the Markt is **Romantikerhaus** (Tues–Sun 10am–5pm; €4), a former residence of philosopher Johann Gottlieb Fichte that's furnished in Romantic style as a backdrop for a small gallery.

The defining edifice on the north side of the Markt is **Stadkirche St Michael** (Mon–Sat 10am–1pm & Mon–Fri 2–5pm). The lofty interior and streamlined pillars within give no hint that the entire chancel rests on a Gothic passageway – the most acclaimed of Jena's wonders and probably the most impressive if only for resilience. The church's greater claim to fame is for a bronze relief of Luther, who preached from its pulpit.

The rest of Jena

In the idle hours between pushing at anatomy's boundaries and rechannelling the River Saale, Goethe pottered in "seclusion in the flower and plant mountains" of the **Botanischer Garten** (daily: June–Aug 9am–6pm; Sept–May 9am–5pm; €3), opposite the Pulverturm on Fürstengraben. He is said to have planted the ginkgo near the Inspecktorhaus in which he lived for most of his five years in Jena between 1817 and 1822, a respite from the daily grind as a Weimar state minister, which gave him the time to craft *Meister Wilhelm* and *Faust*, and indulge scientific pursuits such as his theory of colours (see box, p.271). The scientific legacy of his stay in Jena is the focus of displays in the house as the **Goethe-Gedenkstätte** (April–Oct Wed–Sun 11am–3pm; €1). At the eastern fringe of the garden lies the **Zeiss Planetarium** (Tues–Sun times vary by event; €8; ⓦ www.planetarium-jena .de). The world's oldest public planetarium, opened in 1926, now also shows psychedelic three-dimensional animations soundtracked by Pink Floyd or Queen rock-shows, screened between the standard space explorations.

The planetarium's name doffs a cap to the original lenses of Zeiss, a global precision optic manufacturer founded in Jena in 1846 by Carl Zeiss, who teamed up with physicist and optic pioneer Ernst Abbe, to produce the world's first scientific high-performance microscopes in 1866. Otto Schott, a trim doctor and physicist who developed heat- and chemical-resistant glass, joined the duo in 1891 to found Jenaer Glaswerk Schott & Genossen – today's global glass corporation Schott – and cement Jena's reputation as an optics centre. Their narratives are told in rather didactic fashion with a mock-up of the first factory in the **Optisches Museum** (Tues–Fri 10am–4.30pm, Sat & Sun 11am–5pm, factory by tour, times at ticket desk; €5). More fun are the displays of optic curios such as the peepshows that preceded film. Incidentally, the octagonal temple outside the museum, the **Ernst-Abbe-Denkmal**, studded with bronze reliefs of industry, is the work of Belgian Art Nouveau pioneer Henry van de Velde. Both are on Carl-Zeiss-Platz accessed most easily via glass-roofed mall Goethe Galerie off Leutragraben, opposite the Anatomieturm.

Going south on Leutragraben, it's a fifteen-minute walk via Schillerstrasse to **Schillers Gartenhaus** (Tues–Sun 11am–5pm; €2.50), a romantic residence where the poet Friedrich Schiller spent a decade as university professor during the 1790s. The area's then rural tranquillity proved conducive to the dramatist poet – he settled longest here during an itinerant life in Thuringia and knuckled down to write *Wallenstein* and *Mary Stuart*.

Eating, drinking and entertainment

Jena's "Kniepemeile" (pub mile) is a 200-metre stretch on Wagnergasse, a photogenic alley just across from the Intershop Tower. **Bars** on Krautgasse one block south tend to be a bit livelier. For cocktail sophistication look for the lounge club in restaurant *Scala* (see opposite). The highlight of city **festivals** is open-air music beano Kulturarena (ⓦ www.kulturarena.de), which attracts home-grown and international rock, folk, jazz and world acts from mid-July to late August.

Restaurants and cafés

Alt Jena Markt 9. Historic pub on the Markt which prepares a large menu, including good fish, with prices almost as low as the ceilings upstairs.

Bagels & Beans Leutragraben 6, opposite the Intershop Tower. Provides just what its name suggests, as well as free wi-fi and a couple of terminals for internet access.

Cafe Stilbruch Wagnergasse 1–2. Milkshakes and breakfasts are legendary in this popular bistro with Art Nouveau leanings. There's also a good international menu.

Cleanicum Wagnerstr. 11. Beer and cocktails while you wait for your laundry to finish.

Grüne Tanne Karl-Leibknicht-Str. 1. Solid home-cooking just across the bridge in a riverside guesthouse where Goethe bunked down in 1817–18. Its joy is a river terrace. Closed Sun eve & Mon.

Scala Intershop Tower ℡ 03641/35 66 66, ⓦ www.scala-jena.de. Fine international cuisine in Jena comes with superb views from floor-to-ceiling windows that wrap around the 28th floor of Jena's landmark tower.

Schwarzer Bär Lutherplatz 2 ℡ 03641/40 60. The hotel's restaurant is renowned for traditional dishes revived from old cookbooks – game is a speciality.

Zum Roten Hirsch Holzmarkt 10. An inn whose cocoon of snug panelled rooms dates back five centuries to its founding in 1509 and whose large menu comes at student prices.

Zur Noll Oberlauengasse 20 ℡ 03641 597 70. Cosy restaurant furnished in a sort of modern-rustic style that updates regional cooking with international flavours.

Bars and clubs

Cafe Grünowski Schillergasschen 5. Stripped-down student café and bar in a garden villa just south of Schiller Gartenhaus with an alternative artistic vibe. Usually buzzing on summer eve.

F-Haus Johannisplatz 14 (enter from Krautgasse) ⓦ www.f-haus.de. A university-affiliated place that can get rocking on gig nights. Also hosts clubnights a couple of times a week.

Kassablanca Felsenkellerstr. 13a ⓦ www.kassablanca.de. Clubnights coming from left field – hip-hop, indie, reggae and techno – in a heavily graffitied former train depot near Bahnhof Jena-West (trams #1 or #3).

Med-Club Greitgasse 2 ⓦ www.med-club.de. Lounge bar and club just east of the Holzmarkt for students who prefer their clubs a touch classier. House and funk tunes, plus regular games evenings.

Rosenkeller Johannisstr. 13 ⓦ www.rosenkeller.org. A graffitied passage opposite the Intershop Tower leads to a bastion of student boozing in cellars, with a wide roster of clubnights and live bands.

The Saale Valley

Steep wooded slopes channel the meadows of the **Saale Valley**, which runs to the cultured, former ducal town of **Rudolstadt**, 37km southwest of Jena. That it's largely flat makes this one of the easiest sections of the long-distance **Saale Cycle Route** (ⓦ www.saale-radwanderweg.de), which slaloms along the valley for 200km from Kaatschen-Weichau to Sparnberg on the border of Bavaria. The E3 long-distance hiking route also traverses the area, taking in the **Schwarza Valley**.

By **public transport** trains run from Jena all the way to **Saalfeld**. For **information**, the valley is covered by the regional tourism board of the Thuringian Forest (see p.289) even though it lies outside the official boundaries.

Rudolstadt

The post-World War I dissolution of Germany's petty ducal fiefdoms may have done for the princes of Schwarzburg-Rudolstadt, but their legacy lives on here. Only Weimar trumps **RUDOLSTADT** for the lingering sense of a Residenzstadt of the tin-pot duchies that had hitherto fragmented Thuringia. The same eighteenth-century inter court arts race that elevated Weimar to cultural capital of the German Enlightenment also saw Rudolstadt flourish. Goethe and Schiller shook hands here for the first time in 1788, and the town's **theatre** at Anger 1 (℡ 03672/42 27 66, ⓦ www.theater-rudolstadt.com) was renowned as the most prestigious stage in the area – still is, for that matter.

A powerful statement of power is the hilltop princely residence **Schloss Heidecksburg** (daily: April–Oct 10am–6pm; Nov–March 10am–5pm; collections €2.50–5; ⓦ www.heidecksburg.de). This is palace as self-aggrandizement, from the flamboyant Rococo building that replaced an earlier Renaissance number after a fire – an older portal is on the left as you enter the courtyard – to the fabulous interiors. You get a taste by viewing the various collections on your own: the princes' porcelain and art collections, the latter with Caspar David Friedrich's *Morning Mist in the Mountains*; an armoury; a pleasingly stuffy natural history room of the late 1800s; or a missable town museum. But it's worth taking a **tour** (hourly; 1hr; €6) to see the highlight **Festsaal**, a marbled pastel confection surmounted by a ceiling fresco of Olympus that is arguably the ritziest room in Thuringia. The chinoiserie of the Bänderzimmer also charms. Entrance to the art and porcelain collections is included in the price of the tour. The last piece of frippery is "Rococo en Miniature" (Tues–Sun: April–Oct 10am–6pm; Nov–March 10am–5pm; €3), with precision 1:50 models of state palaces and contemporary life that are so intricate visitors are given magnifying glasses. Outside it is a display of leaf-styled Rococo sleighs fit for a fairytale prince, and there are good views over the Altstadt from the castle belvedere – both are free.

It's worth detouring on the way down to take in the **Stadtkirche St Andreas**, a short way east of the Schloss. Outwardly a rather frumpy church, within it is a time capsule of princely grandiloquence. Much of the revamp is Baroque – that it came soon after the conclusion of the Thirty Years' War may explain the exuberance of the princes' loft that traces a family tree from floor to ceiling, the host of angels that flutter in the vaults, or a pulpit on which a resurrected Christ dances a jig. Among the Renaissance eye-candy is a life-size funeral sculpture of a noble family by the pulpit.

Beyond the Altstadt, gathered around a spacious Markt, you can cross the River Saale to the **Heinrich-Heine-Park**. At its centre two traditional farmhouses and an apothecary plucked from the Saale Valley and reassembled with original folksy furnishings are open as the **Thüringer Bauernhäuser** (April–Oct daily 11am–6pm; €2.50).

Practicalities

The **Hauptbahnhof** is beside the river – walk straight ahead on Bahnhofgasse to reach the Markt. A helpful **tourist office** (Mon–Fri 9am–6pm, Sat 9am–1pm; ℡03672/41 47 43, ⓦwww.rudolstadt.de) is just off it at Marktstrasse 57. Central **accommodation** options are *Adler*, Markt 17 (℡03672/44 03, ⓦwww.hotel -adler-rudolstadt.de; ❹), Goethe's bunkdown in 1817, now renovated to provide modern-country rooms. There's a good affiliated though not official **youth hostel**, *Fröbelhaus* at Schillerstrasse 50 (℡03672/31 36 10, ⓦwww.djh-thueringen .de; dorms from €21.50). With your own transport, *Marienturm*, 2km south in Rudolstadt-Cumbach (℡03672/432 70, ⓦwww.hotel-marienturm.de; ❹), is a good option, offering four-star mod cons and wonderful views of the town from its hilltop – and locals recommend its country-styled restaurant. That of *Adler* is a good central bet for **food**, or *Kartoffelhaus* opposite on the Markt rustles up low-priced rib-stickers.

The Schwarza Valley (Schwarzatal)

Considering it sneaks within the boundaries of the Thuringian Forest National Park and is between two tourist destinations, the **Schwarza Valley** southwest of Rudolstadt is surprisingly little visited. That the canyon twists south via a backroad to Schwarzburg is one factor. Another is the paucity of public transport – trains only go to Bad Blankenburg at the head of the canyon, guarded by the ruins of Schloss Greifenstein, then loop away northeast. The best way to visit this romantic canyon is to hit the hiking trail. Part of the trans-European E3 long-distance route, the track begins at Bad Blankenburg then winds through the pines above the slate-dark Schwarza River, 10km west to Schwarzburg;

allow yourself just over two hours at average pace, stopping at the occasional lookout en route. The reward if you go all the way is **Schloss Schwarzburg** (April–Oct daily 10am–5pm; €2), erstwhile seat of the Rudolstadt princes, where portraits in the Kaisersaal ancestral gallery start dubiously with Caesar. To return to Bad Blankenburg by train change at Rottenbach (hourly).

Saalfeld

SAALFELD, 10km south of Rudolstadt, put its medieval mining past behind it long ago and contents itself as a pretty market town downriver from the Upper Saale Valley. In the foothills of the **Thüringer Schiefergebirge** (Slate Mountains) which hump up south of the Schwarza Valley, it is also a base for activities, its fame bolstered by show **caves** that have given it the mawkish nickname "Feengrottenstadt" (Fairy Grottoes Town).

In the **Altstadt** life revolves around the **Markt**, whose Rathaus is textbook German Renaissance: stolid in stature beneath turrets and cascading gables, and with the requisite oriel windows and octagonal tower. Towering over the Markt to the north are the twin spires of the **Johanniskirche**, whose size says much about Saalfeld's medieval wealth and whose astonishing interior is said to be a medieval representation of Christ's blood drenching the faithful. Divert left en route to the church up Brudergasse and you reach a former Franciscan friary, now the **Stadtmuseum** (Tues–Sun 10am–5pm; €2.50), with displays on local mining and folkcrafts. For a stroll, turn left at the end of Brudergasse on to Obere Torgasse along the former town walls, then left at the triangular fork with Hinter der Mauer, to reach the ruins of **Schloss Hoher Schwarm** (daily 9am–5/6pm; free), medieval seat of the Schwarzburg princes with a garden perfect for a picnic.

However, what makes Saalfeld one of the premier destinations in the Thuringian Forest are the **Feengrotten** (tours every 30min: April–Oct daily 9.30am–5pm; Nov, Dec, Feb & March daily 10.30am–3.30pm; Jan Sat & Sun 10.30am–3.30pm; €7; Ⓦwww.feengrotten.de), just beyond the southwest suburbs at the woods' fringe; take bus #A from the Markt. The "fairy grottoes" cave system was exploited in the sixteenth century as an alum-slate mine, then reopened in 1914 as show caverns that attracted seventeen million visitors in a year. By the 1920s a newly discovered mineral spring – the water bubbles from a fountain in the Brunnentempel (free) – lured speleologists deeper to reveal caverns whose drip-water-features had been oxidized into a kaleido-scope of colours. In 1993 the *Guinness Book of Records* declared them the most colourful on the planet. Well, yes, as far as ochre, rust, cream and grey can be deemed colourful, with the odd flash of green. The system's highlight is the "fairy dome", its carefully lit stalagmite citadels like the Wagnerian stage-set they inspired in the composer's son for a production of *Tannhäuser*, though the Muzak schmaltz played here is faintly hilarious. The centre has added children's attraction the **Feenweltchen** (April–Oct 9.30am–6pm; €5), a "little fairy world" of buildings in the woods.

The **Upper Saale Valley** that twists through pine-covered hills southeast of Saalfeld is a popular destination for **canoeing** and **mountain biking** along the Stausee Hohenwarte, a placid dammed waterway nicknamed the Thuringian Sea. Bike & Boot-Camp Saalfeld, at Am Weidig 3 not far from the Landsratsamt (Ⓣ03671/45 62 90, Ⓦwww.bikeundbootcamp-saalfeld.de), rents bikes by the half-day, and kayaks and Canadian canoes by the day to explore; canoe rental includes transfers to an inlet off the broadest section of the waterway: it narrows as you head upstream.

Practicalities

The **Bahnhof** is on the Saale's east bank fifteen minutes' walk from the centre; follow Bahnhofstrasse then left up Saalstrasse to reach the Markt, where the **tourist office** is at no. 6 (Mon–Fri 9am–6pm & Sat 9am–2pm; April–Oct also Sun 9am–2pm; ☎03671/339 50, ⓦwww.saalfeld.de). For **accommodation**, there's a scattering of private rooms and apartments (❶–❷) booked through the tourist office, and some good-value hotels in the centre: try *Anker* (☎03671/59 90, ⓦwww.hotel-anker-saalfeld.de; ❹) on the Markt for a good old-fashioned country hotel, or basic cheapie *Am Hohen Schwarm* (☎03671/28 84, ⓦwww .schwarmhotel.de; ❸) near the castle ruins. **Camping** is at Bike & Boot-Camp Saalfeld (see p.279). The *Anker's Zur güldenen Gans* **restaurant** is the finest in town, with a terrace in prime position on the Markt. Other good options include *Zur Alten Post*, opposite the Johanniskirche, which supplements traditional regional food with Greek dishes, and unpretentious locals' place *Zum Puppenheimer* at Fleischgasse 5. For an atmospheric evening beer, it's hard to top *Zum Gerhard* (closed Mon), wedged into the medieval town walls on Münzeplatz opposite the Stadtmuseum.

Altenburg

Picking itself up after years of GDR-era neglect, courtly town **ALTENBURG** at Thuringia's eastern limits is known as the "Residenz- und Skatstadt". The former half of the title refers to the one-time seat of the dukes of Saxe-Altenburg. Altenburg's preferred boast, though, is as the cradle of **Skat**. It honed the rules of Germany's favourite card game in the early 1800s, much favoured by intellectuals of the time. One F.A. Brockhaus exclaimed: "My five months' stay in Altenburg gave me more mental and social experience than that gained by many a human being during the whole span of life", a comment to be taken with a pinch of salt, perhaps, since its speaker enthused about editing dictionaries. Today Altenburg is the headquarters of the Skatgericht, court of arbitration on all things Skat, and Germany's largest manufacturer of playing cards, ASS Altenburger. That its nearby airfield is used by budget international airlines means it may also be your introduction to Germany.

The pretty centre-stage of Altenburg, the **Markt**, makes a good impression, nestled beneath a hill and lined with handsome houses in shades of peach, terracotta and cream, and the Renaissance **Rathaus**, whose impressive portal and bulging corner oriel carved with sculptural ruffles are the vision of a Weimar architect. The **Brüderkirche** boxes in the west end of the Markt, borrowing freely from earlier styles and nodding to its own era (1901) with a Jugendstil mosaic of a sermonizing Christ. A block north of the Markt is the **Bartholomäikirche**, where Martin Luther defended his propositions against the papal envoy in 1519; a Gothic child of the Reformation, it preserves a Romanesque core in the crypt. Directly opposite the church on Brühl, the **Seckendorffsche Palais** (1725) cuts a dash in Baroque, and between them a 1903 fountain of brawling gamers honours Altenburg's cherished pursuit. Local lore claims that cards baptized in its waters are lucky – die-hard players can book an official Kartentaufe (card baptism) and Skat tour through the tourist information office.

For all its historic looks, Altenburg is really about its two museums. The first is the ducal **Schloss** east of the centre via Burgstrasse and Theaterplatz. "Even an emperor need not feel ashamed of such a building," Luther whistled upon seeing its walls and towers. The courtyard is an encyclopedia of architectural styles: dumpy Romanesque keep, the Flasche, just predates the slender

Hausmannsturm, which can be ascended for superb views over the complex (Tues–Sun 10am–5pm; €1); and there is a graceful arcaded Renaissance gallery. The castle's rooms (tours on the hour Tues–Sun 11am–4pm; €3) are similarly eclectic: the **Festsaal** is a swaggering revival synthesis crowned by a bright fresco of the marriage of Amor and Psyche by Munich's Karl Mossdorf; the charming **Bachsaal** alludes to the Renaissance; and the highlight **Schlosskirche** is in rich Baroque, its chancel fretted with stellar vaulting. The Schloss's south wing houses the **Schloss- und Spielkartenmuseum** of Meissen china, weaponry and – what else? – playing cards.

A palazzo in the far reaches of the Schlosspark behind contains the **Lindenau-Museum**, private collection of Bernhard von Lindenau (Tues–Sun 10am–6pm; €4), an eighteenth-century statesman who prepared the ground for the state of Saxony and had exquisite taste. As well as superb antique Roman and Greek ceramics there is an excellent gallery of Italian art, most of the 180 pieces early Renaissance works from Florence and Siena: Perugino's *St Helen* is lost in holy reverie; Botticelli produces a swooning portrait of *St Catherine* as a young woman; and there are exquisite small works by Masaccio and Lorenzo Monaco.

Practicalities

The **Hauptbahnhof** is a ten-minute walk north of the centre. The **airport** (ⓦwww.flugplatz-altenburg.de) 5km east is served by buses that coordinate with flight times. The **tourist office** (Mon–Fri 9am–6pm, Sat & Sun 10am–4pm; ⓣ03447/51 28 00, ⓦwww.altenburg-tourismus.de) is at Moritzstrasse 21. **Hotels** include *Parkhotel*, August Bebel-Strasse 16–17 (ⓣ03447/58 30, ⓦwww.parkhotel-altenburg.de; ❹–❺), Altenburg's finest address in a late 1800s mansion opposite the Grosser Teich lake; fairly modern four-star *Altenburger Hof*, Schmöllnsche Landstrasse 8 (ⓣ03447/58 40, ⓦwww.altenburger-hof.de; ❸–❹); and *Astor*, Bahnhofstrasse 4 (ⓣ03447/58 70, ⓦwww.astor-altenburg.de; ❸), bland but convenient for the station. *Parkhotel* has a good **restaurant**, or try the venerable *Ratskeller* at Markt 1. *Kulisse* at Theaterplatz 18 is a tavern decorated with publicity shots from the adjacent theatre and serves pasta and other dishes.

Gotha

Vintage travel books acclaim **GOTHA** as the richest and most attractive town in Thuringia. Leaving aside the question of whether their authors had bothered to visit Weimar or Erfurt 25km east, it remains a handsome if low-key small town whose looks were buffed in the eighteenth century as the courtly residence of the House of Saxe-Coburg, the dynasty better known in Britain as the House of Windsor – the British royals sensed the public mood during war with Germany and rebranded itself in 1917. The legacy of that glorious heyday is **Schloss Friedenstein**, still the main reason to visit, just as it was for Voltaire or Goethe and pals during the Enlightenment, its collections just as erudite. However, the town also serves as a handy gateway to the Thuringian Forest – and if first impressions count there are few better ways to arrive than by its historic tram, the Thüringerwaldbahn (see p.290).

Arrival, information and accommodation

The **Bahnhof** is both on the Erfurt line and the terminus for the dinky Thüringerwaldbahn (see Friedrichroda, p.289). It's sited a long fifteen-minute walk south of the town centre, but you can cut a corner through the Schlosspark at the junction with Parkallee or take tram #3 to Arnoldiplatz, a pedestrianized high street east of Hauptmarkt. The **tourist office** (Mon–Fri 9am–6pm & Sat 10am–3pm, May–Sept also Sun 10am–2pm; ☎03621 507/85 70, ⊛www.gotha .de) at Hauptmarkt 33 stocks brochures on the Thuringian Forest and walking maps of the Rennsteig. **Internet** access is at Gothaer Netc@fe (daily 10am– 10pm) at Gutenbergstrasse 11.

Hotels and pensions

Am Schloss Bergalle 3a ☎03621/85 32 06, ⊛www.pas-gotha.de. One of the best of the many cheap pensions in Gotha, this is a comfortable, homely place close to the front of the Schloss, whose cheapest rooms share amenities. Nice garden, too. ❷

Am Schlosspark Lindenauallee 20–24 ☎03621/44 20, ⊛www.hotel-am-schlosspark.de.

Rooms are in classic-modern style in this smart four-star with a spa on the west side of the park. ❺
Café Suzette Bebelstr. 8 ☎03621/85 67 55, ⊛www.cafe-suzette.com. Simple en-suite rooms above a café near the station. ❷
Waldbahn Bahnhofstr. 16 ☎03621 23 40, ⊛www.waldbahn-hotel.de. A decent second choice if *Am Schlosspark* is full is this four-star handily located near the station. ❹

The Town

Compact Gotha is easily strollable. Figuratively and geographically, the **Altstadt** is very much in the shadow of the **Schloss**. **Hauptmarkt**, its elongated core, sweeps up to the hilltop castle in a gesture of subservience. As befits a courtly Residenzstadt the so-called Wasserkunst, the town's water system, was prettified with belvederes and fountains which gush from grottoes – not Baroque for all its looks but conscious antiquarianism of the late 1800s. Incidentally, court painter Cranach lived at Hauptmarkt 17, its lintel bearing his snake coat of arms. Hauptmarkt flattens into a small square created by a tubby Renaissance **Rathaus**. Its tower (daily 11am–4pm; €0.50) offers an elevated view up the Hauptmarkt's cobbled slope to the Schloss framed by houses.

Schloss Friedenstein and the Schlosspark

There's no doubt about who rules in Gotha. **Schloss Friedenstein** not only takes up half of the town centre, it commands the Altstadt beneath as the largest early-Baroque palace in Germany: 100m by 140m and cornered by massive square bastions that seem to be a response to its being built just after the Thirty Years' War in the 1640s. Its sober looks owe much to the religion of Ernst I, a Protestant nicknamed "the Pious" who chose austere symmetry instead of the flamboyance preferred by his Catholic peers and gave over all but a handful of private quarters to his administration. Set aside a morning for the **Schlossmuseum** (Tues–Sun: May–Oct 10am–5pm; Nov–April 10am–4pm; €5; ⊛www.stiftungfriedenstein.de), and its ducal collections and period rooms. Kicking off on the ground floor is an excellent gallery, notably a room of works from Cranach the Elder; highlights are *Fall and Salvation of Man*, and *Judith at the Table of the Holofernes*, her death already foretold in the background that is enlarged as subsequent *Death of the Holofernes*. Cranach himself looks on at the action from a shrub in the lefthand side of the former. The gallery's star work is *Gotha Lovers* (*Gothaer Liebespaar*), a sumptuous piece by an anonymous master of the 1480s whose foppish beau and coquettish belle epitomize the courtly love of the time. Following rooms shift towards humanism with Dürer prints and Conrad Meit's outstanding statuettes of *Adam and Eve*.

Period rooms above fast-forward through decorative styles, none packing more punch than the **Festsaal**, its ceiling an impasto of sculpted stucco figures and garlands, its table set with the Wedgwood china used at a banquet for King Friedrich III in 1768. Its swagger extends to a stucco portal of Zeus who straddles the family crest mounted on weaponry. The ducal **Kunstkammer** also warrants investigation for its curio cabinet of fancies that caught ducal eyes, and Egyptian and Roman antiquities that benefit from the period setting. The far tower houses exhibits of regional culture and archeology as the **Museum für Regionalgeschichte und Volkskunde** and also a lovely perfectly preserved court theatre, the **Eckhof-Theater**. One of the oldest and last Baroque theatres in Europe – many went up in smoke thanks to the era's use of candlelight and pyrotechnics – it preserves the under-stage pulleys that whisked scenery on to the stage. The venue is as much of an attraction as the drama during Gotha's Ekhof-Festival (Ⓦwww.eckhof-festival.de) in July and August. The **Schlosskirche** in the northeast wing is also worth a look, and you can tour a 300m section of the castle's subterranean **fortifications** (Kasematten; tours Tues–Sun 11am, 1pm & 3pm, April–Oct also 4pm; €3.50), that date from the Schloss's construction, when the Turkish Ottoman steamroller was crushing all opposition east of here.

A trim **Rosengarten** behind the palace and the pretty, original **Orangerie** and **Teeschlösschen** folly to its east are the only manicured parts of a **Schlosspark** (free) that spreads luxuriantly as a mature parkland of English-style naturalistic planting. Leaflets from the Schloss ticket desk pinpoint the requisite Romantic temples. However, after the heavy cultural stuff before, it's pleasant simply to amble around the Grosser Parkteich boating lake; its small island holds the tomb of Duke Ernst II. Go clockwise around the lake to find Thuringia's Neoclassical Merkurtempel.

Eating and drinking

For **food**, *Pagenhaus* beside the Schloss's entry gate (closed Mon) prepares dishes such as lamb with a tomato crust. Otherwise 1903-vintage *Weinschänke* on the corner of Gartenstrasse and Lutherstrasse peps up a regional menu with international dishes, and microbrewery *König Sahl* at Brühl 7 has fresh beers and pub grub. Traditional *Eis-Café Junghaus* opposite the Rathaus or *Café Loesche* at Buttermarkt 6 are the pick of the traditional cafés.

Eisenach

Small in stature, **EISENACH**, 30km west of Gotha, abounds with the big hitters of German culture. It is the birthplace of Johann Sebastian Bach and the refuge from which Martin Luther shaped German Protestantism. Goethe and – with a bit of poetic licence – Wagner get a look in, too, thanks to the **Wartburg**, not just a UNESCO-listed castle whose thirteenth-century court inspired an opera, *Tannhäuser*, but a cradle of culture that's hard-wired into the national psyche. Indeed, such is the heavyweight punch of the small town that everyone rather overlooks the fact that Eisenach is also an amiable place which wears its cultural legacy lightly, and is also a good launch-pad for exploring the Thuringian Forest just south. Its compact **Altstadt** is best enjoyed at walking pace, and as the town is on the must-see list of every coach-tour in Thuringia you may not have any choice about it.

Arrival, information and accommodation

Eisenach's **Hauptbahnhof** lies a short walk east of the Altstadt's edge. The **tourist office** is at Markt 9 (Mon–Fri 10am–6pm, Sat & Sun 10am–4pm; Ⓣ03691/79 23 22, Ⓦwww.eisenach.info). It books accommodation and concert or theatre tickets – keep an eye open for summer concerts in the **Wartburg's**

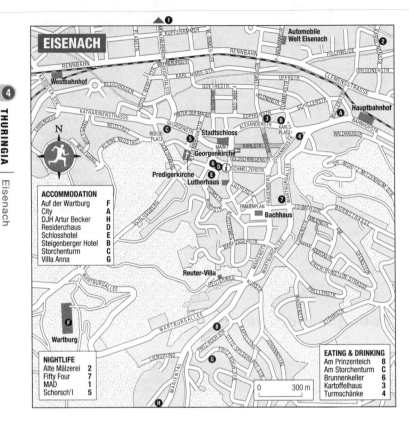

EISENACH

ACCOMMODATION

Auf der Wartburg	F
City	A
DJH Artur Becker	H
Residenzhaus	D
Schlosshotel	E
Steigenberger Hotel	B
Storchenturm	C
Villa Anna	G

NIGHTLIFE

Alte Mälzerei	2
Fifty Four	7
MAD	1
Schorsch'l	5

EATING & DRINKING

Am Prinzenteich	8
Am Storchenturm	C
Brunnenkeller	6
Kartoffelhaus	3
Turmschänke	4

0   300 m

Festsaal, renowned for its superb acoustics. It also sells the **Eisenach Classic Card** (valid 72hr; €18) for free public transport and entry to the museums and Wartburg. Zweirad Hennig (☎03691/ 78 47 38), at Schmelzerstrasse 4–6 west of the Markt, **rents bikes**. **Internet** access is one block north at Goldschmiedenstrasse 14 (Mon–Fri 11am–10pm, Sat & Sun 2–10pm). As befits a town steeped in history and tourism, Eisenach has some appealing accommodation if your budget is up to it – reservations are recommended in season.

Auf der Wartburg Wartburg ☎03691/79 70, ⓦwww.wartburghotel.de. Luxury pile adjoining the Wartburg with equally fabulous views. It exudes country-manor elegance in public areas – individually furnished rooms defer to more modern comforts. ❽–❾

City Bahnhofstr. 25 ☎03691/209 80, ⓦwww .cityhotel-eisenach.de. Good-value modern rooms furnished in pale wood from a three-star near the Hauptbahnhof. ❸

DJH Artur Becker Mariental 24 ☎03691/74 32 59, ⓦwww.eisenach.jugendherberge.de. The official youth hostel in a canary-yellow Art Nouveau pile at the foot of the Wartburg hill;

bus #3 or #10 to "Unterhalb der Herberge". Dorms from €21.

Residenzhaus Auf der Esplanade ☎03691/21 41 33, ⓦwww.residenzhaus-eisenach.de. The medieval tower behind the Markt is a place to live out Rapunzel fantasies: snug in size, with modern bland interior, but a great location for the price. There's one dorm, rooms with shared facilities and en suites. Dorm €20–25, rooms ❸.

Schlosshotel Markt 10 ☎03691/70 20 00, ⓦwww.schlosshotel-eisenach.de. Behind the Lutherhaus, this is a modern courtyard hotel – bland but comfy and with an unbeatable central location. "Komfort" rooms are worth the extra €10. ❺

Steigenberger Hotel Karlsplatz 11 ☎03691/28 0, ⓦwww.eisenach.steigenberger.de. Bright, stylish accommodation from a swish member of the Steigenberger chain in a vintage building. Its *Leander* bar-bistro prepares healthy European–Asian dishes at respectable prices. ➏

Storchenturm Georgenstr. 43a ☎03691/73 32 63, ⓦwww.gasthof-am-storchenturm.de. Hugely popular hostel-pension on a courtyard. Spotless and modern, but retaining the occasional beam from the original storehouse barn. Reservations recommended. Dorms €15.50, rooms ➋

Villa Anna Fritz-Koch-Str. 12 ☎03691/239 50, ⓦwww.hotel-villa-anna.de. Friendly, small hotel in a modernized Art Nouveau villa to the south, whose tasteful modern style has a modest designer slant. ➍–➎

The Wartburg

Few German cities possess so potent an icon as the UNESCO-listed **Wartburg** (daily: March–Oct 8.30am–8pm; Nov–Feb 9am–5pm; ⓦwww.wartburg-eisenach .de), which commands a hilltop south of the Altstadt. The story goes that founder Ludwig der Springer, impressed by the landscape on a hunt, cried, "Wait, mountain [Wart' Burg!], you shall have my castle!", a good yarn that overlooks an early watchtower (Warte). First mentioned in 1080, the castle was beefed up after Landgrave Ludwig II married into the family of mighty Holy Roman Emperor Frederick Barbarossa, and was then tinkered with by members of the dynasty thereafter. Consequently it peels back along its ridge like a picture-book composite of German castles, best appreciated from a lookout uphill from the Torhaus gatehouse. Laid over the architectural encyclopedia is the revivalist fetishizing of the past in vogue during its renovation in the 1840s. Indeed, it is only Goethe's perception that the site was significant to German identity that stopped the complex being left to collapse.

You're free to wander about the twin courtyards or ascend the **Südturm** (€0.50), the only watchtower preserved from the medieval castle, for views over the complex and the Thuringian Forest beyond. The adjacent **Palas**, the oldest and most architecturally impressive building of the Wartburg, is accessed on

▲ The Wartburg, Eisenach

285

The Wartburg: cradle of culture

The Wartburg dominates German culture as much as it commands Eisenach's skyline. It has its own saint for a start, St Elisabeth, a thirteenth-century Hungarian princess, betrothed to Landgrave Ludwig IV, who renounced courtly splendour to pursue an ascetic life caring for the sick. It was some court to snub, too. At the time Wartburg was considered to be one of the richest arts centres in Europe. The finest troubadour of his generation, Walther von der Vogelweide, clashed with *Parsifal* author Wolfram von Eschenbach in the celebrated **Contest of Minstrels** sing-offs; the winner of the six-strong Battle of the Bards met with princely favour, the loser the hangman's noose.

Arguably, the most significant moment in the Wartburg's history, though, was the arrival of **Martin Luther** in May 1521. Excommunicated and declared a heretic for refusing to renounce his doctrine at the Diet of Worms, the renegade priest was kidnapped by order of Saxony Elector Frederick the Wise and protected within the Wartburg's mighty walls. The former cleanly shaven, tonsured monk remained incognito as bearded, woolly haired Junker Jörg (Squire George) while he toiled for fourteen months over the first translation of the New Testament from Greek into the vernacular. For German Protestants that makes the Wartburg a holy of holies. For everyone else, Luther simultaneously propelled German into a modern language.

On October 18, 1817, five hundred students from eleven German universities met to celebrate the Wartburgfest. The jollies morphed into a rallying call for unity delivered to a nation of petty fiefdoms, and the first demand for democratic rights delivered to its ducal rulers. And when students of Jena university hoisted their fraternity flag above the fireplace Germany found the black, red and gold colours for its future national flag.

tours (daily: March–Oct 8.30am–5pm; Nov–Feb 9am–3.30pm; €7, museums only €3.50; English notes on request). Its early Romanesque rooms are canopied by vaults that umbrella from a single column capped with inventive (but reproduction) capitals. The eye-catchers are the quarters that have been rather over zealously restored as a paean to medieval roots: former women's quarters the **Elisabeth Room**, which shimmers in a skin of faux-Byzantine mosaics (1902), or the **Elisabeth Gallery** and **Hall of Minstrels** that inspired Wagner, both frescoed with rich medieval-esque images by Romantic painter Moritz von Schwind. Then there's the gloriously over-the-top **Festsaal**, the venue in which student fraternities laid down a gauntlet to the ruling elite in 1817 (see box above). So impressed was "Mad" Bavarian king Ludwig II by this coffered banqueting hall that he commissioned a replica for Schloss Neuschwanstein.

Women's quarters the **Neu Kemenate** house a small museum (same ticket) of Wartburg treasure and Reformation-era art, notably portraits by Cranach of Martin Luther that introduce the **Lutherstube**. It was in this simple room that excommunicated heretic Luther hid out as Junker Jörg while he toiled over a German translation of the New Testament. They say he hurled his inkpot at a devil that appeared to prevent his labours, which is why a patch of bare masonry is in one corner rather than the ink-spattered wood panels that have been chipped away by centuries of souvenir-hunters.

It's a stiff forty-minute walk from the Altstadt to the Wartburg, much of it uphill: Schlossberg, southeast of the Predigerkirche, is the most direct route, a woodland path off Reuterweg, near Reuter-Villa, the most atmospheric. Bus #10 runs from the Hauptbahnhof via the Markt and tourist mini-trains ascend from the Markt from April to October. A word of warning: crowds are heavy on high-summer weekends.

The central Altstadt

The obvious place to begin a tour of Eisenach town is the spacious **Markt** that is closed on one side by the pastel-peach Baroque box of the **Georgenkirche** (Mon–Sat 10am–12.30pm & 2–5/7pm, Sun 11.30am–12.30pm & 2–5pm). Former choirboy Martin Luther returned here as an outlaw following his excommunication at the Diet of Worms to preach a sermon in 1521, and the organist's son, Johann Sebastian Bach, was baptized in the Gothic stone font in March 1685. The choir at the other end is ringed by epitaphs of the Ludowinger Landgraves who lorded it over Eisenach from Wartburg; founder Ludwig I – known as Ludwig "der Springer" after a jump from a prison window – is behind the altar on the right with a model of the town's first church; Ludwig II who beefed up the castle into a medieval fortress is the bruiser in chainmail. The palatial pile that faces the church is the **Stadtschloss** (Thüringer Museum; Tues–Sun 11am–5pm; €2), a minor residence of the Saxony-Weimar dynasty whose Rococo rooms house municipal displays of Thuringian decorative arts.

The **Predigerkirche** (Tues–Sun 11am–5pm; €2.60), west of the Markt, is a one-time Dominican church erected to honour the canonization of Eisenach's thirteenth-century saint, Princess Elisabeth, which now houses two rooms of Thuringian religious art. Highlights include a sculpture of Heinrich Raspe, the brother-in-law of Elisabeth and benefactor who stumped up the cash for the church, and a willowy *Mourning John* from a southern Harz monastery. Of less artistic merit but enjoyable nonetheless is an altarpiece of the *Holy Family* (1500) composed like a group snapshot, while burghers, one in a Jewish hat, mug behind. A second room holds art exhibitions. For quirky character head west of the Markt where **Schamels Haus**, at Johannesplatz 9, is by common consent the narrowest inhabited half-timbered house in Germany, wedged into a space just 2m wide.

Lutherhaus, Bachhaus and Reuter-Villa

Just uphill from the back of the Georgenkirche, **Lutherhaus** (daily 10am–5pm; €3.50) is something of a misnomer for a residence in which Luther bunked down as a schoolboy with the Cotta family – a wealthy family, too, if their restored Gothic town house is a guide. Small wonder Luther later referred to Eisenach as "*meine liebe Stadt*" (my dear town). As well as reconstructions of the quarters of the fêted lodger, who spent two stints here between 1498 and 1501, are touchscreen terminals (in English) and archive reproductions that attempt to pin down the man and his doctrine in the context of his time.

No less groundbreaking in his sphere, Bach is the subject of the museum five minutes' walk uphill along Lutherstrasse on Frauenplan. It now turns out that **Bachhaus** (daily 10am–6pm; €6; ⓦ www.bachhaus.de) was not the great composer's birthplace as was supposed when the museum was founded in 1906, but that does not distract from a representation of the bourgeois interiors of his era that support a narration of his life story, from Weimar schoolboy to the notoriously tetchy composer who harrumphed between courts in Thuringia and nearby Leipzig. Indeed, displays are as revealing as a portrait of the petty courts that dictated life in the state. Bach, however, is about the music and inevitably the highlights are a room of iPods with explanations of the music in English, and concerts of his music performed on historic instruments; ask about times when you buy a ticket. The statue of Bach outside is also worth a look. Originally erected in the Markt, it was forged in 1884 as an idealized image of the great composer based on the best of the wildly varying portraits painted in his lifetime. So hot was the debate that civic authorities in Leipzig exhumed his skeleton a decade later to settle the issue. Modern academics suggest the composer was rather fleshier in the face.

If you continue ten minutes' walk south on Marienstrasse, Eisenach relaxes into small-town mode as you approach Reuter-Villa at Reuterweg 2. Its accreditation as the **Reuter-Wagner-Museum** (Tues–Sun 11am–5pm; €3) derives from the villa's twin status as a former home of the nineteenth-century writer Fritz Reuter and the home of a huge array of Wagner memorabilia in its period rooms, including his death mask. The composer set his opera *Tannhäuser* in the Wartburg after a visit to Eisenach in 1842.

Automobile Welt Eisenach

Not all Eisenach's heavyweights are cultural. **Automobile Welt Eisenach** (known as AWE), in a 1930s manufacturing plant north of the centre at Friedrich-Naumann-Strasse 10 (Tues–Sun 11am–5pm; €3), celebrates the motors that were manufactured here from 1898 onwards. Worth a look for petrolheads are the carriage-like first Wartburg, which rolled off the production line in 1899, and Wartburg 311 sports coupés. A racy GDR-era marque caught somewhere between Austen Healey and Mercedes, it gets overlooked in the wave of nostalgia for Trabant kitsch. There's also a dinky 1920s Dixi that was destined to be rebranded as a BMW after the Bavarian giant acquired the company moulds in 1929.

Eating, drinking and entertainment

In a word, disappointing. Considering the town's inclusion on the traditional tourist check-list, **restaurants** are thin on the ground – the finest eating options are reserved for prestige hotels. Nor do you come to Eisenach for **nightlife**. The most atmospheric drinking den is *Schorsch'l* at Georgenstrasse 19 (daily from 7pm; Ⓦ www.schorschl.de), which hosts occasional DJs and live gigs. More modern – and the place for cheap cocktails – is *Fifty Four* at Wartburgallee 54. Jazz, blues and rock gigs are at *Alte Mälzerei* (Ⓦ www.jazzclub-eisenach.de) northeast of the centre at Palmental 1; mainstream clubbing at weekends is on offer at *MAD* (Ⓦ www.mad.de) at Am Stadtweg 10.

Am Prinzenteich Mariental. A pleasant little café south of the centre whose lakeside terrace is an attractive spot to break before ascending up to the Wartburg – good barbecues in summer. Closed Mon Jan–April.

Am Storchenturm Georgenstr. 43a. Big portions of regional specialities in a *Gasthof* that's a pocket of rural idyll in the town centre; its beer garden is the best place for a sunny afternoon drink.

Brunnenkeller Markt 10. Restaurant set in chunky stone cellars behind the Georgenkirche, with a long menu of traditional classics.

Kartoffelhaus Sophienstr. 8. More rustic maximalism from this chain of *Gaststätten*, with a menu of chunky potato-based fillers at low prices.

Turmschänke Karlsplatz 28 ☎ 03691/21 35 33. Dishes in the town's gourmet address lean towards Mediterranean, then confound it all with solid *Thüringer Kalbshaxe* (roast veal knuckle) or *Rotwurst*, a nod, perhaps, to its dining room in a medieval defence tower. Menus from €30. Eve only, closed Sun.

Thuringian Forest

Much of Thuringia's acclaim as the green heart of Germany is due to the **THURINGIAN FOREST** (Thüringer Wald). Around two-thirds of the upland region of the state's southwest – 135km from Eisenach west to the A9 east, 35km north to south and 982m at its highest point – is thickly cloaked in pines interspersed with mixed forest or highland meadow, and irrigated by countless streams. Germans have celebrated its landscapes at least since Goethe rambled around

If you go down to the woods: the Rennsteig and other activities

Germany's most popular trail is the **Rennsteig** ridgeway that slices west-east through the Thuringian Forest. Its 168km path along the region's uplands, from **Hörschel** near Eisenach to **Blankenstein** on the River Saale, was a messenger route in the Middle Ages, and in the nineteenth century it acquired a cachet as a symbol of national unity because it formed the border of or ran through a patchwork of petty principalities. It still forms a border of sorts – Thuringians argue over whether the state's best sausages are produced north or south of it. If fit, you could do "Der Runst" in five days' hiking, stopping at villages overnight and dodging the wild boar that root in the woods. It's more enjoyable if you take six. Sections of it make good day-hikes – the route ascends over Grosser Inselberg near Friedrichroda – and the 30km and 15km at either end with the greatest altitude differences, are favoured by cyclists on a parallel mountain bike trail. Kompass's 1:50,000 Rennsteig map (no. 118) covers both routes and is available from tourist offices throughout the region.

An alternative if cycling is to follow part of the north-south 300km **Werratal-Radweg** (Ⓦ www.werratal.de) that tracks the Werra river west of Eisenach to Meiningen and beyond.

The area usually receives a good dump of snow in winter. The focus for **skiing** is a 2km piste on Grosser Inselberg. For ski rental and lessons go to Sport Hellmann (☎036259/508 52, Ⓦ www.sport-hellmann.de) at Lauchagrundstrasse 13, Tabarz. In the east Thuringian Forest, skiing is at Steinach at the Skiarena Siblersattel (Ⓦ www .silbersattel.de). In summer, this renames itself Bikepark (May–Oct Sat & Sun 1–5pm; 2hr €10, 4hr €14; Ⓦ www.silbersattel-bikepark.de) and reinvents the pistes as downhill cycle trails for kamikaze mountain bikers.

Ilmenau, and its romantic villages with cottage workshops do little to dispel the illusion of an area that's a timewarp back a few decades. Indeed, the ambience is more of a draw than sights in the few towns: modest spa-town **Friedrichroda**, sleepy **Schmalkalden**, its Altstadt a fairytale of half-timbered buildings, or former courtly town **Meiningen**, repository of the area's high culture, such as it is.

With your own transport this is touring country, a place to potter around pretty villages. Without, getting around by bus is fiddly; however, the region is superb to explore by foot and bike. With five or six days spare you could take to Germany's favourite long-distance path, the **Rennsteig** (see box above), along the highlands' spine. The forest's boundaries also incorporate the **Hainich National Park** (Ⓦ www.nationalpark-hainich.de) northeast of Eisenach. The main attraction of its 75-square-kilometre lozenge of ancient beech forest is the **Baumkronenpfad** (daily: April–Oct 10am–7pm; Nov–March 10am–4pm; €6), Europe's first canopy-walk which circles up to a 44m lookout. Access is on the C-road west of Bad Langensalza. Regional tourism website Ⓦ www.thueringer-wald.com is handy for planning if your German's up to it.

Friedrichroda

Notwithstanding the Goethe trail from Ilmenau (see p.292), **FRIEDRICH-RODA** is the most accessible access-point for day-hikes in the Thuringian Forest. A busy resort in GDR days, when the monstrous *Berghotel* blighted a hilltop, it suffered when the Berlin Wall came down and has since become a modern incarnation of the rather prim spa resort that wooed 12,000 people a year in the late 1800s. You can fill up water bottles from mineral springs from a fountain pavilion on Marktstrasse, or another, often locked, one in the Kurpark above. Aside from natural cures the time-honoured attraction of Friedrichroda is Europe's largest crystal cave, **Marienglashöhle** (daily: April–Oct 9am–5pm; Nov–March 9am–4pm; €4) 1.5km west of the centre. The showcave's name refers to the gypsum crystal harvested for glitter on statues of the Virgin.

The cave is a stop on the **Thüringerwaldbahn** (tram #4; Ⓦwww .waldbahn-gotha.de), which trundles from Gotha through the countryside to Friedrichroda twice an hour. In summer it's worth staying on board for the most scenic section to tram terminus Tabarz, from where you can board a coordinated tourist-train, the Inselberg-Express (5 daily May to late Oct; €4.50 single, €7 return; Ⓣ036259/57 70), which ascends the Grosser Inselberg (916m) – not the highest summit in the Thuringian Forest and far from the most photogenic owing to an ugly telecoms tower, but unrivalled for its sweeping panorama. From here you could hike along the Rennsteig ridgeway path east over the lesser summits of Trockenberg and Grosser Jagdberg to Heuberghaus (around 4km; 2hr) to hook up with the Thüringer Wald-Express bus (3 daily March–Dec; same Ⓣ & price) back to Friedrichroda.

Friedrichroda's **tourist office** (Mon–Thurs 9am–5pm, Fri till 6pm, Sat till noon; Ⓣ03623/332 00, Ⓦwww.friedrichroda.de) at Marktstrasse 15 can provide maps. The most appealing of the abundant **accommodation** options in town are swish spa-hotel *Ramada Hotel Friedrichroda*, on the far side of the Kurpark at Burchardtsweg 1 (Ⓣ03623/35 26 01, Ⓦwww.ramada-friedrichroda.de; ❺–❻), and traditional house-brewery *Brauhaus* at Bachstrasse 14 (Ⓣ03623/30 42 59, Ⓦwww.brauhaus-friedrichroda.de; ❷) with pleasing old-fashioned rooms. Both serve good food, or try fish-speciality inn *Zue Quelle* (closed Mon) at Schweizer Strasse 30.

Schmalkalden

Once you're past its underwhelming outskirts, **SCHMALKALDEN** is a Thuringian Forest classic that's picture-postcard pretty in an Altstadt of jostling half-timbered buildings. Hard to believe today, but the sleepy small town played a central role in the Reformation. The Schmalkaldic League of Lutheran princes coalesced here as an independent power bloc that opposed the centralization of Catholic Emperor Charles V. Even if they lost the battles of 1546–47, they ultimately won the war after Charles, weary from years of warfare and recognizing the intractable Protestant hardcore within Central Europe, agreed to the Peace of Augsburg in 1555, thereby permitting German states freedom to choose their religion. No history lessons are needed to appreciate **Altmarkt**, its colourful heart fronted as ever by the Gothic **Rathaus** (foyer Mon–Fri 8.30am–4pm, Thurs till 6pm; free) in which the league plotted strategies. The fire of revolution had been sparked by the sermons of Martin Luther preached in 1537 in the adjacent **Stadtkirche St Georg**, built of blushing-pink sandstone and worth a look for the quirky net of stellar vaulting in its chancel. Death scythes down a young girl as a *Memento Mori* on its clock tower as the hour strikes. Mohrengasse leads from Altmarkt via pretty Salzbrücke and Steingasse to Lutherplatz and the chunky sixteenth-century house in which the renegade preacher stayed, **Lutherhaus**, identifiable from its red-painted beams and a Baroque plaque bearing the white rose of the Reformation. Fellow firebrand Philipp Melanchthon stayed at Steingasse 11, today a chemist's. Lutherplatz also represents the start of the **Martin-Luther-Weg** marked by a green "L", a 17km trail that tracks Luther's footsteps on the day the *Schmalkalden Articles* laid down the gauntlet to Charles's Holy Roman Empire in 1537. It makes an enjoyable, easy five-hour trail that ascends meadows to a 742m high-point en route to the village of **Tambach-Dietharz**. Tradition demands walkers drink from the Lutherbrunnen (Luther Well) on the outskirts of the village. Bus #851 makes the return journey a couple of times a day; check times with the tourist office.

Thirty years after the peace deal, Hessen Landgrave Wilhelm IV began work on a courtyard hunting lodge and summer residence on the hilltop above Lutherhaus. **Schloss Wilhelmsburg** (April–Oct daily 10am–6pm; Nov–March Tues–Sun 10am–4pm; €3.50) impresses most as a perfectly preserved slice of the Renaissance, with its displays about the Hessen dynasty and the *Schmalkalden Articles* taking second billing. The **Riesensaal** state room in the east wing with a painted coffered ceiling and murals of the duke among Old Testament and mythological heroes exudes ducal swagger. The Schloss's highlight though, is the galleried **Schlosskirche**. Finished with snow-white stucco decoration, it is one of the first chapels to follow Luther's dictates to elevate the Word above religious eye-candy – the pulpit is strategically placed as a focus above the altar. The organ tucked away above is a pearl of the Renaissance, the oldest playable instrument in Central Europe, with a light flutey tone from its wooden pipes; it features in monthly concerts in summer. A northeast tower screens a twenty-minute 3D film *Ritter del Tafelrunde* (same times; €3), which animates murals discovered in a cellar in the Hessenhof building on Neumarkt: check out reproductions of the scratchy thirteenth-century images of the Arthurian legend – the oldest secular wall murals in Central Europe – in a basement room accessed off the castle courtyard before you go in.

Practicalities

Schmalkalden's **Hauptbahnhof** and **Busbahnhof** are a ten-minute walk west of the centre; coming by train from Erfurt requires a change at Zella-Mehlis, buses arrive from Gotha and Meiningen. A helpful **tourist office** (April–Oct Mon–Fri 9am–6pm, Sat & Sun 10am–3pm; Nov–March Mon–Fri 9am–5pm, Sat 10am–1pm; ☎03683/40 31 82, Ⓦwww.stadt.schmalkalden.de) on the corner of Altmarkt at Mohrengasse 1 provides free booklets that pinpoint every historic beam. Fahrrad Anschütz (☎03683/40 39 09) at Stiller Gasse 17 **rents bikes**. First choices among the central **hotels** are *Patrizier*, Weidebrunner Gasse 9 (☎03683/60 45 14, Ⓦwww.stadthotel-patrizier.de; ❸), an old-fashioned upmarket place, and modern *Teichhotel*, Teichstrasse 21 (☎03683/40 26 61, Ⓦwww.teichhotel.de; ❸), just outside the centre. Both have good **restaurants**, or historic *Gaststätte Zum Kirchhof* behind the Stadtkirche prepares hearty Thuringian snacks such as *Bratwurst* with *Klösse* potato dumplings at low prices. *The Castle* (daily from 7pm), behind Lutherhaus at Schlossberg 1b, is as lively as the bar scene gets.

Meiningen

MEININGEN, 20km south of Schmalkalden, is a surprise in a region fond of half-timbering. There's a touch of aristocratic swagger to the small town on the River Werra. It blossomed as a Residenzstadt of the dukes of Saxe-Meiningen, notably nineteenth-century culture-vulture Georg II. Under the tenure of this friend of Brahms, the town acquired fame Europe-wide for its theatre and orchestra. Enter from the north on boulevard Bernhard Strasse and you're greeted by the duke's city-scale **theatre**, whose massive portico acclaims his noble gift to "the people to befriend and elevate". Civilized stuff, as is adjacent municipal gallery **Galerie Ada** (Tues–Sun 3–8pm; free) with exhibitions of modern and regional works, and the landscaped Englischer Garten behind both.

The heart of ducal culture is **Schloss Elisabethenburg** (Tues–Sun 10am–6pm; €4, combination ticket with Theater Museum €5.50) at the end of Bernhard Strasse, a Baroque building of almost institutional austerity whose traditional U-shape is closed by an odd round wing. Once past an ancestral gallery and a room of Thuringian religious art, a series of faintly shabby rooms hang second-division Old Masters and one premier-league work, a sexually charged encounter between Lot and his daughter by Caravaggio-inspired Spaniard Juseppe Ribera. A Baroque tapestry of Alexander's triumphant entry into Babylon is another highlight. Displays on the second floor furnished in the revival style favoured by Georg II honour the town's musical tradition. Don't miss the lovely Biedermeier **café** (free) at the top, too.

Baumbachhaus (same times & ticket) on Burgstrasse to the left of the Schloss houses a small display of literary figures associated with the court, among them Enlightenment dramatist and poet Friedrich Schiller, who sojourned in Meiningen during his tour of Thuringian courts. The equestrian hall on the other side of the Schloss, in which Duke Georg II practised dressage when not supervising his wife's riding lessons, was the only space able to take the painted backcloths that feature in the **Theater Museum** (tours Tues–Sun 10am, noon, 2pm & 4pm; €3).

The best of the many footpaths that explore the adjacent Werra Valley is the **Premiumwanderweg**, which makes a 12km circuit from the Schloss via neo-Gothic hotel *Schloss Landsberg* (see opposite) and the ruins of thirteenth-century fort Habichtsburg on a wooded hilltop. It begins off Burgstrasse on the lefthand side of the castle and in theory is signposted throughout – check at the tourist office, where you can also ask for directions to **Goetz-Höhle** (tours Tues–Sun: May–Sept 10am–5pm; Oct–April 11am–3pm; €5; ⓦwww.goetz-hoehle.de).

In Goethe's footsteps from Ilmenau

ILMENAU, a somnambulant former glass-making town east of Schmalkalden, has as its celebrated monument a bronze of Goethe on a bench on the Markt. And the reason to visit the town is to tread *"auf Goethes Spurren"* (in Goethe's footsteps) on the **Goethewanderweg** day-hike. The 20km trail's appeal is the variety of scenery en route – you'll need six to eight hours to complete it and come mentally prepared for the occasional stiff uphill section.

The trail begins on the Markt at the **Amtshaus** (Tues–Sun 9am–noon & 1–5pm; €1) with a primer on Goethe's activities in the area as a court official of Weimar-based duke Carl August. From here a trail of signposts marked with a "G" monogram taken from our hero's handwriting direct you west via the peaks of Schwalbenstein – inspired by the view, Goethe knocked off the fourth act of his reworking of Greek tragedy *Iphigenie in Tauris* in a day on its summit – and Emmasteinfelsen to Manebach village. From here it's a long steady ascent up the Kickelhahn (861m), also reached on a short cut by road south of Ilmenau. At its summit is a faux-watchtower lookout and a replica of the hut in which Goethe penned his celebrated *Wayfarer's Night Song*, inscribed in sixteen languages within. The ubiquitous hilltop restaurant is a good spot to pause for lunch. Ten minutes along the trail are displays on Goethe's scientific work in former hunting-lodge **Jagdhaus Gabelbach** (Sat & Sun: April–Oct 10am–5pm; Nov–March 11am–3pm; €2), then it's an easy romp 5km south to the trail terminus at Stützerbach village. Should you wish to return by bus from Stützerbach take #300 – double-check timetables first at the Ilmenau tourist office.

Practicalities

Ilmenau is on a branch line from Erfurt, its Hauptbahnhof east of the centre. The tourist office (Mon–Fri 9am–6pm, Sat 9am–1pm; ⓣ03677/60 03 00, ⓦwww.ilmenau.de) in the Amtshaus at Markt 1 books budget **private rooms** (❶). The **youth hostel** (ⓣ03677 /88 46 81, ⓦwww.ilmenau.jugendherberge.de; dorms from €21) is 2km southeast at Am Stollen 49; bus lines #A, #B or #C go from the train station. Hotels include *Zum Elephant* (ⓣ03677/20 24 41, ⓦwww.e-biz.de/reisen/elephant.htm; ❷) at Marktstrasse 16. For considerably greater comfort and a sauna opt for *Lindenhof*, Lindenstrasse 3 (ⓣ03677/680 00, ⓦwww.hotel-lindenhof.de; ❹–❺).

Europe's largest fissure cave is worth a visit as much for the view of the Altstadt from its entrance on a southeast hillside off Helenstrasse.

Practicalities

The **Bahnhof** and **Busbahnhof** are at the back of the Englischer Garten north of the centre. The **tourist office** (Mon–Fri 10am–6pm, Sat 10am–3pm; ☎03693/446 50, ⓦwww.meiningen.de) is at Markt 14. For **accommodation**, *Sächsischer Hof* (☎03693/45 70, ⓦwww.saeschsischerhof.com; ❺–❻), near the theatre at Georgstrasse 1, aspires to nineteenth-century elegance. "Komfort" standard rooms are good value. On the other side of the Altstadt, *Altes Knasthaus Fronveste*, An der Oberen Mauer 1–3 (☎03693/881 90, ⓦwww.meininger -hotels-mit-flair.de; ❹), is Meiningen's (modest) design hotel in a former prison, and from the same company is the modern-rustic *Schlundhaus*, Schlundgasse 4 (☎03693/813 838, same website; ❹), and luxury castle *Schloss Landsberg* (☎03693/881 90, same website; ❻), 4km northwest, whose neo-Gothic pile was erected after a Meiningen duke visited his sister, Princess Adelheid, at Windsor Castle. Notwithstanding *Schloss-Stuben* in Schloss Elisabethenburg, whose courtyard terrace is pleasant in summer, the best **eating** is in the hotels: *Sächsischer Hof* has regional-historic *Kutscherstube* and gourmet *Die Posthalterei* (Tues–Sat eve & Sun lunch); and *Skyline* prepares an international menu in a metropolitan-styled restaurant atop *Altes Knasthaus Fronveste*, and has a terrace that's a great spot for a swanky sundowner; *Sächsischer Hof* has a historic wine cellar. Traditional dining is in *Schlundhaus* at Schlundgasse 4; they say a former chef invented Thuringian *Klösse* potato dumplings.

Meiningen Theater (☎03693/45 12 22, ⓦwww.das-meininger-theater.de) stages heavyweights of theatre and opera in a gorgeous Neoclassical hall. The best **nightclub** in town is *ELANclub* (ⓦwww.elanclub.de) at Bernhard Strasse 1, though the biggest in central Germany is four-room, multi-bar venue *Kartarena* (Berkeser Strasse 22; ⓦwww.kartarena.de) 3km west in Dreissgacker; pick up a taxi from the Hauptbahnhof.

Mülhausen

Greatness nipped in the bud characterizes **MÜLHAUSEN**. A former medieval free imperial city visited by kings and emperors, it is now bypassed by tourists on a pilgrimage to the Eisenach–Erfurt–Weimar holy trinity, although a lack of visitors only adds to the atmosphere of the Altstadt, a maze-like oval of cobbled alleys ringed by one of the few extent medieval city walls in Germany. Its place in history books is as the hotbed of the Peasants' War of 1525, sparked by its renegade priest Thomas Müntzer. A social radical who despised Lutheran doctrine with the same passion as Catholicism, he led eight thousand farmers into battle against the princes at Frankenhausen with the rallying cry that God was on their side. Utterly defeated then tortured, Müntzer was decapitated in his home town, something which saw him acclaimed as a proto-Marxist hero by GDR authorities and placed on the 5 Mark note. They conveniently overlooked the fact that Müntzer interpreted the defeat as God's judgment on an unworthy populace. Mülhausen may have quietly dropped the "Thomas-Müntzer-Stadt" label, but its early hero remains the star.

There's no finer introduction to Mülhausen than the medieval **town walls** which wrap a 3km belt around the town, studded intermittently with watch-towers. A 375m section of the ramparts is open at the west end of the Altstadt as the **Historische Wehranlage** (April–Oct Tues–Sun 10am–5pm; €3), accessed from the Inneres Frauentor, a chunky former gateway that commanded the principle route into the town, and whose bastions house dry displays of town history. Holzstrasse curls away from here to the **Marienkirche** (Tues–Sun 10am–5pm; €3) in which Thomas Müntzer delivered his final sermon beneath the rainbow banner of his "Eternal League of God". The church houses a memorial to its former firebrand as the **Müntzergedenkstätte** – pick up English notes as you enter – although its displays are less impressive than the five-nave hall church itself, the second-largest in Thuringia after Erfurt's Dom and crowned by a soaring nineteenth-century spire. Look, too, at the southern portal near the entrance, where statues of late fourteenth-century Emperor Karl IV, his wife and a lord and lady of court peer over the balustrade at a street used for processions during Mülhausen's imperial Diets.

Ratsstrasse, at the church's far end, leads to the **Rathaus** (daily 10am–4pm; €4). Added to over the centuries, so that it now straddles the street, the complex has as its core the Grosse Ratsstube, a barrel-vaulted muralled council chamber in which Müntzer ruled the town during the three-month tenure of his revolutionary league. A typically oversized painting from the GDR era depicts him in full oratorical flight. Continue south from the Rathaus and you emerge at pretty Kornmarkt and the **Kornmarktkirche** (Tues–Sun 10am–5pm; €3) for the **Bauernkriegmuseum**, which fleshes out the tale with a narrative of the ill-fated Peasants' War; a large model of the battlefield with a running commentary of events is all good fun. Among a small gallery of twentieth-century artwork inspired by the war, are four characteristically dark works by Expressionist Käthe Kollwitz.

Any of the alleys south from Kornmarkt will take you to spacious Untermarkt and the Divi-Blasii-Kirche. The fame of an early Gothic church founded by the Teutonic Order is as the office of Johann Sebastian Bach during his tenure as organist in 1709 as a precocious 24-year-old. Off the corner of Untermarkt behind the church, town museum the **Museum am Lindenbühl** (Tues–Sun 10am–5pm; €2) has the usual silver and Biedermeier furniture plus exhibitions on regional themes.

Practicalities

The **Bahnhof** is 400m east of the Altstadt, which is reached by Karl-Marx-Strasse. The **tourist office** (Mon–Fri 9am–5pm, May–Oct Sat & Sun 10am–4pm; ☏03601/40 47 70, ⓦwww.muelhausen.de) is opposite the Rathaus at Ratsstrasse 20. **Internet access** is at Mülhauser Internetcafé (Mon–Fri 10.30am–11pm, Sat & Sun 11am–11pm) at Gormarstrasse 64. The tourist office books the usual private rooms (❶–❷). Other **accommodation** options include: *An der Stadtmauer* (☏03601/465 00, ⓦwww.hotel-an-der-stadtmauer.de; ❸), a small three-star just within the north town walls at Breitenstrasse 15, whose best rooms overlook a garden courtyard, and nearby *Mülhäuser Hof*, Steinweg 65 (☏03601/88 86 70, ⓦwww.muehlhaeuser-hof.de; ❹), with modern tasteful if rather snug en suites in the blonde-wood mould. The **youth hostel** at Auf dem Tonberg 1 (☏03601/81 33 18, ⓦwww.muelhausen.jugendherberge.de; dorms from €19) is 2km northwest of the centre – take bus #5 or #6 to "Blobach" from where it's a 500m walk.

While *Mülhäuser Hof* has a highly rated Italian **restaurant**, *Zum Nachbar*, the most appealing eating option is ⚘ *Wirtshaus Antonius Mühle*, Am Frauentor 7 (closed Mon), a historic garden mill, modernized without sacrificing character, and whose house special is an Elle (a 58cm medieval cloth measurement) of *Bratwurst*. A traditional alternative is hotel-restaurant *Zum Löwen* (☏03601/47 10, ⓦwww.brauhaus-zum-loewen.de; ❹), on Kornmarkt, which also serves home-brewed *Pils* and *Weissen* beers.

The Kyffhäuser

Thuringia heaps up unexpectedly in its northern reaches as the **Kyffhäuser**. While it requires an optimist to describe their wooded sandstone uplands as mountains – no peak in a sixty-square-kilometre extension of the Harz range is above 480m – their low-lying nature and lack of development make for pleasant walking country. The range also holds a special place in the nation's psyche as the resting place of Emperor Frederick Barbarossa. Possibly. Fact – or at least historical chronicles – record that the mighty twelfth-century German king and Holy Roman Emperor challenged papal authority to establish German predominance in western Europe before he drowned in the Holy Land in 1190. Legend, however, counters that "Red Beard" slumbers deep within a Kyffhäuser mountain and will one day awaken to lead the united German people to victory against their enemies. It is, as the marketing board never tires of saying, where Barbarossa dreams. In more recent history Thomas Müntzer's peasants' revolution was casually swatted aside on the flanks of the Kyffhäuser in 1525.

Bad Frankenhausen

The most convenient base to ascend into the range is well-aired little spa town **BAD FRANKENHAUSEN**. It's at its best on main square Anger, though the leaning tower of the Oberkirche east via Frauenweg is one for the photo album – 4.22m off vertical. A kilometre uphill a large rotunda crowns the Schlachtberg (Battle Hill) with the **Panorama Museum** (Tues–Sun: April–Oct 10am–6pm; Nov–March 10am–5pm; July & Aug also Mon 1–6pm; €5). That Thomas Müntzer's peasants' war army, the first organized people's rebellion in Germany, was crushed here made the hill a site of secular martyrdom for GDR authorities. In 1989 they unveiled what is claimed as the largest painting in the world – 123m by 14m – to celebrate the regime's fortieth birthday; one of its swan-song acts as it turned out. What could have been another piece of clunking GDR propaganda is salvaged by artist Werner Tübke. The University of Leipzig professor's original plan for a battle-scene morphed into a more ambitious project inspired by the allegorical works of medieval masters Peter Bruegel the Elder and Hironymous Bosch. Audio guides (available in English) sift through the layers of secular and sacred symbolism in Tübke's epic, five years in the making and whose cast of thousands spans from the fifteenth century to his age. Critics hated it, of course, and derided its artistry and politics alike after the *Wende*. No quibbles with its visual impact, though.

Practicalities

Bad Frankenhausen's **Bahnhof** south of the Altstadt lies on a branch line, so requires a change at Sömmerda from Erfurt. The **tourist office** (Mon–Fri 10am–6pm; summer Sat 10am–3pm, Sun 10am–noon; winter Sat 10am–noon; ☎034671/717 16, ⓦ www.kyffhaeuser-tourismus.de) at Anger 14 supplies sketch maps of walks plus details of a 37km route that links all destinations in the area on a three-day circuit. FAV Radwander Zentrum (Mon–Fri 8am–3pm; ☎034671/777 71) at the Bahnhof **rents bikes**. If you can survive without amenities, you can camp for free in a field at the end of Badmühlenweg, 1km west of the centre. Hotel **accommodation** is in traditional *Thüringer Hof*, Anger 15 (☎034671/510 10, ⓦ www.thueringer-hof.com; ❷), and *Alte Hämmelei* (☎034671/51 20, ⓦ www .alte-haemmelei.de; ❷–❸), an old-fashioned rustic-styled place east of Anger at Bornstrasse 33. Both offer solid traditional **food**: *Thüringer Hof* serves a local game goulash and has eleven beers on tap, ideal for its terrace in summer; half-timbered

Alte Hämmelei (Mon–Thurs eve only) is a historic-styled *Kniepe* with a beer garden. Between them at Erfurter Strasse 9, café-restaurant *Schwan* (closed Mon) prepares a slightly more modern menu.

Around Bad Frankenhausen

From Bad Frankenhausen's Panorama Museum you can continue uphill on the Kyffhäuserweg trail (17km; 4–5hr), which ascends via Rathsfeld and Tilleda to the **Kyffhäuserdenkmal** (daily: April–Oct 9.30am–6pm; Nov–March 10am–5pm; €6), jutting above the trees on the hills' brow at 457m. A fabulously absurd piece of imperial pomp, it was unveiled in 1896 as a war veterans' memorial to Wilhelm I who had died a decade previously. The father-figure of Germany's Second Reich, Wilhelm quashed rival fiefdoms to forge a united nation, and in doing so inherited the mantle of Frederick Barbarossa: the monstrous equestrian statue of Wilhelm rides out between war god Thor and History with a pen and laurel wreath, while Barbarossa awakens on his throne beneath like a spare prop from *Lord of the Rings*. Small wonder Hitler paid several visits in the hope the stardust would rub off. Moscow rejected local apparatchiks' offer to dynamite the symbol after the war on the grounds that Germany had to learn from its history. There's a small museum of the memorial within and superb views from the imperial crown 81m up. Much of its pink stone was mined from the **Reichsburg** behind, a fortification that Barbarossa had bolstered into the stronghold of his Hohenstaufen empire. Upper defence the Oberburg has vanished except for a clumsily patched-up tower and what is claimed as the world's deepest well (176m), leaving the Unterburg (free) beneath the monument as the only reference of former scale. It's a lovely picnic spot, too: Goethe and Saxe-Weimar duke Carl August were ticked off by a forest warden for the mess theirs created – you have been warned.

Barbarossa himself is said to doze at a marble table, his red beard growing ever longer, in the **Barbarossahöhle** (tours April–Oct daily 10am–5pm; Nov–March Tues–Sun 10am–4pm; €6; ⓦ www.hoehle), 6km west of Bad Frankenhausen, one of Europe's largest gypsum caves, an 800m section of which is open. Within a fortnight of its discovery by copper miners in 1865, the first tourists came to gawp at its broad caverns. A footpath tracks the Kleine Wipper stream there from Bad Frankenhausen; pick up maps from the tourist office.

On weekdays two morning **buses** ascend to the Kyffhäuserdenkmal via the Barbarossahöhle from Bad Frankenhausen Busbahnhof, southeast of the centre on Esperstedter Strasse; note there is only one morning return and one early afternoon return. A *Gaststätte* at both sites rustles up food.

Travel details

Trains

Altenburg to: Leipzig (hourly; 50min–1hr).
Erfurt to: Eisenach (every 30min; 30–50min); Gotha (every 30min; 15–25min); Ilmenau (hourly; 55min); Jena (hourly; 30min); Leipzig (hourly; 1hr 10min); Meiningen (10 daily; 1hr 30min–1hr 50min); Mülhausen (hourly; 50min–1hr 15min); Weimar (every 20–30min; 15min).

Eisenach to: Erfurt (three hourly; 30–50min); Gotha (hourly; 20min); Meiningen (hourly; 1hr).
Gotha to: Eisenach (hourly; 20min); Erfurt (every 15–30min; 15min); Friedrichroda (every 30min; 1hr); Mülhausen (10 daily; 20min).
Jena to: Erfurt (hourly; 30min); Rudolstadt (hourly; 30min); Saalfeld (every 30min; 25–40min); Weimar (two hourly; 20min).
Weimar to: Erfurt (every 20–30min; 15min); Jena (every 30min; 15–25min).

Northern Bavaria: Franconia

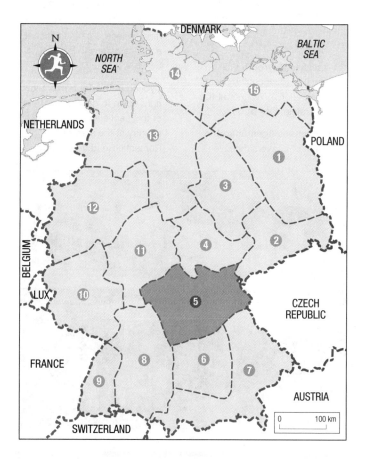

CHAPTER 5 # Highlights

✳ **Nuremberg** The triumphs and tragedies of German history, set against a splendid medieval backdrop. See p.300

✳ **Outdoor activities in the Naturpark Altmühltal** Hike, cycle or canoe your way through this delightful and intriguing Jurassic landscape. See p.311

✳ **Opera in Bayreuth** Plan years in advance if you want to experience Wagner at the Festspiele. See p.317

✳ **Vierzehnheiligen church** A vision of heaven, if heaven's designers were masters of the Rococo. See p.324

✳ **Bamberg's Rauchbier** Smoky and sweetly mysterious, Bamberg's favourite brew is as unique as the city that created it. See p.325

✳ **The Residenz, Würzburg** Balthasar Neumann's Baroque masterpiece is as magnificent a palace as any in Europe. See p.333

✳ **Cycling in the Taubertal** Slow right down to get the most out of this gentle wine-growing country at the start of the Romantic Road. See p.342

▲ Outside bars in Bamberg

Northern Bavaria: Franconia

Entering **Franconia** (Franken) from the north or west can be a disorientating experience for anyone expecting Alps, blue-and-white flags and *Weisswurst*, for Bavaria's northernmost region is not at all the Bavaria of popular cliché. Red and white are the colours of Franconia, the sausage of choice is *Bratwurst* and the unspoilt wooded uplands which cover much of the region rarely rise to mountainous heights, or feature on the itinerary of foreign tourists. In many respects, it has more in common with Thuringia or Hesse than it does with the "real" Bavaria to the south.

Franconia isn't historically Bavarian at all. It owes its name to the Frankish tribes whose territory it originally was, and from the Middle Ages until the early nineteenth century it was highly fragmented. In Lower Franconia and Bamberg, ecclesiastical rule predominated, and the archbishops of Mainz in Aschaffenburg and the prince-bishops of Würzburg and Bamberg ruled their modest fiefdoms in some style, leaving behind the architectural splendour to prove it. In the north and east, Protestantism took root, in Hohenzollern-ruled Brandenburg-Bayreuth and Wettin-ruled Saxe-Coburg and Gotha, whose territories spanned the boundary between Franconia and Thuringia and whose judicious marriage policy ensured its familial links included many of the royal houses of Europe. Outshining all – until its decline at the end of the sixteenth century – was the free imperial city of Nuremberg, seat of the Holy Roman Empire's imperial Diet and one of Europe's great medieval manufacturing and trading centres. Free, too, were the little city-states of Rothenburg ob der Tauber and Dinkelsbühl.

Political diversity ended when Napoleon incorporated Franconia into the newly upgraded Kingdom of Bavaria – previously a mere duchy – in 1806. But it remains a fantastically diverse place to visit. **Unterfranken** (Lower Franconia), centred on **Würzburg**, is wine-growing country, with a feel of the sunny south; it is also the starting point for the **Romantic Road**, a tourist route linking many of Bavaria's most beautiful towns. In **Oberfranken** (Upper Franconia), the Protestant religion and beer predominate. Here, the cultural and historical associations are with **Wagner** in **Bayreuth** and with **Luther** and the British royal family in **Coburg**; everywhere there's a sense of the proximity of the lands of central Germany to the north. **Bamberg** remains a splendid exception, a beer town through and through but opulently Catholic in an otherwise Lutheran region, and one of Germany's most beautiful cities.

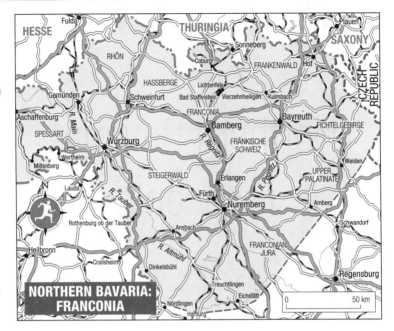

NORTHERN BAVARIA: FRANCONIA

In **Mittelfranken** (Middle Franconia), **Nuremberg** is unmissable for its fascinating and occasionally uneasy blend of medieval splendour and Nazi bombast, while **Rothenburg ob der Tauber** and **Dinkelsbühl** are perfectly preserved medieval gems, if scarcely undiscovered by visitors. Though the towns and cities are the major attractions, Franconia's wooded hills and national parks offer tempting opportunities to escape the crowds, whether by bike, on foot or in a canoe down the lazy Altmühl.

Long-distance **hiking** and **cycle** trails cross the region, while for more rapid progress, the bigger cities have fast main-line **rail** connections and many smaller towns still have a rail link – though the trains serving them can be slow.

Nuremberg (Nürnberg)

Nowhere in Germany gives such a powerful impression of the highs and lows of German history as the former free imperial city of **NUREMBERG**. From 1050 to 1571 – when the custom died out – it was the nearest thing the Holy Roman Empire had to a capital, for it was here that newly chosen emperors held their imperial Diet or Reichstag. At the same time, commercial acumen and artisan skills – above all in metalworking – made Nuremberg one of the wealthiest and most important trading centres in Europe, despite the poverty of its rural hinterland and the lack of a navigable river. And then – happily for today's visitors – the city fell into a long decline, which spared its medieval monuments from ruinous "improvement" or replacement. Despite terrible destruction during World War II, much of Nuremberg remains convincingly medieval in appearance, and when touring the forbidding **Kaiserburg** or exploring surviving lanes of half-timbered houses in the city's **Altstadt**, which is still encircled by its medieval city walls, it's easy to imagine how the Nuremberg of Albrecht Dürer, Veit Stoss or the Meistersingers might have looked. Not surprisingly the museums – from the intimate **Dürer Haus** to the encyclopedic **Germanisches Nationalmuseum** – are compelling.

As for the lows, what's remarkable is how much is still recognizable from Leni Riefenstahl's hypnotic film images of the 1930s Nazi party rallies, not least at the **Zeppelintribüne** where Hitler addressed the massed, uniformed crowds. The dictator purloined the medieval credentials of this most German of all German cities in order to lend credibility to his regime; as a consequence no other city is more closely associated with the Nazi movement – certainly not Munich, where it was actually born. The introduction of driverless trains on the Nuremberg U-Bahn in 2008 prompted the quip that things run better without a Führer – *Führer* also being the German for driver – but the city of the Nuremberg rallies, Nuremberg laws and postwar Nuremberg trials can never be entirely rid of the association. It's greatly to the city's credit that it handles this sensitive legacy with such honesty, and a visit to one or more of Nuremberg's Nazi monuments south and west of the city is an essential counterpoint to the Altstadt's medieval glories. Away from the centre much of Nuremberg is surprisingly industrial and working class, which helps make it a rare stronghold of the left-of-centre SPD party in conservative Bavaria.

Arrival, information and city transport

Nuremberg's **airport** (☎0911/937 00, ⓦwww.airport-nuernberg.de) is on the northern edge of the city at Flughafenstrasse 100; it's linked to the city's **Hauptbahnhof** on the southern edge of the Altstadt by U-Bahn line 2. The main **tourist office** is opposite the Hauptbahnhof at Königstrasse 93 (Mon–Sat 9am–7pm, Sun 10am–6pm; ☎0911/233 61 32, ⓦwww.tourismus.nuernberg.de), with a second one at Hauptmarkt 18 (Mon–Sat 9am–6pm; May–Oct also Sun 10am–4pm; during Christkindlesmarkt Mon–Sat 9am–7pm, Sun 10am–7pm; ☎0911/233 61 35). Either office can sell you a €19 **Nürnberg Card**, valid for two days and offering free use of the city's public transport system, free entry to museums and reductions in shops and for theatre tickets. Nuremberg's **public transport** system (ⓦwww.nuernbergmobil.de) includes trams, U-Bahn and buses. Single tickets cost €1.50, a one-day *TagesTicket* €3.80.

Accommodation

You can search and book **accommodation** through the tourist office website. There are plenty of hotels in the southern Altstadt and near the Hauptbahnhof, with a scattering on the north side of the Pegnitz in the most atmospheric corner of the Altstadt. The prize for the most evocative location in the city, however, for once goes to the youth hostel, right next to the Kaiserburg.

Hotels

Agneshof Agnesgasse 10 ☎0911/21 44 40, ⓦwww.agneshof-nuernberg.de. Smart and welcoming hotel *garni* tucked into a quiet lane in the northwest Altstadt, with 74 rooms, all with bath or shower and WC. On-site facilities include sauna, solarium and jacuzzi. ❺

Deutscher Kaiser Königstr. 55 ☎0911/24 26 60, ⓦwww.deutscher-kaiser-hotel.de. Neo-Gothic architecture and a few turn-of-the-century decorative trappings add a note of class to this central and comfortable three-star hotel. ❺

Drei Raben Königstr. 63 ☎0911/27 43 80, ⓦwww.hotel-drei-raben.de. Very stylish modern hotel in a central location close to the Neues Museum and with a groovy cocktail bar on the ground floor. Rooms have themed decor, with some boasting free-standing bathtubs. ❺

Dürer Hotel Neutormauer 32 ☎0911/214 66 50, ⓦwww.duererhotel-nuernberg.de. The peaceful and

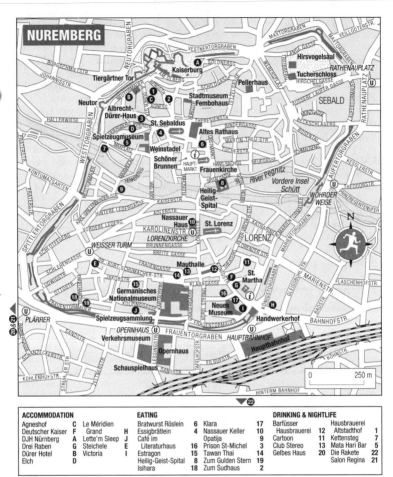

NUREMBERG

ACCOMMODATION				EATING				DRINKING & NIGHTLIFE		
Agneshof	C	Le Méridien		Bratwurst Röslein	6	Klara	17	Barfüsser	Hausbrauerei	
Deutscher Kaiser	F	Grand	H	Essigbrätlein	4	Nassauer Keller	10	Hausbrauerei	12	Altstadthof	1
DJH Nürnberg	A	Lette'm Sleep	J	Café im		Opatija	9	Cartoon	11	Kettensteg	7
Drei Raben	G	Steichele	E	Literaturhaus	16	Prison St-Michel	3	Club Stereo	13	Mata Hari Bar	5
Dürer Hotel	B	Victoria	I	Estragon	15	Tawan Thai	14	Gelbes Haus	20	Die Rakete	22
Elch	D			Heilig-Geist-Spital	8	Zum Gulden Stern	19			Salon Regina	21
				Isihara	18	Zum Sudhaus	2				

central location – close to the Dürer Haus and in the shadow of the city walls – is the x-factor here; rooms have internet connection, en-suite bathroom and minibar, and there's an underground car park. **6**

Elch Irrerstr. 9 ☏ 0911/249 29 80, ⓦ www .hotel-elch.de. Superbly located budget option in a fourteenth-century half-timbered house. Modern comforts include shower and WC, minibar and free wi-fi. There's a restaurant, *Schnitzelria*, on the ground floor. **3**

Le Méridien Grand Bahnhofstr. 1–3 ☏ 0911/232 20, ⓦ www.lemeridien.com. Grand by name and nature, this is the top dog among Nuremberg hotels, with decor that blends Art Deco and Jugendstil touches, a wide range of room types and the best advance prices on the website. **5–8**

Steichele Knorrstr. 2–8 ☏ 0911/20 22 80, ⓦ www .steichele.de. The rooms in the modern hotel extension don't have quite the same atmosphere as the lovely *Weinrestaurant* next door, but all have shower and WC, high-speed internet and satellite TV, and there are 28 singles. **3**

Victoria Königsstr. 80 ☏ 0911/240 50, ⓦ www .hotelvictoria.de. A pleasant mix of tradition and modernity behind a listed nineteenth-century facade. Rooms include some singles, smokers' rooms are available and they also have apartments to let. **4–8**

Hostels

DJH Nürnberg Burg 2 ☏ 0911/230 93 60, ⓦ www.nuernberg.jugendherberge.de.

The spectacular medieval Kaiserstallung with its multistorey attics is the memorable location for Nuremberg's large youth hostel, right next to the Kaiserburg. Dorms from €21.90 with breakfast. **Lette'm Sleep** Frauentormauer 42 ☏ 0911/ 992 81 28, ⊛ www.backpackers.de. Bright and funky, independently run hostel a short walk from the Hauptbahnhof on the fringe of the city's red-light district, with free internet, cooking facilities and no curfew. Dorm beds from €16 per night.

Hauptmarkt and around

It was the Bohemian king and Holy Roman Emperor Charles IV who gave Nuremberg's city fathers permission to expel the inhabitants of its Jewish ghetto in 1349 in order to establish a market. His decision unleashed a pogrom in which at least 562 Jews were burnt to death. For all its gory origins, **Hauptmarkt** remains the focus of the Altstadt and the scene of the world-famous annual **Christkindlesmarkt** or Christmas market. Most of the buildings fringing the square are postwar, but reconstruction from wartime damage was tactful and a few key monuments survive. In the northwest corner of the square stands a multicoloured nineteenth-century copy of the aptly named **Schöner Brunnen**, a flamboyant Gothic skyrocket of a fountain, the fourteenth-century original of which is in the Germanisches Nationalmuseum. The forty figures on it depict Moses, the four Apostles and the seven electors of the Holy Roman Empire among others.

Presiding over Hauptmarkt on its eastern side is the **Frauenkirche** (Mon, Tues & Thurs 8am–8pm, Wed 8am–6pm, Fri 8am–5pm, Sat 9am–7.30pm, Sun 9am–8pm), the rather stubby Gothic church which Charles decreed should be built on the site of the destroyed synagogue and dedicated to the Virgin Mary. The result – the work of Peter Parler, the architect of Prague's St Vitus cathedral – was the first Gothic hall church in Franconia, and though the church was reduced to a shell by World War II bombs, restoration was deft, and it retains a feeling of antiquity along with fragments of the *Kaiserfenster*, or Emperor's Window, the oldest stained glass in the city. The church was intended to serve as the storage place for the imperial crown jewels and its holy relics, but something – probably security concerns – led to the plans being altered, and they were taken instead to Karlstein castle near Prague. Foremost among the Frauenkirche's various treasures – which survived the hail of bombs by being stored underground – is the expressive *Tucher Altar*, the city's greatest pre-Dürer work of art. On the west front of the church, a Glockenspiel dating from 1509 re-enacts Charles's **Golden Bull** decree of 1536, which formalized the status of the seven electors who would choose an emperor, and enshrined in statute the Kaiserburg's role as the venue for the imperial Diet.

From the southeast corner of the square, a stroll to the middle of the **Museumsbrücke** gives picturesque views east towards the **Heilig-Geist-Spital**, a medieval hospice that was extended on two shallow arches over the Pegnitz in the sixteenth century. It's now one of the city's best-known traditional restaurants. The view west takes in the **Fleischbrücke** of 1596, modelled on the Rialto bridge in Venice.

The Rathaus and around

North from Hauptmarkt, Burgstrasse climbs towards the Kaiserburg, with the steep roofs of the fifteenth-century **Kaiserstallung** – built as a grain warehouse but used during imperial Diets as a stable – looming over it. The right-hand side of Burgstrasse is dominated by the splendid Renaissance facade of the **Altes Rathaus**, built between 1616 and 1622 by Jakob Wolff the Younger in the style of an Italian palazzo. Splendid as it is, it screens much older parts of the building, including the **Historischer Rathaussaal** (1332–40), rebuilt after wartime destruction, which was the setting in 1649 for the peace banquet that celebrated the end of the Thirty Years' War. Little of the building is open to general view, but you can visit the creepy **Lochgefängnisse** (tours only: Feb & March Mon–Fri 10am–4.30pm; April–Oct Tues–Sun 10am–4.30pm; during Christkindlesmarkt daily 10am–4.30pm; Jan by appointment only; €3), a medieval jail complex and torture chamber.

Opposite the Rathaus rises the twin-spired **Sebalduskirche** (daily: Jan–March 9.30am–4pm; April, May & mid-Sept to end Dec 9.30am–6pm; June to mid-Sept 9.30am–8pm), the city's oldest parish church, which dates from the early thirteenth century and has been Protestant since 1525. It's unusually large and magnificent for a mere parish church, its style transitional between Romanesque and Gothic, and the interior has a rich array of artistic treasures. The most eye-catching is the tomb of **St Sebald**, in which the casket of the city's patron saint is sheltered by an incredibly delicate Gothic canopy, the work of Peter Vischer the Elder and his sons, who laboured from 1508 to 1519 to complete it. In the east choir there is a Crucifixion group by **Veit Stoss**, the city's most celebrated sculptor. The figures of Mary and St John were created in 1507–08 for the Frauenkirche. Photo plaques in the east choir show the extent of war damage to the church, along with a **Cross of Nails** from Coventry cathedral.

The best surviving Renaissance house in the city is the **Fembohaus**, further up Burgstrasse at no. 15. It houses the **Stadtmuseum** (Tues–Fri 10am–5pm, Sat & Sun 10am–6pm; €5, multivision show €4 extra, free audio guide). Take the lift to the top of the house for the **Tönendes Stadtmodell**, an audiovisual presentation and large-scale model representing the Altstadt in 1939, on the eve of its destruction. The museum's displays on Nuremberg's trading and artistic prowess are all the more compelling for being housed in this splendid house, built for the Dutch trader Philipp van Orl in 1591–96. The Baroque vestibule on the second floor has a wonderful stucco ceiling from 1674 by Carlo Moretti Brentano, the Italian who was also responsible for the stucco work in Munich's Theatinerkirche. The museum also incorporates the richly decorated **Schönes Zimmer** which came from the **Pellerhaus**, an even more magnificent Renaissance house built for Martin Peller (1559–1629), the city's richest merchant in his day. It was largely destroyed during World War II, but the Stadtmuseum has a model, and you can see what survives on **Egidienplatz** east of Burgstrasse; bizarrely, the Renaissance courtyard was incorporated into the 1950s-style Stadtbibliothek, though there are plans for a more thorough rebuild.

The northeastern corner of the Altstadt is the part of town that least resembles its pre-bombing self, and there's a lot of soulless postwar development. One exception to the dreary rule is the **Museum Tucherschloss** at Hirschelgasse 9–11 (guided tours Mon 10am–3pm, Thurs 1–5pm, Sun 10am–5pm; €5), in the summer residence of the patrician Tucher family, built between 1533 and 1544 in an eclectic style blending Gothic, Italian Renaissance and French influences. Its restored interiors reflect the lifestyle of a rich merchant family of the period, and the exhibits include a Renaissance double goblet by Nuremberg silversmith **Wenzel Jamnitzer**. In the garden you can visit the **Hirsvogelsaal**, a splendid Renaissance hall which dates from 1534 and originally formed part of the now-destroyed Hirsvogel mansion.

The Kaiserburg

Simultaneously medieval Germany's parliament and its treasure chest, the **Kaiserburg** (daily: April–Sept 9am–6pm; Oct–March 10am–4pm; €6) lords it over the rooftops of the northern Altstadt. The approach up Burgstrasse takes you past the Kaiserstallung and left past the **Sinwellturm** into the **Ausserer Burghof**; the **museum** and **Palas** are grouped around the Innerer Burghof beyond. Spared the attentions of Renaissance or Baroque builders who might have prettified or domesticated it, the Kaiserburg is a tough-looking fortress, every inch the medieval strongroom. The Kaiserburg grew over the centuries from the original eleventh-century castle erected by the Frankish Salian kings; of their complex, only the **Fünfeckturm** on the west side of the Kaiserstallung survives. Admittance to the **Palas** is by guided tour only, but your ticket includes entry to the **museum**, whose armoury displays and models of the fortress as it was in 1100 and 1300 will pass the time until your tour departs. Though the Palas represents the Kaiserburg at its most domestic, its staterooms lack any real warmth, for it was never actually a private home, and never at any stage possessed its own furniture. Rather, it was a sort of medieval congress centre, whose rooms were only furnished – with items loaned by the patrician families of the city – when they were in use. Highlight of the Palas tour is undoubtedly the Romanesque **Doppelkapelle** of 1180, whose double-height design is deeply symbolic of the social hierarchy of the day, with the emperor at eye level with Christ, lording it physically over his fellow monarchs in the upper chapel, and with lesser fry relegated to the crypt-like lower level. The emperor's balcony is decorated with the Habsburg double eagle. The visit concludes with the unassuming half-timbered building that houses the **Tiefer Brunnen**, the castle's 47m well, whose very existence was a state secret lest it be tainted by throwing an animal carcass down the shaft. Tour leaders demonstrate its impressive depth by lowering a tray of candles to the bottom and by dropping a carafe of water into it and asking you to count the seconds until the splash – it takes around five seconds. Your ticket is also valid for an ascent of the circular **Sinwellturm**, worth the climb for the most panoramic of all views of the city. Afterwards, stroll west through the leafy **Burggarten** to descend to the Altstadt, which you reach at the **Neutor**.

The Dürer Haus and northwestern Altstadt

Among the most photographed of all Nuremberg views is the one east across the little square by **Tiergärtner Tor**, fringed with atmospheric pubs and with the Kaiserburg towering above. On the west side of this open space is the **Albrecht-Dürer-Haus** (Tues–Sun 10am–5pm, Thurs until 8pm; €5, free English audio guide), the fifteenth-century half-timbered house which was the home of the artist from 1509 until his death in 1528. The self-guided tour – supposedly narrated by his wife Agnes – steers you through the details of Dürer's domestic arrangements as well as visiting a mock-up of his studio on the second floor, complete with copper plates and tools used for copperplate engraving. A film explains the significance of his work, which was grounded in realism in a way never previously encountered, as well as recounting episodes from his life, from his youthful travels to Italy to his subsequent fame and commercial success.

Bergstrasse heads southeast from Tiergärtner Tor. At no. 19 is the entrance to the **Nürnberger Felsengänge** (tours at 11am, 1pm, 3pm & 5pm; €4.50), a warren of passageways and chambers hollowed out of the castle hill and used since the Middle Ages to store beer. The existence of such passageways proved invaluable during World War II, when the city's art treasures were hidden underground out of harm's way in the nearby **Historischer Kunstbunker**, Obere Schmiedegasse 52 (tours daily at 2pm; €4.50). At the start of the war, prudent officials equipped this former beer cellar with air-conditioning, moisture-proof storage cells and guardrooms so it could perform its new function.

From here, a turn down Schmiedegasse towards the Sebalduskirche brings you to the **Spielzeugmuseum** at Karlstrasse 13–15 (Tues–Fri 10am–5pm, Sat & Sun 10am–6pm, during Christkindlesmarkt also Mon 10am–5pm; €5), which presents the history of toys from antiquity to Lego and Barbie. Nuremberg was long a renowned toy-making centre, and the exhibition greets visitors with an array of wooden toys before progressing to dolls and dolls' houses and a model railway on the first floor.

From the museum, head west along Weinmarkt and Irrerstrasse to reach **Weissgerbergasse**, the most photogenic and perfectly preserved street of half-timbered houses in the city.

Along the Pegnitz

Though it cuts right through the centre of the city, the banks of the River **Pegnitz** are among the most tranquil spots in Nuremberg. At the western end of the Altstadt the city walls leap across the river in a mighty stone arch; in its shadow, the little **Kettensteig** chain bridge dates from 1824 and is one of the oldest surviving chain bridges in Europe. The next bridge to the east is **Maxbrücke**, which offers lovely views of another of Nuremberg's great medieval set-pieces: the vast half-timbered **Weinstadel** – built between 1446 and 1448 as a lepers' hospital before later becoming a wine store and finally, after World War II, a student hall of residence – and the **Henkersteg**, a covered wooden bridge originally built in 1595 and which got its name – "Hangman's Bridge" – because it led to the **tower** in which the town's hangmen lived from the sixteenth to the nineteenth centuries. As if this architectural ensemble were not picturesque enough, willows hanging low over the water add the final, camera-friendly *pièce de résistance*. Further east still, charming, small-scale **Trödelmarkt** – "junk market" – on an island in the middle of the river proves that postwar German shopping developments can be sympathetic to their surroundings without being dreary.

The southern Altstadt

The commercial realities of modern life intrude south of the Pegnitz, for it's here that Nuremberg's busiest shopping streets are found, along with a startlingly upfront red-light district along Frauentormauer, where prostitutes lean out of upstairs windows to blow kisses at male passers-by. Along with the commercial brashness comes a certain amount of uninspired modern architecture. Yet the southern half of the Altstadt has its share of historic and artistic riches too. On the corner of Karolinenstrasse and Königstrasse is the tall **Nassauer Haus**, a well-preserved, medieval patrician tower house, the lower parts of which date from the early thirteenth century while the upper level with its eye-catching corner towers was built between 1422 and 1433.

Opposite, the Catholic **Lorenzkirche** (Mon–Sat 9am–5pm, Sun noon–4pm) is the southern Altstadt's counterblast to the Sebalduskirche north of the river. In silhouette the two are startlingly similar, but the Lorenzkirche is the later of the two, consisting of a three-aisled basilica with a decorative west front and a late Gothic hall-choir which dates from 1439 to 1477. Like the Sebalduskirche, the Lorenzkirche lost its roof in World War II, but again restoration has been deft and its artworks are exceptional – in particular the beautiful *Annunciation* (1517–18) by Veit Stoss, suspended in midair like a burst of joy in elegantly carved wooden form. There's also an impressively tall, elegant Gothic tabernacle, with a wonderfully lifelike self-portrait by its creator, Adam Kraft, at its base.

Further south along Königstrasse, the **Mauthalle** is another mammoth medieval survivor, built between 1498 and 1502 as a grain warehouse and with five storeys of attics rising above its stone walls. From 1572 onwards it was also the city's weigh- and customs house. The cellar is now a *Hausbrauerei*. On the east side of Königstrasse is the inconspicuous church of **St Martha** (Mon 10am–2pm, Thurs 10am–4pm), remarkable chiefly as the place where the guild of **Meistersingers of Nuremberg** – the artisan folk singers immortalized by Richard Wagner – performed and practised from 1578 to 1620, the church having been secularized during the Reformation. The Meistersingers composed verses based on strict formulae of medieval melody and rhyme; the most famous of them all was Hans Sachs (1494–1576). Nestling in the shade of the mighty Königstor at the southern entrance to the Altstadt is the twee **Handwerkerhof** (Mon–Sat 10am–6.30pm, also open Sun during Christkindlesmarkt), an artisan village whose handicrafts are something of a disappointment given Nuremberg's illustrious tradition – there's some good stuff, but also a lot of *Nürnberger Tand*, the historic expression for pretty things of little real worth.

The Neues Museum and Germanisches Nationalmuseum

Lurking behind the Handwerkerhof and as sleekly incongruous as a digital watch in a costume drama, the **Neues Museum** (Tues–Fri 10am–8pm, Sat & Sun 10am–6pm; €4) is Nuremberg's elegant glass-fronted museum of contemporary art and design, whose collections span everything from Op Art by Bridget Riley to an ERS2 satellite. The art collection includes works by Sigmar Polke, Gerhard Richter and Georg Baselitz, and there's groovy modern furniture aplenty, including a roomful of the defiantly ephemeral Italian Memphis movement of the 1980s. Excellent temporary exhibitions ensure the experience remains fresh and thought-provoking.

The giant among Nuremberg's museums – and the largest museum of its kind in Germany – is a short walk to the west at Kartäusergasse 1. The **Germanisches Nationalmuseum** (Tues–Sun 10am–6pm, Wed until 9pm; €6, English audio guide €1.50; ⓦ www.gnm.de) was founded in 1852 by a Franconian nobleman, Hans Freiherr von und zu Aufsess. The impetus for its establishment was to provide cultural affirmation of the liberal ideal of the nation state at a time when Germany was still a mass of competing kingdoms, dukedoms and landgraviates. The architectural core of the complex is an old Carthusian monastery and its cloisters, but what first strikes visitors is the crisp modernity of the 1993 Museumsforum and the monumental *Street of Human Rights*, a row of white concrete columns inscribed in various languages, by Israeli artist Dani Karavan. The sheer scale of the museum can be daunting: the medieval collections and fine art aside, there's a hangar-like room full of historic musical instruments and entire farmhouse interiors have been reconstructed in the folk art section. It pays, therefore, to be selective. Among the highlights of the prehistoric section is the gorgeously delicate, wafer-thin **Ezelsdorf-Buch Gold Cone**, which dates from some time between 1100 and 900 BC. Highlights of the medieval collections include sculptures by **Veit Stoss** and the Thuringian-born but Würzburg-based **Tilman Riemenschneider**, while the star among the scientific instruments is undoubtedly the **Behaim Globe**, which dates from 1491–93 and is the oldest existing representation of the Earth as a sphere. The glory of Nuremberg's metalworking tradition is admirably demonstrated by the splendidly ornamental **Schlüsselfelder Schiff**, a table centrepiece of a sailing ship from 1503, while its greatest artist, **Albrecht Dürer**, is represented here by seven paintings. Twentieth-century paintings include an Expressionist self-portrait by **Ernst Ludwig Kirchner**. Note that parts of the museum were being refurbished during 2009, so some areas may be closed.

South of the Altstadt: the DB Museum

Brave the pounding traffic along Frauentorgraben to reach the **DB Museum** at Lessingstrasse 6 (Tues–Fri 9am–5pm, Sat & Sun 10am–6pm; €4), with an additional open-air display area around the corner in Sandstrasse. It's Deutsche Bahn's house museum, and tells the story of the railway from its origins in Britain to the thrusting modernity of the ICE high-speed expresses. Highlights include a replica of the **Adler**, the very first German train, which ushered in the age of rail in 1835 when it travelled from Nuremberg to nearby Fürth. You can also see **Ludwig II's royal train** and the saloon coach used by **Bismarck**. The darker side of German railway history is not ignored, with a section of the role of the railway in the Holocaust.

The Reichsparteitagsgelände

If you're even vaguely curious about the role Nuremberg played in the iconography of the Nazi movement, you shouldn't miss a journey out to the **Luitpoldhain** park in the south of the city to see the **Dokumentationszentrum Reichsparteitagsgelände** (Mon–Fri 9am–6pm, Sat & Sun 10am–6pm; €5, free audio guide; tram #9 from Hauptbahnhof). Housed in an ultramodern museum that pierces the side of the **Kongresshalle** – a typically gargantuan piece of Nazi architectural bombast, planned to seat 50,000 but never completed – the exhibition **Fazination und Gewalt** (Fascination and Force) charts the rise of the Nazis with a focus on Nuremberg's role. At the start, skateboarding youths guide you through a short introductory film that juxtaposes the modern city with clips from Leni Riefenstahl's party-rally film *Triumph of the Will*, scenes of war and the Holocaust and the ghastly ruins of Nuremberg in 1945. The Nazis held their party rallies in Nuremberg in 1927 and 1929 for both political and practical reasons: the city's illustrious past and glorious medieval monuments lent Hitler's posturing a spurious air of historical legitimacy, but the Mittelfranken region in which Nuremberg stands was already a Nazi power-base. Silent film footage from this time portrays SA men marching through the Altstadt. Violence associated with the rallies led the city council to ban them, but local Gauleiter (party chief) Julius Streicher – who gained particular notoriety as the publisher of the deranged anti-Semitic newspaper *Der Stürmer* – could already count on the support of the local police chief. A particular strong-point of the exhibition is the filmed interviews with Nurembergers who were witnesses to the events of the 1930s and 1940s; the section on anti-Semitism in everyday life is chilling, and includes anti-Semitic board games and newspaper advertisements from department stores proclaiming their new-found "Aryanized" status.

After the *Machtergreifung* (Nazi seizure of power) in 1933, the **Reichsparteitage** or party rallies became an annual ritual, attracting massive numbers of participants and hangers-on. A vast, self-glorifying **Parteitagsgelände** (party rally ground) was therefore planned, and though much of it – including the colossal **Deutsches Stadion**, which would have accommodated 400,000 spectators – was never built, what survives gives a powerful impression of the gigantism that was designed, in part, to shrink the role of the individual into insignificance and to create an overwhelming experience for the participants that appealed to the emotions, not to reason. The rallies had a wider audience too, for during the 1930s many foreign newspapers sent reporters to cover the event. Leni Riefenstahl used a crew

▲ The Nazi Kongresshalle, Nuremberg

of 170 and some ground-breaking camera techniques to record the 1934 rally for her film *The Triumph of the Will*; the crowning event of the 1935 rally was the special session of the Reichstag convened in Nuremberg to pass the anti-Semitic Nuremberg laws.

A circular **walk** signposted in German and English takes you from the Kongresshalle along the 2km **Grosse Strasse**, the main axis of the complex, deliberately oriented towards the distant Kaiserburg. Still recognizable from old film footage, the **Zeppelintribüne** on the opposite side of the Dutzendteich lake from the Kongresshalle is where Hitler would address the rally – you can climb to the podium where he stood, though the terraced structure is a bit crumbly nowadays – and where Hitler's chief architect, Albert Speer, created his famous **Lichtdom**, or light cathedral, using hundreds of searchlights; the glow was so powerful it could be seen in Prague.

Courtroom 600

The Nuremberg trials of Nazi leaders for the newly created crimes against peace, war crimes and crimes against humanity took place from November 20, 1945, to October 1, 1946, in the specially reconstructed **Courtroom 600** (Schwurgerichtsaal 600) of Nuremberg's war-damaged Justizpalast, now the **Landgericht Nürnberg-Fürth** (Bärenschanzstr. 72; U-Bahn Bärenschanze). Though it's still a working courthouse, it's usually possible to tour the courtroom at weekends, but work to create a more permanent memorial to the trials here means that it is closed to visitors until the beginning of 2010 – check with the tourist office for details.

Tiergarten Nürnberg

Light relief from the weight of historical events is at hand at the city's zoo, the **Tiergarten Nürnberg** (daily mid-March to early Oct 8am–7.30pm; early Oct to mid-March 9am–5pm; €7.50; tram #5 or bus #65), which moved to its present site in 1939 when it was evicted from its previous home by the Dutzendteich to make way for more of Albert Speer's architectural megalomania.

Still, the move was the zoo's gain, for it's unusually beautiful, lushly wooded and dotted with small lakes. The lakes provide a home for sea lions, penguins and otters, but the star of the show is the female polar bear Flocke, born here in December 2007.

Eating, drinking and nightlife

Slim, char-grilled **Nürnberger Bratwürste** are the great Nuremberg delicacy, and though the little sausages are served in high style in quite fancy restaurants, they're never more delicious than when eaten hot from a street stall *Drei im Weckla* – three in a bun; try them from *Bratwursthäusle* by the Sebalduskirche (Mon–Sat 10am–10pm). More substantial savoury dishes are often served with **Nürnberger Klösse**, the somewhat gluey potato dumplings that are, by tradition, prepared using grated raw potato before being boiled. Light they most certainly aren't, but they're good fuel on a wintery day and excellent for soaking up meaty sauces. Nuremberg's sweetly spiced **Lebkuchen** gingerbread – originally a Christmas treat but now available all year round – are on sale at Wicklein at Hauptmarkt 7 or from Schmidt nearby at Plobenhofstrasse 6. You can get gluten-free and diabetic versions from Fraunholz at Bergstrasse 1. Though Nuremberg has many excellent German restaurants, it has plenty of good ethnic choices too; there's no particular concentration of places to **eat** or **drink**, with good options scattered throughout the Altstadt. The same goes for **bars** and **clubs**, though in addition to the Altstadt's offerings there are one or two places worth venturing beyond the city walls for.

Cafés and restaurants

Bratwurst Röslein Rathausplatz 6 ℡ 0911/21 48 60. Big, buzzing, shamelessly tourist-oriented place serving Franconian specialities including – of course – *Bratwurst*, as well as the fancier options such as *Sauerbraten* with *Lebkuchen* sauce. Prices are low, turnover rapid. Open until midnight daily.

Café im Literaturhaus Luitpoldstr. 6 ℡ 0911/234 26 58. Excellent, spacious 1950s-style café with red leatherette seats, good cake and a huge selection of magazines and newspapers, plus regular literary readings. They serve breakfast here from 9am.

Essigbrätlein Weinmarkt 3 ℡ 0911/22 51 31. Simple-sounding but exciting flavour combinations without over reliance on luxury ingredients are the trademark of Andree Köthe, head chef of this gourmet temple in the northwest Altstadt. There's a midday menu for €47, with an evening set menu for €96. Closed Mon & Tues.

Estragon Jakobstr. 19 ℡ 0911/241 80 30. Stylish, gay-friendly restaurant with reasonably priced pasta, salad and veggie dishes from around €6.50, plus more substantial meaty dishes on the weekly changing menu. It's part of a social project, and has a policy of employing people with disabilities.

Heilig-Geist-Spital Spitalgasse 16 ℡ 0911/22 17 61. *Bratwurst* and affordable Franconian specialities are served with plenty of atmosphere in the historic surroundings of the former medieval hospice, and there's Franconian wine to wash it all down.

Isihara Schottengasse 3 ℡ 0911/22 63 95. Esteemed (and rather elegant) Japanese restaurant in the southern Altstadt, with set menus at €35, €38 and €49.

Klara Luitpoldstr. 3 ℡ 0911/240 38 38. The Neues Museum's elegant modern restaurant has an eclectic menu, with everything from Thai curries to *boeuf bourguignon*; main courses à la carte cost around €16, but it also does a €15 three-course set lunch.

Nassauer Keller Karolinenstr. 2–4 ℡ 0911/22 59 67. The cellar of the medieval Nassauer Haus is an atmospheric place to enjoy *Bratwürste* (€6.40 for six) or pork shoulder with potato *Klösse* (€13.50), but first you have to negotiate the extraordinarily low doorway.

Opatija Unschlittplatz 7 ℡ 0911/22 71 96. Elegant restaurant in the *Merian* hotel, with plenty of fish, plus Italian and Balkan influences on the cosmo-politan menu. Main courses €15–26.

Prison St Michel Irrerstr. 2–4 ℡ 0911/22 11 91. Quirky, French restaurant that serves up *moules*, *tarte à l'oignon* and duck *à l'orange* to Francophiles who've tired of *Bratwurst*. €15.90 set menu; open daily until 1am.

Tawan Thai Kornmarkt 4 ℡ 0911/236 96 90. Good Thai food a stone's throw from the Germanisches Nationalmuseum, with main-course dishes from around €9.50 and a few veggie options. Closed Sun.

Zum Gulden Stern Zirkelschmiedsgasse 26 ☎0911/205 92 88. The most atmospheric of all the *Bratwurst* restaurants, in an exceptionally picturesque half-timbered building on the fringe of the red-light district. They stick to what they know here, so expect a short and *Bratwurst*-dominated menu.

Zum Sudhaus Bergstr. 20 ☎0911/20 43 14. The manically cluttered exterior conceals an equally fussy interior, but this faux-rustic restaurant close to the Tiergärtner Tor has a good reputation, with the likes of calf's liver with thyme sauce or venison *Schnitzel* with *Butterspätzle* from around €19.50. Closed Sun.

Bars and clubs

Barfüsser Hausbrauerei Hallplatz 2 ☎0911/20 42 42. Vast *Hausbrauerei* in the cellar of the Mauthalle, with own-brew blonde and black beers and affordable German food; main courses from around €8.50.

Cartoon An der Sparkasse 6 ☎0911/22 71 70. Spacious lesbian and gay café-bar and smokers' club in the southern Altstadt, open until 2am daily.

Club Stereo Klaragasse 8 ☎0911/211 04 55. Hip Altstadt club, with live music and DJ nights embracing everything from indie bands to rap and trash disco.

Gelbes Haus Troststr. 10 ☎0911/28 81 06. Hip cocktail bar west of the Altstadt, with a particularly big selection of whiskies. Open weekdays until 1am, Fri & Sat until 3am.

Hausbrauerei Altstadthof Bergstr. 19 ☎0911/244 98 59. *Hausbrauerei* close to Tiergärtner Tor and the Dürer Haus, that produces four varieties of beer, including a Nuremberg *Rotbier* and a seasonal (and strong) *Maibock*. Daily 11am–1am.

Kettensteg Maxplatz 35 ☎0911/22 10 81. In the summer months there's no more alluring a *Biergarten* in Nuremberg than this, right on the river by the bridge of the same name.

Mata Hari Bar Weissgerbergasse 31 ☎0171/194 95 00. Tiny, lounge-style bar in the northwest Altstadt, with offbeat live music and DJ nights and a big whisky selection. Open until 3am Fri & Sat.

Die Rakete Vogelweiherstr. 64 ☎0911/801 53 15. Live venue and club in the industrial southern suburbs, with everything from hip-hop to reggae and dancehall. U-Bahn Frankenstrasse.

Salon Regina Fürther Str. 64 ☎0911/929 17 99. Newly trendy, vaguely studenty former *Konditorei*, now a café-bar but still preserving its wonderful, early Sixties decor. Daily 10am–1am.

Entertainment and festivals

Pick up a copy of *Plärrer* (€2) for what's on information in German. The Meistersingerhalle, Münchener Strasse 21 (☎0911/231 80 00, ⓦwww.meistersingerhalle .nuernberg.de), is the venue for **classical concerts** and **musicals**; **opera** and **ballet** are staged at the grandiose Opernhaus at Richard-Wagner-Platz 2–10 (☎0911/231 35 75, ⓦwww.staatstheater-nuernberg.de); **drama** is usually staged at the adjacent Schauspielhaus, but rebuilding work means it is being staged in various temporary venues during 2009. Nuremberg's most famous annual event is the **Christkindlesmarkt** (ⓦwww.christkindlesmarkt.de), perhaps the world's most famous Christmas market, which animates the Hauptmarkt from the end of November until Christmas Eve, but the city has a bewildering array of **festivals** throughout the year, including Klassik Open Air – a series of alfresco classical concerts by the city's two orchestras at the Luitpoldhain in July and August, and the somewhat Oktoberfest-like Altstadtfest in September. The city's tourist website has a complete list.

Eichstätt and the Naturpark Altmühltal

Few places illustrate more graphically the contrast between the capital-city airs and country-town scale of a minor German Residenzstadt than **EICHSTÄTT**, tucked into a loop in the Altmühl River in the region known as the Franconian Jura, south of Nuremberg. Even today, the little cathedral and university city is no bigger than a small market town, with a population of less than 14,000. Yet for five centuries, from 1305 until secularization at the beginning of the nineteenth century, its prince-bishops held spiritual and temporal power over a diminutive territory on Franconia's southern fringe. A Catholic stronghold during the Thirty Years' War, it paid for its piety when it was sacked by the Swedes on February 12, 1634. The Baroque reconstruction by the Italians Giacomo Angelini, Mauritio Pedetti and Gabriel de Gabrieli created the capital city in miniature that delights visitors today.

The focus of Eichstätt's "official" quarter is the **Dom**, largely fourteenth-century Gothic, though you'd scarcely know it, so completely do the later Baroque accretions wrap around it on all but the north side facing Domplatz, creating the slightly odd effect of a large ecclesiastical building with no real main facade. Inside, the most notable artwork is the richly carved eleven-metre-high limestone **Pappenheim Altar**, a gift in 1489 from Kaspar Marschall von Pappenheim in thanks for his safe return from a pilgrimage to the Holy Land. A door between the south tower and the Sakramentskapelle leads to the **Mortuarium**, though anything less like a mortuary than this lovely twin-aisled late Gothic hall with its graceful vaulting and stately central pillars is hard to imagine. At the eastern end of the Dom is the entrance to the **Domschatz und Diözesanmuseum** (cathedral treasury and museum; April–Nov Wed–Fri 10.30am–5pm, Sat & Sun 10am–5pm; €2), housed in twelve rooms above the cloisters. Its treasures include the supposed vestments of St Willibald, the Anglo-Saxon who was appointed first bishop of Eichstätt by St Boniface in 740 AD.

The Baroque **Residenzplatz** curves in spectacular fashion around the south and west sides of the Dom. It is a wonderfully uniform urban space, its elegant crescent of houses echoing the style of the **Residenz** opposite (guided tours April–Oct Mon–Thurs 11am & 3pm, Sat & Sun 10.15am, 11am, 11.45am, 2pm, 2.45pm & 3.30pm; €1), which was built in three phases from 1700 to 1777 by Jakob Engel, Gabriel de Gabrieli and Mauritio Pedetti respectively. High points of the tour are Pedetti's impressive staircase and the Spiegelsaal, or hall of mirrors, on the second floor.

Dominating the town from its site high above the Altmühl to the west is the massive **Willibaldsburg**, former seat of the prince-bishops. The castle was established in 1355 by Bishop Berthold von Zollern but owes its present appearance to Elias Holl – architect of Augsburg's Rathaus – who extended it for prince-bishop Konrad von Gemmingen between 1595 and 1612. The bishop established a celebrated botanical garden within the castle walls. Destroyed during the Thirty Years' War, in recent years it has been re-established as the **Bastiongarten**. The castle contains two museums: the **Jura Museum** (April–Sept Tues–Sun 9am–6pm; Oct–March Tues–Sun 10am–4pm; €4), which displays fossils from the region's unusually rich Jurassic limestone deposits, including a rare fossil of an *Archaeopteryx*, a type of prehistoric bird; and the **Museum für Ur- und Frühgeschichte** (same hours & price), which catalogues the region's history from the Stone Age to the early Middle Ages.

Practicalities

Eichstätt's **Bahnhof** is on the Nuremberg–Munich line some distance from town, with shuttle trains completing the last 5km to the Eichstätt-Stadt Bahnhof close to the Altstadt. The **tourist office** is at Domplatz 8 (April–Oct Mon–Sat 9am–6pm, Sun 10am–1pm; Nov–March Mon–Thurs 10am–noon & 2–4pm, Fri 10am–noon; ☎08421/600 14 00, ⓦwww.eichstaett.info), and there's an information centre for the **Naturpark Altmühltal** in the Baroque church of Notre Dame de Sacre Coeur (Easter–Oct Mon–Sat 9am–5pm; Nov–Easter Mon–Thurs 9am–noon & 2–4pm, Fri 9am–noon; ☎08421/987 60, ⓦwww.naturpark-altmuehltal.de).

The great outdoors

Goethe eulogized it. Caspar David Friedrich painted it. Even politicians saluted it when they established the world's first Green Party in 1979. A love of the great outdoors is hardwired into the national psyche, and with more than ninety nature reserves, fourteen national parks and sixteen biosphere reserves to choose from, Germans are not short of unspoilt landscapes in which to hike, cycle, ski, climb, canoe, swim, surf or simply stroll. Go explore.

Rügen's cliffs ▲

Strandkörbe at Binz on the Baltic coast ▼

Coast

Though foreigners have yet to catch on, the German coast is hugely popular at home. The choice for the bucket-and-spade brigade and stylish spa-goers alike is between the Baltic or the North seas. Along the Baltic's long coastline, fringed by powdery beaches and gently shelving shallows, most holidaymakers either take their two weeks on Rügen, famed for its white cliffs, or on quieter Üsedom, Germany's two largest islands, which bask in more hours of sunlight than anywhere else in the country.

Sylt is a very different proposition. The largest of the North Frisian islands, it's celebrated for chic villages and superb wind- and kite-surfing, its wave-washed west coast a 35km sweep of white sand. For more remote island retreats head across the mudflats to the smaller Föhr and Amrum, the latter with one of the finest beaches in Germany.

Mountains

The Bavarian Alps, stretching along its southern border, loom large in the state's identity. Legend has it that the corkscrew peaks of Berchtesgadener Land appeared when angels dropped the best bits of the world. The best-known mountain, however, is Zugspitze, a destination for skiers in winter and for views year-round – the plateau at 2964m is also accessible by cable car.

Though nowhere else compares with the Alps' sheer drama, central Germany's uplands are beloved by locals, in part because of their accessibility from urban centres. Whether it's the sandstone plateaux of the Erzgebirge in Saxon Switzerland, near Dresden; the sleepy Harz mountains, with steam trains and half-timbered villages;

or along the Rennsteig which traverses the Thuringian Forest, you'll find a super-sized adventure playground for hikes, skiing or mountain biking.

Rivers and lakes

Meandering along Germany's waterways is slow travel at its best, with boat operators scheduling regular summer sailings along the country's famed rivers. Choose from the mighty Rhine Valley studded with castles, the meandering Mosel, its banks cloaked by vineyards, the Danube, or the Elbe, which carves majestically through sandstone cliffs in Saxon Switzerland. However, for lazy boating holidays few destinations are finer than the Mecklenburg Lake District – its mosaic of reed-fringed lakes is beloved by canoeists and birdwatchers alike.

▲ Hiking along the Rennsteig, Thuringian Forest

▼ Cycling in the Black Forest

Six activity holidays

▸▸ **Hiking the Malerweg** Five-day circuit through Saxon Switzerland – expect vast panoramas with every step. See p.180
▸▸ **Skiing on Zugspitze** Astounding alpine views, and a good ski-scene based at the fashionable resort of Garmisch-Partenkirchen. See p.402
▸▸ **Mountain-biking in the Black Forest** There are plenty of biking trails across the region, which make a great way to see the area – and without a coach tour in sight. See p.504
▸▸ **Cycling the Elberadweg** An 860km odyssey, and an unparalleled taste of the nation's landscapes, as it tracks the Elbe river from Cuxhaven to Schöna. See p.210
▸▸ **Windsurfing in Westerland, Sylt** Waves on the west coast, flat-water speed-trails on the east. See p.805
▸▸ **Canoeing in the Mecklenburg Lake District** Start at Neustrelitz and spend a week on an expedition through the Land of a Thousand Lakes. See p.853

Lake Obersee, Berchtesgaden, Bavaria ▲

Saxon Switzerland ▼

Six of the best: National Parks

▶▶ **Jasmund** ⓦ www.nationalpark -jasmund.de. On the island of Rügen, celebrated for the white chalk cliffs of the Königstein. See p.836

▶▶ **Müritz** ⓦ www.nationalpark -mueritz.de. Ancient beech forest and marshland area, home to sea eagles and cranes. Lake Müritz is renowned as a boating destination. See p.852

▶▶ **Harz** ⓦ www.nationalpark-harz .de. "Pensioners' mountains", scoff Bavarians, who have the Alps in their back garden. Yet these central uplands brood rather than astound, their crags shrouded in mists and legends of witches on the Brocken (1142m). Hiking and cross-country skiing, plus charming medieval villages and vintage steam trains. See p.241

▶▶ **Saxon Switzerland** (Saechsische Schweiz), ⓦ www.nationalpark -saechsische-schweiz.de. One of the country's most distinctive landscapes, where sculpted sandstone plateaux jut above a mighty river valley. Rock-climbers adore it, but it also provides fine walks and cycling. See p.179

▶▶ **Bavarian Forest** (Bayerischer Wald), ⓦ www.nationalpark-bayerischer-wald .de. The "green roof of Europe" consists of low mountains (1456m) cloaked in pine woods that extend over the Czech border as the largest protected forest in central Europe, populated with deer, otters and pygmy owls, and popular for its mountain-bike trails. See p.414

▶▶ **Berchtesgaden** ⓦ www.nationalpark -berchtesgaden.de. The nation's only alpine park, a sublime area of soaring peaks, impossibly emerald lakes and pristine forest that is home to ibex and eagles – no wonder it is the subject of numerous legends. Provides some of the finest pistes in Germany and stupendous hiking. See p.409

Places **to stay** include the Baroque *Hotel Adler*, Marktplatz 22 (☎08421/67 67, Ⓦwww.adler-eichstaett.de; ❻), and the simpler but attractive *Ratskeller* in the same complex as the Altmühltal information centre (☎08421/90 12 58, Ⓦwww.ratskeller-eichstaett.de; ❷); it also serves food and has a *Biergarten*. The **youth hostel** is below the Willibaldsburg at Reichenaustrasse 15 (☎08421/98 04 10, Ⓦwww.jugendherberge.de; dorms €19.50 with breakfast). The *Ratskeller* aside, good places to **eat** include the attractive *Gasthaus Krone* at Domplatz 3 (☎08421/44 06; closed Wed), which specializes in Altmühltal lamb, and the *Braugasthof Trompete* at Ostenstrasse 3 (☎08421/981 70; open daily), which serves the local *Hofmühl* beer along with Bavarian and Italian food. All are reasonably priced, and there is a smattering of cafés and ice-cream parlours around town.

The Naturpark Altmühltal

The meandering valley of the River Altmühl threads its way from west to east across the three-thousand-square-kilometre **Naturpark Altmühltal**, one of Germany's largest nature reserves. Its Jurassic geology not only yields the remarkable fossils that are on display in the Willibaldsburg's Jura Museum, but also produces fascinating, sculpted landforms, such as the **Zwölf Apostel** at **Solnhofen** west of Eichstätt. The region's blend of scenic and cultural attractions makes it a popular destination for hikers and cyclists alike, and it is crisscrossed with hiking trails and cycle paths. The classic walk is the 200km **Altmühltal Panoramaweg**, which follows the course of the river, linking Gunzenhausen on the edge of the Altmühlsee in the west with Solnhofen, Eichstätt and Kelheim in the east. The gentle 166km **Altmühltal Radweg** for cyclists follows a similar route from Gunzenhausen to Kelheim. The Altmühl itself is one of the slowest-flowing rivers in Bavaria and consequently highly popular with canoeists: Johann Gegg in Dollnstein west of Eichstätt rents out **canoes** by the day (from €17; ☎08422/691, Ⓦwww.boots -verleih.com). For more information on activities in the Naturpark, contact the information centre in Eichstätt (see opposite).

Bayreuth

Though he only lived in the town for a relatively short period towards the end of his life, Richard Wagner casts a long shadow over **BAYREUTH**. For most of the world Bayreuth and Wagner are simply synonymous, as though outside the extraordinary annual social and musical spectacle known as the **Festspiele**, no other Bayreuth existed. Yet the town you actually see owes more to the passions of another remarkable individual, the Markgräfin Wilhelmine (1709–58). The eldest daughter of Friedrich Wilhelm I of Prussia and the sister of Frederick the Great, Wilhelmine was groomed by her Hanoverian mother for marriage into the British royal family. But the plans were thwarted by her father, who – partly for political reasons, partly out of loathing for his wife's British relatives – married her off instead to a minor royal and distant relative, Friedrich von Brandenburg-Bayreuth, the future margrave of the insignificant Franconian micro-state of the same name. Despite its unpromising start, the marriage was a happy one, and with her aspirations to enter the glittering world of the London court thwarted, the intelligent and educated Wilhelmine decided instead to bring worldly sophistication to Bayreuth, embarking on an extravagant building programme whose fruits still grace the town today. Wagner's Festspielhaus may have a superb acoustic, but it's notoriously spartan; Wilhelmine's opera house, on the other hand, is a Baroque gem. Her **Baroque quarter** of town wraps itself around the eastern and

EATING & DRINKING
Café Müller an der Oper 4
Eiscafé San Remo 2
Engins Ponte 1
Goldener Anker C
Podium im Gerberhaus 5
Porsch 3
Richters 6

ACCOMMODATION
Bayreuther Hof E
DJH Bayreuth F
Eremitage D
Goldener Anker C
Goldener Hirsch A
Lohmühle B

BAYREUTH

southern sides of the diminutive **Altstadt** – all small and compact enough to be explored easily on foot. The extensive **Hofgarten** stretches east from the centre to Wagner's **Villa Wahnfried**, while his **Festspielhaus** is on high ground north of the centre. It's also worth venturing out of town to see Wilhelmine's summer pleasure palace, **Eremitage**.

Bayreuth is quite the paparazzi hotspot during the Festspiele in late July and August, when the most surprising celebrities can be seen affecting an interest in the *Ring*. For the rest of the year, it is a quiet and stolidly respectable sort of place, but Wilhelmine's magic ensures it's worth a stay of a day or two.

Arrival, information and accommodation

Hourly trains from Nuremberg serve Bayreuth's **Hauptbahnhof**, north of the town centre, from which a short walk down Bahnhofstrasse brings you to Luitpoldplatz and the **tourist office** at no. 9 (Mon–Fri 9am–6pm, Sat 9am–2pm; May–Oct also Sun 10am–2pm; ☎0921/885 88, ⓦ www.bayreuth-tourismus.de). You can book **accommodation** through the tourist office website, or they'll happily book it for you; they can also sell you a three-day **Bayreuth Card** (€11.50), which grants free museum entry and use of the town's buses. You can also rent an **iGuide** (3hr €8) which takes you on a self-guided tour of the town. **Bike rental** is available at Radgarten, Friedrichstrasse 40 (☎0921/169 19 01).

Bayreuther Hof Rathenaustr. 28 ☎ 0921/50 70 45
60, ⓦ www.bayreuther-hof.de. Good-value, modern
double rooms above a *Gaststätte* west of the
Hofgarten. Prices are higher during the Festspiele. ❹
DJH Bayreuth Universitätsstr. 28 ☎ 0921/76 43
80, ⓦ www.bayreuth.jugendherberge.de. Modern
hostel a short distance southeast of the Hofgarten
and close to the university. Dorms from €18.40
with breakfast.
Eremitage Eremitage 6 ☎ 0921/79 99 70,
ⓦ www.eremitage-bayreuth.de. Individually styled
rooms at this elegant restaurant in the grounds of
Schloss Eremitage, east of town. ❹–❻
🏃 Goldener Anker Opernstr. 6 ☎ 0921/ 650
51, ⓦ www.anker-bayreuth.de. Very

handsome and central hotel, family-run since 1753,
with spacious, individually styled rooms, period
furnishings and bathrooms and an attractive Art
Deco restaurant. There's no lift. ❺
Goldener Hirsch Bahnhofstr. 13 ☎ 0921/15 04
40 00, ⓦ www.bayreuth-goldener-hirsch.de.
Independently run place, comfortable if slightly
dated, in a convenient location between the
town centre and Festspielhaus, and with some
singles. ❹
Lohmühle Badstr. 37 ☎ 0921/530 60, ⓦ www
.hotel-lohmuehle.de. In an old half-timbered
watermill a short walk east of the town centre, with
a good restaurant. Prices are considerably higher
during the Festspiele. ❺

The Baroque city

Wilhelmine's cultural ambitions were nurtured with more than a backward
glance at her beloved brother's court in Berlin. If Frederick the Great entertained Voltaire, then so must she, and if Berlin had an opera house then so, too,
must Bayreuth. Only the best would do, and so Wilhelmine commissioned the
renowned Italian theatre designer Giuseppe Galli Bibiena and his son, Carlo, for
the job. The results left Bayreuth look Berlin in the eye, for the **Markgräfliches
Opernhaus** (daily: April–Sept 9am–6pm; Oct–March 10am–4pm; sound and
light show every 45min; €5) is commonly regarded as one of the most beautiful
surviving Baroque theatres in Europe. The handsome but relatively restrained
exterior gives no hint of the opulence within; once inside, you take a seat and
let the music wash over you. The Opernhaus was inspected – and rejected as too
small – by Wagner, but it is nevertheless still a functioning opera house.

Close by, court architect, Frenchman Joseph Saint-Pierre, built the
Schlosskirche, or court chapel, from 1753 to 1758. Wilhelmine died the year it
was completed and is buried in a vault in the church's delicate Rococo interior,
along with her husband and daughter, Friederike, Duchess of Württemberg.
The octagonal Schlossturm attached to the church dates from 1565 and offers
good views across the town to the Fichtelgebirge from the top (€1 by prior
arrangement; enquire at tourist office). Alongside the church is the **Altes Schloss**,
a fine seventeenth-century Baroque pile whose partial destruction by fire in 1753
gave Wilhelmine the impetus to commission its splendid replacement, the **Neues
Schloss** (April–Sept daily 9am–6pm; Oct–March Tues–Sun 10am–4pm; €5, or €8
with Markgräfliches Opernhaus), a short walk to the south along Ludwigstrasse.
Once again, the job was entrusted to court architect Joseph Saint-Pierre. The
long, low facade is gracious enough, but is on a scale sympathetic to the town,
and it gives no clue to the heights of Rococo refinement within, which reach a
peak of inventiveness and flair in rooms such as the **Spiegelscherbenkabinett**,
where seemingly random fragments of mirror adorn a chinoiserie design – look
out for Wilhelmine herself, portrayed as a tea-drinking Chinese woman receiving
documents from a servant. A gold ceiling and stuccoed mussel shells adorn
the grotto-like neighbouring room where Wilhelmine would retire to read;
Wilhelmine once again puts in an appearance in Oriental guise in the ceiling of
the graceful **Japanisches Zimmer**. Most inventive of all is perhaps the **Palmenzimmer**, where gilded and carved palm trees sprout from the walnut-panelled
walls. The ground floor of the Schloss contains an exhibition on **Wilhelmine's
Bayreuth**, a collection of **Bayreuth faïence** and a branch of the Bavarian state

art collection, displaying seventeenth- and eighteenth-century works including some from the Dutch "golden age" around 1700.

West of the Neues Schloss at Jean-Paul-Platz, Ludwigstrasse intersects with **Friedrichstrasse**, the most elegant street in Bayreuth, full of noble stone houses, one of which houses the renowned **Steingraeber** piano company, whose elegant premises are one of the venues for a piano festival in July.

The Hofgarten and Villa Wahnfried

Behind the Neues Schloss, the **Hofgarten** (free access) was planned in classic Baroque style with parterres, pergolas and a canal as a central axis. It was later redesigned in informal English style, but it still preserves the canal with its right turn and central islands, and the parterre in front of the south wing of the Schloss was restored in 1990.

It's just a short stroll through the Hofgarten to the **Villa Wahnfried**, Richard Wagner's imposing, if not especially big, villa. It was sponsored by his patron, "mad" King Ludwig II of Bavaria, and designed largely by Wagner himself. This was his principal home from 1874 until his death in 1883, though he spent long periods away from it, particularly in Italy, where he died. An inscription on the street facade proclaims: "Here, where my delusions found peace, I name this house named 'Peace from Delusion'." Badly damaged in the closing weeks of World War II, when the side facing the Hofgarten was demolished, it was restored to its original appearance in the 1970s. It now houses the **Richard Wagner Museum** (daily: April–Oct 9am–5pm; Nov–March 10am–5pm; €4; English guidebook €2), a comprehensive but rather dry chronicle of the composer's life, whose glass-case-and-typescript display style is heavy going and which, far from demystifying this famously difficult musical genius, seems content to function as a rather dusty shrine – an impression lent further credence by the fact that the composer is buried, along with his wife Cosima and his favourite dog, in the back garden. The reconstructed drawing room is used for concerts, but as you wander through the museum there's no opportunity to hear any excerpts from the operas whose staging is explained in such exhaustive detail, which seems a shame.

Cosima Wagner's father was the composer **Franz Liszt**, and there's a small museum (daily: July & Aug 10am–5pm; Sept–June 10am–noon & 2–5pm; €1.60) to his memory in the neighbouring house at Wahnfriedstrasse 9 where he died.

The Altstadt and around

After the Baroque grace of Wilhelmine's Bayreuth and the *Sturm und Drang* of Wagner's life, the charm of Bayreuth's **Altstadt** lies in its modesty. Narrow lanes huddle around the **Stadtkirche**, the town's Lutheran parish church, rebuilt after a disastrous town fire in 1605. Surprisingly, the builder, Michael Mebart, chose to rebuild in the original Gothic rather than in a more contemporary style. The church was being restored at the time of writing, and access is limited. On the north side of the church at Kirchplatz 6 is Bayreuth's local history museum, the **Historisches Museum** (July & Aug daily 10am–5pm; Sept–June Tues–Sun 10am–5pm; €1.60), housed in a seventeenth-century schoolhouse and whose exhibits include a display on Hitler's bizarre plans for the town, which as the home of his beloved Wagner and the Festspiele was highly favoured by the regime.

Just to the north is Maximilianstrasse, Bayreuth's main shopping street. In the Renaissance **Altes Rathaus** at no. 33, the **Kunstmuseum Bayreuth** (Tues–Sun

10am–5pm, July & Aug also Mon 10am–5pm; €1.60) shows a changing selection of the municipal art collection and shares the premises with the **Tabakhistorische Sammlung der British American Tobacco** (same hours & ticket), tobacco production being an important local industry. Further west along Maximilianstrasse, it's worth quickly visiting the small but exceptionally pretty **Spitalkirche**, another of Joseph Saint-Pierre's works.

A few minutes' walk from the Altstadt at Kulmbacher Strasse 40, you can tour a handsome nineteenth-century brewery and cooperage at **Maisel's Brauerei- und Büttnerei Museum** (tours daily at 2pm; €4); in addition to the original brewing equipment, there's a vast selection of beer glasses and enamel advertisements. The hour-long tour ends with a glass of Maisel's *Weissbier*.

The Festspielhaus

Richard Wagner first considered Bayreuth as a candidate for the site of his **Festspiele** because of the unusually large stage at the Markgräfliches Opernhaus, but he rejected it as unsuitable after a visit in April 1871. He was, however, taken with the town itself, and so decided to make his home in the town and to build a festival theatre here. Proposals already existed by Gottfried Semper – architect of the Dresden opera house and of the Burgtheater in Vienna – for a grandiose opera house in Munich, but in the event a far more spartan design was selected for the Bayreuth **Festspielhaus** (tours Tues–Sun 10am, 11am, 2pm & 3pm; no tours Nov or during rehearsals, and limited availability during Festspiele; €5; bus #5 from Luitpoldplatz), which stands on a low hill north of the town centre at Festspielhügel 1–2. Wagner – who intended the building to be provisional – was the driving force behind the concept, and his own notes on the blueprints declared "away with the ornaments". True to his word, the builders produced an auditorium with magnificent acoustics but no creature comforts – the orchestra is concealed to preserve sight lines, and to preserve the unique acoustic, the audience sit on wooden benches – thus ensuring that they, too, suffer for Wagner's art.

▲ Bronze of Wagner, Festspielhaus, Bayreuth

Eremitage

East of town, Margrave Georg Wilhelm – Friedrich's uncle – laid out a park and Schloss known as the Eremitage (or Hermitage) from 1715 onwards as a place where he and his court could live a simple life, dressing in monks' habits, sleeping in cells and eating soup from brown earthenware bowls. When Friedrich acceded as Margrave in 1735 he gifted this house, now known as the **Altes Schloss** (guided tours daily: April–Sept 9am–6pm; first two weeks Oct 10am–4pm; €3; bus #2 from Markt) to Wilhelmine. She immediately set about having the Schloss extended, creating a series of magnificent Rococo rooms that eschewed Georg Wilhelm's original austerity without actually eradicating it. The Altes Schloss is closed for restoration until late 2009, but in the meantime a combined tour of the park, water tower and Georg Wilhelm's handsome Marmorsaal is offered. From around 1750, Wilhelmine set about replanning the park, building a crescent-shaped Orangerie as a centrepiece, now known as the **Neues Schloss** (same hours & ticket), focal point of which is the domed, circular Sonnentempel, topped with a gilded representation of Apollo's chariot – with the clear intention of glorifying Friedrich as the Apollo of his day. Trick fountains in the Oberes Bassin play hourly from May to October, and ten minutes later in the Untere Grotte.

Eating and drinking

Good places to **eat** and **drink** are scattered about the centre of Bayreuth, with some of the best restaurants in the hotels.

Café Müller an der Oper Opernstr. 16. ☏0921/507 14 21. Elegant coffee-and-cake haunt next to the Opernhaus that also serves light savoury dishes including pasta and *Bratwurst*. Closed Tues.

Eiscafé San Remo Maximilianstr. 26 ☏0921/608 08 99. Big, bright Italian-run *gelateria* with excellent ice cream and cakes.

Engins Ponte am Canale Grande Opernstr. 24 ☏0921/871 05 03. Large, modern café/bar with pasta and pizza from around €6.50, and a breakfast buffet (9am–2pm) at weekends.

Goldener Anker Opernstr. 6 ☏0921/650 51. The *Goldener Anker*'s smart, Art Deco French restaurant serves the likes of grilled lobster tails with rocket

or tagliatelle with scampi and basil; three courses €39, four courses €54.

Podium Im Gerberhaus Gerberplatz 1 ☏0921/653 83. Music bar with regular live jazz, country and open stage sessions, plus poetry slams and improv nights. Open until 3am Fri & Sat.

Porsch Maximilianstr. 63. ☏0921/646 49. Traditional *Gaststätte* with *Stöckel* beer and affordable German staples such as *Leberkäse* (similar to meatloaf) or *Schnitzel*, until 10pm daily. There's a *Biergarten* in summer.

Richters Friedrichstr. 10 ☏0921/507 58 80. Elegant restaurant, café and cocktail bar using fresh, seasonal local produce, with main courses from around €17.

Festivals

Tickets for the **Festspiele** (ⓦwww.bayreuther-festspiele.de) in late July and August are famously hard to come by: you must write (no emails or faxes) to Kartenbüro, Postfach 100262, D-95402 Bayreuth, in September of the previous year just to apply for tickets, and in practice it will be several years before you stand any chance of actually getting them, since the event is hugely oversubscribed. During the festival itself, any returns are available on the day at the box office from 1.30pm to 4pm; many performances start as early as 4pm because of the great length of Wagner's operas. Bayreuth's other festivals include **Musica Bayreuth** at the Markgräfliches Opernhaus in early May (ⓦwww.musica-bayreuth.de) and the **Fränkische Festwoche** in late May and early June at the same venue. The **Bayreuther Klavierfestival** (Bayreuth Piano Festival; ⓦwww.steingraeber.de) is in July. The **Bayreuther Volksvest** is a folk festival at Whitsun, with fairground rides, beer and live music.

Kulmbach

With a modest Altstadt cowering beneath a mighty hilltop fortress, **KULMBACH** illustrates in built form the power structures of feudal *Mitteleuropa* with great clarity. The fortress in question, the Plassenburg, was the seat of the Franconian branch of the Hohenzollerns from 1338 until they upped sticks for Bayreuth in 1604, and thus Kulmbach – which is otherwise an unpretentious, provincial sort of place with none of Bayreuth's arty airs – can in one respect claim seniority over its southern neighbour.

The **Plassenburg** (daily: April–Sept 9am–6pm; Oct–March 10am–4pm; €10 day-ticket or €4 for each museum) is both a fortress and a royal residence, and once through its forbidding portals it's the latter that is dominant, above all in the arcaded, richly decorated **Schöner Hof**, or "beautiful courtyard", part of a redesign commissioned by Margrave Georg Friedrich following the destruction of much of the castle and town in 1553, after the ambitions of the warlike Margrave Albrecht Alcibiades to unite all Franconia under his rule ended in ignominy, with Protestant Nuremberg and Catholic Bamberg and Würzburg uniting in common cause to thwart him. Construction according to Caspar Vischer's master plan began in 1557 and the results are considered among the masterpieces of the German Renaissance. The Schöner Hof is the venue for concerts in summer.

The castle contains three museums. In the east wing, the **Staatliche Sammlungen** comprises the **Hohenzollern in Franken** exhibition in the early sixteenth-century state apartments (entry by guided tour) and the **Armeemuseum Friedrich der Grosse** (same ticket), which displays weaponry from the Prussian army from 1700 to 1806. The east wing also contains the **Schlosskapelle**, one of the oldest Franconian Protestant churches; the Hohenzollerns took the Protestant side in the Reformation, and later encouraged Protestant Huguenot settlers from France.

In the west wing, the **Landschaftsmuseum Obermain** is a folk museum for the Obermain region with sections on the destruction and subsequent rebuilding of Kulmbach, plus the **Pörbitscher Schatz** – a collection of Augsburg and Nuremberg silverware buried for safekeeping by a Kulmbach patrician family during the Thirty Years' War and only rediscovered in 1912.

The third museum is the **Deutsche Zinnfigurenmuseum**, the world's largest collection of miniature tin figures, with 30,000 of them arranged in a hundred and fifty dioramas that re-create significant events from history, including the world's largest diorama, which depicts Kulmbach's destruction in 1552.

Hiking around Kulmbach

One of Kulmbach's charms is its remote and unspoilt natural setting, sandwiched between the **Naturpark Frankenwald** to the north – thickly forested and cut through with deep valleys – and the **Fränkische Schweiz** ("Franconian Switzerland") to the south and west, whose limestone outcrops and show caves constitute a classic karst landscape. The 500km **Frankenweg** long-distance hiking trail traverses Frankenwald, reaching its highest point, the 794m Döbraberg, before passing through Kulmbach on its way south through the Fränkische Schweiz. An east–west route, the **Mainwanderweg**, passes through Kulmbach on its way from the source of the river in the Fichtelgebirge mountains east of the town to its confluence with the Rhine west of Frankfurt. A similar long-distance route for cyclists, the **Main-Radweg**, also passes through Kulmbach on its way west. The tourist office in Kulmbach can provide information.

A **shuttle bus**, the Plassenburg-Express, links the town's central car park by the tourist office with the Plassenburg twice an hour (€1.80); otherwise, you can make the ascent on foot up Festungsberg from the Altstadt, but there is no car park.

Kulmbach's **Altstadt** tumbles down the lower slopes between the Plassenburg and the modern town centre. **Obere Stadt** is the steep main street, lined with tall, gabled houses, but **Rentamtsgässchen** behind it is more picturesque, with the half-timbered **Roter Turm** and the impressive **Amtshof** of the Langheim monastery, built in the seventeenth century by Leonhard Dientzenhofer, architect of Bamberg's Michelsberg monastery and a member of the Bavarian Dientzenhofer architectural dynasty. At the foot of the Altstadt, the prettily Rococo **Rathaus** presides over Marktplatz, with figures symbolizing wisdom and justice on either side of its gable.

Kulmbach is a renowned brewing centre – its EKU 28 beer was for many years the world's strongest – so it's worth making the short stroll north from the Altstadt to the **Bayerisches Brauereimuseum** at Hofer Strasse 20 (Tues–Sun 10am–5pm; May–Oct open from 9am Sat & Sun; €4.50), where in addition to an exhibit of brewing techniques from around 1900 there's a section on beer in history, from the ancient Egyptians onwards.

Practicalities

Trains from Bayreuth take about 35 minutes to reach Kulmbach's **Bahnhof**, from which it's a short walk to the helpful **tourist office** at Sutte 2 (May–Oct Mon–Fri 9am–6pm, Sat 10am–1pm; Nov–April Mon–Fri 10am–5pm; ℡09221/958 80, ⓦwww.kulbach.de). The *Weisses Ross*, Am Marktplatz 12 (℡09221/956 50, ⓦwww.weisses-ross-kulmbach.com; ❸), is a comfortable, central place to **stay**; the *Kronprinz*, Fischergasse 4–6 (℡09221/921 80, ⓦwww .kronprinz-kulmbach.de; ❸), offers similar levels of comfort and is almost as central. ⚘ *Zunftstube* at Obere Stadt 4 (℡09221/833 77) serves reasonably priced, hearty Franconian **food** and local beer; you could also try the smarter *Stadtschänke*, Holzmarkt 3 (℡09221/45 07), with *Kulmbacher Bratwurst* on the menu along with local *Mönchshof* and *Kapuziner* beers. The *Hausbrauerei, Kulmbacher Kommunbräu*, at Grünwehr 17 (℡0921/844 90), is also a good choice for Franconian food to accompany the in-house beers. Of Kulmbach's various **festivals**, the one not to miss is the Kulmbacher Bierwoche, which starts on the last weekend in July and lasts nine days.

Coburg

The history of **COBURG** is intimately bound up with that of its ducal family, a branch of the Wettin dynasty whose most distinguished member was Elector Friedrich the Wise, champion and protector of Martin Luther. Excommunicated and outlawed in the Holy Roman Empire, Luther stayed at the Veste Coburg fortress above the town for six months during the Diet of Augsburg in 1530 under the protection of Friedrich's brother and successor, Johann the Steadfast. Though he was banned from attending, Luther used messengers to stay in touch with the Diet's negotiations on the fate of the Reformation, which led to the Augsburg Confession, a foundation stone of the Protestant Church. Their loyalty to the Protestant cause cost the Wettins their Electoral status; as mere dukes they thereafter ruled a modest territory from Coburg, extended to include the Saxon duchy of Gotha in 1826, after which they were known as dukes of Saxe-Coburg and Gotha. Modest though their domain was, they pursued a highly successful "marriage offensive", marrying their offspring into the great royal houses of Europe, including those of Belgium, Portugal, Bulgaria and Sweden. The most famous marriage of all was that of Prince Albert, younger son of Duke Ernst I, to his cousin Queen Victoria in 1840.

Though its historic links to Thuringia and Saxony are strong, Coburg's inhabitants voted against union with Thuringia after World War I, and the town became Bavarian. Even so, with the Thüringer Wald just to the north and a postwar history of economic stagnation that is now happily being reversed, this strongly Protestant town has much in common with its near-neighbours in former East Germany. It's a very handsome place, with a small but attractive **Altstadt** – barely 500m across – fringed by some fine examples of Jugendstil. **Schloss Ehrenburg** – the town residence of Coburg's dukes until 1918 – is on its eastern fringe facing **Schlossplatz**, from where it's a stiff 1km walk uphill to **Veste Coburg**, the town's major attraction and one of the largest medieval castles in Germany. Further afield, you might wish to venture east of town to see **Schloss Rosenau**, birthplace of Prince Albert.

Arrival, information and accommodation

Coburg's **Hauptbahnhof** is about ten minutes' walk northwest of the Altstadt, where the **tourist office** is off the Markt at Herrngasse 4 (April–Oct Mon–Fri 9am–6pm, Sat 9am–1pm; Nov–March Mon–Fri 9am–5pm, Sat 9am–1pm; ☏09561/741 80, ⊛www.coburg-tourist.de). Coburg has a reasonable selection of places to **stay**, particularly in the mid-range, with a few options in the Altstadt itself,

DJH Coburg Parkstr. 2 ☏09561/153 30, ⊛www .coburg.jugendherberge.de. Youth hostel in a beautiful nineteenth-century villa 20min walk from the Altstadt, with three- to six-bed dorms and a disco. Dorms €18.10.

Goldener Anker Rosengasse 14 ☏09561/557 00, ⊛www.goldener-anker.de. Spacious and comfortable, if slightly characterless, rooms with bath or shower, WC and wi-fi, close to the Rathaus. ➍

Goldene Traube Am Viktoriabrunnen 2 ☏09561/87 60, ⊛www.goldenetraube.com. Coburg's "grand hotel", with attractive, individually

styled rooms behind a handsome nineteenth-century facade on the edge of the Alstadt. ➎–➐

Münchner Hofbräu Kleine Johannisgasse 8 ☏09561/23 49 23, ⊛www.coburg -muenchnerhofbraeu.de. Plain but simple and attractive rooms above a pub in the Altstadt. ➌

Ringhotel Stadt Coburg Lossaustr. 12 ☏09561/87 40, ⊛www.hotel-stadt-coburg.de. Comfortable three-star hotel handy for the Hauptbahnhof, with a sauna and solarium plus guest parking. Singles, doubles and suites have cable TV, minibar and internet connection. ➍

The Altstadt

Three of the original town gates – the **Spitaltor**, **Judentor** and **Ketschentor** – still guard the entrance to Coburg's compact Altstadt, whose centrepiece is the spacious market place, Markt, with a statue of **Prince Albert** in the centre and, on the north side, the **Stadthaus**, a late Renaissance chancery built under Duke Johann Casimir from 1597 to 1601 and with richly coloured *Coburger Erker* – two-storeyed oriel windows; look out also for the carved heads on the corner facing Herrngasse. On the south side of the square, the stately **Rathaus** cloaks its Renaissance pedigree behind playful Rococo ornament that dates from a 1750 rebuild, but a characteristic *Erker* window remains; its neighbour, the **Sparkasse**, is frothily Rococo. On the east side of the square, the **Hofapotheke**, or court pharmacy, dates from before 1500 and still performs its original function. Just to the south, the fifteenth-century **Münzenmeisterhaus** on Ketschengasse is the oldest and most impressive half-timbered house in Coburg. To the east of here, the splendid Renaissance gable of the **Casimirianum** – a grammar school founded in 1605 – faces the west front of **St Moriz**, Coburg's main Protestant church, a slightly lopsided affair with one tower shorter than the other. Luther preached here during his stay at the Veste Coburg; the interior was given a rather bleak Baroque makeover in the eighteenth century.

On the eastern side of the Altstadt at the foot of the Hofgarten – the park that leads up to the Veste Coburg – is the dignified **Schlossplatz**. On its north side, the neo-Renaissance **Palais Edinburgh** is so named because it was the home of Alfred, Duke of Edinburgh – a son of Queen Victoria – until he inherited the title of Duke of Saxe-Coburg and Gotha from his childless uncle Ernst II in 1893. Next to it stands the elegant **Landestheater**, which dates from 1840; a statue of **Duke Ernst I** – Prince Albert's father – presides over the square's pretty central garden. In summer, Schlossplatz is the venue for **open-air concerts** by big-name acts.

Schloss Ehrenburg

Coburg's dynastic link with Britain is mirrored in the neo-Tudor appearance of **Schloss Ehrenburg** (guided tours hourly Tues–Sun: April–Sept 9am–5pm; Oct–March 10am–3pm; €4), which dominates the south side of Schlossplatz. The facade is the work of Germany's greatest nineteenth-century architect, Karl Friedrich Schinkel, but it conceals a much older structure, commissioned in 1543 on the site of a defunct Franciscan monastery by Duke Johann Ernst and dubbed Ehrenburg – "castle of honour" – by the emperor Charles V because it was completed without compulsory labour; it was subsequently extended under Duke Johann Casimir. Traces of the Renaissance Schloss survive in the south facade, but a catastrophic fire in 1690 swept away much of the rest, and Duke Albrecht commissioned Italian artists to create sumptuous interiors, of which the **Schlosskapelle** and ornate **Festsaal** survive. The latter is known as the **Riesensaal**, or "giants' hall" on account of the 28 atlas figures who seem to shore up the immense weight of its heavy stucco ceiling. In contrast, the **Thronsaal** – a copy of Napoleon's throne room at the Tuileries Palace – and the private apartments date from the nineteenth century and are in French Empire style. Queen Victoria was a frequent guest, and the tour visits the room in which she stayed.

The Veste Coburg

On the east side of Schlossplatz, steps lead up the stone-built **Arkaden** into the spacious **Hofgarten**, through which it's a pleasant – but increasingly steep – twenty-minute walk up to the **Veste Coburg**, the massive fortress that dominates the town; the latter part of the walk is up long flights of steps. Alternatively, bus #5 links the Veste with the town centre.

The "Coberg", or site of the castle, is first mentioned in 1065, and it passed into Wettin hands in 1353. The oldest surviving part of the complex is the slate-roofed, onion-domed thirteenth-century **Blauer Turm**; of the massive stone buildings that form the castle's inner core, the **Hohes Haus**, which dates from the fourteenth and fifteenth centuries, is the oldest. The bastions and towers visible from the exterior create a sombre and forbidding impression, but once you're in the castle precincts its residential function is more readily apparent, and the stonework is softened by trees and greenery.

The Veste's interior houses the ducal art collection, the **Kunstsammlungen der Veste Coburg** (April–Oct daily 9.30am–5pm; Nov–March Tues–Sun 1–4pm; €5, audio guide €1.50; Ⓦ www.kunstsammlungen-coburg.de). You enter via the **Fürstenbau**, which contains the so-called **historic rooms**, apartments created in the early years of the twentieth century for the English-born Carl Eduard, last Duke of Saxe-Coburg and Gotha, who lost his English titles as a result of fighting on the German side in World War I and later became a committed Nazi. The objects on display here include Prince Albert's baby clothes; on the second floor, the wood-panelled **Cranachzimmer** contains a number of paintings by Lucas Cranach the Elder.

The next building, the **Steinerne Kemenate**, or Stone Bower, is accessed directly from the Fürstenbau and is the highlight of the museum. On its second floor is the **Jagdintarsienzimmer** (Hunting Marquetery Room), a *tour de force* of richly ornamented late Renaissance woodcarving, commissioned by Duke Johann Casimir in 1632 and with sixty inlaid panels depicting hunting scenes. The **Georg Schäfer collection** of medieval German art is displayed on this floor, and includes Matthias Grünewald's *Last Supper*, Lucas Cranach the Elder's *St Mary Magdalene and St Elizabeth* from 1515 and Hans Holbein the Younger's *Portrait of Lady Rich*. Among the sculptures, the so-called *Coburg Pietà* (1360–70) is of either Franconian or Thuringian origin. On the first floor is the **Grosse Hofstube**, or banqueting hall, built between 1501 and 1504 and displaying elaborate suits of armour, as well as the **Lutherzimmer** – the rooms in which Martin Luther lived and worked from April to October 1530. In the **Lutherstube**, you can see a portrait of Luther from the workshop of Lucas Cranach the Elder.

The adjacent **Carl-Eduard-Bau** contains the museum's print and glass collections: the former including works by the anonymous Master of the Coburg Roundels, the latter everything from sixteenth-century Venetian glass to beautifully decorative Art Nouveau items. Beyond it, the sixteenth-century **Herzoginbau** houses suits of armour beneath its spectacular rafters and, on its lower floors, hunting rifles and an impressive array of carriages and sledges, including a pair of sixteenth-century wedding carriages and a coach that may have belonged to Queen Victoria.

Schloss Rosenau

Set in an English-style landscaped park east of Coburg, **Schloss Rosenau** (guided tours hourly Tues–Sun: April–Sept 9am–5pm; Oct–March Tues–Sun 10am–3pm; €4; train or bus #8311 or #8322 to Rödental, then BusStadt bus from there) was a ruin when it was acquired by the ducal family in 1805. Rebuilt between 1808 and 1817 in a pretty neo-Gothic style inspired by the young Schinkel, it was here that Prince Albert was born in 1819. In 1845 he returned with his wife, Queen Victoria, who was so enchanted by the picturesque Schloss that she wrote in her diary "If I were not who I am, my real home would be here."

Eating, drinking and entertainment

Coburg's Altstadt has its fair share of good places to **eat** and **drink**, with some atmospheric traditional options alongside more international offerings. Coburg's *Bratwürste* – traditionally cooked over a pine-cone fire – are particularly fine; there's usually a 🍢 stall selling them on Markt. The **Landestheater** at Schlossplatz 6 (☎09561/89 89 89, ⊛www.landestheater-coburg.de) is the place to see opera, operetta, ballet and drama. Somewhat improbably, Coburg hosts Europe's biggest samba **festival** in July (⊛www.samba-festival.de).

Bratwurstglöckle Kleine Johannisgasse 5 ☎09561/752 70. Atmospheric, traditional *Gaststätte*, with painted, vaulted ceilings and a huge menu offering everything from salad to *Schnitzel*. Closed Mon.

Eiscafé Cortina Spitalgasse 29 ☎09561/926 84. Italian-style *gelateria*, established in 1953 and selling frozen yoghurt as well as ice cream. Summer only.

Esszimmer At the *Goldene Traube*, Am Viktoriabrunnen 2 ☏ 09561/87 60. Intimate and luxurious gourmet restaurant, with the likes of foie gras with peach or medallions of salmon with saffron *gelée* and herring caviar; three courses €49, four courses €62. There's also a more informal wine bar, *Weinstübla*.
Goldenes Kreuz Herrngasse 1 ☏ 09561/51 34 07. A classily dark, wood-panelled interior and a menu

of Franconian and seasonal dishes – with apricot dumplings to finish – next to the Stadthaus. Open daily until midnight.
Loreley Herrngasse 14 ☏ 09561/23 55 99. Rustic place behind a delightful *Luftmalerei* (painted) facade opposite Schloss Ehrenburg, with steaks, *Schnitzels*, Coburg specialities and, in season, game. From around €9. Closed Mon.

Vierzehnheiligen and Kloster Banz

Lonely and proud on its hilltop site overlooking the Main Valley on the northwestern edge of Fränkische Schweiz, the pilgrimage church of **Vierzehnheiligen** (daily: summer 6.30am–6.30pm; winter 7.30am–5.30pm) is one of the masterpieces of southern German late Baroque and Rococo. Standing on the pilgrims' route to Santiago de Compostela, the church replaced an earlier structure at the place where during 1445 and 1446 Hermann Leicht, a shepherd at the Cistercian abbey of Langheim near Lichtenfels, had visions of a crying child. The third time the child appeared to him, it was accompanied by the fourteen Holy Helpers – a group of saints whose intercession is often invoked in Catholicism – who told Leicht they wanted a chapel to be built on the site. Soon afterwards the first miracle was reported and the site became a place of pilgrimage.

Vierzehnheiligen was designed by **Balthasar Neumann**, the architect of Würzburg's Residenz. Construction began in 1723 but the church was not consecrated until 1772, nineteen years after Neumann's death. His plans were nevertheless adhered to, and the results impress long before you reach the twintowered church, for it can be seen from a distance as you ascend from the valley. It is built of a particularly warm, gold-coloured stone, but even so the noble exterior is no preparation for the dazzling Rococo vision within, a symphony of white, gold and grey that is sure to lift your spirits, whatever your feelings about the legend that created it. The church is of cathedral-like proportions, its interior focused on Johann Michael Feichtmayr's central **Gnadenaltar**, built on the site of Hermann Leicht's vision and with statues of the fourteen helpers, some eye-catchingly gory: **St Denis**, patron saint of those with headaches, is portrayed with his head tucked under his arm; **St Pantaleon**, with his hands nailed to his head. In the Franciscan monastery next door, there's a **multimedia show** (daily: summer 8am–7.30pm; winter 8am–6.30pm; free) which picks out some of the exquisite architectural detail, and a shop where you can buy an English-language guide (€3).

Facing Vierzehnheiligen across the valley is the former Benedictine monastery of **Kloster Banz**, built from the same honey-coloured stone on a similarly commanding site high above the valley. It was designed by Leonhard Dientzenhofer to replace the previous abbey, wrecked by Swedish troops during the Thirty Years' War; the **church** (guided tours daily by appointment: May–Oct 9am–5pm; Nov–April 9am–4pm; donation requested; ☏ 09573/73 11) was consecrated in 1719, and its interior surprises because it is based on a series of ellipses. Though it's undoubtedly a fine piece of architecture, Banz doesn't dazzle the visitor in quite the way Vierzehnheiligen does, but if you're visiting Vierzehnheiligen with your own transport it's certainly worth a look. If you can't join a tour, the church is usually open as far as the grille; the rest of the abbey is a conference and education centre.

Practicalities

Trains link Coburg (20–25min) and Bamberg (18–30min) with Lichtenfels in the valley below Vierzehnheiligen, from which **bus** #6 (twice daily: April–Oct Mon–Sat; Nov–March Tues, Wed & Thurs only) makes the journey up to the church. There's a large **car park** halfway up the hill to the church, though at off-peak times you should be able to park by the church itself. There's a scattering of places to **eat** and **drink** by the church, including the *Klosterbrauerei Trunk* (℡09571/34 88), where you can tuck into rustic food washed down with dark or lager-style *Nothelfer* – "Holy Helper" – beer. The only buses to Kloster Banz – from Bad Staffelstein, which has a train station on the Bamberg–Coburg line – are school buses (3 daily Mon–Fri, term time only). There's a car park opposite the abbey and a *Gaststätte*, the *Klosterstuben* (℡09573/22 20 58; daily 10am–10pm, closed Tues Nov–April), at the entrance, with *Schnitzel* and goulash for around €8.50.

Bamberg

History has twice been exceptionally kind to beautiful **BAMBERG**, which for centuries until secularization in 1802 was the capital of an independent Catholic prince-bishopric within the Holy Roman Empire. Though occupied twice by the Swedes during the Thirty Years' War, the city was spared the wholesale destruction visited on so many German cities by that conflict. And by some miracle, it came through World War II with barely a scratch too. It thus preserves a wonderfully complete historic townscape, notable not just for its many highlights – the four-spired **Dom**, the splendid Baroque **Residenz** or the absurdly picturesque old **Rathaus** on an island in the river, for instance – but also for its many quaint corners and quiet, narrow lanes, worth exploring for their lost-in-time appeal and atmospheric, traditional brewery-owned *Gaststätten*. Add to this the architectural opulence that resulted from the disdain shown by the Schönborn dynasty of prince-bishops for anything remotely resembling a vow of poverty, and it's no wonder that UNESCO put Bamberg's entire historic centre on its World Heritage list in 1993. Nor is Bamberg merely pretty: at the height of its wealth and power in the Middle Ages, its architectural style influenced a wide swathe of Central Europe, from North Germany to Hungary. Later, it was a centre of the Enlightenment in southern Germany, and in the early nineteenth century G. W. Hegel lived here. So too did E.T.A. Hoffmann, the Prussian author of fantasy and horror tales.

Bamberg is split neatly into three by the parallel courses of the River Regnitz – a short tributary of the Main – and the Main-Donau canal, both of which run south–east to north–west through the city. The **Gärtnerstadt** in the east is of relatively little interest to visitors; **Inselstadt** between the canal and river is the handsome, secular city centre; while for centuries spiritual and temporal power in Bamberg had its seat in the **Bergstadt** – built, like Rome, on seven hills – on the west bank of the Regnitz. Compact enough to be explored fully in a few days, Bamberg is nevertheless a tempting place to linger, thanks to its unique atmosphere and history, hilly views and smoky, distinctive *Rauchbier* (smoked beer). Moreover, the university and a sizeable US presence – there's an American army barracks here – ensure the city never feels parochial. Furthermore, within easy reach of the city **Schloss Seehof** and **Schloss Weissenstein** are a couple of Baroque palaces associated with the prince-bishops that make for pleasant half-day excursions.

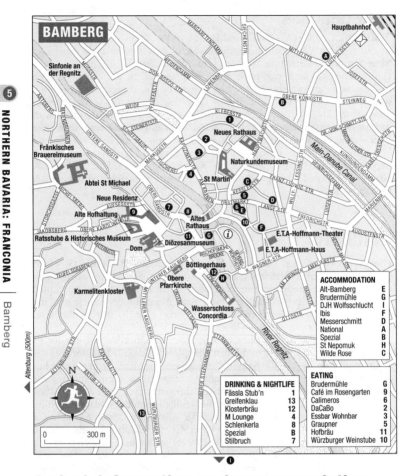

Arrival, information and accommodation

Bamberg's **Bahnhof** is in Gärtnerstadt, a good fifteen minutes' walk from the centre of the Altstadt: numerous buses make the five-minute journey from the train station to the central **bus station** on Promenade in Inselstadt, from where it's a short walk to the **tourist office** on an island in the Regnitz at Geyerswörthstrasse 3 (Mon–Fri 9.30am–6pm, Sat & Sun 9.30am–2.30pm; ☎0951/297 62 00, ⓦwww.bamberg.info). You can book somewhere to **stay** through the tourist office website; hotels are scattered throughout Bamberg, in addition to which the tourist office has a list of **private rooms**. They can also sell you a 48-hour **Bamberg Card**, which for €8.50 entitles you to free travel on city buses and free or reduced-price entry to museums and attractions.

Alt-Bamberg Habergasse 11 ☎0951/98 61 50, ⓦwww.alt-bamberg.de. Plain but attractive rooms above a restaurant in a half-timbered house very centrally located close to the Regnitz. ❸

Brudermühle Schranne 1 ☎0951/95 52 20, ⓦwww.brudermuehle.de. Traditionally styled hotel in an enviable location on the Bergstadt riverside just metres from the Altes Rathaus, with an atmospheric restaurant. ❻

Ibis Theatergassen 10 ☎0951/98 04 80, ⊛www
.ibishotel.com. Modest-sized outpost of the
comfortable budget chain, with the advantage of a
quiet and very central location between the E.T.A.
Hoffmann Theater and the Altes Rathaus. ❸
DJH Wolfsschlucht Obere Leinritt 70 ☎0951/560
02, ⊛www.bamberg.jugendherberge.de. Bamberg's
pretty youth hostel is on the riverside 2km south of
the Altstadt. €18.20 including breakfast. Bus #18
from Bamberg's central bus station.
Messerschmitt Lange Str. 41 ☎0951/29 78 00,
⊛www.hotel-messerschmitt.de. The unintentionally
comic name aside – it means simply "cutler" in
German – this is a lovely, upmarket hotel in an
attractive and historic *Weinhaus*, with masses of
mellow wood and a well-regarded restaurant. ❻
National Luitpoldstr. 37 ☎0951/50 99 80,
⊛www.hotel-national-bamberg.de. Friendly and
comfortable three-star hotel in the Gärtnerstadt,

handy for the Hauptbahnhof and with some singles.
There's limited car parking on site, too. ❸

Spezial Obere Königstr. 10 ☎0951/243 04,
⊛www.brauerei-spezial.de. Simple but
comfortable single and double rooms, most with
shower and WC, above an atmospheric Gärtnerstadt
Brauereigaststätte. ❷

St Nepomuk Obere Mühlbrücke 9
☎0951/984 20, ⊛www.hotel-nepomuk.de.
Stylish, four-star hotel built out over the river, with
a glass bridge linking the Bergstadt and mid-river
wings. Rooms are contemporary in style; the suite
has views downriver to the Altes Rathaus. ❻
Wilde Rose Kesslerstr. 7 ☎0951/98 18 20,
⊛www.hotel-wilde-rose.de. Good, very central
mid-range option in a former brewery in Inselstadt,
with a large *Biergarten* serving the in-house
Wilde Rose Bier in summer. Rooms have shower,
WC and internet. ❹

The Altes Rathaus and around

If a competition had been held to design the most picturesque building
in Franconia, it might have been won by Bamberg's **Altes Rathaus**, an
enchanting combination of Baroque *Lüftmalerei* – the distinctive exterior
wall painting strongly associated with Bavaria, which aims to create architectural and 3D effects – and half-timbered quaintness wedged onto an
artificial islet in the Regnitz, bracketed on either side by the stone arches of
the **Obere Brücke**. Yet picturesque effect wasn't the reason for the curious
site: depending which version you prefer, it was either built mid-river by
stubborn burghers after the prince-bishop refused to donate any land for
its construction, or to mark the division between the sacred and profane
parts of the city and thus demonstrate the independent-mindedness of the
burghers. The half-timbered **Rottmeisterhäuschen** of 1668, which teeters
over the rushing waters on the south side of the islet, is the only part to
preserve its original appearance, but it's not the oldest part of the complex,
for the main body of the Rathaus preserves a fifteenth-century core beneath
an exuberant Baroque and Rococo makeover, which dates from 1744 to
1756. **Johann Anwanders**' lush allegorical paintings on the flanks of the
building have startling depth – watch out for the chubby angel's leg that
really *does* jut out, on the side facing Inselstadt. The Altes Rathaus houses
the **Sammlung Ludwig** (Tues–Sun 9.30am–4.30pm; €3.50), a visual feast
of Strasbourg faïence and Sèvres and Meissen porcelain, including Johann
Joachim Kendler's **Monkey Orchestra** of 1753 – a caricature of human
virtues and vices in porcelain form. The ticket also includes entrance into the
elegant Rococo Room, which dates from 1750 and has an attractive stucco
ceiling by Franz Jakob Vogel.

To the south of the Altes Rathaus, the course of the Regnitz is a cat's cradle of
little bridges and islets. On the largest of these, close to the tourist office, **Schloss
Geyerswörth** was originally a medieval patrician residence, before being rebuilt
in 1580 to 1587 as a bishop's palace. You can get the key to its **tower** from
the tourist office (free) – it's worth the steep climb for one of the best views
over Bamberg, encompassing the Altes Rathaus, Dom, Neue Residenz and
St Michael monastery.

The Inselstadt

Cross the narrow, picturesque **Alter Kanal** by the footbridge behind the Schloss to **Inselstadt**, the historic heart of the secular city. A pleasant stroll along Habergasse and Zinkenwörth brings you to the modest but pretty eighteenth-century **E.T.A. Hoffmann Haus** (May–Oct Tues–Fri 10am–5pm, Sat & Sun 10am–noon; €2) where the composer, critic and author of the eponymous *Tales* lived from 1808 to 1813. The house contains an imaginatively presented exhibition which chronicles his life, work and the opera *Undine*. Retracing your steps north along Zinkenwörth and Habergasse brings you to broad, busy **Grüner Markt**, over which presides the massive Baroque **Pfarrkirche St Martin** (Mon–Wed & Fri–Sun 7.30am–6pm, Thurs 1–6pm; free). The work of brothers Georg and Leonhard Dientzenhofer, completed in 1693, it has a shallow, *trompe l'oeil* dome inside. Tucked behind it on Fleischstrasse is the **Naturkundemuseum** (Tues–Sun: April–Sept 10am–5pm; Oct–March 10am–4pm; €2), the city's natural history museum. Its chief glory is the **Vogelsaal**, in which stuffed birds are still exhibited in the original Neoclassical eighteenth-century display cases. Grüner Markt leads into spacious **Maxplatz**, dominated by the imposing former **seminary**, built between 1732 and 1737 by Balthasar Neumann and now functioning as the city's Rathaus. Maxplatz (or Maximilianplatz to give it its official name) is the focus for numerous events, including Bamberg's **Christmas market**.

There's a studenty vibe to some of the streets between Maxplatz and the river. Follow Heumarkt into Stangstrasse, before heading south down Kapuzinerstrasse to **Am Kranen**, on the banks of the Regnitz where a couple of historic cranes mark the site of the city's main quay from the fourteenth century until 1912; barges sailed downstream from here along the Main and Rhine to the Netherlands and, after 1846, upstream along the Main-Donau canal too. The eighteenth-century slaughterhouse on the riverside – identifiable by a stone effigy of an ox on its gable – dumped its waste and blood directly into the river. The riverside north from here is a particularly picturesque jumble of medieval fishermen's houses, with jetties for gardens and steep red-tiled roofs hanging low over the river. Known as **Klein-Venedig**, or Little Venice, it's seen to best effect from the Bergstadt side of the river.

The Bergstadt

If you cross the river by either the **Obere** or **Untere Brücke**, you enter the lower reaches of the **Bergstadt**, an atmospheric hotchpotch of antique shops, antiquarian booksellers and ancient *Brauereigaststätten*. South of the bridges along Judenstrasse and Concordiastrasse are two of Bamberg's most imposing Baroque houses, the outrageously florid **Böttingerhaus** (1707–13), built for the privy councillor and elector Johann Ignaz Tobias Böttinger, and the more dignified **Concordia** on the riverside, built for the same client by Johann Dientzenhofer between 1717 and 1722. Neither is open to the public.

Standing above the lower town is **Domplatz**, for centuries the nexus of spiritual and temporal power in Bamberg and one of the most splendid urban spaces in southern Germany. It's dominated by the distinctive four-spired silhouette of Bamberg's **Kaiserdom**, or imperial cathedral (daily: April–Oct 8am–6pm; Nov–March 8am–5pm; free). Bamberg's bishopric was established by the Emperor Heinrich II in 1007, but the present cathedral was completed in 1237 in a style that blends late Romanesque and early Gothic elements, and which was influenced by the design of the hilltop cathedral in Laon, France. **Heinrich II** and his consort **Kunigunde** are buried in a fabulously elaborate marble tomb between the east and west choirs, carved by Tilman Riemenschneider between

1499 and 1513. Not to be missed either is Veit Stoss's **Christmas Altar** in the south transept – the Nuremberg carver's last great work, it dates from 1523. The cathedral's most famous monument is the **Bamberger Reiter** of 1235, a stone sculpture of a fine-featured, beardless nobleman on horseback, which has over the centuries been regarded as the embodiment of medieval chivalry. The artist is unknown, and it's not known for certain who the subject was either, though the crowning canopy in the form of a city suggests a saint and thus King Stephen I of Hungary, who completed the task of converting his country to Christianity and was later canonized. The cathedral cloisters house the **Diözesanmuseum** (Diocese Museum; Tues–Sun 10am–5pm; €3), whose prize exhibits are its unique collection of eleventh-century vestments, including Heinrich II's stunning blue-and-gold Sternmantel, made in Regensburg around 1020.

On the east side of Domplatz, the elaborate Renaissance **Ratsstube** houses the **Historisches Museum** (May–Oct Tues–Sun 9am–5pm; Nov–April during temporary exhibitions only; €3), whose rich and varied collection documents the history of Bamberg and the surrounding area. Its treasures include paintings by Lucas Cranach the Elder and Pieter Bruegel as well as an early view of Bamberg – and one of the earliest-ever painted depictions of a German city – in *The Apostles' Farewell* by Wolfgang Katzheimer the Elder. Behind the Ratsstube is the **Alte Hofhaltung**, a meandering complex of fifteenth-century half-timbered buildings that formerly housed the prince-bishops' household.

Zigzagging across the north side of Domplatz is an even more impressive palace, the Baroque **Neue Residenz** (guided tours daily: April–Sept 9am–6pm; Oct–March 10am–4pm; €4), begun in 1613 but extended to its present magnificence under prince-bishop Lothar von Schönborn between 1697 and 1703. The work of Leonhard Dientzenhofer, it has more than forty state rooms, the most impressive of which is the **Kaisersaal**, decorated with sixteen larger-than-life-size portraits of Holy Roman Emperors by Melchior Steidl and with a subtly *trompe l'oeil* ceiling – much shallower than it appears. More intimate but touching are the apartments once occupied by **Otto of Greece**, a member of the Bavarian Wittelsbach royal family who became King of Greece in 1832 but who as a devout Catholic refused to convert to the Orthodox faith and was ultimately forced to abdicate in 1862. He lived out the remainder of his years in Bamberg. After the tour, you can enjoy the paintings of the **Altdeutsche Galerie** – including works by Lucas Cranach the Elder and Michael Wolgemut – at your leisure. The **rose garden** behind the Residenz is absolutely lovely, and boasts sweeping views over the rooftops of the town and up to the Michaelsberg monastery.

The outer Bergstadt

An idyllic walk from Residenzstrasse below Domplatz leads through terraced orchards to the former Benedictine monastery of **St Michael** (daily 9am–6pm, no access during services; free) on a commanding hilltop site with wonderful views over the city. It was founded in 1015 under Heinrich II, but was reconstructed following a catastrophic fire in 1610; the church was complete – in a curious hybrid Gothic style – by 1617. The surrounding Baroque abbey buildings were built by Leonhard Dientzenhofer from 1696 onwards. The monastery also houses the **Fränkisches Brauereimuseum** (April–Nov Wed–Sun 1–5pm; €3), in which Bamberg's own distinguished brewing tradition takes centre stage.

It's worth scaling another of the outer Bergstadt's hills to visit the Obere Pfarre or **Pfarrkirche zu Unserer Lieben Frau** at Eisgrube 4 (daily 9am–5pm, no access during services; free), Bamberg's only purely Gothic church. Built in the fourteenth century, it has a particularly lovely tabernacle in the ambulatory, while Tintoretto's *Assumption* lurks poorly lit to the right of the door as you enter.

Eating, drinking and entertainment

Bamberg's Altstadt has plenty of good places to **eat** and **drink**, including the atmospheric *Gaststätten* associated with its many breweries (known as *Brauereigastätten*). Sandstrasse in the lower Bergstadt has one of the liveliest concentrations of places to drink or hear **live music**: the ♣ *Jazz Club Bamberg*, Obere Sandstrasse 18 (☎0951/537 40, ⓦwww.jcbamberg.de), has regular jazz and cabaret gigs, while the *Blues Bar* (☎0951/533 04) upstairs in the same complex is the place to hear live rock six nights a week. More highbrow cultural tastes are catered to by the E.T.A. Hoffmann Theater, E.T.A.-Hoffmann-Platz 1 (☎0951/87 30 30, ⓦwww.theater-bamberg.de), and by the Bamberger Symphoniker orchestra (☎0951/964 72 00, ⓦwww.bamberger-symphoniker.de), whose home base is at the Konzert- und Kongresshalle Bamberg at Mussstrasse 1 on the banks of the Regnitz.

Cafés and restaurants

Brudermühle Schranne 1 ☎0951/955 20. Cosy, rather traditional riverside restaurant, with hunting trophies on the wall and fish and game on the seasonally changing menu. Main courses from around €13.

Café Im Rosengarten Domplatz 8 ☎0951/98 04 00. Elegant summer-only café in a Baroque pavilion in the Residenz's beautiful rose garden, with the most spectacular views in Bamberg.

Calimeros Lange Str. 8 ☎0951/20 11 72. Slick Tex-Mex place near the Altes Rathaus, something of an Anglo-American hangout, with live sport on TV and tasty and filling *quesadillas*, burritos and burgers. Open until 3am Thurs & Fri and until 4am Sat, otherwise 1am.

DaCaBo Heumarkt 7 ☎0951/297 18 68. Pleasant modern café-bar on a quiet square in Inselstadt, with a big selection of teas and coffees, and set menu or à la carte breakfasts until 4pm. Open from 9am daily.

Essbar Wohnbar Stangsstr. 3 ☎09561/50 99 88 44. Stylish café and restaurant in a boutique hotel in Inselstadt, open from breakfast and serving a cosmopolitan menu, including Thai- and Indian-influenced dishes.

Graunpner Lange Str. 5 ☎0951/98 04 00. Classy *Konditorei* and chocolatier, run by the same team that owns the *Café Im Rosengarten*. The best *Kaffee und Kuchen* stop in Bamberg.

♣ **Hofbräu** Karolinenstr. 7 ☎0951/533 21. Despite the name, this elegant but informal place is more restaurant than bar, with a few French and Italian touches on the menu and contemporary art on the walls. Mains from around €12. Live piano Monday nights.

Würzburger Weinstube Zinkenwörth 6 ☎09561/226 67. Traditional *Weinstube* in a quiet and pretty location close to the Regnitz in Inselstadt, with Franconian wines by the glass, local Bamberg specialities on the menu and main courses from around €10. Closed Tues eve and all day Wed.

Bars, Brauereigaststätten and clubs

Fässla Stub'n Kleberstr. 5 ☎09561/752 70. Smoky, studenty bar in Inselstadt with excellent *Fässla* beer, a regularly changing roster of cheap drinks deals, and great music.

♣ **Greifenklau** Laurenziplatz 20 ☎0951/532 19. Cosy, wood-panelled Bergstadt *Brauereigaststätte*, serving *Bock* and *Weizen* beers as well as its regular *Greifenklau* brew. Closed Mon.

Klosterbräu Obere Mühlbrücke 5. Bamberg's oldest *Brauereigaststätte* is a rambling collection of picturesque buildings on the Bergstadt side of the Regnitz; its *Braunbier* dates back to its origins as the prince-bishops' own brewery, and there's filling, affordable Franconian food available.

M Lounge Kapuzinerstr. 17. Gay (but hetero-friendly) bar and smokers' club in the Inselstadt, open from 8pm.

♣ **Schlenkerla** Dominikanerstr. 6 ☎0951/560 50. The classic place to try *Rauchbier* with a wonderfully historic, beamed interior, simple Franconian food and occasionally grumpy service. Daily 9.30am–11.30pm.

Spezial Obere Königstr. 10 ☎09561/243 04. Rustic, traditional *Brauereigaststätte* in Gärtnerstadt, serving mild *Rauchbier* as well as a *Helles*, with simple food to soak up the beer. The Spezial brewery was founded in 1536.

Stilbruch Obere Sandstr. 18 ☎0951/519 00 02. The most "alternative" of the Bergstadt bars, still fabulously beamy and old but with a laid-back atmosphere, good music selection and *Spezial Rauchbier*. Upstairs is *Blues Bar*, a live music venue; the cellar houses the *Jazz Club Bamberg*.

Around Bamberg: Schlosspark Seehof and Schloss Weissenstein at Pommersfelden

Just northeast of Bamberg at Memmelsdorf, the delightful summer palace of **Schloss Seehof** (April–Oct Tues–Sun 9am–6pm; €3.50; bus #7 or #17 from Bamberg bus station) is further evidence of the prince-bishops' lavish ways. Constructed to plans by Antonio Petrini from 1686 onwards, it fell into disrepair after the secularization of the prince-bishopric and today most of it houses the Bavarian organization responsible for the care and maintenance of historic buildings. Its nine state rooms, however, have been restored, and include the Weisse Saal with magnificent ceiling paintings by Giuseppe Appiani. The eighteenth-century Rococo water gardens with their restored cascade were once famous throughout Germany.

While Seehof was the prince-bishops' "official" summer residence, the immense **Schloss Weissenstein** at Pommersfelden to the south of the city (guided tours daily April–Oct 10am–4pm; €6) was and remains the private home of the Schönborn family, and when they are in residence they fly a standard, just like the British royal family. The Schloss was commissioned by prince-bishop Lothar Franz von Schönborn and built to designs by his court architect, Johann Dientzenhofer, and Johann Lukas von Hildebrandt, the celebrated Austrian Baroque architect and designer of Vienna's Belvedere. The results are magnificent, particularly in Hildebrandt's graceful ceremonial **Treppenhaus**, or staircase, which inspired the still more magnificent example at Würzburg built nine years later. The principal state room, the **Marmorsaal** or marble hall, rises through two storeys and was a tour de force of structural ingenuity in its day, its weighty marble floor resting on the wooden arches of the grotto-like Gartensaal beneath. Schloss Weissenstein is also home to an impressive private **art collection**, including works by Titian, Van Dyck, Rubens, Bruegel and others.

There's an infrequent **bus** (#8227) to Pommersfelden from Bamberg's Bahnhof on weekdays; it also makes a pleasant day's excursion by bike or car. There's a *Gaststätte* (℡09548/224) at the gates to the Schloss, serving light snacks, fresh fish and *Schnitzel*.

Würzburg

Steep, vine-covered hills form the backdrop to **WÜRZBURG**, visible from the centre of the city as a clear reminder that you're no longer in beer country. The centre of the Franconian wine industry was for centuries dominated by the bishopric founded on the banks of the River Main by the English missionary St Boniface in 742 AD and, as in Bamberg, its prince-bishops wielded both spiritual and temporal power. In the late fifteenth and early sixteenth centuries the city nurtured the talent – whilst ultimately spurning the revolutionary politics – of the master woodcarver Tilman Riemenschneider. In the eighteenth century two prince-bishops of the luxury-loving Schörnborn dynasty were responsible for commissioning the city's greatest monument – and Bavaria's most magnificent palace – the **Residenz**, now a UNESCO World Heritage Site. Horrendous damage was visited on Würzburg by Britain's Royal Air Force on March 16, 1945, when the city was subjected to an ordeal by firestorm that laid waste the Altstadt and killed five thousand people; the destruction was so severe the city was afterwards dubbed "The Grave on the Main". Justification for the raid derived supposedly from the city's rail junction, though in truth it had long been on a list of cities with a population of over 100,000 that were earmarked for attack for no specific reason other than their size. After the war, Würzburg recovered with remarkable success, and its war-damaged monuments were slowly and painstakingly restored or rebuilt.

Most of Würzburg's sights are concentrated in the compact area between the **Residenz** and the **River Main**, but you'll need to walk across the Alte Mainbrücke to get the classic view of the Alstadt's pinnacled skyline. Also not to be missed is the **Marienberg fortress**, high above the west side of the river. Würzburg also marks the start of the **Romantic Road** (see box, p.344), the best-known of Germany's various tourist routes, which leads south to the Alps, linking many of Bavaria's most beautiful and historic sights on the way. With its picturesque setting, artistic and architectural treasures and fine wines, the city makes a fitting – and enjoyable – start to Germany's most famous road trip.

Arrival, information and city transport

Würzburg's **Hauptbahnhof** is on the northern edge of the Altstadt, from where Kaiserstrasse leads into the centre. The **tourist office** is in the Falken-haus on Markt (Jan–March Mon–Fri 10am–4pm, Sat 10am–1pm; April, Nov & Dec Mon–Fri 10am–6pm, Sat 10am–2pm; May–Oct Mon–Fri 10am–6pm, Sat & Sun 10am–noon; ☎0931/37 23 98, ⓦwww.wuerzburg.de) and organizes

guided tours of the city in English (meet at tourist office: May–Oct Sat 1pm, 1hr 30min, €6; mid-June to mid-Sept daily except Sat 6.30pm, 1hr, €5). It can also sell you a **Würzburg Welcome Card** (€3), which is valid for one week and entitles you to reductions on museum entry and in various restaurants and *Weinstuben*. Würzburg is compact, but you might want to use **public transport** (Ⓦwww.wvv.de) to reach the Marienberg fortress: from April to October, bus #9 shuttles between the Residenz, Kulturspeicher and Marienberg; the rest of the year trams #2 and #4 will get you most of the way there from Juliuspromenade. A *Kurzstrecke* ticket for up to four stops costs €1.10, a single €2.10 and a one-day *Tageskarte* €4.30.

Accommodation

You can book somewhere to **stay** through the tourist office website; there's plenty of choice in the mid-range, with fewer options for budget travellers or at the top of the market.

Central Hotel Garni Koellikerstr. 1 ☎0931/460 8840, Ⓦwww.centralhotel-wuerzburg.de. Comfortable and good-value if slightly bland rooms in a very central, privately run hotel opposite the Juliusspital, with underground parking. ❸

DJH Würzburg Fred-Joseph-Platz 2 ☎0931/425 90, Ⓦwww.wuerzburg.jugendherberge.de. In a superb location beneath the Marienberg fortress by the river, with accommodation mostly in two- to six-bed rooms. Reception 8am–10pm and there's no curfew. Dorms from €21.60 with breakfast peak season.

Hotel am Congress-Centrum Pleichertorstr. 26 ☎0931/230 79 70, Ⓦwww.hotel-am-congress -centrum.de. Much prettier than its dreary name suggests, this is close to the river on the northern fringe of the Altstadt. Nonsmoking and a/c rooms are available. ❺

🏃 **Hotel Rebstock** Neubaustr. 7 ☎0931/309 30, Ⓦwww.rebstock.bestwestern.de.

Behind a prettily Rococo facade, this is one of the classiest addresses in town, with individually designed rooms and suites, all with bath or shower and high-speed internet. ❼

Pension Zimmer Frei Bahnhofstr. 22 ☎0931/178 55, Ⓦwww.zimmerfrei-wuerzburg.de. Plain but decent rooms on the upper floors of a pub close to the Hauptbahnhof, with modern decor and shared facilities. ❷

Sankt Josef Semmelstr. 28 ☎0931/30 86 80, Ⓦwww.hotel-st-josef.de. Small, cyclist-friendly and nonsmoking hotel, plain but very well kept and handy for the Altstadt's sights. ❹

Zur Stadt Mainz Semmelstr. 39 ☎0931/531 55, Ⓦwww.hotel-stadtmainz.de. Fifteen comfortable rooms with shower, WC and TV, above an atmospheric restaurant on the east side of the Altstadt. There's also a honeymoon suite. ❺

The Residenz

Dominating the Altstadt's eastern flank, the **Residenz** (daily: April–Oct 9am–6pm; Nov–March 10am–4.30pm; €5) is an eighteenth-century status symbol that puts Würzburg firmly into the architectural super league, as it was fully intended to do. Johann Philipp Franz von Schönborn, prince-bishop of Würzburg from 1719 to 1724, transferred his court from the Marienberg to the town, but was not at all satisfied with the modest little Schloss on the site of the present Residenz, and he commissioned Balthasar Neumann to design something more appropriate to his princely status. The proceeds of a lawsuit provided the necessary funds, and Schloss Weissenstein at Pommersfelden – recently completed for the bishop's uncle, Lothar Franz von Schönborn – provided the blueprint. Other architects of the day, including the Viennese Baroque master Lucas von Hildebrandt, provided some of the inspiration. The bishop never lived to inhabit his creation and his immediate successor stopped building work, but it restarted under his brother Friedrich Carl and thus the palace is the coherent creation of a relatively short period of construction.

▲ The Residenz, Würzburg

The results are breathtaking: impressively wide, the Residenz faces a paved *Hof* on three sides. Inside, the highly theatrical **Treppenhaus**, or staircase, stretches across five bays and is topped by a mammoth unsupported vault – a structurally audacious design of which Neumann was so confident he offered to fire a battery of artillery at it to prove its strength. His confidence was vindicated in 1945, when the ceiling withstood the aerial bombardment of the city – which wrecked the north and south wings of the Schloss but left the Treppenhaus intact. The stairs rise through a series of half-landings, their walls richly ornamented with stucco, but everything is merely a setting for **Giovanni Battista Tiepolo**'s magnificent allegorical ceiling fresco, which measures thirteen by eighteen metres and is the largest ever created. It depicts the four continents of Asia, Africa, America and Europe, with the Würzburg court depicted as the centre of the arts in Europe.

At the top of the stairs, the white and pale grey **Weisser Saal** is decorated with tasteful stucco work by Materno Bossi. Completed in 1745, the room provides an entirely deliberate aesthetic breathing space between the Treppenhaus and the most extravagant of the state rooms, the giddily opulent **Kaisersaal**. With its twenty red marble columns, large oval dome and Tiepolo frescoes celebrating Würzburg's position in the Holy Roman Empire, the richly coloured hall provides a memorable setting for classical music concerts. To either side, long processions of rooms lead into the north and south wings. In the north, the delicate stucco ceilings had to be re-created after wartime damage; the **Grünlackiertes Zimmer**, or Green Lacquered Room, is the highlight. The **Southern Imperial Apartments** can only be visited on a free guided tour – enquire in the Weisser Saal – but are well worth seeing for the **Spiegelkabinett**, a riot of painted mirror panels and gold leaf that was re-created after wartime destruction using old photographs and surviving shards of glass as a guide. Afterwards, visit the **Hofkirche** on the south side of the complex (same hours; free), the religious counterpart to the Residenz's secular pomp, again with frescoes by Tiepolo. The south wing also contains the **Martin von Wagner Museum** (Gemäldegalerie Tues–Sun 9.30am–12.30pm, Tues & Thurs also 4–6pm; Antikensammlung Tues–Sat 2–5pm; Sun collections alternate 9.30am–1pm; free), the university's collections of antiquities and art. Highlights of the latter include works by Tilman Riemenschneider and Tiepolo. Stroll in the formal **Hofgarten** (open daily until dusk or 8pm, whichever is earlier; free) afterwards to see the Residenz's southern and eastern facades.

The Dom and around

From the Residenz, Hofstrasse leads west to the heart of the bishops' city. The twin-towered **Dom St Kilian** (Mon–Sat 10am–5pm, Sun 1–6pm; free) was built in the eleventh and twelfth centuries and is one of the largest surviving Romanesque cathedrals in Germany. Its exterior has a pleasing austerity; inside, surviving examples of early eighteenth-century stucco work are balanced by the simplicity of the postwar restoration. Balthasar Neumann's gorgeous **Schönbornkapelle**, built onto the northern transept from 1721 to 1736, competes with the main body of the cathedral for monumental effect and nearly wins: it's a suitably imposing memorial to the self-important Schönborn bishops.

Just opposite is the entrance to the **Museum am Dom** (April–Oct Tues–Sun 10am–6pm; Nov–March 10am–5pm; €3.50; ⓦ www.museum-am-dom.de), which houses the diocesan art collection. The exhibits are hung conceptually, and the result is very far from a dusty collection of religious relics: in addition to sculptures by Tilman Riemenschneider you can see works by Otto Dix and Käthe Kollwitz and art from the former GDR.

More conventional in its appeal is the **Domschatz** (Tues–Sun 2–5pm; €2), an intensely dark treasury a short walk south of the Dom at Domerschulstrasse 2, where the highlights include an impressive eleventh-century lion-head door knocker originally from the Dom, and some well-preserved items from the graves of Würzburg's bishops.

North of the Dom along Schönbornstrasse is the **Neumünster**, whose elegant Baroque facade conceals an eleventh-century Romanesque basilica. The church is built on the site of the graves of the Irish missionary St Kilian and his associates St Kolonat and St Totnan, who were murdered in Würzburg in 689 AD.

Marktplatz and around

Bustling **Marktplatz** is the heart of secular Würzburg, with an eclectic selection of buildings from the medieval to the stylishly modern ranged around its irregular fringes. Much the prettiest is the **Falkenhaus** on the north side, once a *Gasthaus* and now housing the tourist office and municipal library; its sugary external stucco decoration dates from 1751 and looks almost good enough to eat. Looming alongside it is the **Marienkapelle**, a lofty, late Gothic hall church founded in 1377 on the site of the town's synagogue, destroyed in a pogrom in 1349. Tilman Riemenschneider was responsible for much of the church's sculpture; the famous figures of *Adam and Eve* are copies, the originals now being in the Mainfränkisches Museum in the Marienberg, but the tomb of Konrad von Schaumberg is original.

Just west of Marktplatz, the oldest part of the **Rathaus**, the **Grafeneckart**, with its slender Romanesque tower, was originally the seat of episcopal officials, but has served since 1316 as the city's Rathaus. Its northern extension, the late Renaissance **Rote Bau**, was reduced to a shell in 1945 but has been carefully restored. Just beyond the Rathaus, the fifteenth-century **Alte Mainbrücke** crosses the river, lined on either side with Baroque statues of saints – among them St John Nepomuk, who was martyred by being pushed into Prague's Vltava River. Whatever the compromises Würzburg's postwar builders made when they reconstructed the city, from the centre of the bridge the illusion of timelessness is perfect, and the skyline of the Altstadt is a festive huddle of spires and cupolas. North of the bridge, the **Alter Kranen** is a pair of eighteenth-century riverside cranes, the work of Balthasar Neumann's son Franz Ignaz Michael. The **Zollhaus** next to the cranes houses the **Haus des Frankenweins** (see box, p.337).

The Museum im Kulturspeicher and Röntgen-Gedächtnisstätte

North of the Altstadt, a converted dockside warehouse is now the **Museum im Kulturspeicher** (Tues 1–6pm, Wed & Fri–Sun 11am–6pm, Thurs 11am–7pm; €3.50), which houses the municipal collection of art from the nineteenth century to the present day, including works from the Romantic, Biedermeier, Impressionist and Expressionist periods. In addition, the museum houses the Peter C. Ruppert collection of post-1945 Concrete Art, with works by Victor Vasarely, among others.

To the east along Röntgenring is the **Röntgen-Gedächtnisstätte** (Mon–Thurs 8am–4pm, Fri 8am–3pm; free), the laboratory in which Wilhelm Röntgen discovered x-rays in 1895, and whose exhibits include the apparatus he used in his experiments.

Marienberg fortress and the Käppele

Looming above the city on the high west bank of the Main is the **Festung Marienberg**, which was the seat of the prince-bishops from 1253 until Johann Philipp Franz von Schönborn moved his court down into the city in 1719. The walk up through vineyards from the west bank of the river is lovely; otherwise, you can take the bus, or there's ample car parking west of the fortress.

Part medieval fortress, part Renaissance palace and with later Baroque extensions, the sheer scale of the Marienberg is impressive. One of the Baroque additions is the Zeughaus, or arsenal, home since 1947 to the **Mainfränkisches Museum Würzburg** (Tues–Sun: April–Oct 10am–5pm; Nov–March 10am–4pm; €4; ⓦ www.mainfraenkisches-museum.de), which in addition to its sprawling permanent collection mounts engrossing temporary exhibitions. The undoubted highlight is the room devoted to **Tilman Riemenschneider**, the best-known sculptor of the late German Gothic. Born in Thuringia around 1460, he established a flourishing workshop in Würzburg by 1485 which he ran until his death in 1531. The Mainfränkisches Museum has the largest collection of his expressive works anywhere, and it's particularly rewarding to see them up close, rather than at a distance as they might usually be seen in a church. Highlights include his *Mary in Mourning* from Acholshausen, the *Adam and Eve* figures from the Marienkapelle and the two so-called *Candlestick Angels* from 1505. Successful as an artist, Riemenschneider also rose to prominence in politics, becoming mayor of Würzburg in 1520, before falling from grace when the city council formed an alliance with the peasants during the Peasants' War of 1524–25.

Beyond the Zeughaus, the Kernberg – the core of the fortress – contains the **Fürstenbau Museum** (April–Oct Tues–Sun 9am–6pm; €4), whose Brussels tapestries, clerical vestments and religious silver are less engrossing than the chance to see the interior of the building itself – despite being badly damaged by fire in 1945, it retains traces of its original painted decoration. The models of Würzburg as it was in 1525 and 1945 make a fascinating comparison. Afterwards, be sure not to miss the panoramic views of the city from the **Fürstengarten**.

On a neighbouring hillside to the south stands Balthasar Neumann's **Käppele**, a sweetly picturesque pilgrimage church built between 1748 and 1752, whose interior is a riot of Rococo ornament.

Eating, drinking and entertainment

Würzburg has a good selection of places to **eat** and **drink**, with its traditional *Weinstuben* being the most atmospheric places to sample Franconian wine (see box opposite) and food. The Mainfranken Theater Würzburg at Theaterstrasse 21

Franconian wine

Franconian wines are fuller-bodied and often drier than other German wines, their distinctiveness arising in part from the climate, which is less kind than that of the wine-growing regions further west. Summers are warm and dry, but winters are cold, rainfall is high and frosts come early, so slow-ripening varieties like Riesling are less important here. *Müller-Thurgau* – which is also known as *Rivaner* – and *Silvaner* are the significant white-wine grape varieties, with new crosses such as *Bacchus* also coming to the fore. Red wines are grown in the west of the region, around Aschaffenburg, while Würzburg's Stein vineyard has given rise to the generic name *Steinwein*, which is sometimes used to describe all Franconian wines. Most distinctive of all is the squat, rounded **Bocksbeutel** in which Franconian wines are bottled – very different from the tall, slim-necked bottles used by most German wine-makers. Much the most enjoyable way to experience the wines is in one of Würzburg's traditional *Weinstuben*. There's also a wine shop, Vinothek, by the Alter Kranen.

You can also tour the impressive **Staatlicher Hofkeller** cellars by the Residenz, where the €6 price of the tour (March–Dec Sat & Sun hourly 10am–noon & 2–4pm) includes a glass of wine. The city has a busy programme of **wine festivals** throughout the summer months, culminating with the alfresco *Weinparade am Dom* in September; the tourist office has details.

(℡ 0931/390 81 24, ⓦ www.theaterwuerzburg.de) is the main venue for drama, opera and classical concerts.

Alte Mainmühle Mainkai 9 ℡ 0931/167 77. Convivial and classy wood-panelled restaurant right on the Alte Mainbrücke, with a few French and Italian touches to an otherwise Franconian menu. Main courses around €22.

Bürgerspital Theaterstr. 19 ℡ 0931/350 54 41. Sample the wines from this seven-hundred-year-old hospital's own vineyard in its rambling and atmospheric old *Weinstube* – you can sit outside in the eighteenth-century Innenhof in fine weather. The food menu embraces inexpensive Franconian specialities and more creative modern options, and there's also a wine shop.

Café Konditorei Michel Marktplatz 11 ℡ 0931/537 76. The top spot for coffee and cakes in Würzburg, attracting an older clientele.

Odeon Sommer Lounge Am Alten Kranen. Stylish summer-only, open-air Ibiza-style beach bar – complete with palm trees and sand – right on the banks of the Main. Eve only weekdays; from 2pm Sat & Sun. Its parent club, the *Odeon Lounge*, is south of the Alte Mainbrücke at Augustinerstr. 18 (Wed–Sat only).

Papperla Pub – Haus der 150 Biere Bahnhofstr. 22 ℡ 0931/178 55. It's practically sacrilege in such a wine-dominated city, but the vast selection of international beers – including African and South American brands – is the speciality of this bar close to the Hauptbahnhof.

Ratskeller in the Rathaus, Langgasse 1 ℡ 0931/130 21. Steaks and fish are on the menu in a wonderful vaulted space beneath the Rathaus, with Würzburg wines to wash them down.

Rebstock at hotel *Rebstock*, Neubaustr. 7 ℡ 0931/309 30. Franconian wines and gourmet cooking in elegant surroundings at the *Rebstock*'s top-notch restaurant, with menus at €52 and €58. Closed Sun.

Schönborn Marktplatz 30 ℡ 0931/404 48 18. Bustling modern café on Markt, serving breakfast until 4pm, pizzas, soups and light dishes, and with great views over the buzzing market place from its tables upstairs.

Weinstuben Juliusspital Juliuspromenade, cnr Barbarossaplatz 1 ℡ 0931/540 80. Like the *Bürgerspital*, this is a *Weinstube* associated with a hospital, though in this case an enormous Baroque one; there's a wide selection of Franconian wines – including the *Juliusspital*'s own – and *Schnitzels* and Franconian specialities on the menu (from around €11).

Zum Stachel Gressengasse 1 ℡ 0931/527 70. Absolutely gorgeous old *Weinstube* in a building which in part dates back to around 1200, with refined Franconian cooking and local wines. Closed Sun.

Zur Stadt Mainz at hotel *Zur Stadt Mainz*, Semmelstr. 39 ℡ 0931/531 55. Wonderfully over-the-top rustic decor, with deer antlers and wine bottles for decoration and *Schweinshaxe* (pigs' trotter) and beef goulash on the menu. Main courses from around €12.50.

Rothenburg ob der Tauber

The jewel-like hilltop town of **ROTHENBURG OB DER TAUBER** has reason to be grateful for the Peasants' War of 1525 – in which it allied itself with the rebels – and the Thirty Years' War that swept across Central Europe to such catastrophic effect a century afterwards. A former free imperial city that had been thriving and prosperous, Rothenburg dwindled to insignificance after these events, its wealth lost to plunder and reparations and its population halved. As a result of this reverse in its fortune, development came to a standstill, leaving the town with the miraculous legacy of perfectly preserved medieval and Renaissance buildings with which it charms visitors today. The twentieth century's greatest conflict wasn't so kind: aerial bombardment in March 1945 damaged Rothenburg to an extent that would surprise present-day visitors. After the war, the town's numerous fans – including many from abroad – rallied round to ensure its reconstruction was swift and successful, and to all but the most hawk-eyed observers there is little visual evidence of the destruction.

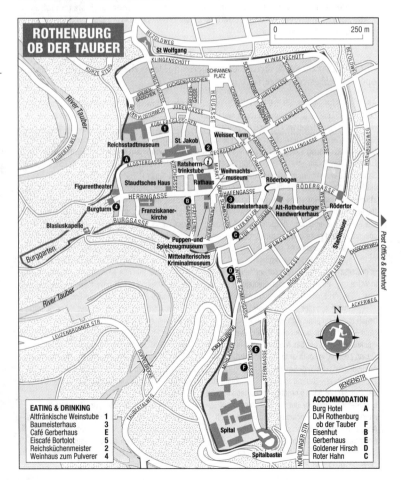

ROTHENBURG OB DER TAUBER

0   250 m

EATING & DRINKING

Altfränkische Weinstube	1
Baumeisterhaus	3
Café Gerberhaus	E
Eiscafé Bortolot	5
Reichsküchenmeister	2
Weinhaus zum Pulverer	4

ACCOMMODATION

Burg Hotel	A
DJH Rothenburg ob der Tauber	F
Eisenhut	B
Gerberhaus	E
Goldener Hirsch	D
Roter Hahn	C

Post Office & Bahnhof

Rothenburg lies on the **Romantic Road** (see box, p.344), accessible by rail (change at Steinach) and close to the Ulm–Würzburg stretch of the A7 Autobahn. As such, it's something of a day-tripper magnet, and the crowds can be oppressive – not only in summer, for the town has an undeniable magic in the weeks leading up to Christmas, too. Yet Rothenburg is not merely a tourist trap: its beauty is undeniable, its restaurants often cosily inviting and its hotels frequently charming. Perhaps the best way to enjoy it is to simply stay overnight, to experience the calm that descends when the shops are closed, the bus tours depart and the crowds have finally thinned.

Arrival, information and accommodation

Rothenburg's **Bahnhof** is a short walk to the east of the Altstadt. The **tourist office** is next to the Rathaus in the fifteenth-century Ratsherrntrinkstube (City Councillors' Tavern) at Marktplatz 2 (May–Oct Mon–Fri 9am–6pm, Sat & Sun 10am–3pm; Nov & Jan–April Mon–Fri 9am–5pm, Sat 10am–1pm; Dec Mon–Fri 9am–5pm, Sat & Sun 10am–3pm; ⓣ09861/40 48 00, ⓦwww.rothenburg.de). As befits such a popular destination, Rothenburg has a good range of **accommodation** – much of it atmospheric and charming – in all price ranges, from classy hotels to simple pensions. There are two **campsites** in nearby Detwang: *Tauber Idyll* (ⓣ09861/31 77, ⓦwww.rothenburg.de/tauberidyll) and *Tauberromantik* (ⓣ09861/61 91, ⓦwww.camping-tauberromantik.de).

Burg Hotel Klostergasse 1–3 ⓣ09861/948 90, ⓦwww.burghotel.rothenburg.de. In an idyllic location right on the town ramparts, with four-poster beds in some rooms and a lovely garden. ⑤

DJH Rothenburg ob der Tauber Mühlacker 1 ⓣ09861/941 60, ⓦwww.rothenburg.jugendherberge.de. Located in two historic buildings – the Rossmühle and Spitalhof – in a great location at the southern tip of the Altstadt. Dorms from €18.70 with breakfast.

Eisenhut Herrngasse 3–5/7 ⓣ09861/70 50, ⓦwww.eisenhut.com. Rothenburg's classiest hotel oozes restrained good taste, from its handsome lobby to its 78 individually styled rooms, which boast period furnishings and modern amenities, including wi-fi and satellite TV. ⑥

Gerberhaus Spitalgasse 25 ⓣ09861/949 00, ⓦwww.gerberhaus.rothenburg.de. Cyclist-friendly hotel with prettily rustic, recently refurbished rooms above an attractive café; there's also a lovely garden – in the shade of the medieval fortifications. ③

Goldener Hirsch Untere Schmiedgasse 16 ⓣ09861/87 49 90, ⓦwww.hotel-goldener-hirsch.de. Elegant and spacious hotel in the southern Alstadt, with period furnishings and views over the Taubertal. ③–⑥

Roter Hahn Obere Schmiedgasse 21 ⓣ09861/97 40, ⓦwww.roterhahn.com. Good-value, pretty rooms in an atmospheric inn which claims to be one of Germany's oldest. ③

The Town

Rothenburg's layout is a variation on the classic cross-shaped medieval street plan, with east–west and north–south streets crossing in the centre at Marktplatz. The River Tauber snakes along the western side of the Altstadt buried in its verdant valley, while the near-complete medieval defences still encircle the town, peppered with picturesque towers. The easternmost of these – and the first you'll see as you approach from the Bahnhof – is the tall **Röderturm** (daily 9am–6pm weather permitting, closed Christmas to end Feb; €2), which you can climb to get your bearings. There's also an exhibition there about the World War II destruction of Rothenburg. Afterwards, an enjoyable way to while away an hour or two is to complete the circuit of the walls; much of the walkway is under cover.

Marktplatz and around

The gulf between Rothenburg's modest present-day status and its former glory is eloquently demonstrated by the magnificence of its **Rathaus**. The splendid Renaissance structure facing Marktplatz dates from 1572 to 1578 and is the work of local architect Leonhard Weidemann; the older Gothic structure behind it was built between 1250 and 1400 and is topped by the spindly **Rathausturm** (April–Oct daily 9.30am–12.30pm & 1–5pm; Nov & Jan–March Sat & Sun noon–3pm; Dec daily noon–3pm; €2), which offers stunning vistas over the town's huddled red rooftops. Be warned, however, the way up gets progressively steeper and narrower and the observation platform feels precarious if you're at all prone to vertigo.

Back on ground level, the gabled **Ratstrinkstube** on the north side of Markt-platz was the scene of the most celebrated – if probably apocryphal – episode of the Thirty Years' War in Rothenburg, the so-called **Meistertrunk** or Master Draught of 1631. The feared Catholic general Tilly, whose troops were occupying the town, promised to spare Protestant Rothenburg destruction if a councillor managed to empty an enormous tankard containing 3.25 litres of wine in a single draught. The former mayor Georg Nusch managed the feat, and Rothenburg was saved. Each year at Whitsun, a festival commemorates the event.

You can learn more about the episode in the engagingly theatrical **Historiengewölbe** (Historic Vaults; mid-March to April daily 10am–4pm; May–Oct daily 9.30am–5.50pm; during Christmas market Mon–Fri 1–4pm, Sat & Sun 10am–4pm; €2), tucked beneath the Rathaus off Herrngasse, which illustrates aspects of the town's history – including its Jewish history – in a kitsch but accessible style; the visit culminates with a look at the grisly dungeons, complete with cells, pillory and rack.

St Jakobs Kirche

Immediately to the north of the Rathaus rises the Protestant parish church of **St Jakob** (April–Oct daily 9am–5.15pm; Nov & Jan–March daily 10am–noon & 2–4pm; during Christmas market Mon–Sat 10am–4.45pm, Sun 10.45am–4.45pm; €2), begun in 1311 but not consecrated until 1485. Its chief glory is the extraordinary **Heilig-Blut-Altar** (1499–1505), so named for the relic it contains – supposedly three drops of Christ's blood – which turned Rothen-burg into a major place of pilgrimage in the Middle Ages. The sinuous, delicate Gothic structure created by local cabinet-maker Erhard Harschner provides a memorable setting for Tilman Riemenschneider's characteristically expressive figures. Centre-point of the altar is his depiction of the Last Supper. Also notable is the richly colourful **Zwölfbotenaltar** or Twelve Apostles' Altar, decorated with fifteenth-century paintings by Nördlingen artist Friedrich Herlin, including one that depicts Rothenburg's Rathaus as it was before fire destroyed the original Gothic building facing Marktplatz.

West along Herrngasse

Stately **Herrngasse** lives up to its name – Lords' Lane – with some of the finest surviving patrician houses in Rothenburg, though at the Marktplatz end it is dominated by the year-round Christmassy commercialism of the Käthe Wohlfahrt store and its associated **Deutsches Weihnachtsmuseum** (German Christmas Museum: April–Christmas daily 10am–5pm; Christmas–March Sat & Sun 11am–4pm; €4), filled with historic Christmas decorations.

Things calm down further west at the austere **Franziskanerkirche**, worth a look for Tilman Riemenschneider's early **St Francis Altar**, which dates from around 1490. At the western end of Herrngasse, the tiny **Figurentheater** (Puppet Theatre; ☎09861/33 33, ⓦwww.figurentheater-rothenburg.com)

nestles in the shadow of the soaring fourteenth-century **Burgtor**, the highest tower in the town walls. Beyond here is the **Burggarten**, a park on the former site of Rothenburg's fortress, destroyed by an earthquake in 1356. From here you get good views of the **Doppelbrücke**, or double bridge, spanning the Tauber to the south, which despite its fourteenth-century design rather resembles a Roman aqueduct. A thirty-minute stroll down through the gardens and along the Taubertalweg brings you to the very odd **Topplerschlösschen** (Fri–Sun 1–4pm; closed Nov; €1.50), a retreat built in 1388 for Heinrich Toppler, the most famous and powerful of Rothenburg's mayors and resembling a small medieval house inexplicably perched atop a stone tower.

The Reichstadtmuseum and northern Altstadt

North of Herrngasse, a former Dominican convent at Klosterhof 5 houses the **Reichsstadtmuseum** (daily: April–Oct 10am–5pm; Nov–March 1–4pm; €3.50). Founded in 1258, the convent closed in 1554 after the last nun died; it passed to the control of the city council and was used as a widows' home. It exhibits a mixed bunch of artefacts of local interest: the original Renaissance stone figures from the Baumeisterhaus, which depict the seven virtues and – altogether more enjoyably – the seven vices, moved here to protect them from decay in 1936. You can also see the cycle of twelve medieval paintings of the Rothenburger Passion from the Franziskanerkirche's rood screen, once thought to be the work of Dürer but now generally believed to be by Martinus Schwarz. Not to be missed is the convent's well-preserved medieval kitchen; there's also a section on Rothenburg's medieval Jewish community.

A stroll north from the museum along Klingengasse brings you to the Klingentor gate and the curious late fifteenth-century **St Wolfgangskirche** (April–Sept daily 10am–1pm & 2.30–5pm; Oct daily 10am–4pm; during Advent Sat & Sun 11am–4pm; €1.50), which is a fortress church with ramparts in the church loft and casemates down below.

The Puppen- und Spielzeugmuseum and Mittelalterliches Kriminalmuseum

There are two museums that are worth a detour just south of Herrngasse. The **Puppen- und Spielzeugmuseum** (Puppet and and Toy Museum; March–Dec 9.30am–6pm; Jan & Feb 11am–5pm; €4), in two historic houses at Hofbronnengasse 11–13, has a collection of more than a thousand dolls from the period 1800 to 1945, as well as tin figures, dolls' houses and wooden toys. At the end of Hofbronnengasse at Burggasse 3–5, the **Mittelalterliches Kriminalmuseum** (Medieval Crime Museum; daily: Jan, Feb & Nov 2–4pm; March & Dec 1–4pm; April 11am–5pm; May–Oct 10am–6pm; €3.80) is an altogether darker affair, with exhibits that include an executioner's mask, an iron maiden and a witch's chair.

The eastern and southern Altstadt

It was the eastern side of Rothenburg's Altstadt that bore the brunt of destruction in 1945, and it's here that the sharp-eyed visitor might spot a few traces of the restorer's art. Yet even here, Rothenburg can be exceptionally picturesque, notably around the quaint **Röderbogen** gateway at the end of Hafengasse, which dates from around 1200. Just beyond it, turn right into Alter Stadtgraben to reach the **Alt-Rothenburger Handwerkerhaus** at no. 26 (Easter–Oct Mon–Sat 11am–5pm, Sun 10am–5pm; during Advent daily 2–4pm; €2.50), an evocative thirteenth-century house stuffed full of peasant-style furniture and craftsmen's tools.

Head south from Marktplatz down Schmiedgasse past the imposing Renaissance **Baumeisterhaus** of 1596 to reach the southern part of the Altstadt. The tourist crowds and souvenir shops are particularly thick on the ground here, for most visitors want to see the absurdly picturesque **Plönlein**, a happily informal little square formed by the intersection of streets from the **Siebersturm** – which leads into the southern Altstadt – and the **Kobolzeller Tor**, beyond which a road winds down to the Doppelbrücke. It's one of the most-photographed views in Germany. The very southern tip of the Altstadt is marked by the formidable defensive complex of the **Spitalbastei**, built in the seventeenth century with two inner courtyards, seven gates and an upper walkway with embrasures.

Eating, drinking and festivals

Rothenburg is full of attractive places to **eat** and **drink**. Franconian **wine** – including local Taubertal wines – is the drink of choice. The local sweet treats are **Schneeballen** – literally snowballs, balled-up masses of biscuit dough which though not light, do have a pleasant, home-baked flavour. Buy them at the Diller bakery, with several branches in town including one at Obere Schmiedgasse 7. Foremost among Rothenburg's **festivals** is the Meistertrunk Festspiel, performed with much attendant parading and music over the Whitsun weekend (ⓦ www.meistertrunk.de).

Altfränkische Weinstube Klosterhof 7 ☏ 09861/64 04. Rothenburg has many snug and cosy old *Weinstuben*, but this twee, rustic and pretty example close to the Reichstadtmuseum probably takes the prize. The food – pork tenderloin with cranberries and salad, *Nürnberger Bratwürste* – is not expensive, and there's a roaring fire if the weather demands. Eve only.
Baumeisterhaus Obere Schmiedgasse 3 ☏ 09861/947 00. Coffee, cakes and a short menu of hot main courses from around €8 are served in evocative surroundings in this Renaissance house, with elaborate wall paintings, vaulted ceilings and a spectacular half-timbered *Hof*.
Café Gerberhaus Spitalgasse 25 ☏ 09861/949 00. *Kaffee und Kuchen*, *Bratwurst* with *Sauerkraut*

and local Taubertal wines in classy but informal surroundings in the southern part of the Altstadt.
Eiscafé Bortolot Untere Schmiedgasse 8. Traditional Italian-style ice-cream parlour in the southern Altstadt.
Reichsküchenmeister Kirchplatz 8 ☏ 09861/97 00. Fish, game and Franconian regional specialities from around €14, beneath the splendidly saggy wooden ceiling of this buzzy hotel restaurant. There's also a more informal *Weinstube*, *Löchle*, with bottles hanging up outside.
Weinhaus Zum Pulverer Herrngasse 31 ☏ 09861/97 61 82. Simple, inexpensive dishes – goulash with *Spätzle*, *Schnitzel* with fries – are served in the beautiful wood-panelled dining room of this *Weinstube* close to the Burgtor. From around €6.80.

Cycling the Taubertal

One very attractive way to get around is to slow the pace right down and explore the gently beautiful Franconian wine-growing countryside by bicycle along the **Liebliches Taubertal Radweg**. The 100km route follows the course of the Tauber from Rothenburg northwest to Wertheim; a tougher route completes the circuit by returning southwest towards Rothenburg along the heights of the Taubertal through Königsheim and Boxberg west of the Tauber. Along the way, there are stunning Tilman Riemenschneider altars at Detwang and Creglingen, a Schloss and museum of the Teutonic Knights at Bad Mergentheim and a Matthias Grünewald Madonna at Stuppach. The route follows forest or farm tracks for much of the way; from May to October the **regional trains** on the west bank of the Tauber between Freudenberg, Wertheim and Schrozberg – 22km west of Rothenburg – carry special luggage vans to cope with cycles, so you don't have to cycle both ways if you don't want to. There's also a baggage service to which some hoteliers sign up, so that you don't need to haul everything with you. There are cycle repair and rental facilities in several of the villages along the route. For more information, contact Liebliches Taubertal e.V, c/o Landratsamt Main-Tauber-Kreis, Gartnerstrasse 1, Tauberbischofsheim (☏ 09341/82 58 06, ⓦ www.liebliches-taubertal.de).

Dinkelsbühl

DINKELSBÜHL, 48km south of Rothenburg ob der Tauber along the Romantic Road, is another medieval gem. Though it lacks the sparkle of Rothenburg's hilly setting, making do with the placid River Wörnitz, some parkland and a few large ponds to set off its perfectly preserved medieval fortifications, it boasts an Altstadt which is, if anything, even more flawless, having escaped damage in World War II. It's also less overwhelmed by tourism. Like Rothenburg, Dinkelsbühl was once a free imperial city; it changed hands eight times in the Thirty Years' War, but after it was occupied by the Swedes in 1632 it was largely spared further damage.

The **Altstadt** measures just 1km from northwest to southeast, and is barely 500m wide from Segringer Tor in the west to Wörnitz Tor in the east. A walk around the outside of the medieval walls is therefore not only instructive but enjoyable. Heading south from the **Wörnitz Tor**, fourteenth century but for its sixteenth-century gabled bell tower, you pass the picturesque, half-timbered **Bäuerlinsturm** before reaching the southern tip of the Altstadt at the **Nördlinger Tor**. Next to it, the impregnable-looking fourteenth-century Stadtmühle houses the **Museum 3.Dimension** (April–Sept daily 10am–6pm; Oct & Christmas–New Year daily 11am–4pm; Nov–March Sat & Sun 11am–4pm; €9), an offbeat but enjoyable museum dedicated to three-dimensional imagery, with everything from stereoscopic art and holographs to a rare collection of Viewmasters, the colour-slide viewing devices that were once a firm favourite as a Christmas gift or holiday souvenir.

West of Nördlinger Tor, the **Alte Promenade** passes a parade of austere, unadorned medieval towers before reaching the **Segringer Tor**, one landmark that was damaged by the occupying Swedes; it was rebuilt in 1655 in Baroque style. Here, the fortifications turn north, reaching the lovely ensemble of the **Faulturm** and **Rothenburger Tor** before swinging southeast again to Wörnitz Tor.

Once within the walls, there's hardly anything to disturb the illusion of medieval perfection. It's just a short walk from Wörnitz Tor to the **Altes Rathaus**, the oldest parts of which date back to 1361. It now houses the **Haus der Geschichte Dinkelsbühl** (May–Oct Mon–Fri 9am–6pm, Sat & Sun 10am–5pm; Nov–April daily 10am–5pm; €4), which presents the history of the town in war and peace over four floors. In addition to artefacts from Dinkelsbühl's imperial heyday, the museum has a gallery showing works that chart the rediscovery of the town by artists in the nineteenth century and later, including a view painted by the Expressionist Karl Schmidt-Rottluff.

Just to the north, the **Münster St Georg** looms over the centre of the Altstadt. The lofty late Gothic hall church was built between 1488 and 1499 to the plans of Nikolaus Eseler, and it's generally reckoned to be one of the most beautiful of its era in southern Germany; the tower is Romanesque, and dates from 1220 to 1230. Facing the church across **Weinmarkt** is a stately parade of five tall, gabled houses, dating from around 1600, the most magnificent being the **Schranne**, a former grain warehouse, and the **Deutsches Haus**, which has a richly decorated, late Renaissance facade – the figures include a representation of Bacchus, the god of wine.

Practicalities

Getting to Dinkelsbühl is bit of a headache out of season if you don't have your own **transport**. Journeys from Rothenburg involve switching from train to bus or bus to bus; there is a handful of direct buses from Nördlingen to the south, from where the journey takes around 45 to 55 minutes. Between May and October

The Romantic Road

Though there are tourist roads that crisscross Germany for everything from wine to fairy tales and half-timbered houses, the **Romantic Road** remains by far the best-known internationally. Created in the 1950s to boost tourism, it threads its way south from the River Main to the Alps as the landscape progressively changes from gentle, rolling agricultural country to the fringes of the mountains. Along the way, it passes by some of Germany's most remarkable and famous visitor attractions: the Residenz in **Würzburg**, the perfectly preserved medieval towns of **Rothenburg ob der Tauber** and **Dinkelsbühl**, the UNESCO World Heritage Site of the **Wieskirche** and "Mad" King Ludwig II's Wagnerian fantasy castle of **Neuschwanstein**. Much the easiest way to travel the Romantic Road is, of course, by car, but if you don't have your own transport the Eurolines-affiliated Europabus (Ⓦ www.touring.de) travels the road daily from May to October between Frankfurt, Füssen and Munich, with special offers for hikers and cyclists and facilities to transport bikes. There's also a 424km **cycle route**, most of it fairly gentle and characterized by well-made local tracks or quiet local roads, or you can follow the route on foot; the GPS data for the entire walk can be ordered from the Romantic Road website, Ⓦ www.romantischestrasse.de.

things are easier: a Eurolines **bus** (Ⓦ www.touring.de) links the various stops along the Romantic Road (see box above). Dinkelsbühl's **tourist office** is in the Haus der Geschichte Dinkelsbühl at Altrathausplatz 14 (May–Oct Mon–Fri 9am–6pm, Sat & Sun 10am–5pm; Nov–April daily 10am–5pm; ☎ 09851/90 24 40, Ⓦ www .dinkelsbuehl.de). The *Deutsches Haus*, Weinmarkt 3 (☎ 09851/60 58, Ⓦ www .deutsches-haus-dkb.de; ❻), is an atmospheric and central **hotel**, with individually designed rooms, some with period furnishings; alternatively, try the cyclist-friendly *Goldenes Lamm*, Lange Gasse 26–28 (☎ 09851/22 67, Ⓦ www.goldenes.de; ❸), in a pair of gabled houses to the south of Weinmarkt, with a pretty garden terrace and parking. The **youth hostel** is in a half-timbered former grain warehouse at Koppengasse 10 (☎ 09851/95 09, Ⓦ www.dinkelsbuehl.jugendherberge.de; dorms €17.10 with breakfast). Both hotels have **restaurants**: the ⚑ *Deutsches Haus* serves refined regional food in a lovely, atmospheric dining room with painted ceilings, with mains starting from around €13; while the menu at the *Goldenes Lamm* features both regional and international dishes. There's a good scattering of cafés and ice-cream places in the Altstadt to satisfy lighter appetites.

Dinkelsbühl's most celebrated festival is the **Kinderzeche** (Ⓦ www .kinderzeche.de), an annual children's and folklore festival that takes place in July. It has its origins in the Thirty Years' War: the story goes that in 1632 a deputation of local children dissuaded the commander of the besieging Swedish forces from ransacking the town by singing. Children in historic costume still form an important element in the festival parades, with music provided by the Knabenkapelle, a famous boys' band.

Aschaffenburg

ASCHAFFENBURG is a last taste – or a first glimpse – of Bavaria for travellers between the Free State and neighbouring Hesse, tucked into the westernmost corner of Franconia at the foot of the wooded Spessart hills. Closer to Frankfurt than it is to Würzburg, from the tenth century onwards it belonged to the archbishopric of Mainz, and was the capital of the largest of a series of scattered parcels of territory belonging to the archbishops – the so-called Oberes Erzstift (upper archdiocese). It was the archbishops' second residence until the dissolution of the archbishopric in 1803; the town finally passed to Bavaria in 1814. Dubbed the "Bavarian Nice" because of its mild climate, Aschaffenburg doesn't quite live up to the comparison – it's too small, and outside the historic core too industrial – but it is an attractive town, which recovered well from grievous damage in the last weeks of World War II, and which has enough sights to justify an overnight stop.

Arrival, information and accommodation

Aschaffenburg's **Bahnhof**, which has high-speed connections with both Würzburg and Frankfurt, is just north of the Altstadt on Ludwigstrasse. The **tourist office** is in the heart of the Altstadt at Schlossplatz 1 (April–Sept Mon–Fri 9am–6pm, Sat 9am–1pm; Oct–March Mon–Fri 9am–5pm, Sat 10am–1pm; ☏06021/39 58 00, ⊛www.info-aschaffenburg.de).

Places to **stay** include the upmarket, historic and reasonably priced *Wilder Mann* at Löherstrasse 52 (☏06021/30 20, ⊛www.hotel-wilder-mann.de; ❹), and its sister hotel, the simpler but comfortable half-timbered *Goldener Karpfen* across the street at Löherstrasse 20 (☏06021/459 09 00, ⊛www.goldenerkarpfen.de; ❸).

The Town

The modest but pleasant **Altstadt** focuses on Schlossplatz, often the setting for open-air events, and dominated by the vast red-sandstone Renaissance **Schloss Johannisburg** (Tues–Sun: April–Sept 9am–6pm; Oct–March 10am–4pm; €4, €6 with Pompejanum), built between 1605 and 1614 under Archbishop Johann Schweikart von Kronberg after its predecessor was destroyed by the troops of the Hohenzollern Margrave Albrecht Alcibidades in 1552. With its four corner towers creating a distinctive and impressive silhouette high on the banks of the River Main, the Schloss is the symbol of Aschaffenburg, instantly recognizable even to drivers rushing past on the A3 Autobahn. Reduced to a shell by the fighting in the spring of 1945, it has been immaculately restored and now houses the eclectic collection of the **Schlossmuseum**. A display at the start of the visit explains the history of the Schloss with the aid of models and shocking photographs of its desolate post-1945 state. Happily, most of the Schloss's contents were stored for safekeeping during the war, and thus it was possible to re-install Archbishop Friedrich Carl von Erthal's restrained, Neoclassical eighteenth-century **apartments** afterwards, one floor higher than their original position. His **art collection** is also on display, and includes Jacob Jordaens' *Allegory on the teaching work of St Augustine* and Rembrandt's *St John the Evangelist* as well as works by Anthony Van Dyck, Lucas Cranach the Elder and Hans Baldung Grien. The museum has a series of remarkable **cork models** of the monuments of ancient Rome, created by the court confectioner and his son between 1792 and 1854. There's also a local history section, with a model of the Altstadt as it was in 1800 and interesting displays on local industries.

A pleasant stroll through the Schlossgarten high above the Main brings you to the remarkable **Pompejanum** (April to mid-Oct Tues–Sun 9am–6pm; €4, €6 with Schlossmuseum), an idealized replica of a Roman villa built for King Ludwig I between 1840 and 1848 by Friedrich von Gärtner, with rooms laid out around a peristyle in Roman fashion, though the central court has a glazed roof in concession to the German winter. The villa has been gradually undergoing restoration, but in the meantime the semi-ruinous state of some of the wall paintings only adds to an already uncanny feeling of authenticity.

On Schlossplatz's south side, the deconsecrated **Jesuitenkirche** (entrance on Pfaffengasse; Tues 2–8pm, Wed–Sun 10am–5pm; €6) is the venue for an interesting array of temporary art exhibitions, with a slight bias towards classic twentieth-century modernism. South of here, the Neoclassical **Stadttheater** fronts a modest little square on the way to the imposing **Stiftskirche** (summer 8am–6pm; winter 9am–5pm; free). Founded in the tenth century, it's an eclectic mishmash of Gothic, Romanesque and Baroque, though the interior is predominantly Romanesque and plain to the point of austerity. It has a noteworthy art collection, however, including Matthias Grünewald's moving *Lamentation*, painted in 1525, and his *Maria Schnee Altar* in the elegant Gothic chapel (Sat & Sun 1–5pm; €1) of the same name; the ticket also allows entry to the Romanesque cloisters.

Next to the Stiftskirche is the **Stiftsmuseum**, Stiftsplatz 1a (Tues–Sun 11am–5pm; €2.50), whose collections encompass archeology, Romanesque and Gothic sculpture and medieval religious painting. Prize exhibits include the mid-thirteenth-century *Aschaffenburger Tafel*, one of the oldest surviving retables of its kind in Germany and originally from the Stiftskirche, and fragments of an altar by Tilman Riemenschneider showing the Nativity.

Aschaffenburg also has a brace of attractive parks. **Park Schöntal** lies on the eastern fringe of the Altstadt and centres on the picturesque ruins of a church that had a brief existence – built in 1544, it was destroyed less than a decade later. To the west of the town on the opposite side of the Main, **Park Schönbusch** (free access) is one of the oldest surviving English-style parks in Germany. Its centrepiece is the archbishops' pretty little Neoclassical summer **Schloss** (guided tours April–Sept Tues–Sun 9am–5pm; €3), furnished in Louis XVI style.

Eating, drinking and entertainment

Good places to **eat** include the rather classy *Wirtshaus Zum Fegerer* at Schlossgasse 14 (☎06021/156 46), in a picturesque corner of the Altstadt, and the pretty *Schlossgass'* next door (☎06021/97 76 30), which is somewhat cheaper, serves traditional local dishes and salads, and has a garden; the cosily old-fashioned *Altstadt Café* at Pfaffengasse 18 (☎06021/282 83) is a good option for lighter choices, including breakfast. Aschaffenburg offers a surprisingly full cultural line-up for its size; the main venue for high **culture** is the elegant Stadttheater at Schlossgasse 8 (box office in the Stadthalle, Schlossplatz 1; ☎06021/270 78). **Live bands** play at *Colos-Saal*, Rossmarkt 19 (☎06021/272 39, ⓦwww.colos-saal.de), with everything from rock to jazz on the programme.

Travel details

Trains

Aschaffenburg to: Frankfurt (every 15–20min; 30min–1hr); Nuremberg (hourly; 1hr 35min); Würzburg (every 20–40min; 40min–1hr 10min).
Bamberg to: Bayreuth (hourly; 1hr 15min); Coburg (hourly; 52min); Lichtenfels (every 20–40min; 15–30min); Nuremberg (every 20–30min; 35min–1hr 10min); Würzburg (every 15–45min; 1hr–1hr 15min).
Bayreuth to: Bamberg (hourly; 1hr 15min); Kulmbach (hourly; 34min).
Nuremberg to: Bamberg (every 15–30min; 40min–1hr); Bayreuth (hourly; 45min–1hr 5min);

Berlin (hourly; 4hr 25min); Coburg (every 2hr; 1hr 40min); Frankfurt (every 30min–1hr; 2hr 5min); Ingolstadt (every 30min–1hr; 30–45min); Lichtenfels (every 20min–1hr; 55min–1hr 10min); Munich (every 10–20min: 1hr–2hr 45min); Regensburg (every 30min–1hr; 50min–1hr 25min); Würzburg (every 15min–1hr; 55min–1hr 10min).
Würzburg to: Aschaffenburg (every 20–40min; 40min–1hr 20min); Bamberg (every 15–45min; 1hr–1hr 10min); Frankfurt (every 20–40min; 1hr 10min–2hr 10min); Nuremberg (every 15–30min; 55min–1hr 15min); Rothenburg ob der Tauber (via Steinach: hourly; 1hr 10min).

Munich and central Bavaria

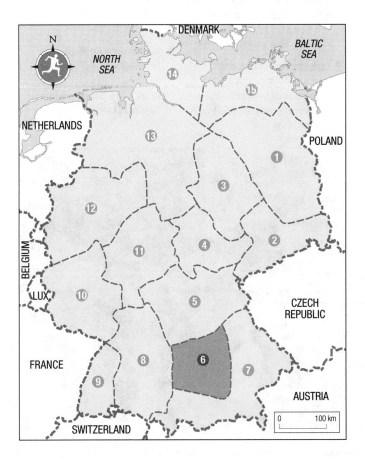

CHAPTER 6   # Highlights

✳ **The Pinakothek der Moderne** Art and architecture in perfect harmony at Munich's impressive temple to modernism. See p.363

✳ **Amalienburg** The Rococo style reaches silvery perfection in this beautiful little hunting lodge built for the Bavarian Wittelsbach dynasty. See p.368

✳ **Oktoberfest** Lederhosen, dirndls and impossibly vast quantities of beer characterize the world's most alcoholic folk festival. See p.373

✳ **KZ Dachau** A visit to the former Nazi concentration camp is a sombre but thought-provoking experience. See p.374

✳ **Kloster Andechs** *Carmina Burana* and Benedictine beer make a winning combination on the shores of the Ammersee. See p.376

✳ **Augsburg's Altstadt** Renaissance architecture meets racy nightlife in Augsburg's beautiful old town. See p.381

▲ Oktoberfest

Munich and central Bavaria

"Laptop and Lederhosen" is the expression the Germans use to explain the paradox of Bavaria, a region firmly rooted in tradition that nevertheless manages to reconcile social conservatism with a dynamic and innovative approach to business that makes it one of the powerhouses of the German economy. Nowhere is the contrast sharper than in its capital city. Munich is as cosmopolitan and sophisticated a city as any in Germany, a citadel of conspicuous consumption much loved by the cashmere-clad *Schickies* for whom it is, self-evidently, the "northernmost city in Italy". Yet at the same time, it's also the beer- and sausage-obsessed centre of all that is traditionally Bavarian, to its detractors a *Millionendorf* – a village with a million inhabitants. Beyond Munich but within easy reach of it, the urbanized and industrialized heartlands of Bavarian Swabia and Upper Bavaria display similar contrasts, with perfectly preserved old towns alongside world-beating manufacturing industries. This is not yet the Bavaria of popular cliché: there aren't even any mountains.

It is, above all, a region of urban glories. As capital of the Duchy that Napoleon expanded and raised to the status of a kingdom, **Munich** has the air – and cultural clout – of a capital city to this day, though its heyday as capital of the kingdom of Bavaria lasted little more than a century. To the west, the Swabian city of **Augsburg** has far older claims to urban greatness, which have left their mark in the city's splendid Renaissance core. In the north, comfortably prosperous **Ingolstadt** balances respect for its historical legacy with pride in its industrial prowess, notably as the home of the car manufacturer Audi. The smaller towns too retain memories of past glories, from the former free imperial city of **Nördlingen** to the picture-book *Residenzstadt* of **Neuburg an der Donau**. Only in the south does the landscape come to the fore, in the rolling lakeland of the **Fünf-Seen-Land**, where the Alps are at last a discernible presence, if only on the horizon.

Getting around this densely populated part of Bavaria is relatively straightforward, with Munich's suburban rail system extending far out into the surrounding countryside and the other major population centres linked to it by Autobahn and rail. Moreover, Munich's airport – Germany's second busiest after Frankfurt – ensures it couldn't be easier to get into, or out of, the region. Yet even here, the Bavarian paradox holds true, for the gleaming, efficient

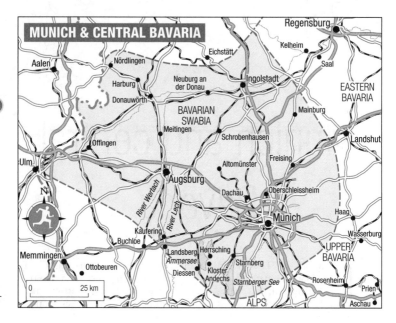

modern airport is named after one of Germany's most reactionary postwar politicians, the long-time Bavarian premier and leader of the conservative CSU party, Franz Josef Strauss.

Munich

If there's such a thing as the German dream, **MUNICH** (München) embodies it. Germany's third – and favourite – city often tops surveys to find the most liveable city on the planet, and it's easy to see why, with lakes and mountains on its doorstep, a fine roster of historic and cultural sights, glittering shops and the air of confidence that comes from being the home of BMW and Siemens. For all Bavaria's conservatism, it's also relatively liberal. If there's a fault, it's perhaps in the very lack of a flaw: with little grunge to offset it, Munich's well-groomed bourgeois perfection can at times seem a little relentless.

Founded in 1158, Munich became the seat of the Wittelsbach dynasty in 1255, but for much of its history it was outclassed by the wealth and success of Augsburg and Nuremberg. Finally, as capital of a fully-fledged Kingdom of Bavaria, established by Napoleon in 1806, it witnessed a surge of construction as Ludwig I and his architect Leo von Klenze endowed it with the Neoclassical monuments commensurate with its status. The turn of the twentieth century brought intellectual kudos: Der Blaue Reiter group of artists flourished, and a young Thomas Mann completed *Buddenbrooks* in the bohemian district of **Schwabing**. War changed everything, and in the chaos after World War I the city gave birth to the Nazi movement, which ultimately brought disaster upon it.

After World War II, Munich assumed Berlin's role as Germany's international metropolis, the haunt of VIPs, celebrities and the leisured rich. Much of the Federal Republic's film output emerged from the Geiselgasteig studios; Wim Wenders graduated from film school here and Rainer Werner Fassbinder held court at the *Deutsche Eiche* hotel. More surprisingly, Munich was one of the birthplaces of the disco movement, as producers like Giorgio Moroder fused strings, synthesizers and soulful vocals to massively commercial effect, though the acts involved either sang in English or were – like Donna Summer – themselves American, and the music's "Germanness" went largely unnoticed. The 1972 Olympic Games should have crowned this golden age, but the murder of eleven members of the Israeli team shocked the world and overshadowed all other events.

Berlin reasserted its old role post-reunification, but Munich has not rested on its laurels: the **Fünf Höfe** shopping complex, **Pinakothek der Moderne** and **Allianz-Arena** have all added lustre to the city in recent years. And, of course, there's always the beer: whether in a historic *Bierkeller*, shady *Biergarten* or in a vast tent at the **Oktoberfest**, Munich's tipple of choice is a world-beater.

Arrival, information and city transport

Munich's **airport** (℡089/975 00, Ⓦ www.munich-airport.de), one of Germany's biggest and most modern, is 28.5km northeast of the city centre. Lufthansa-operated buses (€10.50 single, €17 return) depart every twenty minutes for the Hauptbahnhof. S-Bahn trains on lines #1 and #8 link the airport to the city centre – of the two, S8, which routes via the Ostbahnhof, is quicker to both Marienplatz and the Hauptbahnhof. A taxi to the centre from the airport should cost around €61. There are **tourist offices** at the Hauptbahnhof (April–Oct Mon–Sat 9am–8pm, Sun 10am–6pm; ℡089/23 39 65 55, Ⓦ www.muenchen -tourist.de) and in the Neues Rathaus, Marienplatz 8 (Mon–Fri 10am–8pm, Sat 10am–4pm, closed Sun except during Christmas market), both of which will sell you a city **map** (€0.30) and a **CityTour Card** (1 day €9.80, 2 days €18.80, 3 days €29.50, valid until 6am following day), which offers unlimited use of the city's public transport system and reductions on various attractions and tours – though as these don't include the major museums, whether the card represents good value or not depends how much you expect to use **public transport** (Ⓦ www.mvv -muenchen.de), which includes S-Bahn, U-Bahn, trams and buses. Single tickets for the central zone (which covers most of the places you'll probably want to visit with the exception of the airport and some outlying sights such as Dachau) cost €2.30; a one-day *Tageskarte* for the same zone costs €5. Tickets must be validated in the little blue machines on station platforms before you travel.

Accommodation

Munich is stronger on stylish and luxurious **hotels** than it is on budget offerings, with many of the latter clustering near the Hauptbahnhof, which is also where you'll find a reasonable selection of **backpacker hostels**. **Youth hostels** and **campsites** are, however, in the suburbs. You can book accommodation through the **tourist office** – by phone, on its website or in person – and they won't charge you for their assistance (℡089/23 39 65 55, Ⓦ www.muenchen-tourist.de). There's incredibly heavy demand for hotels during **Oktoberfest**, and if you find anything at all, chances are it will be much more expensive than usual.

Hotels

Carat Hotel Lindwurmstr. 13 ℡089/23 03 80, Ⓦ www.carat-hotel.de. Pleasant three-star hotel close to Sendlinger Tor. It's part of a small chain, and the comfortable if slightly bland rooms boast showers and WC, wi-fi (costs extra), minibar and TV. ⑤

Charles Hotel Sophienstr. 28 ℡089/544 55 50, Ⓦ www.thecharleshotel.com. Polished, luxurious modern outpost of the exclusive Rocco Forte Collection; even the standard rooms are an impressive forty metres squared, and most have views over the old botanical gardens. Prices from around €300. ⑨

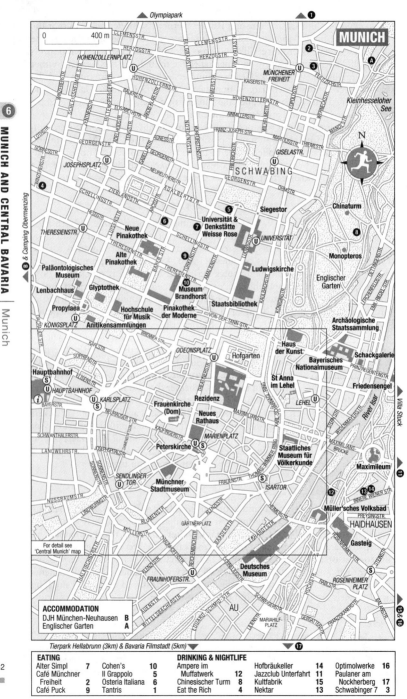

MUNICH

MUNICH AND CENTRAL BAVARIA | Munich

6

Olympiapark

Kleinhesseloher
See

SCHWABING

Chinaturm

Monopteros

Englischer
Garten

N

0   400 m

HOHENZOLLERNPLATZ

MÜNCHENER
FREIHEIT

CLEMENSSTR.
HERZOGSTR.
HOHENZOLLERNSTR.
KAISERSTR.
HOHENZOLLERNSTR.
AINMILLERSTR.
FRANZ-JOSEPH-STR.
GEORGENSTR.
GISELASTR.
GEORGENSTR.
ADALBERTSTR.

JOSEPHSPLATZ

GEORGENSTR.
ZIEBLANDSTR.
SCHELLINGSTR.

THERESIENSTR.

Neue
Pinakothek

Alte
Pinakothek

Paläontologisches
Museum

Lenbachhaus   Glyptothek

Propyläen

Hochschule
für Musik

KÖNIGSPLATZ   Anitikensammlüngen

Propyläen

Museum
Brandhorst

Pinakothek
der Moderne

Staatsbibliothek

Siegestor

Universität &
Denkstätte
Weisse Rose

UNIVERSITÄT

Ludwigskirche

Archäologische
Staatssammlung

Haus
der Kunst

Bayerisches
Nationalmuseum

Schackgalerie

PRINZREGENTENSTR.

Friedensengel

ODEONSPLATZ

Hofgarten

Rezidenz

St Anna
im Lehel

LEHEL

River Isar

Villa Stuck

Hauptbahnhof

HAUPTBAHNHOF

BAYERSTR.

KARLSPLATZ

SCHWANTHALERSTR.

LANDWEHRSTR.

Frauenkirche
(Dom)

Neues
Rathaus

Peterskirche

MARIENPLATZ

SENDLINGER
TOR

Münchner
Stadtmuseum

Staatliches
Museum für
Völkerkunde

ISARTOR

GÄRTNERPLATZ

MÜLLERSTR.

Maximilianeum

Müller'sches Volksbad

HAIDHAUSEN

Gasteig

For detail see
'Central Munich' map

Deutsches
Museum

AU

FRAUNHOFERSTR.

ROSENHEIMER
PLATZ

MARIAHILF-
PLATZ

ACCOMMODATION
DJH München-Neuhausen B
Englischer Garten A

Tierpark Hellabrunn (3km) & Bavaria Filmstadt (5km)

352

EATING				DRINKING & NIGHTLIFE			
Alter Simpl	7	Cohen's	10	Ampere im		Hofbräukeller	14	Optimolwerke	16
Café Münchner		Il Grappolo	5	Muffatwerk	12	Jazzclub Unterfahrt	11	Paulaner am	
Freiheit	2	Osteria Italiana	6	Chinesischer Turm	8	Kultfabrik	15	Nockherberg	17
Café Puck	9	Tantris	1	Eat the Rich	4	Nektar	13	Schwabinger 7	3

Cortiina Ledererstr. 8 ⊕089/242 24 90, ⊛www
.cortiina.com. The doyen of Munich's designer
hotels: super-chic, modest in size and right in the
heart of the Altstadt. Rooms have lots of natural
oak and local Jura stone, and are equipped with
wi-fi and iPod stations. ❻

Deutsche Eiche Reichenbachstr. 13 ⊕089/231
16 60, ⊛www.deutsche-eiche.com. Comfortable
and stylish modern rooms with en-suite showers
and wi-fi, above Munich's most famous gay
Gasthaus, where Fassbinder and Freddie Mercury
were once customers; most but not all hotel guests
are gay or lesbian. ❺

Easy Palace Station Hotel Schützenstr. 7
⊕089/552 52 10, ⊛www.easypalace.de. Basic
rooms without en-suite facilities or more comfortable en-suite rooms, plus dorms (€16.90), in this
vibrant budget option close to the Hauptbahnhof.
There's a sister hostel close to the Theresienwiese
(see below). ❷–❹

Englischer Garten Liebergesellstr. 8 ⊕089/383
94 10, ⊛www.hotelenglischergarten.de. Homely
and attractive Schwabing pension close to the
Englischer Garten; most rooms have en-suite
facilities, and there are some good-value single
rooms. ❹

🏃 Helvetia Schillerstr. 6 ⊕089/590 68 50,
⊛www.helvetia-hotel.com. There's a very
alpine sense of space and neatness about this
stylish, Swiss-themed boutique hotel close to the
Hauptbahnhof. ❺

Hotelissimo Schillerstr. 4 ⊕089/55 78 55,
⊛www.hotelissimo.com. Comfortable and attractive en-suite rooms right by the Hauptbahnhof. Very
good value for the standard of accommodation. ❹

Ibis München City Dachauer Str. 21 ⊕089/55 19
31 02, ⊛www.ibishotel.com. Comfortable and
affordable outpost of the budget chain, close to the
Hauptbahnhof. Rooms are small but have en-suite
shower, TV and WC. ❷–❹

Pension Seibel Reichenbachstr. 8 ⊕089/231 91
80, ⊛www.seibel-hotels-munich.de. Very central
pension within walking distance of the Viktualienmarkt and Marienplatz; some cheaper rooms aren't
en suite. Decor is simple and Bavarian in style, and
the guests a diverse bunch, including many lesbian
and gay visitors. ❸

Platzl Sparkassenstr. 10 ⊕089/23 70 30, ⊛www
.platzl.de. Tasteful, upmarket hotel, with traditionally
styled rooms in the Altstadt, including a wood-
panelled Bavarian suite in rustic style. ❼

Torbräu Tal 41 ⊕089/24 23 40, ⊛www.torbraeu
.de. Elegant, long-established, family-run four-star
hotel right next to the Isartor. The a/c rooms blend
traditional and more contemporary styles, and
there are some triple rooms. ❼

Vier Jahreszeiten Kempinksi Maximilianstr. 17
⊕089/212 50, ⊛www.kempinski-vierjahreszeiten
.de. In a prime position on Munich's most elegant
shopping avenue, the *Vier Jahreszeiten* is the city's
grandest hotel. Rooms and suites are individually
decorated, mixing traditional and contemporary
styles with quirkier touches including original
murals. From around €255. ❾

Hostels

Ao Hostel Arnulfstr. 1 ⊕089/45 23 59 58 00,
⊛www.aohostels.com. Bright, decent, modern
hostel five stops west of the Hauptbahnhof by tram
#17. Dorm beds from €10, plus €3 for bedding, as
well as en-suite singles and doubles (❸); dorms
have private facilities.

DJH München-Neuhausen Wendl-Dietrich-Str. 20
⊕089/20 24 44 90, ⊛www.muenchen-neuhausen
.jugendherberge.de. A short distance from Rotkreuz-
platz U-Bahn in the west of the city, close to
Nymphenburg; accommodation is mostly in four- to
six-bed dorms. €25.10 with breakfast.

DJH München Park Miesingstr. 4 ⊕089/723 65
50, ⊛www.muenchen-thalkirchen.jugendherberge
.de. In the south of the city, close to Hellabrunn
Zoo and Thalkirchen U-Bahn station, from where
it's five stops to Sendlinger Tor. Recently
revamped, it has a cafeteria, bistro, recreation
and internet facilities. Prices in three-, four- and
six-bed dorms from €29.

Easy Palace City Hostel Mozartstr. 4 ⊕089/558
79 70, ⊛www.easypalace.de. Cheerful hostel close
to the Theresienwiese (and thus handy for the
Oktoberfest); dorm beds from´€19 and they also
have apartments, singles and doubles (❸).

Wombat's Senefelderstr. 1 ⊕089/59 98 91 80,
⊛www.wombats-hostels.com. Funky modern
Munich outpost of the well-known Austrian chain,
close to the Hauptbahnhof and with hostel beds
from €19 (breakfast extra). Internet access, free
lockers, and there are laundry facilities as well as a
glass-roofed patio and bar. Open 24hr.

Campsites

Campingplatz München-Obermenzing
Lochhausener Str. 59 ⊕089/811 22 35, ⊛www
.campingplatz-muenchen.de. Close to the end of
the A8 Stuttgart Autobahn in the west of the city.
Mid-March to Oct; they usually have space for
tents here even during Oktoberfest. S-Bahn line #2
to Untermenzing, then #164 bus.

Campingplatz München-Thalkirchen Zentral-
ländstr. 49 ⊕089/723 17 07, ⊛www.camping
.muenchen.de. South of the centre close to
Hellabrunn Zoo, with a shop and snack bar.
Mid-March to Oct. U-Bahn #3 to Thalkirchen.

The Tent In den Kirschen 30 ☎089/141 43 00, ⓦwww.the-tent.com. Low cost, not-for-profit campsite north of Nymphenburg; facilities include internet, bike rental and a *Biergarten*, and you can pitch your own tent or sleep in a cheap dorm tent. June to mid-Oct. Tram #17 to Botanischer Garten, then a 500m walk.

The City

Despite being a city of 1.35 million inhabitants, Munich is compact and easy to get to grips with. A line of boulevards follows the course of the medieval defences to define the **Altstadt**, which still preserves three of its medieval city gates, at **Karlsplatz** (also known as **Stachus**) in the west, **Sendlinger Tor** in the southwest and **Isartor Platz** in the southeast. All are major points of orientation for visitors entering and leaving the city centre, while **Marienplatz**, at the heart of the Altstadt, is the traditional hub of Munich. Immediately north of here is the **Residenz**, the Wittelsbach dynasty's palace. The **Maxvorstadt** stretches north and west from **Odeonsplatz** at the northern tip of the Altstadt and contains many of the city's best museums, including the famous trio of **Pinakothek** art galleries; further north still, the formerly arty and alternative (and now comfortably middle class) district of **Schwabing** fringes the **Englischer Garten**, one of the largest urban parks in Europe. West of Schwabing is the **Olympiapark**, site of the 1972 Olympic Games.

South of the centre, the trendy **Gärtnerplatzviertel** and **Glockenbachviertel** (known collectively as the Isarvorstadt) line the north bank of the Isar, while across the river, **Haidhausen** has some of the best of Munich's nightlife scene. Further afield are the Baroque palace at **Nymphenburg**, **Hellabrunn Zoo** and the **Bavaria Filmstadt**, plus the new and striking football stadium, the **Allianz-Arena**.

Marienplatz and around

When Munich has something to celebrate – from Christmas markets to Christopher Street Day – the focus of the festivities is **Marienplatz**, the small and irregularly shaped piazza at the heart of the Altstadt. As public squares go, it's an amorphous space, with historic buildings scattered around in no particular order, though the gilded *Madonna and Child* atop the **Mariensäule** column, erected in 1638 by the Elector Maximilian I in thanks for the sparing of the city by its Swedish occupiers during the Thirty Years' War, provides a central focus. Monumentality comes courtesy of the immense **Neues Rathaus**, a sooty pile in Flemish Gothic style that has dominated the square since the late nineteenth century. Its **Glockenspiel** draws crowds for the mechanical dancers that perform at 11am, noon and (March–Oct only) at 5pm; to musical accompaniment, jerky musicians and jousting knights perform before the newly-wed Wilhelm V and Renata von Lothringen – who actually married in 1568 – while coopers dance to celebrate the passing of the plague in 1517. You can climb the Rathaus **tower** (May–Oct Mon–Fri 9am–7pm, Sat & Sun 10am–7pm; Nov–April Mon–Fri 10am–5pm; €2) for views of the city. Immediately to the east, the tall gate tower and Gothic hall of the **Altes Rathaus** originally date from 1470 to 1480, but were largely destroyed by bombs during World War II and not fully rebuilt until the 1970s. The Altes Rathaus now houses the **Spielzeugmuseum** (daily 10am–5.30pm; €3), with a charming collection of old-fashioned dolls' houses, model trains and teddy bears. Overlooking Marienplatz from the south is central Munich's oldest church, **St Peter**, popularly known as Alter Peter. The oldest parts of the church date from 1368, though much of its present appearance is the result of a later Baroque rebuild, including the altar which provides an elaborate

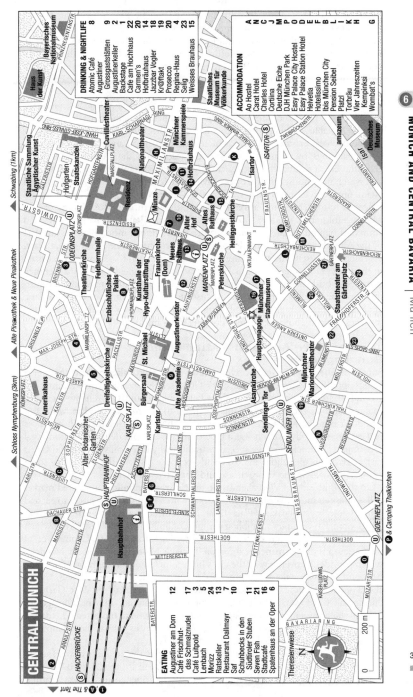

CENTRAL MUNICH

▲ HACKERBRÜCKE

▲ Schloss Nymphenburg (3km)   ▲ Alte Pinakothek & Neue Pinakothek   ▲ Schwabing (1km)

EATING

Augustiner am Dom	12
Café Frischhut– das Schmalznudel	17
Café Luitpold	3
Lenbach	5
Moritz	24
Ratskeller	13
Restaurant Dallmayr	7
Saf	10
Schubecks in den Südtiroler Stuben	11
Seven Fish	21
Stadtcafé	16
Spatenhaus an der Oper	6

DRINKING & NIGHTLIFE

Atomic Café	8
Augustiner	9
Grossgaststätten	1
Augustinerkeller	2
Backstage	22
Cafe am Hochhaus	14
Carmen's	18
Hofbräuhaus	19
Jazzbar Vogler	20
Kröfftakt	4
Prosecco	23
Regina-Haus	15
Selig	
Weisses Brauhaus	

ACCOMMODATION

Ao Hostel	A
Carat Hotel	N
Charles Hotel	C
Cortina	J
Deutsche Eiche	M
DJH München Park	P
Easy Palace City Hostel	O
Easy Palace Station Hotel	D
Helvetia	E
Hotelissimo	F
Ibis München City	B
Pension Seibel	L
Platzl	I
Torbräu	K
Vier Jahreszeiten Kempinksi	H
Wombat's	G

N · 200 m · 0

BAVARIA RING

setting for the late Gothic, seated figure of St Peter by Erasmus Grasser (1492). Its **tower** (Mon–Sat 9am–6pm, Sat & Sun 10am–7pm; €1.50) offers better views than the Neues Rathaus tower – not least because you can see the Rathaus itself. St Peter's near neighbour, the **Heilig-Geist-Kirche**, hides its Gothic origins behind an even more radical Baroque remodelling, the high point of which is a giddily ornamental interior by the Asam brothers, Munich's greatest practitioners of religious Baroque.

The warren of narrow streets northeast of the Altes Rathaus preserves something of the atmosphere of medieval Munich, though much restored and rebuilt. Notable buildings include the **Stadtschreiberhaus** at Burgstrasse 5, Munich's oldest private residence, which dates from 1550 and has lovely Renaissance paintings by Hans Mielich on its facade, and the nearby **Alter Hof**, Burgstrasse 8, a thirteenth-century complex that was the Wittelsbachs' first castle and which now houses the **Infopoint Museen & Schlösser Bayern** (Mon–Fri 10am–6pm, Sat 10am–1pm; Ⓦwww.museen-in-bayern.de), a useful information office for historic buildings in Bavaria. Just to the north, the **Alte Münze** or Old Mint at Hofgraben 4 hides a lovely sixteenth-century Italian Renaissance arcaded courtyard behind its later facades. But the most famous monument in this part of the Altstadt is the much-mythologized **Hofbräuhaus**, one block east at Platzl 9, which dubs itself "the most famous tavern in the world", and is immortalized in the song "*In München Steht ein Hofbräuhau*", written, incidentally, by a Berliner. More ominously, it was here on February 24, 1920, that Hitler proclaimed the 25 theses of the nascent Nazi party at its first big rally. That dubious claim to fame aside, it's a typically big, brassy and bustling Munich beer hall, with a history that stretches back to 1589; the current building dates from 1896.

The southern Altstadt: Viktualienmarkt to Sendlinger Tor

South of the Heilig-Geist-Kirche sprawls the **Viktualienmarkt** (Mon–Fri 10am–6pm, Sat 10am–3pm), the city's famous open-air food market, built on ground cleared of charitable buildings belonging to the Church by decree of Maximilian I in 1807. It's much the best place to get a cheap meal in Munich if you don't mind standing up – the various butchers and snack stalls sell hot slices of *Leberkäs* – literally liver cheese, a type of meatloaf – and delicious, lemony veal *Weisswurst* – Munich's sausage speciality, traditionally eaten only before midday. As well as Bavarian specialities and fruit-and-vegetable displays, the market has some quite fancy stalls selling wine, cheese and imported delicacies.

On the south side of Viktualienmarkt, the **Schrannenhalle** – a restored market hall – offers an indoor version of the market with an emphasis on places to eat and drink. Close by at St-Jakobs-Platz 1, the **Münchner Stadtmuseum** (Tues–Sun 10am–6pm, €4) occupies a rambling complex of buildings, the oldest part of which – the medieval Zeughaus or armoury – dates back to 1491–93. Centrepiece of the museum is the permanent exhibition **Typisch München** (Typically Munich), which provides an overview of the city's history, including a reappraisal of how the city spun its own myths at the time of the museum's foundation in 1888. There's also a section dealing with Munich's role as "secret capital" of West Germany during the Cold War, with a "Chill Out Loden Lounge" in which images of football stadiums and beer tents, laptops and Lederhosen are projected. The darker side of Munich's history is dealt with by a section on its role as the "Hauptstadt der Bewegung" – the capital city of the Nazi movement.

Facing the Stadtmuseum across St-Jakobs-Platz is the striking new **Hauptsynagoge** (guided tours Sun–Thurs at 6pm; free; call ☎089/20 24 0 01 00), a starkly elegant, modern stone-and-mesh cube that opened in 2006 as a fitting

▲ The Hauptsynagoge, Munich

replacement for the grandiose old synagogue destroyed in the summer of 1938 – several months before Kristallnacht. It's one of the largest – as well as the most visually striking – new synagogues in Europe, and serves a community of nine thousand, the second largest in Germany after Berlin. Next to it is the **Jüdisches Museum** (Jewish Museum; Tues–Sun 10am–6pm; €6), which as well as a permanent exhibition on the history of Jewish Munich and on the Jewish faith, often has fascinating temporary exhibitions on such topics as expulsion, persecution and exile.

A short stroll west along Sendlinger Strasse is the **Asamkirche** (daily 8am–5.30pm; free), officially the church of St John Nepomuk, but universally known by the name of its creators, the Asam brothers, who between 1733 and 1746 created the most gaudily theatrical – if by no means the biggest – church interior in Munich, a riot of Rococo opulence just 28m long and 9m wide. The design of the little church was influenced by both Bohemian and Italian Baroque, and it was intended as their own family chapel, which explains its opulence – without a client, all restraints were off. Sendlinger Strasse leads to the tough-looking fourteenth-century **Sendlinger Tor**.

The western Altstadt: The Frauenkirche to Stachus

Munich's main pedestrian shopping area stretches west from Marienplatz along Kaufingerstrasse, lined with the usual German chainstores. Just to the north of it is the **Frauenkirche** (Mon–Wed & Sat 7am–7pm, Thurs 7am–8.30pm, Fri 7am–6pm), whose 98-metre-high twin pepperpot towers (1524–45) soar above the surrounding buildings and are the visual symbols of the city; you can climb the southern tower for yet more views over the city (April–Oct Mon–Sat 10am–5pm; €3). Dating from 1468 to 1488, it was the last big Gothic hall church to be built in the Wittelsbachs' domains, and its austere brick elevations and whitewashed interior – much simplified since its postwar restoration – are pleasingly coherent and simple in a city where fussy Baroque ornament is the usual ecclesiastical style. The onion domes atop the twin towers were intended as a reference to the Dome of the Rock in Jerusalem – actually a mosque, but believed at the time to be King Solomon's Temple. Inside, a mysterious black footprint in the floor beneath the towers is said to have been left by the Devil, stamping in rage after architect Jörg von Halsbach won a wager with him to build a church without visible windows – by pointing out a spot where pillars hid every one.

Kaufinger Strasse continues into Neuhauser Strasse, the eastern end of which is dominated by the Jesuit church of **St Michael**, built under the auspices of Duke Wilhelm V between 1583 and 1597 to replace an earlier church – the first Jesuit church north of the Alps, based on the order's mother church of Il Gesù in Rome – whose tower collapsed before it could even be consecrated. This was the cue to build an even larger and more splendid church, whose financing bankrupted the state and forced Wilhelm to abdicate upon completion. Inside, the twenty-metre-wide, stucco-ornamented barrel-vaulted roof dominates; stylistically it was the prototype for scores of churches built later in southern Germany, though postwar restoration after severe bomb damage was not entirely accurate. The **Fürstengruft**, or crypt (Mon–Fri 9.30am–4.30pm, Sat 9.30am–2.30pm; €2), contains the graves of Wilhelm and another extravagant Wittelsbach, "Mad" King Ludwig II, who commissioned the fairytale castle of Neuschwanstein (see p.396), the mock Versailles of Herrenchiemsee (see p.407) and the more modest, but still opulent, Schloss Linderhof (see p.400).

Midway between St Michael and the Karlstor is the Baroque **Bürgersaal**, a meeting hall for the Catholic Marian congregation, built in 1710. Its crypt venerates Father Rupert Mayer, canonized in 1987 for his anti-Nazi sermons in the late 1930s, preached in defiance of a Gestapo gagging order. Arrested several times, he wound up in Sachsenhausen concentration camp before being transferred to house arrest at Kloster Ettal in southern Bavaria because of his poor health – the authorities were evidently wary of creating a martyr. He died of a stroke a few months after returning to Munich in 1945. Beyond Karlstor, **Karlsplatz**, or **Stachus**, is a crescent-shaped open space dominated by fountains and the vast neo-Baroque **Justizpalast**, which was one of the most important official buildings constructed in Germany during the nineteenth century.

The northern Altstadt

North from Marienplatz you enter Munich's most exclusive shopping district, whose modern face is represented by the slick **Fünf Höfe** mall subtly inserted into the townscape west of Theatinerstrasse and whose more traditional elegance is epitomized by the grand **Dallmayr** delicatessen in Diener Strasse and by the stately facades (and international designer names) of **Maximilianstrasse**, spiritual home of Munich flaneurs. It's dominated at its eastern end by the **Maximilianeum**, the terracotta-clad building high on the opposite bank of the river Isar that houses the Bavarian Land parliament. Like the street itself, it is named after King Maximilian II, during whose reign construction began. At the western end of Maximilianstrasse, the dignified Neoclassical facade of the **Nationaltheater** – reconstructed to the original plans after being gutted during World War II – presides over **Max-Joseph-Platz**.

The Residenz

The Residenz, the enormous royal palace complex of Bavaria's ruling Wittelsbach dynasty who resided here right up until 1918, has its origins in a small fourteenth-century castle, the Neuveste, of which nothing remains. Over the centuries it was gradually transformed into a considerable palace complex by the Wittelsbachs, first as dukes, then from 1623 as electors and finally from 1806 as kings of Bavaria. What survives today is the result of several phases of construction and of post-1945 reconstruction after extensive damage during World War II. The oldest surviving Renaissance part dates from the reign of

Albrecht V (1550–79) and was the work of Jacopo Strada and Simon Zwitzel, elaborated and extended from 1581 onwards by the Dutch architect Friedrich Sustris. Baroque and Rococo extensions followed, notably in the eighteenth century under court architect François Cuvilliés – the diminutive Walloon who also designed Schloss Augustusburg at Brühl. A final major round of construction took place under Leo von Klenze during the reign of King Ludwig I; the additions made by Ludwig II – which included a rooftop winter garden complete with a royal barge on an indoor lake – have not survived.

Its entrance is on the north side of Max-Joseph-Platz, and much of the interior of the palace is open to the public as the **Residenzmuseum** (daily: April to mid-Oct 9am–6pm; mid-Oct to March 9am–5pm; last admittance one hour before closing; €6, or €9 ticket with Schatzkammer, free English audio guide; ⓦwww .residenz-muenchen.de). The most spectacular room you see is also the oldest, the **Antiquarium**, originally built to house Duke Albrecht's collection of antiquities but remodelled under his successors, Wilhelm V and Maximilian I, as a banqueting hall. The results are breathtaking: the 66-metre-long vaulted hall is claimed to be the largest and most lavish Renaissance interior north of the Alps, richly decorated with frescoes, with allegories of fame and virtue by court painter Peter Candid covering the ceiling, while the vaults above the windows and the window jambs are covered with images of the towns, markets and palaces of Bavaria. The **Ahnengalerie**, which was commissioned by the Elector Karl on his accession in 1726, incorporates more than a hundred portraits of members of the Wittelsbach family. It was intended to draw attention to the elector's credentials as a potential emperor – and appears to have done the trick as he was crowned Emperor Karl VII in Frankfurt in 1742. François Cuvilliés' inspired hand is evident in the aptly named **Reiche Zimmer**, or ornate rooms, in which everything from the gilded rocailles on the stucco walls and ceilings to the furniture received the master's attention. The rooms were created between 1730 and 1733. Leo von Klenze's more restrained nineteenth-century **Königsbau** rooms were off limits to visitors at the time of writing due to restoration work.

The collection on display in the **Schatzkammer** (Treasury; same hours; €6, or €9 combined ticket) on the ground floor of the Königsbau was initiated by Albrecht V and is one of the largest royal treasure-houses in Europe; highlights include the ninth-century ciborium of King Arnulf of Carinthia and a dazzling statuette of St George created between 1586 and 1597. The royal insignia of the Kingdom of Bavaria are also on display.

You'll need to re-enter the Residenz complex by the middle entrance on Residenzstrasse and cross the Brunnenhof courtyard to reach the exquisite **Cuvilliés-Theater** (April–June & 1st two weeks Oct Mon–Sat 2–6pm, Sun 9am–6pm; July–Sept daily 9am–6pm; mid-Oct to March Mon–Sat 2–5pm, Sun 10am–5pm; last admission one hour before closing; €3), built from 1751 to 1755 as a court theatre under Elector Max III Joseph; Cuvilliés' extravagance survives only because the elaborately carved tiers of boxes were removed from their original location between the Nationaltheater and Residenz for safekeeping during World War II. The Alte Residenztheater building in which they originally stood was completely destroyed by wartime bombs and replaced by the modern theatre that now stands on the site, but the boxes were re-erected after the war in their present location. It's still used as a theatre.

Odeonsplatz and "Shirkers' Alley"

Directly opposite the entrance to the Brunnenhof on Residenzstrasse, little **Viscardigasse** was known colloquially during the Nazi years as "Drücke-bergergasse" or "Shirkers' Alley", because it was a short cut that could be used to avoid passing the SS honour guard – and having to give the compulsory "German greeting" or Nazi salute to them – stationed day and night on the Feldherrnhalle on nearby **Odeonsplatz**. A **bronze trail** set into the cobbles now recalls those who preferred to "shirk" the SS. Modelled on the Loggia dei Lanzi next to the Palazzo Vecchio in Florence and designed by Friedrich von Gärtner, the **Feldherrnhalle** was built in 1841 to 1844 to shelter statues of two celebrated Bavarian generals – General Tilly (of Rothenburg Meistertrunk fame; see p.340) and Prince Wrede, who helped Napoleon to victory at Wagram before Bavaria switched sides in time to participate in the Congress of Vienna. The Feldherrnhalle occupied a unique position in Nazi iconography, for it was here on November 9, 1923, that Hitler's "Beer Hall Putsch" was stopped in its tracks by police; sixteen of Hitler's associates – later dubbed the "Blood Witnesses" of the movement – were killed. The future dictator was arrested, only to receive an absurdly light sentence for treason from a sympathetic judge; Hitler used the subsequent jail term in Landsberg to write *Mein Kampf.*

Whatever its historical associations, Odeonsplatz is one of Munich's most handsome squares. On the west side, the buttercup-yellow exterior of the **Theatinerkirche St Kajetan** hides an airy white interior. The work of three architects – Agostino Barelli, Enrico Zuccalli and François Cuvilliés – it was modelled on St Andrea della Valle in Rome. Construction began in 1663 but was not completed until a century later, so that the church spans the transition from Baroque to Rococo. Like St Michael, it has a crypt full of Wittelsbachs. On the east side of Odeonsplatz along the north facade of the Residenz is the formal **Hofgarten** (free access), the former palace garden, whose geometric design dates from the reign of Maximilian I (1610–20). Here, the impressive **Staatliches Museum Ägyptisches Kunst** (State Museum of Egyptian Art; Tues 9am–9pm, Wed–Fri 9am–5pm, Sat & Sun 10am–5pm; €5) had its home at the time of writing, though it's due to move to purpose-built new premises by 2010.

Museums along Prinzregentenstrasse

East of the Hofgarten, traffic flashes along broad, straight **Prinzregentenstrasse**. Guarding its western approach is the **Haus der Kunst** (daily 10am–8pm, Thurs until 10pm; €8), a stripped Classical pile commissioned by Hitler, and completed in 1937 as a showcase for the sort of art of which he approved. Its architect, Paul Ludwig Troost, made his name designing the interiors of ocean liners, but missed the mark here, for what was obviously meant to be an imposing building is too squat to have the desired effect: it looks more like the plinth for something much bigger than a finished building. These days it's used for temporary exhibitions of the sort of modern art, design and photography the Nazis would have regarded as "degenerate".

Further along Prinzregentenstrasse is one of the big hitters among Munich's museums, the sprawling **Bayerisches Nationalmuseum** (Bavarian National Museum; Tues–Sun 10am–5pm, Thurs until 8pm; €5; ⓦ www.bayerisches -nationalmuseum.de), behind whose stern facade hides a dizzying array of fine and applied arts from late antiquity to the early twentieth century, much of it stemming from the Wittelsbachs' own collections. The ground floor is devoted to works of the Romanesque, Gothic and Renaissance, from suits of armour to winged altarpieces and carvings by Tilman Riemenschneider; the basement houses the world's largest collection of Nativity cribs, with examples from the Alps and Southern Italy, plus Bavarian furniture of the eighteenth and nineteenth centuries, often decorated with paintings on religious themes. Upstairs, musical instruments from the Wittelsbachs' court, silver table services and antique board games add a luxuriously domestic note, while there's a roomful of Nymphenburg porcelain as well as Rococo sculpture by Johann Baptist Straub and Ignaz Günther.

The Bayerisches Nationalmuseum's near neighbour, the **Schack-Galerie** (Wed–Sun 10am–5pm; €3) houses the art collection built up by Adolf Friedrich Graf von Schack (1815–94), a diplomat who in later life devoted himself entirely to his literary and intellectual pursuits. As an art collector he favoured young and little-known artists, in the process building up a collection of works by artists who were to number among the most important in nineteenth-century Germany, including Anselm Feuerbach and Arnold Böcklin. To this day the collection reflects Count Schack's personal tastes since – with the exception of a handful of losses during World War II – it remains largely unchanged.

On the other side of the River Isar, the last in Prinzregentenstrasse's line-up of art attractions is the **Villa Stuck** (Tues–Sun 11am–6pm; €4), the former home of Franz von Stuck (1863–1928), one of the founders of the Munich Secession and a tutor of Paul Klee and Wassily Kandinsky. The house was conceived as a *Gesamtkunstwerk* – a total work of art unifying life, work, art and architecture, music, theatre and a dash of narcissism. An eclectic mix of Jugendstil and other styles current at the time, the villa provides a suitably lush setting for Stuck's own work as well as a venue for temporary exhibitions on his artistic contemporaries.

Ludwigstrasse and the Maxvorstadt

North from Odeonsplatz stretches arrow-straight **Ludwigstrasse**, lined with early nineteenth-century Neoclassical buildings created during Ludwig I's reign by Leo von Klenze and Friedrich von Gärtner. The street terminates at its north end with the **Siegestor**, a triumphal arch based on the Arch of Constantine in Rome. Badly damaged during World War II, the arch was restored in such a way as to leave the extent of the damage visible. Long, handsome and dignified, Ludwigstrasse was a self-conscious attempt to create a Whitehall or Unter den Linden for Munich, though it's not exactly the liveliest of streets, only really becoming animated near the **Ludwig-Maximilians-Universität** at Geschwister-Scholl-Platz. A touching and innovative memorial in front of the university recalls the bravery and martyrdom of the anti-Nazi student group, Weisse Rose: plaques resembling the doomed students' antifascist leaflets are set

---

The Weisse Rose

Though nowadays it looms large in the mythology of anti-Nazi resistance, the **Weisse Rose** (White Rose) was from beginning to end a modest affair, the initiative of a small group of students – most of whom were studying medicine – and others from their wider circle of friends; the only older member of the group was the Swiss-born philosophy professor **Kurt Huber**. The core of the group, which came together in 1942, consisted of the devoutly Christian **Hans Scholl** – a former Hitler Youth group leader who had become vehemently opposed to Nazi ideology – and the Russian-born medical student **Alexander Schmorell**; Hans's sister **Sophie** also subsequently became involved. At night, the group daubed walls with slogans such as "Hitler, mass murderer" or "freedom", but it is for the six leaflets it produced and distributed – including one that made public the murder of the Jews – that the Weisse Rose is remembered. The last of these proved fateful. On February 18, 1943, Hans and Sophie deposited copies in the atrium of the university, but were spotted by the janitor and subsequently arrested by the Gestapo. Hans and Sophie were tried before the notorious Nazi judge Roland Freisler; they, along with other members of the group, were sentenced to death by guillotine.

into the cobbles almost at random, as though they had just fluttered to earth. Inside, the small **DenkStätte** is an exhibition about the Weisse Rose movement (Mon–Fri 10am–4pm; free).

The district laid out on a grid pattern west of Ludwigstrasse is known as the **Maxvorstadt** and is one of the most urbane in Munich; its browsable mix of antiquarian bookshops, antique shops and cafés repays dawdling.

The Museum Brandhorst

Newest addition to Munich's collection of museums is the **Museum Brandhorst** on the corner of Theresienstrasse and Türkenstrasse (opening spring 2009; Tues–Sun 9am–5pm; Ⓦ www.museum-brandhorst.de). The new museum – an eye-catching polychromatic rectangle by Berlin architects Sauerbruch Hutton – houses the collection of German and international modern art built up by Udo and Anette Brandhorst. The exhibits include works by such major international figures as Andy Warhol, Cy Twombly and Damien Hirst, as well as by major contemporary German artists such as Gerhard Richter and Georg Baselitz. From the outset, the Brandhorsts were interested in the connection between visual and literary art, and thus one of the museum's prize possessions is a collection of 112 first editions of books illustrated by Picasso, which represents most of the artist's output in this field.

The Pinakothek museums

Reason enough for a visit to Munich is provided by the royal flush of Pinakothek art galleries (Ⓦ www.pinakothek.de), each of which is dedicated to a different era in art history. The **Alte Pinakothek** is among the greatest collections of Old Masters in the world, the **Neue Pinakothek** is particularly strong on nineteenth-century German art while the **Pinakothek der Moderne** has seen record-breaking visitor numbers since its debut in 2002.

The Alte Pinakothek

The scars of war are visible on the broken facade of Leo von Klenze's **Alte Pinakothek** (Tues 10am–8pm, Wed–Sun 10am–6pm; €5.50, free English audio guide), at the time of its construction in 1826 to 1836 the largest art gallery in the world. Even today, it can be an overwhelming experience: the collections, which are based on the royal collection of the Wittelsbach dynasty over five hundred years, are arranged geographically and chronologically, encompassing German, Dutch, Flemish, Spanish, French and Italian art, with a timespan from the Middle Ages to the eighteenth century. Things kick off on the west side of the ground floor with **German painting** from the fifteenth and sixteenth centuries. Outstanding works here include Michael Pacher's *Kirchenväteraltar*, created for the Augustine abbey of Neustift in the South Tyrol, Lucas Cranach the Elder's *Adam and Eve* and the same artist's *Golden Age* of 1530, which depicts man's lost earthly paradise. Also on display on the ground floor is Pieter Bruegel the Elder's richly comic *The Land of Cockayne*, which depicts the vices of idleness, gluttony and sloth by showing three prostrate figures evidently sleeping off a good lunch. The main exhibition space is upstairs, beginning with more **medieval painting**: Hans Memling's *The Seven Joys of Mary* (1435–40) is an entire story in one painting, with the story of the Three Magi as its centrepiece; startlingly modern by comparison is Albrecht Dürer's innovative *Self Portrait with a Fur Trimmed Coat* from 1500, which depicts the artist at the age of 28 with flowing locks and aquiline nose – every inch the confident Renaissance man.

Italian art is represented by, among others, Botticelli's vivid *Pietà* of 1490 and an intriguing *Christ with Mary and Martha* by Tintoretto from 1580; but the centrepiece of the Alte Pinakothek's collection is the Rubenssaal, which was intended as the heart of the museum to reflect the importance of the Wittelsbachs' collection of works by Peter Paul Rubens. The room is dominated by the six-metre-high *Last Judgement* of 1617. One of the largest canvases ever painted, it depicts 65 figures, most of them naked, as graves open and the dead are separated into the blessed and the damned. Commissioned for the high altar of the Jesuit church at Neuburg an der Donau, it offended contemporary sensibilities and spent much of its short time at Neuburg draped – though it was the nudity, rather than the depiction of death and damnation, that caused offence. Among **Spanish works** in the collection, El Greco's *Christ Stripped of his Garments*, painted in 1606 to 1608 for Toledo cathedral, is notable for also having caused a scandal. Not only does it depict a scene of humiliation almost never painted in western art, but it also includes Mary Magdalene and the Virgin Mary as onlookers, with the implication that they will at any moment witness Christ's disrobing.

The Neue Pinakothek

Facing the Alte Pinakothek across Theresienstrasse, the **Neue Pinakothek** (Wed 10am–8pm, Mon & Thurs–Sun 10am–6pm; €5.50) picks up where the older museum leaves off, concentrating on art from the nineteenth century to Jugendstil. Like the Alte Pinakothek, it was founded under the auspices of King Ludwig I, but unlike its sister museum its destroyed buildings were not resurrected after World War II. Instead, a modern building was opened to house the collection in 1981.

The tour begins with art from around **1800**, prominent among which are a number of canvases by Goya, before progressing to English painting of the era, including Gainsborough's lovely *Portrait of Mrs Thomas Hibbert*, Constable's *View of Dedham Vale from East Bergholt* of 1815 and Turner's *Ostend* of 1844. Much of the rest of the museum is given over to German art, including works by artists active at Ludwig's court, such as a view of the Acropolis by Leo von Klenze. Another architect, Karl Friedrich Schinkel, is represented by a copy of his fantastical *Cathedral Towering Over a Town* of 1830. More contemplative in tone are Caspar David Friedrich's *Garden Bower* of 1818 and his sensual *Summer* of 1807. Later works include Adolph von Menzel's *Living Room with the Artist's Sister* of 1847 – which shows that the great self-taught Prussian painter was at home with intimate, domestic scenes as he was with his big, official works – and *Munich Beer Garden* by the German Impressionist **Max Liebermann**, painted in 1884.

French **Impressionist** and **Post-Impressionist** works include a Pissarro view of Norwood, a *Portrait of a Young Woman* by Renoir and Manet's *Monet Painting on His Studio Boat* of 1874, as well as one of Van Gogh's *Sunflowers*. There are also several canvases by Cézanne and starkly contrasting works by the Austrians Klimt and Schiele.

The Pinakothek der Moderne

The baton of art history is again picked up by the third of the museums, the **Pinakothek der Moderne** (Tues, Wed & Fri–Sun 10am–6pm, Thurs 10am–8pm; €9.50), which gathers its somewhat disparate collections of classic modern and contemporary art, design and architecture around a striking central rotunda. Stephan Braunfels' clean modern architecture won much praise at the time of the museum's debut, though the building isn't perhaps quite as pleasing as the earlier Kunstmuseum in Bonn, and the layout's complexity means you'll need to hang on to your floorplan if you're to navigate the museum successfully.

All the same, it's a rewarding place to visit. Make a beeline for the **Sofie and Emanual Fohn Collection** on the first floor, which kicks off the museum's impressive selection of modern art with works by artists ridiculed as degenerate by the Nazis, including Kokoschka, Franz Marc and Jawlensky. There follows a gallery devoted to the Expressionist collective Die Brücke – where the highlights include Emil Nolde's gorgeous *Nordermühle* – and a roomful of works by Ernst Ludwig Kirchner. Pride of place goes to Munich's own Expressionists of **Der Blaue Reiter** group, with works by Franz Marc, Kandinsky and others which even pre-World War I were strongly advocating abstraction, and there is considerable space devoted to Max Beckmann, including a scowling 1944 self-portrait. Close by there's a Picasso portrait of a seated Dora Maar from 1940 and a typically big, vivid postwar canvas, *The Painter and His Model*, from 1963.

From 2009 the east wing of the first floor will again display the museum's permanent collection of **contemporary art**, including room installations by Donald Judd, Dan Flavin and Fred Sandback as well as major works by Andy Warhol, Arnulf Rainer and Blinky Palermo. The museum's ground floor is devoted to architecture and to a rotating selection of the graphic works of the **Staatliche Graphische Sammlung**. The basement is a temple to applied **design**, with everything from a streamlined 1930s Tatra car to classic modern furniture by Isamo Noguchi, Arne Jacobsen and Verner Panton. The labelling is somewhat hit-and-miss, however, and in the basement's further reaches there's a general feeling of a department store on a quiet day.

Königsplatz and around

Nowhere expresses Ludwig I's desire to erect an Athens on the Isar better than **Königsplatz**, a short walk to the southwest of the Pinakothek museums. It's a stiff but proper set-piece of Neoclassical architecture, presided over by Leo von Klenze's **Propyläen** gateway of 1846 to 1862, decorated with friezes depicting Greek warriors, and flanked by non-identical twin temples to the arts of antiquity – the Glypothek on the north side, another of Klenze's works, and the Staatliche Antikensammlung on the south side.

Wartime destruction did a great aesthetic favour to the **Glypothek** (Tues, Wed & Fri–Sun 10am–5pm, Thurs 10am–8pm; €3.50, or €5.50 combined ticket with Antikensammlung; English guide €1), for it allowed the museum's curators to strip away Leo von Klenze's fussy and much-criticized interiors and instead present the museum's beautiful collection of antique statuary in surroundings of exquisite austerity. The collection starts as it means to go on with a roomful of early depictions of Greek youths, including a large, rust-coloured **grave statue** of a youth from Attica, dated around 540 or 530 BC. The most famous single sculpture in the museum is the **Barberini Faun**, a remarkable depiction of a sleeping satyr, languid yet athletic, which was probably originally erected in the open space of a Greek sanctuary dedicated to Dionysos. Dated around 200 BC, the sculpture's route to Munich was via the Palazzo Barberini in Rome, from which it acquired its popular name. The largest single collection of sculptures in the museum is the superb group of pediment sculptures from the **Sanctuary of Aphaia** on the island of Aegina, which date from around 500 BC. The Glypothek also has a fascinating selection of **Roman** sculptures from the period of the late Republic, when – in contrast to the aesthetic ideal always depicted in Greek sculptures – there was an attempt to produce genuine likenesses.

The essential counterpoint to the Glypothek's statuary is provided by the more fragile artworks of the **Staatliche Antikensammlung** (Tues–Sun 10am–5pm; €3.50, or €5.50 with Glypothek). Here, you can feast your eyes on astonishingly delicate jewellery in the basement, including many very beautiful Etruscan earrings, a solid-gold diadem from the Greek Black Sea colony of Pantikapeion in what is now Ukraine, dated 300 BC, and a splendid gold funerary wreath from Armento in Italy, dated to 370–360 BC. The ground floor of the museum is devoted to Greek pottery in all its varieties, variously decorated with mythological themes or with scenes from everyday life.

On the western side of the Propyläen, the buildings of the **Lenbachhaus** museum complex flank the continuation of Brienner Strasse. Although it is known above all for its collection of the works of the Munich-based Blaue Reiter group of artists, it has as its core the beautiful Italian-style villa that belonged to the nineteenth-century Munich painter Franz von Lenbach, and the museum also presents works of the Munich school, Jugendstil and Neue Sachlichkeit as well as temporary exhibitions of international contemporary art. The Lenbachhaus itself is closed until 2012 for renovation, and for the time being only the **Kunstbau** (Tues–Sun 10am–6pm; price dependent upon exhibition) on the south side of Brienner Strasse will remain open for temporary exhibitions.

Something about Königsplatz's bleak classical splendour appealed to Hitler, for not only did the Nazis pave it and turn it into a parade ground but they also located the institutions of their party in a scattering of buildings to the east of the square. Most prominent of these were the twin structures flanking Brienner Strasse, which still survive. On its north side was the so-called **Führerbau**, where Hitler had his Munich office and where the Munich agreement to dismember Czechoslovakia was signed in 1938; it's now a school of music and drama. The near-identical building on the south side of Brienner Strasse was the headquarters of the Nazi party – it now houses the administrative offices of various artistic and cultural institutions.

Along the River Isar

South of the Viktualienmarkt, the graceful but densely-packed nineteenth-century apartment blocks of the **Gärtnerplatzviertel** – whose streets radiate out from pretty, circular Gärtnerplatz – and the similar but more amorphous **Glockenbachviertel**, to the west, constitute some of the most sought-after addresses for young professionals in the city, including a high proportion who are lesbian and gay. Though there are few real sights, these districts – collectively known as the **Isarvorstadt** or Isar suburb – offer a strollable mix of quirky boutiques and inviting neighbourhood cafés and bars.

On the opposite bank of the Isar, the **Müller'sches Volksbad** (large hall Mon 7.30am–5pm, Tues–Sun 7.30am–11pm; small hall daily 7.30am–1pm; sauna daily 9am–11pm; swim €3.50) is worth a visit as much for its wonderful Jugendstil architecture as for a swim.

On a narrow island mid-river stands the **Deutsches Museum** (daily 9am–5pm; €8.50; Ⓦ www.deutsches-museum.de), Munich's sprawling museum of science and technology, which houses one of the world's largest collections of its kind, constantly updated and with plenty of interactive exhibits. It honours not just the achievements of science, but the scientists themselves: the **Ehrensaal** on the first floor contains busts of such familiar names as Karl Benz, Rudolf Diesel and Albert Einstein.

The core of the museum's collection was formed by the mathematical and physical instruments of the **Bavarian Academy of Sciences**. Younger visitors in particular will enjoy the astronomy section with its associated **planetarium**, **observatory** and **solar telescope**, with which you can – in complete safety – view real-time images of sunspots. The section on **chemistry** includes reconstructions of a series of historical laboratories, while the **medical** displays are a hypochondriac's nightmare with sections on AIDS, heart disease and cancer, though the section on plants with medicinal uses may provide the antidote. There are sections on mathematics, mass, time and physics, and the beauty of some of the older scientific instruments ensures it's not just one for the nerds. The museum has an outstation, the **Verkehrszentrum**, above the Theresienwiese at Theresienhöhe 14a (same hours; €5; U-Bahn #4 or #5 to Schwannthalerhöhe), which accommodates a sizeable collection of **historic vehicles** and another at Oberschleissheim (see p.375) that houses its **aircraft collection**.

The Englischer Garten and Schwabing

In 1789 the American Sir Benjamin Thompson – later ennobled as Lord Rumford, which explains the origins of Rumfordstrasse in the Isarvorstadt – suggested that a 5km marshy strip along the River Isar be landscaped in English style, and it's thanks to his advice that the people of Munich can enjoy one of the largest city parks in Europe, the **Englischer Garten**. It stretches north from the Haus der Kunst on Prinzregentenstrasse – beside which surfers ride the waves on the **Eisbach** stream when spring meltwater makes the "surf" high enough, and behind which in summer nude sunbathers stretch out on the **Schönfeldwiese**. The landmark **Chinesischer Turm** in the centre of the park was based on the pagoda at Kew Gardens in London; the Englischer Garten's better-known English connection, however, is that it was here in September 1939 that Unity Mitford, the Hitler-obsessed sister of Diana Mosley and the writer Nancy Mitford, shot herself, unable to bear the thought that England and Germany were at war. She failed to kill herself, however, and was shipped home via Switzerland to Britain, where she died shortly after the war, the bullet never having been dislodged from her brain. At the north end of the park, the placid Kleinhesseloher See boating lake borders **Schwabing**, the once bohemian but now safely middle-class neighbourhood where Thomas Mann wrote *Buddenbrooks*. Lenin and the poet Rainer Maria Rilke are among the other famous figures associated with Schwabing. Its literary and artistic heyday ended with World War I, and though the district became a centre of student radicalism in the 1960s it's not these days the sort of place you'd associate with slogans, except perhaps the kind written by advertising copywriters. Nevertheless, it's a pleasant and lively part of town, with some attractive Jugendstil architecture and plenty of café life.

The Olympiapark and BMW Museum

Built on the collected rubble from the bomb-devastated ruins of World War II and thus rising quite literally out of the ashes of the old Munich, the tent-like structures of the **Olympiapark** north of the centre (U-Bahn #3, stop Olympia-Zentrum) were supposed to set the seal on Munich's status as an international metropolis of the first rank. Certainly, Günther Behnisch's amorphous acrylic roofscapes look as fresh and futuristic today as they did in 1972, but the Munich Olympics are inevitably remembered for reasons other than their architecture or, indeed, the achievements of swimmer Mark Spitz or gymnast Olga Korbutt, all totally overshadowed by the murder of eleven members of the Israeli team (see box opposite).

Inevitably, the Olympiapark has to some extent the air of a place from which events have moved on, though on architectural grounds alone it's worth a visit, and there's usually something going on – the pool and ice rink keep things lively, and the Olympiahalle is the venue for concerts by big-name rock acts. You can visit the **Olympiastadion** itself (mid-April to mid-Oct daily 8.30am–8.30pm; mid-Oct to mid-April daily 9am–4.30pm; €2), then ascend the 291m **Olympiaturm** TV tower (daily 9am–midnight; €4.50) for panoramic views over the Olympic complex, the city and beyond.

Just across the Mittlerer Ring highway from the Olympiapark is the **BMW Museum** (Tues–Fri 9am–6pm, Sat & Sun 10am–8pm; €12). The exhibition is divided into seven separate sections: the obligatory worshipping of the BMW brand aside, it does contain some beautiful specimens of the company's output over the past ninety years or so – including both cars and motorcycles. Alongside it is BMW Welt, a glossy combination of showroom and delivery centre for BMW customers. If you're still not sated, you can tour the **factory** behind the complex (Mon–Fri 8.30am–8pm; €6; book in advance on ☏01802/11 88 22).

Nymphenburg

Munich's western suburbs are the setting for **Schloss Nymphenburg** (daily: April to mid-Oct 9am–6pm; mid-Oct to March 10am–4pm; €5 or €10 combined ticket for all Nymphenburg attractions; English audio guide available; tram #12 or #16 to Romanplatz or #17 to Schloss Nymphenburg), the summer palace of the Bavarian electors. It has its origins in the simple cube-shaped building commissioned by the Elector Ferdinand Maria and his consort Henrietta Adelaide to celebrate the birth of their son, designed by Agostino Barelli and begun in 1664. The building was subsequently enlarged by that son – Max Emanuel – to plans by Enrico Zuccalli and Joseph Effner to create the substantial palace you see today. For the full monumental effect of its immensely wide frontage, approach it along the arrow-straight Auffahrtsallee, which straddles the ornamental canal aligned with the centre of the facade.

The massive **Steinerner Saal**, or Great Hall, in the central pavilion is a riot of Rococo stucco work by Johann Baptist Zimmermann, created under the aegis of François Cuvilliés in 1755 and producing an effect that is at once festive and monumental. The room preserves its original Rococo form – since it was completed in 1758, work has been limited to dusting, filling cracks and light retouching. As for the rest of the Schloss, the most famous room is the **Schön-heitsgalerie**, or gallery of beauties, lined with portraits of famous beauties of the day painted for Ludwig I in the 1830s by Joseph Stieler. Among the women portrayed is the dancer Lola Montez – the Elector's infatuation with her pushed Munich to the brink of rebellion, and Ludwig abdicated shortly afterwards. In the south wing of the Schloss, the **Marstallmuseum** (daily: April to mid-Oct 9am–6pm; mid-Oct to March 10am–4pm; €4 or €10 combined ticket) houses a collection of historic state coaches, including a predictably magnificent selection belonging to Ludwig II; upstairs, the **Museum Nymphenburger Porzellan** (same hours & ticket) displays porcelain from the Nymphenburg factory from its foundation by Elector Max III in 1747 until around 1920.

The decorative highlight of Nymphenburg is not in the main palace at all, but in the English-style park at the back of the Schloss, which is where you'll find the graceful little **Amalienburg** (daily: April to mid-Oct 9am–6pm; mid-Oct to March 10am–4pm; €2, or €10 combined ticket), a hunting lodge created between 1734 and 1739 for the Electress Amalia by François Cuvilliés. Its ethereal **Spiegelsaal** is one of the pinnacles of the Rococo style: silver, not gold, is the dominant colour, the delicate stucco work is again the work of Johann Baptist Zimmermann, with themes relating to Diana, Amphitrite, Ceres and Bacchus. The room was used for banquets, balls, concerts and relaxation after the hunt, and it's hard to imagine a more ravishing setting for a party. Three other charming eighteenth-century pavilions in the **Schlosspark** – the **Badenburg**, **Pagodenburg** and **Magdalenenklause** – can also be visited (daily: April to mid-Oct 9am–6pm; €2 each).

The southern suburbs: Hellabrunn Zoo and Bavaria Filmstadt

The southern suburbs of the city contain two attractions of particular appeal to families. **Hellabrunn Zoo** (daily: April–Sept 8am–6pm; Oct–March 9am–5pm; €9; ⓦ www.tierpark-hellabrunn.de; U-Bahn #3 to Thalkirchen, or bus #52 from Marienplatz) was established in 1911 in a relatively natural setting on the meadows alongside the Isar south of the city centre; the attractions include the new Orang-Utan Paradies, and the regular feeding times.

Further south still, the studio tour at **Bavaria Filmstadt** at Geiselgasteig (tours daily on the hour, English-language tour daily at 1pm: April to early Nov 9am–4pm; mid-Nov to March 10am–3pm; €11; ⓦ www.filmstadt.de) is more for fans of cinematic thrills and spills than for dedicated film-buffs, though this is the place where **Das Boot** was made and you do get to see the sets from the film, as well as effects from the children's film fantasy **The Neverending Story**. There's also a live stunt show (€8.50) most afternoons in peak season.

The Allianz-Arena

One of the newest of Munich's attractions is on the northeastern edge of the city alongside the A99 ring road, yet the giant **Allianz-Arena** (Mon–Sat 10am–6pm;

▲ The Allianz-Arena

tours at 10.15am, 11am, 1pm, 3pm & 4.30pm; €9; advance booking only ☎018/05 55 51 01; U-Bahn #6 to Fröttmaning) is worth the trek for fans of architecture as much as for football fans, for it's a spectacular building. Designed by Swiss team Herzog & de Meuron – who also designed London's Tate Modern – and completed in 2005, the 70,000-seat stadium resembles an enormous tyre laid alongside the Autobahn thanks to its air-cushioned facade, which can be illuminated white for the national squad or in the colours of the two soccer teams that play there – red for **Bayern München**, blue for **TSV 1860**.

Eating, drinking and nightlife

Munich is a splendid place to **eat** or **drink**, whether your tastes run to traditional Bavarian *Schweinshaxe* – roasted pig's trotter – or to the latest in fusion cuisine. At the top end of the market the city can boast some genuinely impressive gastronomic temples. The stalwarts of the city's culinary scene are, however, undoubtedly its brewery-affiliated restaurants and **Bierkellers**, where in addition to hearty Bavarian specialities you can sample the city's famous **beer**: well-known brands include Augustiner, Paulaner, Franziskaner and Löwenbräu (both of which belong to the Spaten brewery); the Erdinger and Schneider brands are also popular, though they are brewed outside the city. The classic Munich beer is a *Weissbier* or *Weizenbier* – a cloudy, sharp and refreshing wheat beer, served in half-litre measures in dark (*dunkles*) or light (*helles*) varieties. A visit to a traditional *Bierkeller* or *Biergarten* is a must for any visitor to Munich, but the city also has a chic and sophisticated **nightlife** scene, with everything from glitzy cocktail bars to noisy techno and rock clubs, with Haidhausen, across the river, home to a couple of large club and bar complexes.

Restaurants and cafés

Alter Simpl Türkenstr. 57. Lovely wood-panelled café-bar whose name derives from the famous satirical magazine *Simplicissimus*, many of whose writers or cartoonists were once regulars here. Affordable food includes salads, pasta and meat mains, most under €10; the kitchen is open until well after midnight, though as the evening wears on it becomes more bar-like.

Augustiner am Dom Frauenplatz 8 ☎089/23 23 84 80. Hearty dishes of roast duck with red cabbage or *Bratwürste* with *Sauerkraut* are washed down with Augustiner beers, all at moderate prices, right opposite the Frauenkirche.

Café Frischhut- das Schmalznudel Prälat-Zistl-Str. 8 ☎089/26 82 37. A Munich legend for its heavy, doughnut-like *Schmalznudeln*, this little café near the Viktualienmarkt is equally beloved by early risers and night owls heading home. Daily 7am–6pm.

Café Luitpold Brienner Str. 11 ☎089/242 87 50. Munich is rather thin on grand old *Kaffee und Kuchen* places, but the *Luitpold* – where Thomas Mann and Henrik Ibsen were once customers – is one of the better offerings, though it has long since lost its former architectural glory, at least internally.

Café Münchner Freiheit Münchner Freiheit 20 ☎089/33 00 79 90. Spacious Schwabing café/ *Konditorei* on several floors, with good-value

breakfasts, omelettes, focaccia sandwiches and a few hot Italian dishes, as well as the inevitable tempting cakes. Daily from 6.30am.

Café Puck Türkenstr. 33 ☎089/280 22 80. Relaxed, vaguely Art Deco café with jazzy music, leather sofas and an eclectic selection of affordable eats, from falafel to pasta and *Schnitzel*. The breakfast selection is massive. Daily from 9am.

Cohen's Theresienstr. 31 ☎089/280 95 45. Family-run place in the Maxvorstadt serving up traditional Eastern European Jewish cooking, including *Königsberger Klopse, Pirogi* and *Wienerschnitzel*.

Il Grappolo Adalbertstr. 28 ☎089/39 62 41. Amiable little Italian *vinoteca* with affordable pasta dishes plus more substantial ones like *osso bucco* and swordfish. Informal but pleasant, and popular with academics from the nearby university. Closed Sun.

Lenbach Ottostr. 6 ☎089/549 13 00. Fashionable, Conran-designed, Gault Millau-garlanded and something of a celebrity haunt, yet the prices for *Lenbach's* creative cooking are surprisingly reasonable, with main courses from around €20.

Moritz Klenzestr. 43 ☎089/201 67 76. Searingly authentic Thai dishes are on the menu at this smart restaurant and cocktail bar in the Gärtnerplatzviertel, which attracts a mixed crowd. Open until 3am Fri & Sat, otherwise 2am.

Osteria Italiana Schellingstr. 62 ☎089/272 07 17. Italian food like mamma used to make in lovely, traditional surroundings at this very long established restaurant – it was here in the 1930s that Unity Mitford stalked Hitler over lunch. Main courses around €20.

🏃 Ratskeller Marienplatz 8 ☎089/219 98 90. The labyrinthine cellar of the Neues Rathaus is always full – by no means just with tourists. Serving everything from *Bratwurst* with *Sauerkraut* to elegant seasonal dishes including game, the food is hearty and good. Main courses from around €12.50; there's also a *Weinstube* in the complex.

Restaurant Dallmayr Dienerstr. 14–15 ☎089/213 51 00. This is the restaurant of Munich's celebrated Dallmayr delicatessen: the quality of the produce is unsurprisingly superb, while the creativity of the cooking has helped it win a Michelin star. Main courses à la carte are around €40 and up; there's also a cheaper, but still classy, café/bistro. Closed Sun & Mon.

Saf In Zerwirk, Ledererstr. 3 ☎089/23 23 91 95. Hyper-trendy vegan restaurant where the food is cooked at low temperatures to preserve nutrients; it has a sister restaurant in London. Closed Sun.

Schuhbecks in den Südtiroler Stuben Platzl 6–8 ☎089/216 69 00. One of Munich's gastronomic temples: proprietor Alfons Schuhbeck is a TV chef and national celebrity, who fuses Bavarian and more cosmopolitan influences and makes use of seasonal produce; the wine list runs to four hundred varieties, and the setting is conservative but elegant. Set menus start at €78 for three courses. The more informal and cheaper – but beautiful – *Orlando* next door is run by the same team.

Seven Fish Gärtnerplatz 6 ☎089/23 00 02 19. Stylish, modern wine-bar and fish restaurant, with creative dishes like catfish with *Sauerkraut* and blood-sausage cannelloni from around €23, or you can eat cold appetizers tapas-style from the bar.

Spatenhaus an der Oper Residenzstr. 12 ☎089/290 70 60. The elegantly alpine decor matches the refined Bavarian cooking at this restaurant opposite the opera. Main courses in the informal downstairs restaurant range from €9 to €20; expect to pay a little more in the classier upstairs dining room.

🏃 Stadtcafé in the Stadtmuseum St-Jakobs-Platz ☎089/26 69 49. Buzzy café serving good breakfasts and delectable cakes; there's a beer garden in the Stadtmuseum's *Hof* in summer.

Tantris Johann-Fichte-Str. 7 ☎089/361 95 90. Munich's most renowned restaurant is the place where Bavarians were first introduced to nouvelle cuisine. Classic 1970s decor and an up-to-the-minute gourmet menu: the four-course Saturday

lunch costs €105, after which things start getting seriously expensive. Closed Sun & Mon.

Bierkellers and Biergärten

Augustiner Grossgaststätten Neuhauser Str. 27 ☎089/23 18 32 57. The Augustiner brewery's city-centre flagship is right in the main pedestrian shopping zone, in a very attractive late nineteenth-century building with atmospheric interiors and a garden out back.

Augustinerkeller Arnulfstr. 52 ☎089/59 43 93. The vast beer garden under shady chestnut trees makes this place particularly popular with the locals. There's Augustiner Edelstoff export beer on draught, and simple food including grilled fish or chicken to soak up the alcohol.

Chinesischer Turm Englischer Garten 3 ☎089/38 38 73 27. Vast *Biergarten* at the foot of the eponymous pagoda in the heart of the Englischer Garten, serving *Hofbräu* beers and with an elegant restaurant nearby.

Hofbräuhaus Platzl 9 ☎089/290 13 60. The "most famous pub in the world" is vast and, unsurprisingly, overrun with tourists, but at least one visit is a Munich "must". If the noise and crowds are too raucous, push your way through to the *Biergarten*, a pleasant oasis in the shade of chestnut trees.

Hofbräukeller Wiener Platz ☎089/459 92 50. Imposing neo-Renaissance place in Haidhausen, attracting a wide range of customers including politicians from the nearby Maximilianeum. The *Hofbräu* beer aside, there's also a wide range of inexpensive food.

Paulaner am Nockherberg Hochstr. 77, Giesing ☎089/459 91 30. Naturally cloudy *Nockherberger* beer – which is only available here – plus typical specialities like *Obazda* (soft cheese) and *Leberkäs* – a type of meatloaf – are among the charms of this *Biergarten* attached to a modern beer hall.

Weisses Brauhaus Tal 7 ☎089/290 13 80. Handsome old *Brauhaus* belonging to the Schneider brewery, once Munich-based but since 1944 based in Kelheim and known particularly for its *Schneider Weisse* wheat bear and for the *Weisswurst* sausages it serves. Open until 1am daily.

Bars and clubs

Ampere im Muffatwerk Zellstr. 4, Haidhausen. Hip retro Seventies-styled club in the Muffatwerk cultural complex on the Haidhausen side of the Isar. Eclectic music policy with live bands and DJs.

Eat the Rich Hessstr. 9, Maxvorstadt. The cocktails are served in half-litre measures at this packed party locale near the university, which at least eases pressure on the bar. Tues–Sun 7pm–3am.

Kultfabrik Grafinger Str. 6, Haidhausen. Pioneering "Partygelände" – a sprawling complex of bars and clubs behind the Ostbahnhof that first opened in the late Nineties under the name *Kunstpark Ost* and has since spawned imitators, though it remains under threat of demolition at the end of 2010. Highlights include the rock bar *Titty Twister* and the hardcore techno hangout *Strobe-Club*.

Nektar Stubenvollstr. 1, Haidhausen ☎089/45 91 13 11. Stylish, dress-to-impress blend of lounge, restaurant, cabaret, bar and disco; the stunningly lit *Salon Blanche* is the inner sanctum. Surprise menu €49; closed Mon.

Optimolwerke Friedenstr. 10. Closer to the Ostbahnhof but with about half *Kultfabrick's* twenty-odd clubs, highlights at this *Partygelände*

include *Club Duo*, which plays r'n'b and hip-hop, and *Harry Klein*, a house and electro club that pulls in big-name international DJs.

Regina-Haus Maximiliansplatz 5. City-centre nightlife complex with an outpost of the famed Spanish *Pacha* club empire, the small but trendy electro-club *Rote Sonne* and the *Max und Moritz* disco, which lures a young crowd with cheap drinks. Open Thurs–Sat.

Schwabinger 7 Feilitzschstr. 7, Schwabing. The shanty-town architecture wouldn't win any prizes but this rocky, studenty Schwabing bar has long enjoyed cult status. It's threatened by redevelopment, but locals hope the credit crunch will provide a stay of execution.

The lesbian and gay scene

Munich's **lesbian and gay scene** is one of the biggest and most diverse in Germany after Berlin and Cologne, and is conveniently concentrated in the hip Gärtnerplatzviertel and equally trendy neighbouring Glockenbachviertel, stretching roughly from Viktualienmarkt to Sendlinger Tor. Though neither district is by any means a gay "ghetto", the gay presence is upfront and the atmosphere relaxed. The annual **Christopher Street Day** festivities take place in July (ⓦ www.csd-munich.de) and are great fun, not least for the opportunity to see exotic plumage and traditional Lederhosen on parade in roughly equal measure. For bar listings and information on accommodation, shopping and health advice (in German), pick up the free *Rosa München* guide, regularly updated and available in bars and cafés.

Café am Hochhaus Blumenstr. 29. More bar than café, attracting a young, hip crowd to a prominent site opposite Munich's only Weimar-era skyscraper.

Carmen's Theklastr. 1. Munich's most popular gay and lesbian disco, attracting all age groups with its soundtrack of oldies and chart hits.

Kr@ftakt Thalkirchner Str. 4. Relaxed Glockenbachviertel café-bar that is one of the lynchpins of the Munich lesbian and gay scene.

Prosecco Theklastr. 1. Tiny, camp bar that blends alpine kitsch with every other variety of decorative excess. The music is a mix of German Schlager tunes (schmaltzy German pop) and made-in-Munich Eurodisco hits.

Selig Hans-Sachs-Str. 3. The most stylish gay and lesbian bar in Munich, though despite its name – which means "overjoyed" – some of the customers appear to take themselves a little too seriously.

Live music, theatre and festivals

Munich is a heavyweight on the international classical music scene. The orchestra at the **Bayerische Staatsoper**, principally at the Nationaltheater, is under the direction of the American Kent Nagano, while **Zubin Mehta** is honorary conductor of the Münchner Philharmoniker (ⓦwww.muenchnerphilharmoniker.de). Additional orchestras include the **Symphonieorchester des Bayerischen Rundfunks** (ⓦwww.brnet.de) and its sister orchestra, the **Münchner Rundfunkorchester**. One of the main venues for all these is the Gasteig; the innovative and highly respected **Münchner Kammerorchester** plays at the restored Prinzregententheater. The city's leading **drama** company, the Bayerisches Staatsschauspiel (ⓦwww.bayerischesstaatsschauspiel.de), performs in the modern Residenztheater, the beautiful Cuvilliés Theater in the Residenz, and in the nearby Marstall. For

what's on information, pick up a free copy of *In München* magazine from cafés, bars and venues or the tourist offices' own monthly *München im.. guide.*

The Munich **festival** season kicks off with the annual pre-Lent carnival, known here as *Fasching*; immediately afterwards, the **Starkbierzeit** or festival of strong beer starts and lasts for around four weeks, making the Lenten fast more bearable. In April, the **Frühlingfest**, or spring festival, brings beer tents and fairground rides to the Theresienwiese. From mid-June to mid-July the Olympiapark is the venue for the **Tollwood Sommerfestival** of music, theatre and cabaret (ⓦwww.tollwood.de), which attracts big-name live acts, while the July **Opernfestspiele** includes free live broadcasts of opera performances on a big screen in front of the Nationaltheater. The biggest of all Munich festivals is, of course, **Oktoberfest** (see box opposite).

Cabaret and live music venues

Atomic Café Neuturmstr. 5 ☏089/228 30 52, ⓦwww.atomic-cafe.de. Club and live venue in the heart of the Altstadt, with an emphasis on live gigs by indie bands.

Backstage Wilhelm-Hale-Str. 38 ☏089/126 61 00, ⓦwww.backstage.eu. Live venue west of the Hauptbahnhof along Arnulfstr., with a varied programme of reggae, dancehall, guitar rock, folk, goth, cabaret and more. Tram #17.

Jazzbar Vogler Rumfordstr. 17 ☏089/29 46 62. Live jazz, Latin and soul music in the Gärtnerplatzviertel. There's an entry charge on Mondays and at weekends, and dancing on Saturdays.

Jazzclub Unterfahrt Einsteinstr. 42, Haidhausen ☏089/448 27 94. The big names of the international jazz circuit alternate with new discoveries at this Haidhausen jazz club, where there are also regularly-changing temporary exhibitions of modern art. Open Fri & Sat until 3am, otherwise 1am.

Theatre, opera and classical music venues

Cuvilliés Theater Residenzstr. 1, ☏089/21 85 01. Beautiful Rococo auditorium, used as a stage for drama productions by the Bayerisches Staatsschauspiel.

Deutsches Theater Werner-Heisenberg-Allee 11, Fröttmaning ☏089/55 23 44 44, ⓦwww.deutsches-theater.de. The main venue for big-budget musicals and cheesy tribute shows, recently relocated close to the Allianz-Arena in the suburbs.

Gasteig Rosenheimerstr. 5 ☏089/48 09 80, ⓦwww.gasteig.de. Modern convention centre in Haidhausen that is also Munich's main concert venue, with everything from classical concerts by the Münchner Philharmoniker or Symphonieorchester des Bayerischen Rundfunks to pop, rock and jazz.

Münchner Kammerspiele Maximilianstr. 26–28 ☏08/233 96 60, ⓦwww.muenchner-kammerspiele.de. Principal venue for the Münchner Kammerspiele's productions of serious drama, from Shakespeare to Kafka.

Nationaltheater Max-Joseph-Platz 2 ☏089/21 85 01, ⓦwww.bayerische.staatsoper.de. The beautiful Neoclassical Nationaltheater next to the Residenz is the city's principal stage for opera and ballet; it's the home venue for the Bayerische Staatsoper and its orchestra, the Staatsorchester.

Prinzregententheater Prinzregentenplatz 12 ☏089/21 85 02, ⓦwww.prinzregententheater.de. With a design based on the Bayreuth Festspielhaus – but more opulent and with higher levels of comfort – this is a venue for both classical, jazz and world music as well as drama.

Residenztheater Max-Josephs-Platz 1 ☏089/21 85 01. Modern theatre sandwiched between the Nationaltheater and Residenz; it's the principal stage of the Bayerisches Staatsschauspiel.

Staatstheater am Gärtnerplatz Gärtnerplatz 3 ☏089/20 24 11, ⓦwww.staatstheater-am-gaertnerplatz.de. Opera, operetta, jazz, dance and musicals are all in the repertoire of this beautiful nineteenth-century theatre south of Viktualienmarkt.

Listings

Bicycle rental Mike's Bike Rentals (corner Hochbrückenstr. and Bräuhausstr. ☏0172/852 06 60, ⓦwww.mikesbiketours.com); Radius Bikes (by platform 32 of Hauptbahnhof ☏089/59 61 13, not generally staffed from mid-Oct to mid-April, but call ☏0172/929 65 90, ⓦwww.radiusmunich.com).

Bookshops Hugendubel (Marienplatz 22) has a large English-language section.

The single most important thing to know about **Oktoberfest** (ⓦ www.oktoberfest .de) – Munich's legendary festival of beer and bonhomie – is that it's all over after the first Sunday in the month it's named after. The bulk of the *Fest*, which lasts sixteen days, therefore generally takes place during the last two weeks in September, depending on when the first weekend in October falls. The very first Oktoberfest was indeed held in October – in 1810, to celebrate the marriage of Crown Prince Ludwig to Princess Theresa von Sachsen-Hildburghausen, but over the years, as the festival got longer, the dates were pulled forward into September. The first draught **Mass** (1 litre stein) of **Oktoberfestbier** is always pulled with much (televised) ceremony, after which Bavarian television keeps up a regular live feed from the Theresienwiese, the rather bleak open space named after Ludwig's bride that is the venue for the annual rites. The Oktoberfest is quite a celebrity magnet, with the unlikeliest B-listers donning traditional attire to make their appearance before the cameras – Paris Hilton in a dirndl being one memorable example. To have any chance of joining them in the biggest tents, you'll need to reserve your spaces in advance. You can't do this on the Oktoberfest website, but it does have weblinks and contact details for the individual tents themselves. Without a **reservation**, you won't have much luck in the bigger tents but you might still squeeze into one of the smaller, more intimate ones, which – particularly as the evening wears on and the atmosphere becomes more raucous – can be easier for Oktoberfest newbies to enjoy anyway. There's no doubt that massive and widespread public drunkenness is a regular phenomenon – which doesn't stop the revellers from visiting the enormous **funfair** that runs alongside the beer tents and takes up around half the Theresienwiese's vast acreage. There's simple food – roast chicken, giant pretzels, *Obazda* and the like – to soak up the beer; one additional annual ritual is the intake of breath at the **price** of a *Mass* of beer – at €7.80–8.30 a litre (2009 prices), it may be good, but carousing Oktoberfest-style doesn't come cheap. The Oktoberfest is held on the Theresienwiese – a large open space more than a park – southwest of the Hauptbahnhof (U-Bahn 4 & 5 to "Theresienwiese").

Car rental The following all have rental outlets at the airport: Avis ☎089/97 59 76 00; Budget ☎089/97 59 67 05; Europcar ☎089/973 50 20; Hertz ☎089/97 88 60; National/Alamo ☎089/97 59 76 80; SIXT ☎0180/526 25 25.

Consulates UK, Möhlstr. 10 ☎089/21 10 90; US, Königinstr. 5 ☎089/288 80.

Driving and parking Drivers entering the centre of Munich must display a *Feinstaubplakette* indicating their car's particulate emissions. For more information, call ☎089/23 33 60 10 or email ⓔ verkehrsmanagement.kvr@muenchen.de. Parking at: Marienplatz Garage, Rindermarkt 16; Pschorr-Hochgarage, Altheimer Eck 14a; City Parkhaus am Färbergraben, Färbergraben 5; Königshof-parking, Bayerstr.

Emergency numbers Police ☎110; fire & medical ☎112; medical house calls ☎089/55 55 66; duty doctor at Klinikum Rechts der Isar ☎089/45 75 89 00; dental ☎089/723 30 93 & 723 30 94; women and rape ☎089/76 37 37; AIDS ☎089/544 64 70.

Internet Misc24, Thomas-Wimmer-Ring 1.

Laundry Friedenheimerstr. 11; Schleissheimerstr. 102; Kapuzinerstr. 39; Lindwurmstr. 139; Görresstr. 12.

Left luggage There are coin-operated lockers at the Hauptbahnhof; left-luggage office at Hauptbahnhof ☎089/13 08 34 68.

Pharmacies ⓦ www.apotheker-notdienst.de for information on out-of-hours service, or pick up the *Notdienst-Kalendar* booklet from any pharmacy.

Post office Bahnhofplatz 1 (Mon–Fri 7.30am–8pm, Sat 9am–4pm).

Sightseeing tours Gray Line (☎0700/28 78 68 77, ⓦ www.sightseeing-munich.de); Mike's Bike Tours (☎089/255 43 987, ⓦ www.mikesbiketours .com); Yellow Cab (ⓦ www.citysightseeing.de).

Taxis 24hr service ☎0175/481 28 48. IsarFunk Taxizentrale ☎089/45 05 40, ⓦ www.isarfunk.de.

Around Munich

Munich's efficient public transport network stretches far into the surrounding countryside, making day-trips relatively straightforward. By far the most sombre, but also the best-known destination in the city's hinterland is the former Nazi concentration camp at **Dachau**, north of the city. Also to the north, but altogether more light-hearted, is **Oberschleissheim**, with its palaces and air museum. To the south of the city, the lakes of the **Fünf-Seen-Land** are an obvious lure in summer, given added lustre by the monastery of **Kloster Andechs** and by a remarkable art collection at **Bernried** on **Starnberger See**.

Dachau

Lieber Gott, mach mich stumm, dass ich nicht nach Dachau kumm.
Please God, make me dumb, so I don't wind up in Dachau.

Popular saying

The thing to realize about the former Nazi concentration camp at **Dachau**, now the **KZ-Gedenkstätte Dachau** (Tues–Sun 9am–5pm; free; English audio guide €3; documentary film at entrance in English at 11.30am, 2pm & 3.30pm), is that in contrast to the extermination camps in Poland it was in no way secret. Established on the site of a redundant munitions works as early as March 1933 and a model for all subsequent camps, it was highly publicized, the better to keep the potential malcontents of the Third Reich in line. During its twelve-year existence more than 200,000 people were imprisoned here, of whom 43,000 died. It was finally liberated by US troops on April 29, 1945.

You enter the camp complex through an iron **gate** into which is set the Nazis' bitter joke against its victims – the slogan "Arbeit Macht Frei", which means "work makes you free"; here, as in so many other camps, hard work was no guarantee even of survival. Much of the compound within the perimeter fence now consists of the empty foundations of the old barrack blocks, but two have been reconstructed to give an idea of what living conditions were like, and how they steadily deteriorated during the course of the war as the camp became progressively more overcrowded. The SS guards used any infringement of the barracks' rigid cleanliness regime as an excuse to administer harsh discipline; nevertheless, when the camp was finally liberated typhus was rife.

An **exhibition** in the former camp **maintenance building** describes the full horror of Dachau, including a graphic colour film shot at liberation and grisly details of the medical experiments conducted on prisoners, including hypothermia and altitude experiments conducted on fit young male prisoners in order to determine how long downed Luftwaffe pilots might survive in extreme circumstances, as well as others in which inmates were deliberately infected with malaria or tuberculosis. Behind the maintenance building, the camp **prison** contained cells for important prisoners who were kept separate from the rest of the inmates; these included Georg Elser, the man who tried to assassinate Hitler with a bomb at the Bürgerbräukeller in Munich on November 8, 1939, and Richard Stevens, one of the two British secret agents kidnapped and smuggled across the border from the Netherlands the following day in the notorious Venlo incident.

Though it wasn't an extermination camp Dachau did have a **gas chamber**, screened by trees and located outside the camp perimeter. A crematorium was built in the summer of 1940 because of the rapidly rising numbers of deaths among prisoners; in 1942–43 a larger one was built, and this incorporated a gas chamber. Though it was never used for systematic extermination, former prisoners testify that it was used to murder small groups of prisoners. As in other camps, the fiction of it being a shower room was maintained. A plaque by the crematorium commemorates four women agents of the British SOE who were murdered here on September, 12, 1944.

A place of remembrance as well as a museum, the camp site is peppered with memorials: there are Jewish, Orthodox, Protestant and Catholic memorials at the fringes of the camp, and an expressive **international memorial** in front of the maintenance building.

To get to the KZ-Gedenkstätte, bus #726 shuttles between Dachau's S-Bahn station (line S2 from Munich) three times per hour on weekdays and at peak times on Saturdays; there is no Sunday service. There is parking a short, well-signposted walk from the camp.

Oberschleissheim

The small town of **Oberschleissheim**, just outside Munich, is where the Wittelsbachs built the magnificent Baroque **Neues Schloss** (Tues–Sun: April–Sept 9am–6pm; Oct–March 10am–4pm; €4, or €6 combined ticket with Lustheim and Altes Schloss; Ⓦwww.schloesser-schleissheim.de), designed by Enrico Zuccalli. Work started under Elector Max Emanuel in 1701, but the intervention of the War of the Spanish Succession left the palace an incomplete shell and work was only finally completed in 1719; of the four wings originally planned, only one was built. This however is quite imposing enough, with a glorious sequence of **ceremonial rooms** united by the theme of Max Emanuel's fame. An international team of artists laboured to create the interiors, including the stucco worker Johann Baptist Zimmermann, the ornamental metalworker Antoine Motté and the sculptor Guiseppe Volpini.

The magnificent Baroque **Hofgarten** stretches away from the east front of the Neues Schloss, has never been substantially remodelled and thus is rare in preserving its original Baroque form. At the eastern end of the garden, the little hunting lodge of **Schloss Lustheim** (same hours; €3, or €6 combined ticket) houses a collection of Meissen porcelain.

To the west of the Neues Schloss stands the much smaller Renaissance **Altes Schloss** (same hours; €2.50, or €6 combined ticket) which contains two museums, one comprising images of private piety and public religious festivals from around the world, and another cataloguing the vanished culture of the former Prussian provinces of East and West Prussia, now mainly part of Poland, whose German-speaking inhabitants fled or were expelled as the Red Army swept across Europe in 1945.

Oberschleissheim is also home to the Deutsches Museum's **Flugwerft Schleissheim** (daily 9am–5pm; €6), which houses the museum's collection of historic aircraft.

To reach Oberschleissheim, take S-Bahn 1 (direction Freising) from Munich.

Starnberger See and Kloster Andechs

To the south of Munich, the region known as the **Fünf-Seen-Land** provides a tantalizing glimpse of alpine beauty as well as wide open waters for recreation right on the city's doorstep. Of the two large lakes, **Starnberger See** is known as the Princes' Lake and has the opulent real-estate to prove it; it was on the shores of this lake that "Mad" King Ludwig II and his doctor met their mysterious deaths one night in June 1886. The other large lake, **Ammersee**, is known as the Farmers' Lake, which reflects its somewhat simpler style.

Starnberger See

The region's natural centre is **STARNBERG** on Starnberger See. The town, which is on S-Bahn line #6 from Munich, is one of the wealthiest communities in Germany, and the lake shore is lined with expensive villas. The town itself has a disappointingly suburban feel, but it does have a stunning setting at the north end of the lake, with a backdrop of distant Alps. It makes a handy departure-point for **cruises** on the lake by the boats of **Bayerische Seenschifffahrt** (Easter to mid-Oct; cruises €8.50–15.90 depending on itinerary; ⓦwww .seenschifffahrt.de). The longer Grand Tour departs twice each morning in high season for Bernried at the southern end of the lake, supplemented in the afternoons from June to mid-September by three sailings of the Museum-sschiff Fantasie. These are the most pleasurable way to reach the **Sammlung Buchheim** or **Museum der Phantasie** in Bernried (Tues–Sun: April–Oct 10am–6pm; Nov–March 10am–5pm; €8.50; ⓦwww.buchheimmuseum .de), housed in a beautiful wood-clad building on the lakeside designed by Günther Behnisch, which looks more like a luxurious spa than a museum. It houses the varied collections of the artist and author Lothar-Günther Buchheim, best known as the author of the book on which the hit film *Das Boot* was based. The museum is built along a central axis, which allows the various departments to branch off independently – a clever solution to the problem of displaying a collection whose constituent parts never really make a coherent whole: roomfuls of applied art and unlabelled ethnographic objects feature, along with a good deal of Buchheim's own work, but the core of the collection is a stunning selection of classic twentieth-century German art. Lovis Corinth is represented by his *Dancing Dervish* of 1904, Max Liebermann by some of his lovely drawings, while a few very early works by Max Beckmann contrast with his more familiar later style. There's a caustic Otto Dix portrait, *Leonie*, as well as works by the Expressionists Ernst Ludwig Kirchner, Karl Schmidt-Rottluff and Alexej von Jawlensky.

To **reach** the Sammlung Buchheim other than by boat, take S-Bahn #6 to Tutzing and a bus from there. There's also plenty of car parking at the museum.

Kloster Andechs

Where art presides at the southern end of the Starnberger See, beer and religion reign supreme on **Ammersee**, where the Benedictine monastery of **Kloster Andechs** (ⓦwww.andechs.de) crowns a hilltop on the north side of the village of Erling. The monastery has for centuries attracted pilgrims to see the relics supposedly brought to Andechs by Saint Rasso, an ancestor of the counts of Andechs, in the tenth century. These days it's just as famous for its Benedictine **beers**, which can be sampled in the monastery's *Bräustüberl* restaurant. The abbey **church**, which is not at all as big as its mighty onion-domed tower might lead you to think, makes up for its modest size with the exuberance of its Rococo decoration by the ever-industrious Johann Baptist Zimmermann. Buried beneath the Rococo swirls are traces of the fifteenth-century Gothic church, which was struck by lightening and largely destroyed in the seventeenth century; the Heilige Kapelle still retains its Gothic appearance.

Carl Orff (1897–1982), composer of *Carmina Burana*, is buried at Andechs, and in the summer months the monastery is the venue for the **Orff in Andechs** festival of the composer's work. The abbey website has details.

To **reach** Kloster Andechs, take S-Bahn #5 to Herrsching or #6 to Starnberg Nord, from either of which the infrequent bus #951 will get you to the abbey.

Ingolstadt

With a strategic location on the Danube midway between Nuremberg and Munich, for centuries **INGOLSTADT** was a formidable fortress and from 1392 to 1447 the capital of the Duchy of Bayern-Ingolstadt. Yet despite a rich legacy of historic monuments it's a bustling and remarkably down-to-earth place, with none of the preserved-in-aspic feel that sometimes plagues smaller, more tourist-dominated Bavarian towns. Its streets are tidy and handsome, but the feeling is of solid prosperity rather than overt affluence, with an economy buttressed by oil refineries and by the town's status as the home of the Audi car plant. Ingolstadt's Altstadt – entirely surrounded by greenery on the site of its former defences – is an enjoyable place to while away a day, while beyond the centre are the contrasting delights of the Audi Forum and the Ingolstadt Village outlet mall.

Arrival, information and accommodation

Ingolstadt's **Hauptbahnhof** is approximately 2km south of the Altstadt on the far side of the Danube; frequent buses take around nine minutes to connect it with the centre. The **tourist office** is in the Altes Rathaus at Rathausplatz 2 (April–Oct Mon–Fri 9am–6pm, Sat & Sun 10am–2pm; Nov–March Mon–Fri 9.30am–4.30pm, Sat 10am–1pm; ☎0841/305 30 30, ⓦwww.ingolstadt-tourismus.de). There's a reasonable selection of places to **stay** in the Altstadt. There's also a lakeside **campsite**, *Azur Campingpark*, on the eastern outskirts of town at Auwaldsee (☎0841/961 16 16, ⓦwww.azur-camping.de/ingolstadt).

Adler Theresienstr. 22 ☎0841/351 07, ⓦwww
.hotel-adler-ingolstadt.de. Traditional, family-run
three-star hotel in a very central location close to
the Liebfrauenmünster; all rooms have either bath
or shower plus WC. ❺
Bayerischer Hof Münzbergstr. 12 ☎0841/93 40
60, ⓦwww.bayerischer-hof-ingolstadt.de. In the
quiet southwest corner of the Altstadt, this is a
comfortable three-star option with heavy wood
furniture in the rooms and a typically Bavarian feel
to the decor. ❹

DJH Ingolstadt Friedhofstr. 4 1/2 ☎0841/305 12
80, ⓦwww.ingolstadt.jugendherberge.de. A historic
bastion on the western fringe of the Altstadt makes
for atmospheric location for the youth hostel. Dorm
beds for €17.40 (with breakfast) and single or
double rooms with shared facilities (❶).
Rappensberger Harderstr. 3 ☎0841/31 40,
ⓦwww.rappensberger.de. A stylish blend of
modern comforts in a traditional setting, with a
trendy "slow food" restaurant and a warm
welcome for cyclists. ❺

The Altstadt

The towers of the **Moritzkirche** and its near neighbour the **Pfeifturm**, the former city watchtower, make a central point of reference in the heart of the Altstadt, close to **Schliffelmarkt** where the main east–west and north–south streets cross. From here, Ingolstadt's main shopping street, Ludwigstrasse, heads east to Paradeplatz and the impressive whitewashed **Neues Schloss**, begun in the first half of the fifteenth century by Duke Ludwig the Bearded and completed under the dukes of Landshut after the Ingolstadt line of the Wittelsbachs died out. Since 1972 it has housed the **Bayerisches Armeemuseum** (Bavarian Army Museum; Tues–Sun 8.45am–5pm; €3.50), with more than 35 rooms displaying artefacts from half a millennium of military history, alongside older archeological finds. The exhibits include uniforms of the Bavarian kings, plus booty from the wars against the Turks in the seventeenth and eighteenth centuries, including a beautiful embroidered Turkish tent.

A short walk west of Schliffelmarkt along Theresienstrasse brings you to the late Gothic **Liebfrauenmünster** (daily 8am–6pm), Ingolstadt's largest church, whose red-brick flanks soar impressively above the modest-sized surrounding houses. The largest late Gothic hall church in Bavaria, it's notable mainly for its unusual towers, set at an oblique angle to the west end of the church, and for its vast, steep roof, which conceals seven attic storeys for which 3800 tree trunks were needed.

To the north of Liebfrauenmünster, the Asam brothers' Baroque church of **Maria de Victoria**, Neubaustrasse 1 (March–Oct Tues–Sun 9am–noon & 1–5pm; Nov–Feb Tues–Sun 1–4pm; €2), could scarcely be more different. Built between 1732 and 1736 for the Marian student congregation and lacking either forecourt or towers, the church nevertheless startles with the icing-sugar delicacy of its external decoration. Inside, the eye is drawn irresistibly to Cosmas Damian Asam's ceiling **fresco** on the theme of the Incarnation – the world's largest fresco on a flat surface, it measures 42 by 16 metres. The church's other treasure is the **Lepanto Monstrance** of 1708, which depicts the Christians' naval victory over the Turks at the Battle of Lepanto in 1571 – the last naval battle to be fought between ships driven by oars. On the opposite corner, the gabled **Tillyhaus** at Neubaustrasse 2 is where the feared Catholic commander in the Thirty Years' War, Count von Tilly, died of his battle wounds in 1632.

On the western fringe of the Altstadt at Anatomiestrasse 18–20 is the **Deutsches Medizinhistorisches Museum** (Tues–Sun 10am–noon & 2–5pm; €3), which occupies the Baroque building of the Alte Anatomie or old anatomical institute. Its medical-historical displays include ancient Greek, Roman and Egyptian artefacts as well as a selection of amputation saws, cauterizing irons and bloodletting knives that may not be for the fainthearted. A little to the north beyond the brick Gothic **Kreuztor**, the mid-nineteenth-century fort of Kavalier Hepp houses the **Stadtmuseum** (Tues–Fri 9am–5pm; €3), Ingolstadt's local history museum, along with two others: the **Spielzeugmuseum** (Toy Museum: same hours & ticket) complete with working model railways and the **Europäisches Donaumuseum** (European Danube Museum; same hours & ticket), which focuses on the natural and cultural history of the Danube region.

The Museum für Konkrete Kunst and Reduit Tilly

Close to the river at Tränktorstrasse 6–8, the **Museum für Konkrete Kunst** (Tues–Sun 10am–5pm; €5) is Germany's only museum dedicated to Concrete Art, an abstract art movement that rose to prominence in the 1940s to 1960s, and houses the Gomringer Collection which was acquired by the city in 1981. Artists featured include Josef Albers and Victor Vasarely, and there's a sculpture garden outside the museum.

Facing the Altstadt across the river, the **Reduit Tilly** (Tues–Sun 8.45am–5pm; €3.50 or combined ticket with Neues Schloss €4.50) is the surviving portion of the mighty new fortress built between 1828 and 1848 to replace the old Ingolstadt fortress, destroyed in 1800. Its facade was designed by the Bavarian court architect, Leo von Klenze. The complex now houses a wide-ranging exhibition on Germany's experience in World War I, focusing not just on life in the trenches but on the home front and the changing role of women.

The Audi Forum

As glassy and ultramodern as you'd expect, the **Audi Forum Ingolstadt** (Ⓦ www.audi.de/foren; bus# 15 from centre), north of the Altstadt along Ettinger Strasse, offers everything from an **After Work Jazz Lounge** with regular live music to the opportunity to take a **factory tour** (Mon–Fri 11.30am in English; €6; ☏0800/283 44 44). Housed in an eye-catching circular building, the **Audi Museum Mobile** (daily 9am–6pm; €2) is the company museum, with old and new cars and prototypes on view.

Ingolstadt Village

On the eastern side of Ingolstadt close to exit 61 of the A9 Autobahn, **Ingolstadt Village** (Mon–Sat 10am–8pm; bus #20 from Rathausplatz) is a designer outlet mall done in tasteful, small-town architectural style: beneath its post modern oriels and gables you can browse through more than 75 boutiques, including big names such as Calvin Klein, Rosenthal, Samsonite and Tommy Hilfiger.

Eating and drinking

Places to **eat** and **drink** are scattered throughout Ingolstadt's Altstadt, with a cluster of places near the Neues Schloss and a wider scattering in the western part of the historic centre.

Bar Bistro & Restaurant Rappensberger Harderstr. 3 ☏0841/31 40. The *Rappensberger* hotel's stylish "slow food" restaurant is open until 1am daily, with main courses from around €14.

Café Bistro Hohe Schule Goldknopfgasse 7 ☏0172/442 82 92. Fish, meat and veggie mains from around €8.50 beneath the beautiful painted Gothic ceiling of this nonsmoking café, tucked beneath the former university building.

Gaststätte Daniel Roseneckstr. 1 ☏0841/352 72. Traditional Bavarian cooking and *Herrnbräubier* in Ingolstadt's oldest

Gaststätte, which dates from 1471; choose between the snug and cosy interior or the summer *Biergarten*. Main courses from around €8.

Schlosskeller Paradeplatz 4 ☏0841/354 40. Fine wines and a varied food menu in the wonderful vaulted cellar of the Neues Schloss, which dates from 1419. Closed Mon.

Tagtraum Paradeplatz 3 ☏0841/132 30 12. Arty café/bar opposite the Neues Schloss, with regularly changing art exhibitions, light meals and cakes. Closed Mon.

Neuburg an der Donau

Despite its name, which means "new castle on the Danube", the delightful little town of **NEUBURG AN DER DONAU**, 21km west of Ingolstadt, is scarcely new, though it was only after the foundation of the principality of Pfalz-Neuburg in 1505 that it really gained any importance.

The "official" quarter on a bluff high above the river has a dolls' house prettiness, but is dominated by the impressive Renaissance **Schloss** (Tues–Sun: April–Sept 9am–6pm; Oct–March 10am–4pm; €5), which is the main reason for a visit. It was constructed from 1530 onwards for Pfalzgraf (Count Palatine) Ottheinrich, the principality's first ruler; the splendid arcaded courtyard is decorated with sgraffito while the **chapel** (same hours) was the first purpose-built Protestant church in Germany and has surviving frescoes by Hans Bocksberger dating from 1543. Highlights of the Schloss's interior include the **Rittersaal** or Knights' Hall in the north wing, with its mighty columns and wooden ceiling. A Baroque east wing was added in 1665 to 1670, complete with two round towers that dominate the river and town. The Schloss's west wing contains the **Bayerische Staatsgalerie Flämische Barockmalerei** (same hours; €5), with a hundred and twenty works of Flemish art by masters including Rubens, Van Dyck and Bruegel.

Practicalities

Trains from Ingolstadt take a little over fifteen minutes to reach Neuburg's **Bahnhof**, which is a short walk south of the Altstadt. The **tourist office** is close to the Schloss on Ottheinrichplatz (May–Oct daily 9am–6pm; Nov– April Mon–Thurs 9am–noon & 2–4pm, Fri 9am–noon; ℡08431/552 40, ⓦwww.neuburg-donau.de). The *Gasthaus zur Blauen Traube*, Amalienstrasse 49 (℡08431/83 92, ⓦwww.zur-blauen-traube.de; ❷), is a very central and atmospheric **hotel**, with a **restaurant** (mains from around €12), or you could try the *Neuwirt*, Färberstrasse 88 (℡08431/20 78, ⓦwww.neuwirt-neuburg.de; ❷), in the lower part of town, which also has a restaurant serving Bavarian specialities. Right opposite the entrance to the Schloss, the *Vivat Weinkeller*, Amalienstrasse A61 (℡08431/64 81 13; closed Mon), is a pleasant spot to enjoy Franconian and South Tyrolean specialities, salads, cakes, and German and Austrian wines.

Nördlingen

Fifteen million years ago a meteorite slammed into the Alb plateau close to present-day **NÖRDLINGEN**, northwest of Neuburg on the boundary with Baden-Württemberg. Hitting the earth at a speed of 70,000km per hour, the impact of the meteorite was sufficient to form a crater 25km wide, known today as the **Ries**, and reputedly the best-preserved impact crater on the planet.

Some considerable time later, Nördlingen's medieval church-builders were considerate enough to make the tower of the town's **St Georgskirche** tall enough to provide a suitable vantage-point from which to see the Ries. The view from the ninety-metre-high tower, known as the **Daniel** (daily: April–Oct 9am–7pm; Nov–March 9am–5pm; €2), isn't the only reason to visit the town however, for Nördlingen is another of the **Romantic Road**'s perfectly preserved medieval gems, a former imperial free city like Rothenburg ob der Tauber and Dinkelsbühl, but less touristy than either. The church itself, which was built between 1427 and 1505, is one of the largest and most beautiful late Gothic hall churches in southern Germany, with an airy interior of slender columns and graceful vaulting. Every half-hour between 10pm and midnight the **tower watchman** atop the Daniel issues the traditional cry "So G'sell, so" (roughly "so, follow, so") though there are differing explanations as to precisely why.

Close by, the impressive half-timbered **Tanzhaus** was built as a cloth exchange and ballroom in 1442 to 1444 and features on it a statue of the Emperor Maximilian I, dating from 1513. Directly opposite, Nördlingen's **Rathaus** has been in continuous use as a town hall since 1382; the most beautiful part of the complex is the elegant Renaissance **Freitreppe** (open staircase) built in 1618 by Wolfgang Walberger.

To the north along Baldingerstrasse is the **Heilig-Geist-Spital**, a medieval hospital that now houses Nördlingen's local history museum, the **Stadtmuseum** (mid-March to Oct Tues–Sun 1.30–4.30pm; €4 or €7.50 MuseumsCard for all Nördlingen museums), whose typically eclectic exhibits include a massive diorama of the 1634 Battle of Nördlingen during the Thirty Years' War. Also worth visiting is the nearby **Rieskrater-Museum** in the Holzhof – a sixteenth-century barn – on Eugene-Shoemaker-Platz (Tues–Sun: May–Oct 10am–4.30pm; Nov–April 10am–noon & 1.30–4.30pm; €4). Its displays on the formation of craters in general and the Ries in particular are partly annotated in English. Like Dinkelsbühl, Nördlingen retains its complete circuit of **medieval walls**, which are well worth making a circuit of while you're here.

Practicalities

To reach Nördlingen by **train** from Augsburg or Ingolstadt you have to change at Donauwörth; the journey takes around an hour or an hour and a half, respectively. The town's **Bahnhof** is just east of the Altstadt. The **tourist office** is opposite the Rathaus at Marktplatz 2 (Easter–Nov Mon–Thurs 9am–6pm, Fri 9am–4.30pm, Sat & Sun 10am–2pm; Nov–Easter Mon–Thurs 9am–5pm, Fri 9am–3.30pm; ☏09081/841 16, ⓦwww.noerdlingen.de). You can **stay** right opposite the Daniel at the *Braunes Ross*, Marktplatz 12 (☏09081/29 01 20, ⓔbraunesross@t-online.de; ②), or nearby at the fancier *Kaiserhof Hotel Sonne*, Marktplatz 3 (☏09081/50 67, ⓦwww.kaiserhof-hotel-sonne.de; ③–⑤), both of which also have **restaurants**.

Augsburg

Proud **AUGSBURG** may only be Bavaria's third-largest city, but it's the state's oldest, tracing its origins to the Roman fort of Augusta Vindelicum founded here in the first century AD. The largest city of Bavarian Swabia – a western region linguistically, and historically quite distinct from Bavaria proper – it was one of the wealthiest financial centres in Europe during the Middle Ages, helped by its position on the route south to Italy. Its traders and financiers – the Fuggers and Welsers – were very much the Rothschilds or Vanderbilts of their day, with business connections across the continent and beyond. Augsburg was renowned for its craftsmanship too, above all in metalwork, and the city also produced the father-and-son artists Hans Holbein the Elder and Younger. The city reached a peak of magnificence during the Renaissance, from when much of the city's most impressive architecture dates, notably the splendid **Rathaus** by Elias Holl, who was the municipal architect.

An imperial free city, Augsburg took centre stage in the major religious controversies of the sixteenth century. The city, though with a Catholic bishopric, nevertheless strongly favoured Luther. In 1530 the **Augsburg Confession** – one of the founding documents of the Lutheran faith – was formulated here and presented to the Emperor Charles V at an Imperial Diet. At a subsequent Diet, in 1555, the Peace of Augsburg initiated peaceful coexistence between the religions, in imperial free cities at least, though Ferdinand II attempted to overturn it with his Edict of Restitution in 1629 in the thick of the Thirty Years' War. This had the effect of reversing the power balance between Catholic and Protestant in Augsburg, and the city remains largely – but not overwhelmingly – Catholic today.

Augsburg became Bavarian in 1806, and in the century that followed grew into an important industrial centre. Firms such as MAN and Messerschmitt ensured the city became a target for Allied air raids during World War II, yet the scars were successfully repaired afterwards, and the glory of Augsburg's illustrious past is evident to this day in its **Altstadt** – whose architectural splendour is reason enough for the city to be a worthwhile stop on the **Romantic Road**. The Altstadt runs north–south along the axis of Maximilianstrasse–Karolinenstrasse–Hoher Weg–Frauentorstrasse, with a busy east–west traffic route cutting it into unequal halves. The northern Altstadt is smaller and quieter, centred on the **Dom**; the southern Altstadt, with its magnificent **Rathaus** and the stately mansions of **Maximilianstrasse**, is the hub of the city's shopping and nightlife.

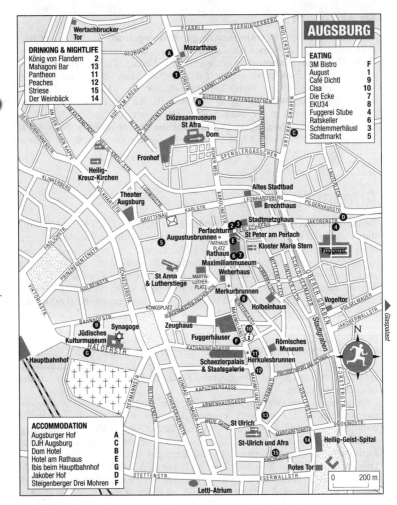

AUGSBURG

DRINKING & NIGHTLIFE
König von Flandern   2
Mahagoni Bar   13
Pantheon   11
Peaches   12
Striese   15
Der Weinbäck   14

EATING
3M Bistro   F
August   1
Café Dichtl   9
Cisa   10
Die Ecke   7
EKU34   8
Fuggerei Stube   4
Ratskeller   6
Schlemmerhäusl   3
Stadtmarkt   5

ACCOMMODATION
Augsburger Hof   A
DJH Augsburg   C
Dom Hotel   B
Hotel am Rathaus   E
Ibis beim Hauptbahnhof   G
Jakober Hof   D
Steigenberger Drei Mohren F

0   200 m

Arrival, information and accommodation

Augsburg's **Hauptbahnhof** – Germany's oldest still in everyday use – is just west of the Altstadt. The **tourist office** is at Maximilianstrasse 57 (April–Oct Mon–Fri 9am–6pm, Sat 10am–5pm, Sun 10am–2pm; Nov–March Mon–Fri 9am–5pm, Sat 10am–2pm; ℡0821/50 20 70, ⊕www.augsburg-tourismus.de). Almost everything you're likely to want to see is within the Altstadt, which is walkable; **public transport** including buses and trams radiates from both the Hauptbahnhof and Königsplatz just west of the Altstadt (single €1.15, *Tageskarte* day-ticket €5.20; ⊕www.stawa.de). You can rent a **bike** from four Mietstationen, including the all-year-round outlet at the Hauptbahnhof (BohusCenter am Hbf, Halderstr. 29; Mon 5.30am–8pm, Tues–Sat 8am–8pm; day rates from €10; ℡0821/456 11 99). Places to **stay** are scattered throughout the city; Augsburg is neither as overtly tourist-oriented nor as expensive as Munich.

Augsburger Hof Auf dem Kreuz 2 ☏ 0821/34 30 50, ⊛ www.augsburger-hof.de. Attractively furnished rooms, including some with a few traditional Bavarian touches, in an old house in the northern Altstadt. ❹

DJH Augsburg Unterer Graben 6 ☏ 0821/780 88 90, ⊛ www.augsburg-jugendherberge.de. Modern hostel on the fringe of the northern Altstadt, with accommodation in four-bed rooms (€19.90 with breakfast) as well as 35 en-suite doubles (❷).

Dom Hotel Frauentorstr. 8 ☏ 0821/34 39 30, ⊛ www.domhotel-augsburg.de. In a central but peaceful location in the northern Altstadt, with a swimming pool and, in summer, breakfast on the patio outside. Rooms range from the blandly modern to beamy and atmospheric. ❹

Hotel am Rathaus Am Hinteren Perlachberg 1 ☏ 0821/34 64 90, ⊛ www.hotel-am-rathaus -augsburg.de. You couldn't be more central than in this discreetly plush hideaway, tucked down a quiet lane behind the Rathaus and with all rooms equipped with bath or shower, WC, wi-fi and cable TV. ❺

Ibis beim Hauptbahnhof Halderstr. 25 ☏ 0821/501 61 50, ⊛ www.ibishotel.com. Close to the Hauptbahnhof and convenient for the Altstadt, this is the more central of two outposts of the budget chain in Augsburg, with comfortable, if bland, en-suite rooms, and keen rates if you book in advance. ❷

Jakober Hof Jakoberstr. 41 ☏ 0821/51 00 30, ⊛ www.jakoberhof.de. Attractive, family-run budget option close to the Fuggerei, with very good value rooms with shared facilities and reasonably priced en-suites. All rooms have wi-fi. ❶–❹

Steigenberger Drei Mohren Maximilianstr. 40 ☏ 0821/503 60, ⊛ www.steigenberger.com. For centuries the *Drei Mohren* has been Augsburg's most celebrated address for visitors, and though the current building is modern, it maintains its traditional "grand hotel" atmosphere, though the rooms are more contemporary and functional than the atmospheric restaurants. ❼–❾

The Rathaus and around

Locals claim that Augsburg's **Rathaus** is the most significant secular Renaissance building north of the Alps, and surveying its tall, dignified elevations from the Rathausplatz – the square at the heart of the Altstadt which it dominates – it's hard to disagree. It was in 1614 that the city council decided to tear down the old Gothic town hall and replace it with something that better reflected the wealth and power of the imperial free city. They commissioned Elias Holl (1573–1646) to design its replacement. The architect – a contemporary of the early English classicist Inigo Jones – had travelled to northern Italy and it's often supposed that, like Jones, Holl was influenced by the work of Andrea Palladio. Certainly, the results anticipate the Baroque style that was to bloom after the Thirty Years' War. Work began on Holl's Rathaus in 1615; the first council meeting was held there in 1620. A little over three centuries later, on February 26, 1944, an air raid reduced it to a shell, but painstaking reconstruction over several decades has gradually restored it to its former glory.

The peak of that glory is the **Goldener Saal** (daily 10am–6pm; €2) on the third floor, a splendidly rich ceremonial hall 32.5m long and 14m high beneath a gilded walnut ceiling. The room fulfils the city council's 1614 design brief perfectly, though in its reconstructed form it wasn't fully restored to its original splendour until 1996 when the final touches were put on its re-created frescoes.

Stylistic companion to the Rathaus is the **Perlachturm** (daily May–Oct 10am–6pm; during Advent Fri, Sat & Sun 2–6pm; €1) just to the north. It's attached to the little Romanesque church of St Peter, but it quite dwarfs the church, since Holl remodelled and raised it to a height of 70m in order to accommodate the bells from the old town hall. It's quite a climb to the top, though you're rewarded with superb views over Augsburg and the surrounding region – as far as the Alps on a clear day. On the way up, photographs show the extent of Augsburg's 1944 destruction.

In front of the Rathaus, the **Augustusbrunnen** fountain is one of three splendid fountains in the Altstadt. It dates from 1588 to 1594 and honours the Roman emperor Augustus, founder of the city.

A little to the west of Rathausplatz along Philippine-Welser-Strasse, the sixteenth-century **Welserhaus**, with its eighteenth-century classical facade, and the gabled house of the patrician **Köpf** family, which dates from 1578, provide suitable neighbours for the beautiful **Maximilianmuseum** (Tues 10am–8pm, Wed–Sun 10am–5pm; €7), a sixteenth-century merchant's house which now houses the city's principal historical and applied art collections. The highlight is the section dedicated to the fabulously skilled silver- and goldsmiths whose work brought Augsburg international renown.

Close by and entered from Annastrasse via Im Annahof is the church of **St Anna** (May–Oct Mon 3–6pm, Tues–Sat 10am–12.30pm & 3–6pm, Sun 10am–12.30pm & 3–5pm; Nov–April Mon 3–5pm, Tues–Sat 10am–12.30pm & 3–5pm, Sun 10am–12.30pm & 3–5pm). Originally a Carmelite monastery, the church has been Protestant since 1525. The late Gothic **Goldschmiedekapelle** (goldsmiths' chapel) is dedicated to St Helen and decorated with beautiful frescoes; at the west end of the church, the showy Renaissance **Fuggerkapelle**, commissioned by Jakob Fugger the Rich for himself and his brothers and built between 1509 and 1512, quite upstages the nave of the church. St Anna is closely associated with Martin Luther, who stayed here in 1518; there's a small museum, the **Lutherstiege** (same hours; free) on the subject. St Anna is undergoing badly needed restoration until 2011 at least, so expect closures and limited visibility of some parts of the church. A little way to the south on Zeugplatz, the **Zeughaus** or city arsenal, is by Elias Holl, dating from 1602 to 1607.

The southern Altstadt

Running south from Rathausplatz, stately **Maximilianstrasse** is, in its entirety, the clearest possible expression of Augsburg's Renaissance wealth, lined with the town palaces of the wealthy. Nowadays the "Maximilian" referred to in the street's name is the Habsburg Emperor Maximilian I, whose fondness for the city led to him being dubbed "Mayor of Augsburg", but it previously referred to another, less popular "Max" – the Bavarian Elector Maximilian Joseph. Its historical importance aside, Maximilianstrasse is a visually impressive link between the Rathaus and the church of St Ulrich und Afra in the south – and it's also the centre of Augsburg's nightlife.

The second of Augsburg's trio of splendid Renaissance fountains, the **Merkurbrunnen**, stands opposite the fourteenth-century **Weberhaus**, or weavers' guild house, at Moritzplatz, a little way south of the Rathaus. The richly coloured paintings on its facade were originally done by Johann Matthias Kager in 1605 but were renewed after World War II. They depict the history of the cloth trade – once very important in Augsburg – and the Battle of Lechfeld in 955 AD, in which the German King Otto held back the Magyar advance into western Europe south of the city.

To the south, the 68-metre-long sgraffito facade of the **Fuggerhäuser** dominates the midsection of Maximilianstrasse. Originally built in 1512 to 1515 as a town palace for Jakob Fugger the Rich, the complex was badly damaged during World War II and rebuilt in simplified form afterwards. During business hours, you can view the lovely Italian Renaissance-style **Damenhof**, or Ladies' Court, through the doors at the back of the Rieger & Kranzfelder bookshop; at the time of writing access to the court – usually possible by the big doors at no. 36 – was restricted due to restoration work.

Further south still, Adrian de Vries' 1602 **Herkulesbrunnen** – the third of Augsburg's Renaissance fountains – stands in front of the most imposing Rococo building in the city, the **Schaezlerpalais**. Built in 1765 as a town palace for Baron Adam Liebert von Liebenhofen, it now houses the paintings of the **Deutsche**

Barockgalerie (Tues 10am–8pm, Wed–Sun 10am–5pm; €7), including works by Angelika Kauffmann, Rubens and Tiepolo. High point of the visit, however, is the beautiful Rococo **Festsaal**, or ballroom, which is used as a concert venue in the summer months – it can't be heated, so it can't be used during the winter. The same ticket also admits you to the **Staatsgalerie** (Tues–Sun 10am–5pm), whose collection of older works includes a 1520 Dürer portrait of Jakob Fugger the Rich.

Maximilianstrasse is brought to a visual stop by the impressive onion-domed bulk of **St Ulrich und Afra**, in size only the second largest church in Augsburg but in terms of its place in the townscape of massively more importance than the Dom. The interior is a really splendid work of late Gothic architecture; begun in 1474, construction continued until 1603, completion of the choir and tower being delayed by the turmoil of the Reformation. The church contains the tombs of St Ulrich – the prince-bishop who defended the city against the Magyars – and of St Afra, while beautiful painted vaulting dating from 1492 to 1496 crowns the chapel of **St Simpert**, burial place of the eponymous saint, who is said to have been a nephew of Charlemagne. In front of St Ulrich und Afra, the pretty little Protestant church of **St Ulrich** represents in built form the workable coexistence Augsburg's Protestants and Catholics reached after the religious turmoil of the sixteenth and seventeenth centuries.

The eastern Altstadt and the Fuggerei

East of Maximilianstrasse at Dominikanergasse 15, the deconsecrated church of St Magdalena now houses the **Römisches Museum** (Tues 10am–8pm, Wed–Sun 10am–5pm; €3.50), where stone memorials, bronzes and Roman coins, ceramics and glass attest to the importance of Augsburg as a Roman provincial city. To the east, the small-scale lanes and waterways of the **Handwerkerviertel** (Artisans' Quarter) have undeniable charm, though the area was quite badly affected by World War II bombs; one of the houses lost was the birthplace of **Hans Holbein the Younger** at Vorderer Lech 20. The building now on the site is home to the

▲ St Ulrich und Afra, Augsburg

Kunstverein Augsburg, which mounts temporary exhibitions of modern art (Tues–Sun 11am–5pm; ⓦwww.kunstverein-augsburg.de).

Further east along Jakoberstrasse is the remarkable **Fuggerei** (daily: April–Sept 8am–8pm; Oct–March 9am–6pm; €4), established for the virtuous poor of Augsburg by Jakob Fugger the Rich and his brothers in 1521 and generally regarded as the world's oldest social-housing scheme. Residents must be Catholic and must say three prayers a day for the founder and the Fugger family; that duty aside, they pay a nominal rent – excluding heating – of €0.88 a year. The Fuggerei's eight lanes of simple, ochre-washed houses constitute a city within a city, complete with seven gates and a church of its own, and it's a charming place simply to wander. An informative **museum** on **Mittlere Gasse** tells the story of the Fuggers in English and German and includes a visit to a house furnished as it would have been historically; you can also visit a modernized show apartment at **Ochsengasse 51** to gain an insight into living conditions at the Fuggerei today. In the former **air raid shelter** nearby, an exhibition tells the tale of the destruction of much of the Fuggerei in the night of February 25–26, 1944, as USAF bombers targeted the Messerschmitt aircraft factory, and of the rapid reconstruction after the war.

Returning west along Jakoberstrasse, a short detour brings you to the **Brechthaus** at Auf dem Rain 7 (Tues–Sun 10am–5pm; €2.50), where the poet and playwright Bertolt Brecht was born on February 10, 1898, though he didn't stay long – the family upped sticks the same year. The building now houses an exhibition on the writer's life and work. Brecht's relationship with Augsburg was a scratchy one, and it was only from the mid-1960s on, as the Cold War began to thaw a little, that the city fathers considered him worthy of recognition. Close by, Elias Holl's splendid **Stadtmetzg** (Butchers' Guild House; 1606–09) guards the way back to Rathausplatz.

The northern Altstadt

The east–west thoroughfare of Leonhardsberg was punched through the Altstadt during postwar reconstruction, and its snarling traffic has the effect of separating the peaceful northern Altstadt – which is dominated by the **Dom** – from the rest of the city. Architecturally, Augsburg's cathedral is an utter hotchpotch: entirely lacking the sublime clarity of St Ulrich und Afra's design, it's more of a picturesque jumble than a coherent building. The spires date from 1150, but much of the rest of the building was rebuilt in Gothic style in the fourteenth century, and it's from this time that the north and south portals – built by sculptors of the Parler school – date. On the south side of the nave, the five **Prophetenfenster** depicting Moses, David, Hosea, Daniel and Jonas date from 1065 and are the oldest figurative stained glass windows in existence. Older still is the bishop's throne or **Cathedra**, which dates from around 1000 AD.

On the north side of the cathedral at Kornhausgasse 3–5, the **Diözesan-museum St Afra** (Tues–Sat 10am–5pm, Sun noon–6pm; €4) contains the cathedral's art treasures. Pride of place goes to the magnificent eleventh-century bronze cathedral doors, which consist of 35 bronze plates illustrating scenes from the Old Testament and allegories of good and evil. There's also some splendid Augsburg silver on display.

A short walk to the north at Frauentorstrasse 20, Augsburg makes the most of its tenuous Mozart connection with the rather enjoyable **Mozarthaus** (Tues–Sun 10am–5pm; €3.50), an imaginatively presented exhibition in the house in which Mozart's father Leopold was born in 1719. The museum is quite engrossing for the light it casts on Leopold's role in the nurturing of his son's talent, and there's English labelling alongside the German.

The synagogue and Glaspalast

Midway between Königsplatz and the Hauptbahnhof at Halderstrasse 6–8, Augsburg's synagogue houses the **Jüdisches Kulturmuseum Augsburg Schwaben** (Tues, Thurs & Fri 9am–4pm, Wed 9am–8pm, Sun 10am–5pm; €4), an engrossing exhibition on the history of Jewish settlement not just in Augsburg itself, but also in the surrounding districts where – thanks to the region's complex political position as an outlier of the Habsburg lands – Jewish communities grew up in quite small rural districts. In the margravate of Burgau as many as a third of the inhabitants of some villages were Jewish. The Augsburg community was extinguished by the Nazis, and the postwar community was dwindling in size as recently as the 1980s, but subsequent immigration from the former Soviet Union has boosted its numbers to 1600 – larger than it was before the Holocaust. The exhibition ends with a glimpse into the synagogue itself, a darkly beautiful blend of Jugendstil and Byzantine influences with a shallow dome picked out in gold.

East of the Altstadt on Amagasakiallee the **Glaspalast**, an imposing iron and glass former textile mill, houses the **H2 Zentrum für Gegenwartkunst** (Tues 10am–8pm, Wed–Sun 10am–5pm; €7), Augsburg's municipal gallery of contemporary art, which exhibits temporary installations by artists. The same ticket admits you to the **Staatsgalerie**, a branch gallery of Munich's Pinakothek der Moderne, which concentrates on post-1945 representations of the human form. The Glaspalast also houses the **Kunstmuseum Walter** (Tues–Fri 10am–5pm, Sat & Sun 11am–6pm; €6), a private collection of classical modern and contemporary art, including 118 works in glass by Egidio Costantini.

Eating, drinking and nightlife

Augsburg's Altstadt has an excellent selection of places to **eat** and **drink** of every style, from traditional German to haute cuisine, and is a particularly good place to eat cheaply and well at lunchtime. The city's surprisingly extensive **nightlife** is mostly of the cocktails and dance music variety, concentrated on the southern end of Maximilianstrasse and the surrounding streets, though there have been threats to its continued viability because of the noise disturbance to residents.

Cafés, restaurants and Weinstuben

3M Bistro In the *Steigenberger Drei Mohren*, Maximilianstr. 40 ☏ 0821/503 60. Attractive French-style bistro open from 9am daily, serving breakfast, French dishes and – bizarrely – curries. There are also daily specials.

August Frauentorstr. 27 ☏ 0821 35279. Classy, modern gourmet restaurant in the northern Altstadt, with the likes of Breton calamari with black curry and *trompettes de mort* to tempt the palate. Five-course menu €86; seven courses €99. They also do a veggie seven-course dinner for €80. Wed–Sat, eve only.

Café Dichtl Bahnhofstr. cnr Schrannenstr. ☏ 0821/52 50 30. Big café-*Konditorei* with impressive cakes, chocolates and a limited menu of inexpensive hot meals. Open daily.

Cisa Anoniushof, Maximilianstr. 55 ☏ 0821/608 44 91. Very stylish, modern café/bar and bistro; open for breakfast from 8am daily, it also serves *Kaffee*

und Kuchen and full meals. There are seats outside in the *Hof* in fine weather.

Die Ecke Elias-Holl-Platz 2 ☏ 0821/51 06 00. Snug, intimate and long-established gourmet restaurant just behind the Rathaus, with refined cooking that embraces German and other influences. Evening set menus €59/68; the two-course €16 lunch is an absolute bargain. Open daily for lunch and dinner.

EKU 34 Hunoldsgraben 34 ☏ 0821/392 94. Vibrantly decorated restaurant in a vaulted cellar in the Altstadt, with regular dinner shows; the food is good but can be over-creative, though they also serve straightforward steaks. Main courses €16 up. Gay friendly, but by no means exclusively gay.

Fuggerei Stube Jakoberstr. 26 ☏ 0821/308 70. Charmingly old-fashioned place at the front of the Fuggerei, serving *Schnitzel, Zwiebelrostbraten* (a traditional beef dish with onions) and the like from around €12 beneath its vaulted ceilings and stone capitals. They also do salads.

Ratskeller Rathausplatz 2 ☏0821/31 98 82 38. Despite its historic setting in the cavernous undercroft of the Rathaus there's a surprisingly bustling, contemporary feel here. It serves a short menu of German classics, plus *Flammkuchen* and Bavarian-style tapas, with cocktails or Riegele beer to wash it down. Daily from 11am; kitchen closes at 11pm.
Schlemmerhäusl Karolinenstr. 2. Tiny delicatessen that serves wholesome, bargain-priced lunches for little more than the price of a burger. Mon–Fri 9am–7pm, Sat until 4pm.

🏃 **Stadtmarkt** Between Fuggerstr. and Annastr. The covered hall of Augsburg's market is a wonderful place for a cheap lunch if you don't mind eating at a counter, with everything from *Bratwurst* and *Schnitzel* to Chinese and Greek food. The queues build up fast, though. Closed Sun.

Bars and clubs

König von Flandern Karolinenstr. 12. *Gasthausbrauerei* in a historic cellar brewing its own *Drei-Heller-Bier*, a *Doppelbock* under the Alligator name and a dark beer; there's also food.

Mahagoni Bar Ulrichsplatz 3. Cocktail bar and dance club that's just about the most happening place in Augsburg at the moment, with a music policy that runs the gamut from rumba and reggae to funk, soul, hip-hop and rock.

🏃 **Pantheon** Maximilianstr. 67. Sophisticated smokers' bar with classy cocktails and Cohiba cigars. Early in the evening it's jazzy and laid-back – people even read books – but it gets noisier later on, and there are regular DJs at weekends. It's in the Villa Sandi, a Renaissance landmark that houses several bars.
Peaches Maximilianstr. 73. Perennially popular cocktail bar, with a spacious outdoor seating area fronting Maximilianstr. in summer.
Striese Kirchgasse 1 ☏0821/309 62. Theatre café-bar with regular live music, close to St Ulrich und Afra.
Der Weinbäck Spitalgasse 8 ☏0821/13 79 11. Lovely *Weinstube* in a quiet corner of the southern Altstadt, with a galleried *Innenhof*, light food and German and international wines by the glass. Closed Sun.

Entertainment and festivals

Augsburg's celebrated Puppenkiste, Spitalgasse 15 (☏0821/450 34 50, 🌐www .diekiste.net), puts on **puppet shows** of particular appeal to children, while the Theater Augsburg, Kennedyplatz 1 (☏0821/324 49 00, 🌐www.theater.augsburg .de), is the home of more adult **drama** and of **opera** and **classical music**. Every summer on the last weekend in June Maximilianstrasse is closed to traffic for Max, a weekend **festival** of live bands and alfresco eating and drinking, while from mid-July to mid-August the Internationaler Augsburger Jazz Sommer (🌐www .augsburger-jazzsommer.de) brings a varied line-up of international jazz acts to the city. Augsburg's biggest folk festival is Plärrer (🌐www.plaerrer-online.de), a combination of funfair and beer tents held twice each year, in spring and autumn.

Travel details

Trains

Augsburg to: Ingolstadt (hourly; 55min); Munich (every 15min; 40–50min); Nuremberg (every 30min–1hr; 1hr 15min–1hr 40min); Stuttgart (every 15–30min; 1hr 40min).
Ingolstadt to: Eichstätt Stadt (via Eichstätt Bhf; hourly; 40min); Munich (every 20min; 35min–1hr); Neuburg an der Donau (hourly; 18min); Nuremberg (every 30min; 1hr 30min–1hr 45min); Regensburg (hourly; 1hr 5min).
Munich: to: Augsburg (every 15min; 40–50min); Berchtesgaden (via Freilassing; every 15–30min; 2hr–2hr 20min); Berlin (hourly; 5hr 40min);

Dachau (every 20min; 20min); Frankfurt (every 30min–1hr; 3hr 10min); Füssen (every 2hr; 2hr 5min); Garmisch-Partenkirchen (every 30min–1hr; 1hr 25min); Herrsching (every 20–40min; 48min); Ingolstadt (every 15–30min; 35min–1hr); Mittenwald (hourly; 1hr 55min); Nuremberg (every 15–30min; 1hr–2hr 45min); Oberammergau (hourly, via Murnau: 1hr 50min); Oberschleissheim (every 20min; 20min); Passau (every 2hr; 2hr 15min); Regensburg (every 30min–1hr; 1hr 30min–2hr); Starnberg (every 20min; 30min); Ulm (every 15–30min; 1hr 20min–1hr 50min); Würzburg (every 30min–1hr; 2hr).

The Alps and eastern Bavaria

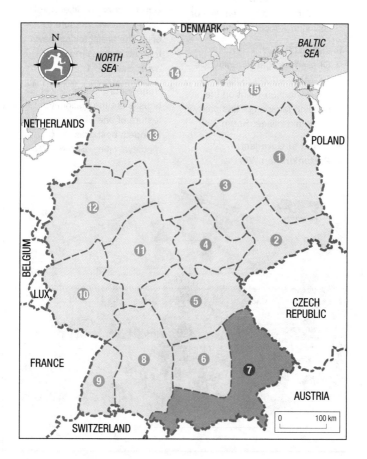

CHAPTER 7 # Highlights

* **Mad Ludwig's palaces** Enter the extravagant fantasy world of "Mad" King Ludwig II at Neuschwanstein, Linderhof or Herrenchiemsee. **See p.396**

* **The Wieskirche** A vision of heaven inspired by a tearful statue of Christ, the Wieskirche is a masterpiece of Bavarian Rococo. **See p.398**

* **Lüftmalerei in Oberammergau** A distinctive Bavarian artform reaches its charming high-point on the building facades of this pretty mountain village. **See p.399**

* **Skiing at Garmisch-Partenkirchen** Whether enjoying the views from the Zugspitze's high-altitude pistes or cutting a dash on the Kandahar run, skiing at Germany's biggest winter resort is a memorable experience. **See p.402**

* **The Eagle's Nest, Berchtesgaden** Hitler hardly used it, but you're sure to enjoy the breathtaking views from his famous mountain eyrie. **See p.411**

* **Regensburg** Gothic tower houses are the distinctive feature of one of Central Europe's best preserved medieval cities. **See p.419**

▲ Lüftmalerei, Oberammergau

The Alps and eastern Bavaria

All the images that foreigners think most typically Bavarian accumulate in profusion in the region south of Munich, where "Mad" King Ludwig's palaces preside over dramatically scenic alpine settings. Here, onion-domed church towers rise above brilliant green meadows, impossibly blue lakes fringe dark forests and the sparkling snow-capped peaks of the **Bavarian Alps** define the southern horizon. And it doesn't disappoint close up: villages are tourist-brochure quaint, while traditional *Tracht* is by no means the fancy dress it can sometimes seem in Munich, and you'll see Dirndls or Lederhosen quite often. Politically and socially, this is Bavaria at its most Catholic and conservative, anchored to its time-honoured lifestyles, crafts and cultural rituals, though sheer numbers of visitors nowadays add a certain cosmopolitan sheen, particularly to major resorts such as **Füssen** or **Garmisch-Partenkirchen** – Germany's highest, and most famous ski centre.

Eastern Bavaria could scarcely be more different: in place of a wall of mountains, it is defined by one of the great cultural and trading thoroughfares of Central Europe, the River Danube. Consequently its ancient cities – notably the perfectly preserved, former imperial free city of **Regensburg** and the prince-bishopric of **Passau** – bear the legacy of Rome and the influence of Italy with considerable grace, while even relatively modest towns such as **Straubing** and **Landshut** preserve architectural wonders from their distant golden ages. Only along its eastern boundary with the Czech Republic do natural wonders again triumph over cultural richness, in the vast, relatively sparsely populated forests of the **Bayerischer Wald** (Bavarian Forest).

Getting around the region is remarkably easy: Regensburg, Passau, Garmisch-Partenkirchen and the Berchtesgadener Land are all linked into the Autobahn network, while train services connect Munich with the major towns and reach into the Alps as far as Füssen, Garmisch-Partenkirchen and Berchtesgaden. Where train services end, buses take over, with services linking at least the most important tourist sites relatively frequently.

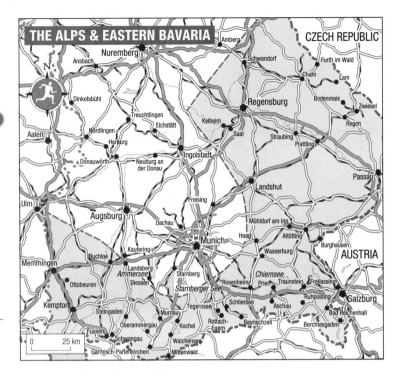

The Bavarian Alps

Bavaria puts on its most spectacular scenic show along its southern boundary. The great, snow-capped rampart of the Alps rears up ahead of travellers heading south from Munich, visible long before you're actually among the mountains. Stretching from the Allgäu in the west to Berchtesgadener Land in the east, it's a region of incomparable natural beauty at any time of year, attracting hikers and cyclists in late spring, summer and early autumn and skiers and snowboarders from Christmas to Easter, in particular to chic **Garmisch-Partenkirchen**, nestling at the foot of Germany's highest mountain, the Zugspitze. In the summer, the region's many lakes provide a secondary focus for visitors, above all for swimming and sailing – notably on **Chiemsee**, the so-called Bavarian Sea. But the attractions aren't limited to scenic wonders. Chiemsee also boasts King Ludwig II's attempt to re-create the palace of Versailles at **Schloss Herrenchiemsee**, while thousands flock to see his famous castle of **Neuschwanstein** – perhaps the most familiar of all Bavarian images – high above the village of **Hohenschwangau** in the **Allgäu**. Completing this theatrical trio of palaces is **Schloss Linderhof** near the village of **Ettal**, which is also remarkable for its Baroque abbey. Nearby **Oberammergau** is home not only to the celebrated Passion Play but to some of the most remarkable examples of Bavarian facade-painting, or *Lüftmalerei*. Bavarian Rococo reaches weightless perfection in the region known as the **Pfaffenwinkel** at the UNESCO-listed Wieskirche at **Steingaden**.

Not all the region's monuments are so light-hearted, however, for **Obersalzberg** above the lively mountain resort of **Berchtesgaden** preserves ominous reminders of Hitler and the crimes of his regime. Yet even here, the sheer scenic magnificence of the Bavarian Alps is hard to ignore – whether from the terrace of the dictator's famous teahouse, the **Eagle's Nest**, or from a boat on the placid waters of the fjord-like **Königsee** far below. A themed tourist road, the 450km **Deutsche Alpenstrasse** (Ⓦ www.deutsche-alpenstrasse.de), links many of the region's most famous sights.

Füssen

The first – or last – stop on the Romantic Road (see p.344) is **FÜSSEN**, in a beautiful setting on the River Lech at the southwest end of the broad Forggensee hard by the Austrian border. The town is dominated by its late Gothic Schloss and by the impressive buildings of the former Benedictine abbey of St Mang, and is much the liveliest place in the district, with a compact Altstadt that fizzes with activity at any time of year. No mere tourist spot, Füssen is also a garrison town, the home to a battalion of the German army's mountain troops. With a direct rail connection from Munich, Füssen is also the most practical base from which to explore the sights of the eastern Allgäu, including the royal castles at Hohenschwangau. It makes an ideal base for hikers and cyclists, with an extensive network of **walking** and **bike trails** fanning out into the surrounding district, including some that cross the border into Austria.

Arrival, information and accommodation

Füssen's **Bahnhof** is just to the northwest of the Altstadt, a short walk from the **tourist office** at Kaiser-Maximilian-Platz 1 (Mon–Fri 9am–5pm, Sat 10am–2pm; ☏08362/3850, Ⓦ www.tourismus-fuessen.de). The tourist office can advise on walks in the area and will help with finding somewhere to **stay**, or you can search and book through their website. The nearest **campsite** is *Camping Hopfensee*, Fischerbichl 17 (☏08362/91 77 10, Ⓦ www.camping -hopfensee.com), on the shores of a small lake to the north of the town.

DJH Füssen Mariahilferstr. 5 ☏08362/77 54, Ⓦ www.fuessen.jugendherberge.de. A 10min walk west of the Bahnhof, with accommodation in two- to six-bed rooms; €19.50 including breakfast.

Fürstenhof Kemptener Str. 23 ☏08362/914 80, Ⓦ www.fuerstenhof-fuessen.de. Family-run hotel *garni* a little west of the Altstadt close to the Eisstadion and Tennishalle; all rooms have shower, WC and TV, and there's car parking for guests. ❸

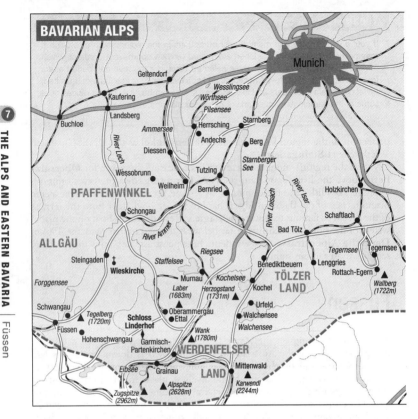

Hotel Hirsch Kaiser-Maximilian-Platz 7
☏ 08362/939 80, ⓦ www.hotelhirsch.de. Very
central, on the edge of the Altstadt and with lots
of character, from the Bavarian-style *Bierstube* to
the individually designed rooms, some with
quirky themes. ❹
Via Hotel Sonne Prinzregentenplatz 1
☏ 08362/80 00 & 90 80, ⓦ www.hotel-sonne.de.
Swanky and central, with stylish modern decor

throughout and several categories of themed
rooms, from small to very large, with en-suite
facilities and internet access; some also have
balconies. ❹–❼
Zum Hechten Ritterstr. 6 ☏ 08362/916 00,
ⓦ www.hotel-hechten.com. This hotel right in the
heart of the Altstadt close to the Hohes Schloss,
has attractive rooms in a simplified Bavarian style,
some with balconies. ❹

The Town

Perched just high enough above Füssen's lively **Altstadt** to dominate the town
from every angle, the white-walled, red-roofed, late Gothic **Hohes Schloss**
(Tues–Sun: April–Oct 11am–5pm; Nov–March 1–4pm; €2, or €3 combined
ticket with museum in Kloster St Mang) was rebuilt around 1500 as a summer
residence for the bishops of Augsburg and the result is one of the most important
late Gothic castle complexes in Germany, with delightful *Lüftmalerei* wall paintings
on the facades of the Innenhof, including numerous "oriel windows" which can
be uncannily convincing when viewed from certain angles. There are also splendid

views over the Altstadt. The Schloss houses the **Staatsgalerie** – an outpost of the Bavarian state art collection showing fifteenth- and sixteenth-century paintings from Swabia and the Allgäu – and the **Städtische Galerie**, which concentrates on the turn-of-the-twentieth-century Munich school and the graphic works of the nineteenth-century artist Franz Graf von Pocci. Highlight of the interior is the Rittersaal, or Knights' Hall, with its magnificent coffered wooden ceiling; as part of your visit you can climb the castle clock tower for the views.

Competing with the Hohes Schloss for dominance, high above the River Lech, the Baroque buildings of the former Benedictine abbey of **Kloster St Mang** now house the **Museum der Stadt Füssen** (same hours & price as Schloss) in a series of rooms in high Bavarian Baroque style; particular highlights are the Fürstensaal or Princes' Hall and the abbey library. The museum's exhibits include numerous lutes and violins, which reflect Füssen's historic importance as a centre for the manufacture of musical instruments – a guild of lute-makers was founded here in the sixteenth century. The Baroque **Annakapelle** features the **Füssener Totentanz** (Dance of Death) mural, completed in 1602 at a time when the plague was raging in the district. The Baroque basilica of **St Mang** itself – now the town's parish church – rests on much older foundations, with tenth-century frescoes in the east crypt.

West of the Altstadt along Kemptener Strasse, the **Bundesleistungszentrum für Eishockey** (Federal Ice Hockey Training Centre; daily 2–3.30pm; disco skating Mon 7.30–9pm; curling Thurs 10am–noon; day-ticket €8) offers a variety of indoor winter sports all year round. National and junior teams use the centre for training, and the centre also hosts ice-hockey matches. Next to the complex is the **Tennishalle Füssen** (☎08362/93 06 02) with three indoor courts.

A short distance to the east of town above Schwangau, the **Tegelbergbahn** cable car (daily 9am–4.30pm; €9.50 single, €16 return; day-pass for skiing €24; Ⓦwww.tegelbergbahn.de) gives access in winter to a long red **ski run** which descends to the valley from the 1720m Tegelberg; in summer it's a popular launch spot for **hang-gliding** and **paragliding**. Three hang-gliding and paragliding schools operate on the mountain: Flugschule Tegelberg (Ⓦwww.abschweb.net); Flugschule Aktiv (Ⓦwww.flugschule-aktiv.de); and Erste DAeC Gleitschirm Schule (Ⓦwww.erste-daec-gleitschirm-schule.de).

Eating and drinking

Many of the most tempting places to **eat** and **drink** in Füssen are in its hotels, though there's also a sprinkling of other places, particularly in the Altstadt.

Eisenschmidt Augsburger Str. 4. Café and cocktail bar just north of the Altstadt, with König Ludwig beers and a menu of pizza, pasta and salads. Open until 3am Sat, otherwise daily until 1am.

Hohes Schloss Reichenstr. 14. Family-run Italian-style ice-cream parlour in the Altstadt, with 36 flavours of ice cream plus Italian coffee.

Il Pescatore Franziskanergasse 13 ☎08362/92 43 43. Traditional Italian restaurant with home-made fresh pasta and pizza, plus fish specialities, in the Altstadt. Closed Wed.

Kurcafé Prinzregentenplatz 4 ☎08362/93 01 80. Long-established *Konditorei* with heavenly cakes and coffee, plus a snug, classy restaurant serving Bavarian dishes alongside salads and pasta.

Steakhaus Füssen Tiroler Str. 31 ☎08362/50 98 53. Steaks, Tex-Mex and Bavarian staples – plus a *Biergarten* – on the south side of the Lech overlooking the river. Closed Mon.

Woaze Weizenbrauhaus Schrannenplatz 10 ☎08362/63 12. Own-brew beer and simple but hearty and affordable Bavarian dishes – *Leberkäs*, *Schnitzel* and the like – plus seasonal specialities including wild mushrooms and asparagus, in a rustic setting in the Altstadt. There's a *Biergarten* in the *Hof*, and a terrace out front in fine weather.

Zum Hechten Ritterstr. 6 ☎08362/916 00. Seasonal regional produce including game and fish, in atmospheric and very Bavarian surroundings in the heart of the Altstadt.

Schloss Neuschwanstein and Hohenschwangau

The vision of the pinnacled and turreted castle of **Neuschwanstein** (frequent guided tours daily: April–Sept 9am–6pm; Oct–March 10am–4pm; €9 or €17 combined ticket with Schloss Hohenschwangau; Ⓦwww.neuschwanstein .de), perched high on its crag and rising above the mist, is perhaps the most reproduced of all tourist images of Germany, a Disney-like fantasy amid a setting of breathtaking alpine beauty. If it all seems too good to be true, that's no surprise, for it is the most celebrated and the most theatrical of all "Mad" King Ludwig II's castles, and has its origins in his desire to rebuild an existing ruin in the authentic style of the old German knights' castles. Ludwig was inspired by the recently restored Wartburg in Thuringia; his architects, Eduard Riedel and Georg Dollmann – who would go on to design Linderhof and Herrenchiemsee – worked from idealized drawings by the theatre designer

Christian Jank. Construction began in 1869, the castle was "topped out" in 1880 and the king was able to move into the (still unfinished) Pallas, or castle keep, in 1884. Ludwig chopped and changed the plans as he went along, incorporating a huge throne room that required ultramodern steel-framed construction methods to make it structurally viable.

The exterior of Neuschwanstein, in a sort of exaggerated Romanesque, is theatrical enough, but the real flights of fancy begin inside, where the decorative schemes are inspired by Wagner's operas *Tannhäuser* and *Lohengrin*. The Byzantine-style **Thronsaal** (Throne Room), inspired by the church of Hagia Sophia in Istanbul, was intended to represent the Grail Hall from *Parsifal* and was completed in the year of Ludwig's death, 1886. Ludwig's **bedroom** is in a heightened Gothic style, with the king's four-poster bed more closely resembling some fifteenth-century church altar than a place in which to sleep. The highlight – and peak of the king's Wagnerian obsession – however, is the **Sängersaal**, or Singers' Hall, which occupies the entire fourth floor and was inspired by the famous hall at the Wartburg that was the scene of the Singers' Contest from *Tannhäuser*. If you've not seen it on your way from the bus, it's worth strolling uphill to the **Marienbrücke** after the tour finishes for the dramatic views down into the Pöllat gorge and across to the castle.

If it weren't literally and figuratively overshadowed by Neuschwanstein, **Schloss Hohenschwangau** (guided tours daily: April–Sept 9am–6pm; Oct–March 9am–3.30pm; €8, or €17 combined ticket with Neuschwanstein), in the valley below Ludwig's castle at the southern end of the village, might be more

"Mad" King Ludwig II

For someone who was so shy and reclusive in life, King Ludwig II has achieved remarkable and lasting popularity in death. Born at Schloss Nymphenburg in 1845, he had spirited good looks not unlike those of his cousin, the Austrian Empress Elisabeth, and cut quite a dash when he came to the Bavarian throne in 1864 at the age of 18. Ludwig was fascinated with the French royal dynasty, the Bourbons, to which his own family was related. This developed into a fixation with the most illustrious of the Bourbons, Louis XIV, whose absolute power contrasted so starkly with the relative powerlessness of the Bavarian monarchy after its defeat alongside Austria in the 1866 war against Prussia, at a time when the young king had only been on the throne for two years. Seemingly overcompensating for this political impotence, the king retreated increasingly into an extravagant fantasy world, becoming steadily more eccentric and – towards the end of his life – rather corpulent. He was a patron of Richard Wagner, whose fantastical operas fired the king's own vivid imagination, and though he disapproved of Wagner's anti-Semitism he continued to support the composer financially, even planning a lavish festival theatre to host the composer's operas in Munich, which was to remain unbuilt. A political reactionary but at the same time a romantic, Ludwig devoted his attention to fabulous but ruinously expensive projects to realize his fantasies in built form: a castle straight from the age of chivalry at **Neuschwanstein**, a homage to the Sun King at **Herrenchiemsee** and an eclectic but breathtakingly opulent "villa" at **Linderhof**. Eventually his spending caught up with him, as foreign banks threatened to foreclose. Ludwig's refusal to react to this crisis in rational fashion prompted the Bavarian government to act unconstitutionally, declaring him insane and removing him from the throne. He was interned at the castle of Berg on Starnberger See, where he and his doctor were discovered drowned in mysterious circumstances on June 13, 1886. Very shortly afterwards his palaces – which had been intensely private places during his life – were opened to the paying public.

widely famous. Standing on a low wooded hill above Alpsee, it was a ruin when Ludwig's father, Maximilian II, bought it in 1832 while still crown prince, and had it rebuilt in a prettily romantic neo-Gothic style. Ludwig II spent much of his childhood here, and it was here that he first encountered the legend of *Lohengrin*, the Swan Knight, as the Schloss is decorated with frescoes on the theme by Michael Neher and Lorenz Quaglio. Schloss Hohenschwangau still belongs to a Wittelsbach trust, not to the state of Bavaria, and part of its charm is that it feels altogether more homely than its showy neighbour.

Practicalities

The frequent OVG **bus** #78 connects Füssen's train station with Hohenschwangau village; in summer, it is also served by the Europa Bus that travels the length of the Romantic Road in both directions (see p.344). If you arrive by car or motorbike, you'll get no further than the village, where you'll have to pay for parking (€4.50 & €2 respectively). **Tickets** for both castles can only be bought at the **ticket centre** at Alpseestrasse 12 in Hohenschwangau village. If you don't fancy the stiff thirty-minute uphill walk to Neuschwanstein, you can take the **shuttle bus** from *Schlosshotel Lisl* (€1.80 uphill, €1 down, €2.60 return) or go by horse-drawn **carriage** (€6 uphill, €3 down); the bus drops you by the Jugend lookout point by the Marienbrücke, from which it's a 600m walk downhill to the Schloss – a lot easier than the ascent on foot, but still scarcely suitable for anyone with limited mobility. There's a **café** in Schloss Neuschwanstein and a restaurant, *Schlossrestaurant Neuschwanstein* (T08362/811 10; daily 11am–6pm), just below the castle gates; otherwise, there's a reasonable selection of places down in the village.

Steingaden and the Wieskirche

The Romantic Road reaches one of its highlights at **STEINGADEN**, which stands in rolling countryside 21km northeast of Füssen in the placid rural district known as the Pfaffenwinkel, or Clerics' Corner – so called because of its numerous churches and monasteries. In most respects it's a fairly modest country town, clustering around the **Welfenmünster** (daily: summer 8am–7pm; winter 8am–5pm; free), a handsome former abbey church that preserves its Romanesque exterior appearance and cloister but is otherwise flamboyantly Baroque. Fine though it is, this is not the church that brings visitors from across the world to Steingaden. They come instead to see the **Wieskirche**, or meadow church (daily: summer 8am–7pm; winter 8am–5pm; free; W www.wieskirche .de), in the tiny hamlet of **Wies** 5km southeast of town. In 1738 farmer's wife Maria Lory spotted tears coming from the eyes of an abandoned figure of a scourged Christ; the site became a place of pilgrimage, and two years later a tiny chapel was built to accommodate the flow of pilgrims. Sheer visitor numbers soon overwhelmed it, however, and so the present church was begun in 1745 to the designs of Dominikus Zimmermann. It was consecrated in 1754. Though the exterior is handsome enough, nothing prepares you for the overwhelming grace and beauty of the interior – a vision of a Rococo heaven in pastel shades, with ceiling frescoes by Dominikus's elder brother Johann Baptist, whose work also graces the monastery of Kloster Andechs and the Wittelsbachs' summer palace at Nymphenburg. The church is generally regarded as one of the pinnacles of the Rococo style, and it was added to UNESCO's World Heritage list in 1983. The church is busy with tour groups in summer, but it's a magical (but freezing cold) experience to visit in midwinter, when you might just have the place to yourself. In the summer months it is also the venue for occasional evening concerts.

Practicalities

Bus #9606 connects Füssen's train station with Steingaden before continuing the short distance to the Wieskirche; in summer, it's also served by the Europa Bus service along the Romantic Road (see p.344). The town's **tourist office** is in the Rathaus at Krankenhausstrasse 1 (Mon–Thurs 8am–noon & 2–5pm, Fri 8am–noon; ⊤08862/200, Ⓦwww.steingaden.de). If you want to **stay**, you could try the *Gasthof zur Post* in the centre of town at Marktplatz 1 (⊤08862/203, Ⓕ60 24; ❷), or the *Gasthof Graf* at Schongauer Strasse 15 (⊤08862/246, Ⓕ64 54; ❷), both of which have **restaurants** serving regional produce, and beer gardens. There's a cluster of places to eat and drink around the Wieskirche.

Oberammergau

Nestling at the foot of the Ammergauer Alpen between the distinctive peaks of **Kofel** (1342m) and **Laber** (1684m), the highly photogenic village of **OBERAMMERGAU** has achieved international fame thanks to the **Passion Play**, which depicts the life of Jesus and is performed by local people every ten years in a purpose-built theatre; the next play is to be performed in 2010 (Ⓦwww.passionsspiele2010.de). It has its origins in a promise by the villagers in the seventeenth century to perform a play if God would spare them the effects of the plague, which was then ravaging the region. You can visit the **Passionstheater** where the play is staged on a guided tour (mid-March to end Oct; English-language tours Tues–Sun at 11am & 2.30pm; €4); in addition to seeing the impressive open-air stage, you'll get to see costumes and props from the last time the play was performed.

For the other nine years in each decade Oberammergau is busy with visitors who come to see its elaborately frescoed houses and to buy the woodcarvings in which its craftsmen specialize. The artform of **Lüftmalerei** or *trompe l'oeil* facade-painting reaches a particularly refined level here, demonstrated most convincingly on the facade of the **Pilatushaus** (mid-May to mid-Oct Tues–Sat 1–6pm; Dec 26–30, Jan 2–6 & Easter 11am–5pm; free) at Ludwig-Thoma-Strasse 10, which was built between 1774 and 1775 and painted by Franz Seraph Zwinck. His work here is considered one of the masterpieces of South German *Lüftmalerei*. The ground floor houses a crafts workshop, while upstairs is **Welten hinter Glas** (Worlds behind Glass), an exhibition of glass paintings. Diagonally opposite at Dorfstrasse 8 is the **Oberammergau Museum** (Tues–Sun 10am–5pm; €4), where you can see more specimens of local woodcarving up close. The museum also hosts regular temporary exhibitions on themes of local artistic or historical interest.

Once you've drunk in the twee prettiness of the painted houses, the obvious thing to do is to don walking boots and ascend the **Kolben Sesselbahn** (daily 9am–4.45pm; single €5.50, return €7.50), a chairlift that ascends to 1276m immediately west of Oberammergau and gives access to the **Königssteig** hiking trail which heads east below the ridge for roughly 5km towards the Kofel before descending to the valley south of Oberammergau, though there's also an easier path that descends to the valley from the **Kolbensattelhütte** at the top of the chairlift. In winter, the downhill route becomes a long blue (easy) **ski** run. On the eastern side of Oberammergau, the **Laber Bergbahn** (daily: winter 9am–4.30pm; summer 9am–5pm; July & Aug until 5.30pm; single €8, return €12.50) ascends the 1684m Laber, from the summit of which a rugged trail descends rapidly to the eastern edge of Oberammergau (about 7km); a somewhat easier but longer route meanders down via a small lake, **Soilesee** (about 11km). In winter, a black (difficult) **ski** run takes the short route back down to Oberammergau (day-pass €21).

Practicalities

Direct **buses** link Garmisch-Partenkirchen with Oberammergau in around forty minutes; if you're coming by **train**, you have to change at Oberau, and if by train from Munich, at Murnau. The **tourist office** is at Eugen-Papst-Strasse 9a (high season May to mid-Oct, Christmas & New Year, early Feb & early March to early April Mon–Fri 9am–6pm, Sat 10am–2pm, Sun 10am–1pm; otherwise Mon–Fri 9am–6pm, Sat 10am–1pm; ☎08822/92 27 40, ⓦwww .ammergauer-alpen.de). The tourist office has details of self-catering flats in which to **stay**, or you could try the charmingly traditional *Hotel Alte Post* at Dorfstrasse 19 (☎08822/91 00, ⓦwww.altepost.com; ❸–❹), or the extremely plush *Hotel Maximilian*, Ettaler Strasse 5 (☎08822/94 87 40, ⓦwww.maximilian -oberammergau.de; ❼). Oberammergau's **youth hostel** is at Malensteinweg 10 (☎08822/41 14, ⓦwww.oberammergau.jugendherberge.de; €17.70) on the southwestern edge of the village, beneath the Kofel. Note that from January to October and again over the Christmas and New Year period, you'll pay a small *Kurbeitrag* or **tourist tax** on the price of your room. Both the *Alte Post* and *Maximilian* have **restaurants** – the *St Benoît* at the latter is quite a gourmet temple; for something simpler, try the *Theater Café* at Othmar-Weis-Strasse 3 close to the Passionstheater, which is open for breakfast.

Ettal and Schloss Linderhof

Slotted into a narrow gap in the mountains between Oberammergau and Oberau and, if possible, even more improbably pretty than Oberammergau, the tiny village of **ETTAL** is utterly dominated by its magnificent Benedictine abbey, **Kloster Ettal** (daily: summer 8am–7.45pm; winter 8am–6pm; free), rebuilt in its present, showily Baroque form between 1744 and 1753 by Joseph Schmuzer, who was required to replace the still-incomplete work of his fellow architect Enrico Zuccalli after the church was devastated by fire in 1744. Despite the overwhelmingly Baroque appearance of his work, bits of the old church were incorporated into the present structure – you pass through a fourteenth-century Gothic portal on your way into the church. The domed interior is quite breathtaking, with frescoes by the Tyroleans Johann Jakob Zeiller and Martin Knoller. After you've admired the church, you can stock up on carvings, candles, liqueurs and Ettaler beer in the abbey shop. **Buses** (#9662 or #9606) take ten to fifteen minutes to reach Ettal from Oberammergau.

Bus #9622 from Oberammergau continues on from Ettal to Ludwig II's **Schloss Linderhof** (daily: April–Sept 9am–6pm; Oct–March 10am–4pm; €7; ⓦwww.linderhof.de) in thirty minutes; the Schloss is in a narrow valley around 11.5km west of Ettal. Originally a hunting lodge belonging to Ludwig's father Maximilian II, the palace was enlarged and re-clad between 1870 and 1878 by Georg Dollmann, who was later to design Schloss Herrenchiemsee. Unlike that palace, Linderhof was actually completed during Ludwig's lifetime. It looks relatively modest from the outside, but the elaborate neo-Rococo interiors are anything but: the riot of gold leaf within reaches a crescendo in the king's staggeringly ornate bedroom, which is the largest room in the house.

The **park** surrounding the Schloss (closed in winter) is delightful, and is particularly known for its **fountains**, which perform every half-hour from April to mid-October. There are several highly theatrical follies in the grounds, including the **Maurische Kiosk** (Moorish kiosk) and the eccentric **Venus–Grotte**, an artificial cave with a lake, fake stalactites and stalagmites and a golden barge with cupid as a figurehead – all inspired by Wagner's opera *Tannhäuser*.

Garmisch-Partenkirchen

As the hyphen in its name suggests, the chic skiing resort of **GARMISCH-PARTENKIRCHEN** was originally not one alpine village but two, which faced each other across the Partnach stream and were united in a shotgun wedding in time for the 1936 Winter Olympics. The Games were an enormous success – so much so that the town was slated to host the 1940 Winter Games after the Japanese city of Sapporo withdrew. In the event, of course, war intervened and the 1940 Games didn't take place, but Garmisch-Partenkirchen has been on the international winter-sports map ever since, which gives the resort a relatively cosmopolitan air. The resort is the venue for the 2011 FIS Alpine World Ski Championships. Though any clear distinction between Garmisch and Partenkirchen has long since vanished, the two halves of the town do have sharply contrasting characters: Garmisch is lively and international, while Partenkirchen better preserves its original alpine charm. Looming over them both is the **Zugspitze**, at 2962m Germany's highest mountain. In summer, the town's mountainous setting attracts hikers and climbers.

Arrival, information and accommodation

Trains from Munich arrive at Garmisch-Partenkirchen's **Hauptbahnhof**, which is slightly closer to the centre of Garmisch than it is to Partenkirchen, though both are within walking distance. The main **tourist office** is next to the Kongresshaus in Garmisch at Richard-Strauss-Platz 2 (Mon–Sat 8am–6pm, Sun 10am–noon; ☎08821/18 07 00, ⓦwww.garmisch-partenkirchen.com); there's a second office at Rathausplatz 1 in Partenkirchen (Mon–Wed 8am–1pm & 2–4pm, Thurs 8am–1pm & 2–5pm, Fri 8am–1pm & 2–3.30pm). They can provide information on walks, sell you walking maps, and have comprehensive lists of holiday flats and a number of bed-and-breakfast places. Several places **rent bikes** in Garmisch-Partenkirchen: the tourist office can point you in the right direction.

Atlas Posthotel Marienplatz 12 ☎08821/70 90, ⓦwww.atlas-posthotel.de. Right in the centre of Garmisch, a traditional-style hotel with plenty of alpine touches in the decor of its spacious, en-suite rooms and suites. Free wi-fi. ❹

DJH Garmisch-Partenkirchen Jochstr. 10 ☎08821/96 70 50, ⓦwww.garmisch .jugendherberge.de. Garmisch's youth hostel is 3km north of town on the edge of the village of Burgrain, with accommodation in four- and six-bed dorms. €22.80 with breakfast in peak season. Closed mid-Nov to Christmas.

🏃 **Gasthof Fraundorfer** Ludwigstr. 24 ☎08821/92 70, ⓦwww.gasthof -fraundorfer.de. Very attractive traditional *Gasthof*

in Partenkirchen, with spectacular *Lüftmalerei* on the facade and pretty alpine-style furniture in its cosy rooms. There's also a restaurant serving Bavarian food. ❸

Gasthof Zum Rassen Ludwigstr. 45 ☎08821/20 89, ⓦwww.gasthof-rassen.de. Another reasonably priced and attractive traditional option in Partenkirchen's charming main street, a little simpler than the *Fraundorfer* and with a rural folk theatre attached. ❷

Hotel Aschenbrenner Loisachstr. 46 ☎08821/959 70, ⓦwww.hotel-aschenbrenner.de. Airy, high-ceilinged rooms and three-star comfort in this hotel *garni* in a handsome old villa a short walk from the heart of Garmisch. ❹

Riessersee Hotel Am Riess 5 ☎08821/75 80, ⓦwww.riessersee-hotel.de. Swanky resort hotel in an idyllic location on a small lake 2km from town, with spa and fitness facilities, pool and well-equipped, comfortable rooms, including some suites. ⑥

The Town

Curving around the southern side of its neat **Kurpark** the centre of **Garmisch** has the bustling air of an international resort, with plenty of places to eat and drink and a **casino** at Am Kurpark 10 (Mon–Thurs & Sun 3pm–2am, Fri & Sat 3pm–3am; French and American roulette from €1, blackjack from €5). The old part of the village clusters around the onion-domed eighteenth-century parish church of **St Martin** west of the Kurpark. It has a Rococo pulpit by the Tyrolean artist Franz Hosp. To the north across the Loisach stream at Loisachstrasse 44 is the **Museum Aschenbrenner** (Tues–Sun 11am–5pm; €3), a collection of dolls, French and German porcelain and nativity scenes. Garmisch is also home to the **Olympia Eissportzentrum** (Olympic Ice Sport Centre; Am Eisstadion 1; daily 11am–4pm; disco evenings Tues 8–10pm; €4.20) at the southern end of Olympiastrasse. In addition to staging ice-hockey tournaments, concerts and the like, it has in- and outdoor skating rinks.

Partenkirchen is less lively but better preserves a sense of history, with an attractive main street, Ludwigstrasse, along which you'll see some eye-catching examples of *Lüftmalerei*. Opposite the parish church at no. 47 is the **Werdenfels Museum** (Tues–Sun 10am–5pm; €2.50), a folk museum with some beautiful examples of religious and folk art, from crucifixion scenes to paintings on glass and furniture. One room is devoted to the local *Fastnacht* or Shrovetide customs. Nearby at Schnitzschulstrasse 19 is the **Richard Strauss Institut** (Mon–Fri 10am–4pm; €2.50), with a multimedia exhibition devoted to the composer who lived in Garmisch-Partenkirchen and who died here in 1949.

At the southern end of Partenkirchen is the **Olympia-Skistadion**, a U-shaped stadium in characteristically self-important Nazi style, rebuilt in this more bombastic form after the 1936 Games, and focused on the new **Skisprungschanze** or ski jump, which in 2007 replaced the one from which the traditional New Year's Ski Jump had taken place. The new jump is illuminated at night and is – the mountains aside – much the most dramatic and impressive landmark in town.

The mountains

To get to the top of the **Zugspitze**, Germany's highest peak, take the **Zugspitzbahn** cogwheel railway (hourly 8.15am–2.15pm) from the **Bahnhof Zugspitzbahn** alongside the Hauptbahnhof at least as far as **Eibsee**, where you're faced with a choice: either continue on the cog railway, or else transfer to the dramatic (and much faster) **Eibseeseilbahn** cable car, which ascends nearly 2000m straight to the summit in a mere ten minutes. If you've decided to stick with the train, the journey takes rather longer: you're deposited on the **Schneefern glacier** on the **Zugspitzplatt** plateau below the peak, which from November to April offers Germany's highest **skiing** (day-pass including ascent €36), with powder snow, a range of red and blue runs and spectacular views, extending in clear weather as far as Italy and Switzerland. For a brief period in midwinter you can also **stay** in an igloo hotel (ⓦwww.iglu-dorf .com; ⑨), which also has a bar and fondue restaurant. From the Zugspitzplatt, you complete the journey to the summit on the ultramodern **Gletscherbahn** cable car. Whichever route you choose, the round trip costs €36 in winter, €47 in summer. In summer, the Zugspitzplatt offers a limited selection of short hikes, including one which crosses the glacier to the Windloch observation point, from

▲ Zugspitzplatt, Garmisch-Partenkirchen

which you have good views of Ehrwald in Tyrol, 2000m below. The descent on foot to Garmisch-Partenkirchen, which includes the Partnachklamm gorge, is only for experienced climbers, and takes six to eight hours. At the summit, there's a second cable-car station – the top of the **Tiroler Zugspitzbahn** (daily 8.40am–4.40pm; €33 round trip; Ⓦ www.zugspitze.at), which ascends from the Austrian side. There's a redundant frontier post between the two stations.

Three other cable cars – the **Alpspitzbahn**, **Kreuzeckbahn** and **Hauseckbahn** – give access to a more extensive skiing area, the **Garmisch Classic** (day-pass €31; Ⓦ www.zugspitze.de) below the 2050m **Osterfelderkopf**, which includes the famous **Kandahar** run, used for World Cup downhill races. Black and red runs predominate. Again, this is hiking and mountaineering terrain in summer, with two challenging climbers' routes – the Ferrata trail and Nordwandsteig – ascending the 2628m **Alpspitze** from the Osterfelderkopf.

The Königshaus on the Schachen

Without doubt the most remote and dramatically situated of all Ludwig II's many residences is the little wooden **Königshaus** (early June to early Oct daily: guided tours at 11am, 1, 2 & 3pm) high on the **Schachenalpe** south of Garmisch-Partenkirchen and close to the Austrian border. Built of wood in the style of a Swiss chalet, its modest exterior gives no clue to the *Thousand and One Nights* extravaganza of the opulent Türkische Saal (Turkish Hall) on the upper floor, though for once much of the rest of the living accommodation could actually be described as simple, with local *Zirbelholz* (Swiss pine) used for some of the furnishings. The Königshaus can only be reached on foot after a fairly long and strenuous walk; the easiest approach is along the well-signposted 10km **Königsweg** from the car park by **Schloss Elmau**, midway between Garmisch-Partenkirchen and Mittenwald, though even this has steep stretches and ascends 850m. It is passable by mountain bike. A more strenuous route ascends via the **Partnachklamm** gorge south of the Olympic ski stadium (about 9km). You can **stay** overnight at the simple *Schachenhaus* just below the Königshaus (☎0172/876 88 68, ⓦwww.schachenhaus.de; ❶), where you can also **eat** hearty, simple meals made from local produce.

Eating and drinking

Garmisch is packed with places to **eat** and **drink**, from fast-food joints and a takeaway fondue and raclette shop to proper restaurants and a superfluity of plush *Kaffee und Kuchen* stops; Partenkirchen's rustic *Gasthöfe* are less showy but arguably more charming. Many of the hotels also have good restaurants that are open to non-residents.

Alpenhof Am Kurpark 10 ☎08821/590 55. Bustling but snug Garmisch steakhouse with a carnivore-friendly menu: sirloin steaks for €12.90, American T-bone €19.90.

Gasthof Fraundorfer Ludwigstr. 24 ☎08821/92 70. *Schnitzels* from €11.80 and a sausage menu in the homely and atmospheric surroundings of one of Partenkirchen's most charming inns, with antlers on the walls.

Konditorei Krönner Achenfeldstr. 1 ☎08821/30 07. Garmisch's plushest café-*Konditorei*, with a chandelier-lit interior and a short menu of hot dishes including baked potatoes alongside the luscious cakes.

Pavillon Café Richard-Strauss-Platz 1 ☎08821/31 77. Bright, glassy café and restaurant at the entrance to the Kurpark, with a full and eclectic food menu that ranges from the German standards to chilli and curry dishes (€7.80 up); it also serves coffee and cake.

Peaches Marienplatz 17 ☎08821/187 27. Brash, lively cocktail bar in the old part of Garmisch, in a complex which also includes a pizzeria and the *Club Music Café* disco (Thurs–Sat).

Poststube Marienplatz 12 ☎08821/70 90. The snug, wood-panelled restaurant of the *Atlas Posthotel* is one of the loveliest settings for a meal in Garmisch; it serves Bavarian specialities from around €9, plus coffee and cake, and there's a glazed terrace running the full width of the front of the building.

Mittenwald and around

Goethe considered the sweetly pretty mountain resort of **MITTENWALD** to be a "living picturebook", and one look at the magnificent *Lüftmalerei* on Obermarkt's houses and the church tower and you're likely to agree. The town is famous for violin making, a trade brought here by local boy Matthias Klotz (1653–1743), who learned it on the other side of the Alps in Italy. The intriguing **Geigenbaumuseum Mittenwald** at Ballenhausgasse 3 (mid-May to mid-Oct, mid-Dec to early Jan & Feb to mid-March Tues–Sun 10am–5pm; Jan, mid-March to mid-May & mid-Oct to early Nov Tues–Sun 11am–4pm; €4), has many splendid examples of the local craftsmen's handiwork, from the Baroque to the present day.

The 2244m **Karwendel** towers over Mittenwald and can be ascended via the dramatic **Karwendelbahn** cable car (daily: summer 8.30am–4.30pm; winter 9am–4pm; €22 return; ⓦwww.karwendelbahn.de); at the top, there is an easy 45-minute **Panoramarundweg**, a circular path around the summit, but the other trails are for experienced – and properly kitted out – hikers and climbers; for information on mountain guides contact the Mittenwalder Bergführer at Im Gries 16 (☎08823/926 96 66, ⓦwww.bergfuehrer-mittenwald.de). Most of the **Karwendelgebirge** massif actually lies across the border in Austrian Tyrol. In winter, the Panoramarundweg remains open, and experienced skiers can enjoy the unprepared powder snow of the 7km **Dammkar Skiroute**. Less-challenging skiing is available at the **Skiparadies Kranzberg** (daily 9am–4.30pm; day-pass €22; ⓦwww.skiparadies-kranzberg.de) west of the town on the 1391m Hoher

Kranzberg; there are blue and red runs and just one black. The same lift gives access to the mountain for hikers in summer. Another popular walk around Mittenwald is into the so-called **Leutschacher Geisterklamm**, a narrow gorge which lies largely within Austrian territory.

Practicalities

Frequent **buses** (30min) and **trains** (20min) connect Garmisch-Partenkirchen to Mittenwald. The **tourist office** is at Dammkarstrasse 3 (ski season Mon–Fri 8.30am–6pm, Sat 9am–noon, Sun 10am–noon; summer Mon–Fri 8.30am–6pm, Sat 9am–noon; spring & autumn low season Mon–Fri 8.30am–5pm; ☎08823/339 81, ⓦwww.mittenwald.de), who can help find **accommodation**, which you can also search for and book through the Mittenwald website. Centrally located hotels include the prettily rustic *Alpenrose* at Obermarkt 1 (☎08823/927 00, ⓦwww .alpenrose-mittenwald.de; ❹), and the swankier *Hotel Post*, Karwendelstrasse 14 (☎08823/938 23 33, ⓦwww.posthotel-mittenwald.de; ❺). Mittenwald's **youth hostel** lies 4km north of the village in a nature reserve at Buckelwiesen 7 (☎08823/17 01, ⓦwww.mittenwald.jugendherberge.de; from €18.40 with breakfast). Mittenwald's **campsite**, the *Naturcampingplatz Isarhorn*, is 3km north of the village and is open all year (Am Horn 4; ☎08823/52 16, ⓦwww.camping -isarhorn.de). The *Alpenrose* and *Post* hotels both have **restaurants**; the local *Kaffee und Kuchen* stop is *Haller Café* at Hochstrasse 16; and there's *après ski* rock music and **drinking** at *Pearl's Bar*, Dekan-Karl-Platz 1 (from 8pm, closed Sun).

The Franz Marc Museum at Kochel am See

North of Mittenwald, the unequal twin lakes of **Walchensee** and **Kochelsee** are separated by the narrow ride of the **Kocheler Berge**. At the village of Kochel am See, the **Franz Marc Museum** (Franz Marc Park 8–10; Tues–Sun: April–Oct 10am–6pm, Nov–March 10am–5pm; €7.50), which houses a substantial collection of works by the celebrated artist of Der Blaue Reiter group along with works by his contemporaries Paul Klee, August Macke, Wassily Kandinsky and Alexej von Jawlensky. There are also important abstract works by the postwar ZEN 49 group. If you have your own **transport**, getting to Kochel am See from Mittenwald is relatively straightforward, as the B11 road takes you directly there with a final twisting flourish as it ascends the Kocheler Berge between Walchensee and Kochelsee; direct **buses** take around fifty minutes and run every two hours or so in summer. The museum has a **restaurant**, *Zum Blauen Reiter*, with views over the lake from its terrace.

Chiemsee and around

A shimmering expanse of silvery waters with a backdrop of distant Alps, **Chiemsee** is often referred to as the Bavarian Sea. Sheer size alone would justify the claim, for the lake covers eighty square kilometres and is tidal. But its origins also make the tag appropriate, for Chiemsee is a remnant of the primeval Thetis Sea which once covered half of Europe. In summer, it's a magnet for active tourism, notably sailing; in winter, much of the lake freezes over, particularly at the placid southern end. The lake's most famous attraction is Ludwig II's Schloss on the island of **Herrenchiemsee**, an extravagant (and unfinished) attempt to re-create the palace of Versailles in a Bavarian setting. The best place to stay for exploring Chiemsee is the lively lakeside town of **Prien**; it's connected by rail to the mountain resort of **Aschau im Chiemgau** to the south, which makes an excellent base for hiking across the border into Austria.

Prien am Chiemsee

The liveliest town on the lake and its main transport hub, **PRIEN AM CHIEMSEE** is the obvious base from which to explore Chiemsee. The town itself is pleasant enough, if not of any great architectural interest. Its church has a prettily Baroque interior and the pastel pink, onion-domed Lourdes Grotte next to it, which serves as the town's war memorial, is a perfect Bavarian church in miniature.

However, the real reason to come to Prien is to get away from it, with plenty of options for exploring the lake area: a narrow-gauge steam railway, the **Chiemseebahn** (late May to Sept; approximately hourly), links the town centre with Prien-Stock on the lakeshore, from where you can embark on a lake steamer for the islands. From Prien, a **cycle route** – the Chiemsee Uferweg – circuits the lakeshore for 60km, sticking close to the shore and in many places passing suitable **bathing** spots. You can **rent bikes** from Chiemgauer Radhaus at Bahnhofsplatz 6 (☎08051/46 31) or Fahrradhaus Prien, Hallwanger Strasse 22 (☎08051/59 34). A second, shorter cycle route heads south from the lake towards Aschau in Chiemgau. A route for **hikers**, the Priental-Weg, also links Prien with Aschau, and there's another relatively short hiking trail hugging the western shore of the lake to the north and south of Prien. From June to October, a hikers' and cyclists' bus (#9586) circuits the lake daily with a trailer to take bikes. If you want to learn to **sail**, head for the Segelschule Prien am Chiemsee, Gladiolenweg 3 (☎08051/34 38, ⓦwww.segelschule-prien.de), which offers courses ranging from one to five days, with prices starting at €80. Prien's tourist office also has information on many other **activities** in the area, from ballooning over the lake to Nordic walking, paragliding, rafting and canyoning. There's

▲ Chiemsee

also a very fancy **beach, pool** and **sauna** complex, **Prienavera**, right on the lakefront at Seestrasse 120 (pool Mon–Fri 10am–9pm, Sat & Sun 9am–9pm; beach May–Sept daily 9am–8pm; ℡08051/60 95 70, ⓦwww.prienavera.de; pool from €3.50 for 2hr).

Practicalities

Prien's **Bahnhof** is right in the centre of the town. The **tourist office** is two blocks west in the Haus des Gastes at Alte Rathausstrasse 11 (May–Oct Mon–Fri 8.30am–6pm, Sat 8.30am–4pm; Oct–May Mon–Fri 8.30am–5pm; ℡08051/690 50, ⓦwww.tourismus.prien.de). Good places to **stay** include the central, three-star *Bayerischer Hof*, Bernauer Strasse 3 (℡08051/60 30, ⓦwww .bayerischerhof-prien.de; ❹), or there's the cheaper, alpine-style *König Ludwig Stub'n*, Seestrasse 95 (℡&ⓕ08051/48 02; ❸), 150m from the lakeside in Prien-Stock. There's a **youth hostel** at Carl-Braun-Strasse 66 (℡08051/687 70, ⓦwww.prien.jugendherberge.de; €19 with breakfast). Prien has two **campsites**: *Panoramacamping Harras*, Harrasser Strasse 135 (℡08051/90 46 13, ⓦwww .camping-harras.de; mid-April to mid-Oct), on a peninsula jutting into the lake; and *Camping Hofbauer*, Bernauer Strasse 110 (℡08051/41 36, ⓦwww.camping -prien-chiemsee.de; Easter–Oct), on the southern outskirts of town on the road to Bernau. The *Bayerischer Hof* and *König Ludwig Stub'n* both have **restaurants**; *Art of Wok* at Postweg 1 (℡08051/963 07 97) serves stir-fries and Thai curries from around €7, and you can stock up on cake, coffee and calories at *Kurcafé Haider* at Marktplatz 6, close to the church.

Herreninsel and Schloss Herrenchiemsee

The largest of Chiemsee's islands, **HERRENINSEL**, is also its greatest visitor magnet thanks to "Mad" King Ludwig II's splendidly deranged attempt to build a copy of the palace of Versailles on it. The result is **Schloss Herrenchiemsee** (guided tours only daily: April to mid-Oct 9am–6pm, last tour 5pm; mid-Oct to March 9.40am–4.15pm, last tour 3.40pm; €7, includes admission to König Ludwig II Museum and Augustiner Chorherrenstift). Construction began in 1878 to the plans of Georg Dollmann, but the Schloss was still unfinished when the king died in 1886, when construction abruptly stopped. The result is a tragicomic testament to Ludwig's obsession with the French "Sun King" Louis XIV, whose image and fleur-de-lys motif are repeated in the Schloss's decor. The tour begins with bare brick, progresses through unimaginable opulence – including, of course, a hundred-metre-long copy of the Hall of Mirrors – and encounters bare brick again on an unfinished staircase, the minimalist *yin* to the lavish main staircase's chandeliered *yang*. Throughout, the decorative theme appears to have been that, when it comes to gold leaf, more is more. Ludwig only spent ten days here, and though the interiors have a festive look this was very far from a festive place when he stayed. Famously misanthropic, the king was also afraid of the dark, and would stay awake by candlelight, retiring to bed during the day. Highlights of the tour include Ludwig's beautiful but ludicrous 60,000-litre bath, which took hours to fill. The exhibits of the **König Ludwig II Museum** (same ticket) include various portraits of the king, furnishings from his apartments in the Residenz in Munich, a model of Gottfried Semper's theatre for Richard Wagner – which was never built – and fascinating images of the winter garden Ludwig had built atop the Residenz in Munich, complete with a lake on which floated a royal barge. At the end, it's hard to escape the conclusion that "Extravagant" would have been a more accurate description of him than "Mad". Your ticket also admits you to the Baroque **Augustiner Chorherrenstift** (daily: April to mid-Oct 9am–6pm; mid-Oct to March 10am–4.45pm), which boasts a splendid Kaisersaal with *trompe l'oeil* frescoes and a museum documenting the building's history, including a section on the meeting that laid the basis for West Germany's postwar constitution, which took place here in 1948. There's also an **art gallery** (daily April to mid-Oct 9am–6pm) devoted to the works of the Munich Secessionist Julius Exter.

Frequent **lake steamers** of the Chiemsee Schifffahrt (€6.50 return; ☎08051/60 90, Ⓦ www.chiemsee-schifffahrt.de) connect Prien with Herreninsel all year round, though in winter sailings can be halted by ice on the lake. The Schloss is a good twenty-minute walk from the landing stage; you buy your tickets at the cash desk close to the landing stage, which is where you'll also find toilets and refreshments.

Fraueninsel

Lake steamers continue northeast from Herreninsel the short distance to the second largest of Chiemsee's islands, **FRAUENINSEL** (€7.60 including stopover at Herreninsel). Much smaller and more built-up than its neighbour – it measures just twelve hectares yet with 250 inhabitants – its attractions are also more low-key. Dominating the island is the tall onion-domed campanile of the Benedictine nunnery of **Frauenwörth**. Founded in the eighth century, the abbey itself isn't generally open to the public, though you can visit its shop (Ⓦ www.frauenwörth .de), which sells liqueurs, *Lebkuchen* and marzipan. The island's fishing village is known for its smoked fish; more than any specific attraction, however, Fraueninsel appeals for its lake views and its traffic-free peace and quiet. From Fraueninsel, the lake steamers continue to **Gstadt** on the "mainland", which is less likely than Prien to be icebound in winter.

Aschau im Chiemgau

South of Prien, the land swiftly assumes an alpine character as you approach **ASCHAU IM CHIEMGAU**, a large but rather scattered village that is a starting point for numerous **hiking trails** up the 1669m **Kampenwand** and beyond it to the 1813m Geigenstein to the south and across the border into Austria. A cable car, the **Kampenwandbahn** (daily: May, June & mid-Sept to Nov 9am–5pm; July to mid-Sept 9am–6pm; Christmas–April 9am–4.30pm; €10.50 single, €15 return; Ⓦ www.kampenwand.de), ascends from the southern part of the village to the high-level trails and superb views over Chiemsee; in winter, the same cable car gives access to a limited network of blue, red and black **ski runs** and chairlifts which together offer the possibility of skiing all the way back down to the valley. Opposite the valley station of the Kampenwandbahn, the impressive bulk of **Schloss Hohenaschau** crowns a small wooded hill. The former seat of the aristocratic Freyberg and Preysing families and of the Cramer-Klett industrial dynasty, the Schloss has been extensively restored in recent years. From April to October there are regular **falconry** demonstrations here (Tues–Sun: April–Oct at 3pm; May–Sept also at 11am; €7).

Trains run approximately hourly from Prien along the Chiemgaubahn branch line, taking just fifteen minutes to reach Aschau's Bahnhof, from where it's a short walk along Kampenwandstrasse to the **tourist office** at no. 38 (☎08052/90 49 37, Ⓦ www.aschau.de), which can help with finding **accommodation** – as well as hotels, there are plenty of holiday apartments. Hotel options include the three-star *Burghotel Aschau* in a picturesque setting in the shadow of the Schloss at Kampenwandstrasse 94 (☎08052/90 80, Ⓦ www.burghotel-aschau.de; ❺), and the nearby *Gasthof zum Baumbach*, Kampenwandstrasse 75 (☎08052/14 81, Ⓦ www.zum-baumbach.de; ❸), some of whose rooms have balconies. Both have

restaurants, though for a truly memorable meal, head for the *Residenz Heinz Winkler*, Kirchplatz 1 (T08052/179 90, Wwww.residenz-heinz-winkler.de), a renowned gourmet destination, with a menu of modern European dishes with the occasional Asian influence, that has boasted three Michelin stars for many years and where a set meal with wine might set you back €160.

Berchtesgaden and around

Shaped like a figure of eight and pushing south deep into Austria's Salzburger Land, the compact territory of **Berchtesgadener Land** contains some of Germany's loveliest alpine scenery and, in the south, its third highest mountain, the 2713m **Watzmann**. Reached most easily via Austria and almost walled in by its mountains, the rugged southern part of the Land has the feel of a separate little country. For much of its history it was an independent bishopric growing fat on its precious salt deposits, in many ways a smaller version of its eastern neighbour, Salzburg; their ways only diverged after the 1803 secularization, with Salzburg ultimately passing to Austria and Berchtesgaden to Bavaria. The region attracted notoriety in the 1930s and 1940s as the preferred holiday-home (and putative last redoubt) of Adolf Hitler, whose **"Eagle's Nest"** has since become one of its most popular attractions. In the summer months, the Nationalpark Berchtesgaden is a paradise for hikers and day-trippers alike; in winter, there's skiing on the **Jenner**, at **Rossfeld** and on the **Hirschkaser** west of Berchtesgaden, though at times the region's scenic beauty can be wreathed in dense, icy fog. Capital and natural focus of the Land is the little town of **BERCHTESGADEN** itself, often known as Markt Berchtesgaden to distinguish it from the wider Land; a second focus for visitors is provided by the prim spa-town of **Bad Reichenhall** in the north.

Arrival, information and accommodation

To reach Berchtesgaden from Munich by **train** you need to change at Freilassing on the Austrian border: from Salzburg, S-Bahn trains make the journey in around an hour. Berchtesgaden's oversized **Hauptbahnhof** – it dates from when this was a major resort for Nazi bigwigs – is in the valley below the Altstadt. The **regional tourist office** is next to the station at Königsee Strasse 2 (June to mid-Oct Mon–Fri 8.30am–6pm, Sat 9am–5pm, Sun 9am–3pm; mid-Oct to May Mon–Fri 8.30am–5pm, Sat 9am–noon; T08652/96 70, Wwww.berchtesgadener-land.info); a walk up Bahnhofstrasse brings you to Maximilianstrasse and the **municipal tourist office** in the Kongresshaus at no. 9 (May–Sept Mon–Sat 9am–6pm, Sun 10am–1pm & 2–6pm; Oct–April Mon–Fri 9am–6pm, Sat & Sun 10am–1pm & 2–6pm; closed weekends during Nov; T08652/944 53 00, Wwww.berchtesgaden .de). There's an information office for the **Nationalpark Berchtesgaden** nearby at Franziskanerplatz 7 (daily 9am–5pm; T08652/694 34, Wwww.nationalpark -berchtesgaden.bayern.de). Berchtesgaden has been a resort for a long time, so there's plenty of **accommodation**, both in the town and scattered throughout the district. As well as hotels there are plenty of holiday apartments, plus a well-equipped **campsite**, *Familiencamping Allweglehen*, Allweggasse 4 (T08652/23 96, Wwww.allweglehen.de).

DJH Berchtesgaden Struberberg 6 T08652/943 70, Wwww.berchtesgaden.jugendherberge.de. In the district of Strub west of the town centre, with views of the Watzmann massif. €17.90 with breakfast.

Haus am Berg Am Brandholz 9 T08652/949 20, Wwww.pension-hausamberg.de. Mountain views and a friendly welcome in a pretty pension perched on a hillside. ❷

Hotel Wittelsbach Maximilianstr. 16 ☎08652/963 80, ⓦwww.hotel-wittelsbach.com. Pleasant, rather old-fashioned three-star hotel with elegant turn-of-the-twentieth-century resort-style architecture and spacious en-suite rooms. ❸

InterContinental Berchtesgaden Resort Hintereck 1 ☎08652/975 50, ⓦwww.berchtesgaden .intercontinental.com. Luxurious – and controversial – modern resort hotel, in a spectacular location on the site of Göring's Obersalzberg holiday home,

complete with on-site spa and a wide range of restaurants and bars. From €255. ❾

Vier Jahreszeiten Maximilianstr. 20 ☎08652/95 20, ⓦwww.hotel-vierjahreszeiten-berchtesgaden .de. Sprawling, grandly atmospheric four-star hotel close to the town centre. It has been in the hands of the same family since 1876, though the modern wings are more extensive than the compact central building. Spacious rooms in an alpine, but not over-rustic style. ❹

The Town

Deep eaves, chalet-style architecture and elaborate *Lüftmalerei* images adorning the facades give the centre of Berchtesgaden a quaintly alpine look, strongly reinforced by the exhilarating mountain views available from much of the town. But the impression of twee rusticity is firmly contradicted by the pretty pink yet surprisingly imposing facade of its **Schloss** (guided tours: mid-May to mid-Oct Mon–Sun 10am–noon & 2–4pm; mid-Oct to mid-May Mon–Fri 11am & 2pm; €7). Built on the site of an Augustinian monastery whose Romanesque cloisters it incorporates, the Schloss was for centuries the seat of Berchtesgaden's ecclesiastical rulers; after secularization it passed to the Bavarian royal family, the Wittelsbachs, whose residence it remains. The splendid Gotische Halle, which dates from around 1400, was once the monks' refectory and contains an outstanding collection of medieval sculpture, including altarpieces by Tilman Riemenschneider. There are also rooms in Renaissance, Empire and Biedermeier styles, in which artworks contemporary with the styles of the rooms are displayed. Next to the Schloss stands the twin-towered former Augustinian church, now the **Stiftskirche**, which was built between 1283 and 1303. Facing the church and Schloss across Schlossplatz is the long, arcaded **Arkadenbau**, whose facade paintings by Josef Hengge are the town's war memorial and include a very rare depiction in public of a soldier in the uniform of the old Wehrmacht.

To the northeast of the Schloss on the banks of the Berchtesgadener Ache is the **Salzbergwerk Berchtesgaden**, the salt mine that was the source of the town's wealth, now open to visitors as the **Salzzeitreise** or Salt Time Journey (daily: May–Oct 9am–5pm; Nov–April 11.30am–3pm; €14; ⓦwww.salzzeitreise.de). The visit commences with a change into protective gear before you journey by train into the mountain; you then slide down a traditional miner's slide into the so-called salt cathedral before being ferried across an underground lake. There's also an underground saline spa facility, the **Salzheilstollen** (from €25; ☎08652/97 95 35, ⓦwww.salzheilstollen.com), where a visit is said to be effective for everything from asthma and bronchitis to depression and disturbed sleep. A more conventional pool and sauna complex, the **Watzmann Therme** (daily 10am–10pm; from €8.80), is closer to the town centre at Bergwerkstrasse 54.

Königsee, the Watzmann and Jenner

Around 4km south of Berchtesgaden proper but connected to it by bus (#839, #841 or #843), the scattered community of **SCHÖNAU AM KÖNIGSEE** is home to one of Germany's most dramatically beautiful (and most photographed) lakes, the eight-kilometre-long, fjord-like **Königsee**, whose wonderfully still, 190-metre-deep waters are the result of glacial action during the last Ice Age and are dominated by the sheer east wall of the **Watzmann** peak. Buses drop you at the car park a short way back from the north end of the lake, and you have to run the gauntlet of a rather tacky cluster of souvenir shops and snack stops to reach the landing stage, but once you board the electric-powered **boats** of the Bayerische Seen-Schifffahrt (daily May–Oct 8am–5.15pm; restricted winter service; €11.80 return to St Bartholomä, €14.80 to Salet; ⓦwww.seenschifffahrt.de) all thoughts of commercial tackiness are left behind as the majestic scenery enfolds before you. The most popular stopoff is the little onion-domed pilgrimage chapel of **St Bartholomä**, nestling on a peninsula at the foot of the Watzmann and reachable only by boat. It's an undeniably picturesque juxtaposition that is among the most photographed views in Germany. The former hunting lodge next door is now a *Gaststätte* (ⓣ08652/96 49 37) serving seasonal game and fresh fish from the lake.

At **Salet** at the southern end of the lake a popular and relatively short walk brings you to a second, smaller lake, **Obersee**, beyond which is Germany's highest waterfall, the 400m **Röthbach-Wasserfall**.

If the Watzmann seems forbidding from the vantage point of the Königsee, the 1874m **Jenner** is altogether more approachable thanks to the **Jennerbahn** cable car at the eastern end of Jennerbahnstrasse, a short walk east of the bus stop and car park for the lake (daily 9am–4pm; €19.80 return to peak, €15.10 to mid-station) which gives access to high-level hiking trails in summer, and in winter to red and blue ski runs (day-pass €26.50) that allow you to ski all the way back down to the valley.

Obersalzberg and the Eagle's Nest

Though its mountain panoramas are as breathtaking as any in the German Alps, its Nazi associations hang over **OBERSALZBERG** like an evil spell from some Grimm tale. Hitler knew and loved the scattered settlement 3km east of Berchtesgaden long before he came to power; after 1933 the new regime expropriated locals to turn the entire mountainside into a sprawling private fiefdom for Nazi bigwigs, many of whom had their holiday homes here. The most notable of the houses was Hitler's **Berghof**, bought and greatly extended with the royalties from sales of *Mein Kampf*; the dictator invited diplomatic guests here – including British prime minister Neville Chamberlain at the time of the Sudetenland crisis in 1938 – to be overawed by the scenic setting and the magnificent panorama from its famous picture-window. As war progressed and Allied air raids on German cities underlined the vulnerability of the site to air attack, a vast system of bunkers was built beneath the mountainside, but in the event the feared "last stand" of the SS never happened here. British bombers badly damaged much of the complex in 1945; afterwards, the ruins were largely demolished. In recent years, a glamorous resort hotel has been built on the site of Göring's house (see opposite), while close to the site of the Berghof stands the **Dokumentation Obersalzberg** (April–Oct daily 9am–5pm; Nov–March Tues–Sun 10am–5pm; €3; ⓦwww.obersalzberg.de; bus #838 from Berchtesgaden), a fascinating exhibition on the rise, fall and crimes of the Nazis and its association with Obersalzberg. As you reach the latter stages of the exhibition, you descend into a decidedly spooky preserved section of the bunker complex.

Frequent buses (mid-May to end Oct; €15 return) depart from the ultramodern terminus on the far side of the car park by the Dokumentation Obersalzberg, ascending the spectacular 6.5km **Kehlsteinstrasse** in the first stage of the ascent to Hitler's celebrated teahouse, the **Kehlsteinhaus**, or **Eagle's Nest** as it is known in English, which is preserved in more or less its original condition. The ascent is very much part of the experience: the narrow, twisting cobbled road – blasted from solid rock in just thirteen months in 1937 and 1938 – ascends 700m and passes

▲ The Eagle's Nest, Obersalzberg

through five tunnels. The buses make the journey at a cracking pace, so anyone prone to vertigo may want to sit on the side of the bus away from the view. You alight next to the tunnel leading to the lift which ascends through solid rock to the teahouse; before you enter, you have to decide which bus you're going to return on and get your ticket stamped accordingly. Once you reach the teahouse itself – now a restaurant – how long you stay depends on the weather conditions: if it's clear, the views are genuinely breathtaking and it's worth wandering across the narrow summit for the views back to the building; if not, a quick glance at the photographic exhibition will suffice. The Kehlsteinstrasse and teahouse were commissioned by Martin Bormann as the Nazi party's fiftieth birthday present to Hitler using funds donated to the party by industrialists, but after an initial rush of enthusiasm in 1938 Hitler rarely visited, fearing lightning strikes and attack from the air. Eva Braun used it more frequently: since she didn't officially exist, she had to make herself scarce during diplomatic visits to the Berghof, and would come here to sunbathe with friends and family.

If you seek a less historically troubling encounter with Obersalzberg's stunning panoramas, take the **Salzberg** cable car (daily: spring & autumn 9.30am–4.50pm; summer 9am–5.20pm; winter 10am–4pm; €8 return) from Berchtesgaden to the **Carl-von-Linde Weg**, a gentle 5.4km hiking trail that offers impressive views of Berchtesgaden, the Watzmann and the 1973m Untersberg on the border with Austria. You can follow the trail northeast from the cable car to reach the Dokumentation Obersalzberg.

The Rossfeld Panoramastrasse

Though the Kehlsteinstrasse is open to buses only, you can take your own car or motorbike 1600m above sea level along the **Rossfeld Panoramastrasse** (car and driver €4.30, each additional adult €1.70, child €1.30; motorbikes €3.50), a toll road which begins just east of the Obersalzberg bus station and is open all year round. Mountain views aside, the road offers a starting point for hikes to the 1692m Purtscheller Haus and to the Eagle's Nest; in winter, it gives access to Rossfeld's blue and red **ski** runs (day-pass €14.50; Ⓦwww.rossfeld.info).

Eating and drinking

Many of Berchtesgaden's hotels have restaurants, but there's also a fair smattering of traditional and attractive places to **eat** and **drink** in the central traffic-free Altstadt.

Bier-Adam Marktplatz 22 ☎08652/23 90. There's a modern interpretation of *Lüftmalerei* on the outside, and affordable veggie dishes and simple meals – *Kasnocken* (cheese dumplings) with salad, *Leberkäse* (meatloaf) with fried egg – on the menu, alongside a few more elaborate dishes. From around €7.50.

Bräustüberl Bräuhausstr. 13 ☎08652/97 67 24. Jolly, lively place next to the Berchtesgadener Hofbräuhaus brewery downhill from the Altstadt, with light snacks and reasonably priced fish dishes and

Bavarian and Austrian specialities to accompany the local beer.

Martin Kruis Hofbäckerei Rathausplatz 2. Gourmet *Kaffee und Kuchen* spot, a little to the north of the Schloss and right opposite the Rathaus. Closed Sat & Sun.

Zum Goldener Bär Weihnachtsschützenplatz 4 ☎08652 /25 90. Old-established and rustic *Gaststätte* in the Altstadt, with quite an extensive menu, including salads, snacks and more substantial goulash and *Zwiebelrostbraten*, from around €8. There are terraces front and back in fine weather.

Bad Reichenhall

North of Berchtesgaden at the point where the Munich–Salzburg Autobahn crosses the narrow neck of Berchtesgadener Land is the conservative spa-town of **BAD REICHENHALL**. In comparison with the scenic splendour of its setting the town's charms can seem a little tame, but despite some unfortunate modern development on its fringes it preserves some genuine turn-of-the-twentieth-century charm around the diminutive **Kurgarten** (daily: summer 7am–10pm; winter 7am–6pm), notably in the Jugendstil **Wandelhalle** (Mon–Fri 9am–12.30pm & 1.30–5pm, Sat & Sun 9am–2pm; free) with its free newspapers, saline spring and outsize chess boards, and in the bizarre **Gradierhaus**, a sort of giant, outdoor wooden air-filter or *Inhalatorium*. Day-trippers head for the southern end of the town to visit the imposing old royal saltworks, the **Alte Saline** (May–Oct daily 10–11.30am & 2–4pm; Nov–April Tues–Fri & 1st Sun in month 2–4pm; €6.50), where there's a museum and mine workings to visit, then ascend 1150m on the **Predigstuhlbahn** (daily: mid-April to mid-Oct 8.30am–7pm; mid-Oct to mid-April 9am–4.30pm; €18 return) to the top of the 1614m **Predigstuhl**. The cable car dates from 1928 and is the world's oldest still in its original condition. At the top, there are impressive **views** north over Bad Reichenhall, and hiking trails head south into the **Lattengebirge** massif, a biosphere reserve.

Hourly **buses** take about 45 minutes to reach Bad Reichenhall from Berchtesgaden; **trains** are quicker but less frequent. The town has a somewhat medicinal air; some of its hotels reflect this, and there's no compelling reason to stay here rather than in Berchtesgaden unless you're taking the *Kur*, though the **tourist office** in the Kurgastzentrum on Wittelsbacher Strasse, a short walk from the Hauptbahnhof (May–Sept Mon–Fri 8.30am–5.30pm, Sat 9am–noon; Oct–April Mon–Fri 8.30am–4.30pm, Sat 9am–noon; ☎08651/60 60, Ⓦwww.bad-reichenhall.de), can advise on **accommodation** if need be. The Altstadt around Rathausplatz and Poststrasse is a better bet for places to **eat** and **drink** than the spa quarter along Ludwigstrasse, though the best option for *Kaffee und Kuchen* is the swanky ☘ **Café Spieldiener** at Salzburger Strasse 5 near the Kurgarten, and *Café Reber* at Ludwigstrasse 10 is famous for its *Genuine Reber Mozartkugeln* – a sort of chocolate-coated marzipan treat – much to the annoyance of confectioners across the border in Mozart's home town of Salzburg.

Eastern Bavaria

Topography has determined the character of Eastern Bavaria every bit as much as the Alps have shaped the south of the state. A vast, uninterrupted belt of forested upland – the **Bayerischer Wald** or Bavarian Forest – guards Bavaria's eastern flank on the border with the Czech Republic. It's a sparsely populated and – compared with much of the rest of Bavaria – still relatively little-visited tract, which was for decades a sort of rural cul-de-sac running northwest to southeast along the Iron Curtain. In contrast, immediately to the west of the Bayerischer Wald, the valley of the Danube runs parallel to the border, and is one of the great natural trade routes of Central Europe. Strung out along it is a series of attractive small cities, each of which has known some glory in its past: **Regensburg**, the largest of them, is a former free imperial city with one of the best-preserved medieval cityscapes in Central Europe; in the south, **Passau** is a former prince-bishopric with more than a touch of Italy in its monuments. Between the two, **Straubing** looks back to a distant golden age as the capital of a strange medieval Duchy that straddled Bavaria and the Netherlands. Not to be forgotten is **Landshut** on the River Isar, the ancestral seat of the Wittelsbach dynasty.

Passau

With a memorable – and flood-prone – location on the Austrian border at the confluence of the rivers Inn, Ilz and Danube, **PASSAU** has a lively, cosmopolitan feel that quite belies its relatively modest size. A city of just 50,000 inhabitants, it has nevertheless long been an important place. There was a Roman fort on the site from around 80 AD, a bishopric was founded here in 739 AD and this was raised to the status of an independent prince-bishopric in 1217, a status it retained for centuries until, secularized and annexed, it shared the fate of the other Bavarian prince-bishoprics at the start of the nineteenth century. Passau also rates a mention in the *Nibelungenlied* (see box, p.520), the epic poem that formed the basis for Wagner's *Ring*, as the heroine Kriemhild is welcomed to the city by her uncle Bishop Pilgrim.

Passau's long history as an independent capital has left it with an impressive array of monuments gracing its Altstadt, which occupies a narrow wedge of land between the Inn and Danube and displays a similar blend of Central European and Italian Baroque architectural influences to that other great ecclesiastical border-town, Salzburg, far to the southwest, though here the ice-cream colours of the houses add a sunny, southern glow that not even Salzburg can match. Add to that a mighty, photogenic fortress and the buzz created by its university and the cruise ships that depart its quays for Vienna, Bratislava and Budapest, and Passau is well worth an overnight stop.

Arrival, information and accommodation

Passau's **Hauptbahnhof** is just west of the Altstadt on Bahnhofstrasse, with one of its two **tourist offices** directly opposite at Bahnhofstrasse 36 (Easter–Sept Mon–Fri 9am–noon & 12.30–5pm; Oct Mon–Thurs 9am–noon & 12.30–5pm, Fri until 4pm; Nov–Easter Mon–Thurs 9am–5pm, Fri 9am–4pm; ☎0851/95 59 80, ⓦwww.tourismus.passau.de); the second is at Rathausplatz 3 (Easter–Sept

Mon–Fri 8.30am–6pm, Sat & Sun 9am–4pm; Oct closes Fri at 4pm; Nov–Easter Mon–Thurs 8.30am–5pm, Fri 8.30am–4pm); both can sell you a **PassauCard** (24hr €13.50, 48hr €18.50, 3-day €22.50) which includes use of local buses, free entry to local museums and reductions on various attractions in the surrounding area and across the border in Upper Austria and the southern Czech Republic. It's possible to find hotel **accommodation** right in the heart of Passau's Altstadt; the nearest **campsite** is *Zeltplatz Ilzstadt* at Halser Strasse 34 (☎0851/414 57), a fifteen-minute walk from the Altstadt on the banks of the Ilz.

7

Altstadt Hotel Bräugasse 23–29 ☎0851/33 70, ⓦwww.altstadt-hotel.de. Right on the banks of the Danube, with a cosy, rather traditional feel and 54 en-suite rooms with TV and minibar. ❹

Deutscher Kaiser Bahnhofstr. 30 ☎0851/955 66 15, ⓦwww.dk-passau.de. Comfortable and reasonably priced hotel *garni* in a central location between the Hauptbahnhof and Altstadt. Cheaper rooms share bathroom facilities. ❸

DJH Passau Veste Oberhaus 125 ☎0851/49 37 80, ⓦwww.passau.jugendherberge.de. In a very atmospheric location within the Veste Oberhaus fortress complex, high above the city. Dorms from €17.40 with breakfast.

Hotel Schloss Ort Im Ort 11 ☎0851/340 72, ⓦwww.schlosshotel-passau.de. Romantically pretty rooms with four-poster or iron-framed beds and a wonderfully atmospheric location close to the meeting of the Inn and

Danube make this a real charmer among Passau's hotels. ❹

Pension Rössner Bräugasse 19 ☎0851/93 13 50, ⓦwww.pension-roessner.de. Plain but comfortable en-suite rooms in a small pension in a quiet part of the Altstadt, close to the Museum Moderner Kunst. ❸

Weisser Hase Heiliggeistgasse 1 ☎0851/921 10, ⓦwww.weisser-hase.de. Plush, historic four-star hotel in a great location at the western edge of the Altstadt. Rooms have bath or shower and WC, flat-screen TV and internet, though the style is rather bland and business-oriented. ❺

Wilder Mann Am Rathausturm ☎0851/350 71, ⓦwww.wilder-mann.com. Pretty, traditional painted furniture graces some of the rooms of this historic hotel close to the Danube riverfront, whose past guests include the Empress Elisabeth of Austria. ❹

The City

The most distinctive feature of Passau's **Altstadt** is its location on a tapering peninsula at the point where the Danube and Inn meet, and the best place to experience the drama of its situation is in the little park at the eastern tip of the peninsula, or **Dreiflüsseeck**. Almost tucked out of sight behind the fifteenth-century **Veste Niederhaus** – the lower part of Passau's massive medieval fortress complex – is the Ilz, very much the junior of the three rivers, which flows into the Danube from the north just before its confluence with the Inn.

The meandering streets west of the Dreiflüsseeck have a particular, quiet charm, without the commercial gloss of the streets further west. Tucked into one of them at Bräugasse 17 is the **Museum Moderner Kunst** (Tues–Sun 10am–6pm; €5). The city's modern art museum is laid out over three floors of one of the Altstadt's most beautiful Gothic houses, and has a small permanent collection of works by the artist Georg Philipp Wörlen (1886–1954) and his circle, though this is often not on view as the museum also hosts surprisingly big-name international touring exhibitions of modern and contemporary art.

A little further west, Passau's **Rathaus** fronts an open square facing the Danube, with the high-water mark from various catastrophic floods marked at the base of its neo-Gothic tower. A plaque commemorates the future Empress Elisabeth of Austria's last stop on Bavarian soil as she made her journey to marry Franz Josef of Austria; known as Sissi, she was born a Wittelsbach. The Rathaus itself is an amalgam of eight buildings of various ages that were united to form a more-or-less coherent whole in the nineteenth century, with the Saalbau on the eastern side dating from around 1400. The Rathaus was one of many victims of a fire that devoured much of Passau in 1662; among the results of the rebuilding work afterwards are the **Rathaussäle** (daily 10am–4pm; closed Nov; €2), a pair of grand Baroque halls on the first floor that are reached via the entrance on Schrottgasse. The larger of the two is decorated with Ferdinand Wagner's 1890 paintings showing the triumphant entry of a rather plump, plain Kriemhild into the city.

Incongruously housed in the *Wilder Mann Hotel* immediately to the west of the Rathaus is the **Glasmuseum Passau** (daily 1–5pm; €5), well worth visiting for its dizzying array of historic glass from ancient times to Jugendstil, Art Deco and beyond. There's a particular emphasis on the glassware of the Central European regions of Silesia and Bohemia.

A short stroll up Schrottgasse and into Schustergasse brings you to Residenzplatz, a small square dominated by the **Neue Residenz**, the residence of the prince-bishops, whose wide, early eighteenth-century Baroque facade is the work of Italian architects and conceals a beautiful Rococo staircase. The palace houses the ecclesiastical treasures of the **Domschatz und Diözesan-Museum** (Cathedral Treasury and Diocesan Museum; Feb–Oct Mon–Sat 10am–4pm; €2). Immediately to the west, the splendid copper-domed **Dom Sankt Stephan** (daily: summer 6.30am–7pm; winter 6.30am–6pm) stands on high ground at the centre of the Altstadt, its twin-towered west front dominating the patrician houses of **Domplatz** and betraying quite plainly the Italian origins of its design by Carlo Lurago. The cathedral owes its present appearance to the same 1662 fire that wrecked the Rathaus, though Lurago's design did incorporate surviving fragments of its Gothic predecessor. The interior is a fabulously opulent essay in rich Italian stuccowork by Giovanni Battista Carlone, with frescoed ceilings by Carpoforo Tencalla. It also boasts the largest cathedral organ in the world; there are regular organ recitals from May to October and again during the Advent season. The square in front of the cathedral is the venue in December for one of southern Germany's classiest **Christmas markets**.

The Veste Oberhaus

Dominating Passau from its hilltop site high above the north bank of the Danube, the **Veste Oberhaus** (mid-March to mid-Nov Mon–Fri 9am–5pm, Sat & Sun 10am–6pm; €5) is one of the largest surviving medieval fortress complexes in Europe, begun shortly after Passau was raised to the status of a prince-bishopric in 1217 but considerably extended and modernized in the second half of the sixteenth century. It now houses the city's local history museum, divided into themed sections: **Faszination Mittelalter** (Fascinating Middle Ages) delves into the medieval life of the castle; **Geheimnis der Bruderschaft** deals with the craftsmen's guilds; and the exhibition **Passau: Mythos und Geschichte** (Passau: Myth and History) explores the history of the city and surrounding region. The castle is also the venue for temporary art exhibitions. From the Veste Oberhaus's **Batterie Linde** there are stunning views over the Altstadt. To **reach** the Veste Oberhaus, ascend the steps opposite the north end of the Luitpoldbrücke or take the shuttle bus from Rathausplatz, which departs every thirty minutes.

Eating, drinking and entertainment

Passau's Altstadt offers plenty of atmospheric places to **eat** and **drink** with no shortage of affordable options for a snack or meal and a reasonable smattering of bars and **nightlife**, including some good **live music** venues. Passau's most prestigious venue for drama, classical music and opera is the Theater im Fürstbischöfliche Opernhaus, housed in the city's beautiful eighteenth-century opera house at Gottfried-Schäffer-Strasse 2–4 (☎0851/929 19 13, ⓦwww.suedostbayerisches -staedtetheater.de). In the summer months, the **tourist boats** of Wurm & Köck

(Höllgasse 26; ☎0851/92 92 92, ⓦwww.donauschifffahrt.de) depart Passau's Danube quays on a variety of excursions long and short, from 45-minute sightseeing trips around the confluence of the three rivers to lengthier cruises downstream to Linz. The more luxurious Danube **cruise ships**, however, tend to be booked through travel agents.

Cafés and restaurants

Eiscafé Veneziana Theresienstr. 4. Summer-only, family-run Italian-style ice-cream parlour in the Altstadt.

🏃 **Heilig Geist Stift Weinschänke**
Heiliggeistgasse 4 ☎0851/26 07. Wood-panelled, Gothic-vaulted and very atmospheric old *Weinhaus*, with the likes of *Schnitzel* or trout from around €11 and up.

Ratskeller Rathausplatz 2 ☎0851/26 30. Reasonably priced hot dishes here include *Tafelspitz* or salmon from around €9.50; the setting is a series of atmospheric vaulted cellars beneath the Rathaus, one of which was the town jail. They also serve beers from the Passauer Löwen Brauerei. Closed Sun eve & all day Mon.

Ristorante Zi'Teresa Theresienstr. 26 ☎0851/21 38. Affordable Italian restaurant in a smart but cosy vaulted setting. Pizzas from €5.60, a massive choice of pasta dishes, plus fish and salads.

Schloss Restaurant Louis XIV at **Schloss Hotel Ort**, Im Ort 11 ☎0851/340 72. *Daube de boeuf* and goat's cheese salad are among the Francophile delights at this smart hotel restaurant close to the Dreiflüsseeck; main courses from €16 up. Eve only, closed Sun & Mon.

Bars and clubs

🏃 **Café Museum** Bräugasse 17 ☎0851/966 68 88. Classy, vaguely Jugendstil café/bar in the vaulted space under the Museum Moderner Kunst, offering organic food and a regular programme of live jazz.

Cultfabrik Schrottgasse 12. Club and live-music venue in the Altstadt, with regular monthly hip-hop and jazz jam sessions. Open Thurs–Sat.

Scharfrichterhaus Milchgasse 2 ☎0851/359 00. Café/bar attached to an art-house cinema, with meat and veggie food, Austrian wines and regular jazz and cabaret.

Zum Alten Bräuhaus Bräugasse 5 ☎0851/490 52 52. Warren-like *Bierhaus* with vaulted ceilings, local *Arcobräu* beer and rustic, simple Bavarian food.

Straubing

STRAUBING stands at the heart of the Gäuboden, a rich grain-producing district that stretches along the Danube midway between Passau and Regensburg. The Lower Bavarian town experienced a relatively brief but glorious heyday between 1353 and 1425 as the capital of the lesser, Bavarian portion of the eccentric independent Duchy of Straubing-Holland, the greater portion of whose territories lay in the present-day Netherlands.

The architectural monuments of this period still preside over **Neustadt**, the planned medieval "new town" that replaced Straubing's original Altstadt as the main focus of the town. The Neustadt is laid out on a grid pattern, with a broad east–west central square that reaches from one side to the other. At its western end it's known as Theresienplatz and is graced by a particularly fine Baroque column, the **Dreifaltigkeitssäule**, or Holy Trinity Column, erected in 1709 during the War of the Spanish Succession. The eastern half is known as **Ludwigsplatz**. The two halves meet at the **Stadtturm**, a 68m fire- and watchtower begun in 1316 and topped out with five copper-clad pinnacles in the sixteenth century. Next to it stands the step-gabled **Rathaus**, a Gothic trading hall bought by the town in 1382 and which still has its historic council chambers behind the present, neo-Gothic facade. Looming over the Straubing skyline to the north is **St Jakob**, the most imposing of the town's medieval churches. The tall, brick Gothic hall church was begun around 1395 and is regarded as a masterpiece of southern German, Gothic church architecture. It was the work of Hans von Burghausen, and there are similarities to St Martin in Landshut – also partly his work – including a soaring, slender brick tower and a relatively simple layout. Inside, there's a beautiful, late Gothic high-altar, and an over-the-top Rococo pulpit that dates from 1752–53 and is the work of Wenzel Myrowsky and Mathias Obermayr.

To the east on Fraunhoferstrasse, the **Gäubodenmuseum** (Tues–Sun 10am–4pm; €2.50) is Straubing's local history museum, the most remarkable part of which is the section housing the Roman treasures found during excavations in 1950. This is the most important find of Roman ceremonial armour anywhere; the horde includes pieces of armour for men and horses, and reflects Straubing's ancient status as the Roman military frontier outpost of Sorviodurum.

In the northeast corner of Neustadt two historic abbeys and their churches straddle Burggasse. The **Karmelitenkirche** is another work by Hans von Burghausen, but its late Gothic exterior hides an exuberant Baroque interior by a member of the Dientzenhofer architectural dynasty. The far smaller **Ursulinenkirche** is more theatrical still, its compact interior the last joint work of the Asam brothers, completed in 1741 on the cusp of the transition from Baroque to Rococo. At the north end of Burggasse, the **Herzogsschloss** (Ducal Castle) dates from Straubing's fourteenth-century glory days and is impressive in its size and monumentality, though these days it's the home of various local government offices and has a rather institutional feel.

Straubing's original centre, **Altstadt**, is a short distance to the east of Neustadt, and is nowadays an odd mix of suburban blandness interspersed with historic monuments. One that's definitely worth seeing is the twin-towered Romanesque basilica of **St Peter** at the eastern end of Petersgasse. Not only is the church itself austerely handsome, but it is set in a stunningly beautiful, rather overgrown medieval graveyard, in which stand three imposing, late Gothic **chapels**. One contains a red-sandstone **monument** to Agnes Bernauer, sweetheart of the future Duke Albrecht III, drowned in the Danube in 1435 on the orders of Albrecht's father Ernst, who did not consider the match suitable. Another contains eighteenth-century frescoes of the **Totentanz** (Dance of Death), by the Straubing artist Felix Hölzl.

Practicalities

Direct **trains** from Passau reach Straubing's **Bahnhof** every two hours or so, taking around forty to fifty minutes to do so. The station is a short walk south of Neustadt. The **tourist office** (Mon–Wed & Fri 9am–5pm, Thurs 9am–6pm, Sat 9am–noon; ☎09421/94 43 07, ⓦwww.straubing.de) is in the Rathaus, which is on the corner of Theresienplatz and Simon-Höller-Strasse in the centre of Neustadt. Appealing, central places to **stay** include the comfortable, old-established three-star *Hotel Seethaler*, Theresienplatz 25 (☎09421/939 50, ⓦwww.hotel-seethaler.de; ❹), and the equally historic, slightly cheaper *Hotel Röhrlbräu*, Theresienplatz 7 (☎09421/43 05 11, ⓦwww.hotel-roehrlbraeu.de; ❸). Straubing's **youth hostel** is fifteen minutes' walk east of Neustadt at Friedhofstrasse 12 (☎09421/804 36, ⓦwww.straubing.jugendherberge.de; from €12.30 with breakfast), and there's a **campsite** north of Neustadt on an island in the river at Wundermühlweg 9 (☎09421/897 94). The *Seethaler* and *Röhrlbräu* both have reasonably priced **restaurants**, the former serving fairly elaborate interpretations of Bavarian specialities with the latter sticking to simpler *Schnitzels* and the like. There's also a reasonable scattering of places in Neustadt serving snacks, ice cream and **drinks**. Straubing's biggest **festival** is the **Gäubodenfest**, which takes place over ten days in August and is Bavaria's second-biggest folk festival after the Oktoberfest, complete with beer tents, funfair rides and cultural events. It kicks off with a **procession**, in which brass brands and traditional peasant costume are much in evidence.

Regensburg and around

Spared from devastation in the twentieth century's wars, timeless **REGENS-BURG** (formerly known as Ratisbon in English, though the name is little used) preserves the appearance of an important medieval trading-city better than just about anywhere else in Central Europe. It's the only major medieval city in Germany to remain intact, and to a remarkable extent the Regensburg you see today preserves its fourteenth-century street layout and much of the architecture – secular and religious – that reflects how it must have looked during its medieval zenith. Straddling routes to Italy, Bohemia, Russia and Byzantium, Regensburg had trading links that stretched as far as the Silk Road. Trade brought cultural interchange too, and the mighty tower houses of the city's medieval merchants – so reminiscent of Italy – are found nowhere else

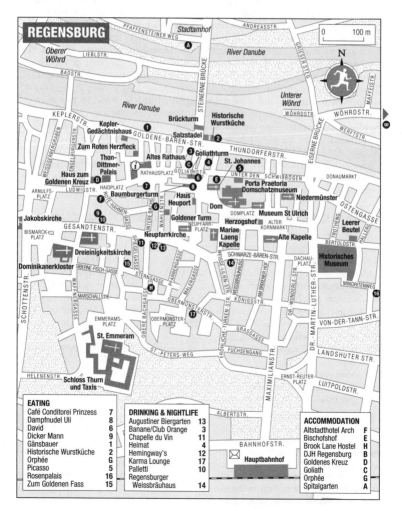

REGENSBURG

EATING

Café Conditorei Prinzess	7
Dampfnudel Uli	8
David	6
Dicker Mann	9
Gänsbauer	1
Historische Wurstküche	2
Orphée	G
Picasso	5
Rosenpalais	16
Zum Goldenen Fass	15

DRINKING & NIGHTLIFE

Augustiner Biergarten	13
Banane/Club Orange	3
Chapelle du Vin	11
Heimat	4
Hemingway's	12
Karma Lounge	17
Palletti	10
Regensburger Weissbräuhaus	14

ACCOMMODATION

Altstadthotel Arch	F
Bischofshof	E
Brook Lane Hostel	H
DJH Regensburg	D
Goldenes Kreuz	B
Goliath	C
Orphée	G
Spitalgarten	A

north of the Alps. No wonder UNESCO added the city to its list of World Heritage Sites in 2006.

The city is actually even older than it looks. The Romans founded a fort here as part of the empire's Limes, or military frontier, in the then-uninhabited region of Donaubogen in 80 AD; it was destroyed in an attack by Marcomanni tribes in 167 AD, only to be re-established as a legion fortress under the name Castra Regina on the site of the present-day Altstadt. As the western Roman Empire died in the fifth century AD, the Roman inhabitants were gradually replaced by Germanic settlers. A bishopric from 739 AD, Regensburg also became a free imperial city in 1245.

Glorious though its architectural heritage may be, this vibrant city is no museum piece. What makes it particularly special is the way its thousand or so historic monuments act as a backdrop for the very contemporary tastes and concerns of its modern citizens, who include large numbers of students. For visitors, Regensburg is a surprisingly multifaceted place: as trendy or timeless, classy or unpretentious as you could want it to be, and well worth a stay of a few days or so.

Finding your bearings in Regensburg is relatively simple. The **Altstadt** runs east–west along the south bank of the **Danube**. Within the Altstadt, the **mercantile** quarters of the medieval city are largely to the west of the **Dom**, while the **eastern** side of the Altstadt is both quieter and more ecclesiastical. The distinction between episcopal and mercantile Regensburg is remarkably sharp even to this day, and where the eastern Altstadt is placid to the point of colourlessness, the streets of the western Altstadt are bustling day and night. **Schloss Emmeram** is on the south side of the Altstadt, beyond which a belt of parkland separates the old town from the **Hauptbahnhof**. To the north of the Alstadt, and linked by the **Steinerne Brücke**, is the **Stadtamhof** on an island.

Meanwhile, **Walhalla** and **Befreiungshalle**, two architecturally remarkable monuments that Ludwig I built to German nationalist sentiment, lie in scenic settings within easy reach of Regensburg.

Arrival, information and accommodation

From Regensburg's **Hauptbahnhof** it's a few minutes' walk along Maxmilianstrasse into the Altstadt. The **tourist office** is in the Altes Rathaus at Rathausplatz 4 (April–Oct Mon–Fri 9am–6pm, Sat 9am–4pm, Sun 9.30am–4pm; Nov–March Mon–Fri 9am–6pm, Sat 9am–4pm, Sun 9.30am–2.30pm; ☎0941/50 74 41, ⓦwww.regensburg.de), where you can rent an English-language audio guide (3hr €8). You can rent **bikes** from Bikehaus at Bahnhofstrasse 18 (☎0800/460 24 60), on the left as you leave the Hauptbahnhof on the northern (Altstadt) side. You may need to use the local RVV **buses** (ⓦwww.rvv.de) if you're heading out to Walhalla (#37), which is on the edge of fare zone 2 (€2.60); a one-day *Tages Ticket* for zones 1 and 2 costs €4. If you're just exploring the Altstadt, however, the best way to do so is on foot.

Regensburg's **hotels** are charming, though budget options within the Altstadt itself are limited; you can **book** accommodation through the tourist website or by calling ☎0941/507 44 12. The tourist office itself is often extremely busy.

Altstadthotel Arch Haidplatz 4 ☎0941/586 60, ⓦwww.altstadtarch.ringhotels.de. Atmospheric Altstadt hotel with a splendidly creaky wooden staircase and plenty of beams. All rooms are en suite, with wi-fi, cable TV and minibar. ❺

Bischofshof Krauterermarkt 3 ☎0941/584 60, ⓦwww.hotel-bischofshof.de. Pretty, traditionally styled and individually decorated rooms fronting a courtyard or quiet lane in the heart of the Altstadt. The setting – in the shadow of the cathedral – is historic and beautiful. ❻–❼

Brook Lane Hostel Obere Bachgasse 21 ☎0941/ 690 09 66, ⓦwww.herberge -regensburg.de. Independently run, cyclist-friendly hostel in the Altstadt, with accommodation in snug dorms (from €15) or spartan singles and doubles (●) furnished in a bland, modern style. Open 24hr.

DJH Regensburg Wöhrdstr. 60 ℡0941/574 02, ⓦ www.regensburg.jugendherberge.de. On an island in the Danube, within easy walking distance of the Altstadt. Dorms €20.40 including breakfast. Closed Christmas to mid-Jan.

🎿 **Goldenes Kreuz** Haidplatz 7 ℡0941/558 12, ⓦ www.hotel-goldeneskreuz.de. In a stunning former imperial lodging-house with a five-hundred-year history, complete with beautiful frescoes and plenty of beams. Tastefully decorated rooms have en-suite facilities and internet. ●

🎿 **Goliath** Goliathstr. 10 ℡0941/200 09 00, ⓦ www.hotel-goliath.de.

Exceptional boutique-style hotel in the heart of the Altstadt, with stylish decor, individually styled, a/c rooms and suites, and with a wonderful roof terrace. ●

🎿 **Orphée** Untere Bachgasse 8 ℡0941/59 60 20, ⓦ www.hotel-orphee.de. Baroque details vie with structural beams and four-poster beds for attention in the rooms of this lovely Altstadt hotel above a classy French bistro, with a smaller, cheaper annexe in nearby Wahlenstrasse. ●–●

Spitalgarten St Katharinenplatz 1 ℡0941/847 74, ⓦ www.spitalgarten.de. Simple but comfortable rooms with shared facilities, next to a shady beer garden just across the Steinerne Brücke from the Altstadt. ●

The Dom and eastern Altstadt

The history of Regensburg's **Dom** (daily: April–Oct 6.30am–6pm; Nov–March 6.30am–5pm) is a familiar German tale of medieval artistic ambition thwarted, with the builders' original vision only fully realized after centuries of delay. Construction of the cathedral began in 1273 after fire ravaged its predecessor, of which the **Eselturm** or Ass's Tower on the north side survives. After 1285, an essentially French high-Gothic style was adopted. The three choirs were completed by around 1320, but apart from the cloisters, construction came to a halt around 1500 with the building incomplete, the twin west towers still lacking their spires. Baroque accretions of the seventeenth century were removed between 1828 and 1841 on the orders of Ludwig I; between 1859 and 1872 the medieval vision was finally completed with the addition of the spires – which somewhat resemble those of Cologne – transept gable and crossing flèche. Despite its six-hundred-year construction history, the result is coherent and graceful, with ribbed vaulting soaring 32m above the nave. Among the artworks, the **Annunciation Group** on the west piers of the crossing stands out. It dates from around 1280 and is the work of the anonymous "Master of St Erminold", and the so-called **Smiling Angel** depicts Gabriel conveying the good news to Mary. Also of note are the five distinctive canopied Gothic altars, while the silver high-altar is a splendid example of Augsburg craftsmanship. Outside, the **west front** is richly decorated with **sculptures**, many of which relate to St Peter, to whom the cathedral is dedicated. The Dom's boys' choir, the famous **Domspatzen** or "Cathedral Sparrows", traces its origins to the school founded by Bishop Wolfgang in 975 AD.

Exit the Dom via the north transept to reach the **Domschatzmuseum** (Treasury Museum; April–Oct Tues–Sat 10am–5pm; Dec–March Fri & Sat 10am–4pm, Sun noon–4pm; €2 or €3 combined ticket with St Ulrich), whose star attraction is the **Emailkästchen**, a glittering reliquary chest decorated with enamel images of mythical creatures, probably made in France around 1400. The museum incorporates the beautiful sixteenth-century Schaumburg altar, which originally stood in the **Obermünster** convent. Watch out too for an illustration on the first floor that shows the cathedral's towers in their stumpy, pre-nineteenth-century state. If you leave the museum on the north side, it's just a short stroll to the **Porta Praetoria**, a substantial chunk of a Roman city gate incorporated into the bishops' brewery in the seventeenth century and uncovered in 1885.

Immediately east of the Dom, the early Gothic thirteenth-century church of **St Ulrich** (April–Oct Tues–Sun 10am–5pm; €2 or €3 combined ticket with

▲ Regensburg cathedral

Domschatzmuseum), originally built as a court chapel, is also now a museum. It displays a millennium's worth of Christian art from the eleventh century to the present; star exhibits include the unique and beautiful **Schmetterlingsreliquiar**, or Butterfly Reliquary, made in Paris around 1310–20, and **Albrecht Altdorfer**'s 1519 painting *Schöne Maria*.

East from St Ulrich fronting Alter Kornmarkt, the **Römerturm** and **Herzogshof**, built around 1200, are surviving parts of a Romanesque Wittelsbach palace. This is the site of the Roman fort of Castra Regina. On the south side of the square, the festive white-and-gold Rococo interior of the **Alte Kapelle** is a delightful contrast to its plain-Jane Carolingian exterior; unsurprisingly, it does a brisk trade in weddings. To the north, the Baroque interior of the **Niedermünster** is, in contrast, rather glum.

The Historisches Museum and Leerer Beutel

East of Alter Kornmarkt at Dachauplatz 2–4, a former Minorite monastery houses the eclectic **Historiches Museum** (Tues–Sun 10am–4pm, Thurs until 8pm; €2.20; English audio guide €2), which has an engrossing section on the Roman origins of the city – scorched tableware and human remains showing signs of violent death attest to the precariousness of life in this distant outpost of empire. The monastery's cloisters and church house an exhibition on the city in the Middle Ages, including sections on the construction of the Dom and the medieval Jewish community, which was expelled in 1519. The top floor is devoted to medieval art, including a room devoted to Albrecht Altdorfer, the leading member of the sixteenth-century Danube school of artists, and a member of the city council that took the decision to expel the Jews.

Close by on Bertoldstrasse is the Leerer Beutel, a fifteenth-century grain warehouse that now houses the **Städtische Galerie** (Tues–Sun 10am–4pm;

€2.20), which focuses on the work of artists from the east of Bavaria. The building is also the venue for live jazz concerts.

The Altes Rathaus and western Altstadt

A secular counterweight to the Dom, the **Altes Rathaus** is the dominant landmark of the western, mercantile part of the Altstadt. The oldest part of the building is its 55m tower, but the most historically significant is the magnificent fourteenth-century Gothic Reichssaal, which was from 1663 to 1806 the fixed venue for the imperial Diet or Reichstag. It can now be visited as part of the **Reichstagsmuseum** (guided tours in English daily at 3pm; in German daily: April–Oct every 30min 9.30am–noon & 1.30–4pm; Nov, Dec & March at 10am, 11.30am, 1.30pm, 2pm, 3pm & 3.30pm; Jan & Feb daily 10am, 11.30am, 1.30pm, 3pm; €7.50). There's also a prison and torture chamber in the basement.

The western Altstadt is the liveliest, and most rewarding part of the city in which to get creatively lost, though the area isn't wanting for landmarks either, with some particularly splendid medieval **tower houses** here. The most impressive of these medieval skyscrapers is the **Goliathhaus**, built in the thirteenth century for the Thundorfer family but deriving its name for the much-retouched sixteenth-century fresco of the eponymous giant that looms over Watmarkt. Magnificent as it is, the Goliathhaus isn't the tallest of the towers: that honour goes to the nine-storey **Goldener Turm** on Wahlenstrasse.

Fringing this cluster of medieval status-symbols to the south is Neupfarr-platz, where the **Neupfarrkirche** replaced the destroyed medieval synagogue; immediately to the west, the white **Ort der Begegnung** (Place of Encounter) by Israeli artist Dani Karavan stands on the actual site of the synagogue, rediscovered in 1995. It outlines the shape of the synagogue, complete with low columns. On the north side of the Neupfarrkirche is the entrance to the subterranean **document Neupfarrplatz** (guided tours Thurs–Sat at 2.30pm; July & Aug also Sun & Mon at 2.30pm; €5), a slice of archeological life which embraces the remains of Roman officers' quarters, traces of the medieval Jewish quarter and a World War II air-raid bunker.

To the west of Neupfarrplatz on the corner of Am Ölberg and Gesandten-strasse, the Lutheran **Dreieinigkeitskirche** has a simple but charming wooden balconied interior and a tall **tower** (April–Oct daily noon–6pm; open evenings in fine weather; €2) that is worth the rather scary climb for the fine views from the top over the city.

The banks of the Danube

Picture-postcard views of the Altstadt are available from the twelfth-century **Steinerne Brücke** at the north end of Brückstrasse; it links the Altstadt to the district of **Stadtamhof** on an island on the north bank of the Danube. Before crossing the river it's worth stopping by the **Brückturm** (April–Oct Tues–Sun 10am–5pm; €2), the last survivor of the bridge's watchtowers, which you can climb for yet more views. Before reaching Stadtamhof, the Steinerne Brücke crosses the narrow neck of the island of **Unterer Wöhrd** and the **Jahninsel**, which is the narrow, easternmost tip of the island of **Oberer Wöhrd**. Stadtamhof itself is pretty, with something of the air of a separate town, which is not altogether surprising, since for much of its history that's precisely what it was.

Back on the Altstadt bank of the river at Keplerstrasse 5, the **Kepler Gedächtnishaus** (Sat & Sun 10.30am–4pm; €2.20) commemorates Johannes Kepler (1571–1630), the celebrated astronomer and contemporary of Galileo, who died here.

Schloss St Emmeram

Occupying a former Benedictine monastery and sprawling like a city within a city on the southern edge of the Altstadt is **Schloss Emmeram**, home of the **Thurn und Taxis** dynasty. The family, whose origins are in northern Italy, held the office of imperial Postmaster General from 1595 and retained it for more than 350 years. The family transferred its court from Frankfurt to Regensburg in 1748, and the Schloss Emmeram has been its home since 1812. You can visit the **interior**, which incorporates Rococo elements from the old Thurn and Taxis palace in Frankfurt, on a guided tour (in English July–Sept daily at 1.30pm; in German: July–Sept Mon–Fri at 11am, 2pm, 3pm & 4pm, Sat & Sun 10am, 11am, and hourly 1–4pm; Nov–March Sat & Sun at 10am, 11am, 2 & 3pm; €11.50). The tour also takes in the abbey's impressive medieval cloisters. The abbey church of **St Emmeram** itself can be visited without joining a tour; its joyful Baroque interior was the work of the Munich-based Asam brothers. The fabulous wealth of the Thurn und Taxis dynasty is eloquently demonstrated by the richness of the collections in the **Fürstliche Schatzkammer** (Princely Treasury; mid-March to early Nov Mon–Fri 11am–5pm, Sat & Sun 10am–5pm; early Nov to mid-March Sat & Sun 10am–5pm; €3.50), where the exhibits range from furniture to porcelain and an impressive collection of snuff boxes.

KOG – the Kunstforum Ostdeutsche Galerie

Just to the west of the Altstadt at Dr-Johann-Maier-Strasse 5, the **KOG – Kunstforum Ostdeutsche Galerie** (Art Forum East German Gallery; Tues–Sun 10am–5pm; €4) focuses on German art in Eastern Europe from the Romantic period to the present, with works by Lovis Corinth and Käthe Kollwitz among others. It also stages exhibitions of contemporary art from Eastern Europe.

Eating, drinking and entertainment

The Altstadt is full of atmospheric places to **eat** and **drink** at all price levels, and you're just as likely to encounter Gothic arches in some cheap pasta place as you are in a gourmet restaurant. The sizeable student population makes its presence felt on the city's **nightlife** scene, too, which has a youthful vitality refreshing in a city of Regensburg's relatively modest size. Regensburg has quite a lively **cultural** scene: you can see live bands, comedy and theatre at the *Alte Mälzerei*, Auerbacher Strasse 12 (℡0941/20 82 20), and live jazz courtesy of the Jazzclub Regensburg (Ⓦwww.jazzclub-regensburg.de), usually at the Leerer Beutel. Theater Regensburg at Bismarckplatz 1 (℡0941/507 24 24, Ⓦwww.theaterregensburg.de) is the main venue for drama, operetta and opera, though its programme of classical music concerts is staged at a number of different locations.

Cafés and restaurants

🏃 Café Conditorei Prinzess Rathausplatz 2 ℡0941/59 53 10. Regensburg's classic *Kaffee und Kuchen* option – pass the mouthwatering displays of pralines in the window to enter Germany's oldest coffeehouse, opened in 1686. The café is on the first floor and there's a *salon de thé* on the second.
Dampfnudel Uli Watmarkt 4 ℡0941/532 97. One of the most popular places in Regensburg for hearty Bavarian food; tiny and inexpensive. Mon–Fri 10am–6pm, Sat 10am–3pm.

David Watmarkt 5 ℡0941/56 18 58. The menu of meat, fish and veggie dishes changes seasonally, and there are wonderful views over the Dom and Altstadt in this classy gourmet restaurant atop the Goliathhaus – and there's a lift. Main courses around €25. Closed Sun & Mon.
Dicker Mann Krebsgasse 6 ℡0941/573 70. Atmospheric fourteenth-century *Gasthof* that claims to be one of the oldest pubs in Germany, with a *Biergarten* in the *Innenhof*. There's a full food menu and the specials are

particularly good value – though it's not exactly an undiscovered treasure.

Gänsbauer Keplerstr. 10 ☏ 0941/578 58. Extremely pretty restaurant with a menu that mixes German and Italian influences; main courses €24 up, set menu €54. Mon–Sat, eve only.

Historische Wurstküche Weisse-Lamm-Gasse 1 ☏ 0941/590 98. Right next to the Steinerne Brücke and looking like somewhere a hobbit might grill sausages, but the smells issuing from this tiny, rustic and historic sausage restaurant – which dates back to the seventeenth century – are mouthwatering.

Orphée Untere Backgasse 8 ☏ 0941/59 60 20. Classy, convivial French bistro, *salon de thé* and patisserie, with the likes of *Coquilles St Jacques* and *coq au vin* on the menu and main courses from around €16.

Picasso Unter den Schwibbögen 1 ☏ 0941/536 57. Informal café/bar in the spectacular setting of the former Salvatorkapelle, which dates from 1476; open for breakfast from 10am, with pasta, salads and light dishes later.

Rosenpalais Minoritenweg 20 ☏ 0941/599 75 79. *Haute cuisine* in the opulent surroundings of a Baroque former banker's mansion in the eastern Altstadt, with the likes of wild salmon with braised radicchio, caramelized fennel and saffron potatoes; four-course menu €56, six courses €75. Tues–Sat eve only.

Zum Goldenen Fass Spiegelgasse 10 ☏ 0941/30 77 99 11. In one of the quieter corners of the southern Altstadt, a traditional *Wirtshaus* in lovely old premises with plenty of beams, wood and stone. The food is rustic – roast calf's heart, wild boar goulash – and there's Augustiner beer, and a *Biergarten* to enjoy it in.

Bars and clubs

Augustiner Biergarten Neupfarrplatz 15. Pretty, leafy *Biergarten* tucked away in the heart of the Altstadt, complete with fountain, and there's a full food menu including meat and fish dishes.

Banane Goldene-Bären-Str. 10. Rock bar on the riverfront with regular live bands; on the same premises is *Club Orange*, a retro 1970s-styled cocktail bar. Open Fri & Sat until 3am, otherwise until 1am.

Chapelle du Vin Spiegelgasse 1 ☏ 0941/599 99 61. Lovely Gothic-vaulted wine bar and bistro in the southern Altstadt.

Heimat Taubengässchen 2. Altstadt bar with a studenty feel, regular live gigs and DJ nights, plus Champions League on TV. Tues–Sat until 2am.

Hemingway's Obere Bachgasse 3–5. Big, vaguely Art Deco-style café and cocktail bar, open from breakfast; there's everything from Thai food to *Schnitzel* and pasta on the affordable food menu, and an emphasis on rum-based cocktails at the bar. Open until 2am Fri & Sat, otherwise 1am.

Karma Lounge Obermünsterstr. 14. Hip bar and club where the decor mixes retro-Sixties and Seventies style with the odd Asian touch. It attracts a mixed trendy/studenty crowd, and there's reduced-price entry for students.

Palletti in the Pustetpassage, Gesandtstr. 6. Attracting an older but rather bohemian crowd, this arty café/bar is a lovely place to stop for an espresso or glass of wine.

Regensburger Weissbräuhaus Schwarze-Bären-Str. 6. *Hausbrauerei* with own-brew light and dark beers, inexpensive main courses – including veggie food – and lighter options from around €6. The gleaming copper microbrewery is the focus of the interior.

Walhalla

High on a hill overlooking the Danube to the east of Regensburg in the village of **DONAUSTAUF**, **Walhalla** (daily: April–Sept 9am–5.45pm; Oct 9am–4.45pm; Nov–March 10–11.45am & 1–3.45pm; €4) is impossible to miss, for it dominates the surrounding countryside. Built by Ludwig I's court architect Leo von Klenze in purest Grecian classical style, this Teutonic Parthenon was a pet project of the future king as far back as 1807, while his father was still an ally of Napoleon. The aim was to house sculptures of "laudable and distinguished" Germans in a building of suitable architectural dignity, and although Ludwig could not finance the building while still crown prince, he commissioned the busts from a number of famous sculptors at a time when Napoleon was still redrawing the map of Europe and German troops were marching with the French emperor to Moscow. Sixty busts were complete by the time Ludwig became king; they included figures of Swiss, Dutch, Austrian and Anglo-Saxon origin – "Germanic" in its widest definition. The building itself was completed by 1842; its name derives from that of the resting place of fallen heroes in Nordic myth. The figures honoured in its spacious interior include monarchs such as Frederick Barbarossa and Catherine the Great of Russia (born in the then-German port of Stettin, now in Poland) and military men such as Blücher, hero of Waterloo, and Radetzky, the Austrian field marshal after whom the Strauss march is named. Writers, artists and thinkers are rather under-represented, but range from Mozart and Goethe to Immanuel Kant and Albrecht Dürer. New figures continue to be added, with Sophie Scholl, heroine of the Weisse Rose resistance movement, one of the most recent, though there are still relatively few women and there are some surprising omissions from recent history: you'll look in vain for Count von Stauffenberg, Heinrich Böll or Willy Brandt, for instance. Presiding over them all, of course, is Ludwig himself. Quite apart from its architectural and historical interest, Walhalla offers lovely views over the expansive Danube plain below. To reach it, take RVV **bus** #5 from Regensburg; it stops at Reifldinger Strasse on the eastern side of Donaustauf, from where a path winds its way up to Walhalla through the woods; alternatively, more frequent buses serve Donaustauf itself, from where it's a short walk along the riverfront. There's also a **car park** at the top of the hill close to Walhalla.

The Befreiungshalle and Donaudurchbruch

Southwest of Regensburg at **KELHEIM**, on a romantic bluff high above the river, the **Befreiungshalle** (Liberation Hall; daily: mid-March to Oct 9am–6pm; Nov to mid-March 9am–4pm; €3; English-language guidebook €3) was Ludwig's monument to the wars of liberation against Napoleon and to the idea of German unity. It was begun in 1842 by Friedrich von Gärtner but completed after Gärtner's death by Leo von Klenze. From the outside, the drum-shaped building looks a little like a Neoclassical gasometer fashioned from painted stucco; the spectacular interior is ringed by 34 winged goddesses of victory with the names of Austrian, Prussian and Bavarian generals picked out in gold above them. A narrow staircase ascends to an internal gallery from which you can better admire the sheer spaciousness of the hall; beyond it, a stone staircase leads to an exterior gallery, well worth the climb for the views over Kelheim and the lovely **Donaudurchbruch**, a narrow, cliff-rimmed stretch of the Danube to the west of the town. You can take a **boat trip** (daily late March to end Oct; every 30min late April to early Oct; less frequent at other times; 40min; single €4.60, return €8.20; Ⓦ www.schifffahrt-kelheim.de) from Kelheim into the gorge as far as the monastery of **Kloster Weltenburg**, wedged scenically between the river and cliffs; the return trip takes only half as long as the journey upstream, but you should allow at least an hour for the round trip. Kelheim is also a good jumping-off point for the **Naturpark Altmühltal** (see p.311).

Trains take around thirty minutes to reach Saal an der Donau from Regensburg; from Saal it's a short **bus** ride into the centre of Kelheim. A footpath ascends to the Befreiungshalle from Kelheim; there's **car parking** near the hall at the top of the hill. If you want to **eat** or **drink** in Kelheim's modestly pretty Altstadt, the obvious place to head for is the *Gaststätte* and *Biergarten* of the **Schneider** brewery in Emil-Ott-Strasse; you can also **tour** the brewery (Tues at 2pm; May–Oct also Thurs 2pm; €4.50).

Landshut

Capital of Lower Bavaria for the past eight hundred years and for a brief period in the thirteenth century Munich's predecessor as the Wittelsbachs' main seat, **LANDSHUT** has architectural splendours that quite outshine its present status as a bustling but essentially medium-sized and provincial town midway between Munich and Regensburg. Its glory days came under the so-called "rich dukes" between 1393 and 1503, when it was the seat of government for the duchy of Bayern-Landshut. The 1475 wedding of one of the dukes, Georg, to Jadwiga (Hedwig in German) – daughter of the Polish king – was one of the most lavish celebrations of the late Middle Ages, and it provides a template for the town's most celebrated festival – the **Landshuter Hochzeit** or Landshut Wedding – to this day.

Laid out along the south bank of the River Isar, Landshut's Altstadt is a grid, defined by two broad, parallel main streets – known confusingly as Altstadt and Neustadt – and by the shorter, narrower side-streets that link the two. Altstadt is lined on either side with stately gabled houses five storeys high, while Neustadt is scarcely less imposing. Dominating everything is the late Gothic hall church of **St Martin** on Altstadt (April–Sept daily 7.30am–6.30pm; Oct–March Mon–Fri 7.30–10.30am & 3–5pm, Sat & Sun 7.30am–5pm; free), begun in 1392 and with an austerely graceful, airy interior. The most remarkable feature of the church is, however, its slender brick skyrocket of a tower, which looms over Altstadt and was completed around 1500. It climbs to a height of 130m and is thus the tallest brick structure in the world.

Further east on Altstadt, the nineteenth-century neo-Gothic facade of the **Rathaus** hides a much older structure, parts of which date from the end of the fourteenth century; the richly ornamented neo-Gothic **Prunksaal** or main hall (Mon–Fri 2–3pm; free) contains the wall paintings depicting the 1475 Landshuter Hochzeit that actually prompted the establishment of the festival that re-enacts it. The room is the venue for live concerts.

Facing the Rathaus across Altstadt is the **Stadtresidenz** (guided tours: April–Sept daily 9am–6pm; Oct–March Tues–Sun 10am–4pm; €3, more during temporary exhibitions), a town palace commissioned by Duke Ludwig X in 1536 but chiefly remarkable for the lovely Italienischer Bau or Italian building which fringes the central courtyard and postdates the duke's travels to Italy: inspired by the Palazzo Te in Mantua, the duke hired Italian architects to build an addition to his palace and the result was the first palace in the Italian Renaissance style on German soil. The **Innenhof**, or palace courtyard, is a lovely, arcaded Renaissance work – a piece of sixteenth-century Italy, with soft, warm Mediterranean colours. High point of the interior is the **Italienischer Saal**, or Italian hall, with its coffered stucco ceilings enriched with frescoes on humanist themes by Hans Bocksberger.

High above the Altstadt and reached via a steep ascent up Alte Bergstrasse is **Burg Trausnitz** (guided tours daily: April–Sept 9am–6pm; Oct–March 10am–4pm), a mighty fortress begun under Duke Ludwig I in 1204. The ancestral castle of the Wittelsbach dynasty, it preserves much of its medieval fabric, including the impressive fortifications, the tall Wittelsbach tower and the castle chapel. The arcaded courtyard, the state rooms with their tapestries and tiled stoves and the famous Narrentreppe or Fools' stair with its frescoes of Commedia dell'Arte buffoons all date from the time of the Renaissance. The **Damenstock** (Ladies' Apartments) contain the **Kunst und Wunderkammer,** or chamber of arts and curiosities, in the characteristically eclectic style of museum collections of the Renaissance, with 750 exhibits spanning natural history, science and European and Oriental art.

Practicalities

Trains take around forty to fifty minutes to reach Landshut's **Hauptbahnhof** from Regensburg. The station is north of the Altstadt on the north side of the River Isar; to reach the centre of town, walk down Luitpoldstrasse and cross the bridge or take a Stadtlinie bus – most of which (except #5, #7, #12 or #14) link the station with either Altstadt proper or Ländtorplatz close by. The **tourist office** is in the Rathaus at Altstadt 315 (March–Oct Mon–Fri 9am–6pm, Sat 10am–4pm; Nov–Feb Mon–Fri 9am–5pm, Sat 10am–2pm; ☎0871/92 20 50, ⓦwww.landshut.de). Atmospheric and comfortable places to **stay**, both in attractive gabled buildings on Neustadt, are the upmarket *Goldene Sonne*, no. 520 (☎0871/925 30, ⓦwww.goldenesonne.de; ⑥), and the cheaper but still very pleasant *Stadthotel Herzog Ludwig* at no. 519 (☎0871/97 40 50; ❹). The **youth hostel** is between the Altstadt and Burg Trausnitz at Richard-Schirrmann-Weg 6 (☎0871/234 49, ⓦwww.landshut.jugendherberge.de; €16.90 with breakfast). The *Goldene Sonne* has a classy **restaurant** serving fish, game and Bavarian staples from around €12 for a main course; alternatively, at the much cheaper but atmospheric and old-fashioned *Gasthof zum Freischütz* at Neustadt 446 (☎0871/264 87; closed Tues) lunchtime prices start as low as €5. There's a fair scattering of places to **drink** in Landshut's lively old town, plus a number of alfresco riverside places in the summer months.

Landshut has quite a rich **cultural** scene, with drama, opera and operetta staged at the Stadttheater Landshut, Ländtorplatz 3–5 (☎0871/922 08 33, ⓦwww .landestheater-niederbayern.de), while the Kammerspiele Landshut, Bauhofstrasse 1 (☎0871/294 65, ⓦwww.kleinestheaterlandshut.de), stages drama and live music. The Kinoptikum cinema, Nahensteig 1 (ⓦwww.kinoptikum.de), occasionally shows English-language films with the original soundtrack and German subtitles (O.m.U). The **Landshuter Hochzeit** takes place every four years in June and July, and features medieval-costumed revelries include jousting tournaments, falconry and medieval music (June 27–July 19, 2009; ⓦwww.landshuter-hochzeit.de).

Travel details

Trains

Berchtesgaden to: Munich (via Freilassing: every 30min–1hr; 3hr 10min).
Füssen to: Munich (every 2hr; 2hr).
Garmisch-Partenkirchen to: Munich (every 30min–1hr; 1hr 20min).
Landshut to: Munich (every 30min; 50min–1hr); Nuremberg (every 2hr; 1hr 50min); Passau (every 2hr; 1hr 25min); Regensburg (hourly; 40min).

Passau: to: Munich (every 2hr; 2hr 15min); Regensburg (every 20min–2hr; 1hr–1hr 25min).
Regensburg to: Ingolstadt (hourly; 1hr 8min); Landshut (hourly; 45min); Munich (hourly; 1hr 33min); Nuremberg (every 30min–1hr; 50min–1hr 30min); Passau (every 2hr; 1hr 2min); Saal a.d. Donau (hourly; 30min); Straubing (hourly; 26min).

Baden-Württemberg

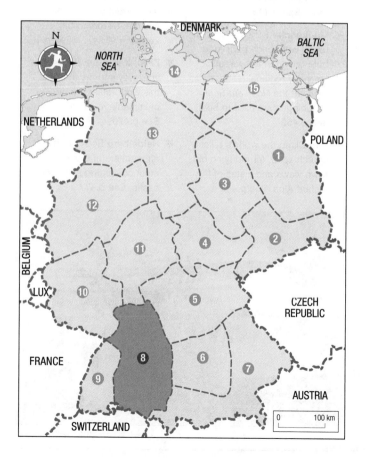

CHAPTER 8

Highlights

✳ **Mercedes-Benz-Museum** Pay tribute to Swabian hardwork and inventiveness at this magnificent automotive museum. **See p.441**

✳ **Tübingen** Punt or paddle the languid waters of this relaxed and venerable university town. **See p.449**

✳ **Maultaschen** These Swabian ravioli were once poor food but now often the yardstick for many regional restaurants; those at the *Hotel am Schloss* in Tübingen are hard to beat. **See p.452**

✳ **Ulm** Climb the world's tallest church spire, for giddying old-town views and vistas of the distant Alps. **See p.453**

✳ **Beuron** Let the dulcet Gregorian chants wash over you at this Baroque monastery. **See p.459**

✳ **Friedrichshafen** Float high above the Bodensee in a Zeppelin, or if your budget won't stretch to it, explore reconstructions and the airship's history at the Zeppelin Museum. **See p.462**

✳ **ZKM, Karlsruhe** Button-push your way into the future at this world-class interactive multimedia museum. **See p.476**

✳ **Heidelberg** Soak up the atmosphere of Germany's most celebrated semi-derelict castle. **See p.477**

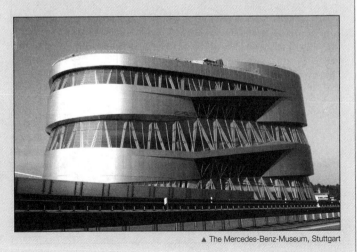

▲ The Mercedes-Benz-Museum, Stuttgart

Baden-Württemberg

Though the Land of **Baden-Württemberg** is the result of cobbling together the states of Baden, Hohenzollern and Württemberg after World War II, it feels like a coherent whole thanks to the strong **Swabian** identity of the people who inhabit the entire federal state. Descended from a Germanic tribe that lived around the Baltic in Roman times, the Swabians subsequently migrated southwest peopling a region north of the **Bodensee** (Lake Constance). In the rest of Germany they're caricatured as hard-working, frugal and rather boring but their industriousness and inventiveness has undoubtedly contributed to the region's wealth. It is Europe's richest area, and the seat of major-league industrial concerns. Unlike Bavaria such prosperity tends not to be flaunted conspicuously, but Swabians have just as strong an identity, built in part around their own food – a pasta-based cuisine including the famous *Spätzle* – a love of good local wine and quirky regional accent. Baden-Württemberg is also influenced by its proximity to France and Switzerland, and its common history with France in particular.

Though Land capital **Stuttgart** is the state's industrial powerhouse, it is small and easily navigable, in an attractive setting between a series of hills, with vineyards running right down to the city's edges. Known for its car industry and attendant museums, the city also boasts the best restaurant and nightlife scene in the region. South of Stuttgart lies the upland plateau of the **Swabian Alb**, a thinly populated agricultural region, encircled by various atmospheric castles, and **Tübingen** and **Ulm**, a couple of interesting and upbeat cities. To its south is the vast **Bodensee** where a huge body of water and Germany's best weather combine to form a popular holiday destination. West of here the hills rise and darken with the Black Forest, Baden-Württemberg's most famous asset – covered in Chapter 9. In the far north of the state, the historic towns of **Heidelberg** and **Karlsruhe** stick out as places worth visiting on your way in or out of the region.

Stuttgart is the main **regional transport** hub, but the whole state – with the exception of the Swabian Alb – is easy to navigate by public transport. Getting to remote places is of course easiest with your own wheels – and given the importance of the motor car industry in the state, this is a part of Germany where roads are kept in premium condition, and you can really let rip on the Autobahn.

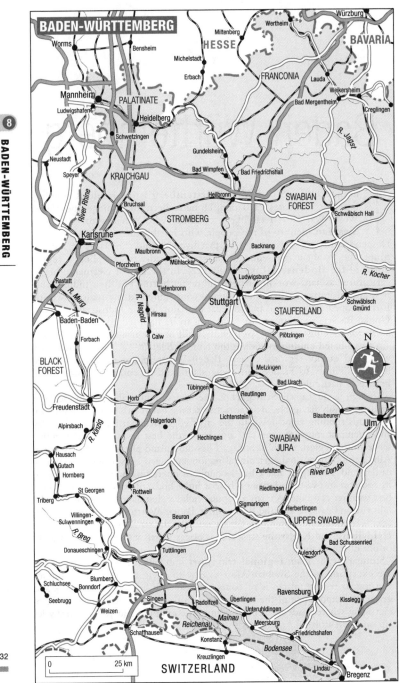

Stuttgart and around

Stuttgart and its environs are the industrial heartland of an otherwise relatively rural Baden-Württemberg. As the headquarters of industrial heavyweights that include Mercedes-Benz, Porsche and electronics giant Bosch, Stuttgart predictably oozes self-confidence and reeks of wealth. However, surprises lurk here too, in the form of parklands, green hills, thermal baths and Renaissance palaces, making the business-orientated town a likeable destination for a weekend or so. It's also a significant regional transport hub and a good place from which to launch day-trips. Other than the northern reaches of the Black Forest (see p.511) or nearby towns like Tübingen (see p.449) and Ulm (see p.453), the most obvious day-trips from Stuttgart are **Ludwigsburg**, with its excessive Baroque palace and, at the other end of the hedonism scale, the old monastery at **Maulbronn**, where the buildings tell a story of a long-forgotten simple monastic life. Both are brilliant, well-preserved and very different snapshots of Germany's past.

Stuttgart

World-leading car-town it may be, but **STUTTGART** is certainly no Birmingham or Detroit. Instead the capital of Baden-Württemberg is surprisingly small (its population is only 600,000), laid-back and leafy, with its multitude of parks and idyllic setting in the palm of a valley – where vineyards thrive – shaping it more than the presence of industrial giants.

The town – and its name – has its origins in a stud farm: a "*Stutengarten*" was established here in 950 AD and a black stallion still graces the city's heraldic crest. It developed as a trade centre and in 1311 became the seat of the Württemberg family. However, the city only really took control of the region once Napoleon made Württemberg a kingdom and Stuttgart its capital in 1805. Eighty years later Daimler and Karl Benz mapped out Stuttgart's future as a motor city.

The town's industrial prowess was duly punished during World War II, when bombs rained on the Altstadt, resulting in a town that today feels rather bereft of history, though there is high culture aplenty in its heavyweight museums, particularly the **Staatsgalerie**'s art collections and in the archeological treasures of the **Landesmuseum Württemberg**. Nevertheless, you're not likely to spend much time in its centre: many of its main sights, most notably the excellent **Mercedes and Porsche museums**, are in the suburbs, along with the city's **parks**, which contain a series of set-piece attractions, including a **TV tower**, **Schloss Solitude** and a good **zoo** – all reachable on the excellent public transport system. There's good hiking among **vineyards** here too, and wine buffs will want to sample some regional treats in Stuttgart's celebrated *Weinstuben*, or wine bars.

Despite the wine, Stuttgart tends, somewhat unfairly, to have a reputation as being a bit dull. Certainly don't arrive expecting the nightlife of Munich, Berlin, Hamburg or Cologne, but considering its size there's plenty going on. Things become lively in April, during the three-week **Stuttgarter Frühlingsfest** which salutes spring with beer and grilled sausages galore; in August when the open-air **Sommerfest** takes over the Schlossplatz with live music and grilled food; and the **Stuttgarter Weindorf** (see p.443) later in the month. Stuttgart also plays host to Germany's largest **Christmas Market** in December, but the town's really big

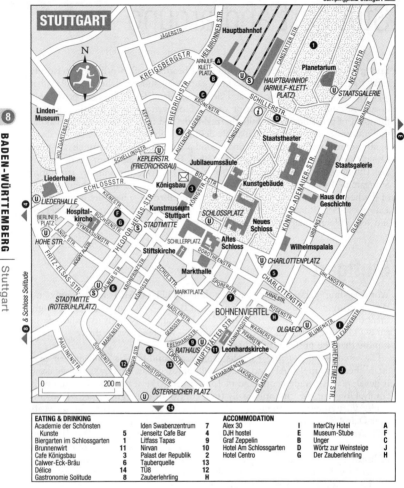

EATING & DRINKING				ACCOMMODATION			
Academie der Schönsten		Iden Swabenzentrum	7	Alex 30	I	InterCity Hotel	A
Kunste	5	Jenseitz Cafe Bar	4	DJH hostel	E	Museum-Stube	F
Biergarten im Schlossgarten	1	Litfas Tapas	9	Graf Zeppelin	B	Unger	C
Brunnenwirt	11	Nirvan	10	Hotel Am Schlossgarten	D	Wörtz zur Weinsteige	J
Cafe Königsbau	3	Palast der Republik	2	Hotel Centro	G	Der Zauberlehrling	H
Calwer-Eck-Bräu	6	Tauberquelle	13				
Délice	14	TÜ8	12				
Gastronomie Solitude	8	Zauberlehrling	H				

event in town is the late September, sixteen-day-long **Cannstatter Volksfest**, the sizeable local equivalent to Munich's Oktoberfest, but as yet undiscovered by invading armies of tourist boozers.

Arrival, information and city transport

Stuttgart's international **airport** (STR; ☎01805/94 84 44, ⓦwww.stuttgart -airport.com) lies 15km south of the city centre. **S-Bahn** lines S2 and S3 run to the **Hauptbahnhof** in the centre of town in around thirty minutes (5am–12.30pm; €2.90). Expect to pay €24 for a **taxi**.

The airport has a **tourist office** (daily 8am–8pm; ☎0711/222 80) booth in the terminal 3 arrivals area, but the main office, Königstrasse 1a (Mon–Fri 9am–8pm, Sat 9am–6pm, Sun 1–6pm; ☎0711/2 22 89, ⓦwww.stuttgart-tourist .de), is opposite the Hauptbahnhof. They can book accommodation and they sell the **StuttCard** (3 days €12) which includes substantial reductions to most museums, sightseeing tours, entertainment, and some shops. The **StuttCard plus** (3 days €18) includes public transport within city boundaries. Otherwise, with a hotel reservation you can get a three-day public transport ticket for €9.90, or the wider metro area for €13.30, available at most hotel receptions.

The city centre is easily walkable, and parks – such as the Schlossgarten – make even longer walks north to Bad Cannstatt a pleasure. Verkehrs- und Tarifverbund Stuttgart (Ⓦwww.vvs.de) run a **public transport** network, with the Hauptbahnhof its main hub. From here the U-Bahn rumbles city-wide and commuter lines of the S-Bahn rail network zip to outer suburbs. A single in zone 1 costs €1.90; a day-pass for two zones – which includes the Mercedes and Porsche museums – costs €5.60 per person, or €9.30 for a group ticket for up to five people.

Accommodation

Accommodation in Stuttgart is overwhelmingly business-orientated, which makes finding something more modest hard, though at weekends their rates are often lowered by as much as a third. At other times the easiest option is to enlist the help of the tourist office.

Hotels and pensions

🕴 **Graf Zeppelin** Arnulf-Klett-Platz 7 ☎0711/204 80, Ⓦwww.steigenberger.com. Five-star place opposite the Hauptbahnhof with *fin-de-siècle* elegance. Rooms come in different styles from classically elegant to clean avant-garde lines. Has its own pool, sauna, gym, restaurant and bar. ⑧

Hotel Am Schlossgarten Schillerstr. 23 ☎0711/202 60, Ⓦwww.hotelschlossgarten.com. Opulence and immaculate service come as standard in one of the city's finest traditional hotels; a park view costs extra, as does breakfast. ⑦

Hotel Centro Büchsenstr. 24 ☎0711/585 33 15, Ⓦwww.hotelcentro.de. Bare-bones hotel, but clean and only a couple of minutes' walk from the pedestrianized centre. There are some bargain singles, if you don't mind sharing a bathroom. ④

InterCity Hotel Arnulf-Klett-Platz 2 Ⓦwww .intercityhotel.com. Sleek rooms in a straightforward business hotel conveniently in the Hauptbahnhof. Huge reductions at weekends. ⑥

🕴 **Museum-Stube** Hospitalstr. 9 ☎0711/29 68 10. Spotless pension above a Croatian restaurant on one of the few central bargains. Not all rooms are en suite. ②

Unger Kronenstr. 17 ☎0711/209 90, Ⓦwww.hotel-unger.de. Classy modern four-star business-hotel in the Altstadt. The breakfast buffet is excellent and there's a fitness studio too. Rates are reduced by about a third on Friday, Saturday and Sunday nights. ⑦

Wörtz zur Weinsteige Hohenheimer Str. 30 ☎0711/236 70 00, Ⓦwww.hotel-woertz.de.

Traditional family-run hotel southeast of the centre where heavy dark-wood furniture provides a bit of time-honoured style . Near U-Bahn Dobelstr. ⑤

Der Zauberlehrling Rosenstr. 38 ☎0711/237 77 70, Ⓦwww.zauberlehrling.de. Suave, family-run, boutique hotel with a hip Bohnenviertel location and extravagant themed decor in every room. This ranges from Japanese minimalism to faded nineteenth-century glamour. ⑥

Camping and hostels

Campingplatz Stuttgart Mercedesstr. 20 ☎0711/55 66 96, Ⓦwww.campingplatz-stuttgart .de. Campground with riverside sites 4km from the city centre in Bad Cannstatt. Two people with a tent and a car pay €12.50. It's 1km southeast of S-Bahn Bad Cannstatt and there's another similar campground nearby.

DJH Stuttgart Hausmannstr. 27 ☎0711/664 74 70, Ⓦwww.jugendherberge -stuttgart.de. Large well-organized hostel, with en-suite two-bed rooms also available, It's a 15min walk southeast of Hauptbahnhof or take bus #42 or tram #15 to "Eugensplatz (Jugendherberge)". Dorms from €22.90.

🕴 **Hostel Alex 30** Alexanderstr. 30 ☎0711/838 89 50, Ⓦwww.alex30 -hostel.de. Cheerful independent hostel southeast of town, close to the Bohnenviertel and near Olgaeck stop on U-Bahn #5, #6 and #7. It has a bar, café, kitchen, tiny terrace and free wi-fi. Dorm beds cost €19, and singles and doubles are available too. Bike rental is offered for €6 per day. ②

The city centre

Central Stuttgart gathers around the **Schlossgarten**, a finger of parkland that runs from the 3km-distant Neckar River alongside the railway tracks and then past the **Hauptbahnhof** to the town centre's main public square: **Schlossplatz**. This is crossed by the spotless main commercial drag **Königstrasse** which leads southwest to the Altstadt, where there are a few remnants of the prewar city.

An excellent place to orientate yourself and start an exploration of Stuttgart is the **Aussichtsplatform** (April–Sept Tues–Sun 10am–9pm; Oct–March Wed & Fri–Sun 10am–6pm, Thurs 10am–9pm; free), at the top of a tower that rises from the **Hauptbahnhof**, crowned by a Mercedes logo. Striking is the amount of greenery on show: vineyards lie just west, while the 8km-long Schlossgarten dominates the east. Here lazy paths weave around a well-used strip that's populated by sunbathers, strollers and roller-bladers at the first hint of sunshine. Of particular interest and in easy walking distance from the Hauptbahnhof is the excellent *Biergarten im Schlossgarten* (see p.444) and the glass pyramid **Carl-Zeiss-Planetarium** (shows Tues & Thurs 10am & 3pm, Wed & Fri 10am, 3pm & 8pm, Sat 2pm, 4pm, 6pm & 7.15pm, Sun 2pm, 4pm & 6pm; €6; ☏0180/511 04 45 22, Ⓦwww.carl-zeiss-planetarium.de), which offers excellent virtual stargazing.

South of the Hauptbahnhof, the **Schlossgarten** offers a peaceful route into the town centre and Schlossplatz past well-tended laws and the grandiose 1912 Opernhaus der Württenbergischen Staatsheater. The alternative is the bustling, but bland, chain-store strip Königstrasse, which runs parallel.

Schlossplatz

Of all Stuttgart's green spaces, **Schlossplatz** is by far the busiest and most noble. Civil servants of the state culture and finance ministries occupy the Baroque **Neues Schloss** built by Friedrich I between 1746 and 1806. It swaggers on the eastern side of the square, its roof lined with allegorical statues and the heraldic stag of the dukes (then kings) of Württemberg prance atop its gate. Inside, the basement of the south wing houses the **Römisches Lapidarium** (Sun 10am–noon & 2–5pm; free), an overflow of the Landesmuseum (see opposite), which brings together Roman reliefs, sculptures and fragments found in the region.

King Wilhelm I of Württemberg's Neoclassical Königsbau rears up opposite, built in the 1850s for court events and stock-market traders in the Börse (stock exchange), who only moved to a more modern dealing-floor in 1991. Today the **Königsbau Passagen**, an upmarket shopping mall that's strong on interior-design shops, occupies the building, while cafés lurk behind its Ionic columns, and entertainment is provided by buskers on the steps.

Schlossplatz's grand centrepiece, however, is the **Jubiläumssäule**, which commemorates the 25th anniversary of King Wilhelm I's accession to the Württemberg throne, and features him enthroned and lauded by fawning nobles in a bombastic relief on the base. Flanking it on either side are capacious Neoclassical fountains with frolicking cherubs. A golden Württemberg stag crowns the dome of the **Kunstgebäude** (Tues & Thurs–Sun 11am–6pm, Wed 11am–8pm; €5; ☏0711/22 33 70, Ⓦwww.wkv-stuttgart.de) on the north side of the square. Temporary displays of big-name artists (past masters include Otto Dix, Munch and Man Ray) and up-and-coming talent hang in spacious exhibition halls.

There's more art across the square in the eye-catching glass box of the **Kunstmuseum Stuttgart**, Kleiner Schlossplatz 1 (Tues, Thurs, Sat & Sun 10am–6pm, Wed 10am–9pm; €5; ☏0711/216 21 88, Ⓦwww.kunstmuseum -stuttgart.de). The exhibitions here are all temporary, but usually revolve around modern or contemporary art; the mobile in front of the building is by Alexander

Calder and purchased for the equivalent of €500,000, causing a stir among frugal Swabians when the city bought it in 1981.

Schillerplatz

One block south of Schlossplatz lies the remaining part of prewar Stuttgart's Altstadt, centred on **Schillerplatz** where a Romantic **statue** of the eponymous hero shows him in an open shirt with his cloak draped casually over a shoulder. The eighteenth-century dramatist and lyric poet enrolled to train as an army doctor at the Hohe Karlsschule and endured seven unhappy years in Stuttgart. The tuition, he confessed to his diary, seemed not just "flawed but altogether harmful". "What bias must be the consequence of such regulated education forced on to pupils from tender childhood to mature youth?" he wondered.

The north side of the square is boxed in by the **Alte Kanzlei**, a Renaissance office-block of the chancellery with god of trade Mercury atop a column; and the adjacent Princenbau claims the honour of welcoming Stuttgart's last king, Wilhelm II, into the world on February 25, 1848.

The renovated **Stiftskirche** is an airy modern space whose glass sails and arty floor-to-ceiling glass strips might have surprised its late Gothic municipal architects Hänslin and Aberlin Jörg. In truth, modernization sees the city's oldest church continuing true to form. Commissioned in 1436 to unite the existing hotch-potch of styles, the father-and-son duo beautifully melded old and new, particularly in the square tower of the twelfth-century Romanesque basilica which morphs into an octagonal bell-tower. In the choir Sem Schlör's **ancestral gallery** of the Württemberg dukes – from city patron Count Ulrich who erected the first stone Schloss in 1265 (far right) to Heinrich of Mompelgard (1519; far left) – is an absorbing German Renaissance masterpiece, each family member brilliantly and imaginatively characterized, including family squabbles. Hand on hip in the centre of the family reunion, Ulrich IV argues his case to his father Eberhard I rather than debate with the impressively bearded Eberhard II beside him. The brothers' co-rule of Stuttgart between 1333 and 1362 exploded into a furious spat about land division. Ulrich IV stepped down in disgust, earning the nickname Eberhard II "Der Greiner" ("the Quarreller"). Look, too, for a late Gothic pulpit on which the four evangelists are hard at work on their gospels, and in the baptistry a beautiful carving of Christ who shelters all society beneath his shroud.

Soul nurtured, feed your senses in the adjacent frescoed Jugendstil **Markthalle** (Mon–Fri 7am–6.30pm, Sat 7am–4pm), with stalls laden with smoked Schwarzwald (Black Forest) hams, doughy *Spätzle*, twee pots of home-made jam and marmalade, a bewildering number of varieties of *Wurst*, German breads and all sorts of strange cheeses to sample. An ideal place to assemble a Schlossgarten picnic.

The Altes Schloss and Landesmuseum Württemberg

Schillerplatz's finest moment is the stolid **Altes Schloss** on its east flank. Two centuries after the original stud farm was established here in 950 AD, a moated stone castle was built to protect it; a stocky corner tower is all that remains of its fourteenth-century replacement. Until Duke Carl Eugen despaired of its "prison-like" conditions and left for Ludwigsburg (see p.445), the Württemberg dukes resided here in the sixteenth-century Schloss, which received a Renaissance makeover courtesy of court architect Aberlin Tretsch. Tretsch excelled in the graceful galleried courtyard that proved too elegant for the intended jousting tournaments, and is more fitting for today's inexpensive summer evening classical concerts. Tretsch also added a Reittreppe, riding ramp, which allowed his master to make a flamboyant entrance into the Rittersaal (Knight's Hall) at full gallop.

The palace now forms a historic setting for the rewardingly eclectic **Landesmuseum Württemberg** (Tues–Sun 10am–5pm; €4.50; ☎0711/279 34 98, ⓦwww.landesmuseum-stuttgart.de). Among the Swabian devotional sculptures a brightly coloured Ulm Passion cycle (1520) catches the eye, but far finer are a pair of carvings by Germany's late Gothic supremo Tilman Riemenschneider, whose finesse and expression need no gaudy make-up. Other treasures include Europe's oldest pack of playing cards (1430) which reveals the era's obsessions, with suits of falcons and hounds, ducks and stags; the state jewellery box includes a necklace with a large 22-carat diamond and a silver filigree tiara fit for a fairytale princess.

The **archeology** section also has much of local interest, particularly a unique haul – including a large chariot with horse harnesses and finely worked jewellery – from the burial mound of a sixth-century BC Celtic prince of Hochdorf near Ludwigsburg. Also in the collection is a lion head that a Bronze Age sculptor carved from a chunk of mammoth tusk, one of the world's oldest pieces of art.

The Landesmuseum ticket is also valid for the **Musikinstrumenten Sammlung** (same hours), in the modernized sixteenth-century wine warehouse and granary, the Fruchtkasten, on Schillerplatz. Occasional concerts bring some of its prodigious collection alive. Formerly castle gardens, spacious **Karlsplatz** opposite now hosts a small Saturday flea market.

The Bohnenviertel and the Haus der Geschichte Baden-Württemberg

An underpass allows you to avoid the furious traffic along Konrad-Adenauer-Strasse to walk east from the centre into the **Bohnenviertel** (Bean Quarter), the traditional blue-collar district that occupies the city blocks between Charlottenstrasse and Pfarrstrasse. Founded in the fourteenth century and largely spared wartime bombs, its cobbled lanes convey a more distant history, and have settled happily into gentrification. The former houses of market gardeners and wine growers are highly prized by jewellers, galleries and antique shops as well as several homey *Weinstuben* – while a modest red-light district occupies the south.

North of the Bohnenviertel, over Charlottenstrasse and back along Konrad-Adenauer-Strasse, curious perspex boxes containing "found objects" blare with videos and music: welcome to the **Haus der Geschichte Baden-Württemberg** (Tues, Wed & Fri–Sun 10am–6pm, Thurs 10am–9pm; €3; ☎0711/212 39 89, ⓦwww.hdgbw.de), a frequently conceptual, occasionally baffling fast-forward through the history of Baden-Württemberg. Its "*Wirtschafts-Wunder*" section salutes regional heroes of industry – Stuttgarter Robert Bosch, now synonymous with power tools, rawl-plug pioneer Fischer, and Matthias Hohner, harmonica king – and, far more fun, the "*Kunststück Schwarzwald*" documents the Black Forest's blossoming from rustic backwater to darling of German tourism (blame nineteenth-century Romantics) in photos and tacky souvenirs.

The Staatsgalerie

North from the Haus der Geschichte along Konrad-Adenauer-Strasse, a curved glass facade by British architect James Stirling announces one of Stuttgart's cultural highlights: the **Staatsgalerie** (Tues, Wed & Fri–Sun 10am–6pm, Thurs 10am–9pm, 1st Sat in month 10am–midnight; €4.50; ☎0711/47 04 00, ⓦwww.staatsgalerie.de).

The gallery, based on the collection of the Württemberg dukes, begins with early German masters. Stars of the Swabian artists are the anonymous Master of the Sterzinger Altar, who paints a sumptuous and delicate *Journey of the*

Magi, and Jerg Ratgeb, the Peasants' War revolutionary. His *Herrenberger Altar* commands the room with a blaze of colour and movement; on its rear are images of the apostles bidding their farewells as they set out to spread the Word abroad. A pair of exquisite Cranachs – saucy nudes and ruthless beauty Judith with the head of Holofernes – lead to the Dutch Old Masters. Hans Memling indulges his vision of Gothic beauty as *Bathsheba at Her Toilet* steps naked from her bath, and Rembrandt again reveals his deft hand with light: wild-haired *Saint Paul in Prison* contemplates the execution sword at his side. One of his celebrated self-portraits peers from the gloom, and there's a tender image of *Tobias Healing his Father.*

Italians gather at the opposite end of the gallery. The counts snapped up Bolognese painter Annibale Carracci's startling *Christ with the Tools of Suffering*. Look, too, for Tiepolo's glorious sketch of a Würzburg palace fresco. Alongside a section on Swabian Classicism, Germany's chief Romantic Caspar David Friedrich shines among nineteenth-century peers, with the magical stillness of *Bohemian Landscape*, painted while a walking tour was still fresh in his mind. Nearby is Beckmann's *Resurrection* (1909), itself resurrected later in the gallery in a disjointed image which expresses the horror of the artist's World War I experience.

Surprising is the room devoted to pre-Raphaelite Edward Burne-Jones; only five of his *Perseus* octet commissioned by future British prime minister Arthur Balfour were finished in oils, the other three remain as sketches.

All the leading lights of French Impressionism are here – Monet's idyllic *Fields in Spring* is incandescent and there's *Sea near Fécamp*, painted at speed on a cliff ledge between tides – as are many of the Expressionists, with vivid canvases by Kandinsky, Kirchner, Nolde and Kokoschka, and Schiele paints a merciless double self-portrait, *Prophets*. Dalí, Duchamp and Matisse lift the mood of these doom-mongers with wacky Surrealism, but the star of the twentieth-century collection is Picasso. Two rooms chronicle his early works from the Blue Period (*Mother and Child* and on its reverse *Crouching Woman*) to iconic Cubisms such as louche *Breakfast in the Open Air* and the most important of his late sculptures, *Bathers*, like African tribal sculptures. Last are works by Warhol, Beuys and Serra, among others, and don't miss the Graphische Sammlung's alternating treasury of graphic arts, from Dürer to twentieth-century greats.

The suburbs

Stuttgart's suburbs spread across the hills that surround the city, leading into parkland and boasting good views of the town along with a few novel buildings dotted around. An aged rack-railway, the **Zahnradbahn**, a short walk south of Stuttgart's centre, makes the **Fernsehturm** (TV tower), one of the most accessible. On the western side of the city stands eighteenth-century **Schloss Solitude**, while to the north is **Höhenpark Killesberg**, of interest for the **Weissenhofsiedlung**, a collection of Bauhaus buildings. Just east of here, and alongside the Neckar River is **Rosensteinpark**, where natural history is given a thorough treatment, from its paleontological beginnings in the Museum am Löwentor to a fine botanic garden and zoo. Over an elbow of the Neckar from Rosensteinpark is **Bad Cannstatt**, an old spa-town 3km northeast of Stuttgart's centre which became incorporated in 1905, but where the feel of a separate town is preserved. Though traditionally known for its mineral baths, these days it is famous as the birthplace of the car and **Mercedes**, which has a terrific museum here. An ex-employee of the company spawned Porsche in the vicinity, and the achievements of that brand are celebrated in the **Porsche Museum** 9km to the north of Stuttgart's centre.

Zahnradbahn and the Fernsehturm

From the Staatsgalerie it's four quick stops on the U-Bahn to Marienplatz station, which is the starting point for the **Zahnradbahn**, a rack railway. Affably known as the "Zacke", Stuttgart's main public transport oddity – and included on passes for the entire network, though using it only requires a *Kurzstrecke* ticket – has been climbing to the suburb of Degerloch since 1884. From the Nägelestrasse station it's a five-minute walk east to the **Fernsehturm** (TV tower; daily 9am–11pm; €5), which hails from 1956 and so is the earliest example of this much-imitated design.

Schloss Solitude

A ridge on the western side of Stuttgart is home to 1760s oval palace, **Schloss Solitude** (April–Oct Tues–Sat 9am–noon & 1.30–5pm, Sun 9am–5pm; Nov–March Tues–Sat 1.30–4pm, Sun 10am–4.30pm; €3.30; ☎0711/69 66 99, Ⓦwww.schloss-solitude.de), which served as main summer residence for the Württemberg court for twenty years or so. It's 7km from the Hauptbahnhof – easily accessed using bus #92 – and is one of Stuttgart's most popular days out, particularly since you can wander at will around the rooms.

Duke Carl Eugen, who built so feverishly in Ludwigsburg (see p.445), commissioned Philippe de La Guêpière to design the palace. The Parisian architect drew a masterpiece, an exquisite oval palace that tempers the final flickers of Rococo with emergent Neoclassicism. Inevitably, despite a ruler-straight 15km road from Ludwigsburg, the swaggering aristocrat bored of his pleasure palace barely six years after its 1769 completion and it was only ever used for rare courtly high-jinks with visiting dignitaries. A 30-year-old Johann Wolfgang von Goethe on a hunting jaunt with the Duke of Weimar in 1779 marvelled at its festive hall, the Weisser Saal, which claims centre stage and has a boastful allegorical fresco about the peaceful good government of Carl Eugen. In one wing are the elegant rooms of his official apartment – the marble Marmorsaal and Palmenzimmer. Like courtiers and visitors, the duke resided in the outbuilding Kavalierbau at the rear, a mirror-image to the administrative Officenbau, which today houses a gourmet restaurant (see p.442).

Höhenpark Killesberg

Lying 2.5km due north of the town centre **Höhenpark Killesberg** was the product of a Nazi work-creation scheme which transformed a disused quarry to host a flower show in 1939. Replanted after the war and jewelled with sparkling water cascades and fountains, Stuttgart's highest park now affords sweeping panoramas over the city from the **Killesberg Turm**, a 43m lookout of winding staircases like an aluminium DNA strand. There are also outdoor pools, children's zoos and restaurants to discover and a shamelessly twee tourist-train for when your legs tire.

The 1950s Messe (trade fair) buildings at the park's southern fringe help locate the Weissenhofsiedlung. In 1927, Stuttgart invited the cutting edge of European architecture to erect show houses for guild show "*Die Wohnung*". They might have frowned at patchy postwar restoration, but Mies van der Rohe, Le Corbusier, Walter Gropius, Hans Scharoun and the other modernist architects involved at the time would be delighted that their clean-lined Bauhäuser still provide homes.

Rosensteinpark and Wilhelma

From the eastern end of Höhenpark Killesberg, Brünner Steg crosses a bundle of S-Bahn lines on a footbridge that leads to the copses of mature trees of **Rosensteinpark**. Wilhelm I spent a decade from 1852 seeding botanical gardens here, which have since grown into heavyweight zoo **Wilhelma** (daily 8.15am–dusk; €11.40; ☎0711/540 20, ⓦ www.wilhelma.de; U-Bahn 14 to Wilhelma or U-Bahn 13 & buses #52, #55, #56 to Rosensteinbrücke). Romantic Moorish fantasies are dotted around the gardens, which feature Europe's largest magnolia grove and four thousand orchids – a perfect backdrop to its nine thousand animal inhabitants.

The zoo and botanic gardens were once simply the gardens of **Schloss Rosenstein** (U-Bahn Mineralbäder), the Neoclassical hilltop retreat by Giovanni Salucci in the southeastern corner of the park. Today this contains the dreary stuffed menagerie of the **Museum für Naturkunde** (Tues–Fri 9am–5pm, Sat & Sun 10am–6pm; €4; ⓦ www.naturkundemuseum-bw.de). Thankfully, an extra €1 on the ticket price buys you a combination ticket that includes the modern and very good **Museum am Löwentor** further west (same hours), a paleontologist's dream of impressive fossils and dinosaur skeletons.

Just beyond the southern edge of **Rosensteinpark**, and a short stroll north by König-Karls-Brücke, lie two large mineral baths beside the Neckar where you can sample the local curative waters: Mineral-Bad-Berg (daily 6am–7.30pm; 2hr €6.50), a mineral pool and sauna where two of Stuttgart's nineteen springs bubble up and pensioners brave winter to swim dutiful lengths in an outdoor pool; slightly more boisterous is Mineral-Bad-Leuze (daily 6am–9pm; 2hr €7) next door.

Bad Cannstatt

During its early years, Stuttgart was level-pegged by **Bad Cannstatt**, especially with the grandeur – now faded – of the riverfront and around the Marktplatz and tight-knit Altstadt streets. The town was treasured above all for the curative powers of the 22-million-litre torrent that gushed from seventeen springs each day, and in the mid-nineteenth century it duly became a fashionable spa town. Emperors decamped court to wallow in its baths, and the great and the good prayed for miracle cures with each glass. Stroll north of the town centre and Wilhelm I of Württemberg on horseback fronts his Neoclassical **Kurhaus**, still a spa for rheumatism, and on its left the Mineral-Bad-Cannstatt (Mon–Sun 9am–9pm; €9.90; ☎0711/216 92 40) caters to a full range of watery pursuits, from frolics to fitness. Behind the Kurhaus is the lovely, restful Kurpark.

Take the path up to it right of the Kurhaus and you'll pass the **Gottlieb-Daimler-Gedächnisstätte**, Taubenheimstrasse 13 (Tues–Sun 10am–4pm; free), a curious shed-cum-greenhouse that served as the workshop of Gottlieb Daimler and apprentice Wilhelm Maybach. Daimler gave up his career in 1882 to tinker here, and though bombs destroyed the adjoining villa, the shed escaped unharmed. His quest to produce a light, fast, internal combustion engine was done so secretively that police raided his workshop for money-counterfeiting on the tip-off of a gardener. In 1883, his single-cylinder four-stroke shattered the repose of Kurhaus spa-goers and by 1885 his patented 264cc "Grandfather Clock" powered a motorbike. A year later the world's first motorboat, the *Neckar*, chugged upriver and his motorized carriage terrorized horses. Daimler moved to a factory on Seelberg in July 1887. The workshop itself – with its workbench tidily laid-out with well-oiled spanners, screwdrivers, vices and drills – seems a little too humble to be the cradle of the world-changing automobile. Models of the first designs put into context the amazing achievements since.

Mercedes-Benz-Museum

While Gottlieb was locked in his shed, Karl Benz had blazed his own motor trail to found Benz & Cie in 1883, the same year as Daimler, though neither was aware of the other's work. The world's two oldest motor manufacturers united in June 1926 as Daimler-Benz long after Daimler had died and Benz retired.

The Mercedes name was introduced in 1902 to honour the daughter of early Austrian dealer Emil Jellinek.

All this is recounted and celebrated by the **Mercedes-Benz-Museum**, Mercedesstrasse 100 (Tues–Sun 9am–6pm; €8; ⊕0711/173 00 00, ⊛www .mercedes-benz.com/museum), in a landmark futuristic building on the bank of the Neckar, 4km northeast of the city centre and five minutes' walk south of the Gottlieb-Daimler-Stadion Bahnhof (S-Bahn S1). It's chock-full of 110 years of immaculate motors and starts with Daimler's pioneering motorbike – a wooden bone-shaker with a horse's saddle – and beside it is the one-cylinder motor-tricycle Motorwagen and motorized carriage Motorkutsche; Benz and Daimler created them independently in 1886, both capable of a not-so-giddy 16kmph. Benz just pipped Daimler to produce the world's first car.

Another trail-blazer is the robust Benz Vélo, the world's first production car, for which twelve hundred of the moneyed elite parted with 20,000 gold Marks. A racy 500K Special Roadster in preening pillarbox red begs for a Hollywood Thirties starlet, but it's the racers that truly quicken the pulse, no more so than the legendary Silver Arrows of the 1920s and 1930s; a cinema shows the sleek machines in action. Just as eye-catching are a pair of experimental record-breakers that look far more futuristic than their dates suggest: in the W125, Rudolf Caracciola clocked up 432.7km per hour on the Frankfurt–Darmstadt Autobahn in 1938 (no one's been faster on a public highway since); and six-wheeler sci-fi vision T80 was powered by an aeroplane engine to 650km per hour in 1939, though World War II killed off the project.

Porsche Museum

As if two motor-car pioneers weren't enough, Stuttgart also lays claim to Ferdinand Porsche. Daimler's 1920s technical director left the company in 1938 to produce sleek racing machines until Hitler demanded his design expertise be applied to creating the Volkswagen. He returned to racing cars later and the company's badge honours the debt to Stuttgart with a rearing horse. The **Porsche Museum**, Porschestrasse 42 (Mon–Fri 9am–4pm, Sat & Sun 9am–5pm; free; ⊕0711/911 56 85; S-Bahn S6 to Neuwirtshaus), in northern suburb Neuwirtshaus, is a crash course in his designs. The museum is reasonably small – with only around twenty vehicles at any one time, but these are frequently switched, making return visits worthwhile for enthusiasts.

Eating and drinking

As a wealthy business centre Stuttgart is well served by good restaurants. If you want to browse for stylish places, try heading to the southern end of **Königstrasse**, around **Eberhardstrasse**, where many restaurants have outdoor seating. For something a bit more earthy and traditional try the Bohnenviertel – particularly **Rosenstrasse** and **Pfarrstrasse**.

Restaurants

Délice Hauptstätter Str. 61 ⊕0711/640 32 22. Intimate, six-table city-centre gourmet restaurant. Master chef Friedrich Gutscher conjures exquisite international flavours and his €70 *Gastrosophisches Menu* is super-fresh and relatively good value. Mon–Fri eve only.

Gastronomie Solitude Schloss Solitude ⊕0711/69 20 25. Pricey modern German gourmet cuisine in the refined Rococo surroundings of Duke Carl Eugen's

palace. Without doubt, in the highest echelons of Stuttgart dining experience. Tues–Sat eve only.

Iden Swabenzentrum Eberhardstr. 1. Pay-by-weight veggie place, offering a buffet of local and organic produce; lots of salads and juices and great home-made soup and cake too. Closed Sun.

Nirvan Eberhardstr. 73. Persian basement restaurant with excellent grilled lamb, poultry and veal (mains around €8). Authentic decor lends atmosphere, as does the belly-dancing on Fridays.

Tauberquelle Torstr. 19 ☎0711/23 56 56. All the Swabian favourites – *Maultaschen, Kasespätzle, Gaisburger Marsch* and *Rostbraten* – are good value (mains €6.50–14.50) and done to perfection at this easy-going city-centre restaurant.

TÜ8 Tübinger Str. 8 ☎0711/223 78 88. Complex housing three restaurants that share the great beers of the resident microbrewery. All three tend towards formulaic themes, but are inexpensive and dependable: *Mäxle* serves Swabian classics; *Spaghettissimo*, vast portions

Wine in Stuttgart

Cradled in a valley with over five hundred vineyards – some of which spill right into the city – Stuttgart naturally enjoys its wine. Local vintners produce a number of white wines, including an elegant Riesling, as well as the popular, full-bodied red Trollinger. Don't be surprised if you haven't heard of Stuttgart's wines though: wine consumption here is twice the national average so local supply only just meets the demand and few wines leave the valley. So, while Frankfurt has its cider taverns and Munich its beer halls, Stuttgart's unique drinking dens are its **Weinstuben** or wine bars – a few of which are listed below. These tend to open in the evenings only, rarely on a Sunday, and are usually unpretentious rustic places. All serve solid and inexpensive Swabian dishes, which invariably include doughy *Spätzle* (noodles) and *Maultaschen*, the local oversized ravioli. More homey still are **Besenwirtschaften**, temporary wine-bars that appear in the front rooms of people's houses to serve the season's vintage with home-cooking, including potato soup (*Kartoffelsuppe*), noodle and beef stew (*Gaisburger Marsch*), or a *Schlachtplatte*, a meat feast served with vegetables. These places traditionally announce themselves with a broom hung outside and their locations vary from year to year. They're all listed in the guide *Stuttgarter Weine* (€1.50) from the tourist office, which is also a good place to pick up information on the *Stuttgarter Weinwanderweg* (☻www .stuttgarter-weinwanderweg.de), the hiking routes that circle through local vineyards along which many *Besenwirtschaften* have set themselves up.

Stuttgart's other great initiative for wine lovers is the **Stuttgarter Weindorf**, when during the last weekend in August the Marktplatz and Schillerplatz fill with wine buffs sampling hundreds of regional tipples. The year's vintages are on sale, and it's a great chance to pick up some rarer wines. A similar event is the Fellbacher Herbst on the second weekend in October, in Fellback, just east of Bad Cannstatt.

Weinstuben

Jägerhof Am Wolfsberg 17, Bad Cannstatt ☎0711/54 43 04. Hearty Swabian cuisine the way it should be and wines from the home vineyard. Closed lunch & Sun.

Kachelofen Eberhardstr. 10 ☎0711/24 23 78. A bastion of beams and lacy tablecloths among the hip bars of Hans-im-Gluck south of Marktplatz. It's the *Weinstube* favoured by Stuttgart's smarter set and serves hearty regional food. Closed lunch & Sun.

Klösterle Marktstr. 71, Bad Cannstatt ☎0711/56 89 62. Swabian specials in the rustic interior of a wonky half-timbered building from 1463, which looks like an incongruous film-set among the modern flats. Closed lunch & Sun.

Melle's In der Villa Berg ☎0711/2 62 23 45. Friendly service, light bites and a blooming garden in a charming *Weinstube* in the Berg park near the top of Unterer Schlossgarten.

Schnellenturm Weberstr. 72 ☎0711/2 36 48 88. *Schwäbischer Sauerbraten* comes in a rich sauce in Duke Christopher's 1564 defence tower transformed into a cosy half-timbered nest. Quality and prices are a little above the average *Weinstube* fare. Closed lunch & Sun.

Stetter Rosenstr. 32 ☎0711/24 01 63. Wine connoisseurs' heaven – at the last count, over 575 wines, nearly 200 regional, were on the list of this Bohnenviertel *Weinstube*. There are no sniffy airs though, just locals exchanging news and tucking into spicy bean soup or rich beef goulash. Mon–Fri 3–11pm, Sat 11am–3pm.

of inexpensive Italian food; *Hacienda*, Tex-Mex favourites.

Zauberlehrling Rosenstr. 38 ☎0711/237 77 70. Relaxed Bohnenviertel restaurant with upmarket German and international cuisine and a €30 three-course regional menu.

Cafés, bars and cheap eats

Academie der Schönsten Kunste Charlottenstr. 5 ☎0711/24 24 36. Marvellous café 5min walk south of the Staatsgalerie. Its quirky mix of 1930s decor and modern painting is a hit with Stuttgart's arty set, who tuck in to healthy sandwiches and salads or weekend brunches – eggs served direct in the pan are delicious – with frothy bowls of cappuccino. Closed Sun eve.

Brunnenwirt Leonhardsplatz 25. Simple sausage kiosk that's become a local institution, legendary in particular for *Currywurst* and *Rote Wurst*.

Café Königsbau Königstr. 28. Excellent café with all the right ingredients in place: the cakes are home-made, including some particularly fine fruit-based offerings; there's seating outside for people-watching on Schlossplatz; while indoors there's a traditional coffee-house atmosphere to enjoy.

Jenseitz Café Bar Bebelstr. 25. Bar and lounge with a 1970s look and great Italian coffees and some light local dishes, including *Flammkuchen*,

the local equivalent to pizza, and good cocktails. Very popular with the gay scene and dependably busy until closing around 1am.

Litfass Tapas Eberhardstr. 35–37. Studenty place with inexpensive Turkish and Swabian food, which gradually transforms into a bar and club with all manner of partying until at least 5am every night of the week.

Palast der Republik Friedrichstr. 27. Offbeat cult place – a former public loo that's now beer kiosk – where when the sun shines, the unconventional hang out in droves, with many ending up sitting on the pavement.

Microbreweries and beer gardens

Biergarten im Schlossgarten Canstatter Str. 18. Large, summer-only beer garden in the Schlossgarten near the Hauptbahnhof. Offers solid traditional canteen food, an array of drinks and a convivial atmosphere with regular live music.

Calwer-Eck-Bräu Calwer Str. 31. Stuttgart's oldest microbrewery with several good standard brews – some organic – and interesting seasonal offerings. The cosy, cheerful atmosphere can be further savoured with a menu of good local offerings: the *Maultaschen* soup (€4.20) is excellent and daily lunch specials (€6.50) include a beer.

Nightlife and entertainment

Though considered rather sedate in the rest of Germany, for its size Stuttgart has a **nightlife** scene it can be proud of, with plenty of busy downtown clubs, particularly along Theodor-Heuss-Strasse, three blocks west of Königstrasse. Stuttgart's wealthy burghers also stimulate a prodigious amount of high culture. One of Germany's finest classical outfits, the Radio-Sinfonieorchester, plus the Stuttgarter Philharmoniker and renowned chamber orchestra Stuttgarter Kammerorchester under American conductor Dennis Russell Davies perform concerts in the **Liederhalle**, Berliner-Platz 1–3 (☎0711/202 77 10, ⊛www.liederhalle-stuttgart.de), also a venue for occasional musicals. Keep your eyes open for must-see concerts of the **Internationale Bachakademie Stuttgart** under director Professor Helmuth Rilling and check the **Stiftskirche** for choral concerts: Stuttgart has one of Germany's densest concentration of top-class choirs. On the stage, the main address is the Staatstheater, Oberer Schlossgarten 6 (☎0711/20 20 90, ⊛www.staatstheater-stuttgart.de), where you'll find opera, theatre and productions by world-acclaimed **Stuttgart Ballet Company** (⊛www.stuttgart-ballet.de); tickets come at bargain prices (from €8) and its restored 1909–12 **Opernhaus** is worth a visit for its galleried hall alone.

The free listings magazine *Moritz* from the tourist office and local bars provides a rudimentary what's-on rundown; for detailed information pick up *Lift Stuttgart*, the city's what's-on bible, or *Prinz* (⊛www.prinz.de/stuttgart.html). The tourist office is the best place for tickets to most events.

Clubs and venues

Dilayla Eberhardstr. 49 ☎ 0711/236 95 27. Dimly lit basement that bustles with a broad spectrum of people dancing to Seventies and Eighties hits or lounging on couches on the last stop of the night: open until 4am weeknights, 6am weekends, only busy after midnight.

Friedrichsbau Varieté Friedrichstr. 24 ☎ 0711/2 25 70 70, ⓦ www.friedrichsbau.de. Good old-fashioned variety shows and cabaret; tickets start at €20. U-Bahn 14 Friedrichsbau/Börse.

King's Club Calwer Str. 21 ☎ 0711/226 45 58, ⓦ www.kingsclub-stuttgart.de. Long-standing and pivotal gay and lesbian basement club with diverse musical tastes and regular theme-nights; enter on Gymnasiumstr. Wed–Sun 10pm–6am, but only busy after midnight.

Kiste Hauptstätter Str. 35 ☎ 0711/553 28 05. Venerable jazz dive with everything from Dixieland to modern jazz packing the place out until 1–2am. Closed Sun.

Perkins Park Stresemannstr. 39 ☎ 0711/256 00 62, ⓦ www.perkins-park.de. Popular with twenty- and thirty-somethings, this club's been spinning records for two decades, making it a local classic. The hippest local DJs play here, and the music can go in virtually any direction. Wed–Sun until at least 3am; 5am on weekends. Covers around €10.

Die Röhre Willy-Brandt-Str. 2 ☎ 0711/200 15 90, ⓦ www.die-roehre.com. Legendary and massively popular local club in an old tunnel, which makes for an industrial feel. Music from across the board, with everything from more mainstream alternative and drum 'n' bass to death metal – played over three dancefloors. Fri & Sat 10pm–5am. Cover €6.

Listings

Banks and exchange American Express, Amulf-Klett-Platz 1; Western Union, Hauptbahnhof behind track 11.

Car rental The international players share an office on platform 16 of the Hauptbahnhof and all companies have a desk at the airport. Avis ☎ 0711/223 72 58; Europcar ☎ 0711/224 46 30; Hertz ☎ 0711/226 29 21; Mages, Pfalateräckerstr. 6 ☎ 0711/46 47 87.

Hospital Katharinen Hospital, Kriegsbergstr. 60 ☎ 0711/27 80.

Post office Main office is in the Königsbaupassagen, northwest of Schlossplatz; there's a branch in the Hauptbahnhof too.

Ludwigsburg

For a heady century the small town of **LUDWIGSBURG** was adorned with grandeur as the seat of the Württemberg dukes and Germany's largest Baroque palace. During that time a planned town was developed on the basis of free land and building materials, and a fifteen-year tax exemption. The elegant Marktplatz at the centre of the town is a reminder of these planned origins with its perfectly balanced streets radiating from a statue of Eberhard Ludwig flouncing atop a fountain.

When Friedrich I's Neues Schloss rose in Stuttgart, 14km to the south, Ludwigsburg suddenly reverted to provincial obscurity, although its Versailles-inspired palace continues to draw visitors and delight those who enjoy all things Baroque – the town returns the compliment by theming as much as it can – including its Christmas market – in this style. Other seasonal high-points include the mid-May **Pferdemarkt**, a traditional horse festival, with much clip-clopping around town; the **Schlossfestspiele** (June to mid-Sept; ⓦ www.schlossfestspiele.de), a classical music, opera, dance and theatre festival; and, in early September, the Venetian-style costume **Carnevale**.

The Residenzschloss

Ludwigsburg's **Residenzschloss** (1hr 30min tours daily: mid-March to mid-Nov 10am–5pm, in English Mon–Sat 1.30pm, Sun 11am, 1.30pm & 3.15pm;

mid-Nov to mid-March 10.30am–4pm, in English daily 1.30pm; €6; ☎07141/18 20 04, ⓦwww.schlossludwigsburg.de) was born out of Duke Eberhard Ludwig's envy of palaces admired on military campaigns abroad. French troops, who in 1697 reduced the ducal hunting lodge here to ashes, provided the required excuse to build a replacement, in the form of a Baroque palace, duly begun in 1706. Just before its completion, the duke demanded two further wings, in part as lodgings for his mistress. The court was furious at his extravagance, but a second, far larger *Corps de Logis* rose to close the square, despite architect's remonstrations about blocking garden views.

However, Eberhard Ludwig was almost modest compared with his successor Duke Carl Eugen. Upon ascending to the duchy throne in 1744, the 16-year-old ruler declared the Residenzschloss his home and established the most vibrant court in Europe where the finest opera, ballet and French comedy was offered, and extramarital dalliances were part of the menu too: the Duke forbade ladies from wearing blue shoes at court except "those who would … devote their honour to him … (and who should) never appear without this distinguishing mark," notes a 1756 court report. Small wonder his wife stomped back to her parents after eight years of marriage.

Out of the over sixty rooms on show of the palace's 452 across eighteen buildings, the older ones tease with hints of the duo's extravagance. A gorgeous allegorical fresco to the arts and sciences for Eberhard Ludwig in the **Ahnensaal** (Ancestors' Hall) leads to Carl Eugen's charming **Schlosstheater**, where classical music is staged in summer in the venue which entertained Mozart, Casanova and Goethe, and Eberhard Ludwig's Schlosskapelle spurns Protestant piety to show off in ritziest Baroque. The east wing's **Satyrkabinett** features cherubs above moustachioed Turkish prisoners of war who lament Eberhard Ludwig's success in the field, and trompe l'ocil frescoes play tricks on the ceiling of the **Ordenshalle**, the festive hall of the ducal hunting order. The new *Corps de Logis* is largely dressed in opulent early Neoclassicism that ranks among Germany's finest, a makeover for Frederick I's summer retreat; no shrinking violet himself, the Stuttgart king became so bloated through wine that he had to be hoisted by block and tackle on to his mount until one could be trained to kneel camel-fashion. The same ticket buys you into small palace museums of theatre and court dress, and a shop retails the hand-painted china of a factory established in 1758 by Carl Eugen.

To the rear, the **Blühendes Barok** (mid-March to early Nov Mon–Fri 9am–6pm, Sat & Sun 9am–7pm; €7.50; ⓦwww.blueba.de), the palace's landscaped gardens, provide a natural breather from the head-spinning opulence inside. Largely landscaped in naturalistic style, punctuated with a castle folly, a Japanese garden, an aviary and a whimsical fairytale garden – complete with kitsch sound effects – they are a relaxing place to lounge and picnic.

Practicalities

Frequent **S-Bahn** (lines S4 & S5) and mainline trains zip from Stuttgart to Ludwigsburg in about fifteen minutes arriving at the **Bahnhof**, a five-minute walk southwest of Marktplatz, itself a five-minute walk southwest of the Schloss gates. From mid-May to October a more stylish way to get here from Stuttgart is **by boat** with the Neckar-Personen-Schifffahrt (☎0711/54 99 70 60, ⓦwww .neckar-kaeptn.de), who offer relaxed two-hour cruises from Bad Cannstatt to Ludwigsburg-Hoheneck: a 25-minute walk east of the Residenzschloss – or quick journey on bus #427.

Ludwigsburg's **tourist office**, Marktplatz 6 (Mon–Sat 9am–6pm, Sun 9am–2pm; ☎07141/910 22 52, ⓦwww.ludwigsburg.de), is central and not far from one or two **hotels** including the clean and bright *Comfort Hotel Ludwigsburg*,

Schillerstrasse 19 (℡07141/941 00, Ⓦwww.hotel-comfort.com; Ⓖ), by the train station, and the similar, nearby *Hotel Favorit*, Gartenstrasse 18 (℡07141/97 67 70, Ⓦwww.hotel-favorit.de; Ⓞ), which also has a sauna and free wi-fi. The Marktplatz has several good cafés, and *Alte Sonne*, Bei der Kath. Kirche 3 (℡07141/92 52 31; closed Sun & Mon), which has an expensive selection of innovative dishes with an international flavour, such as Pinot Noir risotto or Breton-style lamb with Provence goulash, on the menu. Less expensive and opposite the palace gates is *Enoteca*, Schlossstrasse 33 (℡07141/642 26 02), which delivers fine Italian cuisine – antipasti perfect for a summer's lunch or succulent salmon in white-wine sauce – in a quietly ritzy setting.

Maulbronn

Nestled in a relatively isolated valley, 33km northwest of Stuttgart, the small town of **MAULBRONN** is famous for the medieval **Kloster Maulbronn** (℡07043/92 66 10, Ⓦwww.schloesser-und-gaerten.de), which is so well preserved it still exudes monastic contemplation and labour. Founded as a Cistercian monastery in 1140, it was dissolved during the sixteenth century after which it became a Protestant school: fans of former pupil Hermann Hesse may recognize it as the semi-fictional Mariabronn in his book *Narziss und Goldmund*. Parts still serve as a school but only for around fifty pupils.

Initially the most striking feature of the monastery is the wall that encircles it and other defensive fortifications, dating from an era when the region was wild and fairly lawless. Within the compound a tidy collection of Gothic half-timbered

▲ Kloster Maulbronn

buildings reveal themselves, looking much as they would have done five hundred years ago.

The Klosterkirche and around

You can wander the compound free of charge, and there's a useful information board showing the layout and original uses of the buildings outside the **visitor centre** (March–Oct daily 9am–5.30pm; Nov–Feb Tues–Sun 9.30am–5pm). The visitor centre will also sell you a ticket (€5) for some of the most notable buildings in the compound, particularly the church and refectory, and loan you a moderately useful audio guide (€2). The **Klosterkirche** is a typically Cistercian bare-bones affair with no tower and little decoration, though over time works of art and decorations were commissioned to brighten the place up. If anything, decoration was more important in the **refectory** where it was part of a conscious attempt to help distract the mind from the paltriness of meals. Some of the frescoes here were the work of Jerg Ratgeb, who also adorned the ceilings of the **well-house** in the courtyard where monks washed before each meal. Here he depicts events from the monastery's history, as well as a severe self-portrait; he left the work unfinished to become embroiled in the early sixteenth-century Peasants' War, and was quartered in Pforzheim's marketplace for his trouble.

The rest of the monastery

No other buildings are open to the public, but you can walk around the complex – look out for the **Faustturm**, the residence of Dr Faust, a magician who claimed to be able to make gold, and was given a job by an unscrupulous abbot. Faust was a celebrity in his time and the subject of fables in the 1587 *Faustbuch*, published half a century after his death. Contemporary intellectuals certainly took him seriously, and much later various German literary giants – particularly Lessing, Goethe and Thomas Mann – dwelt on him in their exploration of power and absolute knowledge, which served to mythologize Faust. Another striking building in the compound is the **Jagdschloss**, a turreted Renaissance-era affair built by the dukes of Württemberg as a hunting lodge but now part of the school. As you wander between these buildings look out for remnants of a complicated **irrigation system**, which distributed water around the compound and supplied a series of fish ponds.

Practicalities

The journey from Stuttgart to Maulbronn is not as easy as it could be and requires either taking the S4 to Bretten or a train to Mühlacker before taking bus #700 to the monastery from either. Maulbronn is as easy to reach from Karlsruhe, 30km to the east, using trains that follow a branch line to Maulbronn West via Bruchsal. Buses then complete the remaining 4km to the monastery.

The town's **tourist office**, Klosterhof 31 (Mon & Thurs 8am–noon & 1–5.30pm, Tues & Wed 8am–noon & 1–4.30pm, Fri 8am–1.30pm, Sat & Sun 11am–5pm; ☎07043/10 30, ⊛www.maulbronn.de), is in the Rathaus and can help with **accommodation** though there are plenty of places along the main road with "*Zimmer Frei*" signs as well as the good traditional *Hotel Klosterpost*, Frankfurter Strasse 2 (☎07043/10 80, ⊛www.hotel-klosterpost .de; ❹). For **food** try the decent Italian *Klosterkatz*, Klosterhof 21 (☎07043/87 38), atmospherically located in the courtyard of the monastery – one of a couple of options here.

The Swabian Alb and around

Rising as a steep escarpment around 50km south of Stuttgart, the upland plateau of the **Swabian Alb** runs southwest, to all but join the southern Black Forest. A bleak climate and poor soils have made the Alb a sparsely populated and remote region – with a strong local dialect and identity. It's only lightly explored by visitors, who tend mostly to head to the cities around the edge of the range: **Tübingen** to the north on the Neckar River and **Ulm** to the southeast and on the Danube. Both are likeable places with interesting heritages and good restaurants and nightlife. And as regional hubs they also make great bases to explore the Swabian Alb, where the wonderful limestone scenery offers interesting **hiking** and a rash of **romantic castles** which make ideal outings. However, with few direct public transport services between the main points of interest, this is a region where it's best to have your own wheels.

Tübingen

TÜBINGEN, 40km south of Stuttgart, makes its first appearance in the history books in 1078, but the town didn't really blossom until four hundred years later when Württemberg Count Eberhard established a university here. Much of this charming medieval city still remains, with twisting cobbled lanes of bright half-timbered houses gathering below a fortress, but what really marks the place out is the university, one of Germany's best. It injects this venerable city with modern and youthful energy; one-in-four of the town's 70,000 population is directly connected with the university, so a local quip runs that the town doesn't have a university – it is one. Its celebrity scholars include Philipp Melancthon, who taught here before moving to Wittenberg; Goethe, who published his first works here; the philosopher Hegel; astronomer Johannes Keppler; and psychiatrist Alois Alzheimer. More recently Joseph Ratzinger – now Pope Benedict XVI – taught theology here and had a famously hard-line against 1960s student radicalism. A scholarly atmosphere persists around town, but that doesn't mean the students don't know how to let their hair down – the bar scene is good and punting on the Neckar good fun – and everything's much less touristy than in regional rival Heidelberg.

Arrival, information and accommodation

Tübingen's **Hauptbahnhof** and **bus station** lie beside one another an easy five-minute walk from the Eberhardsbrücke accross the Neckar and into the Altstadt. The **tourist office** is at the southern end of the bridge, An der Neckarbrücke 1 (Nov–Sept Mon–Fri 9am–7pm, Sat 9am–5pm; May–Sept also Sun 2–5pm; ☎07071/913 60, ⓦ www.tuebingen.de), and has handy town maps as well as **accommodation** listings and a booking service, which is most helpful for private rooms (❷).

Hotels and pensions

Hotel am Bad Uferweg – Freibad 2
☎07071/797 40, ⓦ www.hotel-am-bad.de. Good mid-range choice, a 2km walk from the centre alongside the river and lido, with clean, simple rooms and wi-fi. ❺

Hotel am Schloss Burgsteige 18
☎07071/929 40, ⓦ www.hotelamschloss.de.

Half-timbered place with overstuffed window boxes just below the Schloss and with fine views over town. Comes with oodles of traditional charm and a great regional restaurant (see p.452). ❹

Hotel Hospiz Neckarhalde 2 ☏07071/92 40, ⓦwww.hotel-hospiz.de. Standard mid-priced hotel whose trump card is its location a mere block from Marktplatz. ❹

Hotel Krone Uhlandstr. 1 ☏07071/13310, ⓦwww.krone-tuebingen.de. Prestigious riverside address by the Eberhardsbrücke with traditional homey rooms furnished with the occasional antique. Has its own sophisticated restaurant and free parking. ❻

Hotel Meteora Weizsäckerstr. 1 ☏07071/227 35, ⓦwww.hotel-meteora.de. Cheerful basic rooms in a spotless mid-priced hotel a 10min walk northeast of town with free on-street parking. Not all rooms are en suite, but single rooms are particularly good value. ❹

Camping and hostels

DJH Tübingen Gartenstr. 22/2 ☏07071/23 002, ⓦwww.jugendherberge.de. Riverside hostel a 5min walk east of the Altstadt with dorm beds for €21.30; rates include a good buffet breakfast. Take bus #22 from the Hauptbahnhof.

Nekar Camping Tubingen Rappenberghalde 61 ☏07071/431 45, ⓦwww.neckarcamping.de. Shaded spots on banks of Neckar around 1.5km west of the Altstadt and reached by bus #9. Two adults with a tent and car pay €12. April–Oct.

Viktor-Renner-Haus Frondsbergstr. 55 ☏07071/55 90 20. Basic hostel 1km north of the Altstadt run by the Internationaler Bund, a youth and social-work organization, which offers no-frills single and double rooms, but no breakfast. Take bus #13, #14, #18 or #19 to "Tübingen Breiter Weg". ❷

The Altstadt

No view better captures idyllic Tübingen, muse of poets and writers, than that from the Eberhardsbrücke. It overlooks the **Platanenallee**, a leafy boulevard on a narrow man-made island – certainly among the most attractive uses for landfill, which formed the basis of its construction. Punts pass serenely by and a row of pink-, mustard- and cream-coloured houses that prop each other up on the opposite riverbank look on. Behind them the old town rises up to gather around two focal squares, the **Holzmarkt** and the **Markt** from which various small streets fan out, some climbing to **Schloss Hohentübingen**.

The Hölderlinturm

Among the buildings that overlook the Neckar beside the Eberhardsbrücke, the **Hölderlinturm** (Tues–Fri 10am–noon & 3–5pm, Sat & Sun 2–5pm; €2.50) stands out as a part of the town's medieval fortifications. Named after the acclaimed poet Friedrich Hölderlin, who spent his last 36 years here, it houses memorabilia of his life and of the carpenter's family who nursed him. Much of his most original and complex work was produced here, when he was on the brink of madness. He moved to the tower from Tübingen's first hospital, the Burse on Bursagasse, the road behind, which is now student halls.

Punting the Neckar

Tübingen's stretch of willow-lined Neckar is too shallow for commerce – one factor in the town's lack of industrialization – but has also formed the basis for one of the quintessential Tübingen activities: poling a *Stocherkahn*, or punt, up and down the river.

The big event is the annual Tübingen punt race – held in May or June – where student fraternities battle it out in front of thousands of spectators. At other times in summer punting down the river with a group of friends, a picnic or crate of beer, seems as popular a student activity as any. You can join them by renting out rowing boats, pedalos and canoes – from €7.50 per hour – from Bootsvermietung Märkle, Eberhardsbrücke 1 (mid-April to Oct; ☏07071/315 29, ⓦwww.bootsvermietung-tuebingen.de), in front of the tourist office. Or let them do the work by renting the traditional twelve-seater *Stocherkahn* with a guide for €48 per hour.

Holzmarkt

A staircase at the eastern end of Bursagasse leads up to Neckargasse, which quickly curves its way up to one of Tübingen's principal squares: the **Holzmarkt**, which is dominated by Count Eberhard's Gothic, late fifteenth-century **Stiftskirche St Georg** (daily: April–Oct 9am–5pm; Nov–March 9am–4pm). Magnificent star vaulting spreads across nave and aisle roofs, and a pulpit buds from a single stem into carvings of Mary, Pope Gregory and early Christian fathers. In a choir (€1) dappled by beautiful stained glass, university founder Count Eberhard is upstaged by the mausoleum of Countess Mechthild (the work of Ulm's Hans Multscher), one of thirteen members of the House of Württemberg buried here. For two hundred years the dynasty made the town their second residence, and they hide their tombs from prying eyes behind a graceful Gothic rood-screen. Albrecht Dürer's pupil Hans Schäufelein created its centrepiece altar. The entrance ticket to the choir also provides admission to the church tower for views over the Holzmarkt and the roofscape of this part of the Altstadt.

Opposite the church's main entrance, a plaque on **Cottahaus** remembers three nights Goethe lodged here with his publisher Johann Friedrich Cotta in September 1797. Not that it was all literary business – a plaque on the adjacent student dormitory replies scurrilously, "*Hier kotzte Goethe*" ("Goethe puked here"). In earlier days, delinquent students might have found themselves on bread and water in the **Karzer**, Münzgasse 20 (prison; 20min tours; Sat & Sun 2pm; €1), for such blatant cheek. Now tourists inspect the graffiti-and-soot silhouettes they created to while away the hours during their incarceration. Tübingen also claims Hermann Hesse among its literary luminaries – the student dropout worked as a bookbinder and seller in the Buchhandlung Heckenhauser on the north side of Holzmarkt before he nurtured his own literary genius.

The Markt

From the Holzmarkt the half-timbered Kirchgasse leads west in an attractive preamble to Tübingen's extraordinary **Markt**. The town's heart and main hangout is liveliest during Monday, Wednesday and Friday markets when traders' stalls gather around the series of jolly cherubs and women who depict the seasons on the **Neptunenbrunnen**. Competing for attention behind is the Gothic **Rathaus** (1433) with its neo-Renaissance frescoes of local heroes painted to celebrate the university's four-hundredth birthday in 1877. The real Renaissance is represented here in the form of an astronomical clock (1510), above a Baroque balcony that juts out like an opera box.

Marktgasse on the lower side of the Markt runs into a network of old streets, lanes and passages that once served as a wine-growing neighbourhood. These bygone days are the subject of the **Stadtmuseum**, Kornhausstrasse 10 (Tues–Sun 10am–6pm; €2.50), at the end of the Marktgasse, in which nine hundred years of city history are carefully documented.

Schloss Hohentübingen

Back at the Markt, the walk uphill naturally leads to the handsome street of Burgsteige where several antique shops encourage loitering en route to Schloss Hohentübingen, the Württemberg dukes' Renaissance successor to an eleventh-century castle, as the 1604 triumphal arch with their coat of arms at the entrance attests. A couple of viewpoints on the outer perimeter offer fine views over the red-roofed Altstadt, while inside much of the Schloss houses university departments. However one wing contains a **Museum of Archeology and Egyptology** (March–Sept Wed–Sun 10am–6pm; Oct–April Wed–Sun 10am–5pm; €4; ☎07071/297 73 84), which is a bit disappointing even if its main treasure is one of the world's earliest sculptures: a horse carved from a mammoth tusk by an Upper-Paleolithic sculptor.

Eating, drinking and entertainment

Tübingen is a place that rewards strolling around to find somewhere good to eat or drink. The area around Haagasse west of Am Markt and the Marktplatz itself are good places to try for both cafés and bars. The **Landestheater**, Eberhard-strasse 6 (℡07071/159 29, ⊛www.landestheater-tuebingen.de), puts on plays and classical concerts.

Restaurants

Hotel am Schloss Burgsteige 18 ℡07071/929 40. Said by many to serve the best *Maultaschen* in the Land; and there's certainly an excellent selection of these regional giant ravioli, with 23 varieties – including veggie options – on the menu. Many are seasonal, like the trout or asparagus, but all are under €10, and there are fine views from the outdoor terrace too.

Ratskeller Haagasse 4 ℡07071/213 91. Upmarket traditional dishes served behind, rather than in, the Rathaus. Great for meat dishes, such as the excellent pork medallion in a Cognac cream sauce, but also known for its giant pancakes.

Weinstube Forelle Kronenstr. 8 ℡07071/240 94. Traditional wine bar and local favourite which oozes old-world charm; its walls are painted with cherubs, vines and heraldic crests. Known for its regional ingredients and cooking, the trout (*Forelle*) in almond butter is particularly good, as is the game. There's also a good selection of salads and some good local wines.

Die Würstküche Am Lustnauer Tor 8 ℡07071/927 50. No-nonsense roasts and doughy Swabian noodles are on the menu in this country-style restaurant in the west of town. Sensational *Maultaschen* too. Inexpensive and very popular, though it's spread over two floors, so getting a seat is rarely a problem.

Cafés and beer gardens

Neckarmüller Gartenstr. 4 ℡07071/278 48. Far and away the best beer garden in town, attached to a microbrewery. Also does good basic dishes, particularly bargain lunches, veggie choices and good *Maultaschen*. Mains average €10 and it's open – and usually heaving – nightly until 1am.

Tangente Jour Münzgasse 17 ℡07071/245 72. Café near the Stiftskirche and with great Altstadt atmosphere, which specializes in breakfast and light meals – excellent bagels and seasonal salads – but also serves several local beers until 1am.

Bars and clubs

Blauer Turm Lounge Friedrichstr. 21. Easy-going basement lounge with relaxed leather sofas and ambient house music until around 11pm when DJs start playing sets, the tempo picks up and the dancefloor gradually fills. Entry rarely exceeds €3.

Jazzkeller Haagasse 15 ℡07071/55 09 06. Mellow basement bar with a variety of DJs and live music, often jazz but also with an excellent hip-hop night on Thursdays. Open Wed–Sun 9pm–late.

Marktschenke Am Markt 11. Pleasant little bar on the marketplace that's popular mainly for its location: it spills out onto the square and is a good place to start a night out. Open until at least 1am.

Tangente Pfleghofstr. 10 ℡07071/230 07. Studenty place in the centre that's built for hard partying and heavy drinking; open until 3am and legendary for its raucous karaoke.

Zoo Tübingen Schleifmühleweg 86 ℡07071/97 73 00. Popular pub, beer garden and disco, about 1km west of the Altstadt. Has a very provincial atmosphere, but is highly likeable for it, and for its young, upbeat crowd.

Around Tübingen

Tübingen lies within view of the northwestern edge of the Swabian Alb, where sections of the limestone have been more resistant to erosion than the surrounding land, resulting in steep escarpments and craggy outcrops. Many of these cry out for fortresses and castles to be built on them, and over the years, that's exactly what has happened. The most impressive today are the Gothic palaces built by the Romantic movement for pure show – and in that sense are no more authentic than Disney palaces – but their impressive locations are undeniable and many come with some interesting history of their own.

Schloss Lichtenstein

From its high-peak vantage point, the photogenic **Schloss Lichtenstein** (tours: Feb, March & Nov Sat & Sun 9am–noon & 1–5pm; April–Oct Mon–Sat 9am–noon & 1–5pm, Sun 9am–5.30pm; €4; ☎07129/41 02, ⓦwww .schloss-lichtenstein.de) lies on an escarpment at the edge of the Swabian Alb where views of the flat river-valley below and the ready visibility of the plains around Tübingen, 32km away, provide a feeling that you are on the edge of a mountain range. The many gabled and turreted Schloss itself was constructed in the 1840s, with its design based largely on the exaggerated literary descriptions of an earlier fortress on the site, provided by fairytale writer Wilhelm Hauff. Grand views aside, the castle's most impressive feature is its armoury. The castle is a thirty-minute walk from the village of Lichtenstein, which is connected by various bus services to Tübingen – with changes at Reutlingen; the journey takes around 45 minutes.

Burg Hohenzollern

Rising dramatically from an isolated crag 31km southwest of Tübingen **Burg Hohenzollern** (daily: mid-March to Oct 9am–5.30pm; Nov to mid-March 10am–4.30pm; €2.50 or €5 with tour; ☎07471/24 28, ⓦwww.burg -hohenzollern.de) is one of Germany's finest fairytale castles. The Romantic edifice with its medieval-looking battlements and towers was designed by Friedrich August Stüler (a pupil of Schinkel), again incorporating details of an earlier fortress on the site. The St-Michael-Kapelle with its ornate stained glass is a survivor from the original.

The castle lies 4km south of the town of **HECHINGEN** (ⓦwww.hechingen .de), which you'll need to pass through if arriving by train from Tübingen (frequent; 20min). A shuttle bus to the castle leaves from Hechingen's train station only once a day at 11.20am, returning at 4.10pm.

Ulm

ULM lies on the southern side of the Swabian Alb, around 95km southeast of Stuttgart and 85km east of Tübingen, but it's the city's location on the Danube that has shaped it most. In the Middle Ages it enabled Ulm to build great wealth from trading, boat building and textile manufacture. It became an imperial city in 1376 and then leader of the Swabian League of cities, which it used to throw its weight about on the European stage. Over time though, corruption, wars and epidemics whittled away at the city's greatness; then, in just thirty minutes in December 1944 its glorious **Altstadt** disappeared beneath 2450 tonnes of explosive. Luckily its giant Münster came out relatively unscathed, and parts of the Altstadt have been reconstructed, but Ulm has also used the opportunity to experiment with some bold modern buildings too. This sets the scene for a city that is as forward-looking as it is nostalgic and one that celebrates its **festivals** with an almost Latin passion (see p.455). The best place to appreciate Ulm's skyline is on the eastern side of the Danube in the modern and uninteresting **Neu Ulm** – a city in its own right and in Bavaria.

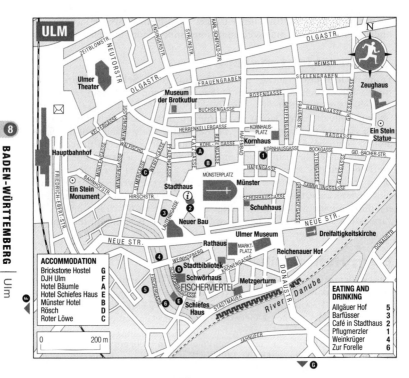

▼Ⓖ

Arrival, information and tours

Ulm's **Hauptbahnhof** lies just west of the town centre and opposite a workaday shopping precinct that separates it from the focal Münsterplatz, location of the **tourist office** at no. 50 (Mon–Fri 9am–6pm, Sat 9am–1pm; ☎0731/161 28 30, ⓦwww.tourismus.ulm.de), which sells the **Ulm Museum Card** (€6), for entry to eight city museums including all those detailed below.

A quick way to get a handle on the city and see it from one of its most attractive angles is to take a **boat cruise** on the Danube with the MS *Donau* (May–Oct Mon–Fri 2pm, 3pm & 4pm, Sat & Sun 2pm, 3pm, 4pm & 5pm; 50min; €7; ☎0731/627 51). A far more active version is offered by Sportiv Touren (☎0731/970 92 90, ⓦwww.sportivtouren.de) whose two-and-a-half-hour **canoe tour** costs €24. On land, you can rent **bikes** and tandems from Radstation, Friedrich-Ebert-Strasse (☎0731/150 02 31).

Accommodation

The best first port of call for **accommodation** is the tourist office who offer a reservation service along with extensive listings. It's relatively easy to find inexpensive Altstadt lodgings, though many places you might be offered are a little off the beaten track in Neu Ulm.

Hotels and pensions

Hotel Bäumle Kohlgasse 6 ☎0731/622 87, ⓦwww.hotel-baeumle.de. Renovated five-hundred-year-old building in the shadow of the Münster, with good-value standard hotel rooms. Free broadband and parking. Also has a rustic wood-panelled restaurant. Ⓐ

Hotel Schiefes Haus Schwörhausgasse 6 ☎0731/96 79 30, ⓦwww .hotelschiefeshausulm.de. Famously wonky, half-timbered place from 1443 with wood-beam ceilings and floors that are so crooked that the bed legs are different lengths. ❻
Münster Hotel Münsterplatz 14 ☎0731/641 62, ⓦwww.muenster-hotel.de. Cheerful, great-value and very central, if basic, hotel: not all its clean and tidy rooms are en suite, but some have Münster views. ❸
Rösch Schwörhausgasse 10 ☎0731/657 18. Clean and basic pension in a modern Fischerviertel house. ❷
Roter Löwe Ulmer Gasse 8 ☎0731/14 08 90, ⓦwww.akzent.de. Modern hotel located between the Hauptbahnhof and Münster and with its own swimming pool and sauna. ❻

Hostels

Brickstone Hostel Schützenstr. 42 ☎0731/602 62 00, ⓦwww.brickstone-hostel.de. Friendly, clean and independent hostel, over the river in Neu Ulm with kitchen facilities and dorm beds in four-bed rooms from €21. From the Hauptbahnhof take bus #7 direction Willy-Brandt-Platz and get off at stop "Schützenstrasse".
DJH Ulm Grimmelfinger Weg 45 ☎0731/38 44 55, ⓦwww.jugendherberge-ulm.de. Good, clean and well-organized hostel – with large social areas – in wooded surroundings on the edge of town, 3.5km southwest of the Hauptbahnhof and accessible via bus #4 or #8 (stop "Schulzentrum"). Dorm beds cost €21.10 and there's the option of a buffet breakfast too.

The Altstadt

The vast sweep of **Münsterplatz** provides Ulm with its focal point, and when there's not some sort of event taking place here (see box below) it provides space for a Wednesday- and Saturday-morning market. The dimensions of the square are matched by the gigantic **Münster** beside, which protrudes from town like a Gothic rocket and provides an easy orientation point wherever you are. The streets south of the Münster contain the Fischerviertel, Ulm's most immediately attractive old quarter, where fisher-folk once lived. Ulm's **Rathaus** and two best **museums** lie just south of here.

Ulm's festivals

Few summer weekends go by when there's not something going on in Ulm, and particularly on its central Münsterplatz which hosts the June **Stadtfest** and a famously grand **Christmas market** in December. But the city's biggest annual bash is **Schwörwoche** (Oath Week) in late July, which centres on the Danube, and celebrates an annual mayoral address in which a pledge to honour the town's 1397 constitution is reiterated. This rather solemn affair takes place at 11am on *Schwörmontag* – the penultimate Monday in July – but is bookended by a couple of livelier celebrations. The enchanting **Lichtserenade** (Light Serenade) in which candle-lit lanterns are floated down the Danube takes place on the previous Saturday, and the big event, **Nabada**, starts at 3pm on *Schwörmontag* when all manner of vessels and raucous crew navigate their way a couple of kilometres downstream to a fairground. Water pistols feature heavily in the celebrations – and local department stores discount them on the day.

The Danube is also the focus of other traditional frolics whose origins go back to the fifteenth century and are held every four years (next in 2009 and 2013): **Fischerstechen** (Fishermen's Jousting) takes place on the river on the second and third Saturday in July and a **Bindertanz** (Coopers' Dance) is held on a pair of July Fridays the same year. Finally, the banks of the Danube also host a biannual July event, **Donaufest** (even years), which celebrates the music and culture of the communities along the river's length; Austrians, Hungarians, Serbians and Romanians arrive to sing, dance, and sell snacks and handicrafts.

The Münster

Quickly commissioned and begun in 1377, the year after Ulm received its independence, its flamboyant Gothic **Münster** (daily: Jan & Feb 9am–4.45pm; March & Oct 9am–5.45pm; April–June & Sept 9am–6.45pm; July & Aug 9am–7.45pm) reflected the city's incredible ambitions. Though only a parish church, it was designed for a standing congregation of twenty thousand – more than twice the population of city at the time – and plans included far and away the world's tallest spire.

From any angle the dimensions of the powerful openwork spire impress. Following the guiding principle of Gothic church architecture to draw the observer's eyes to the heavens, medieval architect Matthäus Böblinger exaggerated the principle a little too much for the workmanship of the day, for in 1492 stones rained from the tower mid-build onto a Sunday congregation. Böblinger fled Ulm in disgrace and his spire was fudged until nineteenth-century Romantics rediscovered the medieval plans and applied their superior know-how: it finally reached 161.6m in 1890. Views of the Black Forest and, on clear days, the Alps, are possible, framed by stone filigree as you gasp up 768 lung-busting steps (€4) up to a height of 143m.

On entering and adjusting to the relative gloom inside the church, it takes a moment for its giant dimensions to sink in. Again, the eye is drawn upwards by the Münster's lofty 41.6m-high nave. And halfway along it, the **pulpit** does this too: in its cobweb-fine carving a smaller staircase corkscrews up to a perch that would be unreachable by humans, and so symbolizes that the words come from a higher place. Futher along the elegant 26m-high **tabernacle** is also eye-catching as is the vast 1471 fresco that covers the entire high chancel arch with a sermon on damnation and the Last Judgement.

However, the most extraordinary workmanship in the church lies just behind, in the **choir**, which is spangled with light from some equally exquisite medieval stained glass – temporarily removed and so saved during World War II. The late Gothic choir-stalls include some of the finest examples of German wood-carving and illustrate the city's medieval charter of civil rights – symbolically reiterated in the annual *Schwörwoche* (see p.455). Jörg Syrlin the Elder's vivacious ten sibyls are a nod to classical humanism, while opposite are representations of poets and scholars from Greek and Roman antiquity.

Give yourself time to really soak in all the detail and atmosphere here, and try to attend a thirty-minute **organ concert** (Mon–Sat noon; €2) when eight thousand pipes test the church's phenomenal acoustics.

The Fischerviertel

Leaving the Münsterplatz behind, a downhill walk from the tourist information office – inside American architect Richard Meier's Postmodern Stadthaus – brings you to a snug riverside district where narrow lanes crisscross streams and which once served as the home of medieval artisans, whose legacies are still visible: pulleys that hoisted goods to top-floor warehouses still dangle at the ready, a pretzel is carved in a baker's door-frame at Fischergasse 22, a boatman at Fischergasse 18. But the quirkiest and most time-worn place of all is the 1443 **Schiefes Haus**, which slumps into the stream on its piles, every bit the crooked house of its name, and is now a hotel (see p.455). Moments north is the **Schwörhaus** (Oath House), where Ulm residents gather on *Schwörmontag* (see p.455) to hear their mayor pledge a 1397 city oath "to be the same man to rich and poor, without reservation, in all common and honourable matters". Meanwhile, just south of the Schiefes Haus you can climb onto the 1480 riverside defence wall and walk downstream to another crooked building: the fourteenth-century defensive tower of the **Metzgerturm**, the "Leaning Tower of Ulm", which is two metres off the vertical.

The Rathaus and around

From the Metzgerturm it's a brief walk uphill to the Rathaus and attendant square. Catching the eye here is the all-glass pyramid of the **Zentralbibliothek** (Central Library) – designed by Gottfried Böhm and completed in 2004. Opposite lies Syrlin's startling Fischkastenbrunnen (fish-crate fountain), which depicts three saints dressed as knights, in which fishmongers once kept their produce fresh.

But it's the sixteenth-century **Rathaus** itself that demands most attention, with its decorative frescoes that salute Ulm's medieval heyday as an imperial merchant: tubby Danube merchant-ships gather beneath the crests of trading partners; vices and virtues are caricatured; and tributes paid to emperors and electors. Inside hangs a replica of Albrecht Ludwig Berblinger's hang-glider. The "**Tailor of Ulm**", crash-landed into the Danube in 1811, eighty years before his pioneering countryman Otto Lilienthal took to the air. Ulm has since warmed to its tailor as an eccentric hero – a plaque on Herdbrücke marks the spot where Berblinger took off – but in his day Berblinger was mocked mercilessly. Worn down by ceaseless jibes, his business in tatters, he died bankrupt in 1825, a drunkard and gambler. Ironically, his design has since proved to be workable, and only the lack of thermals on the day caused failure and ruin.

Kunsthalle Weishaupt and the Ulmer Museum

The square on the north side of the Rathaus, Hans-und-Sophie-Scholl-Platz, is named for two local students who organized anti-Nazi resistance by overtly distributing handbills, for which they were executed. Overlooking it is the striking modern building of **Kunsthalle Weishaupt** (Tues, Wed & Fri–Sun 11am–5pm, Thurs 11am–8pm; €6; ☎0731/161 43 60, ⓦwww.kunsthalle-weishaupt.de), which is most extraordinary at night when its illuminations makes it resemble a giant ice-cube. Inside, it's equally striking, its giant, bright clear rooms containing the vivid colours of vast modern and Pop Art canvases: Warhol, Klee, Macke, Kandinsky and Picasso are among those represented.

The Kunsthalle is joined by a bridge to the **Ulmer Museum** (Tues, Wed & Fri–Sun 11am–5pm, Thurs 11am–8pm; €3.50, free Fri; ☎0731/161 43 30, ⓦwww.museum.ulm.de), the town history museum, and a combination ticket (€8) allows you to visit both. Much of it is a crash course in Ulm and Swabian arts from the Middle Ages to the present, with particular reference to the Renaissance. Illustrations depict a powerful city dominated by a stumpy Münster and enclosed within river fortifications. Among archeological exhibits don't miss the stunningly old and atavistic *Löwenmensch*, a 28cm-tall carving of a human form with a lion's head from 30,000 BC.

Eating, drinking and entertainment

The Fischerviertel and the streets just north of Münsterplatz are both ideal for finding somewhere to **eat** and for **bar-hopping**. For events, pick up the monthly listings magazine *Spazz* at the tourist office, which also sells tickets.

Restaurants

Allgäuer Hof Fischergasse 12 ☎ 0731/674 08. Fine old-fashioned *Gastätte*, with dark wood panelling, where mobile phones are banned. Uniquely almost everything on the menu is served on vast sweet or savoury *Pfannkuchen* (crêpes); prices are modest with most mains around €10.

Pflugmerzler Pfluggasse 6. The full menu of Swabian cooking, all excellently prepared, in a cosy restaurant hidden on an alley off Hafenbad north of the Münster. Closed Sat eve & Sun.

Zur Forelle Fischergasse 25 ☎ 0731/639 24. One of Ulm's best addresses is certainly one of its most charming. This snug 1626 Fischerviertel house – which has a Napoleonic cannonball lodged in one wall – is a place where the tall have to stoop. An Ulm dish worth trying is the spicy herb and salmon soup with garlic. Among the mains (average €15) try the *Gaisburger Marsch* (a hearty beef, potato and *Spätzle* stew), to fill an empty stomach, or the trout (*Forelle*) speciality if you want to tantalize a

more delicate palate. Einstein and Karajan both dined here on their visits to Ulm, and it's popular enough to merit booking ahead.

Cafés and pubs

Barfüsser Lautenberg 1 ☎ 0731/602 11 10. Ulm's best beer-hall and microbrewery, with a range of traditional food to complement the beers. Mains cost €7–13; or simply have an excellent home-made pretzel.

Café in Stadthaus Münsterplatz 50 ☎ 0731/600 93. Stylish, modern café with Münster views and good light meals for €7.50–15.50, but best of all are its excellent home-made cakes.

Weinkrüger Weinhofberg 7 ☎ 0731/649 76. Rustic wine-bar and restaurant in a cosy half-timbered old bathhouse and tannery. Has over ninety different wines by the glass and is one of a clutch of places with a beer garden in the vicinity. Its traditional German mains cost €8–15.

Upper Danube Valley

On its southeastern side the Swabian Alb tends to fall away more gradually, but in many places the Danube has cut a tremendous gorge through the rock, producing steep cliffs and spectacular scenery, particularly in the **Upper Danube Valley**. Much of this is protected as the Naturpark Obere Donau, which is centred on this forested and steep-sided limestone valley and particularly colourful in spring when wildflowers bloom and during its magnificent autumn foliage, all best appreciated on hikes that head up to the many viewpoints above the valley.

With a railway along much of its length, the region is very accessible for day-trips from Ulm. However, this very quiet region also has plenty of inexpensive accommodation, encouraging longer exploration, particularly by bike following the Donauradweg (**Danube cycle path**) that begins at the source of the Danube at the unassuming provincial town of Donaueschingen and follows the Danube for 199km to Ulm. There's plenty of smaller **wildlife** along the route to watch, particularly on the marshy right bank of the Danube between Ehingen and Ulm, which teems with waterfowl.

Blaubeuren

BLAUBEUREN, 20km west of Ulm, is not in the Danube Valley but rather the source of the tributary Blau River, which joins the Danube in Ulm's Fischerviertel. Nevertheless it's a good first-stop on a journey to the higher reaches of the Danube, and a good day-trip from Ulm, particularly if you have time to **hike** in the rocky hills that cradle the town.

The town's key sights are a half-timbered former **monastery** that was only in use for 25 years before the Reformation and beside it the **Blautopf**, the source of the Blau. The rich blue waters of this twenty-metre-deep pool are transformed into green then yellowy brown by rain. Beside it is the **Hammerschmiede**, a mid-eighteenth-century mill and smithy which is at the trailhead of a number of hikes.

Hourly trains from Ulm (11min) pull into Blaubeuren's **Bahnhof**, on the southern edge of town, about a five-minute walk from the signposted **tourist office**, Aachgasse 7 (Fri 2–5pm, Sat & Sun 10am–noon & 2–5pm; ☎07344/92 10 25, ⓦwww.blaubeuren.de), who have good information on local hikes, but given their limited hours, you're as well to get this from Ulm's tourist office in advance.

Sigmaringen

The small regional town of **SIGMARINGEN** is known for and entirely dominated by the vast Gothic **Schloss Sigmaringen** (tours daily: Feb–April & Nov 9.30am–4.30pm; May–Oct 9am–4.45pm; €6; ⓦwww.hohenzollern.com), another castle that dates from the Romantic movement, and in a league with the best of them. Built as a medieval fortress, it was brutally sacked in the Thirty Years' War, then subject to a large domestic fire in the late nineteenth century, so today only two towers from the original structure remain. Owned by a branch of the Hohenzollern family, the Schloss provided a useful foothold during the Prussian unification of Germany in the nineteenth century. Its impressive armoury is testament to the military might that underpinned this and the grizzly highlight of the castle tours.

Sigmaringen's **train station** lies on the eastern side of the town centre and an easy five-minute walk from the **tourist office**, Schwabstrasse 1 (Mon–Fri 10am–6pm, Sat & Sun 10am–4pm; ☎07571/10 62 24, ⓦwww.sigmaringen .de), which sits in a huddle of houses in the Altstadt below the Schloss. Among the accommodation options here is the *Traube*, Fürst-Wilhelm-Strasse 19 (☎07571/645 10, ⓦwww.hotel-traube-sigmaringen.de; ❸), a half-timbered old-fashioned place with cheerful rooms and a reliable, inexpensive regional restaurant with a particularly good line in salads.

Beuron

Some of the most dramatic sections of the Upper Danube Valley lie around the village of **BEURON**, 28km west of Sigmaringen. Beuron gathers around an enormous Baroque **monastery**, which is of scant interest but for the chance to attend a **service** (Mon–Sat 11.15am & 6pm, Sun 10am & 3pm) at the monastery church and hear monks who are world famous for their expert **Gregorian chanting**.

Beuron is also at the centre of some great **hiking** territory. Obvious and rewarding destinations include the **Knopfmacherfelsen**, a viewpoint 6km from town, and **Burg Wildenstein**, an eleventh-century stronghold in a precarious spot above the Danube that's now one of Germany's most atmospheric ⚲ **youth hostels** (☎07466/411). Dorm beds cost €21.70 and include breakfast; half- (€26.60) and full-board (€30.50) are also possible – useful since there's nothing else in the vicinity.

Beuron's **tourist office**, Kirchstrasse 18 (Mon–Fri 9am–noon & 1–4pm; ☎07579/921 00, ⓦwww.beuron.de), is a very modest affair, but has some information on hiking routes. More useful is the large map on a board in the car park opposite, where you can get a good idea of the various well-marked local routes.

The Bodensee

As a giant body of water with a balmy dry climate, the **Bodensee**, or **Lake Constance**, has long been Germany's Riviera. It hugs the country's southwest border with Austria and Switzerland and to the south the Alps rear up, creating a fine backdrop. Most German towns along the lake are on the north shore and include the Bavarian town of **Lindau**, the transport hub of **Friedrichshafen** and the archetypal medieval lakeside settlement **Meersburg**. The upbeat city of **Konstanz** on its southern shore is the most cosmopolitan place on the lake, and is easily the best base with regular ferry services across the lake and to nearby **islands** making for easy, rewarding day-trips. Given the good weather, the Bodensee region is known above all for outdoor activities, particularly hiking and cycling on lakeside trails that connect its small towns, vineyards, orchards and beaches. Watersports are also popular, but most visitors simply sunbathe, swim and mess around in the water, which averages a pleasant 20°C in the summer providing a respite from the humidity. Summer is the most popular holiday season, but such popularity brings congested roads and booked-up hotels, making spring perhaps a better time to visit, when fruit trees blossom, while autumn is the prime time for those interested in the wine harvest.

Travelling on and around the Bodensee

With a circumference of 273km the Bodensee is a respectable body of water that can produce truly sea-like conditions – waves pound the shores during poor weather and shipwrecks litter the lake bed. However these days, travelling around the Bodensee has become safe and most visits to the region will involve catching a ferry or two – indeed should, as sailing the lake is part of the experience.

The lake's lifeline service is the **car ferry** between Konstanz and Meersburg, a fifteen-minute crossing, 24 hours a day (hourly midnight–5am; every 15min 5.30am–9pm; every 30min 9pm–midnight; car with driver €7.20; ☏07531/80 30, ⓦ www.sw.konstanz.de). Another useful service is the fifty-minute crossing on **Der Katamaran** between Konstanz and Friedrichshafen (hourly 5am–6pm or later; €9.50 one-way; ☏07541/971 09 00, ⓦ www.der-katamaran.de). Otherwise the network of services between lakeside towns is organized by a number of companies, particularly **BSB** (ⓦ www.bsb-online.com) and **OBB** (ⓦ www.bodenseeschiffahrt.de).

Thankfully things are simplified by **Euregio Bodensee**, a regional public transport system of ferries, buses and trains in Germany, Austria and Switzerland. Various day-tickets (ⓦ www.euregiokarte.com) are offered for a network that's divided into zones: a €27 day-pass gives you a run of the entire system and is sold at tourist offices, train stations and ferry terminals. Use of the network is also included in the price of the main **Bodensee Erlebniskarte**, which provides admission or substantial discounts to a range of regional attractions. It's available from tourist and ferry offices between April and October and costs €69 for three days, €89 for seven, €119 for fourteen; prices roughly halve without public transport included.

The 268km-long **Bodensee-Radweg** (ⓦ www.bodensee-radweg.com) is a network of cycle paths around the lake; bikes are allowed on most ferries and trains – allowing for adaptable itineraries if the weather turns or you get tired.

Lindau

Bavaria begins – and the German shore of the Bodensee ends – at the idyllic resort of **LINDAU**, hard by the Austrian border and with the Austrian town of Bregenz clearly visible across the lake. Though the modern town sprawls for several kilometres along the mainland shore, it's the picture-postcard medieval Altstadt on an island in the lake, with its sunny, south-facing harbour, mild climate and luxuriant summer vegetation that makes Lindau a fully-fledged tourist honeytrap. Crowded it may be, but it's sweet for all that, with barely an eyesore in sight.

Arrival, information and accommodation

Lindau's old town is linked to the mainland by rail and road causeways. There are vast **car parks** along the north shore of the island, while the charmingly old-fashioned **Hauptbahnhof** is on the western side of the island close to the harbour, with the **tourist office** opposite at Ludwigstrasse 68 (mid-March to to mid-Oct Mon–Fri 9am–1pm & 2–6pm, Sat 2–6pm; mid-June to mid-Sept also Sun 10am–2pm; mid-Oct to mid-March Mon–Fri 9am–noon & 2–5pm; ☏08382/26 00 30, ⓦwww.lindau.de).

The swankiest places to **stay** in Lindau are generally along the harbour. There are plenty of **apartments** or **private rooms** available in Lindau too – ask at the tourist office; the **campsite** is right by the Austrian border at Fraunhoferstrasse 20 (☏08283/722 36, ⓦwww.park-camping.de; mid-March to mid-Nov).

Bayerischer Hof Seepromenade ☏08382/91 50, ⓦwww.bayerischerhof-lindau.de,. A classic alpine grand-hotel on the harbour with handsome, spacious rooms in traditional style. **❼**

DJH Lindau Herbergsweg 11 ☏08382/967 10, ⓦwww.lindau.jugendherberge.de. The town's youth hostel is on the mainland in the district of Reutlin. Bus #1 or #2 from Altstadt to ZUP, then bus #3, stop Jugendherberge. From €21.90.

Gasthof Inselgraben Hintere Metzgergasse 4–8 ☏08382/54 81, ⓦwww.inselgraben.de.

Affordable and cyclist-friendly Altstadt choice. **❸**

Reutemann Seepromenade ☏08382/91 50, ⓦwww.reutemann-lindau.de. A little more informal than its sister hotel, the *Bayerischer Hof*, but still stylish and with arguably the better, more central location on the harbour. **❻**

Spiegel-Garni In der Grub 1 ☏08382/949 30, ⓦwww.hotel-spiegel-garni.de. Very pleasant hotel in the Altstadt, with rooms that range from the simple to the extravagantly alpine in style. **❹**

The Altstadt

Smart hotels and café terraces line the **harbour**, which is busy with yachts and excursion boats in summer and whose entrance is guarded by a tall lighthouse and an outsized Bavarian lion, placed there in the mid-nineteenth century. Beyond it, a spectacular backdrop of snow-capped Alps rises above the far shore. On the quay, the thirteenth-century **Mangturm** – the predecessor to the present lighthouse – has an almost Venetian look, complete with its colourful tiled roof. A little way back from the harbour stands the fourteenth-century **Rathaus**, the splendour of its stepped gables a reflection of Lindau's medieval importance as a trading centre and former free imperial city, though the colourful frescoes on the exterior – which depict the Reichstag, the imperial Diet held here in 1496 – date from the nineteenth century.

On the north side of the Rathaus, Maximilianstrasse – Lindau's main thoroughfare – runs roughly east–west across the island and is lined with tall, gabled houses, their oriel windows and Gothic arcades hinting at their antiquity. Head east to reach Marktplatz and the patrician, Baroque **Haus zum Cavazzen**, built in

1729 and reckoned to be the most beautiful of its kind on the Bodensee. It now houses the charming **Stadtmuseum** (April–Oct Tues–Fri & Sun 11am–5pm, Sat 2–5pm; €5), whose collection of religious paintings includes some extraordinary *Spottbilder* – satirical paintings from the time of the Reformation. The museum also displays glass painting, toys, furniture from the Rococo, Biedermeier and Jugendstil periods, and has a couple of rooms full of prettily painted peasant furniture and spinning wheels.

Opposite the museum, the town's main Protestant and Catholic churches stand placidly side-by-side, the hurled insults (and worse) of the Reformation and Counter-Reformation apparently forgotten. But the most interesting of Lindau's churches is the unassuming little eleventh-century **Peterskirche** on Schrannenplatz at the western end of In der Grub, parallel to Maximilianstrasse one block north, which in addition to serving as the town's war memorial also contains the *Lindauer Passion* – the only known surviving wall frescoes by Hans Holbein the Elder. Opposite the church the fourteenth-century **Diebsturm**'s absurdly picturesque appearance, complete with glittering multicoloured roof tiles, belies its prosaic function – it once served as both a jail and as part of the town's defences.

Eating, drinking and entertainment

Night-time diversions include the Marionettenoper at the Stadttheater, Fischergasse 37 (Puppet Theatre; ☎08382/94 46 50, ⓦwww.lindauer-mt.de), which puts on perfomances of classic operas using puppets, and a modern **casino**, the Spielbank Lindau, by the causeway to the mainland at Chelles-Allee 1 (☎08283/277 40, ⓦwww.spielbanken-in-bayern.de; daily 3pm–2/3am), though you'll need to be at least 21 if you want to play.

Alte Post Fischergasse 3 ☎08382/934 60. The pretty dining room serves *Schnitzels*, *Tafelspitz* and the like from around €12, and there's a sunny terrace in summer.

Ratsstuben Ludwigstr. 7 ☎08382/66 26. Specializes in fish from the lake, including eel and trout. Closed Mon & winter.

Reutemann Seepromenade. The elegant terrace here is a prime lakefront spot for *Kaffee und*

Kuchen and more substantial dishes.

Treibgut Metzgergasse 17. The spacious, pub-like place is good for a drink and has occasional live music.

Zum Sünfzen Maximilianstr. 1 ☎08382/58 65. Lindau's most atmospheric and traditional place to eat.

Friedrichshafen

Lying at the lake's widest point and with the longest promenade of any Bodensee town, **FRIEDRICHSHAFEN**, 22km west of Lindau, has the feel of a seaside resort. But the town leads a double life, as both a rather showy resort and the lake's only industrial town. It was bombed to smithereens during World War II thanks to its aviation industry, but this also made it the setting for one of the world's most intriguing aeronautical events, for it was here that Count Ferdinand von Zeppelin manufactured and launched his cigar-like airships. On July 2, 1900, his *LZ1* first drifted over the lake and three decades later, Friedrichshafen promoted itself as a hub of international travel. Airships made scheduled flights to Stockholm, Rome, Cairo and Leningrad; a Zeppelin buzzed to New York every three weeks; and the truly rich could leave Friedrichshafen to step off at Rio de Janeiro after twelve days in the clouds.

Arrival, information and accommodation

Some **trains** stop at Hafenbahnhof beside the Zeppelin Museum and port, but all pull in at the central Stadtbahnhof on the western side of the small town centre. Usefully bike rental is available at the Stadtbahnhof for €8 per day; just beside is the town's **tourist office**, Bahnhofsplatz 2 (May–Sept Mon–Fri 9am–6pm, Sat 9am–1pm; April & Oct Mon–Thurs 9am–noon & 2–5pm; Nov–March Mon–Thurs 9am–noon & 2–4pm; ☏07541/300 10, ⓦwww.friedrichshafen.de), which has a raft of regional information and lists of the good range of local accommodation.

Hotels and pensions

Buchhorner Hof Friedrichstr. 33 ☏07541/20 50, ⓦwww.buchhorn.de. Bright rooms with views over the Bodensee in the best address in town: a century-old traditional place, but with the modern conveniences of a sauna, steam room and whirlpool. The freshest fish is prepared in an acclaimed restaurant (mains around €20) and there's a charming *Weinkeller* for an aperitif. ⑥

City-Krone Schanzstr. 7 ☏07541/70 50, ⓦwww.hotel-city-krone.de. Bright and very central four-star place where terracotta tones and rattan furnishings add warmth to modern styles. Also has a small swimming pool, sauna and a restaurant with a good international menu. ⑥

Gasthof Rebstock Werastr. 35 ☏07541/950 16 40, ⓦwww.gasthof-rebstock-fn.de. A family-run house with modest homey rooms 750m northwest of the Stadtbahnhof, with its own beer garden and bikes for rent too. ⑥

Goldenes Rad Karlstr. 43 ☏07541/28 50, ⓦwww.goldenes-rad.de. Best Western hotel one block behind the harbour. The modern rooms are a bit bland but there's a fitness centre and sauna. ⑥

Maier Poststr. 1–3 ☏07541/40 40, ⓦwww.hotel-maier.de. Rustic and elegant family-run hotel in Fischbach, a sleepy district at the western edge of town, about 5km from the centre. Its restaurant is first class for game, herring and pike-perch (mains €12–23). ⑥

SEEhotel Bahnhofplatz 2 ☏07541/30 30, ⓦwww.seehotelfn.de. Comfortable designer pad and spacious business choice by the Stadtbahnhof, with spa and steam room. ⑦

Campsites and hostels

CAP Rotach Lindauer Str. 2 ☏07541/734 21. Small campsite on the lakefront, 2km east of the Hafenbahnhof and frequently linked by #7 bus to both stations. Two adults in a tent pay €15.

DJH Friedrichshafen Lindauer Str. 3 ☏07541/724 04, ⓦwww.jugendherberge-friedrichshafen.de. Popular and sociable hostel opposite *CAP Rotach*. Almost always fully booked so advance reservation is recommended. Dorms from €21.30.

The Zeppelin Museum

Friedrichshafen's most celebrated association has produced its chief site: the **Zeppelin Museum**, Seestrasse 22 (July–Sept daily 10am–6pm; May, June & Oct Tues–Sun 10am–6pm; Nov–April Tues–Sun 10am–5pm; €7.50; ☏07541/380 10, ⓦwww.zeppelinmuseum.de). Located on the promenade on the eastern side of the town centre, the collection celebrates Friedrichshafen's quirky entry into the annals of aviation history, with the advent and production of giant gas-powered rigid airships. With most museum signage in German, the English-language audio guide (€3) is extremely useful. The museum's centrepiece is a 33m section of the *Hindenburg* where you can nose around a Bauhaus-style lounge in which a pianist would play as the clouds slid by, and peek into one of its 25 tiny cabins. Also on view are the remains of the *Graf Zeppelin* engine, battered from storage. Spare a thought for the engineers cocooned in its bubble for three-hour stints to nurse a constant 50°C temperature. More fascinating is archive film footage of the Zeppelin era showing the enthusiastic reception they received wherever they appeared and how hundreds of people were needed to land the things.

Trace its highs and lows before you inspect relics of the disaster: the charred jacket of radio operator Willy Speck; memorial ribbons – simple laments from

Look, no wings!

In the late nineteenth century **Count Ferdinand von Zeppelin**, a maverick figure with an impressive walrus moustache and military honours, turned his attention – and most of his wealth – to airships. His pioneering *LZ1* drifted above the Bodensee in 1900, to great enthusiasm and jubilation. Later the Zeppelins acquired their first real use as bombers and scouts in World War I.

In 1928 the pride of the fleet, *Graf Zeppelin*, hummed across the Atlantic in four days, fifteen hours and forty four minutes; the year after that she circumnavigated the globe in just twelve days' air-time and a golden age of luxurious airships had arrived. Once times improved to well under two days, a scheduled service to New York was set up, with passengers paying around 1200 Reichsmark for a return ticket – around seven months' worth of the average wage of the time.

No matter that she had made 590 flights, 114 of them ocean-going, the *Graf Zeppelin*'s days were numbered as soon as 245m sister-ship *Hindenburg* erupted into a fireball in New Jersey on May 6, 1937, killing 36 passengers and crew (61 survived); later analysis suggests that a static spark from earthed mooring-lines ignited the varnish on the linen skin and the blaze spread to the airship's hydrogen tanks. Ironically the airship had been designed to use inert and non-combustible helium, but the US withdrew permission to use this fuel.

The disaster, along with easier progress elsewhere in the aviation industry, put Zeppelins out of favour for a long time, although there has been a good deal of research and development since and they're now often seen over the Bodensee. These airships are non-rigid, filled with helium, and run by the Deutsches-Zeppelin-Reederei, Allmannsweiler Strasse 132, Friedrichshafen (from €190 for 30min; ☎0700/93 77 20 01, @www.zeppelinflug.de). These ships are only a tenth the size of the originals and climb to 2000m to take twelve well-heeled passengers for jaunts above the Bodensee.

families; bombastic requiems from the Nazis who hijacked the service to enshrine its victims as martyrs of the Third Reich; and a clock stripped to bare metal forever stuck at 7.25.

Oddly, the top floor of the museum is devoted to regional art from Gothic to modern. Otto Dix, who moved to lakeside village Hemmenhofen in 1936, provides bite among whimsical canvases and is in withering form in *Vanity*, an update of the old-masters' favourite with a brassy nude shadowed by a bent crone.

The Uferpromenade to the Schlosskirche

Nowhere is the Bodensee's regional moniker, the "Swäbische Meer" (Swabian Sea), more apparent than at the bustling harbour in front of the Zeppelin Museum. Ferries come and go with a roar of engines bound for Switzerland or to Konstanz and Lindau; passengers amble with ice creams; and fishermen unload crates of *Felchen*, a Bodensee delicacy somewhere between salmon and trout. The 22m **Moleturm** tower on a breakwater provides an elevated view of the action. Boats – rowing, motor and pedaloes – are for rent from €5 per hour at the smaller harbour to its west beside the **Uferpromenade**, full of summer strollers admiring a lake view that is speckled with sails, the white-capped Swiss Alps behind. It's especially scenic at sunset – when the snow glows in the dusk.

The **Zeppelindenkmal** stands like an exclamation mark in the formal gardens behind the path, although the bronze obelisk to Friedrichshafen's shepherd is more stately than the mawkish **Zeppelinbrunnen** behind: the copy of a 1909 fountain by Munich sculptor Bruno Diamant depicts a naked child cradling a blimp atop the world.

At the western end of Uferpromenade, cultural centre **Graf-Zeppelin-Haus** (Ⓦwww.gzh.de) juts in acute angles, a replacement for a swish spa-hotel of the late nineteenth century that had been home to a French commandant for eleven years after the war. The path meanders into neat residential backstreet Olgastrasse. At its end, beside a neo-Renaissance pier, is the Schloss of the Württemberg dukes, fashioned from a Benedictine priory in 1654, still in the family's hands and strictly private. Behind it are the landmark onion-domes of Christian Thumb's Baroque **Schlosskirche** (daily mid-April to Oct 9am–6pm), with a stucco garden on its roof that was re-created during postwar restoration.

Eating

For picnic items try the Saturday **farmers' market** on Adenauerplatz, with all sorts of home-made sausages and cheeses to sample, plus Italian mozzarella and fresh regional fruit. All the best places for a sit-down meal are along Friedrichshafen's **seafront**, although many of the better hotels (see p.463) also have excellent restaurants.

Glückler Olgastr. 23 ☏07541/221 64. Small *Weinstube* where zander, Bodensee *Felchen* and trout are on the menu and a baffling variety of the house special Breton galettes, from simple butter to a feast of cheese, ham, onions, tomato and Roquefort liberally laced with garlic. Prices are moderate, mains average ₣11.

Kurgarten Graf-Zeppelin-Haus, Olgastr. 20 ☏07541/320 33. Views of yachts on the Bodensee accompany international dishes – steak and scampi or good veggie choices like spinach-stuffed mushrooms or courgette ratatouille (mains around €14) eaten on the Seeterrasse and in the modern

conservatory of Friedrichshafen's finest restaurant. The *Panoramacafé* above is appropriately named.

Lammgarten Uferstr. 27 ☏07541/2 46 08. Inexpensive restaurant where €8 will buy you fresh *Felchen* plucked from the Bodensee, and *Schnitzel*, served on a leafy terrace behind the yacht marina.

Museums-Restaurant Hafenbahnhof ☏07541/333 06. You'll need patience to claim a table on the terrace above the harbour's comings and goings. The menu here is internationally eclectic, ranging from Swabian specials to Norwegian salmon.

Meersburg

With a foreboding and wonderfully ramshackle castle looming over a narrow lakefront strip of half-timbered houses, **MEERSBURG**, 17km to the west of Friedrichshafen, is something of a living snapshot of a fairytale Germany. Small wonder then that in peak season, coach parties and day-trippers crush in. But arrive early or linger till dusk to watch the town watchman do his rounds and you'll truly appreciate the magic. There are also a couple of quirky sights – the **Pfahlbauten** open-air museum and **Basilika Birnau** – that are worth exploring in the area. Good local festivals include the **Winzerfest** in the first weekend in July when wine, food and song enliven Meersburg's streets and the **Bodensee Weinfest**, the second weekend in September, when you can sample the latest vintage.

Arrival, information and accommodation

Meersburg doesn't have a train station, but **buses** #7395 and #7394 from Friedrichshafen arrive here every thirty minutes, dropping passengers at the top of the Altstadt and at the ferry terminal just west of the old town. From here it's a stiff uphill walk up Steigstrasse to the **tourist office** at Kirchstrasse 4 (May–Sept Mon–Fri 9am–6.30pm, Sat 10am–noon; Oct–April Mon–Fri 9am–noon and

2–4.30pm; ☎07532/44 04 00, ⓦwww.meersburg.de). They can provide full **accommodation** listings including a number of the private rooms which are the main budget option; some advertise themselves with *Zimmer Frei* signs along Unterstadtstrasse, which runs just behind the sea front.

🏃 **Gasthof zum Bären** Marktplatz 11 ☎07532/432 20, ⓦwww.baeren -meersburg.de. Window boxes are overstuffed with geraniums at this romantic old place which harks back to the thirteenth century. Rooms are good value considering they're in the heart of the Altstadt, even if they're a little snug. ⑤

Hotel Löwen Marktplatz 2 ☎07532/430 40, ⓦwww.hotel-loewen-meersburg.de. Opposite and very similar to the *Bären*, also family-run and with

cosy wood-clad interiors, a good restaurant and snug wine-bar. ⑤

Seehotel Off Uferpromenade 51 ☎07532/447 40, ⓦwww.hotel.off.mbo.de. Lakeside option beside vineyards, which is run on feng shui and eco-friendly principles. Most rooms have a private balcony and lake views. ⑤

Seehotel zur Münz Seestr. 7 ☎07532/435 90, ⓦwww.seehotel-zur-muenz.de. Lakefront accommodation with fairly standard rooms, though many have balconies and overlook the lake. ⑤

The Altstadt

Impressively entered from the modern town and main road via the medieval **Obertor** gate, almost all Meersburg's Altstadt is pedestrianized. A short way downhill from the gate is the small **Marktplatz**, from where Steigstrasse runs down past rows of touristy shops to the lakefront and pleasant **Seepromenade**. Meanwhile a lane parallel to Steigstrasse leads to the **Altes Schloss** and **Neues Schloss**, the formidable old castle and Baroque palace that dominate the upper town.

The Altes Schloss

The austere **Altes Schloss** (daily: March–Oct 9am–6.30pm; Nov–Feb 10am–6pm; €8.50; ☎07532/800 00, ⓦwww.burg-meersburg.de), with its origins dating back to the Merovingian king Dagobert I in 628 AD, claims to be Germany's oldest castle. It's certainly archetypal: moats, dungeons, a great hall, manifold turrets, old armour and weaponry, portraits of glowering ancestors and general heavy atmosphere are all present. The public can visit thirty furnished rooms decorated in the style of various eras, right up to the cheery and flowery Biedermeier quarters of Annette von Droste-Hülshoff (1797–1848). Arguably Germany's greatest female poet, she lived here when the castle belonged to her brother-in-law, Baron Joseph von Lassberg, finding inspiration for her Romantic angst-racked verses in the castle's severity. The bedroom where she died on May 24, 1848, and her study are both treated with shrine-like reverence.

The Neues Schloss

The general cheerlessness of the Altes Schloss finally inspired the powerful prince-bishops of Konstanz – who'd had it as their summer residence since 1268 – to build a more civilized palace next door in the eighteenth century. Baroque supremo Balthasar Neumann was drafted in for the purpose and the **Neues Schloss** is the pastel-pink result. It was only enjoyed for fifty years until secularization in 1802, but the views from gardens over roofs to the shimmering Bodensee continue to enchant, and are openly accessible. They tend to top the municipal gallery (April–Oct daily 10am–1pm & 2–6pm; €4; ☎07532/440 49 00, ⓦwww.schloesser-und-gaerten.de) inside, though its exhibits on local flying-boat pioneer Claude Dornier are of interest to aeronautical fans.

Eating

The **cafés** and **restaurants** along Meersburg's seafront and Unterstadtstrasse behind are good for local fish. In the upper town *Zum Bären* and *Hotel Löwen* (see opposite) are both great for traditional food.

Cafe Gross Unterstadtstr. 22. ☎07532/60 55. Worth seeking out for the best home-made cakes in town.

Café im Barrockschloss Neues Schloss ☎07532/800 00. It seems fitting and elegant to enjoy coffee and cakes on the terrace of the Baroque Schloss.

Gutschänke Seminarstr. 4 ☎07532/80 76 30. Patience and quick feet will win you a table on the terrace for idyllic views and

a summer lunch of light bites – try the rich home-made *Leberwurst* (liver sausage). Mains average €9.

Zum Becher Höllgasse 4 ☎07532/90 09. Cosy and cheerfully cluttered, rustic wine-bar serving the finest cuisine in Meersburg with good traditional food: the *Rostbraten* with *Spätzle* (€17) is excellent, as are the local fish dishes. A big wine list complements the food and it's good for just a drink too. Closed Mon.

The Pfahlbauten Museum and Basilika Birnau

Some 8km northwest of Meersburg are two sights – a reconstructed prehistoric hamlet and a Baroque church – that are reachable by the hourly #7395 bus between Friedrichshafen and Überlingen. The well-publicized **Pfahlbauten Museum** (April–Sept 8am–6pm; Oct 9am–5pm; March & Nov Sat & Sun 9am–5pm; €5.50; ⓦwww.pfahlbauten.de) features open-air reconstructions of Stone and Iron Age dwellings whose forms are based on archeological remains found here. Jolly and obligatory German-only tours take you round the structures which are famously supported on huge stakes driven into the lake. Sadly, they're not quite true to life though, since lake levels were lower then, putting these structures firmly on dry land.

A twenty-minute uphill walk through vineyards from the Pfahlbauten takes you to the fine Rococo **Basilika Birnau** (Wed 7.30am–5.30pm, Sun 7.30am–7pm), designed by, among others, Peter Thumb, painter Gottfried Bernhard Göz and sculptor Josef Anton Feichtmayr. The furiously lurid interior is a riot of optical illusions, including a mirror in the cupola. One curious altar to the right of the main one is dedicated to St Bernard of Clairvaux, whose words were said to be as sweet as honey. A cherub, sucking a finger he's dipped in a bees' nest illustrates this.

Konstanz

Hard on the Swiss border on the southern side of the lake, the likeable university town of **KONSTANZ** came out of the war almost unscathed – it was deemed too close to neutral Switzerland to be bombed – ensuring its **Altstadt** is well preserved. Though with Roman origins, today's settlement dates largely from the Middle Ages when the town thrived as a Free Imperial City, gaining fame particularly between 1414 and 1418 when the Council of Konstanz met here to heal the Great Schism in the Catholic Church in a restructuring that replaced three popes with one. Altstadt sightseeing aside, Konstanz also makes a good base for **day-trips** to nearby islands, particularly **Mainau** and **Reichenau**. With one in seven of the population students, Konstanz is a bustling town, and the **restaurant and bar scene** correspondingly lively in what's otherwise a very staid region.

The town's biggest annual festival is **Seenachtsfest** in August when the lake mirrors a firework bonanza.

Arrival, information and local transport

Although smaller **passenger ferries** dock at the town's waterfront, **car ferries** from Meersburg arrive 4km northwest of town in the suburb of Staad, from which bus #1 runs to the city centre. Konstanz has two **train stations**, which lie almost beside one another and between the harbour and Altstadt: the **Deutscher Bahnhof** is the southern terminus of the Schwarzwaldbahn, from Offenburg via Triberg and Willingen; the **Schweizer Bahnhof** has connections to many Swiss destinations. **Tourist information** is in the north end of the German station at Bahnhofplatz 13 (April–Oct Mon–Fri 9am–6.30pm, Sat 9am–4pm, Sun 10am–1pm; Nov–March Mon–Fri 9am–12.30pm & 2–6pm; ☎07531/13 30 30, ⓦwww.konstanz.de/tourismus), as is Kultur-Rädle, Bahnhofplatz (☎07531/290 75 31), who offer **bike rental** from €10 per day. The hub of the local **public bus** system (ⓦwww.sw.konstanz.de) is also here: single tickets cost €1.80, day-passes €3.50; but you'll travel free with a Gästekarte, which your host will provide if you stay in town for two nights or more.

Accommodation

Most of Konstanz's central hotels are in atmospheric historic buildings, so expect things to be a bit cramped and pricey. Cheaper options, like campsites, the hostel and most private rooms that you can book in the tourist office, are a good way out of the centre.

Hotels and pensions

Barbarossa Overmarkt 8–12 ☎07531/220 21, ⓦwww.barbarossa-hotel.com. Central mid-range place, with some real time-honoured class – frescoes adorn the outside walls and Kaiser Friedrich I signed a peace treaty with the Italians here in 1183 – but cramped bathrooms. ❺
Graf Wisenstr. 2 ☎07531/128 68 90. Basic pension near the station. Some rooms are en suite, but don't expect much. ❷
Hotel-Sonnenhof Otto-Raggenbass-Str. 3 ☎07531/22257, ⓦwww.hotel-sonnenhof-konstanz .de. Basic, but well-priced hotel in a quiet residential street and just yards from the Swiss border at the southern end of town. ❸
Schiff am See William-Graf-Platz 2 ☎07531/310 41, ⓦwww.ringhotel-schiff.de. Comfortable waterfront option, close to car ferry, with reasonably spacious but fairly standard rooms and a good traditional restaurant. ❻
Steigenberger Inselhotel Auf der Insel 1 ☎07531/12 50, ⓦwww.steigenberger.com.

Prestigious five-star place in an old thirteenth-century Dominican monastery overlooking the Bodensee, with all the trimmings, including a fitness centre, sauna and 24hr room service. ❾

Hostels and camping

Campingplatz Bruderhofer Fohrenbühlweg 45 ☎07531/313 88, ⓦwww.campingplatz-konstanz .de. One of two pleasant neighbouring campgrounds on the lakeshore 3km northeast of the centre and around 1km from the car-ferry dock. Getting here can be a bit awkward without your own transport (it's a walk from bus #4), but lakeshore cyclepaths make ideal if you've a bike. Two-person tent site with car parking costs €12.
DJH Konstanz Zur Allmannshöhe 18 ☎07531/322 60, ⓦwww.jugendherberge-konstanz.de. Excellent hostel uniquely occupying an old water-tower, but it's a fair way out of town and even a good walk from the car-ferry docks. Take bus #1 (to Allmannsdorf-Post) or #4 (to Jugendherberge). Dorm beds cost €21.30.

The waterfront

Straddling the Rhine and overlooking the Bodensee, the **waterfront** is a major feature of Konstanz, and the town has made the most of it by constructing a pleasant **promenade** dotted with aged buildings, attractive greenery and eye-catching statues. It starts beside the train stations and heads north towards the Rhine where some of the town's oldest fortifications survive.

The southern end of the promenade is its newest, thanks to a regeneration programme that has seen old warehouses stylishly converted into a small restaurant district beside the clattering sails of the yacht harbour. Also at this end of town is **Sea Life**, Hafenstrasse 9 (July to mid-Sept daily 10am–7pm; May, June & mid-Sept to Oct daily 10am–6pm; Nov–April Mon–Fri 10am–5pm, Sat & Sun 10am–6pm; €11.75; ☎07531/12 82 70, ⓦ www.sealifeeurope .com), an aquarium belonging to the international chain, that showcases the rather lacklustre sea creatures of the Rhine and Bodensee, but is largely geared to kids.

North, beyond an underpass that leads to the Markstätte and the Altstadt, lies the most striking building on the waterfront, the **Konzilgebäude**, a conference and concert hall which dates back to a 1388 granary and warehouse, but gets its name as the probable site where the Council of Konstanz convened to elect Pope Martin V in 1417. Also recalling the Council is **Imperia**, the imposing 9m-high rotating statue of a voluptuous woman, which was erected at the end of the pier opposite the building in 1993. It's based on a prostitute vividly described in a Balzac novel about the days of the Council of Konstanz, though in truth the infamously powerful lady lived in a later time.

Back near the beginning of the pier another statue commemorates airship inventor Count Ferdinand von Zeppelin (see p.464), who was born on a tiny island, simply called the **Insel**, that lies just north of the leafy Stadtgarten park at the end of this section of promenade. The Insel was long inhabited by a Dominican priory – Jan Hus spent time incarcerated in its cellars – but is now given over to the five-star *Inselhotel*.

The Rheintorturm, Archäologisches Landesmuseum and beyond

A short walk north, the **Rheintorturm**, a fifteenth-century defensive tower with a conical red-tile roof, and the adjacent **Rheinbrücke** mark the place where the Rhine and the Bodensee meet. The bridge leads north over the Rhine to a row of handsome Art Nouveau villas. Opposite, a former convent on Benediktinerplatz houses the **Archäologisches Landesmuseum** (Tues–Sun 10am–6pm; €3, free on first Sat of month; ☎07531/980 40, ⓦ www.konstanz.alm-bw.de), the state's archeological collection where finds are neatly arranged by era. Many of the most impressive exhibits are Roman, particularly some wonderful second-century bronzes from Lopodunum – today's Ladenburg between Heidelberg and Mannheim. Among them are proud lion-heads, all sorts of deities and fantastical creatures like sea leopards. The collection also contains items of local interest, particularly details of some of the many shipwrecks in the Bodensee, remnants of a local fifteenth-century merchant ship and some canoes that date back to 650–750 AD. There's also some information on Pfahlbauten and the culture that surrounded them – more accurately but less vividly presented than over the lake near Meersburg (see p.467).

From the archeology museum an underpass dips under the Rheinbrücke to head east along Konstanz's finest promenade. It's nowhere near as busy as that in the centre, and a particular pleasure on a bike. A network of paths combine to head around the peninsula and up to the ferry terminal at Staad and to the island of Mainau. Along the route are many good places to **swim and sunbathe** including the private beach **Strandbad Horn**, Eichhornstrasse 89, the most popular beach at the tip of the peninsula, where you can also rent windsurfers (€8 per hr). Bus #5 comes here from the town centre.

The Altstadt

Just southeast of the confluence of the Rhine and Bodensee, lies the oldest part of the **Altstadt**, which retains a snug atmosphere in its twisting network of tight alleys, dotted with local shops, wine bars and restaurants. It's an easy place to enjoy at an ambling pace, ducking in and out of appealing lanes, which grow progressively broader to the south of the focal **Münsterplatz**.

The Münsterplatz

Romans laid the foundation stones in this part of town and their work can be viewed through a glass panel in the midst of **Münsterplatz**, the square that surrounds Konstanz's main church. Built of soft local sandstone, the **Münster** (Mon–Sat 9am–6pm, Sun 10am–6pm) has spent much of its recent past under repair, but finally most of the scaffold shroud is off to reveal an elegant Romanesque and Gothic structure. Its fine oak **main doors** deserve a closer look for the well-preserved medieval carvings of New Testament scenes. Inside a medley of styles complement each other well. The oldest part is the Carolingian crypt, but most of the Romanesque structure dates from between the twelfth and fifteenth centuries, though the vaulted Gothic side-aisles and main choir-stalls are clearly a later vintage, as are the glittering Baroque high-altar and nineteenth-century neo-Gothic spires which can be climbed (Mon–Sat 10am–5pm, Sun 12.30–5.30pm; €2) for a fine view over town. One unusual thing to look out for is the "**Schnegg**" – which gets its name from an old-fashioned slang word for snail — a late fifteenth-century spiral staircase in the northern transept that's ablaze with decoration. The church was the main meeting-place of the Council of Konstanz. This is where **Jan Hus** stood trial – he's thought to have stood in the central isle at about row 24 to hear his judgement – instead of getting the safe passage home that he'd been guaranteed to lure him here, the council had him burnt at the stake for heresy.

The rest of the Münsterplatz is surrounded by fine old town houses from as far back as the fifteenth century, so it comes as a surprise to see them reflected in the glass of the alarmingly modernist **Kulturzentrum am Münster** in which the **Städtische Wessenberg-Galerie** (Tues–Fri 10am–6pm, Sat & Sun 10am–5pm; €3) puts on often engaging temporary exhibitions on regional art and history.

The Markstätte and around

From the Münsterplatz various old pedestrianized lanes snake south and east providing several options to loop back to the waterfront, though the busiest route goes south along Wessenbergstrasse, which becomes Hussenstrasse, then east along Konzilstrasse to the **Markstätte**, the large, elongated marketplace and commercial hub of town. There's plenty of bustle and atmosphere along the way, but only two real attractions. The **Hus-Museum**, at the southern end of Hussenstrasse, no. 64 (June–Sept Tues–Sun 11am–5pm; Oct–May Tues–Sun 11am–4pm; free), occupies the house where the would-be reformer stayed prior to his imprisonment. Events that took place over a hundred years later in Wittenberg showed he was a man well before his time, and, just as Luther became a figurehead of German nationhood, so too did Hus become vital to Czech identity. Hence the museum is run by a Czech Jan Hus society, but its exhibition is a bit thin. Much better is the **Rosgartenmuseum**, Rosgarten-strasse 3 (Tue–Fri 10am–6pm, Sat & Sun 10am–5pm; €3; free first Sun of month and after 2pm Wed; ☎07531/90 02 46, ⓦ www.rosgartenmuseum-konstanz.de), the town history museum in an old butchers, grocers and pharmacists guildhall. Its eclectic collection of regional art and history contains maps and models that help bring medieval Konstanz alive, while its greatest treasure by far is Ulrich Richental's *Chronicle of the Council of Konstanz*, a beautifully illustrated work of the great event, which of course includes a lurid burning of Hus.

Eating and drinking

Konstanz has some great **cafés** and small **restaurants** tucked away in pedestrian streets south of the Münster, but in summer you'll likely be drawn to all the activity at the harbour, where there's first-class people-watching and often a bit of oompah music in the lakefront **beer garden** too.

8

Brauhaus Johann-Albrecht Konradigasse 2. Atmospheric little microbrewery that's worth seeking out for its good array of beers and well-priced pub food.

Hafenhalle Hafenstr. 10. The biggest of the harbour-side restaurants, with good local fish and game on the menu of the fairly smart restaurant and with simple canteen food in its beer garden. Great for breakfast, particularly on Sun when there's live Dixieland and jazz.

Niederburg Weinstube Niederburggasse 7 ☏07531/213 67. Tiny, rustic, backstreet wine bar with hundreds of regional wines, served until midnight.

Staader Fährhaus Fischerstr. 30. A bit off the beaten track, beside the ferry terminal in Staad, but worth the trek if you're after creative and excellent local fish dishes priced around the €13 mark (closed Tues).

Steg 4 Hafenstr. 8 ☏07531/174 28. Restaurant with good stone-oven pizzas in an old warehouse by the ferry harbour.

Nightlife

As a student town, there's a fair bit going on in Konstanz, with the best source of listings the German-only website ⓦwww.party-news.de. The big event is **Rock Am See** (☏07531/908 80, ⓦwww.koko.de), a big open-air outdoor music festival in late June. Rivalling it, but playing to a very different crowd, are a number of classical music festivals throughout the summer, particularly the **Bodensee Festival** in May and the **Konstanzer Internationale Musiktage**, between mid-June and mid-July. As Germany's oldest active theatre, with dependably good productions, the **Stadttheater Konstanz**, Konzilstrasse 11 (☏07531/90 01 50), deserves a mention, though it's **Konstanz Casino**, Seestrasse 12 (☏07531/815 70), that draws the crowds: it has all the usual table games, a €3 cover, and a jacket-and-tie dress code.

Das Boot Am Hafen ⓦwww.dasboot.de. For something unique and local, check out the events and club nights on this old ferry.

Cuba Libre Hussenstr. ☏07531/567 03. Busy Latin-themed cocktail bar with salsa dancing and a sociable vibe.

K9 Obere Laube 71 ☏07531/167 13, ⓦwww .k9-kulturzentrum.de. Venue with an incredibly eclectic range of events and musical performances; often good for world music.

The Bodensee islands

The two most obvious jaunts from Konstanz are to the islands of **Mainau** and **Reichenau**. Both have thrived thanks to rich soils, near-tropical climate, thriving flora and tourism, but that's where the similarities end. Mainau is far smaller and the busier of the two, and little more than an elaborate landscaped garden. Meanwhile the sedate market-garden haven of Reichenau, with several small hamlets, ancient monastic churches and a bucolic pace that's catching, has far more to explore. Both islands are connected to the mainland by causeways and are within easy striking distance of Konstanz by ferry and by bike on well-marked cycle-paths.

BADEN-WÜRTTEMBERG | Konstanz

Mainau

With its thriving palm groves, orange orchards and flower gardens, the tiny island of **MAINAU** (daily: April–Oct 7am–8pm; Nov–March 9am–6pm; €11.90; ☎07531/30 30, ⓦ www.mainau.de), 6km north of Konstanz, seems to have wafted in from the Mediterranean. Yet it lies at the foot of the Alps, making the setting as idyllic and romantic as the island is popular. Over two million people visit per year, which can easily be a bit much, but if formal gardens are your thing, don't miss out but try to come early or late in the day to avoid the worst crowds. Other good times include the **Count's Island Festival**, around the last weekend of May, and an outdoor music festival in July.

For five hundred years Mainau was owned by the Teutonic Knights during which time they erected a Baroque Schloss and Schlosskirche. The crowd-pleasing **gardens** didn't arrive until 1853, courtesy of new owner Grand Duke Friedrich I of Baden. His current descendant, Count Bernadotte, an aristocratic Swede, continues the tradition with a dazzling year-round horti-cultural spread: in spring the island is carpeted in tulips, on the eastern slopes rhododendrons and azaleas erupt into colour and floral fireworks explode in an orchid show; in summer the Italian rose-garden hits peak form and opulent fuchsias bloom; and in autumn there's a riot of dahlias. Whatever the season, tropical butterflies flit in a vast butterfly house while banana trees and bamboos fill the lush tropical garden.

Mainau is easily reached **by bike** from Konstanz along well-signposted paths – though bikes are not allowed on the island – and **by bus** #4 from the Stadt-bahnhof. More attractive is the journey here by various **boats** and ferries en route to Meersburg and elsewhere that leave from Konstanz's harbour. There are several bistros and **cafés** on the island but it's worth seeking out the excellent *Schwedenschenke* (March, April & Oct Mon–Wed & Sun 11am–6pm, Fri & Sat 9am–11pm; May–Sept daily 9am–11pm; ☎07531/30 31 56). This is a good-value restaurant by day – renowned for its Swedish meatballs – but by night transforms into an elegant flagship of *haute cuisine* and is excellent for fresh local perch and trout in a romantic setting.

Reichenau

Though the causeway that joins **REICHENAU** to the mainland is only 2km long, the island's sleepy atmosphere makes it feel a world apart from Konstanz only 8km west. It was this sense of remoteness coupled with a very forgiving climate and easy vegetable cultivation that encouraged Benedictines to found a monastery here in 724 AD. It grew to become one of Europe's premier places of learning in the tenth century and was particularly famous for its massive library and scriptorium, where monks would sit in rows patiently producing extraordinarily intricate and beautiful manuscripts. Examples of these can be seen, and copies purchased, in the **Museum Reichenau** (April–June, Sept & Oct Tues–Sun 10.30am–4.30pm; July & Aug Tues–Sun 10.30am–5.30pm; Nov–March Sat & Sun 2–5pm; €3) in the central village of Mittelzell. The museum also has an excellent section on the island's history – in English too – which provides the best introduction to the island's three surviving tenth-century monastic churches. The most impressive is the **Münster** around the corner from the museum.

Reichenau measures only 4.5km by 1.5km and is fairly flat and traffic free, which makes it ideal to explore by **bike**. One good idea is to rent a bike in Konstanz and ride to the island along well-marked cycle paths, explore its quiet roads, then take one of the frequent **ferries** back to Konstanz from the quay on the southwestern side of the island. The island is also served by the frequent

Christmas markets

Christmas in Germany is celebrated with such gusto and sense of tradition that you'd think it was invented here. Each December small wooden huts twinkling with lights spring up across the country to showcase local handicrafts and delicacies. But it's not just shopping: the markets are as much about the pleasure of splitting a bag of roasted chestnuts with friends and soaking up the Christmas spirit – along with a mug or two of steaming Glühwein.

Ice skating on a frozen lake near Munich ▲

A traditional, carved Santa Claus ▲

Stollen on sale in Dresden ▼

A brief history

The first Christmas market almost certainly went unrecorded, but the 1294 market in Vienna has to be one of the earliest. Around this time the idea caught on among Czechs, and it was just over the border in Bautzen in 1384 that a Christmas market was first recorded in Germany. In Frankfurt stall holders set up alongside its Mystery Plays in 1393, making it the oldest of the larger markets.

The earliest markets mainly sold meat, but over time they grew to include local handicrafts. This trade got a terrific boost from the sixteenth-century teachings of Martin Luther who suggested the birth of Christ would be a better time to exchange gifts than the traditional saints' days of St Nicholas (December 6), or St Martin (November 11). But despite having roots in religious veneration, the markets – usually held by the city's main church to attract church-goers – soon competed with the churches themselves. As early as 1616 a Nuremberg priest complained that he'd had to abandon a Christmas Eve service because all of his congregation were at the market.

Today, Germany's markets attract 160 million visitors a year and market-related revenues are around €5 billion: impressive for what's fundamentally a craft-and-bake sale.

Food and drink

Traditional Christmas delicacies are often based around warming sensations – gingery cakes and spiced punch – but the variety of both across the country is staggering. Many towns keep their recipes a closely guarded secret, even trademarked, with Nuremberg's **Lebkuchen**, a soft spiced gingerbread that's been produced since the fourteenth century, the most famous. In the Rhineland and Westphalia **Spekulatius** – cardamon and cinnamon biscuits – are common, while the heavy **Stollen** fruitcake is particularly associated with Saxony.

The seasonal drink of choice is **Glühwein** (mulled wine) – usually red but occasionally white – and its non-alcoholic cousin *Kinderpunsch*. *Feuerzangenbowle*, red wine flavoured with a flaming rum-dipped block of sugar, and *Eierpunsch* – a sort of eggnog – are also popular.

▲ A *Räuchermänchen* incense holder

▼ Dortmund's Christmas market

Crafts

In a country where real Christmas tree candles and wooden ornaments prevail, it's no surprise to find traditional handmade crafts dominating most Christmas markets. Items like straw stars, candles and glass baubles are easy to find, but wooden crafts are the most popular and include crib figurines, toys, marionettes and nutcrackers. Particularly charming are the wooden **Weihnachtspyramide** – in which the heat from candles rotates a nativity scene – and the jovial little **Räuchermänchen** – figures that serve as incense holders and puff smoke from their mouths.

▼ Gingerbread hearts on sale

Christmas for kids

Christmas markets are obviously great for kids, and you'll usually find a **carousel**, a few games or rides and sometimes an **ice rink**. Other draws often include street performers, nativity plays, puppet theatres and concerts; and there's always a **nativity scene** – sometimes populated by a petting zoo of sheep, donkeys and goats. But Germany's best kid's Christmas market is doubtless that of the **Europa-Park** theme park (see p.505) which goes all-out for the occasion.

A Christmas tree decoration for sale ▲

A mug of Glühwein ▼

Christmas in the city

Though small towns often have the most atmospheric markets (listed at Ⓦ www.germany-christmas-market.org .uk), some of the big cities have great, easily accessible Christmas festivities:

▶▶ **Bremen** As well as the attractive main market, Bremen has a medieval maritime market, where you can fire crossbows, have your fortune told and watch magic and outdoor performances of the *Stadtmusikanten* fairytale.

▶▶ **Cologne** Located by the cathedral, which also forms the motif for many of its *Spekulatius* biscuits. Other novelties include Rhine cruise-ship markets and the medieval Chocolate Museum market, with entertainers and stall-holders in period costume. Look out for local speciality *Meth*, a honey wine.

▶▶ **Dresden** Dresden's invention of *Stollen* is celebrated in the jovial Stollenfest, in which a four-tonne version journeys through the city before being carved into more bite-sized portions.

▶▶ **Frankfurt** The Römerberg market, with its giant Christmas tree, vintage carousel and half-timbered facades, is atmospheric and fun.

▶▶ **Hamburg** Great for market-hopping, with a cheerful circus-themed market featuring wandering performers; the stylish Winterzauber market with ice bar, skating rink and puppet theatre; the Finnish-themed Fleetinsel market; and the irreverent Santa Pauli market in the red-light district.

▶▶ **Munich** The Marienplatz market is wonderfully atmospheric and great for handicrafts, but Münchener Freiheit is more relaxed and has better food.

▶▶ **Nuremberg** The delightful huddle of red-and-white striped canvas on a square below the castle is deservedly popular, but on weekends it can feel like its two million visitors have arrived all at once. The *Lebkuchen* is its hallmark, but look out for *Nürnberger Zwetschgamännla*: little figures made from prunes.

bus #7372 from Konstanz which loops around the island and past the **tourist office** (May–Sept Mon–Fri 8.30am–12.30pm & 1.30–6pm, Sat 9am–noon; Oct–April Mon–Fri 8.30am–noon & 2–5pm; ☎07534/920 70, ⓦwww .reichenau.de), which lies close to Museum Reichenau.

Northern Baden-Württemberg

Northern Baden-Württemberg is chiefly of interest for **Karlsruhe** and **Heidelberg**: two lively **university** cities at the northern end of the old state of Baden that both make appealing stop-offs for visitors travelling between the Rhineland and Black Forest. Though known for and centred around a palace, the Rhine-side location has given Karlsruhe an industrial base and a modern dynamism that has spawned an exceptional contemporary art and technology museum, the **ZKM**, whose glut of stimulating installations put it among the world's best. **Heidelberg** is more removed from modernity and one of Germany's tourist honeypots, well preserved in past because it was a provincial backwater for a long time, as a mighty ruined castle attests to. It's particularly popular with Americans who spared the city from wartime bombing and now can follow in the steps of Mark Twain, who was enchanted by the city's Altstadt when he visited.

Karlsruhe

Only 15km from France, **KARLSRUHE** is one of Germany's youngest cities and a bright and busy place, with some good museums and Baroque palaces. Meaning "Karl's rest", Karlsruhe was created in 1715 by Margrave Karl Wilhelm of Baden as a place to escape his dull wife and spend time with mistresses. It grew as capital of Baden from 1771 and developed as a liberal town where arts and sciences flourished, as did the university that still gives the town a happening feel. After the war it lost out to Stuttgart as regional capital, but as seat of Germany's two highest courts it still plays a significant national role and it is also an important industrial base. With admittedly few top-flight attractions, Karlsruhe does have several excellent **museums** – particularly the **ZKM** with its contemporary art and high-tech installations – and lies at the heart of a well-priced regional public transport network, which puts it within easy reach of the Northern Black Forest and Baden-Baden (see p.487). One unusual event in town to look out for is the **Trachten and Folklorefest**, when folk groups from all over Europe converge in the June of even-numbered years.

Arrival, information and accommodation

The **Hauptbahnhof** lies 3km southwest of the central Marktplatz to which it's joined by line #3 of a tram-cum-light-rail service (single ticket €2, 24hr €4.80 or €6.50 for groups of up to six people). These services are the hub of a system that extends all the way to Baden-Baden and Bruchsal, with regional day-tickets

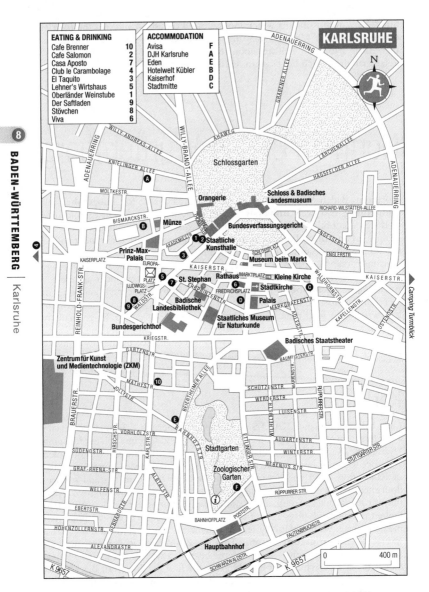

KARLSRUHE

EATING & DRINKING
Cafe Brenner	10
Cafe Salomon	2
Casa Aposto	7
Club le Carambolage	4
El Taquito	3
Lehner's Wirtshaus	5
Oberländer Weinstube	1
Der Saftladen	9
Stövchen	8
Viva	6

ACCOMMODATION
Avisa	F
DJH Karlsruhe	A
Eden	E
Hotelwelt Kübler	B
Kaiserhof	D
Stadtmitte	C

only €9. The **tourist office** (☎0721/37 20 53 83, ⊛www.karlsruhe-tourism
.de) has branches at both the station (Bahnhofplatz 6; Mon–Fri 9am–6pm, Sat
9am–1pm) and on the Marktplatz (Karl-Friedrich-Strasse 9; Mon–Fri 9.30am–
7pm, Sat 10am–3pm). Both offer the **Karlsruhe WelcomeCard** (€9.50 for two
days including public transport and discounted museum entry) and *Karlsruhe
Extra*, a listings magazine. They also sell tickets to local events, rent audio tours
for town (€8) and have **accommodation** listings, which include a particularly
good stock of business-level hotels.

Hotels and pensions

Avisa Am Stadtgarten 5 ☎0721/349 77, ⓦwww.hotel-avisa.de. Dependable if unexciting hotel two blocks northeast of the train station with clean and tidy, if small, modern rooms and reasonable breakfast buffet. **④**

Eden Bahnhofstr. 15–19 ☎0721/181 80, ⓦwww.eden-ka.de. Large hotel beside the large, leafy Stadtgarten midway between Hauptbahnhof and centre – and a 10min walk from either. The modern rooms are sizeable and reasonable value, the breakfast buffet large and varied. **⑥**

🏃 **Hotelwelt Kübler** Bismarckstr. 37–43 ☎0721/14 40, ⓦwww.hotel-kuebler.de. Hotel complex with a variety of rooms from standard mid-range affairs to the eccentric themed rooms in the *Allvitalis Traumhotel*. The complex also includes a spa and the *Badisches Brauhaus*, a microbrewery with an evening buffet. **⑤**

Kaiserhof Karl-Friedrich-Str. 12 ☎0721/917 00, ⓦwww.hotel-kaiserhof.de Swish family-run city centre place with a bit of Baroque character, though the rooms are mostly bright and modern. Has a sauna and excellent breakfast buffet. **⑥**

Stadtmitte Zähringerstr. 72 ☎0721/38 96 37. Central pension, with a bit of *fin-de-siècle* elegance, small rooms and friendly host. **❸**

Camping and hostels

Camping Turmblick Tiengerer Str. 40 ☎0721/49 72 36, ⓦwww.azur-camping.de. Big well-organized campground 5km east of centre in district of Durlach, with tennis courts and an outdoor swimming pool next door.

DJH Karlsruhe Moltkestr. 24 ☎0721/282 48, ⓦwww.jugendherberge-karlsruhe.de. Multistorey hostel an easy 5min walk northwest of the centre, connected to the Marktplatz by trams #2, #4 and #6 to Europaplatz. Dorms €20.10 and most are en suite.

The Town

At the town's centre stands Karlsruhe's **Schloss**, now home to the **Badisches Landesmuseum**, which was originally designed in the Francophile Baroque style of the 1750s, but was destroyed during World War II and rebuilt with Neoclassical additions. The formal palace is surrounded by more relaxed **gardens** – including a botanical one – which are a popular hangout with students from the university campus just to the southeast. A trip up the **Schloss tower** (free to visitors of the Badisches Landesmuseum) best reveals Karlsruhe's unusual circular road layout: from the centre, roads radiate out in an attempt to resemble a fan – the work of local architect Friedrich Weinbrenner, though postwar rebuilding has made the design less obvious. The **Marktplatz**, two blocks south of the Schloss, remains another key focal point, and was similarly the vision of Friedrich Weinbrenner, whose work was deeply influenced by Roman styles, as the Neoclassical forms around the Marktplatz attest. Stretching west of here is the main commercial street Kaiserstrasse, around the western end of which lie two fine museums: the **Staatliche Kunsthalle** and the **Stadtmuseum**, a top-flight art museum and city museum respectively. The city's most impressive museum is the **ZKM**, 2km southwest of the centre, and best reached by public transport.

The Badisches Landesmuseum

Occupying Karlsruhe's Schloss, the **Badisches Landesmuseum** (Tues–Thurs 10am–5pm, Fri–Sun 10am–6pm; €4, free after 2pm Fri; ☎0721/926 65 20, ⓦwww.landesmuseum.de) is effectively the vault of Baden's royal family. Along with their jewelled crown, sword and sceptre, there's a bevy of medieval art and sculpture and a prodigious number of war trophies from Ludwig Wilhelm's seventeenth-century Ottoman campaigns. Known as the *Türtenbeute* (Turkish spoils), these are testament to the sophistication of the Ottoman Empire of the time: the embroidery, books, jewellery, leather and wood crafts are exquisitely made and the hoard of grim and powerful weapons demonstrate what an impressive feat victory over the Turks was. Of more local interest is the museum's strong collection of regional archeology: finds include Assyrian ivory carvings and impressive Roman sculptures, with two stand-out nautical gods.

The Staatliche Kunsthalle

Immediately southwest of the Schloss, one of Germany's finest art galleries, Karlsruhe's **Staatliche Kunsthalle**, Hans-Thoma-Strasse 2–6 (Tues–Fri 10am–5pm, Sat & Sun 10am–6pm; €6; ☎0721/926 33 70, ⓦwww.kunsthalle-karlsruhe .de), is strong on works by late Gothic masters such as Cranach the Elder, Dürer, Burgkmair and Baldung as well as Matthias Grünewald, whose emotional *Crucifixion* gets centre stage. Equally accomplished are the Dutch, Flemish and French sections – the latter features Delacroix and Courbet as well as Impressionists Degas, Manet, Monet, Pissarro, Renoir and Sisley. Local talent is represented by a glut of nineteenth-century work by Black Forest native Hans Thoma who served as gallery director for twenty years, while members of Der Blaue Reiter group also get a look in, particularly Beckmann, Marc and Kokoschka.

The Stadtmuseum and Museum am Markt

Once nationally important as the residence of the last chancellor of the Second Reich, who announced the abdication of the Kaiser and paved the way for the Weimer Republic, the **Prinz-Max-Palais** is now of purely local interest as Karlsruhe's **Stadtmuseum** (Tues, Wed, Fri & Sun 10am–6pm, Thurs 10am–7pm, Sat 2–6pm; free). It's the best place to see the city as it was originally intended in 1834 via a splendid collection of prints and maps. Also here is the Daisienne, the 1818 work of a local inventor, claimed to be the world's first bicycle.

At the other end of Kaiserstrasse, on Marktplatz's northern side, the **Museum am Markt**, Karl-Friedrich-Strasse 6 (Tues–Thurs 11am–5pm, Fri–Sun 10am–6pm; €2, free after 2pm Fri; ☎0721/926 65 78), is worth a look if you're a fan of twentieth-century industrial art and design for its collection of elegant and accomplished Art Nouveau, Art Deco and Bauhaus pieces.

Zentrum für Kunst und Medientechnologie

The hulking, slightly ominous-looking, detached building 2km southwest of Karlsruhe's Schloss (take tram #2) was once a munitions factory, but like so many defunct industrial buildings it has leant itself superbly to becoming an exhibition space. The Zentrum für Kunst und Medientechnologie, or **ZKM**, Lorenzstrasse 19 (Wed–Fri 10am–6pm, Sat & Sun 11am–6pm; ☎0721/81 00 12 00, ⓦwww.zkm.de), occupies the building's vast airy halls, and includes cafés and restaurants, space for regular and dependably great temporary exhibitions as well as three excellent museums; a combined day-ticket to all costs €14.

Art and gadgetry collide in the **Medienmuseum** (€5, free after 2pm Fri), which is chock-full of entertaining electronic gimmicks that synthesize various elements of music, film, photography and design into creative and interactive art installations which can easily take all day to explore. Activities include using electronic dice to create a pastiche of a waltz by irreverently cobbling together bars of Mozart, using a vast image library to create collages; and shooting small movies using geometric shapes. All this is of course based on computer technology, so as a tribute you can see the maze of tubes and cables of the world's oldest operable computer (1941) and some of the 1950s and 1960s old optical illusions of the **Neuer Tendenzen**, or Nouvelles Tendances, an avant-garde school of art that pioneered this style. If all this hasn't left you fuzzy headed enough, the top floor of the museum is replete with various video games from every era, which you can play.

After all this, the **Museum für Neue Kunst** (Museum for Contemporary Art; €5, free after 2pm Fri) could easily be an anticlimax, but its thoughtful exhibits are engaging, and include 1960s Pop Art, but are usually dominated by contemporary art that reflects on aspects of modern-day Germany.

Finally, at the other end of the ZKM, and accessed by a separate entrance, is the **Städtische Galerie**, Lorenzstrasse 27 (€2.60; ☎0721/133 44 01, ⓦwww .staedtische-galerie.de), the most staid of the museum trio, yet still accomplished. It focuses on local and postwar German art, but is usually most worthwhile for its temporary exhibitions, which try for broad popular appeal – such as exhibitions of graphic novels.

Eating, drinking and entertainment

For a university city Karlsruhe is relatively quiet in terms of **eating** and **nightlife**, but does have a few busy spots like Ludwigsplatz on the western side of town and the bohemian southern end of Waldstrasse. Karlsruhe is particularly known for the **Badisches Staatstheater**, Baumeisterstrasse 11 (☎0721/355 74 50 ⓦwww .staatstheater.karlsruhe.de), which puts on dependable theatre productions, opera and classical concerts. One for the kids is the **Marotte Figurentheater**, Kaiserallee 11 (ⓦwww.marotte-figurentheater.de), an excellent puppet theatre.

Restaurants

Casa Aposto Ludwigsplatz. Good Italian restaurant with €4.90 lunch specials as well as good pizzas, pastas and salads. The home-made Italian ice-cream is also first class and the outdoor seating on a convivial square makes it a place to linger.

El Taquito Waldstr. 22–24. All the usual Tex-Mex favourites averaging an inexpensive €6 per dish and served indoors or outside in a quiet courtyard. Also offers a reasonable Saturday brunch (noon–3pm, €8.50).

Lehner's Wirtshaus Karlstr 21. Hip place but still good for its range of inexpensive traditional favourites; set lunches are good value at €4.90 as is the crispy *Flammkuchen* at €7. A good place for breakfast too, served from 10am.

Oberländer Weinstube Akademiestr. 7. Venerable wine bar and bistro with eight hundred wines and a gourmet menu to match – most mains cost around €20. Closed Sun & Mon.

Viva Rathaus-Passage, Lammstr 7. Laudable self-service vegetarian place, with excellent salads and several hot options too. Pay by the weight of your plate, which can mean that if you pile it high, you're in for a shock. Closed Sat eve & Sun.

Cafés, bars and clubs

Café Brenner Karlstr 61a. A coffee house since 1896 and good place for that mid-afternoon sugar rush from its selection of great cakes.

Café Salomon Hans-Thoma-Str. 3 ☎0721/921 20 80. Small café opposite the Staatliche Kunsthalle with a good line in bagels, soups and some cakes.

Club le Carambolage Kaiserstr. 21 ☎0721/37 32 27, ⓦwww.club-carambolage.de. Wacky club with truly experimental decor – everything from stuffed mountain-goats to antique wheelchairs – opposite the university campus so fairly studenty. Organizes lots of themed nights and open daily until at least 3am.

Der Saftladen Waldstr. 54. Another bohemian place on this stretch of Waldstrasse, with first-class smoothies and coffees; good for a bowl of muesli early in the day too.

Stövchen Waldstr. 54. Cheerful pub with sociable beer garden and a low-budget menu – which includes dishes for as little as €3 so attracts students in droves.

Heidelberg

Nestled in a wooded gorge of the River Neckar, the university town of **HEIDELBERG** boasts a roster of sights that publicists of larger rivals would pay handsomely for. Goethe waxed lyrical about its ideal beauty, looks which so bewitched Turner that he captured it for posterity, and even Benjamin Disraeli fell for its "exceeding loveliness". "Here," he sighed, "the romantic ruggedness of the German landscape unites in perfect harmony with the delicate beauty of Italy." So effective was this PR, that today three million tourists a year are enticed to it, and for many Heidelberg remains the must-see of the Grand European Tour that it was for the nineteenth-century Romantics.

Ironically, they had stumbled upon a town down on its luck. French troops ravaged Heidelberg during the War of the Palatinate Succession in 1688 and Louis XIV returned five years later to deliver a blow of such force that writer Nicolas Boileau suggested Jean-Baptiste Racine inform the Académie Française "Heidelberger deleta". To cap its tale of woe, Palatinate elector Charles Philip left in favour of Mannheim after the Protestant stronghold refused to embrace Catholicism, in doing so demoting ravaged Heidelberg to just another provincial town.

Arrival and information

Arriving at its **train station**, a twenty-minute walk west of the Altstadt (or a ten-minute ride on buses #11 or #33 or tram #1), first impressions of Heidelberg fail to live up to the hype. At least it's useful as the location of the very busy main **tourist office**, outside the Hauptbahnhof at Willy-Brandt-Platz 1 (April–Oct Mon–Sat 9am–7pm, Sun 10am–6pm; Nov–March Mon–Sat 10am–6pm; ☎06221/194 33/142 40, ⓦwww.cvb-heidelberg.de). There's also a smaller branch, open in the summer only (same hours) at Neckarmünzplatz and beside the Schloss Bergbahn terminus. Both can sell you the two-day **HeidelbergCARD** (€12), which provides free entry or discounts to all sights, including the Schloss tour.

Accommodation

More than anywhere else in Germany, getting accommodation throughout the summer in Heidelberg can be extremely difficult, particularly if you are looking for lodgings at the lower end of the scale. The best bet is to reserve well ahead of time – and don't expect any assistance from the overworked tourist office.

DJH Heidelberg Tiergartenstr. 5 ☎06221/41 20 66, ⓦwww.jugendherberge -heidelberg.de. Big busy hostel a 3km walk west of the centre on the other side of the Neckar River. Take bus #33 from the train station. Dorms €22.30.

▲ Heidelberg

Der Europäischer Hof – Hotel Europa Friedrich-Ebert-Anlage 1 ☏ 06221/51 50, ⓦ www .europaeischerhof.com. Individually decorated rooms (doubles start at €334 in summer), suites furnished with antiques and gourmet restaurant *Die Kurfürstenstube* combine to create the premier address in town. ❾

Hirschgasse Hirschgasse 3 ☏ 06221/45 50, ⓦ www.hirschgasse.de. The connoisseur's choice counts Mark Twain and Count Otto von Bismarck among past guests. The style is luxury country – four-posters and Laura Ashley – and its north-bank location is spared summer hordes. ❼

Holländer Hof Neckarstaden 66 ☏ 06221/605 00, ⓦ www.hollaender-hof.de With luck, you'll bag a river view in this good-value, elegant number beside the Alter Brücke. ❻

Hotel Central Kaiserstr. 75 ☏ 06221/206 41, ⓦ www.hotel-central-heidelberg.de. Sparkling and airy, but rather bland modern hotel near the train station; one of the best-value places in town that's likely to have a bed. ❸

Pension Jeske Mittelbadgasse 2 ☏ 06221/237 33, ⓦ www.pension-jeske-heidelberg.de. Bright and central Altstadt place, cheerfully decorated and usually full – and generally unwilling to take reservations so turn up early on the day. It has some cheap triples and singles too. Breakfast not included. ❷

Weisser Bock Grosse Mantelgasse 24 ☏ 06221/900 00, ⓦ www.weisserbock.de. Small but comfortable rooms high in atmosphere in a backstreet charmer with a lovely dining room. ❺

🏃 **Zum Ritter St Georg** Hauptstr. 178 ☏ 06221/13 50, ⓦ www.ritter-heidelberg .de. Nostalgic charm from the Romantik chain in Heidelberg's most magnificent patrician's mansion, with a handful of cheaper, non-en-suite rooms. ❻

The Schloss

Heidelberg's devastation proved its salvation: to Romantic eyes, the mighty red **Schloss** (daily 8am–5.30pm; €5, grounds free from 6pm until dusk) sited magnificently on a bluff and mailed in ivy was not simply a ruin but a wistful embodiment of melancholy and decay. Even that scurrilous wit Mark Twain described it as "deserted, discrowned, beaten by the storms, but royal still, and beautiful". And today it is one of the most significant tourist draws in Germany.

From elegant **Kornmarkt** you can ascend to Heidelberg's star attraction on the Bergbahn funicular or up a steep staircase. Far better though, is to take adjacent Burgweg and marvel at the massive towers. The Dicker Turm (Fat Tower), blasted by French explosives despite walls 7m thick, is impressive, but the southeast Pulverturm is the darling of romantics past and present. French sappers split in two the mighty bulwark, the cleaved section slid into the moat and the powder tower became the **Gesprengter Turm** (exploded tower). It's best admired from the terrace which once bloomed with Frederick V's Hortus Palatinus ornamental gardens (1616), the wonder of their age. The Wittelsbach ruler commissioned them to charm his uppity English bride, 19-year-old Elizabeth Stuart, daughter of James I, and to surprise her, says local lore, he erected overnight the Elisabethentor (1615) to the west of the terrace. Poor Frederick. Few of his attempts to impress succeeded. Four years later, against better advice, the impetuous 24-year-old was crowned King of Bohemia and so declared a threat by the mighty Habsburg dynasty. The clash proved a disaster, both for him – his forces were routed by Emperor Ferdinand II, and the "Winter King" was stripped of all his titles – and for Europe, igniting the tinderbox of resentments that became the Thirty Years' War.

The Schlosshof

Impressive though they are, the Schloss fortifications are only a warm-up act for the **Schlosshof**, reached via the Torturm gatehouse and the only building to survive explosives. Look for a crack in the left-hand door's iron ring – the bite of a witch after Ludwig V pledged his new castle to anyone able to chomp the ring in two – then enter the courtyard, where the Gothic **Ruprechtsbau** (4–6 daily tours; €4) has an angelic keystone, said to be a memorial to the master builder's

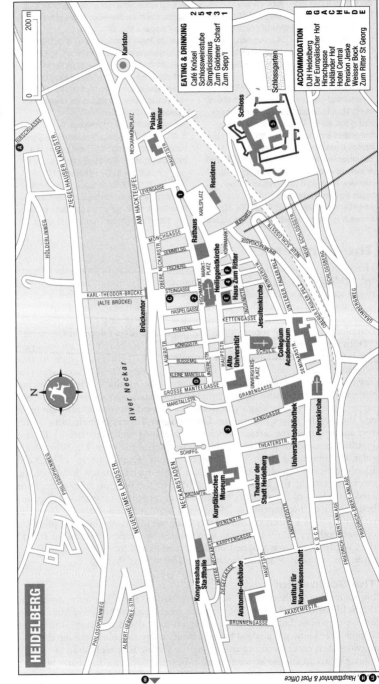

HEIDELBERG

EATING & DRINKING

Café Knösel	2
Schlossweinstube	5
Simplicissimus	4
Zum Goldener Scharf	3
Zum Sepp'l	1

ACCOMMODATION

DJH Heidelberg	B
Der Europäischer Hof	G
Hirschgasse	A
Holländer Hof	C
Hotel Central	H
Pension Jeske	F
Weisser Bock	D
Zum Ritter St Georg	E

Karlstor

Palais Weimar

NECKARMÜNZPLATZ

HIRSCHGASSE

ZIEGELHAUSER LANDSTR.

HÖLDERLINWEG

LEYERGASSE

AM HACKTEUFEL

HAUPTSTR.

Residenz

KARLSPLATZ

Schloss

5

MÖNCHGASSE

Rathaus

OBERE NECKARSTR.

SEMMELSG.

FISCHERG.

MARKT-PLATZ

Heiliggeistkirche

KORNMARKT

BURGWEG

NEUE SCHLOSSSTR.

GRABENGASSE

STEINGASSE

Brückentor

KARL-THEODOR-BRÜCKE
(ALTE BRÜCKE)

FISCHMARKT

HASPELGASSE

E 4 F
Haus Zum Ritter

INGRIMSTR.

KETTENGASSE

UNTERE FAULER PELZ

OBERE FAULER PELZ

PFAFFENG.

KÖNIGSTR.

Jesuitenkirche

ZWINGERSTR.

SCHLOSSBERG

River Neckar

BUSSEMG.

KLEINE MANTELG.

UNTERE STR.

HAUPTSTR.

Alte Universität

UNIVERSITÄTS-PLATZ

SCHULG.

SEMINARSTR.

Collegium Academicum

N

GROSSE MANTELGASSE

MARSTALLSTR.

GRABENGASSE

SANDGASSE

3

Peterskirche

PHILOSOPHENWEG

NEUENHEIMER LANDSTR.

SCHIFFG.

NECKARSTADEN

THEATERSTR.

Universitätsbibliothek

BAUAMTG.

Kurpfälzisches Museum

Theater der Stadt Heidelberg

BIENENSTR.

LANDFRIEDSTR.

FRIEDRICH-EBERT-ANLAGE

PLÖCK

ALBERT-ÜBERLE-STR.

UNTERE NECKARSTR.

ZIEGELGASSE

KARPFENGASSE

Kongresshaus Stadthalle

Anatomie-Gebäude

HAUPTSTR.

BRUNNENGASSE

AKADEMIESTR.

Institut für Naturwissenschaft

FRIEDRICH-EBERT-ANLAGE

0   200 m

late sons, and fancy Renaissance fireplaces and castle models. Springs from the Königstuhl hill behind fed the 16m well in the Brunnenhaus loggia opposite. Its marble pillars were swiped from Charlemagne's Ingelheim castle, although the Holy Roman Emperor had himself snatched them from a Roman palace.

However, it's the Renaissance palace buildings that impress the most. The magnificent shell of the **Ottheinrichsbau** (1559) has a four-tier chorus of allegorical sculptures, including planetary deities, Old Testament heroes and the Virtues. The basement contains the quirky and charmingly cluttered **Deutsches Apotheken Museum** (daily 10.15am–6pm; same ticket as Schloss), with eighteenth- and nineteenth-century dispensaries from the area. The **Glässener-Saal-Bau** (Hall of Mirrors), a Romanesque take on cutting-edge Renaissance, links the Ottheinrichsbau to the show-piece **Friedrichsbau**, where the ancestral gallery of swaggering sculptures traces the House of Wittelsbach from a highly dubious claim on Charlemagne to its builder Friedrich V, a lineage legitimized in the centre by Justice. Join a tour to see the original statues, a beautiful, late Gothic Schlosskapelle and rooms re-created in period style.

The descent back to Heidelberg's centre ends at the **Fassbau** and its cottage-sized wine cask, the **Grosses Fass** (1751) – around 130 oak tree trunks created the 221,725-litre whim of Elector Karl Theodor, and many a quadrille was danced atop its platform. Before it stands a statue of the rule's court jester, keeper of the vat and legendary boozer Clemens Perkeo. He was named, they say, for his response to offers of wine – "Perche no?" (Why not?). From the **Grosser Altern** (Grand Terrace) before the Friedrichsbau there's a gorgeous view of the Altstadt's roofscape. Return at night to sympathize with Twain: "One thinks Heidelberg by day the last possibility of the beautiful, but when he sees Heidelberg by night, a fallen Milky Way … he requires time to consider the verdict," he sighed.

The Town

If the view of the Schloss's ensemble from **Karlsplatz** seems impressive by day, at night it is sensational. The square, below the Schloss and east of Kornmarkt, is flanked by a pair of Baroque palaces: a grandiose ducal number by Rémy de la Fosse (now university-owned); and the Palais Boisserée, home of flamboyant French art collectors Sulpiz and Melchior, who twice hosted Goethe during his forty-year love affair with Heidelberg.

A short walk west lies the central **Marktplatz** where, with public executions and stocks long gone, crowds linger over beer and coffee instead. At its centre, the Gothic **Heiliggeistkirche** with a Baroque mansard roof upholds a medieval tradition once common country-wide with traders' stalls snuggled between its buttresses. Founder Ruprecht III is entombed in the north aisle, and scraps of medieval frescoes hint at the garden which once bloomed on the church roof before being stripped in a 1693 orgy of French looting. The only house left standing after the 1693 sack is the **Haus Zum Ritter** opposite, with its flamboyant Renaissance facade, an uncharacteristic extravagance by a Calvinist cloth merchant.

North, the **Brückentor** gateway topped by jaunty Baroque helmets guards the graceful arch of **Alte Brücke**. Goethe hailed the bridge of "such beauty as is perhaps not to be equalled by any other in the world", and from here is a classic vista of the Altstadt. The view is only trumped by the panorama from Philosophenweg. Visit the north-bank hillside path named after its debating students at sundown and you can watch the Schloss blush deeper still, a play of light Turner captured beautifully in *Heidelberg Sunset*.

Universitätsplatz and the Kurpfälzisches Museum

The Baroque **Alte Universität** (April–Sept Tues–Sun 10am–6pm; Oct Tues–Sun 10am–4pm; Nov–March Tues–Sat 10am–2pm; €2.50) on Universitätsplatz is the ritziest building of Germany's oldest university, founded in 1386 by Ruprecht III, and a palace compared with the modern Neue Universität in the same square. One ticket admits you into the small Universitätsmuseum, a grand nineteenth-century assembly hall Alte Aula and the Studentkarzer (student prison; entrance on Augustinergasse). The usual pranks – drunkenness, extinguishing street lamps, chasing pigs – earned students up to two weeks inside the university jail, but an insult to the law could spell up to four weeks. Since it could be taken at the miscreant's convenience (and even then, offenders were bailed for exams), small wonder a stint inside was *de rigueur* for all self-respecting graduates, who have left their marks in graffiti and candle-soot silhouettes.

East on Schulgasse the **Jesuitenkirche**'s spacious hall features restrained Rococo stucco, and south along Grabengasse the **Universitätsbibliothek** (Mon–Sat 10am–6pm; free), a blur of students in term-time, houses scholarly exhibitions. Back on main street Hauptstrasse is the **Kurpfälzisches Museum** at no. 97 (Tues–Sun 10am–6pm; €3). The pick of the regional exhibits of the classy history museum housed in a professor's Baroque mansion is Tilman Riemenschneider's Altar of the Twelve Apostles, which has shed its suffocating polychrome coat to emerge as an expressive masterpiece of late Gothic.

Eating

Alongside all the usual choices are Heidelberg's student taverns – particularly *Zum Sepp'l*.

Café Knösel Hopelgasse 20 ☏ 06221/223 45. Old-world charmer which has sold its *Studentenkuss* (student's kiss), a chocolate praline, since 1830. *Kaffee und Kuchen* doesn't come much better than this.

Schlossweinstube Schloss ☏ 06221/979 70. Pricey but top-notch German cuisine beneath the atmospheric vaulting in the Schloss. Closed lunch, & all day Wed.

Simplicissimus Ingrimstr. 16 ☏ 06221/18 33 36. The gourmet address in Heidelberg. Decor is quietly elegant, the French cuisine is superb and the three-course *Tagesmenu* is a bargain (€29). Closed lunch, & all day Tues.

Zum Goldener Schaf Hauptstr. 115 ☏ 06221/208 79. Lots of lamb and regional delights, many with a generous helping of doughy home-made *Spätzle* in an atmospheric tavern; mains around €12.

Zum Sepp'l Hauptstr. 213. Student haunt since the 1630s with much of this history of revelry preserved in bric-a-brac and sepia fraternity photos. Still atmospheric and used by fraternities, even if most patrons are tourists. Food is the hearty traditional German kind, and mains priced around €12. If it looks too full, try the almost identical *Zum Roten Ochsen* a few doors down.

Travel details

Trains

Friedrichshafen to: Freiburg (hourly via Basel; 2hr 40min); Ulm (hourly; 1hr 13min).
Heidelberg to: Karlsruhe (frequent; 45min).
Karlsruhe to: Baden-Baden (frequent; 20min); Freiburg (frequent; 1hr).
Stuttgart to: Frankfurt (hourly; 2hr); Friedrichshafen (hourly; 2hr 20min); Heidelberg (hourly; 40min); Karlsruhe (hourly; 40min); Konstanz (hourly; 2hr 40min); Ludwigsburg (frequent; 10min); Munich (frequent; 2hr 20min); Tübingen (frequent; 1hr); Ulm (frequent; 1hr).

Buses

Meersburg to: Friedrichshafen (frequent: 40min).

The Black Forest

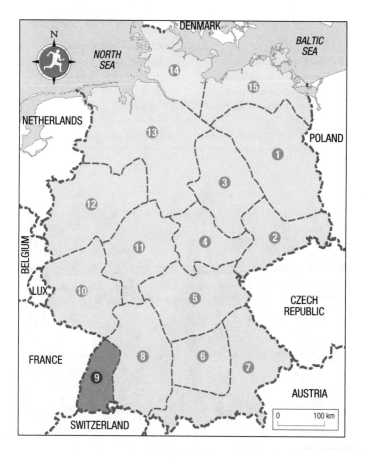

The Black Forest

Map legend:
- DENMARK
- NORTH SEA
- BALTIC SEA
- NETHERLANDS
- POLAND
- BELGIUM
- LUX
- CZECH REPUBLIC
- FRANCE
- AUSTRIA
- SWITZERLAND
- N
- 0 100 km

THE BLACK FOREST

CHAPTER 9 **Highlights**

* **Baden-Baden** Avoid losing your head in the elite company of Baden-Baden's casino, and then let the town's spas rejuvenate you. See p.487

* **Triberg** Home to the world's largest cuckoo clock, and a good place to buy your own piece of timeless Black Forest kitsch. See p.496

* **The Schwarzwälder Freilichtmuseum** Peep into the region's rustic past in this open-air museum. See p.496

* **Freiburg** Ascend the Schauinsland cable car for incredible views, then walk or mountain-bike back to Freiburg on fine woodland trails. See p.498

* **Todtnau** Ski, mountain-bike or rattle down a summer bobsleigh track at this all-season resort. See p.504

* **Europa-Park** Germany's biggest amusement park offers myriad rides to keep the kids entertained. See p.505

▲ Baden-Baden

The Black Forest

A s the setting of countless Grimm Brothers' fairy tales, the **Black Forest** happily plays up to its image as a land of cuckoo clocks, cherry gâteaux, outlandish traditional garb, hefty half-timbered farmhouses and hill after hill of dark, even fir forest. But even a brief exploration soon reveals more of the character of a region that's part of the state of Baden-Württemburg (see p.429) but shaped as much by its history as a long-disputed borderland between Germany, France, and Switzerland – and where something of each is in evidence.

As far back as Roman times this series of rounded granite summits, which structurally and topographically forms a counterpart to France's Vosges on the other, western, side of the Rhine Valley, has been defined as a border region. It formed the rather impenetrable eastern boundary of the Roman Empire, when it was known as *Marciana Silva* – using the Germanic word for borderland and the Roman for forest. The region took centuries to populate and was always considered a rather oddly traditional, if not slightly backward, part of Germany. Inevitably the Black Forest first rose to commercial prominence for its vast timber reserves, and forestry became so much part of life here that it naturally spawned woodwork – providing farmers something to do in the winter – and so the famous cuckoo-clock industry, the associated precision engineering, and the manufacture of musical instruments followed. These all continue to provide jobs, though the regional mainstay is now gentle rural tourism, which continues year-round thanks to winter sport and spa facilities. Inevitably this means you won't find yourself alone exploring this attractive region, but it's a long way from overrun and escaping the crowds at the various hot-spots is easy, particularly if you're keen to explore the countryside on foot or by bike.

Relative to its fame, the Black Forest region is not terribly big – about 150km long and maybe 50km wide – and so easily explored by car in just a few days, though of course that rather misses the chance to drop down a gear and enjoy the heart of one of Germany's treasured regions where good scenery is matched by many time-honoured traditions. Dozens of small attractive towns and villages with a modest provincial or rural lifestyle, make slower touring a delight, but arguably the best way to explore is to base yourself in one of the two largest towns and strike out from there. Easily the most genteel base is **Baden–Baden**, the grand old nineteenth-century spa town in the north of the region, a place for dignified recuperation and pampering. If you're heading south, then the way to travel from here is along the **Schwarzwaldhochstrasse**, a scenic drive par-excellence, which will introduce you to some of the best scenery the Black Forest has to offer. The drive leads into the heart of the central Black Forest and the head of the attractive **Kinzig Valley** which, along with the adjoining **Gutach Valley**, offers an easy

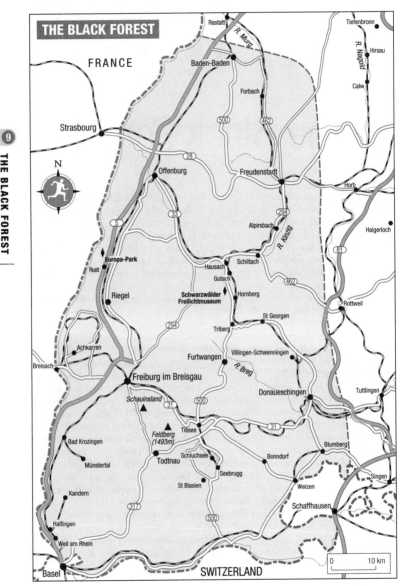

glimpse of traditional village life. South of here, the Black Forest is dominated by the attractive and upbeat university town of **Freiburg**. Exploring its usually sun-soaked narrow streets is fun, but its main attraction is as a handy base from which to **hike** and **bike** and explore the entire southern Black Forest. The area includes first-rate wine-growing areas on the French border and the minor ski and lake resorts of the **Feldberg** region just to the south, where deep valleys are flanked by rounded peaks that top out at around 1500m.

Baden-Baden

The smart and dignified grande dame of German spas, **BADEN-BADEN** lies cradled in the palm of idyllic and gentle wooded hills, 42km south of Karlsruhe. In the nineteenth century this was the St Tropez of high society and something of this era's privilege lives on in the dusty elegance of its villas, hotels and boutiques and in the manicured gardens where immaculately groomed socialites promenade.

The Baden margraves who built the thermal baths in 1810 around the same springs that once lured Roman bathers – in particular Emperor Caracalla – nearly two millennia earlier would be thrilled. The baths were immensely popular in nineteenth-century Germany, and the margraves' architect Friedrich Weinbrenner designed a Neoclassical spa quarter. Barely thirty years later, dapper Parisian impresario Jacques Bénazet added a casino and catapulted Baden-Baden from spa town to elite playground as an international who's-who flocked to play, promenade and soothe rheumatic joints: Tolstoy, Strauss, Queen Victoria, Kaiser Wilhelm I, Dostoyevsky, Bismarck, Tchaikovsky, Brahms and the Vanderbilts all journeyed to Europe's glittering summer capital. Mark Twain came too, but had mixed feelings, describing it as "an inane town, filled with sham and petty fraud and snobbery". The town emerged from World War II without a scratch and now effortlessly blends its halcyon days with modern-day pampering, and in the absence of any heavyweight sights it provides a near perfect setting for a recuperative weekend break. Social highlight of the year is the August **Iffezheim races**, Germany's Ascot, which has been going strong since 1858 and which encompasses two events: the **Frühjahrsmeeting** over the last week of May; and the grander **Grosse Woche** in the last week in August, when the country's elite dress to the nines and don flamboyant hats.

Arrival, information and local transport

Karlsruhe-Baden **airport** (☎07221/66 20 00, ⓦwww.badenairpark.de) lies 15km west of Baden-Baden and is connected by hourly **buses** (Mon–Fri 6.52am–8.26pm). **Taxis** cost around €30. **Trains** pull into a station 5km northwest of the centre in the suburb of Oos and are linked to the centre by bus #201. The **tourist office**, Kaiserallee 3 (Mon–Sat 9am–5pm, Sun 2–5pm; ☎07221/27 52 00, ⓦwww .baden-baden.de), is in the Trinkhalle (see p.489), just west of the centre.

Baden-Baden is very walkable, and promenading is de rigueur, but there's also a good **bus system** run by Stadtwerke Baden-Baden (☎07221/27 71, ⓦwww.stadtwerke-baden-baden.de) whose two-zone, €2 ticket covers all city destinations and whose day-ticket extends to Karlsruhe.

The SchwarzwaldCard

Staying overnight in most hotels and pensions in the Black Forest entitles you to a *Gästekarte* which will include a number of reductions at various local attractions. Those with a "Konus" logo also include free public transport in the region. Another money-saving option, particularly if you plan a busy itinerary, is the three-day **SchwarzwaldCard**, which includes free admission to 150 attractions, including museums, cable cars, boat trips, spas and pools; the full list of partners is at ⓦwww .blackforest-tourism.com. Available at most of the region's tourist offices, the adult pass costs €32, or €55.50 for a version that includes a day at Europa-Park (see p.505), and there are also kids and family versions (€21/45 and €99/189 respectively; the latter covers two adults and three children).

THE BLACK FOREST | Baden-Baden

9

487

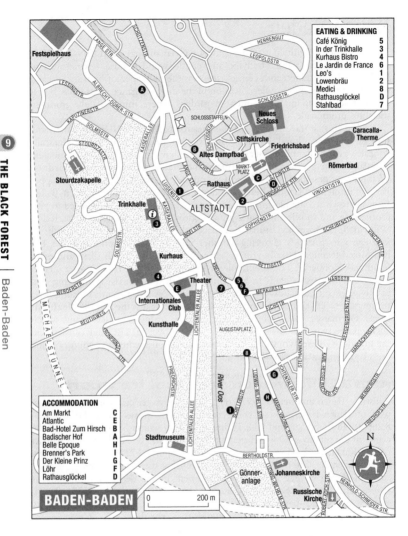

EATING & DRINKING
Café König	5
In der Trinkhalle	3
Kurhaus Bistro	4
Le Jardin de France	6
Leo's	1
Lowenbräu	2
Medici	8
Rathausglöckel	D
Stahlbad	7

ACCOMMODATION
Am Markt	C
Atlantic	E
Bad-Hotel Zum Hirsch	B
Badischer Hof	A
Belle Epoque	H
Brenner's Park	I
Der Kleine Prinz	G
Löhr	F
Rathausglöckel	D

BADEN-BADEN   0   200 m

N

Acommodation

Accommodation in Baden-Baden is inevitably swish, with the emphasis on classic luxury, which means it tends to be pricey. Staying on a budget is hard, but the tourist office can provide lists of **private rooms** (③).

Am Markt Marktplatz 18 ☏ 07221/270 40, ⓦ www.hotel-am-markt-baden.de. Friendly, family-run pension on the charming Marktplatz – ask for a room with a view. Fairly basic, but hands-down the town's best budget choice. ④
Atlantic Sofienstr. 2a ☏ 07221/36 10. Traditional number opposite the theatre whose rooms are

comfortable if a little dated. It's worth paying the extra €12 for views and a balcony over Lichtentaler Allee. ⑦
Bad-Hotel Zum Hirsch Hirschstr. 1 ☏ 07221/93 90, ⓦ www.heliopark-hirsch.de. Thermal spring water flows from the taps in antique-furnished rooms at this historic hotel in the central Altstadt.

Its fine public rooms include an especially splendid ballroom. **❼**

Badischer Hof Lange Str. 47 ☎07221/93 40, ⓦwww.steinberger.com. Landmark place that was long *the* social centre of the rich and famous and whose thermal pools, steam baths and saunas make it the luxury historic hotel of choice for spa-goers – some rooms even have thermal spa water on tap. **❽**

Belle Epoque Maria-Viktoria-Str. 2c ☎07221/30 06 60, ⓦwww.hotelbelleepoque.de. An 1870s villa every inch the retreat of Second Empire aristocrats. Sixteen luxurious rooms are furnished top to bottom in rich antiques and cleverly hide all their mod cons from view. Rooms are themed; book early – advance reservations are a must – and you can choose between the styles of Empire, Louis XV, Biedermeier, Victorian, Louis Philippe and Louis XVI. **❾**

Brenner's Park Hotel Schillerstr. 4–6 ☎07221/90 00, ⓦwww.brenners.com. The queen of Baden-Baden addresses in its own park before Lichtentaler Allee has all the effortless elegance of the town's heyday and remains world class.

Lounges are furnished in Second Reich antiques, rooms have flowery fabrics and chandeliers. There's also an excellent modern spa and gym complex and the *Park-Restaurant* is a gourmet address. Doubles cost €310 but you can pay as much as €1650 for a suite in high season. **❾**

Der Kleine Prinz Lichtentaler Str. 36 ☎07221/34 63, ⓦwww.derkleineprinz.de. Occupying two elegant city mansions, this sister hotel to the *Belle Epoque* has an upmarket rustic air and is decorated with prints of Antoine de Saint-Exupéry's charming hero. Every room has a special feature – whirlpool, fireplace, balcony, tower – and the quality of the service and its restaurant are outstanding. **❽**

Löhr Lichtentaler Str. 19 ☎07221/30 60. Central hotel, and by local standards cheap, with clean but nondescript en-suite rooms. Has wi-fi. **❹**

Rathausglöckel Steinstr. 7 ☎07221/906 10, ⓦwww.rathausgloeckel.de. Family-run hotel with neat and small pine-furnished en-suite rooms with the occasional nineteenth-century touch. Some have views over the town's roofs. **❹**

The Town

Baden-Baden is split in two by the north–south flowing Oos. On its west bank gather all the grand nineteenth-century buildings and follies that were built as social centres and as points between which to promenade. Set amongst parkland here the grand drinking hall, or **Trinkhalle**, home of the tourist office, is the natural place to start exploring, along with another landmark building, the **Kurhaus**, an entertainment venue that includes a famous casino. Extending south from them is **Lichtentaler Allee**, the promenading high-street which passes the **Kunsthalle**, a heavyweight contemporary art museum, the **Stadtmuseum** and an elegant rose garden before becoming a more natural riverside walk to the suburb of **Lichtental**.

The rest of the town centre is grouped on the right bank of the Oos, home to the relatively modern **Altstadt** and all the commercial areas, as well as the famous **baths**. Behind them sloping meadows and forests rise up, surrounding **Burg Hohenbaden** above town.

The Trinkhalle and Stourdza-Kapelle

Fronted by a sixteen-column parade, the **Trinkhalle** (Sun–Thurs 10am–2am, Fri & Sat 10am–3am) features a 90m portico that shelters fourteen nineteenth-century frescoes depicting local legends. Mark Twain fumed at the "tranquil contemptuousness" of the young female clerks who served spa waters to nineteenth-century spa-goers; you needn't negotiate them today for a drink from the tap in the centre of the hall. Plastic cups for the purpose are available from the adjoining café for a small charge.

Behind the Trinkhalle, the Benazetweg path idles up the Michaelsberg to the **Stourdza-Kapelle** (entry by appointment: daily 10am–6pm; ☎07221/285 74) amid redwoods and rhododendrons. Michael Stourdza, having settled in Baden-Baden after his exile as last ruler of Moldovia, commissioned Munich master architect Leo von Klenze to build this requiem for his 17-year-old son, killed in a Paris duel in 1863. Pathos in the dignified marble interior comes from frescoes of the dead prince and his parents.

The Kurhaus

Nowhere better captures Baden-Baden's aristocratic pretensions than the **Kurhaus** (℡ 07221/35 30, ⓦ www.kurhaus-baden-baden.de), which almost single-handedly made the town what it is today. Weinbrenner's 1820s centre-piece for his fledgling spa resort is an exercise in restraint, dignity and poise: strictly Neoclassical in style, it is guarded by eight Corinthian columns and set behind a manicured lawn with cheerful flowerbeds.

The Kurhaus **interior** is far less solemn. In 1855, Edouard Bénazet commissioned Parisian craftsmen to spice up the **casino** he inherited from father Jacques – the portrait of that first *roi de Bade* takes pride of place in the casino lobby – fusing Versailles opulence and *belle époque* glamour in an attempt to outdo both. In its **Wintergarten**, Second Empire-style fountains shimmer in gilt mosaic, Hsien-Feng porcelain vases line the walls and a gold-trimmed roulette table winks seductively in the light. As striking, the adjacent **Roter Saal**, ablaze with strawberry silk wall-coverings from Lyon and a riot of gilt trim, is modelled on Versailles, while the Renaissance-style **Florentinesaal** drips crystal from chandeliers and once rang to concerts by Brahms and Clara Schumann. Small wonder Marlene Dietrich whistled that it was the most beautiful casino in the world. You can marvel at the shameless opulence on twenty-minute tours (daily every 30min; April–Sept: 9.30–11.30am; Oct–March 10–11.30am; €4), but far better to drink in the Bond-movie glamour during the evening shuffle of cards and clatter of roulette balls (daily 2pm onwards; €3; ID required). For women dresses or skirts are obligatory, while men need a jacket and tie (€8 and €3 respectively to rent), and while smart jeans are permitted, sports shoes certainly aren't. Minimum stakes begin at €2, but night owls can watch Saudi sheiks play the final hand of baccarat around 5am, when all stake limits (usually €25,000) are waived. Needless to say, there's an ATM inside, but beware: an aide to Tsar Nicolas II arrived in 1902 with twenty million roubles' worth of booty swiped from royal treasure chests and left penniless a week later; and Dostoyevsky is said to have written *The Gambler* after he lost his shirt here.

The bandstand and Lichtentaler Allee

The small **bandstand** in front of the Kurhaus was once the stage for concerts by Strauss and Brahms. Nowadays, however, it usually plays host to light jazz to entertain summer strollers who follow in the footsteps of the fashionable spa-goers who once shamelessly posed along the adjacent avenue of chestnut trees, now lined by expensive boutiques.

But the promenade of choice for the leisured classes was **Lichtentaler Allee**, a 2.5km-long parkland avenue south of the Kurhaus and beside the Oos where you can still readily imagine the click of ebony walking-canes on cobbles and the swish of silk dresses. In 1860 at the instigation of Edouard Bénazet this simple avenue of oaks was elevated to an English-style garden of global specimen trees. Queen Victoria took the air here and Mark Twain grudgingly admired its "handsome pleasure grounds, shaded by noble trees and adorned with sparkling fountain jets". Today, perfectly clipped grass is carpeted with crocuses in March, busts of luminary guests punctuate the gardens and palatial villas look on in elegant shades of cream.

The Theater and the Kunsthalle

The first notable building on Lichtentaler Allee, the neo-Baroque **Theater**, modelled on the Paris Opera House, opened in 1863 for the première of Berlioz's *Béatrice et Bénédict* conducted by the French composer. Beside it, Weinbrenner's 1820 summer palace for Queen Friederike of Sweden has been claimed by the **International Club** as headquarters for the social event of the year, the Iffezheim horse races, while further south is the **Kunsthalle** (Tues & Thurs–Sun 11am–6pm, Wed 11am–8pm; €5), home to dependably high-profile international contemporary art exhibits. Its bold modern concrete-and-glass annex, by Richard Meier, is home to **Sammlung Frieder Burda** (Tues–Sun 10am–6pm; €9; ☎07221/39 89 80, ⓦwww.sammlung-frieder-burda.de), one of Germany's most extensive private modern art collections: a high-octane display of German Expressionism, Cubist Picassos and Abstract Expressionists such as Pollock and de Kooning.

The Stadtmuseum, Gönneranlage and Russische Kirche

South of the grand airs of the Kunsthalle, Lichtentaler Allee relaxes into such an easygoing pace that you'd never guess the traffic of the B500 thunders in a tunnel beneath your feet. At the southern end of the most formal part of the park, the **Stadtmuseum**, Lichtentaler Allee 10 (Tues–Sun 10am–6pm, Wed 10am–8pm; €4; ☎07221/93 22 72), skips through Roman roots to dwell on the vintage roulette wheels and spa cures that made Baden-Baden a glamorous nineteenth-century playground. Beside the museum, the arterial Bertholdstrasse crosses the park and a five-minute stroll beyond, across the Oos on a neat footbridge, lies the **Gönneranlage**, a secret garden behind thick beech hedges where over four hundred varieties of rose thrive in the benevolent microclimate to create a heady perfume. Pergolas, statues and fountains add structure.

The area around here, known as the Südstadt, was the traditional expat quarter and one of the outstanding mementoes of this era is the Byzantine-style **Russische Kirche** (Feb–Nov daily 10am–6pm; €0.50), which lies south along Lichtentaler Allee from the Gönneranlage, on a brief detour from Maria-Viktoria-Strasse. Crowned by a gold onion-dome, the church was built in the 1880s for a then sizeable population of expatriate Russian diplomats, nobles and writers. Its heavily frescoed interior is the work of Grigor Grigorijevitsch Gagarin, painter to the tsars.

Lichtental

A half-hour walk – or ride on bus #201 – from the Gönneranlage through parkland paths beside the Oos brings you to the southern suburb of **Lichtental**. Here the thirteenth-century **Kloster Lichtental** huddles in peaceful contemplation around a triangular courtyard of gnarled trees, screened off from the world by a high wall. The thirty nuns in residence here are famous both for their religious handicrafts and a powerful spirit distilled in the convent – both are on sale in a small shop (Mon–Sat 9am–12.30pm & 2.30–5.30pm) – while the prize of their Cistercian abbey founded in 1245 is the **Fürstenkapelle** (tours: Tues–Sun 3pm, except first Sun of month; €2), chapel of the Baden margraves until 1372. Those with sturdy legs can stroll 3km further on Geroldsauer Strasse to an idyllic waterfall snuggled in the woods – a café provides sustenance for the return journey – otherwise walk from the focal Brahmsplatz up Maximilianstrasse to the **Brahmshaus** at no. 85 (Mon, Wed & Fri 3–5pm, Sun 10am–1pm; €2). Tiny rooms where the German composer sweated over symphonies 1 and 2 and wrestled with his monumental *Deutsches Requiem* are as he knew them during his 1865–74 sojourn here.

The Altstadt

Back in the centre of Baden-Baden and just over the river east of the Kurpark and gathered around the Rathaus, lies the **Altstadt**, which is none too old, thanks to the actions of one General Duras. Leading the French troops in the Palatinate War of Succession, he swooped upon Baden-Baden in 1689 – while Margrave Ludwig Wilhelm commanded forces in Hungary – and reduced it to ashes, executing Louis XIV's order to reduce disputed borderlands into a *glacis*, or wasteland. Ludwig Wilhelm deserted his ravaged town for Rastatt in 1705 and Baden-Baden began a century-long rebuild. Though its layout is far older, most of the Altstadt buildings are a product of this rebuild – as their cream, coffee and pink facades attest.

Above this network of bustling streets, the **Marktplatz** has a forgotten feel, its shuttered villas lining up like a stage set for an Italian operetta. The square's **Rathaus** started life as a seventeenth-century Jesuit college and quietly glosses over its fourteen years as a casino and restaurant from 1810 before the Kurhaus opened for business. Opposite is the **Stiftskirche Liebfrauen**, whose landmark spire is a crash course in its history: a Romanesque square tower sprouts an octagonal Gothic cap then buds into Baroque cupolas. Inside, lurking in the gloom, is a superb late-Gothic (1467) 5.6m crucifix sculpted from a single block of sandstone, the masterpiece of Nikolaus Gerhaert von Leyden, an influential Dutch sculptor who pioneered an expressive realism. Crudely showing off before it in styles from Renaissance to Rococo are tombs of Baden-Baden margraves. The finest is a swaggering apotheosis of Ludwig Wilhelm; marshal's baton in hand, he is lauded by Courage (left), Justice (right) and Wisdom (above) and stands above the apparatus of war with which he routed Turkish forces to earn his nickname, "Turkenlouis". Don't overlook an intricate tabernacle to the left of the choir – carved two decades after Gerhaert's work, it hides polychrome saints among knotted vines and twisted branches, and its anonymous sculptor signs his work on the base with a self-portrait holding set-square and compasses.

Behind the church, occasional wisps of steam drift over the cobbles from grilles in front of the Tuscan-styled **Altes Dampfbad** (Tues–Fri 3–6pm, Sat & Sun 11am–5pm; free). From 1848, spa-goers gasped for air in its steam baths; now its lofty rooms host temporary exhibitions of culture, many with a local theme. To its left, the Schlossstaffeln stairway zigzags up to the **Neues Schloss**. The Baden margraves claimed the highest point in town for a more central seat to replace Burg Hohenbaden from 1479 until they fled to Ratstatt. Snapped up by the al-Hassawi group in 2003, there's been no public access to the Renaissance palace or the fine views from its gardens since, though there will be, once renovation work is complete.

The Bäderviertel

The narrow alleys at the northeastern end of the Altstadt open up to reveal the large buildings and parkland of the **Bäderviertel** (Baths Quarter). Baths were established here by the Romans in around 75 AD, as part of their town Aquae Aureliae, as local spring waters were thought to ease aching joints. Something of this time can still be seen in the **Römische Badruinen**, Römerstrasse 11 (mid-March to mid-Nov daily 11am–1pm & 2–5pm; €2), where the ancient bathhouses are preserved – computer animation provides a reconstruction to help make sense of the crumbling walls you can see from raised floors above them. The ruins are hidden in the basement of the famous **Friedrichsbad** (daily 9am–10pm, last entry 8pm; ☎07221/27 59 20, ⓦwww.roemisch-irisches-bad .de), the undisputed queen of German spas. By happy coincidence the wraps came off the splendid neo-Renaissance bathing hall five years after Kaiser Wilhelm I outlawed gambling in 1872, and the baths cashed in on the casino's temporary halt. And just as Bénazet had brought opulence to local gambling, so Grand Duke Friedrich I's spa elevated bathing. Outside, the Friedrichsbad looks like a minor palace, fronted by busts of Baden-Baden spa heroes including Friedrich I crowned with green copper cupolas; inside it is a paean to a golden age of antiquity, a colonnaded beauty of elegant arches and columns in tones of terracotta and stone. Speciality of the house is the Roman-Irish bath (€21, or €29 including a brush massage; towel rental included), a three-hour-long course of showers, baths, steam rooms and saunas of ever-decreasing temperatures. By stage ten, you drift dazed in a pool, watched by a ring of cherubs on an ornamented cupola; at stage sixteen you collapse, prune-like and dozy, in a resting area for a snooze. As Twain noted, "Here at the Friedrichsbad you lose track of time within ten minutes and the world within twenty." Leave your inhibitions at the door, however – bathing is mixed (except Mon & Thurs when sexes are segregated) and nude. Children under 14 are not allowed, those over only with parents.

Just across the square is the more modern **Caracalla Spa** (daily 9am–10pm, last entry 8pm; 2hr €13, 3hr €15, 4hr €17; ☏07221/27 59 20, ⊛www.caracalla .de), named in honour of the Roman emperor who nurtured Baden-Baden's bathing culture. It contains modern pools (one outdoor) between 18 and 38°C as well as steam baths and saunas (the only nude area of the complex). The three springs – the Friedrichsquelle, Fettquelle and Murquelle – that spout from fountains in the upstairs foyer can be viewed without admission, and many people simply come here to knock back a glass of their curative warm and salty water; it's not a taste that's forgotten in a hurry though.

Burg Hohenbaden

Aloof and magnificent on a bluff 3km north of the town centre, a 45-minute walk from central Baden-Baden, the ruins of **Burg Hohenbaden** (May–Sept 10am–10pm; free), the eleventh-to-fifteenth-century seat of the Baden margraves, has long been a favourite destination for a stroll: from its usurper, the Neues Schloss, take a path which meanders uphill through deciduous woods and meadows speckled with wildflowers (or bus #215 Augustaplatz or the Caracalla Spa). Its keep perches on a knuckle of rock to the rear, guarded in front by the fourteenth-century Unterburg, but the treat of the mighty fortress ruined by fires in 1584 and 1597 is simply to explore: there are vast cellar vaults to peer into; mantelpieces cling surreally halfway up walls; and stairways begin their spiral to long-crumbled towers. Sweeping views over the Black Forest and Rhine plains make the climb worth all the effort, and a **restaurant** (☏07221/269 48; closed Oct–April) rustles up inexpensive German staples and pastas. Behind the castle a path clambers through protected woods to **Battert** (Battery), a cliff popular with local climbers.

Eating and drinking

Baden-Baden is obviously good for gourmet food and high-brow entertainment, and there are places to find a bit of nightlife too, particularly in the hotels: try the *Jockey Bar* in *Badischer Hof*, or the *Oleander Bar* in *Brenner's*, but dress up for the occasion.

Restaurants

Le Jardin de France Lichtentaler Str. 13 ☏07221/300 78 60. Baden-Baden's elegant gourmet restaurant is in a courtyard off Lichtentaler Strasse, with a decor of antiques and flowers that's every bit as exquisite as the creative, modern French dishes served (mains €28–38). The service is immaculate and reservations required. Closed Tues lunch & Mon.

Medici Augustaplatz 8 ☏ 07221/20 06. *Belle époque*-style restaurant which has welcomed Bill Clinton and Nelson Mandela yet serves moderately priced (mains €8–16) items like zander filet with pancetta, tomato and aubergine torte and, the house special, a Thai chicken curry. Closed Mon.
Rathausglöckel Steinstr. 7 ☏ 07221/906 10. Traditional favourites like venison goulash (€9.50) and winter-warmer potato soup (€7) are served in this cosy sixteenth-century house on a side street off the Marktplatz.
Stahlbad Augustaplatz 2 ☏ 07221/245 69. Aristocrat among local restaurants where traditional Black Forest dishes like trout, goose or venison steak are elevated to new heights with the addition of exquisite French flavours. In the right season, look out too for the first-class fettuccini Alfredo with white truffles. Most mains are in the €15–30 range. Closed Mon.

Cafés and bars

Café König Lichtentaler Str. 12 ☏ 07221/235 73. The place for *Kaffee und Kuchen* and a throwback to the elegant days pictured on the black-and-white prints on its walls.

The delicate *Schwarzwälder Kirschtorte* (Black Forest gâteau) is the finest you'll eat and there's quiche, soups and salads for lunch. Closed eve.
In der Trinkhalle Kaiserallee 3 ☏ 07221/05 30 29. Idyllic café in a wing of the Trinkhalle that's perfect for a lazy cappuccino or light lunch on the suntrap terrace or a leather Chesterfield inside.
Kurhaus Bistro Kaiserallee 1 ☏ 07221/90 70. Attached to the Kurhaus (see p.490) and so a cut above the usual bistro, with signed photos covering the walls of dignitaries who have sampled its international menu, which follows the seasons. Dishes are in the €8–21 range.
Leo's Luisenstr. 8–10 ☏ 07221/380 81. Heaving bistro and wine bar that's Baden-Baden's hippest hangout; the restaurant – all chocolate-coloured woods and black-and-white photos – serves international dishes (average €15) in wonderful sauces nuanced with the likes of Dijon mustard and rosemary. Open until 3am.
Lowenbräu Gernsbacher Str. 9 ☏ 07221/223 11. A Bavarian beerhall wafted west to bring jollity to the town's poise. Perhaps a bit formulaic, but the beer garden and hall are both cheerful and the food dependable and solid, with mains averaging €15.

Entertainment

Outside the **casino** (see p.490) much of the rest of the entertainment centres on the 2500-seater **Festspielhaus**, Beim Alten Bahnhof 2 (☏ 07221/301 31 01, ⓦ www.festspielhaus.de), which boasts two distinguished house orchestras: the Baden-Badener Philharmonie (ⓦ www.philharmonie.baden-baden.de) and the SWR Sinfonieorchester (ⓦ www.swr-freiburg.de) and often welcomes international stars such as the London or Berlin Philharmonics. It also stages ballet and opera. The **Kurhaus** is another venue for smaller classical concerts and often jazz. Tickets to everything can be bought from a box office in the Trinkhalle (daily 10am–6.30pm; ☏ 07221/93 27 00), where you can pick up the what's-on booklet *Baden-Baden Aktuell*.

The Kinzig and Gutach valleys

The Kinzig and Gutach valleys are quintessential Black Forest landscapes; they're also the birthplace of all the most eccentric folk costumes, and cuckoo clocks are sold here by the tonne. From Baden-Baden the region is most attractively accessed along the twisty and scenic **Schwarzwaldhochstrasse** (see box opposite), which leads to the northeastern end of the steep-sided and densely forested **Kinzig Valley**, the horseshoe-shaped hub of the Black Forest's largest valley system, which is dotted with a series of picturesque small towns. Particularly appealing are the monastery and brewery town of **Alpirsbach**, and the quaint gathering of half-timbered houses at **Shiltach**. For generations this remote valley made its money logging and farming and its modest and fairly sleepy communities celebrate this heritage with various evocative museums, including the open-air **Schwarzwälder Freilichtmuseum**, one of the region's

There are various routes from Baden-Baden into the heart of the Black Forest, but the most attractive is probably the magnificent **Schwarzwaldhochstrasse** – the Black Forest Highway or B500 – which climbs from Baden-Baden through an idyllic combination of pines and meadows, valleys and peaks to Freudenstadt. The route may only be 60km long but it's worth taking about half a day over the drive, allowing for time to break the journey at the various car parks, viewpoints and belvederes which dot the route to take in fine views of the upper Rhine valley and France's Vosges.

Before you go, try to pick up a brochure on the Schwarzwaldhochstrasse at the tourist office in Baden-Baden. Other scenic-drive brochures to look out for include the **Badische Weinstrasse**, a north–south route between Baden-Baden and Freiburg that joins various wine-making areas, and one for the **Deutsche Uhrenstrasse**, which provides a cuckoo-clock tour of the central Black Forest.

premier sights, just up the feeder valley of the River **Gutach**. Further up the Gutach Valley is **Triberg**, the Black Forest's most tourist-oriented town, packed with cuckoo-clock shops and coach parties and probably worth avoiding unless you're after a chirping time-piece – in which case you'll certainly want to visit the good, nearby clock museum at **Furtwangen** too.

Train lines run along the bases of both the Kinzig and Gutach valleys, and are supplemented by a bus network, making getting around the valleys easy. Following the 91.5km **Kinzigtalradweg**, a marked cycle-route from Offenburg to Lossburg, is one way to absorb some of this region at the pace it deserves.

Alpirsbach

Strung out along a road in a tight valley, the small town of **ALPIRSBACH**, some 69km south of Baden-Baden, lacks any real heart, but is an attractive enough place thanks to a medieval golden age which left it with the Romanesque Benedictine monastery **Kloster Alpirsbach** (mid-March to Oct daily 10am–5.30pm; Nov to mid-March Thurs, Sat & Sun 1–3pm; €3; ☏07444/951 62 81, ⓦwww.schloesser-und-gaerten.de). Its hulking **Klosterkirche**, built of regional red sandstone in the eleventh century, has an empty interior, but is worth a look for its nave capitals, a tribute to the early Christian fixation with good and evil. Its **museum** includes various items from the sixteenth century, including the clothes of former pupils, who studied here once the monastery had been dissolved. The monks' chilly Dormotorium and a Calefectorium are the subject of hour-long **tours** in German (mid-March to Oct Mon–Sat 11am, noon, 1.30pm, 2.30pm & 3.30pm, Sun hourly 12.30pm–3.30pm; Nov to mid-March Thurs, Sat & Sun 2pm; €8), as is the brewery museum of the adjacent **Alpirsbacher Klosterbräu** (daily 2.30pm; €6) in which a variety of local beers are introduced (in German).

Alpirsbach's **tourist office**, Hauptstrasse 20 (☏07444/951 62 81, ⓦwww .alpirsbach.de), is beside the train station a short walk from the centre of town and has plenty of hiking and cycling information as well as accommodation listings.

Schiltach

From Alpirsbach, the Kinzig flows 9km southwest to the tiny, postcard-perfect town of **SCHILTACH**. It's a quiet place, gathered around the gurgling river where an old lumber mill has been reconstructed for the **Schüttesägemuseum**

(Sawmill Museum; late March to Oct daily 11am–5pm; Nov to late Dec Sat & Sun 11am–5pm; free) in the centre of town, where black-and-white photos of loggers illustrate the region's history. The town's focus, a steeply sloping Marktplatz a couple of minutes' walk upstream, is encircled by half-timbered buildings dating no earlier than the mid-sixteenth century. Murals on its Rathaus explain why: look out for the witch who was allegedly responsible for a conflagration which reduced the town to ashes in 1533.

Schiltach's **tourist office**, close to the sawmill museum at Hauptstrasse 5 (May–Sept Mon–Fri 9am–noon & 2–5pm, Sat 10am–noon; Oct–April Mon–Thurs 9am–noon & 2–5pm, Fri 9am–noon; ☏07836/58 50, ⓦwww.schiltach .de), has the usual accommodation listings and can point you in the direction of a couple of good local walks. *Zum Weyssen Rössle*, Schenkenzeller Strasse 42 (☏07836/387; ❹), a couple of minutes' walk east of the Marktplatz, is a good old-fashioned **hotel**, though with free wi-fi, and a **restaurant** (mains around €10; closed Mon) where the German cooking is far more adventurous than the rustic decor would suggest.

The Schwarzwälder Freilichtmuseum

Just short of the workaday town of Hausach, 14km west of Schiltach, the Kinzig is joined by the Gutach tributary. This small stream is responsible for the broad 25km-long Gutach Valley – which stretches south to Triberg and beyond and famous for its *Bollenhut*, a black hat with red pompoms worn as a traditional folk costume by women and reproduced in tourist literature throughout the region.

Just over 1km south of the Gutach's confluence with the Kinzig lies the **Schwarzwälder Freilichtmuseum** (daily: March–July & Sept–Oct 9am–6pm; Aug 9am–7pm; €6; ☏07831/935 60, ⓦwww.vogtsbauernhof.org), an open-air museum focused on an old farm – the Vogtsbauernhof – that has been here since 1570. Its huge roof is typical of the local traditional building style and the sort of place that caused Jerome K. Jerome to comment: "The great charm about a Black Forest house is its sociability: the cows are in the next room, the horses are upstairs, the geese and ducks in the kitchen, while the pigs, children and chickens live all over the place."

The 26 other buildings in the complex – which include a sawmill, granary, bakery, distillery, smithy and chapel – have been moved here from elsewhere to create a rather phoney little village. But great effort has gone into authentically furnishing them all and costumed guides doing craft demonstrations help bring the place alive and broaden the appeal.

Triberg

From where it meets the Kinzig Valley, the Gutach Valley progressively narrows then climbs to a point some 1000m above sea level after 20km, where the air is so pure it once made the town of **TRIBERG** a health resort. But this was long ago, and today the town is obsessed with only one thing: the cuckoo clock. Thousands are on sale here and the tourist traffic the industry spawns can be nightmarish; but if you embrace the kitsch and are in the market for a clock, it can be fun.

The long, thin **Marktplatz** that follows the main road through town is its natural focus, with a large pilgrimage church, or Wallfahrtskirche, looming over it decked out in florid Baroque. But the busiest end of town is uphill from here at a bend in the main road, where clock shops are squeezed together. They're an attraction in themselves (see box opposite), and certainly as well visited

The cuckoo clock

The origins of the **cuckoo clock** are uncertain. Though the first known description comes from Saxony in the mid-sixteenth century, it's thought they were probably first made in Bohemia. Certainly it was only about a hundred years later – in the 1730s – that cuckoo clocks began to be made in the Black Forest, with Schönwald near Triberg being the site of the earliest workshops. The quality of the craftsmanship and engineering quickly captured the imagination and the European market, and the cuckoo clock has roosted here ever since. Local shops sell a bewildering array, but as the over-eager shop assistants will inform you, it all boils down to three designs – the **chalet**, the **hunting theme** and the simple **carved cuckoo**. The technology in each is much the same, clocks with small pine cones dangling below them require daily winding while those with larger cones need only weekly attention. There's more labour-saving on hand, thanks to the digital revolution which hasn't been allowed to bypass this traditional craft: some models are battery- and quartz-driven, and play recordings of an actual cuckoo on the hour; others are even light sensitive so both you and the bird can get some sleep. Prices vary according to the size of the clock. Good-sized clocks can be bought for under €100, but for a real talking piece you'll need to pay almost twice that – and some creations fetch thousands.

The choice is overwhelming, competition keen and almost all shops offer shipping services, but one shop you might want to visit is the **Uhren-Park**, Schonachbach 27 (Easter–Oct Mon–Sat 9am–6pm, Sun 10am–6pm; ⓦ www.uhren-park.de), on the main road 2.7km south of Triberg, which charges a €1.50 fee to see what it claims is the largest cuckoo clock in the world – though there's a rival claimant on the other side of town. For a less commercialized insight try the excellent **Deutsches Uhrenmuseum** (daily: April–Oct 9am–6pm; Nov–March 10am–5pm; €4; ⓣ07723/920 28 00, ⓦ www .deutsches-uhrenmuseum.de), 16km south of Triberg in Furtwangen, which has an inspiring glut of timepieces in myriad styles from just about every era; naturally these include many elaborate and aged cuckoo clocks.

▲ Traditional Black Forest cuckoo clock

as the town's two other main attractions nearby. The better of the two is the **Schwarzwaldmuseum**, Wallfahrtstrasse 4 (Nov–Easter Tues–Sun 10am–5pm; May–Oct daily 10am–6pm €4.50; ⓣ07722/4434, ⓦ www.schwarzwaldmuseum .de), a cache of local curios. Of course clock-making apparatus is here in force, but so too are various other mechanical instruments including what claims to be Europe's largest barrel-organ collection and a model Schwarzwaldbahn. As interesting is the collection of local folk costumes, including, of course, the *Bollenhut*, and there are sections on mining and winter sports, both traditionally a major part of life hereabouts.

The town's other main sight is a bit of a disappointment, even though it calls itself Germany's longest **waterfall**. In reality this is a series of seven smaller falls over a distance of 163m, but their natural beauty is completely compromised by the presence of the strolling masses on wide pavements alongside. Between April and October the charge for walking them is €2.

Practicalities

Despite its remote location, Triberg is well integrated into the rail system on the route of the Schwarzwaldbahn between Offenburg and Konstanz. Its **train** and **bus** stations lie a fifteen-minute walk downhill of its centre and the helpful **tourist office**, Wahlfahrtstrasse 4 (daily 10am–5pm; ℡07722/86 64 90, ⓦwww.triberg.de). They have plenty of English-language information on the area and accommodation listings which include a good number of traditional farmhouse bed-and-breakfasts (❷), much the best local option if you have your own transport; they also announce themselves with "*Zimmer frei*" signs along country roads.

Adler Hauptstr. 52 ℡07722/45 74. Café and hotel with hands-down some of the best cakes in the region, which can be enjoyed in a little courtyard away from the main road. The rooms are spacious and well turned out, and the breakfast buffet tremendous. ❸
DJH Triberg Rohrbacher Str. 35 ℡07722/41 10, ⓦwww.jugendherberge-triberg.de. Somewhat institutional but comfortable hostel on a ridge at the southeastern edge of town a 3km walk from the Bahnhof. Dorms are mostly six-bed and cost from €18.70.
Gästehaus Maria Spitz Weihermatte 5, Schonach ℡07722/54 34. Hillside farmhouse

3.7km west of Triberg where cattle graze beneath your bedroom window and you can enjoy freshly baked bread for breakfast, and milk and eggs direct from the barn. ❷
Parkhotel Wehrle Gartenstr. 24 ℡07222/860 20, ⓦwww.parkhotel-wehrle.de. Triberg's most prestigious lodging in this four-star number where Hemingway once stayed on a fishing trip. As well as the old-fashioned charm of a house built in the 1600s and individually decorated rooms with rustic frills, there's a health centre with a pool and a garden. The restaurant is one of the best in the area, with its traditional game dishes (mains around €28) among the best. ❻

Freiburg

Blessed with Germany's sunniest climate and wooded hills that virtually rise out of a picture-postcard Altstadt, **FREIBURG** – officially Freiburg im Breisgau – is an immediately likeable place. Its accessible size makes it easy to explore and the sizeable university helps make it an upbeat, lively place. Though the town centre is quickly covered, the city's role as a regional transport hub makes Freiburg a good base for a few days' exploration of the hills around the town and the southern Black Forest, putting the town's good **cafés**, **restaurants** and **nightlife** at your disposal after a day in the mountains.

The town also plays host to several lively festivals: **Fastnet** is celebrated with various fire rituals and particular gusto on the eve of Shrove Tuesday, and preceded by a jester parade the day before. Other celebrations fill the summer, with the late June and early July **Internationales Zeltmusikfest**, hosting many musical genres, but particularly jazz; while the late July **Weintagen** and mid-August **Weincost** both celebrate local wines. The city also has a big ten-day **Volksfest** as part of the May **Frühlingsfest**, and the October **Herbstfest**.

Arrival, information, tours and city transport

Basel's **Euroairport**, 74km to the south, is connected to Freiburg by the buses Freiburger Reisedienst (55min; €20; ☎0761/50 05 00, ⓦwww.freiburger -reisedienst.de), which pull into the **bus station** beside the **Hauptbahnhof** on the western edge of the Altstadt. From here it's an easy five-minute walk to the **tourist office** on Rathausplatz (June–Sept Mon–Fri 9.30am–8pm, Sat 9.30am–5pm, Sun 10am–noon; Oct–May Mon–Fri 9.30am–6pm, Sat 9.30am– 2.30pm, Sun 10am–noon; ☎0761/388 18 85, ⓦwww.freiburg.de), departure point for the informative ninety-minute English-language **walking tours** of Freiburg Kultour (April–Oct Mon–Fri 10.30am, Sat 10am; Nov–March Sat 10am, Sun 10.30am; €7; ☎0761/290 74 47, ⓦwww.freiburg-kultour.com). Walking is the best way to explore the city, though Freiburg's **bus** and **tram**

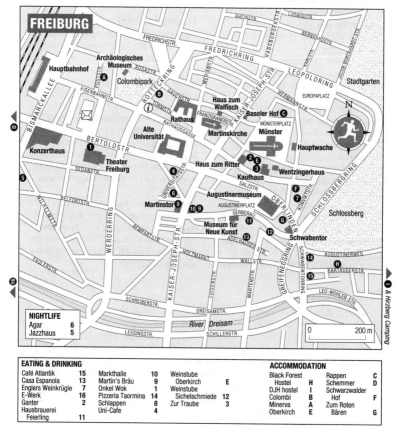

service run by VAG (@www.vag-freiburg.de) is excellent. For **bike rental**, try Mobile, Wenzingerstrasse 15 near the Hauptbahnhof (☎0761/292 79 98, @www.mobile-freiburg.com), who offer bikes for €15 per day.

Accommodation

Freiburg has the full range of **accommodation** choices from a pleasant campground and hostel on the edge of town to central options to suit every budget. However, competition for beds can be keen, so if you're having trouble head straight for the tourist office and get them to do the legwork for a €3 fee.

Hotels and pensions

Colombi Am Colombi Park ☎0761/2 10 60, @www.colombi.de. Tradition, taste and luxury are combined to create this *grande dame* of Freiburg's hotels. Amenities include a pool, steam baths, sauna and gourmet restaurant; its park-side location is central yet quiet. **8**

Minerva Poststr. 8 ☎0761/38 64 90, @www .minerva-freiburg.de. Hotel in an elegant Art Nouveau building a 5min walk from the Altstadt. Rooms are spotless and modern, and there's a sauna and free wi-fi. **5**

Oberkirch Münsterplatz 22 ☎0761/202 68 68, @www.hotel-oberkirch.de. Open the curtains to Münster views in this traditional family-run place. Its rooms – including some well-priced singles – have a rustic feel, and the German restaurant is classy. **6**

Rappen Münsterplatz 13 ☎0761/313 53, @www .hotelrappen.de. Old-fashioned place in the thick of things with its own *Weinstube* and café on Münsterplatz and with a dash of Black Forest cosiness inside. Rooms are straightforward but some have fine Münster views. Free wi-fi. **4**

Schemmer Eschholzstr. 63 ☎0761/20 74 90, @www.hotel-schemmer.de. Tidy little hotel in a town house a short walk from the Hauptbahnhof and the cheapest central deal, though not all the modest rooms have their own bathroom. **2**

Schwarzwalder Hof Herrenstr. 43 ☎0761/380 30, @www.shof.de. Small and smart hotel a stone's throw from Münsterplatz whose rooms all have solid wood flooring, minimalist elegance and free internet connections. **6**

🏃 **Zum Roten Bären** Oberlinden 12 ☎0761/878 70, @www.roter-baeren.de. Germany's oldest hotel, inside Schwabentor, welcomed its first guests in 1120, two hundred years before the Münster's spire was sketched on to parchment. Scattered antiques continue to give it a venerable feel, while all facilities have been brought up to date. **6**

Hostels and camping

🏃 **Black Forest Hostel** Kartäuserstr. 33 ☎0761/881 78 70, @www.blackforest -hostel.de. Laid-back bohemian place with sociable vibe and large communal areas – which include a kitchen – as well as internet and bike rental. Offers singles, doubles and dorm beds from €13. **2**

DJH hostel Kartäuserstr. 151 ☎0761/676 56, @www.jugendherberge-freiburg.de. Massive and hugely popular hostel that's often packed with school groups despite a rather inconvenient location beyond the eastern fringes of town and 3km from the Altstadt: take tram #1 to Römerhof then follow signs for the remaining 10min walk. Dorms €24.90.

Hirzberg Camping Kartäuserstr. 99 ☎0761/350 54, @www.freiburg-camping.de. Well-organized and leafy, but tightly packed campground where two adults with a tent pay €15.50 and where you can also rent tents (€9). It's 1.5km east of Altstadt and near the Stadthalle stop of tram #1.

The Altstadt

Freiburg's **Altstadt** was founded in 1091 and – despite suffering twenty minutes of bombardment in the war in which over eighty percent of the town was levelled – still preserves a quaint and historic feel. One curious feature that makes the place more interesting are its *Bächle*, little streams sunken into the pavement on most streets. Originally providing water for animals and fire fighters, today they're largely decorative, though plenty of people use them to cool their heels on a summer's day.

The Altstadt fans out around a magnificent **Münster** and focuses on a series of squares, which don't take much more than a morning to explore.

The Münster

Built from the region's signature dark red sandstone, Freiburg's magnificent Gothic **Münster** was lucky to come out of the war almost unscathed. Work on the church began in around 1200 when Freiburg's population was around four thousand, its giant dimensions saying a lot about local civic ambitions of the time, particularly since it wasn't a bishopric so all funding had to come from local coffers. One of the first parts of the church to be built was the **west porch**, now the most magnificent entrance with impressive rows of carvings that produce something of a poor-man's Bible, but include no less than 125 images of Maria, to whom the church is devoted.

Within, the gloominess of the church interior serves to enhance the dazzling affect of the incredible **stained glass**: note the forerunner of today's banner advertising in the panes at the base of the windows. Here the boots of the cobblers' guild and the pretzels of the bakers show exactly who sponsored the church.

This reliance on local funding was one reason why the Münster took four hundred years to build, which resulted in a medley of styles. The earliest sections – easily identifiable by small windows and thick walls – are Romanesque and copy elements of Basel's Münster – while later Gothic sections belong to a period when local architects looked to copy Strasbourg for inspiration and built with huge arches and giant windows.

Of the many pieces of ecclesiastical art dotting the church, those in the **ambulatory** are particularly noteworthy. Recesses here are lined with the altarpieces of rich church patrons – look out for one by Hans Holbein the Younger – while at their centre is the exquisite **high altar** painted between 1512 and 1516 by Hans Baldung Grien, a pupil of Albrecht Dürer.

Rising high above all this is the Münster's 116m **tower**, with octagonal summit. At this height it was seen to metaphorically reach out to God, while its filigree stonework, completed in 1330, makes it Germany's first openwork spire, its carvings inspired by mysticism. The workmanship can be admired while climbing it (Mon–Sat 9.30am–5pm, Sun 1–5pm; €1.50) en route to views over town, the surrounding hills and all the way into France.

Münsterplatz

Surrounding Freiburg's chief church, the **Münsterplatz** is home to a bustling daily market but is largely the work of modern builders since much of it was levelled during World War II and not rebuilt in the original style. One notable exception is the blood-red **Historisches Kaufhaus** on the southern side, a 1530 trading hall. Three of the four Habsburg emperors decorating the facade visited Freiburg, back in the days when the town gave itself to them for protection, making it a part of the Austrian empire. Of the two Baroque palaces either side of the Kaufhaus the **Wentzingerhaus** (1761) to the east is the more remarkable. Once the town house of sculptor Christian Wentzinger it now houses the **Museum für Stadtgeschichte** (Tues–Fri 10am–5pm, Sat & Sun 10.30am–5pm; €2; ☏0761/201 25 15), which offers a few interesting insights into Freiburg's history. As impressive are the mansion's elaborate frescoes and fine Rococo staircase railings; Wentzinger also left lovingly crafted allegorical statues of the four seasons in the back garden.

Augustinerplatz and around

Alleys between buildings on the southern side of Münsterplatz lead through to Schusterstrasse, one of Freiburg's best-preserved – or rather reconstructed – medieval streets where pavement mosaics announce tradesmen and shops. The next street south, Salzstrasse, is a broader thoroughfare and flanked by

Freiburg's Museumticket

Freiburg has five municipal museums (ⓦ www.museen.freiburg.de): the Augustiner-museum, Museum für Neue Kunst, Adelhausermuseum, Archäologisches Museum Colombischlössle and the Museum für Stadtgeschichte. The **Museumticket**, available at any of them and the tourist office, costs just €4.20 for a one-day pass for entry to all of them.

Augustinerplatz, a relaxed square around which lie three reasonable museums. The **Augustinermuseum** (Tues–Sun 10am–5pm; €2; ☎0761/201 25 31) is based on the extensive medieval art collection of a former monastery and has in its ecclesiastical art collection several old masters, including paintings by Cranach the Elder and Hans Baldung Grien. Also worth a look is the exceptional stained-glass collection, which includes some of the earliest of the Münster windows, placed here for preservation, while copies are in situ. A section on folklore is also of interest if you are about to explore the Black Forest.

Regional culture also influences the Expressionist and Abstract art of the **Museum für Neue Kunst**, Marienstrasse 10 (Tues–Sun 10am–5pm; €2; ☎0761/201 25 81), just southeast of Augustinerplatz. It's particularly strong on German Expressionism and its counterpoint the New Objectivity. Behind the museum the thirteenth-century Schwabentor, one of Freiburg's main town gates, is worth a look before backtracking to the **Adelhausermuseum**, an ethnographic museum with some interesting gems scoured from the seven seas that will be inaccessible until its renovation is complete in the spring of 2010.

The University Quarter

From Augustinerplatz, the old-tannery street Gerberau leads west to the town's other surviving main gate, the **Martinstor**, which marks the beginning of a network of streets that spreads west into a university quarter. The arterial Kaiser-Joseph-Strasse, which passes through the gate and runs north through town, is little more than a strip of chain and department stores, and better passed over in favour of walking the parallel Universitätstrasse to the west. There are no real set-piece sights here, but the bustling atmosphere and pavement cafés make it a place to linger. At its northern end Universitätstrasse empties into Rathausplatz, where the Renaissance **Neues Rathaus** – whose carillon plays daily at noon – is linked to the 1559 Altes Rathaus. Looming over both is the **Martinskirche**, a former Franciscan monastery church that was badly battered in World War II, but meticulously rebuilt. West of the Rathausplatz, Rathauspassage is a lively narrow street that leads to the edge of the Altstadt where things quickly open up around the **Columbiapark**, Freiburg's most central park. Here the Colombischlössle villa houses the **Archäologisches Museum**, Rotteckring 5 (Tues–Sun 10am–5pm; €2; ☎0761/201 25 71), which has a collection of Stone Age, Celtic and Roman remains, and is, like Freiburg's other municipal museums, hardly unmissable, but deserving of a quick look.

Eating and drinking

As befits a place with students and fine weather, there are lots of relaxed **cafés** with pavement seating for lazing around in and cheerful **bars** with beer gardens in which to unwind. The **restaurant** scene is a shade less vibrant, though there are options enough.

Cafés and cheap eats

🏃 **Markthalle** Martinsgässle 235 & Grünewalderstr. 4. Food court that bustles with locals visiting different kiosks for quality regional Swabian, Mexican, Indian, Asian, French and Italian dishes. It's standing only, so hardly a place for a relaxed bite, but the food is excellent value and service quick. The entrance can be tricky to find: the side entrance lies at the end of an alley just east of the Martinstor, the main entrance is barely more obvious and off Grünewalderstrasse.

Onkel Wok Bertoldstr. 53 ☎0761/767 15 67. Hectic Asian place with an open kitchen and great, freshly prepared food that keeps it busy around the clock. Fill up from as little as €4.

Uni-Cafe Niemensstr. 7 ☎0761/38 33 55. Cult, local, see-and-be-seen place, one of a cluster of cafés on this pedestrianized corner of the university district.

Restaurants

Casa Espanola Adelhauser Str. 9 ☎0761/202 30 40. Fairly basic tapas bar of the sort found everywhere in Spain but rarely outside. The tapas are top-notch – and the clay dishes of fat prawns in sizzling garlic oil a particular treat – and there's an extensive Iberian wine selection.

🏃 **E-Werk** Ferdinand-Weiss-Str. 6a ☎0761/28 70 70. Gourmet restaurant at the back of a bar of the same name. The menu is oft-changing but always creative and with a bit of Mediterranean flair; a bit pricey but there are several set-meals in the €20–30 price range.

🏃 **Pizzeria Taormina** Schwabentorring 4 ☎0761/341 60. Modest pizzeria serving the best pizzas in Freiburg and at very reasonable prices.

Zur Traube Schusterstr. 17 ☎0761/321 90. This romantic, refined six-hundred-year-old member of Freiburg's culinary elite provides a short, but exquisite menu of game, meat and fish dishes (mains €13–32) prepared with classic French flavours. Closed Tues & Wed.

Bars and microbreweries

Café Atlantik Schwabentorring 7. Scrappy dive with cheap food and lively goings-on, with bands occasionally playing and the place open until at least 2am.

Englers Weinkrügle Konvikstr. 12 ☎0761/38 31 15. Cosy wood-panelled *Weinstube* with very good and reasonably priced regional food (mains average €11).

Ganter Münsterplatz 18–20 ☎0761/343 67. Belonging to the town's largest brewery with a commanding location on the Münsterplatz, there's a good range of beers, including an unfiltered *Urtrunk*, and also hearty meals, though they're nothing special.

Hausbrauerei Feierling Gerberau 46 ☎0761/24 34 80. Cheerful microbrewery with wood-and-copper interior and Freiburg's best beer garden. Serves a good range of pub food – mains average €9 and include giant *Schnitzels* as well as a handful of veggie options. Its sour *Patrizier-Bräu* beer has a bit of a cult following, but is an acquired taste.

🏃 **Martin's Bräu** Kaiser-Joseph-Str. 237 ☎0761/387 00 18. Cosy cellar microbrewery, with a great selection of beers, including several wheat beers and a tasty smoky *Rauchbier*. The basic pub-grub is nothing special (mains average €10), but at least the kitchen closes late at 11.30pm.

Schlappen Löwenstr. 2 ☎0761/334 94. Laid-back studenty pub with jazz-themed decor that's known for its huge range of absinthe and whiskies. Also reasonable for simple food like *Flammküchen* – done here to perfection – with dishes in the €4–9 range.

Weinstube Oberkirch Münsterplatz 22 ☎0761/202 68 68. Excellent traditional place with outdoor seating on the Münsterplatz. Food is of a traditional regional variety, served in large portions and including good poultry dishes (around €12), particularly pheasant. Also has rooms; see p.500.

Weinstube Sichelschmiede Insel 1 ☎0761/350 37. A quirky delight in one of the loveliest corners of Freiburg. There are lots of nooks full of country clutter to nestle into and its food is a triumph of good-value home-cooking.

Entertainment and nightlife

There's plenty going on in Freiburg and the **nightlife** tends to morph out of some of the more popular and late-opening cafés and bars, making it best to just investigate one or two and go with the flow. To see what's on pick up the monthly listings magazine *Freiburg Aktuell*. Tickets to most events are sold by BZ-Kartenservice, Bertholdstrasse 7 (☎01805/55 66 56, ⓦwww.badische-zeitung.de).

Clubs and venues

Agar Löwenstr. 8 ☎0761/38 06 50. One of Freiburg's longest-standing clubs with three bars and a large dance floor. Theme nights are regularly organized and it's particularly busy on Sunday nights when cover (usually around €5) is waived for the over-30s.

Jazzhaus Schnewlinstr. 1☎0761/349 73, ⓦwww.jazzhaus.de. Club in an old wine cellar that hosts all manner of musical events, from world music concerts through blues, jazz, rock and hip-hop to busy, fairly mainstream weekend club nights – all attracting a wide age-range. Big names occasionally play here, when tickets run to around €10–30, otherwise the cover is about €6. Open until at least 3am most nights.

Konzerthaus Konrad-Adenauer-Platz 1 ☎0761/388 15 52, ⓦwww.konzerthaus.freiburg .de. Modern concert hall and arts venue and home to regular performances by the Freiburger Barockorchester (ⓦwww.barockorchester.de).

Around Freiburg

The hills of the Black Forest almost rise out of Freiburg's Altstadt giving the town a hugely convenient outdoorsy playground for hikers and mountain bikers. The largest of these forested peaks, the **Shauinsland**, has its summit 7km south of the city and beyond that lies a series of rounded and densely forested mountains around the Feldberg (see p.507), which include the ski resort of **Todtnau**. To the west the land flattens around the Rhine and the French border, making the cluster of hills called the **Kaiserstuhl** stick out in what's otherwise a clear run up to the impressive Vosges mountains on the horizon. This stretch of the Rhine Valley is also home to the **Europa-Park**, Germany's largest theme-park, which is packed with rides and commercial joy.

Getting to all these places by **public transport** from Freiburg is reasonably straightforward, though in most cases you'll have to change services en route, but it's all frequent enough to make them easy day-trips. Services are coordinated by RVF (☎0761/20 72 80, ⓦwww.rvf.de) and their €10 REGIO24 ticket is a useful day-pass that covers all the places detailed in the rest of this chapter. The group version of the ticket covers up to five people travelling together for €17 per day.

Shauinsland

Translating as "look at the land", the 1286m mountain of **Shauinsland** is true to its name, lying as it does on the edge of the Black Forest range. The stellar views are also easily reached, thanks to the **Shauinslandbahn** (daily: Jan–July 9am–5pm, July–Sept 9am–6pm, Oct–Dec 9am–5pm; return €11.50; ☎0761/451 17 77, ⓦwww.bergwelt-schauinsland.de), a cable car that makes the lengthy journey up a snap. At the top a short trail leads the remaining five-minute walk to a lookout tower and the top of several well-marked trails. These offer first-class hiking and mountain biking – partly because almost the entire 14km journey back to Freiburg is downhill – with great views along the way. Despite good signposting a map is useful, since many trails crisscross the mountain; pick this up at the tourist office or a bookshop before you strike out. To get to the Shauinslandbahn take tram #2 to its Günterstal terminus, then bus #21.

Todtnau

The quiet little mountain town of **TODTNAU**, 32km southeast of Freiburg and 25km beyond the Shauinslandbahn, bustles with activity in winter when it becomes a gateway to a network of ski lifts around the Feldberg (see p.507).

One lift, up the Hasenhorn (☎07671/96 980, ⓦwww.hasenhorn-rodelbahn
.de), carries **toboggans** (half-day ticket €16; rental €6) and continues to attract
a steady trickle of visitors in summer thanks to the presence of a 2.9km roller-
coaster-cum-bobsleigh track (single ride €8.50) and a couple of excellent
downhill **mountain-bike** trails aimed at experienced riders who can buy or
rent any equipment they need at the base-station shop.

From Freiburg you need to change at Kirchzarten or Titisee (see p.506) for
Todtnau; either way the journey takes around an hour but travels through some
fine scenery.

Kaiserstuhl

The **Kaiserstuhl** is something of a geological oddity: a small group of
hills of volcanic origin on an otherwise flat plain around the Rhine 25km
northwest of Freiburg. Their isolated position have made them ripe for local
legends: that Frederick Barbarossa died here en route to the Holy Land,
and it is said to be shaped to seat him on his second coming. But until that
happens the land offers great hiking and biking along with splendid views
of the Black Forest region and the Rhine Valley framed by France's Vosges
mountains. Thanks to its volcanic soil and clement microclimate, an array
of fruit orchards – striking when blooming in spring – and vineyards thrive
here, with the area noted for *Spätburgunder* (Pinot Noir) and *Grauburgunder*
(Pinot Gris). Many of the steep local slopes are densely terraced and several
rustic wine-bars tempt for a tipple.

An easy way to explore is to take the **Kaiserstuhlbahn**, a rail loop of the
hills, easily picked up at the town of **Riegel am Kaiserstuhl**, itself a fifteen-
minute hop from Freiburg by train. Riegel is also the start of the 15km
Winzerweg, a hiking trail northeast to southwest across the Kaiserstuhl,
through a series of vineyards and past several taverns to the train station at the
small town of Achkarren. Another way to explore is by bike, following the
64km **Kaiserstuhltour**, a loop of the region which makes a good day out for
reasonably fit cyclists and which is signposted from Breisach, a regional town
on the French border 27km west of Freiburg.

Europa-Park

Though not that well-known beyond Germany's borders, the **Europa-Park**
(daily mid-March to early Nov 9am–6pm; Dec 11am–7pm; €31.50; ☎01805/77
66 88, ⓦwww.europapark.de) is one of Europe's premier theme-parks and a
sure-fire kid-pleaser, with about fifty rides in an area around the size of eighty
football pitches and set amid a number of villages themed by European country.
Located 35km north of Frieburg near the village of Rust, it's particularly
convenient for drivers heading between Strasbourg or Karlsruhe and the Swiss
Alps. For those reliant on public transport, it's a simple matter of taking a train
to Ringsheim and then a shuttle bus to the park.

The southern Black Forest

From Freiburg the Southern Black Forest rises rapidly to the southeast,
becoming much wilder, which is best appreciated along the deep, dark
canyon of the **Höllental**. Its raw, jagged and shaded cliffs begin 15km east
of Freiburg and are followed by the B31 and Höllentalbahn, a train line that

▲ Traditional Black Forest festival

winds through a creative network of tunnels and viaducts; when it was built in 1887 much of the engineering involved was ground breaking. All this is best appreciated along the **gorge footpath**, which makes for a good four-hour hike back from the train station at **Titisee**, the first town along it. However, the quiet, resort town of Titisee itself is defined more by its location beside an eponymous lake, popular with older holidaymakers. Younger visitors are more likely to head up the **Feldberg**, the highest peak in the area, for skiing and hiking. Only smaller settlements dot its slopes, and the area of more densely wooded hills just south of here is also thinly populated, with the modest lakeside resort town of **Schluchsee** and small spa resort of **St Blasien** the only exceptions. Trains offer the most obvious and attractive way into the area, but its **bus network** is also well organized, reasonably frequent, and included in the price of a ski pass or accommodation – where you'll be given a Gästekarte. The towns below also form a good scenic loop that can be driven from Freiburg in a day.

Titisee

The relaxed but rather touristy lake-resort of **TITISEE** lies 29km from Freiburg, via the Höllentalbahn or the B31, and offers a quick way into the mountains. There are plenty of well-marked hiking, cycling and cross-country skiing routes in the area, making it easy to leave the crowds and lake front souvenir shops behind, and there's always the option of messing around on the quiet scenic lake with short cruises offered and rowing boats for rent. The most obvious walk is the easy 6km hike around the lake and the 1192m Hochfirst; only the most basic of maps is needed to tackle these, available free from the **tourist office**.

Practicalities

Titisee's lakefront **tourist office**, Strandbadstrasse 4 (May–Oct Mon–Fri 9am–6pm, Sat & Sun 10am–1pm; Nov–April Mon–Fri 9am–noon & 1.30–5pm; ☏07651/980 40, Ⓦwww.titisee-neustadt.de), is in the Kurhaus, a signed five-minute walk from the **train station**. Their local **accommodation** listings include the DJH hostel, Bruderhalde 27 (☎07651/238, ⓦwww .jugendherberge-titisee-veltishof.de; dorms €18.70), a fine hostel 2km south of the tourist office – take bus #7300 or a thirty-minute walk. Other lodgings include the well-priced *Gästehaus Wiesler*, Bruderhalde 8 (☎07652/16 18, ⓦwww.gaestehaus-wiesler.de; ❷), in a romantic spot ten minutes' walk southwest of town and close to the lake with its dated but spotless wood-clad rooms. A notch up, but also good value is the *Parkhotel Waldeck*, Parkstrasse 4–6 (☎07651/80 90, ⓦwww.parkhotelwaldeck.de; ❸), with its small colourful rooms and good spa which includes a pool, hot tubs and saunas. The top of the local pile is *Treschers Schwarzwaldhotel*, Seestrasse 10 (☎07651/80 50, ⓦwww.schwarzwaldhotel-trescher.de; ❼), a sprawling lakeside place with even better amenities and a good **restaurant** known for its excellent local trout; reservations recommended. The *Parkhotel* also has a good restaurant, and there are plenty of places to browse around the lakefront.

Feldberg

At 1493m the **Feldberg** is the Black Forest's highest mountain, but it's hardly a soaring peak. Instead its huge bulk rears into a bald, rather flat, treeless dome. Nevertheless, the area is protected as a nature reserve where wildflowers flourish as do unusual fauna like mountain hens and goat-like chamois. The scattered presence of traditional Black Forest farmhouses and the occasional alpine hut add to the charm. But most houses in the area are part of the small villages that provide for the major regional **downhill-skiing centre** on the mountain. One such is the village of **FELDBERG**, little more than a group of roadside houses on a 1234m-high pass, but which includes the **Haus der Natur** (July & Aug Mon–Fri 8.30am–5.30pm, Sat & Sun 10am–noon; ☎07676/93 36 66), at the base of the Feldberg chairlift, which has various displays on natural history. There's also good **cross-country skiing** here, with some trails using the excellent summertime **Feldberg-Steig**, a highly recommended 12km hiking loop that links five alpine huts around the upper reaches of the Feldberg. Much of it passes over open ground, offering open vistas which many other Black Forest hikes lack.

Practicalities

The nearest **train station** to Feldberg is Feldberg-Bärental on the branch line from Titisee. **Buses** provide a frequent service for the final 6km to the village of Feldberg. **Tourist information** is provided by the Haus der Natur. The Feldberg chairlift costs €6.90 for a return trip in summer, while in winter it's part of a network of 28 ski lifts and covered by a day pass (€23).

The modern DJH hostel is at Passhöhe 14 (☎07676/211, ⓦwww .jugendherberge-feldberg.de; dorms from €23.60). Other options include *Haus Waldvogel*, Köpfleweg 25 (☎07676/480, ⓦwww.cafe-waldvogel.de; ❸), which has plush modern rooms on a sunny spot on the pass as well as excellent home-made cakes in its café and a reasonable **restaurant**. But given the general lack of services and nightlife in Feldberg, for a longer stay it might be better to stay in the valley in the more well-rounded village of **ALTGLASHÜTTEN**, 8km away, at the *Sonneck Hotel*, Schwarzen-bachweg 5 (☎07676/211, ⓦwww.sonneck-feldberg.de; ❸), a chalet with smart modern rooms opposite the village tourist office and again with a good regional restaurant.

Schluchsee

A far larger body of water than the Titisee and farther off the beaten track, 10km to its south, is the more relaxed **Schluchsee**. It's a quiet, calm and clean lake and several communities bask in its peace along its eastern shore. The largest, also called **SCHLUCHSEE**, has a reasonable beach, managed as the Aqua Fun Strandbad (late May to mid-Sept daily 9am–7pm; €3.80; ☎07656/77 32), the most popular place to swim on the lake. The town is also the local hub for sailing and windsurfing as well as the boat trips of Thomas Toth, which circle the lake at hourly intervals (May to late Oct 10am–5pm; €6; ☎07656/92 30, ⓦwww.seerundfahrten.de) and stop at various points where you can hop on and off. Meanwhile, on land, you might try the easy two-hour walk up to the **Riesenbühlturm** (1097m) for lake views, and on to the **Vogelhaus**, Unterfischbach 12 (June–Aug Tues–Sun 1–4pm), 1km northeast, where for 25 years Helga Reichenbach has been crafting all manner of traditional Black Forest costume and handicrafts; you can pick up a mini-*Bollenhut*. The walk starts off Dresselbacher Strasse just northeast of town and continues up a forestry track just to the right of a sports centre; maps of this and other local walks are available from the tourist office.

Practicalities

Schluchsee lies at the end of a branch line 16km from the town of Titisee and served by local **trains** which arrive at the lakefront and a couple of minutes' walk from the **tourist office**, Fischbacher Strasse 7 (Mon–Thurs 8am–6pm, Fri 9am–6pm; July also Sat 10am–noon; Aug also Sat & Sun 10am–noon; ☎07656/77 32, ⓦwww.schluchsee.de), on the town's central square. The office has **accommodation** listings – and several reading rooms with free wi-fi – but generally finding somewhere to stay is easy, and most of the best places to eat are in the hotels.

DJH Schluchsee-Wolfsgrund Im Wolfsgrund 28 ☎07656/329, ⓦwww.jugendherberge-schluchsee -wolfsgrund.de. Very popular with groups for its great location on peninsula jutting into lake a 10min walk west along the shore from the Schluchsee train station. Dorm beds from €18.70.
Mühle Unterer Mühlenweg 13 ☎07656/209. A picture-book traditional Black Forest house nestled among pine trees to the west of town but whose simple rooms feature modern comforts. Balconies brim with blooms and the restaurant is a picture of rusticity. Its menu is fairly basic – traditional *Schnitzels* and the like – but good quality, and the breakfast buffet excellent. ④

Parkhotel Flora Sonnhalde 22 ☎07656/974 20, ⓦwww.parkhotel-flora .de. Sprawling but charming four-star family-run hotel where personal touches abound. It has a country-style elegance and lake views as well as a pool and sauna, and breakfasts are first class. ⑥
Schiff Kirchplatz 7 ☎07656/975 70, ⓦwww .hotel-schiff-schluchsee.de. Traditional hotel in the centre of Schluchsee with modest and dated but perfectly comfortable rooms and a lakeside terrace attached to its restaurant which serves good regional food; mains from €10. ②

St Blasien

Nestled in a tight, forested valley, the small spa-town of **ST BLASIEN**, 15km south of Schluchsee, is odd for being dominated by its main sight, the grandiose **Dom St Blasien**, a church that's well out of proportion with the rest of the mountain town. Wandering St Blasien's handful of central streets doesn't take long, though admiring its various wooden sculptures – product of the town's annual woodcarving festival – adds a few minutes. Another place to dwell is **Museum St Blasien** (Tues–Sun 2.30–5pm; €1.60), the town's oddball local history museum above the tourist office.

The local radon-rich waters draw visitors year-round and the town forms a good hiking and skiing base too, which the tourist office has a good stock of information on, though much of this action is 9km away in the incorporated village of **Menzenschwand**. Here the **Radon Revital Bad**, In der Friedrichsruhe 13 (daily 10am–9pm; €8.50 for 4 hours; ☎07675/92 91 04, Ⓦwww.radonrevitalbad.de), is a very smart spa and sauna complex offering watery bliss, while in winter **ski lifts** are fired up on nearby slopes to power a small ski area. Sport Gfrörer, Hinterdorfstrasse 8 (☎07675/92 38 10), rents out ski gear, and bikes in summer.

The Monastery and Dom

St Blasien first found itself on maps in the ninth century when a Benedictine monastery was founded here, but its golden hour came in the eighteenth century when under powerful prince-abbot Martin Gerbert the **Dom St Blasien** was built (daily: May–Sept 8am–6.30pm; Oct–April 8.30am–5.30pm). Modelled on Rome's St Peter's, much of its Italian-inspired design was brought here by French architect Michel d'Ixnard who effectively introduced monumental Neoclassicism to Germany. Its stand-out feature is its huge cupola, which at 36m wide is Europe's third largest, but inside it's not the twenty powerful supporting Corinthian pillars that overwhelm as much as the dazzlingly white interior. Light floods in through the cupola, reflecting off the light stonework and brilliant stucco to give an impression of white marble; only close examination proves otherwise. The church also has superb acoustics, which are best appreciated during its free classical music concerts (June to early Sept Tues & Sat 8.15pm). The rest of the **monastery** is now a Jesuit-run boarding school and one of Germany's top private schools.

Practicalities

St Blasien is linked to Seebrugg, the southernmost settlement on the Schluchsee, by **bus** #7319 (hourly; 20min). The **tourist office**, Haus des Gästes at Am Kurgarten 1–3 (May–Sept Mon–Fri 10am–noon & 3–5pm, Sat 10am–noon; Oct–April Mon–Fri 9am–noon & 2–5pm; ☎07672/414 30, Ⓦwww.st-blasien.de) is in the shadow of the Dom and beside a small park in the centre of town. They can help with booking **private rooms** (❷–❺) in the area, some of which are very smart indeed. Less so, but friendly is the **DJH hostel**, Vorderdorfstrasse 10 (☎07675/326, Ⓦwww.jugendherberge -menzenschwand.de; dorms €22.10), in an old wooden farmhouse in Menzenschwand. Back in St Blasien proper, one of the best deals is the *Dom Hotel*, Hauptstrasse 4 (☎07672/22 12, Ⓦwww.dom-hotel-st-Blasien.de; ❷), which almost lies on the doorstep of the Dom and offers smart, simple and spotless rooms. A slicker choice is the *Hotel Klostermeisterhaus*, Im Süssen Winkel 2 (☎07672/848, Ⓦwww.klostermeisterhaus.de; ❹), around the back of the Dom in an early nineteenth-century villa, where the rooms are sleekly furnished with bare wood. Its stylish restaurant serves modern cuisine: try grilled zander with spinach or roast beef and a risotto with red lentils (closed Mon & Tues; mains €10–25). For simpler and less expensive food the *Dom Hotel* is a good choice and serves hearty dishes such as *Wurstbettle*, a plate of home-made black sausage and liver sausage with hunks of bread, in a cheery *Gaststätte* full of Black Forest knick-knacks.

Travel details

Trains

Baden-Baden to: Freiburg (frequent; 45min); Freudenstadt (frequent; 1hr 40min); Karlsruhe (frequent; 20min); Konstanz (hourly; 2hr 45min); Ringsheim (hourly; 1hr); Stuttgart (frequent; 1hr 10min).

Freudenstadt to: Alpirsbach (hourly; 17min); Haslach (hourly; 50min); Schiltach (hourly; 27min); Triberg (5 daily; 1hr 30min).

Freiburg to: Feldberg-Bärental (hourly; 47min); Freudenstadt (hourly; 2hr); Karlsruhe (frequent; 1hr); Konstanz (frequent; 2hr 30min); Ringsheim (hourly; 25min); Schluchsee (hourly; 1hr); St Blasien (hourly; 1hr 32min); Stuttgart (hourly; 2hr); Titisee (frequent; 40min); Triberg (hourly; 1hr 30min).

Bus

Freiburg to: Todtnau (hourly; 1hr 15min).

Rhineland-Palatinate and Saarland

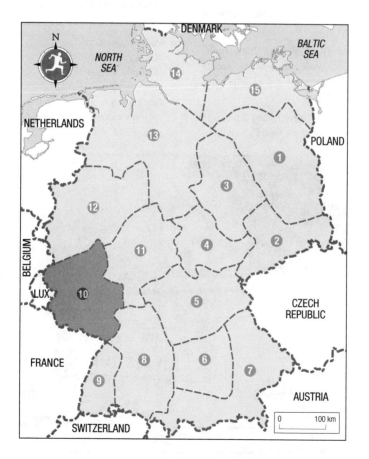

CHAPTER 10

Highlights

✳ **Worms** The tales of the *Nibelungenlied* are the star in this attractive town with a fascinating museum on the subject. See p.517

✳ **Mainz** Dirty your hands with printer's ink as you get to grips with early printing technology in the town where it was invented. See p.521

✳ **The Romantic Rhine** The classic castle-hopping route along the Rhine Gorge. See p.524

✳ **The Nürburgring** Zip around one of the world's most infamous motor-racing circuits. See p.535

✳ **Bernkastel-Kues** Cosy up in a half-timbered *Weinstube* and try some of the Mosel's fine wines. See p.538

✳ **Trier** Northern Europe's most impressive Roman remains. See p.539

✳ **Völklinger Hütte** The rusting carcass of the Saarland's steel industry has been preserved as a fascinating monument to the region's industrial heritage. See p.544

▲ Mural advertising wine tasting in the Mosel Weinstrasse region

Rhineland-Palatinate and Saarland

T he Rhine and its tributaries have almost single-handedly shaped both the **Rhineland-Palatinate** (Rheinland-Pfalz) and the **Saarland**. While large portions of both states are rural and remote, their three main watery arteries – the Rhine, Mosel and Saar – have bustled with traffic, and commerce, for generations. Vital as trade routes, the Rhine and Mosel have been studded by strategically placed fortifications and towns since Roman times. Many have been repeatedly destroyed and rebuilt in competition for the land, particularly with the French who have at one time or another had most of the region in their possession and left a mark on the region's culture and food. Viticulture along all three rivers is also important and the region's wines are of international quality.

If you travel along the Rhine as it snakes its way across the plain around the eastern, then northern border of the region, the first cities you reach of any significance along the broad river are a trio of imperial cathedral cities: **Speyer**, **Worms** and **Mainz**, which grow in magnitude and importance as you move downstream. Beyond them, the Rhine is squeezed through the famed Rhine Gorge or **Romantic Rhine**, so called for its array of fairytale castles, largely built by aristocrats in the eighteenth century, but nonetheless hugely evocative of earlier times. This leg of the river finishes around the city of **Koblenz**, beyond which the Rhine becomes far less interesting en route to Bonn. However, it is at Koblenz that the Rhine meets the Mosel, and the area around the Mosel Valley southwest of here, known as the **Mosel Weinstrasse** for its wines, is a Romantic Rhine in miniature, with some stand-out castles, particularly the fairytale **Burg Eltz**, along with the exceptionally cute small town of **Bernkastel-Kues**. South of here the steep sides of the valley fade away around **Trier**, a city with spectacular Roman remains that lies just shy of the confluence with the Saar, which departs the landscape of castles and wines to travel through what in the early twentieth century was one of Europe's leading industrial regions. These days most of that lies closed, decaying and rusting, but at least the **Völklinger Hütte** ironworks has been recognized for what it is – a fascinating snapshot of a bygone era – and preserved as such. It's on the doorstep of the Saarland's modest capital **Saarbrücken**, which has the buzz of a little international flair about town.

In general **roads** and **trains** follow the main rivers around the region, so getting between the main cities and points of interest is straightforward. There's plenty off the beaten track too, and all three rivers have marked **cycle routes**. If that

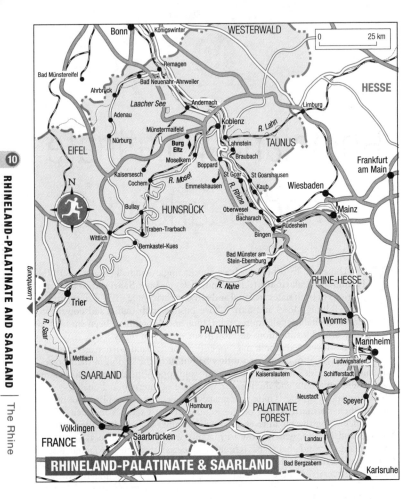

seems too much like hard work, you can always hop on and off the many **boats** that cruise up and down the Rhine and Mosel, with or without a bike in tow.

The Rhine

On its journey around Rhineland-Palatinate, the Rhine readily divides into two geographic areas. The **Upper Rhine**, a section of the river said to begin in Switzerland's Basel, is characterized by a large, flat flood-plain across which the broad river snakes. Along this part of the river the three main cities of

Speyer, **Worms** and **Mainz** dominated in imperial times when they all received gigantic cathedrals and were regularly visited by the imperial parliament. Today their clout is far less and they've been absorbed into adjacent metropolitan regions: Speyer and Worms into the Rhein-Neckar metropolitan region – which includes Karlsruhe, Heidelberg and Mannheim; Mainz into the Rhein-Main Metropolitan region – which includes Wiesbaden, Frankfurt and Aschaffenburg to the north. Though each of the trio of cities has an Altstadt and important historical legacy, each is fairly businesslike and with a contemporary attitude.

Not so the towns of the **Romantic Rhine** – the nickname for the Rhine Gorge some 40km west of Mainz – which are stuck in something of a time warp that's based in part on their commodification for the tourist industry. But it's an undeniably dramatic and attractive section of river which is only enhanced by its many castles and vineyards and which stretches some 65km as far as the sprawling and semi-industrial city of **Koblenz**.

Speyer

The pleasant market-town **SPEYER**, 25km southwest of Heidelberg, is a fairly quiet place these days, but things were very different in the Middle Ages when it regularly hosted imperial parliaments and was a key player in the Holy Roman Empire – as the presence of a giant Romanesque **Dom** suggests. From the cathedral the pedestrianized **Maximilianstrasse** cuts through the small Baroque Altstadt and is lined by most of its cafés and shops while on its other sides the Dom is surrounded by gardens which separate it from the Rhine and also the **Technik Museum**, a first-class transport museum.

Arrival, information and accommodation

Speyer's **Hauptbahnhof** and adjacent **bus station** lie about 1km north of the centre along Bahnhofstrasse. The **tourist office**, at Maximilianstrasse 13 (April–Oct Mon–Fri 9am–5pm, Sat 10am–3pm, Sun 10am–2pm; Nov–March Sat 10am–noon; ☎06232/14 23 92, ⓦwww.speyer.de), offers all the usual services as well as listings of **accommodation**, of which there is a reasonable range and quantity, given the size of the town.

DJH Speyer Geibstr. 5 ☎06232/615 97, ⓦwww.jugendherberge.de. Modern hostel beside the Rhine and a short walk from the Technik Museum. Dorm beds cost €18.40, and all twin rooms have private bathrooms. **②**

Domhof Im Bauhof 3 ☎06232/132 90, ⓦwww.domhof.de. Venerable ivy-clad hotel just beside the Dom with classy, antique-studded rooms and a top-class breakfast buffet. **⑤**

Hotel am Technik Museum Am Technik Museum 1 ☎06232/671 00, ⓦwww.hotel-am-technik-museum.de. Motel-style and quality rooms and some campsites (€19) for campervans and tents in a handy location opposite the Technik Museum and the large, modern, local pool complex. **④**

Trutzpfaff Webergasse 5 ☎06232/29 25 29, ⓦwww.trutzpfaff-hotel.de. Centrally located hotel on a quiet street a block south of the tourist office, with straightforward, bright and simple rooms, and a *Weinstube*: see p.517. **③**

The Kaiserdom

With its square towers and copper dome soaring above town, Speyer's vast and dignified **Kaiserdom** (Imperial Cathedral; April–Oct daily 9am–7pm; Nov–March Mon–Sat 9am–7pm, Sun noon–7pm) is the world's best-preserved

Romanesque church, as confirmed by its status as a UNESCO World Heritage site. The project was begun in 1030, though it took until 1858 to get it to its present form. Over the years the building has witnessed a good deal of drama: in 1689, locals stacked their furniture in the church for safekeeping as French troops bore down on the town, though to no avail, as the soldiers broke in and torched the lot anyway. The heat effectively destroyed the western end of the church. During the French Revolution there was more chaos in the church as locals ran riot inside. Unsurprisingly, then, the interior is almost devoid of furnishings, which serves to emphasize the building's mighty proportions – though what is there is rather mediocre and of nineteenth-century vintage. This makes the beautiful **crypt** a highlight, where the presence of rows of elegant tombs of Salian emperors, kings and queens helps explain the scale of the church.

Maximilianstrasse

Along **Maximilianstrasse** Speyer's two-thousand-year pedigree and Roman origins are most evident. The unusually broad and straight road was built with triumphalist parades of Roman troops in mind and later used for the same purpose by medieval emperors. However, the backdrop would have looked very different, even in the Middle Ages, for marauding French troops fairly comprehensively destroyed the Altstadt in 1689, and what's on view today is a pastel Baroque rebuild.

On the corner of Maximilianstrasse and facing the Dom is the small but very good **Historisches Museum der Pfalz** (Tues–Sun 10am–6pm; €4; ☎06232/620 22 22, Ⓦwww.museum.speyer.de), which is known above all for its outstanding *Goldener Hut von Schifferstadt*, a piece of odd, conical Bronze Age headwear, and, in its little wine museum, a jellied **third-century wine**, thought to be the world's oldest. Various sparkling imperial treasures of the Domschatz (Cathedral Treasury) also call the museum home.

At its other, western, end Maximilianstrasse terminates at the 55m-high **Altpörtel** (April–Oct Mon–Fri 10am–noon & 2–4pm, Sat & Sun 10am–5pm; €1), a twelfth-century city gate that was once one of 68 towers in town, but is now alone in crowning what remains of Speyer's fortifications.

The Technik Museum

Away from Maximilianstrasse, the Dom is surrounded by gardens through which an attractive, signed kilometre-long walk southeast leads to the **Technik Museum** (Mon–Fri 9am–6pm, Sat & Sun 9am–7pm; €12; ☎06232/670 80), Speyer's other big draw. Its glut of vintage vehicles, and other minor marvels of transport engineering, are completely overshadowed by the many **aeroplanes** perched on pedestals around the museum. Most are open for you to clamber around and while the most spectacular is the Boeing 747 – a video inside shows how complicated it was to mount it here – the most intriguing are the many curious Eastern Bloc designs. There's also the fairly rare chance to wander around the claustrophobic confines of a submarine. And for those hard-to-please children, there's also a playground and an IMAX cinema.

Eating and drinking

Speyer punches above its weight in matters of **food** and **drink**, and there are plenty of good cafés with outdoor seating along Maximilianstrasse; and even the canteen at the Technik Museum makes for a good pit-stop.

Backmulde Karmeliterstr. 11–13 ☎06232/715 77. Arguably the finest restaurant in town and located a block south of the Altpörtel. Specializes in French dishes and seafood as well as gourmet versions of traditional local recipes, using fresh local ingredients. You might find items like quail stuffed with lamb or oysters in champagne on the oft-changing menu for around €25–30, though the daily three-course menu weighs in at a more reasonable €40. The wine list is huge.

Domhof Brauerei Grosse Himelsgasse 6 ☎06232/740 55. Local microbrewery, located close to the Dom and with Speyer's best beer garden. The food is hearty, local and inexpensive, with most mains around €10.

Maximilian Korngasse 15. Hip café at the Altpörtel with good breakfasts, light lunches and inexpensive dinners; simple pasta mains and the like cost around €6.

Trutzpfaff Webergasse 5. Pleasant *Weinstube* where well-priced mains cost around €10; the local dish *Saumagen* (pig's stomach stuffed with meat, potatoes and herbs then boiled, sliced and fried) is excellent but might sound gory enough to turn you towards the good selection of veggie dishes.

Zum Alten Engel Mühlturmstr. 1a. Cosy and convivial restaurant in an atmospheric antique-furnished vaulted cellar. Its outstanding regional dishes are mostly meaty, like the liver dumplings and *Sauerbraten*; mains run €7–20. Closed Sun.

Worms

Midway between Speyer and Mainz – both 50km away – **WORMS** is one of Germany's oldest cities, famous as the fifth-century home of the Burgundian kingdom, as extensively celebrated in the **Nibelungenlied**, about which Worm has an excellent multimedia **museum**. But the city has flourished during several periods since as well, first under Charlemagne, who made it his winter residence, and particularly during the Salian dynasty (1024–1125) when the city's grand Romanesque **Dom** was built. Worms also occasionally served as a seat for the imperial parliament, its most famous session here being when it sat in judgement on Martin Luther in 1521.

For many centuries Worms was also home to a powerful **Jewish community**, which began to grow to prodigious size in the eleventh century and became – together with Mainz and Speyer – one of Germany's foremost Jewish communities. It survived the fifteenth century when many other cities expelled their Jews, only to be all but eradicated by the Third Reich. Nevertheless important reminders of this community remain, above all in its Jewish **graveyard** and rebuilt **synagogue**.

All this is fairly quickly explored leaving you to wander the pedestrian streets of Worms' Altstadt, which has been attractively rebuilt following almost total destruction during World War II. The old town always has a reasonably lively bustle about it, but is best in late summer during the mid-August **Nibelungen Festspiele**, a two-week festival of theatre based on the epic, and the Backfischfest, a wine festival that follows, during which fried fish is the accompaniment of choice.

Arrival, information and accommodation

From Worms' **Hauptbahnhof** and adjacent **bus station** you can use the spires of the Dom to guide you southeast along pedestrianized Wilhelm-Leuschner-Strasse and then towards Neumarkt, the square that lies adjacent to the Dom, where you'll find the **tourist office** (April–Oct Mon–Fri 9am–6pm, Sat 9.30am–1.30pm, Sun 10am–2pm; ☎06241/250 45, ⓦwww.worms.de) at no. 14. They offer a useful free English-language walking-tour brochure and listings of **accommodation**, of which there is a reasonable range.

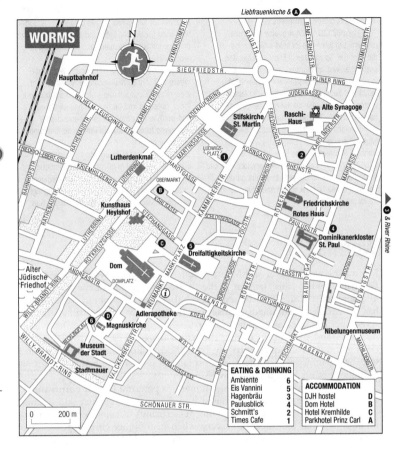

DJH Worms Dechaneigasse 1 ☎06241/257 80, ⓦwww.jugendherberge.de. Modern hostel with a good range of rooms including not only dorms (€18.40) but also singles and twins. Virtually all are en suite. ❺

Dom Hotel Obermarkt 10 ☎06241/90 70, ⓦwww.dom-hotel.de. Functional business hotel a block from the cathedral with sizeable, international-standard rooms and free parking. ❺

Hotel Kriemhilde Hofgasse 2–4 ☎06241/911 50, ⓦwww.hotel-kriemhilde.de. Modest inn close to the Dom, with straightforward, uncluttered but fairly small rooms. ❸

Parkhotel Prinz Carl Prinz-Carl-Anlage 10–14 ☎06241/30 80, ⓦwww.parkhotel -prinzcarl.de. Swish hotel in a former nineteenth-century barracks just north of the town centre. Rooms are spacious and cheerful. The breakfast buffet is excellent. ❻

Dom St Peter and around

Rearing up high enough to offer a handy orientation point from anywhere in the city and even far beyond, **Dom St Peter** (daily: April–Oct 9am–5.45pm; Nov–March 9am–4.45pm) is the pride of Worms' Altstadt. Largely built during the eleventh century in late Romanesque style, many of its walls are constructed in an unusual manner: flat on one side and curved on the other, particularly the earliest exterior walls, but it's easier to see the design inside in the east choir, the church's oldest part. Other highlights to look out for include the impressively big and opulent high altar (1742) by Balthasar Neumann and the fourteenth-century chapel of St. Nichola, with its Gothic baptismal font and impressive stained-glass windows. The Dom is also famous as the location of the Diet of Worms almost five hundred years ago, when Luther came before the Reichstag, who demanded he recant; it also figures in the *Nibelungenlied*, but that's just a flight of fancy, since it wasn't built until hundreds of years after the demise of the Burgundians.

A good place to get a feel for the city's eventful past is the town museum, or **Museum der Stadt**, Wecklingplatz 7 (Tues–Sun 10am–5pm; €2), located in the former Andreastift Kirche, beside some surviving sections of city wall, and an easy walk south of the Dom. The collection is a good one, beginning in Neolithic times, with a strong Roman section, and providing an interesting overview of Worms' turbulent history.

Though by no means a crucial part of a visit to Worms, the **Kunsthaus Heylshof** at Stephansgasse 9 (May–Sept Tues–Sun 11am–5pm; Oct–April Tues–Sat 2–5pm, Sun 11am–5pm; €2.50; ☎06241/220 00, ⓦ www.heylshof.de), in the park just north of the Dom, is worth ducking into for its respectable private collection of fine and applied arts. The European paintings – from the fifteenth to nineteenth centuries – include a particularly touching *Madonna and Child* by Rubens and there's a rather anomalous but satisfyingly quirky collection of beer glasses and steins.

Jewish Worms

Southwest of the Dom and over the circular road Willy-Brandt-Ring, lies the old cemetery, the **Alter Jüdische Friedhof** (daily: July & Aug 9am–8pm; Sept–June 9am–dusk), the most impressive reminder of Worms' once sizeable Jewish community who, in the Middle Ages, called the city Varmaiza. By 1933 the community exceeded a thousand; now the figure is around a hundred, with most more recent settlers from former Soviet territories. The graveyard opened for business in 1076 and has the unkempt look typical of most traditional Jewish graveyards. Among the crooked headstones, a few stand out for their larger piles of memorial pebbles and messages: one belongs to Rabbi Meir of Rothenburg who died in 1293, imprisoned for trying to lead a group of persecuted Jews to Palestine. His captor, Rudolf of Habsburg, was the first of the dynasty on the German throne. Rothenburg's is the only stone in the graveyard to point to Jerusalem in the customary fashion, though why the others don't is unknown.

Most of Worms' Jewish community would have spent much of their lives in the Jewish ghetto on the northeast edge of the Altstadt, which is centred on **Judengasse**, a ten-minute walk from the cemetery along Lutherring – where there's a large statue celebrating the reformer and his associates. Little of the ghetto's history is evident around Judengasse, except for the **Alte Synagoge** (April–Oct Mon–Fri & Sun 10am–12.30pm & 1.30–5pm, Sat 1.30–5pm; Nov–March Mon–Fri & Sun 10am–12.30pm & 1.30–4pm, Sat 1.30–4pm; free), a 1961 replacement for an eleventh-century one destroyed by Nazis. Around the side, the twelfth-century *mikveh*, used for ritual bathing, survived more or less intact. Alongside the synagogue, the Raschi Haus, named for the renowned rabbi-scholar who studied in Worms, houses the **Jüdisches Museum**, Hintere Judengasse 6 (April–Oct Tues–Sun 10am–12.30pm & 1.30–5.30pm; Nov–March Tues–Sun 10am–12.30pm & 1.30–4.30pm; €1.50; ☎06241/853 47 07), a modest enterprise with some general information about Jewish customs and beliefs along with a few exhibits about Worms' Jews.

The Nibelungen Museum

Dedicated to the *Nibelungenlied*, the great German epic poem (see box below), the **Nibelungen Museum**, a five-minute walk east of the Dom at Fischerpförtchen 10 (Tues–Fri 10am–5pm, Sat & Sun 10am–6pm; €5.50; ☎06241/20 21 20, ⓦwww.nibelungenmuseum.de), is easily Worms' most engaging and satisfying attraction. Housed in a chunk of the town's extant medieval fortifications – two towers and a portion of wall – it uses the building to good effect. The first-class multilingual audio guide is the most important of a number of audiovisual tools that recount the *Nibelungenlied*; others include excerpts from Fritz Lang's film and music from Wagner's opera. But the museum goes well beyond simply narrating the tale, by trying to put it into context – exploring myths of medieval honour and valour and the way in which the tale was twisted into emotive Nazi propaganda that portrayed Germans as a Nordic race – and their enemies as barbarians from the east. From the top of one of the towers there's a good view over the surrounding landscape.

Eating and drinking

The choices for **eating** and **drinking** in central Worms are hardly exciting, but there are a few good options worth tracking down.

Restaurants

Ambiente Weckerlingplatz 6 ☎06241/304 98 88. Quality Italian, as good for a quick pizza (€6–12) as for more imaginative dishes like the venison-and-chestnut tortellini (€12.20). The quality's tip-top and the service cheerful.

Paulusblick Paulusstr. 17 ☎06241/30 91 95. Elegant restaurant serving *Neue Deutsche Küche*, with the addition of some exotic flavours. Gourmet items like duck-breast, rump steak and parrot fish (most mains around €20) are graced by the likes of satay or mango sauces. There's also helpful advice about the good selection of local wines on the list.

The Nibelungenlied

Written at the end of the twelfth century, the **Nibelungenlied** is *the* German epic tale and is based on legends surrounding the destruction of the Burgundian kingdom: Roman allies who ran Worms for about twenty years in the fifth century AD before being driven out by the Huns. It's a captivating tale with a glut of mythic beings like dragons and giants, and much drama in the form of love, hate, riches, treachery, revenge and lots of death.

Nibelung himself was the mythical king of Nibelungenland (Norway), who, with twelve giants, guarded a hoard of treasure. **Siegfried**, prince of the Netherlands and hero of the first part of the poem, kills Nibelung and his giants and pinches the hoard as a dowry for his new wife **Kriemhild** of Burgundy. Siegfried then helps Kriemhild's brother, **Gunther**, King of Burgundy, to gain the hand of **Brunhild** of Iceland. This is no mean feat since the immensely powerful Brunhild will only marry a man who can beat her at the javelin, shot put and long jump. Siegfried helps Gunther to cheat – using his rather handy cloak of invisibility – and win Brunhild over. After the marriage, Kriemhild indiscreetly lets Brunhild know how she'd been tricked, which infuriates her so much that she arranges for Gunther's aide, **Hagan** (the poem's chief villain), to murder Siegfried, grab the treasure, and toss it in the Rhine. The plan is to recover it later, but by the end of the poem everyone's dead, so the treasure's lost.

The second part of the poem tells of Kriemhild's subsequent marriage to Attila the Hun (called **Etzel** in the poem). Kriemhild invites the Burgundians to the Hunnish court, where Hagan lets rip once again and ends up killing Etzel's son. Aghast, Kriemhild decapitates Gunther and Hagan with her own hands, only to be killed herself.

Cafés, pubs and microbreweries

Eis Vannini Am Marktplatz. This kiosk in the Marktplatz serves a bewildering array of delicious flavours of Italian ice cream, making it an essential stop on any summertime trip to Worms.

Hagenbräu Am Rhein 3. If it's microbrewery beer and inexpensive hearty German food you crave (mains €5–10) head down to this Rhine-side locale a 5min walk from the centre.

Schmitt's Karolingerstr. 71. Traditional inn with various reasonable *Schnitzels* (€5–15), salads and the like, and if on arrival it doesn't really grab you, there are several other options on this small pedestrian street – some with outdoor seating.

Times Café Ludwigsplatz 1. Sympathetically cosy and dependably busy café with good breakfasts, quick items like burgers, *Flammkuchen* and salads (each around €9) and daily lunch specials for around €5. Also has a few good cakes and is popular for cocktails until late.

Mainz

The largest town and capital of Rhineland-Palatinate, **MAINZ**, with its rapid transport links with Frankfurt some 40km northeast, has a very different, more urban feel to the rest of the rural state. The city has also made a rather heavyweight contribution to German history: starting as a strategically important settlement at the confluence of the Main and Rhine, by the eighth century it had developed into the main ecclesiastical centre north of the Alps, and its archbishop was one of the most powerful electors in the Holy Roman Empire. The city also entered the history books when Mainz resident **Johannes Gutenberg** made their mass production possible with the invention of the printing press in the fifteenth century.

Like much of the Rhineland, Mainz has had a spell in French hands as the city of Mayence (1792–93 and 1798–1814), which it survived quite well. It was less fortunate during World War II when bombers pounded a good portion of the city into submission. Nevertheless enough of the half-timbered **Altstadt** and the **Dom**, around which the main sights are centred, survived or was rebuilt to make its compact centre attractive to explore. Bustling adjacent **Marktplatz** is home to the **Gutenberg Museum**, while the only attractions outside the immediate centre are relatively minor draws, appealing most to those with an interest in Roman times: the **Landesmuseum** and the **Museum für Antike Schiffahrt**.

Mainz's many **Weinstuben** offer a good place to refresh your palate and rest your legs at the end of the day, while the liveliest time to be in town is during the **Mainzer Johannisnacht** on or around the last week of June when half a million revellers come to a giant Volksfest.

Arrival, information and accommodation

Mainz's **Hauptbahnhof** lies 1km west of the Altstadt and the **tourist office**, Brückenturm am Rathaus (Mon–Fri 9am–6pm, Sat 10.30am–2.30pm; ☏06131/28 62 10, ⊛www.info-mainz.de), which is tricky to find – in an isolated position elevated above the street beside a pedestrian bridge. They sell the **MainzCard** (€6), which provides unlimited public transport for two days and various discounts on admission to town attractions. English-language **tours** also leave from the tourist office at 2pm on Saturday – more often in the summer, but times vary.

Accommodation in Mainz tends to be a bit pricey, particularly in the more pleasant Altstadt – budget options around the Hauptbahnhof tend to be a bit tatty. The tourist office runs an online bookings service and **room reservations** hotline (☏06131/28 62 12).

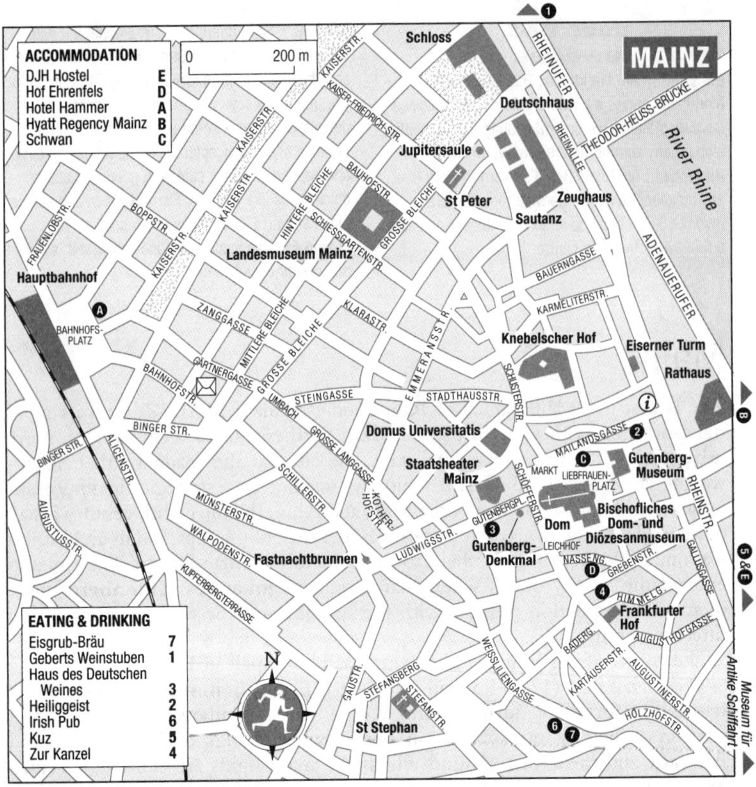

DJH hostel Otto-Brunfels-Schneise 4 ⓣ06131/853 32, ⓦwww.jugendherberge.de. Modern hostel 2km southwest of the centre with beds from €18.40; take bus #61 or #62 from the Hauptbahnhof..

Hof Ehrenfels Grebenstr. 5–7 ⓣ06131/971 23 40, ⓦwww.hof-ehrenfels.de. Fifteenth-century convent with Dom views that's long since been converted into a smart hotel, though with modest rooms, and a nice *Weinstube*. ⑤

Hotel Hammer Bahnhofplatz 6 ⓣ06131/ 96 52 80, ⓦwww.hotel-hammer.com. One of the best of the hotels around the Hauptbahnhof: elegant, well managed and with a sauna too. ⑤

Hyatt Regency Mainz Malakoff-Terrasse 1 ⓣ06131/73 12 34, ⓦwww.mainz.regency.hyatt .com. Luxurious and sophisticated five-star hotel in a striking modern building a 10min walk southeast of the Dom. It has all manner of amenities, including a busy beer garden, pool and fitness centre. Some units even open out onto the Rhine. ⑦

Schwan Liebfrauenplatz 7 ⓣ06131/14 49 20, ⓦwww.mainz-hotel-schwan.de. Family-run hotel in a sixteenth-century Altstadt building with some really pleasant rooms: they're all spacious and a Baroque touch gives them a bit of style. Its *Weinstube* claims to be the oldest in the region. ⑤

The Dom

Mainz's majestic six-towered Romanesque **Dom** (Mon–Fri 9am–6.30pm, Sat 9am–4pm, Sun 12.45–3pm & 4–5pm) isn't the first cathedral on the site, but a twelfth-century replacement for one that burnt down in 1066, one day before its consecration. Outside, one notable feature is the unusual way in which many of its red sandstone walls adjoin surrounding houses – which tends to make the church look bigger. Inside, the church is rather spartan and gloomy and, though some of the tombstones of archbishops and various other notables are interesting enough, most of the real treasures are tucked away in the **Dommuseum** (Tues–Fri 10am–5pm, Sat & Sun 10am–6pm; €3, €5 with the Gewölbehallen; ☎06131/25 33 44, ⓦwww.dommuseum-mainz .de), accessed from adjoining cloisters. Its treasures include sparkling reliquaries and some intricate fifteenth- and sixteenth-century tapestries, but most of the cathedral's artwork is stored in the adjacent **Gewölbehallen** (€2.50, €5 for both). The highlights here are a thirteenth-century rood screen from the Master of Naumburg, which vividly depicts sin and salvation, an early fourteenth-century pewter baptismal font and some Rococo choir stalls from an impressive collection of more church furnishings.

The Gutenburg Museum and Druckladen

The real highlight of a visit to Mainz is the **Gutenburg Museum** at Liebfrauen-platz 5 (Tues–Sat 9am–5pm, Sun 11am–3pm; €5; ☎06131/12 26 44), which celebrates the work of the city's most famous son. It was in the early fifteenth century that Johannes Gutenberg, a goldsmith by trade, began work on developing a printing press. Working in secret he effectively pioneered several technologies simultaneously: the development of moveable metal type; the moulds to produce them; oil-based inks that would take to the type and then the page; and the technology of the actual printing press, which adapted the techniques used in wine presses and the like.

It's fair to say that the results changed the world forever, enabling information to spread more quickly and be controlled less easily, and meaning literacy became important in all levels of society. The results proved to be remarkably democratizing and one of its earliest unforeseen effects was to smooth the passage of the Protestant Reformation, with the knock-on effects of popularizing written German and galvanizing the development of a Germanic identity.

The museum itself is mainly a tribute to the technology, but it goes far beyond Gutenberg and the historical presses of the time, with displays encompassing earlier Asian printing and some hand-copied manuscripts, which became a dying art. But the museum's greatest single showpiece is a copy of Gutenberg's first major work, the 1455 **forty-two-line Bible**, named for the number of lines on each page.

The hands-on extension of the Gutenberg Museum is the **Druckladen** (Printing Shop; Mon–Fri 9am–5pm, Sat 10am–3pm; by donation of around €3–5; ☎06131/12 26 86, ⓦwww.druckladen.mainz.de), where you can hand-set type to produce posters, cards and the like. It's a fun setup, with a relaxed atmosphere, and you're encouraged to get stuck in by enthusiastic staff who will happily guide you through the process. Even if that doesn't appeal or sounds too messy (aprons are provided), it's worth browsing the range of hand-printed items available for sale.

The Landesmuseum and Museum für Antike Schiffarht

Based at the site of a Roman military camp from 12 BC, and an easy five-minute walk north of the Altstadt, Mainz's **Landesmuseum**, Grosse Bleiche 49–51 (Tues 10am–8pm, Wed–Sun 10am–5pm; €4, free on Sat), covers local and regional history quite broadly, but is most impressive for its Roman collection. This includes first-century tombstones of soldiers and civilians, as well as the strikingly ornate **Jupitersäule**, a triumphal column from the time of Nero.

Around the same distance south of the Altstadt, the **Museum für Antike Schiffahrt**, Neutorstrasse 2b (Tues–Sun 10am–6pm; free; ⓣ06131/28 66 30), is also of interest for its Roman remains. Based on a find of five wooden ships used by Roman Rhine patrols, impressive full-size replicas provide a wonderful insight into the past.

Eating, drinking and entertainment

In some corners of Mainz's Altstadt the **Weinstuben** sit cheek by jowl, making them an essential part of the Mainz experience as the first choice for traditional meals.

Though Frankfurt is within striking distance for a night out, there's a surprising amount going on in Mainz. For opera and drama try the **Staatstheater**, Gutenbergplatz 7 (ⓣ06131/285 12 22, ⓦwww.staatstheater-mainz.de), while trendier, more low-key and more diverse performances are found at **Frankfurter Hof**, Augustinerstrasse 55 (ⓣ06131/22 04 38, ⓦwww.frankfurter-hof-mainz.de), and at *Kuz* (see below). For listings, look out for free local monthly magazines *Fritz* and *Mainzer*; the tourist office sells tickets to most bigger events.

Weinstuben and restaurants

Geberts Weinstube Frauenlobstr. 94 ⓣ06131/61 16 19. Simple and traditional wine-tavern in one of Mainz's oldest buildings, hugely popular for its local dishes, particularly fish but also game; mains run around €25 and can be washed down with a fine choice of wines. Closed Sat & Sun lunch.

Haus des Deutschen Weines Gutenbergplatz 3 ⓣ06131/22 13 00. While living up to its name, with hundreds of wines from all over Germany, there's also good-quality and reasonably priced food here (mains €13–18). Particularly good is the fresh or marinated salmon, a traditional Rhine dish, and the venison, but many items on the menu are local and often seasonal. It's also a good place to just drink wine – with *Spundekäse*, a cheese, onion and cream dip with crusty bread the accompaniment of choice.

Heiligeist Rentengasse 2. The Gothic vaults of a fifteenth-century hospital have been turned into this attractive and inexpensive bistro whose

mains (€6–15) are international but include several Italian options.

Zur Kanzel Grebenstr. 4 ⓣ06131/23 71 37. Delightful restaurant with debonair service and candlelit seating in a courtyard. The French and regional cuisine is hardly experimental, but of high quality with mains priced around €17.

Microbreweries, bars and clubs

Eisgrub-Bräu Weissliliengasse 1a. Microbrewery with an accomplished range of its own beers and a good line in inexpensive food, including breakfast, lunch and dinner buffets for €4–8.50.

Irish Pub Weissliliengasse 5 ⓣ06131/23 14 30. Convivial pub with live music almost every night and so always busy.

Kuz Dagobertstr. 20b ⓣ06131/28 68 60, ⓦwww.kuz.de. Mainz's most dependably happening club with a sociable beer garden and busy events which often feature live music, particularly world music. Usually busy until at least 4am on weekend nights; covers around €8.

The Romantic Rhine

Upstream from Mainz, the banks of the Rhine gradually rear up to form a deep, winding 65km-long gorge popularly known as the **Romantic Rhine**, thanks to a series of quaint towns and a bewildering number of castles. Of course much of this romance is pure fabrication, first by the German Romantics, who rebuilt many of the castles in the nineteenth century, and subsequently by the tourist and wine industries, but nevertheless the gorge's unique geological, historical and cultural features have ensured it a place on UNESCO's list of World Heritage Sites.

The gorge itself is composed of a type of slate sedimentary rock, folds in which produced the Hunsrück mountains to the west and the Taunus mountains to the east, while the Rhine carves a passage between the two, creating steep walls that rise up to two hundred metres above the river, and its own sheltered, sun-trap microclimate. Many of the riverbank's slopes were terraced for agriculture from an early age, the south-facing ones in particular providing near-perfect conditions for viticulture. This, together with booming trade along the river, brought wealth to the string of small riverside settlements whose rulers built a series of castles to protect their interests and levy tolls. This racket was lucrative enough to make the area an important region in the Holy Roman Empire and a focus for much of the Thirty Years' War, which left many of the castles in ruins, as did French campaigns that briefly claimed this region as part of France until Prussia turned the tables in the early nineteenth century. The Prussians then spearheaded the reinvention of the region as a quintessential part of Germany, rebuilding legendary castles and featuring it in much of the art of the time. Wagner, for example, uses this stretch of the Rhine as the setting for his powerful *Götterdämmerung*. Since then, the tourist industry has lapped all this up, which means that coach parties are an integral part of the scenery. However, don't let this put you off: many of its castles are certainly worth a look as are its many *Weinstuben* for a taste of the excellent local vintages. The annual **Rhine in Flames** festival – which also takes place in Koblenz (see p.531) – is another draw, with spectacular firework displays taking place at St Goar in September.

The full range of **transport** options exist for this length of the Rhine: you can drive, follow cycle paths or take the train up either side of the river, and car ferries link several places. But probably the most relaxing way to travel and appreciate the scenery is to take a **boat** – and several companies offer hop-on, hop-off services along this stretch of the river – many conveniently beginning in Mainz, Rüdesheim (see p.577) or Koblenz. If you're pressed for time a day-trip is all you'll need to get a feel for the place, but if you're keen to explore some of the castles, it's worth adding a day or two to your itinerary.

Cruising the Romantic Rhine

There's little to choose between the half-dozen or so operators that offer cruises along the Romantic Rhine, so the convenience of their hub will tend to be the deciding factor. Most also take bikes and allow you to hop on and off, making it possible to create your own itinerary. The price of a round trip between Koblenz and Bingen – the entire Romantic Rhine – comes in at around €30 and takes three hours and thirty minutes in each direction. Virtually all services stop at every dock along the way, but double-check if you have particular destinations in mind – look too at the frequency of services, which becomes important if you want to make short stops at various places along the way.

Bingen-Rüdesheimer ☎06721/141 40, ⊛www.bingen-ruedesheimer.com. Offers trips from Bingen and Rüdesheim as far as St Goar – so covering the lower half of the gorge.

Hebel Line ☎06742/24 20, ⊛www.hebel-linie.de. Based in Boppard, with a couple of daily sailings to Bingen and Rüdesheim and back.

Köln-Düsseldorfer ☎0221/208 83 18, ⊛www.k-d.com. The big player with five daily sailings between Koblenz and Bingen, with most continuing to or starting in Mainz too. Bikes welcome.

Loreley-Line ☎06773/341, ⊛www.loreley-linie.com. Boppard-based company with six daily sailings to the Loreley and back for only €11 return.

Bingen to Bacharach

From the towns of **Rüdesheim** in Hesse (see p.577) and **Bingen**, which watch each other from opposite banks of the Rhine (and are connected by a car ferry) some 30km west of Mainz, the Rhine Gorge starts to emerge and its first sentinels come into view, with three castles worth a visit on the 17km journey to Bacharach, the next settlement of any size.

All three castles lie on the south, or left, bank of the river. The first and the most spectacular is **Burg Rheinstein** (mid-March to mid-Nov daily 9.30am–5.30pm; mid-Nov to mid-March Mon–Thurs 2–5pm, Sun 10am–5pm; €4; ☎06721/63 48, ⓦ www.burg-rheinstein.de), a compact pile with blackened towers, which was given a complete makeover in 1820 to transform it into a neo-Gothic summer residence – setting a trend for the rest of the valley. The pastel and rather twee interior rooms feel as though they belong in a very different building. Various boats stop below the castle, or you can follow a signed thirty-minute walk from the train station at the village of **Trechtingshausen**, 2km west. Another, shorter, walk from here leads up to the landmark Rhineland **Burg Reichenstein** (mid-March to mid-Nov daily 9.30am–5.30pm; mid-Nov to mid-March Mon–Thurs 2–5pm, Sun 10am–5pm; €4; ☎06721/63 48, ⓦ www.burg-reichenstein.de), whose brooding form looms above the village. The atmospheric interior is appropriately cluttered with hunting trophies, armoury and timeworn furnishings.

A further 6km towards Bacharach sits the fairly obviously nineteenth-century **Burg Sooneck** (April–Sept Tues–Sun 9am–6pm; Oct, Nov & Jan–March Tues–Sun 9am–5pm; €2.60; ☎06743/60 64), mainly of interest for its Biedermeier furniture and paintings. Again, many boats will stop just below the Burg, otherwise the nearest train station is Niederheimbach, a signposted thirty-minute walk away.

▲ Bacharach on the Rhine

Bacharach

Pretty, half-timbered **BACHARACH**, 22km from Bingen, huddles behind a fourteenth-century wall which you can walk along for a brilliant overview of the town. The town's streets radiate from the **Peterskirche** (daily 9.30am–6pm), whose bawdy capitals are worth a look: serpents suck at the breasts of a guilty woman to warn against adultery. From here any of the centre's alleyways are good for a wander, full of quirky buildings like the celebrated **Altes Haus** at Oberstrasse 61, which is so wonky it seems to lean in all directions at once. Many of them house *Weinstuben*, where you should try local favourite *Hahnenhof* Riesling. If your legs are up to it afterwards, take a short walk up to **Burg Stahleck**, a twelfth-century castle reached via a path beside the Peterskirche. It once served as the seat of the Count Palatine of the Rhine, and now provides rather fabulous youth hostel accommodation.

Practicalities

Bacharach's **tourist office**, Oberstrasse 45 (April–Oct Mon–Fri 9am–5pm, Sat & Sun 10am–1pm; Nov–March Mon–Fri 9am–noon; ☎06743/919 303, ⓦwww .rhein-nahe-touristik.de), is at the centre of town beside the Peterskirche and most of the local **accommodation** is close by. The least expensive options include the pleasant *Campingplatz Sonnenstrand*, Strandbadweg 9 (☎06743/17 52, ⓦwww .camping-sonnenstrand.de; April–Oct), about 500m south of town along the main road, and the wonderfully atmospheric hostel in the medieval *Burg Stahleck* (☎06743/12 66, ⓦwww.diejugendherbergen.de; dorms from €17.40). Its rooms sleep one to six people and almost all are en suite. The *Rhein Hotel*, Langstrasse 50 (☎06743/12 43, ⓦwww.rhein-hotel-bacharach.de; ⓞ), is an excellent family-run half-timbered hotel with spotless rooms alongside the town's ramparts, which also offers good regional food in its **restaurant** (closed Tues), with most mains around €12. Other good places to eat include the *Altes Haus*, in one of the Rhine region's most famous buildings at Oberstrasse 61 (☎06743/12 09), whose trout and salads are good for a light bite, but the hungry should choose the *Wildschwein* (wildboar) in a *Spätburgunder* sauce seasoned with rosemary; most mains are around €13. Another worthwhile old favourite is the cosy *Kurpfälzische Münze*, Oberstrasse 72 (☎06743/13 75), with its snug interior that bursts with character. The *Münzteller* (€11) – a large plate of hams, cheeses and breads – is a summer treat. Finally, if you're on the lookout for a good *Weinstube*, try *Zum Grünen Baum*, Oberstrasse 63, which serves a fifteen-wine sampler for €13.50.

Kaub

KAUB, 4km from Bacharach but on the opposite bank of the Rhine and linked by a car ferry (€1.50) that runs in all but high-water conditions, is famed for the unusual **Burg Pfalzgrafenstein** (April–Sept Tues–Sun 10am–1pm & 2–6pm; Oct–Nov Jan–March Tues–Sun 10am–1pm & 2–5pm; €4.10 including ferry from Kaub) situated on the river in front of the town, which Victor Hugo described as "A ship of stone, eternally afloat upon the Rhine, and eternally lying at anchor …" Indeed, the castle does appear to be "moored" on an islet, where it was built by Ludwig the Bavarian in 1325 to levy tolls on Rhine shipping. The gun bastions and lookouts are seventeenth-century additions.

The chief claim to fame of Kaub itself is as the site where Prussian general Blücher constructed a vital pontoon bridge in a Napoleonic campaign. The general later became famous for his timely intervention that won the day at Waterloo. The town house the general used as his headquarters in Kaub is now the **Blüchermuseum**, Metzgergasse 6 (April–Oct Tues–Sun 11am–4pm;

Nov–March Tues–Sun 2–5pm; ☎06774/400), where a clutter of military memorabilia is very evocative of the time.

Oberwesel

Some 5km north of Kaub, and back on the left bank, the charming wine-town of **OBERWESEL** boasts the best-preserved medieval fortifications in the region. A 3km-long medieval wall, dotted with guard towers, surrounds most of the Altstadt and would be picture-perfect, were it not for the railway lines that clumsily separate the town from the river.

The Altstadt is quickly explored, but its local history museum, the **Kulturhaus**, Rathausstrasse 23 (Tues–Fri 10am–noon & 2–5pm, Sat & Sun 2–5pm; €2.50; ☎06744/71 47 26), is worth a closer look for its collection of nineteenth-century engravings that romanticized this stretch of Rhine and a series of photos that celebrates a quirky local tradition: a local lady has been crowned a *Weinhexe* – a good witch who protects the wine harvest – every April since the 1940s.

The town's **tourist office**, Rathausstrasse 3 (April–June, Sept & Oct Mon–Fri 9am–1pm & 2–6pm, July & Aug also Sat 10am–2pm; Nov–March Mon–Fri 9am–1pm & 2–5pm; ☎06744/71 06 24, ⓦwww.oberwesel.de), is just up the street and close to the Rathaus, while opposite is one of the best **places to stay**: the *Hotel Römerkrug*, Marktplatz 1 (☎06744/70 91, ⓦwww.hotel-roemerkrug.rhinecastles .com; ❹). This dignified half-timbered residence has old-fashioned rooms with wooden beams and four-poster beds, as well as all the usual modern amenities. The **restaurant** (closed Wed; Sat & Sun only in winter) has much the same atmosphere and a fairly predictable range of German favourites, most priced around €15.

St Goar

Around 7km downstream of Oberwesel lies the smaller but far more popular town of **ST GOAR**. Much of this bustle is thanks to St Goarhausen and the Loreley on the opposite riverbank and linked by a **car ferry** (daily around 6am–9pm but times vary; €1.50). However, its own sprawling, ruined **Burg Rheinfels** (March–Sept daily 9am–6pm; Oct daily 9am–5pm; Nov–Feb Sat & Sun 11am–5pm; €4; ☎06741/383) is one of the most evocative Rhine castles and so equally worthwhile. In 1255 the then-new castle survived a fourteen-month siege by the nine thousand troops of the Rhineland City League, and under the Hesse Landgraves it blossomed into a magnificent Renaissance fortress which frustrated 28,000 troops of Louis XIV during the 1692 War of Palatinate Succession. Ironically, it fell in 1794 without a shot being fired. Seduced by the promise of "*Liberté, égalité, fraternité!*" commandant General von Resius yielded to French troops and was later executed for his naïveté. No wonder, because the French immediately demolished the only castle they were unable to take by force in the war to leave spectacular labyrinthine ruins. The castle is a twenty-minute uphill walk from its car park by the youth hostel, or a short trip on the Burgexpress shuttle (April–Oct every 20min; €3). In town, the **Heimatmuseum** (daily 9.30am–noon & 1–5.30pm; free) is worth a look for models of the early castle.

Practicalities

St Goar's **tourist office**, Heerstrasse 86 (April & Oct Mon–Fri 9am–12.30pm & 1.30–5pm; May–Sept Mon–Fri 9am–12.30pm & 1.30–6pm, Sat 10am–noon; Nov–March Mon–Thurs 9am–12.30pm & 1.30–5pm, Fri 9am–2pm; ☎06741/383, ⓦwww.st-goar.de), lies a couple of minutes' walk downstream of the car ferry.

The town's budget **accommodation** option is the *DJH St Goar*, Bismarckweg 17 (℡06741/388, ⓦwww.jugendherberge.de; dorms €14.40), an old-fashioned hostel by the harbour. More central is the *Hotel zur Loreley*, Heerstrasse 87 (℡06741/16 14, ⓦwww.hotel-zur-loreley.de; ❸), with standard but spotless and bright rooms and good regional **restaurant** with a vast local wine selection and mains for around €12. An even better bet for food is up the road at the smart, traditional *Zum Goldenen Löwen*, Heerstrasse 82 (℡06741/28 52), which offers top-notch German cuisine at only slightly higher prices. There's lots of fish – meaty zander, or light *Felchen* from the Bodensee – but true culinary adventurers should try the regional delicacy *Pfälzer Saumagen* (pig's stomach stuffed with cabbage) or *Braten vom Spanferkal* (roasted suckling pig).

St Goarshausen and the Loreley

Over the Rhine from St Goar, **ST GOARSHAUSEN** is famous above all for a giant rock outcrop above town called the **Loreley**. Legends claim an alluring siren would sit here, combing her blonde locks and bewitching sailors with her beauty and plaintive song. Then, distracted from their job, the sailors would be lured to their deaths in the awkward currents of this stretch of Rhine – as it thins to its narrowest point between Switzerland and the North Sea. The maiden is portrayed in bronze at river-level, but more impressive is the view from the outcrop itself. If you can't face the thirty-minute climb, drive up or take a shuttle bus (April–Oct hourly; €1.45) from the tourist office in St Goarshausen. At the summit, the **Loreley Besucherzentrum** visitors' centre (March to mid-Nov 10am–6pm; €2.50; ℡06771/59 90 93, ⓦwww.loreley-touristik.de) has some engaging displays on the region's geography and natural history and a little on the history of tourism in the Rhine Valley.

Also above St Goarshausen is the thirteenth-century customs castle **Burg Katz** (closed to the public), which the counts of Katzenelnbogen built to trump the Trier archbishops' castle then known as Burg Peterseck, 3km downstream above Wellmich. The latter was colloquially renamed **Burg Maus** as a play on both the name and game that was being played. These days Burg Maus is known for its falconry displays (mid-March to late Oct Tues–Sun 11am & 2.30pm; €8; ⓦwww.burg-maus.de).

Practicalities

St Goarshausen's **tourist office**, Bahnhofstrasse 8 (April–Oct Mon–Fri 9am–5pm, Sat 10am–noon; ℡06771/91 00), is by the train station. Generally St Goar is the better bet for **accommodation**, though an interesting alternative is to stay up on the Loreley rock at the best local campsite, *Campingplatz auf der Loreley*, Auf der Loreley 5 (℡06771/80 26 97, ⓦwww.loreley-camping.de), or at the *Berghotel auf der Loreley*, Auf der Loreley (℡06771/809 20, ⓦwww.berghotel -loreley.de; ❸), a modern place with small rooms but a great setting. The hotel also has a reasonable **restaurant** and a fine outdoor terrace, but there's better food in town at the *Loreley Weinstuben*, Bahnhofstrasse 16 (℡06771/70 68), a snug unpretentious restaurant with all sorts of fresh fish or try the wine-laced *Rieslingschnitzel* (€8). Another good, but slightly pricier option is the riverfront restaurant *Rheingold*, Professor-Müller-Strasse 2 (℡06771/450), which does a great *Rheinischer Börsetopf* – a rich meatball-and-vegetable stew – and has fine views of Burg Rheinfels from an upstairs terrace that's preferable to its shame-lessly chintzy dining-room.

Boppard

Strung along the outside of a horseshoe bend in the Rhine, 21km south of Koblenz and 14km upriver of St Goar, **BOPPARD** is a sizeable and attractive place, which is reasonably touristy, even if it has few real sights. Its great assets are its riverfront **promenade** and a chairlift that takes visitors to the **Vierseenblick**, a point above town where a couple of hikes start. Boppard also produces some good Rieslings.

The town centres on its right-angled Marktplatz, home to a Friday-morning market and the late Romanesque **Severuskirche** in which tender medieval frescoes venerate its patron saint. The square south of the church is the busiest and adjoins main shopping-street Oberstrasse. Crossing it is Kirchgasse, a short walk along which brings you to the **Römer-Kastell**, a preserved part of Boppard's fourth-century Roman walls. Of the 28 watchtowers that once graced the military camp, four have been preserved and illustrations on information boards in the Römer-Kastell help conjure up how things would once have looked.

Back on Oberstrasse, and a couple of minutes' walk west along it, is Karmeliterstrasse, named after a Carmelite monastery that once stood here. Its church, the **Karmelitenkirche**, is noteworthy for particularly egalitarian carvings on its Gothic choir stalls which celebrate farmers alongside monks and prophets. Local farmers have taken this to heart, and for as long as anyone can recall have placed the season's first ripe grapes in a niche outside alongside the **Traubenmadonna**, or Grape Madonna, to receive her blessing.

The Rhine is just north of here, and you can stroll along Boppard's riverfront promenade back east towards the town centre. Rearing up a little beyond the Marktplatz, the **Alter Burg** is easily the most impressive building on the front. Built in 1340 as a stronghold and tollhouse for the Elector Balduin of Trier, it now houses the **Museum der Stadt Boppard** (April–Oct Tues–Sun 10am–12.30pm & 1.30–5pm; free; ☎06742/103 69). This local-history collection makes much of local cabinetmaker Michael Thonet (1796–1871), the inventor of bentwood furniture. By soaking layered strips of veneer in hot glue then bending them into shape in metal moulds he created elegantly curved furniture that became all the rage in the mid-nineteenth century. His curved-frame chairs – effectively two hoops joined together – are the best known, having graced thousands of European cafés since the turn of the twentieth century.

The view from the hills just north of Boppard is known as the **Vierseenblick**, or Four Lakes View, because the four sections of the Rhine visible from here look unconnected. Optical illusions aside, the views are very fine, and the pleasant wooded terrain is home to a few good hikes which are detailed in brochures available from the tourist office. The most adventurous, the Klettersteig, takes in some precipitous sections with the aid of chains and ladders. The Vierseenblick can be reached by a **chairlift** (April–Oct daily 9.30am–6.30pm; €6.20 return) at the northern end of town, or a 5km walk – signposted to **Gedeonseck**, the name of a viewpoint with an attendant café and restaurant.

Practicalities

Boppard's **tourist office** (May–Sept Mon–Fri 8am–6pm, Sat 9am–1pm; Oct–April Mon–Fri 8am–4pm; ☎06742/38 88, ⓦwww.boppard.de) lies on the Marktplatz and has all the usual information as well as organizing wine tastings (April–Oct; €5) at various local vineyards. **Accommodation** options include *Weinhaus Heilig Grab*, over the road from the Hauptbahnhof at Zelkesgasse 12 (☎06742/23 71; ❸), a historic winehouse with two hundred years of tradition and a lovely shady garden with a few basic rooms. A pleasant and more luxurious waterfront alternative is *Bellevue*, Rheinallee 41 (☎06742/10 20, ⓦwww.bellevue-boppard.de; ➎), which still exudes 1887 grandeur and where the choicest antique-decorated rooms overlook the Rhine. Gourmet meals in its elegant *Chopin* **restaurant** come with piano accompaniment (mains around €17). For heartier food and lower prices try the *Severusstube*, Untere Marktstrasse 7 (☎06742/37 18), a snug inn with wood beams where dishes including the rack of lamb or half-kilo *Schweinehaxe* should satisfy the largest of appetites for €7–12.

Braubach and the Marksburg

BRAUBACH, just two tight horseshoe bends downstream of Boppard but on the opposite bank, is a half-timbered delight. But it's best known for its magnificent **Marksburg** (tours daily: Easter–Oct 10am–5pm; Nov–Easter 11am–4pm; €4.50; ⓦwww.marksburg.de), one of the Rhine gorge's most impressive castles with as fine a hilltop setting as any. It's also one of the few never to have been destroyed, making its huddle of towers and turrets authentically medieval. Tour highlights include an atmospheric Gothic grand hall and an armoury that bristles with weapons and grisly torture instruments. The Marksburg can be reached by a forty-minute bus journey (#570) from Koblenz's Hauptbahnhof to Braubach's Bahnhof, then by following a signed walking route uphill for twenty minutes.

Schloss Stolzenfels

Over the river and 3km upstream of the Marksburg, the series of set-square-perfect crenellated battlements belongs to **Schloss Stolzenfels** (April–Sept Tues–Sun 9am–6pm; Jan–March, Oct & Nov Tues–Sun 10am–5pm; €2.60; ☎0261/516 56, ⓦwww.schloss-stolzenfels.eu), the Prussian rebuild of a thirteenth-century castle that French troops had reduced to rubble in 1689. The ruins were given to Friedrich Wilhelm IV who entrusted the task of rebuilding the structure as a summer residence to celebrated architect Karl Friedrich Schinkel, who used original plans and local styles but added touches from other sources, particularly Moorish architecture. The results are almost a caricature of mid-nineteenth-century Romanticism: an oversized toy castle where medieval fantasies are even played out in the lavish neo-Gothic living quarters where Queen Victoria was once a guest. The Schloss lies just 5km south of Koblenz and is reached by bus #650 from its Hauptbahnhof to its car park, a fifteen-minute walk from the castle gates.

Koblenz

Founded as Roman settlement Confluentes at the confluence of the Rhine and Mosel rivers in 10 BC, **KOBLENZ**, some 100km downstream of Mainz, marks the transition from the Rhine Gorge to the gentler landscapes of the Middle Rhine, which continues down to Bonn 70km away. Its strategic location has meant it has been fought over and conquered several times, most notably by the Swedes in the Thirty Years' War, the French in 1794, and the Russians in 1814, and turned over to Prussia in 1822 only to be comprehensively destroyed by British Lancaster bombers towards the end of World War II. In its rebuilt form – a mix of old-looking and modern – it's a relaxed if unexciting town with few sights. However, as the northern gateway to the Romantic Rhine – several cruises down both the Rhine and Mosel start here (see p.525) – and with a good collection of bars and restaurants in its likeable pedestrian centre it makes a good base.

The best time to be in town is during the annual **Rhein in Flammen** (Rhine in Flames; Ⓦwww.rhein-in-flammen.de) festival in August, a firework bonanza, best appreciated from **Festung Ehrenbreitstein** fortress above town or one of a convoy of boats on the river.

Arrival, information and accommodation

Koblenz's **Hauptbahnhof** lies a little over 1km southwest of the Altstadt and is the location of the major **tourist office**, Bahnhofplatz 17 (April & Oct daily 9am–6pm; May–Sept daily 9am–7pm; Nov–March Mon–Fri 9am–6pm, Sat & Sun 9am–2pm; Ⓣ0261/313 04, Ⓦwww.koblenz.de). There's another tourist office in the central Rathaus, Jesuitenplatz 2 (April & Oct Mon–Fri 9am–6pm, Sat & Sun 10am–6pm; May–Sept Mon–Fri 9am–7pm, Sat & Sun 10am–7pm; Nov–March Mon–Fri 9am–6pm, Sat & Sun 10am–4pm; Ⓣ0261/13 09 20), which offers all the same information, ticketing and **accommodation** booking services. These can be useful since the town is a hub for large coach parties and some of its hotels quickly fill as a result.

Hotels and pensions

Diehl's Hotel Rheinsteigufer Ⓣ0261/19 70 70, Ⓦwww.diehls-hotel.de. A bit dated maybe, but riverside location, views of the Rhine and good facilities, which include a pool and sauna, make up for it. ❺

Hotel Brenner Rizzastr. 20–22 Ⓣ0261/91 57 80, Ⓦwww.hotel-brenner.de. Elegant, friendly and great-value hotel a 5min walk south of the Altstadt with spotless, if dated, rooms and a garden. ❸

Hotel Jan van Werth Von-Werth-Str. 9 Ⓣ0261/365 00, Ⓦwww.hoteljanvanwerth.de. Budget place midway between the Hauptbahnhof and Altstadt with bright, pine-furnished rooms, some of which share a bathroom. Singles are half the price of doubles. ❷

Kleiner Riesen Kaiserin-Augusta-Anlagen 18 Ⓣ0261/30 34 60, Ⓦwww.hotel-kleinerriesen.de. Traditional place southeast of the town centre and one of the few places to stay that fronts the Rhine. The rooms are a bit chintzy, but there are several public rooms and atmosphere is relaxed. ❺

Hostels and camping

Campingplatz Rhein-Mosel Schartwiesenweg 6 Ⓣ0261/827 19, Ⓦwww.camping-rhein-mosel.de. Spacious campground opposite the Deutsches Eck and Festung Ehrenbreitstein and with good views of both. A passenger ferry across the Mosel gives campers a convenient way to get to the Altstadt. Two adults with a car and tent pay €14.50 per night.

DJH Koblenz Festung Ehrenbreitstein Ⓣ0261/97 28 70, Ⓦwww.diejugendherbergen .de. Easily one of Germany's most remarkable hostels, deep inside the Festung Ehrenbreitstein citadel, yet with modern facilities and incredible views from its terrace over the Rhine, Mosel and Koblenz, particularly when there's a good sunset. Many rooms have a private bathroom, and beds start at €17.40 per night and some twin rooms are available. Guests get discounts on the chairlift and free entrance into the Ehrenbreitstein complex. ❷

The Deutsches Eck and around

Exploration of town is best started at the point where the town was founded on a promontory at the Rhine–Mosel confluence called the **Deutsches Eck** (bus #1 from the Hauptbahnhof). A large statue of Kaiser Wilhelm I on horseback presides over it and behind him there's yet more Germanic pedigree in the form of the **Deutschherrenhaus**, once the thirteenth-century headquarters of the Teutonic Knights. It now houses the **Ludwig Museum** (Tues–Sat 10.30am–5pm, Sun 11am–6pm; €2.50; Ⓣ0261/300 40 40, Ⓦwww.ludwigmuseum.org) of modern and contemporary art whose collection primarily focuses on postwar French art, but where temporary exhibitions are far more eclectic.

South of here, the **Rheinpromenade** is a pleasant promenade that stretches for around 3km along the banks of the Rhine, and worth strolling for its riverside views, though the heart of town lies in the other direction.

The Altstadt

As you walk down the thin strip of parkland west from the Deutsches Eck, the picturesque and brightly painted **Altstadt** comes into view along the banks of the Mosel. If you turn inland just before the Balduinbrücke you arrive at the **Florinsmarkt**, the first of several squares that form focal points in the Altstadt. Its **Florinskirche** is known above all for the *Augenroller*, a figure below its clock who rolls its eyes and sticks its tongue out every half-hour (June–Aug daily 11am–5pm). The square's also home to the **Mittelrhein-Museum** (Tues–Sat 10.30am–5pm, Sun 11am–6pm; €2.50; ☎0261/129 25 20, ⓦwww.mittelrhein -museum.de), a regional history museum of interest to those keen to flesh out their experience of the Romantic Rhine with some historical background. Particularly revealing are some of the nineteenth-century paintings that helped to establish the Romantic myth. Also of interest are the many works of leading Rococo painter Januarius Zick, who lived in Koblenz. A network of alleys leads south from the Florinsmarkt to the **Liebfrauenkirche** (daily 9am–6pm), Koblenz's main church which, despite its Baroque onion-domed towers, is of Romanesque origin. Inside, the Gothic choir and chancel are the stand-out features. The Liebfrauenkirche is surrounded by a square where plenty of attractive restaurants and cafés have outdoor seating, but another, more significant square, **Am Plan**, lies just south of the row of houses on its southern side and is accessed by an alley. This civic space has had a particularly bloody past, with a spell as a butcher's market and as the town's main place for executions and medieval tournaments. At its southwestern corner, at the crossroads of two main shopping streets, Marktstrasse and Am Plan (which becomes Altengraben to the west and Entenpfuhl in the east), lie the **Vier Türme**: four seventeenth-century buildings which have become celebrated for their ornate facades.

Festung Ehrenbreitstein

Watching over Koblenz's Altstadt on the east bank of the Rhine, the gigantic fortress **Festung Ehrenbreitstein** (daily 10am–5pm; €1.10; ☎0261/974 24 40) has a commanding position over everything in town. So mighty was it that it proved impregnable until 1801 when Napoleonic troops comprehensively destroyed it. Today's version is an impressive Prussian rebuild from 1832 that houses various enterprises including a hostel, restaurants and the **Landesmuseum** (mid-March to mid-Nov daily 9.30am–5pm; €4; ☎0261/667 50, ⓦwww.landesmuseumkoblenz.de), which explores the region mainly from the point of view of the industries that shaped it: trade, tobacco, wine, photography and automobile manufacture – the latter in a tribute to August Horch, founder of Audi who hailed from Winningen, 10km upstream along the Mosel from Koblenz.

From Koblenz, Festung Ehrenbreitstein is reached by a **passenger ferry** from the **Rheinpromenade** (Easter to mid-Nov Mon–Fri 8am–6.55pm, Sat & Sun 8.30am–6.55pm; €1.30), or by bus; take bus #9 or #10 to Obertal then it's a ten-minute walk, or you can get off early at the base of a **chairlift** (Easter to late May, Sept & Oct 10am–5pm, June–Sept 9am–5.50pm; €5.80 return) to Ehrenbreitstein.

Eating and drinking

Koblenz's Altstadt is small enough to allow easy browsing for places to **eat** and **drink** and its selection is quite good: the presence of a few unusual non-traditional places is particularly welcome.

Restaurants

Elsa's Cuisine Paradies 2 ☎0261/133 88 68. Exotic departure from the usual traditional German offerings, with all sorts of African bush meat on the menu – bison, crocodile, ostrich, kangaroo – and accompanied by some good French sauces. The gastronomic safari doesn't come cheap though, with mains running €11.50–26.

Guarida An der Liebfrauenkirche 19 ☎0261/91 46 98 00. Spanish place with plenty of outdoor seating in the shadows of the Liebfrauenkirche. The tapas (most around €4.50) menu is lengthy and excellent, and some larger meals, salads and omelettes are available too.

Pizzeria La Mamma Am Plan 7 ☎0261/177 60. Excellent Italian place with candle-lit outdoor seating on one of Koblenz's main squares. Great for pizzas (€6–10), of course, but also a range of other dishes including some excellent mussels in white-wine sauce in the winter months.

Cafés and bars

Affenclub Münzstr. 16. One-time gay and lesbian bar, that's long since become popular across the board, and always packed to the gunnels until the early hours – sometimes as late as 6am. And, as for the monkeys (*Affen*) – the theme is executed with the help of plenty of greenery and soft toys dangling all over the place.

Cafe Miljöö Gemüsegasse 12. Stylish traditional café with greenery and a sophisticated feel, which is good for breakfast, salad lunches and home-made cakes later on.

Irish Pub Burgstr. 7. Convivial pub with regular live music on weekend nights; a favourite with local English-speakers.

Weindorf Julius-Wegeler-Str. 2. A small group of wine taverns around a mock village square off the Rheinpromenade: a touristy but fun place to sample local food and wine, with the reasonable quality mains ranging €6–17.

The Mosel and the Saar

Though both are significantly smaller than the Rhine, together the **Mosel** and its tributary the **Saar** drain most of the Rhineland-Palatinate and the Saarland, and so form focal-points for these states, making them key to understanding the region: its slower pace along the Mosel, and its post-industrial realities along the Saar. The attractions along them, particularly the Mosel, may be broadly similar to those of the Rhine – castles, fine wines, meandering river scenery, absorbing old towns – but somehow they're more accessible: the scale is more manageable; the sights often less busy. The final leg of the Mosel, in the run up to its confluence with the Rhine at Koblenz, is as scenic as any regional river, a classic mix of castles, vineyards and minor half-timbered towns along the **Mosel Weinstrasse**. Beyond this mini-Romantic Rhine, the venerable city of **Trier** entices with a glut of Roman ruins, while just to the south the Mosel is joined by the Saar, a very different river along which the mood noticeably alters as you pass into the Saar coalfield, a former European hub of heavy industry. The landscape is still recovering from its industrial pounding, but where most see blight the town of **Völklingen** has had the foresight to celebrate its industrial heritage by turning their ironworks **Völklinger Hütte** into a museum and an incredible venue for the arts. The big city on its doorstep, **Saarbrücken**, is a better base though, and has some good museums.

The Mosel Weinstrasse

Along its final 195km-long stretch between Koblenz and Trier the Mosel cuts a sinuous and attractive deep gorge, home to some of Germany's steepest vineyards and best full-bodied wines. The route that follows the banks of the river is known as the **Mosel Weinstrasse**, or Mosel Wine Road. This links a

The Eifel, the tranquil region immediately north of the Mosel Valley, is known for sleepy villages, gentle hills and bare heathland, but famous for the incongruous **Nürburgring** (☏02691/30 26 30, ⓦwww.nuerburgring.de), a racetrack that's one of motorsport's most hallowed pieces of tarmac.

Among aficionados, its **Nordschleife** (north loop), completed in 1927, is widely considered the toughest, most dangerous and most demanding purpose-built racetrack in the world. With 73 curves along its 22.8km length it proved so hard to master that over the years it's claimed dozens of lives, including those of four Formula One drivers. Jackie Stewart dubbed it "The Green Hell", though he chalked up three wins here, including one of his finest ever in the rain and fog of 1968. Some eight years later Niki Lauda's near fatal crash here caused race organizers to move things to the Hockenheimring near Mannheim in 1977, though the building of the **Südschleife** in 1984 brought Formula One back and it now alternates with the Hockenheimring as the venue for the annual German Grand Prix.

Other motorsports and novelty events, such as old-timer races, also regularly use the track, but when these aren't on it's possible to drive the Nordschleife (€21; generally daily 9am–dusk, but check the website first). Despite common misconceptions to the contrary, German road law applies: speed limits exist, though not everywhere, and passing on the right is prohibited. For an inside view of the real deal and speeds of up to 320kmph, book a seat in the **BMW Ring-Taxi** (March–Nov Mon–Fri 10am–noon; ☏02691/93 20 20, ⓦhttp://bmw-motorsport .com/ms/ringtaxi.html), who charge €200 for up to three people and will take kids taller than 150cm. It's popular and often booked up months in advance, though last-minute cancellations are not unheard of.

The Nürburgring is situated 90km southwest of Cologne and 60km northwest of Koblenz. The nearest train station is at Mayen from which bus #344 leaves (daily Mon, Wed & Fri at 9.15am, returning at 3.04pm). On other days Adenau is the nearest hub (bus connections at 11.20am, 3.20pm & 5.20pm; return journeys at 12.17pm, 4.17pm and 6.17pm).

solid selection of traditional attractions, which include the faultless medieval castle **Burg Eltz**, the half-timbered wine town of **Cochem**, **Traben-Trarbach** with its attractive Jugendstil villas and **Bernkastel-Kues**, the Weinstrasse's most colourful town and best base.

It's an easy stretch of river to explore and its many bridges make access to both banks straightforward. The northern half of the river, as far as the town of Bullay, is served by **rail**, the southern portion, to Trier, covered by frequent **Moselbahn buses** (☏0651/968 00, ⓦwww.moselbahn.de). **Boats** offer another way of travelling the valley: Köln-Düsseldorfer (☏06742/22 32, ⓦwww.k-d.com) covers the northern leg between Koblenz and Cochem; the Mosel-Schiffs-Touristik (see p.537) concentrates on the middle leg around Traben-Trarbach and Bernkastel-Kues; while the Personen-Schiffahrt Gebrüder Kolb (☏02673/15 15, ⓦwww.moselfahrplan.de) offers regular sailings from Trier to Bernkastel-Kues.

All these forms of transport make it easy to explore sections of the **Moselhöhenweg**, the long-distance **hiking** trail that follows the top of both sides of the valley, or **cycling** legs of the **Mosel-Radweg** long-distance cycle path which comes all the way from Metz in France, but is most popular along the 210km stretch from Trier to Koblenz. It can be done as a week's easy cycle, but with all forms of transport allowing the carriage of bikes, it's also easy just to do sections as day-trips.

Burg Eltz

Tucked in a hidden valley, 29km southwest of Koblenz, **Burg Eltz** (late March to Oct 9.30am–5.30pm; €8; ☎02672/95 05 00, ⓦwww.burg-eltz.de) is a hot contender for title of Germany's finest castle. The setting is absolutely perfect, with the fortification standing on a seemingly purpose-built knuckle of rock at the centre of a wooded and otherwise deserted small valley, and the structure itself is archetypal romantic castle. Its first stones were laid in the twelfth century, and though there have been plenty of later additions, with the greatest portion built between the mid-fifteenth and mid-sixteenth centuries, the compact turreted pile has never been destroyed or rebuilt. However, it did have its share of close shaves: it was once under siege for two years in the early fourteenth century and during the general destruction of the area by the French in 1689 it was only saved by the good fortune of having a family member in the French army. With such an attractive setting and exterior, tours of the **interiors** are a bit of an anticlimax, despite being well preserved. Its **treasury** contains all manner of family booty with some well-crafted gold and silver, and its armoury features some painful and unwieldy-looking items.

Burg Eltz is a little tricky to reach. The easiest way if you have your own transport is from the village of **Münstermaifeld**, 34km southwest of Koblenz and a turn-off from the Moselweinstrasse at Hatzenport 5km away, from where it's an 800m walk from the car park (shuttle bus €1.50). But a far more attractive route is from the town of **Moselkern**, 32km southwest of Koblenz: follow signs to the *Ringelsteiner Mühle*, an inn with a car park 2km behind town along

▲ Burg Eltz

the Eltztal road, from where an attractive trail follows the valley to the castle – reachable on foot in about 45 minutes. Moselkern has its own train station with regular connections to Koblenz and Trier, and a dock at which all passing passenger boats stop.

Cochem

COCHEM, 55km along the Mosel as it winds from Koblenz, is as attractive a half-timbered town as any on the Mosel, but tends to be let down by the sheer number of its visitors. It's known above all for its **Reichsburg** (daily mid-March to Nov 9am–5pm; €4.50; ☏02671/225, ⓦwww.reichsburg-cochem .de), a turreted medieval-style castle built high above town in 1877, though following the original ground-plans of a castle that's been here since the eleventh century. The walk up to the castle is clearly signposted from town and takes around fifteen minutes; its antique-dotted, mock-medieval interior can only be explored on forty-minute guided tours (frequent; German-only, but translation sheets provided). The town's other main attraction is the **Pinnerkreuz chairlift** (daily: mid-July to Aug 9.30am–7.30pm; Easter to mid-July & Sept to mid-Nov 10am–6pm; €5.50 return; ☏06541/98 90 63), which begins a short walk west of the tourist office, and offers not only great views of the valley but also the chance for a pleasant downhill hike back to town between vineyards.

Practicalities

Trains pull in on the north bank just downstream of town, within easy walking distance of the **tourist office** at Enderplatz 1 (all year Mon–Fri 9am–1pm & 2–5pm; May to mid-July also Sat 9am–5pm; mid-July to Oct also Sat 9am–5pm, Sun 10am–noon; Nov–April Sat 9am–3pm; ☏06541/600 40, ⓦwww.cochem .de). A good place to **stay** and **eat** is the centrally located *Alte Thorschenke*, Brückenstrasse 3 (☏02671/70 59, ⓦwww.castle-thorschenke.com; ❺), which dates from 1332 though most of its rooms – some with four-poster beds – are in a modern 1960s wing. Its restaurant has all the usual German dishes, with most mains around €13.

Traben-Trarbach

The twin town of **TRABEN-TRARBACH**, straddling the Mosel 55km south of Cochem, is notable for its attractive collection of Jugendstil villas. Though lacking any kind of heart, there are a couple of appealing promenades on either side of the broad river, which is used for occasional speedboat and waterskiing competitions, though more frequently by the boats of the Mosel-Schiffs-Touristik (May to mid-July Sat & Sun; mid-July to Oct daily; €10 one-way; ☏06531/82 22, ⓦwww.moselpersonenschifffahrt.de), which sail five times a day to Bernkastel-Kues, 24km away by boat, though 8km on foot, giving you the option of taking the boat one-way, then a scenic if reasonably strenuous walk back.

The town itself doesn't take long to look around: **Traben**, on the north side of the Mosel, where the tourist office, bus and train station are, is the more workmanlike, though fans of Jugendstil design will want to have a look at the riverside **Hotel Bellevue**. It was the work of Berlin architect Bruno Möhring who gave it its hallmark turret, domed tower gables and high-pitched roof as well as elaborate timberwork and oak lobby. Step inside to admire the stained glass. There's another chance to admire his work while crossing the bridge to Trarbach where **Brückentor**, which he designed, acts as a sentinel at the bridge's end.

Trarbach, on the southern bank of the Mosel, has a couple of pretty but unspectacular pedestrian streets, which are quickly seen en route to its Marktplatz from where a steep footpath leads up to the **Grevenburg**, the ruined fourteenth-century castle that watches over town. There's not much left of the castle, but considering it was laid siege to six times and destroyed seven, that two walls remain is a small wonder. From them you can make out a spot on the opposite bank that has seen similar activity: Louis XIV built a fortress here in the late seventeenth century, which only survived a few decades before its dismantling.

Practicalities

Traben's **tourist office**, Am Bahnhof 5 (April–June & Nov Mon–Fri 10am–6pm; July–Oct Mon–Fri 10am–6pm, Sat 11am–3pm; Dec–March Mon–Fri 10am–noon & 2–4pm; ☎06541/839 80, ⓦwww.traben-trarbach .de), beside the train station, organizes local **wine tours** and will help book **accommodation**. Choices include a DJH hostel, Hirtenpfad 6 (☎06541/92 78; dorm beds €17), a little over 1km northeast of the train station. Much closer is the modern family-run *Central Hotel*, Bahnstrasse 43 (☎06541/62 38, ⓦwww.central-hotel-traben.de; ❸), a solid mid-market option, while the most atmospheric place to stay is the *Hotel Bellevue*, Am Moselufer (☎06541/70 30, ⓦwww.bellevue-hotel.de; ❼), which has classy antique-furnished rooms and provides free bike rental, a fitness centre, spa, sauna and pool and a **restaurant** to delight gourmands (mains average €20) with regional and international dishes. Another good place to eat in interesting surroundings is at the *Brücken-Schenke* (☎06541/81 84 35) in the Brückentor, where you can choose from a menu of standard German dishes and enjoy fine river views; most mains are around the €10 mark.

Bernkastel-Kues

The twin town of **BERNKASTEL-KUES** nestles by a serpentine bend in the Mosel, just 8km on foot from Traben-Trarbach through woods and steep vineyards, but the terrain is such that the road takes 17km to link the two and the river an even twistier 24km. With this scenic backdrop, Bernkastel-Kues is a half-timbered gem. Predictably, it's rather touristy, but with some of the wonkiest houses you'll ever see and wall-to-wall with wine taverns to help distort their dimensions even more, it's a place that shouldn't be passed up. There's always a cheerful buzz about town, and things are liveliest in the first weekend in September when gallons of the local *Bernkastelr Doctor* wine are downed with spirited results – even the fountain in the middle of the Marktplatz flows with wine.

Easily the more attractive part of town, tiny **Bernkastel**, on the east bank of the Mosel, gathers behind the **Pfarrkirche St Michael**, a fourteenth-century church that once formed part of the town's defence. A short way behind, the tiny focal **Marktplatz** is surrounded by half-timbered houses with decorative gables and is so well preserved that if it weren't for the other visitors and souvenir shops, you'd think you'd walked into a medieval street scene – even a ring on the Rathaus which miscreants were chained to is intact. Just uphill from here is the faintly absurd **Spitzhäuschen**, a tiny, precarious-looking, top-heavy house that's Bernkastel at its most extreme.

From Bernkastel's Marktplatz, the main Mandatstrasse brings you to the back of town and becomes Burgstrasse as far as the signed start of a 3km hiking trail to **Burg Landshut** (open access), the ruined eleventh- to thirteenth-century castle that surveys this stretch of the Mosel. It served the archbishops of Trier and is worth the hike for tremendous valley views of cascading hillsides streaked by vineyard greens. The hike takes about 45 minutes and climbs steeply on easy woodland paths, but if you don't fancy that you can hop aboard a shuttle bus (April–Oct hourly 10am–6pm; €3.50) from tourist information instead.

In comparison to Bernkastel, the far larger town of **Kues** is rather workaday, though it does have one sight that makes crossing the river worthwhile: the **St-Nikolaus Hospital**, Cusanusstrasse 2 (Sun–Fri 9am–6pm, Sat 9am–3pm; free; T06531/22 60), a poorhouse founded in 1458 by theologian Nikolaus Cusanus who was born in the town and rose to great ecclesiastical heights as a cardinal in Rome. There's a Gothic chapel and cloister to explore and its library is also of interest for Cusanus's extraordinary collection of thousand-year-old manuscripts though it's only accessible on a guided tour (April–Oct Tues 10.30am, Fri 3pm; €4). Also here, in the cellars, is the **Mosel-Weinmuseum** (daily: mid-April to Oct 10am–5pm; Nov to mid-April 2–5pm; €2; T06531/41 41), which has a wine bar where you can taste as many of the local wines as you like for €9.

Practicalities

Though not on the rail network, Bernkastel-Kues is served effectively enough by connecting **buses** from the train station at Wittlich 16km away, or by boat from Traban-Trarbach (see p.537). Its **tourist office**, Am Gestade 6 (May–Oct Mon–Fri 8.30am–12.30pm & 1–5pm, Sat 10am–5pm, Sun 10am–1pm; Nov–April Mon–Fri 8.30am–12.30pm & 1–3pm; T06531/40 23, Wwww.bernkastel.de), is on the waterfront by the bridge in Bernkastel, and has a **hotel** reservations board with a free phone – handy since the town is often near-full. The **campsite** *Campingplatz Kuewer Werth*, Am Hafen 2 (T06531/820, Wwww.camping-kueser-werth.de), is 2km upriver by the yacht harbour in Kues. The DJH **hostel**, Jugendherbergstrasse 1 (T06531/23 95, Wwww.diejugendherbergen.de; €15.40), is as far out of town, up by Burg Landshut on the Bernkastel side. In town, the most atmospheric places to stay are on the Bernkastel side and include elegant *Zur Post*, Gestade 17 (T06531/967 00, Wwww.hotel-zur-post-bernkastel.de; ❹), with its small rooms and sauna, and *Doctor Weinstuben*, Hebegasse 5 (T06531/5080, Wwww .doctor-weinstuben.de; ❺), which occupies an attractive half-timbered mid-seventeenth-century building with many woodcarvings. The rooms here are also small, but the rustic atmosphere spot on and its *Weinstube* is as good a place to **eat** traditional German food as any in town. Otherwise try to avoid the places on the main drag, where the food tends to be a bit overpriced and the staff overworked; that said, the *Ratskeller*, on the main square, is a good one.

Trier

South of Bernkastel-Kues the landscape around the Mosel gradually begins to open up, so that **TRIER**, 50km downstream, sits among gently rolling hills. But most visitors pay little attention to the landscape, for the city has northern Europe's greatest assemblage of **Roman remains**. Founded as Augusta Treverorum in 15 BC, Trier grew to become the capital of the western Roman Empire by the third century AD. As Rome declined, Trier fell into the hands of various tribes, including the Huns under Attila, until eventually the Franks asserted themselves at the end of the fifth century, ushering in a period of relative stability which saw the city gain independence from Ostfrankenreich in 1212

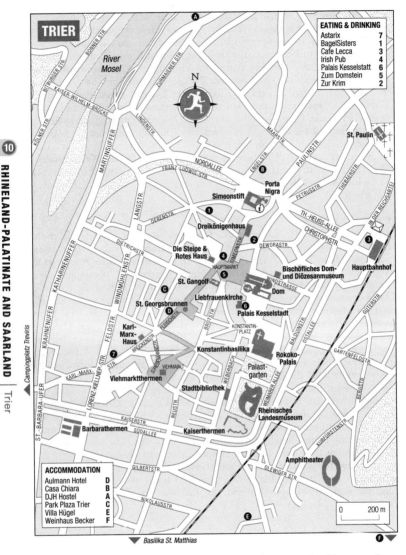

TRIER

River
Mosel

EATING & DRINKING

Astarix	7
BagelSisters	1
Cafe Lecca	3
Irish Pub	4
Palais Kesselstatt	6
Zum Domstein	5
Zur Krim	2

N

St. Paulin

Porta
Nigra

Simeonstift

Dreikönigenhaus

Die Steipe &
Rotes Haus

HAUPTMARKT

St. Gangolf

St. Georgsbrunnen

Karl-
Marx-
Haus

Liebfrauenkirche

Palais Kesselstadt

KONSTANTIN-
PLATZ

Konstantinbasilika

VIEHMARKT

Viehmarktthermen

Stadtbibliothek

Bischöfliches Dom-
und Diözesanmuseum

Dom

Hauptbahnhof

Rokoko-
Palais

Palast-
garten

Rheinisches
Landesmuseum

Barbarathermen

Kaiserthermen

Amphitheater

0   200 m

ACCOMMODATION

Aulmann Hotel	D
Casa Chiara	B
DJH Hostel	A
Park Plaza Trier	C
Villa Hügel	E
Weinhaus Becker	F

Basilika St. Matthias

and become an archbishopric in 1364. This brought a second golden age when its archbishops became prince-electors and so vital imperial power-brokers.

But Trier is not a city that lives entirely on its past, and the **vineyards** around town along with a large student population help liven things up, while the proximity to Luxembourg and France provides a cosmopolitan feel that makes it an immediately likeable and easy-going place and good base for day-trips, not just along the Mosel Valley but also to Völklinger Hütte (see p.544) and Saarbrücken (see p.545). And if you're driving don't forget to nip over to Luxembourg for the cheap fuel – price differences have spawned a minor industry just over the border.

Arrival, information and accommodation

From Trier's **Hauptbahnhof** it's an easy five-minute walk west to the Porta Nigra and adjacent **tourist office** (May–Oct Mon–Thurs 9am–6pm, Fri & Sat 9am–7pm, Sun 9am–5pm; Nov–April Mon–Sat 9am–5pm, Sun 10am–1pm; ☎0651/97 80 80, @www.tourist-information-trier.de), which sells the **Trier Card** (individual €9; family €15 for two adults and three children), which, among other things, includes free public transport and a 25 percent discount to all its Roman monuments. But if it's the latter you're interested in, the **kombi-ticket** to the four big attractions – the Porta Nigra, Kaiserthermen, Amphitheater and Barbarathermen – can be bought at any of them for €6.20. Trier's tourist office is also the starting point for two-hour English-language **walking tours** of the city (April–Oct Sat 1.30pm; €6) and has a schedule of **wine tours** put on by various local vintners. Finally, they can help with booking **accommodation** – which is plentiful in Trier, if a little pricier than usual and regularly booked up – in person, via their hotline (☎0651/978 08 16), or website.

Hotels and pensions

Aulmann Hotel Fleischstr. 47–48 ☎0651/976 70, @www.hotel-aulmann.de. Straightforward rooms in a good three-star place in the pedestrianized centre of town. ❻

Casa Chiara Engelstr. 8 ☎0651/27 07 30, @www.casa-chiara.de. Friendly, family-run place, with scrupulously clean rooms and good breakfasts, a couple of minutes' walk from the Porta Nigra. ❺

Park Plaza Trier Nikolaus-Koch-Platz 1 ☎0651/999 30, @www.parkplaza-trier.de. Big, central chain hotel, with predictable four-star comforts and service, including a Roman-themed pool and sauna area, use of which costs extra, as does breakfast. ❺

Villa Hügel Bernhardstr. 14☎0651/93 71 00, @www.hotel-villa-huegel.de. Upscale Art-Nouveau villa and highly recommended for its cheerful rooms and facilities which include a pool, sauna and a sun terrace with lovely valley views. ❻

Weinhaus Becker Olewiger Str. 206 ☎0651/93 80 80, @www.weinhaus-becker.de. Stylish pension in the wine-producing suburb of Olewig, 2km from the centre, but an easy walk from the amphitheatre. It has a decent restaurant and can usually organize some wine-tasting. ❹

Hostels and campsites

Campingplatz Treviris Luxemburger Str. 81 ☎0651/820 09 11, @www.camping-treviris .de. Pleasant family-run campground with shaded sites on the banks of the Mosel around 2km southwest of town; two adults with a tent pay €19.05.

DJH Trier An der Jugendherberge 4 ☎0651/14 66 20, @www.diejugendherbergen.de. Spotless riverside hostel, 1km northeast of the centre. Rooms have their own bathroom and no more than six beds (€18.40 per night); from the Hauptbahnhof take bus #12.

The Porta Nigra and Hauptmarkt

Incredibly, Trier's northern city gate, the **Porta Nigra** (daily: March & Oct 9am–5pm; April–Sept 9am–6pm; Nov–Feb 9am–4pm; €2.10; ☎0651/754 24) dates back to the second century. Its name – Black Gate – comes from its blackening by the passage of time, but it's more remarkable for its ingenious design, with the entire structure supported by just its own weight and a few iron rods. In the eleventh century the gate was converted into a church – St Simeonkirche – and named in honour of a resident Greek hermit. A monastery, the **Simeonstift**, was attached to the church, but now partly houses the **Stadtmuseum** (March–Oct daily 9am–5pm; Nov–Feb Tues–Fri 9am–5pm, Sat & Sun 9am–3pm; €2.60; ☎0651/718 14 59, @www.museum-trier.de), a well above-average local history museum which has not only a good Roman section, but also some fine textiles and East Asian sculptures.

Simeonstrasse is the broad, straight pedestrian road that leads south from the Porta Nigra to the **Hauptmarkt** at the centre of the Altstadt. At Simeonstrasse 19 is the **Dreikönigenhaus**, an unusual thirteenth-century Gothic town house whose original entrance was on the first floor at the top of a retractable staircase that could be withdrawn in times of trouble. The bustling **Hauptmarkt**, home to a market most days, is focused on the brightly coloured Petrusbrunnen fountain, and encircled by grand houses. Among these are the vivid **Rotes Haus** and the eye-catching **Steipe**, a one-time banqueting hall and now a **Spielzeugmuseum** (Toy Museum; April–Oct daily 11am–6pm; Nov–March Tues–Sun 11am–5pm; €4; ☎0651/758 50), a cheerful collection of miniature trains and dolls.

The Karl-Marx-Haus and the Viehmarktthermen

From the western corner of the Hauptmarkt, Fleischstrasse leads south into a dense network of Altstadt lanes and directly to the **Karl-Marx-Haus**, Brückenstrasse 10 (April–Oct Mon 1–6pm, Tues–Sun 10am–6pm; Nov–March Tues–Sun 10am–1pm & 2–5pm; €3; ☎0651/97 06 80), where the political philosopher (1818–83) was born and grew up. The bourgeois mansion attests to Marx's affluent background, and his father was a well-respected local lawyer of Jewish descent, but this background is little discussed in the museum, whose collection includes volumes of poetry, original letters, photographs and a collection of rare first editions of his work, as well as an exhibit on the development of socialism.

From the Karl-Marx-Haus a right turn onto Stresemannstrasse quickly brings you to the large **Viehmarktplatz** where in medieval Trier livestock were traded. The incongruous glassy cube at the centre is a 1980s construction to protect the **Viehmarktthermen** (opening hours vary, usually Tues–Sun 9am–5pm; €2.10; ☎0651/994 10 57), the smallest and oldest of Trier's Roman bath complexes. It was a surprise discovery during excavations for a parking

▲ Porta Nigra, Trier

garage, and worth a quick look through the window, though your energies are better saved for the Kaiserthermen.

The Dom

A block east of the Hauptmarkt and in front of a large square of its own, Trier's **Dom** (daily: April–Oct 6.30am–6pm; Nov–March 6.30am–5.30pm) is largely Romanesque, with building work on its austere facade beginning in the early eleventh century (and continuing for almost two hundred years). Its most important relic, a robe supposedly worn by Christ at his crucifixion, is rarely on show, but kept secure in the extravagant Baroque **Heiltumskapelle**. Nevertheless, the **Domschatz** (Cathedral Treasury; April–Oct Mon–Sat 10am–5pm, Sun 2–5pm; Nov–March Mon–Sat 10am–4pm, Sun 2–4pm; €1.50) still has some interesting items displayed, including a portable tenth-century altar designed to carry the sandal of St Andrew. Outside on the south side of the Dom, cloisters join it to the **Liebfrauenkirche** (daily: April–Oct 7.30am–6pm; Nov–March 7.30am–5.30pm), an early Gothic church whose twelve pillars represent the apostles. Meanwhile on the north side of the Dom, the **Bischöfliches Dom und Diönzesanmuseum**, Windstrasse 6–8 (April–Oct Mon–Sat 9am–5pm, Sun 1–5pm; Nov–March Tues–Sat 9am–5pm, Sun 1–5pm; €2; ☎0651/710 52 55), the museum of the bishopric, is worth a visit for the fourth-century Roman fresco removed from the palace that once stood where the Dom was built.

Konstantinbasilika and the Rheinisches Landesmuseum

South of the Dom, and every bit as impressive, the **Konstantinbasilika**, Konstantinplatz (April–Oct Mon–Sat 10am–6pm, Sun noon–6pm; Nov–March Tues–Sat 11am–noon & 3–4pm, Sun noon–1pm), has ended up as another of Trier's churches but was originally intended as a giant throne-hall for the Emperor Constantine in the fourth century. Much later it was converted into a Protestant church for use by the prince-electors who resided in the neigh-bouring **Rokoko-Palais** (closed to the public), a garish, pink Baroque affair that couldn't contrast more with the sombre church. South beyond them both are suitably formal gardens, which pave the way south to the Kaiserthermen past the **Rheinisches Landesmuseum**, Weimarer Allee 1 (Mon–Fri 9.30am–5pm, Sat & Sun 10.30am–5pm; Nov–April Tues–Fri 9.30am–5pm, Sat & Sun 10.30am–5pm; €5.50; ☎0651/977 40, ⓦwww.landesmuseum-trier.de), a Roman-archeology museum par excellence, with an engrossing scale-model of fourth-century Trier which puts what survives in context, and a well-presented hoard of glassware, coins, tombstones and mosaics.

The Kaiserthermen and the Amphitheater

Trier's **Kaiserthermen**, Weimarer Allee 2 (Imperial Thermal Baths; daily: March & Oct 9am–5pm; April–Sept 9am–6pm; Nov–Feb 9am–4pm; €2.10; ☎0651/442 62), were not only the largest of several in town, but also the largest in the Roman world. Little of the buildings remain, but their foundations and underground heating system are intact. As you wander around, information panels help you to visualize the scale of this fourth-century complex, which remains impressively large even today.

The scale impresses too at Trier's **Amphitheater** (daily: March & Oct 9am–5pm; April–Sept 9am–6pm; Nov–Feb 9am–4pm; €2.10; ☎0651/730 10), a ten-minute walk southeast along Olewiger Strasse from the underpass at the southeast corner of the Kaiserthermen. This 20,000-capacity arena was built around 100 AD – making it Trier's oldest Roman structure – for gladiatorial and animal fights and is well preserved, so it is easy to imagine its dank cellars hanging heavy with tension and the stench of sweat and blood as participants waited to be brought before baying crowds.

If you still have the time and interest, then a couple of more secondary Roman sights are worth exploring, an easy fifteen-minute walk back along Olewiger Strasse, which becomes Südallee further west. Alongside the road and readily visible are the **Barbarathermen**, a second-century Roman bath now under renovation, while close to the end of the road, the **Römerbrücke** is a bridge which still uses five Roman-era pylons to support its weight.

Eating, drinking and entertainment

Though many of the Altstadt's restaurants are fairly touristy, Trier's university population ensures there's still a circuit of good inexpensive and lively places to **eat**. Also worth investigating are **wine bars** in the basements of some of the best restaurants – with whom they share a kitchen – which are excellent places for sampling a few regional wines. For an evening's entertainment of a different sort, investigate **TuFa**, Wechselstrasse 4–6 (℡0651/718 24 14), a former towel factory that now serves as a venue for both conventional and off-beat music, drama and dance performances.

Restaurants

Palais Kesselstatt Liebfrauenstr. 10 ℡0651/402 04. Upmarket restaurant where the food matches the extravagance of the Baroque decor of a former Count's residence. The gourmet menu changes with the seasons (mains €16–25), and there's a choice of wines from the restaurant's own estates. For less of the formality and simpler food but the same good wines, try the basement *Weinstube* where mains average €12.

Zum Domstein Hauptmarkt 5. Innovative place with both standard regional dishes (mains around €15) – such as trout in a Riesling sauce – as well as quirky choices in the basement *Römischer Weinkeller* where Roman dishes are served. The recipes – which almost all involve very rich sauces – are those of the court cook for the Emperor Tiberius, and are particularly good value at lunch when mains cost around a third less. This is also a good place for a spot of wine tasting: three different glasses together cost only €7.

Zur Krim Glockenstr. 7 ℡0651/739 43. Split between an earthy bar up front and a stylish restaurant at the rear – with tapas the speciality throughout. The quality is first class, the prices reasonable (most around €6) and the mussels outstanding.

Cafés and bars

Astarix Karl-Marx-Str. 11. Large laid-back student bar with good inexpensive pizzas and casseroles for around €5. The entrance is down an alley.

BagelSisters Pferdemarkt 8. Fun café with not just great bagels and muffins but also a quirky selection of breakfasts, including the "hangover" – a bottle of beer and an aspirin – which sets the tone of the place, as well as some superb daily soups.

Café Lecca Bahnhofsplatz 7. Stylish café outside the Altstadt but close to the Hauptbahnhof that is great for breakfast and cakes. It's renowned for its fantastic Sunday brunch buffet (€9.50). With free wi-fi too.

Irish Pub Jakobstr. 10. Cosy pub and favourite with local Anglophones – including American soldiers from nearby bases – and those keen on watching the English premier league.

Völklinger Hütte

The town of **VÖLKLINGEN**, 71km from Trier but just 10km downstream along the Saar from Saarbrücken, is one of those one-time industrial power-houses – and now picture of industrial malaise and decline – that most people would usually give a wide berth to when they can. However, its huge and rusty decaying old ironworks, the **Völklinger Hütte** (daily: April–Oct 10am–7pm; Nov–March 10am–6pm; €12, free Tues after 2pm; ☏06898/910 01 00, Ⓦwww.voelklinger-huette.org), only a couple of minutes' walk from the Hauptbahnhof, have become celebrated to an extent that UNESCO has even made it a World Heritage Site. It's preserved as one of the last of its generation, a quiet reminder of a grimy and now-disappearing period of European history. Opened in 1873, the ironworks' huge size and the complexity of the site are what immediately impress most. By its mid-1960s heyday the workforce peaked at around 17,000, before slowly decreasing until production finally ceased in 1986.

It's now hard to imagine the place at full throttle with all the noise, dust and dirt involved, but the excellent multilingual audio guide and useful signs (in English too) do their best to bring all this alive, and a candid exhibition on the lives and health problems of the workers sets the tone for an honest appraisal of the site's history. Numerous spaces in the ironworks serve as temporary exhibition galleries for photography and art, with the raw backdrop often adding an unexpected poignancy to the pieces displayed. **Concerts** also take place here, with jazz a regular feature of Friday nights.

Saarbrücken

The modern town of **SAARBRÜCKEN** is not a place to go out of your way for, but is nevertheless a lively university town whose closeness to the French border comes across in its attitudes and food. The background to this is the subject of the town's local history museum, **Historisches Museum Saar**, which is the most rewarding of the city's museums, though it's a close-run thing with the **Museum für Vor- und Frühgeschichte** which boasts a hoard of ancient Celtic treasures. The city centres on **St Johann**, a town incorporated into Saarbrücken two hundred years ago and whose marketplace, **St Johanner Markt**, still preserves much of its history, as well as harbouring a lively restaurant and café scene. From here the main shopping street Bahnhofstrasse heads north and is paralleled by a promenade along the River Saar from which bridges lead over to an area known as **Alt-Saarbrücken** on the south bank. Most of Saarbrücken's few real sights are clustered here, including the remains of an eighteenth-century Schloss, built during the city's heyday under Prince Wilhelm Heinrich (1718–68) and designed by court architect Friedrich Joachim Stengel, who was also responsible for several Baroque town houses and churches in the surrounding area.

Arrival, information and accommodation

Saarbrücken's **Hauptbahnhof** opens onto the broad pedestrian boulevard Reichsstrasse, which twists south to become five-hundred-metre-long chain-store street Bahnhofstrasse south as far as focal square St Johanner Markt. Just short of this and west along Betzenstrasse is the town's Rathaus, location of the **tourist office** (Mon–Fri 9am–6pm, Sat 10am–4pm; ☏01805/72 27 27, Ⓦwww.die-region-saarbruecken.de). Getting here and around the compact centre generally is easy enough on foot. With Saarbrücken attracting few casual visitors, most of its **accommodation** is geared to business travel; as always the tourist office can help finding and booking private rooms (❷).

Am Triller Trilerweg 57 ☎0681/58 00 00,
ⓦwww.hotel-am-triller.de. Swish modern hotel
in Alt-Saarbrücken with well-kept but rather
nondescript rooms and excellent facilities which
include a pool, sauna and fitness centre and wi-fi
throughout the hotel. ⓖ

DJH Saarbrücken Meerwiesertalweg 31
☎0681/330 40, ⓦwww.www.diejugendherbergen
.de. Sparkling modern hostel in the university
district northeast of the centre and on the green
edges of town. Rooms have only two or four beds
and all are en suite; prices start at €18.40. To get
here take tram S1 to Johanneskirche and then bus
#101 or #150 to stop "Jugendherberge".

Madeleine Cecilienstr. 5 ☎0681/322 28,
ⓦwww.hotel-madeleine.de. Family-run,
mid-range choice with small bright rooms in a
great central location opposite the Rathaus. Free
bike rental and completely organic breakfasts
sweeten what's already a good deal and rates
even drop a little during the week. ❸

Schlosskrug Schmollerstr. 14 ☎0681/367 35,
ⓦwww.hotel-schlosskrug.de. Bland but clean and
well-run budget option a 5min walk east of the
centre. Not all of the rooms have their own
bathroom, but at around €30 the singles are real
bargains. ❷

St Johann

A town in its own right from 1353, **St Johann** was made part of Saarbrücken by the Prussians in 1815, but its focus remains its long elongated square Sankt-Johanner-Markt, home to the city's oldest buildings and with an ornate Stengel-designed fountain its centrepiece. At no. 24, the **Stadtgalerie** (Tues & Thurs–Sun 11am–7pm, Wed noon–8pm; free; ☎0681/936 83 21, ⓦwww.stadtgalerie.de) is worth a look for its oft-quirky contemporary art exhibitions.

A larger municipal collection of modern art is also on this side of the Saar, in the **Moderne Galerie**, which is part of the **Saarland Museum**, Bismarckstrasse 11–15 (Tues & Thurs–Sun 10am–6pm, Wed 10am–10pm; €1.50; ☎0681/996 40, ⓦwww.saarlandmuseum.de), a fifteen-minute walk southeast from Sankt-Johanner-Markt through residential streets. The German Impressionist section – Liebermann and the like – is strong and neatly put into context by the work of some French contemporaries. It's also good on Expressionism, with Kirchner's *Bathers in a Room* one of its most celebrated paintings.

Alt-Saarbrücken

From Sankt-Johanner-Markt it's an easy five-minute walk southwest along the pedestrian Saarstrasse and the Alte Brücke footbridge over the Saar to **Alt-Saarbrücken**. Here, beyond the thundering and unsightly A620 Autobahn, the generally Baroque quarter begins with a Gothic **Schlosskirche**, Am Schlossberg 6 (Tues & Thurs–Sun 10am–6pm, Wed 10am–10pm; free; ☎0681/950 76 38), which is worth a look. It had its stained glass blown out in the war, to be replaced by obviously 1950s panes, and now holds a museum of religious art from the thirteenth century onwards which includes some noteworthy fifteenth-century pieces. Behind the church is the heart of Alt-Saarbrücken's residential quarter and its fine pastel town houses constitute some of Stengel's best work.

A short walk uphill from the Schlosskirche, the grand **Schlossplatz** provides a rather lifeless forecourt for the **Saarbrücker Schloss**, a largely Renaissance and Baroque edifice, again by Stengel, with a glass extension – by Gottfried Böhm – that looks every inch the 1980s addition that it is. It's worth wandering around the outside of the building for the views over town. Inside the excellent **Historisches Museum Saar** (Tues, Wed, Fri & Sun 10am–6pm, Thurs 10am–8pm, Sat noon–6pm; €2.50; ☎0681/506 45 01, ⓦwww.historisches-museum.org) specializes in exhibitions about the region and its turbulent twentieth-century history. Beside it the **Museum für Vor- und Frühgeschichte**, Schlossplatz 16 (Tues–Sat 9am–5pm, Sun 10am–6pm; free; ☎0681/95 40 50, ⓦwww.historisches-museum.org), is of particular interest for the hoard of jewellery that was found in the grave of a Celtic princess buried around 400 BC on what's now the French border 25km southeast of Saarbrücken. At the same address is the Saarlandmuseum's collection of fine and applied art: the **Alte Sammlung** (Tues & Thurs–Sun 10am–6pm, Wed 10am–10pm; €1.50; ☎0681/95 40 50, ⓦwww.saarlandmuseum.de), which includes pieces that date back to the eleventh century but is strongest on medieval pieces and on sixteenth- to nineteenth-century portraiture. Of particular regional interest is its tapestry collection – including many fine examples from Alsace and Lorraine, and Luxembourg.

Eating, drinking and entertainment

The obvious focus for **eating**, **drinking** and **nightlife** is the Sankt-Johanner-Markt and the small streets around it, but there are more places in the Nauwieser quarter just north of the Rathaus that are less mainstream and favoured by local students.

The main venue for high culture is the grand Neoclassical **Staatstheater**, Schillerplatz 1 (☎0681/30 920, ⓦwww.theater-saarbruecken.de), which is regularly graced by ballet, drama, opera, musicals and concerts. A more novel option is to hop on one of the frequent trains to Völklingen – just nine minutes away – and attend events at its old ironworks (see p.544).

Restaurants

Hashimoto Cecilienstr. 7. Near-gourmet Japanese restaurant with a good range of dishes including first-glass sushi. Three courses begin at around €21; prices are lower at lunch.

La Bastille Kronenstr. 1b. Small, cosy French restaurant on a side street by the marketplace. The seasonal menu is reasonably priced with mains starting around the €10 mark.

Tierlieb Cecilienstr. 12. Vegetarian restaurant amid a clutch of interesting Bohemian cafés and bistros. Good for lunch when the daily special costs only €4.90 and including items like paella and crêpes.

Cafés and bars

Café Kostbar Nauwieserstr. 19. Courtyard place with very laid-back feel and good inexpensive food for around €6, including many vegetarian dishes such as fried potatoes with tsatziki, salad and bread. Particularly good for breakfast or a great Sunday brunch (€10). Most of the food is organic and locally sourced.

Chez Tintin Kappenstr. 9. Belgian pub with first-rate *frites* – served with mayo and fried onions – as well as excellent *Flammkuchen* and dozens of malty beers.

Gasthaus Zum Stiefel Am Stiefel 2. Saarbrücken's oldest house (1702) with a *Brauhaus* atmosphere, popular beer garden and good portions of hearty local food – such as *Dibbelabbes*, a leek, meat and potato casserole and *Hoorishe*, potato rissoles – all easily washed down with the local *Bruch-Bier*.

Kulturcafé St Johanner Markt 24. Part of the Stadtgalerie, the café walls are lined with art, while the outdoor seating is in premium people-watching position; but both will have to compete for your attention with the excellent cakes.

Karateklub Meier Nassauerstr. 11. Laid-back and sociable pub – one of a couple on the block – with spartan furnishings, loud rock and the constant flicker of silent films on the wall. Occasional live music too.

Travel details

Trains

Koblenz to: Frankfurt (frequent; 2hr); Saarbrücken (hourly; 2hr 30min); Speyer (hourly; 2hr 10min); Trier (hourly; 1hr 30min); Worms (hourly; 1hr 45min).

Mainz to: Frankfurt (frequent; 30min); Koblenz (hourly; 50min); Saarbrücken (frequent; 2hr 30min); Speyer (hourly; 1hr); Stuttgart (hourly; 1hr 30min); Trier (hourly; 2hr 30min); Worms (frequent; 30min).

Saarbrücken to: Frankfurt (8 daily; 2hr); Speyer (frequent; 2hr); Stuttgart (hourly; 2hr); Trier (hourly; 1hr 10min); Völklingen (frequent; 9min); Worms (hourly; 2hr 30min).

Speyer to: Heidelberg (frequent; 50min); Stuttgart (hourly; 1hr 10min); Worms (frequent; 1hr 10min).

Trier to: Frankfurt (hourly; 3hr); Speyer (hourly; 3hr); Stuttgart (hourly; 4hr); Völklingen (hourly; 1hr); Worms (hourly; 3hr 30min).

Hesse

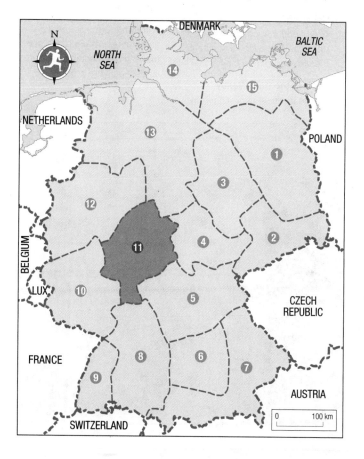

CHAPTER 11

Highlights

✳ **Apfelwein** Frankfurt's cider is best enjoyed alfresco on summer nights in old Sachsenhausen. See p.561

✳ **Mathildenhöhe** The spirit of Jugendstil lingers on at Darmstadt's remarkable artists' colony. See p.567

✳ **Hessisches Staatstheater** Grand opera at not-so-grand prices at Wiesbaden's beautiful theatre. See p.573

✳ **Cycling the Lahn Valley** Gentle inclines, cyclist-friendly hotels and beautiful towns and countryside make the Lahn Valley a cyclist's joy. See p.580

✳ **Rhön Biosphere Reserve** Hike, paraglide or simply enjoy the spectacular views in this pristine upland landscape. See p.590

✳ **Wilhelmshöhe** Old masters and eighteenth-century water tricks in a remarkable garden landscape. See p.595

▲ The Hessisches Staatstheater, Wiesbaden

Hesse

For many visitors – and particularly those stepping off an intercontinental flight at Frankfurt airport – Hesse is their first taste of Germany. It can be a disconcerting experience, for at first sight there's little about Frankfurt's steel-and-glass modernity or its easy internationalism to summon up half-remembered childhood notions of a Hansel-and-Gretel Germany.

For much of its history Frankfurt was a free imperial city, proudly independent of the competing micro-states that characterized the rest of the region. The modern Land of Hesse was created by the occupying Americans after World War II, who joined the Prussian province of Hesse-Nassau – itself an amalgamation of the old Electorate of Hesse-Kassel, the comic-opera statelet of Hesse-Homburg and the Duchy of Nassau – to the former Grand Duchy of Hesse-Darmstadt.

Confusing? Perhaps. But the complexity of its history helps explain the richness and diversity of Hesse's attractions. If it's big-city buzz that you crave, then **Frankfurt** – Germany's fifth largest city and the financial capital of the Eurozone – has much to offer, including a heavyweight selection of museums and evocative monuments to its literary, imperial and Jewish pasts. Along the Rhine, you can unwind in the **Rheingau**'s wine country or embrace the day-tripper brashness of **Rüdesheim**. To the south, laid-back **Darmstadt** is unmissable for fans of Jugendstil, and also a base for visiting a brace of UNESCO World Heritage sites – the **Messel** fossil site and the monastery at **Lorsch** – close by. The genteel spa-towns of Land capital **Wiesbaden** and **Bad Homburg** make the perfect antidote to Frankfurt's urban stress. Away from the Rhine-Main region, Hesse is archetypal Germany, with a rolling and often forested landscape that reaches near-mountainous heights in the **Taunus** and **Rhön**. Other than Frankfurt, the towns are mostly small, but they're an appealing bunch, from picture-book cathedral towns such as **Fritzlar**, **Limburg an der Lahn** and **Wetzlar** to the proud university town of **Marburg** or the handsome former prince-bishopric of **Fulda**. Smaller than them all, yet well worth a visit, is the tiny ducal seat of **Weilburg**. In the north, **Kassel** lures visitors for the *documenta* contemporary art fair, but then surprises with its exceptional Baroque gardens and excellent museums. Wherever you go, there are reminders of the world-famous figures who left their mark on German history and culture, and who were born here, made their home in Hesse or passed this way: of **Goethe** in Frankfurt; of the **Brothers Grimm** – whose fairy tales capture the imagination of children worldwide – in Marburg and Kassel; and of **St Boniface** – the English bishop who became the patron saint of Germany – in Fritzlar and Fulda. For British and Commonwealth visitors, there are reminders of Germany's complex relationship to the British royal family, particularly in Darmstadt.

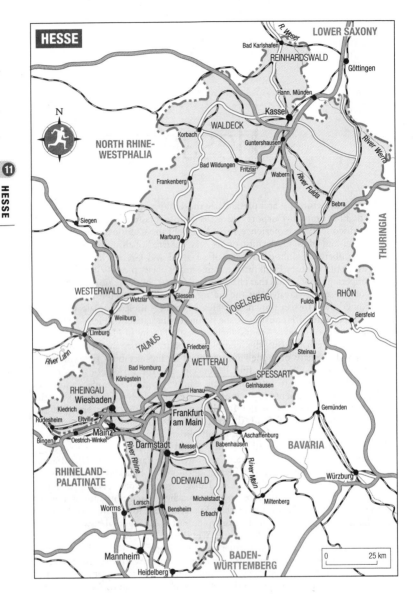

Getting into and **around** Hesse is easy. Frankfurt's airport has more inter-continental connections than any other in Germany, with high-speed ICE trains linking the airport direct to many cities. Public transport in the main Rhine-Main conurbation is integrated, making ticketing and information easy; elsewhere, you can explore the Lahn Valley with ease by car, bike or train, while outlying Fulda has fast trains to Frankfurt, and Fritzlar is easily reached by rail or bus from Kassel.

Frankfurt am Main

Thrusting, dynamic **FRANKFURT** is the beating heart of Germany's financial sector and home to the European Central Bank. It has an impressive skyline bristling with eye-catching skyscrapers, earning it the nickname Mainhattan, while business travellers flock here for the trade shows, which include the world's largest book fair. It's an important transport hub too, with Germany's busiest Autobahn intersection and its largest international airport, which is linked directly to the high-speed ICE rail network.

For all its high-octane modernity, Frankfurt has played a long, often distinguished role in German history. In the Middle Ages it was a free imperial city, and even today its fierce civic pride echoes that doughty medieval independence. In 1562 it succeeded Aachen as the city in which Holy Roman Emperors were crowned, a role it retained until 1792, and in 1848 it was the setting for the first democratically elected German national assembly. A century later, it narrowly lost out to Bonn in the competition to become capital of the new Federal Republic of Germany. Frankfurt also has a proud Jewish history: the Rothschild banking dynasty originated here, and though the Jewish tradition was all but wiped out under the Nazis it has of late made a spirited comeback.

First impressions of limousines, office towers and briefcases can suggest Germany's fifth largest city is all work and no play, and among business travellers it sometimes commands more respect than affection. Though Frankfurt's charms can occasionally be elusive, they're real, from alfresco *Apfelwein* imbibing in the Sachsenhausen district to museum-hopping on the Museumsufer or Ibiza-style DJ bars atop city-centre car parks in summer. Spend time discovering them and you'll find this sophisticated, cosmopolitan city repays your investment with interest.

Arrival, information and city transport

Frankfurt's **airport** (☏069/69 00, ⓦwww.airportcity-frankfurt.com) is a short distance west of the city. S-Bahn trains from the Regionalbahnhof in terminal one take just eleven minutes to reach Frankfurt's **Hauptbahnhof**, which is itself ten minutes' walk west of the Hauptwache. There's a **tourist office** in the station's main reception hall (Mon–Fri 8am–9pm, Sat & Sun 9am–6pm; ☏069/21 23 88 00, ⓦwww.frankfurt-tourismus.de); there's also a second one in the Altstadt at Römerberg 27 (Mon–Fri 9.30am–5.30pm, Sat & Sun 10am–4pm). Both sell the **Frankfurt Card** (1 day €8.70, 2 days €12.50) which gives fifty percent discounts on museums plus unlimited, free use of the public transport system and discounts at various other venues, including theatres, restaurants, cafés and bars. **Sightseeing tours** start daily at 10am and 2pm from Römerberg tourist office (€26 with English commentary; ☏069/21 23 89 53 for information).

Frankfurt's public **transport** is integrated with the rest of the Rhine-Main region as part of the RMV network (ⓦwww.rmv.de), which makes accessing the neighbouring cities of Wiesbaden, Darmstadt and Bad Homburg by S-Bahn easy. Within the city, buses, trams and U-Bahn make navigation straightforward, though frequency of service drops noticeably in the evening. If you're only travelling a kilometre or so you can buy a *Kurzstrecke* ticket (€1.50), otherwise single tickets cost €2.30 and a *Tageskarte* €5.80 – the latter is valid until public transport shuts down for the night, and you can use it on night buses. Announcements on public transport are in both German and English.

FRANKFURT AM MAIN

0 — 250 m

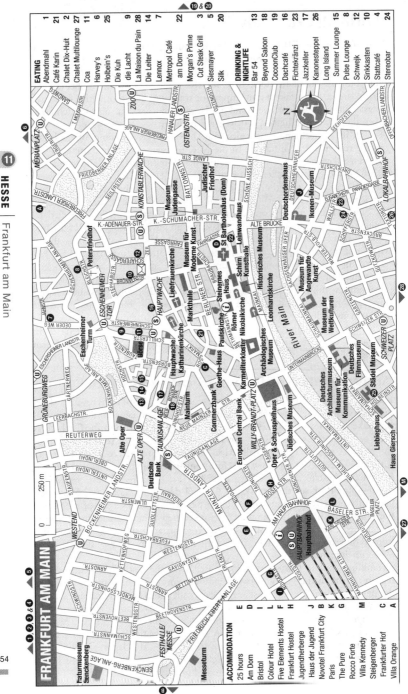

ACCOMMODATION
25 hours	E
Am Dom	D
Bristol	I
Colour Hotel	L
Five Elements Hostel	F
Frankfurt Hostel	H
Jugendherberge	J
Haus der Jugend	B
Novotel Frankfurt City	K
Paris	G
The Pure	M
Rocco Forte	
Villa Kennedy	C
Steigenberger	
Frankfurter Hof	A
Villa Orange	

EATING
Abendmahl	1
Café Karin	21
Chalet Dix-Huit	2
Chalet Multilounge	27
Coa	11
Harvey's	6
Holbein's	25
Die Kuh	9
die Lacht	28
La Maison du Pain	14
Die Leiter	7
Lennox	22
Metropol Café	
am Dom	3
Morgan's Prime	5
Cut Steak Grill	20
Siesmayer	
Silk	

DRINKING & NIGHTLIFE
Bar 54	13
Beyond Saloon	18
CocoonClub	19
Dachcafé	16
Fichtekränzi	23
Jazzkeller	17
Kanonesteppel	26
Long Island	
Summer Lounge	15
Pulse Lounge	8
Schwejk	12
Sinkkasten	10
Stattcafé	4
Stereobar	24

Accommodation

You can book **accommodation** through the tourist office website or their accommodation hotline (☎069/21 23 08 08); if you reserve in person at the tourist information offices, however, they charge a €3 fee. Frankfurt's **hotels** are largely aimed at business travellers, though a new breed of more individual, smaller hotels is challenging the expense-account blandness at all price levels. Room rates – which can be high during the week – take a tumble at weekends, making this a good time to visit the city.

Hotels

25 Hours Niddastr. 58 ☎069/256 67 70, ⓦwww.25hours-hotels.com. Hyper-trendy denim-themed hotel attached to the German headquarters of the Levi's jean company, close to the Hauptbahnhof. Rates are 25 percent lower if you're under 25, and cheaper at weekends. ⑤

Am Dom Kannengiessergasse 3 ☎069/28 21 41, ⓦwww.hotelamdom.de. Small, quiet family-run place in a very central location in the shadow of the Dom. All rooms have shower or bath and wi-fi. ⑥

Bristol Ludwigstr. 15 ☎069/24 23 90, ⓦwww.bristol-hotel.de. Attractive modern boutique-style hotel close to the Hauptbahnhof, with wi-fi, 24hr bar and parking. Good value for the high standard of accommodation it provides. ④

Colour Hotel Baseler Str. 52 ☎069/36 50 75 80, ⓦwww.colourhotel.de. Bright, modern two-star hotel whose funky design and vibrant colours make a virtue of its comfortable austerity. It also has singles, from €29. ②

Novotel Frankfurt City Lisa-Meitner-Str. 2 ☎069/79 30 30, ⓦwww.novotel.com. Comfortable, contemporary outpost of the business-oriented chain, close to the Messe and offering excellent weekend deals. ②–⑤

Paris Karlsruher Str. 8 ☎069/273 99 63, ⓦwww.hotelparis.de. Comfortable budget option close to the Hauptbahnhof. All rooms have shower, WC and cable TV. ③

The Pure Niddastr. 86 ☎069/710 45 70, ⓦwww.the-pure.de. Minimalist all-white designer hotel north of the Hauptbahnhof – pricey during the week, but rates tumble at weekends. ⑥

Rocco Forte Villa Kennedy Kennedyallee 70 ☎069/71 71 20, ⓦwww.villakennedy.com. Twice voted best business hotel in Europe, the city's plushest hotel occupies a historic late nineteenth-century villa on the Sachsenhausen side of the river, and has weekend rates from around €240. ⑧–⑨

Steigenberger Frankfurter Hof Am Kaiserplatz ☎069/215 02, ⓦwww.frankfurter-hof.steigenberger .de. Frankfurt's prime example of a traditional grand hotel, with imposing nineteenth-century architecture, an excellent, central location and good deals on advance rates. ⑦

Villa Orange Hebelstr. 1 ☎069/40 58 40, ⓦwww.villa-orange.de. Classy Nordend hotel, with tasteful, conservatively modern decor and – in some rooms – the bathrooms are very elegant, with free-standing baths. ⑦

Hostels

Five Elements Hostel Moselstr. 40 ☎069/24 00 58 85, ⓦwww.5elementshostel.de. Bright new Bahnhofsviertel hostel. Beds in five-bed dorms from €18; there are also quads, twins and doubles (②).

Frankfurt Hostel Kaiser Str. 74 ☎069/247 51 30, ⓦwww.frankfurt-hostel.com. Bustling backpacker hostel on the upper floors of a nineteenth-century building close to the Hauptbahnhof. It has singles (€50), doubles (②) and dorms (including women-only dorms; beds from €18) and a groovy ambience. The tiny lift might be a struggle if your backpack is particularly big.

Jugendherberge Haus der Jugend Deutschherrnufer 12 ☎069/610 01 50, ⓦwww .jugendherberge-frankfurt.de. Frankfurt's modern youth hostel is on the Sachsenhausen side of the river to the east of the city centre. Accommodation is in singles, doubles, or four-, eight- or ten-bed dorms; beds from €17.

The City

The centre of Frankfurt is easily recognizable on a map, surrounded by a crescent of green spaces called *Anlagen* that follow the course of the old fortifications. The major shopping streets intersect at the **Hauptwache**, while the skyscrapers of the financial district straddle the **Taunusanlage** and **Gallusanlage** to the west. Further west still is the **Bahnhofviertel** around the main train station, which is where many of the hotels are located. Frankfurt's major historic sites are close to the north bank of the River Main, where the carefully reconstructed

Römerberg provides the focus; across the river is **Sachsenhausen,** home to the city's celebrated *Apfelwein* taverns and to most of its museums. Further afield, the lively residential districts of **Bornheim, Bockenheim** and **Nordend** are chiefly of interest to visitors for their good eating and drinking.

The Römerberg and around

Steep gables, half-timbered facades and the picturesque sixteenth-century **Gerechtigkeitsbrunnen** or Justice Fountain make spacious **Römerberg,** the old central square, the focal point of Frankfurt's Altstadt and the very image of a medieval town square. It's the perfect setting for the city's Christmas market, just as it has been the scene for major events since the Middle Ages. What you see is, however, in part an illusion. The old town went up in flames during an air raid on the night of March 22, 1944, and the much-photographed **half-timbered houses** on the east side are modern reconstructions. On the west side, the stately **Römer** – Frankfurt's Rathaus – is genuine enough, though it was grievously damaged during the war. Its three central gables were "improved" by the addition of neo-Gothic elements in the nineteenth century, but the oldest bits of the rambling complex date back to 1322. Cross the main courtyard – accessed via Limpurgergasse on the south side – to visit the **Kaisersaal** (daily 10am–1pm & 2–5pm; €2) on the first floor, with its 52 nineteenth-century portraits of kings and emperors of the Holy Roman Empire, from Charlemagne to Franz II. It was here that the Electors would hold their concluding banquet after the selection of a new emperor, and the reconstructed hall is still used for VIP receptions. It has a touch of postwar blandness about it, however, and the graceful Renaissance staircase you climb to reach it is rather more appealing.

The one genuine half-timbered house on Römerberg is **Haus Wertheim** in the southwest corner, which dates from around 1600 and was spared destruction in the 1944 raid. Opposite, the bunker-like **Historisches Museum Frankfurt** (Tues & Thurs–Sun 10am–6pm, Wed 10am–9pm; €4) has the decency to half-hide behind the pretty little thirteenth-century Gothic **Nikolaikirche,** which was used as a spectator stand during imperial coronations. The Historisches Museum's forbidding concrete exterior conceals a much older complex of buildings beyond, which incorporates the twelfth-century Romanesque **Saalhof chapel** – originally a court chapel and the oldest building in Frankfurt – in whose cellar emperors stored the imperial crown jewels when they were in Frankfurt. The museum's permanent and temporary exhibitions do a good job of tracing the city's history from 784 to the present day: along with the usual archeological exhibits and a display of the municipal silver, there's a giant model of the Altstadt as it was before its destruction, a section charting the city's experiences under the Nazis and a sizeable collection of medieval religious art, including some lovely woodcarving by Tilman Riemenschneider.

The Dom and eastern Altstadt

Away from the showpiece of the Römerberg, only isolated buildings were rebuilt after World War II. One is the **Steinernes Haus,** east of Römerberg at Markt 44. Built in 1464 for a patrician family from the Rhineland, it now houses the **Frankfurter Kunstverein** (Tues–Sun 11am–7pm; €6), which hosts temporary art exhibitions. Between here and the Dom is the hated **Technisches Rathaus,** a crass lump of 1970s concrete that tramples over the historic setting and scale of the Altstadt. Current plans are to tear it down so that the old street pattern and some of the lost houses can be reinstated. Facing it to the south, the **Schirn Kunsthalle** (Tues & Fri–Sun 10am–7pm, Wed & Thurs 10am–10pm; €8, ⓦ www.schirn.de) ignores the scale of the old town just as blatantly, but is much more sympathetic in style. It's the city's main venue for large-scale touring exhibitions of fine and applied art. On the south side of the museum along **Saalgasse**, a row of tall, gabled houses in postmodern style cleverly reproduces the scale and feel of the Altstadt without aping medieval methods or materials. At the eastern end of Saalgasse on Weckmarkt, another medieval patrician house – the **Leinwandhaus** – is the new home to the **Caricatura** museum of satirical and comic art (Tues–Sun 10am–6pm; €5).

Dominating everything else in the eastern Altstadt is the west tower of the **Kaiserdom** (daily except Fri am 9am–noon & 2.30–6pm), not in fact a cathedral at all but the city's principal Catholic church, dedicated to St Bartholomew and the venue for ten imperial coronations between 1562 and 1792. Much of the church dates from the thirteenth and fourteenth centuries; the tower, built to the designs of Madern Gerthener between 1415 and 1513 but left incomplete for 350 years when its top was added, was for centuries the dominant feature of Frankfurt's skyline. Inside, the tower hall contains a 1509 **crucifixion** group by the Mainz sculptor Hans Backofen, while the Marienkapelle houses the lovely **Maria-Schlaf altar** from 1434. The **Wahlkapelle** where emperors were elected is surprisingly modest. It was used for this purpose from 1356, at a time when the coronations were still taking place in Aachen. The first emperor to be crowned in Frankfurt was the Habsburg Maximilian II. The cathedral cloisters house the **Dommuseum** (Tues–Fri 10am–5pm, Sat & Sun 11am–5pm; €3), which in addition to displaying seventh-century Merovingian grave goods and the cathedral's ecclesiastical treasure also hosts interesting exhibitions of contemporary art.

A little to the north of the Kaiserdom at Domstrasse 10, the **MMK Museum für Moderne Kunst** (Tues–Sun 10am–8pm; €8, free on last Sat of month; Ⓦwww .mmk-frankfurt.de) houses the city's collection of modern and contemporary art in a striking postmodern building by the Austrian architect Hans Hollein, whose design owes something to the Expressionist architecture of the 1920s. The collection spans the period from the 1960s to the present day, from American Pop Art and Joseph Beuys to works by Gerhard Richter, Bruce Naumann and a younger generation of artists including Julian Schnabel. A short walk east along Battonn Strasse brings you to the excellent **Museum Judengasse** (Tues & Thurs–Sun 10am–5pm, Wed 10am–8pm; €2), an outpost of the Jüdisches Museum built on the site of the cramped medieval ghetto. You can wander among the surviving foundations and cellars of the medieval houses which once stood here. In 1560, around a thousand of Frankfurt's 12,000 inhabitants were Jewish; by 1600 the community had grown to 2700. Shortly afterwards rioting citizens plundered Judengasse and expelled the Jews, but they were escorted back by imperial troops and afterwards the imperial crest was fixed to the ghetto gates as a sign of the Emperor's protection. The families who trace their roots to this street include the Rothschilds, whose name derived from a house called Rotes Schild.

West of Römerberg: the Leonhardskirche and Jüdisches Museum

A short stroll west along the river from the Römerberg, the beautiful Catholic **St Leonhardskirche** escaped the worst of the wartime air raids and thus preserves the smell and feel of antiquity in a way that the other Altstadt churches don't. It's late Romanesque, with some lovely late Gothic details, including a suspended vault depicting the Scourging of Christ.

Continuing west along the Mainkai brings you to the **Jüdisches Museum** (Tues & Thurs–Sun 10am–5pm, Wed 10am–8pm; €4; Ⓦwww.juedischesmuseum .de), which occupies a Neoclassical mansion that once belonged to the Rothschilds. Its displays on the history of Frankfurt's Jewish community are a little dry and the progression from one section to another isn't always clear, but there are English-language texts to help make sense of it all. In the early nineteenth century Frankfurt's professional classes played a key role in the birth of the Jewish Reform movement, which introduced preaching and prayers in German, organ accompaniment for choirs, and rescinded the strict separation of men and women. On the eve of the Nazi takeover, the city's Jewish community numbered 30,000, among them the young Anne Frank. In the years 1938 to 1942 more than seven hundred despairing Frankfurt Jews took their own lives; deportations of the rest to the ghettoes of Łódź, Minsk and Riga began late in 1941. The postwar community, founded in 1948, has grown in recent years and now has more than seven thousand members.

North of Römerberg: the Paulskirche, Goethe-Haus and Neustadt

Immediately to the north of the Römer the circular Neoclassical **Paulskirche** (daily 10am–5pm; free) has a proud place in German history, for it was in this, the city's principal Lutheran church, that on May 18, 1848, the first democratically elected German national assembly met, only to collapse in little more than a year, its demise hastened by a wave of nationalist sentiment allied to the Schleswig-Holstein question and by the machinations of Prussia and Austria. The interior is very plain following postwar reconstruction, with touch-screen panels that bring its historical significance to life.

A little to the west, the refectory and cloisters of the thirteenth-century **Karmelitenkloster** contain wonderful wall paintings by the Swabian artist and revolutionary Jerg Ratgeb portraying the Passion of Christ and the story of the Carmelites. Ratgeb was executed by quartering in Pforzheim in 1526 for his part in the Peasants' War. The same complex also houses the **Archäologisches Museum Frankfurt** (Tues–Sun 10am–5pm; €6), which in addition to its permanent collection of local, classical and oriental antiquities hosts regular temporary exhibitions.

Close by, on the boundary between the Altstadt and the modern city centre, is the **Goethe-Haus** (Mon–Sat 10am–6pm, Sun 10am–5.30pm; €5, English audio guide €2; ⓦ www.goethehaus-frankfurt.de), where Johann Wolfgang von Goethe – commonly regarded as Germany's greatest writer – was born on August 28, 1749. Even if you're not familiar with *Faust* or *The Sorrows of Young Werther* it's an engrossing museum, for it creates a powerful impression of bourgeois family life in eighteenth-century Frankfurt. Take a good look at the bottom four steps of the main staircase: following the destruction of the house by bombs in 1944 on the anniversary of Goethe's death, the ruins rose no higher than these. Postwar reconstruction was loving and astoundingly effective.

Just to the north, the Baroque **Katharinenkirche** where the Goethe family worshipped overlooks the **Hauptwache**, a graceful little eighteenth-century guardhouse that now houses a café. West of it, chic **Goethestrasse** is lined with luxury boutiques, while to the east stretches **Zeil**, one of the busiest shopping streets in Germany and the scene of Baader-Meinhof's rather farcical debut in April 1968, when Andreas Baader, Gudrun Ensslin and others set fire to two department stores, only to be arrested shortly afterwards. Architecturally Zeil is a mix of dull postwar buildings and attention-grabbing newer developments. The brash new **Palais Quartier** mall incorporates skyscrapers and – rather more improbably – a reconstruction of the destroyed Baroque **Thurn und Taxis Palais** around the corner on Grosse Eschenheimer Strasse. At the end of this street, the pinnacled fifteenth-century **Eschenheimer Turm** looks too Disney-perfect to be true, but it's a perfectly genuine survivor of the city's medieval defences. Like the cathedral tower, it's partly the work of Madern Gerthener.

Mainhattan: the financial district

A giant illuminated Euro symbol stands in front of the **European Central Bank** at Willy-Brandt-Platz, marking the start of Frankfurt's banking quarter. At the foot of the bank there's an information centre, café and shop (Mon–Fri 9am–6.30pm, Sat 10am–2pm) where the souvenirs on sale include briquettes made from recycled Euro notes – literally, money to burn.

For the full canyon-like **Mainhattan** effect of towering skyscrapers, take a stroll up Neue Mainzer Strasse. Much the most interesting architecturally is the 299m **Commerzbank** by British architect Norman Foster. Completed in 1997, it's the tallest office building in Europe and looks its best at night, when its pinnacles glow an unearthly yellow, creating a geometric lightshow whose resemblance to the Art Deco style of Fritz Lang's *Metropolis* is surely intentional. You can't visit the Commerzbank, but you can ascend to the viewing platform of its neighbour, the 200m **Maintower** (summer Mon–Thurs & Sun 10am–9pm, Fri & Sat 10am–11pm; winter Mon–Thurs & Sun 10am–7pm, Fri & Sat 10am–9pm; €4.60). The views are most magical at sunset, and there's a smart restaurant one floor down from the platform.

A few minutes' walk to the north, the handsome neo-Renaissance **Alte Oper** straddles the Taunusanlage at the western end of Grosse Bockenheimer Strasse. The opera house was a ruined shell for many years after World War II before finally being restored in the early 1980s. To the east on Börseplatz, bronzes of a bull and bear symbolize rising and falling markets in front of the **Börse**, Germany's principal stock exchange (introductory talks on floor and Xetra trading Mon–Fri 10am & 11am; free; Ⓦ www.deutsche-boerse.com).

The Westend and Bockenheim

Skyscrapers pepper the western fringes of the Taunusanlage, but the **Westend** was originally a smart residential district. A stroll west from the Alte Oper along Kettenhofweg underlines the extent to which this is still a discreetly desirable – and wonderfully central – place to live. At its western end on Senckenberganlage is the **Naturmuseum Senckenberg** (Mon, Tues, Thurs & Fri 9am–5pm, Wed 9am–8pm, Sat & Sun 9am–6pm; €6; Ⓦ www.senckenberg.de; English audio

▲ Frankfurt's skyline

guides), whose giant dinosaur skeletons are a rainy-day godsend for parents with small children. Scary monsters aside, the museum's natural history collection is remarkably comprehensive, and includes a section on the fossil finds from the Grube Messel (see p.570), worth seeing before you visit the site itself.

To the north, beyond Bockenheimer Warte, the **Palmengarten** (daily: Feb–Oct 9am–6pm; Nov–Jan 9am–4pm; €5) is a splendid botanical garden of the old school, with prodigious flower beds and a series of hothouses accommodating plants of various habitats, from mangrove swamp to semi-desert and alpine. West of Bockenheimer Warte, **Bockenheim** itself is one of Frankfurt's most appealing districts – a mix of turn-of-the-century apartment blocks with modern additions and, around Kirchplatz in the west, the charming original village centre, which has some good places to eat and drink.

Sachsenhausen and the Museumsufer

South of the river, the modest, winding lanes of **Alt-Sachsenhausen** perform the "Alstadt" task of providing inexpensive eating and easy bar-hopping between unpretentious *Apfelwein* taverns, though it all looks rather tired by day. Gateway to the district is the Baroque **Deutschordenshaus**, a former monastery at the southern end of the Alte Brücke that now houses the **Ikonen Museum** (Tues & Thurs–Sun 10am–5pm, Wed 10am–8pm; €3), whose permanent collection of Orthodox religious icons is supplemented by regular temporary exhibitions.

To the west along Schaumainkai stretches the so-called **Museumsufer**, an impressive line-up of museums and art galleries. First up is the **Museum für Angewandte Kunst** (Museum of Applied Art; Tues & Thurs–Sun 10am–5pm, Wed 10am–9pm; €5), an airy white building by American architect Richard Meier. The collection highlights the magnificence of the craft skills of Renaissance Nuremberg and Augsburg; there are also superb Islamic ceramics and a crowd-pleasing section of modern classics, from the WG24 Bauhaus lamp to an Eileen Gray table and more recent pieces by Ron Arad, Philippe Starck and Verner Panton. The sections dealing with contemporary design have good labelling in English. At Schaumainkai 29–37, the **Museum der Weltkulturen** (Tues & Thurs–Sun 10am–5pm, Wed 10am–8pm; entry fee varies depending on exhibition) is the city's ethnological museum, and presents temporary exhibitions of art from the Americas, Africa, Asia and Oceania.

The focus of the **Deutsches Filmmuseum**, Schaumainkai 41 (Tues, Thurs & Fri 10am–5pm, Wed & Sun 10am–7pm, Sat 2–7pm; €2.50), is the technical development of moving pictures. The exhibits – which are labelled in German only – start with early peep-show devices such as the Mutoscope and Magic Lantern before progressing to the pioneering work of the Lumière brothers and to modern special effects. Temporary exhibitions explore the cultural side of cinema history. The **Deutsches Architekturmuseum** next door (Tues & Thurs–Sun 11am–6pm, Wed 11am–8pm; €6) features a house-within-a-house used in the staging of temporary exhibitions. The permanent exhibition traces the development of building from the paleolithic hut to the skyscraper, and there's good labelling in English.

At Schaumainkai 53, the **Museum für Kommunikation** (Tues–Fri 9am–6pm, Sat & Sun 11am–7pm; €2.50; English audio guide €1.50 or pick up a free leaflet) presents the history of post and telecommunications with real flair, from the horse-drawn mail coaches which switched from wheels to sleighs in winter to the vintage postal vans and buses, a wartime Enigma-code machine and an amusing display of brick-like, early mobile phones.

The undoubted star of the Museumsufer is the **Städel Museum** (Tues & Fri–Sun 10am–6pm, Wed & Thurs 10am–9pm; €10, English audio guide €4;

@ www.staedelmuseum.de), which has a world-class collection of fine art from seven centuries. Nineteenth- and twentieth-century art is on the first floor. The Städel lost seven hundred works as a result of the Nazi campaign against "degenerate" modern art, and one of the most interesting features of the collection is the way in which works lost during the Third Reich have subsequently been re-acquired. Thus, you can see Franz Marc's *Dog Lying in the Snow*, painted in 1910–11 and acquired in 1919, which was confiscated in 1937 and repurchased in 1961, or Max Beckmann's *Still Life with Saxophones*, repurchased in 1955. Other modernist gems include Picasso's *Portrait of Fernande Olivier*, considered a definitive work of Cubism. The upper floor of the museum is devoted to European art from the Middle Ages to the Baroque: Tischbein's *Goethe in the Roman Campagna*, painted in 1787, is the best-known likeness of the writer, while there is a heavyweight selection of early German painting, including Lucas Cranach the Elder's *Venus* and works by Stephan Lochner and Albrecht Dürer. Non-German masters include Tiepolo's *Saints of the Crotta Family* and Rembrandt's *Blinding of Samson*. There's good labelling in English.

Housed in a grandiose nineteenth-century villa at Schaumainkai 71, the sculpture collection of the **Liebieghaus** (Tues & Fri–Sun 10am–5pm, Wed & Thurs 10am–9pm; €8) encompasses the art of classical antiquity along with splendid examples of the medieval German "beautiful" style and works of the Renaissance, Mannerist and Baroque periods. Among the highlights are Hans Multscher's alabaster *Holy Trinity* of 1430 from Ulm and Matthias Steinl's gorgeously theatrical *Maria Immaculata* from Vienna, created in 1688. The museum regularly stages excellent themed exhibitions, while the villa's upper floors give an insight into the heavy historicist decor favoured by the city's nineteenth-century elite. Close by, the westernmost of the Museumsufer's museums, the **Museum Giersch** (Tues–Fri noon–7pm, Sat & Sun 11am–5pm; €4) presents exhibitions of art from the Rhine-Main region.

Eating, drinking and nightlife

What's left of Frankfurt's Altstadt – around Römerberg – doesn't really perform the culinary function that similar districts in Cologne or Düsseldorf do. You'll have more luck finding good places to **eat** and **drink** in Sachsenhausen, where you can tuck into *Handkäs mit Musik* – cheese marinated in oil and vinegar, which is absolutely delicious if done well – or *Frankfurter Grüne Sosse* – a refreshing, creamy sauce made with yoghurt or sour cream, eggs, and a bewildering variety of fresh green herbs, usually served with boiled meat; wash it all down with a sharp glass of *Ebbelwoi*, also known as *Apfelwein*, the Frankfurt version of cider. More elegant and expensive restaurants cluster around the Börse, Alte Oper and Grosse Bockenheimer Strasse, also known as *Fressgass* or "Scoff Lane". There are also some good places just beyond the city centre in Bockenheim, Bornheim and Nordend. The city's multinational population ensures there's a vast choice of ethnic cuisines. Some of Frankfurt's best **clubs** are found in the rejuvenated strip of docklands east of the Altstadt, while the **lesbian and gay scene** clusters in the streets north of Zeil – for lesbian and gay listings, pick up a free copy of *Gab* magazine from bars or cafés.

Cafés and restaurants

Abendmahl Florastr. 24 ☏ 069/70 25 55. Informal Bockenheim restaurant with excellent-value Spanish and German cooking, including the best home-made *alioli* this side of Andalucia. The name is a pun; it means "evening meal", but is also the German for Holy Communion. Closed Sun. U-Bahn Kirchplatz.

Café Karin Grosser Hirschgraben 28. Popular café just around the corner from the Goethe-Haus. It serves breakfast until 6pm, and has plenty of outside seating in fine weather.

Chalet Dix-Huit Grempstr. 18 ☏069/70 28 14. Tiny, pretty French restaurant in the old, villagey part of Bockenheim, with crêpes from €12 and more substantial dishes from €18. Closed Sun.

Chalet Multilounge Speicherstr. 49–51 ☏069/15 24 91 71. More Heidi Klum than Heidi, this chic alpine-themed café/bar on the Westhafen does great breakfasts, including delicious omelettes, plus pizzas, noodle dishes and salads.

Coa Schillerstr. 4 ☏069/92 03 99 66. Pan-Asian food including stir-fries, curries and noodle dishes in a minimalist setting close to the Börse. Main courses from €6.50, including plenty of veggie choices, and there's a second branch at Kaiserstr. in the Bahnhofsviertel.

🏃 **Harvey's** Bornheimer Landstr. 64 ☏069/48 00 48 78. Stylishly revamped, high-ceilinged neighbourhood bar-restaurant, with a versatile menu and plenty of seating outside. Between Nordend and Bornheim. Mon–Fri until 1am, Sat 2am, Sun midnight.

Holbein's Holbeinstr. 1 ☏069/66 05 66 66. The Städel's bistro is an airy modern place, great as a culinary pitstop while pounding the Museumsufer and with a sunny terrace. Tues–Sun until midnight.

🏃 **Die Kuh die Lacht** Schillerstr. 28 ☏069/27 29 01 71. The name means "the cow that laughs", and the friendly service and excellent burgers – including veggie options – are sure to induce a smile. From around €6.

La Maison du Pain Schweizer Str. 63. Sachsenhausen's best breakfast place is a classy, overtly Francophile affair, with prodigious pastries, cakes and breads, plus salads and tartines.

Die Leiter Kaiserhofstr. 11 ☏069/29 21 21. Plush Franco–Italian restaurant just off Fressgass, full of debonair financial sector types, with a pretty terrace in summer and main courses from €18. Closed Sun.

Lennox Jahnstr. 51 ☏069/90 55 03 91. Elegant little Nordend place with accomplished cooking that blends Italian and modern German influences; there's a €31 set menu, pasta and veggie mains start at €12 and meat dishes from €18.

Metropol Café am Dom Weckmarkt 13–15. This relaxed café in the shadow of the Dom is one of the best bets for a meal or snack in the Altstadt, with organic produce, good cakes and a pleasant outdoor terrace. Open from breakfast until late.

Morgan's Prime Cut Steak Grill Clemensstr. 10–12 ☏069/70 79 36 77. Upmarket steak place on the eastern fringe of Bockenheim, close to U-Bahn Bockenheimer Warte and the Palmengarten.

🏃 **Siesmayer** Siesmayerstr. 59 ☏069/90 02 92 00. Frankfurt's most alluring spot for *Kaffee und Kuchen*, on the fringe of the Palmengarten, with a sunny terrace fronting

the park. It's also a great place for an alfresco lunch. Open daily.

Silk At *Cocoon*, Carl-Benz-Str. 21 ☏069/90 02 00. Decadent gourmet restaurant at Sven Väth's *Cocoon* club, where you eat a succession of luxurious nibbles Roman-style on day-beds to the accompaniment of a DJ.

Apfelwein taverns, bars and clubs

Bar 54 Grosse Bockenheimer Str. 54 ☏069/92 88 68 48. Small but very smart Fressgass bar, close to the Alte Oper and with a bewildering variety of cocktails.

Beyond Saloon Neue Rothofstr. 13 ☏069/36 60 19 24. Huge, slick modern DJ-bar close to the Opera, attracting a lively after-work crowd of the city's young suits. Occasional live music too.

CocoonClub Carl-Benz-Str. 21 ☏069/90 02 00, ⊛www.cocoonclub.net. Techno superstar Sven Väth's home base is one of Germany's best-known superclubs, with a roster of big-name international techno, house and electro DJs and a brace of on-site restaurants. Open from 10pm.

Dachcafé Zeilgalerie, Zeil ☏069/92 02 03 40. Rooftop café and cocktail bar atop the Zeilgalerie shopping mall, offering regular salsa nights and excellent alfresco views of the city's skyline from its terrace. Open until midnight Sun–Thurs, later at weekends.

Fichtekränzi Wallstr. 5. ☏069/61 27 78. One of the nicest of Sachsenhausen's *Apfelwein* taverns, with a wood-panelled interior, a spacious garden and a menu of Frankfurt specialities. Daily from 5pm; the garden closes around 1hr before the bar.

Kanonesteppel Textorstr. 20 ☏069/61 18 91. Traditional Sachsenhausen tavern, with *Grüne Sosse* and *Handkäs mit Musik* to anchor down the 0.3 litre *Gerippte* of *Apfelwein*, a simple interior and a garden.

🏃 **Long Island Summer Lounge** Parkdeck 7, Parkhaus Börse ☏069/29 72 36 96. Very stylish summer-only bar atop a financial district car park, with two pools, four bars and children's play area. The trendy *Long Island City Lounge* on the ground floor is open all year round.

Pulse Lounge Bleichstr. 38a. Sprawling bar, restaurant and club that's among the most stylish lesbian and gay venues in Germany. The cocktails usually hit the mark, and the back garden is one of the best alfresco spots in the city.

Schwejk Schäfergasse 21. As tacky and camp as *Pulse* is slick and stylish, this small but incredibly popular gay bar is nevertheless enormous fun. Open until 2am Fri & Sat.

Sinkkasten Brönnerstr. 5–9. Live rock and jazz, karaoke, oldies nights and Latin disco nights are all on the programme at this versatile, long-established place just off Zeil.

Stattcafé Grempstr. 21. Vaguely bohemian in a city that can seem relentlessly bourgeois, this is a nice place to unwind over a glass of wine in the prettiest part of Bockenheim, with daily specials chalked on a board and seating outside. U-Bahn Kirchplatz.

Stereobar Abtsgässchen 7 ☎069/61 71 16. Groovy Sachsenhausen DJ bar with affordable prices and occasional live bands.

Entertainment and festivals

Frankfurt's **arts** scene is lively and well patronized, with the Forsythe ballet company in particular enjoying an international reputation, and with an Anglophone expatriate community helping support continental Europe's largest English-language theatre. The **cinemas** at the Filmmuseum (Schaumainkai 41; ☎069/961 22 02 20, ⓦwww.deutsches-filmmuseum.de) and the Mal Seh'n Kino (Adlerflychtstrasse 6; ☎069/597 08 45, ⓦwww.malsehnkino.de) both occasionally show English-language films with the original soundtrack and German subtitles (OmU).

Major **festivals** include the traditional **Mainfest** and the **Museumsuferfest** cultural festival, both of which take place on the banks of the River Main in August; September brings wine tasting to Fressgass in the form of the **Rheingauer Weinmarkt**. For free monthly **listings** information (in German), pick up a copy of *Frizz* – available from many cafés, bars and other venues. There's also a paid-for monthly, *Prinz* (ⓦwww.frankfurt.prinz.de; €1.50).

Alte Oper Opernplatz ☎069/130 44 00, ⓦwww.alteoper.de. Classical concerts by the HR-Sinfonieorchester, Frankfurter Museumsorchester and others – including big-name touring orchestras – are the mainstay of the programme at the magnificently restored opera house.

Bockenheimer Depot Carlo-Schmid-Platz 1 ☎069/21 23 75 55, ⓦwww.ballett-frankfurt.de. The main local venue for performances by Frankfurt's internationally renowned ballet company, under the aegis of American William Forsythe.

The English Theatre Gallusanlage 7 ☎069/24 23 1620, ⓦwww.english-theater.org. The city's English-speaking theatre, with a populist programme of musicals and established box-office favourites.

Festhalle Messe Frankfurt Ludwig-Erhart-Anlage 1 ☎069/75 75 64 04, ⓦwww.messefrankfurt.com. The graceful old main hall of the trade-fair grounds is also the venue for big-name rock concerts, ice shows and other large-scale spectacles.

Jazzkeller Kleine Bockenheimer Str. 18a ☎069/28 85 37, ⓦwww.jazzkeller. Old-established jazz club that attracts an international line-up of live acts. Regular Wednesday jam sessions from 9pm, plus Friday Latin dance nights.

Oper Frankfurt Willy-Brandt-Platz 1 ☎069/212 02, ⓦwww.oper-frankfurt.de. The classical opera repertoire, in a modern auditorium opposite the European Central Bank.

Papageno Musiktheater In the Palmengarten ☎069/134 04 00, ⓦwww.papageno-theater .com. Operetta, opera and ballet venue in the Palmengarten, with separate children's performances of classics such as *The Nutcracker*.

Schauspielfrankfurt Willy-Brandt-Platz 1 ☎069/21 23 70 00, ⓦwww.schauspielfrankfurt .de. The city's main stage for theatre, in the same complex as Oper Frankfurt.

Tigerpalast Heiligkreuzgasse 16–20 ☎069/920 02 20, ⓦwww.tigerpalast.com. Glossy, old-style variety shows, with everything from clowns and magicians to acrobats and tightrope walkers.

Listings

Boat trips Frankfurter Personenschiffahrt (☎069/133 83 70, ⓦwww.primus-linie.de) runs fifty- and hundred-minute sightseeing cruises on the Main, plus longer excursions to Rüdesheim or Aschaffenburg.

Books British Bookshop, Börsenstr. 17, and Hugendubel, Steinweg 12, have good selections of English books.

Car rental Major rental agencies are represented at the airport. There are also the following desks at

the Hauptbahnhof: Avis ☎069/27 99 70 10;
Europcar ☎069/242 98 10; Hertz ☎069/23 04 84;
SIXT ☎01805/25 25 25.

Consulates Australia, Main Tower 28th floor, Neue
Mainzer Str. 52–58 ☎069/90 55 80; Ireland
Reuterweg 49 ☎069/977 88 38 83; UK honorary
consulate: Barclays Capital, Bockenheimer Landstr.
38–40 ☎069/71 67 53 45; US, Giessener Str. 30
☎069/753 50.

Driving As in other major German cities, you'll
need a *Feinstaubplakette* displaying the particulate
pollution produced by your car if you want to drive
into the centre of Frankfurt.

Emergency Doctor or fire brigade ☎112, police
☎110, women's emergency number ☎069/70 94 94.

Internet PTT Multi Media Store, Baseler Str. 35,
opposite the Hauptbahnhof's southern exit.

Pharmacy Centrum Apotheke, Zeil 96 (☎069/29
51 29), is the most central pharmacy offering an
out-of-hours service.

Post office Zeil 90 (Mon–Wed 9.30am–8pm,
Thurs–Sat 9.30am–9pm); Hauptbahnhof (Mon–Fri
7.30am–7pm, Sat 8am–4pm).

Taxis Ranks at the Hauptbahnhof and Hauptwache,
or call: ☎069/25 00 01, 23 00 01, 23 00 33 or
73 30 30.

Darmstadt and around

Jugendstil, the German version of Art Nouveau, is the reason most people visit
DARMSTADT, thanks to Grand Duke Ernst Ludwig (1868–1937), Queen
Victoria's grandson and an inspired patron of the arts. Under his aegis the
Mathildenhöhe artistic colony flourished in the years before World War I.
Shortly after Ernst Ludwig's death, much of his family was killed in a plane crash
en route to a wedding in London, but a connection to Britain lives on, since
the Battenbergs – whose British relatives judiciously rechristened themselves
Mountbatten in 1917 – were princes of Hesse too, with a family seat at Schloss
Heiligenberg south of the city. There's also a Russian link: Ernst Ludwig's sister
married Tsar Nicholas II to become Tsarina Alexandra Fyodorovna, notorious
for her friendship with Rasputin.

Though the city lost its Altstadt to a nightmarish 1944 air raid, much of
the city is attractive still, its townscape softened by the gardens left behind by
the Hesse-Darmstadt dynasty. Central Darmstadt's bland shopping streets can
safely be skipped in favour of the cluster of monuments around the **Schloss**
and **Herrngarten**. The city's most significant attraction, **Mathildenhöhe**
is to the east, while south of the centre there are more formal gardens in
Bessungen. Away from the main sights, much of Darmstadt – particularly the districts fringing its parks – has a villagey charm. Students at the
Technische Universität ensure an easygoing nightlife, while the city is popular
with families downshifting from the hurly-burly of Frankfurt. The laid-back
ambience is catching; in summer a day or two here is liable to induce a certain
feel-good languor.

Within easy reach of the city are the UNESCO World Heritage sites at
Messel – a remarkable fossil-pit east of town – and the monastery of **Lorsch**,
which dates from Charlemagne's time.

Arrival, information and accommodation

Fast trains from Frankfurt take fifteen minutes to reach Darmstadt's Jugendstil
Hauptbahnhof, west of the centre. From the station, trams #3 and #5
(€1.45) take around seven minutes to reach Luisenplatz, where the **tourist
office** is at no. 5 (Mon–Fri 9.30am–7pm, Sat 9.30am–4pm; ☎06151/279
99 99, ⓦ www.darmstadt.de). It can help with accommodation and sell you
a **Darmstadt Card** (€9), valid for two days and entitling you to free public
transport and reduced-price entry to museums. As in Frankfurt, **hotel** prices
are generally lower at weekends.

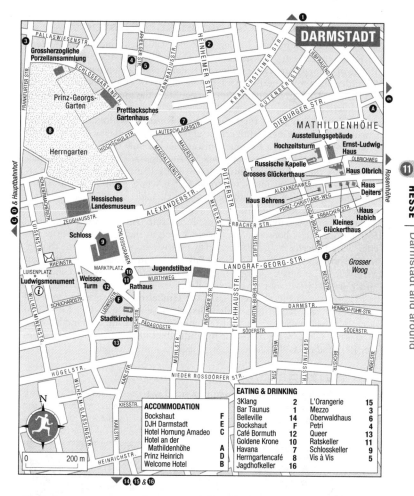

MATHILDENHÖHE
Ausstellungsgebäude
Hochzeitsturm
Ernst-Ludwig-Haus
Russische Kapelle
Grosses Glückerthaus
Haus Olbrich
Haus Behrens
Haus Deiters
Haus Habich
Kleines Glückerthaus

Grosser Woog

ACCOMMODATION

Bockshaut	F
DJH Darmstadt	E
Hotel Hornung Amadeo	C
Hotel an der Mathildenhöhe	A
Prinz Heinrich	D
Welcome Hotel	B

EATING & DRINKING

3Klang	2	L'Orangerie	15
Bar Taunus	1	Mezzo	3
Belleville	14	Oberwaldhaus	6
Bockshaut	F	Petri	4
Café Bormuth	12	Queer	13
Goldene Krone	10	Ratskeller	11
Havana	7	Schlosskeller	9
Herrngartencafé	8	Vis à Vis	5
Jagdhofkeller	16		

0   200 m

Hotels

Bockshaut Kirchstr. 7–9 ☎06151/996 70, ⊛www.bockshaut.de. Attractive, country-style rooms above a traditional inn next to the Stadtkirche. ❹

DJH Darmstadt Landgraf-Georg-Str. 119 ☎06151 /452 93, ⊛www.djh.hessen.de. Modern hostel on the fringe of the Grosser Woog, a short walk from the Mathildenhöhe. Accommodation is in two-, four- or six-bed rooms. Dorm beds from €23.90 including breakfast.

Hotel an der Mathildenhöhe Spessartring 53 ☎06151/498 40, ⊛www.hotel-mathildenhoehe.de. Comfortable three-star hotel close to Mathildenhöhe that is a lot more attractive than its rather brutalist external appearance suggests. ❺

Hotel Hornung Amadeo Mornewegstr. 43 ☎06151/92 66, ⊛www.hotel-darmstadt.com. Big, bright rooms and a peaceful, if characterless location between the Hauptbahnhof and Herrngarten. ❸

Prinz Heinrich Bleichstr. 48 ☎06151/813 70, ⊛www.hotel-prinz-heinrich.de. Traditionally furnished hotel a few minutes' walk west of the Herrngarten. ❸

Welcome Hotel Karolinenplatz 4 ☎06151/ 391 40, ⊛www.welcome-hotel-darmstadt.de. Stylish, business-oriented hotel on a very central site fringing both Karolinenplatz and the Herrngarten. A/c rooms have flat-screen TVs and wi-fi, and there are cheap weekend rates. ❸–❺

Luisenplatz, the Schloss and Altstadt

Napoleon raised Darmstadt's Landgraves to the status of Grand Dukes of Hesse and Rhine in 1806. A Neoclassical column, the **Ludwigsäule**, commemorates the first of them, Grand Duke Ludwig I. It dominates **Luisenplatz**, which with **Mathildenplatz** to the north still suggests the dignity of a capital city in miniature. The Baroque **Kollegiengebäude** on Luisenplatz is the former Hessian Ministry of the Interior.

East of Luisenplatz looms the red-sandstone **Residenzschloss**, a mishmash of ages and styles. In the eighteenth century, French architect Rémy de la Fosse was commissioned to design a Baroque replacement, but only two wings were built. One of these dominates the north side of Marktplatz. The older Renaissance wing houses the **Schlossmuseum** (Mon–Thurs 10am–1pm & 2–5pm, Sat & Sun 10am–1pm, visit by guided tour only; €2.50), whose paintings, furniture and *objets d'art* – including Jugendstil pieces from Mathildenhöhe – give an insight into life at the Darmstadt court.

Facing the Schloss across Marktplatz, the Renaissance **Altes Rathaus** dates from 1598 and nowadays houses a *Hausbrauerei*; a little to the south, the fourteenth-century **Stadtkirche** is a rather bleak affair, heavily restored after wartime damage, but it's worth a visit for the magnificent 9m alabaster memorial to Magdalena zur Lippe, wife of Landgrave Georg I. The streets hereabouts, which once constituted Darmstadt's old town, are now rather soulless. For a glimpse of what was lost cross the footbridge over Holzstrasse to reach the **Hinkelsturm**, a surviving tower of the old city walls, which houses the **Altstadtmuseum** (April–Oct Sat & Sun 2–4pm; €2), where you can see a video of the vanished Altstadt and a model of the city as it was. Close by, the handsome **Jugendstilbad** (daily 10am–10pm; €2) dates from 1909 and offers the chance to swim in grandiose surroundings.

The Herrngarten and around

Facing the Schloss across **Karolinenplatz** stand two stately nineteenth-century buildings: the Neoclassical court theatre, now the Hesse state archive, and the **Hessisches Landesmuseum Darmstadt**, which is closed for refurbishment.

▲ Friedensreich Hundertwasser's Waldspirale building

The Landesmuseum's collection embraces everything from fine art to Jugendstil and fossils from the Grube Messel; until it reopens in 2011, temporary exhibitions at various venues will display parts of the collection.

The informal, English-style **Herrngarten** north of here, features a memorial to Goethe, who was a member of the literary circle known as the **Darmstädter Kreis**. In the northeast corner of the park is the Rococo **Prinz-Georg-Garten** (daily: March–Oct 7am–7pm; Nov–Feb 8am–5pm; free), whose formal design dates from 1764 and combines ornament with practicality: courgettes and chillies grow amid sundials, flowerbeds and neatly pruned fruit trees. Two eye-catching buildings fringe the garden. On the east side, the **Prettlack'sches Gartenhaus** dates from 1710 and has a prettily painted exterior. On the north side, the Baroque **Prinz-Georg-Palais** provides a light-flooded setting for the **Grossherzoglich-Hessische Porzellansammlung** (Mon–Thurs 10am–1pm & 2–5pm, Sat & Sun 10am–1pm; €2.50). The grand ducal porcelain collection includes Ludwig I's Sèvres dinner service and some delightful Meissen, as well as items from the local Hoechst, Frankenthal and Kelsterbach works and some intriguing English pieces. The streets fringing the park have a sleepy charm, with half-timbered cottages and shuttered windows creating a village-like setting. To the north across Rhönring stands the extraordinary **Waldspirale** apartment complex, a typical work of the eccentric Austrian architect Friedensreich Hundertwasser, who died in 2000. Trees grow on roofs, onion domes and majolica catch the light and – a Hundertwasser trademark – there isn't a straight line in sight.

Mathildenhöhe, Rosenhöhe and the Grosser Woog

From Karolinenplatz, a traffic-free promenade heads east to **Mathildenhöhe**, the artists' colony founded by the Grand Duke Ernst Ludwig in 1899 (see box, p.568). A grove of neatly clipped plane trees, the **Platanenhain**, stands at the entrance and provides shade for summer *boules* players. The first building is the tiny, richly decorated **Russische Kapelle** (Tues–Sun 10am–4pm; donation requested) built for Ernst Ludwig's relatives, the Russian royal family. Behind it soars the 48.5m **Hochzeitsturm** or Wedding Tower (March–Oct Tues–Sun 10am–6pm; €1.50), designed by Joseph Maria Olbrich as the city's wedding present to the Grand Duke in 1908 and the colony's most prominent landmark. It's an impressive work of architecture, reflecting the eclectic roots of the style: daringly modern for its time yet with copper-clad gables that recall North German brick Gothic. Take the lift to the top to enjoy views which extend to Frankfurt and the Taunus on a clear day, then descend via two richly decorated rooms: the Hochzeitszimmer or Wedding Room and the opulent Fürstenzimmer. The tower still functions as Darmstadt's registry office. Alongside it, the **Austellungsgebäude** (Tues–Sun 10am–6pm, Thurs until 9pm; €8, or €11 combined ticket with Museum Künstlerkolonie; Ⓦ www.mathildenhoehe.info) was built for the 1908 exhibition and is now the venue for major touring art and design exhibitions. The much smaller but more richly decorated **Ernst-Ludwig-Haus** nearby was built for the 1901 exhibition and functioned as the artists' ateliers. It now houses the **Museum Künstlerkolonie** (Tues–Sun 10am–5pm; €3, or €5 including temporary exhibitions), a fascinating exhibition on the history and work of the colony. There's a model of the area in the foyer, while the displays document the four great exhibitions and the work of individual members of the colony. Highlights include the dining room Peter Behrens created for the Berlin department store Wertheim in 1902. Afterwards, stroll among the villas to the south of the main complex, many of which have been taken over for institutional purposes. Particularly noteworthy

The **Matildenhöhe** artists' colony in Darmstadt was founded by Grand Duke Ernst Ludwig with the aim of making the city a cultural centre unique in Germany. The artists who joined it built their own houses and lived and worked here, in a district that covered a cluster of streets. The Grand Duke was a passionate art lover, inspired by the English Arts and Crafts movement, one of whose members, Mackay Hugh Baillie Scott, refashioned two rooms of the Grand Duke's residence in 1898. Shortly afterwards, the Grand Duke's office was designed by the German Jugendstil artist Otto Eckmann, and Jugendstil – literally the "style of youth" – became the colony's trademark style. Of the seven founding members, the best known are the Austrian architect Joseph Maria Olbrich, who as leader of the colony was responsible for the concept of the first two big exhibitions, and the pioneering modernist Peter Behrens. Four major exhibitions – in 1901, 1904, 1908 and 1914 – spread the fame of the colony and its innovative work, which embraced architecture, interior design, furniture and applied arts. Olbrich left for Düsseldorf in 1907, where he designed the Tietz department store (see p.640); he died shortly afterwards. His role as leader of the colony was taken by Albin Müller, but the 1914 exhibition was cut short by the outbreak of World War I, which brought the colony's brief heyday to an end.

are the **Kleines Haus Glückert** at Alexandraweg 25, the **Haus Olbrich** at no. 28 and the **Haus Behrens** at no. 17. East of Mathildenhöhe, the Expressionist, brick-built 1924 **Löwentor** is topped by the lions from the 1914 exhibition and marks the entrance to **Rosenhöhe**, a former vineyard reworked as an English-style park in the early nineteenth century. The grounds are peppered with buildings, from the 1950s artists' ateliers to a pretty Biedermeier tea house and the Neoclassical mausoleum in which many of the Hesse-Darmstadts are buried. The highlight is the formal rose garden created for Ernst Ludwig. West of Rosenhöhe on Landgraf-Georg-Strasse, the **Freibad Grosser Woog** (Mon 9am–8pm, Tues–Fri 8am–8pm, Sat & Sun 9am–6pm; €2.50) offers open-air swimming at the lake of the same name. You can also rent boats (€2.50).

South of the Altstadt: the Orangerie and Bessungen

The southern suburb of Bessungen (tram #3 from the centre) is home to more verdant delights, where splendid formal Baroque gardens stretch in front of Rémy de la Fosse's elegant 1721 **Orangerie**, which is occasionally used for concerts. **Bessungen** itself still has the air of a village, especially along Bessunger Strasse, where there's a pretty eleventh-century church and an eighteenth-century hunting lodge, the **Bessunger Jadghof**. To the north is another park, the informal Prinz-Emils-Garten.

Eating, drinking and entertainment

A cluster of places between the Schloss and Stadtkirche aside, the most promising area for places to **eat** and **drink** in Darmstadt is north and east of the Herrngarten in the Martinsviertel, with another scattering of good options in Bessungen. The Staatstheater Darmstadt at Georg-Büchner-Platz (☎06151/335 55, ⓦwww .staatstheater-darmstadt.de) is the main venue for **drama**, **concerts** and **opera**, while in July and August the Darmstädter Residenzfestspiele brings classical music to historic venues across the city, including the Orangerie, Kollegiengebäude and Mathildenhöhe.

Cafés and restaurants

3Klang Riegerplatz 3 ☎06151/669 88 43. Stylish, very popular café/bar in the Martinsviertel, serving breakfast until 3pm, a lunch menu of salads and pasta and with outdoor seating in summer.

Belleville Forstmeisterstr. 5 ☎06151/66 40 91. Charming French restaurant next to the Jagdhof in Bessungen, with main courses from around €14. Closed Mon. Tram #3, #7 or #8 from the centre.

Bockshaut Kirchstr. 7–9 ☎06151/996 70. Reasonably priced regional cooking plus lighter choices, in an atmospheric, traditional-style *Gasthaus* close to the Stadtkirche and Rathaus. There's a shady terrace, and a simpler smokers' bar, *Datterichs Äbbelwoi Stub*.

Café Bormuth Marktplatz 5 ☎06151/170 90. Sumptuous cakes and a large selection of reasonably priced breakfasts, though it's not quite as swanky as it was in its 1950s prime.

Havana Lautenschlägerstr. 42 ☎06151/71 04 59. Labyrinthine Cuban/Hispanic restaurant close to the Technische Universität, with a long menu, classic and Latin cocktails and a very pretty garden at the back. The kitchen stays open until midnight; the bar is open until 2am Friday and Saturday.

Herrngartencafé Schleiermacherstr. 29 ☎06151/504 77 73. Classy café in the centre of the Herrngarten, with an open-air stage featuring live bands on Sunday mornings in summer.

L'Orangerie Bessungerstr. 44 ☎06151/396 64 46. Michelin- and Gault-Millau-garlanded gourmet restaurant in Bessungen, with a cool, spacious dining room and Italian-influenced cooking. Veggie menu €38, otherwise set menus from €48. Daily for lunch and dinner. Tram #3.

Mezzo Pallaswiesenstr. 19 ☎06151/29 59 38. Modern Italian restaurant with substantial salads from €10, meat main courses around €20 and a tree-shaded garden at the front.

Oberwaldhaus Dieburgerstr. 257, am Steinbrücker Teich ☎06151/71 22 66. This ivy-covered and rather splendid restaurant is a popular excursion stop, 4km by cycle or bus from the centre of Darmstadt. There's *Schnitzel*, steak and fish on the menu, and numerous paths into the woods outside along which to walk off your meal. Open daily until midnight.

Vis à Vis Fuhrmannstr. 2 ☎06151/967 08 06. Attractive Martinsviertel deli and café, serving breakfasts, soups, coffee and snacks. Mon–Sat 10am–6pm.

Bars and clubs

Bar Taunus Kranichsteinerstr. 42 ☎06151/96 75 66. Trendy, minimalist smokers' bar serving cocktails, cheap pasta dishes and with outdoor seating in the middle of Taunusplatz in summer.

Goldene Krone Schustergasse 18 ☎06151/213 52. Disco, theatre and live rock bands in the Altstadt's only surviving medieval house.

Jagdhofkeller Bessungerstr. 84 ☎06151/66 40 91, ⊛www.jagdhofkeller.com. Jazz, *chanson* and stand-up comedy in the gorgeous setting of the Jagdhof's cellar, originally used to store game.

Petri Arheilger Str. 50 ☎06151/971 04 30. Relaxed neighbourhood bar near the Herrngarten, with a beer garden, light food and *Apfelwein*. Open 6pm–midnight; *Biergarten* until 11pm.

Queer Schulstr. 15. Darmstadt's gay bar – small but lively, and open daily until 3am.

Ratskeller Marktplatz 8 ☎06151/264 44. *Hausbrauerei* in the old Rathaus, open daily until 1am and serving its own-brew *Pils*, dark *Spezial*, *Bock* and *Hefe* beers. There's traditional food – including *Schweinshaxe* and *Schnitzel* – from around €7.

Schlosskeller in the Studentinnenkeller, Residenzschloss ⊛www.schlosskeller -darmstadt.de. DJ bar and live-music venue in the cellars of the Residenzschloss; there's also a *Biergarten* in one of the Schloss's courtyards in summer.

Around Darmstadt: the Grube Messel and Kloster Lorsch

Darmstadt is a good base for forays into the unspoilt southern Hesse countryside, much of which forms part of the **Geo-Naturpark Bergstrasse-Odenwald**. To the east, the city gives way to woodland and, beyond, to a remarkable archeological site, the **Grube Messel**. To the south, the Bergstrasse passes through one of Germany's mildest climate zones on its way to Heidelberg. Protected from easterly winds by the uplands of the Odenwald, the region produces almonds, cherries, peaches and apricots, and in spring is a profusion of blossom. The major attraction, however, is Charlemagne's abbey at **Lorsch**.

The Steinbrücker Teich and Grube Messel

From *Oberwaldhaus* (see p.569) by the **Steinbrücker Teich** lake, 4km from Darmstadt and easily reached by bus, car or cycle, footpaths and cycle trails lead off into the surrounding forest; you can also rent rowing boats on the lake (☎0177/357 51 63, ⓦ www.freizeitpark-darmstadt.de). A few kilometres further east is the **GRUBE MESSEL**, a redundant oil-shale pit on the site of an ancient volcanic crater-lake which has yielded such rich fossil finds that it is now a UNESCO World Heritage Site. The fossils date from the Eocene period around 49 million years ago, when the climate in what is now Hesse was subtropical; the present-day descendants of many of the species found here – including opossum, anteaters, flightless birds and crocodiles – are now only found far from Germany. The fossils are in exceptionally good condition, often preserving food residue in their stomachs: the macrocranion – a relative of the modern hedgehog – has been found with fish bones in its stomach, while the stomachs of the world's oldest-known bats preserve the scales of moths and butterflies. One theory for the unusual richness of the finds is that poisonous gas from the crater lake – a so-called maar volcano – killed the bats. Messel is particularly famous for its fossils of ancient horses, which were tiny compared with their modern descendants.

Trains reach Messel's **Bahnhof** in around eleven minutes from Darmstadt; the Grube Messel is a short walk to the south. To visit the site **by car**, take the side turning off the road to Messel, just north of the junction with the Darmstadt–Dieburg road. From the car park, a short path leads to the **Infostation** (April–Oct daily 11am–4pm; ⓦ www.grube-messel.de); there is an **observation platform** (free access at all times) a little beyond it overlooking the pit, and a bigger visitor centre is planned. If you want to visit the pit itself you'll have to join a guided tour (April–Oct; 1hr €7, 2hr €9, €15 surcharge for English-language groups; ☎06159/71 75 35). There's a small **museum** at Langgasse 2 in the old centre of Messel north of the train station (April–Oct Tues–Sat 2–5pm, Sun 10am–noon & 2–5pm; Nov–March Sat 2–4pm, Sun 10am–noon & 2–4pm; free); it's worth visiting this and the Senckenberg Museum in Frankfurt before seeing the pit.

Kloster Lorsch

What it lacks in size, the mysterious **Torhalle** at the former Benedictine abbey of **Lorsch** – another UNESCO World Heritage Site – more than makes up in beauty and historical significance. The royal abbey was built between 767 and 880 AD, and the Torhalle dates from the latter part of this period. With its well-preserved, festive red-and-white stone facade rising above three very Roman-looking arches, it certainly looks like a gatehouse, hence its popular name, but it's actually not at all certain what the original function of the little building was, though archeological investigation suggests that it stood within the main gate of the abbey, whose precincts covered a much greater area than that which you now see. The hall upstairs is a palimpsest of wall paintings, from two layers of Carolingian origin to traces of Romanesque and more substantial later Gothic work. The tough-looking twelfth-century abbey **church** behind the Torhalle is built on what remains of a much larger and older building; the grounds also contain a herb garden and an imposing medieval tithe-barn.

There's free access to the abbey precincts; to visit the Torhalle's interior (guided tour; €2.50) enquire at the **Museumszentrum Lorsch** (Tues–Sun 10am–5pm; €3) across Nibelungenstrasse from the abbey. It has a section on the abbey's history (German only; English leaflet €0.50) plus well-curated displays on tobacco – a major crop in the area until the twentieth century – and an intriguing section on domestic life, with reconstructed period interiors including a 1920s so-called Frankfurt Kitchen, regarded as the prototype of the fitted kitchen.

To reach Lorsch by **train** from Darmstadt change at Bensheim onto the Worms line; the journey takes a little over twenty minutes. The abbey is in the centre of town opposite the half-timbered Rathaus, around which cluster a few **eating** and **drinking** options: the *Weisses Kreuz*, Marktplatz 2 (☎06251/58 66 54; closed Mon) serves hearty German food while *Café am Kloster*, Nibelungenstrasse 2, dispenses breakfasts and light meals.

Wiesbaden

With its grand hotels, opulent villas and antique shops, few places in Germany exude the confident style of *Kaisers Zeiten* – the age of the Kaisers – quite as strongly as **WIESBADEN**, about 40km west of Frankfurt. The Romans had a fort here, the hot springs have been popular for centuries and the city served as capital of an independent Duchy of Nassau from 1815 until it was subsumed into Prussia after the 1866 Austro-Prussian war. But it was in the Wilhelmine era following German unification in 1871 that Wiesbaden experienced its heyday as a fashionable spa, favoured by Kaiser Wilhelm II himself, and it's from this period that much of its grandiose architecture dates. It came through two

world wars in better shape than most large German cities, and its status grew post-1945 as capital of the newly created Land of Hesse and as the European headquarters of the US Air Force: the Berlin airlift was coordinated from here in 1948. It's also a centre for the *Sekt* – or German champagne – industry.

Idyllically situated at the foot of the rolling Taunus and with lavish parks and greenery, Wiesbaden combines the attractions of a health resort with those of a city. The traffic-free **Altstadt** is easily explored on foot and is fringed to the east by **Wilhelmstrasse** – the kilometre-long avenue known as the "Rue" – with the **Kurhaus** on its eastern side. Within easy reach to the north, the **Neroberg** is popular for fresh air and views, while south of the centre the suburb of **Biebrich** boasts a Baroque Schloss and park. Offering everything from bracing walks and spa facilities to good restaurants, luxurious shopping and high culture – all of it overlaid with an atmosphere of faded glamour and genteel convalescence – the "Nice of the North" is unique among major German cities.

Arrival, information and accommodation

S-Bahn trains from Frankfurt take about 45 minutes to reach Wiesbaden's monumental **Hauptbahnhof**, south of the centre, from where buses (#4, #14, #27, #45) head north to Dern'sches Gelände. From here it's a short walk to the **tourist office** at Marktplatz 1 (Mon–Fri 10am–6pm, Sat 10am–3pm; April–Sept also Sun 11am–3pm; ☏0611/172 97 80, ⓦwww.wiesbaden.de). It can help with **accommodation** and sell you a **Wiesbaden Tourist Card** (€11.90), valid for two days and entitling you to free travel on public transport in Wiesbaden and Mainz and cut-price entry to museums. You can **rent bicycles** from Der Radler at the Hauptbahnhof (Mon–Fri 7am–7pm; May–Sept also Sat 8am–1pm; ☏0171/222 78 88).

DJH Wiesbaden Blücherstr. 66 ☏0611/486 57, ⓦwww.djh-hessen.de. Modern hostel to the west of the city centre, with singles (€30), doubles (❷) and dorm beds from €19.50, including breakfast. Bus #14 from Hauptbahnhof.

Fürstenhof Sonnenberger Str. 30–32 ☏0611/724 20, ⓦwww.fuerstenhof-wiesbaden.de. Sprawling, rather faded but characterful hotel in a good location on the edge of the Kurpark. Cheapest rooms don't have a shower, while the more expensive ones are in Jugendstil style. ❸–❻

Hotel de France Taunusstr. 49 ☏0611/95 97 30, ⓦwww.hoteldefrance.de. Elegantly contemporary, modest-sized boutique-style hotel on one of Wiesbaden's smartest shopping streets. Rooms have flat-screen TV, free wi-fi and either bath or shower. ❻

Hotel Hansa Bahnhofstr. 23 ☏0611/90 12 40, ⓦwww.hansa.bestwestern.de. Comfortable mid-range hotel dating from 1898, part of the Best Western network and close to the Museum Wiesbaden. Rooms have bath or shower and TVs, and there are nonsmoking rooms on request. ❻

Hotel Klemm Kapellenstr. 9 ☏0611/58 20, ⓦwww.hotel-klemm.de. Comfortable, three-star hotel with nineteenth-century architecture, a peaceful garden and a quiet, central location. ❹

Nassauer Hof Kaiser-Friedrich-Platz 3–4 ☏0611/13 30, ⓦwww.nassauer-hof.de. The best hotel in town – a grand hotel of the old school with every conceivable luxury and a plum position close to the Kurhaus. A member of the Leading Hotels of the World. Doubles from €268. ❾

Town Hotel Spiegelgasse 5 ☏0611/36 01 60, ⓦwww.townhotel.de. Bright, attractive hotel with crisp, modern decor and a very central location; rooms have hardwood floors, flat-screen TV and high-speed internet. The hotel also has mountain bikes for guests' use. ❸

The Altstadt and Kaiser-Friedrich-Therme

Most of the sights of Wiesbaden's Altstadt cluster around Schlossplatz, where the modest, early seventeenth-century **Altes Rathaus** is the oldest building in the city, and its more imposing neighbours are testament to the city's rapid rise during the nineteenth century. The Neoclassical **Stadtschloss** on the north side was built in 1840 as a town residence for Duke Wilhelm of Nassau and was later a favourite residence of the Kaiser. It now houses Hesse's state parliament. On the east side, the **Neues Rathaus** is an odd-looking affair, having lost much of its neo-Renaissance facade during World War II; the facade facing Dern'sches Gelände to the south is original. Next to the Neues Rathaus rise the red brick spires of the neo-Gothic **Marktkirche**, the city's main Lutheran church and a distinctive landmark.

To the north and west of Schlossplatz, the maze of pleasant, narrow lanes is enlivened in summer by café terraces, particularly along **Goldgasse**, at the end of which at Langgasse 38–40 stands the **Kaiser-Friedrich-Therme** (daily 10am–10pm, Fri & Sat until midnight; women only on Tues; summer €3.50 per hr/winter €5), whose imposing Irish-Roman Bath – a Jugendstil pool and sauna richly ornamented with frescoes and ceramics – opened in 1913 on the site of a hot spring known to the Romans. The complex is nudist. Just south of the Kaiser-Friedrich-Therme is the **Heidenmauer**, a fragment of a fourth-century defensive wall that is the most visible remnant of Wiesbaden's Roman past. To the north, steam issues from the pavilion housing the **Kochbrunnen** or boiling fountain – aptly named, as the water bubbles up at a piping 66°C. Grand hotels and former hotels surround the Kochbrunnenplatz on which the spring emerges.

The "Rue", the Kurhaus and around

Wilhelmstrasse – the so-called "Rue" – runs north–south through the city, its western side a flaneur's paradise of upmarket boutiques, elegant cafés and hotels, many of them long established behind florid late nineteenth-century facades. On the eastern side, the gardens and the central pond **Warmer Damm** provide a verdant setting for the **Hessisches Staatstheater**, a turn-of-the-twentieth-century pile built at the behest of Kaiser Wilhelm II by the renowned Viennese theatre architects Fellner and Helmer, and a rarity in a large German city for preserving its graceful auditorium in its original neo-Baroque style. The extravagant neo-Rococo foyer, built in 1902, now functions as a breathtakingly opulent bar. Even if you don't go to a performance, it's worth asking whether any of the tourist office's themed guided tours is due to visit. The theatre's entrance is in the colonnaded group of buildings surrounding the **Bowling Green** to the north. Dominating these is the Neoclassical **Kurhaus**, built at the Kaiser's request between 1904 and 1907 and housing a splendid concert hall, the **Friedrich von Thiersch Saal**, as well as the plush **Casino Wiesbaden** (daily: slot machines noon–4am, table games 2.45pm–3/4am; €2.50; over-18s only, proper attire required including jacket and, usually, a tie for men; ⓦ www.spielbank-wiesbaden.de).

In summer, a broad café terrace sits on the edge of the English-style **Kurpark** at the back of the Kurhaus. A pleasant walk east from here through parkland brings you to the **Thermalbad Aukammtal** (Mon, Wed, Thurs & Sun 8am–10pm, Tues 6am–10pm, Fri & Sat 8am–midnight; €8.50), a modern spa with indoor and outdoor pools and extensive sauna facilities.

North from the Kurpark: Taunusstrasse and the Neroberg

Antique dealers and art galleries set the tone in discreetly luxurious **Taunusstrasse**, which begins at the Kurpark's northwestern corner and leads to another garden, the **Nerotal-Anlagen**. Fringed by villas, the little park contains a statue of **Bismarck** looking every inch the Prussian warrior-statesman, complete with spiked *Pickelhaube* helmet.

At the far end of the park, a charmingly old-fashioned funicular railway, the **Nerobergbahn** (May to mid-Sept daily 9.30am–8pm; April & mid-Sept to Oct Wed noon–7pm, Sat & Sun 10am–7pm; €2.20 single, €3 return) ascends the slopes of the 245m Neroberg; a steep, zigzag path also gives access to the hill. There are wonderful views over the city from the little **Nerobergtempel** near the top and there's a beautiful Bauhaus-style lido, the **Opelbad** (May–Sept 7am–8pm; €7), whose open-air pool overlooks vineyards and has a café. From the summit, paths wind down through the woods to the gold-domed Orthodox **Russische Kirche** (April–Oct daily 10am–5pm; Nov–March Sat noon–4pm, Sun 10am–4pm; €1), built between 1848 and 1855 in memory of Elisabeth Michailovna, the young wife of the Duke of Nassau and niece of the Tsar, who died in childbirth in 1845, less than a year after arriving in Wiesbaden; her sarcophagus is inside. Nearby a lovely, rather overgrown **Russian cemetery** contains the grave of the painter Alexej von Jawlensky and a who's who of the Baltic German aristocracy – members of the old ruling caste of Russian-dominated Estonia and Latvia who, while preserving their German identity, converted to the Orthodox faith.

The Neroberg is a part of the wooded **Taunus** range (see p.578), which sweeps along Wiesbaden's northern boundary and is crisscrossed by hiking and cycling trails, a few of which depart from the base of the Nerobergbahn.

South of Warmer Damm: villas and the Museum Wiesbaden

Grand villas fringe Warmer Damm, including the **Villa Söhnlein**, also known as the "Little White House", built in 1906 by the *Sekt* merchant Wilhelm Söhnlein for his American wife in imitation of the Washington original, and the Pompeian **Villa Clementine**, the scene of the forced repatriation in 1888 of the 12-year-old Crown Prince of Serbia, whose mother had settled in Wiesbaden after separating from the Serbian king, Milan I. From the southeast corner of Warmer Damm, a stroll uphill on **Gustav-Freytag-Strasse** underlines the opulence of nineteenth-century Wiesbaden, with villas in every conceivable style from Neoclassical to half-timbered and Jugendstil. The jumble of porticoes, shutters, castellated roofs and gables is more impressive the higher you climb: a right turn into Solmsstrasse brings you to one of the most imposing, the **Solmsschlösschen**, a neo-Gothic fantasy built in 1890 for Prince Albrecht zu Solms-Braunfels.

Turn downhill along Humboldt Strasse and Rheinstrasse to reach the **Museum Wiesbaden** (Tues 10am–8pm, Wed–Sun 10am–5pm; €5; Ⓦ www.museum -wiesbaden.de), the high point of which is the collection of paintings by the Russian-born but Wiesbaden-based Expressionist, Alexej von Jawlensky (1864–1941). Jawlensky was a key member of the Munich Blaue Reiter group before World War I and is best known for his richly coloured portraits of women, represented here by *Lady with a Fan* from 1909. His work is more varied than commonly recognized, and the collection includes vibrant landscapes and still lifes as well as later works charting his move towards abstraction. There are also some late works by Karl Schmidt-Rottluff and paintings by Ernst Ludwig Kirchner, Emil Nolde and Max Beckmann. More contemporary art – including large-scale installations – is exhibited upstairs. The museum's local history section will transfer to a new Stadtmuseum on a nearby site by 2011; it and the natural history section are being refurbished during 2009.

The southern suburbs

The best-known – if not necessarily the most prestigious – German *Sekt* producer is **Henkell**, and by booking in advance you can tour its neo-Rococo **Sektkellerei**, Biebricher Allee 142 (Mon–Thurs 10am & 2pm, Fri 10am; €7 per person; ☏ 0611/632 09, Ⓦ www.henkell.de; bus #4, stop Landesdenkmal). The tour lasts one and a half hours and includes three free tastings. The riverside suburb of **Biebrich** itself (bus #4) feels like a separate town, graced by a Baroque **Schloss** that sprawls along the banks of the Rhine and was built between 1700 and 1750 for the Dukes of Nassau. It's not generally open to the public, but the lovely park behind it is worth a stroll, and Biebrich is a stopping-off point for **boat trips** of the KD line (☎0611/60 09 95, ⓦwww.k–d.com).

Eating, drinking, nightlife and entertainment

The narrow lanes of Wiesbaden's Altstadt offer plentiful **eating** and **drinking** options. Classier establishments tend to be just outside the Altstadt, and there's a reasonable scattering of **cafés** and **bars**, both in the Altstadt and on Taunusstrasse and Wilhelmstrasse. Wiesbaden transforms one of its car parks into trendy lounge-bar *Sonnendeck* in summer (Karstadt Parkhaus, Kirchgasse 35–43; ⓦwww.sonnendeck -wiesbaden.de); you can see cabaret and comedy live at *Thalhaus*, Nerotal 18 (☎0611/185 12 67, ⓦwww.thalhaus.de) or live bands at *Schlachthof*, Gartenfeld-strasse 57 (☎0611/97 44 50, ⓦwww.schlachthof-wiesbaden.de). Classical **concerts**, including performances by the Hessisches Staatsorchester Wiesbaden, take place in the Friedrich-von-Thiersch-Saal in the Kurhaus (☎01805/74 34 64), while the Bowling Green in front of the Kurhaus is often the venue for open-air concerts in summer. The main venue for high **culture** – including opera, ballet and drama – is the Hessisches Staatstheater (☎0611/13 23 25, ⓦwww.staatstheater-wiesbaden .de). It's a good place to catch reasonably priced opera in suitably grand surroundings. Wiesbaden's big annual cultural event is the **Maifestspiele** in May, Germany's second oldest theatre festival.

Cafés and restaurants

Café Maldaner Marktstr. 34 ☎0611/30 52 14. Grand café and *Konditorei*, established in 1866 and the classic Wiesbaden *Kaffee und Kuchen* stop.
Ente Kaiser-Friedrich-Platz 3–4 ☎0611/13 30. Michelin-starred haute cuisine in the elegant surroundings of one of Germany's most long-established gourmet haunts, at the *Nassauer Hof*. Set menu from €115, or main courses à la carte from around €35. Closed Sun.
Feinkost Feickert Wilhelmstr. 14 ☎0611/990 75 13. Informal bistro attached to Wiesbaden's best delicatessen, with a short menu of light, daily specials. Mains from around €8. Closed Sun.
Frickel Marktstr. 26 ☎0611/30 20 29. No-frills fish restaurant attached to the old, established fishmongers of the same name.
Fritz Kunder Wilhelmstr. 5 ☎0611/44 13 59. Every spa town has its sweet treat to take away the taste of the waters; Wiesbaden's is the *Wiesbaden Törtchen*, a sophisticated affair of pineapple jelly and bitter dark chocolate, available from this elegant *Konditorei*.
Käfers Kurhausplatz 1 ☎0611/53 62 00. Classy without being stuffy, this elegant brasserie in the Kurhaus is open daily until 2am, and has a beer garden in the Kurpark. Main courses from €20.
Lumen Marktplatz ☎0611/30 02 00. Huge, light-flooded café/bar in the centre of Marktplatz, with a

spacious garden terrace in summer. Open from breakfast, and until 2am Fri & Sat.
Orangerie Kaiser-Friedrich-Platz 3–4 ☎0611/13 30. The *Nassauer Hof*'s German restaurant has a pretty winter garden and serves refined daily specials plus a €35 Sunday lunch buffet. Open daily.
Restaurant M *Hotel de France*, Taunusstr. 49 ☎0611/204 87 65. Creative haute cuisine in elegant modern surroundings, with set menus from €36–52, a decent selection of German and international wines and, in summer, tables on the street outside. Closed Sun.
Turm Auf dem Neroberg 1 ☎0611/959 09 87. Strategically placed café atop the Neroberg, with a sunny terrace, cocktails and full food menu including *Flammkuchen* – Alsace-style pizza.

Bars and clubs

James Joyce Sonnenberger Str. 14 ☎0611/204 89 96. Irish pub with live music, sport on TV and British and Irish beers, plus the likes of fish and chips or sausage and mash for homesick expats.
Park Café Wilhelmstr. 36 ☎0611/341 32 46. Classy DJ bar and disco, open from 7pm weekdays and 5pm Saturday and Sunday and with a music policy embracing hip-hop, r'n'b, dancehall and soul.
Ratskeller Schlossplatz 6 ☎0611/30 00 23. Hearty Bavarian cooking washed down with König

von Bayern beer in the spacious *Bierkeller* of the Neues Rathaus.

Spital Kranzplatz ☎0611/52 88 30. Trendy bar/lounge close to the Kochbrunnen, with a stylish mix of historic and modern decor, DJs, outdoor terrace and food. Open from breakfast.

Weinhaus Kögler Grabenstr. 18 ☎0611/37 67 37. Wiesbaden's oldest *Weinstube* is a charmingly traditional affair, with good dry Rieslings, inexpensive German food, plus salads.

Zócalo Taunussstr. 9 ☎0611/52 41 60. Mexican bar/restaurant and club open until 5am Friday and Saturday, with a Latin, r'n'b and hip-hop music policy and salsa lessons on Saturday nights. Popular with Americans.

The Rheingau

West of Wiesbaden, the gently sloping north bank of the Rhine between the Taunus and the river constitutes one of Germany's most prestigious wine-growing regions, the Rheingau, known for its Riesling and *Spätburgunder* or Pinot Noir. The English term *Hock* for German wines derives from Hochheim near Wiesbaden, whose wines found favour with Queen Victoria. It's a region of photogenic, vine-clad hillsides and pretty villages, and boasts one unmissable attraction, the hauntingly beautiful Gothic monastery at **Eberbach**. At the western end of the region, the day-tripper magnet of **Rüdesheim** balances brash commercialism with a range of fine- and wet-weather attractions.

The Rheingau wine routes and Kloster Eberbach

Separate but broadly parallel itineraries – the **Rheingauer-Riesling Route** for cars, the **Riesling Radwanderweg** for cyclists and the **Rieslingpfad** for hikers – meander west from Wiesbaden past vineyards, villages and historic landmarks, with plenty of opportunities to stop off along the way to sample the local wines, including seasonal *Strausswirtschaften* run by the wine-makers themselves.

The cyclists' route stays closest to the river while the hikers' route hugs the higher and more scenic ground on the fringe of the Taunus, but all three thread their way through wine-growing villages – **Eltville**, **Kiedrich**, **Oestrich-Winkel** among them – and pass **Kloster Eberbach** (daily: April–Oct 10am–6pm; Nov–March 11am–5pm; €3.50, English audio guide €3.50; ⓦwww.kloster-eberbach.de). Tucked discreetly into the narrow Kisselbach Valley above the Kiedrich–Hattenheim road, the abbey was established by the Cistercian order in 1136. The first monks brought with them from Burgundy the wine-making expertise with which the abbey is still associated – the expression *Kabinett* or cabinet, which refers to high-quality German wines, derives from the abbey's *Cabinetkeller* or cellar, and there's a wine shop (daily 10am–6pm) in the old hospital. The abbey's well-preserved medieval interior is compelling; a left turn as you reach the cloister takes you to the star-vaulted chapter house with its single central pillar and thence into the memorably austere church. Antique wine-presses fill the immense, damp, lay refectory on the west side, but it's the 72-metre-long monks' dormitory on the east side – which dates from 1250–70 and is one of the most splendid, secular, early Gothic rooms in Europe – that is the highlight. Interior scenes of the big-screen version of Umberto Eco's *The Name of the Rose* were filmed at Eberbach.

Practicalities

Cycling, walking or driving are the most enjoyable and flexible ways to **tour** the Rheingau, but there is also a **bus** (#172) linking Eltville's **Bahnhof** with Kiedrich and Kloster Eberbach. There are **tourist offices** at Rheingauer

Strasse 28 in Eltville (Mon, Tues, Thurs & Fri 10am–1pm & 2–6pm, Wed 2–6pm, Sat 10am–1pm; Nov–March closes 5pm weekdays; ☎06123/909 80, ⓦwww.eltville.de), and at the Rathaus in Kiedrich (Mon–Thurs 8am–4.30pm, Fri 8am–12.30pm; ☎06123/90 50 10, ⓦwww.kiedrich.de), who have lists of reasonably priced **accommodation** in the area. The Rheingau has a busy programme of wine-related **festivals** all year round, from a gourmet festival in early March to Kiedrich's Rieslingfest in June and the Riesling Gala at Kloster Eberbach in November. Tourist offices have details.

Rüdesheim

After the beauty of the Riesling route's landscape, first impressions of **Rüdesheim** can come as a shock, above all on noisy, crowded **Drosselgasse**, the narrow lane leading up from the river into which tour groups are funnelled for a pre-packaged, over-amplified facsimile of German joviality. Having suffered wartime bombardment, it's not even consistently pretty.

Yet there are quaint and peaceful corners, and beneath the veneer of plastic oompah there is a perfectly genuine wine-growing village worth exploring. At the western end of the village, the twelfth-century **Brömserburg** castle provides an atmospheric setting for the **Rheingauer Weinmuseum** (March–Oct daily 10am–6pm; €5, English audio guide included in price; ⓦwww.rheingauer -weinmuseum.de), whose exhibition begins with a huge collection of old wine presses before progressing through viticulture's origins in the ancient world and its arrival in the Rhineland. There are amphorae from the eastern Mediterranean, old brandy stills and antique goblets, punch bowls and Jugendstil wine coolers. The vertigo-inducing battlements offer views over vineyards towards the **Niederwald Denkmal**, a bellicose bit of Wilhelmine-era nationalistic statuary that offers wonderful views over the Rhine. You can reach it on foot along the track that begins next to the Romanesque **Boosenburg** tower close to the Weinmuseum, but many visitors opt for the cable-car ride on the **Seilbahn Rüdesheim** (March–Nov daily 9.30am to between 5pm and 7pm; also during Christmas market; €4.50 single, €6.50 return or €10 for "Ringtrip" including boat trip back from Assmannshausen; ⓦwww.seilbahn-ruedesheim.de). Down on the river between Rüdesheim proper and its sister settlement of Assmannshausen are the picturesque ruins of the medieval **Burg Ehrenfels**, which faces the equally romantic **Mäuseturm** on an islet in the river and was used to collect river tolls before being wrecked by the French in 1688 during the War of the Palatine Succession.

Back in the village itself along Oberstrasse, the half-timbered **Brömserhof** dates from 1542 and now houses a quirky collection of musical automata, **Siegfried's Mechanisches Musikkabinett** (March–Dec daily 10am–6pm; €5.50); there's another saggy half-timbered beauty, the early sixteenth-century **Klunkhardshof**, in a narrow lane off Markt. At the eastern end of the village at Ingelheimer Strasse 4, you can see a short multi-vision show and buy a wide variety of brandies produced locally by the Asbach distillery at the **Asbach Besucher Center** (March–Dec Tues–Sat 9am–5pm; free; ⓦwww.asbach.de).

Practicalities

Rüdesheim's **Bahnhof** is at the western extremity of the village, from where a walk along the riverfront Rheinstrasse leads to the **tourist office** at Geisenheimer Strasse (April–Oct Mon–Fri 8.30am–6.30pm, Sat & Sun 10am–4pm; Nov–March Mon–Fri 11am–3pm; during Christmas market daily 11am–3pm; ☎06722/90 61 50, ⓦwww.ruedesheim.de). Rüdesheim is a stop for the KD line's **boat trips** (☎06722 /38 08, ⓦwww.k-d.com), or you can take castle- or

Loreley-themed trips with the Bingen-Rüdesheimer fleet (℡06722/29 72, Ⓦwww.bingen-ruedesheimer.com); for more on boat trips along the Rhine see box on p.525.

Accommodation is fairly plentiful, but Rüdesheim gets busy in summer. Try the cyclist-friendly *Burg Hotel*, Oberstrasse 7 (℡06722/23 94, Ⓦwww .rheinromantikhotel.de; ❷–❸), in a quiet and pretty location close to the Boosenburg, or in town *Zum Grünen Kranz*, Oberstrasse 42–44 (℡06722/483 36, Ⓦwww .gruenerkranz.com; ❸), with modern, renovated rooms above a historic restaurant, or the attractive, low-key *Gasthaus Zur Lindenau*, Löhrstrasse 9 (℡06722/33 27, Ⓦwww.zur-lindenau.de; ❸). Rüdesheim's **youth hostel** (℡06722/ 27 11, Ⓦwww.djh-hessen.de; €17.90 with breakfast) is in a scenic setting above the town with excellent views and walks through the vineyards. *Zum Grünen Kranz* and *Zur Lindenau* both have typical *Weinstuben* where you can **eat** and **drink** local food and wines; for a special meal, head out of town to the Michelin-starred *Gourmet Restaurant Burg Schwarzenstein*, Rosengasse 32, in Johannisberg (℡06722/995 00; closed Mon & Tues), where the views of the Rhine Valley are as memorable as the French-influenced cuisine, with menus from €48.

The Taunus

North of Frankfurt, skyscrapers and Autobahns swiftly give way to the unspoilt, wooded hills of the **Taunus**. Tantalizingly close to the city, the Taunus range is never very high, but it offers a refreshing foretaste of what much of rural Hesse away from the Rhine-Main conurbation is actually like. The affluent spa-town of **Bad Homburg** – at the foot of the Taunus yet still within sight of the Frankfurt skyline – is the region's obvious gateway, with easy access to the heights of the **Hochtaunus range** and to the reconstructed Roman fort at **Saalburg**.

Bad Homburg

BAD HOMBURG disputes with Wiesbaden the dubious distinction of being the spa where Russian novelist Fyodor Dostoyevsky frittered away his fortune at the roulette wheel and thus found inspiration for *The Gambler*. Literary associations aside, the town shares with its larger sister a certain genteel quality and a rather longer history than its Wilhelmine airs and graces would suggest: from 1622 to 1806 it was the seat of the Lilliputian landgraviate of Hesse-Homburg, and it has the Schloss to prove it. In the nineteenth century Kaiser Wilhelm II was a regular visitor and the Prince of Wales – the future British king Edward VII – popularized the Homburg hat.

Arrival, information and accommodation

S-Bahn trains take 21 minutes to link Frankfurt to Bad Homburg's **Bahnhof**, south of the Kurpark and shopping zone. From the station, head up Bahnhofstrasse to Louisenstrasse and turn left; from here it's a gentle stroll uphill to the **tourist office** in the Kurhausgalerie (Mon–Fri 8.30am–6.30pm, Sat 10am–2pm; ℡06172/17 81 10, Ⓦwww.bad-homburg.de). You can rent **bikes** at Snow + Bike Action, Ober-Eschenbacher Strasse 22 (℡06172/94 20 94). Bad Homburg is an easy day-trip from Frankfurt; if you **stay**, you'll pay a small *Kurtaxe* as part of your room bill. Hotel rates dip at weekends and rise if there's a trade fair in Frankfurt.

DJH Bad Homburg Mühlweg 17 ℡06172/239 50, Ⓦwww.djh-hessen.de. The town's youth hostel is next to the Schlosspark. Dorms €24 with breakfast.

Landksrone Audenstr. 4 ℡06172/215 00, Ⓦwww.hotel-landskrone.de. Cheap and central place with rooms above a restaurant. ❸

Steigenberger Kaiser-Friedrich-Promenade 69–75 ☎06172/18 10, ⍟www.bad-homburg.steigenberger .de. If money's no object head for this luxurious choice. Weekdays ❽, weekends ❻.

Villa am Kurpark Kaiser-Friedrich-Promenade 57 ☎06172/180 00, ⍟www.villa-am-kurpark.de. An attractive Jugendstil villa opposite the Kurpark. Weekdays ❼, weekends ❺.

The Schloss and around

Long, straight Louisenstrasse links the historic quarter at the top of the hill with the spa quarter lower down. The former centres on the **Landgrafenschloss** (guided tours hourly Tues–Sun: March–Oct 10am–4pm; Nov–Feb 10am–3pm; €4 or €6.50 with English wing), a largely Baroque affair created in 1678 for the one-legged Landgrave Friedrich II, known as "Silver Leg" and the inspiration for Kleist's drama *The Prince of Homburg*. The Schloss apartments reflect not just the taste of the Landgraves but also those of the Hohenzollerns, for Bad Homburg was the imperial family's preferred summer residence before 1918. The **Englischer Flügel**, or English wing (separate tour), contains the collections of Elizabeth, daughter of the British king George III, who married Landgrave Friedrich VI in 1818. The slender, 48m **Weisser Turm** is the sole surviving part of the original medieval castle; you can climb it (March–Oct Mon 9am–3pm, Tues–Sun 9am–4pm; Nov–Feb daily 9am–3pm; €1) for views of the surrounding countryside. The attractive **Schlosspark** (daily until dusk; free) mixes formal beds with informal, English-style landscaping. To the north of the Schloss, Bad Homburg's diminutive **Altstadt** is little more than a huddle of red roofs clustering around the surviving vestiges of the medieval defences; rather more impressive is the elegant quarter along Dorotheenstrasse east of the Schloss, where the Baroque **Sinclair Haus** (Tues 2–8pm, Wed–Fri 2–7pm, Sat & Sun 10am–6pm; price varies depending on exhibition) is the venue for temporary art exhibitions.

The Kurpark

Bad Homburg's **spa quarter** centres on the verdant **Kurpark** one block north of Louisenstrasse; it was the creation of the nineteenth-century garden designer Peter Joseph Lenné and is one of Germany's largest town parks. At the entrance on Kaiser-Friedrich-Promenade a bust of Friedrich III – Emperor of Germany for just 99 days in 1888 – faces his English consort Victoria, eldest daughter of Queen Victoria, across formal flowerbeds. The focal point of the park is the imposing copper-domed **Kaiser-Wilhelms-Bad**, built in 1887–90 and now home to the **Kur-Royal Day Spa** (daily 10am–1pm; ⍟www.kur-royal.de), which offers a variety of steam treatments, beauty therapies and massage. The **Casino Bad Homburg** alongside it (Mon–Wed & Sun 2.30pm–3am, Thurs–Sat until 4am; admission €2.50, minimum stake €2; ☎06172/170 10, ⍟www .casino-bad-homburg.de) is modest-looking from the outside but smart within; jeans and sports shoes aren't allowed and men are required to wear a jacket and tie. It was established by the French Blanc brothers in 1841, one of whom went on to establish the casino at Monte Carlo, and the casino consequently styles itself "Mother of Monte Carlo". The Kurpark repays gentle exploration; among its attractions are the **Siamesischer Tempel**, donated in 1907 by King Chulalongkorn, and the **Russische Kirche**, whose opening was attended by the last Tsar of Russia and his Hesse-born wife. There are more **spa facilities** on the eastern side of the park including the **Seedammbad** (Mon 1–9pm, Tues–Fri 7am–9pm, Sat & Sun 8am–8pm; €6) with in- and outdoor pools, sunbeds and a whirlpool bath, and the similar but more gimmicky **Taunus Therme** (daily 9am–11pm/midnight; 2hr €12.50) with extensive, themed outside areas.

Eating and drinking

Schreinerei Pfeiffer, next to the *Landskrone* hotel on Audenstrasse (☎06172/201 68; eves only), is an atmospheric place to **eat** and **drink**, with reasonably priced *Schnitzels*, salads and light meals served in a former carpenter's workshop; a more elegant menu is served at *Casa Rosa*, Kaiser-Friedrich-Promenade 45 (☎06172/91 73 99; daily lunch & dinner), a gourmet Italian with an elegant garden, pasta dishes from €7.50 and main courses from around €16. For a drink in lively surroundings, head for *Prinz von Homburg*, Audenstrasse 7, which is open until 2am and has DJs and live music. The town's deconsecrated Anglican church on Ferdinandsplatz is the venue for **live jazz** and **cabaret**; enquire at the tourist office to find out what's on.

Naturpark Hochtaunus and Saalburg Roman Fort

If you head north out of Bad Homburg along the B456 you're immediately into the **Naturpark Hochtaunus** (ⓦwww.naturpark-hochtaunus.de), the second-largest protected nature reserve in Hesse. The highest, conifer-clad peaks are along a ridge – the **Hochtaunusklamm** – which runs northeast to southwest for 40km; highest of all is the 879m **Grosser Feldberg**, which is climbed by a minor road that twists its way up from Oberursel, west of Bad Homburg. It's crowned by an observation tower and is busy with skiers on winter weekends when the somewhat unreliable snow allows. In summer the entire Hochtaunus-klamm is popular with hikers; the 591m **Herzberg** close to Bad Homburg has a number of trails.

For more than a hundred and fifty years from the first century AD, the Hochtaunusklamm formed part of the **Limes**, the military frontier separating the Roman Empire from the Germanic tribes to the north and east. There's a reconstructed fort just off the B456 at **Saalburg** (March–Oct daily 9am–6pm; Nov–Feb Tues–Sun 9am–4pm; €3; ⓦwww.saalburgmuseum.de; bus #5 from Bad Homburg Bahnhof), where in addition to the usual archeological displays you'll get a vivid impression of what a lonely military outpost of the empire might have actually looked like to the five to six thousand troops stationed there. Saalburg is a stop on the **Deutsche Limes–Strasse**, which links up sites along the old frontier from Bad Hönningen near Koblenz to Regensburg.

Along the River Lahn

North of the Taunus and on Hesse's western border, the River Lahn – a tributary of the Rhine – meanders its way through a placid landscape of gentle upland beauty, threaded with historic and interesting small towns. The **Lahntalradweg** cycle route ensures the valley is deservedly popular with cyclists, and many hotels proclaim their cycle-friendliness, and the Lahn's waters are popular with canoeists. But the valley can be explored just as easily by car or train. Highlights along the way include the delightful small cathedral cities of **Limburg an der Lahn** and **Wetzlar**, and the diminutive but pristine Residenzstadt of **Weilburg**.

Limburg an der Lahn

Perched on a crag overlooking the River Lahn in full view of traffic speeding along the Frankfurt–Cologne Autobahn, **LIMBURG**'s impeccably picturesque Dom acts as a sort of billboard in stone for the charms of this beguiling little city, for though the attention-grabbing cathedral is undeniably Limburg's major draw, tucked behind it is a half-timbered Altstadt of modest size but considerable age and beauty.

Count Konrad Kurzbold founded a collegiate chapter of eighteen canons in 910 AD on a superb defensive site high above the river, but the present **Dom** (daily 8am–7pm; free) dates from the thirteenth century, its construction financed by the wealth accumulated by local merchants during the Crusades. Its seven spire-topped towers aside, what makes the Dom's appearance so singular is the fusion of late Rhenish Romanesque and early French Gothic details and its brick red-and-white colour scheme, the result of a 1960s project that restored the exterior to its original medieval colour scheme. Colour is a feature of the interior too, subtly enlivened by original frescoes that are among the best preserved from the time in Germany. The depiction of Samson uprooting a tree is particularly prized. The baptismal font in the south aisle is a mass of Romanesque sculptural detail, while the figurative supports of Konrad Kurzbold's tomb in the north transept predate the Dom.

Tucked almost unnoticed behind it is Limburg's **Schloss** (no public access to the inside), a jumble of half-timbered and stone buildings whose overall effect is more picturesque than martial; the oldest part dates from the early thirteenth century. A short walk downhill on Domstrasse brings you to the **Diözesanmuseum** (mid-March to mid-Nov Tues–Sat 10am–1pm & 2–5pm, Sun 11am–5pm; €2), whose treasures include the *Staurothek*, a tenth-century Byzantine cross reliquary, and a reliquary of similar age from Trier said to contain a portion of St Peter's staff.

Occupying the long slope down from the Dom to the fourteenth-century **Alte Lahnbrücke**, Limburg's **Altstadt** is a coherent mass of tall, gabled medieval houses, many of them half-timbered and sagging in an appealing fashion. There are splendid examples dating back to the thirteenth century, including the **Werner Senger Haus** at Rütsche 5, which dates from around 1250, and where you can stay (see below). Not everything is wood – the impressive, Gothic step-gabled **Steinernes Haus** at Fischmarkt 1 dates from 1350 and is a notable exception; the former **Rathaus** opposite has a Gothic vaulted cellar and a grand hall on the ground floor, nowadays home to the town's art collection (Mon 8.30am–noon, Tues 7am–noon, Wed 8.30am–2pm, Thurs 8.30am–noon & 2–6pm, Fri 8.30am–noon & 2–4pm, Sat & Sun 11am–5pm; €2). To enjoy the classic **view** of the Dom looming high above the river, stroll across the Alte Lahnbrücke.

Practicalities

Limburg's **Bahnhof** is in the modern part of the town centre, a couple of minutes' stroll from the **tourist office** at 2 Hospitalstrasse (April–Oct Mon–Fri 9am–5pm, Sat 10am–noon; Nov–March Mon–Thurs 9am–5pm, Fri 9am–1pm; ☏06431/20 32 22, ⓦwww.limburg.de). There's currently nowhere to rent **bikes** in Limburg, but Lahn Tours (Lahntalstrasse 45, Roth/Lahn; ☏06426/92 80, ⓦwww.lahntours .de) organizes cycle tours in the Lahn Valley. From April to October, the *Wappen von Limburg* **cruises** down river to Balduinstein in Rheinland Pfalz, passing through four locks along the way (Tues, Wed, Sat & Sun; 4hr; €13; ☏06431/263 23, ⓦwww.lahnschiffahrt.de).

Accommodation options include the comfortable but characterless *Hotel Huss*, Bahnhofsplatz 3 (☏06431/933 50, ⓦwww.hotel-huss.de; ❹), in an ugly modern building close to the Bahnhof; the upmarket *Dom Hotel* on the fringe of the Altstadt at Grabenstrasse 57 (☏06431/90 10, ⓦwww.domhotel.net; ❺); or the simpler accommodation at the beautiful ⚐ *Werner Senger Haus*, Rütsche 5 (☏06431/69 42, ⓦwww.werner-senger-haus.de; ❸). Limburg's **youth hostel**

is some distance from the centre at Auf dem Guckucksberg (℡06431/414 93, ⓦwww.djh-hessen.de; €18.80 with breakfast), and there's a **campsite** on the riverside at Schleusenweg 16 (℡06431/226 10, ⓦwww.lahncamping.de; April–Oct). Both the *Dom Hotel* and *Werner Senger Haus* have excellent **restaurants**, as does the *Nassauer Hof* by the Alte Lahnbrücke (℡06431/99 60; eve only except Sun, closed Mon; menu €25). Limburg's status as a day-tripper favourite ensures plenty of *Kaffee und Kuchen* places in the Altstadt.

Weilburg

Even the landscape genuflects to the feudal authority of **WEILBURG**'s Schloss, for the River Lahn loops so tightly around the immaculate little town that its Altstadt is almost an island and the **Schloss** (guided tours on the hour: March–Oct Tues–Sun 10am–5pm; Nov–Feb Tues–Sun 10am–4pm; €4; last tour 1hr before closing) presents very different faces according to your vantage point: stern and overbearing from the river, it appears gracious from its sunny terraced Baroque **Schlosspark** (daily until dusk; free) and prettily Renaissance once in the *Hof* or central courtyard. A castle has existed here since the tenth century, but the present Schloss was built between 1535 and 1575 for the counts of Nassau-Weilburg, with a further phase of construction in the eighteenth century creating the massive Marstall or stable block to the north along with the formal layout of the **Marktplatz**, dominated by the **Stadtkirche**, designed by Julius Ludwig Rothweil, which has the town's Rathaus built on to it. It's regarded as the most important Baroque Protestant church in Hesse.

Facing the main entrance to the Schloss on Schlossplatz is the **Bergbau- und Stadtmuseum Weilburg** (April–Oct Tues–Sun 10am–noon & 2–5pm; Nov–March Mon–Fri 10am–noon & 2–5pm; €3), which in addition to the more predictable local museum exhibits has a reconstruction of an iron ore mine – an important industry in the area until the 1950s. Weilburg's other great curiosity is the **Schiffstunnel**, a short cut through the neck of Weilburg's meander that was cut for river traffic between 1844 and 1847 and is unique in Germany. You can take a boat trip through the tunnel in summer months – the tourist office has details. On the eastern side of town in a commercial zone at Viehweg 6 you can see an exhibition of the Chinese **Terracotta Army** (Tues–Sun 10am–5pm; €9.50), but though the sheer scale is impressive – there are more than 350 soldiers alone – the figures are only copies.

Practicalities

Weilburg is on the Koblenz–Giessen line with direct trains from Limburg. The **Bahnhof** is on the north side of the river to the east of the Altstadt: cross either of the two main bridges to reach the Altstadt. The **tourist office** is at Mauerstrasse 6–8 (April–Oct Mon–Fri 9am–6pm, Sat 10am–noon; Nov–March Mon–Fri 10am–5pm, Sat 10am–noon; ℡06471/314 67, ⓦwww.weilburg .de). Places to **stay** include the *Schlosshotel Weilburg*, occupying the Marstall at Langgasse 25 (℡06471/509 00, ⓦwww.schlosshotel-weilburg.de; ④), which has a **restaurant**, *Alte Reitschule*; or the simpler but comfortable *Hotel Weilburg*, east of the Altstadt at Frankfurter Strasse 27 (℡06471/912 90, ⓦwww.hotel -weilburg.de; ③). Weilburg's **youth hostel** is west of the Altstadt in the suburb of Odersbach, Am Steinbühl 1 (℡06471/71 16, ⓦwww.djh-hessen.de; €20.50 with breakfast). The best place for a light **meal** or *Kaffee und Kuchen* is the lovely terrace of the *Schlosscafé* in the Schlosspark; there's also an ice-cream café, *Bella Italia*, on Vorstadt in the Altstadt, with a terrace overlooking the river. In June and July, the courtyard of the Schloss is the venue for classical **concerts** (ⓦwww.weilburger-schlosskonzerte.de).

Wetzlar

WETZLAR was once a place of some importance. In the mid-fourteenth century it rivalled Frankfurt in size, while from 1693 until its dissolution in 1806 it was the seat of the Reichskammergericht, the highest court of the Holy Roman Empire. This drew Goethe, who came here in 1772 as a legal trainee and it was here he developed an attachment to Lotte Buff, who was to inspire the character of Lotte in *The Sorrows of Young Werther*.

The hilly, half-timbered **Altstadt** stands aloof from the rather tacky modern commercial quarter on the other side of the river. It's dominated by the eccentric **Dom**, which is, in effect, two churches in one, for not only is it shared by separate Protestant and Catholic congregations, but it combines two quite separate designs. As Wetzlar grew in size and prosperity during the thirteenth century, envious looks were cast at the splendid new churches in Limburg and Marburg, and plans were hatched for a new, more imposing building to replace the Romanesque Stiftskirche, barely forty years old at the time. But the project ground to a halt, and what should have been a soaring, twin-spired Gothic hall church was stopped in its tracks halfway, with one tower complete but the other barely begun. What makes the half-Romanesque, half-Gothic result odder still is that the older half is cold and grey, while the Gothic church is constructed in cheerful red standstone.

Downhill from the Dom at Fischmarkt 13 is the much-rebuilt fourteenth-century **Rathaus** which served as the Reichskammergericht; a stroll south along Krämerstrasse and across Eisenmarkt brings you to Hofstatt and the **Reichskammergerichtmuseum** (Tues–Sun 10am–1pm & 2–5pm; €2.50, or €5 ticket for all Wetzlar museums), in the mid-eighteenth-century Avemannsche Haus, which chronicles Wetzlar's associations with the court in a house that was let to court officials and their families. Opposite at Kornblumengasse 1, another fine eighteenth-century house is occupied by the **Sammlung Lemmers-Danforth** (same hours & price), a collection of European furniture from the fifteenth to the eighteenth centuries, with paintings, clocks and ceramics.

Though not without modern intrusions Wetzlar has, like Limburg, many impressive groups of half-timbered houses. One such is uphill from Hofstatt on **Kornmarkt**, where Goethe lived at no. 7 in the summer of 1772. A short stroll from here, at Lottestrasse 8–10 in a complex which once belonged to the Teutonic Knights, the **Stadt- und Industriemuseum** (same hours & price as above) charts Wetzlar's history as a free imperial city and, later, an industrial centre: the area's ironworking industry is represented by a collection of ovens. The same complex contains **Viseum** (same hours & price), a slick modern exhibition on optics – an important industry in Wetzlar, whose most famous brand name is the camera company Leica. The half-timbered building next door is now the **Lottehaus** (same hours & price), furnished in period style and with a number of exhibits relating to *The Sorrows of Young Werther*, including a first edition, translations and parodies.

Practicalities

Wetzlar is on the Koblenz–Giessen line with frequent trains from Limburg and Weilburg. The **Bahnhof** is north of town by the Forum Wetzlar shopping mall on the far side of the B49 highway: cross under the highway and head down the traffic-free shopping precinct to reach the river. The Altstadt is on the opposite bank, with the **tourist office** at Domplatz 8 (May–Oct Mon–Fri 9am–5pm, Sat 10am–2pm; Nov–April Mon–Fri 9am–5pm, Sat 10am–noon; ⊕06441/99 77 50, ⊛www.wetzlar.de). Places to **stay** include the cyclist-friendly *Domblick* on the west side of the Lahn at Langgasse 64 (⊕06441/ 901 60, ⊛www.domblick .de; ❹); the smart and central *Wetzlarer Hof*, Obertorstrasse 3 (⊕06441/90 80,

@www.wetzlarerhof.de; ➍); and the pleasant, traditional *Bürgerhof* on the edge of the Altstadt at Konrad-Adenauer-Promenade 20 (☎06441/90 30, @www .buergerhof-wetzlar.com; ➍). Wetzlar's **youth hostel** is on the south side of town at Richard-Schirmann-Strasse 3 (☎06441/710 68, @www.djh-hessen.de; €21 with breakfast). The *Wetzlarer Hof* and *Bürgerhof* both have **restaurants**; other places to eat and drink in the Altstadt include the inexpensive *Ristorante Wirt am Dom* at Domplatz 9 (☎06441/425 22), with lunchtime pasta specials from €6, and the classy *Werther's Freuden* on Kornmarkt (☎06441/569 39 90), with a huge antipasti selection, French, German and Italian wine, salads and *Flammkuchen*.

Marburg

"Other towns have a university; **MARBURG** is a university" – so runs the saying, and there's a grain of truth to it, for the prestigious Philipps University utterly dominates the life of the town. It's the oldest Protestant university in the world, founded in 1527 by Landgrave Philipp the Magnanimous without imperial or papal recognition because of the Landgrave's Protestant faith. Notable figures associated with it include Nobel Prize-winning physiologist Emil von Behring, the philosopher Martin Heidegger and the political theorist Hannah Arendt.

Physically, the town is dominated by the splendid hilltop **Landgrafenschloss**, a reminder of Marburg's former status as the seat of the Hessian Landgraves, visible from all over town and a handy navigation aid. Below, the perfectly preserved medieval **Oberstadt** (upper town), which centres on the steeply sloping Markt, tumbles downhill towards the River Lahn. The lower town, the **Unterstadt**, curves around Oberstadt following the course of the Lahn, its chief glory being the Gothic hall church dedicated to St Elisabeth of Hungary.

Arrival, information and accommodation

The **Hauptbahnhof** is north of the centre on the opposite side of the Lahn; from here it's a good ten-minute stroll to the **tourist office** at Pilgrimstein 26 (Mon–Fri 9am–6pm, Sat 10am–2pm; ☎06421/991 20, @www.marburg.de). Places to **stay** are mainly in Unterstadt with a more limited supply in Oberstadt.

DJH Marburg Jahnstr. 1 ☎06421/234 61, @www.djh-hessen.de. The town's youth hostel in a pretty and peaceful setting south of the centre on the riverside. Dorms from €19.50 with breakfast.

Hostaria del Castello Markt 19 ☎06421/243 02, @www.del-castello.de. Pretty rooms above a restaurant in an impressive half-timbered building in the heart of the Oberstadt. ➌

Marburger Hof Elisabethstr. 12 ☎06421/59 07 50, @www.marburgerhof.de. Good-value, sprawling hotel between the Hauptbahnhof and town centre, with everything from snugly comfortable singles to fancy suites. ➋–➏

Waldecker Hof Bahnhofstr. 23 ☎06421/600 90, @www.waldecker-hof-marburg.de. Cyclist-friendly hotel right by the Hauptbahnhof, with gym and leisure facilities, wi-fi and comfortable, if scarcely trendy, rooms. ➍

The Oberstadt and Landgrafenschloss

Characterized by meandering lanes, elaborate roofscapes and plenty of steps, Oberstadt – the hilly "upper town" – focuses on elongated, lively **Markt**. Fringed by multistorey half-timbered houses that sag at giddy angles and with a step-gabled, early sixteenth-century stone **Rathaus** on the southern, downhill side, it's as lovely a town square as any in Germany, its café terraces buzzing contentedly in fine weather. At Markt 16, the **Haus der Romantik** (Tues–Sun 11am–1pm

& 2–5pm; admission varies, but usually €2) commemorates the *Marburger Romantikkreis* group, whose members included the Brothers Grimm and which met from 1800 to 1806 to discuss the political and philosophical trends of the day. The museum also presents changing exhibitions on the Romantics. Just off the northeast corner of Markt on Schlosssteig – which was called Judengasse or Jew Lane until 1933 – are the glassed-in remains of the town's **medieval synagogue**, demolished in 1452 and excavated between 1993 and 1998. To the west of Markt along Nikolaistrasse, the terrace in front of the Gothic Lutheran **Pfarrkirche** offers superb views over the huddled rooftops. The oldest parts of the church date from the thirteenth century, and it has a distinctive, twisted spire. To the south of Markt, the overbearing neo-Gothic mass of the **Alte Universität** dominates the lower approaches to Oberstadt. It was built in the late nineteenth century on the foundations of a thirteenth-century former Dominican monastery which the university had long since outgrown.

From almost any vantage point, however, the Oberstadt is dominated by the mighty **Landgrafenschloss** (April–Oct Tues–Sun 10am–6pm; Nov–March Tues–Sun 10am–4pm; €4), which is reached up the Schlosstreppe off the north end of Markt and then up steep, cobbled Landgraf-Philipp-Strasse. Pause for breath on the way to admire the impressive gable of the **Landgräfliche Kanzlei**, built in 1573. There has been a fortress atop the Gisonenfelsen crags since 900 AD, though most of what you see today – the slate-hung Renaissance **Rentkammer** on the south front as you climb the hillside – is essentially Gothic, and the splendour of its proportions reflects its status as the residence from 1292 onwards of the first Landgraves of an independent Hesse. Nineteenth-century "restoration" robbed it of some of its original fabric – including its medieval roof timbers – but what survives is impressive enough. You enter via the **Saalbau** on the north side of the Hof; upstairs is the **Fürstensaal**, one of the largest secular Gothic rooms in Germany, with an elaborately beautiful wooden Renaissance doorway by Nikolaus Hagenmüller dating from 1573. Equally impressive is the thirteenth-century **Schlosskapelle** (court chapel) on the south side, reached across an upstairs landing from the Saalbau and preserving a refined full-length fresco of St Christopher and the original (and beautiful) coloured floor tiles. The east wing or **Wilhelmsbau** contains the **Museum für Kulturgeschichte** (same ticket) whose extensive collections of folk and religious art include Catholic and Protestant folk costumes or *Tracht*, still a common sight in Marburg as recently as the 1950s, though nowadays they're seen only on special occasions. To the west of the Schloss, the small but pretty **Schlosspark** is the venue for concerts and open-air film shows in summer.

The Unterstadt

From Markt, one of Oberstadt's gentler inclines leads north down Wettergasse, Neustadt and Steinweg to the medieval core of **Unterstadt**. The houses here are no less beautiful than in the upper town, but they're more modest in scale. However, there's nothing modest about the **Elisabethkirche** (daily: April–Sept 9am–6pm; Oct 10am–5pm; Nov–March 10am–4pm; €2.50 to visit choir and transepts; no admittance during services), the oldest pure Gothic hall church in Germany. It was built in less than fifty years between 1235 and 1283, which explains the unusual purity and coherence of its twin-towered design. The church was built by the Teutonic Knights on the site of the grave of St Elisabeth of Hungary, the young widow of Landgrave Ludwig IV of Thuringia, who died in Italy on his way to the Crusades. After his death Elisabeth eschewed courtly life, founding a hospital and devoting herself single-mindedly to the care of the sick.

Elisabeth also died young, and was rapidly canonized, and the church built over her tomb became one of the most important places of pilgrimage in medieval Europe. The rich furnishings include the brightly coloured **Französische Elisabeth** on the left side of the nave, which dates from 1470 and depicts a regal-looking Elisabeth holding a model of the church. A relief at the base of her **tomb** in the north transept depicts the grief-stricken sick and poor mourning her corpse. Somewhat incongruous among the gorgeously coloured monuments to medieval virtue is the austere tomb of **Paul von Hindenburg**, the last president of the Weimar Republic and the man who appointed Hitler – the man he had belittled as a "Bohemian corporal" – chancellor in 1933.

The severe-looking buildings that cluster around the Elisabethkirche include the **Kornspeicher**, a grain store built by the Teutonic Knights in 1515. It now houses the **Mineralogisches Museum** (Wed 10am–1pm & 3–6pm, Thurs & Fri 10am–1pm, Sat & Sun 11am–3pm; €1), with a glittering array of crystals in glass cases. Altogether more engrossing is the **Universitätsmuseum für Bildende Kunst** at Biegenstrasse 11 (Tues–Sun 11am–1pm & 2–5pm; €2 or €4 combined ticket with Schloss), where in addition to paintings by Tischbein and Winterhalter and a tiny Paul Klee etching, you can see works of local interest, including some by Otto Ubbelohde, illustrator of the Grimm fairy tales, and some rather *völkisch* art by Carl Bantzer, who was feted by the Nazis, though he maintained a certain distance from them.

You can enjoy Marburg's scenic **setting** by renting a pedalo or rowing **boat** from Trojedamm on the east bank of the Lahn (April–Oct 10am–8pm; ☏0162/64 70 72) or by heading up to the **Kaiser Wilhelm Turm** high on the ridge of the Lahnberge east of town (March–Oct Mon & Wed–Sun 2–6pm; Nov–Feb Mon & Wed–Sun 2–5pm; €1; bus #7), where there are breathtaking views from the observation platform at the top.

Eating and drinking

As befits a student town, there are plenty of affordable places to **eat** and **drink** in Marburg: kebab places abound, and elsewhere the emphasis is more on value than gourmet swank. Lively during term time, Marburg pays for the dominance of the university during the holidays when it can be a fairly quiet place, with some restaurants and bars closing.

Alte Ritter Steinweg 44 ☏06421/628 38. One of Marburg's classiest culinary offerings, with the likes of goose liver parfait with onion confit, top-notch German wines and main courses from around €15.

Café Vetter Reitgasse 4 ☏06421/258 88. Classic café-*Konditorei* with a rambling layout and sunny terrace. They also do snacks, full meals and a low-cost student breakfast, for which you'll need to show ID.

Delirium with Frazzkeller Steinweg 3. Enjoyably grungy student bar with cheap drinks and a rock music soundtrack; *Frazzkeller* – the smokers' bar – is grungier still. Daily 8pm–2am.

Elisabeth Gasthausbrauerei Steinweg 45 ☏06421/183 05 44. Trendy *Hausbrauerei* close to the Elisabethkirche, with a bistro serving food, a *Bierkeller* (closed Mon) and own-brand light and dark beers.

Felix Barfüsserstr. 7 ☏06421/30 73 36. One of a number of modern café/bars in Oberstadt selling pizza, burgers and salads at very student-friendly prices. There's a long cocktail list, too. Open until 2am Fri & Sat.

KostBar Barfüsserstr. 7 ☏06421/16 11 70. Trendy place offering salads, veggie and pasta dishes with a few inventive touches; main courses from around €9. They also do organic breakfasts.

Venezia Neustadt 5 ☏06421/656 50. Italian-style *gelateria*, established in 1957 and with jolly, kitschy murals to cheer up the interior. You can also buy ice cream to take away.

Weinlädele Schlosstreppe 1 ☏06421/142 44. Enjoy regional wines and light, inexpensive food including *Maultaschen* and *Flammkuchen* in this informal wine tavern's beamy interior or outside with views over Markt.

Entertainment

Both the Fürstensaal at the Schloss and the Elisabethkirche are **concert** venues; you can hear **live bands** at *KFZ*, Schulstrasse 6 (☎06421/138 98, ⓦwww.kfz -marburg.de), and **live jazz** at *Cavete*, Steinweg 12 (☎06421/661 57, ⓦwww .jazzini.de). Marburg's art house **cinema** is Filmkunst am Steinweg, Steinweg 4 (☎06421/672 69, ⓦwww.marburgerfilmkunst.de), with three screens. The Hessisches Landestheater, Am Schwanhof 68–72 (☎06421/256 08, ⓦwww .hlth.de), is the place to see **drama**.

Fulda and around

With the uplands of the Vogelsberg to the west and the impressive sweep of the ancient, volcanic Rhön mountains rising to over 900m in the east, there's a touch of wild grandeur to the spacious landscape around **FULDA**. And there's more than a hint of pomp about the old prince-bishops' Residenzstadt itself, with a stately official **Barockviertel**, or Baroque quarter, crowning a low-rise hill, adding a stately flourish to the fringes of its attractive, walkable **Altstadt**, immediately to the south. Relatively remote from Hesse's other major cities, Fulda has never grown especially large, but it has a bustling, self-sufficient air that makes it an enjoyable place to spend a few days. On the city's fringe **Schloss Fasanerie**, the summer residence of the prince-bishops, makes a worthwhile excursion if you have your own transport, while further afield the beautiful uplands of the **Rhön Biosphere** reserve can be reached easily from Fulda by bus.

Arrival, information and accommodation

Fast, frequent ICE trains connect Frankfurt with Fulda's **Hauptbahnhof**, on the eastern side of the Altstadt and just a few minutes' walk from the **tourist office** in the Baroque Palais Buttlar at Bonifatiusplatz 1 (Mon–Fri 8.30am–6pm, Sat & Sun 10am–2pm; ☎0661/102 18 13/4, ⓦwww.tourismus-fulda .de). It can rent you a handy English-language **audio guide** (€5) to take you on a two-hour guided walk through the city and sell you a **Museums Pass** (€9.50) offering free entry to the major museums. Fulda's **hotels** are scattered throughout the Altstadt.

Arte Altstadt Hotel Doll 2–4 ☎0661/25 02 98 80, ⓦwww.altstadthotel-arte.de. Stylish modern design touches and a prime location in the southern Altstadt; rooms have internet connection and there's an underground car park. ❹

DJH Fulda Schirrmannstr. 31 ☎0661/733 89, ⓦwww.djh-hessen.de. Youth hostel 2km from the centre on the southwestern outskirts of town. Dorms from €20.40 with breakfast.

Goldener Karpfen Simpliziusbrunnen 1 ☎0661/868 00, ⓦwww.hotel-goldener -karpfen.de. Classy family-run hotel on a pretty square in the southern Altstadt, with tasteful, tradi-tional furnishings and a *Weinstube* – and Goethe for a former guest. ❻

Hotel am Schloss Kanalstr. 1b ☎0661/250 55 80, ⓦwww.hotel-am-schloss-fulda.de. Rambling, cyclist-friendly hotel in a historic half-timbered house just moments from the Stadtschloss and Dom. ❷

Hotel Garni Hirsch Löherstr. 36 ☎0661/380 90 95, Ⓔhotel-hirsch@lycos.de. Attractive rooms at bargain rates in an atmospheric half-timbered house, handy for the southern Altstadt's nightlife. ❷

Maritim am Schlossgarten Pauluspromenade 2 ☎0661/28 20, ⓦwww.maritim.de. Smart, business-oriented hotel in a quiet but very central location on the Schlossgarten, and incorporating the magnificent Baroque Orangerie. ❻

The Barockviertel

Fulda's **Barockviertel** was built in the early eighteenth century as the city recovered financially from the Thirty Years' War, and it lends Fulda the air of a comic-opera capital city, with all the necessary grandeur and dignity for the role, but on a human scale. The first of the Barockviertel's landmarks to be built was the **Dom**, which faces spacious, paved Domplatz. The work of the Bamberg architect Johann Dientzenhofer, it was constructed between 1704 and 1712 but still contains elements of its predecessor, the Ratgar Basilica, which was the largest Carolingian church north of the Alps. With its twin towers and central dome the cathedral looks more southern than central German; the airy, white stucco interior is relatively restrained by the standards of the style, though the high altar, which portrays the Assumption of the Madonna, provides a theatrical but graceful focal point, smothered in gold leaf. The crypt contains the tomb of St Boniface, the English-born apostle to the Germans and patron saint of Germany, who was murdered while proselytizing in Frisia in 754 AD.

The wealth and importance of Fulda's Catholic bishopric is vividly illustrated by a visit to the **Dommuseum** (April–Oct Tues–Sat 10am–5.30pm, Sun 12.30–5.30pm; Nov to mid-Jan & mid-Feb to March Tues–Sat 10am–12.30pm & 1.30–4pm, Sun 12.30–4pm; €2.10, English-language leaflet €0.50), where the sheer weight of eighteenth-century ecclesiastical bling is almost overwhelming. Amid the Baroque excess the Silver Chapel and its ghoulish skull reliquary of St Boniface stand out; there are also some lovely medieval woodcarvings, and a painting by Lucas Cranach the Elder, *Christ and the Adulteress*, dating from 1512.

Overlooking the Dom to the north is the simple but lovely **Michaelskirche** (daily: April–Oct 10am–6pm; Nov–March 2–5pm; free), the Carolingian burial chapel of Fulda's Benedictine Abbey, parts of which date back to 822 AD; it was extended into a Roman cross form in the tenth and eleventh centuries. The rotunda is particularly beautiful.

Fulda's most delightful secular Baroque monuments face each other across the beautiful **Schlossgarten** (daily: April–Oct 7am–10.30pm; Nov–March 7am–9pm) opposite Domplatz. The **Orangerie**, now part of a hotel (see p.587), is perhaps the most elegant of all, a refined pleasure-palace designed by Maximilian von Welsch betwen 1722 and 1725. The **Apollosaal** in the centre of the building with its ceiling frescoes is impressive – nowadays it's the hotel's breakfast room, but if there's not an event on nobody minds too much if you take a look. The formal part of the Schlossgarten is planted with sweet-smelling heliotrope in summer and centres on a fountain.

The **Stadtschloss** on the south side of the Schlossgarten is also the work of Johann Dientzenhofer, who from 1706 to 1717 extended and rebuilt the existing Renaissance Schloss and incorporated the twelfth-century **Schlossturm**, which faces the Schlossgarten and can be climbed for an exhilarating view over the park, city and surrounding landscape (same hours; €1.50, or €3.50 with Historische Räume). Built as the prince-bishops' residence, the Schloss now functions as Fulda's Rathaus, but you can visit the **Historische Räume** (Sat–Thurs 10am–6pm, Fri 2–6pm; €3 or €3.50 with Schlossturm), which preserve their Baroque appearance. The coolly elegant, stucco Kaisersaal on the ground floor opens onto the Schlossgarten and is decorated with portraits of Habsburg emperors; upstairs, a procession of rooms displaying eighteenth-century Fulda and Thuringian porcelain leads to the delightful **Spiegelkabinett**, or cabinet of mirrors; on the second floor is the **Fürstensaal**, a splendid reception room whose stucco ceiling is decorated with paintings on mythological themes by the Tyrolean artist Melchior Steidl. Opposite the Stadtschloss the Hauptwache is reminiscent of its Frankfurt namesake and now houses a café/bar.

The Altstadt

The charms of Fulda's largely traffic-free **Altstadt** are low key in comparison with the pomp of the Barockviertel, but it's an animated and interesting district to explore, with plenty of quaint corners and civilized places to eat and drink.

A stroll down Friedrichstrasse from the Stadtschloss brings you to the towering but rather dull **Stadtpfarrkirche**, the last Baroque structure to be built in Fulda, between 1770 and 1786. Tucked behind it is the picturesque half-timbered **Altes Rathaus** (1500–31) with a galleried ground floor and a memorable roofline – the attic windows eschew the usual dormers for a series of look-at-me pinnacles.

Just to the south, another Baroque pile – a former seminary – now houses the **Vonderau Museum** (Tues–Sun 10am–5pm; €3), Fulda's biggest museum and principal wet-weather refuge. The core of the museum is essentially a local history collection, whose curiosities include the reconstructed Drogerie zum Krokodil – a Jugendstil pharmacy – and the Fulda-Mobil, a curious bubble car that was built in Fulda in the 1950s and 1960s. There are also sections on natural history, and a collection of paintings and sculptures of local importance. Opposite the museum is Andreas Gallasini's 1733 **Alte Universität**. Founded by prince-bishop Adolph von Dalberg, the university was dissolved in 1805 after secularization brought the prince-bishops' rule to an end.

The southern and western fringes of the Altstadt in particular preserve many half-timbered houses and here – in contrast to the banal shopping quarter north of the Alte Universität – restoration has been sensitive. In Kanalstrasse, the 14m **Hexenturm** is a surviving remnant of the medieval city wall.

Eating, drinking and entertainment

Fulda's Altstadt is liberally peppered with places to **eat** and **drink**, with the thickest cluster of **bars** around Karlstrasse and Kanalstrasse at the southern end of the Altstadt. The Schlosstheater, Schlossstrasse 5 (☎0661/102 14 80, ⓦwww .schlosstheater-fulda.de), is the place for **drama**, **opera** and **classical music**; big-budget spectaculars are staged at the Esperantohalle on Esperantoplatz (☎0661/24 29 10, ⓦwww.esperantohalle.de); there are regular organ concerts in the Dom, while in summer the courtyard of the Stadtschloss is the venue for concerts by big-name pop acts.

Restaurants, cafés and bars

Café Palais Bonifatiusplatz 1 ☎0661/250 92 63. Strategically located next to the tourist office, this is a stylish modern café with a big terrace, modern art and good cakes. Open for breakfast.

Café Thiele Conditorei Mittelstr. 2 ☎0661/727 74. Founded in 1892, this is the cream of Fulda's *Kaffee und Kuchen* stops, with a vast selection of around fifty different types of cake.

Felsenkeller Leipzigerstr. 12 ☎0661/727 84. *Biergarten* of the Hochstift brewery, on the brewery premises just north of the Barockviertel, with a menu of reasonably priced *Schweinshaxe* and *Schnitzel*.

Goldener Karpfen Karlstr. 31 ☎0661/868 00. Elegant hotel restaurant serving a refined menu, such as a rack of venison with chanterelles and sliced dumplings. There's a two-course €18 set lunch; evening à la carte main courses are €16–36.

Hohmanns Brauhaus Florengasse 31. Big *Gasthausbrauerei* in the southern Altstadt with splendid copper microbrewery, a short menu of seasonally changing specials, and dark and *Hefeweizen* beers.

Krokodil Karlstr. 31 ☎06421/628 38. Lively beer and cocktail bar in the fabulous premises of the former Krokodil pharmacy.

🏃 **Schwarzer Hahn** Friedrichstr. 18 ☎0661/24 03 12. Local beer *Rhöner Landbier* and good German food – including *Tafelspitz* (boiled beef) with superb Frankfurter *Grüne Sosse* – are served in pleasantly fussy surroundings here. Main courses from around €9.50.

Viva Havanna Bonifatiusplatz 2 ☎0661/227 11. Exuberantly decorated Cuban café/bar in the Hauptwache opposite the Stadtschloss, with rum cocktails, and tapas or tortadillas to eat. Open until 3am Fri & Sat, otherwise 1am.

Around Fulda: Schloss Fasanerie and the Rhön Biosphere Reserve

Seven kilometres south of Fulda is **Schloss Fasanerie** (April–Oct 10am–5pm, guided tours on the hour; €6, or €10 with porcelain collection; Ⓦ www.schloss -fasanerie.de; no public transport). A modest country house was built on the site in 1711, but in 1739 it was massively extended by the prince-bishops' architect Andreas Gallasini to create a magnificent Baroque summer residence. It has a chequered history: after the dissolution of the prince-bishopric it fell into a ruinous state before becoming the residence of the Elector Wilhelm II of Hesse-Kassel, whose architect Johann Conrad Bromeis rebuilt the interior in elegant Neoclassical style. The lofty **Kaisertreppe**, or main staircase, is decorated with portraits of Habsburg emperors; in summer, the splendid **Grosser Saal** – the largest room in the Schloss – is the venue for classical music concerts. The Schloss is also home to a collection of priceless **porcelain** (€6, or €10 with Schloss tour), which includes the Electors' 1800-piece dinner service.

East of Fulda and accessible by hourly buses (#26; €3.70), the 950m **Wasserkuppe** is the highest mountain of the Rhön and the highest point in Hesse. The landscape was formed by volcanic activity in the Tertiary period. The Rhön region – which stretches into Thuringia and Bavaria – has been declared a UNESCO Biosphere Reserve to safeguard its pristine upland landscapes, so it comes as a surprise to find the summit of the Wasserkuppe so cluttered. There's a useful **information centre** (Tues–Sun 10am–4pm; ☎06654/91 83 40, Ⓦ www.rhoen.de) and an aerodrome as well as the **Deutsches Segelflugmuseum** (daily: April–Oct 9am–5pm; Nov–March 10am–4.30pm; €3; Ⓦ www.segelflugmuseum.de), packed with full-size and model gliders: the summit has been the main centre for gliding in Germany since the 1930s. Beyond the cluster of buildings, you'll see paragliders launching themselves off the grassy summit – there's a **school** (☎06654/75 48, Ⓦ www.wasserkuppe.com) should you want to join them. A circular walk around the summit offers breathtaking views south over neighbouring peaks and west towards Fulda. On the northwest side at **Märchenwiesenhütte** there's a summer **toboggan** run (€2) and, in winter, blue, red and black **ski runs**. You can rent ski gear on site. The Rhön is splendid **hiking** country: the 215km Fulda Weg and the 89km **Rhön Rennsteig Weg** – which links the Rhön and Thüringer Wald – start here. Unsurprisingly, it's also a popular destination for bikers.

Fritzlar and around

Half-timbered old towns aren't unusual in Hesse, yet even by the standards of the region, **FRITZLAR**'s **Altstadt** is magical, surrounded by its medieval defences and with a central **Marktplatz** of such theme-park quaintness you pinch yourself to believe that the houses – which are perfectly genuine – weren't built that way merely to attract tourists. The most eye-catching is the crooked **Gildehaus**, or Kaufhäuschen, which was built around 1475 and was the guildhouse of the Michaelsbruderschaft, one of the first German trade guilds, which survived into the mid-nineteenth century.

Fritzlar's most impressive house, however, is the mammoth **Hochzeitshaus** a little to the west of Marktplatz. Built in 1580 to 1590, it's the largest half-timbered house in North Hesse and is home to the **Regionalmuseum** (March–Dec Tues–Fri 10am–noon & 3–5pm, Sat & Sun 10am–noon, from May–Oct also

Sat 3–5pm; €2), whose eclectic local history displays embrace everything from geology and prehistory to folklore, though some sections are closed during ongoing restoration work on the building.

South of Marktplatz, Fritzlar's stone and slate-hung **Rathaus** dates from 1109 and is claimed to be the oldest in Germany still fulfilling its original function; facing it, the **Dom** (Mon–Fri 8am–6pm, Sat & Sun 9am–7.30pm; free) is successor to the modest wooden church founded by St Boniface in 723 AD. It's a handsome blend of Romanesque and Gothic, nowhere more magical than in the Romanesque **crypt** (Mon 2–5pm, Tues–Fri 10am–noon & 2–5pm, Sat 10–11.30am & 1.30–4.30pm, Sun 1.30–4.30pm; Nov–April Mon–Fri closes 4pm; €2.50), which contains the tomb of St Wigbert, a contemporary of St Boniface. The same ticket gives access to the fourteenth-century **cloisters** and the **Domschatz**, whose treasures include the jewelled *Heinrichskreuz* from 1020.

Afterwards, climb the lofty **Grauer Turm** (April–Oct daily 9am–noon & 3–5pm; €0.25) on the town walls for views across the Altstadt's rooftops.

Practicalities

Fritzlar is linked to Kassel by train and bus; the **Bahnhof** is south of the Altstadt on the south side of the River Eder, while buses arrive on the north side of the Altstadt on Kasseler Strasse. The **tourist office** is in the crazily twisted Spitzchenhäuschen at Zwischen den Krämen 5 (Mon 10am–6pm, Tues–Thurs 10am–5pm, Fri 10am–4pm, Sat 10am–2pm; ☎05622/98 86 26, ⊛www.fritzlar .de), halfway between the Marktplatz and Dom. There's a scattering of places to **stay** in the Altstadt: the *Kaiserpfalz*, Giessener Strasse 20 (☎05622/99 37 70, ⊛www.kaiserpfalz.com; ❸), is the most upmarket and modern, but has an oddly institutional feel. Alternatively, try the more central, prettier *Zur Spitze*, Marktplatz 25 (☎05622/18 22, ⊛www.zur-spitze.de; ❸), or the *Domgarten*, south of the Dom at Neustädterstrasse 9 (☎05622/917 60, ⊛www.hotel -domgarten.de; ❸). All three hotels have **restaurants**; for coffee and cake, try the friendly *Hetzler* at Marktplatz 16–18, open daily until 6pm.

Edersee

West of Fritzlar, change buses at **Bad Wildungen** towards Waldeck to reach the shore of the **Edersee**, one of the Sauerland reservoirs whose **dams** were the targets of the famous World War II **Dambuster raids** in May 1943. Not that you'd know it today: the dam was rapidly repaired after the raid and looks as solid now as it must have done before the attack. You can stroll from one side to the other, and it's certainly a beautiful spot, on the fringe of the **Sauerland Nationalpark**; the meandering lakeshore is hugged by low, wooded hills, and from either side of the dam you can take a **boat trip** (April–Oct; fares from €4; ⊛www.personenschifffahrt-edersee.de) on the lake. On the Waldeck (eastern) shore you can rent **electric boats** from Bootsverleih Kretschmann (from €2 per hr). There's also a **restaurant**, *Zum Grossen Hecht*, serving salads, fish dishes and baked potatoes. On the west side of the dam there's a **tourist office** (daily 11am–5pm; ☎05623/99 98 50, ⊛www.edersee.com) for information on **sports** and **leisure** activities or finding somewhere to **stay**.

West of the dam, on the road to Bringhausen, a bouncing bomb sits in front of the **Sperrmauer Museum Edersee** (daily 11am–5pm; ⊛www.ausstellung -edersee.de). The museum tells the story of the Edersee raid, though don't expect a straightforward tale of stiff-upper-lip British patriotism – the destructive (and deadly) effects of the raid and the use of slave labour to repair the dam are also covered.

Kassel

KASSEL is the largest city in northern Hesse, and a rather nicer place than it's generally given credit for. Internationally, it's renowned for the *documenta* contemporary art exhibition, which rolls in every five years, takes over the city and is next due back in 2012. Between times it's as if Kassel falls off the radar. True, the city centre is dull – as single-mindedly devoted to shopping as any *Fussgängerzone* (pedestrian zone) in Germany – but the city's interesting museums include one devoted to the **Brothers Grimm**, the **parks** are among the most extraordinary eighteenth-century garden landscapes in Europe, and at **Schloss Wilhelmshöhe** there's a first-rate collection of Old Masters. And for those who don't relish hanging out in shopping centres, the leafy, attractive **Vordere Westen** quarter – between the city centre and Wilhelmshöhe – has all the sinuous Jugendstil architectural details and relaxed café life you could wish for.

For visitors, Kassel is a linear city, with most of the sights at either end of **Wilhelmshöher Allee** – in the east are the city centre's museums and a beautiful park, **Karlsaue**; in the west there's the exceptional landscape and art collection of Wilhelmshöhe. Hotels and places to eat and drink are scattered between the two.

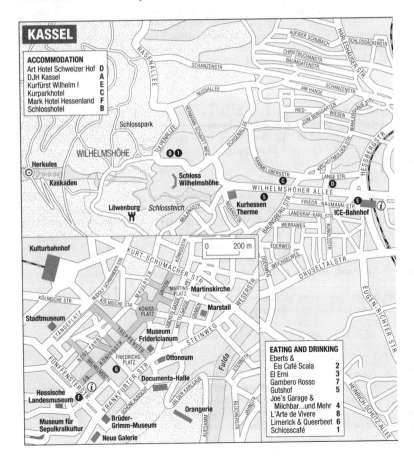

KASSEL

ACCOMMODATION
Art Hotel Schweizer Hof	D
DJH Kassel	A
Kurfürst Wilhelm I	E
Kurparkhotel	C
Mark Hotel Hessenland	F
Schlosshotel	B

EATING AND DRINKING
Eberts & Eis Café Scala	2
El Erni	3
Gambero Rosso	7
Gutshof	5
Joe's Garage & Milchbar...und Mehr	4
L'Arte de Vivere	8
Limerick & Queerbeet	6
Schlosscafé	1

Arrival, information and accommodation

Fast, frequent ICE trains arrive at **Kassel-Wilhelmshöhe station**, which is midway between Schloss Wilhelmshöhe and the city centre and where there's a **tourist office** (Mon–Fri 9am–6pm, Sat 9am–1pm; ☎0561/340 54, ⊛www.kassel -tourist.de); there's another tourist office in the Rathaus at Obere Königsstrasse 8 (Mon–Fri 9am–6pm, Sat 9am–2pm; ☎0561/70 77 07). Either office can sell you a €10 **KasselCard**, valid for one or two people for 24 hours and offering free public transport and reductions on museum entry. **Public transport** is provided by NVV (⊛www.nvv.de); a *Kurzstrecke* ticket for up to four stops costs €1.60, single tickets €2.40, or a *Tageskarte* €5.70). There's a scattering of **hotels** close to Wilhelmshöhe, but wherever you stay in Kassel you're likely to be hopping on and off tramline #1, which runs along Wilhelmshöhe Allee and links the city centre with the west of the city.

Art Hotel Schweizer Hof Wilhelmshöher Allee 288 ☎0561/936 90, ⊛www.arthotel -schweizerhof.de. The decor is a little more gaudy than the "art hotel" label would suggest – there's an awful lot of Swiss-flag red – but this is nevertheless a smart and comfortable option, in a convenient location close to Wilhelmshöhe. ❹

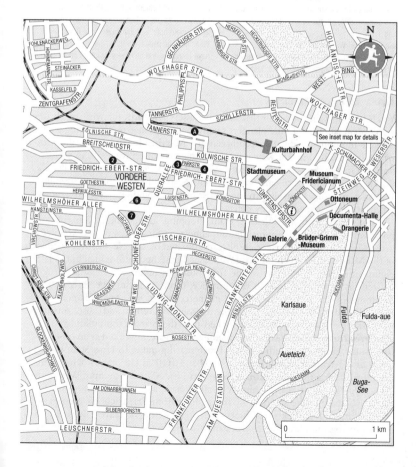

DJH Kassel Schenkendorfstr. 18 ☎0561/77 64 55, ⑩www.djh-hessen.de. The city's youth hostel is close to the Vordere Westen's bar and restaurant scene. Dorms from €20.20 with breakfast.

Kurfürst Wilhelm 1 Wilhelmshöher Allee 257 ☎0561/318 70, ⑩www.kurfuerst.bestwestern .de. Tastefully refurbished nineteenth-century hotel next to Bahnhof Wilhelmshöhe, with a bedframe wittily balanced atop its corner tower and comfortable, en-suite rooms with wi-fi and TV. ❻

Kurparkhotel Wilhelmshöher Allee 336 ☎0561/318 90, ⑩www.kurparkhotel-kassel.de. Modern, slightly anonymous hotel with tastefully decorated rooms and a convenient location close to Wilhelmshöhe. ❻

Mark Hotel Hessenland Obere Königsstr. 2 ☎0561/918 10, ⑩www.markhotels.de. Three-star hotel, convenient for the city-centre museums and trams to Wilhelmshöhe. Public areas are in a lovely 1950s style; rooms are not so stylish, but are spacious and comfortable. ❸

Schlosshotel Schlosspark 8 ☎0561/308 80, ⑩www.schlosshotel-kassel.de. Four-star comfort in a modern hotel just across the road from the Wilhelmshöhe palace complex. Some of the rooms have balconies and all have satellite TV and wireless internet. ❺

The city centre

You'll look in vain for much that's old in Kassel's **Altstadt**, for what the RAF didn't obliterate in 1943 the planners swiftly eradicated afterwards, sparing a few isolated monuments: the fourteenth-century **Martinskirche** on Martinsplatz, whose towers and interior were rebuilt in a strangely inventive 1950s interpretation of Gothic; the sixteenth-century Weser Renaissance **Marstall**, rebuilt as a market hall (Thurs & Fri 7am–6pm, Sat 7am–2pm) and a great place to assemble a picnic; and the **Druselturm** on Druselplatz, a spindly thirteenth-century survivor from the medieval city defences.

Leading west from the Altstadt, main shopping street Obere Königsstrasse preserves its handsome proportions, but almost nothing of its prewar architecture. It leads to the vast Friedrichsplatz, dominated by the Neoclassical portico of the **Museum Fridericianum** (Wed–Sun 11am–6pm; €5) which in the late eighteenth century was one of the first museums in Europe to display royal collections to the public – in this instance, those of Landgrave Friedrich II of Hesse-Kassel, whose statue stands in the centre of the square named after him. Nowadays the Fridericianum is a *documenta* venue and hosts touring exhibitions of contemporary art. Tucked into the rear of the building is the **Zwehrenturm**, another surviving medieval city gate, reworked as an observatory in the early eighteenth century. Brave roaring traffic to cross Steinweg to reach the **Ottoneum**, built between 1604 and 1607 as Germany's first theatre but now housing the **Naturkundemuseum** (Tues–Sun 10am–5pm, Wed until 8pm; €2.50), whose natural history displays have a touch of whimsy about them and include the skeleton of an elephant from Friedrich II's menagerie and the Holzbibliothek – a library-like presentation of leaves, flowers and seeds. Nearby, the ultramodern **documenta-Halle** is a hive of activity during the *documenta* exhibitions.

Karlsaue and the museums

From the *documenta*-Halle, steps lead down to the **Karlsaue**, an eighteenth-century park on a vast scale, whose groomed lawns and well-drilled trees and water features stretch into the distance from the elegant, yellow-painted **Orangerie**, built in the early eighteenth century as a summer residence for Landgrave Karl and now home to the **Astronomisch-Physikalisches Kabinett** (Tues–Sun 10am–5pm; €3), whose collection of clocks, globes and scientific instruments from the sixteenth to eighteenth centuries is fascinating and beautiful. Pride of the collection is the *Augsburger Prunkuhr*, a staggeringly opulent clock built in Augsburg in 1683. A side pavilion houses the **Marmorbad** (Tues–Sun 10am–5pm; €4 with English audio guide), which contains sinuous mythological sculptures in Carrara marble by Pierre Etienne Monnot (1657–1733). At the southern end of the park is the **Insel Siebenbergen** (Easter to early Oct Tues–Sun 10am–7pm; €3), renowned for its flowering plants.

On a low hill on the north side of the Karlsaue, **Schöne Aussicht** ("beautiful view") was once lined with Baroque mansions. One survivor, the Palais Bellevue, now houses the **Brüder-Grimm-Museum** (Tues–Sun 10am–5pm, Wed until 8pm; €1.50), which charts the careers of the brothers Jacob and Wilhelm Grimm, their association with Kassel and the extraordinary international success of their children's tales. The brothers studied law at Marburg, and were subsequently appointed librarians at the court of the Elector in Kassel before falling from favour and moving to Göttingen, where they again fell foul of the local ruler. In their lifetimes the brothers were widely respected for their grammatical works, and in 1840 they were summoned to Berlin by Friederich Wilhelm IV of Prussia. There they remained for the rest of their lives, working on their German dictionary. The museum is scheduled to close for refurbishment at the end of 2009. Its near neighbour, the **Neue Galerie**, contains the city's collection of art from 1750 to the present, including works by Tischbein, Lovis Corinth, the German Expressionists and Joseph Beuys. The gallery has been closed since 2006 for rebuilding, but was scheduled to reopen in the autumn of 2009.

The **Museum für Sepulkralkultur** (Tues–Sun 10am–5pm, Wed until 8pm; €4) at Weinbergstrasse 25–27, a little to the west of Schöne Aussicht, is about as bright and cheery as any museum on the theme of death and burial could be. Pick up an English-language leaflet at the start as labelling is in German. At Brüder-Grimm-Platz 5, the eclectic collections of the **Hessisches Landesmuseum** (closed for refurbishment at time of writing) range from pre- and early history to a surprisingly engrossing wallpaper museum and a more conventional museum of applied art on the top floor, including displays of eighteenth-century Kassel porcelain. Finally, make sense of Kassel's complex history with a visit to the **Stadtmuseum** at Ständeplatz 16 (Tues–Sun 10am–5pm; €1.50), which is worth a visit to see the model of the city as it was in its elegant eighteenth-century heyday. The city's later development sowed the seeds for its destruction in World War II, for it was an important industrial centre during the nineteenth century.

Wilhelmshöhe

The exuberance of the palace and parks of **Wilhelmshöhe** is visible even from the city centre, for the flamboyant Baroque **Bergpark** climbs the hill in front of you along Wilhelmshöher Allee. The steepness of the incline foreshortens the view, and it's only once inside the park that you realize Wilhelmshöhe is as vast as it is spectacular. Pick up a map from the **information office** close to the terminus of the #1 tram (daily: April–Oct 9.30am–5.30pm; Nov–March 9.30am–4.30pm).

▲ Herkules-Oktagon and Kaskaden

Created on the whim of Landgrave Karl in the first decade of the eighteenth century by the Italian Francesco Guerniero, Wilhelmshöhe is dominated by the **Herkules-Oktagon** (viewing platform mid-March to mid-Nov Tues–Sun 10am–5pm; €3), a fantasy castle topped by a pyramid on which stands an 8.25m-tall figure of **Hercules**, the work of the Augsburg coppersmith Jacob Anthoni. The choice of subject reflected Karl's not-so-modest view of his own qualities. From the foot of the Oktagon, the stepped **Kaskaden** (cascades) descend for 400m; from May to early October (Wed & Sun at 2.30pm), this is the scene of the best free show in Hesse, the **Wasserkünste**, as water is released at the top and slowly flows downhill. It takes around ten minutes to descend the Kaskaden, then disappears, reappearing over the **Steinhöfer** waterfall and under the picturesque **Teufelsbrücke** before finally re-emerging below Schloss Wilhelmshöhe to power a spectacular 52-metre-high **water jet**. The entire performance takes an hour, so that you can comfortably follow its progress downhill. From June to September, there's an illuminated evening performance on the first Saturday of the month. Bus #22 ascends to the Oktagon; #23 travels through the lower reaches of the park.

The lower reaches of the park are dominated by **Schloss Wilhelmshöhe**, a massive Neoclassical pile built between 1786 and 1801 to plans by Simon du Roy for Landgrave Wilhelm IX. The central **Corps de Logis** houses the **Gemäldegalerie Alte Meister** (Tues–Sun 10am–5pm; €6), a heavyweight collection of Old Masters originally amassed by the Landgrave Wilhelm VIII of Hesse-Kassel and ranking with the best in Germany. Laid out over three floors, it is particularly strong in Flemish and Dutch works. The third floor of the museum is a treasure-trove of works by Rubens, Van Dyck, Jacob Jordaens and

Rembrandt, with highlights including Rembrandt's tender *Jacob Blessing Ephraim and Manasseh* from 1656 and Rubens' *Flight into Egypt*, a delicate and modest-sized panel painting that lacks the theatrical swagger of his famous altarpieces. The second floor displays Dutch painting of the sixteenth and seventeenth centuries, while German works on the first floor include a small Cranach portrait of a rather stout Martin Luther, dated 1543, Dürer's 1499 *Portrait of Elsbeth Tucher* and a number of works by Johann Heinrich Tischbein the Elder, court painter to the Hesse-Kassels, including a portrait of Wilhelm VIII himself. The first floor also displays Italian, Spanish and French art, including canvasses by Titian and Tintoretto. The ground floor and basement of the Corps de Logis are occupied by the **Antikensammlung** of Classical antiquities, as well as a series of cork models of the monuments of ancient Rome created at the end of the eighteenth century by Antonio Chichi. One of the side wings of Schloss Wilhelmshöhe is the **Weissensteinflügel** (guided tours Tues–Sun: March–Oct 10am–5pm; Nov–Feb 10am–4pm; €4), the only part of the Schloss to preserve its original Neoclassical domestic interiors.

Elsewhere in the park, the **Löwenburg** (guided tours same hours & price as Weissensteinflügel) is a picturesque mock-medieval castle containing the Hesse-Kassel armoury, a chapel and a number of rooms furnished in mock-antiquarian styles.

Eating, drinking and nightlife

Good places to **eat** are thin on the ground in the city centre but plentiful in the **Vordere Westen**, which is where you'll also find many of Kassel's best **bars**; though it's not the liveliest city in Germany for nightlife, there are some stylish and enjoyable options. The Staatstheater Kassel on Friedrichsplatz (☎0561/109 42 22) is the place to see **drama**, **ballet** and **classical music** in Kassel.

Eberts Friedrich-Ebert-Str. 42 ☎0561/739 92 30. Stylish café in the elegant Jugendstil surroundings of a former officers' mess; open from breakfast.
Eis Café Scala Friedrich-Ebert-Str. Traditional family-style Italian *gelateria*, a couple of doors down from *Eberts*.
El Erni Parkstr. 42 ☎0561/71 00 18. Popular Spanish restaurant in the Vordere Westen, with a tree-shaded terrace fronting Querallee.
Gambero Rosso Gräfe Str. 4 ☎0561/28 53 81. Fresh pasta and wines direct from the Italian producers at this modest-sized restaurant and wine bar in the Vordere Westen. Closed Sun.
Gutshof Wilhelmshöher Allee 347 ☎0561/325 25. Classy restaurant in the grounds of a TV studio close to Wilhelmshöhe, with the likes of *Tafelspitz* (boiled beef) with horseradish and Calvados sauce for around €15.
Joe's Garage Friedrich-Ebert-Str. 60 ☎0561/186 86. Trendy Vordere Westen rock bar with an American gas station theme and twice-monthly live bands during the winter months.

L'Arte de Vivere Friedrichsplatz 10 ☎0561/766 84 46. Modern Italian trattoria and bar opposite the Fridericianum; pizza from €6, pasta from €7 and meat-based main courses around €15.
Limerick Wilhelmshöher Allee 116 ☎0561/77 66 49. Not an Irish pub, but a spacious café/bar on a corner site in the Vordere Westen, with Italian food from around €6 and a big selection of beers.
🏃 **Milchbar … und Mehr** Friedrich-Ebert-Str. 64. Stylish Vordere Westen café with classic 1950s decor and music, a scooter in the window and a large mural of Marilyn Monroe. Open from breakfast.
Queerbeet Wilhelmshöher Allee 116 ☎0561/766 89 79. The Vordere Westen's gay bar, tucked into modest premises next to *Limerick* and with an outside terrace in summer. Eve only; open until 3am Fri & Sat, otherwise 1am.
Schlosscafé Schlosspark ☎0561/325 43. A pretty spot for a cool drink after a visit to Schloss Wilhelmshöhe, with a sunny terrace, the *Schlosscafé* is the pick of the Bergpark's refreshment stops.

Travel details

Trains

Darmstadt to: Frankfurt (very frequent; 15–40min); Heidelberg (every 30min; 35min–1hr).

Frankfurt to: Aschaffenburg (every 15–20min; 28min–1hr 10min); Bad Homburg (very frequent; 21min); Berlin (hourly; 4hr 10min); Bonn (15 daily; 1hr); Cologne (every 20min–1hr; 1hr 23min–3hr 36min); Darmstadt (very frequent; 15–40min); Frankfurt airport (very frequent; 11min); Fulda (every 14–30min; 32min–1hr 35min); Hamburg (every 20min–1hr; 3hr 37min); Heidelberg (every 30min–1hr; 53min–1hr 20min); Kassel-Wilhelmshöhe (every 20min; 1hr 5min–1hr 23min); Limburg an der Lahn (every 20min–1hr; 1hr 3min–1hr 22min); Mainz (very frequent; 30–40min); Mannheim (every 20min–1hr; 38min–1hr 32min); Marburg (every 30min–1hr; 56min–1hr 20min); Munich (every 30min–1hr; 3hr 10min–4hr); Nuremberg (every 30min–1hr; 2hr 5min); Rüdesheim (11 daily; 50min–1hr 5min); Stuttgart (every 15min–1hr; 1hr 20min–1hr 30min); Wetzlar (every 30min–1hr; 57min–1hr 16min); Wiesbaden (very frequent; 45min); Würzburg (every 20min–1hr; 1hr 10min–1hr 50min).

Fulda to: Frankfurt (every 15–20min; 55min–1hr 20min); Kassel-Wilhelmshöhe (every 15–20min; 30min–1hr 30min).

Kassel (Hauptbahnhof) to: Fritzlar (1 daily; 38min).

Kassel (Wilhelmshöhe) to: Frankfurt (every 20min; 1hr 23min–2hr); Fulda (every 14–30min; 30min–1hr 35min).

Limburg an der Lahn to: Frankfurt (every 30min; 1hr–1hr 20min); Weilburg (every 30min–1hr; 24–36min); Wetzlar (every 30min–1hr; 42min–1hr 11min).

Wiesbaden to: Frankfurt (very frequent; 40–55min); Mainz (every 15–30min; 11min).

North Rhine-Westphalia

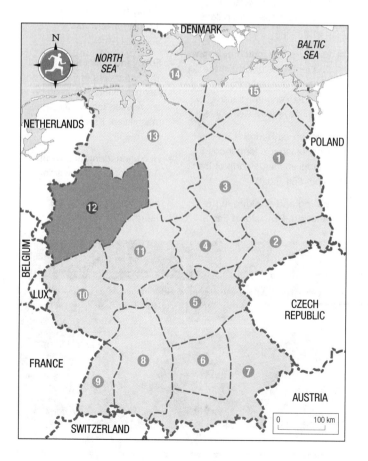

CHAPTER 12

Highlights

✶ **Cologne** The great metropolis of western Germany is fascinating, free spirited and enormous fun to visit.
See p.603

✶ **Schloss Augustusburg** Piety takes a back seat to pleasure at this dazzling Rococo archbishop's palace.
See p.620

✶ **Haus der Geschichte, Bonn** The remarkable story of the postwar German miracle, told in an engaging and imaginative way. See p.625

✶ **Aachen cathedral** Charlemagne's former court chapel is unique north of the Alps. See p.630

✶ **Eating and drinking in the Altstadt, Düsseldorf** Far more than merely "the longest bar in the world", Düsseldorf's Altstadt has an almost Mediterranean élan on fine summer nights. See p.642

✶ **Landschaftspark Duisburg-Nord** Industrial heritage meets nature and science fiction at this remarkable, recycled steelworks.
See p.647

✶ **Folkwang collection, Essen** The superstars of French and German nineteenth-century art, housed temporarily at the magnificent Krupp villa.
See p.652

✶ **Hermannsdenkmal, Detmold** A winged, bearded warrior rises romantically above the wooded ridge of the Teutoburger Wald. See p.666

▲ Bar in Düsseldorf's Altstadt

North Rhine-Westphalia

With its population of around eighteen million actually exceeding that of the neighbouring Netherlands, **North Rhine-Westphalia** (Nordrhein-Westfalen) is by far Germany's most populous Land, though it's by no means the biggest geographically. As the name suggests, it's an artificial construction, cobbled together by the occupying British after World War II from the Prussian provinces of the Rhineland and Westphalia. Perhaps that explains why, for all its size and economic clout, it lacks the sort of breast-beating regional patriotism found in Bavaria. Instead, loyalties tend to be more local: to the city – particularly in the Land's great metropolis, **Cologne** – or to the region, as in the **Ruhrgebiet**, which straddles the historic boundary between Rhineland and Westphalia.

Occupied at various times by the French and British and with Charlemagne's capital, **Aachen**, at its western tip, North Rhine-Westphalia is an outward-looking, European-minded place. Several of its cities have played a decisive role in European history: in the north, the handsome cathedral city of **Münster** was the scene for the signing of the Treaty of Westphalia which ended the Thirty Years' War, while in the south the university city of **Bonn** – birthplace of Beethoven – strutted the world stage more recently as capital of West Germany during the Cold War. Though it lacks the alpine drama of Germany's south, North Rhine-Westphalia has its share of scenic beauty, along the mighty **Rhine**, in the charming **Siebengebirge** and in the wooded, peaceful **Sauerland**.

Urban attractions are nevertheless to the fore, particularly in thriving, multicultural **Cologne** and glamorous **Düsseldorf**, its near-neighbour, rival and the Land's capital. The increasingly post-industrial cities of the Ruhr conurbation – such as **Duisburg**, **Essen**, **Bochum** and **Dortmund** – also have their charms, not least in their inventive reworking of their rich industrial heritage. Further afield, the ham-and-pumpernickel wholesomeness of the smaller Westphalian towns like **Soest**, **Paderborn**, **Detmold** and **Lemgo** couldn't be less like the Ruhr, while along the **Lower Rhine** – around Kalkar and Xanten – the proximity of the Netherlands makes itself felt in place names, architecture and landscape.

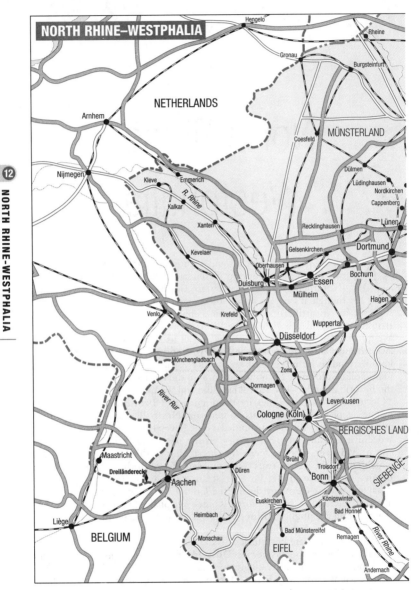

NORTH RHINE–WESTPHALIA

Getting into and **around** the region is easy. Three major **airports** – at Cologne-Bonn, Düsseldorf and Dortmund – are well-connected internationally, while there's a dense web of **public transport** links, with the core of the region well-served by rail, U-Bahn and bus. This is also one of the easiest parts of Germany to explore by **bicycle**, with well-equipped Radstations at many train stations and well-signposted cycle paths along which to explore the countryside.

602

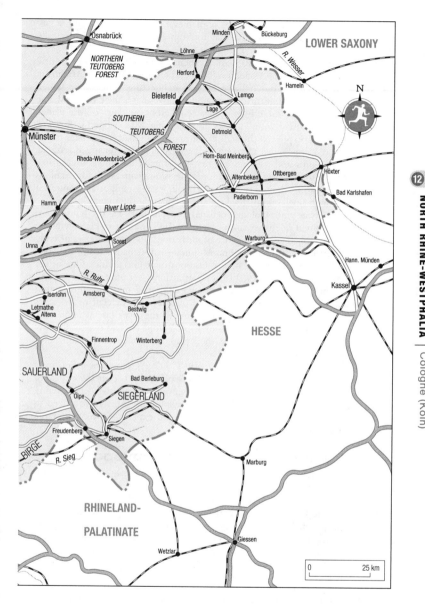

Cologne (Köln)

For centuries **COLOGNE** was *the* German metropolis. The city's origins are Roman: the Emperor Claudius's fourth wife Agrippina – Nero's mother – was born here, and after their marriage he raised the city to *Colonia* status, from which it derives its name. Later, while upstarts like Munich or Berlin were still a twinkle in the eye of their founders, early medieval Cologne was the largest city north of the Alps, ruled by powerful archbishops and benefiting economically from its strategic location astride the Rhine.

This illustrious history has left its mark. Cologne may not be the most beautiful big city in Germany – it was visited too early and too often by the RAF during World War II for that – but it has a unique architectural inheritance which creates a powerful sense of historical continuity. Above all it is the **cathedral**, one of the most famous and instantly recognizable religious buildings on the planet, that Cologne is identified with. The city also has a highly developed sense of its own distinctiveness, expressed through the strong *Kölsch* dialect, the beer of the same name, and a fun-loving approach to life most apparent during **Karneval**. Though its museums and galleries are first-rate, there's nothing museum-like about Germany's fourth city: it's the nation's television centre, with four stations based here, and is also – despite rivalry from Berlin – still an important centre for the art world, with small commercial galleries peppering the inner city.

During the postwar years, Cologne radiated moral authority as the home town of Chancellor Konrad Adenauer and of Heinrich Böll, the Nobel Prize-winning author who was dubbed the "conscience of the nation". Its archbishop – currently the ultra-conservative Cardinal Joachim Meisner – is Germany's senior Catholic cleric. Yet at the same time, this is one of Europe's most liberal cities. One in ten of its one million residents are lesbian or gay, making it a pink citadel to rank with Amsterdam or San Francisco. And though arguments over the construction of a splendid new mosque in the Ehrenfeld district – ten percent of the city's population are Muslim – have threatened to dent the city's liberal reputation, when a group of far-right politicians from across Europe tried to exploit the row in 2008, they were forced to abandon their planned conference in the face of spirited local opposition.

The local tourist office's slogan *Köln ist ein Gefühl* ("Cologne is a Feeling") neatly sums up the city's appeal. You could tick off its sights over the course of a long weekend or so, but if you want to discover how multi-faceted, trendy, fascinating and downright enjoyable this marvellous city really is, you need to get away from the river and the tourist haunts and explore some of the city's quarters where the locals actually live.

Arrival, information and city transport

Cologne-Bonn **airport** (☎02203/40 40 01, ⓦwww.koeln-bonn-airport.de) is southeast of the city, connected by S-Bahn trains every twenty to thirty minutes, taking fifteen minutes to the **Hauptbahnhof**, which is right in the centre of the city alongside the Dom. The city's **tourist office** is right opposite the Dom at Unter Fettenhennen 19 (Mon–Sat 9am–8pm, Sun 10am–5pm; ☎0211/221 304 00, ⓦwww.koeltourismus.de); it offers online accommodation booking through its website, though the tourist office staff can also help in person. The office also organizes **walking tours** (Sat 1pm; €9), will rent you an electronic **iGuide** (4hr €8; 8hr €12) and has a fun souvenir shop in the basement. Cologne is an enjoyable city to explore on foot, but sooner or later you're likely to make use of the **public transport system** (ⓦwww.kvb-koeln.de), which includes S-Bahn and U-Bahn metro networks – the latter emerging above ground at various points to become tramways, extending as far out as Bonn–Bad Godesberg (see p.626). A €1.60 *Kurzstrecke* ticket is valid for up to four stops; to travel further within the city you'll need a €2.40 *CityTicket*, or a €6.90 *TagesTicket*, which can be used from the moment it is validated until 3am the following day. However, if you're anticipating museum-hopping, the **Köln WelcomeCard**, available from the tourist office (24hr €9; 48hr €14; 72hr €19) – which gives twenty percent off municipal museums, reduced entry to many others and unlimited use of the public transport system – is a worthwhile alternative; a family or group card costs respectively €18, €28 or €38. For €5 more than the individual card, you can get the **Pink WelcomeCard**, which in addition to the standard benefits offers reductions in various lesbian and gay bars, shops and businesses.

Accommodation

Cologne has scores of **hotels** in just about every category, though they can still get pretty busy if there's a major trade-fair in town, when prices also take an upward hike across the board. There are plenty of hotels right in the heart of the **Altstadt**, with a cluster of budget and mid-priced options north of the Hauptbahnhof and several swanky business-oriented offerings across the river in **Deutz**. The **Belgisches Viertel** has some stylish small hotels which make a sensible base if Cologne's nightlife or shopping are your priority.

Hotels

Altera Pars Thieboldgasse 133–35 ☎0221/27 23 30, ⍟www.alterapars-koeln.de. Comfortable, gay-friendly hotel above a restaurant, just off Neumarkt and handy for the Rudolfplatz bar scene. ❹

Ariane Hohe Pforte 19–21 ☎0221/759 88 02 10, ⍟www.hotelariane.de. Pleasant, mid-range hotel on the Rosenmontag parade route, with wi-fi in all areas, and a personal trainer available for guests. All rooms are en suite; you have to ask if you want a TV in your room. ❹

Breslauer Hof am Dom Johannisstr. 56 ☎0221/27 64 80, ⍟www.hotel-breslauer-hof.de. Bright, comfortable if slightly characterless rooms – all en suite – and a very central location just across from the Hauptbahnhof make this family-owned hotel very good value. ❸

Chelsea Jülicher Str. 1 ☎0221/20 71 50, ⍟www.hotel-chelsea.de. "Art hotel" in the Belgisches Viertel, with an astonishingly eccentric roof line, artworks by artists who actually have a connection to the place and a good café on the ground floor. The rooms are crisp, modern and minimalist in style, with bath or shower; some have balconies, and the most distinctive are built into the roof structure.❹

Dom Hotel Domkloster 2a ☎0221/202 40, ⍟www.koeln.lemeridien.de. The *grande dame* of Cologne's hotels offers tasteful and luxurious accommodation behind a handsome nineteenth-century facade facing the Dom. Advance rates are very good value. ❼

Eden Hotel Früh am Dom Sporergasse 1 ☎0221/27 29 20, ⍟www.hotel-eden.de. There's a funky, youthful feel to this modern boutique-style hotel next to the Früh Brauhaus, and it's just across from the Dom. ❺

Esplanade Hohenstaufenring 56 ☎0221/921 55 70, ⍟www.hotelesplanade.de. Retro-modern touches in the decor and a great location on the western fringe of the city centre make this a good choice for clubbers or shoppers. ❺

Excelsior Hotel Ernst Domplatz/Trankgasse 1–5 ☎0221/27 01, ⍟www.excelsior-hotel-ernst.de. Truly palatial city-centre hotel with a 140-year history. A member of the Leading Hotels of the World group, it's recently refurbished with a conservative but up-to-date ambience. Doubles from €265. ❾

Hopper et cetera Brüsseler Str. 25 ☎0221/92 44 00, ⍟www.hopper.de. Excellent, Belgisches Viertel boutique hotel in a converted monastery, with bright and stylish – if not particularly huge – rooms, a churchy mural in the restaurant and a waxwork monk in the lobby. ❻

Hopper St Antonius Dagobertstr. 32 ☎0221/166 00, ⍟www.hopper.de. The *Hopper et cetera's* slightly grander sister has bigger rooms, a more sombre colour palate and a quiet location a few minutes' walk north of the Dom. It's popular with media and music business types. ❻

Im Wasserturm Kaygasse 2 ☎0221/200 80, ⍟www.hotel-im-wasserturm.de. The most luxurious and architecturally audacious of Cologne's modern designer hotels really does occupy a converted nineteenth-century water tower, and numbers Brad Pitt and Madonna among its customers. ❽

Maritim Heumarkt 20 ☎0221/202 70, ⍟www.maritim.de. Eye-catching modern architecture and a huge atrium distinguish this smart chain hotel on the south side of Heumarkt. It's also one of the city's most gay-friendly. ❼

Müller Brandenburger Str. 20 ☎0221/912 83 50, ⍟www.hotel-mueller.net. Family-run budget option on a quiet side-street north of the Hauptbahnhof, with a bar and patio garden. ❸

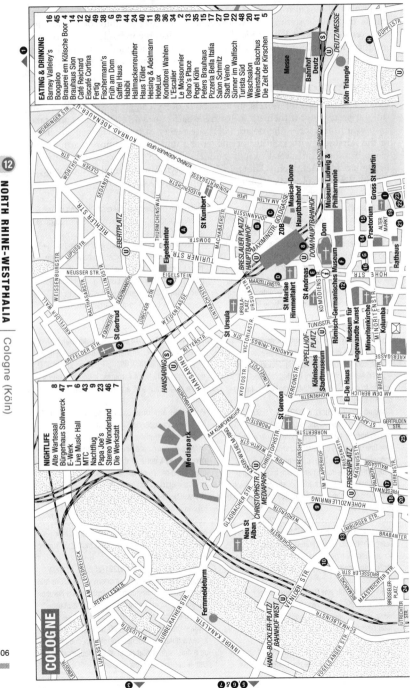

COLOGNE

NIGHTLIFE

Alte Wartesaal	8
Bürgerhaus Stollwerck	47
E-Werk	1
Live Music Hall	6
MTC	43
Nachtflug	9
Papa Joe's	23
Stereo Wonderland	46
Die Werkstatt	7

EATING & DRINKING

Barney Valleley's	16
Boogaloo	45
Brauerei em Kölsche Boor	4
Brauhaus Sion	14
Café Reichard	12
Eiscafé Cortina	42
Fertig	49
Fischermann's	38
Früh am Dom	G
Gaffel Haus	19
Habibi	44
Hallmackenreuther	24
Haus Töller	40
Heising & Adelmann	11
HoteLux	39
Konditorei Wahlen	36
L'Escalier	34
Le Moissonnier	2
Osho's Place	13
Pegel Köln	35
Peters Brauhaus	15
Pizzeria Bella Italia	17
Salon Schmitz	27
Stadt Venlo	10
Sünner im Walfisch	22
Turista Süd	48
Waschsalon	20
Weinstube Bacchus	41
Die Zeit der Kirschen	5

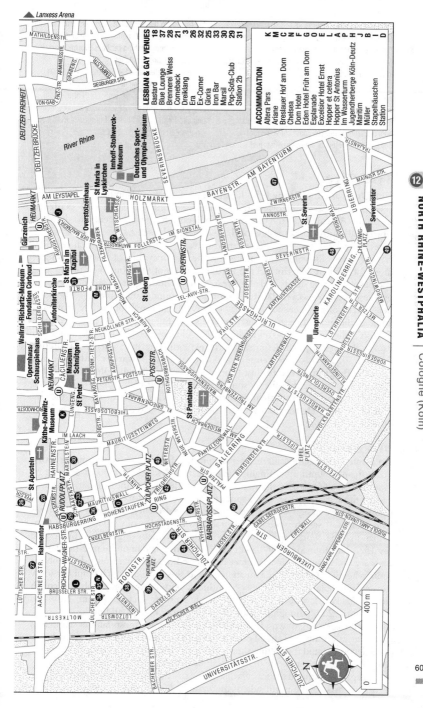

Stapelhäuschen Fischmarkt 1–3 ☎ 0221/272 77 77, ⓦ www.koeln-altstadt.de/stapelhaeuschen. Twee, atmospheric small hotel in one of the Altstadt's rare surviving medieval houses, right next to Gross St Martin. ❸

Hostels

Jugendherberge Köln-Deutz Siegesstr. 5, Deutz ☎ 0221/81 47 11, ⓦ www.koeln-deutz .jugendherberge.de. The most convenient of Cologne's HI hostels is a modern affair just across the river from the Altstadt in Deutz. Accommodation is in two- or four-bed rooms, all of which have shower, WC and washing facilities. Dorms from €23.30, including breakfast.

Station Marzellenstr. 44–56 ☎ 0221/912 53 01, ⓦ www.hostel-cologne.de. Funky, privately run hostel just a few minutes' walk north of the Dom. There are free safes or lockers, plus laundry facilities and free internet access. Dorm beds from €17; singles €30; en-suite doubles ❷.

The City

The **Dom** and the **Rhine** – both just metres from the Hauptbahnhof – are the obvious main points of orientation. Strictly speaking the entire **city centre** is Cologne's Altstadt, since the crescent of boulevards fringing the centre to the west, north and south marks the line of the old medieval fortifications, some of whose gates survive. But the area often referred to as the **Altstadt** – and which certainly has the most old-world atmosphere – is the tight network of lanes and squares around **Gross St Martin** and the **Rathaus**, south of the Dom. West of this area, the main shopping streets – **Hohe Strasse** and **Schildergasse** – run north–south and east–west respectively. West of **Neumarkt** around **Rudolfplatz** is a fashionable district of designer shops and gay bars, while the **north** of the city centre has some of the most interesting museums and sights, but is otherwise relatively quiet. So, too, is the **Severinsviertel** in the south. Cologne's neighbourhoods are known as *Veedel* or *Viertel*; two definitely worth exploring are the studenty **Zülpicher Viertel**, southwest of the centre – also known as the **Kwartier Lateng** – and the chic **Belgisches Viertel** just to its north. Further afield, **Köln-Ehrenfeld** is arty, multicultural and home to some of the city's best clubs, while north of the centre, the **Zoo** and **botanical garden** offer an escape from the noise of the city. Across the river, **Deutz** has more greenery, plus the classic views across the river to the city's skyline.

The Dom

So iconic, so perfectly realized does the profile of Cologne's awe-inspiring **Dom** (daily 6am–7.30pm; free; English-language tour Mon–Sat 10.30am & 2.30pm, Sun 2.30pm, €6) appear that it's a surprise to learn that the familiar silhouette lacked those soaring, 157-metre spires for most of its history. Construction of the Dom – whose design was inspired by the colossal French cathedrals of Beauvais and Amiens – was prompted by the transfer of the relics of the Three Magi from Milan in 1164. Work began in 1248, with the fifty-metre-high choir consecrated by 1322, but stopped in 1560 and remained incomplete until the mid-nineteenth century, when neo-Gothic architect Ernst Friedrich Zwirner finished the job. It's only when you get up close you appreciate its sheer size, at which point the sooty towers resemble vast waterfalls of Gothic sculpture. You can climb the **south tower** (daily: May–Sept 9am–6pm; March, April & Oct 9am–5pm; Nov–Feb 9am–4pm; €2.50), though be warned – there are 509 steps, and no lift.

Once inside, the downside of it being Germany's most famous church is apparent, as grumpy, red-robed officials struggle to maintain some sort of ecclesiastical decorum amid the seething mass of visitors. But look up and you'll forget the crowds, for the genius of the design lies in the way sheer height lends such delicacy and elegance to the structure of what is, by any measure, an enormous building. Five windows on the north side of the nave date from 1507 to 1509, though the

▲ The Dom, Cologne

Dom's oldest window, the *Bible Window*, dates from around 1265 and is in the Chapel of the Three Magi in the ambulatory. The cathedral's treasures include the very **Shrine of the Three Magi** that first inspired its construction; gorgeously gilded and bejewelled, the reliquary dates from around 1190 to 1225 and is behind the high altar. Close by, the so-called **Plan F** is one of seven surviving medieval drawings of the cathedral. It depicts the design of the towers, and was of great help to their nineteenth-century builders. On the north side of the ambulatory, the

Gero Crucifix is the oldest remaining monumental crucifix in the western world; it dates from 970, and originally stood in an early predecessor to the Dom. The most recent addition to the Dom's artworks is the striking 19-metre-high abstract window by Cologne-based artist **Gerhard Richter**, installed in the south transept in 2007. Archbishop Meisner is not a fan, and ruffled feathers when he suggested it might be more at home in a mosque.

The partly subterranean **Domschatzkammer** (daily 10am–6pm; €4) is accessed from the exterior of the cathedral on the north side, and has something of the air of a bank vault, which is hardly surprising given the priceless works of religious art it contains, or the fact that one of them – the jewelled, seventeenth-century **Sumptuous Monstrance** – was badly damaged by thieves in 1975. The treasury occupies a series of thirteenth-century vaults, and its artefacts are beautifully lit and presented: particularly eye-catching are the gilded silver **bishop's crosier** dating from 1322 and the so-called **St Peter's Crosier**, which is Roman and dates from the fourth century AD. Also on display is the original wooden structure of the **Shrine of the Three Magi**, while on the museum's lower level it's possible to see a fragment of the Roman city wall and the finds from two sixth-century Frankish tombs.

The Roman city

Riches from Cologne's Roman past are housed in the **Römisch-Germanisches Museum** on the south side of the Dom (Tues–Sun 10am–5pm; €6, or €7.50 combined ticket with Praetorium), whose most famous exhibit is the third-century **Dionysos mosaic** discovered on the site as an air-raid shelter was being dug in 1941. It originally formed the floor of a dining room leading off the peristyle or courtyard of a grand villa, and is startling in its completeness, size and beauty. The imposing mausoleum of the Roman soldier Lucius Poblicius, which dates from 40 AD, rises from the museum's lower level to utterly dominate the staircase. Though there are plenty of impressive chunks of Roman stone in the museum, it's often the smaller, more everyday objects that are the most revealing, from the locally produced second-century glassware to the personal effects of Cologne's Roman citizens, which include mirrors, razors, hairpins and some delightful children's toys. Incidentally, the modest heap of stones in front of the Dom's west front is what survives of the Roman city's **North Gate**.

A few minutes' walk to the south, an inconspicuous doorway on Kleine Budengasse west of Alter Markt leads to the remains of the **Praetorium** (Tues–Sun 10am–5pm; €2.50, or combined ticket with Römisch-Germanisches Museum), the Roman palace of the governors of Lower Germania and the most important Roman building in the region.

Museum Ludwig

A very modern contrast to the Roman city's glories is provided by the **Museum Ludwig** (Tues–Sun 10am–6pm, until 10pm first Fri of the month; €9), sandwiched between the Roman museum, Dom and river. Though it has a fascinatingly complex contemporary roofscape, the museum is a self-effacing work of architecture that doesn't try to compete with the glories of the Dom. Inside, a succession of handsome and light-flooded spaces provides a wonderful setting for an exceptional collection of modern art. The museum's particular strong point is Pop Art of the 1960s and 1970s, and you can feast your eyes on works by David Hockney, Roy Lichtenstein and Robert Rauschenberg, admire Claes Oldenburg's *Giant Soft Swedish Light Switch* or Duane Hanson's lifelike *Woman with a Purse*, and see Warhol's celebrated works depicting Brillo and Campbell's soup boxes. The museum also has a roomful of works by Max

Beckmann, several Expressionist canvases by Karl Schmidt-Rottluff and Emil Nolde's stunning *Nach Sonnenuntergang* of 1915. Steps lead down from the back of the Museum Ludwig to the riverside, where an inconspicuous **monument** recalls the Nazis' lesbian and gay victims. You can also cross the river here by the footpath along the south side of the **Hohenzollern railway bridge**.

Gross St Martin and the Rathaus

One of Cologne's great architectural glories is the collection of twelve **Romanesque churches** that have survived – albeit variously battered and rebuilt – to the present day. The most imposing, if not necessarily the most beautiful, is **Gross St Martin**, south of the Dom (Tues–Fri 10am–noon & 3–5pm, Sat 10am–12.30pm, 1.30–5pm, Sun 2–4pm), a former Benedictine monastery whose monumental square tower was the dominant feature of the city's skyline until the Dom acquired its towers. The narrow lanes that huddle around it convey the atmosphere of medieval Cologne better than anywhere else in the city, though many of the **Martinsviertel**'s "medieval" houses only date from the mid-1930s, when the Nazis spruced up the hitherto unsanitary and poverty-ridden quarter. Genuinely old specimens include the much-photographed **Stapelhäuschen** in front of the church. Altogether more splendid are the Renaissance **Haus St Peter** on Heumarkt and the incredibly tall, double-gabled **Zur Brezel/Zur Dorn** on Alter Markt, which dates from 1580 to 1582.

The sprawling **Rathaus** (Mon, Wed & Thurs 8am–4pm, Tues 8am–6pm, Fri 8am–2pm; free) occupies much of the space between Alter Markt and Rathausplatz. Seriously damaged during World War II, the complex now presents a dizzying array of styles, from Gothic to 1970s. Miraculously, the beautiful Renaissance **Rathauslaube**, or porch, built between 1569 and 1573 to the plans of Wilhelm Vernukken of Kalkar, was only lightly damaged during the war. Another surviving feature is the eight-sided, fifteenth-century Gothic **tower**. Highlights of the interior include the **Hansa Hall** dating from 1330 and the rich Renaissance decoration of the Senatssaal or Senate Hall, which escaped destruction by being removed for safekeeping during the war. In front of the Rathaus, the foundations of the medieval **synagogue** and **Jewish quarter** are currently the subject of further excavations, which will link with the Praetorium to form a new subterranean archeological museum by 2011.

The Wallraf-Richartz Museum and around

The south side of Rathausplatz is dominated by the clean modern lines of the **Wallraf-Richartz-Museum/Fondation Corboud** (Tues, Wed & Fri 10am–6pm, Thurs 10am–10pm, Sat & Sun 11am–6pm; €6–9 depending on exhibitions), beautifully laid out and curated in such a way that it offers a coherent lesson in art history. It has an important collection of medieval Cologne art, Flemish and Dutch masters, and French and German art of the nineteenth and early twentieth centuries. Medieval highlights include Stefan Lochner's *Virgin in the Rose Bower* (c.1440–42), as well as works by Albrecht Dürer and Lucas Cranach the Elder, and the depiction of the legend of St Ursula in fifteen paintings on wood by the Kölnischer Meister of 1456. Rubens' gory *Juno and Argus* of 1610 is one of the highlights of the second floor, where you can also see Van Dyck's *Jupiter as Satyr with Antiope* from 1620 and a late Rembrandt self-portrait among a considerable trove of Flemish and Dutch masters. The top floor's highlights include some typically symbolic works by Caspar David Friedrich, Wilhelm Leibl's lovely *Girl at a Window* of 1899 and *The Lady of Frankfurt* by Leibl's French contemporary and associate, Gustave Courbet. Other works include Max Liebermann's *The Bleaching Ground* and several Impressionists, including a 1915 Monet *Water Lilies* that is already well on the way to abstraction.

Just behind the museum on Martinstrasse, the **Gürzenich**, a fifteenth-century banqueting hall, is another much-mauled but impressive survivor from Cologne's medieval heyday, and is closely associated with Cologne's carnival festivities (see box, p.619). The neighbouring church of **St Alban**, left a ruin as a war memorial, is currently undergoing restoration. A short walk to the south is another of the city's Romanesque churches, **St Maria im Kapitol**, which is hemmed in by houses and so despite its size it's as self-effacing as Gross St Martin is bombastic. The oldest parts of the church – which was built as a convent on the site of a Roman temple – date from the middle of the eleventh century. It has a trefoiled choir based closely on the plans of the Church of the Nativity in Bethlehem. The city's last surviving Romanesque merchant's house, the step-gabled **Overstolzenhaus**, is nearby at Rheingasse 8. A few minutes' walk to the west of St Maria im Kapitol at Cäcilienstrasse 29–33, the deconsecrated **Cäcilienkirche** provides a suitable setting for the **Museum Schnütgen**'s collection of medieval religious art (Tues–Fri 10am–5pm, Sat & Sun 11am–5pm; €3.20).

The **Rheinauhalbinsel** jetty on the riverside is home to two museums, the child- and chocoholic-friendly **Schokoladenmuseum** (Tues–Fri 10am–6pm, Sat & Sun 11am–7pm; €7.50) and the more worthy but imaginatively presented **Deutsches Sport & Olympia Museum** (same hours; €5), whose highlights include displays relating to the 1936 Berlin and 1972 Munich Olympics, as well as winter sports, football and boxing.

Kolumba and around

Standing atop the war-shattered remains of the church of St Kolumba and incorporating them into its design, **Kolumba**, Kolumbastrasse 4 (daily except Tues noon–5pm; €5; @www.kolumba.de), houses the art collection of the Diocese of Cologne. Though the theme of the collection is spiritual, this is no narrow display of conventional religious iconography, as the inclusion of kinetic sculptures by Rebecca Horn and of work by Joseph Beuys demonstrates. One of the museum's greatest treasures is Stefan Lochner's *Madonna with the Violet*; it's arguable, however, that the stunning building itself is at least as memorable as the collection, which it displays with lavish spaciousness, and there are superb views of the Dom from its upstairs windows. Right across the street, the sweeping curve of the **Disch Haus** – a Weimar-era office building – has been beautifully restored and provides an excellent architectural foil to the museum.

Close by at **Glockengasse 4711** (Mon–Fri 9am–7pm, Sat 9am–6pm; free) are the premises of the famous manufacturer of *Kölnisches Wasser* – Eau de Cologne – which derives its brand name from the number allocated to the house on Glockengasse by occupying French troops in 1796. The French connection is acknowledged by the carillon on the building's south facade, which plays the *Marseillaise* every hour on the hour. Inside, there's a small museum and a fountain of cologne, which you can dip into free of charge.

The northwest Altstadt

A short walk to the north of Glockengasse at An der Rechtschule, the **Museum für Angewandte Kunst** (Tues–Sun 11am–5pm; €4.20) presents the city's substantial collection of applied art, including the work of such big-name international designers as Charles Eames and Philippe Starck, alongside fine art by Mondrian, Kandinsky and others. To the west at Zeughausstrasse 1–3, a winged, gilded Ford car atop the medieval city armoury announces the **Kölnisches**

Stadtmuseum (Tues 10am–8pm, Wed–Sun 10am–5pm; €4.20; free English audio guide), which takes an engrossing journey through Cologne's long history. Among its exhibits is a huge model of the city based on Mercator's 1571 plan, which shows quite extensive areas within the walls were given over not to buildings, but to vineyards. There's also a model of one of the extraordinary log rafts that were once floated down the Rhine to satisfy the enormous demand for timber. They could be 300m long and had accommodation on board for the four to five hundred people needed to crew them. In the Middle Ages, seagoing ships could go no further upriver than Cologne, and the city's prosperity was greatly aided by the *Stapelrecht* – a law that stipulated merchants had to offer their goods for sale to the citizens of Cologne before they were allowed to transship them. It persisted until 1831. The museum also has displays on Cologne in the Nazi era, which is covered in more depth at the **El-De Haus** around the corner at Apellhofplatz 23–25 (Tues–Fri 10am–4pm, Sat & Sun 11am–4pm; €3.60; English audio guide €2). Here, the crimes of the Nazi regime in Cologne are documented in the city's former Gestapo headquarters. The exhibition squarely demolishes the idea that the Nazis enjoyed no support in Cologne, and among the most chilling exhibits are the letters written by two elderly female residents of a retirement home, denouncing their young parish priest.

West of the El-De Haus is **St Gereon** (daily 10am–6pm; closed during Sun mass), the most memorable of all Cologne's Romanesque churches thanks to the spectacular decagon at its heart, a monumental space which blends late Romanesque and early Gothic elements. It was reworked into its current form in the early thirteenth century, when the oval core of the church was already nine hundred years old. Some of its medieval frescoes have survived, making its interior less austere than some Cologne churches. Nearby, the well-preserved **Römerturm** at the eastern end of Friesenstrasse was the northwest corner tower of the city's Roman fortifications. It dates from around 50 AD, and is decorated with mosaic-like stone patterns. The bars and restaurants of the attractive **Friesenviertel**, which stretches west along Friesenstrasse and south along Friesenwall, are the stamping ground of trendy media types; the district also preserves some of the tall, narrow town houses that were once characteristic of Cologne's inner city.

Rudolfplatz and around

At the western extremity of the Ring, the series of roads that mark the old city walls, one surviving medieval gate presides over bustling **Rudolfplatz**. By day this square hosts an organic farmer's market, while the surrounding shopping streets are among the city's best – **Ehrenstrasse** is young and trendy, while the boutiques of **Pfeilstrasse** and **Mittelstrasse** are chic and expensive. At night, this area is the main hub of the city's nightlife, and also of its lesbian and gay scene. At the eastern end of Mittelstrasse, a bronze of Germany's first postwar chancellor (and former Cologne mayor) Konrad Adenauer stands in front of the Romanesque church of **St Aposteln**. There's a small exhibit on the church's history – including wartime damage and reconstruction – inside. St Aposteln faces out over **Neumarkt**, the western limit of the central pedestrian zone and an important transport hub. High above the Neumarkt Passage on the north side of the square is the small **Käthe Kollwitz Museum Köln** (Tues–Fri 10am–6pm, Sat & Sun 11am–6pm; €3), which exhibits the largest existing collection of lithographs, drawings and watercolours by the antiwar artist, who was increasingly preoccupied by themes of death after her son was killed in Flanders in World War I. Her compassion for wider human suffering is evident throughout the museum.

The Belgisches Viertel, Zülpicher Viertel and Severinsviertel

West of the Ring, the beautiful Jugendstil apartment buildings of the **Belgisches Viertel** escaped wartime bombing and are now among the most sought-after in the city. Cologne's most fashionable district, it's a great place to linger over a *Milchkaffee* or glass of wine between extensive bouts of window-shopping in the area's numerous small boutiques. From Zülpicher Platz, Zülpicher Strasse heads southwest to define the so-called **Kwartier Lateng**, which in recent years has become a funky strip of student-friendly bars, restaurants and shops, thanks in part to its proximity to the university. On Chlodwigplatz at the southern tip of the Ring, the medieval **Severinstor** leads into the **Severinsviertel**, presided over by yet another Romanesque church, the **Severinskirche**, and with something of the air of a separate town – if you've seen the Mercator plan in the Stadtmuseum, you'll understand why, for in the Middle Ages the Severinsviertel, though within the city walls, was separated from Cologne's centre by extensive vineyards. At Severinstrasse 15, the tall, gabled **Haus Balchem** dating from 1676 is one of the best-preserved historic merchant's houses in the city.

Beyond the centre: Ehrenfeld, the Zoo and Deutz

A stroll northwest from bustling Friesenplatz, on the liveliest section of the Ring, along Venloer Strasse and into **Ehrenfeld** is instructive for anyone wishing to get to grips with Cologne's multicultural character. A working-class neighbourhood that has latterly acquired a bohemian overlay, it's one of the most cosmopolitan corners of the city, with everything from Turkish travel agents and baklava bakeries to a Provencal café and an Asian tea shop. Many of its residents are of Turkish origin, and it's here that Cologne's new central **mosque** will be built. Old industrial areas west of Venloer Strasse have been partly reworked as studio space for artists, and the area also has many gay and lesbian residents. It wasn't always so tolerant: towards the end of World War II, the Nazis staged mass executions here of slave labourers and of *Edelweisspiraten* – members of an anti-authoritarian youth movement who refused to participate in the Hitler Youth.

Stumbling blocks of history

You first notice them almost by accident, as the sun catches the pavement and something glitters underfoot. Yet once you've spotted your first **Stolperstein** – the name means, literally "stumbling block", you'll keep stumbling over more. The little brass plaques, memorials to individual victims of the Nazis which usually stand in front of the house from which that victim was taken, are the work of Gunter Demnig, a Berlin-born but Cologne-based artist, who in the past eighteen years has laid 17,000 *Stolpersteine* in Germany and others in Poland, Austria, Hungary, the Czech Republic and the Netherlands. They are particularly thick on the ground in the Zülpicher Viertel and Belgisches Viertel, close to the Roonstrasse synagogue; you'll sometimes stumble across a dozen or more in front of a single house. Incredibly moving, they're the antithesis of the big, official monuments to the Holocaust: they record the name, birth-date and fate – as far as it is known – of an individual. Chillingly, in many cases, the story is the same: deported and *verschollen* – missing, presumed dead. The placement of the stones outside the homes of the victims means the fate of entire families is often recorded. While many of the individuals remembered by the stones are Jewish, there are also *Stolpersteine* for political opponents of the regime, for the murdered Sinti and Roma, and for the Nazis' gay victims.

North of the centre, Cologne's child- (and parent-) friendly **Zoo** at Riehler Strasse 173 (daily: March–Oct 9am–6pm; Nov–Feb 9am–5pm; €13; U-Bahn Zoo/Flora) and its sweetly old-fashioned **Botanischer Garten** (daily 8am–dusk; free) are pleasant escapes from the bustle of the city on a fine day. The latter has tropical and arid hothouses, formal flowerbeds and a kitchen garden. A cable car, the **Kölner Seilbahn** (April–Oct daily 10am–6pm; €4 single, €6 return) connects the Zoo with the **Rheingarten** park on the opposite side of the river in **Deutz** – the views en route are spectacular. The Rheingarten provides ample space for lazing in the sun as well as boasting an exclusive spa, the **Claudius Therme** (daily 9am–midnight; 2hr from €14).

Deutz's **riverside** offers the classic view of Cologne's **skyline** across the Rhine. More dramatic still are the views from the observation platform atop the steel and glass **KölnTriangle** skyscraper, at Ottoplatz 1 on the eastern end of the Hohenzollernbrücke (May–Sept Mon–Fri 11am–10pm, Sat & Sun 10am–10pm; Oct–April Mon–Fri noon–6pm, Sat & Sun 10am–6pm; €3), though light bouncing off the platform's glass screens sometimes thwarts attempts to get reflection-free photographs.

Eating and drinking

The **Altstadt** is the first port of call for most visitors looking for somewhere to **eat** or **drink**, and it's here that the traditional *Brauhäuser* are thickest on the ground, serving up hearty portions of eccentrically named Cologne specialities to help soak up the dainty glasses of local beer *Kölsch* (see box, p.616). Many of Cologne's most interesting and fashionable places to eat and drink are, however, on the western fringe of the centre, where **Hohenzollernring**'s raucous strip of bars, restaurants and cinemas provides the focus, but with maximum charm found in the streets of the **Belgisches Viertel** to the west. Studenty Zülpicher Strasse – the so-called **Kwartier Lateng** or Latin Quarter – is good for bars, but is above all the city's most fertile hunting-ground for cheap eats.

Restaurants and cafés

Café Reichard Unter Fettenhennen 11 ☎0221/257 85 42. The classic *Kaffee und Kuchen* stop – and the seats on the terrace have a superb view of the west front of the Dom.

Eiscafé Cortina Hohenstaufenring 22. Classic 1950s-style Italian *gelateria* with huge windows and a terrace fronting the Ring. The frozen yoghurt is particularly delicious.

Fertig Bonner Str. 26 ☎0221/801 73 40. Hearty portions of French-accented bistro food, from confit of duck to tuna steak with thyme, dished up in informal surroundings south of the Severinstor.

Fischermann's Rathenauplatz 21 ☎0221/801 77 90. Asian and Mediterranean influences blend in the cooking of this trendy restaurant and cocktail bar; main courses from around €13.

Habibi Zülpicher Str. 28. Huge portions of cheap, wholesome falafel-based meals make this Kwartier Lateng café a Cologne institution, complete with Arab pop music and a studenty clientele.

Heising & Adelmann Friesenstr. 58–60 ☎0221/130 94 24. Smart Friesenviertel restaurant and cocktail bar favoured by media types; the garden at the back is much in demand in fine weather. Eve only, closed Sun.

Konditorei Wahlen Hohenstaufenring 64. Absolutely classic, plushly old-fashioned coffee-and-cake place – cossetting, comfortable and civilized.

L'Escalier Brüsseler Str. 11 ☎0221/205 39 98. Highly respected gourmet restaurant dishing up surprisingly affordable, seasonal dishes – including a bargain €19.50 two-course lunch with wine – to an appreciative public in the Belgisches Viertel. Closed Sun.

Le Moissonnier Krefelder Str. 25 ☎0221/72 94 79. Superlative French cooking – at a price – at this renowned restaurant in the north of the city. Main courses from around €33, or there's a four-course weekday menu for €62.50. Closed Sun & Mon.

Osho's Place Venloer Str. 5–7 ☎0221/800 05 81. Bright, modern veggie place, with Asian-influenced food, monthly sushi evenings and a regular Sunday brunch buffet.

Pizzeria Bella Italia Freisenwall 52 ☎0221/277 46 22. Clubbers swear by this astonishingly cheap-and-cheerful Italian, which stays open until 2am on Fri and Sat nights; pizzas from around €3.

Waschsalon Ehrenstr. 77. Washing machines reworked as decor dominate this busy café, which offers a large range of breakfast options, though the bill can mount rapidly if you're too free with the drinks and extras.

🏃 **Die Zeit der Kirschen** Venloer Str. 399 ☎0221/954 19 06. Creative, modern European cooking in elegant surroundings – with a peaceful garden out back – make this modish Ehrenfeld restaurant well worth the short U-Bahn trip. Main courses around €15. Closed Sat lunch. U-Bahn Venloer Str/Gürtel.

Café-bars, Brauhäuser and bars

Barney Valleley's Kleine Budengasse 7. The inevitable Irish bar and expat hangout, complete with hurling or Premiership football on TV and Guinness and Murphy's on draught.

Boogaloo Roonstr. 19. Hip Zülpicher Viertel bar with artfully distressed retro decor and a soul to latin music policy.

Brauerei em Kölsche Boor Eigelstein 121–23 ☎0221/13 52 27. Traditional *Brauhaus* a little off the beaten track, and hence less obviously touristy than some of the more central offerings, with *Gaffel Kölsch* to wash down the hearty and reasonably priced Rhineland dishes.

Brauhaus Sion Unter Taschenmacher 5–7 ☎0221/257 85 40. Cavernous *Brauhaus* belonging to the Sion brewery, rebuilt after wartime destruction in finest 1950s "traditional" style; more sedate than some, with sausages and local dishes like *Dicke Bohnen* on the menu.

Früh am Dom Am Hof 12 ☎0221/361 22 11. Much the most atmospheric (and frequently the busiest) of the big Altstadt *Brauhäuser*, with a labyrinthine interior. The cheeky waiters and general bustle are all part of the experience, as are the Cologne *Brauhaus* staples like *Kölsche Kaviar* and *Halver Hahn*.

Gaffel Haus Alter Markt 20–22 ☎0221/257 76 92. A plum position on Alter Markt – complete with sunny terrace – and a dark, cluttered interior characterize this Altstadt *Brauhaus*, which, as the name suggests, has *Gaffel Kölsch* on draught as well as inexpensive local food.

🏃 **Hallmackenreuther** Brüsseler Platz 9 ☎0221/51 79 70. Wonderful retro-Sixties decor and a peaceful location overlooking a leafy square make this trendy Belgisches Viertel bar a winner.

Haus Töller Weyerstr. 96 ☎0221/258 93 16. Lovely, long-established *Brauhaus* close to Barbarossaplatz, nothing like as touristy as the Altstadt haunts but with plenty of atmosphere; there's draught Päffgen Kölsch to drink and Rhineland specialities such as *Sauerbraten* to eat. Closed Sun.

HoteLux Rathenauplatz 22. Mad, vibrant and tiny Soviet-themed vodka bar with lurid red decor, Polish and Russian vodkas and "Soviet" cocktails. Open until 3am Sat & Sun.

Pegel Köln Brüsseler Str. 10. Stripped-down, rather industrial-feeling DJ bar in the Belgisches Viertel, closed Sun.

Peters Brauhaus Mühlengasse 1 ☎0221/257 39 50. Big yet surprisingly cosy and intimate Altstadt *Brauhaus*, serving a bewilderingly large choice of Cologne delicacies to anchor down the eponymous Kölsch.

Salon Schmitz Aachener Str. 28 ☎0221/139 55 77. Elegantly decorated Belgisches Viertel bar that attracts a good looking, trendy thirty-something crowd. There's food available from the beautiful former butcher's shop next door.

Stadt Venlo Venloer Str. 29. The 1960s decor makes this quirky Belgisches Viertel DJ bar a real period piece, yet it's extremely hip, attracting a studeny crowd and playing an offbeat selection of music, including New Wave and Reggae.

Kölsch – the local accent on beer

Kölsch is not only the name of the local Cologne dialect – one of the strongest regional accents in all Germany and positively mystifying to foreign visitors – but also of the city's deliciously refreshing, hoppy, top-fermented beer, traditionally drunk in tall, slim 0.2 litre glasses known as *Stangen*, though these days there's a certain amount of glass-size inflation going on to please German and foreign visitors accustomed to drinking their beer in larger measures. Brewery-owned or -affiliated *Brauhäuser* (or *Bierhäuser*) represent the traditional core of Cologne's eating and drinking scene, and there's a whole range of colourfully named local dishes to accompany the *Kölsch*, from *Kölsche Kaviar* – in reality blood sausage – to *Halver Hahn* – a cheese roll rather than the "half a chicken" the name suggests – and *Hämmche* – pig's trotter. The characteristically self-aggrandizing behaviour of the cheeky *Köbes* or waiters rounds off a highly distinctive, regional beer culture.

Sünner im Walfisch Salzgasse 13 ☎0221/257 78 79. *Matjes* herrings and *Brauhaus* classics soak up the beer in the classy setting of this gabled medieval house, moved to its present site in 1935.
Turista Süd Severinstr. 3. Amiable, low-key Spanish tapas bar in the Severinsviertel.

Weinstube Bacchus Rathenauplatz 17 ☎0221/21 79 86. Charmingly unpretentious neighbourhood *Weinstube*, with a pretty terrace at the front, a good selection of German and international wines, and locals playing board games inside. They also serve food. Eve only.

The lesbian and gay scene

Cologne's **lesbian and gay scene** is one of the biggest in Europe, catering not just to the one in ten city residents who identify as lesbian or gay but also to regular weekend visitors from Düsseldorf, the Ruhr and further afield. Though **club** nights take place at venues all over the city, there are two main focuses for the bar scene: the traditional bars attracting an older, mostly male clientele to the **Altstadt** area between Alter Markt and Heumarkt – also the focus for the summer's Christopher Street Day celebrations – and the rather larger and more fashionable scene focused on **Rudolfplatz**. Pick up a free copy of the monthly *Rik* magazine from bars for comprehensive **listings** (in German) and good, clear maps to help you find it all. **Christopher Street Day** (Ⓦwww.csd-cologne.de) all but takes over the city in late June and early July, regularly attracting between 750,000 and a million people to see the colourful parade that snakes its way through the city on the final day. What follows is a selection of the most popular venues and club nights.

Lesbian and gay cafés, bars and clubs

Bastard Friesenwall 29. Café/bar in a *Hinterhof* close to Ehrenstrasse's shopping, and especially popular for its outside seating on two levels.
Blue Lounge Mathiasstr. 4–6. Bar and dance club attracting a mixed clientele, particularly popular with lesbians.
Brennerei Weiss Hahnenstr. ☎0221/257 46 38. Traditional restaurant which gradually becomes more bar-like as the evening goes on, and is popular with both gay men and lesbians.
Comeback Alter Markt 10. One of the nicer of the Altstadt's gay bars, with a touch of theatricality and a terrace fronting the square outside.
Dreiklang at ARTheater, Ehrenfeldgürtel 127, Ⓦwww.artheater.de. Long-running club night for lesbians, gay men and gay-friendly heteros, with a similarly eclectic music policy, spinning everything from indie, Brit- and Deutsch-Pop to house. Third Fri of the month. U-Bahn 3 or 4 to Venloer Gürtel.

Era Friesenwall 26. The smartest of the Rudolfplatz area's many gay-oriented café-bars, and a good spot for a late breakfast.
Ex-Corner Schaafenstr. 57–59. The absolute lynchpin of the Rudolfplatz scene, this is one gay bar that is busy even during the week, when much of the Cologne scene is otherwise quiet. Cruisy, but jolly with it.
Gloria Apostelnstr. 11. One of the main gay and lesbian club venues is this 1950s theatre, complete with a beautiful café at the front.
Iron Bar Schaafenstr. 45. Excellent, spacious cocktail bar in the Rudolfplatz district that also serves surprisingly good German wines.
Marsil Marsilstein 27. Small but perfectly formed, *Marsil* is the most chic gay men's bar in the city, and regularly attracts a good-looking crowd.
Pop-Sofa-Club at *Teatro*, Rudolfplatz Ⓦwww.pop-sofa-club.de The most successful lesbian club night in Cologne; check the website for upcoming dates.
Station 2b Pipinstr. 2. Cologne's biggest leather and fetish bar, open until 5am Fri & Sat.

Nightlife, entertainment and festivals

As befits a major city and media centre, Cologne is a superb place for **live music**, with everything from small clubs featuring up-and-coming bands to stadium-style venues for the monsters of the international rock circuit, as well as **jazz**, **opera** and **classical music**. The **club scene** is characterized by regularly changing themed nights, often in converted theatres or industrial premises. Kino Off Broadway, 24 Zülpicher Strasse (☎0221/23 24 18, Ⓦwww.off-broadway.de), frequently shows English-language **films** in the original version with German subtitles, while if your German is up to it the city has a thriving **theatre** scene, with around sixty venues. Cologne's **football** team, FC Köln (Ⓦwww.fc-koeln.de), plays at the RheinEnergieStadion in Müngersdorf, west of the city. The city's German-language **listings magazine**, *Stadt Revue*, costs €2 from bookshops and newsstands.

Cologne's biggest festival is without doubt **Karneval**, which is celebrated with as much ritual and dedication to frivolity here as it is in Rio, filling the streets and bringing normal life to a standstill, never mind that the February weather in the Rhineland is nothing like as tempting as in Brazil. In recent years, the **Christopher Street Day** parade (see p.617) has evolved into a summer equivalent of Rosenmontag, with the fun by no means restricted to the lesbian and gay community. In the run-up to **Christmas**, a traditional market fills Roncalliplatz on the south side of the Dom, with others on Alter Markt, Heumarkt, Neumarkt and Rudolfplatz.

Clubs, cabaret and live music

Alte Wartesaal Johannisstr. 11, Hauptbahnhof ☎0221/912 88 50. Elegant old former station waiting-room that now provides a plush and intimate venue for various club nights.

Bürgerhaus Stollwerck Dreikönigenstr. 23 ☎0221/991 10 80, Ⓦwww.buergerhausstollwerck.de. Community arts centre in a vast former chocolate factory in the Severinsviertel, the venue for small-scale drama, comedy and cabaret.

E-Werk Schanzenstr. 37 Ⓦwww.e-werk-cologne.com. Beautifully restored nineteenth-century power station northeast of the centre that's now a spacious live music venue and disco.

Lanxess Arena Willy-Brandt-Platz, Deutz ☎0221/80 20, Ⓦwww.lanxess-arena.de. Purpose-built stadium-style venue – the largest of its kind in Germany – for major rock concerts and other large-scale events.

Live Music Hall Lichtstr. 30 ☎0221/954 29 90. Club and live music venue in an industrial zone in Ehrenfeld. At Saturday's *Rockgarden* there's free beer 10pm–midnight. U-Bahn 3 or 4 to Venloer Gürtel.

MTC Zülpicherstr. 10 ☎0221/240 41 88, Ⓦwww.mtcclub.de. One of Cologne's more intimate live venues, with a varied roster of bands playing everything from psychobilly to acoustic hip-hop.

Musical Dome Köln Goldgasse 1 ☎0221/734 41 50, Ⓦwww.musical-dome.de. Purpose-built venue for big-name international musicals.

Nachtflug Hohenzollernring 87 ☎0177 4000 901, Ⓦwww.nachtflug.com. City-centre disco with a regularly-changing programme of events, including the evergreen pan-sexual after-hours club *Greenkomm*, from 7am the first Sunday of the month.

Papa Joe's Buttermarkt 37 ☎0221/257 79 31, Ⓦwww.papajoes.de. This Altstadt jazz club claims to be Germany's oldest, with a sister bar on Alter Markt.

Stereo Wonderland Trierer Str. 7. DJ bar and music venue in the Kwartier Lateng, with regular live bands and a music policy that spans everything from punk chanson to electro.

Die Werkstatt Grüner Weg 1b ☎0221/356 39 15, Ⓦwww.werkstatt-koeln.de. Hip club and live venue in Ehrenfeld, with DJs spinning trash pop, punk and electro. U-Bahn 3 or 4 to Venloer Gürtel.

Theatre, opera and classical music

Hänneschen – Puppenspiele der Stadt Köln Eisenmarkt 2–4 ☎0221/258 12 01. Long-established and very famous puppet theatre, whose performances are in the local *Kölsch* dialect, which even native German-speakers struggle to understand.

Kölner Oper Offenbachplatz ☎0221/22 12 84 00, Ⓦwww.buehnenkoeln.de. One of the city's major postwar landmarks, Cologne's opera house presents classic and less well-known operas as well as children's opera in the Yakult-Halle, and occasional Jewish klezmer shows.

Philharmonie Franziusstr. 7 ☎0211/66 96 99 90, Ⓦwww.koelner-philharmonie.de. The city's major classical concert hall is the home for two orchestras, the Gürzenich-Orchester and the WDR-Sinfonieorchester, as well as providing a venue for jazz and pop concerts.

Schauspiel Köln Offenbachplatz ☎0221/22 12 84 00. The city's major stage for theatre is part of the same complex as the opera house. It also hosts ballet and other music-related performances. A glittering new theatre is planned to replace the existing 1950s building over the next few years.

The so-called "fifth season" is officially launched each year at 11.11am on November 11, but **Karneval** (Ⓦ www.karneval.de) doesn't really get underway properly until the New Year, with around six hundred Karneval-related events – including balls and *Sitzungen* or sessions, where *Bütten* or carnival speeches are made – taking place between then and Ash Wednesday. The season reaches its climax with the **Tolle Tage** or "crazy days", beginning on the Thursday before Ash Wednesday with **Weiberfastnacht** or Women's Day. This is a bad day to wear a tie if you're a man, because it will get snipped off, the symbolism of which is somewhat obvious. The **Rosenmontag** procession on the following Monday is the undoubted highpoint of Karneval, with wonderfully silly costumes and floats, presided over by the *Prinz* (the master of ceremonies), the *Bauer* (a farmer) and the *Jungfrau* or maiden, who is represented by a man in drag (though this aspect was suppressed by the Nazis). Around a million people turn out to see the **Rosenmontag** procession, which takes around four hours to wind its way through the city centre, as sweets (*Kamelle*), bouquets (*Strüsjer*) and other goodies are thrown at the *Jecke* – the "fools" or spectators – from the passing floats, and all and sundry cry *Kölle Alaaf!* – the carnival greeting, which is a dialect derivation of "*Köln über alles*" or, freely translated, "up with/long live Cologne". In parallel with the official carnival events, there's a lively alternative scene, including a gay and lesbian element.

Listings

Banks and exchange There are currency exchange facilities in the airport's terminals, while most bank ATMs recognize major debit or credit cards.
Bookshops Thalia and Mayersche on Neumarkt are both large bookshops which have English-language sections, as does Ludwig in the Hauptbahnhof.
Car rental Avis, airport ☎ 02203/402 243, Hauptbahnhof ☎ 0221/913 00 63; Alamo, airport ☎ 02203/40 24 59; Europcar, airport ☎ 02203/95 58 80, Hauptbahnhof ☎ 0221/139 27 48.
Helicopter tours Lifeflight, Marienburger Str. 44 (☎ 0700/54 33 35 44, Ⓦ www.lifeflight.de) offers helicopter sightseeing trips over Cologne from €143.10.
Pharmacies in Hauptbahnhof (☎ 0221/139 11 12); Gürzenich Apotheke, Gürzenichstr. 6 (☎ 0221/ 277 22 74); Hof Apotheke, Wallrafplatz 1 (☎ 0221/258 04 71). There's also a pharmacy at the airport.
Post office Breite Str. 6–26 (Mon–Fri 9am–7pm, Sat 9am–2pm).

River cruises Boats of the KD Köln-Düsseldorfer fleet (☎ 0221/208 83 18, Ⓦ www.k-d.de) anchor in front of Gross St Martin and offer a variety of excursions all year round, including dinner cruises and trips south past Bonn and the Siebengebirge. Boats belonging to Kölntourist (☎ 0221/12 16 00, Ⓦ www.koelntourist.net) follow similar itineraries.
Sightseeing tours Tourist Shuttle (Ⓦ www.hop-on-hop-off.de; €10), Cologne Coach Service (☎ 0221/979 25 70, Ⓦ www.ccs-busreisen.de; €10) and Kölner City Tour (☎ 0221/270 45 66, Ⓦ www.cityfahrten.de; €10) offer sightseeing bus trips with English commentary, or there's a miniature tourist train, Wolters Bimmelbahn (☎ 02234/772 26), which offers a variety of themed itineraries.
Swimming Agrippabad, Kämmergasse 1 (daily until at least 9pm; €5; ☎ 0221/279 17 30) has indoor and outdoor zones and is close to the *Wasserturm* hotel.
Taxis Taxi-Ruf Köln ☎ 0221/28 82.

Brühl

The industrial southern fringes of Cologne seem an unlikely setting for an outburst of fantasy, frivolity and surrealism, yet all are on display in copious quantities in the otherwise unassuming commuter-belt town of **BRÜHL**.

It was in 1725 that the elector and archbishop of Cologne, Clemens August, first commissioned a new palace on the ruins of a medieval moated palace, but the results – by Westphalian builder Johann Conrad Schlaun – were judged insufficiently fabulous for a member of the Wittelsbach dynasty, and so the Bavarian court architect François de Cuvilliés was commissioned to vamp things up. The result is **Schloss Augustusburg** (guided tours in German; Feb–Nov Tues–Fri 9am–noon & 1.30–4pm, Sat & Sun 10am–5pm; €5), a Rococo Xanadu of extraordinary panache that is one of Germany's most magnificent palaces and, since 1984, a UNESCO World Heritage site. The moment you see the breathtakingly lavish, ceremonial **Treppenhaus** (staircase) by Balthasar Neumann with its frothy rocailles and vivid stucco marble effects, you'll understand why this was Clemens August's favourite residence, for as you ascend the staircase the sheer exuberance of the design becomes apparent, even as you try to decide precisely how far over the top it all is. Napoleon, who visited in 1804, is said to have remarked that it was a pity the Schloss wasn't on wheels so he could take it with him. The dizzying reception rooms at the top of the staircase continue in a similar vein, while the **gardens** (7am–dusk; free), with their parterres and fountains, offer an outdoor equivalent to the indoor excess. An avenue leads across the park to the little lodge of **Jagdschloss Falkenlust** (same hours as Augustusburg; €3.50), which though smaller in scale is similar in spirit, and for which you don't have to join a tour. Clemens August used it for entertaining and for trysts with his mistresses.

Brühl's other cultural claim to fame is the **Max Ernst Museum** at Comestrasse 42 near the station (Tues–Sun 11am–6pm, first Thurs of month until 9pm; €5; Ⓦwww.maxernstmuseum.de), which opened in 2005 to commemorate the work of the Brühl-born Dadaist and Surrealist artist Max Ernst (1891–1976). In addition to early works and most of the artist's graphic output, the collection includes 36 so-called "D Paintings" which were birthday presents or love offerings to his wife, the artist Dorothea Tanning.

Less cerebral, but highly enjoyable, the **Phantasialand** theme park (April–Oct daily 9am–6pm; also Wed–Sun in Dec and Sat & Sun in Jan, but hours vary; day-ticket €25.50; Ⓦwww.phantasialand.de) is widely regarded as one of Europe's best. Its elaborately landscaped rides compare with Disney and include the African-themed, looping roller-coaster *Black Mamba* and *Talocan*, a suspended top-spin ride with an Aztec theme. It's not all adrenaline-pumping thrills, however, and there are more sedate rides for younger children as well as a brace of log flumes and a beautiful old-fashioned carousel. In the evening there's also a glossy dinner show, *Fantissima*.

Practicalities

Brühl is easily reached from the centre of Cologne, either by **tram** #18 or by **train** from Cologne's Hauptbahnhof, which takes just thirteen minutes. Given its extreme proximity to both Cologne and Bonn, there's little real reason to **stay** here, though should you wish to the town's **tourist office** at 1 Uhlstrasse (Mon–Fri 9am–7pm, Sat 9am–4pm, Sun 1–5pm; ℡02232/793 45, Ⓦwww .bruehl.de) can point you in the right direction. The pleasant, traffic-free town centre is small-town stuff and sedate even compared with Bonn, but there's a scattering of decent places to **eat** and **drink**, with Bahnhofstrasse close to Schloss Augustusburg a good place to look. If you're heading to Phantasialand, the easiest way to get there is to hop on the **shuttle bus** from Brühl Bahnhof or the Stadtbahn (tram) stop Brühl-Mitte.

Bonn

The placid university town of **BONN** was "provisional" capital of West Germany for fifty years, from 1949 until the Bundestag and many government departments began relocating to Berlin in 1999. Bonn was dubbed "Federal Capital Village" for the sheer improbability of its choice as capital; likelier candidates included Frankfurt, which even built a parliament building to fulfil its anticipated role. But Bonn prevailed, and it was changed by the experience, so that by the time the federal government moved to Berlin it was no longer quite the "small town in Germany" of John Le Carré's Cold War spy story. The two houses of the German parliament may no longer reside here, but several ministries do, along with the United Nations and the headquarters of Deutsche Telekom, T Mobile and Deutsche Post.

Bonn's pleasant, traffic-free **Altstadt** benefits from its associations with Ludwig van Beethoven, who was born here, while the setting – at the beginning of a particularly scenic stretch of the Rhine – is a delight, and easily explored on foot, but the modern city stretches far along the Rhine. Sandwiched between the city proper and its spa-town suburb of **Bad Godesberg** is the old government quarter, the **Bundesviertel**, and its strip of modern museums along the so-called **Museumsmeile**, planned before the Berlin Wall fell but that, in the event, proved to be a generous goodbye-present to the city..

Facing Bonn across the Rhine are the inviting, wooded hills of the **Siebengebirge** – a hugely popular destination for walkers and day-trippers alike, right on Bonn's doorstep.

Arrival, information and city transport

Bonn's **Hauptbahnhof** is on the south side of the Altstadt, close to the **tourist office** at Windeckstrasse 1 (Mon–Fri 9am–6.30pm, Sat 9am–4pm,

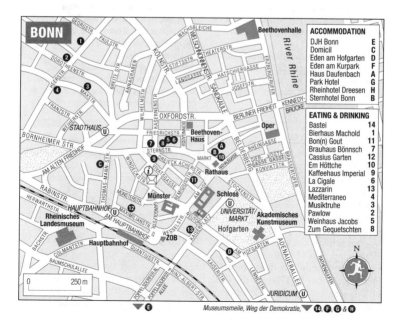

BONN

ACCOMMODATION	
DJH Bonn	E
Domicil	C
Eden am Hofgarten	D
Eden am Kurpark	F
Haus Daufenbach	A
Park Hotel	G
Rheinhotel Dreesen	H
Sternhotel Bonn	B

EATING & DRINKING	
Bastei	14
Bierhaus Machold	1
Bon(n) Gout	11
Brauhaus Bönnsch	7
Cassius Garten	12
Em Höttche	10
Kaffeehaus Imperial	9
La Cigale	6
Lazzarin	13
Mediterraneo	4
Musiktruhe	3
Pawlow	2
Weinhaus Jacobs	5
Zum Gequetschten	8

Museumsmeile, Weg der Demokratie, ▼ ⑭, ⑰, ⑱ & ⑲

Sun 10am–2pm; ☎0228/77 50 00, ⓦwww.bonn-region.de). There's a second tourist office opposite the Bahnhof in Bad Godesberg (Mon–Fri 10am–6pm, Sat 10.30am–5pm; ☎0228/184 26 90). If you're staying in Bonn, it's worth buying the **Bonn Regio WelcomeCard** (24hr €9, 48hr €14 or 72hr €19) – it gives free or reduced entry to museums and attractions in and around Bonn, reductions on selected Cologne attractions and unlimited use of the VRS Rhein-Sieg **public transport** system as far as Cologne. U-Bahn lines 16, 63 and 67 link the centre to the Museumsmeile and Bad Godesberg; if you're exploring the scenic Siebengebirge hills on the opposite bank of the Rhine, take line #66 towards Bad Honnef. **Bicycles** can be rented from Bonn's **Radstation** (Mon–Fri 6am–10.30pm, Sat 7am–10.30pm, Sun 8am–10.30pm; ☎0228/981 46 36), which is in Quantiusstrasse behind the Hauptbahnhof.

Accommodation

Bonn's **hotels** tend to be mid- or upmarket, with budget options rather thin on the ground.

DJH Bonn Haager Weg 42 ☎0228/28 99 70, ⓦwww.bonn.jugendherberge.de. Bonn's youth hostel is on the Venusberg hill south of the centre, on the edge of the Kottenforst nature reserve; to reach it, take bus #621 (direction Ippendorf-Altheim) and get off at the Jugendherberge bus stop. Reception open 7am–1am. Dorm bed €23.
Domicil Thomas-Mann-Str. 24 ☎0228/72 90 90, ⓦwww.domicil-bonn.bestwestern.de. Stylish, modern hotel set around a garden courtyard in an attractive street of nineteenth-century houses a few minutes' walk from the Hauptbahnhof. ❼
Eden am Hofgarten Am Hofgarten 6 ☎0228/28 97 10, ⓦwww.eden-bonn.de. Good-value, mid-range hotel in a peaceful setting on the western side of the Hofgarten, with some proper singles as well as comfortable doubles. ❹
Eden am Kurpark Am Kurpark 5a ☎0228/95 72 70, ⓦwww.eden-godesberg.de. Very pleasant sister hotel of the *Eden am Hofgarten*, located opposite Bad Godesberg's Stadtpark; rooms have wi-fi, en-suite showers and TVs. ❹

Haus Daufenbach Brüdergasse 6 ☎0228/969 46 00, ⒻAX63 79 45. Old-fashioned but cheap and very central accommodation above a *Weinhaus* off the Markt; cheaper rooms share facilities. ❷
Park Hotel Am Kurpark 1 ☎0228/36 30 81, ⓦwww.parkhotelbonn.de. Comfortable hotel in Bad Godesberg, with a central location opposite the Stadtpark and 25 single rooms in addition to its doubles and suites. Prices are higher if there's a conference or exhibition in town. ❺
Rheinhotel Dreesen Rheinstr. 45–49 ☎0228/820 20, ⓦwww.rheinhoteldreesen.de. In an idyllic riverside location with wonderful views towards the Siebengebirge, this slightly faded historic hotel is comfortable, upmarket and traditional, with a splendid beer garden, the *Kastaniengarten*. ❼
Sternhotel Bonn Markt 8 ☎0228/726 70, ⓦwww.sternhotel.de. Elegant hotel with a winning location in the very heart of the city and a choice between classic-style or contemporary rooms. ❻

The Altstadt

Before 1989, the market stalls in front of the prettily Rococo eighteenth-century **Rathaus** were a potent symbol of the West German capital's lack of metropolitan swagger and, by implication, of the extent to which the Federal Republic had turned its back on the Nazi era's megalomania; visiting VIPs including Charles de Gaulle and John F. Kennedy appeared before Bonners on the Rathaus steps. Now stripped of symbolic importance, **Markt** remains the liveliest of the irregularly shaped squares that punctuate the Altstadt's meandering streets. To the north at Bonngasse 20 is the appealingly creaky **Beethoven-Haus** (April–Oct Mon–Sat 10am–6pm, Sun 11am–6pm; Nov–March Mon–Sat 10am–5pm, Sun 11am–5pm; €5; ⓦwww.beethoven-haus-bonn.de) where Ludwig van Beethoven was born in an attic room in 1770. At the time, the city was the capital of the Electorate of Cologne, and Beethoven's father and grandfather had both been employed by

▲ Statue of Beethoven, Bonn

the archbishop-electors as court musical director and court singer respectively. Beethoven's father had promoted him as a Mozart like child prodigy in Bonn, and by his early teens, Ludwig was already working as a court musician. In 1787 he travelled to Vienna to have lessons with Mozart, and in 1792 returned there to study under Haydn. The dissolution of the Electorate two years later – and hence the disappearance of his court position – turned what had been a study trip into permanent exile. Pick up the English-language leaflet or an audio guide (€2) to get the most from the museum's displays, which include family portraits, a Broadwood piano identical to the one presented to Beethoven by its London maker in 1817 and the ear trumpets the composer used as his hearing steadily deteriorated. In the so-called **Digitale Beethoven Haus** next door (same ticket & hours) you can use workstations to carry out Beethoven-related internet and intranet searches or experience a twenty-minute 3D multimedia presentation of scenes from *Fidelio*.

From the Markt, Markt Brücke and Remigiusstrasse lead past **Remigius-Platz** – a café-fringed square that hosts a flower market – to wide, sunny **Münster-platz**. Here, **Beethoven's statue** stands in front of the Baroque palace that's now occupied by the post office; in Ernst Julius Hähnel's stern 1845 likeness, the composer looks every inch the genius. On the south side of Münsterplatz, the **Münster** (daily 7am–7pm; free) is a harmonious, unmistakably Rhenish fusion of Romanesque and Gothic, largely dating from the eleventh to thirteenth centuries and oddly lacking in monumentality despite its high central spire. The choir served as the prototype for subsequent Rhineland churches, but the peaceful, memorial-lined Romanesque **cloister** (daily 9am–5pm; free) is more appealing.

Around the Hofgarten

East of Münsterplatz, the immense Baroque facade of the Electors' **Schloss** – now the university – extends the full width of the **Hofgarten**, a broad expanse of lawn fringed by small museums. In the Koblenzer Tor of the Schloss itself is the **Aegyptisches Museum** (Tues–Sun noon–6pm; €3.50), which contains the university's Egyptology collection, with displays relating to everyday life in ancient Egypt as well as mummies and religious artefacts. On the south side of the park, a Neoclassical pavilion that was partly the work of Karl Friedrich Schinkel houses the **Akademisches Kunstmuseum** (Tues & Thurs 4–6pm, Sun 11am–4pm, longer hours during special exhibitions; €3), a collection of original and plaster copies of antique classical sculptures. At the southern corner of the park is the **Arithmeum**, Lennéstrasse 2 (Tues–Sun 11am–6pm; €3), a beautifully presented exhibition that traces the history of arithmetic, from the clay tablets used in ancient Mesopotamia through various increasingly ingenious and beautiful mechanical calculating machines to the silicon chip. There's plenty of information in English, and the light-filled museum building is a delight.

From the western end of the Hofgarten, broad Poppelsdorfer Allee connects the Schloss with the Poppelsdorfer Schloss or **Schloss Clemensruhe**, the Electors' Rococo summer palace, completed in the eighteenth century by Balthasar Neumann and now part of the university. In summer it is the venue for concerts, while its gardens are now the **Botanische Gärten Bonn** (April–Oct Sun–Fri 9am–6pm; Nov–March Mon–Fri 9am–4pm; €2 on Sun, otherwise free), one of the oldest and largest plant collections in Germany. The **glasshouses** (April–Oct Mon–Fri 10am–noon & 2–4pm, Sun 10am–5.30pm; Nov–March 10am–noon & 2–4pm) contain the world's largest water lilies.

The gracious **Südstadt** district east of the Schloss is full of grand houses that testify to Bonn's nineteenth-century status as one of Germany's wealthiest cities. North of the Schloss at Colmantstrasse 14–16, the **Rheinisches LandesMuseum** (Tues & Thurs–Sun 10am–6pm, Wed 10am–9pm; €7; English audio guide available) takes a modern, thematic approach to its eclectic collections of regional interest. The most famous exhibit is the 42,000-year-old skull of a man discovered in a quarry at Neandertal near Düsseldorf in 1856; subsequently, *Neanderthal* – using the old German spelling of the place name – became the accepted term for the extinct species of pre-modern human to which he belonged. As well as the skull and other bones, you can see a modern reconstruction of his face. The museum has extensive Roman displays and a collection of medieval religious art, including the expressive fourteenth-century *Roettgen pietà*. There's also a fascinating collection of paintings and drawings exploring the allure of the "Romantic Rhine" in German and Anglo-Saxon art – works on display include J.M.W. Turner's *Hochkreuz and Godesberg* from 1817.

The Museumsmeile

From the Hofgarten, a boulevard named for three of Germany's political giants leads south through the **Bundesviertel** or former government district. It begins as Adenauer Allee, continues as Willy-Brandt-Allee and then becomes Friedrich-Ebert-Allee, named after the Weimar-era socialist who was Germany's first democratic president.

The western side of this avenue constitutes the **Museumsmeile**, an impressive strip of museums that ensures Bonn's heavy-hitter status among Germany's cultural centres. First up is the **Museum Koenig** (Tues & Thurs–Sun 10am–6pm, Wed 10am–9pm; €3; U-Bahn Museum Koenig), a stately sandstone pile that was the venue for the first elected postwar national assembly on September 1, 1948. The museum's zoological exhibits have been given a child-friendly makeover, though the lack of English labelling limits its rainy-day appeal slightly – pick up the English-language leaflet at the entrance. Displays are grouped by habitat and include African savannah, rainforest and the Arctic; the Vivarium in the basement has live lizards, snakes and fish, as well as the *Zwergmaus* – a particularly tiny rodent.

A little way to the south, the **Haus der Geschichte der Bundesrepublik Deutschland** (Tues–Sun 9am–7pm; free; ⓦ www.hdg.de; U-Bahn Heussallee/ Museumsmeile) charts the history of the Federal Republic of Germany in a lively and entertaining way; as you leave the U-Bahn the first thing you see is the luxurious railway carriage used by chancellors Konrad Adenauer and Ludwig Erhard but originally built for Nazi bigwig Hermann Göring. Pick up the English-language guidebook (€6) as the labelling is in German only. Rubble marks the start of the story in 1945, with grim footage of concentration camps and of destroyed German cities; it continues through the beginnings of democratic politics and of artistic rebirth to the 1950s *Wirtschaftswunder* – the "economic miracle" – where exhibits include a BMW Isetta bubble car, nicknamed the "cuddle ball" or "motorized raincoat" for its modest dimensions. Upbeat displays on consumerism, US cultural influence and the changing role of women balance grimmer ones on the Berlin Wall, the 1960s Auschwitz trials and Baader-Meinhof/RAF terrorism, and the museum balances coverage of the West with a look at parallel developments in the East.

The most architecturally refined of the area's museums is the **Kunstmuseum Bonn** (Tues & Thurs–Sun 11am–6pm, Wed 11am–9pm; €5; ⓦ www.bonn .de/kunstmuseum), whose starkly beautiful modernist interior provides a fitting home for its collection of works by August Macke and the Rhine Expressionists. Macke, who was born in 1887 and killed in action in France in 1914, grew up in Bonn but was no mere "regional" artist, as his gorgeous, colour-filled canvases demonstrate: poignantly, the most confident are the 1914 *Tightrope Walker* and *Turkish Café*. The museum's upper floor is devoted to post-1945 German art, with works by heavyweights including Gerhard Richter, Georg Baselitz and Joseph Beuys.

Next door, the **Kunst- und Ausstellungshalle der Bundesrepublik Deutschland** (Tues & Wed 10am–9pm, Thurs–Sun 10am–7pm; admission price varies according to exhibition; ⓦ www.bundeskunsthalle.de) provides a venue for large-scale touring art exhibitions and is big enough to host several simultaneously. Don't miss the striking roof garden, dominated by three ceramic-clad light spires. Further south at Ahrstrasse 45, the **Deutsches Museum Bonn** (Tues–Sun 10am– 6pm; €4; ⓦ www.deutsches-museum-bonn.de; U-Bahn Hochkreuz/Deutsches Museum) is a resolutely contemporary museum of science and technology whose themed displays allow you to find out how a car airbag works, learn about medical research and see various Nobel Prize–winning discoveries. There's also a Transrapid hoverrail train.

The Weg der Demokratie

Between the Museumsmeile and the Rhine, the **Weg der Demokratie** ("the Path of Democracy") is a signposted walk through sites associated with Bonn's period as federal capital. It starts and finishes at the Haus der Geschichte (see above), and while the full itinerary is too exhaustive for all but the most obsessive fans of German democracy, a stroll through the district underlines the former capital's low-key style, with leafy avenues and government buildings interspersed with suburban housing. The main landmarks are along Görresstrasse a couple of blocks east of Willy-Brandt-Allee, where Günther Behnisch's glassy 1992 **Plenarsaal** replaced an earlier home of the Bundestag – the lower house of the German parliament – only to be rapidly superseded by the new Berlin Reichstag. The adjacent **Bundeshaus** is a Bauhaus-style 1930s teacher-training college that was adapted for parliamentary use to counter Frankfurt's rival claims; the **Bundesrat** – the upper house of the German parliament – sat in its north wing until 2000. To the north, along Adenauer Allee, the 1860-built

Palais Schaumburg was from 1949 the official residence of the German chancellor; it was here in 1990 that representatives of East and West Germany signed the treaty on monetary, economic and social union, and it remains the chancellor's Bonn residence. Further north, the elegant white **Villa Hammer-schmidt** is the president's official Bonn residence.

Bad Godesberg

For much of the twentieth century diplomacy and **Bad Godesberg**, south of the centre, were synonymous, for its gracious villas found favour as embassies during Bonn's time as federal capital. The compact town centre is a slightly odd mix of spa-town prettiness and crass postwar development, fringed by leafy parks. Facing one of these on Kurfürstenallee is the graceful late eighteenth-century **La Redoute**, a concert hall and ballroom where the young Beethoven played for Haydn. Looming above the town centre, the solitary surviving tower of the thirteenth-century **Godesburg** castle now accommodates an upmarket restaurant; you can climb the **tower** (daily 10am–6pm; €2; collect key from restaurant) for sweeping views over the town towards the river and Siebengebirge. East of Bad Godesberg's U-Bahn station, stately Rhein Allee leads to the banks of the **Rhine**, and some wonderful opportunities for walking, cycling and rollerblading with magnificent views of the **Siebengebirge** hills on the opposite bank. It was on the Bad Godesberg riverbank at the **Rheinhotel Dreesen** that Adolf Hitler and British prime minister Neville Chamberlain had their first meeting during the Sudeten German crisis in September 1938; Chamberlain stayed in the hilltop *Petersberg* hotel across the river, which can be clearly seen from the Dreesen. Following the river to the south brings you to the **Panoramabad Rüngsdorf** (May–Sept daily 6.30am–8pm; €3), an attractive riverside open-air swimming pool and sunbathing meadow; further south still, you can take the **ferry** (€1) to Königswinter (see p.628).

Eating and drinking

Central Bonn and Bad Godesberg both have their fair share of places to **eat** and **drink**, with some of the most interesting options in the Nordstadt, a formerly working-class district that is nowadays the city's bohemian quarter.

Restaurants

Bastei Von-Sandt-Ufer 1 ☎0228/368 04 33. Landmark restaurant and *Biergarten* on the Bad Godesburg riverside, with fabulous views of the Siebengebirge and seasonally changing Mediterra-nean-influenced menus. Daily until midnight.

Cassius Garten Maximilianstr. 28 ☎0228/65 24 29. Bright, modern, sprawling vegan and veggie place opposite the Hauptbahnhof, with reasonably priced organic food. Open from breakfast onwards.

Em Höttche Markt 4 ☎0228/69 00 09. Gorgeously traditional *Gasthaus* right next to the Rathaus, with a history dating back to 1389 and a versatile menu of Rhineland specialities that includes both substantial main courses and lighter dishes.

La Cigale Friedrichstr. 26 ☎0228/184 12 50. Elegant French-style brasserie and wine bar in the Altstadt's pedestrian zone, with weekly-changing menu. Closed Sun.

Mediterraneo Heerstr. 121 ☎0228/969 19 95. Pleasantly informal Nordstadt restaurant, with hearty sub-€10 pasta dishes and plenty of fish from around €14 and up, and with a pretty terrace in summer.

Weinhaus Jacobs Friedrichstr. 18 ☎0228/63 73 53. Old-fashioned, slightly kitschy Altstadt *Weinhaus* with inexpensive German wines and filling traditional dishes such as *Saumagen* and *Tafelspitz* from around €11. Eve only, closed Sun.

Cafés and bars

Bierhaus Machold Heerstr. 52 ☎0228/963 78 77. Smart and historic Nordstadt *Bierhaus*, with own-label Machold beer, veggie and children's menus and a regular Sunday lunch buffet.

Bon(n) Gout Remigiusplatz 2–4 ☎0228/65 89 88. Stylish, modern café with a sunny terrace fronting the flower market, with good breakfasts, reasonably priced salads and daily specials.

Brauhaus Bönnsch Sterntorbrücke 4 ☎0228/65 06 10. Altstadt *Bierhaus* serving its own Bönnsch beer along with typical Rhineland cuisine and daily-changing specials. Fri & Sat open until 3am.

Kaffeehaus Imperial Vivatsgasse 8 ☎0228/965 78 14. Classic Viennese-style café-*Konditorei* in elegantly Jugendstil premises, with sumptuous cakes and outdoor seating in the shadow of the thirteenth-century Sterntor.

Lazzarin Kaiserplatz 6. Italian-style ice-cream parlour with a big outdoor terrace in a plum position at the beginning of the Poppelsdorfer Allee.

Musiktruhe Maxstr. 40 ☎0228/969 19 95. Amiably grungy Nordstadt blues and rock bar, with occasional live bands, billiards and darts, and a decent selection of bottled beers. Daily from 8pm.

Pawlow Heerstr. 64 ☎0228/65 36 03. Cult Nordstadt café/bar, by day a place to breakfast late or linger over a *Milchkaffee*, by night livelier, when the music is eclectic and the action spills into the street outside.

Zum Gequetschten Sternstr. 78 ☎0228/63 81 04. Traditional Rhineland *Brauhaus* in the Altstadt, with *Kölsch* and *Jever* on draught, serving Cologne and Rhineland specialities and, in summer, an outside terrace.

Nightlife and entertainment

Bonn isn't exactly renowned for **nightlife**, but **live bands** play at *Kult 41*, Hochstadenring 41 in the Nordstadt (☎0228/908 57 07, ⓦwww.kult41.de), while *Nachtrauschen*, Belderberg 15 (☎0228/336 86 05, ⓦwww.nachtrauschen.com; Tues & Fri–Sun), is a city-centre club that spins electro and commercial dance music. Beethoven features prominently on the city's **cultural** scene, with an annual Beethovenfest (ⓦwww.beethovenfest.de) in September; venues include the Beethovenhalle, Wachsbleiche 17 (☎0228/722 23 33), home of the Klassische Philharmonie Bonn, and the more intimate Beethoven-Haus (see p.622). The **Oper der Stadt Bonn**, by the river at Am Boeselagerhof 1 (☎0228/77 80 00, ⓦwww.theater.bonn.de), is the venue for opera, drama and dance. For what's on listings, there's a monthly local magazine, *Schnüss* (€1.90), or pick up the free *Live!* magazine, which also covers Cologne.

The Siebengebirge

Facing Bonn and Bad Godesberg across the Rhine, the extinct volcanic domes of the **Siebengebirge** are perfect mountains in miniature. None rises higher than 500m, yet the hills are steep-sided and thickly wooded enough to create a plausible impression of alpine ruggedness. Much mythologized and immortalized in song, the Siebengebirge were rescued from destruction by quarrying in the nineteenth century and now comprise one of Germany's oldest nature parks. There are in fact many more hills – 42 in all – than the name, which means seven mountains, would suggest, and several are topped by ruined fortresses, which merely adds to their mystique. The entire range is crisscrossed by hiking trails, including the 320km **Rheinsteig** long-distance path which passes through on its way from Bonn to Wiesbaden. Given their picturesque charm and extreme proximity to the Rhineland's big cities, the Siebengebirge are, not surprisingly, highly popular.

Of all the hills, the most visited is the 320m **Drachenfels** (or "dragon rock"), which rises above the riverfront resort of Königswinter. Though it's not one of the higher hills, the reasons for its popularity are not hard to divine: it has a castle-topped prettiness, and rises high above the banks of the Rhine to give breathtaking views from its summit north over Bonn and Cologne – you'll see Cologne cathedral on a clear day – and south over the town of Bad Honnef. Most significantly of all, there's a cog railway – the **Drachenfelsbahn** (Jan, Feb & Nov Mon–Fri noon–5pm, Sat & Sun 11am–6pm; March & Oct daily 10am–6pm; April daily 10am–7pm; May–Sept daily 9am–7pm; €9 return, €7.50 single; ⓦwww.siebengebirge.com) – to ease the ascent. To enjoy the Drachenfels to the full, it's a good idea to take the train to the summit for the views from the castle ruins, then take the meandering footpath downhill, pausing halfway at **Schloss Drachenburg** (April–Oct Tues–Sun 11am–6pm; Nov–March 11am–4pm; €2.50; @www.schloss-drachenburg.de), a fantastically spooky neo-Gothic mansion from whose terrace there are spectacular views downriver. The Schloss is currently undergoing long-term renovation, but there's access to some of the freshly renovated interiors plus a small exhibition giving a behind-the-scenes look at the work of the restorers. A little further downhill, the **Nibelungenhalle** (mid-March to Nov daily 10am–6pm; Nov to mid-March Sat & Sun 11am–4pm; €4) is no less extraordinary or gloomy. Built in Jugendstil style in 1913 to commemorate the centenary of Wagner's birth, the little temple leads to a short tunnel – the **Drachenhöhle** – which is adorned by a 13-metre-high dragon representing the beast supposedly slain here by Siegfried in the tale of the same name which forms part of Wagner's opera cycle, the *Ring of the Nibelung*. The tunnel leads in turn to a **reptile zoo** (same ticket & hours), whose attractions include snakes and crocodiles. There's a cluster of places to **eat** or **drink** close to the Nibelungenhalle; if you don't fancy the descent on foot from the top of the Drachenfels, there's a station on the cog railway close to Schloss Drachenburg.

At the foot of the Drachenfels, the small town of **Königswinter** itself has a neat waterfront lined with imposing hotels and a spanking modern **Sea Life** aquarium (daily 10am–6pm; €13; @www.sealifeeurope.com). It nevertheless has the air of a place that has seen better days, and given the speed and efficiency of the U-Bahn link from Bonn there's no particular reason to **stay** here unless your budget will stretch to a night or two of five-star luxury at the spectacular mountaintop *Steigenberger Grandhotel Petersberg* (T02223/740, @www.grandhotel-petersberg.steigenberger.de; ●), which has a long history as a diplomatic retreat.

From Bonn's city centre the Bonner Personen Schifffahrt from the quay Brassertufer "Am Alten Zoll" (€7 single; T0228/63 63 63, @www.b-p-s.de) can get you here by **boat** in 25 minutes. Alternatively from Bad Godesberg there's a car and passenger ferry that shuttles back and forth across the river (€1).

Aachen

Few places can claim such proudly European credentials as **AACHEN** (known as Aix-la-Chapelle in French, Aken to the Dutch). Its hot thermal springs were known to the Celts and Romans, but it wasn't until Charlemagne took up residence in 768 AD that the city briefly took centre stage as the capital of his vast Frankish empire. At its height, this encompassed much of what formed – more than a millennium later – the original core of the European Union. But it didn't long survive his death, and nor did Aachen's political importance, though for six centuries afterwards the city remained the place where German emperors were crowned. Charlemagne's chief legacy is the magnificent domed court chapel – now the city's cathedral and a UNESCO World Heritage Site – that is still the most splendid thing in the city.

During World War II, Aachen was the first German city in the west to fall to Allied invasion, after a six-week battle in the autumn of 1944 that laid waste to much of it. However, the **cathedral** escaped destruction and the heart of the city, at least, retains a pleasing sense of history. These days, Germany's most westerly city is a lively, medium-sized place, its municipal boundary forming the international frontier at the point where Belgium and the Netherlands meet, creating an easy-going and cosmopolitan feel, with the student population supporting a vibrant nightlife scene and the spa bringing in a steady stream of more genteel visitors. Skip the bland streets between the Hauptbahnhof and the Elisenbrunnen, for Aachen's ancient treasures lie beyond Schinkel's colonnade in the north of the **Altstadt**. The **centre** is compact and walkable, with the main **spa** facilities and some **museums** a little way to the east. There's a second spa-quarter south of the Hauptbahnhof, while further afield a trip to the **Dreiländereck** where Germany, Belgium and the Netherlands meet makes for a relaxing afternoon in pleasant, rural surroundings.

Arrival, information and accommodation

Aachen's **Hauptbahnhof** is on the south side of the city centre, from where it's a five-minute walk north to Friedrich-Wilhelm-Platz and the Elisenbrunnen, a Neoclassical spa colonnade by Karl Friedrich Schinkel which houses the **tourist office** (Easter–Christmas Mon–Fri 9am–6pm, Sat 9am–3pm, Sun 10am–2pm; Christmas–Easter Mon–Fri 9am–6pm, Sat 9am–2pm; ☏0241/180 29 60, Ⓦwww.aachen-tourist.de). City buses depart from the **Bushof** a few hundred metres to the northeast at the corner of Kurhausstrasse and Peterstrasse; though Aachen's historic centre is compact and walkable, a one-day *Tages-Ticket* (€6.10) may be useful if you're staying outside the centre. You can also get a one-day

EATING, DRINKING & NIGHTLIFE
Am Knipp	5
Bar Museo	15
Café Kittel	6
Domkeller	13
Gallo Nero	14
Leo van den Daele	12
Malteserkeller	4
Molkerei	3
Musik Bunker	16
Ocean	2
Postwagen	11
Ratskeller	9
Starfish	1
Vertical	10
Zum Goldenen Einhorn	8
Zum Goldenen Schwan	7

ACCOMMODATION
Benelux	C
Da Salvatore	E
Drei Könige	B
Euroregionales Jugendgästehaus	H
Hesse	F
Residenz Hotel Domicil	G
Sofitel Aachen Quellenhof	A
Stadtnah	D

0   200 m

Euregioticket (€14.50) valid for the Aachen region and for cross-border travel far into Belgium and the Netherlands. Alternatively, rent a **bike** from the Radstation on the square in front of the Hauptbahnhof (Mon–Fri 5.30am–10.30pm, Sat, Sun & public hols 10am–6.30pm). You can book **hotels** in both Aachen and neighbouring Dutch or Belgian towns through the tourist office website.

Hotels

Benelux Franzstr. 21–23 ☎0241/40 00 30, ⓦwww.hotel-benelux.de. In a fairly quiet location midway between the Hauptbahnhof and Dom, with some bright, spacious rooms. ❺

Da Salvatore Bahnhofsplatz 5 ☎0241/313 77, ⓦwww.zimmer-in-aachen.de. Simple, inexpensive but pleasant rooms above an Italian restaurant, strategically located opposite the Hauptbahnhof. ❷

Drei Könige Am Markt/Büchel 5 ☎0241/483 93, ⓦwww.h3k-aachen.de. Modest-sized, boutique-style hotel in an unbeatable central location, with vibrantly coloured rooms, wireless internet and satellite TV. ❻

Hesse Friedlandstr. 20 ☎0241/47 05 40, ⓦwww.hotelhesse.de. Recently renovated three-star hotel facing a small green a few minutes' walk west of the Hauptbahnhof, with tastefully decorated, if slightly bland rooms. ❸

Residenz Hotel Domicil Lütticher Str. 27 ☎0241/705 12 00, ⓦwww.domicilaachen.de. Stylish small hotel in an attractive nineteenth-century villa southwest of the city centre, with singles, doubles, apartments with kitchens plus some garden studios. ❺

Sofitel Aachen Quellenhof Monheimsallee 52 ☎0241/913 20, ⓦwww.sofitel.com. A classic grand hotel with a contemporary twist, the *Quellenhof* is right on the Kurpark between the casino and conference centre, and is the choice of visiting VIPs. ❼

Stadtnah Leydelstr. 2 ☎0241/47 45 80, ⓦwww.hotelstadtnah.de. A good-value, simple option above a bistro opposite the Hauptbahnhof. ❸

Hostel

Euroregionales Jugendgästehaus Maria-Theresia-Allee 180 ☎0241/71 10 10, ⓦwww.aachen.jugendherberge.de. Modern hostel south of the city centre, with accommodation in twin or family rooms and four-, eight-, or multi-bed dorms. Take bus #2 from stop "Miseror" a few 100m west of the Hauptbahnhof; turn left out of the station main entrance to reach it; alight at stop "Ronheide". Dorms €23.20; doubles ❷.

The Dom and Schatzkammer

Though its slightly eccentric exterior hints at the building's unique riches, the dark, Byzantine interior of Aachen's **Dom** (Mon–Sat 11am–7pm, Sun 1–6pm; guided tours in English daily at 2pm, enquire at Schatzkammer, €3) nevertheless comes as a surprise. As you enter the cathedral through the massive, twelve-hundred-year-old bronze doors you're immediately presented with its great glory, the octagonal **palace chapel** built for Charlemagne and inspired by the churches of San Vitale in Ravenna and Little Hagia Sophia in Istanbul. It was the first domed church north of the Alps and though it was the work of Otto von Metz, Charlemagne himself contributed his own ideas to the design. If you can, take the **guided tour** as much of the interior is off limits for casual visitors and you'll only gain the most superficial impressions without it. In particular, it's only on the tour that you'll see the modest marble **Imperial Throne** in the upper gallery which was used for coronations for six centuries, from Otto I in 936 to Ferdinand I in 1531. At the time of writing, ongoing restoration work meant parts of the octagon were obscured from view. The vast twelfth-century gilded **Barbarossa chandelier**, which hangs low in the centre of the octagon, catches the eye, along with the nineteenth-century mosaics inside the dome high above, but the octagon's marble **pillars** are altogether more ancient, having been brought to Aachen from Rome and Ravenna with the permission of Pope Hadrian I. So prized are they that French troops hauled 28 of them off to Paris in 1815, where four can still be seen in the Louvre. As the burial place of Charlemagne and a place of pilgrimage, the cathedral was embellished over the centuries with various chapels, and in the fourteenth century a soaring, light-filled Gothic **choir** – the so-called "Glass House of Aachen" – was added to ease the crush of visiting pilgrims. It houses the gilded thirteenth-century **shrine** that contains Charlemagne's remains. The choir's original **stained glass** was destroyed by hail in 1729; the present windows are post-1945, and replaced glass destroyed during World War II.

With such a long history, the Dom's **Schatzkammer**, just around the corner on Johannes-Paul-II Strasse (April–Dec Mon 10am–1pm, Tues, Wed & Fri–Sun 10am–6pm, Thurs 10am–9pm; Jan–March Mon 10am–1pm, Tues–Sun 10am–5pm, first Thurs in month until 10pm; €4), has more than its share of treasures – indeed, it's regarded as the most important religious treasury north of the Alps. The gilded silver **bust of Charlemagne** looking every inch the emperor is perhaps the most recognizable of the hundred or so exhibits, though as it dates from 1349 – half a millennium after his death – it's scarcely a reliable guide to what he might have looked like. Other treasures include the fabulous **Lothar cross** dating from around 1000 AD, and, richly adorned with gemstones, the extraordinary **Dreiturmreliquiar** – a triple-pinnacled fourteenth-century Gothic creation in gold – and a second-century Roman marble **sarcophagus** carved with scenes from the rape of Persephone.

The Rathaus and Altstadt

A short stroll north of the Dom and scarcely less imposing, Aachen's Gothic **Rathaus** looms over the Markt, the city's central square. Dating from the early fourteenth century, the building incorporates surviving sections of Charlemagne's palace, including twenty metres of the Granus tower on the east side, plus later accretions. The side facing the Markt is decorated with statues of fifty German emperors with another four on the east facade; 31 of them were crowned in Aachen. Above the main entrance, Charlemagne is to the right of Christ with a model of the Dom, with Pope Leo III – who consecrated it – to the left. Inside, the splendid **Krönungssaal** on the first floor (daily 10am–1pm & 2–5pm; €2) is where newly crowned emperors held their coronation banquets. Today it's where the Charlemagne Prize for services to European unification is awarded, and on the stairs you'll see photo portraits of past winners; more improbable recipients include Tony Blair and Henry Kissinger. The hall is decorated with mid-nineteenth-century **frescoes** on themes from Charlemagne's life by Aachen-born painter Alfred Rethel. Of the original eight frescoes, only five survived wartime damage. Copies of the imperial **crown jewels** are also on view; the originals are in Vienna.

A short walk down Krämerstrasse on the east side of the Rathaus at Hühnermarkt 17 is the **Couven Museum** (Tues–Fri 10am–6pm, Sat & Sun 11am–6pm; €5; ⓦ www.couven-museum.de), a handsome old town house that is now a museum of bourgeois interiors from the Rococo to the Biedermeier. The Festsaal on the first floor is particularly lovely, with five tall windows giving views across to the Rathaus; so too is the elegant early nineteenth-century Biedermeier furniture on the top floor. The reconstructed pharmacy on the ground floor alludes to the history of the house itself; there was a pharmacy on the premises as early as 1662.

Back on Markt, the café terraces give fine views of the Rathaus while the houses surrounding the square are a mishmash of everything from venerable Gothic to postwar modern. Just north of Markt in the fifteenth-century Haus Rupenstein on Pontstrasse is the **Internationale Zeitungsmuseum** (International Newspaper Museum; Tues–Fri 9.30am–5pm; free). It was in this street in 1850 that Paul Julius Reuter founded his famous news agency, and the museum traces four hundred years of newspaper history through exhibits that include a rare surviving copy of Émile Zola's 1898 *"J'accuse"* letter to *L'Aurore* on the subject of the Dreyfus case, copies of the Nazi newspaper *Völkischer Beobachter* and a display showing how world media reported the reunification of Germany. There's also a copy of *Aachener Nachrichten*, the first post-Nazi German newspaper, published in January 1945 while war still raged. Beyond the museum, Pontsstrasse is one of the liveliest streets in the Altstadt, stretching as far as the mighty **Ponttor**, a survivor of the medieval city's outer defences.

The Kurviertel and around

Northeast of the Altstadt along Monheimsallee, Aachen's elegant Wilhelmine **Kurviertel** (spa district) is dominated by the portico of the **Neues Kurhaus**, which houses the swanky **Casino Aachen** (daily 3pm–3am, until 4am Sat; €5; Ⓦ www.casino-aachen.de), for which you're expected to dress smartly, though men don't need a tie. Behind the Kurhaus, the pretty **Stadtgarten** was the work of the great Prussian garden designer Peter Joseph Lenné (1789–1866). On the far side of the park, the modern **Carolus Thermen** spa complex (daily 9am–11pm; admission without sauna from €10, with sauna from €20; Ⓦ www.carolus-thermen .de) offers a full range of mineral water pools, steam baths and a Finnish-style sauna, with beauty treatments available and a choice of healthy restaurants.

Further east on grungy Jülicher Strasse, the **Ludwig Forum für Internationale Kunst** (Tues–Fri noon–6pm, Sat & Sun 11am–6pm; €5; Ⓦ www .ludwigforum.de; buses #1, #11, #21 or #52 from Bushof) is a former 1920s umbrella factory whose glass-roofed building provides an ideal setting for regularly changing exhibitions of contemporary art, with masses of space for large-scale installations. The permanent collection is strong on American Pop Art, including Duane Hanson's life-size *Supermarket Lady* complete with shopping trolley and junk food, Robert Rauschenberg's *Spray Shield Marathon* and Andy Warhol's *Portrait of Peter Ludwig*. There are also works by Sigmar Polke, Jean-Michel Basquiat and Roy Lichtenstein.

South of the Kurviertel, Monheimsallee becomes Heinrichsallee, then Wilhelmstrasse where, at no. 18, the **Suermondt-Ludwig-Museum** (Tues, Thurs & Fri noon–6pm, Wed noon–8pm, Sat & Sun 11am–6pm; €5; Ⓦ www .suermondt-ludwig-museum.de) has an altogether more eclectic art collection. The presentation is a little old-fashioned in places, but there's sublime medieval religious wood carving, some seventeenth-century Dutch and Flemish masters and a selection of twentieth-century German art on the ground floor that includes works by Max Slevogt, Max Beckmann, Lovis Corinth and Karl Schmidt-Rottluff. Highlights include Lucas Cranach the Elder's gory *Judith with the Head of Holofernes*, and there's some excellent modern stained glass. East of Wilhelmstrasse in a quiet residential district at Bismarckstrasse 68, a museum of local history occupies a partly thirteenth-century castle, **Burg Frankenberg**, but its opening hours (Sun 11am–2pm; €1) are extremely limited.

Dreiländereck

One popular short trip out of town is by bike to the meeting of the German, Dutch and Belgian borders, about 5km west of Aaachen. If you're coming by car, the **Dreiländereck** is most easily reached via Vaals on the Dutch side, but the approach that cyclists take – along Dreiländerweg through rolling countryside – is pleasant by car too, though you'll need to park by the *Gasthäuser* some way back from the frontier and walk the rest of the way. The route veers right just before **Gut Fuchstal** and then winds up through woods to the frontier; you emerge just south of the meeting point itself, which is marked by a post – touchingly, it's very hard to work out which country you're in without reference to it. From 1816 to 1919 a fourth "country" abutted the other three. The tiny wedge-shaped territory of **Neutral Moresnet** was created after the Congress of Vienna to settle a territorial dispute between the Netherlands and Prussia. It was abolished by the Versailles Treaty after World War I and is now part of Belgium.

Eating and drinking

Good places to **eat** and **drink** are scattered throughout Aachen's historic core: there's a concentration of atmospheric, traditional eating places in and around Markt, while Pontstrasse is where you'll find the liveliest of Aachen's bar scene. The local sugary treats are *Aachener Printen*, a type of gingerbread; sample it at *Leo van den Daele* or from *Nobis* at Münsterplatz 3 near the cathedral.

Restaurants

Am Knipp Bergdriesch 3 ☎0241/331 68. Northern Altstadt stalwart with enchantingly pretty interior and *Flammkuchen* and German staples on the menu, though, despite claiming to be Aachen's oldest restaurant, it isn't quite what it seems – the building is a postwar reconstruction. Eve only, closed Tues.

Gallo Nero Kaiserplatz 6 ☎0241/401 49 30. Classy, Michelin-listed Italian restaurant east of the Altstadt, with high ceilings, a mezzanine and the likes of *Saltimbocca alla Romana* at surprisingly reasonable prices. Closed Mon.

Postwagen Krämerstr. 2 ☎0241/350 01. Wonderfully atmospheric seventeenth-century restaurant attached to the Rathaus serving good, hearty traditional dishes such as *Himmel en Erd* – blood sausage with mashed potato and apple.

Ratskeller Markt 40 ☎0241/350 01. Creative gourmet cooking in the elegant surroundings of the Rathaus's refurbished cellars, with the likes of crisp-roast Barbary duck breast with braised chicory or ragout of Provençal vegetables with courgette spaghetti; set lunch €30; eve €37.50.

Zum Goldenen Einhorn Markt 33 ☎0241/326 93. Historic *Gasthaus* facing the Rathaus, with classy ambience and a mix of local and Italian specialities on its menu.

Zum Goldenen Schwan Markt 37 ☎0241/316 49. Traditional *Gasthaus* that's just as atmospheric and historic as its neighbour the *Einhorn*, but cheaper, and with the emphasis firmly on traditional food, such as Rhineland-style *Sauerbraten* for €9.

Cafés and bars

Bar Museo Wilhelmstr. 18 ☎0241/253 93. Trendy glass-fronted café-bar next to the Suermondt museum, with regular Friday DJ nights until 5am, good-value food and occasional dining events in the museum's imposing entrance hall.

Café Kittel Pontstr. 39 ☎0241/365 60. Café-bar at the start of the northern Altstadt's nightlife strip, open from breakfast onwards and with a pretty beer garden in summer.

Domkeller Hof 1 ☎0241/342 65. Lovely old pub-type place close to the Rathaus, with a huge outside terrace in summer and live music on Mondays.

Leo van den Daele Büchel 18 ☎0241/357 24. The dark, woody interior behind the glossy black-and-gilt shopfront is the classic place to stop for coffee and cakes in Aachen; they do inexpensive lunches too.

Molkerei Pontstr. 141 ☎0241/ 489 82. One of a number of stylish café-bars that cluster around the Apollo cinema at the north end of Pontstrasse, busy much of the time and serving affordable food and cocktails to a fairly young crowd.

Ocean Pontstr. 164 ☎0241/401 93 30. Trendy café-bar in the thick of the Pontstrasse action whose leafy outdoor terrace makes it a prime spot for alfresco lounging in fine weather.

Vertical Kockerellstr. 13 ☎0241/900 67 41. Classy little wine-bar with high stools, a few tables outside in fine weather and thirty wines by the glass, many from prestigious wineries, plus hot and cold food. Closed Sun.

Nightlife and entertainment

The imposing Neoclassical Theater Aachen on Theaterplatz (☎0241/478 42 44, ⓦwww.theateraachen.de) is the main venue for serious **drama**, **musicals** and **concerts**; the Eurogress congress centre in the Kurviertel, Monheimsallee 48 (☎0241/913 10, ⓦwww.eurogress-aachen.de), is the venue for large-scale events, from **rock** and **classical concerts** to ice spectaculars. For what's on information, pick up a free copy of the local listings magazine, *Klenkes*.

Clubs and venues

Malteserkeller Malteserstr. 14 ☎0241/257 74, ⓦwww.malteserkeller.de. Live jazz on Wednesdays and Saturdays in this brick cellar near the Pontsstrasse, with a more eclectic music policy and DJ nights at other times.

Musik Bunker Rehmannstr. 2 ☎0241/53 21 80, ⓦwww.musikbunker-aachen.de. Live rock venue in the extraordinary setting of a vast World War II air-raid shelter.

Starfish Liebigstr. 19 ☎0241/93 89 00, ⓦwww.starfish-aachen.de. Aachen's biggest dance club is northeast of the centre, just off Jülicher Str., with four dancefloors each with a different music style, from mainstream house to classic rock, disco, hip-hop or ragga.

Wuppertal

Around 40km northeast of Cologne in the hilly Bergisches Land, **WUPPERTAL** is not so much a city as an amalgam of towns strung out along the narrow, wooded valley of the River Wupper; they united in 1929 and shortly afterwards adopted the name Wuppertal. Known internationally for its unique suspended-monorail system, the **Schwebebahn**, and for Pina Bausch's **Tanztheater Wuppertal** – one of the world's most renowned modern dance troupes – it's also the place where Aspirin was invented, and was a major centre of the German textile industry. Despite some down-at-heel stretches the city is redeemed by its hilly, leafy site and by the survival of a large number of buildings from its nineteenth-century heyday, particularly in **Elberfeld**, which is the larger and more attractive of the two main centres, the other being **Barmen**, a little to the east.

Arrival, information and accommodation

Elberfeld's Hauptbahnhof is on Döppersberg at the start of the traffic-free shopping zone. The tourist office is opposite (Mon–Fri 9am–6pm, Sat 10am–2pm; ☎0202/194 33, ⓦwww.wuppertal.de); there's also an **information point** in the Rathaus at Barmen (Mon–Wed & Fri 8am–1pm, Thurs 8am–5pm; ☎0202/563 66 88).

Art Fabrik & Hotel Bockmühle 16–24, Barmen ☎0202/283 70, ⓦwww.art-fabrik-hotel.de. Wuppertal's most interesting hotel is the arty and reasonably priced *Art Fabrik*, in a converted textile mill that once belonged to the Engels family. ❸

Astor Schlossbleiche 4–6, Elberfeld ☎0202/45 05 11, ⓦwww.hotel-astor-wuppertal.de. A tasteful and comfortable place near the tourist office. ❸

DJH Wuppertal Obere Lichtenplatzerstr. 70, Barmen ☎0202/55 23 72, ⓦwww.wuppertal .jugendherberge.de. The city's youth hostel is at the foot of a wooded nature reserve south of Barmen town centre. Dorms from €17.50.

Ibis Hofaue 4, Elberfeld ☎0202/870 44, ⓦwww .ibishotel.com. Central but not very distinctive. ❸

Elberfeld

Wedged between the river and the high ground to the north, **ELBERFELD**'s tight knot of shopping streets contains a few dignified old civic buildings. One of these, the handsome former Rathaus from 1842, houses the **Von der Heydt Museum** (Tues, Wed & Fri–Sun 11am–6pm, Thurs 11am–8pm; €3), with an impressive collection of big-name fine art from sixteenth- and seventeenth-century Flemish and Dutch masters to the French and German Impressionists and a roll call of modern movements, including Expressionists, Fauvists, Cubists and Futurists. The graphic works include prints and drawings by Otto Dix, Karl Schmidt-Rottluff and Ernst Ludwig Kirchner, while postwar highlights include a couple of typically geometric works by Victor Vaserely, a Joseph Beuys self-portrait and works by Wuppertal-based British artist Tony Cragg; the bronzes in front of the museum are also by him. The museum also has an important collection of works by the Elberfeld-born nineteenth-century neo-Idealist Hans von Marées.

West of the centre along Friedrich-Ebert-Strasse, the delightful **Luisenviertel** is a small-scale district of former weavers' houses, their simple slate-hung or clapboard facades giving them a remarkably North American appearance. The district's architectural focus is spacious Laurentiusplatz with its Neoclassical early nineteenth-century church of **St Laurentius**, but the pretty **Luisenstrasse** just to the north is more enjoyable, with its individual antique, jewellery and clothes shops and relaxed cafés, bars and restaurants. From here, ascend steep **Ortenbrucher Strasse** or the evocatively named **Tippen-Tappen-Tönchen** steps – so named for the noise the workers' wooden clogs made on them – to reach the Nordstadt or **Ölberg**, another miraculously preserved nineteenth-century residential district whose steep streets and elaborate facades provoke comparisons with San Francisco or Montmartre. It's popular with film-makers looking for intact period street; the director Tom Tykwer, who made the 1990s hit *Run, Lola, Run*, is a native of Wuppertal. Though it's by no means uniformly gentrified, the Ölberg does have an arty, bohemian side, and in summer the area's artists hold regular Sunday **art fairs** on Otto-Böhne Platz, where you can buy paintings, sculpture, prints, ceramics, jewellery and books – check ⓦwww.unternehmen-nordstadt.de for dates. The most grandiose of the district's old apartment houses are along its main artery, Marienstrasse. While the Ölberg was traditionally working class, the **Briller Viertel** immediately to the west was where the city's prosperous textile magnates built their elaborate villas, many of which still survive. The streets have grandiose, Prussian names and are if anything even steeper than those of the Ölberg; struggle up arrow-straight Sadowastrasse to reach the shady Nützenberg park, topped by the **Weyerbusch Turm** (visits by appointment daily 8am–3pm; ☎0202/563 62 91), one of a number of similar hilltop observation towers in the city funded by wealthy industrialists in the nineteenth century. Descend again via **Roonstrasse**, the district's most photographed street, a picturesque ensemble of gables, turrets, balconies and steps.

Barmen

Compared with Elberfeld's intact nineteenth-century streetscapes the charms of **BARMEN** are modest, but there's enough to see there to justify a trip on the **Schwebebahn** (tickets as for other cities in the VRR network; see Essen, p.648). The system, which is suspended from massive girders above the course of the River Wupper, was an ingenious solution to the problem of providing a rapid-transit system in an extremely narrow valley where space was at a premium. It was the idea of Cologne engineer Eugen Langen, and was built in the 1890s; Kaiser Wilhelm II took an inaugural ride in 1900 and it opened to the public a few months afterwards. It takes some getting used to as the trains are noisy and sway from side to side in slightly disconcerting fashion, but the system has a good safety record, and on weekend afternoons you can take a "*Kaffeefahrt*" on one of the original 1900 trains, departing from Vohwinkel station. Alight at Adler Brücke to reach the **Historisches Zentrum** (Tues–Sun 10am–6pm; €4) which comprises a rather dry and old-fashioned museum in the **Engels Haus**, commemorating the revolutionary Friedrich Engels, son of a wealthy local textile magnate, born nearby in 1820, and the altogether more engrossing **Museum für Frühindustrialisierung** (Museum of Early Industrialization). This tells the story of Wuppertal's rise to become Germany's cotton metropolis during the nineteenth century by way of various looms, artefacts and photographs. As the displays – which include a Spinning Jenny, a brace of Arkwright machines and a Crompton Spinning Mule – attest, the industry was initially dependent on technological and trading links with Britain, though by the end of the century the city was producing its own looms. As in the UK, in the first half of the nineteenth century children formed the majority of the workforce in Wuppertal's mills; the city's great export success was a form of blue-and-white gingham used to clothe slaves. Nowadays the industry plays only a subsidiary role in Wuppertal's economy, though the city continues to produce specialist fibres for medical and other applications.

Eating, drinking and entertainment

By far the best place for **eating** and **drinking** in Wuppertal is the Luisenviertel. The Historische Stadthalle, Johannisberg 40 (℡0202/24 58 90, ⓦwww.stadthalle .de), is a magnificent **concert hall** built in 1900 and with its original, opulent interiors, is the home base for the Sinfonieorchester Wuppertal. When it's not touring, Pina Bausch's **Tanztheater Wuppertal** is based at the Schauspielhaus on Bundesallee (tickets ℡0202/569 44 44, ⓦwww.pina-bausch.de).

Alaturka Luisenstr. 63a, Elberfeld ℡0202/30 84 13. An excellent Turkish restaurant with belly dancing, a pretty courtyard with climbing roses and plenty of veggie choices. Closed Mon.

Café du Congo Luisenstr. 118, Elberfeld ℡0202/31 62 13. Good for salads from around €7 or more substantial mains in funky, informal surroundings, with a pretty terrace across the street.

Caribe on the corner of Brunnenstr. and Wülfratherstr. A pleasant spot on the Ölberg for a drink, with a big beer garden and reasonably priced food.

Domhan Marienstr. 36. A beer and whisky bar with occasional live music.

Katzengold Cnr Luisenstr. & Untergrünewalder Str. ℡0202/30 45 26. Informal but popular neighbourhood hangout with chalked-up daily specials.

Düsseldorf

Chic **DÜSSELDORF** is not just North Rhine-Westphalia's capital but also its Knightsbridge or Upper East Side – a sophisticated, cosmopolitan city of swish hotels and designer labels, which is very different from the industrial Ruhr. This worldly flair is evidently nothing new, for when Napoleon passed through in 1806 he thought the city "a little Paris". First mentioned in the twelfth century, the village at the mouth of the River Düssel owed its subsequent rise to the counts of Berg, whose Schloss dominated the Altstadt until it burned down in 1872. It blossomed under Elector Johann Wilhelm of Pfalz-Neuburg (1658–1716), known as Jan Wellem, and by the time Napoleon arrived the city had already spread in planned fashion beyond its historic core.

Though its surface glitter is underpinned by the business acumen of its banks and corporate headquarters, fashion houses and advertising agencies, it's the confident ease with which Düsseldorf enjoys its prosperity that strikes visitors most forcefully, from the Altstadt's bars and restaurants to the chi-chi boutiques on stately Königsallee. The city has latterly acquired some cutting-edge architecture to match its established reputation for modern art: Joseph Beuys, the *enfant terrible* of the postwar art scene, was a professor at the city's esteemed Kunstakademie, and the city's galleries are impressive. It has a strong rock music tradition too, the most famous local musical export being synthesizer pioneers Kraftwerk. And it was in a Düsseldorf nightclub in the 1980s that supermodel Claudia Schiffer was discovered. The city's greatest son was, however, neither rock star nor fashion plate, but the Romantic poet **Heinrich Heine**, who is commemorated by a museum. For all its glitz, Düsseldorf is an easy city to enjoy, but its pleasures don't necessarily come cheap. You'll probably notice the price differential if you arrive here after Cologne or the Ruhr.

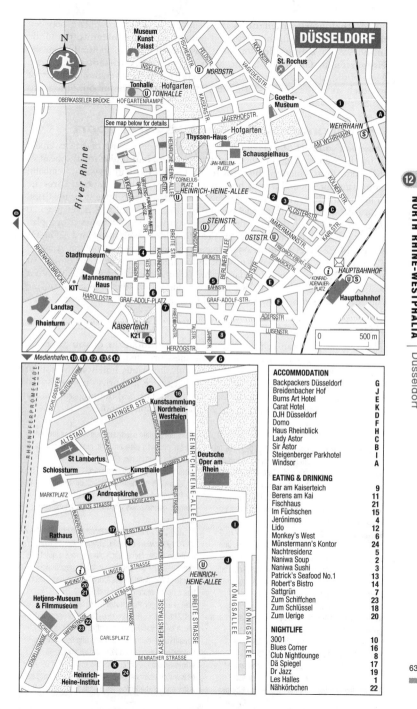

ACCOMMODATION

Backpackers Düsseldorf	G
Breidenbacher Hof	J
Burns Art Hotel	E
Carat Hotel	K
DJH Düsseldorf	D
Domo	F
Haus Rheinblick	H
Lady Astor	C
Sir Astor	B
Steigenberger Parkhotel	I
Windsor	A

EATING & DRINKING

Bar am Kaiserteich	9
Berens am Kai	11
Fischhaus	21
Im Füchschen	15
Jerónimos	4
Lido	12
Monkey's West	6
Münstermann's Kontor	24
Nachtresidenz	5
Naniwa Soup	2
Naniwa Sushi	3
Patrick's Seafood No.1	13
Robert's Bistro	14
Sattgrün	7
Zum Schiffchen	23
Zum Schlüssel	18
Zum Uerige	20

NIGHTLIFE

3001	10
Blues Corner	16
Club Nightlounge	8
Dä Spiegel	17
Dr Jazz	19
Les Halles	1
Nähkörbchen	22

The **Rheinuferpromenade** is the main pedestrian thoroughfare between the vibrant **Altstadt** in the north and the trendy **Medienhafen** to the south. Inland, swanky **Königsallee** (or Kö as it is known) runs north–south from the **Hofgarten** to Graf-Adolf-Strasse, with the peaceful **Carlstadt** to the west. Most of the city's sights are located between Kö and the river, though many of its hotels are to the east or south, and you may want to venture out of town to see **Schloss Benrath**.

Arrival, information and city transport

Düsseldorf's **airport** (☎0211/42 10, ⊛www.dus-int.de) is north of the city, linked in five to twenty minutes by frequent trains to the **Hauptbahnhof**, southeast of the centre, from which the **bus**, **tram** and **U-Bahn** system (⊛www.rheinbahn .com) fans out – useful if your hotel is any distance from the Altstadt. **Fares** are in line with other cities of the VRR network – travel up to three stops for €1.30 on a *Kurzstrecke* ticket or throughout the city on a €2.20 Class A ticket. A €5.20 *TagesTicket* is valid all day from the moment you validate it. If, however, you plan to visit museums or galleries, go for the **Düsseldorf WelcomeCard** (24hr €9, 48 hr €14, 72 hr €19) which offers free or reduced entry plus unlimited use of public transport. You can buy it in some hotels and museums or at one of the two **tourist offices**, opposite the Hauptbahnhof (Immermannstrasse 65b; Mon–Sat 9.30am–7pm; ☎0211/17 20 28 44, ⊛www.duesseldorf-tourismus.de), or in the Altstadt at the corner of Marktstrasse and Rheinstrasse (daily 10am–6pm).

Accommodation

The tourist offices can help with finding **accommodation**, or you can book through their website. There's a glut of business-oriented **hotels** in Düsseldorf, mainly three stars or higher, with some truly luxurious hotels at the top of the market; genuine budget options are rather scarce, and prices rise across the board when there's a major trade fair or event on. The best hunting-ground for all prices is in the streets north and west of the Hauptbahnhof.

Hotels

Breidenbacher Hof Königsallee 11 ☎0211/16 09 00, ⊛www.breidenbacherhofcapella.com. The most über glitzy of all Düsseldorf's five-star hotels opened in 2008, though it harks back to the original *Breidenbacher Hof* of 1812. The style is traditional grand hotel with the luxury vamped up to the max. Doubles start at €410. ❾

Burns Art Hotel Charlottenstr. 60 ☎0211/779 29 10, ⊛www.hotel-burns.de. Crisp, clean lines and sober colours distinguish the rather masculine decor of this "art hotel" between Königsallee and the Hauptbahnhof. Weekend rates are lower, and they also have apartments to rent. ❻

Carat Hotel Benrather Str. 7a ☎0211/130 50, ⊛www.carat-hotels.de. Solid four-star comfort in a great location close to Carlstadt's shops and galleries and the Altstadt's nightlife. ❻

Domo Scheurenstr. 4 ☎0211/384 45 30, ⊛www.nk-hotels.de. Comfortable, good-value pension on the fifth floor of a tower between Königsallee and the Hauptbahnhof – don't be put off by the slightly seedy surroundings, as the hotel itself is perfectly pleasant, and also offers two- and three-bed apartments. ❷

Haus Rheinblick Mühlenstr. 15–17 ☎0211/32 53 16, ⊛www.hotel-haus-rheinblick.de. Small, slightly old-fashioned *hotel garni* in the heart of the Altstadt, offering very good value for its extremely central location. ❸

Sir and Lady Astor Kurfürstenstr. 18/23 ☎0211/17 33 70, ⊛www.sir-astor.de. Stylish, intimate twin boutique hotels facing each other across a quiet street near the city centre. *Sir Astor*'s decorative theme is "Scotland meets Africa", while *Lady Astor* has a richer, more opulent feel. ❹–❻

Steigenberger Parkhotel Königsallee 1a ☎0211 13810, ⊛www.duesseldorf.steigenberger .de. A dependable deluxe address with tasteful, conservative decor and a prime site between the Hofgarten, Altstadt and Königsallee shops. ❼

Windsor Grafenberger Allee 36 ☎0211/17 33 70, ⊛www.sir-astor.de. Sister hotel to the *Sir and Lady Astor* east of the Hofgarten, handsomely decorated in traditional style behind an attractive Jugendstil stone facade. ⑤

Hostels

Backpackers Düsseldorf Fürstenwall 180 ☎0211/302 08 48, ⓦwww.backpackers -duesseldorf.de. Friendly, spacious hostel south of the centre, with accommodation in four- or six-bed dorms, free internet access and no curfew. Reception open 8am–9pm. Dorms from €22.

DJH Düsseldorf Düsseldorfer Str.1, Oberkassel ☎0211/55 73 10, ⓦwww.duesseldorf .jugendherberge.de. Impressive modern hostel in the swanky suburb of Oberkassel west of the Rhine; to reach it, take the U-Bahn to Luegeplatz, from where it's a 7min walk. Accommodation is in twin, four- or six-bed rooms, with some family rooms available. Dorms €24.80.

The Altstadt

All that remains of the castle of the counts of Berg is a stumpy tower on riverside Burgplatz. Today the **Schlossturm** (Tues–Sun 11am–6pm; €3) houses a **museum** on Rhine shipping and is topped by a café. Along with the distinctive spire of the nearby church of **St Lambertus** (Mon–Thurs 8.30am–6pm, Fri 11am–6pm, Sat 7am–6pm, Sun 9am–6pm; free) it forms the visual focus of the agreeably walkable **Altstadt**. The church's spire owes its twisted shape to the use of unseasoned timber when it was rebuilt after a lightning strike in 1815. Inside, the highlights are the rocket-like fifteenth-century Gothic tabernacle and the splendid Renaissance memorial to Duke Wilhelm V.

Düsseldorf's favourite Elector, **Jan Wellem**, sits plump and pleased with himself astride his horse in front of the Renaissance **Rathaus** to the south on Marktplatz. Legend has it that there wasn't enough metal to cast Gabriel di Grupello's splendid equestrian likeness – created towards the end of Jan Wellem's life – and that locals were forced to donate their best silver to complete it. To the east and south, the streets are animated day and night as tourists and locals descend on a vast array of bars, cafés and restaurants.

Schulstrasse on the Altstadt's southern fringe is home to two museums. The **Hetjens Museum** (Tues & Thurs–Sun 11am–5pm, Wed 11am–9pm; €3) houses an impressively eclectic collection of ceramics from ancient times to the present day; star exhibits include a spectacular seventeenth-century blue faïence dome from Multan in Pakistan. Highlights of the **Film Museum** (same hours & price; €4 during special exhibitions) next door include the tin drum from Volker Schlöndorff's 1978 film of the same name, plus costumes from Peter Greenaway's *The Cook, The Thief, His Wife and Her Lover* and Werner Herzog's *Nosferatu*. To the east, **Carlsplatz** defines the Altstadt's southeastern tip and bustles six days a week with an excellent **food market**.

Swing north from here along Mittelstrasse, and a five-minute amble brings you to the **Mahn- und Gedenkstätte Düsseldorf** (Tues–Fri & Sun 11am–5pm, Sat 1–5pm; free) at Mühlenstrasse 29, a somewhat text-heavy chronicle of Nazi crimes in Düsseldorf, though there's an English-language leaflet available on request. Altogether more uplifting is the Baroque **Andreaskirche** (Wed, Thurs & Sat 3–5.30pm, Fri 4–6.30pm, Sun 2–4pm) on nearby Andreasstrasse, built for the Jesuits in the early seventeenth century and with an icing-sugar stucco interior that's worth a visit to see the low-key **mausoleum** containing Jan Wellem's tomb.

The Hofgarten and around

To the east of the Andreaskirche at Grabbeplatz 4, the bunker-like **Kunsthalle** (Tues–Sat noon–7pm, Sun 11am–6pm; €5.50; ⓦwww.kunsthalle-duesseldorf .de) is the first of an impressive string of museums and art galleries fringing the

Hofgarten, a graceful, lake-studded park laid out in the eighteenth century and later extended by Napoleonic decree. The Kunsthalle hosts big-name temporary exhibitions of modern art and is also home to the **Kunstverein**, which promotes the work of less established artists, and to the **Kom(m)ödchen**, a political cabaret. Facing it across Grabbeplatz is the sinuous, glossy black facade of the **K20 Kunstsammlung Nordrhein-Westfalen** (usually Tues–Fri 10am–6pm, Sat & Sun 11am–6pm; Ⓦ www.kunstsammlung.de), which houses an outstanding collection of modern art including around a hundred works by Paul Klee as well as important pieces by Picasso and Joseph Beuys. The museum was closed pending completion of a new extension at the time of writing; it is scheduled to reopen in autumn 2009.

A stroll through the western fringes of the Hofgarten past the imposing Kunstakademie and Expressionist 1926 **Tonhalle** (see p.644) brings you to the **Museum Kunst Palast** (Tues–Sun 11am–6pm; €10; Ⓦ www.museum-kunst-palast.de), worth a visit for its eclectic collection of modern and not-so-modern art, though the thematic displays – which juxtaposes twentieth-century artists Franz Marc or Alexej von Jawlensky with medieval woodcarvers – will irritate some. Highlights include Rubens' *Assumption of the Virgin Mary* and *Venus and Adonis*, and works by painters of the nineteenth-century Düsseldorf school, whose pleasing landscapes give light relief from the occasionally heavy-handed moral themes. Not to be missed is the **Glasmuseum Hentrich** on the building's lower floors, with an encyclopedic glass collection that encompasses the Romans, Tiffany, Gallé, Lalique and some superb contemporary Czech and German fine art glassware. Much of the display is grouped by glassmaking technique, which makes a visit informative as well as fun. Next door, the **NRW Forum** (Tues–Thurs, Sat & Sun 11am–8pm, Fri 11am–midnight; €5.50; Ⓦ www.nrw-forum.de) hosts excellent temporary exhibitions on subjects of contemporary cultural interest, from fashion to photography and advertising.

Halfway across the Hofgarten, the **Theatermuseum Düsseldorf**, Jägerhofstrasse 1 (Tues–Sun 1–8.30pm; €3), is one for enthusiasts – and German speakers – only, while the somewhat dusty presentational style of the **Goethe-Museum Düsseldorf** (Tues & Thurs–Sun 11am–5pm, Wed 11am–9pm; €3), on the park's eastern fringe at Jacobistrasse 2, will try the patience of all but the most diehard of the great man's fans, though it's housed in a delightfully pretty Rococo Schloss.

Königsallee and Carlstadt

A little of the Hofgarten's leafy charm continues south from the park along **Königsallee**, the lavish 82-metre-wide boulevard laid out along the course of the city's old fortifications at the beginning of the nineteenth century. The eastern side is probably Germany's prime spot for flaneurs or fashion victims, its 812m length an A to Z of international designer names from Armani to Ermenegildo Zegna, not forgetting Germany's own Jil Sander. A block east on Grünstrasse, the extrovert **Stilwerk** mall is filled with upmarket interiors stores. Separated from all this by two avenues of trees and an ornamental moat, Königsallee's western side fringes the banking district and is more sober in style, though even here there is some glitz. The copper-roofed Jugendstil **Kaufhof** at the north end is the city's most imposing department store. It was designed for the Tietz chain in 1907–09 by Joseph Maria Olbrich, a leading light of the Viennese Secession and of Darmstadt's Mathildenhöhe *Künstlerkolonie* (see p.568).

West of Königsallee, the broad, straight avenues of the banking quarter have an almost North American feel, an impression heightened by two Weimar-era skyscrapers – the 1924 **Wilhelm-Marx-Haus** on Heinrich-Heine-Allee and the 1922 **Haus der Stummkonzern** at Breite Strasse 69, both of which blend Expressionist and brick Gothic elements to good effect.

Stretching towards the Rhine west of Kasernenstrasse, the delightful **Carlstadt** is more modest in scale, preserving among its antiquarian bookshops, art galleries and delicatessens some of the handsome eighteenth- and nineteenth-century houses that have long made it a favoured residential district. One such house at Bilkerstrasse 12–14 houses the **Heinrich-Heine-Institut** (Tues–Fri & Sun 11am–5pm, Sat 1–5pm; €3) in the same street in which the poet was born in 1797. The author of some of the loveliest verse ever written in the German language, Heine was the son of prosperous, assimilated Jewish parents, and his Judaism was a theme not only during his lifetime – he converted to Christianity in 1825, declaring his act a "ticket of admission to European culture" – but also long after his death. Heine's books were among those burned by the Nazis in 1933 as they began to fulfil his prophecy that "There, where one burns books, one also burns people in the end." But not even they could ban his most popular work, the *Loreley*, which was tolerated – in poem form and in the musical setting by Friedrich Silcher – as a "folk song". Heine was deeply influenced by the spirit of the French Revolution, which he imbibed during the years of the French occupation of Düsseldorf. A radical and a trenchant critic of German feudalism, he spent much of his life in exile in Paris, and died there in 1856. Pick up an English-language leaflet at the start, as the museum's displays are in German only.

Carlstadt is fringed to the south by small lakes. On the north side of one of them, at Berger Allee 2, the **Stadtmuseum Düsseldorf** (Tues–Sun 11am–6pm; free, €3 for temporary exhibitions), housed in the eighteenth-century Spee'sches Palais and its eye-catching modern extension, presents an engrossing overview of Düsseldorf's history, with labelling in English and German. Exhibits include a model of the long-vanished Schloss and a French passport dating from the Napoleonic occupation. You'll also see packaging from the Henkel company, whose Persil washing powder is Düsseldorf's most famous brand name.

On the south side of another lake, the Kaiserteich, the former Rhineland parliament now houses **K21 Kunstsammlung Nordrhein-Westfalen** at Ständehausstrasse 1 (Tues–Fri 10am–6pm, Sat & Sun 11am–6pm; €6.50; Ⓦ www .kunstsammlung.de), which is the city's main contemporary art gallery, picking up where K20's collection of classical modernism leaves off. Installations, video art and photography are interspersed with works in oil or charcoal; among the artists featured are Nam June Paik, Andreas Gursky and the Liverpool-born, Wuppertal-based Tony Cragg. The conversion of the grandiose neo-Renaissance nineteenth-century parliament into a clean, white space with a vast atrium and over-arching glass roof is an audacious work of modern architecture.

The Rheinuferpromenade and Medienhafen

Düsseldorf regained its riverside in 1995 when the traffic-choked B1 highway was finally diverted into a tunnel. In its place, the **Rheinuferpromenade** makes for delightful strolling south from the Altstadt towards the **Medienhafen**, a revamped dockside district that's now one of the city's most visually striking.

Admire the dignified stone facade of Peter Behrens' 1912 **Mannesmann-Haus** building before pausing for artistic and liquid refreshment at **KIT** (Kunst im Tunnel; Tues–Sat noon–7pm, Sun 11am–6pm; €4; Ⓦ www.kunst-im-tunnel.de), an inspired venue for contemporary art sandwiched between the two arms of the road tunnel, with a cool café/bar at ground level. To the south, beneath the Rheinkniebrücke, the **Apollo Varieté** (☎0211/828 90 90, Ⓦ www.apollo -variete.de) organizes alfresco tango evenings in summer. Beyond the bridge, the obligatory **TV tower** (Rheinturm Düsseldorf; daily 10am–11.30pm; €3.50) looms above the North Rhine-Westphalia parliament, with an observation deck 168m above the river, a revolving restaurant and illuminated portholes forming the world's largest decimal clock.

Over the past decade or so, the redundant harbour south of the parliament has been reinvented as the hip **Medienhafen**, with advertising agencies alongside slick nightclubs, restaurants and eye-catching buildings by celebrity architects. Particularly distinctive are the wobbly silver-and-white **Neuer Zollhof** towers by Frank Gehry; also notable is the **Stadttor**, which resembles a steel-and-glass Arc de Triomphe astride the entrance to the road tunnel. Though it's all undeniably developer-led, the Medienhafen is anything but sterile, and in the nightlife stakes at least is beginning to give the Altstadt a run for its money.

Beyond the centre: Schloss Benrath

Southwest of the centre (tram #701 from Jan-Wellem-Platz or S-Bahn 6), the pretty, pink ensemble of **Schloss Benrath** is arranged symmetrically around a large pond. Built between 1755 and 1770 for the Elector Carl Theodor by his French court architect Nicholas de Pigage in a style that is on the cusp between Rococo and Neoclassical, the complex has a doll's house neatness that belies its size. The central **Corps de Logis** (mid-April to Oct Tues–Sun 10am–6pm; Nov to mid-April Tues–Sun 11am–5pm; €7, or €10.50 joint ticket with museums) can only be visited on a guided tour. Once inside, it's apparent that the Schloss's modest external appearance disguises a sumptuous palace. The rooms display the same grace and lightness of touch as the exterior, though the circular domed hall aspires to monumental status. The prettily feminine garden rooms are particularly delightful. The two service wings flanking the Corps de Logis both contain museums: the enjoyable **Museum für Europäische Gartenkunst** (Museum of European Garden Design; same hours as Corps de Logis; €5) occupies the east wing while the rather less exciting **Museum für Naturkunde** (Museum of Natural History; same hours; €5) is in the west wing. There's a classy café, and in summer the grounds are used for concerts.

Eating, drinking and nightlife

The Altstadt is the obvious first port of call for **eating** or **drinking**. Traditional *Brauhäuser* (microbreweries) dispense the distinctive, local top-fermented *Altbier*, while in summer elegant restaurant terraces give Berger Strasse a Mediterranean flair. Bolkerstrasse is the epicentre for raucous mainstream bars, while Ratinger Strasse to the north is more bohemian and charming. Elsewhere, Immermann-strasse is good for Japanese and other Asian restaurants while the Medienhafen has some stylish options for eating and drinking.

Cafés and restaurants

Berens am Kai Kaistr. 16 ☏ 0211/300 67 50. The Bauhaus-style severe decor ensures all attention is focused on the haute cuisine at this Medienhafen restaurant; main courses start around €33, there's an €85 menu and 500 bottles on the wine list. Closed Sun.

Fischhaus Berger Str. 3 ☏ 0211/854 98 64. Excellent, bustling fish restaurant with sumptuous fresh seafood displays, brusquely efficient waiters and, in summer, a pleasant terrace at the front. Main courses from around €11.

Jerónimos Hohe Str. 23 ☏ 0211/600 32 86. Classy Spanish-style tapas place with a devoted local following; tapas from €3.80 plus more substantial, fishy main courses. Closed Sun.

Lido Am Handelshafen 15 ☏ 0211/15 76 87 30. Memorably set on an ultra-modern "island" in the Medienhafen, this stylish bistro offers modern European food with a French accent and plenty of seafood. Two-course *Tagesmenü* €32.50, three courses €41.

Monkey's West Graf-Adolf-Platz 15 ☏ 0211/64 96 37 26. Trendy, see-and-be-seen restaurant/bar in the banking district, with shoulder of venison with hazelnut *Spätzle* on the menu and main courses from around €23. Eve only at weekends; kitchen open until midnight.

Münstermann's Kontor Hohe Str. 11 ☎0211/130 04 16. Hugely popular Carlstadt lunch spot, attached to a long-established delicatessen, with daily specials chalked up on a blackboard.

Naniwa Oststr. 55 ☎0211 16 17 99. Simple Japanese canteen selling cheap noodle dishes and soups; the sister restaurant across the street has more expensive sushi, sashimi and tempura.

Patrick's Seafood No.1 Kaistr. 17 ☎0211/617 99 88. Elegant French seafood restaurant in the Medienhafen, with modern art on the walls and *bouillabaisse* on the menu. Closed Mon, eve only Sat & Sun.

🏃 **Robert's Bistro** Wupperstr. 2 ☎0211/30 48 21. Wonderfully unpretentious French bistro close to the Medienhafen, with authentic choices such as confit of duck and *andouillette*; main courses from €14. Closed Sun & Mon.

Sattgrün Graf-Adolf-Platz 6 ☎0211/876 33 90. Organic and largely vegan place near the banking district, with €12.90 brunch menu. Closes at 8pm weekdays and earlier on Sat; closed Sun.

Brauhäuser and bars

🍺 **Bar am Kaiserteich** Ständehausstr. 1 ☎0211/17 13 20. The cocktail bar at K21 is one of the most stylish in the city, with bubble-inspired decor creating the impression that you're sitting at the bottom of a giant drink. Also serves food.

Im Füchschen Ratinger Str. 28 ☎0211 137 470. Civilized *Hausbrauerei* with excellent beer, traditional atmosphere and affordable food, with main courses from €8.50.

Nachtresidenz Bahnstr. 13 ☎0211/136 57 55, ⓦ www.nachtresidenz.de. Huge city-centre club in a converted cinema, playing house, Latin, soul and disco and with a "dress to impress" door policy.

Zum Schiffchen Hafenstr. 5 ☎0211/132 421. A touch more refined than most of the Alstadt *Brauhäuser*, serving *Frankenheimer Alt*; its proudest boast is that Napoleon stopped by in 1811.

Zum Schlüssel Bolkerstr. 41–47 ☎0211/82 89 50. Vast traditional Altstadt *Hausbrauerei* serving hearty regional food alongside the *Altbier*; main courses from around €9.

Zum Uerige Berger Str. 1 ☎0211/86 69 90. Labyrinthine, atmospheric Altstadt *Hausbrauerei* that spills outside in summer. It's not sophisticated, but the bitter *Altbier* is good and there's simple food to mop it up.

Nightlife and entertainment

Again the Medienhafen is a good spot for **nightlife** and **clubs**. Düsseldorf's **lesbian and gay** scene suffers from the city's proximity to Cologne, but there are a few convivial places in addition to the rather glum men-only offerings near the Hauptbahnhof.

You can see the full panoply of performance in Düsseldorf, with everything from opera to cabaret and variety. The **theatre** tradition is strong: the great actor-director Gustav Gründgens, the subject of Klaus Mann's unflattering novel *Mephisto*, was born here, while in the postwar years the Düsseldorfer Ensemble attracted such internationally renowned actors as Anton Walbrook and Elisabeth Bergner. In February, the city celebrates the climax of **carnival** with as much fervour as Cologne; in July the **Grösste Kirmes am Rhein** – an odd blend of folk festival and shooting fair – fills the riverbanks with old-fashioned funfair rides, and in September the **Altstadtherbst** brings dance, music and drama to various Altstadt venues, with a theatre tent on Burgplatz.

Clubs and live music

3001 Franziusstr. 7 ☎0211/66 96 99 90. Trendy club in the Medienhafen with cheap Thursday student night "Milchbar".

Blues Corner Ratinger Str. 50 ☎0211/32 89 90, ⓦ www.bluescorner.de. Live rock, blues and acoustic sets in a convivial, arty bar in the north of the Altstadt.

Club Nightlounge Corneliusstr. 1. Convivial but low-key little gay bar just south of Graf-Adolf-Strasse. Open 3pm–5am.

Dä Spiegel Bolkerstr. 22 ☎0211/323 74 90. Noisy bar with regular live music; gigs kick off at 10pm Wed–Sat.

Dr Jazz Flingerstr. 11 ☎0211/136 57 19. Basement bar in the Altstadt with regular live

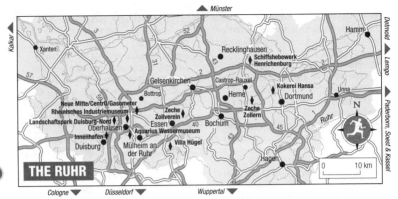

music, including jazz, world music and rock 'n' roll. Thurs–Sat from 8pm.

Les Halles Schirmerstr. 54 ☎211/440 26 74. Vaguely "alternative" club and restaurant in a former freight depot, with inventive decor that mixes the opulent and the industrial.

Nähkörbchen Hafenstr. 11 ☎0211/323 02 65. The "little sewing basket" is an enjoyable, sing-along-style gay bar in the southern half of the Altstadt. Eve only on weekdays, open at weekends from lunchtime.

Theatres, concert venues and cabaret

Deutsche Oper am Rhein Heinrich-Heine-Allee 16a ☎0211/892 5211, ⓦwww.rheinoper.de. Both opera and ballet are presented at Düsseldorf's opera house, which premieres several new productions each season.

Düsseldorfer Marionettentheater Palais Wittgenstein, Bilkerstr. 7 ☎0211/32 84 32, ⓦwww.marionettentheater-duesseldorf.de. Puppet theatre presenting opera and children's classics like *Beauty and the Beast* as well as more serious pieces.

Düsseldorfer Schauspielhaus Gustav-Gründgens-Platz 1 ☎0211/36 99 11, ⓦwww.duesseldorfer -schauspielhaus.de. Düsseldorf's major theatre, which also presents modern dance, in an iconic, white modernist building just off the Hofgarten.

Kom(m)mödchen Bolkerstr. 44 ☎0211/32 56 06, ⓦwww.kommoedchen.de. Renowned political cabaret that attracts performers with a national reputation.

Roncalli's Apollo Varieté ☎0211/828 90 90, ⓦwww.apollo-variete.de. Old-style variety shows, with everything from acrobats to clowns, jugglers and magicians.

Tonhalle Ehrenhof 1 ☎0211/89 96 123, ⓦwww.tonhalle.de. Concert hall with excellent acoustics. The home base of the Düsseldorfer Symphoniker orchestra.

Zakk Fichtenstr. 40 ☎0211/973 00 10. Politically engaged cultural centre in a converted factory east of the Hauptbahnhof, with rock and reggae concerts, poetry, comedy and women-only events.

Duisburg

Straddling the Rhine at the point where the Ruhr empties into it, **DUISBURG** is the western gateway to the Ruhrgebiet and, with a population of half a million, its third largest city. Though the surviving medieval defences point to a long history, it was the industrialization of the Ruhr in the nineteenth century that transformed it into a major city, the largest inland port in Europe as well as a centre for steel, coal and engineering. From the mid-1960s onwards, Duisburg's heavy industries went into decline, but the city has faced its challenges with drive and imagination, restructuring its economy towards technology and services and hiring the British architect Norman Foster to oversee its physical transformation. These days its engrossing museums, reworked industrial landscapes and funky, revitalized docks are worth a day or two of anyone's time.

Arrival, information and accommodation

Duisburg's **Hauptbahnhof** is at the eastern edge of the city centre, a short way from Königsstrasse and the **tourist office** at no. 86 (Mon–Fri 9.30am-6pm, Sat 10am–1pm; ℡0203/28 54 40, ⊛www.duisburgnonstop.de), which can help with accommodation.

City Hostel Friedenstr. 85 ℡0203/935 63 62, ⊛www.hostel-duisburg.de. Hostel a short distance south of the city centre, with beds in four- to ten-bed dorms from €20 including bedding.
City Hotel Hohe Str. 14–16 ℡0203/604 59 99, ⊛www.cityhotel-duisburg.de. New budget hotel close to the Hauptbahnhof and Königsstrasse. Reception open 7–11am and 5–10pm; phone ahead at other times. ❷

Duisburger Hof Neckarstr. 25a ℡0203/300 70, ⊛www.Steigenberger.de. Duisburg's most luxurious hotel since 1927, full of four-star elegance and just off the central König-Heinrich-Platz. ❺–❼
Goldener Hahn Hohe Str. 25a ℡0203/317 74 05, ⊛www.hotelgoldenerhahn.de. Family-run place close to the Hauptbahnhof with comfortable, if slightly characterless, rooms above a restaurant. ❸

⑫

⊛

The reinvention of the Ruhr

A tough working-class cop with a complex personal history and a fondness for drink sounds like an unlikely rescuer for a depressd industrial region. Yet when Duisburg *Kriminalhauptkommissar* **Horst Schimanski** burst into German homes in the television series *Tatort* in 1981, initial outrage at his unorthodox methods quickly turned not just into adulation, but also to a resurgence of interest in the Ruhr's history and identity. Played by Götz George as a soft-centred macho with a combat jacket and huge moustache, Schimmi's rise to cult status was greatly aided by the show's atmospheric use of gritty Ruhr locations, and the show is credited with having rallied the region's morale, badly battered by the decline of its coal and steel industries from the 1960s onwards. Gradually the idea arose that the **Ruhrgebiet** – or **Ruhrpott** as it's affectionately known by its inhabitants – could be cool too.

Germany's largest urban area, the Ruhrgebiet consists of a string of interlinked towns and cities stretching east of the Rhine along the often surprisingly green valley of the Ruhr. It straddles both the historic boundary between Rhineland and Westphalia and the confessional divide – Dortmund was traditionally Protestant, whereas Essen was the seat of a Catholic abbey and later home to a large Jewish community. The Ruhr's cities nevertheless have a shared history of sleepy provincialism abruptly transformed by coal and steel in the nineteenth century. It has also always been an important **footballing region**, with teams like Gelsenkirchen's Schalke and Borussia Dortmund numbered among the nation's most successful, but in recent years its cultural credentials have been burnished too. Rather than demolish and forget its redundant steelworks and mines, the Ruhr reinvented them as design centres, art galleries or museums, in the process creating some of the most strikingly original visitor attractions in Europe. Eyebrows may have been raised when the region was awarded the coveted **European Capital of Culture** title for 2010, but they will arch in astonishment when confronted with the edgy and exciting venues that will host the year's events.

The Ruhr's image became a touch trendier still when it took over as the host for the immensely successful **Love Parade** after Berlin tired of hosting the annual techno-fest in 2007. Any suggestion that the Ruhr version couldn't match the original was laid to rest in Dortmund in 2008 when 1.6 million techno fans partied on the Bundesstrasse 1 highway, shattering all previous attendance records. As for Schimanski, the grizzled cop in the combat jacket is regularly back on screen in one-off specials, and is now so closely identified with Duisburg that there were even proposals to name the university after him.

For information on the European Capital of Culture 2010, see ⊛www.ruhr2010.de. There was no Love Parade scheduled for 2009; the next is to be held in Duisburg in 2010, with Gelsenkirchen the venue for 2011; see ⊛www.loveparade.de.

NORTH RHINE-WESTPHALIA | Duisburg

The City

Duisburg's main thoroughfare is tree-lined Königsstrasse, a standard-issue shopping precinct enlivened by the imposing civic buildings that fringe revamped König-Heinrich-Platz and by Niki de Saint-Phalle's jolly **Lifesaver fountain**, which adds a splash of colour further west. Turn left here down Düsseldorferstrasse to reach the **Stiftung Wilhelm Lehmbruck Museum** (Tues–Sat 11am–5pm, Sun 10am–6pm; €6), which houses a remarkable collection of modern sculpture in a pair of calm, pavilion-like structures set in a sculpture park. At the heart of the collection is the work of Duisburg-born Wilhelm Lehmbruck (1881–1919), regarded as one of the pioneers of twentieth-century sculpture and whose work, which focuses on the female form, is represented here by numerous busts, full-length figures and paintings. There are also works by a roll call of big international names, from Alexander Calder to Barbara Hepworth and Jean Tinguely, as well as a selection of German Expressionist paintings.

West of the *Lifesaver* statue the course of the old fortifications marks the edge of Duisburg's **Altstadt**, though there's not much of any great age save the **Salvatorkirche**, the city's main Protestant church, completed in 1415 and the final resting place of Flemish-born cartographer Gerhard Mercator (1512–94). The church forms an impressive architectural ensemble alongside the vast, early twentieth-century Rathaus next door.

Nearby, the square brick **Schwanentor** bridge marks the course of the **Innenhafen**, the former dock that is now the focus of the city's regeneration. Next to the bridge, boats depart on two-hour **cruises** through Duisburg's extensive harbour (March to mid-Oct daily 11.30am, 1.30pm & 3.30pm; mid-Oct to Nov Wed, Sat & Sun 12.30pm & 2.30pm; €9.50; Ⓦ www .wf-duisburg.de). You can follow the Innenhafen on foot northeast from the bridge to the **Kultur- und Stadthistorisches Museum Duisburg** (Tues–Thurs & Sat 10am–5pm, Fri 10am–2pm, Sun 10am–6pm; €3), which has a collection relating to the life and work of Mercator. Beyond it, a preserved section of medieval city wall leads to the **Garten der Erinnerungen**, one of the best areas of the revitalized dock, a strikingly tough post-industrial garden designed by Israeli artist Dani Karavan. Isolated chunks of dock architecture are preserved like whitewashed specimens among the highly sculptural lawns and planters. The rabbits love it – come at dusk and they're leaping all over the place. East of the garden, a row of preserved warehouses marks the liveliest part of the Innenhafen, lined on both sides with big restaurants, cafés and bars. A giant yellow brick giraffe standing outside one of the buildings on the south side marks the entrance to the **Legoland Discovery Centre** (daily 10am–5pm; adults €12.95, children €9; Ⓦ www .legolanddiscoverycentre.de), where the child-friendly attractions include Lego reproductions of the Ruhr's landmarks, a jungle made of plastic bricks and the chance to test skyscraper models for earthquake resistance. Close by, a massive former grain warehouse is now the **Museum Küppersmühle für Moderne Kunst** (Wed 2–6pm, Thurs, Sat & Sun 11am–6pm, Fri by appointment only; €6), Duisburg's museum of contemporary art, whose cool white spaces host touring exhibitions and have housed the Ströher collection of German art since the 1950s, with works by major figures such as Georg Baselitz, Anselm Kiefer, Sigmar Polke and Gerhard Richter. Plans for a startling vertical extension of the building by Swiss architects Herzog & de Meuron – designers of London's Tate Modern and of the Allianz Arena in Munich – will, if realized, transform the Küppersmühle into Germany's most important museum of contemporary art.

The Landschaftspark Duisburg-Nord

North of the centre is Duisburg's most original attraction, the **Landschafts-park Duisburg-Nord** (Mon–Thurs 10am–5pm, Fri–Sun 10am–9pm; free access to site, group guided tours in English from €75 on request to the visitor centre; ☏0203/429 19 42, ⓦwww.landschaftspark.de). Until 1985 it was a giant steelworks belonging to the Thyssen group; since its decommissioning, nature has reclaimed large parts of the two-square-kilometre site, with rose gardens planted in former ore-hoppers and trees growing up and through the rusty blast furnaces, one of which can be climbed for a vertigo-inducing – though perfectly safe – closer look. The atmosphere is eerie, almost post-apocalyptic, yet there's no doubt that it works, both as a peaceful urban park and an awe-inspiring piece of industrial archeology. It's also a concert venue and activity centre, with alpine climbing gardens and Europe's largest artificial diving centre housed in a flooded gasometer. At weekends a stunning light installation turns it into pure science-fiction after dark. To get there, take tram #903 or #902 from Duisburg's Hauptbahnhof, stop Landschaftspark Nord, from where it's a short walk along Emscherstrasse.

Eating and drinking

The best area for a place to **eat and drink** is the eastern end of the Innenhafen, with a row of slick and trendy places on both sides of the basin.

Brauhaus Schacht 4/8 Düsseldorferstr. 21 ☏0203/28 10 00. Reasonably priced food is available along with beer from the microbrewery housed in the neo-Renaissance, former Reichsbank building.

Drei Giebel Haus Nonnengasse 8 ☏0203/223 89. Traditional German cooking in the historic surroundings of the city's only surviving medieval house.

Faktorei 21 Philosophenweg 21 ☏0203/346 83 79. Hip, spacious bar/restaurant with monthly disco-classic nights and an Italian-influenced menu.

Mezzomar Am Innenhafen 8–10 ☏0203/363 59 57. Big Italian bar and restaurant on the north side of the Innenhafen, dishing up pizzas, steaks and seafood along with the drinks.

Mississipi Schifferstr. 190 ☏0203/348 63 20. Vast American-style bar/diner on the north side of the Innenhafen, with Cajun and Tex-Mex dishes, salads and a good-value breakfast buffet.

Entertainment and nightlife

Duisburg's main temple to high **culture** is the Theater der Stadt Duisburg on König-Heinrich-Platz (☏0203/300 91 00, ⓦwww.theater-duisburg.de), which hosts drama, opera and classical concerts; the Theater am Marientor at Plessingstrasse 20 (☏0203/282 50, ⓦwww.theater-am-marientor.de) puts on anything from operetta to cabaret, dance and musicals. There's regular live jazz, funk and world music at *Djäzz*, Börsenstrasse 11 (ⓦwww.djaezz.de), and a rockier edge to the sounds at *Kultkeller*, Steinsche Gasse 48.

Essen

For many Germans, **ESSEN**'s best-known son is Heinz Rühmann (1902–94), Germany's greatest screen comic, whose extraordinary film career spanned the Weimar Republic, Third Reich, Cold War and post-reunification eras and whose best-loved film – the school comedy *Die Feuerzangenbowle* – still enjoys *Rocky Horror*-style cult status more than sixty years after it was first shown. For the rest of the world, however, the city's name is synonymous with that of the **Krupp** family, the powerful steel-to-armaments dynasty whose rise mirrored the city's own ascent to industrial greatness during the nineteenth century, and whose commercial genius and questionable political judgement accurately reflect the experience of Germany in the first half of the twentieth century.

For visitors expecting vistas of belching chimneys, first impressions of Essen can be surprising, for it's an unashamedly commercial city, with a modest forest of office towers and a truly vast central shopping zone. Though it contests with Dortmund the status of biggest city in the Ruhr – both have populations just under 600,000 – Essen is the one with the unmistakable big-city feel, and it's this, as much as its central position in the region, that makes it the Ruhr's "secret" capital. It's an enjoyable place to spend a day or two, with plenty of high culture, a smattering of interesting sights that includes one UNESCO World Heritage Site, and a lively nightlife scene.

Basic orientation is straightforward: the **city centre** is immediately north of the Hauptbahnhof, with the main **cultural zone** to the south; further south still is some of the most enticing eating, drinking and sightseeing, while the gritty north preserves reminders of the city's industrial greatness.

Arrival, information and city transport

Essen's **tourist office** is opposite the north exit from the **Hauptbahnhof** at Am Hauptbahnhof 2 (Mon–Fri 9am–5.30pm, Sat 10am–1pm; ☎0201/194 33, ⓦwww.essen.de). To get to grips with this large city, you'll need to master the extensive **public transport** system, which includes bus, tram and U-Bahn (ⓦwww.evag.de) as well as trains to the suburbs and neighbouring cities. Ticketing is integrated with other Ruhr communities through the **VRR regional transport network**: you can travel up to three stops for €1.30 on a *Kurzstrecke* ticket or throughout the city on a €2.20 Class A ticket. A €5.20 *TagesTicket* allows 24 hours of unlimited travel. *NachtExpress* night buses serve outlying districts after normal services have ceased, departing hourly from the Hauptbahnhof.

Accommodation

Essen's **hotels** are geared more to the business traveller than the leisure visitor and are widely scattered through the city.

Ambassador Viehofer Str. 23 ☎0201/24 77 30, ⓦwww.ambassador-essen.de. Comfortable, slightly bland hotel right in the central pedestrian zone, with private parking and some roomy singles. Handy for the city centre's nightlife scene. ❹

Arosa Rüttenscheider Str. 149 ☎0201/722 60, ⓦwww.hotel-arosa-essen.de. Classy modern hotel in a great location right on the Rü, but it's also close to the Messe, so watch out for price hikes during conferences and exhibitions. ❹–❻

DJH Essen Pastoratsberg 2 ☎0201/49 11 63, ⓦwww.djh.de. Essen's youth hostel is in the pretty half-timbered suburb of Werden, south of the Baldeneysee and reached by S-bahn to Essen-Werden, then bus #190.

Margarethenhöhe Steile Str. 46 ☎0201/438 60, ⓦwww.margarethenhoehe.com. Boutique-style hotel in a historic building in the garden suburb of Margaretenhöhe, southwest of the centre, with best rates available at weekends. ❹–❼

Mövenpick Am Hauptbahnhof 2 ☎0201/170 80, ⓦwww.moevenpick-essen.com. Slick, central business-class hotel, with tasteful modern decor, spacious, a/c rooms and remarkably good deals if you pick your dates. Rates do not include breakfast. ❸–❼

Parkhaus Hügel Freiherr-vom-Stein Str. 209 ☎0201/47 10 91, ⓦwww.imhoff-essen.de. Attractive hotel-restaurant in a leafy setting next to the Villa Hügel, overlooking the Baldeneysee and with regular S-Bahn trains into town. ❺

Zum Deutschen Haus Kastanienallee 16 ☎0201/23 29 89, ⓦwww.hotel-zum-deutschen -haus.de. The views aren't the loveliest, but this is a good budget option, very central and with a tradi-tional German restaurant. Cheapest rooms share facilities, and there are some singles. ❷–❸

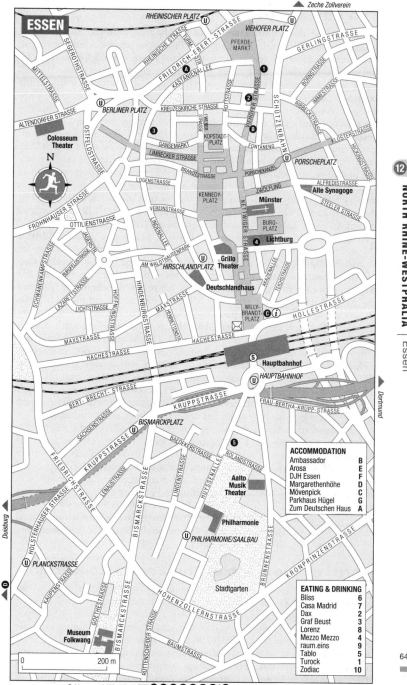

ESSEN

12

Zeche Zollverein

RHEINISCHER PLATZ

VIEHOFER PLATZ

PFERDE-MARKT

GERLINGSTRASSE

SEGEROTHSTRASSE
MITTELSTRASSE
FRIEDRICH-EBERT-STRASSE
RHEINISCHE STRASSE
TURMSTR.
KASTANIENALLEE
BORNSTRASSE
IMMELSTRASSE

BERLINER PLATZ

KREUZESKIRCHE STRASSE

RIBBECKSTRASSE
KLOSTERSTRASSE
HICKINGSTRASSE

ALTENDORFER STRASSE

Colosseum
Theater

N

OSTFELDSTRASSE

GÄNSEMARKT
LIMBECKER STRASSE

KOPSTADT-
PLATZ

ROTTSTRASSE
WEBER STRASSE
VIEHOFER STRASSE
SCHÜTZENBAHN

FONTÄNENG

PORSCHEPLATZ

BRANDTSTRASSE
PORSCHEKANZEL

ALFREDISTRASSE

LOGENSTRASSE

KENNEDY-
PLATZ

ZWÖLFLING

Alte Synagoge

FROHNHAUSER STRASSE
OTTILIENSTRASSE
VEREINSTRASSE
LINDENALLEE

Münster

KETTWIGER STRASSE

STEELER STRASSE

SCHWANENKAMPSTRASSE
JÄGERSTR.
BURGFELDSTRASSE
LAZARETTSTRASSE
LICHTSTRASSE
HOFFNUNGSTRASSE
HINDENBURGSTRASSE
MAXSTRASSE
HEBELSTRASSE

AM WALDTHAUSENPARK
HIRSCHLANDPLATZ

Grillo
Theater

BURG-
PLATZ

Lichtburg

AKAZIENALLEE
TEICHSTRASSE

Deutschlandhaus

WILLY-BRANDT-PLATZ

HOLLESTRASSE

MAXSTRASSE
HACHESTRASSE

HACHESTRASSE

Hauptbahnhof

HAUPTBAHNHOF

Dortmund

BERT-BRECHT-STRASSE

KRUPPSTRASSE

FRAU-BERTHA-KRUPP-STRASSE

SACHSENSTRASSE
FRIEDRICHSTRASSE
HOLSTERHAUSER STRASSE

BISMARCKPLATZ

KRUPPSTRASSE

LENAUSTRASSE
BAEDEKERSTRASSE

LINDENSTRASSE

ROLANDSTRASSE

HUYSSENALLEE

BISMARCKSTRASSE

Aalto
Musik
Theater

Philharmonie

BRUNNENSTRASSE

KRONPRINZENSTRASSE

Duisburg

PLANCKSTRASSE

KAUPENSTRASSE
GOETHESTRASSE

PHILHARMONIE/SAALBAU

Stadtgarten

HOHENZOLLERNSTRASSE

BISMARCKSTRASSE
RÜTTENSCHEIDER STRASSE

Museum
Folkwang

BAUMSTRASSE

0   200 m

Baldernaysee & Villa Hügel ▼ ❻,❼,❽,❾,❿,Ⓔ,Ⓕ & Ⓖ

ACCOMMODATION

Ambassador	B
Arosa	E
DJH Essen	F
Margarethenhöhe	D
Mövenpick	C
Parkhaus Hügel	G
Zum Deutschen Haus	A

EATING & DRINKING

Bliss	6
Casa Madrid	7
Dax	2
Graf Beust	3
Lorenz	8
Mezzo Mezzo	4
raum.eins	9
Tablo	5
Turock	1
Zodiac	10

The city centre

A sign on the roof of the **Handelshof** building opposite the Hauptbahnhof welcomes you to "Essen, the shopping city". Essen's city centre has long functioned as a financial and service centre for the rest of the Ruhr, and much of its character still derives from a handful of early twentieth-century commercial buildings – imposing rather than beautiful – which by their sheer solidity testify to the confidence of Essen's business class in the years before the Depression. In the midst of the banking quarter along Lindenallee, the 1929 **Deutschlandhaus** is perhaps the pick of them, a slim, elegant Bauhaus proto-skyscraper with graceful rounded corners and a small internal shopping arcade. A cluster of Weimar-era monuments is also found along **Kettwigstrasse**, the city's main shopping street, which leads north from the Hauptbahnhof. Here, the 1928 **Baedekerhaus** at no. 35 recalls the pioneering guidebook publisher Karl Baedeker, who was born in Essen in 1801; the neighbouring Peek & Cloppenburg store was the Jewish-owned Blum drapery until forcibly "Aryanized" under the Nazis in the 1930s, a fate shared by the much-loved 1928 **Lichtburg** cinema opposite: Germany's largest, it hides a beautiful 1950s auditorium behind its no-nonsense Bauhaus facade.

Rather overshadowed by all this commercial bombast is Essen's **Münster** (Mon–Fri 6.30am–6.30pm, Sat 9am–7.30pm, Sun 9am–8pm; no access for visitors during Mass; free), founded as a convent in 852 AD by Altfrid, bishop of Hildesheim, and with a sturdy octagonal tower dating from around 1000 AD, which survived both the fire that destroyed the rest of the church in 1275 and the World War II bombing raids. The Münster's low, attenuated profile is partly an accident of topography and partly the result of its curious physical attachment to a second church, the tiny **Johanniskirche**, reached across the tenth-century atrium or *paradies* at the cathedral's west end. The Münster's **Schatzkammer** (Tues–Sat 10am–5pm, Sun 11.30am–5pm; €3) is well worth a look: its treasures include the jewel-encrusted *Lilienkrone* – the crown reputedly used to crown Otto III in Aachen in 983 AD – as well as a series of fabulous gilded crosses dating from the tenth and eleventh centuries. The cathedral's most famous treasure, however, is the **Goldene Madonna**, a graceful gilded wood figure which dates from around 980 AD and which has its own chapel in the main body of the cathedral.

A few hundred metres to the east – marooned by speeding traffic – stands the **Alte Synagoge** (Tues–Sun 10am–6pm; free), one of Germany's largest. Designed by Edmund Körner and built in 1911–13, its splendour reflects the former importance of Essen's Jewish community, which at its apogee in 1933 numbered 4500. Essen's Jews were politically liberal and many were prominent in business; after 1933, Nazi boycotts and Aryanization badly affected the community and by the summer of 1939 it had already dwindled through emigration to 1650. The synagogue survived being burnt on Kristallnacht and again after an electrical fire in 1979; nowadays it houses an exhibition on the history of the community, with plentiful English-language labelling.

North of the centre: The Zeche Zollverein

Essen's working-class northern suburbs would be an improbable place to visit were it not for the **Zeche Zollverein**, Gelsenkirchener Strasse 181 (visitor centre April–Oct daily 10am–7pm; Nov–March Sat–Thurs 10am–5pm, Fri 10am–7pm; free), an enormous Bauhaus-style coal mine and coking plant dating from the early 1930s and declared a UNESCO World Heritage Site in 2001 in recognition of its significance as an example of industrial architecture. Today, the sprawling complex houses everything from museums and art installations to restaurants and artists' studios; there's even a swimming pool open in summer. A visit begins with

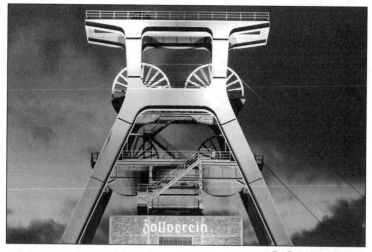

▲ The Zeche Zollverein, Essen

a journey up a long escalator into the former coal-washing plant; en route, there's plenty of time to admire the retro-futuristic grandeur of the architecture – it's all very Flash Gordon. The visitor centre is here, and a new permanent home for the **Ruhr Museum** will open in the building in the autumn of 2009.

Nearby, the former boiler house was redesigned by Norman Foster to house the **Red Dot Design Museum** (Tues–Thurs 11am–6pm, Fri–Sun 11am–8pm; €5; Ⓦ www.red-dot.de), the world's largest exhibition of contemporary design, with everything from saucepans and power tools to packaging and furniture. Perhaps inevitably, it sometimes has the feel of a department store where you can't actually buy anything – though there is a gift shop at the entrance – while some of the selections are questionable: can a gas-guzzling SUV, however ingenious, really be a design classic? Nevertheless the displays are engrossing and make inventive, often witty use of the dramatic, vertigo-inducing space.

The Zollverein complex becomes less crowded the further you venture from the visitor centre, and by the time you reach the distant **coking plant** it's positively deserted. It's worth the trek, however, to see Ilya and Emilia Kabakov's eccentric art installation **The Palace of Projects** (April–Oct Wed–Sun noon–8pm; Nov– March Wed–Sun noon–4pm; €4), which documents various of their projects, in the dark, echoing former salt store. The plant itself is gargantuan, though without familiar architectural reference points it's difficult to grasp the sheer size of the place. Human scale is restored in December and January, when an ice rink opens in the shadow of the coke ovens.

To reach the Zeche Zollverein, take tram #107 (direction Gelsenkirchen) from the city centre and alight at the "Zollverein" stop.

South of the centre: culture, art and the Krupp dynasty

South of the Hauptbahnhof, two of Essen's cultural jewels fringe the leafy Stadt-garten: the **Philharmonie** and the more eye-catching **Aalto-Musiktheater**, a characteristically white, elegant structure by the Finnish modernist Alvar Aalto, which opened in 1988.

Just to the south, the **Museum Folkwang** at Kahrstrasse 16 (closed for rebuilding; for latest information see ⓦ www.museum-folkwang.de) is usually reason enough for a trip to Essen, its exceptional collection of nineteenth- and twentieth-century French and German art including works by Caspar David Friedrich, Monet, Cézanne, Van Gogh, Emil Nolde and Max Beckmann. At the time of writing the museum is closed pending a radical rebuild by British architect David Chipperfield; it should however be open again in time for the Ruhr's 2010 European Capital of Culture festivities.

In the meantime, until August 2009, highlights from the Folkwang's collection can be seen at the **Villa Hügel** (Tues–Sun 10am–6pm; €3; S-Bahn to Essen-Hügel), the Neoclassical mansion built between 1868 and 1873 to his own designs by industrialist Alfred Krupp in a lush, forested setting south of the city. The mansion is reached by a meandering path through the park from the station, and is considerably bigger than photographs suggest; inside, the rooms are monumental in scale, if a little ponderous in style. Pick up a leaflet in English at the entrance (€0.50), as you'll be lost without it. Next to the main house, the former guesthouse now hosts an exhibition on the history of the **Krupp** dynasty (same hours and ticket; English leaflet €0.50), which attained greatness in the nineteenth century under the leadership of Alfred Krupp (1850–87), only to acquire notoriety during the Third Reich under Gustav Krupp and his son Alfried Krupp von Bohlen und Halbach for their use of slave labour in the manufacture of armaments. An upstairs room deals with this dark chapter in the company's history, but the displays are in German only.

If all this has left you in a sombre mood, the obvious antidote is a cruise on the **Baldeneysee** (mid-April to early Oct: 4–5 sailings daily; €8.50; ⓦ www .baldeneysee.com), an artificially widened stretch of the Ruhr that makes for a popular summer excursion as well as a focus for rowing and sailing. The lake is fringed by low, wooded hills and is rather picturesque.

Eating, drinking and entertainment

For laid-back drinking and cosmopolitan eating, head south to Rüttenscheider Strasse ("Rü" for short; U11 to Rüttenscheider Stern or Martinstr. or trams #101 or #107). There's a more raucous, younger edge to bars in the city centre, particularly around Viehofer Platz and Kennedy Platz.

Restaurants

Casa Madrid Rüttenscheider Str. 182. The nicest of the tapas places on Rü. Paellas and seafood aside, there are good veggie pickings and the odd German dish. Mon–Sat noon–3pm & 5pm–midnight; eve only Sun.

Lorenz Rüttenscheider Str. 187 ☏ 0201/799 46. Chic, lively café-bar and restaurant in a prime position on the Rü. The menu fuses Asian and Mediterranean influences; mains around €20.

Mezzo Mezzo Kettwigerstr. 36 ☏ 0201/22 52 65. Casual but classy modern Italian in the Lichtburg cinema, with mountainous bruschetta and excellent, if pricey, fish specials.

raum.eins Rüttenscheider Str. 154. Pleasantly informal bar-restaurant with Mediterranean-influenced food and a tree-shaded terrace.

Tablo Huyssenallee 5, Essen-Südviertel ☏ 0201/811 95 85. Critically acclaimed, stylish, modern Turkish restaurant close to the Philharmonie and Aalto-Musiktheater.

Zodiac Witteringstr. 43 ☏ 0201/770 12. Charming veggie place in Rüttenscheid, a little off the beaten track but worth the trek for its luxuriant plant life and reasonably priced food.

Cafés and bars

Bliss Im Girardet-Haus, Girardet Str. 2–38. Boistrous Rüttenscheid bar with cocktails from €6.50, a big range of whiskies and a surprisingly elegant restaurant next door.

Dax Viehofer Str. 49. Big, stylish, gay-friendly café and cocktail bar with huge windows and a long bar. Mon–Fri 9.30am–1am, later at weekends.

Graf Beust Kastanienallee 95. Groovy city-centre *Brauhaus*, open until 2am at weekends and eschewing the usual old German trappings in favour of a quirkier, fun ambience.

Turock Viehofer Platz 3. Grungy, trendy student-friendly city-centre rock club with regular live bands and, in summer, a big outdoor terrace.

On the trail of the Ruhr's industrial heritage

Though the Ruhr has experienced the same structural difficulties faced by similar "rust belt" regions in the US, UK and northern France, it has risen to the challenge of what to do with redundant but often gargantuan industrial sites in a very different way. Fierce local pride ensured that instead of bulldozing the sites many were preserved in acknowledgement of the historical significance and tourist potential of these so-called "cathedrals of industry". Today, a 400km road route and a well-signposted 700km cycle trail together form the **Route der Industriekultur** (Industrial Heritage Trail; ⊛ www.route-industriekultur.de) linking former steelworks, coal mines and slagheaps to offer a fascinating insight into the technology of heavy industry, with a healthy injection of contemporary culture. Thus, light installations turn redundant steelworks into gargantuan artworks, landscaping and sculpture transform slagheaps into viewing platforms and industrial buildings have been reworked as concert halls, exhibition spaces and museums. Many of the most significant attractions are dealt with in the individual city sections in this chapter, but others of interest are listed below. You can **rent bikes** from cycle stations at some of the main sites, at certain train stations or by contacting RevierRad at Mülheim's Hauptbahnhof (☎0208/848 57 20, ⊛ www.revierrad.de); for an additional fee you can opt for a one-way rental, picking up the bike in one place and leaving it in another.

Aquarius Wassermuseum ⊛ www.aquarius-wassermuseum.de. Built by August Thyssen in 1892–93 to provide a nearby ironworks with water, this spectacular mock-medieval water tower soars above the Mülheim suburb of Styrum and now houses a water-themed museum on 14 levels. Tues–Sun 10am–6pm, €3; S-Bahn, S1 from Dortmund, Bochum, Essen, Düsseldorf, Duisburg; S3 from Oberhausen, Essen, Hattingen to Mülheim-Styrum, then a 10min walk.

Gasometer ⊛ www.gasometer.de. This 117m-high gasometer next to Oberhausen's CentrO shopping mall was built to service a nearby steelworks in 1929 and has been reworked to provide a spectacular exhibition space for large-scale works of art, as well as a viewing platform with panoramic views over the western Ruhr. Tues–Sun 10am–6pm; €6; bus or tram from Oberhausen Hauptbahnhof to Neue Mitte.

Kokerei Hansa ⊛ www.industriedenkmal-stiftung.de. This giant coking plant in the north of Dortmund was built in the 1920s and has been preserved as a gigantic sculpture; an adventure trail leads visitors into the imposing compressor house with its huge engines, and to the coal tower, from which there are panoramic views over Dortmund. April–Oct Tues–Sun 10am–6pm; Nov–March Tues–Sun 10am–4pm; €3, or €5 with tour; U-Bahn 47 from Dortmund Hauptbahnhof to Parsevalstrasse, then 5min walk.

Rheinisches Industriemuseum Oberhausen ⊛ www.rim.lvr.de. The former Altenberg zinc-works now houses a permanent exhibition on heavy industry, with everything from giant ingot moulds, mill rollers and a steam locomotive to a 53-tonne steam hammer. Tues–Sun 10am–5pm, €4; adjacent to Oberhausen Hauptbahnhof.

Schiffshebewerk Henrichenburg ⊛ www.schiffshebewerk-henrichenburg.de. Opened in 1899 by Kaiser Wilhelm II, the imposing Henrichenburg ship-lift at Waltrop north of Dortmund lifted barges 14m from the lower to the upper reaches of the Dortmund–Ems Canal until replaced by a bigger, faster lift in 1970. Attractions include a working steam engine, a model of the lift and preserved boats and barges. Tues–Sun 10am–6pm; €3.50; bus #231 from Recklinghausen Hauptbahnhof, stop Kanalstrasse.

Entertainment and nightlife

The Grillo Theater on Theaterplatz (℡0201/812 22 00, ⓦwww.theater-essen .de) is the home of classical **drama**, while the Colosseum Theater, Altendorfer Strasse 1 (℡0201/887 23 33, ⓦwww.stage-entertainment.de), hosts musicals and other spectaculars. The Aalto Theater, Opernplatz 10 (℡0201/8122 200, ⓦwww .theater-essen.de), shows **opera** and **ballet**; the Philharmonie, Huyssenallee 53 (℡0201/812 28 12, ⓦwww.philharmonie-essen.de), is the city's main concert hall. *Zeche Carl*, Wilhelm-Nieswandt-Allee 100 (℡0201/834 44 10, ⓦwww.zechecarl .de), is a former mine reinvented as a **cabaret** and **live music** venue and dance club, while *Essence*, Viehofer Strasse 38–52 (℡0201/ 747 48 63, ⓦwww.club -essence.de; Sat from 10pm), is a classic big club, hosting guest DJs from the likes of the Ministry of Sound.

Bochum

Wedged between Essen and Dortmund, the Ruhr's fourth largest city can't even get a flattering write-up in song. Herbert Grönemeyer, Germany's most revered singer-songwriter, started his career at Bochum's Schauspielhaus theatre and described the city fondly as "no beauty" on his album *4630 Bochum*. Yet if its visual appeal is modest, **BOCHUM** makes up for it with its engrossing museums, vibrant nightlife and – if your German is up to it – the aforementioned theatre, which enjoys a nationwide reputation.

The **Deutsches Bergbau-Museum** (German Mining Museum; Tues–Fri 8.30am–5pm, Sat & Sun 10am–5pm; €6.50) is the world's largest devoted to the subject, housed in a huge brick pile just north of the centre. Dominating the complex is the 63-metre-high winding tower that once graced Dortmund's Germania mine. You can climb it after you've toured the museum's displays, which include a stretch of show mine beneath the building. A couple of blocks to the east at Kortumstrasse 147, the **Museum Bochum** (Tues & Thurs–Sun 10am–5pm, Wed 10am–8pm; €3), houses the municipal collection of modern and contemporary European art, with particular emphasis on Eastern Europe, works on paper and photography; the collection includes individual pieces by Francis Bacon, Cy Twombly and Nam June Paik.

Practicalities

Bochum's **Hauptbahnhof** is on the eastern edge of the city centre, close to the **tourist office** at Huestrasse 9 (Mon–Fri 9am–6pm, Sat 10am–4pm; ℡01805/26 02 34, ⓦwww.bochum-tourismus.de). If you're here for the nightlife, the pick of the **hotels** is the trendy *art Hotel Tucholsky*, right in the thick of it at Viktoriastrasse 73 (℡0234/96 43 60, ⓦwww.art-hotel-tucholsky .de; ❹). The business-oriented *Plaza*, Hellweg 20 (℡0234/130 85, ⓦwww .plaza-bochum.de; ❹), is just a few minutes' walk away, with some singles. Hostel beds are available at *Aleppo*, Nordring 30 (℡0234/58 83 80, ⓦwww .hotelaleppo.de; dorms from €22), close to the Bergbaumuseum.

Places to **eat and drink** are thick on the ground in the **Bermudadreieck**, an inverted triangle of streets between Südring and Konrad-Adenauer-Platz at the southern tip of the city centre that offers a raucous and enjoyable mix of al fresco beer, live bands, DJ bars and affordable ethnic restaurants; there are more than sixty venues in all, many with regular student nights. The most famous is probably *Mandragora* on Konrad-Adenauer-Platz, where Kraftwerk and Gröne-meyer are among the greats to have played live. Hangover-cure central is the stylish 🎭 *Tucholsky* café in the hotel, with a huge breakfast selection, pasta and veggie dishes and big salads.

Bochum's **cultural** jewel is the Schauspielhaus Bochum, housed in an elegant 1950s building south of the Bermudadreieck at Königsallee 15 (☎0234/33 33 55 55, ⓦwww.schauspielhausbochum.de), with a programme that embraces everything from new writing to Shakespeare.

Dortmund

Perched at the Ruhr's eastern extremity, **DORTMUND** is a former free imperial city and Hanseatic League member that grew rich in the Middle Ages from its position on the Hellweg, a major trading route, before falling into decline after the Thirty Years' War. Its later development was similar to that of its sisters, as provincial obscurity was transformed by coal, steel and beer: at one point only Milwaukee brewed more. All three industries declined in the late twentieth century and there's now just one brewer, the Dortmunder Actien-Brauerei. Information and biotechnology are the economic motors of the "new" Dortmund, which seems to have mastered the transition from heavy industry rather well. Though the old Union brewery with its giant illuminated "U" still looms on the skyline, it's overshadowed by the city's funky new skyscrapers and there are plans to convert it into a centre for creative industries. The surviving medieval street pattern and a scattering of worthwhile sights ensure that Dortmund preserves a sense of its history – not just for the distant Hansa days, but also of the sleepy market town of later centuries and the industrial behemoth it subsequently became.

Arrival, information and accommodation

Shuttle buses (5am–10.30pm, hourly; €5.50) connect the **airport** (☎0231/92 13 01, ⓦwww.dortmund-airport.de) with the **Hauptbahnhof** on the north side of the city centre. The **tourist office** (Mon–Fri 9am–6pm, Sat 9am–1pm; ☎0231/18 99 92 22, ⓦwww.dortmund.de) is opposite at Königswall 18a. If you're visiting museums outside the centre you may need to use **public transport**, which includes trams, buses and U-Bahn and is integrated with neighbouring cities (short-hop *Kurzstrecke* tickets €1.30; singles €2.20; one-day *TagesTicket* €5.20). You can **rent bikes** from the Hauptbahnhof (Mon–Fri 6am–9pm) or – with advance notice – at weekends through the tourist office. The city's **hotels** are geared to business visitors and are scattered throughout the city.

Ibis Dortmund City Märkische Str. 73 ☎0231/18 57 70, ⓦwww.ibishotel.com. Comfortable, if bland, modern budget hotel southeast of the centre and about a 15min walk from the best of the Kreuzviertel. It has three rooms equipped for people of limited mobility. ❷

Jugendgästehaus Adolf Kolping Silberstr. 24–26 ☎0231/14 00 74, ⓦwww.djh-wl.de/dortmund. Large, modern HI hostel right in the city centre, with plenty of doubles and four-bed rooms and a small number of singles. Open 24hr; check-in from 1pm. Dorms from €23.

NH Königswall 1 ☎0231/905 50, ⓦwww.nh-hotels .com. Slick, modern business hotel next to the Hauptbahnhof. All rooms are suites, with separate living room, plus microwave and wireless internet, and there are some exceptional deals available for advance booking. ❹

Pullman Dortmund Lindemannstr. 88 ☎0231/911 30, ⓦwww.pullmanhotels.com. Upmarket modern hotel close to Westfalenpark, the Signal Iduna stadium and the Kreuzviertel's bar and restaurant scene, with spacious, tastefully decorated rooms, internet access, a fitness centre, sauna and solarium. ❹

Union Arndtstr. 66 ☎0231/55 00 70, ⓦwww.hotel-union-do.com. Pleasant family-run hotel in a peaceful residential area 10min walk east of the centre, with some good-value singles. ❹

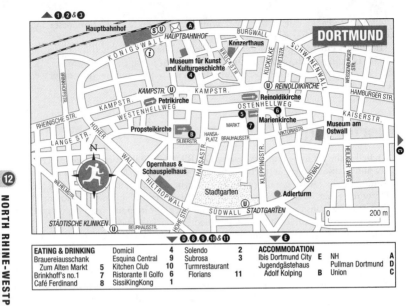

EATING & DRINKING						ACCOMMODATION			
Brauereiausschank		Domicil	4	Solendo	2	Ibis Dortmund City	E	NH	A
Zum Alten Markt	5	Esquina Central	9	Subrosa	3	Jugendgästehaus		Pullman Dortmund	D
Brinkhoff's no.1	7	Kitchen Club	10	Turmrestaurant		Adolf Kolping	B	Union	C
Café Ferdinand	8	Ristorante Il Golfo	6	Florians	11				
		SissiKingKong	1						

The city centre

Dortmund's compact, walkable **centre** is surrounded by a ring of streets following the course of the medieval walls, of which one vestige, the reconstructed **Adlerturm** survives, and which contains a **museum** of the city's history (Tues–Fri 10am–1pm, Sat noon–5pm, Sun 10am–5pm; €1.50).

The city's hub is along Ostenhellweg, where a handful of prewar stone buildings provides the backdrop for two of Dortmund's surviving medieval churches: the looming, thirteenth-century **Reinoldikirche** – considered the city's principal church and named after the city's patron saint – and the twelfth-century Romanesque **Marienkirche** (Tues–Fri 10am–noon & 2–4pm, Sat 10am–1pm) facing it across the street to the south. The former is imposing and preserves a feeling of antiquity, but the latter is the more interesting, not least for the radiant red, gold and blue Gothic altar triptych painted by local boy Conrad von Soest in 1420 and considered one of the masterpieces of German medieval art. It depicts scenes from the life of Christ and the Virgin Mary. What survives is incomplete: the panels were butchered in the eighteenth century to fit it into a new, Baroque high altar, which itself fell victim to a World War II air raid. Less battered by history is the Berswordt altar in the north aisle, which dates from 1395 and depicts the Crucifixion. The sixteenth-century choir stalls portray human weaknesses – adultery, theft, excess, vanity and disobedience – in light-hearted fashion.

Further west along Westenhellweg, the fourteenth-century Gothic **Petrikirche** (Tues–Fri noon–5pm, Sat 11am–4pm) lost its Baroque accretions to wartime bombs, leaving a plain, coherent setting for its chief treasure, an extraordinary sixteenth-century Flemish altar originally carved for the city's Franciscan monastery. The largest surviving Flemish altar of the period, it's also one of the largest works of Gothic church art anywhere. The nearby **Propsteikirche** – which remained Catholic after the Reformation – is similarly austere following wartime destruction, but houses a winged altar dating from 1470 to 1480.

Two worthwhile museums fringe the city centre. Near the Hauptbahnhof on Hansastrasse, the **Museum für Kunst und Kulturgeschichte** (Museum for Art and Cultural History; Tues, Wed, Fri & Sun 10am–5pm, Thurs 10am–8pm, Sat noon–5pm; €3, or €5 *Tageskarte* valid for other city museums) is eclectic and engrossing, housed in the rotunda of an Art Deco former bank building. Friezes at the entrance depict the crises of the early 1920s, including the hyper inflation and the French occupation of the Ruhr, while inside there's a section on the city's history, a collection of religious art and paintings by Lovis Corinth, Max Liebermann and Caspar David Friedrich, among others. There's a strong emphasis on applied arts, the result of the museum's origins as a pedagogic institution, charged with the task of improving the quality of Germany's manufactured goods. There's everything from Meissen porcelain and Tiffany glass to groovy modernist furniture by Marcel Breuer and Verner Panton. On the eastern edge of the centre at Ostwall 7, the **Museum am Ostwall** (same hours & price) must, externally at least, be one of the dullest-looking gallery buildings in Europe, but things perk up considerably inside: the exhibition spaces are actually quite good, with a big double-height central space ideal for exhibiting large-scale works, while upstairs the museum presents a changing selection from its impressive permanent collection of classic modern art. You might see Emil Nolde's stormy *Herbstmeer*, a Max Beckmann view of Bandol in the south of France dating from his Nazi-era exile, or Schmidt-Rottluff's *Vorfrühling*. More recent works include pieces by Jean Tinguely and Joseph Beuys.

North of the centre

North of the Hauptbahnhof and traditionally the wrong side of the tracks, Dortmund's **Nordstadt** is a sprawling mix of docks, industry and close-packed nineteenth-century housing. It has lately acquired an arty, hip overlay, but it's no place for carefree strolling: it's too big, and parts of it are decidedly dodgy. However, it does repay selective exploration. Close to the northern exit from the Hauptbahnhof, the **Mahn- und Gedenkstätte Steinwache**, Steinstrasse 50 (Tues–Sun 10am–5pm; free; pick up an English text at the entrance), houses an exhibit on the Nazi terror in Dortmund in a former Gestapo prison. Dortmund's prosecutors were openly pro-Nazi even before Hitler came to power, siding with fascist thugs against the local police in a notorious 1932 case, in which the police, not their Nazi attackers, were put on trial. During the Third Reich, thirty thousand people were imprisoned in this building; in one of the cells you can see the names of some of the prison's many inmates scratched into the wall.

To the north, at Steigerstrasse 16, the **Brauerei-Museum** (Tues, Wed, Fri & Sun 10am–5pm, Thurs 10am–8pm, Sat noon–5pm; €1.50) is housed in the former machine hall of the Hansa-Brauerei and focuses on the commercialized, large-scale beer production for which Dortmund became famous in the nineteenth and twentieth centuries, in particular the glory years after 1950.

South of the centre

A ten-minute walk south of the centre along Hohe Strasse, the leafy **Kreuzviertel** (U-Bahn Saarlandstr.) has the visual appeal much of the city centre lacks, particularly around Arnecke Strasse, Vincke Platz and Liebigstrasse. Here, lovely Jugendstil facades rise above relaxed neighbourhood cafés and bars, making this a good part of town to let the pace slip. Suitably refreshed, continue south to the **Westfalenpark** (daily 9am–11pm; €2), home to several attractions, from a cookery book museum to the German Rose Society and its three thousand-plus varieties of roses. It's overshadowed by the city's 212m **TV tower** (Tues–Fri noon–11pm, Sat & Sun 10am–11pm; €1.70), which you can ascend for spectacular outdoor panoramas and which also has a classy revolving restaurant. West of the park, **Signal Iduna Park**, the 80,000-seat home of Borussia Dortmund, rises behind the **Westfalenhalle**, the city's largest live music and exhibition venue.

The Zeche Zollern and dasa

Two of Dortmund's more engrossing industrial heritage sites can be reached easily by train from the Hauptbahnhof. **Zeche Zollern**, Grubenweg 5 (Tues–Sun 10am–6pm; €3.50; Bahnhof Bövinghausen), is, like Essen's Zollverein, an architecturally distinguished former coal mine. In this case the buildings are a mixture of revival and Jugendstil, and provide a setting for permanent and temporary exhibitions of the LWL Industrial Museum documenting working life in a colliery in the first half of the twentieth century. The quirky but surprisingly rewarding **dasa** (Deutsche Arbeitsschutzausstellung or German Occupational Safety and Health Exhibition; Friedrich-Henkel-Weg 1–25; Tues–Sat 9am–5pm, Sat & Sun 10am–5pm; €3; Dorstfeld-Süd station) takes an imaginative approach to what might seem a dry subject – the development of health and safety at work. It's all highly interactive, and covers everything from traditional factory work to an aircraft cockpit.

Eating and drinking

Eating and **drinking** in Dortmund divides between city-centre Italians and traditional brewery-owned places, and the more relaxed Kreuzviertel, where boundaries between café, bar and restaurant tend to blur.

Restaurants

Brauereiausschank Zum Alten Markt Markt 3 ☎0231/57 22 17. Traditional trappings and old Westphalian specialities from around €13 are the order of the day at this brewery-owned city-centre beer hall.

Brinkhoff's No. 1 Markt 6 ☎0231/52 58 15. Similar to *Zum Alten Markt* but more opulently dark and with a menu that ranges from *Matjes* herring to €12 *Schnitzels* and €15 steaks. Daily 11am–midnight.

Esquina Central Kreuzstr. 69 ☎0231/13 40 58. Laid-back, intimate Kreuzviertel tapas bar (from €2.50). Daily from breakfast onwards.

Kitchen Club Saarlandstr. 102 ☎0231/589 77 06. Bright, busy canteen-style neighbourhood restaurant with good-value mains including plenty of veggie options, from around €7.

Ristorante Il Golfo Rosental 12 ☎0231/57 12 75. Don't be misled by the slick decor or wine-bar trappings, for this is essentially a solidly traditional Italian place. Open until 2am most nights.

Turmrestaurant Florians Florianstr. 2 ☎0231/138 49 75. Haute cuisine at the top of the city's TV tower, with sky-high prices to match, including a six-course *dégustation* menu for €96.

Bars and cafés

Café Ferdinand Liebigstr. 23 ☎0231/86 46 12. Spacious, informal, modern neighbourhood café-bar in the Kreuzviertel, with affordable salads, meat and fish dishes for around €13–14.

Domicil 7 Hansastr. ☎0231/862 90 30. A stylish blend of café-bar and serious jazz venue, with a bit of world music thrown in, all in a landmark Weimar-era building in the city centre.

SissiKingKong Landwehrstr. 17, Nordstadt ☎0231/728 25 78. Battered but groovy Seventies furniture, trendy ambience and music make this quirky café-bar a favourite among the city's arty crowd. There's also a short, eclectic food menu.

Solendo Speicherstr. 2a ☎0231/882 13 82. Summer-only Ibiza-style beach bar – complete with sand and deckchairs – in the unlikely setting of the city's docks.

Subrosa Gneisenaustr. 56, Nordstadt ☎0231/86 46 12. Battered, kitschy opulence, live bands and football on TV are the attractions of this studenty Nordstadt bar.

Nightlife and entertainment

As with restaurants and bars, **nightlife** is split between the big city-centre venues and quirkier offerings elsewhere – including some great offbeat choices in the Nordstadt. Dortmund has a lively **club scene**: big-name DJs guest at the stylish *zuHOUSE.Club* in the old Thier brewery in Hövelstrasse, which is also home to the DJ bars *Liquid Lounge* and *Mendoza* and to *Sixx.PM*, which has a more eclectic music policy. The modern *Konzerthaus Dortmund* at Brückstrasse 21 (☎0231/22 69 62 00, ⊛www.konzerthaus-dortmund.de) is the home of the Philharmonie für Westfalen, while **opera and ballet** is staged at the Opernhaus on Platz der Alten Synagoge (☎0231/502 72 22, ⊛www.theaterdo .de). Big-ticket rock and pop concerts, ice spectaculars and the like take place at the Westfalenhalle, Rheinlanddamm 200 (☎01805/16 05 16 14). Tickets for **Borussia Dortmund** games can be bought at ⊛www.bvb.de, by calling ☎01805/309 000, from the ticket office at Rheinlanddamm 207–209 or from various city-centre outlets, including Karstadt Sport.

⑫

The Lower Rhine

North of Duisburg the Rhineland's heavy industry gives way to a peaceful, agricultural region dotted with small towns, the place names and flat terrain reflecting the proximity of the Dutch border. Under the Holy Roman Empire the **Duchy of Cleve** counted for something – famously supplying the English king Henry VIII with one of his wives – but these days the region is mainly of interest as an excursion from the Ruhr, with hourly trains from Duisburg making historic **Xanten** a magnet for day-trippers. Beyond it, placid **Kalkar** preserves a more low-key charm.

Xanten

With its Disney-like Roman reconstructions, teeming shops hawking clothes or assorted trinkets and with a miniature tourist train doing endless circuits of the old town in the height of summer, it's easy to spot the tacky side of **XANTEN**, 45 minutes by train from Duisburg, which owes its name to a corruption of the Latin dedication *"ad sanctos"* ("to the saints"). Yet as the Roman connection suggests, it's one of the oldest towns in Germany, the mythical birthplace of Siegfried – the hero of the *Nibelungenlied* (see box, p.520) – and still encircled by its **medieval defences**. The town's chief architectural glory is the imposing twin-towered **Dom St Viktor** (April–Oct Mon–Sat 10am–6pm, Sun 2–6pm; Nov–March Mon–Sat 10am–5pm, Sun 1–5pm), walled off from the rest of the Altstadt in the wonderfully peaceful **Immunität**, or cathedral close, which is fringed by handsome houses and walled gardens, as if shunning the tourist hubbub outside. The Immunität's intriguing name reflects the fact that the area encircling the cathedral is independent of civil law. The cathedral itself, which has a splendid five-aisle late Gothic nave, contains the grave of the eponymous St Victor, a Roman-Christian legionnaire martyred in the fourth century. Like much of Xanten, the cathedral was grievously damaged in the final months of World War II; repairs were completed by 1966. A new **Museum St Viktor** is under construction to house the cathedral's treasures.

On the far side of the B57 road and about a ten-minute walk from the cathedral, the reconstructed Roman defences of the **Archäologischer Park** (daily: March–Oct 9am–6pm; Nov 9am–5pm; Dec–Feb 10am–4pm; €6.50, less in winter; €8/9 with RömerMuseum and Grosse Thermen) give an undeniably powerful impression of the sheer size of the Roman settlement of Colonia Ulpia Traiana, which achieved urban status under Emperor Trajan around 100 AD. Once inside the park, you'll find the isolated re-creations of Roman architecture either intriguing or kitsch. There's a Pompeiian-style restaurant where you can eat Roman dishes, though the modern German and Italian options are cheaper. Vast though it is, the Archäologischer Park covers less than half the site of the Roman town, and you'll have to cross the B57 again to reach the new **RömerMuseum** (same hours; €5, or joint ticket with Archäologischer Park), built on the site of the Grosse Thermen, the Roman town's public bath complex. It's arguably the more rewarding of the two sites, the modern building's imposing dimensions corresponding to the size of the original.

Practicalities

From Xanten's **Bahnhof** outside the medieval walls, Bahnhofstrasse leads directly to the **tourist office** at Kurfürstenstrasse 9 (April–Oct Mon–Fri 9am–1pm & 2–6pm, Sat 10am–4pm, Sun noon–4pm; Nov–March Mon–Fri 10am–1pm & 2–5pm, Sat 10am–1pm; ☏02801/983 00, Ⓦwww.xanten.de). Xanten's tourist hordes disappear at 6pm sharp and a delightful evening calm descends on the town, making an overnight **stay** a good way to experience the place at its peaceful best. The modern **youth hostel** at Bankscher Weg 4 (☏02801/985 00, Ⓦwww.xanten.jugendherberge.de; dorms from €20.40) is some distance from the Altstadt alongside the **Freizeit Zentrum Xanten**, an extensive water-park offering everything from bathing beaches to water skiing and diving. You can also stay in an **apartment** (❷) in the fourteenth-century *Klever Tor*, which is part of the town's medieval defences; contact the tourist office for information. Hotel options include *Hövelmann's*, right in the centre at Markt 31–33 (☏02801/40 81, Ⓦwww.hotel-hoevelmann.de; ❹), and the grand, historic *Hotel van Bebber*, Klever Strasse 12 (☏02801/66 23, Ⓦwww.hotelvanbebber.de; ❺), which has an attractive **restaurant** with game dishes from around €20 and a cheaper *Bierkeller, De Kelder*. Other eating options include the picturesque *Gotisches Haus*, at Markt 6, and *Café de Fries*, Kurfürstenstrasse 9, the fanciest of the cafés catering to the day-trip trade.

Kalkar

Hourly buses take about twenty minutes to connect Xanten's Bahnhof with **KALKAR**. With a strollable Altstadt dotted with stepped gables and a central market square dominated by the fifteenth-century brick Gothic **Rathaus**, it's an attractive place; as sleepy as Xanten is lively, it's worth a visit for the artistic and architectural riches left from its fifteenth- and sixteenth-century heyday. The late Gothic church of **St Nikolai** just off Markt (Mon–Sat 10am–noon & 2–6pm, Sun 2–5pm) contains a dazzling array of nine Gothic altars, including a splendid high altar commissioned in 1488 that took three craftsmen twelve years to complete. No less imposing is the wonderful *Sieben-Schmerzen-Altar* in the right aisle, carved by the Kleve craftsman Henrik Douverman, who came to Kalkar in 1515. Behind the Rathaus, the brick gabled house **In gen Stockvisch** dates from 1500 and is now the **Städtisches Museum** (Tues–Sun 10am–1pm & 2–5pm), with displays of local interest and a small collection of nineteenth- and twentieth-century art. West of town and connected to it by bus from Markt, the neo-Gothic **Schloss Moyland** (April–Sept Tues–Fri 11am–6pm, Sat & Sun 10am–6pm; Oct–March Tues–Sun 11am–5pm; €7; Ⓦwww.moyland.de) houses the private art collection of the van der Grinten brothers, close associates of Joseph Beuys, whose works form the core of the collection.

Kalkar's other outlying attraction, **Wunderland Kalkar**, Griether Strasse 110–20 (day-ticket €32.50; Ⓦwww.wunderlandkalkar.eu), is an odd combination of resort hotel and amusement park on the site of a nuclear power station that was abandoned without ever being commissioned. It is geared more towards overnight stays than day-trips.

Practicalities

The nearest **campsite** is north of Kalkar at the *Freizeitpark Wisseler See* (Ⓣ02824/963 10, Ⓦwww.wisseler-see.de). Central places to **stay** in town include the *Hotel Stillleben*, Markt 25 (Ⓣ02824/97 15 97, Ⓦwww.hotel-stillleben.de; ❹), and *Hotel Siekmann*, Kesselstrasse 32 (Ⓣ02824/924 50, Ⓦwww.hotel-siekmann -kalkar.de; ❸), which has a **restaurant** serving meaty mains from around €10; alternatively, try the classy *Ratskeller* under the Rathaus at Markt 20 (Ⓣ02824/ 24 60; closed Mon), with mains for around €13, or the *Brauhaus Kalkarer Mühle*, Mühlenstege 8 (Ⓣ02824/932 39; closed Mon in winter), in a preserved eighteenth-century windmill on the fringe of the Altstadt.

Soest

Set in rich farming country fifty minutes by train east of Dortmund, idyllic **SOEST** was another medieval Hanseatic League member on the Hellweg, with trade links reaching as far as Russia. Cologne's archbishops founded a *Pfalz* or residence here around 960–965 AD, and were for centuries the town's overlords; Soest's fifteenth-century struggle to be rid of them triggered its decline and by 1500 its glory days were over, leaving an enchanting townscape of half-timbered houses and striking, sage-green sandstone churches whose charm even wartime bombs couldn't erase. Most of what's worth seeing is within the surviving **medieval defences**, a circuit of which makes a pleasant way to spend an hour or two.

Arrival, information and accommodation

Soest's **Bahnhof** is just north of the Altstadt; from here Brüderstrasse meanders south towards the Dom and Grosser Teich. The **tourist office** is in the watermill at Teichsmühlengasse 3 (Mon–Fri 9.30am–4.30pm, Sat 10am–3pm; summer also Sun 11am–1pm; Ⓣ02921/66 35 00 50, Ⓦwww.soest.de). It provides information on the **Saarland** (see box, p.662) as well as on Soest itself. There are some atmospheric places to **stay**.

DJH Soest Kaiser-Friedrich-Platz 2 Ⓣ02921/162 83, Ⓦwww.djh.de/soest. Soest's youth hostel is immediately south of the Altstadt, easily reached on foot. Dorms from €19.10.

Domhof Wiesenstr. 18 Ⓣ02921/981 04 36, Ⓦwww.hotel-domhof.de. Not as atmospheric as some of Soest's other hotels, but very central and tranquil. ❷–❸

Hotel Drei Kronen Jakobistr. 37 Ⓣ02921/136 65, Ⓦwww.hotel3kronen.de. Affordable accommodation in a venerable old tavern in one of the Altstadt's most attractive streets. ❸

Im Wilden Mann Am Markt 11 Ⓣ02921/150 71, Ⓦwww.im-wilden-mann.com. Occupying a striking half-timbered house on the main square, with a bustling restaurant on the ground floor, this is the most central and best known of Soest's historic inns. ❹

Pilgram Haus Jakobistr. 75 Ⓣ02921/18 28, ⒺInfo@pilgramhaus.de. Next to the town wall, this charming old place claims to be the oldest inn in Westphalia, dating from 1304. ❹

The Town

Soest's distinctive green sandstone is seen to best effect in the sublime **St Maria zur Wiese**, a tall, graceful late Gothic hall church, begun in 1313 and among the loveliest in Germany. Inside, you experience an almost overwhelming rush of colour from the green stone and vast stained-glass windows, one of which – the *Westfälische Abendmahl* – dates from around 1500 and shows Jesus and the disciples tucking into a Germanic Last Supper of beer, pork, pumpernickel and ham. For all its magnificence it has never been the town's main church, and its soaring (and fragile) twin spires rise above modest, villagey houses on the opposite side of the **Grosser Teich**, the town's millpond – still with an intact watermill – from the main body of the Altstadt.

Closer encounters with the mysterious green stone can be had at the nearby **Grünsandstein Museum**, Walburgerstrasse 56 (Mon–Sat 10am–5pm, Sun 2–5pm; free), which has some beautiful specimens of Gothic carving to supplement its geological displays. The stone's colour varies from yellow-green to almost blue, depending on its mineral content; it was deposited on the shore of a warm sea ninety million years ago.

South of St Maria zur Wiese near the Grosser Teich, Hohe Gasse leads to the late Romanesque **St Maria zur Höhe**, known as the Hohnekirche, which dates from around 1230 and is as squat as the younger church is lofty. It too has a beautiful interior, with rich frescoes showing Byzantine influence and the strange *Scheibenkreuz*, a cross on a carved wooden background that dates

The Sauerland

Modest by Alpine standards, the swathe of unspoilt wooded hills known as the **Sauerland** nevertheless represents a precious taste of the great outdoors for the millions who live in North Rhine-Westphalia's major cities, as well as attracting holidaymakers from further afield. The region, which strays across the Land boundary into western Hesse, is above all popular for activities, from **hiking, mountain biking** or **Nordic walking** in the summer to **skiing** in the winter, while its artificial lakes – the target of the famous RAF "Dambuster" air raids during World War II (see p.591) – offer a focus for all kinds of water-based activities, from canoeing and fishing to swimming, sailing and windsurfing. You can take a sedate coffee-and-cake excursion aboard a comfortable cruise boat on the Möhnesee, while at the Sorpe dam you can take a tour through the weir.

Five natural parks together comprise almost three-quarters of the region's territory, crisscrossed by a number of themed hiking-trails such as the **Sauerland-Höhenflug** – a high-altitude route that takes in four 800m peaks – and the 240km **Waldroute**, which links the towns of Iserlohn, Arnsberg and Marsberg to provide a close-up view of the region's forests and fauna. For mountain-bikers, the 1700km **Bike Arena Sauerland** is the draw, supported by cyclist-friendly hotels and guesthouses certified by the local tourist board, SauerlandTourismus (☏01802/40 30 40, ⓦwww.sauerland .com). For information on cycle routes check ⓦwww.bike-arena.de. With its beautiful scenery and (relatively) open roads, the Sauerland is also something of a centre for motorcycle touring.

Given its wholesome fresh air and exercise appeal, it's no surprise that the Sauerland was the birthplace of the **youth hostel** movement, with the world's first housed in the castle at **Altena**, southeast of Dortmund (ⓦwww.djh-wl.de/burg .altena; dorms from €19.10). **Möhnesee** is the closest of the Sauerland lakes to Soest; a bus service – the #R49 – takes around 25 minutes to connect Soest Bahnhof with the lakeside town of **Körbecke**. For more information, visit the helpful web portal ⓦwww.sauerland.com.

from 1200 and resembles the end of a beer barrel. Just to the east of here along Osthofenstrasse, the sixteenth-century **Osthofentor** – sole survivor of the town's ten gates – houses a **museum** (April–Sept Tues–Sat 2–4pm, Sun 11am–1pm & 3–5pm; Oct–March Wed 2–4pm & Sun 11am–3pm; €2) with displays on Soest's medieval heyday as well as the remnants of the municipal armoury. The ticket also admits you to the **Burghofmuseum** (Tues–Sat 10am–noon & 3–5pm, Sun 11am–1pm) in Burghofstrasse in the southern Altstadt, with yet more local history. It's worth pausing en route to admire the five-storied half-timbered houses at 42 and 48 Osthofenstrasse; most of the medieval houses on this side of the Grosser Teich are modest, but these are exceptions.

Similarly impressive is the **Haus zur Rose** on Markt, the town's central square, with its beautiful, coloured fan decorations. Crowning a modest rise nearby, the **St Patrokli Dom** (Mon–Wed & Fri 10am–5.30pm, Thurs 10am–2.30pm & 3.45–5.30pm, Sat 10am–5pm, Sun noon–6pm) is the town's thousand-year-old principal church, an architectural show of strength by the Cologne archbishops. It preserves beautiful Romanesque frescoes of St Patroclus, the town's patron saint, but otherwise shows obvious traces of postwar restoration. Opposite, the Protestant **Petrikirche** is another green-tinged Romanesque survivor, with a couple of Crucifixion frescoes on the columns of the nave attributed to the Gothic painter Conrad von Soest – a Dortmund man, despite his name. He was also responsible for the lovely retable in the tiny **Nikolaikapelle**, tucked behind the Dom on Thomästrasse. It's usually locked, but the tourist office offers guided tours along with the Petrikirche and Dom. Soest's central architectural ensemble is completed by the Baroque **Rathaus**, which stands between the Dom and Petrikirche and is painted a rich terracotta. If you've not had your fill of half-timbered houses, it's fun to get creatively lost in the Altstadt's picturesque lanes, some of which have colourful names, such as Elendgasse ("Misery Lane").

Eating, drinking and entertainment

There's no shortage of good places for eating and drinking in Soest, though as a popular day-trip destination it's not particularly cheap. The hotels mentioned all serve food, with the **restaurant** at the *Pilgram Haus* being particularly imaginative. For café lounging, *Konditorei-Café Fromme* at Markt 1 is the central, see-and-be-seen spot, while *Bontempi im Park* on the Grosser Teich is relaxed, serving Italian food, ice cream and cake. Soest claims to be the birthplace of **pumpernickel**, the sticky, black rye bread so beloved of Germans; you can buy it from Haverland Pumpernickel Bäckerei on Nöttenstrasse just off Markt. The high point of Soest's calendar is the **Kirmes** fair which fills the Altstadt in early November; the Altstadt is also the setting for a **Christmas market** in December.

Paderborn

Religion and power meet at **PADERBORN**, where Charlemagne discussed his coronation as emperor with Pope Leo III in 799 AD. Its bishopric blossomed in the Middle Ages into a prince-bishopric and in 1929 into an archbishopric. The compact cathedral city remains a strongly religious place, with a theology faculty that traces its roots back to the Jesuit university founded by Prince-Bishop Dietrich von Fürstenberg in 1614. Its religious monuments, combined with its unique geographical location at the source of Germany's shortest river, make it an engrossing place for a short visit, well worth an overnight stop.

Arrival, information and accommodation

Paderborn/Lippstadt **airport** (℡02955/770, 🌐www.airport-paderborn.com) is southwest of the city, linked by bus (#400, #460 & #NE 16) to the **Hauptbahnhof** (buses #2, #4, #8, #9 to Rathausplatz) west of the centre on Bahnhofstrasse. This continues as Westernstrasse, the city's main shopping street, to Marienplatz and the **tourist office** at no. 2a (April–Oct Mon–Fri 10am–6pm, Sat 10am–2pm; Nov–March Mon–Fri 10am–5pm, Sat 10am–2pm; ℡05251/88 29 80, 🌐www .paderborn.de), which can help with finding accommodation.

DJH Paderborn Meinwerkstr. 16 ℡05251/220 55, 🌐www.djh-wl.de/paderborn. In a sprawling old building right on the fortifications. Dorms from €17.60.

Galerie-Hotel Abdinghof Bachstr. 1 ℡05251/122 40, 🌐www.galerie-hotel.de. The nicest place to stay in Paderborn, in a sixteenth-century *Brauhaus* facing the Paderquellgebiet. The pretty rooms are named after famous artists and all have either bath or shower and WC. ④

Hotel Aspethera Am Busdorf 7 ℡05251/288 81 00, 🌐www.hotel-aspethera.de. A more expensive option next to the Busdorfkirche, this place hides an eighteenth-century wine cellar beneath its modern exterior. ⑤

Hotel zur Mühle Mühlenstr. 2 ℡05251/107 50, 🌐www.hotelzurmuehle.de. A good, comfortable central choice, with fourteen single and ten double rooms, all with bath or shower. ④

Stadthaus Hathumarstr. 22 ℡05251/188 99 10, 🌐www.hotel-stadthaus.de. This very pleasant three-star hotel occupies an imposing old house close to the Adam und Eva Haus. ⑤

The Town

Paderborn stands at the point where powerful springs bubble up from a limestone aquifer to form Germany's shortest river, the 4km-long Pader. The area around the source, the **Paderquellgebiet**, is a delightful water garden right in the heart of the city. An air raid on March 27, 1945, left Paderborn a smoking ruin, yet paradoxically the destruction had some positive consequences, enabling the city authorities to open up the hitherto densely built-up and rather malodorous Paderquellgebiet, while in 1963 demolition of war-damaged houses led to the sensational rediscovery of the **Carolingian Königspfalz**, the palace where Charlemagne held the first Frankish assembly on Saxon soil in 777 AD. Its foundations can now be seen between the cathedral and the Ottonian Kaiserpfalz, a rather successful 1970s resurrection of the Carolingian palace's eleventh-century successor, incorporating whatever of the actual palace survived. It houses the **Museum in der Kaiserpfalz** (Tues–Sun 10am–6pm; €2.50), where you can see documentary footage of the 1960s excavations plus archeological displays and before-and-after images of Paderborn's wartime destruction. Between the museum and cathedral stands the most substantial survivor of the palace complex, the eleventh-century **Bartholomäuskapelle** (daily 10am–6pm; free). It was the first hall church north of the Alps and reputedly the work of Greek builders. The interior is austere but elegant: there's almost no decoration except for the capitals on its six slender columns.

The distinctive square tower and copper-clad spire of the cathedral, or **Dom**, dominate Paderborn's skyline. The construction of this monumental thirteenth-century hall church spanned the stylistic transition from Romanesque to Gothic: the great west tower is Romanesque, the nave – which has two sets of transepts – Gothic. The best way to enter the cathedral is down the steps from Markt on the south side through the **Paradies**, which in the Middle Ages served as a shelter for pilgrims en route to Santiago de Compostela. Inside, it's the richness of the various tombs that catches the eye, particularly the splendid black-and-white Mannerist memorial to prince-bishop **Dietrich von Fürstenberg** by Heinrich Gröninger. The **cloisters** contain the celebrated sixteenth-century

Hasenfenster or *Hare Window*, which with great artistic cunning depicts three leaping hares who share just three ears, though each hare somehow has a pair. At the cloister's northern exit is a moving **memorial** to the victims of the World War II air raids and in particular to the fourteen killed by a bomb which landed in the cloister on March 22, 1945. Mosaics by Paderborn artist Agnes Mann depict three young boys trapped in the burning city. The cathedral is dedicated to St Liborius, an early Christian bishop from Le Mans whose remains were transferred to Paderborn in 836 AD. The obscure Gallo-Roman cleric is the focal point of the annual nine-day **Libori** festival in late July, when the golden shrine containing his reliquary is paraded through the streets and the city centre becomes a riotous mix of nuns and beer, attracting a million visitors.

In front of the cathedral on the south side, the uncompromisingly modernist **Diözesanmuseum** (Tues–Sun 10am–6pm; €4; Ⓦ www.erzbistum-paderborn .de) presents its collection of religious art with considerable flair – Baroque angels from the destroyed 1736 *Libori Festaltar* soar above your head, while in the crypt-like cellar the treasures include the shrine of St Liborius itself.

Beyond the museum, the city centre focuses on **Markt** – with its carefully restored gabled houses facing the cathedral – and **Rathausplatz**, dominated by the three flamboyant Weser Renaissance gables of the city's greatest secular building, the **Rathaus**. It dates from 1616 and was another of prince-bishop Dietrich's building projects. Just to the west, the gabled facade of the **Heising'sches Haus**, built for Burgomeister Heinrich Stallmeister around 1600, is almost as showy.

South of the Rathaus stand more fruits of Dietrich's building mania in the shape of the reconstructed **Gymnasium Theodorianum** and the formerly Jesuit **Marktkirche** next door, which has a sumptuous high altar, re-created after complete wartime destruction and finally completed in 2004. To the east, the beautiful cloisters of the eleventh-century **Busdorfkirche** are worth a look, while the city's finest half-timbered house, the **Adam und Eva Haus** on Hathumarstrasse, contains a small museum of local history (Tues–Sun 10am–6pm; free), with graphic film footage of Paderborn after the air raids.

As for the rest of Paderborn's centre, it's a mishmash of surviving and reconstructed historic buildings interspersed with postwar austerity housing and a few regrettable eye-sores, and it's only intermittently picturesque. A popular **walk** from the city centre takes you along the park-like banks of the Pader towards **Schloss Neuhaus**, the former residence of the prince-bishops; on the way, you'll pass the **Heinz Nixdorf MuseumsForum**, Fürstenallee 7 (Tues–Fri 9am–6pm, Sat & Sun 10am–6pm; €6; Ⓦ www.hnf.de), which claims to be the world's largest computer museum and takes a broad perspective on its subject, the exhibits beginning with the development of writing in Mesopotamia around 3000 BC.

Eating, drinking and entertainment

Places to **eat and drink** are scattered throughout the city centre. *Kulturwerkstatt* at Bahnhofstrasse 64 (Ⓣ 05251/317 85) is the city's busiest **live music** venue, part of a complex that also includes dance and rehearsal studios, a café and cinema. The city's temple to high culture is the Paderhalle on the north side of the city centre at Heiersmauer 45–51 (Ⓣ 05251/10 39 40, Ⓦ www.paderhalle.de)

Caféhaus & Bistro Plückebaum Am Abdinghof 32. Good-value light bites in a slightly sedate café close to the Paderquellgebiet.
Deutsches Haus Kisau 9 Ⓣ 05251/221 36. Steaks, salads and €9 *Schnitzels* in a traditional, woody setting northwest of the Paderquellgebiet.

Kupferkessel Marienstr. 14 Ⓣ 05251/236 85. The Michelin-listed *Kupferkessel* is the city's most elegant restaurant, with mains from around €16. Closed Sun.
La Petite Galerie At the Abdinghof, Bachstr.1 Ⓣ 05251/122 40. Quiches, cakes and more

substantial mains in arty surroundings, with a leafy terrace outside.

Ostermann Café am Dom Markt 4. Paderborn's most sumptuous coffee-and-cake place, right opposite the cathedral.

Paderborner Brauhaus Kisau 2. The city's biggest beer garden, just to the northwest of the Paderquellgebiet.

Ratskeller Rathausplatz 1 ℡ 05251/20 11 33. Westphalian *gutbürgerlich* cuisine in the atmospheric cellar of the city's Rathaus.

Detmold

High above **DETMOLD** on the forested ridge of the Teutoburger Wald, a solitary, wing-helmeted warrior raises his sword above the canopy of trees. The **Hermannsdenkmal** (March–Oct 9am–6.30pm; Nov–Feb 9.30am–4pm; €1.30; ⓦ www.hermannsdenkmal.de) was the vision of one dogged obsessive, the sculptor Joseph Ernst von Bandel, a bust of whom stands outside the hut he occupied while struggling to complete the 53.46-metre-high monument, begun in 1838 and finally completed with financial support from the Prussian state in 1875. The copper-green warrior commemorates Arminius (or "Hermann"), chieftain of the Cherusci, who united local tribes in 9 AD to annihilate three Roman legions at the battle of Teutoburger Wald and thus struck an early blow for German unity. Though the impetus for Hermann's construction was blatantly nationalistic, these days he cuts a romantic figure, and there's no denying the beauty of the views from the platform at his feet.

A path descends through the woods east of the monument to reach the **LWL–Freilichtmuseum** on the town's southern outskirts (April–Oct Tues–Sun 9am–6pm; €5; ⓦ www.lwl-freilichtmuseum-detmold.de), Germany's largest open-air museum, which assembles an evocative collection of rustic half-timbered buildings from across the region, along with a forge, a bakery, and rare breeds of domestic animals. To the south of the Hermannsdenkmal at Ostertalstrasse 1, the **Vogelpark Heiligenkirchen** (mid-March to mid-Nov 9am–6pm; €6; ⓦ www.vogelpark-heiligenkirchen.de) is a family-friendly aviary and zoo with over a thousand species, including plenty of exotica; the daily feeding of the parrot chicks at 3pm is a highlight for children. More avian attractions are found nearby at the **Adlerwarte Berlebeck** (mid-Feb to mid-Nov 9.30am–5.30pm; €5), where you can see eagles and other birds of prey in free flight. Detmold's final outlying attraction is the **Externsteine** (€1 parking, but free access to site on foot), a series of strange sandstone pinnacles southeast of town with an intriguing religious significance: thought to have originally been a pagan site, the rocks were allegedly adopted by Christians in the Middle Ages as a substitute for the pilgrimage to Jerusalem.

All these attractions are linked to Detmold at weekends by **bus** #792; access on weekdays is more problematic without a car, though bus #701 passes the Freilichtmuseum and will get you to the foot of Hermann's hill, the Grotenburg, and to the Adlerwarte.

After the natural and nationalistic thrills of the surrounding district, Detmold's genteel **Altstadt** can seem rather tame, yet it's an undeniably pretty town with hundreds of historic buildings in a variety of styles from slate-hung and half-timbered to Jugendstil. Lange Strasse, the main street, is handsome enough, but for sheer cuteness it's hard to beat the row of half-timbered seventeenth-century artisans' cottages in quiet **Adolfstrasse**, east of Markt off Schuler Strasse. The centre of the town is dominated by the **Fürstliches Residenzschloss** (daily: April–Oct 10am–5pm; Nov–March 10am–4pm; €4), a fine example of the Weser Renaissance style, which you can visit on one of the hourly guided tours. The seat of the princes of Lippe – an extinct principality of which Detmold was the capital – the Schloss is still in the hands of the family; its chief artistic glory is a set of Brussels tapestries depicting the battles of Alexander the Great. Facing the Schloss across the watery Schlossteich, the **Lippisches Landesmuseum** (Tues–Fri 10am–6pm, Sat & Sun 11am–6pm; €4.50) is partly housed in the five-storey, sixteenth-century Kornhaus, where the wonderful timber structure provides an atmospheric setting for displays on local and peasant life, from room reconstructions and painted furniture to weaponry and regional costume – notable for the women's eccentric headgear. The top floor eschews the *völkisch* with a display of classic modern furniture tucked under the eaves.

Practicalities

Detmold is 30km from Paderborn, to which it is linked by train. The **Bahnhof** is northwest of the Altstadt: turn left into Bahnhofstrasse then right into Paulinenstrasse, following it to its junction with Bruchstrasse; follow this to Markt, where you'll find the **tourist office** in the Rathaus (April–Oct Mon–Fri 9am–6pm, Sat & Sun 10am–2pm; Nov–March Mon–Fri 9am–5pm, Sat 10am–2pm; ℡05231/97 73 28, ⓦwww.stadtdetmold.de).

Good places to **stay** include the classy *Detmolder Hof*, Langestrasse 19 (℡05231/98 09 90, ⓦwww.detmolderhof.de; ❼), the comfortable but slightly less swish *Lippischer Hof*, Willy-Brandt-Platz 1 (℡05231/93 60, ⓦwww .hotellippischerhof.de; ❹), and the attractive *Stadthotel* by the station at Bahnhofstrasse 9a (℡05231/616 18 00, ⓦwww.stadthotel-detmold.de; ❹). Detmold's **youth hostel** is close to the Freilichtmuseum at Schirmannstrasse 49 (℡05231/247 39, ⓦwww.djh-wl.de; dorms from €16.70).

The *Detmolder Hof* and *Lippischer Hof* both have good **restaurants**; alternatively, the *Speisekeller im Rosental*, opposite the Landestheater at Schlossplatz 7 (℡05231/222 67; closed Mon & Tues lunch), serves creative modern cuisine, with mains from €20. There are lighter choices and Ayurvedic teas at the *Grabbe Café*, Unter der Wehme 7, in the former home of the Detmold-born dramatist and satirist Christian Dietrich Grabbe (1801–36).

Lemgo

LEMGO, 11km north of Detmold, preserves a beguiling small-town atmosphere that harks back to its Hanseatic League prime, its streets a photogenic blend of Weser Renaissance pomp and picturesque half-timbering. Not everything in the town's history is as charming as its architecture. Converting to Protestantism after the Reformation, from 1583 to 1681 Lemgo was gripped by an anti-witchcraft frenzy that was cynically exploited by politicians – most notoriously by Hermann Cothmann (1629–83), the so-called *Hexenbürgermeister* or "witch mayor", who presided over the last, bloodiest, wave of trials. The last woman prosecuted for witchcraft, Maria Rampendahl, survived, but 254 men and women were not so fortunate.

Cothmann's former home at Breite Strasse 19 is a stunning example of Weser Renaissance architecture, built in 1571 and distinguished by a spectacular high gable and carvings that depict the virtues – including, ironically, charity. It houses the **Städtisches Museum Hexenbürgermeisterhaus** (Tues–Sun 10am–5pm; €3), where you can see instruments of torture, watch a film (English on request) and learn more about some of the individuals caught up in the trials. Around the corner on Stiftstrasse, the appealingly saggy Gothic **Marienkirche** (Tues–Sun: summer 8am–6pm; winter 8am–4pm) is notable for a rare, early seventeenth-century "swallow's nest" organ clinging to the church wall. Back on Breite Strasse, the Gothic **Wippermannsches Haus** from 1576 may have lagged behind the architectural fashion of its day, but it's another beauty.

To the north, on Markt, the **Rathaus** is no coherent set-piece but rather a delightful jumble of buildings dating from 1325 to 1612, with the star turn being the **Apothekenerker**, an exuberant Renaissance oriel window attached to the municipal pharmacy and decorated with images of eminent physicians from Hippocrates to Paracelsus. On the south side of the complex, the op-art zigzags on the **Zeughaus** (armoury) dazzle, while the terracotta-coloured **Ballhaus** (ballroom), which just predates the Thirty Years' War, completes the ensemble. Looming above the lot are the mismatched spires of the **Nikolaikirche**, which is currently undergoing restoration.

From the Rathaus, a stroll east along **Mittelstrasse** takes you past elaborate, multicoloured half-timbering, the **Planetenhaus** with its astral decoration and the gorgeous **Haus Alt Lemgo** being particularly fine examples. East of the Altstadt at Hamelner Strasse 36, the **Junkerhaus** (April–Oct Tues–Sun 10am–5pm; Nov–March Fri–Sun 11am–3pm; €4) is the eccentric work of nineteenth-century sculptor and artist Karl Junker; its elaborately-carved interior is spooky enough to conjure up thoughts of those Lemgo witches. A little to the south at Schlossstrasse 18, the moated late sixteenth-century **Schloss Brake** – a former residence of the Counts zur Lippe – houses the **Weserrenaissance Museum** (Tues–Sun 10am–6pm; €3; ⓦ www.wrm.lemgo.de), which displays a fine collection of Renaissance paintings, furniture, silverware and other *objets* that helps put the town's architectural splendour in context.

Practicalities

A frequent **bus** service (#790; every 30min) links Detmold with Lemgo's **Bahnhof**, which is at the southern entrance to the Altstadt. To reach the **tourist office** at Kramerstrasse 1 (Mon–Fri 9am–5pm, Sat 9am–1pm; ☏05261/988 70, ⓦ www.lemgo.de) follow Breite Strasse north from the car park just east of the station. You can **stay** in sixteenth-century splendour at the *Hotel Stadtpalais*, Papenstrasse 24 (☏05261/25 89 00, ⓦ www.hotel-stadtpalais.de; ❹), in comfortable but simpler surroundings at the *Hansa Hotel*, Breite Strasse 14–16 (☏05261/940 50, ⓦ www.hansa-hotel.de; ❸), or in more modern style south of the Altstadt at the *Lemgoer Hof*, Detmolder Weg 14 (☏05261/976 70, ⓦ www.lemgoer-hof .de; ❹). There's also a **campsite**, *Campingpark Lemgo*, just east of the Altstadt at Regentorstrasse 10 (☏05261/148 58, ⓦ www.camping-lemgo.de). The *Stadtpalais* has a **restaurant**; for lighter choices try the *Picasso* café and teahouse at Breite Strasse 56, and there's ice cream at *Eiscafé Cortina* at no. 44.

Münster

Bicycles rule in cultured, studenty **MÜNSTER**, which with twice as many bikes as people, is Germany's most cycle-friendly city. Its history is intertwined with that of its bishopric, the name Münster deriving from the monastery founded at Charlemagne's behest in 793 AD, while in the twentieth century Bishop Clemens August von Galen was one of the few prominent clerics to publicly defy Nazi rule. In the Middle Ages Münster was a Hanseatic city; during the

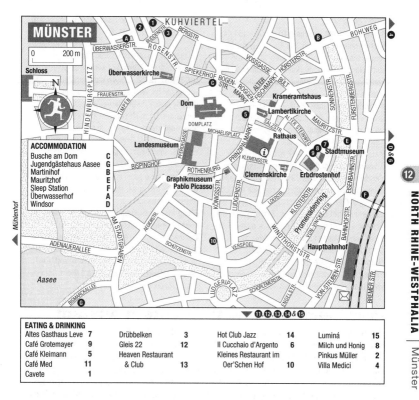

MÜNSTER

0   200 m

Schloss

N

ACCOMMODATION

Busche am Dom	C
Jugendgästehaus Aasee	G
Martinihof	B
Mauritzhof	E
Sleep Station	F
Überwasserhof	A
Windsor	D

Überwasserkirche

Dom

Landesmuseum

Graphikmuseum
Pablo Picasso

Krameramtshaus
Lambertikirche
Rathaus
Stadtmuseum
Clemenskirche   Erbdrostenhof

Promenadenring

Hauptbahnhof

Aasee

EATING & DRINKING							
Altes Gasthaus Leve	7	Drübbelken	3	Hot Club Jazz	14	Luminá	15
Café Grotemayer	9	Gleis 22	12	Il Cucchaio d'Argento	6	Milch und Honig	8
Café Kleimann	5	Heaven Restaurant		Kleines Restaurant im		Pinkus Müller	2
Café Med	11	& Club	13	Oer'Schen Hof	10	Villa Medici	4
Cavete	1						

Reformation it experienced a brief but bloody tyranny under an extreme Anabaptist sect, but soon returned to the Catholic fold. In 1648, it was the venue for the signature of the Peace of Westphalia; later, during the Napoleonic wars, the city was briefly the capital of the French *département* of Lippe, before in 1816 becoming capital of Prussian Westphalia. Built – or rather rebuilt – on a human scale, Münster is easy and fun to explore on foot: defined by the continuous green **Promenadenring** that follows the line of the old defences, the **Altstadt** contains the main sights. Beyond it, you'll find fresh air and space to picnic around the **Aasee** lake southwest of the centre, and cool bars and restaurants on the **Stadthafen**'s waterside strip. Watch your step though, for those cyclists are not to be messed with.

Arrival, information and accommodation

Münster-Osnabrück airport (℡02571/94 33 60, ⓦwww.flughafen-fmo .de) is at Hüttruper Heide north of the city; frequent buses (25–45min; €5.60) connect it to the **Hauptbahnhof**, from where you can **rent bikes** from Radstation (Mon–Fri 5.30am–11pm, Sat & Sun 7am–11pm; ℡0251/484 01 70). City **buses** depart from the stops in front of the Hauptbahnhof. From the station, follow Windthorststrasse across the Promenadenring into Stubengasse, which in turn becomes Heinrich-Brüning-Strasse: the **tourist office** is at no. 9 (Mon–Fri 9.30am–6pm, Sat 9.30am–1pm; ℡0251/492 27 10, ⓦwww .tourismus.muenster.de).

Hotels

Busche am Dom Bogenstr. 10 ☎0251/464 44, ⓦwww.hotel-busche.de. You'll scarcely get more central than this long-established, family-run place close to the Dom. Rooms are furnished in traditional Westphalian style and include some singles. ❺

Martinihof Hörstenstr. 25 ☎0251/41 86 20, ⓦwww.hotel-martinihof.de. Very central and reasonably priced hotel above a pub, with 54 rooms, mostly with shower and WC. ❸

Mauritzhof Eisenbahnstr. 17 ☎0251/417 20, ⓦwww.mauritzhof.de. Central and classy modern boutique-style hotel with 39 individually designed rooms, including seven suites, some with a balcony or terrace. Free wi-fi. ❻

Überwasserhof Überwasserstr. 3 ☎0251/417 70, ⓦwww.ueberwasserhof.de. Attractive modern decor, good bathrooms and comfortable rooms, handy for the Kuhviertel's bar scene. ❻

Windsor Warendorfer Str. 177 ☎0251/13 13 30, ⓦwww.hotelwindsor.de. Comfortable, if conservatively furnished three-star hotel east of the centre, with a locally renowned restaurant. Bus #2 or #10, stop "Danziger Freiheit". ❹

Hostels and camping

Campingplatz Münster Laerer Werseufer 7 ☎0251/31 19 82, ⓦwww.campingplatz -muenster.de. Well-equipped site 5km east of the city centre, with internet access, shop and restaurant. Open all year.

Jugendgästehaus Aasee Bismarckallee 31 ☎0251/53 02 80, ⓦwww.djh-wl.de. Münster's HI hostel is southwest of the centre facing the Aasee lake, with accommodation in two- and four-bed rooms including some adapted for wheelchair users. Bus #10 or #4, stop "Jugendgästehaus Aasee". Dorms €25.20.

Sleep Station Wolbecker Str. 1 ☎0251/482 81 55, ⓦwww.sleep-station.de. Friendly, well-run backpacker hostel in a convenient position right next to the Hauptbahnhof, with accommodation in single or double rooms and four-, five-, six- or eight-bed dorms. Check-in 9am–12.30pm & 5–9pm. Dorms from €15; doubles ❷.

Prinzipalmarkt and the eastern Altstadt

With its steep stone gables and natty arcades, elegant, curving **Prinzipalmarkt** is as fine a street as any in Germany. But it isn't quite what it seems, for wartime bombs devastated Münster and by 1945, ninety percent of the city's core was a ruin. Faced with the alternatives of starting afresh or trying to recapture some of the city's lost beauty, the authorities opted for the latter. Major monuments were rebuilt exactly as they had been, but others were reconstructed in a loose pastiche of historic forms. The mix works well.

Flanked by the Renaissance **Stadtweinhaus** (1615) and Gothic **Haus Ostendorff**, Münster's fourteenth-century **Rathaus** was reduced to its lower storeys by the wartime bombs, but rapidly rebuilt afterwards, and the delicate finials topping its high gable once again amaze visitors as they must have done when first built. Step inside to see the **Friedenssaal** (Tues–Fri 10am–5pm, Sat & Sun 10am–4pm; €1.50), the room in which on October 24, 1648, the Catholic half of the **Peace of Westphalia** was brokered – the Protestant faction was based in Osnabrück. Regarded as the first triumph of modern diplomacy, it brought the Thirty Years' War to an end, recognized the sovereignty of the Netherlands and Switzerland and put Catholic and Protestant faiths on an equal legal footing. The room's magnificent sixteenth-century wood panelling and the 37 portraits of the delegates are original, having escaped wartime destruction by being stored outside the city.

To the north, the sooty openwork spire of the late Gothic **Lambertikirche** is hung with a grisly garnish of three iron cages in which the bodies of Anabaptist leader Jan van Leiden and his lieutenants were exhibited in 1535 after their torture and execution under prince-bishop Franz von Waldeck. Leiden, who had proclaimed himself king of the "New Zion" in Münster, presided over a colourful, but bloody, brief period in which polygamy was a duty, money was declared obsolete and all property communal. The spire is nineteenth century, but the body of the church was built between 1375 and 1450 and is notable for the relief of the tree of Jesse above the main portal.

It was from a pulpit in the light-filled interior that on August 3, 1941, Bishop von Galen denounced the Nazis' euthanasia programme against the mentally ill. During the evenings, a watchman blows a copper horn from the church tower (Wed–Mon 9pm–midnight, every 30min).

Tucked behind the Lambertikirche at Alter Steinweg 6/7 is the brick gabled **Krameramtshaus**, a former guildhall dating from 1589 that houses a library and research institute specializing in the Netherlands and Flanders.

As you head east, stop briefly to admire the Baroque **Erbdrostenhof** and **Clemenskirche**, both the mid-eighteenth-century work of court architect Johann Conrad von Schlaun, en route to the **Stadtmuseum** at Salzstrasse 28 (Tues–Fri 10am–6pm, Sat & Sun 11am–6pm; free), which offers a well-displayed, exhaustive overview of the city's history, though labels are in German only. The grimmer exhibits are leavened with more light-hearted displays, like the original 1950s interior of the former *Café Müller*. Just beyond the Promenaden-ring at Windthorststrasse 26, the **Museum für Lackkunst** (Tues noon–8pm, Wed–Sun noon–6pm; €3, free Tues; ⓦwww.museum-fuer-lackkunst.de) houses a unique collection of lacquerwork, including examples from China, Japan and the Islamic world.

The Domplatz and around

Situated at the heart of the Altstadt, the immense **St Paulus Dom** (Mon–Sat 6.30am–6pm, Sun 6.30am–7.30pm) is the largely thirteenth-century successor to the church built by the Frisian monk Liudger in the eighth century. Take a gentle circuit of the building before entering the west transept via the **Paradise** porch, which features late Romanesque sculptures of Christ and the Apostles, with Jesus sitting as supreme judge above the gate to heaven – rather appropriately, since this space once had a judicial function. On the right, black-and-white photographs show the extent of wartime damage, with the west front almost obliterated, the roof gaping and one of the towers in a state of collapse. Inside, the Dom impresses more through its unusual width than its modest height, and it is pleasingly austere save for some splendid memorials and a sixteenth-century **astronomical clock** in the ambulatory, constructed between 1540 and 1542 by the printer Theodor Tzwyvel, the Franciscan friar Johannes Aquensis and the wrought-iron craftsman Nikolaus Windemaker. Decorated with paintings by Ludger tom Ring, the clock is divided into 24 hours, charts the position of the planets and is accurate until 2071. A chapel in the ambulatory contains the tomb of Bishop von Galen, the "Lion of Münster", who died in 1946 and was beatified in 2005. The Dom's artistic treasures can be seen on the north side of the cloisters in the **Domkammer** (Tues–Sun 11am–4pm; €3); they include an eleventh-century head reliquary of St Paul and a jewel-encrusted thirteenth-century cross reliquary.

Facing the cathedral across Domplatz with its main entrance in Pferdegasse, the eclectic **Landesmuseum für Kunst und Kulturgeschichte** (Tues, Wed & Fri 9am–7pm, Thurs 9am–9pm, Sat & Sun 10am–6pm; €9) houses a sprawling collection of fine and applied art from the medieval to the modern, though ongoing building work means parts of the complex are subject to closure and not everything may be on view at any one time. **Medieval** works on the ground floor include Conrad von Soest's *Saints Dorothea and Odilia*, created for the Walburgis convent in Soest, and splendid late medieval carvings by Münster-born Heinrich Brabender, the great master of Westphalian sculpture at the turn of the sixteenth century, represented here by his *Entry of Christ in Jerusalem*, carved for the Dom around 1516. Upstairs, the **Renaissance** is represented by paintings by Münster's own tom Ring dynasty, but also by the *Wrangelschrank*, a spectacular inlaid cabinet made in Augsburg in 1566 and decorated with scenes from Roman wars. It was once the property of Swedish field marshal Carl Gustav Wrangel. The extensive **modern art** collection includes Impressionist paintings by Max Liebermann and Lovis Corinth and Expressionist works from the Brücke and Blaue Reiter groups, with an emphasis on the work of Westphalian-born August Macke. Opposite the Landesmuseum at Pferdegasse 3, the university's fossil and mineral collections were due to be back on display in a new **GeoMuseum** during 2009. South of Domplatz the **Graphikmuseum Pablo Picasso** at Königsstrasse 5 (Tues–Sun Mon 10am–6pm; €10; ⓦ www.graphikmuseum-picasso-muenster.de) presents a changing selection of graphic works by Picasso and his contemporaries, plus some worthwhile temporary exhibitions.

The western Altstadt

Northwest of the cathedral, a lane leads across the diminutive river Aa to the **Überwasserkirche**, or church over the water, badly trashed by the Anabaptists in 1534. Its medieval sculptures were smashed and buried, but exhumed during excavations of the transept in 1898, and are now on view in the Landesmuseum. The delightfully small-scale district beyond the church, known as the **Kuhviertel**, is one of Münster's liveliest quarters, with a good choice of places to eat or drink.

On the western fringe of the Altstadt, the stately **Schloss** is another of Johann Conrad von Schlaun's Baroque confections, built as the prince-bishops' residence between 1767 and 1787. Nowadays it houses the university. Three times a year, the space in front of it hosts a giant market and funfair, the **Send**. At other times, the **Botanischer Garten** (summer 7.30am–5pm; free) in the grounds is worth a stroll.

South of the university, spacious **Aasee** is Münster's chief recreation ground, with boats to rent and an attractive shoreline for a picnic. On the north side of the lake, the **Freilichtmuseum Mühlenhof** (April–Sept daily 10am–6pm; March & Oct daily 11am–4pm; Nov–Feb Mon–Fri & Sun 11am–4pm; €4) is a rustic assembly of buildings from rural Westphalia, including an eighteenth-century windmill.

Eating, drinking and entertainment

Münster punches its weight when it comes to **eating** and **drinking**. There's a traditional or studenty vibe to the Kuhviertel's offerings, while slick modernity is the rule along the Stadthafen's Kreativkai. The Städtische Bühnen, Neubrückenstrasse 63 (☎0251/590 91 00, ⓦ www.stadttheater.muenster.de), is the city's main **cultural** venue, with everything from drama or operetta to classical concerts by the Sinfonieorchester Münster; serious drama is performed on a more intimate scale at the Wolfgang Borchert Theater in the Stadthafen (☎0251/400 19, ⓦ www.wolfgang-borchert-theater.de). The cinema on Warendorfer Strasse (☎0251/303 00) sometimes shows English-language **films**.

Restaurants and cafés

Altes Gasthaus Leve Alter Steinweg 37 ☎0251/455 95. "Münster's oldest *Gaststätte*" is in fact a postwar reconstruction of the destroyed seventeenth-century original, but it's nevertheless an atmospheric place offering reasonably priced Westphalian specialities, and the kitchen stays open until 11pm.

Café Grotemeyer Salzstr. 24 ☎0251/424 77. Smart Viennese-style café-*Konditorei* with heavenly cakes and live piano music on Friday and Saturday afternoons from 4pm.

Café Kleimann Prinzipalmarkt 48 ☎0251/430 64. Classic coffee-and-cake pit stop, with a prime site facing the Lambertikirche and a largely elderly clientele. Closed Sun.

Café Med Hafenweg 26a ☎0251/674 95 95. Good pizzas, big salads and an informal atmosphere attract a lively, young crowd to this vast dockside café-bar, though the service sometimes struggles to cope with the rush.

Drübbelken Buddenstr. 14–15 ☎0251/421 95. The "olde worlde" atmosphere is laid on with a trowel at this darkly *gemütlich* Kuhviertel place, in a half-timbered house with open fire and hearty Westphalian food – including pork belly, home-made *Bratwurst* and beef in onion sauce.

Il Cucchaio d'Argento Warendorfer Str. 177 ☎0251/39 20 45. The refined gourmet Italian cooking at the *Windsor* hotel has attracted a string of celebrity visitors over the years. Sun–Fri lunch & dinner, Sat eve only.

Kleines Restaurant im Oer'Schen Hof Königstr. 42 ☎0251/484 10 83. One of Münster's top gourmet offerings in the elegant surroundings of an eighteenth-century house, with creative, seasonal dishes that blend Westphalian, Mediterranean and Asian influences.

Luminá Hafenweg 2–6 ☎0251/133 32 72. Modern Italian on the approach to the Stadthafen, a bit more refined than most of the waterside offerings and with good-value lunch specials. Open from breakfast.

Villa Medici Ostmarkstr. 15 ☎0251/342 18. Upmarket Italian with creative cooking and an elegant dining room enlivened with well-chosen modern art. Five course *menu dégustation* €47. Closed Sun & Mon.

Bars and clubs

Cavete Kreuzstr. 37–38, Kuhviertel. Münster's classic student pub, with a fabulously grungy, grotto-like interior, and pizza and noodle dishes to soak up the beer or cocktails.

Gleis 22 Haftenstr. 34 ☎0251/492 58 57. Studenty live music venue and club close to the Hauptbahnhof, with DJ nights spanning everything from electro to British indie or drum'n'bass.

Heaven Restaurant & Club Hafenweg 31 ☎0251/609 05 85. Spacious dockside restaurant that transforms itself into a fairly mainstream disco on Friday and Saturday nights, with guest DJs spinning house, electro, soul and hip-hop.

Touring Münsterland

With its placid rural landscapes and gentle inclines, the countryside around cyclist-friendly Münster is ideal for exploring by bike. Around 4500km of well-signposted **cycle paths** crisscross the region, including a stretch of the Boulogne-to-St Petersburg R1 cycleway and several themed routes. In effect, the hub of the network is the 4.5km Promenadenring in Münster itself, with more than 1500 cyclists per hour making it a veritable superhighway of cycling. Of the themed routes, the 47km **Skulpt(o)ur** that links public artworks in and around Münster is the shortest while the 1400km **100 Schlösser Route**, which links castles and palaces in the surrounding region, is the longest. Highlights of the 100 Schlösser Tour can be visited on a 140km circuit south and west of Münster and include the lovely *Wasserburg* (moated castle) of **Hülshoff** (mid-March to Nov 11am–6.30pm; €4.50), family seat of the nineteenth-century author Annette von Droste-Hülshoff, at Havixbeck 10km west of Münster; the Münsterland Museum in the equally picturesque **Burg Vischering** at Lüdinghausen (April–Oct Tues–Sun 10am–12.30pm & 1–5.30pm; Nov–March closes at 4.30pm; €2.50); and **Schloss Nordkirchen**, the so-called "Westphalian Versailles", with spectacular gardens (free access) and open-air concerts in the courtyard in summer. All these destinations can also be visited **by car**, and **buses** also depart Münster's Hauptbahnhof for Havixbeck, but getting to the others from Münster by public transport is difficult. Lüdinghausen has a station on the Dortmund–Coesfeld rail line; to reach Nordkirchen you'll need to take the train from Dortmund to Selm and then a bus.

Another themed route, the 170km **Friedensroute**, links places between Münster and Osnabrück associated with the Peace of Westphalia, including Telgte, setting for the fictional 1647 meeting of writers and intellectuals that was the subject of Günter Grass's novel *The Meeting at Telgte*. For more information on the routes, and on packages including accommodation and accompanied tours, contact Münsterland Tourismus at An der Hohen Schule 13, Steinfurt (☎02551/93 92 91, ⓦwww.muensterland-tourismus .de, though the website is currently in Dutch and German only). They can also provide information on accommodation and horseriding packages.

Hot Club Jazz Hafenweg 26b ☎0251/68 66 79 10. Live music venue on the Stadthafen with a programme that embraces jazz, funk, soul, blues and Latin music.

Milch und Honig Alter Steinweg 37 ☎0251/396 78 56. Stylish lounge and cocktail bar next to the *Altes Gasthaus Leve*, with a soundtrack

of electro, house and dance classics, plus live jazz on Thursdays from 9pm.

Pinkus Müller Kreuzstr. 4, Kuhviertel ☎0251/451 51. Vast *Gaststätte* owned by Münster's sole surviving brewery, with traditional trappings and Westphalian food to accompany the beer.

Travel details

Trains

Aachen to: Cologne (every 20–30min; 35min–1hr); Dortmund (every 30min; 2hr 38min); Duisburg (every 30min; 1hr 45min); Düsseldorf airport (hourly; 1hr 40min); Düsseldorf (every 15–30min; 1hr 32min); Frankfurt airport (3 daily; 1hr 35min); Frankfurt (3 daily; 1hr 50min); Liège (8 daily; 45min–1hr 10min).

Bonn to: Berlin (6 daily; 4hr 45min); Bochum (16 daily; 1hr 25min); Cologne (every 10–20min; 20–30min); Dortmund (every 30min–1hr; 1hr 35min); Duisburg (every 20min; 1hr 8min); Düsseldorf airport (hourly; 1hr 7min); Düsseldorf (15 daily; 50min–1hr); Essen (every 1–2hr; 1hr 20min); Frankfurt (10 daily; 2hr); Koblenz (every 10–20min; 30min–1hr 5min); Mainz (hourly; 1hr 30min); Munich (3 daily; 5hr 40min–7hr 10min); Münster (1–2 hourly; 2hr 10min); Trier (6 daily; 2hr 12min); Wuppertal (approx. hourly; 50min–1hr 17min).

Cologne to: Aachen (every 20–30min; 30min–1hr); Amsterdam (6 daily; 2hr 40min); Berlin (every 30min–1hr; 5hr 5min–8hr 15min); Bochum (every 15min; 58min–1hr 12min); Bonn (extremely frequent; 20–30min); Brussels (8 daily; 2hr 20min); Dortmund (every 20–30min; 50min–1hr 25min); Duisburg (up to every 10min; 37–55min); Düsseldorf airport (every 20–30min; 30–37min); Düsseldorf (extremely frequent; 20–50min); Essen (up to every 10min; 45min–1hr 37min); Frankfurt airport (every 14–30min; 55min);

Frankfurt (every 20min–1hr; 1hr 10min–2hr 20min); Koblenz (every 10–20min; 50min–1hr 40min); Mainz (every 30min–1hr; 1hr 50min); Munich (14 daily; 4hr 40min); Münster (every 20min; 1hr 45min–2hr); Wuppertal (up to every 10min; 25–35min)

Dortmund to: Cologne (every 20–30min; 1hr 10min–1hr 25min); Münster (every 20–30min; 30–50min); Paderborn (hourly; 1hr 5min–1hr 10min); Soest (every 20–30min; 35–50min).

Duisburg to: Münster (every 30min; 1hr 10min–1hr 20min); Xanten (hourly; 45min).

Düsseldorf to: Aachen (every 20–30min; 1hr 20min–1hr 30min); Bonn (21 daily; 45min–1hr); Cologne (extremely frequent; 20–50min); Dortmund (extremely frequent; 45min–1hr 30min); Essen (extremely frequent; 23–40min); Münster (approx. hourly; 1hr 20min).

Essen to: Cologne (extremely frequent; 50min–1hr 40min); Dortmund (extremely frequent; 20–40min); Duisburg (extremely frequent; 10–20min); Düsseldorf (extremely frequent; 25–45min); Münster (every 20–30min; 1hr).

Münster to: Berlin (3 daily; 3hr 40min); Dortmund (every 30min–1hr; 30min–55min); Duisburg (every 20–30min; 1hr–1hr 20min); Essen (every 20–30min; 55min–1hr 5min); Paderborn (every 30min; 1hr 30min).

Wuppertal to: Bonn (approx. hourly; 58min–1hr 15min); Cologne (up to every 15min; 30–45min); Düsseldorf (up to every 15min; 20–30min).

Lower Saxony and Bremen

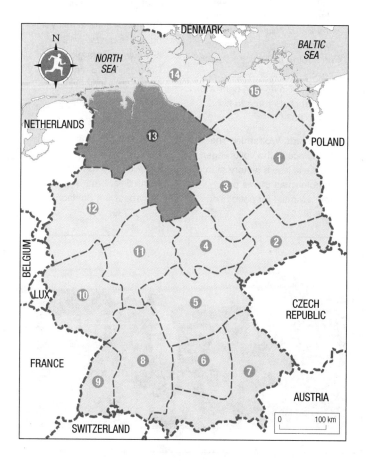

CHAPTER 13

Highlights

✳ **Hannover** One of the finest Baroque gardens in Europe, good galleries and a grungy drinking district that lets rip at weekends – the state capital proves culture comes in bars as well as museums. See p.679

✳ **Follow the Fairytale Road** Hameln of Pied Piper fame and Baron Münchhausen's Bodenwerder are two stops on a route that swoops south beside the River Weser – an attraction in its own right with a great cycle-route to boot. See p.697

✳ **Autostadt, Wolfsburg** The birthplace of the Volkswagen Beetle is less a factory than a motor-mad theme park that's a must for petrolheads. See p.711

✳ **Celle** Carved timbers by the tonne in a picture-book pretty courtly town within easy reach of Hannover. See p.713

✳ **Lüneburg** Wonky red-brick buildings in a small town that exudes provincial contentment. See p.717

✳ **Bremen** A state in its own right, this buzzy, small city swings from glorious Renaissance to medieval village via Art Nouveau fantasy. See p.726

✳ **Bar-hopping in Bremen** A strip of beer gardens on the river with a vibe that's more Mediterranean than North Sea. What's not to like about the Schlachte? See p.735

▲ Royal gardens, Hannover

Lower Saxony and Bremen

f **Lower Saxony** is little known by foreign visitors, it is probably because it lacks the sort of definitive city- or landscape that helps to cement other German Länder in the mind. It is a neutral ground; the second largest state in Germany after Bavaria, it shares more borders than any other federal state. Architecturally, too, it represents a middle ground that segues from the half-timbered country to a red-brick coast. It's tempting to put this lack of identity down to history. **Niedersachsen**, as Germans know it, only came into being in 1946 through the postwar redrawing of the map by the British military administration. The area's focus was the one-time kingdom (then Prussian province) of Hannover, onto which was grafted former city-states Oldenburg, Schaumburg-Lippe and Braunschweig. Yet Lower Saxony has deeper roots. Though misleading for a state that lies above, not below, present-day Saxony, the moniker is a reflection of the Saxon tribe that populated the region long before Germany existed as a defined entity. This was the stamping ground of mighty Saxon duke Henry the Lion (Heinrich der Löwe), a European super-power of the twelfth century, and the state would probably have retained the name "Saxony" had his humbling not led to the slow migration of the Saxon powerbase up the Elbe to the state that now bears its name.

The watchword when touring, then, is diversity – both of attractions and in scenic shifts that morph from brooding highlands in the Harz (see p.238) via the rolling **Lüneburg Heath** to the salty air and mudflats of the North Sea coast. All landscapes benefit from a low population density. The only city worth the name is state capital **Hannover**, and even this city of gardens and art is small fry with just over half a million people. The second urban hub lies around **Braunschweig**, which preserves the monuments from its era as the powerbase of Henry the Lion. But even this most industrialized part of the state defies easy categorization. Within half an hour in either direction lie destinations as distinct as **Wolfsburg**, definitively modern, and the daydreaming former Residenzstadt, **Wolfenbüttel**. The latter is as good an introduction as any to the small medieval towns dotted throughout the state. Places such as UNESCO-listed provincial town **Hildesheim**, or **Celle**, whose picture-book, half-timbered Altstadt stands in contrast with the red-brick in **Lüneburg**. Divided by the Lüneburg Heath, the duo sum up the transition from beam to brick – country to coast – in a nutshell. **Hameln** of Pied Piper fame is another world again in an Altstadt characterized by Weser Renaissance

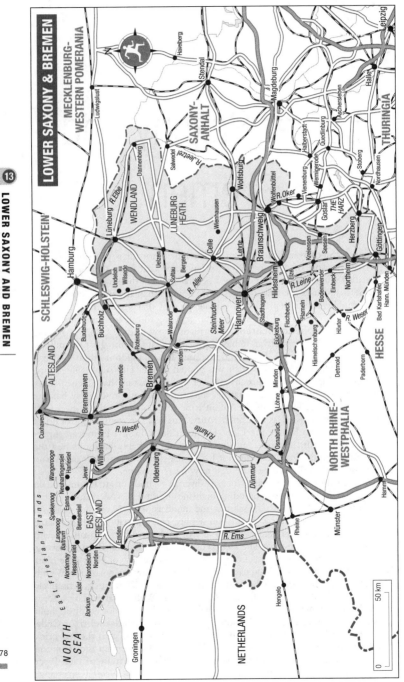

LOWER SAXONY & BREMEN

MECKLENBURG-
WESTERN POMERANIA

SCHLESWIG-HOLSTEIN

SAXONY-
ANHALT

THURINGIA

HESSE

NORTH RHINE-
WESTPHALIA

NETHERLANDS

NORTH
SEA

East Friesian Islands

EAST
FRIESLAND

ALTESLAND

WENDLAND

LÜNEBURG
HEATH

THE
HARZ

Leipzig

Havelberg

Stendal

Ludwigslust

Dannenberg

Salzwedel

R. Jeetzel

Wolfsburg

Magdeburg

Halle

Tscherslaben

Halberstadt

Quedlinburg

Stoberg

Nordhausen

Wernigerode

Ilenburg

Goslar

Herzberg

Seesen

Göttingen

R. Oker

Wolfenbüttel

Braunschweig

Hildesheim

Kreiensen

Einbeck

Northeim

Bad Karlshafen

Hann. Münden

R. Weser

Höxter

Bodenwerder

R. Leine

Elze

Hameln

Detmold

Paderborn

Hamm

Münster

Rheine

R. Ems

Hengelo

Groningen

Borkum

Juist

Norderney

Nessmersiel

Baltrum

Spiekeroog

Langeoog

Wangerooge

Neuharlingersiel

Harlesiel

Esens

Bensersiel

Jever

Wilhelmshaven

Cuxhaven

Bremerhaven

Worpswede

Bremen

R. Weser

R. Hunte

Oldenburg

Emden

Norddeich

Norden

Dümmer

Osnabrück

Löhne

Minden

Bückeburg

Stadthagen

Fischbeck

Hämelschenburg

Hannover

Steinhuder
Meer

Verden

Walsrode

Rotenburg

Buchholz

Buxtehude

Hamburg

Lüneburg

R. Elbe

Uelzen

Soltau

Bergen

Undeloh

Wilsede

Celle

Wienhausen

Leifte

R. Aller

N

0   50 km

styles as well as its hilly hinterland, the Weserbergland, which swoops south along the Fairytale Road to buzzy university town **Göttingen**. Separated northwest on the flatlands where North Rhine-Westphalia bites a chunk out of the state is **Osnabrück**, capital of the western state whose history of peace-broking may have contributed to its accreditation as the happiest city in Germany.

Though included within this chapter, former Hanseatic trading city **Bremen** and its North Sea port **Bremerhaven** represent a state in their own right – independent and fiercely proud of it.

Eastern Lower Saxony

The eastern half of the state is the most densely populated part of the Land, and the hub around which all life (and transport revolves) is **Hannover**, long mocked as a dull federal capital, known only as host of the world's largest trade fair. This seems an insult to its vibrant arts and nightlife and royal Baroque garden that ranks among the finest in Europe. The variety of sights within an hour of Hannover are intriguing, making this classic touring country. **Braunschweig**, the second city, is a former stamping-ground of mighty Saxony duke Henry the Lion as well as a good launchpad for rev-head's wonderworld **Wolfenburg**, home both of that quintessentially German brand Volkswagen and a splendid science centre, and sleepy former ducal seat **Wolfenbüttel**. South, in the foothills that roll up to the Harz range, **Hildesheim** is a gentle, provincial place with a UNESCO-listed ecclesiastical heritage. Pied Piper town **Hameln**, west, marks the start of a classic route south that swings around meanders of the Weser River valley, offering superb cycling and canoeing and taking in such picture-book half-timbered towns as **Hann. Münden**. What stops the area south to Frankfurt from falling asleep in a surfeit of sunshine and small-town life is **Göttingen**, a bar-hopping university town par excellence.

North of Hannover the landscapes flatten as you roll past half-timbered Residenzstadt **Celle** and over rugged heathland to **Lüneburg**, prettified as a member of the Hanseatic League and a first inkling of the coast beyond.

Hannover (Hanover) and around

"Is Hannover the most boring city in Germany?" news weekly *Der Spiegel* once asked. In a word, no, though the capital of Lower Saxony can appear every bit a faceless modern metropolis. When five of the world's ten largest trade fairs roll into town, up to 800,000 businesspeople wheel, deal, then disappear, the majority probably unaware that they had been in a state capital which, from 1815 to 1866, ruled a kingdom in its own right. Eighty eight air raids reduced the city from elegant aristocrat to war-torn widow and, with ninety percent of the centre reduced to rubble, the city patched up where possible but largely wiped clean the slate.

It was some past to write off, too. The seventeenth-century dukes of Calenburg turned the head of the former Hanseatic League member when they took up summer residence at nearby village Höringehusen, and in 1679 Ernst August ushered in a golden age for his royal capital. Court academic Gottfried Wilhelm Leibniz wowed Europe with his mathematical and philosophical theories and the arts blossomed, as did a Baroque garden seeded by the regent's wife Sophia, Hannover's prize, which ranks among the finest in Europe. More significantly for history, Sophia's parentage as granddaughter of James I of England saw her son, plain old Georg Ludwig, metamorphose into George I of Great Britain in 1714 to begin the house of Hannover's 120-year stint on the British throne.

Even if the city's EXPO2000 exhibition turned out to be something of a damp squib – it attracted less than half the forty million people hoped for – that it happened at all sums up a vigorous, ambitious city. It's a place with the bottle to reinvent itself through street art, from the *Nanas* at Hohen Ufer to the wacky bus- and tramstops commissioned to cheer up drab streets before EXPO. Similarly, there are some vibrant art museums and a grungy bar and nightlife scene that is anything but boring. What it lacks is a landmark. Wartime destruction, then postwar planning, conspired to erase the coherence of Hannover's Altstadt. North of the pocket that has been rebuilt stretch broad avenues of high-street shopping, south across the arterial ring-road lie the **Maschsee** lake and the best **art galleries**. The celebrated **gardens** are northwest of the centre, beyond the lively nightlife district centred around the **Steintor**.

Arrival, information and city transport

The **Hauptbahnhof** and **bus station** behind it lie in the heart of the city, at the head of the pedestrianized high streets. Hannover international **airport** (Ⓦ www.hannover-airport.de) is 9km northwest of the centre, linked by S-Bahn S5 to the Hauptbahnhof; a taxi will cost around €20. A hugely helpful **tourist office** (Mon–Fri 9am–6pm, Sat & Sun 9am–2pm; ☎0511/12 34 51 11, Ⓦ www.hannover-tourism.de) is directly opposite the Hauptbahnhof at Ernst-August-Platz 8. As well as the usual information services, it can book accommodation for €2.50 per booking and sells the **HannoverCard**, which provides free travel on all public transport and discounts of around twenty percent on most sights and many opera and theatre tickets. A one-day card costs €9, a three-day card €15. Also on sale is an English-language booklet (€2) of sights on the *Roter Faden*, the 4.2km "Red Thread" painted on pavements that links the city's principle sights. An excellent touchscreen Infopoint outside the tourist office provides details on everything from hotels to nightlife, with links to maps – a godsend for late arrivals. **Public transport** within Zone 1 – all you'll ever need – costs €2 for a single and €3.90 for a *TagesTicket*, or €7.80 for a TagesGruppenTicket that covers up to five people. **Bike rental** is from a Fahrradstation (Mon–Fri 6am–10.45pm, Sat & Sun 8am–10.45pm) on the east side of the Hauptbahnhof.

Accommodation

Unsurprisingly for a city famous for its trade fairs, hotels in Hannover are business-orientated. Be aware too that beds are hard to come by when trade-fair expense accounts roll into town. Worse, prices double, triple then asphyxiate – prices quoted below are for standard times, so book ahead or check with the tourist information office rather than trust it to chance. The nearest campsite is *Naherholungspark Arnumer See* (☎05101/855 14 90, Ⓦ www.camping-hannover.de), a pleasant spot beside a lake 9km south in the village-suburb of Arnum. Bus #300 gets you there (eventually) from the bus station.

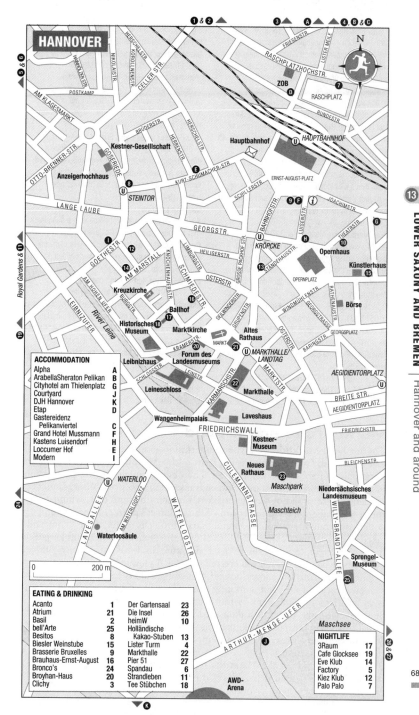

HANNOVER

❶ & ❷ ▲   ❸ ▲   Ⓐ ▲   ▲ ❹, Ⓑ & Ⓒ

N

❺ & ❻

RASCHPLATZHOCHSTR.

ZOB Ⓓ

❼

RASCHPLATZ

AM KLAGESMARKT

POSTKAMP

Kestner-Gesellschaft

Hauptbahnhof 🚉 Ⓤ *HAUPTBAHNHOF*

Anzeigerhochhaus

⑧ Ⓤ

STEINTOR

ERNST-AUGUST-PLATZ

Ⓔ

LANGE LAUBE

❾ Ⓕ *(i)*

GEORGSTR.

Ⓖ

Royal Gardens & ⑰

⑫

Ⓤ

⑩

Opernhaus

KRÖPCKE

Künstlerhaus

⑭

⑬

⑮

OPERNPLATZ

Kreuzkirche

Börse

⑯

Ballhof

⑰

Historisches Museum ⑱

Marktkirche

Altes Rathaus

⑲

ACCOMMODATION

Alpha	A
ArabellaSheraton Pelikan	B
Cityhotel am Thielenplatz	G
Courtyard	J
DJH Hannover	K
Etap	D
Gastereidenz Pelikanviertel	C
Grand Hotel Mussmann	F
Kastens Luisendorf	H
Loccumer Hof	E
Modern	I

Leibnizhaus

⑳ Forum des Landesmuseums

Ⓤ *MARKTHALLE/LANDTAG*

MARKT ㉑

Leineschloss

㉒

Markthalle

AEGIDIENTORPLATZ

Ⓤ

Wangenheimpalais

Laveshaus

FRIEDRICHSWALL

FRIEDRICHSTR.

Kestner-Museum

BLEICHENSTR.

Ⓤ *WATERLOO*

Neues Rathaus ㉓

Maschpark

Niedersächsisches Landesmuseum

Maschteich

Waterloosäule

0   200 m

Sprengel-Museum

㉕

EATING & DRINKING

Acanto	1	Der Gartensaal	23
Atrium	21	Die Insel	26
Basil	2	heimW	10
bell'Arte	25	Holländische	
Besitos	8	Kakao-Stuben	13
Biesler Weinstube	15	Lister Turm	4
Brasserie Bruxelles	9	Markthalle	22
Brauhaus-Ernst-August	16	Pier 51	27
Bronco's	24	Spandau	6
Broyhan-Haus	20	Strandleben	11
Clichy	3	Tee Stübchen	18

Maschsee

NIGHTLIFE

3Raum	17
Cafe Glocksee	19
Eve Klub	14
Factory	5
Kiez Klub	12
Palo Palo	7

AWD-Arena

Ⓚ

Alpha Friesenstr.19 ⓣ0511/34 15 35, ⓦwww
.hotelalpha.de. No minimalist understatement for
the Mediterranean-themed *Alpha*. Charming or
chintzy depending on taste, but unarguably on a
quiet street behind the Hauptbahnhof. ⑥

ArabellaSheraton Pelikan Pelikanplatz 31
ⓣ0511/909 30, ⓦwww.sheraton.de/hannover.
North of the Hauptbahnhof by Listerplatz U-Bahn,
this is the chief executive's choice, a marriage of
slick modern design and first-class comforts. ⑥–⑦

Cityhotel am Thielenplatz Thielenplatz 2
ⓣ0511/32 76 91, ⓦwww.smartcityhotels.com.
Retro modernism at a budget price from a young
hotel that's well located near the Hauptbahnhof
– expect Verner Panton-style chairs and aluminium
globe lights in renovated rooms, though others are
a little frumpy. ③–④

Courtyard Arthur-Menge-Ufer 3 ⓣ0511 36 60
00, ⓦwww.marriott.de. Pay an extra €15 and
mornings come with glorious views down the
Maschsee – the only place in Hannover with one.
Otherwise standard classic-modern decor and all
the mod cons you'd expect of a Marriott hotel. ⑥

DJH Hannover Ferdinand-Wilhelm-Fricke-Weg 1
ⓣ0511/131 76 74, ⓦwww.djh-niedersachsen.de.
An enormous place among the greenery south of
the AWD-Arena on the west bank of the Maschsee.
Take the S-Bahn to Hannover-Linden-Fischerhof.
From €27.90.

Etap Rundestr. 7 ⓣ0511/235 55 70, ⓦwww
.etaphotel.com. The usual functional en suites of
the budget chain – best treated as a crash pad but

a good price considering the central location. One
of the few bargains during a trade fair, too. ②

Gästeresidenz Pelikanviertel Pelikanstr. 11
ⓣ0511/399 90, ⓦwww.gaesteresidenz
-pelikanviertel.de. Great-value apartments
furnished in simple, modern Scandinavian fashion
in an old brick warehouse with 24hr check-in. It's
located 1km north of the centre, midway on tram
line #3, #7 or #9. ③

Grand Hotel Mussmann Ernst-August-Platz 7
ⓣ0511/365 60, ⓦwww.grandhotel.de. Once a
grand station hotel, the *Mussmann* has reinvented
itself as a quietly stylish number with parquet
floors and marble bathrooms in high-ceilinged
rooms. ⑥–⑦

Kastens Luisenhof Luisenstr. 1–3 ⓣ0511/304
40, ⓦwww.kastens-luisenhof.de. With a guestbook
that features names such as Pavarotti and the
Queen Mother, five-star, classic modern elegance
and calm rule supreme at Hannover's oldest and
most exclusive hotel. ⑥–⑦

Loccumer Hof Kurt-Schumacher-Str. 14–16
ⓣ0511/13 11 92, ⓦwww.loccumerhof.com.
Friendly, modern hotel in the centre that offers
quirky rooms themed by elements and countries; a
clock alarm of the Dalai Lama singing in the "Tibet"
room is typical of their idiosyncratic touches.
Others are in comfortable business style. ⑤

Modern Goethestr. 2 ⓣ0511/897 39 90,
ⓦwww.hotel-modern-hannover.de. Fairly cheap
and cheerful small hotel in the grungy heart of the
Steintor bar district. ③

Marktkirche and around

The medieval **Marktkirche** – the southernmost example of north Germany's
love affair with Gothic brick – is the heart of the **Altstadt**, perched on a barely
noticeable hill above the Leine River. The church's mighty tower powers up
98m as a launch pad for a spire – and ends instead in a pinprick. Why Hannover
residents are so proud of this landmark is a mystery because their whimpering
turret is a fudge, a miniature version of the architect's plans enforced by empty
coffers and builders who, a contemporary chronicle relates, were "faint and
taken of the sickness". After almost total wartime obliteration, a faithful rebuild
has swept the interior clean of later furniture to leave the austere purity
conceived when the church was erected in 1366. A Gothic Passion altar survives
from the Reformation purges; behind, St George suffers his trials in medieval
stained glass, and to the left, sprouting from a base like a gramophone trumpet,
is an oversized fifteenth-century font featuring the Marktkirche's second saint,
St James, with the staff and scallop shell of Santiago de Compostela pilgrims.
Don't leave without taking a look at the entrance doors with which Bauhaus
sculptor Gerhard Marcks delivers a sermon on the "discordia and concordia" of
modern German history.

On the south side of the Markt the rebuilt **Altes Rathaus** is a sideshow to
the Marktkirche despite step gables that bristle with finials and layers of glazed
and red brick, two styles favoured by the Baltic cities Hannover aped after it

signed up to the Hanseatic League in 1386. Among the princes and heraldic arms depicted in a plaster frieze on the Schmiedestrasse flank, two medieval burghers are locked in a game of *Luderziehen*, a sort of medieval tug-of-war using fingers.

Around Holzmarkt and Hohen Ufer

In the late 1800s, Jerome K. Jerome acclaimed Hannover for "handsome streets and tasteful gardens side by side with a sixteenth-century town where old timbered houses overhang the narrow lanes; where through low archways one catches glimpses of galleried courtyards". A faint echo of this is in **Kramerstrasse**, off the Markt, and **Burgstrasse** – the most photographed streets in Hannover are a parade of seductively neat half-timbered houses, gloriously swaying fakes all, rebuilt as Hannover residents hankered after the medieval intimacy that 88 air raids wiped off the map in 1943.

The half-timbering on Kramerstrasse frames **Leibnizhaus** on Holzmarkt, the rebuilt Renaissance mansion of philosopher Gottfried Wilhelm Leibniz, whose facade is fresh-from-the-wrapper neat. Leibniz asserted cheerfully that his job as ducal librarian to the Guelphic dukes in the late 1600s left spare hours for his leisure pursuits: inventing differential and integral calculus independently of Newton; honing theories of metaphysics; idly dreaming up the concept of cataloguing as an offshoot of a utopian universal library of thought; advancing theories of linguistics. His sharp mind also elevated his employer, Ernst August, to an elector after he unearthed tenuous links between the dukes and noble Italian stock of Este. During office hours, the university-owned building is open for a look at the polymath's work – letters to contemporaries such as Newton, Huygens and Bernoulli, plus essays and calculations showcased in the foyer.

The concrete bunker adjacent houses the **Historisches Museum** (Tues & Thurs 10am–7pm, Wed & Fri–Sun 10am–5pm; €5, free Fri), an enjoyable take on the town museum. Models and maps follow Hannover from a kernel trading outpost on the Leine onwards, including postwar footage of the devastation wrought by the Allies and details on EXPO2000. On the ground floor, among

▲ Niki de Saint-Phalle's *Nanas* sculptures

the remnants of the former sixteenth-century armoury, a Rococo stagecoach straight from Walt Disney's *Cinderella* outshines the three other carriages that are on loan from the House of Hannover. The museum incorporates into its fabric the solid Beginenturm (1357), a relic of the city fortifications that girdled the city in Hanseatic days.

Adjacent **Hohen Ufer** promenade stretches along the River Leine, its name a nod to the "high banks" above the floodline that inspired the first citizens to found "Honoevere" in the tenth century. Opposite, three buxom belles pirouette like extras from a scene in *The Yellow Submarine* as imagined by Picasso. For sober Hannover residents, the psychedelic **Nanas** sculptures created by New York artist Niki de Saint-Phalle were not simply derogatory, they were expensive, too – with characteristic pragmatism, it was pointed out the *Nanas*' DM150,000 price tag could have paid for three rapid-response cars for doctors – and the people demanded Hannover's Experiment Strassenkunst (Street Art Experiment) conducted in the early 1970s be brought to a hasty conclusion. Inevitably, the bulging *Nanas* are now treasured as colourful icons of a largely faceless city. There's more of the artist's work in the Sprengel-Museum and the Herrenhäuser Garten.

Britons will recognize the lion-and-unicorn crest on Duke Georg Ludwig's (King George I) former stables gateway Tor des Marstalls on the Historisches Museum's north side (see box below). Beyond the gateway and across Burgstrasse is a sweet courtyard, **Ballhof**, lined with restaurants and galleries. Hannover had most definitely arrived when Henry the Lion, all-powerful duke of Saxony, convened court on this spot in 1163, but it's the seventeenth-century sports hall (now the Lower Saxony State Theatre) in which Duke Georg Wilhelm swiped at shuttlecocks that gives Ballhof its name.

Hannover and the British connection

It was 1700 and the English were in a bind: Queen Anne was old and her last child sickly. Parliament had scoffed previously at talk of a link between the Crown and the House of Hannover. But the legitimate claim of exiled Catholic James Edward, "the Old Pretender", had concentrated Protestant minds. In 1701 the Act of Settlement declared the crown to "the most excellent princess Sophia, electress and duchess-dowager of Hannover" on the grounds that Electress Sophia von der Pfalz was a granddaughter of King James I, adding a caveat that "the heirs of her body being Protestant". No matter that her son spoke no English, nor that his slow pedantic manner was spectacularly unsuited to the tumultuous life of the contemporary English court. Georg Ludwig, Duke of Brunswick-Lüneburg, elector of Hannover, became George I in 1714 to begin 120 years of joint rule by the House of Hannover.

Of the four Georgian kings of Great Britain, George III was the first to take any interest in his new territory. George I and II were content to appoint a "prime minister" to rule as their representative, accidentally taking the first step towards the modern British political system. Indeed it was only with English-speaking George III that the Hannoverian dynasty got hands on but by then it was too late. A now-powerful parliament and fate – social unrest, the loss of the American colonies not to mention the king's mental illness – got in the way. Those woes conspired to make him the most abused monarch in British history. Shelley wrote about "an old, mad, blind, despised and dying king", and liberal historians of the next century competed in their condemnation of him. Yet it was not bad press that did for joint rule. Salic law forbade the accession of women to head the kingdom of Hannover, newly declared at the Congress of Vienna in 1814. So when William IV died in 1837, Ernst August took up the crown in Hannover while his niece, Victoria, settled on to the throne in London.

Around the Neues Rathaus

Friedrichswall, an arterial road that traces the former city walls, demarcates the southern edge of the Altstadt. Stuttering chunks of the medieval defences remain like Morse code from the past: on the path between Georgswall and Osterstrasse, for example, or incorporated into the fabric of the Volkshochschule. The latter lies opposite the **Neues Rathaus** (Mon–Fri 8am–6pm, Sat & Sun 10am–5pm; free), and what a town hall it is. Its neo-Renaissance hulk, tempered by a dash of neo-Gothic gravitas and crowned by a dome of preposterous dimensions, received the stamp of approval from a design competition committee chaired by Vienna's Otto Wagner. It also so impressed Kaiser Wilhelm II that he officiated at its opening in 1913. Over six thousand piles prevent the fantastical behemoth sinking into marshy ground, and, although architect Hermann Eggert locked horns over the interior (and lost), the Jugendstil entrance hall retains something of the exterior's grandiose scale, with a domed ceiling like a secular cathedral. Small wonder that it was here the birth of Lower Saxony was announced in 1946. Four models of the city trace Hannover's meteor-like path, from ascendant golden age with the arrival of the Guelph dukes in 1639 to the low of a postwar city reduced to rubble. In addition one of Europe's two inclined lifts (€2.50) judders around the cupola to the Rathausturm, with spectacular views of the city and countryside beyond.

A modern counterpart to the Neues Rathaus's ego architecture, the **Norddeutsches Landesbank** headquarters just east of here is a vision of 1960s science-fiction made real – all glass tunnels and rhomboids stacked at uneasy angles. Opposite, a shroud of ivy is fast covering the shell of the **Aegidienkirche**, left as a requiem to war dead since it was smashed on October 9, 1943; a peace bell gifted by Hiroshima hangs in the rebuilt Baroque tower and tolls on August 6 to mark the date of the twin city's obliteration.

On the other side of the Neues Rathaus is the **Kestner-Museum** (Tues–Sun 11am–6pm, Wed till 8pm; €4, free on Fri) and a six-millennia tour through applied arts. The exhibits are founded on the collection of August Kestner, an art-loving chargé d'affaires of the Vatican. He was the most successful son of Charlotte Kestner, née Buff, who so captured the heart of a 23-year-old Goethe that she became immortalized in his *The Sorrows of Young Werther*, much to the chagrin of her future husband, who believed himself "grievously exposed and prostituted". Thomas Mann rendered a later, painfully polite meeting between Goethe and Charlotte as *Lotte in Weimar*. Inside, Kestner's collection of Egyptian, Greek, Etruscan and Roman antiquities is updated with Art Nouveau and twentieth-century design classics.

West of the Neues Rathaus

In a pledge to ennoble a city badly neglected by kings engrossed in British affairs, incoming duke Ernst August entrusted his court architect Georg Ludwig Friedrich Laves with the task of dressing Hannover in finery appropriate for the capital of a newly declared kingdom. The 28-year-old architect had a thing for Neoclassical pomp, revealed west of the Neues Rathaus in a "Laves Mile", which opens with **Laveshaus** at Friedrichswall 5; suitably, the house Laves built for himself is home to the Lower Saxony Chamber of Architects. A little further along Friedrichswall is **Wangenheim-Palais**, residence of Hannover king George V. On Leinstrasse a block north, Laves called on the architectural authority of Classical Greece for his **portico** to the Leineschloss, his most grandiose creation, which miraculously escaped the wartime bombs and is the public face of the Lower Saxony parliament – housed behind here in the palatial **Leineschloss**, a masterpiece from the drawing board of Remy de la

Fosse. Laves also designed the 42m **Waterloosäule** (Waterloo Column) west via Lavesallee, a memorial to local troops who marched in an alliance of Prussian, German and British forces to strike a knockout blow to Napoleon's ambitions. Yet for all the grandeur of these southern edifices, the work Laves hoped would shore up his place in history is the **Opernhaus** (Opera House; see p.690), marooned from its counterparts northeast near the Hauptbahnhof. When Ernst August saw the plans he spluttered that he could never agree to the "utterly absurd idea of building a court theatre in the middle of a field".

The Maschsee and Niedersächsisches Landesmuseum

Directly behind the Neues Rathaus, the leafy **Maschpark** and its **Maschteich** lake are a prelude to the 2.4km long **Maschsee** lake, flanked to the east with a boulevard of trees and to the west by the meandering Leine. Hannover's nineteenth-century council had envied the Binnenalster lake in Hamburg and finally got its own artificial lake through a Nazi work-creation scheme. Today Maschsee is a focus for summer days, whether taking a cruise from quays on all banks (mid-May to Oct 11am–5/6pm; €3 up to three stops, €6 round trip; ⓦ www.uestra-reisen .de) or messing about in a sailing or rowing boat rented from a quay opposite the Sprengel-Museum, dining in a couple of superb restaurants or spending lazy days on the Strandbad beach at the southeast corner. It takes around thirty minutes to walk north to south along a foot-, cycle- and rollerblade path on the east bank – bus #267 plies a route down the east bank, or U-Bahn Altenbekener Damn lies one block across, midway down.

Culture hereabouts comes from the **Niedersächsisches Landesmuseum** (Tues–Sun 10am–5pm, Thurs till 7pm; €4; ⓦ www.nlmh.de) on Willy-Brandt-Allee. Founded in the mid-1800s, the grande dame of Lower Saxony museums has multiple personalities over its three levels. An aquarium and reptile house claim the ground floor alongside fairly musty ethnographical displays. Exhibits above track European civilization from prehistory to Roman and Saxon – the crowds inevitably gather around Roter Franz, a 300 BC bog corpse named for his red hair – and there are the usual dinosaur skeletons and stuffed mammals in the natural history department. But it's the gallery of art in the second-floor Landesgalerie that steals the show. A Gothic Passion altar by Meister Bertram fizzes with the artist's characteristic vivacity, and there's a flowing *Mary and Child* by Tilman Riemenschneider, the genius of late Gothic; nearby, Cranach studies his friend Martin Luther, alive and dead. Botticelli and Tiepolo star among the Italians, and the Dutch and Flemish masters are well represented: Bartolomeus Spranger teeters on the verge of Baroque with his saucy Bacchus tweaking the nipple of Venus; and look for Rubens' *Madonna and Child*, modelled, it's thought, on his first wife, Isabella Brant, and eldest son, Albert. Caspar David Friedrich provides a Phases-of-the-Day cycle, *Morning*, *Noon*, *Dusk* and *Evening*, and Monet glimpses Gare St-Lazare through thick swirls of steam. Excellent collections of Max Slevogt, Lovis Corinth, Worpswede's Paula Modersohn-Becker and Max Liebermann represent German Impressionism and early Expressionism.

The Sprengel-Museum

Works in the Landesmuseum are an overture to the superb twentieth-century art in the **Sprengel-Museum** (Tues 10am–8pm, Wed–Sun 10am–6pm; €7; ⓦ www.sprengel-museum.de) located five minutes' walk south. Blockbuster exhibitions bolster rotating exhibits of the gallery's veritable who's who of classical modernists which is hung in its clean-lined modern space. Curators rotate the permanent collection, but you can expect all the big guns of Der Blaue Reiter group – Macke, Kandinsky and especially Klee, who gets a room to himself – plus savagely bitter canvases from Beckmann and displays of Munch and Kokoschka that are a tutorial in Expressionism. Their angst-wracked doom-mongering is balanced by the empathetic humanism of sculptor Ernst Barlach and surrealists such as Magritte and Ernst, or a wealth of Picasso's Cubist works. Some of the world's largest collection of sculptures by Niki de Saint-Phalle, the American artist who dreamed into being Hannover's *Nanas*, will also be on display.

The western Altstadt and around Steintor

Northwest of the Markt, just past Hannover's oldest house at Burgstrasse 12, a former farmhouse on whose wonky half-timbers spinning rosettes and twisted rope motifs are picked out in gold and red, a passage cuts right to **Goldener Winkel** (Golden Corner), an idealized vision of inner-city housing imagined by Fifties town-planners. The rebuilt Gothic **Kreuzkirche** at its centre holds a Passion triptych by Cranach, the only joy of the otherwise blank canvas. Architectural aficionados will also enjoy a pair of buildings a couple of blocks north around the Steintor U-Bahn station, beyond the bar district around Reuterstrasse, a grungy marriage of Szene bars and pole-dancing clubs. The bulging, twisted **Üstra-Tower** at Goethestrasse 13 is an architectural double-take by Bilbao Guggenheim architect Frank Gehry; and north on Goseriede, the **Anzeiger Hochhaus** is a touch of 1920s class, with a brick facade favoured by its Expressionist architect Fritz Höger, better known for his Chilehaus in Hamburg. It's especially impressive when picked out in neon at night. Now home to a media company, it has an almost church-like foyer, while up in its copper cupola an art-house cinema replaces the original planetarium. Next to it at Goseriede 11 is the **Kestnergesellschaft** (Tues–Sun 10am–7pm, Thurs till 9pm; €5; Ⓦ www.kestner.org). In a Jugendstil former swimming hall, acclaimed arts patron the Kestner Institute stages blockbuster exhibitions of modern art: past names have included Warhol and Picasso, Anton Corbijn, Joseph Beuys and the Chapman brothers.

The Georgengarten and Wilhelm-Busch-Museum

Hannover only truly looks the part of historic royal capital in the gardens laid out a fifteen-minute walk northwest of Steintor. Of the quartet of gardens planned during the ducal tenure, **Welfengarten** abutting the city is the most forgettable, though popular with students who laze between lectures in the Welfenschloss at its east side, a preposterous piece of Gothic Revival with faux battlements.

More romantic is the **Georgengarten** beyond, whose neat lawns and mature trees are a model of the naturalistic English style that Romantics conceived as a "walk-in painting". In the middle of the park, the Baroque Georgenpalais houses the **Wilhelm-Busch-Museum** (Tues–Sat 11am–5pm, Sun 11am–6pm; €4.50; Ⓦ www.wilhelm-busch-museum.de), devoted to the Hannover-born nineteenth-century artist who dreamed of emulating Rubens but stumbled into immortality as the father of the modern cartoon strip with *Max und Moritz*. Alongside Busch's works are four centuries of satirical art, and every three months an exhibition of a luminary of the graphic arts; past masters have included Goya and Hogarth. The lake beyond is crossed by a bridge by Laves.

The Grosser Garten and Berggarten

The original garden is the beautiful Baroque **Grosser Garten** (daily: April–Oct 9am–7/8pm; Nov–March 9am–5pm; summer €3 or €4 combined ticket with Burggarten, free Nov–March; Ⓦwww.herrenhaeuser-gaerten.de), beyond the Georgengarten. Fired with inspiration after a visit to Versailles and aided by French master-gardener Martin Charbonnier, Electress Sophie, the consort of Ernst August, hailed by Leibniz as the greatest female mind of her age, transformed the kitchen garden of the royal summer palace into a horticultural masterpiece. "The Herrenhäuser garden is my life," she admitted, with good reason since the royals' open-air ballroom was thirty years in the making, finally complete in 1710. But what a stage: a precision-planted paean to the Age of Reason, surrounded by a moat that was plied by Venetian gondolas. At the northern end, an orangerie and frescoed festival hall are a relic of the palace flattened by Allied bombs. The heart of the garden beyond is the formal Grosse Parterre, with pouting allegorical statues among the neat box hedge – the Cascade viewing platform provides an elevated view. Its grotto (9am–4pm; €2 in winter) received a shot of cultural adrenaline for EXPO2000 from Niki de Saint-Phalle, she of the *Nanas*, who inlaid Gaudí-esque ribbons of mosaic in rooms themed as *Spirituality*, *Day and Life*, and *Night and the Cosmos*, all bulging with her trademark cartoony sculptures.

In summer Shakespeare and Molière are still staged in the **Gartentheater** east, a splendid piece of decadence whose troupe of nude statues surrounding the stage scandalized the odd foreign dignitary. West of the Grosse Parterre is a maze, and beyond it is a horticultural history-book of styles from Baroque to Rococo, Dutch to Low German, in plantings of fleur de lys, crescents and knots. Further down, as a centrepiece to neat beech wedges which radiate from fountains to corner temples, is the Grosse Fontäne ("Wasserkunst" fountain displays April–Sept 11am–noon & Mon–Fri 3–5pm, Sat & Sun 2–5pm). Sophia tasked the greatest engineering minds, Leibniz included, with the problem of how to power a fountain to rival the Sun King's. The pump was cracked by English know-how; in 1720 a plume of water spurted 36m high and Europe marvelled. The weight attached to this symbol of prestige has not decreased – the pump now has oomph to fling a jet 80m and the city continues to boast of having the highest fountain of any garden in Europe.

The **Berggarten** (same times; €2) on the other side of Herrenhäuser Allee is meagre stuff afterwards. It was intended to house rare blooms in its greenhouses, some of which remain to house the largest permanent display of orchids in Europe. Laves's garden library, the Bibliothekspavillon, which is framed as you walk up Herrenhäuser Allee, flanks the other side of the entrance. He also designed a mausoleum of the Hannover kings which lies in front of a rhododendron thicket that blooms in late May to earn its name, Paradies (Paradise). The latest attraction, opened in 2007, is **Sea Life** (daily 10am–6pm; €12.95; Ⓦwww.sealifeeurope.com), a kiddie-friendly aquarium and rainforest bubble that's at its best in a tunnel beneath a "Caribbean Sea".

The Baroque complex west of the Berggarten is the Fürstenhaus royal palace; at the time of writing it was only open to group tours.

Eating

A little touristy, Kramerstrasse and Knochenhauerstrasse are nevertheless good to browse for restaurants in the centre. To prepare a picnic for the gardens head to delicatessens in the Markthalle (see opposite) and organic supermarket Denn's Biomarkt at Marktstrasse 45 (closed Sun).

Restaurants

Atrium Karmarschstr. 42 ☎0511/300 80 40. The atrium is that of the Altes Rathaus, the food is Mediterranean in an airy courtyard which weds a historic setting to smart bistro-style dishes – a fine lunch spot. Closed Sun.

Basil Dragonerstr. 30 ☎0511/62 26 36. One of Hannover's flagship restaurants, its clientele as sophisticated as the setting canopied by lofty brick vaults of a Royal Prussian stables. Menus that range freely across Eurasian and New World continents are created from whatever is freshest that season. Take tram #1 or #2 north of the Hauptbahnhof to "Dragonerstrasse". Eve only, closed Sun.

bell'Arte Kurt-Schwitters-Platz 1 ☎0511/809 33 33. Stylish restaurant of the Sprengel-Museum beloved by an arty, older crowd for an excellent Italian menu and a classic panorama over the Maschsee from its terrace. Closed Mon.

Besitos Goseriede 4 ☎0511/169 80 01. Funky courtyard place in the Steintor area that segues from Spanish restaurant serving tapas and mid-priced grilled fish and meats to a cocktail bar. There's a touch of industrial chic to its main room and a courtyard space in summer.

Biesler Weinstube Sophienstr. 6 ☎0511/32 10 33. Lamb from the Lüneburg Heath in rosemary juice and roast zander epitomize the classic upmarket dishes prepared using the finest fresh ingredients in one of the city's oldest restaurants. Closed Sat lunch & all day Sun; Aug & Sept closed Mon.

Brasserie Bruxelles Ernst-August-Platz 10 ☎0511/353 08 08. Well-provided Belgian dishes – beef risoles with cherries and chips with everything – in a beautiful Jugendstil brasserie. Closed Sun.

Broyhan-Haus Kramerstr. 24 ☎0511/32 39 19. Named for a Hannover brewer of the 1500s, this is as traditional a tavern as you could want. Expect the likes of leg of boar in hazelnut sauce and pork fillet in a rich red-wine sauce on a menu that changes once a century.

Clichy Wiessekreuzstr. 31 ☎0511/31 24 47. Behind an unpromising exterior on a side street behind the Hauptbahnhof lies a classy, small

French restaurant that comfortably marries tradition with modern decor – fish of the day is ever reliable. Closed Sun.

Die Insel Rudolf-von-Bennigsen-Ufer 81 ☎0511/83 12 14. The gourmet international menu is hailed by many locals as Hannover's finest (mains around €22), decor is understated class and the location is beach-side at the south end of the Maschsee – the sybaritic summer lunch par excellence.

Pier 51 Rudolf-von-Bennigsen-Ufer 51 ☎0511/807 18 00. A glass box on a pier midway down the east bank of the Maschsee that's both a hip restaurant preparing modern international dishes and a cool Manhattan-styled bar. Has a great terrace and a beer garden with wicker *Strandkörbe* beach-seats in summer.

Spandau Engelbosteler Damm 30 ☎0511/12 35 70 95. Popular retro-modern place near the university, 10min north of Steintor, that serves fresh pan-global dishes at student prices: tasty Thai veggie curries.

Cafés and snacks

Der Gartensaal Trammplatz 2. At the rear of the Neues Rathaus overlooking the Maschteich lake and as elegant a lunch spot as you can find in Hannover. Cooking is modern German: grilled *Rotbarsch* in Pernod sauce.

Holländische Kakao-Stuben Ständehausstr. 2–3. Be prepared to wait for a table on Saturdays because it can feel as if all Hannover has come to this Dutch-styled historic café, all Delft tiles and blue-and-white china. Award-winning gâteaux and eleven varieties of cocoa make the wait worthwhile. Closed Sun.

Markthalle Karamarschstr. 49. Not a café per se, but a pan-global food hall of *Imbiss*-style places that are an excellent spot for a quick, quality bite.

Tee Stübchen Am Ballhof 10. Enchanting family-run throwback to nineteenth-century café society, all pea-green panelling and snug candle-lit niches. Over forty teas, all served in bowl-like cups, and tasty, home-made apple cake.

Entertainment and nightlife

The **Steintor** area has morphed from red-light district to "Partymeile" centred on the bar-clubs of parallel Reuterstrasse and Scholvinstrasse – still fairly tawdry but fun for bar-hopping. Bars on Goseriede are less seedy or, for elegant drinking, try the stylish lake-side bars of restaurants *Pier 51* and *Die Insel* (see above) – both are the stuff sundowners are made of. The tourist office stocks the usual **listings** freesheets, or for a more comprehensive run down pick up glossy weekly *Prinz* (€1) at newsagents. Café-bistro *Café Konrad* at Knochenhauerstrasse 34 and cocktail bar *Caldo* at Bergmannstrasse 7 are good sources of information on the Hannover **gay scene**.

The tourist office has a **ticket desk** for all entertainment and sports events in the city. The highlight of the year is the largest **Schützenfest** (marksmen's festival; ⓦ www.hannover.de/schuetzenfest) in Germany, held over ten days over the end of June and into July. Similar but more restrained is the **Maschsee** festival over nineteen days from the last Wednesday in July. Late May to early June brings world music beano; the **Masala Festival** (ⓦ www .masala-festival.de).

Bars

Acanto Dragonerstr. 28. Bar and club, where classic funk and soul, house and Latin are spun for an older crowd beneath high brick vaults drenched in washes of colour – one of Hannover's most glamorous venues.

Brauhaus-Ernst-August Schmiedestr. 13. The brewery for unfiltered *Pils Hanöversch* and a local institution that sprawls over several rooms, some of which host live music and DJs several times a week – open till 5am at weekends.

Bronco's Schwarzer Bär 7. Funky retro-chic bar and club 1km west of the centre with rich velour wallpapers and leather couches. Party tunes lure a friendly crowd onto a small dancefloor.

heimW Theaterstr. 6. Metropolitan chic in a stylish lounge-bar with teardrop lights, located in one of the classiest districts of Hannover.

Lister Turm Walderseestr. 100. Hannover's largest beer garden has room for six-hundred drinkers outside its historic pile at the west edge of the Eilenriede park near Lister Platz U-Bahn – unbeatable for a traditional booze-up in summer, but the food is hit and miss.

Strandleben Weddingenufer. Deckchairs, parasols and sand between the toes at Hannover's best city beach, on a bend of the Leine River south of the Georgengarten, neutral ground for hipsters and counter culture alike. The soundtrack is chilled funk, Brazilian and nu-jazz grooves. Follow signs for Faust e.V. Closed Oct–April.

Nightclubs

3Raum Ballhofstr. 5 ⓦ www.3raum-ballhof.de. Bar-cum-club that also stages occasional concerts for a discerning thirty-something set: an eclectic music policy includes nu-jazz, old-skool funk, boogaloo and Latin, and contemporary soul.

Cafe Glocksee Glockseestr. 35 ⓦ www .cafe-glocksee.de. A mainstay of indie nights that also schedules a mixed programme of everything from electro to Fifties rock 'n' roll via reggae, plus occasional gigs.

Eve Klub Reuterstr. 3–4 ⓦ www.eve-klub.de. Good-time grooves from the Sixties and Seventies interspersed with the occasional house and hip-hop classic pack out the dancefloor in a small retro-styled place.

Factory Engelbosteler Damm 7 ⓦ www .mensfactory.de. Founded in 1990, this is a grand-daddy of German techno clubbing, located 15min north of Steintor. Techno and hard house pound out for a straight and gay clientele.

Kiez Klub Scholvinstr. 4 ⓦ www.kiez-klub.de. Local DJs bring a record box of dirty house and electro for an up-for-it crowd. One of the best of the Steintor area.

Palo Palo Raschplatz 8a ⓦ www.palopalo.de. Sweaty, small club behind the train station with a diet of largely soul and r'n'b. Occasionally has bands.

Live music and theatre

Faust Zur Bettfedernfabrik 3 ☎ 0511/45 50 01, ⓦ www.faustev.de. Indie rock, ska-punk, reggae, metal, world music – you name it this alternative cultural centre in a disused factory in Lindennord south of Georgengarten programmes the lot, alongside modern dance and art exhibitions plus club nights in concert hall 60er-Jahre-Halle and bar *Mephisto*.

GOP Varieté Georgstr. 36 ☎ 0511/301 86 70, ⓦ www.gop-variete.de. Aerobatic spectaculars and magic, song-and-dance numbers and comedy in classic cabaret nights.

Jazz-Club Am Lindener Berge 38 ☎ 0511/45 44 55, ⓦ www.jazz-club.de. Acclaimed venue that programmes a variety of jazz sounds. Past guests include Jan Garbarek and Lionel Hampton.

Opernhaus Opernplatz 1 ☎ 0511/99 99 00, ⓦ www.staatstheater-hannover.de. The grande dame of Hannover high culture programmes opera and ballet as well as classical concerts.

Pavillon Lister Meile 4 ☎ 0511/235 55 50, ⓦ www.pavillon.de. A former shopping-centre behind the bus station, now a cultural centre that programmes theatre and music – it hosts the Masala world-music festival each year – and hosts a buzzy café-bar, *Café Mezzo*.

Schauspielhaus Prinzenstr. 9 ☎ 0511/99 99 00, ⓦ www.staatstheater-hannover.de. The leading stage for premieres and new productions, and the umbrella body for modern works staged at the two-theatre Ballhof.

Listings

Car rental Rental outfits unite operations in a side-office of the Reisezentrum in the Hauptbahnhof. All also maintain a desk at the airport: Avis ☎ 0511/32 26 10; Hertz ☎ 0511/31 40 36; SIXT ☎ 0180/25 25 25; Europcar ☎ 0511/363 29 93.

Cinema Multi-screen Cinemaxx (🌐 www.cinemaxx .de) is behind the Hauptbahnhof on Raschplatz. Art house and repertory is screened in the Anzeiger Hochhaus (☎ 0511/144 54) at Goseriede 9 – screenings are three or four times daily, listings are posted on the door.

Hospital Marienstr. 37 ☎ 0511/304 31.

Internet in the pedestrainized shopping streets is TeleKlick, Schillerstr. 23 (daily 8.30am–midnight); Merkur Spielothek Center (Mon–Sat 8am–3am,

Sun 11am–3am) has Star Trek-style booths in the Steintor bar district at Goseriede 8.

Markets A Sat flea market (7am–4pm) sprawls among the *Nanas* on Hohen Ufer behind the Historiches Museum – tatty, cheerful fun that can even turn up the occasional bargain.

Police Raschplatz 1, behind Hauptbahnhof ☎ 0511/32 94 12.

Post Ernst-August-Platz 2, in front of Hauptbahnhof.

Sports The AWD Arena (🌐 www.awd-arena.de) on the west bank of the Maschsee was modernized into a 53,000-seater for the World Cup 2006. It hosts matches of Bundesliga Hannover 96, one of Germany's oldest football clubs, plus occasional rugby. Tickets are best sourced through the tourist office.

Around Hannover: Steinhude and Dino Park

Hannover residents have long found the village of **STEINHUDE**, 25km west, irresistible. The reason is an unlikely combination of smoked eels and summer thrills, and the source of both is the Steinhude Meer. The largest lake in northwest Germany, all 32 square kilometres of it, has raised the village from fishing backwater into the sort of chirpy tourist resort that would have set the eel fishermen of old muttering darkly. Smoked eel cured to secret recipes of herbs and smoke remains Steinhude's culinary must-do – the bronzed fish are stuffed between hunks of bread in numerous cafés. The story of their fishermen is told alongside that of local weavers in exhibits of domestic and working life at the **Fischer- und Webermuseum**, Neuer Winkel 8 (May–Oct Tues–Sun 1–5pm; March, April & Nov Sat & Sun 1–5pm; €2; 🌐 www.steinhuder-museen.de). Occasional displays of net-mending and fish-smoking skills are staged (times at entrance). A block behind, **Insektenmuseum Steinhude** (March–Nov 15 daily 11am–6pm; Jan & Feb Sat & Sun 11am–4pm; €2; 🌐 www.schmetterlingsfarm .de) is a joint butterfly park and insect zoo. However, Steinhude is more for messing about in, on or alongside the water. At the end of Lindenhopsweg, northeast of a pretty centre of half-timbered houses and restaurants, **Badeinsel** lives up to its name (Baths Island) with a stretch of fine beach and shallow water that locals swear is a cure-all. South of Steinhude's centre, ferries depart for cruises around the lake (April–Oct; €7; 🌐 www.steinhuder-personenschifffahrt .de) from the Steinhuder Strandterrassen quay, pausing at Insel Wilhelmstein, a perfectly square island Count Wilhelm von Schaumberg constructed in the shallow lake in the mid-1700s. Your ticket also buys you into a dinky fortress that guards its centre. An evocative way to arrive in summer is aboard a tradi-tional Auswanderern sailing yacht (€6 return) – boards advertise trips or ask at the **tourist office** (April–Oct Mon–Fri 9am–noon/1pm & 2–5/6pm, Sat from 10am, Sun 1–5pm; Nov–Feb Mon–Fri 9am–noon; ☎ 05033/950 10, 🌐 www .steinhuder-meer.de) at Meerstrasse 2.

If you have kids to entertain, **Dino Park Münchehagen** (Feb 2–Nov 4 daily 10am–6pm; €9.50; 🌐 www.dinopark.de), at the lake's southwest corner on the B441, is worth a visit. Conceived as a hybrid attraction where open-air museum meets *Jurassic Park*, its 220 life-size fibreglass dinosaurs lurk in the woodland around a set of genuine dinosaur tracks – paleontologists suggest the fossilized prints belong to a diplodocus, an iguanodon and possibly a carnivorous allosaurus which plodded across what was a tropical lagoon some 140 million years ago.

To reach either destination by **public transport**, take a Regional Express or S-Bahn (S1 or S2) train to Wunstorf, then catch bus #710 or #711 from the Bahnhof to Steinhude Badeinsel or bus #716 to "Entrance Saurier Park". The total journey time for both is about 45 minutes; @www.regiobus.de has timetables.

Hildesheim

For centuries **HILDESHEIM**, 30km southeast of Hannover, starred on the check-list of every cultured Grand Tour of Europe. It was medieval Germany writ large, its two Romanesque churches among the finest on the continent and its Altstadt a half-timbered fairytale. So a night of firebombs on March 22, 1945, which ravaged the centre as the Allies targeted prestige cities to sap German morale during the war's end-game, struck particularly hard. The town salvaged what it could and erected typically monstrous postwar rebuilds until, in 1984, the council took the unprecedented decision to re-create the former townscape. Uncharitably, then, the architectural highlights of Hildesheim are conscious antiquarianism at best, glorious fakes at worst. Yet UNESCO deemed the efforts worthy of its World Heritage list, an unexpected fillip to a beautification programme that seems likely to continue. Aside from the architecture, Hildesheim is a relaxed university town, pleasant, certainly, but also fairly provincial.

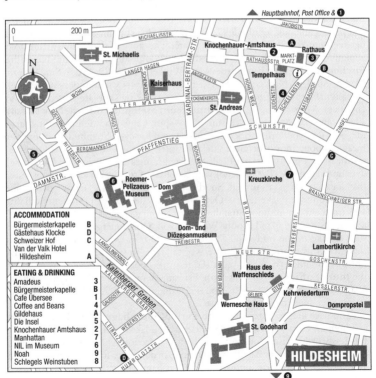

Arrival and information

Hildesheim lies at a rail junction of the Hannover and Braunschweig lines, its **Hauptbahnhof** around 500m due north of the centre. The **tourist office** (Mon–Fri 8.30am–6pm, Sat 8.30am–3.30pm; ☎05121/179 80, ⓦwww .hildesheim.de) is just off the Markt at Rathausstrasse 18–20. Without a bicycle it'll take either determination or a long day to cover all of Hildesheim's sights, which are spread over a wide area. Most are covered in the tourist office's pamphlet guide *Hildesheimer Rosenroute* (€2) – follow the white roses painted on the pavements. **Bike rental** is available from Fahrrad Ritzel, Osterstrasse 31 (Mon–Fri 9am–5pm, Sat 9am–1pm); **internet access** is at *Il Giornale* (daily 3–7pm), an Italian ice and coffeeshop off the Markt at Judenstrasse 3–4.

Accommodation

Budget **accommodation** is not Hildesheim's forte and the town suffers trade-fair price-hikes from nearby Hannover. Notwithstanding **private rooms** (❷) booked through the tourist office, your best option for a cheap bed is the youth hostel. The **campsite**, *Am Müggelsee* (☎05121/531 51, ⓦwww.mueggelsee-hildesheim .de; May–Oct), 2km from the centre beside its eponymous lake, is no closer but slightly more convenient by bus; take #1 to stop "Kennedydamm". If you're driving, it's at the B6–B1 junction.

Bürgermeisterkapelle Rathausstr. 8 ☎05121/140 21, ⓦwww.hotelbuergermeisterkapelle.de. This pleasant old-fashioned family hotel just off the Markt has received a tentative makeover in decor without anything to scare off an older clientele. ❹–❺

DJH Hildesheim Schirrmannweg 4 ☎05121/427 17, ⓦwww.djh-niedersachsen.de. Though in a bucolic location it's a fair schlep from the centre and not served by direct transport. From the train station, take bus #1 to "Schuchstrasse", then change to a Bockfeld-bound bus #4 and alight at "Triftstrasse", from where it's a 15min walk uphill. From €20.20.

Gästehaus Klocke Humboldtstr. 11 ☎05121/17 92 12, ⓦwww.gaestehaus-klocke.de. Unfussy

rooms with high ceilings and pine floors in a miniature mansion with creaky staircases and stained glass. It's located on a quiet residential street in the southern Altstadt, a short walk from St Godehard. ❸

Schweizer Hof Hindeburgplatz 6 ☎05121/390 81, ⓦwww.hotelschweizerhof.de. Rather tired block on a busy square that could do with refurbishment. A functional fall-back, nonetheless. ❹

Van der Valk Hotel Hildesheim Markt 4 ☎05121/30 00, ⓦwww.vandervalk.de. Modern flair meets old-world charm in a glamorous design and spa hotel spread over three reconstructed houses on the Markt – bear in mind that front rooms get the town market from 5am on Wednesday and Friday as well as views. ❺–❻

The Markt and Andreasplatz

Playing the game of superlatives, the great nineteenth-century academic, philosopher and all-round Prussian brainbox Wilhelm von Humboldt, who had seen a fair bit of Europe in his function as a diplomat, declared Hildesheim's **Markt** the most beautiful in the world. Hyperbole, perhaps, but the one-time mercantile showpiece of the city is once again pure camera-fodder since its rebuild in 1984, the only sign of which is rather over-polished "medieval" buildings. The stone **Rathaus** at its rear was able to be patched up to return its handsome Gothic form – a medieval iron rod to measure an ell of cloth remains embedded in stone blocks at the rear corner. A copper trumpeter sounds a horn daily at noon, and a carillon chimes at noon, 1pm and 5pm. The **Tempelhaus** patrician's house on the south side of the Markt was similarly revived through repairs. Its turreted facade is thought to derive from a Crusader's description of the Holy Land, while its name refers to a Jewish temple that stood here before its build in the 1400s.

The Renaissance oriel tacked on its front narrates the parable of the Prodigal Son. Continuing clockwise, conjoined Wedekindhaus, Lüntzelhaus and Rolandstift are all replicas, the former smothered in carvings, as is the Bäckeramtshaus (bakers' guildhouse) that opens the west side of the square. The source of all the "oohs" is the colossal **Knochenhauer Amtshaus** (butchers' guildhouse) at its side. The current incarnation was completed in 1989 to the same plans and carpentry methods as the Gothic original, deemed through time-honoured tradition as "the most beautiful half-timbered building in the world". One reason is the playground of folkloric images – old and new – carved on gables that cascade from a peak 26m up. It's one of the few reconstructed buildings you can go inside as the home of a **Stadtmuseum** (Tues–Sun 10am–6pm; €2.50; ⓦwww .rpmuseum.de) in the upper floors and a café (see p.696).

The firebombs that obliterated the Markt also did for **Andreasplatz** southwest, formerly considered its rival. In late 2007, a council motion was passed to reconstruct iconic medieval house, **Umgestülpter Zuckerhut** ("Sugarloaf House") – its inverted half-timbered stack should return to a corner by early 2010. Until then there's the **Andreaskirche**, rebuilt from its foundations with the four naves and ambulatory planned by the medieval builders but which proved beyond their technical know-how. The reason to visit is for views from the tower (May–Oct Mon–Sat 11am–4pm, Sun noon–4pm, last entry 3.30pm; €1.50).

St Michaelis Kirche

Of all Hildesheim's reconstructed ecclesiastical monuments it is **St Michaelis** that receives most accolades. The UNESCO-listed church on a low hill west of Andreasplatz rises like a miniature city of towers and copper roofs, a vision of Jerusalem as conceived by its founder Bishop Bernward to venerate a fragment of the Holy Cross. The erudite bishop, a tenth-century aristocrat who tutored Emperor Otto III, lived just long enough to see his three-aisled basilica stand in 1022 as what turned out to be the pinnacle of Ottonian architecture, a bridging style that pioneers Romanesque. Bernward was canonized for his effort in 1192 – he lies in the crypt at the western end – and to commemorate the event a rood screen was carved to depict Bernward with a model of his church among angels and holy dignitaries. A superb work, it ranks among the masterpieces of German sculpture of the time. The church's other highlight is a ceiling of the Tree of Jesse inspired by manuscript illuminations. Yet what impresses as much is the architectural dignity of the basilica, achieved through its classically inspired adherence to quadrilateral measures. The nave is as wide as two transepts, and the church pioneers the so-called Lower Saxon style of alternating pillars and bulky columns, creating quadrangles to frame the transepts. Renovation is scheduled for completion in 2010, a millennium after building work began.

The Dom and Roemer- und Pelizaeus-Museum

UNESCO's second salute to Hildesheim was the World Heritage accreditation of its **Dom**, seemingly caught in a temporal back-eddy within its romantic courtyard. Never mind the fudge of styles that obscures the early eleventh-century structure, its fame is twofold. Foremost in artistic merit are its rear bronze doors. Bishop Bernward commissioned the doors, each over 4.7m high and 1.2m wide, in 1015 for the St Michaelis Kirche only for his successor, Bishop Godehard, to remove them as a processional portal for the new cathedral. Their sixteen-cell biblical cartoon-strip, cast from a sculpted sand mould, narrates the Old Testament from the creation of man to the fratricide of Cain, then the New

Testament of Christ, with an almost Expressionist kinetic energy and wealth of background detail that is unparalleled in contemporary casting. Bernward also commissioned the Christussäule (Christ pillar) in the south transept soon after the doors' completion, and the same energy infuses the life story of Christ as it spirals up the 4m column. The well-travelled bishop clearly modelled his creation on Rome's victory pillar, the Trajan Column, although the top "Romanesque" capital is a clumsy attempt at beautification from the late 1800s. Also worth a look is Germany's oldest wheel-shaped chandelier (c.1055), forged by Godehard as a representation of the heavenly city of Jerusalem and hovering symbolically over the altar. Other artistic treasures from the era, notably a couple of gold crucifixes, are displayed in rotating exhibitions in the **Dom Museum** (Tues–Sat 10am–1pm & 1.30–5pm, Sun noon–5pm; €4). Look, too, for a gem-studded cross inlaid with gold filigree said to have been that of Saxon duke Henry the Lion. The second source of the Dom's fame is the thousand-year-old **rosebush** in its cloisters (Mon–Sat 9.30am–5pm, Sun noon–5pm; €0.50). The story goes that Emperor Louis the Pious, son of Charlemagne, who raised Hildesheim to a bishopric in 815 AD, awoke while hunting one summer to find his Marian relics frozen fast to a rosebush. Detecting the hand of the divine, he vowed forthwith to found a diocese on the spot. Whether this is the same bush is a matter of some conjecture. Even if it is, what you see is growth that sprouted after the original was burned along with the cathedral in 1945 – a somewhat miraculous revival, perhaps, but a rosebush is still only a rosebush.

A former friary just southwest of the Dom serves as one wing of the **Roemer- und Pelizaeus-Museum** (Tues–Sun 10am–6pm; €8; ⓦ www.rpmuseum.de), a well-lit display of antiquities that would do credit to any European capital. Indeed, in 1912 the manager of Berlin's Egyptian Museum acclaimed its most famous exhibit, the life-size tomb statue of Hem-iunu, an Egyptian vizier c.2400 BC, as "the best figure I know of in Egypt", adding, "What a shame it will be relegated to the provinces." The pharaoh's man-boobs are an indication of his prestige. The museum's strength is a re-creation of a tomb and the largest collection of Egyptian jewellery in Germany. Smaller pieces, such as a four-thousand-year-old model granary in which labourers fill grain sacks, also intrigue and there are displays from ancient Peru and imperial Chinese porcelain.

The southern Altstadt

While the bombs rained on the centre, the southern Altstadt was spared, preserving a pocket of old Hildesheim. The charm begins at the bottom of Brühl with early seventeenth-century **Wernersche Haus**, its beams carved with images of the virtues and vices, local heroes – bearded Charlemagne, Louis the Pious and St Bernward with his church. Hinterer Brühl behind is also worth a look for its contemporary streetscape. Opposite the house, **St Godehardikirche** is a well-preserved basilica erected in the fourteenth century in honour of the bishop who had been canonized earlier that century. He is depicted in the tympanum beside Christ. The interior is modelled on St Michaelis, its advance being the knotted capitals of its alternating Lower Saxon-style pillars.

Northeast of the church the former Jewish ghetto – the **Lappenburg** district – is a photogenic nest of residential streets. Armourers' guildhouse **Haus des Waffenschmieds** on Gelber Stern depicts its trade and what may – or may not – be two Hebrew kings, while Kesslerstrasse beyond is a lovely jumble of half-timbering. The **Kehrwiederturm** that punctuates the skyline is a relic of the city's medieval fortifications, one celebrated in a legend about a noble virgin who used it as homing beacon to return through thick forest from her beloved knight.

They say he was struck by lightening for his subterfuge romance. The yarn probably derives from a local tradition of annual donations to virtuous virgins, hence the maiden who proffers a laurel wreath on the city coat of arms.

Schloss Marienburg

Not in Hildesheim but an easy day-trip from it, **Schloss Marienburg** (Easter–Oct daily 10am–6pm, tours every 45min; €6.50; Ⓦwww.schloss-marienburg .de), 15km northwest of the centre, is as romantic a castle as you could wish for. It was intended both as a birthday gift from Hannoverian king Georg V to his wife Queen Marie in 1857, and a fantastical homage to the history of his Guelphic dynasty realized by one of Germany's finest neo-Gothic architects, Conrad Wilhelm Hase. Prussian annexation of his kingdom meant the ruler never got to enjoy his romantic summerhouse – Marie lived there in semi-imprisonment for just under a year before she followed him into exile in Austria – but ancestral owner Prince Ernst August VI von Hannover occasionally resides here. The fantasy medieval aesthetic continues in an interior whose decor swings between neo-Gothic swagger – state halls such as the Rittersaal banqueting hall, furnished with silver chairs that Georg II commissioned from Augsburg goldsmiths in 1720, for example, or a spectacular queen's library which umbrellas from a central pillar – and genuine romance, with the Salon der Prinzessinen (Princesses' Salon), a dream-like children's bedroom whose window is painted with scenes from *Sleeping Beauty*, apt for a palace that mouldered until 1945. Access by public transport is via Nordstemmen, linked to Hildesheim by frequent trains, from where it's a 3km walk north. To make a day of it, you could cycle 14km west on a good track – allow about 1hr 30min each way. The tourist office in Hildesheim can provide advice and maps of the route. There's a restaurant at the Schloss.

Eating and drinking

Small bar districts are on Friesenstrasse off Hindenburgplatz and at the north end of Osterstrasse, near the junction with Wallstrasse.

Restaurants

Amadeus Marktstr. 17 ☎05121/98 19 66. Brasserie-styled *Gaststätte* behind the Rathaus whose epic portions and low prices make it a popular choice for a student nosh-up. Menu ranges from German to Italian.

Gildehaus *Van der Valk Hotel Hildesheim*, Markt 4 ☎05121/30 00. Classy dining in the town's premier hotel, with a seasonal international menu inspired by local dishes and an elegant dining room that is a comfortable union of modern and traditional styles.

Die Insel Dammstr. 30 ☎05121/145 35. Traditionally styled mid-range restaurant and café that prepares a large menu of solid German staples for an older clientele. Not cheap, but you're paying for the eponymous location on "The island" where the canals meet – it's worth waiting for a terrace table. Closed Mon.

Knochenhauer Amtshaus Markt 7 ☎05121/288 99 09. Roast piglet in *Bock* beer marinade and

Bratwurst plates are among the traditional dishes rustled up in the rebuilt butchers' guildhouse – touristy but what a location. That it gets the morning sun makes the smorgasbord breakfasts popular.

NIL im Museum Roemer- und Pelizaeus-Museum, Am Steine 1 ☎05121/40 85 95. The glass-walled restaurant and café of the museum, beloved by an older, arty set for its stylishly laid-back vibe and modern Mediterranean-flavoured cooking.

Noah Hohnsen 28 ☎05121/69 15 30. Stylish glass-walled Mediterranean bistro and café with a terrace over the Hohnsensee lake – legendary for weekend brunch buffets. It's located a 20min walk south of St Godehardikirche along Weinberg, then right at the junction with Hohnsen.

Schlegels Weinstuben Am Steine 4–6 ☎05121/331 33. Tucked away behind the Roemer- und Pelizaeus-Museum this timewarp back to the 1500s has historic rooms as a backdrop for high-class, fresh regional cooking and a wine bar. Eve only, closed Sun.

Cafés and bars

Burgermeisterkapelle Rathausstr. 8. For old-fashioned charm try the wine bar in a sixteenth-century chapel beneath the eponymous hotel.

Cafe Übersee Cnr Almsstr. and Wallstr. Quietly cool café and bar with wicker chairs and parasols outside and a modern interior; recommended for its cheap breakfasts. Occasionally hosts weekend gigs.

Coffee and Beans Scheelenstr. 14. Modern coffee bar just off the Markt that's popular with students

for good espresso and its long menu of bagels and muffins. Closed Sun.

Havanna *Van der Valk Hotel Hildesheim*, Markt 4. Hotel bar with a nice eye for cocktail glamour; think crushed red velvet and black-glass chandeliers meets traditional whisky bar and a pianist at weekend evenings.

Manhattan Wollenweberstr. 78. Over 300 cocktails and 250 whiskies in what *Playboy* magazine once listed among the coolest cocktail bars in Germany. Closed Sun & Mon.

Hameln (Hamelin)

Like Bremen with its town musicians, **HAMELN** must say a daily prayer in praise of fairytales. The rat-turned-child-catcher not only gave the town international fame but a ready-made promotional angle. Fountains of pipers gush rodents and thousands of white rats painted on the pavements lead visitors around the sights. Even the Marktkirche has a Pied Piper window. Whatever the yarn would have you believe, the town has more than its fair share of children, too, because the ploy works. Such is its popularity – the town receives over 3.5 million tourists per year – Hameln isn't always the "pleasanter spot you never spied" that American Robert Browning describes in his jaunty poem of the tale. It is a good-humoured place, however, with few pretentions to greatness other than its historic Altstadt. It also serves as gateway to the lovely hill-and-river country of the Weserbergland south.

Arrival and information

Hameln's **Bahnhof** is a fifteen-minute walk west of the Altstadt centre: follow Bahnhofstrasse to Diesterstrasse and turn left. En route you'll pass the **tourist office** (Mon–Fri 9am–6/6.30pm; May–Sept Sat 9.30am–4pm & Sun 9.30am–1pm, Oct–April Sat & Sun 9.30am–1pm; ☎05151/95 78 23, ⓦwww.hameln .com). **Bike rental** is from Troches Fahrradshop (☎05151/136 70) near the

The Pied Piper legend

Hameln, June 1284: a stranger in multicoloured clothes strikes a deal with the town council over payment to lift a plague of rats that has infested the town. He pipes the rodents to their deaths in the Weser, yet the council renege on payment. The stranger returns while the citizens are in church, and, dressed in a hunter's costume, exacts his revenge – 130 children follow his pipe from the town and are never seen again. Just two boys remain, one lame the other deaf. Germany's most famous legend was recognized in a stained-glass panel in the church as early as 1300. Academics agree the yarn is rooted in history – it is surely not coincidence that Hameln town records commence with the tragedy, which is reported as straight news a century later in a manuscript and given a date – June 26, 1284 – but hard facts remain elusive. The most plausible theory proposes nothing more fantastical than an exodus of citizens, Hameln "children" all, during colonization of eastern nations such as Pomerania and Prussia – the finger is often pointed at Count von Schaumberg who moved to Olmutz, now Chechnya. In the Grimm Brothers' account, compiled from eleven sources, the children found a town in Transylvania. However, the presence of rats has led some scholars to propose a mass migration during the Black Death, a baton taken up by a theory that suggests the tale remembers an early plague in which the piper represents Death.

Bahnhof at Kreuzstrasse 7. Flotte Weser (mid-April to mid-Oct; Ⓦ www.flotte
-weser.de) operates river cruises on the "River Weser, deep and wide/[which]
washes its wall on the southern side" as Browning put it; some go south through
the hilly Weserbergland as far as Bad Karlshafen. All depart from a quay on the
Weser Promenade south of the centre.

Accommodation

Despite a wide spread of accommodation, Hameln's popularity means it's worth
calling ahead in high season. There's space for a few tents among the caravans of
Fährhaus an der Weser (Ⓣ 05151 674 89, Ⓦ www.campingplatz-faehrhaus-hameln
.de) at Uferstrasse 80, on the west bank of the Weser a fifteen-minute walk from
the centre. Amenities include a Greek restaurant and a pool-side bar.

Alte Post Hummenstr. 23 Ⓣ 05151/434 44,
Ⓔ ottokater@aol.com. B&B in a historic *Gaststätte*
located on a quiet side-street. ❷

Christenhof Alte Marktstr. 18 Ⓣ 05151/950 80,
Ⓦ www.christinenhof-hameln.de. Classy, small
hotel with a nod to romance in its classic business
style. Also has a small counter-current pool in a
historic brick cellar and a sauna. ❹

City Hotel Neue Marktstr. 9 Ⓣ 05151/72 61,
Ⓦ www.city-hotel-hameln.de. Best of a clutch
of budget hotels on a pretty street across from
Ostertorstr. – old-fashioned, quiet, and all rooms
en suites. ❸

DJH Hameln Fischbecker Str. 33 Ⓣ 05151/34 25,
Ⓦ www.djh-niedersachsen.de. Has a riverside
location among woods north of the centre; it's an
easy 20min walk from the Markt or you can take
bus #2 to "Wehler Weg" from the Bahnhof. From
€19.10.

Jugendstil Wettorstr. 15 Ⓣ 05151/955 80,
Ⓦ www.hotel-jugendstil.de. Period character in
high-ceilinged, characterful modern rooms make
this an appealing four-star in a large Art Nouveau
block north of the Altstadt. Owners claim former
guests include Klimt and Toulouse-Lautrec. ❺

Zur Krone Osterstr. 30 Ⓣ 05151/90 70,
Ⓦ www.hotelzurkrone.de. Beams of the renovated
seventeenth-century house bring character to front
rooms in this friendly central three-star. Those in
the modern block behind are classic modern. ❹

The Town

Whatever the fun of fairytales, small-town Hameln is also known for its Weser
Renaissance style, a home-grown version of the Italianate acclaimed for its
elaborate facades. The best can be found along Osterstrasse, a street that opens with
a ritzy display of carving on the **Rattenfängerhaus** at no. 28, a former councillors'
house from 1602. Its "Ratcatcher House" moniker refers to the inscription on its
side that relates the tale. The Rattenfängerhaus looks positively sober compared to
the **Lesithaus** at no. 9, a confection of candy pinks, cream and sherbet yellows from
whose sugary oriel Lucretia gazes distractedly, her modesty just about covered by a
slip of cloth. It seems likely that local architect Cord Tönnies drew up the plans for
the merchant's home to trump its older neighbour, the **Stiftsherrenhaus** whose
half-timbered facade is a riot of cartwheeling rosettes, twisted rope motifs and
biblical and astrological personalities, a very contemporary union of religion and
superstition. Together they house **Museum Hameln** (Tues–Sun 10am–4.30pm;
€3), with the usual town history displays perked up by a small section on the piper
legend. Among its facsimiles is the earliest depiction of the narrative from the early
fifteenth century with a jester-like piper standing above a tiny town as a crowd of
kids march up a hill – one version of the yarn has the children disappear inside
the cave depicted and returned after a substantially inflated payment. Residential
streets off the opposite side of the Osterstrasse are worth a look for charming half-
timbered buildings.

At the end of Osterstrasse is seventeenth-century banqueting hall the Hochzeithaus,
a "Wedding House" with a contrapuntal carillon to accompany a witty narration
of the piper legend (1.05pm, 3.35pm & 5.35pm). The house holds the modern

Erlebniswelt Renaissance (Experience Renaissance; in theory daily 10am–6pm; €9), whose multimedia displays place Weser Renaissance within the context of contemporary developments in science and the arts – fun but also fairly meaningless if your German is sketchy; English-language audio guides are planned.

Osterstrasse concludes at the **Markt**, town centre and venue for performances of the town's legend by an eighty-strong local troupe (May to mid-Sept Sun noon; free). The **Marktkirche** is a postwar rebuild that is missable except for a stained-glass window of the piper tale, a replica of an original said to have been crafted within a lifetime of the event. Directly opposite is **Dempsterhaus**, with a flouncing Weser Renaissance facade created for a town mayor. Five minutes' walk from here via Ritterstrasse is the **Pulvertrum**, one of the last defence towers of the town's medieval fortifications – when beefed up into the strongest defences in the Kingdom of Hannover, they gave Hameln a reputation as a "Gibraltar of the North". It now houses a glass factory (Mon–Sat 10am–1pm & 2–5/6pm, Sun 10am–5pm; €3) with glass-blowing demonstrations – visitors can try under supervision – and a shop.

Eating and drinking

Hameln's dining scene is lifted by the historic appeal of many of its restaurants – as ever pubs and cafés rustle up cheap, basic meals.

Restaurants

Ambrosia Neue Marktstr. 18 ☏05151/253 93. A lovely traditional house just off Osterstrasse adds a historic backdrop for Greek and Italian dishes.

Kartoffelhaus Kupferschmiedestr. 13 ☏05151/223 83. Potatoes with everything in a lavishly decorated half-timbered house. The speciality is the *Bürgerhus*, a meat-feast of pork, turkey and rump steak with vegetables and, of course, *Bratkartoffeln*.

Rattenfängerhaus Osterstr. 28 ☏05151/38 88. A famous *Gaststätte* that provides good *Bürgerlich* cooking in a traditional Hameln house – thankfully, the rat-themed cooking is in name only (although there may be some truth in the name of fifty percent proof *Schnapps Rattenkiller*). Touristy but none the worse for it.

Cafés and bars

El Solin Münsterkirchhof. In a pretty square off Bäckerstrasse, the Hameln outpost of a regional chain follows the template of St Tropez café-bar style – nice terrace for summer evenings. Also prepares cheap Italian dishes.

Merengue Mo Neue Marktstr. 12. Cocktail and whisky bar on a quiet backstreet with a clubby vibe.

Museumcafé Osterstr. 8. Cheap, light lunches and snacks such as club sandwiches and *croque monsieurs*, plus the inevitable *Rattenfängertorte* (Ratcatcher cake) in one of Hameln's finest buildings.

SumpfBlume Am Stockhof 2. A self-described "culture and communication station" translates into a riverside café by the Flotte Weser quay that serves Tex-Mex and sandwiches. In the eve it becomes a bar, club and live music venue that's open till 2am at weekends – its terrace is first choice for a sundowner.

Down the Weser River

South of Hameln a great touring route swings alongside the Weser for much of the way to **Hann. Münden** along the B83, swooping around broad meanders and hauling up over wooded hills as you roll south along the arterial valley of the Weserbergland. The journey is as much an attraction as the destinations, which makes this stretch one of Germany's most popular **cycle routes**, the Weserradweg (Ⓦwww.weser-radweg.info & Ⓦwww.weserradweg.de) – 150,000 cyclists a year can't all be wrong. It's also acclaimed **canoeing** country, but a swift current means you're best to make the journey in reverse, heading north from, say, Bad Karlshafen. With careful juggling of timetables you can make most of the journey from Hameln by ferries of the Flotte Weser line (Easter–Oct; ⓦ www.flotte-weser.de), which go to Bodenwerder on Wednesday, Friday and Sunday, and from Höxter 30km south, linked by local buses to Bad Karlshafen, on Tuesday to Sunday; the ferry quay in Hameln and all tourist offices in the area stock up-to-date timetables. Bus transport is fiddly: daytime-only bus #520 from Hameln goes via Bodenwerder to Holzminden to hook up with train services to all destinations south.

Bodenwerder

Hameln has a piper, **BODENWERDER**, 20km south, has Baron Münchhausen. The aged baron who told fantastical tales of feats such as riding cannonballs, travelling to the moon and pulling himself out of a swamp by his own hair (or bootstraps depending on who tells the story) is founded upon local baron Karl Friedrich Hieronymous von Münchhausen. The literary hero he became (see box below) looms large in what is an otherwise unremarkable one-street village. The odd cannonball in the **Münchhausen Museum** (daily 10am–noon & 2–5pm; €2) opposite the Rathaus struggles to live up to the narrative fantasy. More enjoyable are illustrations of the tall tales that are showcased near portraits of the real baron. Elsewhere several bronzes of his exploits will entertain the kids. A fountain outside the museum has our hero astride the prize horse that was shot in half in battle – he didn't realize until water poured from its body as it drank (he sewed the horse up again). Another fountain on the pedestrianized main street depicts the baron riding his cannonball to spy out Turkish positions, while one block behind him he hauls himself from a pond by his hair. The yarns are staged in front of the Rathaus on the first Sunday of the month from May to October (from 2pm; free). Every third Sunday of the month, the **Grotto pavilion** where Hieronymous von Münchhausen told his stories in his hunting room is opened to visitors – visits are coordinated through the **tourist office** (March–Oct Mon–Fri 9am–12.30pm & 2–5pm, Sat & Sun 10am–12.30pm; Nov–Feb Mon–Fri 9am–noon; ☎05533/405 41, ⓦwww.muenchhausenland.de) by the museum at Märchhausenplatz 2. A board outside lists accommodation options.

Bad Karlshafen

Snuggled into woodland on a meander 60km south of Bodenwerder, idyllic **BAD KARLSHAFEN** is a surprise after the half-timbered towns north. If its handsome white villas on broad streets seem to have been beamed across the border from France it is because the miniature Baroque town was planned by seventeenth-century Huguenot refugees from Languedoc and Dauphine who were guaranteed sanctuary and tax-free trading by Landgraf Karl von Hesse-Kassel. With the earl's death and the silting up of its canal at the confluence of the rivers Weser and Diemel, the town founded on wool and linen trading withered on the vine, and all that's left is the villas around a harbour in which lighters once tied up. The **Deutsches Hugenotten-Museum** (mid-March to Oct Tues–Fri 10am–noon & 2–6pm, Sat & Sun 11am–6pm; €3), at Hafenplatz 9, fills in the background with displays about the tyranny that followed Louis XIV's revocation of religious tolerance – there are some grisly copperplates of persecution – before tackling the town itself upstairs. There's also a model of the town that never materialized in the foyer of the Rathaus on the other side of the harbour – it and the colossal Invalidenhaus, a military hospital, at the end of elegant Conradistrasse, hints at the planners' ambitions.

Practicalities

The Rathaus also holds the **tourist office** (May–Sept Mon–Fri 9am–5.30pm, Sat 9.30am–noon, Sun 2.30–5pm; Oct–April Mon–Fri 9am–noon & 2–6pm; ☎05672/99 99, ⓦwww.bad-karlshafen.de). This provides maps of walking trails – arguably the best of the three planned routes is a river circuit to Helmarshausen 2km south via ruined Romanesque castle Krukenburg (daily 10am–6pm; free). Local **canoe operator** Kanu Schumacher (☎05642/76 82, ⓦwww.kanu -schumacher.de), just up from the campsite on the far side of the bridge over the Weser, rents Canadian canoes by the hour – tributary River Diemel is a lovely spot to dip an oar – and provides transfers back from destinations all along the Weser. Overnight expeditions go to Hann. Münden.

With an idyllic atmosphere and a good spread of **accommodation**, Bad Karlshafen makes a splendid overnight on the route south. First choice for atmosphere is *Zum Schwan* (☎05672/10 44, ⓦwww.hotel-zum-schwan -badkarlshafen.de; ❹), a grand old-fashioned place in a Baroque mansion at harbourside Conradistrasse 3–4. Alternatives include traditional *Hessicher Hof*, Carlstrasse 3–4 (☎05672 10 59, ⓦwww.hess-hof.de; ❸), and *Zum Weser-dampfschiff*, Weserstrasse 25 (☎05672/24 25, ⓦwww.weserdampfschiff.de; ❸), whose terrace restaurant (closed Mon) overlooking the Weser just pips the Baroque splendour of *Zum Schwan* in summer. *Campingplatz Bad Karlshafen* (☎05672/710, ⓦwww.campingplatz-bad-karlshafen.de) is spread along the river bank on the opposite side.

Hann. Münden

As the marketing blurb mawkishly puts it, **HANN. MÜNDEN**, 40km south of Bad Karlshafen, is sited "where the Werra and Fulda kiss" to flow into the Weser River. Naturalist Alexander von Humboldt, who knew a thing or two about the world having explored Russia and Latin America, declared it "one of the seven most beautifully sited towns in the world". Never mind the scenery, it's the **Altstadt** that wows in Hannoverisch Münden, to give it the full and rarely used title; a picture-book-pretty jumble of over seven hundred half-timbered houses beside those burbling rivers. A tourist office booklet guides you around every carefully carved beam.

As ever, the place to begin explorations is the **Markt** if only for a stone **Rathaus** whose chunky Weser Renaissance facade is an exercise in solidity among this streetscape of beams. At noon, 3pm and 5pm, a glockenspiel clunks out a ditty to accompany the tale of Dr Johann Andreas Eisenbart, a local hero who toured markets in eighteenth-century Germany and won fame for a technique that cured cataracts with a needle. Jealous peers and his weakness for self-publicity have conspired to make his name synonymous with charlatan. During office hours you can usually nose inside the Rathaus's Renaissance debating hall.

The other building of note is a walloping **Welfenschloss** beside the Werra River, a sober Weser Renaissance palace that houses the inevitable **town museum** (Wed–Fri 10am–noon & 2.30–5pm, Sat 10am–4pm, Sun 10am–12.30pm; €1.70) – access to frescoed ducal chambers is by tour through the tourist office. A semicircular tower near the entrance is the most impressive of the town's medieval defences. Others are revealed by walking around the Schloss's pale apricot walls to reach the Werrabrücke over the river, from where you get a lovely view back into an Altstadt of swaying houses. The best view of the town's rippling roofs is from a castellated viewing tower known as the **Tillyschanze** (May–Oct Tues–Sun 10am–8pm; Nov–April Fri–Sun 11am–8pm; €1.10), sited on a hillside west, a twenty-minute walk from the Altstadt.

Practicalities

Hann. Münden lies on the Göttingen–Kassel rail line; its **Bahnhof** and also the ZOB **bus station** are east of a centre that is reached via Bahnhofstrasse. The **tourist office** (May–Sept Mon–Fri 8am–5.30pm, Sat 10am–3pm, Sun 11am–3pm; Nov–April Mon–Thurs 9am–4pm, Fri 9am–1pm; ☎05541/733 13, ⓦwww.hann.muenden.de) is in the Rathaus. There's some good **accommodation** in town, no address finer than four-star *Alter Packhof* overlooking the Fulda River at Bremer Schlagd 10–14 (☎05541/988 90, ⓦwww.packhof.com; ❹–❻). In a renovated town house on one of the town's most photogenic squares, *Aegdienhof*, Aegidiistrasse 7–9 (☎05541/984 60, ⓦwww.fahrrad-hotel.de; ❷), is a bargain for the arty touches it brings to its rustic minimalism – friendly owners, too. *Rathausschänke*, Ziegelstrasse 12 (☎05541/88 66, ⓦwww.hotel-rathausschaenke.de; ❸), is a good fall-back. The **youth hostel** (☎05541/88 53, ⓦwww.djh-niedersachsen.de; from €18.90) is 1km north off the B80 at Prof-Oelkers-Strasse 10; take bus #190 from the Bahnhof. The **campsite** (☎05541/122 57, ⓦwww.busch-freizeit.de) on the river island on the west side of the Altstadt couldn't be more central.

The first choice for **food** is the excellent Italian-influenced cooking at *Reblaus* (☎05541/95 46 10), on the corner of Tanzwerderstrasse and Ziegelstrasse, which also has a large terrace on Kirchplatz. Brewery-restaurant *Rats-Brauhaus*, Markt 3 (closed Mon; ☎05541/95 71 07), prepares traditional dishes in the Rathaus cellars, or for a snack *Imbiss-café Ritter der Rotwurst*, Lange Strasse 29 (closed Sun), rustles up award-winning *Bratwurst* alongside tasty home-made soups.

Göttingen

GÖTTINGEN calls itself the "City of Science" (Stadt die Wissenschaft); it has nurtured forty Nobel Prize winners and institutions such as the German Aerospace Centre and the Max-Planck-Institutes. But don't let that put you off. For most visitors – and probably the majority of locals – the town is more about its café and bar culture than high culture. The root cause of both is the same: the **Georg-August Universität**. Founded in 1734 by Hannover elector Georg August, also known as King George II of Great Britain, the university grew into one of the intellectual think-tanks of Europe and boasted a roll-call of distinguished professors, among them Brothers Grimm Jakob and Wilhelm. It also brings a city-sized vibrancy to a medium-sized town. One in five of the 130,000-strong population is a student, nurturing a free-thinking liberalism that harks back to the Göttingen Seven, an academic grouping that dared to question the authority of Hannover king Ernst August in 1837. Students and easy-going attitudes also mean nightlife – perhaps the primary reason to visit whatever the value of the Hanseatic heritage.

Arrival, information and accommodation

The **Bahnhof** is at the western edge of the centre, most of which is pedestrianized. The **tourist office** (Mon–Fri 9.30am–6pm, Sat 10am–6pm; April–Oct also Sun 10am–4pm; ☎0551/49 98 00, ⓦwww.goettingen-tourismus.de) is in the Rathaus on the Markt at its bull's-eye. It sells the **GöCard** (one-day €5, three-day €12) ticket for free public transport and discounts on museum entry and city tours. **Bikes** can be rented from Velo-Voss in a bike-park (Fahrrad-Parkhaus; Mon–Sat 6am–10pm, Sun 8am–10pm) beside the Bahnhof – note that the police routinely hand out fines for riders who ignore the no-cycling signs in the pedestrian centre. **Internet access** is available in call-centre Preisparadis at Weender Strasse 98 (daily 9.30am–midnight).

All options for cheap **accommodation** are outside the centre.

Central Jüdenstr. 12 ☎0551/571 57, ⓦwww .hotel-central.com. Central, indeed, and a modest design number to boot wringed from an older hotel. Nice small garden, too. ⑤

DJH Göttingen Habichtsweg 2 ☎0551/576 22, ⓦwww.djh-niedersachsen.de. Dated hostel 3km south reached by bus #6 from the Bahnhof or Kornmarkt off the Markt. From €23.20.

Gebhards Goetheallee 22–23 ☎0551/496 80, ⓦwww.gebhardshotel.de. The five-star prestige address in Göttingen features traditional elegance in public areas and up-to-date comfort in its rooms. The *Georgia Augusta-Stuben* restaurant is excellent. ⑥–⑦

Kasseler Hof Rosdorfer Weg 26 ☎0551/72 08 12, ⓦwww.kasselerhof.de. On a quiet southwest residential street beyond the Altstadt ring road, this is a good-value, friendly hotel with Ikea-esque en suites. ③

Leine Groner Landstr. 55 ☎0551/505 10, ⓦwww.leinehotel-goe.de. A 15min walk behind the Bahnhof and described as a "boarding house", which translates into spacious if rather functional split-level rooms with small kitchenettes. ④

Stadt Hannover Goethe-Allee 21 ☎0551/54 79 60, ⓦwww.hotelstadthannover.de. Classic-modern family-run three-star in a central location. ⑤

The Town

Geographically, historically, socially, the focus of the small Altstadt is a **Markt** dominated by its **Altes Rathaus**. Its chunky Gothic stems from a fifteenth-century renovation of a progenitor merchants' guildhall. The 1880s wall-paintings in the debating hall (same times as tourist office) allude to that trading past with shields of Hanseatic League members and add the sort of allegorical faux-medievalisms beloved by an empire busy rediscovering its past; four decades earlier, the same zeitgeist had inspired university professors Jakob and Wilhelm Grimm to compile traditional folk-tales. At the centre of the Markt the **Ganseliesel** is, as the tourist board never tires of quipping, "the most kissed girl in the world". By tradition, graduating doctoral students kiss the demure goose-trader who stands canopied in a wrought-iron thicket. Behind the Altes Rathaus rise the octagonal spires of the **St Johanniskirche**. The highest, at 62m, was probably the tallest student digs in Germany when it housed theology students – probably the noisiest, too, with the bells so close. Before you leave the Markt area **Barfüsserstrasse** on the opposite side of the Altes Rathaus is worth a look for a couple of houses from Göttingen's sixteenth-century heyday. Finest is the colourful Junkernschänke on the corner of Jüdenstrasse; among its biblical panoply are portraits of the owner and his wife carved on the corner post.

Arterial pedestrian high-street Weender Strasse heads north of the Markt towards the **St Jacobikirche**. Once you've recovered from the shock of its interior – geometric stripes zigzag up its columns, a trick of the Middle Ages to create the illusion of distance and movement – there's a fine high altar by a mystery master. Fully open, it presents the coronation of the Virgin as queen of heaven before an assembly of saints, among them church patron St James with scallop shell worn. When closed, you see either a sumptuous narrative of Christ, its scenes divided by pillars like rooms in a Gothic castle, or the life story of the patron, depending on which of the two sets of wings is shut. The tower provides views over the Altstadt's roofscape in summer (daily 11am–6pm; €2). A block behind the church, the town's sole surviving Renaissance manor house at Ritterplan 7–8 houses the obligatory **town museum** (Tues–Fri 10am–5pm, Sat & Sun 11am–5pm; €1.50).

A green belt of landscaped gardens girdles the town in place of the ramparts that were constructed in the mid-1300s, then inched up for two centuries thereafter. Indeed, the Altes Rathaus would have been larger had funds not been diverted to the defences. A stroll around the centre takes just over an hour. At 7 o'clock on a circuit, you'll find the last tower on the rampart, the **Bismarckhäuschen** (Tues 10am–1pm, Thurs & Sat 3–5pm, or by appointment ☎0551/48 58 44; free). Hearsay has it that the 18-year-old Otto von Bismarck was banished to its dumpy garret for student high-jinks in 1833 – it is a replica of his study that is on display. Certainly Göttingen proved an unhappy year for the future Iron Chancellor. A Prussian aristocrat and snob, Bismarck looked down on his liberal colleagues, and seems to have whiled away most of his single year there not studying law but duelling and boozing with an aristocratic fencing fraternity.

Eating and drinking

Restaurants

Gaudi Rote Str. 16 ☎0551/531 30 01. Airy and arty upmarket place in a mews, which serves modern Mediterranean food and tapas.
Gauss Obere Karspüle 22 ☎0551/566 16. Uphill from St Jacobikirche, the finest restaurant in town prepares weekly seasonal menus of contemporary German cuisine, served in a stone-walled dining room or summer terrace. Eve only, closed Sun & Mon.
Rathskeller Markt 9 ☎0551/564 33. Everything the Rathaus restaurant should be – bags of atmosphere in a cellar muralled with medieval-inspired

images, and unashamedly traditional in service, menu and portion sizes.
Zum Schwarzen Bären Kurze Str. 12 ☎0551/582 84. *Gaststätte* that has been serving traditional dishes in its beamed rooms since 1637 – the menu changes every century or so. Closed Mon.
Zum Szültenbürger Prinzenstr. 7 ☎0551/431 33. Another historic *Gaststätte*, this a cosy tavern decorated with images of old Göttingen in a single snug dining-room. The menu offers good-value home-cooking. Closed Mon.

Cafés

Cello Coffee Bar Weender Str. 87. "The world of espresso" – twelve types of coffee – as well as fresh smoothies and ten varieties of bagel. Its rose-filled garden is a great spot for breakfasts. Closed Sun.

Cron & Lanz Weender Str. 25. A favourite for coffee and cake is this splendidly old-fashioned café that's been going strong since the 1860s thanks to the gateaux and pralines of its *Konditorei*. Closed Sun morning.

GroMo Goetheallee 13. Exhibitions by local artists serve as decoration for a relaxed café and bar that specializes in "Grosses Monster Crepes".

Bars

ADe! Prinzenstr. 16. Despite a stylistic revamp (it was previously called *Zum Altdeutschen*), still an atmospheric cellar-like student dive-bar that's lit by candles.

JT Casino Am Wochenmarkt. The bar of the Junges Theater whose cool junk shop chic, epitomized by Coca-Cola bottle lampshades, woos an older mid-thirties crowd.

Kleiner Ratskeller Jüdenstr. 30. Not quite the same bastion of student boozing of yore but a lovely, historic little *Kneipe* nevertheless. Mains on a menu of student fodder average €7.

Mr Jones Goetheallee 8. Airy modern café-bar that overlooks the Leine canal – a refined spot for large cocktails while DJs play a good-times funk and jazz soundtrack at weekends.

Pools Barfusserstr. 13. No glitz in a no-frills student place that's all the better for a grungy vibe; there are battered sofas in the courtyard in summer and a dive bar over two levels is soundtracked to dirty funk and indie.

Sausalitos Hospitalstr. 35. Housed in a half-timbered former mill near the Bismarck-häuschen, this typically knockabout member of the Tex-Mex bar chain maintains a "beach" beer garden in summer.

Nightlife

A student town par excellence, Göttingen punches far above its weight for **clubbing**. Local pop-culture magazine *Pony* is your best source of what's on; there's often a copy knocking about in student bar *Pools* (see above). As ever weekends offer the greatest choice, but you should find something somewhere week-round. Wednesday night is student night – expect reduced or free entry to nightclubs and cheap drinks.

Alpenmax Weender Landstr. 3–7 ⓦ www .alpenmax.de. The only club in town currently open on Monday and certainly the only one styled as an alpine ski-hut.

Blue Note Wilhelmsplatz 3 ⓦ www.bluenote -goettingen.de. Basement cellar club that specializes in nights of "Tropical" party classics and salsa, and has some jazz gigs.

JT Keller Am Wochenmarkt 6 ⓦ www.jt-keller.de. Friendly basement club whose music policy ticks all boxes depending on who's in – check the website. Weekenders at the start of each month are always fun.

Savoy Berliner Str. 5 ⓦ www.club-savoy.de. Mainstream house-music club in a warehouse-style place with a penchant for glitterball glamour and themed nights – Porno-Karaoke, anyone?

Braunschweig

After nearly a millennium of habit **BRAUNSCHWEIG** routinely tags itself "Die Löwenstadt". The lion refers to Saxon duke Henry the Lion (Heinrich der Löwe), a twelfth-century giant of early Europe who commanded the last great independent duchy of fledgling Germany. His territory comprised a great swathe north to Kiel – he founded Lübeck and Lüneburg among other towns – and much of present-day Bavaria; Munich is another of his creations. His capital, however, was Braunschweig, and the high points of the state's second largest city after Hannover are intrinsically bound up with its founder despite an illustrious history that again flared into brilliance in the mid-1700s as a ducal Residenzstadt. As the epicentre of Lower Saxony's industry whose historic centre was badly damaged in 1944, Braunschweig is not the most instantly appealing destination in the state. As a major transport junction it is one you're sure to pass through, however, and there are a couple of appealing day-trips to Wolfenbüttel (see p.710) and Wolfsburg (see p.711) within half an hour.

Arrival, information and transport

The **Hauptbahnhof** and the adjacent ZOB **bus station** lie a hefty 1.5km southeast of the centre: trams #1 or #2 or any bus bound for the "Rathaus" will whisk you into a fairly dispersed centre. Single **tickets** come in two forms: they either cost €1.70 or are priced by time: a one hour thirty minute Einzelfahrschine costs €2, a day-long Tageskarte is €5 – the €7.30 day-ticket for a group of up to five is a steal. Extend the zone to take in nearby Wolfen-büttel and day-ticket prices rise to €7.30 and €10.80 respectively. **Bike rental** is from the Hauptbahnhof. The **tourist office** (Mon–Fri 10am–7pm, Sat 10am–4pm; May–Sept also Sun 10am–12.30pm; ☎0531/470 20 40, ⓦwww .braunschweig.de/touristinfo) is at Vor der Burg 1 opposite the Dom at the town's centre. **Internet access** is available at TeleKlick (daily 10am–11pm) at Münzstrasse 9. From May to September you can rent canoes to paddle on the Oker in the Burgerpark south of the centre at Bootstation Braunschweig (☎0531 270 27 24, ⓦwww.bootstation.de) just east of JF Kennedy-Platz. It also runs day-tours as far as Wolfenbüttel (5hr; €37.50).

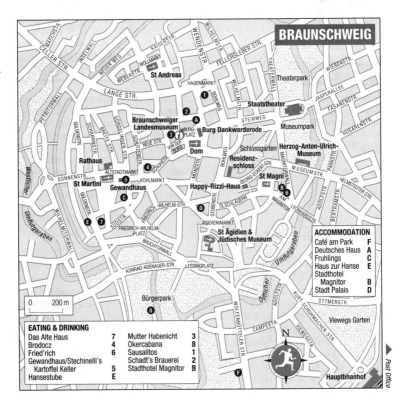

Accommodation

You've got a decent spread of mid-range and upmarket options for an overnighter, though budget options are limited.

Café am Park Wolfenbütteler Str. 67 ⊕0531/730 79, Ⓦwww.hotel-cafeampark.de. Pleasant cheapie south of the centre with white walls and pine furniture in spotless en suites – no frills, just bright and efficient. ❸

Deutsches Haus Ruhfäutchenplatz 1 ⊕0531/120 00, Ⓦwww.deutscheshaus .ringhotels.de. A grand traditional hotel that's now showing its age in rooms of dated dark-wood furniture and tasselled lampshades. Comfy enough, and central location. ❹–❼

Frühlings Bankplatz 7 ⊕0531/24 32 10, Ⓦwww.fruehlingshotel.de. Friendly place in a late 1800s building in the centre that is slowly being renovated from the bottom up into a quietly stylish number – those at the top are fine if dated. Some large suites have kitchenettes. ❹

Haus zur Hanse Güldenstr. 7 ⊕0531/24 39 00, Ⓦwww.haus-zur-hanse.de. Slick designer place which blends centuries-old beams of its court brewery building with modern style and reproduction antiques. The restaurant is excellent (see p.709). ❺

Stadthotel Magnitor Am Magnitor 1 ⊕0531/471 30, Ⓦwww.stadthotel-magni.de. A former half-timbered storehouse in the historic Magniviertel whose design hotel marries functional business decor to stripped-down designer style. Also has a good restaurant. ❺

Stadt Palais Hinter Liebfrauen 1a ⊕0531/24 10 24, Ⓦwww.palais-braunschweig.bestwestern.de. Local outpost of the Best Western chain and all you'd expect – modern, comfortable and with seamless service. ❻

Burgplatz

If Braunschweig has a holy of holies it's **Burgplatz**, the heart of the Altstadt – or what's left of it – and the well-spring of its growth from which Henry the Lion ruled an empire. The Saxon lion king commissioned the leonine *Burglöwe* statue at its centre as a vainglorious symbol of his power and jurisdiction. The original, said to be the first freestanding monument cast north of the Alps since the Roman occupation, is in **Burg Dankwarderode** (Tues, Thurs & Sun 11am–5pm, Wed 1–2.30pm & 4–8pm; €3), a squat structure that boxes in the square's east side. Its out-of-the-wrapper-neat Romanesque is an 1880s guess at Henry's palace based on excavations. Its ground floor displays the medieval collection of the Herzog-Anton-Ulrich-Museum (see p.708), the star pieces among some eye-catching reliquaries being the *Burglöwe* that Heinrich cast in 1166 and a cloak said to have belonged to his son, Otto IV. The Rittersaal above (Tues & Thurs–Sun 10–11am, Wed 2.30–4pm) is a splendid piece of imperial pomp that alludes to the knights' halls of medieval fable.

In 1173 Heinrich returned from pilgrimage to the Holy Land and commissioned a mighty **Dom** as a repository for his souvenir relics and a burial place to honour his magnificence. His tomb lies at the heart of a basilica, the ruler cradling a model of his church on a slab (1235) that depicts him beside his English queen, Mathilde. Inspired by a German ruler who masterminded expansion east and never shy of a PR coup, Hitler ordered the tomb be opened in the 1930s, only to discover a small man with black hair, probably due to Henry's Italian lineage. Other members of the Welf dynasty lie in sarcophagi in the crypt (€1). The absence of decoration elsewhere in the church only heightens the impact of muddy thirteenth-century frescos in the choir. Accidentally uncovered in 1845, their pictorial bible is imbued with all the smoke and mystery of the early Church. The colossal seven-arm candelabra inset with cloisonné enamel in front is another legacy of Henry – it was commissioned to sit over his tomb as a symbol of resurrection.

The most impressive of the facing buildings that ring Burgplatz are **Huneborstelsches Haus** and **Von Veltheimisches Haus**. Carved with a playground of folkloric images, they are early 1900s rebuilds pieced together from older timbers. At their side, the **Braunschweigisches Landesmuseum** (Tues–Sun 10am–5pm, Thurs till 8pm; €2.50) plods through regional history and has an earlier replica *Burglöwe* in its foyer.

West and north of Burgplatz: Altstadtmarkt and Neustadt

Altstadtmarkt, which started as a mercantile township of the fledgling settlement in the mid-1100s, served as a counterweight to the governmental authority on Burgplatz and flourished as a venue of trade fairs and parades as Braunschweig blossomed into a commercial medieval power. Hence the L-shaped Gothic **Rathaus** (Tues–Fri & Sun 10am–1pm & 2–5pm; free), which wraps around the far corner. A town museum within skips through the centuries up to the 1960s using odds and ends of civic pride, from fashions to council silverware and early copperplates of the town. It rather takes second place to the Grosse Dornse council chamber on the first floor, or the view from its elegant balcony on which councillors gazed out at the citizens beneath, their authority confirmed by its statues of Welfen dukes – Heinrich and Mathilde are at the end opposite the church of St Martini.

Only drapers' warehouse and trading hall the **Gewandhaus** which shuts in the opposite side can match the Rathaus in size. Its bulk reflects the prestige of the most distinguished guild in the city. A rich one, too, if the Renaissance facade added to the east end is any guide. At the opposite end is a former customs house rebuilt after the war whose carved beams are worth a look. Square backdrop **St Martini Kirche** (Tues–Fri 10am–1pm & 3–5pm, Sat 10am–5pm, Sun 10am–noon & 3–5pm) was both that of patricians and the first church erected after the Dom, which served as a model before its rethink into Gothic. It hosts occasional art exhibitions.

A couple of sights warrant the walk to the **Neustadt** district north of Burgplatz. First is the Alte Waage weigh-house, a chunky half-timbered structure rebuilt in 1994. Beyond is the St Andreaskirche whose Baroque tower (April–Oct Wed–Sun 3–5pm; €2) seems like a fairytale garret for Rapunzel. Extended to 93m high in 1740, it permits a view over the city – with 389 steps, the old cliché about breathtaking rings true.

East of Burgplatz: the Magniviertel and Herzog-Anton-Ulrich-Museum

Only the ducal **Residenzschloss** will detain you on the route east of Burgplatz – it reappeared in 2007 after a total postwar rebuild and is slated to house a Schlossmuseum. For the moment the area's focus is the historic **Magniviertel**. A picturesque corner of half-timbered houses on cobbled lanes, it is one of the few corners of the city to have escaped wartime destruction and is, inevitably, gentrified as a popular bar and restaurant district. It's located behind the Schloss's right-hand corner beyond **Happy-Rizzi-Haus**, a candy-coloured complex by New York Pop Art artist James Rizzi – local opinion is divided over whether the cartoony complex is whimsically wacky or better suited to a kindergarten.

Henry the Lion receives all the attention, but Braunschweig duke Anton Ulrich deserves much credit for masterminding a golden age of culture in the mid-1600s. His eclectic tastes are reflected by the diversity of the **Herzog-Anton-Ulrich-Museum** (Tues & Thurs–Sun 10am–5pm, Wed 1–8pm; €3;

@ www.museum-braunschweig.de), northeast of the Magniviertel on Museum-strasse, a jackdaw's hoard presented as Germany's first public museum in 1754, four decades after the duke's death. He had impeccable taste. Among the German artworks are several Cranachs, including *Hercules and Omphale*, a warning about lust that sees the tempted hero bagged like the partridges in the background. The duke also had an eye for Dutch works – Rubens and especially Rembrandt – and porcelain, including the world's largest private collection of Fürstenburg china, as well as fine Chinese lacquerwork. Elsewhere are European bronzes and furniture and antiquities. Whether all is on display depends on the progress of a €25 million renovation that will add a new wing by 2010, at which point the museum's current older building will undergo restoration for three years.

Eating and drinking

Magniviertel's main street, Am Magnitor, is the first choice to browse for restaurants and bars, especially in summer.

Restaurants

Das Alte Haus Alte Knochenhauer Str. 11 ☎ 0531/480 35 03. Slick, modern place with a small seasonal menu of Mediterranean flavours – expect thyme crusts to lamb, and olive and tomato sauces. Eve only, closed Sun & Mon.

Brodocz Stephanstr. 1 ☎ 0531/422 36. Fairly smart fish and vegetarian restaurant in the pedestrian centre whose bargain-priced lunch menu is served in a pretty, half-timbered courtyard. Closed Sun.

Fried'rich Am Magnitor 5 ☎ 0531/417 28. Sweet Magniviertel restaurant and wine bar that has a good reputation among locals – fish dishes come recommended on a menu of light German cooking. Eve only & closed Sun Jan–mid April.

Gewandhaus/Stechinelli's Kartoffel Keller Altstadtmarkt 1–2 ☎ 0531/24 27 77. Two cellar restaurants at either end of the former drapers' hall; the first is a traditional restaurant (closed Sun) which prides itself on its *Schnitzel*, the latter rustles up cheap, filling dishes with the potatoes of its name.

Hansestube *Haus zur Hanse*, Güldenstr. 7 ☎ 0531/24 39 00. Widely hailed as the best restaurant in town. It serves both a seasonal Mediterranean and a traditional menu some of whose dishes come with Braunschweig speciality *Mumme* sauce created

from malt extract. The hotel's more modern *Boom* bistro-bar is less formal.

Mutter Habenicht Papenstieg 5 ☎ 0531/459 56. An old favourite for low-cost eating that's been going strong since 1870. Nothing on a traditional menu is priced over €15 and there's a choice of rooms and small beer garden at the rear.

Stadthotel Magnitor Am Magnitor 1 ☎ 0531/471 30. The *Magnitor* has a good restaurant that peps up regional specialities such as *Sauerbraten* with international flavours. Nice summer terrace on the main square, too.

Bars

Okercabana Bürgerpark. Robinson Crusoe with cocktails in a great city beach on the River Oker, 10min walk behind the Volkswagen Halle on Adenauer Strasse. Lounging central for families and hipsters alike by day, it segues into a laid-back night-spot with DJs at weekends. May–Sept daily from noon.

Sausalitos Hagenmarkt. Reliably lively member of the Tex-Mex chain, with a similar menu of cocktails, burgers and burritos and a pleasant beer garden on the leafy square.

Schadt's Brauerei Am Marshall 2. Unpretentious *Hausbrauerei* just north of Burgplatz that brews a *Pils, Weizen* and a seasonal beer.

Nightlife and entertainment

The largest of Braunschweig's **nightclubs** is *Jolly Joker* (@ www.jolly-joker-de) at Broitzemer Strasse 220. Depending on the night you'll either get a playlist of party classics or hip-hop, soul and r'n'b from a weekend programme buttressed by student midweekers and occasional gigs. Other venues include *Brain Klub*, Bruchtorwall 21 (@ www.brain-bs.de), playing a leftfield mix or indie rock from Thursday to Saturday, and posey lounge-bar *Cube Eleven*, Böcklerstrasse 30–31 (@ www.cube11.com), host of a regular Saturday house club.

While occasional stadium-rockers visit the Volkswagen Halle on Adenauer Strasse (ⓦwww.volkswagenhalle-braunschweig.de; tickets from tourist office), the city's main **cultural venue** is the Stadthalle on Leonhardsplatz (ⓣ01805/80 57 30, ⓦwww.stadthalle-braunschweig.de); expect musicals or dance and classical concerts. The Staatstheater (ⓣ0531/123 40, ⓦwww.staatstheater-braunschweig .de), Am Theater, is the main stage for drama and opera.

Wolfenbüttel

Legendary libertine Giacomo Casanova spent "the most wonderful week of my entire life" there and Wilhelm Busch, father of the modern cartoon-strip, declared the place "marvellous". Yet still **WOLFENBÜTTEL** is not as well known as it deserves. Having escaped war and mass tourism, this small town, with an ensemble of over six hundred half-timbered houses, has an almost fairytale quality, a blend of aristocracy and an erudite mindset that sees its museums publish websites in Latin. Partly to blame is the ducal House of Braunschweig which declared Wolfenbüttel a Residenzstadt in 1432. Under the Guelphic dukes' three-century tenure, high culture flowered and the royal town metamorphosed into the first planned town in Renaissance Germany. And when the dukes shifted back to Braunschweig in 1753 they sent Wolfenbüttel into a deep sleep from which it seems yet to awake – one reason to go.

When urban planners designed the town in the late 1400s, they created discrete districts for society's different strata. For the aristocracy, that neighbourhood was **Dammfestung** huddled at the feet of the largest **Schloss** in Lower Saxony (Tues–Sat 10am–5pm; €3). Behind its facade, a model of elegant Baroque only slightly thrown off-kilter by a Renaissance tower, the private apartments of the last duke, the flamboyant Anton Ulrich, he of the Braunschweig museum, are a sumptuous display of rich wall coverings and frothy stucco lightened with cheeky everyday touches such as a commode or a powdered wig. The treasure is coffee-room the **Intarsienkabinett**, whose oval marquetry panels are inlaid with delicate ivory scenes.

Outside, a dusky pink Zeughaus seems incongruous as the armoury that once held the most powerful cannons in Germany. **Lessinghaus** (Tues–Sun 10am–5pm; €3) opposite pays homage to its most celebrated resident, Gotthold Ephraim Lessing. The pioneering Enlightenment dramatist penned *Nathan the Wise* in his *maison de plaisance* when not working as ducal librarian of the **Herzog August Bibliothek** (same hours & ticket) at the back of Schlossplatz. For a moment in history, Duke August the Younger pored over the largest library in Europe, and his 800,000-tome collection, bound in leather hides and shelved in a hall of marble pillars, is a bibliophile's dream. Pride of place among such treasures as Descartes' *Tractatus de homine*, Cicero's *De officiis*, Renaissance globes and beautiful *livres de peintre* goes to what was the world's most expensive book when it was bought at auction for DM32.5 million (€16.62 million) in 1983, the *Welfen Evangeliar*, a gospel that Saxon duke Henry the Lion commissioned for the Braunschweig Dom in 1188, though only a facsimile is on display.

Along Löwenstrasse off Schlossplatz, Wolfenbüttel relaxes as you enter the **Freiheit** district, where court employees wedged themselves between royal and civic districts. Beyond Wolfenbüttel's narrowest house at Kleiner Zimmerhof 15 you can discover a remnant of a canal system carved through Wolfenbüttel by Dutch engineers and known as "Little Venice". Southeast of here the dukes' planned town, Heinrichstadt, appears as a formal grid of streets. Its heart is **Stadtmarkt**, with its bronze of August the Younger leading his horse. One-time home to courtiers and wealthy townsmen, it was modelled on piazzas of the Italian Renaissance, and the **Fachwerkhäuser** (half-timbered houses) along the north side are particularly elegant. Among them, blushing furiously and with hearts interweaved on its gable, is one of the most joyful register offices in Germany (1736).

More attractive architecture lies on streets that radiate north and east: Kanzleistrasse, where the ochre **Kanzlei** houses archeological exhibits of the **Braunschweigisches Landesmuseum** (Tues & Fri 10am–1pm, Wed, Thurs & Sun 10am–5pm; €2.50), and off it, Harzstrasse. East of Stadtmarkt, Reichsstrasse features a parade of houses from around 1600 and the **Hauptkirche** (Tues–Sun 10am–noon & 2–4pm; €1 donation requested), which was completed in 1608 as the first in Germany to follow Luther's credo against visual distraction. Certainly the bright interior where the dukes lie in state is a model of simplicity. But without such restraints for his facade, Schloss architect Paul Francke lets rip with a concoction that peps up plain Gothic with frilly Weser Renaissance.

Practicalities

Wolfenbüttel falls within the public transport zone of Braunschweig, linked by buses and Regional Bahn trains, and most visitors treat the town as a day-trip from there. The **Hauptbahnhof** lies five minutes' walk south of the historic centre, Stadtmarkt, home to the **tourist office** (Mon–Fri 9am–6pm, Sat 10am–2pm; ☎05331/862 80, ⓦwww.wolfenbuettel-tourismus.de) at no. 7. Wolfenbüttel's best **hotel** is *Parkhotel Altes Kaffeehaus*, Harztorwall 18 (☎05331/88 80, ⓦwww .parkhotel-wolfenbuettel.de; ❻), sited in the Stadtgraben parkland a little southeast of the Stadtmarkt, or *Forsthaus*, Neuer Weg 5 (☎05331/271 88, ⓦwww.hotel -forsthaus.eu; ❷), the half-timbered guesthouse where Wilhelm Busch holidayed, on the main road ten minutes' walk north of the centre. The former has two good **restaurants** plus a historic wine cellar, *Alte Kaffehaus*. Otherwise the *Ratskeller* at Stadtmarkt 2–4 (closed Mon; ☎05331/88 27 46) comes up trumps for traditional German cooking, as does Bavarian-styled inn *Bayrischer Hof* (☎05331/50 78, ⓦwww.bayrischer-hof-wf.de; rooms ❸) on the corner of Brauergildenstrasse and Reichsstrasse. Nearby *La Domenica* (☎05331/59 53) at Okerstrasse 16 gets the nod for Italian.

Wolfsburg

Around 120,000 people live in **WOLFSBURG**, but make no mistake, this is Volkswagen's town. The village of the mid-1930s was reinvented almost overnight when Hitler's Ford-inspired dream of a Volkswagen (literally "people's car") was made actual in 1937 when a sprawling factory began churning out the "Beetles" of Ferdinand Porsche. Aided by the economic pick-me-up of a postwar British military contract, an exception to enforced de-industrialization elsewhere, Volkswagen thrived, a fairy godmother of the economy's rags-to-riches Cinderella story. Such was the bad press that met a threat to slim down operations at the world headquarters, Volkswagen was forced to shelve the plan.

All of which makes **Autostadt** (daily 9am–6pm; €15 or €23 with phaeno; ⓦwww.autostadt.de), behind the train station, reached by a footbridge over a canal, a rev-head's paradise. VW's intended car collection centre has morphed into a futuristic theme park of museums, rides and a 360-degree cinema. The five-storey ZeitHaus salutes pioneers of automotive history (Karl Benz's 1886 tricycle, a Rolls-Royce Silver Ghost and Auto Union "Silver Arrow" racing cars) and also its icons (the millionth Mini, John Lennon's Beetle featured on the cover of *Abbey Road*, and a gorgeous 1930 Cadillac convertible). In architectural pavilions behind, Volkswagen indulges in entertaining self-promotion for its brands: Bentley's craftsmanship; Lamborghini's oomph; reliable Skoda; futuristic Audi; and the quality and safety of Volkswagen. However, Autostadt's star attraction is the factory itself, which at 8.4 square kilometres is four times larger than Monaco; only from a footbridge before Autostadt do you sense its scale. The most popular tours (daily 10.15am–4.15pm; every 45min; 2hr; €11) are made by mini-train around a few sections. Others ascend the company's landmark cylindrical glass tower (€8) in which shiny cars await collection. Hands-on attractions such as a 4WD terrain course (GeländeParcours; €25) are provided as "training" activities. Should you need another motor fix – unlikely – more classic VWs are in the AutoMuseum Volkswagen ten minutes' walk southwest (Dieselstrasse 35; daily 10am–5pm; €6).

Wolfsburg isn't all motor-mad. To promote an image as a city of science, it commissioned the **phaeno** museum (Tues–Fri 9am–5pm, Sat & Sun 10am–6pm; €12; ⓦwww.phaeno.com), beside the Hauptbahnhof, which is unmissable thanks to its building by architect Zaha Hadid – a sort of futuristic take on Corbusier's modernism. Beneath its steel-girdered roof lies a playground of 250 interactive scientific experiments, zoned into themes such as wind and water, biology, technology or energy. Forty were designed by artists, making for exhibits that are often as aesthetic as they are educational – the *Feuertornado* (fire tornado) which creates a 7m flaming whirlwind is particularly impressive.

Wolfsburg's centre south of here would be spectacularly dull without the **Kunstmuseum Wolfsburg** (Tues 11am–8pm, Wed–Sun 11am–6pm; €6; ⓦwww.kunstmuseum-wolfsburg.de), which lies two uninspiring kilometres down pedestrianized Porschestrasse, its cool glass-and-steel structure not unlike Autostadt. Its focus is contemporary art: changing displays of a permanent collection that includes big names such as Warhol, Damien Hirst, Jeff Koons and Gilbert and George, plus big-name temporary exhibitions.

History hereabouts is confined to the Weser Renaissance **Schloss Wolfsburg** 1km northeast of Autostadt. Its **Stadtmuseum** (Tues & Sat 1–5/6pm, Wed–Fri & Sun 10am–5/6pm; €2.50) chronicles the history of the young city it christened and also houses a gallery of modern German art (Tues 10am–8pm, Wed–Fri 10am–5pm, Sat & Sun 10am–6pm; €2.50).

Practicalities

The central **Hauptbahnhof** is on the Hannover and Braunschweig lines and houses the **tourist office** (daily 9am–6pm; ☎05361/89 99 30, ⓦwww.wolfsburg -marketing.de) and a **bike rental** outfit. Though Wolfsburg is best treated as a day-trip, overnight options include *Gasthaus Alter Wolf*, Schlossstrasse 21 (☎05361/865 60, ⓦwww.alter-wolf.de; ❸), an old-fashioned hotel and restaurant by the Schloss, and *City-Hotel Journal*, Kaufhofpassage 2 (phone in advance if arriving on Sun; ☎05361/848 49 77; ❸), in a mall off the pedestrian high-street. For a splurge the *Ritz-Carlton* in Autostadt (☎05361/60 70 00, ⓦwww.ritzcarlton.com; ❽) is one of the state's most luxurious addresses, home to a superb gourmet restaurant, *Aqua* (eve only Tues–Sat). There's a central if dated **youth hostel**, at Lessingstrasse 60 (☎05361/133 37, ⓦwww.djh-niedersachsen.de; from €21.20), and a good **campsite**, *Am Allersee* (☎05361/633 94, ⓦwww.camping-allersee.de) signposted 1.5km east of Autostadt. Among **cafés** throughout Autostadt are noodle bistro *ANAN* in the ZeitHaus, and *TachoMeter* in the KundenCenter, whose *Currywurst* is manufactured in a dedicated VW butchery. In the main hall, trattoria *Barolo*, food hall *Lagune*, and Asiatic and New World fusion restaurant *Chardonnay* (closed Sun & Mon eve) cater to most tastes. In Wolfstadt centre, the Kunstmuseum has a stylish bistro-café, *Awilon* (closed Mon), that's popular for weekend brunch, or *Paulaner Botschaft* opposite rustles up the usual sturdy Bavarian fodder.

Celle

CELLE is just half an hour from Hannover but the distance in atmosphere is centuries. While the bombs rained on the state capital, this small town emerged unscathed, a charming miniature of the seventeenth-century townscape lost in Hannover. As one of the finest half-timbered towns in Germany, Celle gets more than its share of tourists; indeed it's worth an overnight visit just to enjoy it free of day-trippers. However, it remains – just – more market town than museum piece. It also positively hums with quiet prosperity, and for that some thanks must go to the dukes of Braunschweig-Lüneburg. Banished from Lüneburg, the nobles crossed to the other side of the Lüneburg Heide in 1378 and made Celle an aristocratic Residenzstadt for nearly three centuries, encouraging the prosperity that built its streetscape. Celle is a testament that feudalism starts as a street plan: the ducal Schloss lies at the western edge of the Altstadt, whose parallel streets east run up towards it, a gesture of submission to the ducal yoke.

Arrival, information and accommodation

On the Hannover line, Celle's **Hauptbahnhof** lies fifteen minutes' walk west of the Altstadt via Bahnhofstrasse, which emerges at the rear of the Schloss. The **tourist office** (May–Sept Mon–Fri 9am–6pm, Sat 10am–4pm, Sun 11am–2pm; Oct–April Mon–Fri 9am–5pm, Sat 10am–1pm; ☎05141/12 12, ⓦwww.region-celle.de) is at Markt 14–16. **Bike rental** is from Fahrradverleih Am Bahnhof (Mon–Fri 9am–1pm & 3–6pm, Sat 9am–1pm) at Bahnhofstrasse 26–27. **Internet access** is at no. 14 at pool-bar *Interpool*. Celle has a good range of **accommodation**, with many hotels stuffed into historic buildings. The downside of its proximity to Hannover, however, is that it suffers similar price rises during trade fairs. The nearest campsite is *Campingpark Silbersee* (☎05141/321 23, ⓦwww.campingpark-silbersee.de), 4km north of the centre in Vorwerk suburb (bus #6).

Borchers Schuhstr. 52 ☎05141/91 19 20, ⓦwww.hotelborchers.com. Pleasant enough modern hotel in the Altstadt, some of whose nineteen rooms open directly onto a garden. ⑤
Celler Hof Stechbahn 11 ☎05141/20 11 41, ⓦwww.wallbaumhotels.de. A half-timbered house on one of Celle's finest streets hides seventy rooms with mod cons from the Wallbaum chain. You're paying mostly for a central location opposite the Stadtkirche – keep the window open and its trumpeter provides a reveille at 9.30am. ⑤
DJH Celle Weghauserstr. 2 ☎05141/532 08, ⓦwww.djh-niedersachsen.de. Popular with school groups, and a 25min walk from the Bahnhof or take bus #3 and alight at "Jugendherberge". From €17.70.

Fürstenhof Hannoversche Str. 55–56 ☎05141/20 10, ⓦwww.fuerstenhof-celle.de. Celle's premier address, housed in a Baroque palace just south of the Schloss. The decor is inspired by local themes – royalty, hunting, equestrian or heathland, and calm and five-star sophistication reign. ⑦–⑧
Götz Hannoversche Str. 28 ☎05141/278 80 72. The cheapest hotel in Celle has basic pine-furnished en suites – though nothing special, they are clean and perfectly acceptable for a bunk-down on a budget. Front rooms can be noisy. ②–③
Schifferkrug Speicherstr. 9 ☎05141/37 47 76, ⓦwww.schifferkrug-celle.de. Comfortable small en suites, most renovated, in a traditional inn behind the Schloss that dates from 1685 as the guildhouse of river boatmen. Pretty, small garden, too. ③–④

The Schloss and museums

The moated pile the Braunschweig-Lüneburg dukes built for themselves sits aloof from the Altstadt proper, a beautifully proportioned Renaissance **Schloss** (Tues–Sun 10am–5pm; €3) which stands on the same spot where Duke Otto the Severe erected a medieval tower residence in the 1200s to found a town. Inside, living quarters and halls where the last duke, Georg Wilhelm, gave audience from his bed are a document of Baroque high-life, largely thanks to rich stucco confected by an Italian master, Giovanni Battista Tornielli. There's also an apartment in which exiled queen Caroline Mathilde of Denmark, youngest sister of Britain's King George III, lived out her final years as a semi-prisoner until 1775. Her crime was to fall for the court doctor after her husband, Danish King Christian VII, lost his wits. Her lover, who had became de facto ruler, lost his head. Tours (April–Oct Tues–Sun hourly 11am–3pm; Nov–March daily 11am & 3pm, Sat & Sun 1pm; €4; notes in English available) take in the living quarters and also the palace's finest spaces such as the **Schlosskapelle**. Its stern Gothic – a sole survivor of the original castle – is drowned out by a cacophony of Renaissance colour, not least in the paintings by Antwerp Mannerist Marten de Vos, whose allegorical *Temptation of the Holy Church* is to the left of the entrance. Tours also take in a lovely miniature **court theatre** if no rehearsals are ongoing on the oldest Baroque stage in Germany, created in 1674 to stage commedia dell'arte and operetta. Tickets for performances (☎05141/905 08 75, ⓦwww.schlosstheater-celle.de) are sold from a kiosk just behind the Rathaus at Markt 18.

Opposite the Schloss, the **Bomann-Museum** (Tues–Sun 10am–5pm; €3; ⓦwww.bomann-museum.de) documents rural and town lifestyles and includes reconstructed farmsteads. The glass-skinned cube it stands next to is the **Kunstmuseum Celle** (Tues–Sun 10am–5pm; €5 or free Fri; ⓦwww.kunst .celle.de), whose night-time illumination of exhibits in the window – and colours that wash over its facade – prompts its billing as the world's first 24-hour museum. Its largely post-1960s permanent art collection of works by modern giants such as Joseph Beuys reflects the tastes of the Hannover connoisseur, Robert Simon. Some space is also reserved for temporary exhibitions.

The Altstadt and around

Celle's old town lies east as parallel streets that run up to the Schloss. All are worth a stroll for the row upon row of half-timbered buildings erected over two hundred years from the sixteenth century onwards to bequeath a streetscape that's among North Germany's most historic. Your introduction is likely to be **Stechbahn**, a broad artery and one-time ducal games-ground that leads from the Schloss into the Altstadt. Duke Otto the Magnanimous is said to have come a cropper here during a joust in 1471 – a horseshoe outside the court chemist, Löwenapotheke, marks where he fell. The **Stadtkirche** (Tues–Sun 10am–6pm) opposite received a makeover during renovation of the Schloss under the mastery of Tornielli, who here matches his craftsmanship with exquisite artistry: a stucco garden of flowers on the barrel-vaulted roof, twelve apostles stride from pillars and in the choir he provides an intimation of paradise in the flowers that smother the original Gothic vaults. A pictorial Bible that wraps around the gallery and one of the finest and frilliest Baroque organs in North Germany, which was played by Johann Sebastian Bach himself, completes the picture. A 234-step tramp up the tower (April–Oct daily 10am–noon & 1–6pm; €1) provides both views of Celle's roofscape and a platform for a town trumpeter (9.30am & 5.30pm). At the end of Stechbahn, tourists pose for a holiday snap wearing the neck manacles that shamed miscreants in public in the 1700s, and quite overlook the venerable Gothic **Rathaus** beside it, remodelled in Weser Renaissance style in 1571.

So to that **half-timbering**: the finest streets fan out east and south from the Rathaus. Upper storeys jut over the narrow streets to eke extra space and beams are carved with a carnival of allegorical figures and God-fearing maxims – "He who trusts in God has built well" is a favourite – in a typically late-medieval marriage of folklore and religious piety. **Zöllnerstrasse**, the continuation of Stechbahn eastwards, is a pictorial textbook of sixteenth-century beam decoration: its development traces from early step- or branch-and-tendril motifs, via zigzag ropework and rosettes to squiggles that ape clasps on furniture.

Turn right from the end of Stechbahn instead, however, for **Hoppenhauer Haus** (1532) on the corner of Poststrasse and Rundestrasse, one of the ritziest pieces of carving in town, its scrollwork and rural scenes created as a statement of prestige by a ducal official. Grosser Plan further south is worth a look for a handsome – and usually quieter – wedge-shaped piazza. Some of the most enjoyable carving lies on less grand streets north of Zöllnerstrasse. Look at Neue Strasse 11 for a bawdy monster that defecates coins in a sermon about the fate that awaits the avaricious in hell.

The area southeast of the Altstadt was the town's Jewish ghetto, though you'd never know until you step inside the **synagogue** at Im Kreise 23–24 (Tues–Thurs noon–5pm, Fri 9am–2pm, Sun 11am–4pm; free). The oldest in North Germany, it occupies a half-timbered house that survived Kristallnacht in 1938. Its original interior was destroyed during that Nazi purge and, poignantly, some articles for its replacement were donated by survivors of the nearby Bergen-Belsen concentration camp (see p.716), who worshipped here after liberation. A small museum within has an exhibition of local Jewish life. From here it's a five-minute walk to the **Französischer Garten** which borders the southern Altstadt. The name probably derives from the French gardeners employed by Celle duke Georg-Wilhelm; the mature parkland itself is in naturalistic English style.

Eating and drinking

Café Müller am Französischer Garten Südwall 33. Take the lovely gardens south of the centre, add in a grand villa, light lunches and excellent gateaux and you have an elegant spot for a break from the centre.

Central Café Am Heiligen Kreuz 5 ☎05141/223 20. Everything from Argentinean steaks to good fish offered on a wide-ranging menu of lighter modern German cooking. In summer a leafy beer garden is a great place for a beer – of which there are six on tap.

Endtenfang Hannoversche Str. 55–56 ☎05141/20 10. The *Fürstenhof* boasts one of the finest chefs in the region, Hans Sobotaka, whose gourmet creations such as saddle of venison with walnuts and hibiscus jus, parsley roots and baked apple jelly, have earned him a Michelin star. Four-course dinner menus cost €65, simpler lunch menus are €39. Sister restaurant *Palio* serves superb Italian. Closed Sun & Mon.

Fachwerk Schuhstr. 25 Maximalist wallpaper, leather sofas, tapas and cocktails in a lounge bar that's the antidote to the heritage shtick elsewhere. Closed Mon.

Raths-Weinschenke Zöllnerstr. 29. Located in a verdant courtyard, Celle's oldest and cosiest *Weinstube* is a charmer, with half-barrel seats in a tiny interior. Foodwise expect cheese plates and quiche. Eve only except Sat, closed Sun & Mon.

Ratskeller Markt 14 ☎05141/290 99. A little pricey, but quality regional cuisine – look for lamb grazed on the Lüneburger Heide – and dining beneath the Gothic arches of the oldest restaurant in North Germany (1378) is probably worth paying extra for. Closed Sun eve.

Schifferkrug Speicherstr. 9 ☎05141/34 47 76. A hotel restaurant that's an old Celle favourite, with a historic ambience to go with an upmarket traditional menu featuring Lüneburg lamb.

Weinkeller Postmeister von Hinüber Zöllnerstr.
25 ☎ 05141/284 44. Historic cellar restaurant that
prepares quality Mediterranean-flavoured contemporary cooking from seasonal produce. Eve only,
closed Sun & Mon.

Zum Ältesten Haus Neue Str. 27
☎ 05141/48 73 99. More lamb-based regional
favourites – moorland mutton goulash or lamb chop
– alongside solid German dishes in a traditional
half-timbered tavern.

The Lüneburg Heath

Between Celle and Lüneburg lie the open heathlands of the **LÜNEBURG HEATH** (Lüneburger Heide). Minimally populated with farming villages of Lower Saxony red-brick and beams, the area has been mostly drained of its original moorland to stand as an uncultivated rolling landscape area famed for the heather that lays a carpet of dusty purple blooms from mid-August, auguring in a month of village fêtes to crown a Heather Queen: the week-long Heather Blossom Festival at Amelinghausen from the middle Saturday in August is the largest. Being mixed with broom, gorse and juniper, the heather also produces excellent honey and adds flavour to the shaggy Heidschnucke lambs, which are grazed here year-round by shepherds with a weakness for traditional floppy hats and waistcoats. The favoured grazing ground is conservation area the **Natur-schutzpark Lüneburger Heide**, centred on the Wilseder Berg, a hill that at 169m is easily the highest point in the park. Alongside sheep, you can spy from its summit a couple of the huge megaliths that dot the area, known locally as **Hünengräber** (giants' graves). The hill is accessed from pretty village Undeloh just off the A7 west of Lüneburg, but limited public transport makes visiting tricky without a bike or a car – tourist offices in Celle and Lüneburg are your best sources of information or, for pre-planning, area tourism website ⓦwww.lueneburger-heide.de is useful, though there's not much in English.

Nowithstanding tracks that crisscross the heather, the most popular attraction of the area is **Vogelpark Walsrode** (daily: March–Oct 10am–5/7pm; Nov–Feb 10am–4pm; €14; ⓦwww.vogelpark-walsrode.de) – Europe's largest bird park stages free-flight displays to buttress attractions of its raised treewalk, penguin enclosure and rainforest house. It's at the western fringe of the heath, 2km from the Bahnhof at Walsrode; bus #51 goes direct from the station.

Bergen-Belsen

The heath's place in history is bound up with World War II. Field Marshal Montgomery accepted unconditional German surrender here on May 4, 1945. And on the opposite side of raw heathland from Walsrode, just south of Belsen, the Allies first reeled at Hitler's "Final Solution" in the **BERGEN-BELSEN** concentration camp 22km northwest of Celle. Established to hold prisoners of war in 1940 – around eighteen thousand Russian prisoners from the eastern front perished of hunger, cold and disease here in 1941–42 – the camp became infamous as the SS detention camp in which fifty thousand Jews died, most of starvation and disease under its commanding officer, the "Beast of Belsen" Josef Kramer. An exhibition centre at the **Belsen Gedenkstätte** (daily 9am–6pm; free; ⓦwww.bergen-belsen.de) tracks the camp's history, including its use postwar as a "displaced persons' camp" for Jews emigrating to Israel. Even though a documentary of the liberation tackles the atrocities with thought-provoking interviews, the footage, which was screened in UK cinemas, remains genuinely shocking. Much of the area is being reclaimed by silver birch and pine – the buildings were razed by the British to prevent a typhus epidemic – but that doesn't make a walk where the Allies discovered around twelve thousand unburied corpses on April 15, 1945, any less disturbing. Camp paths and the track of the outer fence cut like scars through the forest, barrack foundations remain free of trees. Similarly blunt statements of the dead within mass graves appal even though the statistics are infamous. A haunting personal dimension is the memorial to teen diarist Anne Frank, who succumbed to typhus weeks before the liberation in March 1945.

Bus #11 travels twice a day from Celle Bahnhof to the Bergen-Gedenkstätte but double-check the return – limited to one direct in late afternoon at the time of writing, two with a change.

Lüneburg

Despite the richness of its architecture, **LÜNEBURG** is founded on the prosaic. Local salt mines were already being worked by the monks of St Michaelis here in 956 AD, and when Lüneburg's citizens wrested independence from the Guelphic princes in 1371 and signed up to the mercantile Hanseatic League, exports of its "white gold" via Lübeck catapulted the town into the highest echelons of affluence. In its Renaissance heyday, Lüneburg was Europe's largest salt producer, only to shrink suddenly into obscurity as its Hanseatic market waned. Salt production ceased in 1980. The flip-side of stagnation is preservation, however. Without funds for building, Lüneburg has had to make do with an Altstadt full of Hanseatic step-gables and brickwork like twisted rope. Indeed, salt continues to shape the town – subsidence of underground deposits causes the Altstadt to lean at decidedly woozy angles. Lüneburg's Altstadt is ordered around two squares: **Am Markt**, the civic heartland above its historic port, the Wasserviertel; and elongated **Am Sande** at its southern end.

Arrival, information and accommodation

Lüneburg's **Hauptbahnhof** and ZOB **bus station** lie east of its centre, with the Altstadt accessible from either end of Bahnhofstrasse in front. The **tourist office** (all year Mon–Fri 9am–6pm; May–Oct Sat 9am–4pm, Sun 10am–4pm; Nov–April Sat 9am–2pm; ☎04131/207 66 20, ⓦwww.lueneburg.de) is in the Rathaus on Am Markt. **Bike rental** is at the Hauptbahnhof. Alongside a decent quota of mid-range hotels, **private rooms** (❶–❷) and holiday homes offer **accommodation** in historic Altstadt houses, often handy as a base from which to explore the Lüneburg Heath. All beds can be booked through tourist information (☎0800/220 50 05). You can pitch a tent at *Rote Schleuse* (☎04131/79 15 00, ⓦwww.camproteschleuse.de) by the river Ilmenau 4km south of the centre; it's signposted off the main road south from the centre towards the B4.

Altstadt Gästehaus Drewes Wale Auf der Altstadt 43 ☎04131/70 91 70, ⓦwww.altstadt -gaestehaus.de. Sixteenth-century brewery whose cosy rooms have been opened up to create five apartments with kitchenettes – modern, without sacrificing period character. Call ahead to ensure the owner is around. ❹

Bergström Bei der Lüner Mühle ☎04131/30 80, ⓦwww.bergstroem.de. Four-star facilities include a pool and gym in a well-sited hotel in the Wasserviertel overlooking the river. Some suites

retain the historic character of its renovated mill complex. It also has a good waterside café and restaurant. ❺–❻

Bremer Hof Lüner Str. 12–13 ☎04131/22 40, ⓦwww.bremer-hof.de. Well located near the Wasserviertel, with room prices varying according to style: traditional-charming in a historic merchant's house or comfy-bland in a modern block behind. Those with a shower are cheaper. A fine restaurant specializes in local lamb. ❹–❻

DJH hostel Soltauer Str. 133 ☏ 04131/418 64, ⓦ www.djh-niedersachsen.de. South of the centre near the university. Bus #5011 or #5012 to "Scharnhornstrasse" drop you close by, but services are meagre in the evening. From €22.50.

Scheffler Bardowicker Str. 7 ☏ 04131/200 80, ⓦ www.hotel-scheffler.de. Rooms are a little dull compared to the bags of character in the public areas, but this is a perfectly acceptable family-run hotel, well located just off the Markt. ❹

Das Stadthaus Am Sande 25 ☏ 04131/444 38, ⓦ www.das-stadthaus.de. A hotel since 1880 on Lüneburg's southern square, this has been renovated into a rather characterful place with modern art on the walls and reproduction antique beds. Front rooms have balconies. ❹

Around the Markt

No building expresses Lüneburg's former standing better than the **Rathaus**, begun in the thirteenth century and extended over five hundred years. The buttoned-up frontage is Baroque at its most balanced, refined from the dull early variant but not yet smothered by Rococo froth, and here topped by a peal of Meissen china bells that ring out the ditties of Lüneburg composer J.A.P. Schulz. Within are rooms of Germany's finest Renaissance town hall (tours in German daily 10am, 11.30am, 1.30pm & 3pm; €4.50). City fathers saved the firework display of gilt and paintwork for the Court of Justice (Gerlichtslaube), with its inscription promising equal judgement for rich and poor and stained glass of "nine good heroes", although it is run a close second by the beamed roof of the Prince's Hall (Fürstensaal). The real treasure is the Council's Great Chamber (Grosse Ratstube): not nearly so flashy as previous rooms, but whose carving by Westphalian master Albert von Soest is first-rate German Renaissance. One tympanum depicts the agonies of the damned in particularly vivid detail.

Outside on **Am Markt**, the fountain, crowned by Roman moon goddess Luna, and half-crescents on the Rathaus's exterior suggest a romantic derivation of Lüneburg – actually a conceit dreamed up with the intellectual flowering of the Renaissance for a name that is just a corruption of the Lombard *hiluni* or refuge. The gables carved as dolphins on **Heinrich-Heine-Haus** to the right of the Rathaus date from the same era. The house was home to the Romantic poet's parents – Heine is said to have penned his famous *Lorelei* here in the 1820s – but he was scathing about the cultural backwater that was contemporary Lüneburg, and pined in one letter for the "*Makkaroni und Geistesspeise*" (literally, macaroni and spiritual food) of Berlin.

Behind the Rathaus, via Waagestrasse, some of the most photogenic residential streets in Lüneburg lie off Auf dem Meere, making up in kooky charm what they lack in civic grandeur. Salt subsidence that has caused the streetscape to sway drunkenly also affected St Michaelskirche; its pillars lean dangerously like a Gothic-horror film-set. If you go the other way from Am Markt, up Bardo-wicker Strasse on its northeast corner, you arrive at sailors' and artisans' church **St Nikolai**. Although its 93m spire is a product of overzealous renovation in the late 1800s, the French-style high Gothic nave fretted with star vaulting is genuine, best interpreted as a statement of pride by a merchant population at the high point of its prosperity. It's a sentiment repeated in the ambulatory on an altarpiece of the town from c.1444 – the earliest portrait of Lüneburg is recognizable by the crooked spire of St Johannis (see opposite) – and a nearby work that sees Abraham breaking bread outside medieval Lüneburg rather than the Promised Land.

The sailors' church lies en route to the **Wasserviertel** below. The clamour of Hanseatic trade in the port on the River Ilmenau has long been replaced by the civilized buzz of dockside restaurants, although a 1330s cargo crane (renovated in the late 1700s) and a former herring warehouse topped with a cargo-lighter weathervane bear witness to its former life. A wander through streets above reveals fine merchants' houses; those on Rotenhahnstrasse are the oldest.

Around Am Sande

Grosse Bäckerstrasse leads off the south side of Am Markt to conclude at elongated square **Am Sande** for a lesson in step-gables, many leaning dangerously due to salt subsidence. The square's most impressive building, the twin-gabled **Schwarzes Haus** (Black House), now the Chamber of Commerce and Industry, was built in 1548 as a brewery, during an era when malt rivalled salt in civic importance, and Lüneburg boasted over eighty breweries. The old **Kronen-Brauerei** (Tues–Sun 1–4.30pm; free), on Heiligengeiststrasse off the west end of the square, retains a traditional brewery over several floors; pick up leaflets in English to guide you through the process of traditional beer-making.

Am Sande is dominated by the brick church of **St Johannis**, or rather its 108m spire that is off-kilter by 2m; a dubious tale relates that a haycart thwarted a suicide jump by the distressed architect, who later slipped off his bar stool while celebrating his luck and died. Five naves create a spacious interior whose pillars frame a late medieval altar, its panels a sermon of Passion and Resurrection. More impressive is an organ that fills the rear wall, which inspired a young keyboardist named Johann Sebastian Bach to great things and remains one of the biggest and most sonorous in North Germany. Times of daily concerts are posted by the church door. Just by the church's corner, a neo-Gothic **watertower** (April–Oct daily 10am–5pm; Nov–March Tues–Sun 10am–5pm; €3.70) provides aerial views of Am Sande.

From Am Sande, Heiligengeiststrasse leads southwest to eventually emerge at Lambertiplatz, beyond which is the once all-important salt works. On a street just off here, in one half of a former warehouse (the rest is occupied by a supermarket), the **Deutsches Salzmusem** (April–Sept Mon–Fri 9am–5pm, Sat & Sun 10am–5pm; Oct–March daily 10am–5pm; €5; ⓦ www.salzmuseum .de) explains more than you're ever likely to want to know about salt production;

▲ Am Sande, Lüneburg

enter through the train carriage. The salt infatuation continues further south in salt-water baths of spa and pools centre **Salztherme** (Mon–Sat 10am–11pm, Sun 8am–9pm; from €7.90; Ⓦwww.kurzentrum.de) ten minutes further south of Lambertiplatz via Sülztorstrasse.

Eating

The Wasserviertel is first choice for dining and drinking alfresco, and Schröder-strasse, off the Markt, is lined with cafés for a quick bite.

Bremer Hof Lüner Str. 12–13 ℡04131/22 40. The restaurant of the hotel prepares a good country-modern menu that's strong on local specialities such as Lüneburger Heide lamb with apples and cranberries, served in a lovely historic dining room.
Kronen-Brauhaus Heiligengeiststr. 39 ℡04131/71 32 00. No-nonsense *Bürgerlich* such as pork and beef steaks with *Bratkartoffeln* at low prices in a cheerful *Hausbrauerei* off Am Sande.
Schallander Am Stintmarkt 10 ℡04131/328 00. Claiming the largest section of riverfront in Lüneburg's Wasserviertel, this cheap place offers ciabattas, pasta and salads as well as the usual meat and spuds.

Sushi Bar Schröderstr. 8 ℡04131/24 83 48. Not just sushi, but pan-Asian dishes such as Thai curries and stir-fries. A popular spot for lunch among locals.
Zum Alten Brauhaus Grapengeisserstr. 11 ℡04131/72 12 78. One of Germany's oldest sausage houses, this dark, atmospheric restaurant centred around a galleried merchant hallway prepares the full range of brewery classics. Closed Sun am.
Zum Heidkrug Am Berge 5 ℡04131/241 60. Modern gourmet cuisine inspired by regional flavours and beautifully presented by a former Michelin-star-winning chef, Michael Röhm. Closed Sun–Tues.

West Lower Saxony and Bremen

Though the western half of the state is the least interesting in scenery, it is here that you first sense the coast as you progress up Germany. Much of the northwest incorporates East Frisia (Ostfriesland), which owes as much to Holland in landscape as it does in its dialect, Plattdeutsch, also known as Low German as a nod to its coastal plains. Definitively flat and notoriously damp, the area is sparsely populated, with only the cheerful university and episcopal centre **Osnabrück** qualifying for the title of city (and then only just). Germany peters out as the East Frisian islands arc around the coast like a barrage in the North Sea. Favoured by Germans as escapist nature retreats and with broad sandy beaches, the little-developed islands are spectacularly unsuited for fast-moving modern tourism, largely due to transport that is dependent on shifting tides and long-stay accommodation in holiday houses. Western destinations in Lower Saxony such as one-time ducal town **Oldenburg** or artists' village **Worpswede** are best treated as day-trips from **Bremen**, a state in its own right and no less proud of its independence today as it was throughout a mercantile history in the Hanseatic League. A feather in its cap is that the Markt was accredited World Heritage status by UNESCO in 2004. Once brusque and utilitarian, its port **Bremerhaven** is quietly reinventing itself through billion-euro investments in museums and architecture.

Osnabrück

Welcome to the happiest town in Germany. A poll found citizens of **OSNABRÜCK**, the largest city in western Lower Saxony, more content than those anywhere else in the nation, inspiring a marketing campaign in *Stern* magazine in 2006 that declared *"Ich komm zum Glück aus Osnabrück"* (I'm lucky to be from Osnabrück). A friendly small-scale city of modest good looks, kept alive by its university, it has much to be happy about despite a notoriously damp climate. In 1648 after more than four years of negotiations here and in Münster 60km south, Catholic and Protestant signatures dried on the Peace of Westphalia and the political and religious inferno of the Thirty Years' War was finally doused. Osnabrück has treasured its diplomacy of peace ever since. Her two great sons, Justus Möser and Erich Maria Remarque, dreamed of ennobled, free workers and railed against war's insanity respectively, and today Osnabrück proudly declares herself "Die Friedenstadt" (Peace City), host of Nobel Peace Prize winners Henry Kissinger and the Dalai Lama and home of the Federal Fund for Peace Research and international child-relief agency Terre des Hommes. Perhaps it's no surprise that its finest museum-gallery pays homage to a Jewish artist murdered at Auschwitz.

Maps reveal the city's origins as an episcopal town gathered around a Dom founded by Frankish king Charlemagne, and the Neustadt huddled around the church of St Johann. When the two merged in the thirteenth century, Osnabrück blossomed as a staging post on a trade crossroads, its clout shored up by membership of the North Sea-based Hanseatic League. Wartime damage has claimed much of that history, and unlike its rival Münster, Osnabrück scorned a complete rebuild. Old-world charm among the bland pedestrianized centre is focused around the renovated **Markt** and **Dom** areas.

Arrival and information

Osnabrück shares an international **airport** with Münster, midway between the two cities about 40km southeast. Minibus #X150 shuttles to the Hauptbahnhof (40min); expect to pay around €50 for a taxi to the centre. The **Hauptbahnhof** is just outside the city walls to the southeast. Another station north of the centre, Bahnhof Hasetor, is for local trains going north. A helpful **tourist office** (Mon–Fri 9.30am–6pm, Sat 10am–4pm; ☎0541/323 22 02, ⓦwww.osnabrueck.de) is just off the Markt at Bierstrasse 22–23. Alongside the usual souvenirs and cycling maps, it sells the **Kulturkarte day-ticket** (€7.50), which provides free entry into all museums. The oval Altstadt is easily walkable, but a bike may be useful should you go out of town; **bike rental** is at Fahrrad Praxis, Martinstrasse 9 (☎0151/14 91 73 76), or Radstation Osnabrück at the Hauptbahnhof, Theodor-Heuss-Platz 2 (☎0541/25 91 31). The biggest **festival** of the year is Maiwoche, a ten-day extravaganza of music and entertainment, usually from the second Friday in May.

Accommodation

Most **accommodation** is in or around the Altstadt, with the exception of the youth hostel. The nearest **campsite**, *Campingplatz Attersee* (Zum Attersee; ☎0541/12 41 47, ⓦwww.camping-attersee.de), is around 7km west of the city near junction 71 of the A1; take bus #13 to "Zum Attersee".

DJH Osnabrück Iburger Str. 183 ☎0541/542 84, ⓦwww.jugendherberge.de. In the city's southern limit, near the Schölberg park; take bus #21 to "Kinderhospital". From €20.50.

Dom Kleine Domsfreiheit 5 ☎0541/35 83 50, ⓦwww.dom-hotel-osnabrueck.de. Nothing flashy, just a small, welcoming hotel well located behind the Dom with inoffensive decor of pale-wood furniture and pastel walls. ❹

Intour Maschstr. 10 ☎0541/96 38 60, ⓦwww
.intourhotel.de. Popular family-run three-star on a
quiet side-street west of the Altstadt, a 10min walk
from the Hegertor bars, with simple, good-value
accommodation. ❷–❸

Nikolai Kamp 1 ☎0541/ 33 13 00. No looker from
the outside and easy to overlook above a shopping
centre, this home of 1980s decor is nevertheless
bright and central. ❹

Penthouse Backpackers Möserstr. 19
☎0541/600 96 06, ⓦwww.penthousebp.com.
North of the station on the top floor of an office
block – hence the name – this is a friendly, small
hostel, cheerfully shabby and with an outdoor
terrace for barbecues. Eight- and ten-bed dorms,
bright rooms, two en suite, laundry and free
internet and breakfasts. Dorms €14–18, rooms ❷.

Steigenberger Hotel Remarque Natruper-Tor-
Wall 1 ☎0541/609 60, ⓦwww.hotelremarque
.de. Just outside the Altstadt, the premier
address in Osnabrück maintains an air of
relaxed elegance for all its modern decor.
Deluxe rooms, with wet-room showers, are
worth the little extra. ❺

Walhalla Bierstr. 24 ☎0541/349 10,
ⓦwww.hotel-walhalla.de. The connoisseur's three-
star choice, smack in the heart of town. Decor
is suitable for a 300-year-old half-timbered inn
– think warm-hued fabrics and old beams – albeit
on the historic side in terms of space. ❺–❻

The Dom

In 780 AD, Charlemagne thrust his standard into the Hase's banks and vowed to
bring Christianity to the Saxons on the far bank. Just as his pioneering mission
grew into a town, so his church has swelled into the **Dom** that sits on its own
square near Osnabrück's birthplace. Begun as a Romanesque basilica, it was
built at a leisurely pace over five hundred years with each era stamping its mark,
not all successfully. Renaissance builders enlarged the girth of the southwest
tower rather than re-forge a prize bell, which was cast too large for it. Its smaller
sister tower remains to lend the facade a lopsided appearance.

The interior speaks of strength and dignity in powerful Gothic columns and
arches that parade to a luminous choir where the relics of French saints Crispin
and Crispinian, who renounced Roman nobility for humble cobbling to spread
the word, were venerated as Charlemagne's gift. The star pieces are the bronze
font in the baptistry, cast in 1226, and Lower Saxony's largest Triumphkreuz (1240),
a blaze of gilded evangelist symbols. There's also a fine, Gothic stone Madonna in
the north transept, a picture of serenity as she tramples a serpent, and through iron
gates that play *Alice in Wonderland* tricks with perspective, a late Gothic triptych
(1517) is hidden in a chapel off the square ambulatory. More masterpieces,
including an ivory comb said to be Charlemagne's, are in the **Diözesanmuseum**
(Tues–Sun 10am–6pm; €5). Among the Romanesque crucifixes studded with
coloured jewels, Roman cameos and bishopric rings are devotional carvings by the
Master of Osnabrück, the anonymous sculptor behind the city's most distinguished
works of the Middle Ages.

The Markt

The spiritual heart of Osnabrück, the **Markt** is a triangle of cobbles lined
with Hanseatic-style step-gables in ripe shades of saffron and terracotta. On its
long side, kings and emperors glower from a stolid **Rathaus**, for all their looks,
nineteenth-century newcomers that replaced allegorical statues as Germany
swaggered into a new empire, its confidence so high that Kaiser Wilhelm I is
cast as the right-hand man of Charlemagne in the centre. However, Osnabrück
has reason to be proud of its Gothic hall. Protestant factions met here for over
four years to broker their half of the Peace of Westphalia (the Catholics were
in Münster) and unpick the knotted conflicts of the Thirty Years' War that
had brought German cities to their knees. Once signed by both, city fathers
stood on the Rathaus steps on October 25, 1648, and proclaimed the carnage
over, a declaration greeted at first with disbelief by the crowd, then by tears

and a spontaneous outburst of hymns. As a contemporary pamphlet relates: "Osnabrück and all the world rejoices, the joyful people sing, Flags fly bravely … I am only sorry for the poor swordsmiths for they have nothing to do." Envoys of the Protestant Swedish and German factions stare gloomily above the bench seats on which they hammered out the deal in the Friedenssaal (Mon–Fri 8am–6pm, Sat 9am–4pm, Sun 10am–4pm; free) and a replica of the famous deed is in the Schatzkammer alongside the Rathaus's treasure, the fourteenth-century Kaiserpokal – the story goes that incoming councillors had to prove their worth by downing in one a draught from this gold goblet.

Right of the Rathaus is the Stadtwaage guilds' weights and measures office and next to it Gothic church the **Marienkirche** (April–Sept 10am–noon & 3–5pm; Oct–March 10.30–noon & 2.30–4pm), whose haggard Christ splayed on a medieval Triumphkreuz commands attention, as does a Passion altar from Antwerp in the choir. Look, too, in the ambulatory for the tombstone slab of Justus Möser (1720–94). When not poring over the finances of the town's last prince-bishop, this articulate heavyweight of the German Enlightenment pioneered a vision of a state whose citizens were free of the dictates of sovereign rulers. Hailed as both a people's champion and an intellectual star, Möser is honoured with a memorial before the Dom. Before you ascend the tower for a view over the Markt, there's a Stations of the Cross cycle by Renaissance hero Albrecht Dürer, created five years before the Passion altar in 1510, centuries ahead in artistry.

Another favourite son is Erich Maria Remarque, author of World War I classic *All Quiet on the Western Front*. If your German's up to it, a text-heavy museum (Tues–Fri 10am–1pm & 3–5pm; Sat & Sun 11am–5pm; free) opposite the Marienkirche chronicles his life.

Around the Markt

Behind the Rathaus, the conjoined high-streets of **Krahnstrasse** and **Bierstrasse** house the best of the buildings that survived Allied bombs. A former inn Erich Maria Remarque acclaimed for its *"erstklassig Essen"* (first-class eating), now a hotel (see opposite), *Walhalla* hosts a troupe of saints and cherubs on its beams, beneath which the devil is caught squatting on a chamberpot. Gourmet restaurant *La Vie* next door (see p.724) is an elegant piece of Neoclassicism, and at Krahnstrasse 7 **Haus Willmann** is a class act, with a relief of Adam and Eve and roses carved in outline. More historic charm is in the nest of streets behind Bierstrasse known as the **Hegetorviertel**, a triangular area that squirrels away Osnabrück's best shopping and a bar district. All alleys thread south to the eponymous **Hegetor** gate in the former city walls, a Neoclassical salute to soldiers who fought at Waterloo. Before it on Bucksmauer is the Bucksturm where medieval guards kept watch, first for marauding invaders then over prisoners. North of the Hegertorviertel, at the end of Bierstrasse, is the Gothic **Dominikanerkirche** (Tues–Fri 11am–6pm, Sat & Sun 10am–6pm; €3; ⓦwww.osnabrueck.de/kunsthalle) – its Dominican monks long gone, and now a spectacular canvas for modern art exhibitions.

The museums and south Altstadt

Although the defence walls have disappeared, their embrace is felt as you face the ring road that replaces the old defences. Across Heger-Tor-Wall lies the **Kulturgeschichtliches Museum** (Museum of Cultural History; Tues–Fri 11am–6pm, Sat & Sun 10am–6pm; €5; ⓦwww.osnabrueck.de/kgm), a chronicle of local history in, among other things, weaponry, folk costume and sculpture. Its archeology wing features Roman items unearthed from a garrison town near Detmold where Germanic tribes triumphed in battle and took a decisive step towards a fledgling country. A better reason to visit is its extension **Felix-Nussbaum-Haus** (same ticket & hours), principally for the dialogue between architecture and art created by Daniel Libeskind. The architect behind Berlin's acclaimed Jewish Museum here creates a savagely oppressive building, its angular rooms slashed by windows, its long corridors sloping upwards to constrict the visitor in echo of the disorientation and oppression of Osnabrück-born Jewish painter Felix Nussbaum. His Surrealism-lite darkens into cadaver-like figures with the onset of Nazi persecution, when he was forced into hiding in Brussels and began to use pencil and charcoal for fear the oils might reveal his hideaway. More crushing is the despair of his final works: *Self-portrait with Jewish Identity Card* and *Triumph Of Death*, painted just before his death in Auschwitz in 1944. Paradoxically, the period saw **Villa Schlikker** behind (same ticket) serve as a local Nazi headquarters. It now houses a section on the "Topography of Terror" as part of a permanent display of life in the twentieth century.

South along Heger-Tor-Wall is a yellow **Schloss** of mid-1600s vintage – prince-bishop Ernst August I pointed to Rome's Palazzo Madama as a model for his architects and Germany received one of its first Baroque palaces. Its current incarnation is as a university. Opposite is Osnabrück's finest private building, the **Ledenhof**, created by a merchant who abutted a Renaissance manor and tower to a Gothic warehouse. Its psychedelic stripes and a facade like a stage flat are all original.

Eating, drinking and nightlife

The most central bar-scene is in the west Altstadt streets by the Hegertor, the so-called Hegertorviertel. Nightclub *Alando-Palais* (Ⓦwww.alando-palais.de), near the Hauptbahnhof at Pottgraben 58, hosts nights of house, soul, classics and charts in a glitzy ballroom from Thursday to Saturday. Booklet *Mosquito* from bars and the tourist office is a good source of listings, also at Ⓦwww.mosquito-os.de.

Restaurants

La Vie Krahnstr. 1–2 ℡0541/33 11 50. Head chef Thomas Bühner creates Mediterranean-influenced gourmet creations in this smart restaurant – not simply one of the finest addresses in North Germany, but a regular name in the finest creative cooking in Germany. Degustation menus cost €108. Eve only, closed Mon.

L'Italiano Herrenteichstr. 28 ℡0541/80 27 03. Glossy modern Italian, its restaurant furnished in dark woods and ruby lacquer, its terrace canopied by trees beside the Hase canal. All the usuals – pizza from €7 – plus Argentinean steaks.

Pferde haben keine Flügel Am Kamp 81–83 ℡0541/202 79 10. The most atmospheric option among the chain restaurants on the high street is this tapas bar, rough-walled and candle-lit. Plates cost around €5.

Rampendahl Hasestr. 35 ℡0541/245 35. Full traditional meals in the eve and a couple of plates for lunch in a brewery that produces a good range of *Pils* and dark beers.

Ratskeller Am Markt 30 ℡0541/233 88. "Quality and tradition" is the motto, which means the town-hall restaurant is a credit to its ilk. Expect hearty traditional dishes and regional specials. Closed Sun.

Weinkrüger Marienstr. 18 ℡0541/233 53. Above-average German cooking in a half-timbered house whose capacious interior has been fashioned into a cosy space of booths and beams. Eve only Mon–Fri.

Cafés and bars

Café Läer Krahnstr. 24. "*Die kunst zu geniessen*" ("the art of enjoyment") is the self-declared mantra of this cool split-level café in a Gothic mansion. Cakes are highly rated by locals and there are tasty organic quiches and fresh soups.

Café Leysieffer Krahnstr. 41. "*Himmlische*" (heaven-sent) is how Osnabrückers describe praline specials at the most famous café in town. Don't even glimpse the gateaux if you had a light lunch in mind.

Café Melange Marienstr. 9. A café with a space to suit all moods, from the chunk of rough medieval tower reinvented in Mediterranean style to a cottagey corner for tea. The menu ranges from chilli con carne to cakes. Closed Thurs.

Grüner Jager Am den Katherinenkirche 1. Good old student boozer that rambles through several rooms – love that faux baronial hall – and has a large glass-roofed beer hall.

Sausalitos Kommendereistr. 32. The usual quesadillas and cocktails from a perennially popular member of the Tex-Mex chain, housed in a candlelit barn behind the university.

Zwiebel Heger Str. 1. Snug, rather quirky *Kneipe* whose wood-panelled walls are pickled from over a century of drinking. Also rustles up snacks such as jacket potatoes.

Around Osnabrück

Osnabrück is sandwiched between two layers of woodland and meadows designated in 2004 as the UNESCO-listed **Geo Park TERRA.vita** (Ⓦwww .naturpark-terravita.de). With a network of 2300km of walking trails and 1500km of tracks, the area to the north is ideal for a bike day-trip (see p.721 for bike rental); the tourist office stocks maps of the area. The premier attraction is **Varusschlacht Museum und Park Kalkriese** (April–Oct daily 10am–6pm; Jan–March Tues–Sun 10am–5pm; €7; Ⓦwww.kalkriese-varusschlacht.de) at the park's northern edge, 20km north of Osnabrück – too far to cycle; **bus** #X275 from Osnabrück provides an erratic service to the museum and park (scheduled for a couple of times a day). When a British major and amateur archeologist unearthed a treasure-trove of silver Roman coins in summer 1987 he stumbled upon the site where Germanic tribes triumphed over their Roman overlords in 9 AD – a key skirmish in the so-called "Battle of the Teutoburg Forest", long thought to have taken place near Detmold, southeast. It was as much a defeat for ruler Publius Quinctilius Varus, a "greedy, self-important, amateurish weakling", according to Roman records, as it was a triumph for the fledgling German identity. Both the Second Reich and Hitler mythologized the victorious Arminius as a symbol of national strength, quietly overlooking that little was – nor still is – known about the Germanic commander. In 2000 the battlefield opened as an archeological park that's at its best in a rusted-steel tower. Here a museum narrates the political tectonics of the conflict and displays archeological finds, including a superb Roman cavalry mask. Its viewing platform provides a view over the battlefield itself where the legions were ambushed between woodland and marsh. As well as a replica section of Germanic rampart that ripples away across the field, the site has three themed pavilions for different perspectives on the area. A museum restaurant provides pseudo Roman and Germanic dishes, although this is perfect picnic territory.

Bad Essen and around

For a day-tour by car, continue east to **BAD ESSEN**, a quietly prosperous small town gathered around half-timbered Kirchplatz, a lovely market square where time seems to have stopped around three hundred years ago. Two kilometres north, just west of Harpenfeld, **Schloss Hünnefeld** (Wed–Fri by appointment, Sat 2–5pm, Sun 11am–5pm; €3; ℡05472/49 62, Ⓦwww.schloss-huennefeld.de) is a handsome Dutch-style Wasserschloss with a sweet **café** (Wed–Fri 3–6.30pm, Sat & Sun 11am–6.30pm) and Baroque gardens. A kilometre east is **Schloss Ippenburg**, a former residence of the Herrenhäuser family of Hannover-garden fame – they open to the public several times between April and September as Germany's largest private garden show; visit Ⓦwww.ippenburg.de for dates. From here, 3km east of Bad Essen, then 5km south through Barkahusen to reach the **Sauerierspuren** uphill off the main road. Its sandbank of fossilized footprints was laid when dinosaurs plodded across what was a tropical wetland – life-size fibreglass models loom above the site – and marks the start of a 4km forest circuit. Bad Essen is served by bus #275 from Osnabrück; the **tourist office** is at Lindenstrasse 39 (Mon–Fri 9am–5pm, Sat 9am–noon, Sun 2–5pm; T05472/949 20, Wwww.badessen.info). Foodwise, classy **hotel** *Höger's* (T05472/946 40, Wwww.hoegers.de; ❹), on Kirchplatz, also has a restaurant.

Tecklenburg

Southwest of Osnabrück, at the far end of the Teutoburger Wald, **TECKLEN-BURG** is small and uncomplicated with an Altstadt of wonky half-timbered buildings and cobbled lanes that is pure camera-fodder. Should you tire of loafing in cafés on the idyllic Markt, you can peruse displays of toys and folk culture in the **Puppenmuseum** (Sat & Sun 2–5pm; April–Oct also Tues & Thurs 2–5pm; €2) – follow the enamelled cobbles from the Markt – or ascend to the ruins of a sixteenth-century **Schloss** above the town. Partly rethought as Germany's largest open-air theatre, it hosts the Tecklenburger Festspielsommer from May to September; recent productions including *Footloose*, *Cinderella* and *Mozart Das Musical* typify its repertoire of crowd-pleaser musicals.

Tecklenburg is linked by regular **trains** from Osnabrück. The **tourist office** is on the Markt (Mon–Fri 9am–5pm; April–Oct also Sat & Sun 11am–4pm; T05482/938 90, Wwww.tecklenburg-touristik.de). For eating, head to traditional hotel *Drei Kronen* (T05482/225, Wwww.hoteldreikronen.de; ❹) in the central Altstadt of Tecklenburg.

Bremen

Never mind that the donkey, dog, cat and cockerel celebrated in the folk tale (see box below) forgot all about their goal as soon as they had a roof over their heads, brochures and innumerable souvenirs cheerfully proclaim **BREMEN** "*die Stadt der Stadtmusikanten*" (the Town of the Town Musicians). A more eloquent insight into what makes Bremen tick is that it is the smallest Land of the Federal Republic, a declaration of Bremeners' independence that is a leitmotif of a 1200-year history. In the twentieth century alone, Bremen proclaimed itself a socialist republic in 1918, and in 1949 it was the only former Land except Hamburg to wrest back its city-state accreditation. Small wonder that Germans view it as a stronghold of provocative politics. Blame the port. The oldest and largest in Germany after Hamburg, it has encouraged free-thinking attitudes as part and parcel of the wealth the city enjoyed after it received free-market rights in 965 AD, just two hundred years after Charlemagne's Bishop Willehad planted

---

Bremen's awesome foursome

It was the Grimm Brothers, during their collation of Lower Saxony folk tales, who popularized the age-old story of the **Bremener Stadtmusikanten** (Town Musicians of Bremen). The story goes that a donkey, dog, cat and cockerel, fearful of the slaughterhouse and cooking pot in their elderly years, journeyed to Bremen to seek a future as musicians. At nightfall they sought shelter in a house only to discover it occupied by thieves. Undeterred our heroes formed an animal pyramid, the cockerel at the top and donkey at its base, and unleashed their first performance – a caterwaul of brays, barks, meows and crowing. The robbers flee from the banshee outside their door and the four settled down to live happily ever after.

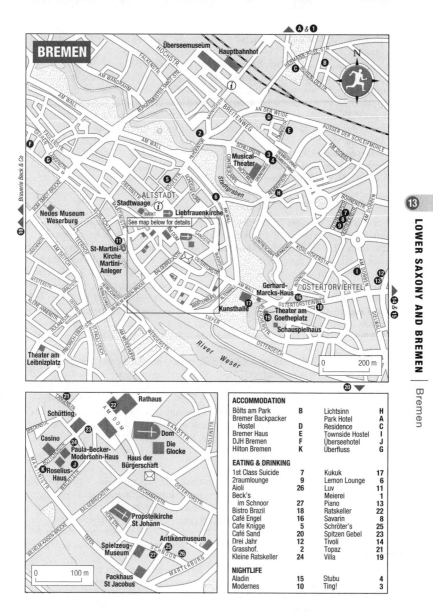

BREMEN

Überseemuseum
Hauptbahnhof

Musical-
Theater

ALTSTADT
Stadtwaage
Neues Museum
Weserburg
Liebfrauenkirche
See map below for details

St-Martini-
Kirche
Martini-
Anleger

Gerhard-
Marcks-Haus
OSTERTORVIERTEL
Kunsthalle
Theater am
Goetheplatz
Schauspielhaus

Theater am
Leibnizplatz

River Weser

0   200 m

Brauerie Beck & Co

Rathaus
Schütting
Casino
Paula-Becker-
Modersohn-Haus
Roselius-
Haus
Dom
Die
Glocke
Haus der
Bürgerschaft

Propsteikirche
St Johann

Antikenmuseum
Spielzeug-
Museum

Packhaus
St Jacobus

0   100 m

ACCOMMODATION			
Bölts am Park	B	Lichtsinn	H
Bremer Backpacker Hostel	D	Park Hotel	A
		Residence	C
Bremer Haus	E	Townside Hostel	I
DJH Bremen	F	Überseehotel	J
Hilton Bremen	K	Überfluss	G

EATING & DRINKING			
1st Class Suicide	7	Kukuk	17
2raumlounge	9	Lemon Lounge	6
Aioli	26	Luv	11
Beck's im Schnoor	27	Meierei	1
Bistro Brazil	18	Piano	13
Café Engel	16	Ratskeller	22
Cafe Knigge	5	Savarin	8
Café Sand	20	Schröter's	25
Drei Jahr	12	Spitzen Gebel	23
Grasshof.	2	Tivoli	14
Kleine Ratskeller	24	Topaz	21
		Villa	19

NIGHTLIFE			
Aladin	15	Stubu	4
Modernes	10	Ting!	3

---

a crucifix among the Saxons and Bremen was officially born. By the eleventh century, when Bremen was being acclaimed a Rome of the North, the grumbles of a merchant class about its ecclesiastical governors crescendoed until, emboldened by the city's admission to Europe's elite trading-club, the Hanseatic League, in 1358, they flared into open hostility. Its legacy is one-up manship in bricks and mortar – the Rathaus and chivalric *Roland* statue, both on UNESCO's World Heritage list, and the nearby Dom, are a squabble in stone.

Self-confidence and a university have made Bremen a liberal city free of conservative hang-ups. Few southern German cities would allow an architectural fantasy like **Böttcherstrasse** to be dreamed up in their midst. As appealing, Bremen feels far smaller than a place with a population of one million – only around half that number live within the confines of the city (as opposed to its municipal boundaries) – and the centre feels more like a large town than city-state. The majority of sights are within the **Altstadt** elongated along the north bank of the Weser, bound to the north by its former moat. When the city burst outside its defences in the nineteenth century, it created the **Ostertorviertel**, known as "das Viertel", and the home of a lively bar district that's only bettered in summer in the beer gardens that occupy former harbour promenade, the **Schlachte**.

Arrival, information and city transport

For once, the **airport** (Ⓦwww. airport-bremen.de) is close to the city centre, just 6km south; tram #6 zips you to the Hauptbahnhof in fifteen minutes; a taxi costs €13–15. Both the **Hauptbahnhof** and **bus station** are a ten-minute walk northwest of the Altstadt. Alongside a **tourist office** at the Hauptbahnhof (Mon–Fri 9am–7pm, Sat & Sun 9.30am–6pm; ☎01805/10 10 30, Ⓦwww .bremen-tourism.de), there's a large bureau just off the Markt on the corner of Liebfrauenkirchhof (Mon–Fri 10am–6.30pm, Sat & Sun 10am–4pm). Both sell the **ErlebnisCARD** (24hr €7.90, 48hr €9.90) for free public transport and up to fifty-percent discounts on admissions; each card covers one adult and two children under 14. Group cards (24hr €16, 48hr €19.90) for up to five people are good value.

The Altstadt is eminently walkable, but for attractions outside the centre you may need **buses** and **trams** (singles €2.15–2.70 depending on zone; *Tageskarte* day-card €5.70); the tourist board's ErlebnisCARD is better value. Travel information and tickets are available at an information booth at the bus station (Mon–Fri 7am–7pm, Sat 8am–6pm, Sun 9am–5pm). Being a university city, Bremen is also a cyclists' city – **bike rental** is from a cycle centre and workshop beside the Hauptbahnhof at Bahnhofsplatz 14 (Mon–Fri 10am–6pm, Sat 10am–2pm).

Accommodation

As ever, there's a clutch of **hotels** around the station, some fairly expensive for their facilities. Alongside two good independent **hostels**, Bremen has an excellent youth hostel. The nearest **campsite**, *Camping am Stadtwaldsee* (☎0421/841 07 89, Ⓦwww.camping-stadtwaldsee.de), occupies a spacious waterside site at the head of the Bürgerpark in the north of the city; take Universität-bound tram #6 to station NW1, then bus #28 to "Station Campingplatz".

Hotels

Bölts am Park Selvogtstr. 23 ☎0421/34 61 10, Ⓦwww.hotel-boelts.de. Family pension on a leafy street behind the Hauptbahnhof, which maintains the aura of a former residential house of the 1930s. Room decor is more modern. **❹**

Bremer Haus Löningstr. 16–20 ☎0421/329 40, Ⓦwww.hotel-bremer-haus.de. On a quiet side-road near the station, this is a rather elegant small hotel whose modernized rooms are good value for money. It also boasts a good restaurant with a garden terrace. **❹–❺**

Hilton Bremen Böttcherstr. 2 ☎0421/369 60, Ⓦwww.hilton.co.uk/bremen. Art Deco notes such as the staircase and Himmelsaal (ask for the key) seep in from Bremen's most famous street. Otherwise this business hotel is stylish – the skylit atrium is a knock-out – and comfortable with all the service of a superior four-star. **❻–❼**

Lichtsinn Rembertistr. 11 ☎0421/36 80 70, Ⓦwww.hotel-lichtsinn.de. A welcoming mid-range hotel moments from the Wallanlagen whose classic style makes a welcome change from the bland chains. Many rooms are individually decorated – one has a folk-painted four-poster. ⑤

Park Hotel Im Bürgerpark ℡0421 340 80, ⓦ www.park-hotel-bremen.de. A member of the "Leading Hotels of the World" – and with prices to match – the queen of Bremen's hotels is a palace of luxury in marble and parquet, with to-die-for views across the landscaped Bürgerpark and an ornamental lake. Superior rooms are worth the little extra, suites are sensational. Doubles from €255 ⑨.

Residence Hohenlohestr. 42 ℡0421/34 87 10, ⓦ www.hotelresidence.de. Despite its link to the City Partner chain, this small, family-run hotel behind the Hauptbahnhof retains a distinct character with individual decor in rooms, most modernized. Good breakfast buffet, too. ④–⑥

Überseehotel Wachtstr. 27–29 ℡0421/360 10, ⓦ www.ramada-treff.de. Not as expensive as you'd expect for a location just off the Markt, and with all the mod cons of a four-star member of one of Germany's leading hotel chains. ⑤–⑥

Überfluss Langenstr. 72 ℡0421/32 28 60, ⓦ www.hotel-ueberfluss.de. Bremen's only design hotel and far from cheap. You're paying for streamlined style and a location just 7m

above the river – waterfront rooms are worth the extra €15. ⑦

Hostels

Bremer Backpacker Hostel Emil-Waldmann-Str. 5–6 ℡0421/223 80 57, ⓦ www.bremer -backpacker-hostel.de. Friendly hostel on a quiet side-street 5min walk from the Hauptbahnhof. Bright and modern throughout, and not a bunk bed in sight in its six- and four-bed dorms. Dorms €17–19, rooms ②.

DJH Bremen Kalkstr. 6 ℡0421/163 820, ⓦ www.jugendherberge.de. The official hostel is in a modern building beside the Weser River – an 1816-vintage hostel-ship is moored outside (same contacts & price) – just west of Burgermeister-Smidt-Brücke in the western Altstadt. It's a 20min walk from the Hauptbahnhof or take tram #1 bound for Huchting and alight at "Am Brill". From €23.50.

Townside Hostel Am Dobben 62 ℡0421/780 15, ⓦ www.townside.de. A new hostel, in a large house moments from the Ostertorviertel bar scene. Dorms, including a women-only one, sleep four to seven, and all the usual facilities such as laundry and free wi-fi. Dorms €20–23, rooms ②.

The Markt

There's no better introduction to Bremen than one of the finest squares in North Germany. From the Hanseatic Cross set in cobbles to the flash patricians' houses, the UNESCO-listed **Markt** is a paean to mercantile prowess in Rococo and Renaissance. No surprise that a citizenry dedicated to declaring its independence from the Church created the **Rathaus** that dominates the square; the story goes that councillors determined its size by huddling voters into a rectangle in the early 1400s. That Gothic original, with trademark Hanseatic striped brickwork, is largely smothered beneath a flamboyant Weser Renaissance facade that makes this one of the prized buildings of North Germany. No piece is more extravagant than the balustrade. Among its allegorical images are the hen and chicks that found refuge from the flooded Weser on a sandbank and inspired Saxon fishermen to found a town – or so the story goes – and reliefs that mock the clergy as a crowing cock with sceptre and crown or depict a bare-chested man riding a bishop. Rooms within (tours Mon–Sat 11am, noon, 3pm & 4pm, Sun 11am & noon; €5; tickets from tourist office on Liebfrauenkirchhof) live up to the looks outside: there's an ornate Renaissance staircase; model trading-ships that salute the Hansa heritage; and in the Güldenkammer, gilded Jugendstil leather wall-hangings from Worpswede artist Heinrich Voegler.

Almost as renowned as the town hall is a warren of domed cellars that rambles beneath the Rathaus and Markt. Happiness, suggested Romantic poet Heinrich Heine, is escaping a North Sea storm to hunker down in the "peaceful warmth of the good Ratskeller of Bremen", and Goethe paid tribute to Bremen as a wine city of the north. The **Ratskeller** remains the world's foremost cellar of German wines (over 650 varieties) – you can admire some of the vast barrels in which it's stored over a meal (see p.735) or on a one-hour tour (March–Oct Fri 4pm; €9.50; tickets from Liebfrauenkirchhof tourist office), washed down with a glass of wine – just don't expect the cellar's *Rüdesheimer Apostelkeller*, the oldest drinkable wine in Germany, which was bottled in 1727.

Beside the Ratskeller's entrance, Bremen's fab four, the **Stadtmusikanten** (Town Musicians), pose in the pyramid that terrified a band of thieves and won them a home according to the folk tale popularized by the Brothers Grimm (see box, p.726) and re-enacted in the Domshof (daily May–early Oct noon & 1.30pm). Created by Bauhaus sculptor Gerhard Marcks in 1951, the bronze is Bremen's icon; they say it grants any wish made while holding the donkey's legs. Behind rise the spires of **Unser Lieben Frauen Kirche**, its stark three-nave interior a victim of Reformation purges.

The city's traditional hero is chivalric knight **Roland**, Charlemagne's nephew and star of the medieval French epic *Chanson de Roland*. Since 1404, the symbolic guardian of civic rights has stood before the Rathaus and brandished a sword of justice at the Dom to champion the citizens' independence from the archbishops. The shield, tacked on as an afterthought, reminds Bremen's burghers, "Freedom I give unto you that Karl [Charlemagne] and many other princes granted to this town." Bremeners say that as long as their 5.5m-high protector stands on his 10m plinth, the city's liberty is assured. Bar Napoleon, who occupied from 1810 to 1813 but respected the free-city status, and Hitler (who didn't), they've been right.

The jury is still out on whether Wassili Luckhardt's Land parliament building, **Haus der Bürgerschaft** (tours Mon–Fri 9am–5pm; free), is a brave interpretation of traditional Hanseatic styles or just a concrete horror of the Sixties. More appealing is the Renaissance **Schüttung** mansion, the former guildhall of merchants (now the chamber of commerce), which squares up to its municipal counterpart opposite. So irked were Bremen's councillors by its ritzy looks, they commissioned the Rathaus's facade. Nearby at Langenstrasse 13, the **Stadtwaage** is a former city weights and measures office that bristles with Weser Renaissance pillars, by the city architect who revamped the Rathaus.

St Petri Dom

The indirect cause of the Markt's showpiece architecture is the medieval **Dom** directly east. The archbishops erected its 98m towers in the thirteenth century as a sermon on the absolute authority of divine power – only for the independent burghers to reply with their *Roland*. Incidentally, by tradition young men must sweep the steps while wearing top hat and tails and women polish the doorhandles while playing a barrel organ in penance for being unwed at thirty, a ritual maintained with booze-fuelled good humour. Within is an elegant sandstone organ gallery (1518) by Münster's Hinrik Brabender – a furiously bearded Charlemagne holds a contemporary model of the Dom with his bishop, Willehad, who converted the progenitor Saxon village on a sandbank in 787 AD. If the high choir above is open, you can ascend to see its painted ceiling and hunt out a church mouse carved on a south pillar, a joke by a stonemason. The Dom's eleventh-century forerunner survives in crypts at either end of the church, that in the east retaining a contemporary Enthroned Christ and Romanesque capitals that put pagan symbols of a wolf and snake cheek by jowl with a Christian flower of salvation. The star piece of Romanesque sculpture is the baptismal font (1220) in the west crypt. The **Dom Museum** (May–Oct Mon–Fri 10am–4.45pm; Nov–April Mon–Fri 11am–3.45pm; all year Sat 10am–1.30pm, Sun noon–4.45pm; free) contains more sculpture alongside a panel by Cranach, archbishops' silk robes and ceremonial crosiers. You can also ascend one tower for an aerial view of the Markt (same times; €1).

Beneath the southern cloister – a peaceful spot in the central city entered from outside the Dom – is the **Bleikeller** (Lead Cellar; same hours as museum; €1.40). A careless roofer, a Swedish general killed during the Thirty Years' War, a mystery countess and a student who lost a duel are among the eight mummies that gape from glass-topped coffins, desiccated by super-dry air on Bremen's highest sandbank, according to one theory. Whatever the truth, they've been a ghoulish attraction for at least three centuries.

Böttcherstrasse

Bremen boasted the first coffee shop in Germany (1673) and half the country's beans still enter through its port, Bremerhaven. So it's fitting that a Bremen coffee baron funded the transformation of **Böttcherstrasse** southwest of the Markt into an eccentric fantasy. Ludwig Roselius, who made his fortune through decaffeinated coffee, Kaffee Hag – the story goes he stumbled upon the secret using beans that had been soused in sea water – commissioned a team of avant-garde artists, notably sculptor Bernhard Hoetger, to jazz up the alley's Gothic houses with cutting-edge Jugendstil, Art Deco and Expressionist styles. Soon after the makeover of his 110m "Kunst Schau" (Art Show) in 1931, the Third Reich condemned it as degenerate. Only Roselius's wily suggestion that it should stand as a warning against further cultural depravity saved it from demolition. Today prime retail estate, Böttcherstrasse still astounds for the invention of its impulsive brick work, the artistry of its sculpture and wrought iron and its weird glob lights – it's especially enigmatic when spotlit at dusk.

Its overture is Hoetger's gilded relief **Lichtbringer** (Bringer of Light), which bathes the street's entrance in a golden glow. Hoetger also drew the swoopy lines of the **Paula-Modersohn-Becker Museum** (Tues–Sun 11am–6pm; €5; ⑩www.pmbm.de), which contains Roselius's collection of the artist from nearby Worpswede (see p.738), including a self-portrait painted on her sixth wedding anniversary in the self-containment of pregnancy, a year before she died in 1907. Upstairs are sculptures and ceramics by Hoetger; he also cast the bronze sculptures for the foyer. The same ticket gets you into Roselius's revamped Gothic merchant's house, **Roselius-Haus** (same hours). Here, panels by Cranach and Westphalia's late-Gothic master Conrad von Soest fight a losing battle against rich wallpaper and fiddly furniture. A *Pietà* by Tilman Riemenschneider fares better in an isolated alcove, a typically powerful work by Germany's greatest late-Gothic sculptor, which infuses Gothic piety with Renaissance humanism.

Where medieval craftsmen plied their trades in Handwerkerhof behind, Hoetger lets rip a kaleidoscope of Expressionist brickwork – circles, stripes and impassioned splurges – a bust of Roselius and a fountain which immortalizes Bremen's caterwauling musicians. A courtyard space opposite the **casino** (Böttcherstr. 3–5; 3pm–3am; €2.50; jackets and ties required for men) fills several times a day for a Meissen china glockenspiel which chimes out ditties (May–Dec hourly noon–6pm; Jan–April, except when frosty, noon, 3pm & 6pm) while panels bearing the images of craggy transatlantic pioneers, from Leif the Viking to Count Ferdinand von Zeppelin via Columbus, revolve in salute to the adventurous zeal of Bremen's Hanseatic merchants. Further down, **Atlantis-Haus** (now the *Hilton* hotel) has a spectacular Art Deco staircase that spirals up within blue glass bricks and bubbles in approximation of the lost city; and almost opposite, **Robinson-Crusoe-Haus** has carvings of the castaway for no other reason than that Defoe mentions in passing that his father is "a foreigner of Bremen".

Along the Weser River

Böttcherstrasse emerges at the Gothic **St-Martini-Kirche** (May–Sept 10.30am–12.30pm & 2–4pm), which sits on the river, so its merchant congregation could nurture their souls without straying far from the ships that nourished their wallets. A window in the south aisle commemorates assistant preacher and Bremen son Joachim Neander. Wowed by a sermon he'd come to mock, the teenager renounced his larrikin past and became the best hymnal poet of the Calvinists – the church bells peal his *Lobe den Herren* (Praise the Lord). Alas his fame has been hijacked by his namesake, Neanderthal man, through a bizarre chain of events: the prototype human was unearthed in the Neandertal valley near Düsseldorf, named after the Neanderhöhle Grotto where our hero briefly lived as a hermit.

Beneath the church is a quay for **river cruises** from the Hal Över Schreiber (Ⓦwww.hal-oever.de) and Weisse Flotte (Ⓦwww.weisse-flotte.de) lines. Among options are city harbour tours (€9), trips downriver to port Bremerhaven (see p.737; €21 return) and to North Sea stump Helgoland (May–Sept; €35 return). It was the river port that propelled Bremen into the big time – hence the replica trading cog of Hanseatic merchants moored here in summer. The focus of the town's commercial activity was the **Schlachte** west of the quay. By the late 1700s, over three hundred dockers and porters toiled on a 400m harbour lined by inns. The river's silting forced the creation of sea-port Bremerhaven in the late 1800s, leaving the leafy harbourside promenade free as a strip of restaurants and bars. When up to two thousand revellers descend on summer weekends, the vibe is far more Mediterranean than North Sea.

Formerly warehouses for coffee imports, the **Neues Museum Weserburg**, Teerhof 20 (Tues, Wed & Fri 10am–6pm, Thurs 10am–9pm, Sat & Sun 11am–6pm; €5; Ⓦwww.nmwb.de), on the tip of river island Teerhofinsel, houses modern art exhibits grouped by various collectors' take on the 1960s, including Fluxus and Pop Art, as well as works of the past decade. A fifteen-minute walk further upstream on the south bank is **Brauerie Beck & Co**, which maintains a half-millennium tradition of brewing in Bremen. Though famous internationally, Beck's is a relative newcomer, having been founded by a local entrepreneur in

▲ Cafés along the Schlachte, Bremen

1873. Two-hour tours (Thurs–Sat 2pm in English, plus 12.30pm, 2.30pm & 5pm; April–Dec also Thurs–Sat 11am; Jan–April €7.50, May–Dec €8.50; Ⓦ www.becks .de) take in a museum, the former stables and the brewhouse where Germany's premier export beer is produced, all washed down with a free brew – German connoisseurs rate red-labelled Haake-Beck highly.

The Schnoorviertel

Southwest of the Dom, the traditional quarter of fishermen, sailors and craftsmen on the Weser's banks is both the oldest residential district in Bremen and an urban village. Named after the narrow main street **Schnoor** (*schnur* translates as "string"), it survived postwar modernists who mooted ripping the area down, and benefited from a preservation order that saw restoration of its cottages. Today the Schnoor is a photogenic quarter of upmarket boutiques, galleries and restaurants – touristy, certainly, but charming nonetheless. The area's gateway is **Lange Wieren**, the "long wire" that leads to the string of the Schnoor. Here barn-like **Propsteikirche St Johann** was built as a church by the medieval Franciscan order; vows of poverty meant a spire was too great an extravagance. Beyond, Schnoor peels away as cute half-timbered cottages painted in chalky pastels.

Alley Wüste Stätte halfway down on the right is home to the quaint **Hochzeitshaus** (Marriage House) at no. 5. The tiny house stems from a medieval decree that couples from the surrounding area who married in Bremen had to spend a night in the city. The two-bed, one-room hotel (Ⓣ 0162/104 49 54, Ⓦ www.hochzeitshaus-bremen.de; ❾) is hailed locally as the smallest hotel in the world. More miniature still is Wüste Statte 3: an outside ladder leads to a door on the upper floor rather than waste inside space on a staircase. Further along at no. 10, where pre-Reformation pilgrims bedded down before they embarked for Santiago de Compostela – hence the statuette of St James outside – the St Jacobus Packhaus is Bremen's only remaining Altstadt warehouse. Spruced up for EXPO2000, it spins through city history, using costumed actors in places, as **Bremer Geschichtenhaus** (Mon noon–6pm, Tues–Sun 11am–6pm; €4.90; Ⓦ www.bremer-geschichtenhaus.de). The latest attraction in the area is the **Antikenmuseum** (Wed–Sun noon–5pm; €3) uphill at the end of Schnoor. Its small but superb œuvre of Grecian vases stands up to comparison with pieces in any major city in the country.

The Kunsthalle and Ostertorviertel

Bordering the Schnoorviertel to the northeast, Ostertorstrasse (East Tower Street) ends at Am Wall (literally "at the rampart"). If their names don't give it away, a map reveals the latter's semicircular route along a defensive wall that encircled the Altstadt until removed by Napoleon. The ramparts have been landscaped to create the **Wallanlagen gardens** around the former zigzagging moat – an easy escape from the city in summer.

Bremen hoards its art treasures in the **Kunsthalle** (Tues 10am–9pm, Wed–Sun 10am–5pm; €5; Ⓦ www.kunsthalle-bremen.de) at the eastern end of Am Wall. Temporary exhibitions claim most space downstairs, although changing displays from a collection of over 220,000 prints, from Dürer to Degas via big guns like Tiepolo, Goya, Picasso and Beardsley, are not to be missed. Upstairs, Cranach titillates under the pretence of mythology with one of German art's first erotic nudes, *Nymphquelle*. There's also a joint effort by Rubens and Jan Bruegel, *Noli Me Tangere*, a highlight among the Dutch and Italian works. The Kunsthalle's pride is a gallery of French and German Impressionism. Delacroix prepares the ground with the largest collection outside France and lives up to Baudelaire's accolade to him as the last great artist of the Renaissance and the first of the modern. Thereafter are most of the big guns of French Impressionism – Renoir, Manet and two early Monets – followed by Cézanne and Van Gogh, whose *Poppy Field* throbs with natural vitality. Pick of their German counterparts are Lovis Corinth and Max Liebermann, who get a room of their own, Max Beckmann and insightful works by Paula Modersohn-Becker, who outshines everyone else among the otherwise whimsical Worpswede group.

The "Kulturmeile" (Culture Mile) continues in the Neoclassical guardhouses that replaced the eastern gate in the city defences. **Gerhard-Marcks-Haus** (Tues–Sun 10am–6pm; €5; Ⓦwww.marcks.de) showcases modern and avant-garde sculpture – temporary exhibits of heavyweights such as Joseph Beuys, Georg Kolbe and France's Aristide Maillol sit alongside occasionally quirky works by the eponymous sculptor who crafted the Bremen musicians statue; his tubby *Trumpeter* is a delight. **Wilhelm-Wagenfeld-Haus** opposite (Tues 3–9pm, Wed–Sun 10am–6pm; €3.50) documents design in all its guises – industrial, graphic, packaging and fashion. On Goetheplatz east, flagship play- and opera-house **Theater am Goetheplatz** and the restored **Villa Ichon** are a testimony to booming Bremen in the late 1800s. The latter is by far the grandest of the *fin-de-siècle* villas in the Ostertorviertel erected by businessmen and bankers, particularly fine along Mathildenstrasse. The area today has reinvented itself again as a nightlife centre that gets grungier the further you go along Ostertorsteinweg.

Outside the Altstadt

The modern city is a jolt after the Altstadt. Closest of its widely scattered sights is the **Übersee-Museum** on Bahnhofsplatz (Tues–Fri 9am–6pm, Sat & Sun 10am–6pm; €6.50). In the 1890s, Bremen merchants staged a grand exhibition of curios to show off their global reach. The ethnological museum it fathered groups around a pair of courtyards as a comprehensive if rather didactic tour of the continents which sparks into life when exhibits are liberated from showcases: a Japanese garden and African village; a Polynesian paradise in huts, boats and palms; and a lovely early twentieth-century coffee merchant's shop, all faded tins on tidy shelves.

Behind the Hauptbahnhof lies over two square kilometres of landscaped lawns, cattle-grazed meadows and woodland. This is the **Bürgerpark** (Ⓦwww .buergerpark.de), a lovely place to while away an afternoon in a rowing boat – **boat rental** is available from a kiosk (April–May 14 Mon–Sat 2–6pm, Sun 10am–6pm; May 15–Sept 14 Mon 2–6pm, Tues–Sun 10am–6pm; Sept 15–Oct 3 Mon–Sat 2–5pm, Sun 11am–5pm) on the southwestern Emmasee – or over a picnic. Other eating options are one-time summerhouse *Meierei* at the centre, and beer garden *Waldbühne* in the northeast. The parked UFO beyond the latter at the park's northeastern tip (tram or bus #6 to "Universität" stop) is child-friendly science centre **Universum Bremen**, Weiner Strasse 2 (Mon–Fri 9am–6pm, Sat & Sun 10am–7pm; €15.50; Ⓦwww.universum-bremen.de), whose hands-on exhibits tackle the big questions of humanity, the earth and space. If you like this, you may also enjoy a visitor centre at **Astrium** (tours Fri 5pm, Sat 1pm & 3pm; April–Dec also Sun 11am; €16.50; tickets are from tourist information), headquarters of the German space agency, which runs tours of the International Space Station module being assembled in a hangar at the city airport.

Further out still, the **Focke-Museum** (Tues 10am–9pm, Wed–Sun 10am–5pm; €4; Ⓦwww.focke-museum.de; tram #4 or #5) is largely overlooked, which is a shame for a complex whose well-presented exhibits span over a millennium of local history and culture. Bremen's obsession with the Weser River and trade is a leitmotif: exhibits chronicle the Hanseatic seafarers and the elegant glassware and Fürstenberg porcelain prized by the merchant elite are displayed, appropriately, in an aristocrat's Baroque summerhouse. The original Rathaus statues of Charlemagne and the prince-electors are also here, balanced by displays of rural life in one of three historic half-timbered barns rebuilt in the parkland. Ten minutes' walk further – up Schwachhauser Heerstrasse then along Horer Heerstrasse – is the **Rhododendronpark** (daily 7am–sunset; free; tram #4), a landscaped parkland that looks its best in May and June, when over two-thousand varieties of rhododendron turn on the fireworks. Glasshouse botanika (Tues–Fri 9am–6pm, Sat & Sun 10am–6pm; Nov–Feb till 4pm; €8; Ⓦ www.botanika.net) adds a whistle-stop tour of east Asian flora.

Eating and drinking

Bremen's culinary scene features as many upmarket restaurants as there are traditional. It divides neatly into four areas: the **Altstadt** and especially the **Schnoorviertel** are the choice for traditional restaurants; lively waterfront promenade **Schlachte**; **Ostertorsteinweg**, lined with bistro-style restaurants for cheap eats; and ten minutes north is **Auf den Höfen**, an intimate yard of restaurants and bars. **Drinking** and **nightlife** is focused in the latter three. Though dominated by chains, the Schlachte is great for beer garden bar-hopping in summer, while "das Viertel" along Ostertorsteinweg segues from restaurants to a grungy student vibe as you progress. As well as fish, one local delicacy to try is *Braunkohl mit Pinkel*, cabbage and sausage seasoned with bacon and onions.

Restaurants

Aioli Schnoor 3–4 ☏0421/32 38 39. Tapas plates and larger Spanish main dishes are served to a soundtrack of lazy jazz in an atmospheric old town house.

Beck's im Schnoor Schnoor 36 ☏0421/32 31 30. Above-average traditional dishes in the historic *Gaststätte* of the brewery.

Grasshof Contrescarpe 80 ☏0421/147 49. Parisian brasserie meets gourmet cooking in a bistro attached to an equally excellent delicatessen, a choice lunchspot for an arty forty-something set. Expect to pay around €20 a main. Lunch only, closed Sun.

Kleine Ratskeller Hinter dem Schütting 11 ☏0421/32 61 68. Charming *Gaststätte* near the entrance of Böttcherstrasse that serves traditional dishes as well as the likes of salmon in a fennel-butter sauce. Good choice of beers, and live accordion on Saturdays. Closed Wed & Sun.

Luv Schlachte 15–18 ☏0421/165 55 99. Restaurant and lounge-bar at the west end of the strip that is all things to all people; both a beer garden and a contemporary bar, and a home to lobster as well as *Currywurst*. Nice breakfast spot, too.

Meierei Im Bürgerpark ☏0421/340 86 19. Smart dining in a Swiss chalet-styled summerhouse in the Bürgerpark, serving international dishes – a popular spot for Sunday lunch then a stroll. Closed Mon.

Ratskeller Am Markt ☏0421/334 79 27. A tourist attraction in its own right, the veritable *Ratskeller*

is a joy, with excellent traditional local dishes – this is the best place to sample *Braunkohl mit Pinkel* – and waiters in traditional garb. It's also home to gourmet French restaurant *L'Orchidée* (dinner only, closed Sun & Mon).

Savarin Auf den Höfen 12–15 ☏0421/769 77. Small and friendly restaurant that prepares a great-value menu ranging from stews to Spanish-style cooking and pastas.

Schröter's Schnoor 13 ☏0421/326 67. German cuisine with a Mediterranean twist – lamb with a herb and mustard gratin, pike-perch with balsamic tomatoes – in a small restaurant with a rear side-room of chunky beams.

Topaz Kontorhaus am Markt-Langenstr. 2–4 ☏0421/776 25. Ladies who lunch do so in this smart wine bistro: expect the likes of tuna tartare with avocado, a house-special *Wiener Schnitzel*, and lemon cheesecake cooked to a secret recipe of the owner's mother. Set menus are good value at €9. Mon–Fri till 9pm, Sat lunch only.

🏃 **Villa** Goetheplatz 4 ☏0421/362 85 57. On the lower floor of Villa Ichon – entry at the back – this award-winning place has great food and bags of style: fine international dishes such as giant prawns in cognac in snug tiled rooms or an idyllic garden in summer. Closed Sat lunch & Sun.

Cafés and bars

1st Class Suicide Auf den Höfen. Funky little bar at the end of the alley hosted by a speed metal guitarist.

2raumlounge Auf den Höfen. Not as sophisticated as it likes to think, but a decent lounge bar-club nonetheless with a mainstream soundtrack of chart tunes.

Bistro Brazil Ostertorsteinweg 83. Owners claim they mixed North Germany's first *caipirinha* in 1983, and it's still the pick in a cocktail bar with four happy hours (6–10pm) and an older clientele.

Café Engel Ostertorsteinweg 31. One-time chemist's now a laid-back gastropub at the heart of the Viertel that serves tasty pastas.

Cafe Knigge Sögstr. 42–44. Bremen's bastion of *Kaffee und Kuchen* features vintage style and rich cakes and pralines.

Café Sand Strandweg 106. Beach culture comes to Bremen as a cool conservatory bar-café on the south bank of the Weser – a passenger ferry shuttles from a quay on Osterdeich, near the junction with Sielwall (single €1.20, return €2). Weekends only in winter.

Drei Jahr Fehrfeld 58. Chandeliers and vintage furnishings in a relaxed retro-styled wine- and cocktail bar in the Viertel. Decent food menu, too.

Lemon Lounge Am Wall 164. A former strip-club at the top of a spiral staircase that's still slightly seedy – arguably part of the attraction of this small clubby bar. Mon–Sat from 8pm.

Kukuk Am Wall 207. The minimalist bistro at the rear of the Kunsthalle prepares the likes of spaghetti with truffle sauce and lamb rack with a bean ragout for an older, arty crowd.

Piano Fehrfeld 64. Lazy paced café-bar in the Ostertorviertel whose menu of pizzas, pastas and steaks, all priced under €10, is popular with everyone from families to friends.

Spitzen Gebel Hinter dem Schütting 1. A splendid cocoon of old wood and brass in the oldest *Bürger-haus* in Bremen (1348) with just enough space for a few tables. House speciality is a liqueur named "*Sluk ut de Lamp*" distilled to a secret recipe. Closed Sun.

Nightlife and entertainment

Glossy newsstand titles *Prinz* (€1) and *Bremer* (€2.50) provide more comprehensive listings than freesheets stocked in the tourist offices. **Clubbing** in Bremen is good value – entry is usually around €6–8. A strip of clubs lies on Rembertiring, east of the Hauptbahnhof, although many Bremeners dimiss its chart sounds as teenie-fodder. Most clubs only open on Friday and Saturday. For **classical music**, keep an eye on concerts staged in the city's churches, usually the Dom.

Nightclubs

Aladin/Tivoli Hannoversche Str. 9–11 Ⓦwww.aladin-bremen.de. Rock, metal and goth clubs and acts, plus oldies' nights in a venue going strong since 1977.

Modernes Neustadtswall 28 Ⓦwww.modernes .de. Bremen's best nightclub, one of the few with midweek nights, is in a former cinema in the Neustadt south of the Weser. Expect nights of indie or classic disco, funk and party house plus the occasional gig midweek, all ventilated by a sliding domed roof.

Stubu Rembertiring 21 Ⓦwww.stubu.de. A multi-room palace to mainstream clubbing spread over five themed rooms; their soundtrack ranges from hip-hop and r'n'b to Sixties via chart sounds and electro. Always packed with a young party crowd.

Ting! Rembertiring 1 Ⓦwww.ting-club.de. Electro and breaks from visiting DJs, plus nights of dancehall and reggae on Fridays and the occasional rock and metal thrash on Wednesdays. One of the more appealing options on the strip.

Music and theatre

Die Glocke Domsheide 4–5 ☎0421/33 66 99, Ⓦwww.glocke.de. Bremen's grand old concert hall, renowned for fine acoustics and host to both the Bremener Philharmoniker and the acclaimed Deutsche Kammerphilharmonie, Bremen's chamber orchestra. Some jazz gigs scheduled.

Schlachthof Findorffstr. 51 ☎0421/37 77 50, Ⓦwww.schlachthof-bremen.de. World music, cabaret and theatre, and art and photography exhibitions in a cultural centre north of the Hauptbahnhof created from a former abattoir. Its bar screens all Werder Bremen games (free).

Theater am Goetheplatz Goetheplatz ☎0421/365 33 33, Ⓦwww.bremertheater.com. The most prestigious stage in town hosts heavyweight opera, operettas and dance. Affiliated Neues Schauspielhaus (Oster-torsteinweg 57a; same contacts) is the city's leading dramatic stage – expect modern classics and avant-garde.

Theater am Leibnizplatz Am Leibnizplatz ☎0421/50 03 33 (Tues–Sat 3–6pm only), Ⓦwww.shakespeare-company.com. Home of the renowned Bremen Shakespeare Company, whose trademarks are bare stage or nonrepresentational productions.

Listings

Bookshops and media Thalia's megastore at Obernstr. 50 maintains the largest foreign-language section in Bremen. Presse & Buche at the Hauptbahnhof carries a small stock of international newspapers.

Car rental All operators maintain a desk at the airport and share an office at the Hauptbahnhof: Hertz ☎ 0421/55 53 50; Europcar ☎ 0421/55 74 40; SIXT ☎ 01805/25 25 25; Budget ☎ 0421/597 00 16.

Hospital Rotes Kreuz Krankenhaus, St-Paul-Deich 24.

Internet Two call-shops at Bahnhofstr. 10–11 provide internet access (Mon–Sat 10am–10pm, Sun noon–10pm). In the centre, there's access in the basement of Thalia bookstore at Obernstr. 50, and in the Ostentorviertel at Lift

Internet (daily 2pm–midnight, later Fri & Sat) at Weberstr. 18.

Markets An antiques, crafts and junk market takes over the waterfront west of the Schlachte on Saturday until early afternoon.

Police Am Wall 200 ☎ 0421/36 20.

Post office Bahnhofplatz 21 (outside the Hauptbahnhof).

Sport Former Bundesliga champions and league cup-winners Werder Bremen, frequent competitor in the Champions League, play in the Weser Stadion (ⓦ www.weserstadion.de) 1km east of the centre off Osterdeich. Tickets (€10–45) are hard to come by, but you can try at Werder Bremen Ticket-Center at Franz-Böhmert-Str. 1c (Mon–Fri & match days 9am–6pm). Fixtures are published in English at ⓦ www.werderbremen.de.

Around Bremen

Within an hour's travel of Bremen is a trio of day-trips to suit all tastes: **Bremerhaven**, fast reinventing itself from container port to tourist destination; bucolic artists' colony **Worpswede**; and the erstwhile ducal town of **Oldenburg**. With the possible exception of Worpswede, none warrants an overnight stay and frequent transport links mean you're never stuck for a return, however long you tarry.

Bremerhaven

As its port silted, Bremen petitioned the King of Hanover to acquire the land between the Geeste and Weser rivermouths and so found **BREMERHAVEN** in 1827. It's no charmer, the centre thrown up after 95 percent of the port was obliterated by air raids, and has long had a utilitarian air. No wonder considering that Bremerhaven has the world's longest quay (4.9km) and is Germany's premier fishing port. Yet "Fischstadt" is raising its game. Central harbours have been renovated as a focus for two superb museums and billion-euro architecture projects: the **Atlantic Hotel Sail City** (viewing platform €3), modelled on Dubai's signature *Burj Al-Arab* hotel; and behind it a glass ellipse that will hold climate and climate-change museum **Klimahaus** (ⓦ www.klimahaus-bremerhaven.de) by mid-2009.

Reason enough for a visit is the **Deutsches Auswanderen Museum** at the Neuer Hafen harbour basin (daily 10am–6pm, till 5pm Nov–Feb; €10.50; ⓦ www.dah-bremerhaven.de), a European Museum of the Year in 2007 that documents the seven million New World émigrés who departed from its wharf between 1830 and 1974. Receive a boarding card of a former émigré and you pass through stage-set dioramas to follow a transatlantic odyssey that took the first passenger steamers twelve weeks. Most fascinating is a "Gallery of the Seven Million", a faux-library that weaves into the larger narrative real-life stories of emigrants. In addition a cinema screens poignant documentaries on the immigrant experience and there's a free research centre with a database of German emigrants. Imaginative, thought-provoking, occasionally moving and more relevant than ever in an era when debates about immigration are so divisive, this is highly recommended.

Before the museum opened in 2005, Bremerhaven's pride and joy was its **Deutsches Schifffahrtsmuseum** (Tues–Sun 10am–6pm; April–Oct also Mon; €6; ⓦwww.dsm.museum), on adjacent harbour Alter Hafen. Its maritime displays in a modern complex are diverting, notably a section on the windjammers built in Bremerhaven until 1928 and a showpiece fourteenth-century Hanseatic cog undergoing slow renovation. Most of the eleven historic vessels in an adjacent harbour are open in summer (free with ticket or €1), including a wartime submarine (same times; €3). A so-so sand beach, **Weser Strandbad**, lies just south.

Other diversions in the vicinity are the child-friendly **Zoo am Meer** (daily: April–Sept 9am–7pm; March & Oct 9am–6pm; Nov–Feb 9am–4.30pm; €6.50; ⓦwww.zoo-am-meer-bremerhaven.de), opposite the emigration museum, and **cruises** (daily March–Dec; €8.50; ⓦwww.hafenrundfahrt-bremerhaven.de) from Neuer Hafen to the port and Columbus Quay from which millions of emigrants departed (and a young GI named Elvis Presley arrived on October 1, 1958).

The fishing port **Fischereihafen**, 2.5km south of the harbours (bus #505 or #506), is garnering minor redevelopment: there's a glut of fish restaurants, fishing ship *Gera* (daily Mar 24–Nov 4 10am–6pm; €1.50) and the Atlanticum seawater **aquarium** (daily 10am–6pm; €4; ⓦwww.atlanticum.de). If you walk here from the shipping museum you pass the **Historisches Museum** (Tues–Sun 10am–6pm; €4; ⓦwww.historisches-museum-bremerhaven.de) at the bridge over the Geeste River after 500m. Alongside town history, it contains a research database of four million emigrants available to visitors.

Practicalities

The Hauptbahnhof is in the southeast of the city, a twenty-minute walk from the harbours northwest: take Friedrich–Ebert-Strasse then pedestrianized Bürgermeister-Smidt-Strasse. Hal Över timetables cruises from Bremen, though they're best made one-way, as a return will only give you two hours in Bremerhaven. The main **tourist office** is at the bridge by the emigration museum (Mon–Fri 9.30am–6pm, till 5pm Nov to mid-March, Sat & Sun 10am–4pm; ☎0471/94 64 61 20, ⓦwww.bremerhaven-touristik.de). Another at the Fischereihafen (Am Schaufenster 6; daily mid-March to Oct 9.30am–7pm; ☎0471/94 64 61 27) rents bicycles. For **eating**, it's hard to beat *Seute Deern* for maritime flavour: the world's largest sail trader, built in 1919, is moored outside the Deutsches Schifffahrtsmuseum. The finest fish restaurant is *Natusch* at Fischereihafen (Am Fischbahnhof 1; ☎0471/710 21).

Worpswede

When Impressionist artists Fritz Mackerson and Otto Modersohn discovered it in the 1880s, **WORPSWEDE**, 26km north of Bremen, was just another village that eked out a living on the Teufelsmoor (Devil's Bog). Within ten years of the pair setting up their easels, inspired by its pastoral scenes silvered by birch and huge cloudscapes, it had morphed into an artists' colony, and today there are ateliers scattered throughout a village that is the cultured day-trip par excellence. Of these early pioneers – Fritz Overbeck, architect and painter Heinrich Voegler, poet Rainer Maria Rilke, and Bernhard Hoetger of Böttcherstrasse fame – it's Paula Modersohn-Becker (Otto Modersohn's wife) who shines in the **Grosse Kunstschau** (mid-March to Oct daily 10am–6pm; Nov to mid-March Tues–Mon 10am–5pm; €4; ⓦwww.grosse-kunstschau.de), a Hoetger-designed gallery at the village centre. Keep an eye open too for Voegler's pre-Raphelite-inspired *Sommerabend* (Summer Evening) which depicts the artists loafing on his patio. **Worpsweder Kunsthalle** (same hours; €3.50; ⓦwww.worpsweder-kunsthalle.de) below stages exhibitions of community works, new and old. Hoetger's eccentric

Kaffee Worpswede beside the main gallery was derided by villagers immediately as "*Café Verrückt*" (Café Crazy): small wonder considering its fusion of traditional, Expressionist and tribal styles – don't miss the tent-like interior. As quirky is the **Kaseglöcke** ("Cheesebell"; Feb–Dec Tues–Sun 11am–4/5pm; €2) in the woods behind, a fairytale cottage with furnishings by Hoetger and Modersohn-Becker, which was created for the colony's first tour guide.

The creative hotbed then was Voegler's home and studio, **Barkenhoff** (daily 10am–6pm; €4; @www.barkenhoff-stiftung.de), at Ostendorfer Strasse 10 – follow Lindenallee uphill from the Grosse Kunstschau, then take a path left off the right bend. Beyond a front garden recognizable from *Summer Evening*, the house features his works that switch from Jugendstil to early Expressionism. A short stroll nearby ascends through cornfields on the Weyerberg hill (on the right as you walk along Lindenallee) to the Niedersachsenstein war memorial, shaped as a stylized eagle. Another option for an outing is an idyllic **river cruise** aboard traditional barges known as *Torfkahn* (May–Oct; 1hr 30min; €9.50). The nearest operator to the village is Hammehütte Neu Helgoland (@04792/76 06, @www.hammehuette.de) at Hammeweg 19, 1.5km west of the centre, which also rents canoes. Details of others are at the tourist office.

Practicalities

Bus #670 runs to Worpswede from the Bremen bus station at frequent intervals, as does nightbus #N3 on Friday and Saturday. From May to October the historic Moor Express **train** (@04792/93 58 20, @www.moorexpress.net) operates from Bremen Hauptbahnhof four times a day. **Bike rental** is on the main road from Eckhard Eyl (@04792/23 23) at Findorffstrasse 28. The **tourist office** (April 15–Oct 14 daily 10am–5pm; Oct 15–April 14 Mon–Fri 10am–5pm, Sat & Sun 10am–2pm; @04792/93 58 20, @www.worpswede.de), in the centre at Bergstrasse 13, sells information packs (€2) with an area map and booklets of ateliers and appealing **accommodation**. Among your options are: lovely half-timbered *Haus im Schluh*, Im Schluh 37 (@04792/95 00 61, @www.haus-im-schluh.de; ❸–❹), a former residence of Voegler, some of whose work is on display; *Village*, Bergstrasse 22 (@04792/935 00, @www.village-worpswede.de; ❻), with elegant split-level suites; design hotel and restaurant *Der Eichenhof*, in a traditional house at Ostendorfer Strasse 13 (@04792/26 76, @www.eichenhof-worpswede.de; ❻–❼); and area giant *Worpsweder Tor* (Findorffstrasse 3; @04792/989 30, @www.hotel-worpsweder-tor.de; ❺–❻), whose style alludes to the colony's Art Deco heyday. The **youth hostel** (@04792/13 60, @www.jugendherberge.de; from €17.70) is a short walk west of the centre at Hammeweg 2. *Kaffee Worpswede* (@04792/10 28) prepares a first-class menu of modern German cuisine – expect the likes of duck in mustard sauce with sour-cream and truffle spinach – or for something cheaper there's a good **restaurant** overlooking fields in Hoetger's Art Deco Bahnhof.

Oldenburg

Once a proud ducal city-state that flourished in the late 1700s after a century of Danish neglect, **OLDENBURG** contents itself as the capital of the Weser-Ems region. A fire in 1676 reduced much of the town to ashes, and only at southern square Schlossplatz is there a tangible sense of former greatness through the pastel yellow Renaissance **Schloss**, its facade enlivened by an exotic menagerie. Until 1921 the U-shaped palace was a residence of the Oldenburg branch of the Holstein-Gottorp family tree, one of Europe's most regal dynasties. No occupant was more influential for Oldenburg than Duke Peter Friedrich Ludwig. Thanks to that eighteenth-century arts patron, the **Landesmuseum für Kunst und**

Kulturgeschichte (Museum of Art and Cultural History; Tues–Fri 9am–5pm, till 8pm Thurs, Sat & Sun 10am–5pm; €3; ⓦwww.landesmuseum-oldenburg .niedersachsen.de), an otherwise pedestrian plod through local history from the Middle Ages, boasts impressive first-floor palace rooms, such as the marble-clad Mamorsaal ballroom. The star piece is the Idyllenzimmer anteroom, with a cycle of coquettish nymphs by Johann Heinrich Wilhelm Tischbein. A pal of Goethe, he was brought to Oldenburg as the duke's court artist.

The same ticket provides entry to galleries (same times) on the far side of the ring road opposite the Schloss. The **Prinzenpalais** hangs Worpswede Impressionists and Expressionists of Die Brücke group in a Neoclassical building commissioned by the duke as a palace residence. The Italianate **Augusteum** opposite – Oldenburg's first art museum when completed in 1867 – contains his Italian and Dutch Old Masters. Another of Duke Peter's creations, the **Schlossgarten** spears south behind the latter as a naturalistic park. Further down from the galleries is the **Landesmuseum für Natur und Mensch** (Tues–Fri 9am–5pm, Sat & Sun 10am–5pm; €3 or €4 combination ticket with Schloss; ⓦwww.naturundmensch.de). Ostensibly a repository of natural history and archeology which originated from a ducal collection, it feels closer to a modern art gallery thanks to pure white walls and creative installations such as a plasticized slab of peat to display three 2300-year-old corpses preserved by tannins of the surrounding moorland. The rest of the Altstadt is unexceptional, although the Lambertikirche on the Markt opposite the Schloss is worth a look. Bristling with nineteenth-century spires outside, its interior springs a surprise with a china-like rotunda modelled on the Pantheon.

Practicalities

Oldenburg's **Hauptbahnhof** is isolated northeast of the centre. Take the "Stadt Mitte" exit to reach Bahnhofstrasse, then at its end turn left onto Gottorpstrasse and continue south towards the Schloss. The **tourist office** (Mon–Fri 10am–6pm, Sat 10am–2pm; ☎0441/36 16 13 66, ⓦwww.oldenburg-tourist.de) is in the centre at Kleine Kirchenstrasse 10, just up from the Lambertikirche on the Markt. There's also a service point in the Hauptbahnhof (Mon–Fri 6am–10pm, Sat 7am–10pm, Sun 8.30am–10pm). Both book accommodation. Locals' choice for good **eating** is *Klöter* (lunch only, closed Sun; ☎0441/129 86) attached to a delicatessen on Herbertgang off Lange Strasse north of the centre. Wallstrasse, the heart of the bar scene a block south, is chock-full of cafés and pizza joints. The Markt is a more relaxing spot for café culture and a home to the *Ratskeller*, with reliable traditional cooking.

Travel details

Trains

Braunschweig to: Hannover (every 40min; 30–45min); Wolfenbüttel (every 45min; 10min); Wolfsburg (every 30min; 15–30min).
Bremen to: Bremerhaven (every 40min; 35–50min); Hamburg (every 30min; 1hr); Hannover (every 30min–1hr; 1hr); Oldenburg (every 40min; 30min); Osnabrück (every 45min; 50min–1hr 15min).
Göttingen to: Hann. Münden (hourly; 35min).

Hannover to: Braunschweig (every 45min; 30–45min); Bremen (every 40min; 1hr); Celle (every 15–30min; 20–45min); Goslar (hourly; 1hr–1hr 20min); Göttingen (every 20–40min; 35min–1hr); Hameln (every 30min; 45min); Hildesheim (every 30min; 25–35min); Lüneburg (hourly; 1hr); Osnabrück (every 2hr; 1hr 30min); Wolfsburg (every 15–30min; 30min–1hr).
Osnabrück to: Bremen (hourly 50min–1hr 10min); Hannover (hourly 1hr 5min–1hr 30min); Münster (every 30min; 25min).

Hamburg and
Schleswig-Holstein

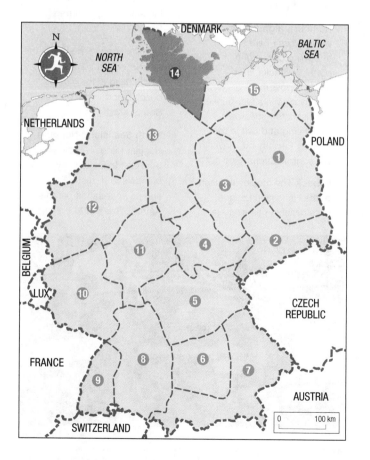

CHAPTER 14

Highlights

✳ **Hamburg** Both a rollicking port city and a boom-town media capital with thriving art and gourmet scenes, Germany's liberal second metropolis has a restless energy that makes it arguably the nation's most life-affirming city. See p.744

✳ **Hamburg nightlife** From world-class opera to throbbing club-nights in portside shacks, from showstopper musicals to grungy gigs in a war bunker, sophisticated style-bars to dancing at dawn in the Sunday Fischmarkt. Revel in the contradictions. See p.771

✳ **Lübeck** The medieval queen of the Hanseatic League is as ravishing as ever – a small-town symphony that's as cultured as it is charming. And all with a decent beach on its doorstep. See p.776

✳ **Schleswig** The former Viking stronghold of northern Europe has mellowed into an idyllic small town on a fjord with a blockbuster museum to boot. See p.794

✳ **Sylt** Never mind the weather, this North Sea watersports wonderland is the gliziest beach resort in the country. See p.803

✳ **North Sea island-hopping** Regular ferries let you skip from Sylt to its low-key sister-islands south, rustic Föhr and powder-sands paradise Amrum. See p.808

▲ Hamburg nightlife

Hamburg and
Schleswig-Holstein

D on't look for national stereotypes on Germany's north coast. If the homespun south can seem affiliated to the other side of the Alps, the northernmost regions of Germany – dynamic city-state **Hamburg** and **Schleswig-Holstein** – have the cool reserve of northern climates. Indeed for most of an area defined by a sandy coast and flat countryside the temperament is closer to Britain than Bavaria – perhaps no surprise, since the Angles from Schleswig-Holstein sailed west to England in the fifth century as part of the Anglo-Saxon invasion. No surprise, either, that after centuries of tug-of-war between present-day Germany, Sweden and Denmark, the coastal north feels distinctly Nordic, nor that the sea has bred the live-and-let-live attitudes typical of many coastal communities. Whether in cosmopolitan Hamburg, Germany's media capital and its second metropolis, the commercial ports of Schleswig-Holstein, such as Land capital **Kiel**, or the resorts on the Baltic, Germany's seaboard exudes an easy-going liberalism to make land-locked southerners appear prudish.

The air of a separate country is compounded by a predominantly fish diet – something of a relief after the meat-feast inland – and a switch to the red-brick architecture handed down by the **Hanseatic League** (see box, p.776). From its headquarters at the axis of the Baltic and North seas, the medieval superpower stretched an arm across present-day Europe – from Sweden to the Alps, Britain to Estonia – and provided a blueprint for the brick Gothic style throughout the Baltic region. Four centuries after the league was wound up, towns throughout the area continue to flaunt their "Hansestadt" title, and its legacy is a distinct local identity as you travel east from league-leader **Lübeck**, one of Germany's finest small towns and reason enough itself to visit the region.

Notwithstanding the cultural heavyweights of Hamburg and Lübeck, or industrial port Kiel, this is holiday country. Largely free of urban development, Schleswig-Holstein is characterized instead by the expansive land- and skyscapes that have long captivated artists such as Emil Nolde. With your own transport, you could lose a week on a circuit from Hamburg, bowling through a series of small towns where coast meets country; places like cultured backwater **Eutin** or erstwhile Viking stronghold **Schleswig**, home to a blockbuster art museum that ticks all boxes. Powder beaches have enshrined the **North Frisian islands** off the western coast into playgrounds celebrated by Germans but largely overlooked by foreigners in the stampede south. People-watching in **Sylt**, or simply loafing around anywhere in wicker *Strandkörbe* seats, are a defining part of the German coastal experience. Even metropolis Hamburg finds space for beach bars from May to September, complementing a year-round nightlife that is as much a reason to visit as some of the finest galleries and museums in the country.

Without a car, Hamburg is your best transport hub, although rail links from Lübeck serve east-coast destinations as far as Kiel. Remember, too, that ferry services off the west coast permit island-hopping down the trio of North Frisian islands – the relaxed beach holiday in a nutshell.

Hamburg

HAMBURG suffers from image schizophrenia. To many of its tourists, Germany's second metropolis is simply sin city – a place of prostitutes and strip shows in the Reeperbahn red-light district – while in its homeland it is revered as a cosmopolitan, stylish city-state, rapaciously commercial and home to the highest head-count of millionaires in the country. Either way the cause is the same: through one of the greatest ports in Europe it has sucked in wealth – and probably vice – ever since a canny piece of diplomatic manoeuvring in 1189 led Emperor Friederich I (also known as Emperor Barbarossa) to grant tax-free imports down the Elbe. Hamburg never looked back. The good times began to roll in the early Middle Ages after it fostered links with Hanseatic leader Lübeck and the city paused only to congratulate itself when declared a Free Imperial City by Emperor Maximilian I in 1510.

Today a restless boom-town, forever reinventing itself, Hamburg still flaunts its "Freie und Hansestadt" (Free and Hanseatic Town) title. And that umbilical link to maritime trade continues in a sprawling container port that grounds the city, adding a workaday robustness to the sophistication that comes with its postwar role as Germany's media capital. Though the port makes Hamburg fairly grimy in places, seedy even, it adds an earthy flavour to the rich cosmopolitan stew. It brings dive bars to a city renowned for its arts and theatre; nurtures a strong counter-culture movement alongside hip media types; and helps support a nightlife that is as depraved as it is refined. Even the drizzle that blankets the city for days at a time can't dampen the spirit of Germany's most life-affirming city.

The surprise, then, is that Hamburg is so manageable. Despite a population that nudges towards 1.8 million, just under a fifth of which has immigrant roots, Hamburg has the lowest population density of any European city. Only around a third of the land area is urban development, the rest is parks and water. Canals that once carried produce now provide breathing space among the offices as they thread from the mercantile heart on the Elbe's banks to the Alster lakes. The city's 2302 bridges are more than Venice, Amsterdam and London combined.

Most of the main sights are located in the **city centre**, a seamless semicircular spread of architecture north of the Elbe, but for local character look to outlying residential districts: **St Georg** east of the Hauptbahnhof, which is shaking off a red-light past to emerge as a gentrified, gay-friendly area centred on the restaurants and bars of Lange Reihe; or exclusive quarters that fringe the **Aussenalster** lake – Rotherbaum and Harvestude on the west shore are renowned for a streetscape of smart, late 1800s villas, and are still Hamburg's

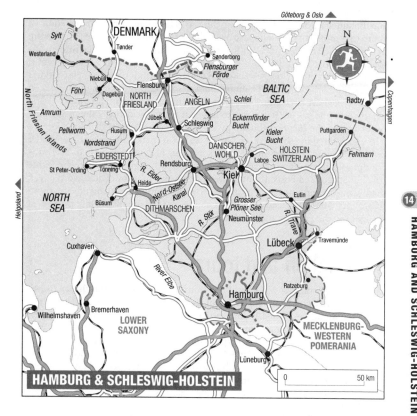

HAMBURG & SCHLESWIG-HOLSTEIN

0   50 km

des res among the well-heeled. West of the centre are **St Pauli**, the former port district of **Reeperbahn** fame, and to its north, the scruffy but rapidly gentrifying **Schanzenviertel** and **Universitätsviertel**. Together, these three form the heartland of Hamburg nightlife. Things become progressively quieter (and more expensive) as you shift downriver through the western riverside suburbs from **Altona** and **Övelgönne** to **Blankenese**, where city tycoons occupy some of the most expensive real-estate in Germany.

Arrival

Served by domestic and international carriers, Hamburg **airport** (☎040/507 50, ⓦwww.ham.airport.de) is around 8km north of the centre. The canary-yellow Airport Express leaves from a stop outside Terminal 1 (every 10–15min 4.45am–midnight; 25min; single €5, return €8; ☎040/227 10 60, ⓦwww .jasper.de), for the Hauptbahnhof. Alternatively bus #110 links the airport to S/U-Bahn station Ohlsdorf (every 10min 5.40am–12.40am), and bus #52 goes to Bahnhof Altona (every 30min 5.50am–10.30pm). A taxi to the Hauptbahnhof costs around €25.

The most useful of Hamburg's four **train stations** are the Hauptbahnhof, a fifteen-minute walk east of the Rathaus and a short way west of St Georg, and Bahnhof Altona in the west of the city. Depending on their direction of approach, some services also call at Bahnhof Dammtor north of the centre or Bahnhof Harburg in the south of the city. The ZOB (**bus station**) is just southeast of the Hauptbahnhof on Adenauerallee. Though far from dangerous compared with other European cities, Hamburg demands basic city sense around the Kirchenallee exit of the Hauptbahnhof despite efforts to clean up the area in the past decade. A large police presence keeps hassle at a minimum but this – and nearby Hansaplatz – are not places to linger at night. Incidentally the main safety issues around the Reeperbahn are pickpockets and belligerent drunks.

If you're arriving **by car** be aware that car parks are expensive in the centre – a large harbour-side car park east on Hafenstrasse, east of St-Pauli-Landungsbrücken, is a cheaper alternative – although most hotels provide parking at reduced costs. If you leave a car in the suburbs check and recheck that your chosen spot is legitimate. Towing companies demand a ransom of around €400 to release cars from a pound in Rothenburgsort on top of charges for the parking incurred in the pound itself.

Information and tours

Hamburg Tourismus (Ⓦwww.hamburg-tourism.de) operates four **visitor information centres**: at the Hauptbahnhof, Kirchenalle exit (Mon–Sat 8am–9pm, Sun 10am–6pm); St-Pauli-Landungsbrücken, between piers 4 and 5 (April–Oct Mon–Thurs & Sun 8am–7pm, Fri & Sat 8am–8pm; Nov–March Mon–Wed 9.30am–6pm, Thurs–Sat 9.30am–7pm, Sun 9am–6pm); and terminals one and two of the airport (daily 5.30am–4pm). All provide free **maps** and can book just about anything in town, from hotels (€4 booking fee per person) to tickets for theatres and sightseeing tours by bus or foot. The central information hotline is ℡040/30 05 13 00; for hotel bookings call ℡040/30 05 13 51, for tickets ℡040/30 05 16 66.

All bureaux sell the **Hamburg CARD**, which provides free public transport and free entry or discounts on municipal museums, plus ten to thirty percent reductions on harbour cruises, city tours, theatre tickets and in selected restaurants. Single tickets are: €8 for a one-day card, valid from 6pm the previous day; €18 for a three-day; and €33 for a five-day card. Group tickets for up to five people of any age are a bargain at €11.80, €29.80 and €51 respectively.

For boat tours of the port and lake, see p.761 and p.755. GPS e-guides are available for rent from visitor information centres. There's a world of **bus tours** available in English. Options include: Top-Tour (daily every 30min 9.30am–5pm; €14; Ⓦwww.top-tour-hamburg.de), a hop-on, hop-off double-decker that begins at the Kirchenallee stop of the Hauptbahnhof and circuits around the city to St-Pauli-Landungsbrücken; Maritim-Tour from the same company (April–Oct daily 10am, 12.30pm & 3pm; Nov–March Sat & Sun same times; €14; Ⓦwww .maritim-tour.de) begins at St-Pauli-Landungsbrücken 2 and also at the Haupt-bahnhof then tours the port area, including the south bank and out to Övelgönne; Gala-Tour (daily 10am & 2pm; €19; Ⓦwww.gala-tour.de), a two-and-a-half-hour, city-wide tour of the metropolis, including the lake suburbs, port and Altona. Numerous **walking tours** are on offer, generally themed along the lines of Hanseatic history, The Beatles, cuisine, the port and the Reeperbahn's bawdy past. Contacts are printed on the back of tourist office maps. Hamburg Rundflüge provides **scenic flights** over the city from the airport (daily; from €49 or €89 for 30min depending on group size; ℡040/70 70 88 90).

City transport

Public transport is run by HVV (ⓦwww.hvv.de) as a coordinated system of **U-** and **S-Bahn trains** and **buses**. The former are as clean and efficient as you'd hope of German transport, organized into colour-coded routes – three underground (U) and six express commuter (S) routes – and operating every five minutes from 5am to 12.30am. In addition, three long-distance commuter lines (AKN) snake into outlying regions. **Night buses** operate between midnight and 5am; in theory conductors can pre-book a taxi for your stop. All forms of public transport are priced by zone, although most of the time you're unlikely to go outside central zone A. Current **prices** for all public transport are: €1.30 for a single ticket; €6 for day-ticket (Tageskarte) or €5.10 if bought after 9am; three-day tickets are €15. A 9am Group Ticket (Gruppenkarte) for up to five people of any age costs €8.60. Note, too, that three children under 15 can travel for free on an adult single ticket, and that the Hamburg CARD (see opposite) provides free travel. An alternative way to reach the western suburbs – and a bit of sightseeing in its own right – is by the Elbe **river ferries** from St-Pauli-Landungsbrücken. Boats to Altona or Övelgönne leave from Brücke 3 every fifteen minutes; prices are the same as those for trains and buses. Non-municipal tourist services of the ATG Alster-Touristik line make circuits around quays on the Aussenalster in both directions; boats leave from Jungfernstieg from late March to early October between 10am and 6pm.

Walking in the city centre requires stamina but is pleasant enough away from the major thoroughfares. As an idea of distances, from the Rathaus to St Michaelis church takes about twenty minutes at a brisk pace. **Cycling** is the fastest and most flexible means of travel over short distances within the centre thanks to a good network of cycle routes off the main roads, demarcated by red-paved lanes. **Bike rental** is available from the Hauptbahnhof, or try Fahrradladen St Georg (ⓣ040/14 39 08) at Schmilinskystrasse 16 in neighbouring district St Georg. You can take a bicycle on to any rapid-transit rail service (U-, S-, A-Bahn) and many buses free of charge from Monday to Friday outside of rush hour (6–9am & 4–6pm) and all day at weekends. Bicycles are also permitted on board ferries at all times.

Taxis wait 24 hours a day at ranks on the Kirchenallee side of the Hauptbahnhof and outside St-Pauli-Landungsbrücken. To pre-book a taxi, try Taxi Hamburg (ⓣ040/66 66 66).

Accommodation

The downside of a booming economy is that accommodation in Hamburg is among the most expensive in Germany. Ever progressive, the city boasts a quota of **design hotels** that are big on the wow factor. At the other end of the scale is a scattering of **hostels** that are reliable sources of cheap beds, though you'll need to make a reservation.

Which area you stay in depends as much on your plans for the city as your budget. Upmarket hotels in the city centre provide sights on your doorstep, but can leave you marooned from the nightlife centres. Gentrified, gay-friendly St Georg has a clutch of cheaper hotels around the Hauptbahnhof, although the proximity of a minor red-light district means you should be wary of any bargain hotel not recommended here or by the tourist information offices. Quieter, and certainly more elegant, are those hotels on the Aussenalster lake, home to the city's two *grande-dame* addresses, and in surrounding suburbs northeast.

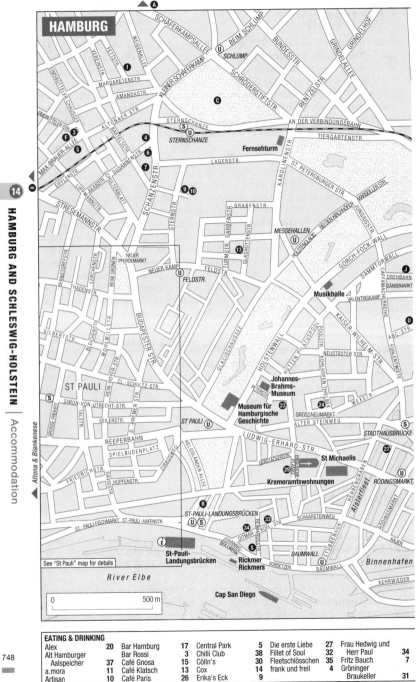

HAMBURG

See "St Pauli" map for details

River Elbe

0 ——————— 500 m

Cap San Diego

EATING & DRINKING

Alex	**20**	Bar Hamburg	**17**	Central Park	**5**	Die erste Liebe	**27**	Frau Hedwig und
Alt Hamburger		Bar Rossi	**3**	Chilli Club	**38**	Fillet of Soul		Herr Paul	**34**
Aalspeicher	**37**	Café Gnosa	**15**	Cölln's	**30**	Fleetschlösschen	**35**	Fritz Bauch	**7**
a.mora	**11**	Café Klatsch	**13**	Cox	**14**	frank und frei	**4**	Gröninger
Artisan	**10**	Café Paris	**26**	Erika's Eck	**9**			Braukeller	**31**

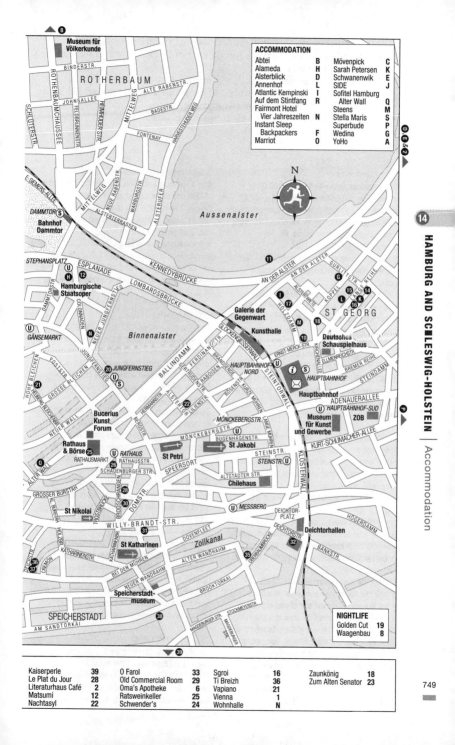

ACCOMMODATION

Abtei	B	Mövenpick	C
Alameda	H	Sarah Petersen	K
Alsterblick	D	Schwanenwik	E
Annenhof	L	SIDE	J
Atlantic Kempinski	I	Sofitel Hamburg	
Auf dem Stintfang	R	Alter Wall	Q
Fairmont Hotel		Steens	M
Vier Jahreszeiten	N	Stella Maris	S
Instant Sleep		Superbude	P
Backpackers	F	Wedina	G
Marriot	O	YoHo	A

Museum für Völkerkunde

BINDERSTR.

ROTHERBAUM

ROTHENBAUMCHAUSSEE

SCHLÜTERSTR.

JOHNSALLEE

FELDBRUNNENSTR.

HEIMHUDER STR.

MITTELWEG

ALTE RABENSTR.

BADESTR.

FONTENAY

HARVESTEHUDER WEG

E-SIEMERS-ALLEE

DAMMTOR Ⓢ

Bahnhof Dammtor

MITTELWEG

NEUE RABENSTR.

WARBURGSTR.

ALSTERUFER

ALSTERTERRASSEN

Aussenalster

N

STEPHANSPLATZ

ESPLANADE

DAMMTORSTR.

Ⓤ Ⓗ 12

Hamburgische Staatsoper

COLONNADEN

NEUER JUNGFERNSTIEG

KENNEDYBRÜCKE

LOMBARDSBRÜCKE

AN DER ALSTER

11

AN DER ALSTER

GURLITTSTR.

KLOSTER REIHE

Ⓖ

15 14

ALSTERTWIETE

KOPPEL

Ⓛ

16 Ⓚ

ST GEORG

Ⓤ GÄNSEMARKT

N

Binnenalster

JUNGFERNSTIEG

GLOCKENGIESSERWALL

Galerie der Gegenwart

Kunsthalle

Ⓘ 17

Ⓜ

ZUM DAMM

18

Ⓤ 10

Deutsches Schauspielhaus

ERNST-MERCK-STR.

KIRCHENALLEE

ELLMENREICHSTR.

BREMER REIHE

STEINDAMM

HÖHE BLEICHEN

POSTSTR.

GROSSE BLEICHEN

21

NEUER WALL

GR. BURSTAH

NEUER JUNGFERNSTIEG

BERGSTR.

HERMANNSTR.

ALSTER FLEET

20 Ⓤ Ⓢ

BALLINDAMM

DER FERDINAND-STR.

BRANDSTR.

GR. FREITAGS-PL.

RABOISEN

LILIENSTR.

22

MÖNCKEBERGSTR.

ROSENSTR.

KURZE MÜHREN

LANGE MÜHREN

HAUPTBAHNHOF NORD Ⓤ

STEINTORWALL

Ⓘ Ⓢ

HAUPTBAHNHOF

Hauptbahnhof

ADENAUERALLEE

HAUPTBAHNHOF-SUD

Museum für Kunst und Gewerbe

ZOB

STEINDAMM

BREMER REIHE

KURT-SCHUMACHER-ALLEE

Bucerius Kunst Forum

Rathaus & Börse 25

Ⓤ RATHAUS

RATHAUSSTR.

RATHAUSMARKT

SCHAUENBURGER STR.

St Petri

MÖNCKEBERGSTR.

BUGENHAGENSTR.

Ⓤ

St Jakobi

STEINSTR.

Ⓤ STEINSTR.

Ⓠ

ALTER WALL

26

SPEERSORT

ALTSTÄDTER STR.

Chilehaus

KLOSTERWALL

GROSSER BURSTAH

NL. BURSTAH

DOMSTR.

28

30

St Nikolai

Ⓤ MESSBERG

DEICHTOR-PLATZ

WILLY-BRANDT-STR.

31

DOVENFLEET

DEICHTORSTR.

Deichtorhallen

HÖGERDAMM

St Katharinen

Zollkanal

ALTER WANDRAHM

32

BANKSTR.

36

37

CREMON

KATHARINENSTR.

BEI DEN MÜHREN

NEUER WANDRAHM

OBERBAUMBRÜCKE

35

SPEICHERSTADT

Speicherstadt-museum

BROOKTORKAI

38

AM SANDTORKAI

MAGDEBURGER STR.

STOCKMEYERSTR.

39

Ⓓ, Ⓔ & ②

Ⓟ

Ⓑ

NIGHTLIFE

Golden Cut	19
Waagenbau	8

Kaiserperle	39	O Farol	33	Sgroi	16	Zaunkönig	18
Le Plat du Jour	28	Old Commercial Room	29	Ti Breizh	36	Zum Alten Senator	23
Literaturhaus Café	2	Oma's Apotheke	6	Vapiano	21		
Matsumi	12	Ratsweinkeller	25	Vienna	1		
Nachtasyl	22	Schwender's	24	Wohnhalle	N		

St Pauli and the Schanzenviertel are the hubs of Hamburg nightlife and offer a good spread of cheaper options. Altona west of St Pauli is still fairly close to the action but more refined.

The nearest **campsite** is *Camping-Buchholz* (☎040/540 45 32, ⓦwww .camping-buchholz.de), 5km northwest of the centre at Kieler Strasse 374 – the A4, and linked by train – S-Bahn Hamburg-Stellingen (S3 and S21), U-Bahn Hagenbecks Tierpark (U2) – as well as bus and nightbus.

Hotels

City centre

Alameda Colonnaden 45 ☎040/34 40 00, ⓦwww.hotelalameda.de. Nothing flashy, just a spotless, helpful small hotel whose spacious rooms are a bargain considering the location in Hamburg's most exclusive shopping district. ❹

Marriott ABC Str. 52 ☎040/350 50, ⓦwww.hamburgmarriott.com. Comfortable central business hotel with spacious classic-modern rooms. ❻–❽

SIDE Drehbahn 49 ☎040/30 99 90, ⓦwww .side-hamburg.de. A five-star temple of interior design with space-age sofas above the courtyard foyer and Zen-like minimalist style in rooms of marble, glass and dark wood. Its *Bar Fusion* is the place to mingle with the beautiful people. ❽

Sofitel Hamburg Alter Wall Alter Wall 40 ☎040/36 95 00, ⓦwww.sofitel.com. Try to secure a room overlooking the Alster Fleet in this neutral-toned, minimalist-styled luxury outpost of the Sofitel chain. Also has a spa. ❽

Around the Alster lakes

Abtei Abteistr. 14 ☎040/44 29 05, ⓦwww .abtei-hotel.de. A small period-piece of the Relaix & Chateaux group that peps up its late 1800s decor with subtle modern pieces. Located 5min walk from the Aussenalster's northwest ferry quay. ❼–❽

Alsterblick Schwanenwik 30 ☎040/22 94 89 89, ⓦwww.hotel-alsterblick.de. A comfortable, quietly charming small hotel which makes full use of the elegant architecture of this late 1800s villa on the Aussenalster banks. ❻

Atlantic Kempinski An der Alster 72–79 ☎040/288 80, ⓦwww.kempinski.atlantic.de. This grand five-star of the old school was created for ocean-liner passengers – its foyer is a paean to Twenties glamour. Deluxe and Superior rooms are worth the extra over disappointing Standard-grade – the Atlantic Suite starred in Bond movie *Tomorrow Never Dies* – and facilities are as luxurious as you'd expect. Doubles from €295. ❾

Fairmont Hotel Vier Jahreszeiten Neuer Jungfernstieg 9–14 ☎ 040/349 40, ⓦwww.fairmont.com/hamburg. Less of a hotel than a Hamburg institution, this five-star founded in 1897 is one of the most prestigious addresses in the city. It feels like a turn-of-the-twentieth-century country house, and the service is just as immaculate. Doubles from €250. ❾

Schwanenwik Schwanenwik 29 ☎040/220 09 18, ⓦwww.hotel-schwanenwik.de. Modest small hotel well located by the lake and within walking distance to St Georg, though the decor is a little frumpy. Bus #6 to Mundsburger Brücke. ❹

St Georg

Annenhof Lange Reihe 23 ☎040/24 34 26, ⓦwww.hotelannenhof.de. A cheap and cheerful gay-friendly pension on St Georg's main strip; rooms feature bright walls, wood floors and moments of historical architectural character; those at the front are largest but noisiest; good value nonetheless. ❸

Sarah Petersen Lange Reihe 50 ☎ 040/24 98 26, ⓦwww.galerie-hotel-sarah-petersen.de. Five rooms in an eighteenth-century house with an eclectic mix of art and antiques and named after its artist owner – think homely comfortable rather than designer art hotel. ❹–❼

Steens Holzdamm 43 ☎040/24 46 42, ⓦwww.steens-hotel.com. Anonymous in style, big in location, just up from the acclaimed *Atlantic Kempinski*. A clean and safe choice for those on a budget. ❹–❺

🏃 **Wedina** Gurlittstr. 23 ☎040/280 89 00, ⓦwww.wedina.de. Four styles, from minimalism to standard modern hotel, in four wings of an understated hip hotel close to the action on Lange Reihe. Those in Green, Yellow or Blue house have the most character. All provide good breakfasts and access to a lovely garden. ❺–❼

St Pauli and Schanzenviertel

🏃 **East** Simon-von-Utrecht-Str. 31 ☎040/30 99 32 05, ⓦwww.east-hamburg .de. An über-hip design number carved from a former iron foundry that's big on the wow factor in public areas: the fluid organic forms make it feel like being inside a Dalí painting. The decor elsewhere is tasteful interior design-style and there's a luxury spa. **❼**–**❽**

Etap Simon-von-Utrecht-Str. 64 ☏040/31 76 56 20, ⓦwww.accorhotels.de. The usual functional member of the budget chain, but a good fall-back at an excellent price for the location. **❷**–**❸**

Hafen Seewartenstr. 9 ☏040/311 11 30, ⓦwww.hotel-hafen-hamburg.de. This walloping former seamen's bunk-down is in a superb location above the port. Lowly "Seaman's" and "Lieutenant's" classes are a little disappointing, but "Captain's" class in a new wing is more modern. Reservations and two-night minimum stay for a port view. **❺**–**❼**

Kogge Bernhard-Nocht-Str. 59 ☏040/31 28 72, ⓦwww.kogge-hamburg.de. Wacky themed decor in a friendly "rock 'n' roll hotel" – the streetside Show Room is one for exhibitionists. All rooms are on the small side and above a bar, though this is all about its location in the Reeperbahn's grungy heart. **❷**

Mövenpick Sternschanze 6 ☏040/334 41 10, ⓦwww.moevenpick.com. Created from a historic watertower in 2007, so with more character than other chain franchisees; bare brick walls in public areas and relaxed modern decor in the rooms. Well located for nightlife in the Schanze. **❻**

St Annen Annenstr. 5 ☏040/317 71 30, ⓦwww.hotel-st-annen.de. Pleasant, small business hotel with a touch of designer flair and a location on a quiet square that's close – but not too close – to the Reeperbahn nightlife. Nice garden, too. **❹**–**❻**

Stella Maris Reimarusstr. 12 ☏040/319 20 23, ⓦwww.stellamaris-hamburg.de. Though facilities are shared, cabin-sized "Seaman's rooms" are a steal for their location in the port-side Portuguese quarter. Higher-grade rooms in this friendly three-star are larger and en suite. **❷**–**❹**

YoHo Moorkamp 5 ☏040/284 19 10, ⓦwww.yoho-hamburg.de. Tagged "The Young Hotel" and targeting the post-backpacker market, this provides hip designer style on a budget. The caveat is there's not space to swing a suitcase in some doubles. Under-26s **❸**, others **❹**.

Altona and western suburbs

25 Hours Paul-Dessau-Str. 2 ☏040/85 50 40, ⓦwww.25hours-hotels.com/hamburg. Colour, pattern and the odd knowing wink of kitsch characterize a funky hotel from the team behind Hamburg's first design hotel. Location is rather isolated: Bahrenfeld S-Bahn is a 15min walk. **❻**

Louis C Jacob Elbchaussee 401–403 ☏040/02 25 50, ⓦwww.hotel-jacob.de. An idyllic location on the Elbe and classic old-world elegance combine to grant this refined hideaway membership to the exclusive "Leading Small Hotels of the World" club. Its gourmet restaurant is sensational (see p.768). Doubles from €255. **❾**

Hostels

The majority of hostel accommodation is in the nightlife areas of St Pauli and the Schanzenviertel.

Auf dem Stintfang Alfred-Wegener-Weg 5, St Pauli ☏040/31 34 88, ⓦwww.jugendherberge.de/jh/hamburg-stintfang. The best of Hamburg's youth hostels, renovated into a modern, bright place with superb port views from its communal lounge. Inevitably popular with school groups, which means school rules, though open 24hr. Check-in from 1pm. Dorms €15.90–19.90, rooms **❷**.

Backpackers St Pauli Bernstorffstr. 98, St Pauli ☏040/235 170 43, ⓦwww.backpackers-stpauli.de. Small hostel run by St Pauli locals with an alternative attitude – a chance to get off the backpacker circuit. Check-in is at The Globe bar. Six- and eight-bed dorms €19.50–23, rooms **❸**.

Instant Sleep Backpackers Max-Brauer-Allee 277, Schanzenviertel ☏040/43 18 23 10, ⓦwww.instantsleep.de. Though a little spartan, enlivened only by splashes of bright colour, Hamburg's first independent hostel is well placed for the nightlife of the Schanzenviertel. Laundry and kitchen facilities, free internet and storage, and not a bunk bed in sight. Dorms €15.50–18.50, rooms **❷**.

Schanzenstern Altona Kleine Rainstr. 24–26, Altona ☏040/39 91 91 91, ⓦwww.schanzenstern.de. An upmarket hostel, colourful and friendly, with a dorm, rooms and a couple of apartments. Dorm €19, rooms and apartment **❸**.

Superbude Spaldingstr. 152, St Georg ☏040/380 87 80, ⓦwww.superbude.de. This new, funky place is halfway between hostel and budget design hotel. Bright colours and quirky details such as beer-crate seats abound, plus there's a Wii games room and super-friendly staff. Dorm €16–22, rooms **❸**–**❹**.

The city centre

If their semicircular shape doesn't drop a heavy hint, names of the roads that end in "wall" give away the path of the defences that girdled the city until Napoleon added a new prize to his empire. The boundary still defines the city centre, officially comprised of the **Altstadt** (bordered to the north by the Alsterfleet canal) and the **Neustadt** (everywhere else in the centre). If the demarcation between these two is unnoticeable today, it is somewhat academic historically, too. Just 380 years after Charlemagne rode out across a sandy hummock between the Elbe and the Alster in 808 and built the "Hammaburg" ring fort on the site of a Saxon village, Count Adolph III of Schauenburg began to draw up the new boundaries for the fledgling city.

However, districts can be distinguished within the seamless spread of architecture. As ever, the heart of the city is the **Rathaus**. The Great Fire of 1842 then Allied bombs a century later wiped most historic architecture from the streetscape, but the jumble of postwar styles has its own dynamism. What little survived fire and war is in the city's oldest quarters south of the Altstadt, at its most historic in **Deichstrasse**. Beyond it are the port warehouse district, **Speicherstadt** and adjoining **HafenCity**, that feature some of the most distinctive harbour architecture in Europe – old and new. The hub of current port activity is St-Pauli-Landungsbrücken a fifteen-minute walk west. The area north of the Rathaus is characterized by luxury shopping boutiques and the lovely Alster lakes that define the centre, while east towards the Hauptbahnhof are principal shopping high-streets Steinstrasse and Mönckebergstrasse. The Kunsthalle near the Hauptbahnhof represents the start of Hamburg's **Kunstmeile**, the "Art Mile" that is home to the city's blockbuster cultural museums.

The Rathaus and around

Forty-four years after the Great Fire of 1842 razed the Altstadt, city fathers began work on their morale-booster, a monument to inspire Hamburg's citizens and embody her phoenix-like revival. If the neo-Renaissance Rathaus oozes civic self-confidence today, it must have positively swaggered when the final stone was laid in 1897. It isn't shy about boasting either: above a parade of German emperors are statues of the tradesmen who won the city's prosperity; protectress Hammonia casts an imperial gaze from above the balcony; and triumphant classical figures and wreaths of plenty adorn the bases of two flagpoles crowned with gold ships. Hard to believe, then, that only four thousand oak poles prevent this bombastic pile from subsiding into the sandbank beneath. The senate and city government still dictate policy from the Rathaus's 647 rooms, a taste of whose opulence can be seen on 45-minute guided tours (every 30min Mon–Thurs 10am–3pm, Fri 10am–1pm, Sat 10am–5pm, Sun 10am–4pm; in English, daily 10.15am, also Thurs 3.15pm & Fri–Sun 1.15pm; €3). With a coffered ceiling and oversized murals of the city's founding, the Great Hall is a knockout.

At the right-hand shoulder of the Rathaus, the **Bucerius Kunst Forum** (Tues–Sun 11am–7pm except Thurs till 9pm; €5; Ⓦ www.buceriuskunstforum .de) hosts temporary art exhibitions, while on the other side of the Alsterfleet canal, the arcades of **Alsterarkaden** aspire to St Mark's Square in Venice, which served as a model when they were built in 1843. Now home to smart boutiques, it forms the window-dressing of a triangle of haute-couture shopping and arcades that extends back to Gansemarkt. At the back of the Rathaus, on Adolphsplatz, you'll find the **Börse**, the current incarnation of Germany's first stock market, and a revealing symbol of mercantile priorities at the heart of government.

The historic Altstadt

Lost among the offices south of Adolphsplatz is the **Trotsbrücke**, Hamburg's oldest bridge. That it marks the transition to the site of the first settlement on the other side of the Alsterfleet explains its statue of Count Adolph III of Schauenburg, the savvy nobleman who expanded the city and pulled off the 1189 tax concession that kick-started Hamburg's ascendancy. Like all good businessmen, he clinched the deal with a sweetener – a donation to the crusade of Emperor Frederick I. Opposite him is St Ansgar, the "Apostle of the North", who slotted in fourteen years as Hamburg's first archbishop from 831 between spreading the gospel to Vikings and Danes.

A short distance from the bridge, in the Altstadt proper, are the skeletal remains of **St Nikolai**. The Great Fire did for the original, then a century later Allied air command destroyed its replacement and Hamburg left the remnants as a peace symbol to remember victims of oppression and war. A hint of the church's former glory is there in Germany's third highest spire, a 144m neo-Gothic number that Sir George Gilbert Scott – an Englishman, ironically – modelled on the steeples of the Dom in Cologne and Freiburg's Münster, and a documentation centre (daily 10.30am–5.30pm; €3.50) with sobering images of the wartime destruction. The same ticket gets you into a glass lift up the tower's blackened skeleton (daily: June–Aug 9.30am–8pm; April, May, Sept & Oct 10am–7pm; Nov–March 10.30am–5.30pm) for a panoramic view.

Nearby **Deichstrasse** provides a glimpse of Hamburg before that destructive century. In this quiet corner off Willy-Brandt-Strasse stands a row of gabled houses that were the homes and warehouses of seventeenth- and eighteenth-century merchants. One of the more remiss among them was probably to blame for the 1842 conflagration which is said to have started at no. 42. Poet and playwright Friedrich Hebbel, who lived on Deichstrasse, reported that the blaze lasted three days – the sandstone portal of no. 25 still bears the scars. Slip down a passage between the houses and you reach the Nikolaifleet, one of the most evocative spots in the city; you don't have to stretch the imagination far to visualize the canal filled with ships, their crews heaving produce from the holds into warehouses via pulleys at the gables' peaks. Good views of the river frontage

Operation Gomorrah, July 1943

The port that nourished Hamburg also made it a prime target for the Allies. In retaliation for earlier Luftwaffe raids, British and US raids wiped ten square kilometres of Hamburg off the map and obliterated eighty percent of the harbour during a week of relentless sorties at the end of July 1943. Over seven thousand tonnes of high explosives and incendiaries rained onto the city, killing nearly 40,000 people; by way of comparison, the famous Luftwaffe raid on Coventry killed 538.

As the flames sucked in oxygen, typhoon winds blasted western residential districts and the Germans had to create a new word to describe the apocalypse – *"Feuersturm"* (firestorm). Winds of nearly 1000°C set asphalt streets ablaze, trees were uprooted, cars flung into superheated air. "Every human resistance was quite useless," reported Hamburg's police chief later. "People jumped into the canals and waterways and remained swimming or standing up to their necks for hours … Children were torn away from their parents' hands by the force of the hurricane and whirled into the fire."

Third Reich architect Albert Speer later revealed that Hitler and Hermann Göring had been shocked at the devastation. Even Air Chief Marshal Arthur "Bomber" Harris conceded that the attacks on the Reich's second city were "incomparably more terrible" than anything previously launched at Germany. Operation Gomorrah was well named.

▲ The view from St Nikolai's spire to the Rathaus and the Aussenalster lake

are also available from Hohe Brücke at the end of Deichstrasse. Also here is a plaque that commemorates where the flood waters finally stopped rising on the night of February 16, 1962. This catastrophe, caused by a storm surging down the Elbe, claimed over three hundred lives.

Unmistakable due to its twin-lantern Baroque spire that defines Hamburg's waterfront, **St Katharinen church** was the focus of the medieval merchants' quarter; inside are a crucifix and a demure effigy of its saint, who clutches the spiked wheel on which she was tortured for daring to out-debate the pagan sages of Emperor Maxentius. Local folklore narrates that the replica of St Katharine's gold crown, which wraps around the spire, was smelted from the booty of pirate Klaus Störtebeker, the bane of Hanseatic merchants until, according to legend, he was double-crossed and executed in Hamburg in 1401. They say the folk hero's decapitated body rose and walked from the scaffold.

The east Altstadt

Continue east up Dovenfleet alongside the Zollkanal and you enter the **Kontorhaus** (Counting House) quarter and the red-brick edifices of the business district. The mightiest of all is the eccentric **Chilehaus** (1924). Taking inspiration from the ships in the docks opposite, Expressionist architect Fritz Höger fused traditional building in brick with sleek Twenties style. And the ten-storey Chilehaus certainly has style despite locals' quips about a flat iron. If you look back at it from where Burchardplatz meets Pumpen, Höger's ocean liner becomes apparant: the building's end forms a high bow, a Chilean condor acts as a figurehead and decks with railings jut out on either side. Its merchant owner, Henry Barens Sloman, earned his wealth through thirty years of saltpetre trade with Chile, hence the building's name.

A giant among organs takes pride of place in the fifteenth-century church of **St Jakobi** on Steinstrasse. It is the largest surviving work of Arp Schnitger, a rising star of organ-building when he created it in 1693, who is now recognized as the best the Baroque era produced; his instruments are prized for their craftsman-ship as much as their tone. Johann Sebastian Bach tickled its keys in 1720 while considering a position as resident organist. That it survives at all is a wonder. In World War I its case-pipes were melted for munitions and after a 1944 air raid, all that remained of the church was its Gothic facade and a stump of tower. The organ escaped the devastation in a basement store alongside St Jakobi's art treasures: the high altar of the Coopers' Guild, depicted at work in the stained glass above; the Fishers' Guild altar; and the fine altar of St Lukas. Look, too, for a sight of old Hamburg in a 1681 cityscape, the skyline pricked by Hamburg's spires as today.

St Jakobi borders shopping high-street Mönckebergstrasse that leads to **St Petri**, site of nine hundred years of ecclesiastical history. Today's neo-Gothic building stands on the foundations of a fourteenth-century church destroyed by fire in 1842. This was only the final insult because Napoleon's troops used the church as a stable and prison during their occupation of Hamburg from 1808 to 1814. In the northern gallery off the soaring nave is a tender sandstone *Madonna and Child* of 1470, attributed to the sculptor behind the *Darsow-Madonna* in Lübeck's Marienkirche. The church is also home to Hamburg's oldest artwork, a bronze lion's-head door-knocker cast in 1342. A calf-burning climb takes you to a peak in the church tower (Mon–Sat 10am–4.30pm; €2) where you peer out through portholes for views of the Rathaus, the Alster lakes and the Elbe; anyone who suffers vertigo may want to think twice.

Around Jungfernstieg, and Alster cruises

As the port characterizes the south of the city, the **Binnenalster** and **Aussen-alster** lakes define the centre. Created when the Alster rivulet was dammed in the thirteenth century, the lakes were ignored until the 1800s, when they caught the eye of the city's wealthy burghers, who colonized the area around them and strolled their banks. During a Sunday constitutional, families paraded their unmarried daughters ("Jungfern") beside the Binnenalster's banks on **Jungfernstieg**. It's no coincidence the street is a slick couture number, while behind it are the class acts of Hohe Bleichen, ABC-Strasse and Grosse Bleichen. Less flashy are the arcades that line – and name – **Colonnaden**, a pleasing slice of late nineteenth-century pomp.

Eligible offspring in tow or not, the Alsterwanderweg path remains a popular walk around the Aussenalster lake (see p.762) – the best picture-postcard view of city spires and the frontage along Binnenalster is from Lombardsbrücke. Alterna-tively, **boat tours** of the ATG Alster-Touristik line (every 30min mid-March to

early Oct daily 10am–6pm, until 5pm until early Nov; ☎040/357 42 40, ⓦwww
.alstertouristik.de) depart from the quay on Jungfernstieg; options include a
fifty-minute Alster-Rundfahrten (€10) which circuits the lakes; a two-hour Kanal-
Fahrten (times vary by season; €13) that also tours the waterways of rich suburbs
northeast of the lake; and the Dämmertörn, which departs at twilight (May–Sept
8pm; €15). *St Georg*, a historic steamer operated by Verein Alsterdampschiffahrt,
departs from the same wharf (March 21–Nov 2 daily every hour 10.45am–5.45am;
45min; €9; ☎040/792 25 99, ⓦwww.alsterdampfer.de). Also leaving from this
quay is the Fleet-Fahrten cruise through the Alster locks to the Speicherstadt and
HafenCity (late March to Oct daily 10.45am, 1.45pm, 4.45pm; €15; 2hr).

Arguably more fun is to pick up a **pedalo**, **canoe** or **sailing dinghy** at rental
outfits dotted all around the Aussenalster: Segelschule Pieper (☎040/24 75 78,
ⓦwww.segelschule-pieper.de), opposite the *Atlantic Kempinski*, has a good range
of craft, or Bootshaus Silwar (Eppendorfer Landstrasse 148b; ☎040/47 62 07,
ⓦwww.bootshaus-silwar.com), in northern suburb Epplesdorf, rents canoes,
should you want to paddle into canals off the lake. Whichever way you travel,
expect views of handsome villas peeking between the trees.

Museums of the Kunstmeile

Hamburg stores its finest collections of art on the "**Art Mile**" that arcs south
behind the Hauptbahnhof towards the Elbe, officially just outside the central
boundary. With work from classics to cutting-edge, pure art to decorative design
and photography, there's something for everyone here, plus two world-class
collections in the Kunsthalle and Museum für Kunst und Gewerbe.

The Kunsthalle

The Kunstmeile kicks off with the world-class **Kunsthalle** (Art Hall; Tues–Sun
10am–6pm, Thurs till 9pm; €6; ⓦwww.hamburger-kunsthalle.de), just north
of the Hauptbahnhof on Glockengiesserwall, a feast of paintings and sculpture,
from medieval to modern, which takes around half a day to digest properly.
North Germany's premier artist pre-1400, Meister Bertram, gets star billing
among the German medieval artists for his Grabow altarpiece, once the high
altar of St Petri. This 36-panel work blazes with sumptuous colour and lively
detail, especially the *Creation of the Animals*. Look, too, for charismatic portraits
by Cranach, and Rembrandt's early *Simeon in the Temple*, which overshadows all
the Dutch land- and seascapes before it.

Nineteenth-century Germans are well represented, including the finest works
of short-lived Philipp Otto Runge. The big draw, however, is their Romantic-
in-chief, Caspar David Friedrich, and his *Rambler above the Sea of Fog* and *Ice
Sea*, two variations on his favourite themes of solitude and the power of nature.
From the same period but a world away in style are Manet's scandalous courtesan
Nana, enjoyable works by fellow Frenchmen Toulouse-Lautrec and Renoir, and
the warped eroticism of Munch's dark *Madonna*, more whore than holy. German
Impressionism follows, as well as vigorous works by Expressionists of Der Blaue
Reiter and Die Brücke groups, as well as non-affiliates Beckmann and Klee.

The **Galerie der Gegenwart** (Gallery of Contemporary Art; same hours
& ticket), a white cube with a central, light-filled atrium designed by Oswald
Mathias Ungers, is reached through a tunnel from the Kunsthalle. It's worth
taking a break in the latter's charming, period-piece *Café Liebermann* before
continuing into the collection of post-1960s international art and installations.
Modern giants rub shoulders with up-and-coming names: from established
figures such as Andy Warhol, David Hockney, Joseph Beuys and Richard Serra
in the basement, via recent American work on the second floor, including Jeff

Koons' cheeky kitsch, to key figures of German painting such as Georg Baselitz and Sigmar Polke on the third floor.

The Museum für Kunst und Gewerbe

In a scruffy area of St Georg south of the Hauptbahnhof, the neo-Renaissance palace that houses the **Museum für Kunst und Gewerbe** (Museum of Art and Crafts; Tues–Sun 10am–6pm, Thurs till 9pm; €8; ⓦ www.mkg-hamburg.de) is a treat. Over three spacious, well-ordered floors is a treasure-trove of decorative arts from antiquities to a who's who of modern interior design, alongside superb Renaissance and Baroque exhibits, fashions, graphics and photography, plus *objets d'art* from the Islamic world and East Asia, including a Japanese teahouse that hosts the obligatory ceremony (3rd weekend of the month; €2.50).

The museum's pride and joy is its early European keyboards in the Schumann wing, the finest collection of its sort in the world, including the extravagantly decorated clavichords on the ground floor, notably a beautiful instrument by Venetian master Giovanni Celestini with a thicket of leaves and roses in cyprus and parchment inlaid on its soundboard. Ask about the times of daily concerts when you buy your ticket.

If time's tight be sure not to miss the period rooms, including a Hamburg piano room in Louis XVI style and a cabin-like nook that a lawyer who was nostalgic for his sea journey to Brazil commissioned from St Petri and Rathausmarkt architect Alexis de Chateauneuf. Less charming but more valuable are the magnificent Jugendstil and Art Nouveau rooms that were assembled by the museum's first director at the 1900 World Exhibition in Paris. Justus Brinckmann conceived his acquisitions of furniture, wall hangings, textiles, lamps, decorative objects, even books, as a "*Gesamtkunstwerk*" (integrated artwork) and generously allowed the city council to pick up the bill for what was the largest purchase of contemporary works ever made by a German museum. There's also fluid furniture from Henry van de Velde, the Belgian who pioneered Art Nouveau, and a blocky showcase by Gauguin – the only piece of large furniture the artist produced – which is decorated with portraits of his children, Jean and Aline. Pop Art design is an enjoyable bit of space-age kitsch, and there's a charming old-fashioned café on the ground floor.

The rest of the Kunstmeile

The art continues south in exhibitions presented in a line of private galleries along Klosterwall – **Kunsthaus**, Klosterwall 15 (Tues–Sun 10am–6pm; price varies) and **Kunstverein** and **Akademie der Kunst** (both Klosterwall 23; same times) – before it concludes at the **Deichtorhallen**, Deichtorstrasse 1–2 (Tues–Fri 11am–6pm, Sat & Sun 10am–6pm; €6.50; ⓦ www.deichtorhallen.de). The former halls of a fruit and veg market, now six thousand square metres of exhibition space divided between contemporary art and photography, house blockbuster retrospectives of contemporary German artists and international names such as Andy Warhol, Roy Lichtenstein, Helmut Newton and Arne Jacobsson. Also here is the Hamburg High-Flyer (p.759) helium balloon.

St Michaelis church and the Krameramtswohnungen

A city icon, **St Michaelis**, at the western edge of the city centre by Ludwig-Erhard-Strasse, is Hamburg's finest church and its favourite. No wonder because more than any other building, the "Michael" mirrors the city's fighting spirit. Burned down after a lightning strike in 1750, it was rebuilt in Baroque style under Ernst Georg Sonnin (then renowned as a mathematician and mechanic more than a master builder) only to be incinerated again in 1906 when a workman started a blaze with his blowtorch. In 1945, the Allies obliterated the roof and decor of church number three. Reconstructed again to Sonnin's plans, it is now the finest Baroque church in North Germany.

With white-washed walls alleviated only by capitals picked out in gold, it's a typically plain Protestant affair; Martin Luther, whose portly statue stands outside, would have approved of its light-filled space and restraint. With his elevation of the spoken word, he would also have admired a pillar-free nave that provides a two-and-a-half-thousand-strong congregation with a clear view of the preacher in a pulpit like a chariot.

A "Multivision" show (daily 12.30–3.30pm; €2.50 or combined ticket €4) whizzes through the city's history, while a so-so museum in the vaults (11am–4.30pm; €1.50) traces the church through various stages of construction and destruction in images and mementoes. Here, too, you can pay homage at the grave of CPE Bach, who succeeded Telemann as its musical director; St Michealis **organ concerts** are rated second after those in St Jakobi by the city's aficionados. Perhaps the most rewarding attraction is the **viewing platform** 82m up (daily: May–Oct 9am–7pm; Nov–April 10am–5.30pm; €2.50), which provides one of the best views over Hamburg: the 360-degree panorama takes in Speicherstadt, the container port and shipping on the Elbe, the Alster lakes, and the five spires of the churches and Rathaus, which punctuate the skyline like exclamation marks. Forfeit the lift for the 449 stairs down and you are rewarded with a close-up view of the church's bells.

Hidden through an archway on Krayenkamp a moment east of the church is the **Krameramtswohnungen**, a cluster of almshouses where the shopkeepers' guild (the Krameramt) housed widows of its departed members. It's an atmospheric nook where seventeenth-century brick and half-timbered buildings huddle so close to the tiny alley the widows could have nattered across the street without shouting. It's also on the must-see list of every tour group and the almshouses sold out to tourist shops and souvenir galleries long ago. Still, a museum (April–Oct Tues–Sun 10am–5pm; €1) provides an authentic impression of the cramped conditions.

Around St Michaelis church

Northwest of St Michaelis, Peterstrasse, reached via Neanderstrasse off Ludwig-Erhard-Strasse, is a rare glimpse of historical streetscape. The gabled Baroque town houses that line this cobbled street were reconstructed brick by brick after a city-wide rescue effort. It's a pleasing corner of the city, a glimpse of Hamburg's architectural heritage that's all the more enjoyable because your only company is likely to be locals gossiping on a bench. Peterstrasse 41 is a small museum of manuscripts, scores and souvenirs (Tues, Thurs & Sun 10am–4pm; €4) that honour Johannes Brahms, who was born nearby in 1833. Hamburg did little else for its local son, however: teenage Brahms is said to have made ends meet as a pianist in dancehall dives at the port and at 29 his aspiration of being the city's conductor were dashed; he eventually harrumphed off to Vienna. It was probably guilty conscience that led the city to erect the neo-Baroque Musikhalle on nearby Johannes-Brahms-Platz.

Looking lost among the traffic on Holstenwall is the stately building that houses the **Museum für Hamburgische Geschichte**, or Hamburgmuseum (Tues–Sun 10am–5pm, Sun till 6pm; €7.50; ⓦwww.hamburgmuseum.de). No surprise that the port looms large in its potted history of Hamburg and its citizens – there are models of the city's fleets, both Hanseatic merchant ships and trans-atlantic liners, and an opportunity to explore the bridge of a 1909 cargo steamer against a backdrop of the first footage of the port shot in colour. Equally engaging are the re-created historic Hamburg interiors on the second floor, none more evocative of former mercantile pomp than the seventeenth-century quarters of a prosperous merchant from Deichstrasse. Elsewhere are well-displayed exhibits of medieval religious sculpture salvaged from the churches, town fashions, an enormous model of Solomon's Temple – less a historical fact than an insight into the ideals of Baroque architecture – and on the top floor a 1:32 1950s model railway which whirrs into action at regular intervals (daily 11am, noon, 2pm & 3pm, plus Sun 4pm). Most exhibits have annotations in English, and its charming café is a pleasant spot to pause.

Opposite the museum, looming above the treetops, is a 37m-high monument to Otto von Bismarck – the largest in Germany. The Iron Chancellor's characteristic strong-arm tactics wrestled back Schleswig and Holstein from Denmark in 1864, allowing Hamburg to resume its boast of being a "gateway to the world", which is why Bismarck gazes downriver towards the North Sea. The statue stands at one end of Wallanlagen, the first in a line of parks which ring the town as a leafy bulwark in place of the fortifications ripped away by Napoleon. The highlight is Planten un Blomen, in the centre north of the Musikhalle, a botanic garden and Europe's largest Japanese garden.

Speicherstadt and HafenCity

Not just the name, **Speicherstadt** (Warehouse Town), but also the atmosphere of cobbled streets, gables and turrets combine to make the area on the other side of Zollkanal (Tax Canal) a world apart from the city opposite. The red-brick architecture – a deliberate nod to Hanseatic days – of the largest continuous warehousing in the world sprang up from 1885 to 1927, providing storage for a city that had recently signed up to the fledgling Customs Union (1888) of the Second Reich. An entire residential district was razed, and nearly 24,000 people displaced to make way for it. Trade has leached away to deeper water, but things haven't changed much in concept. Today's importers still hoard goods tax-free until market prices provide a tidy profit and so strict are preservation orders on the area that goods are hoisted by block and tackle. Carved up by canals, its warehouses are piled high with crates and Middle Eastern carpets (it still houses Europe's largest stock), and the air is tinted with occasional whiffs of malt and coffee.

With such striking architecture, simply nosing around is much of the pleasure, especially from dusk, when spotlit warehouses rising sheer from the waterways is one of Hamburg's most evocative sights. However, you can also experience the area at water-level on **boat trips** that depart from St-Pauli-Landungsbrücken and the Binnenalster quay on Jungfernstieg. For an aerial view over the warehouses and downriver to the port, head to the **Hamburg High-Flyer** helium balloon (daily 10am–10pm; 15min €15, 30min €22), which ascends to 150m on a tether outside the Deichtorhallen, wind permitting.

A growing number of warehouses have been recycled into museum spaces. On the front there's Europe's largest model railway, **Miniatur Wunderland** (Mon–Fri 9.30am–6pm, Tues till 9pm, Sat & Sun 8am–8pm; €10); the **Hamburg Dungeon** (daily: Jan–May & Sept–Dec 11am–6pm; June–Aug 10am–6pm; €16.95), a franchise of the camp horror-fest; at the rear of the block, **Spicy's Gewürzmuseum**, Am Sandtorkai 32 (year-round Tues–Sun 10am–5pm plus Mon June–Oct; €3), which provides a powerful hit of olfactory exotica to reflect Hamburg's status as a leading spice importer; and ten minutes' walk east the intriguing **Dialog im Dunkeln**, Alter Wandrahm 4 (Tues–Fri 9am–5pm, Sat & Sun 11am–7pm; €14; reservations required; ☎0700 44 33 20 00), in which blind guides lead sighted visitors through darkened scenarios to re-experience familiar environments.

For detail on the area's history head a short way east to St Annenufer and the **Speicherstadtmuseum** (April–Oct Tues–Fri 10am–6pm, Sat & Sun 10am–6pm; Nov–March Tues–Sun 10am–5pm; €3) which displays photos of the area's development. A more relevant attraction for Germany's principal seaport is the **International Maritime Museum** (Tues–Sun 10am–6pm; €10) to the southeast, with ten storeys of all things maritime. As impressive as the breadth of coverage – from navigation, sail and shipbuilding to oceanography via art and bone models crafted by prisoners of war, plus a pair of Nelson's cannons at the entrance – is that most exhibits are the personal collection of Peter Tamm, former CEO of Europe's largest newspaper publisher, Hamburg-based Axel Springer Verlag.

HafenCity

Ever ambitious, Hamburg is shoring up its economic clout with a €5bn redevelopment of derelict docklands that will extend the centre by forty percent south and east of Speicherstadt. By its completion in 2025, the area is expected to provide sufficient office space for 40,000 people and 5500 apartments. Notwithstanding that **HafenCity** currently makes the famous building site at Potsdamer Platz, Berlin, seem like minor roadworks – its 1.55-square-kilometre area is fifteen times bigger – Europe's largest construction site is rapidly resolving into showpiece steel-and-glass offices and modernist apartments that are cantilevered over former quays. At present it looks best from Marco-Polo-Terrassen.

The figurehead over the Elbe at the symbolic convergence of river, city and harbour will be the **Elbphilharmonie**. A bold design by Swiss architects Herzog & de Meuron of London's Tate Modern fame, it places a futuristic tower of glass on the shell of a brick industrial warehouse. Until the concert hall opens in 2011, former boilerhouse Kesselhaus (Tues–Sun 10am–6pm; free) provides information on both the project and HafenCity, plus occasional tours of the development.

The port

The massive stone blocks of **St-Pauli-Landungsbrücken** are an exercise in solidity for a city fond of brick. Four years after work on the quay began in 1906 the first ocean-going liner processed up the Elbe to moor alongside; the occasional cruise-ship still docks nearby, dwarfing everything else around. The centre of the

Destination America

Such is the hubris of boom-town Hamburg that its role as the principal emigration point in Germany is largely overlooked. Yet the unprepossessing patch of wasteland opposite HafenCity was the last piece of Europe experienced by millions of Europeans and Russians. Nearly five million people embarked at Hamburg for a new life in the New World – almost 1.9 million people left during the peak period of mass migration between 1891 and 1914, when poverty and pogroms proved the final straw for many in southern and eastern Europe. A cholera epidemic that claimed ten thousand lives in three months prompted city authorities to demand that the emigration shipping lines relocate from the docks at St Pauli to Veddel island opposite Speicherstadt. The last brick Emigrant Hall to house the masses is the centrepiece of the **Ballinstadt museum** (daily 10am–6pm; €9.80), whose interactive exhibits seek to re-create the emigrant experience with dioramas that combine contemporary exhibits and personal narratives. Most emigrants were bound for the United States, so what may be of more interest to American visitors is a research area that provides access to the records of émigrés from 1850 to 1934, plus a partner database with 34 million records. Genealogy researchers are on hand to assist.

action today is the floating wharf where ferries come and go to up river districts or across the river; the Stintfang balcony behind the U/S-Bahn station provides good views of the nonstop bustle on the water.

The wharf is also the embarkation point for **boat tours** (Hafenrundfahrt) of Germany's largest harbour (the ninth biggest in the world), a must on any visit to Hamburg. In high season all manner of craft – from two-storey catamarans to replica Mississippi paddle-steamers – set off every half-hour to spend an hour or two nosing among the vast container port and dry docks opposite or through the canals of Speicherstadt and HafenCity upriver. Prices range from €10 to €15 depending on duration. It's worth checking if an English commentary is available; many operators have an audio loop and Rainer Abicht (ⓦwww .abicht.de) schedules daily tours in English at noon from March to November (€12; 1hr). A second wharf for harbour tours is adjacent to the lightship east (see below). If your budget is tight, opt for municipal ferries operated by HADAG which are priced as other forms of public transport, so free with a Hamburg-CARD. Ferry #62 provides a great trip downriver before it terminates at the south-bank docks at Finkenweder, or you can disembark at Neumühlen/Övelgönne then walk back along the river. Ferry #73 skips along wharves on the south bank before heading deep into the container docks.

East of the wharves

Near the wharves, the three-masted 1896 barque **SS Rickmer Rickmers** (daily 10am–6pm; €3) is an insight into the self-contained world of working ships a century ago. Four years' restoration work buffed her up from the mouldering hulk that lay in Lisbon until 1983; she was a reparation gift from the British to the Portuguese Navy, snatched during World War I off Chile to the disgust of her Hamburg owners. From the beautifully varnished belay pins to the signalling flags neatly shelved in the navigator's quarters, the 92m windjammer is complete except for her 25 crew, and you sense their ghosts in the personal possessions in cabins or scratches scored by trouser buttons in the benches of the officers' mess. Upstream is the far less romantic **Cap San Diego** (Überseebrücke; daily 10am–6pm; €5), the "White Swan of the South Atlantic", which ran all manner of cargo to South America. You can nose around from her deck to her engine room, and there are exhibitions on the history of the Hamburg South Shipping Line and emigration from Hamburg.

A last slice of maritime history is further upriver – a permanently moored **British lightship** full of maritime junk opposite U-Bahn station Baumwall (Mon–Sat 11am–1pm & Sun 9am–10.30pm; free) which doubles as a restaurant-bar with jazz sessions (Sun noon & Mon eve) and a hotel (ⓣ040/36 25 53, ⓦwww.das-feuerschiff.de; ⓞ).

West of the wharves

The circular building immediately on the west side of St-Pauli-Landungs-brücken is the gateway to the **Elbtunnel** (24hr for cyclists and pedestrians; free). A marvel of engineering when completed in 1911 so workers could cross to Steinwerder in bad weather. The 462m tunnel beneath the river takes you to the scruffy south bank for a different perspective of the wharf opposite.

Running behind here on the north side, **Hafenstrasse** was the battle ground for fierce fighting between squatters and real-estate developers keen to exploit the "tenderloin of the port's border" during the 1980s. It's still in limbo as a wellspring of counterculture where graffiti declaims "*Kein mensch ist illegal*" (No one is illegal) and protest banners hang like battle colours. Ten minutes' walk further you pass the late nineteenth-century auction halls of the notorious **Sunday Fischmarkt**

The Fischmarkt, a party just for the halibut

Official records reveal the **Fischmarkt** as the city's oldest market, but that rather misses the point. Hamburg's Sunday market retains the same hours as when it began in 1703 – from 5 to 9.30am (from 7am Nov–March) – yet its focus shifted from sales to celebration long ago. And just as it's doubtful that modern traders pack up to go to church as their predecessors did, so fish now takes second place to a mind-boggling sprawl of wares, from genuine bargains to tat, from fruit and veg to livestock. The story goes that in the early 1960s The Beatles received a police warning for chasing a live pig they bought here among the stalls.

Even that is civilized stuff compared to the action in the iron Fischauktionshalle. Where Altona's fishing fleet once sold its catch, late-night casualties from St Pauli cross paths with early birds, as everyone sinks a beer and bellows along to live rock bands while bemused tourists look on. Unless you're in a sympathetically booze-fuelled frame of mind, such raw exuberance at such an early hour can be hard to stomach. Fortunately, cafés on the first floor are a safe haven from where to watch the chaos over a buffet breakfast.

(see box above). That schizophrenic institution characterizes a mixed area undergoing rapid change: on the "Elbemeile" beyond Stilwerk, a conglomerate of hip interior designers housed in a former malthouse and stylish restaurants rub shoulders with fish wholesalers – Hamburg in a nutshell.

The inner suburbs

The regions that border the centre are a mixed bag of residential districts. Light on traditional sights, they are instead areas to shop, dine or party alongside locals according to where you go: from the seriously wealthy streets behind the Aussenalster lake to the grungy nightlife in St Pauli and Schanzenviertel, or gentrified village districts downriver.

Around the Aussenalster

The lakeside enclaves around the **Aussenalster** north of the centre are among the flashest in Hamburg. **Rotherbaum** and **Harvestehude** remain as prestigious now as when they emerged in the late 1800s as the des res of business tycoons, their smart villas still jaw-droppingly affluent and home to high society and foreign consulates. The favoured hangout is **Pöseldorf**, an exclusive area located just behind Fährdamm wharf in the northwest. Between lunch with Hamburg's media high-rollers and browsing the boutiques and galleries in Milchstrasse, there is superb Jugendstil architecture in the side streets to discover – nowhere else in Hamburg boasts such a diverse mix of large white villas, courtyards and mews. Also in the area is the **Museum für Völkerkunde**, housed in a handsome building at Rothenbaumchaussee 64 (Museum of Ethnology; Tues–Sun 10am–6pm, Thurs till 9pm; €5). An engaging collection of ethnology, it's strong on Africa and the Pacific, and offers an illuminating approach to its subjects, with interesting asides on cross-cultural exchange. The nearest U-Bahn is Hallerstrasse but it's a pleasant walk up the west shore once you're free of the main road. Allow three hours for a straightforward eight-kilometre circuit of the lake – or you can hop on one of the tourist ferries operated by ATG Alster-Touristik which call at various quays (every 30min; late March to early Oct 10am–6pm).

St Pauli and the Schanzenviertel

Here it is then, the Sündermeile (Sin Mile) counterweight to the Kunstmeile on the opposite side of the city. Hamburg's citizens are miffed that the **Reeperbahn**'s red lights still attract so much attention abroad. While the "Kiez" is a far cry from the road where immigrant ropemakers weaved hemp warps for the docks (*Reep* is rope), and its seedy underbelly attracts more than the usual quota of dubious characters – a few don't seem far removed from Tom Waits's lowlife from his torch song "Reeperbahn" – the area has come a long way from the rough dockers' quarter of brawling bars where sailors spent shore leave. Commercial investment has driven out the excessive prostitution and hard drugs that characterized the late 1970s and reinvented the Reeperbahn as a nightlife centre where theatre venues trade on tourist-friendly titillation and small clubs provide some of the best nights out in town. A no-nonsense police force keeps crime figures among the city's lowest, too.

The street-spanning neon along **Grosse Freiheit** recalls the area's rollicking Sixties heyday, popularized during The Beatles' residence (see box, p.764). The street's name – Great Freedom – alludes to a liberal area of free trade and religion in the seventeenth century rather than loose morals. **Spielbudenplatz** on the

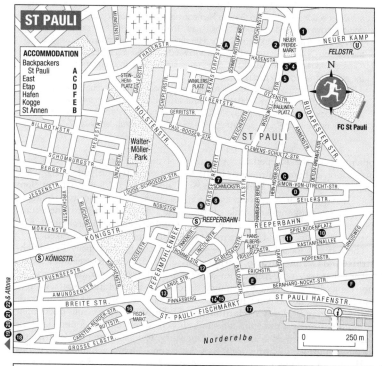

EATING & DRINKING					NIGHTLIFE			
Amphore	15	Hamburg del Mar/		Schauermann	14	Angie's	11	Golden Pudel Club	16
Au Quai	20	Lago Bay	19	Strand Pauli	17	Blankenese Kiez		Grosse Freiheit 36	7
Café Geyer	12	Henssler & Henssler	18	Summum Bonum/		Internat	8	Grüner Jäger	2
Christiansen's	13	Le Canard Nouveau	22	Zoë 2	1	China Lounge	9	Grünspan	6
East	C	Meanie Bar	10	Toast	5				
Fischereihafen	21	Nil	3	Die Welt ist schön	4				

They arrived in Hamburg as ramshackle amateurs in August 1960. They left two years and five visits later as a fledgling Fab Four. The Beatles have always acknowledged the debt they owe Hamburg. As John Lennon put it: "It was Hamburg that did it. We would never have developed so much if we'd stayed at home." Its red-light district area was also an eye-opener for the teenagers: "I was born in Liverpool, but I grew up in Hamburg," Lennon quipped.

Many of the shrines are still there to make St Pauli as holy as Liverpool for Beatles pilgrims. The boys' first address in the city was a squalid, windowless cell in a cinema, Bambi Kino (Paul-Roosen-Strasse 33), that was convenient for gigs in the grimy *Indra* club (Grosse Freiheit 64). Here they earned thirty marks a day each by entertaining sailors and strippers for four and a half hours on weekdays, six on Saturdays. The venue's manager, Bruno Koschminder, was unimpressed after their first lame performance and demanded they "*Mach shau!*" (Put on a show). Lennon duly hung a toilet seat around his neck and George Harrison played in his Y-fronts. They transferred to nearby *Kaiserkeller* (Grosse Freiheit 64) and found haircuts from Hamburg's hip Existentialists, the Exis, and a new drummer, Ringo Starr, then playing for Rory Storm and the Hurricanes. This stint was truncated when Paul McCartney and former drummer Pete Best hung a lit condom outside their room then spent a night in the Spielbudenplatz police station accused of arson before being deported. In truth, the tour was at a close anyway because 17-year-old George Harrison had been deported for being underage and the boys returned to Liverpool, billed as "The Beatles: Direct From Hamburg". In 1961 the band returned to Germany for a 98-day run at the epicentre of all things beat, the *Top Ten Club* (Reeperbahn 136), and afterwards a seven-week stint at the *Star Club* (Grosse Freiheit 39). The latter has gone up in smoke and only a memorial etched in the style of the old billboard is a reminder.

Elsewhere, Beatles devotees can re-create a publicity shot of John Lennon in the doorway of Jägerpassage 1 (off Wohlwillstrasse 22) that featured on the cover of solo album *Rock'n'Roll* and diehards can follow in the boys' footsteps and buy their first cowboy boots from Paul Hundertmark Western Store (Spielbudenplatz 27–28).

other side of the Reeperbahn is the hub of the area's regeneration. Its latest incarnation as home to musicals in the **Operettenhaus**, Spielbudenplatz 1, and waxwork figures in the **Panoptikum**, Spielbudenplatz 3 (Mon–Fri 11am–9pm, Sat 11am–midnight, Sun 10am–9pm; €5), follows the pattern set two centuries ago when tightrope walkers, snake charmers and acrobatic riders performed stunts. Nearby on the corner of Taubenstrasse, a **condomerie** (noon–midnight; free) that peddles saucy tourist tat as a pseudo-museum typifies the area's makeover.

The focus of local boozing is the seedy streets south, principally **Friedrichstrasse** and **Gerhardstrasse**. **Herbertstrasse**, skulking off the latter and screened off at either end, is the Amsterdam-style red-light district proper. Women, though not expressly prohibited, are strongly discouraged from visiting – attacks from prostitutes are not unknown. A block west, on the corner of Balduinstrasse and Erichstrasse, **Harry's Hamburger Hafenbasar** (Tues–Sun noon–6pm; €2.50) operates as a museum-cum-junk shop of global exotica founded on the souvenirs of a former sailor, Harry Rosenberg. His daughter presides over the joyous abundance of curios, from faux-Asian tourist tat to genuinely interesting African masks and sculpture, much of which is for sale. Don't expect to find any bargains, mind. The **Erotic Art Museum** at nearby Bernhard-Nocht-Strasse 69 (Sun–Thurs noon–10pm, Fri & Sat noon–midnight; €8), displays high-class smut from the sixteenth century onwards, including sketches and sculptures by the likes of Jean Cocteau and Henry Miller, in a former port warehouse, though its future was uncertain at the time of writing.

St Pauli segues north into the **Schanzenviertel**. A former working-class district that nurtured the city's alternative culture, the Schanze has evolved into the haunt of young media types and students, with a good spread of cheap eats, bars and boutiques and a hip, laid-back vibe; its varied bar-scene is the locals' choice over the rather tacky options off the Reeperbahn. From Neuer Pferdemarkt where Feldstrasse meets Budapester Strasse, the region fans out around its spine street, Schanzenstrasse, its core being the plaza where Schulterblatt meets Susannenstrasse. More interesting independent boutiques lie in the rapidly gentrifying streets just north of Feldstrasse U-Bahn station.

Altona and Övelgönne

A little pleased with its prosperity perhaps, **Altona** is the Schanzenviertel gentrified. It is the first in the series of ever more exclusive districts west of the centre, an erstwhile working-class district of immigrant settlers that has been colonized by Hamburg's Schickie-mickies (yuppies) and, with them, all the requisite fashion outlets, interiors stores and bars – a sort of Hamburg-style Notting Hill. At least part of the appeal is that Altona retains the feel of the separate town it was until the Nazis dragged it within Hamburg's jurisdiction in 1937. Before then, the free city of Altona was an upstart to its larger neighbour, an irritating one, too, since it poached Hamburg trade when Napoleon mounted a continental blockade against England in 1806.

South of the Bahnhof, a Baroque fountain on Platz der Republik hints at past glories as you head towards the **Altonaer Museum**, Museumstrasse 23 (Tues–Sun 10am–6pm, till 9pm Thurs; €6). Models of fishing boats, plus a claustrophobic cabin from one, and ships' figureheads flag up the settlement's maritime roots, and there's an enjoyable showcase of eighteenth-century life in Schleswig-Holstein through rebuilt farmhouse rooms. One block further south, aristocratic street **Palmaille** provides more evidence of the past as a Mediterranean-style esplanade – its Neoclassical villas in smart creams and greys are the legacy of shipping magnates and heads of trading dynasties, its name is that of *palla a maglio*, Italy's take on croquet. Just east, Altonaer Balkon offers sweeping views of shipping along the mighty Elbe at the outer edge of Hamburg's port.

The waterfront beneath is a throwback to a bygone era of neat gardens and gas lanterns. This is **Övelgönne**, one of the most prestigious addresses in Hamburg and one of its most charming corners. Twenty or so restored craft nod at their moorings as an open-air harbour museum, while a short way downstream is the city's finest beach, where passing container ships provide waves and the beautiful people pick at a sausage and potato salad at the *Strandperle* café (see p.770). Incidentally, the rock on the foreshore beyond is a 220-tonne glacial erratic from Sweden that was dredged from the shipping channel.

Return towards the centre along the river and you're on the **Elbemeile**, a former fishing docks that is rapidly morphing into an epicentre of gourmet Hamburg. Part of this redevelopment is the cutting-edge Dockland office building on the Fischereihafen; from the top of its glass-and-steel wedge (steps up on the outside) – intended to suggest the superstructure of cruise liners – you get great views downriver.

Blankenese

Though **Blankenese** is the next Elbvororte (Elbe suburb) west of Övelgönne, the distance in atmosphere is leagues. The feel is more coastal village than city suburb, even though the sea captains have long made way for captains of industry – probably the only people who can afford some of the most expensive real estate in Germany. For the tourist, there's little to tick off, which is a relief after the high culture of Hamburg, and Blankenese demands little more than exploring a nest of paths and ambling along the riverfront.

It'll take strong legs, though. Blankenese is a suburb of stairways – 58 in total, with nearly five thousand steps – which spill off Blankenese Hauptstrasse then trickle like tributaries down to the Elbe, threading through the half-timbered cottages, nineteenth-century villas and modern glass-and-wood statements shoehorned onto the hillside. A surprisingly fine beach fronts the river, which is nearly 3km wide at this point and is best admired from Süllberg hill. Go west along Strandweg, past a varied selection of restaurants and cafés, and the sand becomes purer, the beaches more isolated, and you find the bizarre summer scene of beach balls and bikinis as the container ships chug past. Away from the river, east of the Bahnhof and signposted off Elbchaussee, **Hirsch-Park** is a tranquil area of oak and beech woodland with rampant rhododendron bushes and a deer park – a pleasant spot to idle.

Eating and drinking

Hamburg has blossomed into the great gourmet centre of Germany. Alongside first-class modern German cooking you'll find good seafood and a cosmopolitan range of cuisines that strays far beyond the inevitable Italian. Of particular note are the restaurants in the Portuguese quarter of Ditmar-Koel-Strasse just east of St-Pauli-Landungsbrücken, and a handful of sushi restaurants that showcase super-fresh fish from the North Sea. Hamburg's role as a prosperous media metropolis has also nurtured a community of discerning diners with a penchant for eating in style – traditional restaurants are thin on the ground compared to the rest of Germany – and a voracious appetite for the next big thing. For a comprehensive guide consider investing in a local restaurant guide such as *Szene Essen & Trinken* (€6), available at larger newsagents and sometimes tourist information centres.

A taste of Hamburg

Cosmopolitan flavours rule in Hamburg, fusion food is a favourite. Nevertheless, many restaurants offer at least one time-proven traditional dish on the menu.

Aalsuppe The soup is largely vegetable despite the seeming reference to eel; "aal" means "all" in Low Saxon, apparently, though most chefs now add eel to avoid arguments.

Alsterwasser Fortunately not the water of the Alster lakes but shandy in a fifty-fifty ratio of beer and lemonade.

Bohnen, Birnen und Speck Literally, green beans, pears and bacon – a tasty, light dish that's ideal for summer.

Hamburger The world's favourite fast-food began as a port street-snack and was introduced to the States by emigrants in the late 1800s. Ironically another immigrant food, the doner kebab, is far more popular in the "home" town.

Labskaus A sailor's hash that minces corned beef, potatoes and beetroot and is topped with a fried egg and rollmop herring. The result: a bright pink stodge that locals swear cures hangovers. One theory also attributes the dish as the linguistic derivation of the Liverpudlian nickname "Scouser".

Rotes Grütze Rich soupy dish made of red berries swimming in cream, is popular in summer.

There are two caveats to this rosy picture. First, your options are more limited in the city centre, especially in the evenings. Streets such as Deichstrasse and Colonnaden or squares such as Grossneumarkt and nearby Fleetmarkt provide choice in one location, as does the fore-mentioned Portuguese district. The larger museums also boast excellent cafés. Otherwise head to outlying residential districts: Lange Reihe in St Georg has a spread of options to suit all budgets, the Schanzenviertel north has student-budget dining, and the Elbemeile from the Fischmarkt to Övelgönne is the latest gourmet hotspot. The second caveat is that, notwithstanding the Schanze, eating out in Hamburg is notably more expensive than in other German cities.

Restaurants

City centre

Alt Hamburger Aalspeicher Deichstr. 43
☎040/36 29 90. A seventeenth-century *Bürgerhaus* provides the historic setting for a popular restaurant serving traditional cuisine – touristy and not particularly cheap, but the quality is consistently high.
Cölln's Brodschrangen 1–5 ☎040/36 41 53. Bismarck was a regular at this elegant gourmet restaurant of snug historic rooms and tiled walls. Expect expensive German haute cuisine with a local flavour: the fillet steak in port-wine sauce and sole with North Sea shrimps are local legendo. Closed Sat lunch & Sun.
Fillet of Soul Deichtorstr. 2 ☎040/70 70 58 00. Laid-back cool in a hip retro-industrial styled hall at the Deichtorhallen. Lamb with cumin yoghurt and mint couscous are typical of the gastro-pub style dishes, all served to a clubby soundtrack. Lunches are excellent value. Closed Mon.
Le Plat du Jour Dormbusch 4 ☎040/32 14 14. Top-notch classic French cuisine in a wood-panelled dining room ruled by waiters in black-and-whites. Menus are good value at €27. Closed Sun.
Matsumi Colonnaden 96 ☎040/34 31 25. Gourmet-quality Japanese food and sushi that's rated by many connoisseurs as the best in Hamburg – pieces cost €5, traditional Japanese sets €25. Closed Sun.
O Farol Ditmar-Koel-Str. 12. Down-to-earth, occasionally boisterous place in the Portuguese quarter by the port, with bench seating and a menu that includes the fish stew *caldeirada*. Closed Mon lunch.
Old Commercial Room Englische Planke 10 ☎040/36 63 19. Oyster, lobster and caviar starters in a renowned seventeenth-century seafood restaurant opposite St Michaelis church. Its decor has a nautical theme – cabin-style walls, a figurehead and a compass on the ceiling – and photos of famous guests fight for space among nostalgic images of port life.

Ratsweinkeller Grosse Johannisstr. 2
☎040/36 41 54. A cut above the usual Ratskeller, but still as traditional as you could want, both in decor – vaulted ceilings, heavy wood tables and crisp white tablecloths – and top-notch fish plates. Closed Sun eve.
Zum Alten Senator Neanderstr. 27
☎040/371 44 70. Classic Hamburg dishes – highly rated by locals – are served in a modern dining room of blonde wood and designer lampshades off the tourist circuit.

St Georg and around

Cox Lange Reihe 68 ☎040/24 94 22. The first home of haute cuisine in St Georg and as popular as ever. Leather banquettes and crisp white tablecloths make a nod to French brasserie styles, and the short menu brings interesting global flavours to contemporary German cooking. Closed lunch Sat & Sun.
Golden Cut Holzdamm 6 ☎040/85 10 35 32. Pan-European and Asian cuisine in an über-cool retro-modernist lounge bar; think vintage chairs, bronze-petalled tulip lamps and minimalist sofas. Diners bypass the famously picky door policy for the associated club, though still dress to impress. Closed lunch Sun–Tues.
Sgroi Lange Reihe 40 ☎040/28 00 39 30. The sophisticated gourmet address of St Georg, where star chef Anna Sgroi crafts Italian-influenced cuisine; mains cost around €34, which makes the €26 lunch menus good value. Closed Sat & Sun lunch and all day Mon.
Zaunkönig St Georgs Kirchhof 3 ☎040/24 67 38. Serves contemporary light takes on German classics – arguably the best food on this quiet square.

St Pauli, Schanzenviertel and the Universitätsviertel

Artisan Kampstr. 27, Schanzenviertel
☎040/42 10 29 15. A cool retro-modernist café by day with gourmet bites for around €10 chalked

up on the blackboard, which morphs into a home of creative cuisine in the eve, with set menus from €32. Closed Sun & Mon.

East Simon-von-Utrecht-Str. 31, St Pauli ☎040/30 99 30. Pricey Asian fusion food in the restaurant of a design hotel with wow factor (see p.750); dining is in a lofty brick hall of sculptural pillars. If money's tight, opt for lounge bar *Yakshi* which has similar style and inventive cocktails.

Nil Neuer Pferdemarkt 5, Schanzenviertel ☎040/439 78 23. Located in a former shoe-shop, this intimate galleried space serves as the bastion of quality eating for an older Schanze clientele. Its modern German cuisine is keenly priced at around €18 a main. Eve only, closed Tues.

Schauermann Hafenstr.136–138, St Pauli ☎040/439 78 23. Smart dining without the fuss nor stinging prices in a contemporary restaurant with harbour views and witty waiters. Consistently excellent, it has evening three-course menus from €36. Tricky to find: go around the corner (towards the river) from the west end of Bernhard-Nocht-Str. Closed Sat lunch & all day Sun.

Vienna Fettstr. 2, Universitätsviertel ☎040/439 91 82. Cosy place with rustic decor that serves excellent German and Austrian dishes – the garden is a charmer in summer. Closed Mon.

Altona and the Elbemeile

Au Quai Grosse Elbstr. 145 ☎040/38 03 77 30. Hip riverfront dining, from the arch-pun of the name to the style of Zen minimalism fused with industrial chic to the Mediterranean-modern French cuisine. Its "Club La Nuit" (Thurs–Sat) attracts a poser crowd for classic house and champagne washed down with awesome river views. Closed Sat lunch & all day Sun.

Fischereihafen Grosse Elbstr. 143 ☎040/38 18 16. Set among the fish wholesalers and by common consent the best fish restaurant in town. The style is reassuringly traditional, both in decor and menu: North Sea sole drizzled with butter is

consistently superb or there's a mixed fish platter with smoked eel and North Sea shrimp.

Henssler & Henssler Grosse Elbstr. 160 ☎040/38 69 90 00. Sashimi and excellent sushi – straight and Californian fusion-style – as well as grills served up in a large casual dining room. Closed Sun.

Le Canard Nouveau Elbchaussee 139 ☎040/88 12 95 31. One of Hamburg's best restaurants, with a clean and modern style, which is visited as much for a location overlooking the Elbe as the exquisite Mediterranean-modern cuisine. Mains cost around €35 but then most diners here aren't worried about budgets; two-course business lunches are excellent value at €24. Closed Sun & Mon.

Zum Alten Lotsenhaus Övelgönne 13 ☎040/880 01 96. Decent fish and traditional favourites such as *Labskaus* and *Rote Grütze* in an old-fashioned place whose tiers of terraces overlook the historic boats and docks.

Blankenese

Ahrberg Strandweg 33 ☎040/86 04 38. A lovely Edwardian-style fish restaurant with an extended river terrace. Daily fish specials alongside standards such as shrimp and potato soup.

Jacobs Elbchaussee 401 ☎040/82 25 50. The restaurant of the elegant *Louis C. Jacobson* hotel is one of Hamburg's culinary figureheads, offering sensational river views to accompany the exquisite French cuisine crafted by Thomas Martin. Staggeringly expensive even by local standards but arguably the premier gourmet address in town.

Witthüs in Hirsch-Park, Elbchaussee 499 ☎040/86 01 73. Glorious alfresco dining and snug rooms in a thatched house make this a local legend. Cakes and nibbles in the café make way for an evening restaurant with the likes of calf's liver with apple and onion. Café Mon–Sat 2–6pm, Sun 10am–6pm, restaurant Tues–Sun from 7pm.

Cafés and cheap eats

City centre

Alex Alsterpavillon, Jungfernstieg 54. Pricey and chain-café fodder, but there's no faulting the superb balcony seats over the Binnenalster.

Café Paris Rathausstr. 4. Moments from the Rathaus, this French bistro in a former merchants' headquarters accommodates a cosmopolitan crowd for brunch, *moules frites* or simply drinks. Worth visiting for its tiled interior alone. Closed Sat & Sun eve.

Fleetschlösschen Brooktorkai 47. Junk-shop chic, Motown on the stereo and light bistro dishes – such as salmon with tomato and crème fraîche or fish coconut curries – in a tiny, former harbour tax office with some seating canal-side in summer. A gem.

Frau Hedwig und Herr Paul Ditmar-Koel-Str. 24. Stripped decor, Portuguese nibbles and big beanbags to flop into – part café, part bar, all stylishly relaxed by the Landungsbrücken.

Kaiserperle Am Kaiserkai 47. Good-value Italian cooking from a wharfside bistro in HafenCity with views of shipping on the river. Closed Mon.

Schwender's Grossneumarkt 1. A locals' favourite in the centre and a pleasant spot to eat alfresco in summer. There's a good-value lunch menu and a long German wine list, too.

Ti Breizh Deichstr. 39. Delicious crêpes and buttery galettes washed down with cider in a cute Breton café-restaurant that overlooks the Nikolaifleet.

Vapiano Hohe Bleichen 10. An outlet of a modern chain that rustles up above-average, under-budget Italian at double-quick speed – good for a bite on the go and absurdly popular. Note you receive a café "credit card" then pay on leaving.

Wohnhalle *Fairmont Vier Jahreszeiten* hotel, Neuer Jungfernstieg 9–14. A legend city-wide for its British high tea and luxurious cakes in sumptuous Beidermeier surroundings.

St Georg and around

a.mora An der Alster, Atlantic-Steg. On the quay before the *Atlantic* hotel, this unites views over the Aussenalster with lounger-style eating from the hip *Bar Hamburg* team. Heaven for brunch on sunny weekends.

Café Gnosa Lange Reihe 93. The quaintly old-fashioned café of 1930s vintage is the wellspring of St Georg's gay community; a good first port of call for the Hamburg scene.

Literaturhaus Café Schwanenwik 38 ☎040/220 13 00. Outstanding breakfasts, light lunches then a serious evening à la carte – expect dishes like *gnocchi* with monkfish and a tomato-olive pesto –

all served in glamorous neo-Baroque rooms lit by glass chandeliers that are stylish without ever showing off. Good bar, too. Closed lunch Sat & Sun.

St Pauli, Schanzenviertel and the Universitätsviertel

Café Geyer Hein-Köllisch-Platz 4, St Pauli. Proof that St Pauli is not all grungy is this friendly locals' café-bar with a nice line in relaxed urban cool. Great for weekend breakfasts or cheap fish and *Schnitzels*.

Café Klatsch Glashüttenstr. 17, St Pauli. Artistically battered little café on the interesting side of the Schanze that serves all-day breakfasts and snacks.

Erika's Eck Sternstr. 98, Schanzenviertel. Bargain-priced fillers in an old-fashioned place intended for workers at the nearby abattoir but whose hours have won it a fan base among clubbers – a Hamburg institution. Open daily 5pm–2pm the next day, except Mon from midnight, Sat & Sun till 9am.

Oma's Apotheke Schanzenstr. 87, Schanzenviertel. Nothing fancy, just tasty cheap grub such as steaks and jacket potatoes in a *Kneipe* that retains the vintage fittings of the chemist's that originally occupied the space.

Altona and Blankanese

Filmhauskneipe Friedensallee 9, Altona. Ever-popular gastro-pub with a modern-rustic style – rough pine tables and splashes of colourful art – and a menu of tasty German and Italian dishes.

Kujüte SB12 Strandweg 79, Blankanese. Just five tables and checked upholstery give this place a beach-shack vibe – a lovely spot for a light lunch of pasta, herring or salad.

Bars and pubs

With everything from dubious dive-bars above the port to glossy hangouts of the local jet-set via Szene drinking dens and laid-back pubs, Hamburg's drinking scene ticks all boxes. Like any major city, the turnover is fairly rapid, and hip bars can swing into and out of fashion within a few years. Either way, your drinking options are limited in the city centre and locals vouch instead for St Pauli, especially the Schanzenviertel. The tacky Reeperbahn bar scene on Friedrichstrasse and Gernhardtstrasse is largely derided as tourist fodder, though can be unsophisticated fun if you don't mind stag parties. The distinction between fashionable bar and nightclub can blur, with many of the former boasting a dancefloor and booking DJs at weekends. Similarly many cafés become laid-back bars at night – often good options for a relaxed drink. Wherever you go, opening hours generally extend till at least midnight and often run until 5am at weekends in the nightlife districts.

City centre

Bar Hamburg Rautenbergstr. 6–8. Near the *Kempinski Atlantic* hotel, this attracts an immaculately groomed crowd of young professionals,

wannabe actresses and models, plus the occasional jet-set celeb (stand up, Mick Jagger) to sip cocktails and spirits while DJs spin jazzy lounge beats. All very glossy.

Chilli Club Am Sandtorkai 54. Actually a café-restaurant serving modern Asian food but with the best waterfront terrace in HafenCity. DJs spin on Saturday nights.

Die erste Liebe Michaelisbrücke 3. Handy for a central drink, this café-bar softens its hip minimalism with old pillars and chunky wooden tables. Also serves pasta and sandwiches.

Gröninger Braukeller Willy-Brandt-Str. 47. Vast old-fashioned cellar *Hausbrauerei* whose shiny copper vats brew superb *Pils* and *Weizen* beers – top-ups keep coming until you put a beer mat over your glass. It also rustles up rib-sticking pub grub in man-size portions.

Nachtasyl Alstertor 1. A bar within the Thalia Theater that manages to appeal to everyone from businessmen to forty-something intellectuals. Love that flock wallpaper.

St Pauli and the Schanzenviertel

Amphore St Pauli-Hafenstr. 140, St Pauli. A great little café-bar that's all about the view over the docks illuminated below, but which also has nice touches like blankets for drinkers on the terrace. Home-made food and delicious hot chocolate.

Bar Rossi Max-Brauer-Allee 279, Schanzenviertel. Arguably the most popular *Szene* bar-cum-club in the Schanze, decked out in retro style and sound-tracked by house and techno from DJs. Rammed at weekends with a dressy twenty-something crowd – get here before 11pm if you want a seat.

Christiansen's Pinnasberg 60, St Pauli. A Manhattan-style cocoon of dark wood and red leather with an astounding drinks list; more cocktails than you knew existed and over a hundred whiskies. Mon–Sat from 8pm.

frank und frei Schanzenstr. 93, Schanzenviertel. Large lazy pub with a touch of old-fashioned charm – a slice of the Schanze from years back.

Fritz Bauch Bartelsstr. 6, Schanzenviertel. Good old boozer with bright coloured walls and an older clientele who never quite stopped being students.

Meanie Bar Spielbudenplatz 5, St Pauli. Seventies retro rules in one of the few bars on the Reeperbahn strip with local credibility. DJs spin a mixed box of old skool beats, alt-rock, indie and punk for an unpretentious crowd throughout the week. Daily from 9pm.

Summum Bonum/Zoë 2 Neuer Pferdemarkt 17, Schanzenviertel. Junk shop chic taken to the max – battered sofas and granny's tassled lamps within carefully distressed walls.

Summer beach-bars

That locals have idled away their weekends on river beaches since the late 1800s at least may help explain why no town in Germany does the Stadtstrand (city beach) with such flair as Hamburg. The Elbe views help, of course, as does sand on the river-banks. But even away from the river, bar owners import sand to create a little piece of coastal paradise, scattering deck chairs among the potted palms and adding a soundtrack of lazy funk and chilled house beats. The city's beach clubs – nine at the last count – operate daily in summer (roughly May–Sept) from midday to midnight. Those on the river with views of the container port are quintessentially Hamburg.

Central Park Max-Brauer-Allee 277, Schanzenviertel. A surprising slice of beach lifestyle at the Schulterblatt crossroads provides sand between the toes and deckchairs in the urban heart of the Schanze.

Hamburg del Mar Van-der-Smissen-Strasse 4, Altona. Less flashy than neighbour *Lago Bay*, which means more space, more sand and (usually) a more laid-back vibe. The *Strandkörbe* on a terrace that juts into the river are a superb spot to while away an evening.

Lago Bay Van-der-Smissen-Strasse 4, Altona. White sand, white sofas and an open tent with a glass chandelier make this a passable attempt at St Tropez sophistication. Young families come for the small swimming pool by day, club nights are scheduled at weekends.

Strand Pauli Hafenstr. 89, St Pauli. Less styled than other beach bars but probably more charismatic in a nicely shabby way – urban retro meets island castaway – and the views of the docks opposite are unbeatable. Hamburg in a nutshell.

Strandperle Schulberg 2, Altona. The first and for many locals still the best of the Hamburg beach bars: no fuss, just a shack and a deck on the beach beyond the boats at Övelgönne where the beautiful people from Altona hang out and top up tans.

▲ Beach bar *Strand Pauli*

Toast Wohlwillstr. 54, Schanzenviertel. Laid-back and friendly home from home for a mixed group of in-the-know creatives. Great drinks list and buzzing on Fridays.

Die Welt ist schön Neuer Pferdemarkt 4, Schanzenviertel. An intimate, clubby bar, less posey than some of its neighbours, and where it always feels like 2am. There's a chill-out lounge upstairs – another on the roof, too, in summer – and a small courtyard garden. From 6pm.

Altona

Eisenstein Friedensallee 9, Altona. Glamorous restaurant and bar housed in the industrial space of a former factory – rather posey, but impressive nonetheless. Tasty pizzas and pasta alongside more substantial international dishes.

Elbeterassen Övelgönne 1. With deckchairs and an elevated unobstructed view over the river, this is the stuff sundowners are made of.

Nightlife and entertainment

Freesheets in visitor information centres provide what's-on basics; they're especially useful for a rundown of which blockbuster musicals have settled in for a long run. For comprehensive information and a breakdown of the myriad activities such as clubbing, bands, art-house cinema and the gay scene, look to local listings magazines such as *Szene* (€3) or *Prinz* (€1). Flyers in bars and cafés in districts such as St Pauli and the Schanzenviertel are an alternative source of information. Visitor information centres at the Hauptbahnhof and St-Pauli-Landungsbrücken have ticket bureaux that can handle most mainstream venues or try Ticketmaster-affiliate Kartenhaus at Schanzenstrasse 5 (Mon–Fri 10am–7pm, Sat 10am–2pm; ☎040/43 59 46, Ⓦwww.kartenhaus.de).

Clubs

Many live music venues also programme club-nights: *Docks* hosts regular clubs in the Kiez and *Uebel und Gefährlich* offers one of the most memorable nights out in the Schanzenviertel area. Be aware, too, that many clubs operate from Thursday to Saturday only, so double-check websites or local listings before you go. Either way, weekend clubbing in Hamburg doesn't get going until after midnight.

Angie's Spielbudenplatz 27–28 ⓦ www.schmidts .de. A famous nightclub of the old school where a dressed-up crowd is powered along by soul and funk from guests of long-serving host Angie Stardust and her band.

Blankenese Kiez Internat Grosse Freiheit 10 ⓦ www.blankenesekiezinternat.de. Currently the name to drop for deep house, electro and minimal bleeps.

China Lounge Nobistor 14 ⓦ www.china-lounge.de. Though not as cool as it would like to think, a good option on the Reeperbahn that's more stylish than many mainstream venues. There's hip-hop and r'n'b in a tiny basement, house and electro on the main floor and a chill-out lounge above.

Golden Cut Holzdamm 6 ⓦ www.goldencut.org. One of the few options in St Georg, this provides grown-up sophisticated clubbing for an older crowd – dress up to get past the doorman. House, soul and jazzy lounge tunes.

Golden Pudel Club Fischmarkt 27, Altona ⓦ www.pudel.com. A party crowd sardines into one room for everything from throbbing electro to

Jamaican dancehall and spills onto the street around this oversized shack – very trashy, very random. Rocks on Saturday nights, when the nearby Fischmarkt provides a perfect carry-on.

Grosse Freiheit 36 Grosse Freiheit 36 ⓦ www.grossefreiheit36.de. Crowd-pleaser clubbing throughout the week: expect nights of Eighties and Nineties, salsa, indie classics, house and the occasional goth-industrial hammer-fest.

Grüner Jäger Neuer Pferdemarkt 36 ⓦ www.gruener-jaeger-stpauli.de. A pretension-free bar-club that provides a good-times mix of Sixties soul, cheesy Eighties and Nineties rock and pop or indie depending on the night, all spun in a hunting lodge gone disco.

Grünspan Grosse Freiheit 58 ⓦ www.gruenspan.de. The self-proclaimed "Rockcenter No 1" provides club nights and midweek concerts in a galleried hall.

Waagenbau Max-Brauer-Allee 204 ⓦ www.waagenbau.com. Breaks, super-heavy funk, dubstep, drum 'n' bass and electro, plus reggae on Mondays in a grungy favourite of the Schanzenviertel scene.

Live music: rock, blues and jazz

Rock club *Grünspan* hosts occasional international acts: past guests include the likes of Babyshambles, Mogwai, Röyksopp and Chimaira.

Birdland Gärtnerstr. 122, Eimsbüttel ☎ 040/43 27 37 95, ⓦ www.jazzclub-birdland.de. Hamburg's premier jazz venue provides a fantastic range of styles in an intimate space lined with portraits of the greats.

Docks Spielbudenplatz 19 ⓦ www.docks.de Rock gigs plus trance, drum 'n' bass and techno club nights at weekends in a bastion of the St Pauli scene. Dodgy acoustics, mind.

Fabrik Barnerstr. 36, Altona ☎ 040/39 10 70, ⓦ www.fabrik.de. A long-running venue carved from a former machine factory. Rock, blues, funk, world and jazz acts, with one or two major

international names a month, attract an older clientele of knowledgeable musos.

Hafenklang-Exil Grosse Bergstr. 178, Altona ⓦ www.hafenklang.org. A café, bar and venue with an underground vibe and an eclectic programme of small concerts that defies categorization. Drum 'n' bass fans should also check out its club nights.

Kaiserkeller Grosse Freiheit 36 ☎ 040/31 77 78 11, ⓦ www.grossefreiheit36.de. The venue forever linked with The Beatles still champions up-and-coming rock acts and welcomes a major international act once or twice a month.

Gay and lesbian Hamburg

It should come as no surprise that a liberal metropolis such as Hamburg has a thriving gay and lesbian scene. Its epicentre is the **St Georg** district, with a number of mainstream gay cafés and bars sited along main-drag Lange Reihe. *Café Gnosa* at no. 69 is the daytime lynchpin and best source of information for what's on. There's usually a copy of local gay listings magazine *Hinnerk* (ⓦ www.publigayte .com) knocking around. The best clubbing tends to be found in the one-nighters that shift between venues, many in St Pauli; again consult listings and local knowledge. Hamburg also has a separate but important leather scene – the annual Hamburg Leather Party, organized in the second week of August by fetish club *Spike* (ⓦ www .spike-hamburg.de), is a major event on the scene's European calendar.

Logo Grindelallee 1, Rotherbaum ☎ 040/36 26 22, Ⓦ www.logohamburg.de. Touring international alt-rock acts alongside Hamburg names in a venue near the university.
Uebel und Gefährlich Feldstr. 66 Ⓦ www.uebelundgefaehrlich.com. The gritty Hamburg

Szene in a nutshell, this is one of the city's most interesting venues, partly for its being on an upper floor of a concrete war bunker in the Schanzenviertel, but also for a roster of hip alternative acts – always worth checking out. Kicking club-nights, too.

Live music: classical, opera and musicals

Hamburg has a well-deserved reputation for high culture that is maintained by one of the country's most prestigious orchestras – the Philharmonisches Staatsorchester – and what many critics argue is the finest opera house, the Staatsoper, currently under the baton of Australian Professor Simone Young, critics' Conductor of the Year in 2006. The city's churches also host frequent classical music concerts, notably St Jakobi and St Michaelis, which stage acclaimed organ recitals and choral works.

Allee Theater Max-Brauer-Allee 76 ☎ 040/30 05 16 66, Ⓦ www.alleetheater.de. Opera rarities and selected classics from the seventeenth to nineteenth centuries.
Laeiszhalle-Musikhalle Johannes-Brahms-Platz 1 ☎ 040/34 69 20, Ⓦ www.laeiszhalle.de. Home of the NDR-Sinfonie-Orchester, whose international reputation was cemented under former conductor Günter Wand.

Staatsoper Dammtorstr. 28 ☎ 040/35 68 68, Ⓦ www.hamburgische-staatsoper.de. In the world's opera top-ten for most critics, its reputation bolstered under the stewardship of Simone Young. Also serves as a concert venue for the Hamburg Philharmonic (until 2011) and has an acclaimed ballet company run by American John Neumeier. Reservations recommended – advance ticket saloo from Grosse Theaterstr. 25.

Theatre, musicals and cabaret

Hamburg's weakness for show-stopper musicals in the New York and London mould provides an antidote to high culture. Tourist information can book tickets for whichever mega-budget production has settled in for a very long run – bear in mind that familiar international names will have been translated into German.

Deutsches Schauspielhaus Kirchenallee 39 ☎ 040/24 87 13, Ⓦ www.schauspielhaus.de. The largest stage in Germany is also one of the leading centres of the dramatic arts. Expect innovative productions of classics and modern plays.
The English Theatre Lerchenfeld 14 ☎ 040/227 70 89, Ⓦ www.englishtheatre.de. Largely thrillers and comedy, interspersed with the occasional classic, performed by a professional team since 1976.
Neue Flora Stresmannstr. 159a ☎ 01805/44 44, Ⓦ www.stage-entertainment.de. Musicals in the corporate crowd-pleaser vein: recent productions include *Dirty Dancing* and Disney's *Tarzan*.
Operettenhaus Spielbudenplatz 1 ☎ 01805/44 44, Ⓦ www.stage-entertainment.de. Big song-and-dance-number musicals just off the Reeperbahn.
Pulverfass Reeperbahn 147 ☎ 040/24 78 78, Ⓦ www.pulverfasscabaret.de. Sequins, ostrich

feathers and heavy make-up in variety shows performed by international drag queens. Gloriously camp with a frisson of the risqué.
St-Pauli-Theater Spielbudenplatz 29 ☎ 040/41 71 06 66, Ⓦ www.st-pauli-theater.de. A charming small theatre with a mixed programme of quality cabaret and comedy.
Schmidt Spielbudenplatz 27–28 ☎ 040/30 05 14 00, Ⓦ www.schmidts.de. Cabaret and variety. Schmidts Tivoli (same contacts) has hosted *Heisse Ecke*, a romanticized musical about Reeperbahn lowlife, in the same venue since 2003.
Theater im Hafen Ferry from St-Pauli-Landungsbrücken, Brücke 1 (included in ticket price) ☎ 01805 44 44, Ⓦ www.stage-entertainment.de. A tent-like venue on the south bank that has hosted Disney's *The Lion King* for many a year.

Cinema

"OmU" is the all-important acronym to find original-language films with German subtitles; evening newspaper *Hamburger Abendblatt* indicates original-language films with "OF" in its listings on Thursday and Saturday. Tickets cost €6–8 and most cinemas offer midweek discounts. CinemaX, Dammtordamm 1 (Ⓦwww.cinemaxx.de), the city's largest and most central multiplex, located just west of Binnenalster, screens Hollywood blockbusters. Nearby Streits, Jungfernstieg 38 (Ⓦwww.cinestar.de), has less choice but its mainstream American and British films are always in English. Hamburg is well-served for art-house cinema: 3001, Schanzenstrasse 75–77 (Ⓦwww.3001-kino.de), and Abaton, Allendeplatz 3 (Ⓦwww.abaton.de), screen quality international releases and shorts, old and new. Three-screen Zeise Kinos, Friedensallee 7–9 (Ⓦwww.zeise.de), in a former ship factory, is another good option for European art-house and late-night screenings.

Shopping and markets

Pedestrianized Mönckebergstrasse, also known as the "Mön", and parallel Spitalerstrasse are the hub of **high-street shopping**; look out for Görtz and Sport Karstadt on the Mön, formerly Europe's largest shoe and sports shops respectively – the latter even has a space for jogging and ice-skating on the roof. Hamburg tourism is far prouder of its seven **arcades**, accessed from Jungfernstieg, Poststrasse and Grosse Bleichen, which contain a wide range of retailers, cafés and restaurants. Known as the **Hanseviertel**, the area is a triangle of designer couture, which stretches north from the Rathaus to Gansemark. More edgy fashions plus vintage and secondhand boutiques lie in the **Schanzenviertel**. Interiors addicts should head to the wonderful Stilwerk conglomerate of small designers opposite the Fischmarkt on Grosse Elbstrasse.

The best weekly **markets** are morning-only affairs in Isestrasse (Tues & Fri), Goldbeuker (Tues, Thurs & Sat) and Grosseneumarkt (Wed & Sat). The mother of all markets is the Sunday **Fischmarkt** in St Pauli (see p.762).

For **books and newspapers** Thalia's megastore at Spitalerstrasse 8 maintains the largest foreign-language section in Hamburg; a second, smaller outlet is at Grosse Bleichen 19. English Books and British Foods in the Schanzenviertel (Stresemannstrasse 169–167) is chock-a-block with secondhand tomes and has a food outlet as well. Presse & Buche at the Hauptbahnhof has a decent stock of international newspapers.

Listings

Car rental Hertz, Kirchenalle 34–36 (Hauptbahnhof) ☎040/280 12 01; Europcar, Bronkampsweg 58a ☎040/306 82 60; SIXT, Hauptbahnhof Wandehalle ☎040/32 24 19; Budget, Hamburger Str. 166–68 ☎040/819 76 10. All operators maintain a desk at the airport.

Consulates Canada, Ballindamm 35 ☎040/460 02 70; New Zealand, Domstr. 19 ☎040/442 55 50; Ireland, Feldbrunnenstr. 43 ☎040/44 18 61 13; South Africa, Palmaille 45 ☎040/38 01 63 93; UK, Harvestehuder Weg 8a

☎040/448 03 20; US, Alsterufer 27–28 ☎040/41 17 13 00.

Hospitals and medical Marien Krankenhaus, Alfredstr. 9; Universitätsklinikum, Martinstr. 52. Round-the-clock emergency doctors at ☎040/22 80 22.

Internet Callshop & Internet Café, Ernst-Merck-Str. 9 (behind Hauptbahnhof), daily 9am–midnight; Saturn department store, Mönckerbergstr. 1, Mon–Sat 9.30am–8pm; Match Games, Rothenbaumchaussee 61 (Rothenbaum), daily 2pm–midnight.

Laundry St Pauli Waschsalon, Hein-Hoyer-Str. 12, 6am–10pm; Schnell & Sauber, Neuer Pferdemarkt 27, 6am–11pm.

Left luggage All train stations have lockers for upto 72hr.

Police At the Hauptbahnhof, Kirchenallee exit, and on Spielbudenplatz, St Pauli.

Post Dammtorstr. 14; Alter Wall 38; Mönckebergstr. 7.

Sports Bundesliga club Hamburger SV play in a modern 50,000-seater stadium northwest of the centre, the AOL Color Line Arena. Ticket availability varies by fixture – visitor information centres should be able to advise or try Kartenhaus (see p.771). The city's second team is FC St Pauli, a local team with an obsessive fanbase. It plays in the Millerntor-Stadion just south of Feldstrasse U-Bahn; advance tickets are bought at the stadium's fanshop (Mon–Sat 10.30am–6pm, Thurs till 8pm, Sat till 4pm; ☎040/31 78 74 51). The AOL Color Line Arena also hosts handball matches of local team HSV Handball.

Swimming Alster-Schwimmhalle, Ifflandstr. 21 (Mon–Fri 6.30am–11pm, Sat & Sun 8am–11pm), and St Pauli Budapester Str. 29 (Tues–Sat 2–6pm, Sun 10am–6pm), are the most central pools, in the east and west respectively. For locations and opening times of options elsewhere visit website ⓦ www.baederland.de.

Schleswig-Holstein

Schleswig-Holstein is all about location. The most northerly Land in Germany is a product of the forces around it: west and east the North and Baltic seas; north and south Denmark and Germany. The former is realized as fine sand beaches and marram-grass dunes, candy-striped lighthouses, commercial ports on Baltic fjords, and changeable weather as fronts barrel rapidly east. The latter have squabbled over the peninsula for centuries to shape the Land's character as a classic European borderland. Initially divided at the River Eider as Danish Schleswig and Holy Roman Empire-owned Holstein, the peninsula came under Danish rule from the fifteenth century until the mid-1800s, when nationalist fervour inspired renewed calls for independence among its German-speaking population. This posed the Schleswig-Holstein Question, which vexed some of the finest diplomatic minds in Europe. As British prime minister Lord Palmerston is said to have despaired: "The Schleswig-Holstein Question is so complicated only three men in Europe have ever understood it. The first was Prince Albert, and he is dead; the second is a German professor, and he is in an asylum; and the third was myself, and I have forgotten it." The final ingredient in the mix is a local dialect akin to Dutch, Plattdeutsch, almost as impenetrable to Germans as it is to foreigners. A friendly "Moin moin!" (hello) always wins a smile in the North Frisian islands.

Although the Land capital is **Kiel**, a brusque, working port at the head of the canal of the same name, the title sits most comfortably on **Lübeck**, a one-time city-state whose tale is as rich and complex as any plotline by local son Thomas Mann. At its kernel lies one of the most enigmatic old towns in Germany, with a heritage and sense of cultural worth handed down from over four hundred years at the head of medieval trading-cartel the Hanseatic League, the first pan-European superpower in the region. The lumpy lakeland of **Holsteinische Schweiz** (Holstein's Switzerland) – the name derives from a nineteenth-century hotel near Bad Malente rather than its low moraine hills – ripples north past Kiel towards **Schleswig**, a daydreaming small town rooted in a Viking past that exudes provincial charm but is worth a visit for the most engrossing museum collections in the state.

While the gentle Baltic coast is notched by fjords, the west is wind-blown and wild, a corner of flatlands and colour-wash skyscapes that have inspired artists such as Expressionist Emil Nolde. However, it's the effortless sandy beaches that have seen the **North Frisian archipelago** raised to the status of celebrated holiday playground. **Sylt**, a sort of German Hamptons, is the most sophisticated island, not least in Kampen, one of the chic-est retreats in the country. **Föhr** and **Amrum** are sleepy backwaters that are all about walks, cycle rides and sand castles on the beach. That you can island-hop between them – or join guided walks across the mud flats – just makes a visit even more enjoyable.

Lübeck

Few towns on the North European coast capture the glory of their medieval selves like **LÜBECK**. For over two centuries as flagship of the Hanseatic League (see box below), it was one of the richest and most powerful cities in Europe, a Venice of the Baltic that lorded it at the head of a medieval trading-cartel with nearly two hundred members which challenged policy of the Holy Roman Emperor himself. Mercantile wealth found its expression in magnificent architecture erected during the Hansa heyday: from the oldest Rathaus in Germany – an expression of civic

The Hanseatic League

When the European Union was just a twinkle in history's eye, the **Hanseatic League** acted as a powerful pan-European bloc whose reach stretched from England to Russia, from Scandinavia to the German Alps. Such was its power, it issued ultimatums to sovereign states and launched its own fleet when diplomacy failed.

Saxon duke **Henry the Lion**'s guarantee of mercantile independence from the Church in 1159 established Lübeck as a base for North German trading guilds (**Hanse**; Hansa in English), and prompted mutual security deals at a time when there was no national government to safeguard trade. The momentum for a league proper began in 1241, when Lübeck, with easy access to Baltic trade routes, struck a deal with Hamburg on the North Sea to tie up exports of Lüneburg salt – a smart move in an era when states waged war over the "white gold". As their influence grew in a fragmented Europe, towns from Belgium to Poland signed up to benefit from the collective bargaining power, and league colonists established Hansa outposts in cities as far away as Aberdeen and Novgorod, trading league bills of exchange to the chagrin of commercial centres such as London. Throughout, Lübeck remained the headquarters for annual meetings and was the arbiter in Hansa law.

The league's primary directive to maintain trade routes inevitably led to its emergence as a political and military force. The merchant cartel fixed prices of essential commodities such as timber, fur, tar, flax and wheat. And after an international fleet of Hansa members united in 1368, Danish king Valdemar IV was forced to cede Scandinavian trade rights (and fifteen percent of his own profits) to the medieval superpower. The victory proved a high-water mark. Strong-arm tactics inevitably bred resentment, particularly among the great seafaring countries like England and Holland which had been deliberately excluded to favour the league's chosen markets. Both nations nurtured fleets to defeat the competition. New World trade routes leached away more influence and the chaotic Thirty Years' War in the 1600s was the final nail in the coffin for a league that was already crumbling from internal tension. Only nine members attended the last annual meeting in 1669, and when the league was formerly wound up in 1862 only Lübeck, Hamburg and Bremen remained, which perhaps explains why each still declares itself a Hansastadt.

independence from the bishopric – to powerful churches crowned by soaring spires or a streetscape of merchants' mansions. The highly decorative red-brick Gothic pioneered here served as a blueprint for the entire North European coastline, and it's a measure of the enduring splendour that Lübeck was the first town in North Europe to make it onto UNESCO's list in 1987. The league imploded in the late 1600s, puncturing Lübeck's status as a regional superpower, but by then its artistic legacy was as valuable as its architectural one.

The flipside of stagnation is preservation, and the delicately crumbling past is the town's main draw – Lübeck appeal lies as much in side streets where houses lean at crazy angles as its architectural show-stoppers. It is no stuffy museum town, however. While it can be terrifyingly cultured, a vibrant university life balances the rich diet of opera and classical music served in the concert halls, and 20km north lies the chirpy resort of **Travemünde** for sand between your toes.

Arrival and city transport

The **Hauptbahnhof** lies five minutes' walk west of the Holstentor and visitor information centre. The **bus station** (ZOB) is just outside. Lübeck **airport** (T0451/58 30 10, Wwww.flughafen-luebeck.net), 7km south of the centre, is served by international flights of budget airlines as well as domestic services to Frankfurt. A dedicated shuttle bus coordinates with international flights, otherwise bus #6 goes from the airport to the bus station (5am–11.50pm); expect to pay around €15 for a taxi. Taxi ranks are outside the Hauptbahnhof, or try Lübecker Funktaxen (T0451/811 21) or Radi's Taxi (T0451/442 44). Finnlines (Wwww .finnlines.de) operates **ferry services** to Travemünde from several Finnish ports and to Lübeck from St Petersburg, while DFDS Tor Line (Wwww.dfdstorline .com) sails to Lübeck from Riga, Latvia. The largest **car parks** in Lübeck are by the Musik- und Kongresshalle on Willy-Brandt-Allee.

Although **local transport** is free with a Happy Card (see below), it's easier to negotiate Lübeck's compact Altstadt on **foot**. **Bikes** can be rented from Laufrad (Beckergrube 29) and Buy Cycle (Wahmstrasse 28), both in the Altstadt. The fastest route **to Travemünde** is a rail branch line from the Hauptbahnhof that runs to three stations: ferry terminal Bahnhof Skandinavienkai; Hafenbahnhof, in the town centre; and Strandbahnhof near the beach. Cruises operated by Könemann Schiffahrt are a more scenic option from April to October (see p.779).

Information and tours

There are two **tourist offices** in Lübeck: the excellent municipal Welcome Center halfway between the Hauptbahnhof and Holstentor, Holstentorplatz 1 (Jan–May & Oct–Dec Mon–Fri 9.30am–6pm, Sat 10am–3pm, plus Sun 10am–2pm in Dec; June–Sept Mon–Fri 9.30am–7pm, Sat 10am–3pm, Sun 10am–2pm; T0451/889 97 00, Wwww.luebeck-tourism.de); and the private Lübecker Verkehrsverein (Mon–Sat 9am–1pm & 2–6pm, from 10am & 3pm in winter; T0451/723 39, accommodation T0451/702 02 78, Wwww.luebecker -verkehrsverein.de) in the Hauptbahnhof. There's also an outpost of the Welcome Center in **Travemünde** Strandbahnhof (Jan–Easter, Nov & Dec Mon–Fri 9.30am–5.30pm; Easter–June, Sept & Oct Mon–Fri 9.30am–5.30pm, Sat 10am–3pm, Sun 11am–2pm; July & Aug Mon–Fri 9.30am–5.30pm, Sat & Sun 10am–5pm; Wwww.travemuende-tourism.de). All information centres provide maps (€0.90), can book hotel accommodation and sell the **HappyCard**, which provides free local transport and free entry or discounts to most attractions; a 24-hour card costs €6, a 72-hour card €12. In addition three-day Kombikarten are available for combined entry to two (€7) or three (€10) municipal museums.

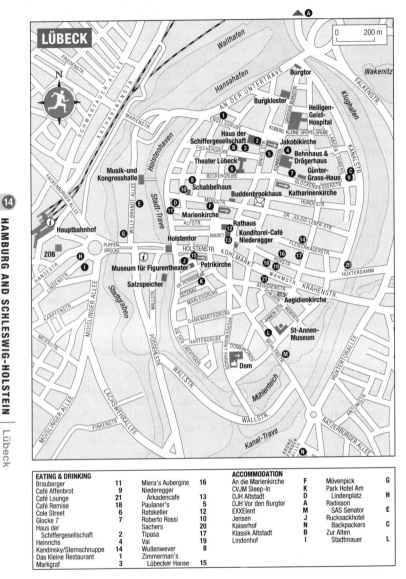

LÜBECK

EATING & DRINKING				ACCOMMODATION			
Brauberger	11	Miera's Aubergine	16	An die Marienkirche	F	Mövenpick	G
Café Affenbrot	9	Niederegger		CVJM Sleep-In	K	Park Hotel Am	
Café Lounge	21	Arkadencafe	13	DJH Altstadt	D	Lindenplatz	H
Café Remise	18	Paulaner's	5	DJH Vor den Burgtor	A	Radisson	
Cole Street	6	Ratskeller	12	EXXElent	M	SAS Senator	E
Glocke 7	7	Roberto Rossi	10	Jensen	J	Rucksackhotel	
Haus der		Sachers	20	Kaiserhof	N	Backpackers	C
Schiffergesellschaft	2	Tipasa	17	Klassik Altstadt	B	Zur Alten	
Heinrichs	4	Vai	19	Lindenhof	I	Stadtmauer	L
Kandinsky/Sternschnuppe	14	Wullenwever	8				
Das Kleine Restaurant	1	Zimmerman's					
Markgraf	3	Lübecker Hanse	15				

The Welcome Center also stocks the German-language *Lübeck Rundum* book (€2.90) of shopping, restaurants, tours and tips.

Guided **walking tours** of the Altstadt in English depart from the Welcome Center (June–Sept Sat 11.30am; €6). The Welcome Center also rents out computerized guides "led" by novelist brothers Thomas and Heinrich Mann (4hr €8.50; 8hr €12.50); bring a passport or credit card as deposit. Lübecker Verkehrsverein is your best source of other tours in English on themes such as the Hanseatic past or Lübeck's charming courtyards.

Cruises

Cruises around the Altstadt moat are run by three companies from wharves around the Holstenbrücke or on either bank by the Musik- und Kongresshalle: City Schiffahrt (☏0451/706 38 59, ⓦ www.cityschiffahrt.de), Quandt Linie (☏0451/777 99, ⓦ www.quandt-linie.de); and Stühff Fahrgastschifffahrt (☏0451/707 82 22). Each has daily departures (March–Oct 10am–6pm, every 30min; around 1hr €8), the latter pair at reduced times during other months, when City Schiffahrt ceases operating. Since they operate identical routes on near-identical craft, you're best to walk the wharf and hop aboard the next departure.

Könemann Schiffahrt operates longer trips downriver **to Travemünde** (daily April–Oct 15 10am & 2pm, July–Sept also 5.45pm; €9 one-way, €15 return; ☏0451/280 16 35, ⓦ www.koenemannschiffahrt.de). Departures are from Drehbrücke, north of the other wharves at the end of Engelsgrube. Wakenitz Schifffahrt Quandt (☏0451/280 16 35, ⓦ www.wakenitz-schifffahrt-quandt.de) and Personenschiffahrt Reinhold Maiworm (☏0451/354 55) operate lovely two-hour trips down the Wakenitz River to Rothenhausen (March–Nov 2 daily; also July & Aug Sat & Sun every 2hr; €9 one-way, €15 return), where you can connect to a second ferry to Ratzeburg (see p.789); they depart from Moltebrücke, east of the Altstadt on the other side of the moat.

Accommodation

Rooms are at a premium during high season and early December, when the crowds pour in for the Christmas markets. The town also boasts a decent stock of budget options. Private houses (❷–❸) squirrelled away in the Altstadt offer good-value rooms or apartments and charm in abundance – booking is through tourist offices. The municipal tourist information website is an excellent one-stop shop for research. The nearest **campsites** are *Campingplatz Schönböcken* 4km west of Lübeck at Steinrader Damm 12 (☏0451/89 30 90, ⓦ www.camping-luebeck.de) – bus #7 stops outside – and in *Travemünde Strandcamping Priwall* (April–Sept; ☏04502/28 35, ⓦ www.strandcamping-priwall.de), a short walk from the beach on the east bank of the river at Dünenweg 3.

Lübeck

Hotels

An die Marienkirche Schüsselbuden 4 ☏0451/79 94 10, ⓦ www.hotel-an-der-marienkirche.de. This small, private hotel offers contemporary Scandinavian-style furnishings in a superb location. ❹

EXXElent Mühlenbrücke 7–9 ☏0451/702 06 07, ⓦ www.hotel-exxelent.de. Small designer number with canal views outside and period detail within, bringing historic character to minimalist rooms. Its lounge-bar is favoured by the fashion-conscious. ❺

Jensen An der Obertrave 4–5 ☏0451/70 24 90, ⓦ www.hotel-jensen.de. Tidy, classic rooms and views over the Stadt-Trave canal in a renovated harbour-side merchant's house with a good restaurant, *Yachtzimmer*. ❹–❺

Kaiserhof Kronsforder Allee 11 ☏ 0451/70 33 01, ⓦ www.kaiserhof-luebeck.de. A grand old place created from two patrician homes of the late 1800s. Upmarket rooms offer a level of comfort above their price. ❺–❻

Klassik Altstadt Fischergrube 52 ☏0451/70 29 80, ⓦ www.klassik-altstadt-hotel.de. Comfy, traditional rooms themed after writers and artists, friendly service and a location in the heart of the Altstadt. Good buffet breakfasts, too. ❻

Lindenhof Lindenstr. 1a ☏0451/87 21 00, ⓦ www.hotel-lindenhof-luebeck.de. Pleasant, modern family-run three-star that's one of several mid-range hotels behind the bus station – a good fall-back. ❹–❺

Mövenpick Willy-Brandt-Allee 1–5 ☏0451/150 40, ⓦ www.moevenpick-luebeck.de. Designer style is not as sumptuous as the *Radisson* opposite – standard rooms are very ordinary – but four stars nevertheless. ❻–❼

Park Hotel Am Lindenplatz Lindenplatz 2
℡0451/87 19 70, ⓦwww.parkhotel-luebeck.de.
Pleasant, family hotel near the station with a hint of
1920s swagger in its proportions; classic-modern
decor in the spacious rooms and a small garden
behind. ④–⑤

Radisson SAS Senator Willy-Brandt-Allee 6
℡0451/14 20, ⓦwww.senatorhotel.de. The
smartest outfit in the centre is this business-style
hotel with wings propped above the harbour and all
the facilities you'd expect from a five-star member
of the chain. ⑦–⑧

Zur Alten Stadtmauer An der Mauer 57
℡0451/7 37 02, ⓦwww.hotelzuraltenstadtmauer
.de. Good-value family-run cheapie in the southeast
Altstadt with clean budget rooms of pine furnishings, some with shared facilities. ③–④

Hostels

CVJM Sleep-In Grosse Petersgrube 11
℡0451/399 94 10, ⓦwww.cvjm-luebeck.de.

A great Altstadt location for the YMCA hostel in a
renovated late-Gothic house. A second YMCA
Hotel am Dom (Dankwartsgrube 43; ℡0451/399
94 30; ③) near the cathedral has rooms only.
Dorms €12.40, rooms ③.

DJH Altstadt Mengstr. 33 ℡0451/702 03 99,
ⓦwww.djh-nordmark.de. The smaller and most
central of Lübeck's two youth hostels, comfy
enough in a simple way and in a great location in
one of Lübeck's most prestigious streets. Dorms
from €18.70.

DJH Vor den Burgtor Getrudenkirchhof 4
℡0451/334 33, ⓦwww.djh-nordmark.de.
A large fall-back just west of the Altstadt's
Burgtor gate, but often swamped by school
groups. Dorms from €17.60.

Rucksackhotel Backpackers Kanalstr. 70
℡0451/70 68 92, ⓦwww.rucksackhotel-luebeck
.de. Pleasant independent hostel in the east
Altstadt in the funky Werkhof complex, with two- to
eight-bed dorms. Dorms €7.50–17, rooms ②.

Travemünde

Columbia Hotel Casino Travemünde Kaiserallee 2
℡04502/30 80, ⓦwww.columbia-hotels.de.
Classic-modern style, spacious rooms and the
architectural fabric of the former casino – a luxury
address of traditional elegance. ⑦–⑧

Grand Spa Resort A-Rosa Aussenallee 10
℡04502/307 00, ⓦwww.a-rosa.de. The spa
house of the resort's nineteenth-century heyday
behind the beach now houses a luxury spa resort

of calm designer decor and faultless service – the
swishest address in the area by a long shot.
The *Buddenbrook's* restaurant is excellent. Doubles
from €278. ⑨

Strandperle Kaiserallee 10 ℡04502/30 89 89.
Decent mid-range hotel in a house behind the
beach in a quiet location 5min walk from the
centre. ④

The Altstadt

The city moat preserves the **Altsadt** as a compact oval of streets. The twin axes
around which all life revolved in Hanseatic Lübeck were league headquarters
the Rathaus and the river port, and the pair remain a focus for most sights, while
linking streets are characterized by the des res mansions of merchant patricians.
The humble residential east Altstadt – today the student district – was that of
artisans. While you can tick off the big sights, the joy of the Altstadt is that it is
sufficiently compact to explore down whichever street looks interesting. Indeed,
stumbling upon the city's enchanting courtyard "villages" is part of the fun.

From the Holstentor to the Petrikirche

There's no finer introduction to Hanseatic Lübeck than the iconic **Holstentor**.
If city fathers wanted first impressions to count, they must have been thrilled
with the imposing structure presented by a municipal architect in the fifteenth
century. Its two fat towers, capped by cone-like turrets and joined by an arch
with stepped gables, are so impressive as a portrait of solidity the gateway
featured on the old 50DM note. Actually the Holstentor leans in all the wrong
places like a collapsing sand castle. Despite its wood piles, it gently sagged into
the marshy ground beneath during construction from 1466 to 1478 and has
been bolstered twice – it was a close call whether it would be demolished

▲ The Holstentor, Lübeck

entirely in the nineteenth-century revamp. The facade remains one of Lübeck's finest, with trademark rows of black and red bricks beneath the legend "SPQL" within, a vainglorious nod to the Romans' SPQR acronym Senatus Populus Que Romanus ("the senate and people of Rome"). One tower holds a town museum (Jan–March Tues–Sun 11am–5pm; April–Dec daily 10am–6pm; €5) within its three-metre-thick walls – a model of the Altstadt c.1650 outshines every Hansa-era model ship and torture instrument beforehand.

The peaked facades beyond are the warehouses that stored salt from fellow Hanseatic Leaguer Lüneburg during the seventeenth and eighteenth centuries; cross Holstentorbrücke and you can see where gable-mounted hoists lowered the "white gold" into ships' holds for export to Scandinavia.

Grosse Petersgrube, right from Holstentorbrücke, reveals other strata to Lübeck's architectural heritage, with a handsome crescent of Gothic, Baroque and Rococo. Towards the top, on side street Kolk, the **Museum für Puppentheater** (daily 10am–6pm; €4) houses around five thousand puppets – the largest collection in the world, it claims – gathered mainly from Europe, Asia and Africa, some of which feature in performances at its Marionettentheater. The big draw of the area is the **Petrikirche**, a walloping five-nave Gothic church whose spire towers over everything else in this corner of the Altstadt. Badly damaged by air raids in 1942 (see box, p.782), it was patched up to serve as a gallery (Tues–Sun 11am–4pm; free) – the space is as much an attraction as the contemporary art exhibitions it holds. A lift (daily: April–Sept 9am–9pm; Oct–March 10am–9pm; €3) takes you to a platform 50m up with a great view of the flying buttresses of the Marienkirche, like sails among the waves of terracotta roofs.

The Rathaus and around

The Holstentor is a statement of prosperity tempered by the dictates of defense. The **Rathaus**, however, is unfettered pride. It was begun to celebrate the town's new status as a Free City of the Holy Roman Empire from 1226, making it one of the oldest town halls in Germany and certainly one of the most beautiful, despite some concrete monstrosities that share the square. The current building

The night before Palm Sunday, 1942, war finally caught up with Lübeck as the Allies unleashed the first major bombing campaign on a German town. A U-boat training school and docks for Swedish iron ore provided a fig leaf of legitimacy, but in reality the raid was in retaliation for the Luftwaffe Blitz on British urban centres. The target was the Altstadt itself, its timbered buildings a trial run for a newly developed incendiary bomb. Nearly a fifth of the town was destroyed in two days of raids, and Lübeck might have gone the way of Dresden had a German Jewish exile working as a liaison officer not tipped off his Swiss cousin about plans to raze the Altstadt entirely to sap public morale in 1944. That cousin was Carl-Jacob Burkhart, president of the Red Cross. Thanks to his efforts Lübeck was nominated as an official entry harbour for gifts to Allied POWs, and Bomber Command looked elsewhere for targets. Burkhart was later made an honorary citizen of Lübeck.

is a product of four centuries of home improvements. The first incarnation rises at the back of the Markt as three copper-clad turrets like candle-snuffers and a "show facade" that is punched by two holes so it survives winds off the Baltic Sea. On to its front is tacked a pure Renaissance lobby of Gotland sandstone, as white as icing after a recent scrub. The Langes Haus on the side was built as a festive hall sometime in the fourteenth century. But the star piece is the Neuen Gemacht (New Chamber) above, added in 1440. With staccato turrets, windholes and heraldic crests of other Hansa members, it unites the best of the earlier Rathaus and throws in for good measure a stone staircase in Dutch Renaissance style on Breite Strasse. The pick of the interior rooms (tours Mon–Fri 11am, noon & 3pm, Sat & Sun 1.30pm; €4) is the swirling Rococo Audienzsaal where the Hanseatic League court passed sentence. Allegorical paintings portray the ten virtues of good government, and an oak door by local master-craftsman Tönnies Evers shows King Solomon pondering his judgement. The story goes that felons slunk out with heads hung low by the smaller door while the innocent left through the larger door with heads high.

Lübeck is to **marzipan** what Dijon is to mustard, and opposite the Rathaus at Breite Strasse 89 is *JG Niederegger-Café* – shop, café and, in a Marzipan Salon above, a museum (Mon–Fri 9am–7pm, Sat 9am–6pm, Sun 10am–6pm; free) that combines modest history and a puff piece on the company with gloriously silly marzipan sculpture. Lübeck tourist authorities would love to believe a yarn that a town baker confected the delicacy during a siege with his last four ingredients – sugar, almonds, eggs and rose water. Another tall tale that describes it as the bread of St Mark (marcus panis) explains the sugary loaves on sale inside. Facts – or at least guild records – show Lübeckers have imported almonds, the principal ingredient, since at least 1530, and today Lübecker marzipan is guarded with strict purity laws.

The Marienkirche

The **Marienkirche** behind the Rathaus is not only Lübeck's most impressive church, it's also the finest brick church in northern Germany. The merchant elite, their independence from the Church guaranteed by Saxon overlord and town founder Henry the Lion, had a point to prove when they built it during the thirteenth and fourteenth centuries – it's no coincidence the church melds into the heart of civic power, nor that its two spires dwarf those of the bishop's Dom south. A minor collapse mid-build provided an excuse to modify the original Romanesque plans and switch instead to fashionable French Gothic; flying buttresses explode like ribs from the side aisles to the nave.

If its scale impresses from the outside – it's the third-biggest church in Germany – the interior inspires awe. Gothic frescoes of Christ and saints add colour to otherwise plain walls; the pastel images only resurfaced when a fire caused by the 1942 air raid licked away the coat of whitewash. Two bells that fell from the south tower during the raid remain shattered on the floor as a poignant memorial to war dead. Also lost in the fire was the instrument of Lübeck's favourite organist, Dietrich Buxtehude, whose improvisatory, fugal concerts were a sensation during a forty-year tenure from 1667. Such was their renown that a young organist, Johann Sebastian Bach, from Arnstadt 200 miles south, took four weeks' leave to investigate them in 1705. A variation on the story has it that Bach journeyed to take up Buxtehude's position but had a change of heart on learning his daughter's hand was part of the package. The new Buxtehudeorgan, the world's largest mechanical organ, stars in concerts.

There's superb visual art too. Behind the chancel in the Marientiden-Kapelle, beneath the final words of a Buxtehude cantata in stained glass, a double-winged triptych altar from Antwerp depicts the life of St Mary in cobweb-fine carving. In the ambulatory nearby, a pair of sandstone Passion reliefs by Münster's Hinrik Brabender draws visitors mostly for a tiny mouse in the Last Supper scene. Apparently, like the ravens of London's Tower, Lübeck was secure so long as a rose bush bloomed beside the Marientiden-Kapelle. A mouse gnawed at its roots to create a nest, the plant wilted, and soon afterwards, in 1201, Danish king Waldemar II conquered the city for a quarter of a century. Smooth from wear, the tiny mouse is said to bring wealth to whoever touches it with their left hand. The Briefkapelle is worth a look for its leafy capitals beneath star vaulting, and if you're visiting at noon, Jesus blesses a parade of figures on the astronomical clock, a grumpy fisherman pulling up the rear with hands thrust in his pockets. As amusing is the folk tale about the church's build told on a plaque beside a bronze devil outside.

Buddenbrookhaus and Mengstrasse

Perhaps inevitably, plain old Mengstrasse 4 no longer exists and in its place there is forever **Buddenbrookhaus** (daily: April–Dec 10am–6pm; Jan–March 11am–5pm; €7; ⓦ www.buddenbrookhaus.de). Thomas Mann housed the declining merchant family of his Nobel Prize-winning debut *Buddenbrooks* in this, his grandparents' house – he was born and lived nearby at Breite Strasse 38. All that remains of the original is its late Baroque facade, but that hasn't stopped its postwar replacement from becoming a shrine to Mann and his novelist brother Heinrich, with a museum about the family and their exile during the Nazi years, and above, the Landschaftsimmer (landscape room) and Speisesaal (dining room) furnished as Mann saw in his mind's eye. Such veneration is a far cry from the outrage expressed by Lübeck citizens upon the book's release in 1900. Many perceived themselves in his cast of decadent characters and Mann's description of Lübeck as a "mediocre trading centre on the Baltic Sea" probably won few friends.

Downhill from Buddenbrookhaus, **Mengstrasse** holds some of Lübeck's grandest merchants' houses on a street that unites the two axes around which Lübeck revolved – Hansa government and harbour. One of the finest buildings houses *Schabbelhaus* (Mengstrasse 48–52; see p.788), one of Lübeck's most famous restaurants, named after a master pastry chef who made his fortune by creating a "Hanseat" biscuit in Lübeck colours. He bequeathed the house to the city to save the property as a period piece, exactly the sort of self-aggrandizing Mann satirized. Further down, at no. 64 is the shop where Germany's oldest wine importer, Carl Tesdorpf (Mon–Fri 9am–6pm,

Sat 9am–2pm), has operated since 1678. Medieval salt-ships returned with casks of Bordeaux red, so they could be matured in local cellars as *Lübecker Rotspon* – Napoleon's officers acclaimed it far superior to the Bordeaux at home. The merchant holds supplies in a superbly equipped period cellar – a must for any wine buff.

Around the Jakobikirche

The defining sight at the north end of Breite Strasse is the spire of **Jakobikirche**. The original congregation of sailors and fishermen means its Gothic is far less flashy than that of the Marienkirche, although there are similar pastel frescoes on the pillars, including a large St Christopher – folklore that claimed anyone who saw it would last out the day was probably a ruse to guarantee attendance. Elsewhere a splintered lifeboat from the training barque *Pamir*, which sunk with all hands in 1957, is the centrepiece of a memorial to drowned mariners in the north chapel, at whose front is a superbly carved spiral staircase from 1606, which loops up to an equally splendid 1504 organ. The older Stellwagen organ in the transept is the one listed among northern Europe's most historical instruments. The church's trump card is the **Brömbse Altar**, a subtle masterpiece by Hinrik Brabender. The artist carved himself into the Crucifixion scene – he wears a beret next to Mary Magdalene – while the benefactor, mayor Heinrich Brömbse and his wife pay homage from the wings.

Opposite is the **Heiligen–Geist–Hospital** (Tues–Sun 10am–5pm, till 4pm winter; free), Germany's oldest hospital (c.1260) and a pensioners' home. Its interior features superb frescoes: a fourteenth-century *Christ in the Mandorla* on the north wall with portraits of the hospice's patrons girdling the Son like an inner circle and an early fifteenth-century rood screen of the life of St Elizabeth. At the back is the Langes Haus men's ward where pensioners lived in tiny huts until 1970, though they didn't enjoy a daily prescription of three litres of home-brew like their counterparts did until 1775.

On the opposite side of the church is the Renaissance-gabled **Haus der Schiffergesellschaft** on Breite Strasse 2. It was purchased by the Shippers' Guild in 1535, and their members' widows still benefit from the lease money earned through the restaurant inside, a bosun's locker of maritime knick-knacks with rough tables, long wooden benches and the obligatory model ships, some over 2m long. If you can face the crowds, the self-styled "world's classiest pub" offers highly atmospheric dining.

The northern Altstadt

A clutch of less-visited sights in old Lübeck's far corner can be combined in a scenic loop that begins in **Engelsgrube**; its name refers to trade with England rather than angels ("Engel"). Alleys burrow behind the street-front introduce the mews that bring romance to the refinement of Lübeck's streetscape (see box opposite). **Hellgrüner Gang 28**, halfway along side-street Engelswich, is the most enchanting of the ninety or so that remain; duck down its low tunnel and you emerge into a secret "village" of dead ends and courtyards whose cobbles are worn smooth. Dunkelgrüner Gang a block north is also worth a look.

Hidden away on Kleine Burgstrasse in a quiet corner of the Altstadt is the **Burgkloster** (Tues–Sun: April–Dec 10am–5pm; Jan–March 11am–4pm; €5). The monastery was built to honour a battle oath that summoned Mary Magdalene to evict the Danes on July 22, 1227, if the *Chronicella Novella* of Dominican historian Hermann Korner can be believed. Its whitewashed interior serves as a blank canvas for a cultural centre with temporary art exhibitions alongside two permanent displays: a Hanseatic merchant's stash of gold coins,

Courtyard charm

The romantic courtyards and mews secreted behind the street fronts are one of Lübeck's most charming features. Though much of this housing was – and some still is – charitable, many developments were a ploy by landlords who developed the space between houses as the population exploded by over 25 percent in the 1600s. By the end of the century, Lübeck's streetscape was riddled with 190 passageways like woodworm holes, into which were shoehorned tiny Buden (literally, booths) for artisans and labourers; the smallest in Lübeck, at Hartengrube 36, was 3.5m wide, 5m high and 4.5m deep. Charity seemed lacking even in some almshouses: during meetings in Haasenhof, widows enjoyed soft chairs while spinsters were only permitted wooden stools.

Today ninety or so courtyards remain. The most picturesque in the Altstadt are Hellgrüner and Dunkelgrüner Gang off Engelswich in the northwest, and Der Füchtingshof and Glandorpsgang off Glockengiesserwall in the east (see p.786). Tourist information organizes the occasional courtyard tour – useful as entrance gateways can be locked – and some houses are available as idyllic holiday accommodation, again sourced via tourist information. Ones for the photo album include:

• Der Kolk und seine Gruben (off Kolk, opposite Puppet Museum)
• Von Höveln Gang (Wähmstrasse 73–77)
• Lüngreens Gang (Fischergrube 38)
• Schwans Hof (Hartengrube 18)
• Von Dornes Hof (Schulmacher Strasse 19, between Fleischhauerstrasse and Hüxstrasse)
• Haasenhof (Dr Julius Leber-Strasse 37–39)
• Grützmacherhof and Blohms Gang (20m north of An der Obertrave–Effengrube junction)

around 24,000 from over eighty international mints, and a photographic record of Jewish life in the town. The latter was shattered during Nazi rule, and you can visit the Gerichtsaal (Magistrate's Hall) upstairs where Third Reich "justice" was handed down to union workers and Jews.

Along Königstrasse

Spine-street Königstrasse runs north–south almost the length of Lübeck. Adjacent to the Jacobikirche, there's a bronze of nineteenth-century poet Emanuel Geibel, figurehead of Munich's lyric poets who penned a ditty about the Mercury statue on the Puppenbrücke before the Holstentor. A rough translation reads: "On Lübeck's bridge is standing/ The god Mercury proud and fine/ In every part, toned muscles form/ A statue Olympian/ In god-like contemplation/ To clothes he won't succumb/ So to all those people passing/ He bares his naked bum."

Königstrasse continues as an aristocratic Baroque parade that includes **Drägerhaus** and **Behnhaus** at nos. 9–11, merged to create a museum of art and culture (Tues–Sun: April–Dec 10am–5pm; Jan–March 11am–4pm; €5). Behind the pinched frontage, the Drägerhaus opens out into an exercise in balanced refinement that speaks volumes about Lübeck high-life c.1800 and serves as a backdrop for displays of Classical furniture and *objets d'art*. The Behnhaus houses the town's gallery of Impressionist and Expressionist art beyond the largest hallway in town. Stand-out sections include a room by local son Friedrich Johann Overbeck, ringleader and most steadfast of the Nazarene artists who strived for high art through Italian Renaissance inspiration, and works by Ernst-Ludwig Kirchner, Max Beckmann and Edvard Munch.

"I always carried a piece of Lübeck inside me, wherever I had to go," said Willy Brandt, the German chancellor and twentieth-century statesman celebrated in **Willy-Brandt-Haus**, Königstrasse 21 (daily 11am–6pm; free). Though intended as a homage to a local son, the museum is also a compelling document of the social tides that have swept through modern Germany, especially in sections that tackle the Ostpolitik which thawed icy relations with the GDR and won Brandt the Nobel Peace Prize – the certificate is displayed here.

A short way beyond on the corner of Glockengiesserstrasse is the museum-church **Katharinenkirche** (April–Sept Tues–Sun 11am–1pm & 1.30–5pm; free), a thirteenth-century Franciscan monastery whose renown is for its trio of chunky sculptures by Ernst Barlach on the facade. On the left, titled *Woman in the Wind*, *The Beggar* and *The Singer*, their vivacious style reveals the influences of medieval carving and social empathy that shaped the Expressionist's works. Barlach would have cast all nine in a "Community of Saints" cycle had he not been condemned as "degenerate" by the Nazi regime in 1932, leaving Bauhaus sculptor Gerhard Marcks to finish the job after the war. Inside, Tintoretto's monumental *The Resurrection of Lazarus* is half-hidden in the gloom on the west wall, a souvenir picked up by a Lübeck merchant from Venice.

The eastern Altstadt

Away from the grand architecture around the harbour area and main thoroughfares – the prestigious addresses coveted by the town's moneyed elite – Lübeck relaxes into cobbled backstreets – a pleasant spot to amble. Glockengiesserstrasse, off Königstrasse, holds three of the town's most celebrated seventeenth-century almshouse courtyards. Unmissable by its Baroque portal, **Füchtingshof**, Glockengiesserstrasse 23–27 (daily 9am–noon & 3–6pm), was a merchant's bequest to house mariners' widows; today 28 pensioners enjoy the charming mews of manicured flowerbeds and dusty pink walls. Further along is **Glandorps-Hof**, the oldest of the charitable Höfe, and next to it is Glandorps-Gang (no. 39–41).

On the same street at no. 21, the **Günter Grass-Haus** (daily: April–Dec 10am–5pm; Tues–Sun Nov–March 11am–5pm; €4) is an intriguing small collection for fans of a colossus of German modern literature who lives near Lübeck. Light on traditional literary exhibits, its displays showcase instead the Nobel Prize winner's etchings and bronze sculpture to tease out common themes in his writings and graphics.

If you walk south along St-Annen-Strasse, you pass one wing of the university and student-friendly bars before arriving at the **Aegidienkirche** (Tues–Sun 10am–4pm) in a peaceful square. The smallest of the five Gothic churches in the Altstadt, it would barely rate a mention were it not for a Renaissance choir gallery by Tönnies Evers the Younger, son of the Rathaus Audienzsaal woodcarver, and a highly prized organ with a fine, early Baroque front. It may be no coincidence that the church is traditionally that of craftsmen.

St-Annen-Strasse nearby hosts the **St-Annen-Museum** (April–Sept Tues–Sun 10am–5pm; Oct–March Tues–Sun 10am–4pm, Sat & Sun 11am–5pm; €5) with a first-rate gallery of ecclesiastical art from the fifteenth and sixteenth centuries in the cloisters of a former Augustinian convent. A room of predellas and altarpieces commissioned by Lübeck guilds is a sumptuous balance of wealth and piety, but even these pale next to a brilliant Passion altar by Flemish master Hans Memling that glows with inner radiance. Elsewhere, the original Baroque statues from the Puppenbrücke – Mercury included – strike a pose in a charming courtyard and

Lübeck lays out its domestic past to the late 1800s in living and dining rooms of flashy merchants; don't miss a 1736 grand hall with a kitchen tucked beneath a carved balcony.

The Dom

Cross Mühlenstrasse to reach Fegefeuer (purgatory), heed a warning plaque of sinners simmering in Hölle (hell) and, good pilgrim, you are rewarded with Paradies (paradise) – the vestibule of the **Dom** in whose tympanum Christ sits as supreme judge. Saxon duke Henry the Lion laid the foundation stone of his only surviving monument in town in 1173, only for mercantile Lübeck to cock a snook at the newly arrived bishopric from Oldenburg and found a civic centre around what became the Rathaus and Marienkirche. True, its Romanesque basilica with tacked-on Gothic choir can't match the latter for scale or flamboyance, but its bulk and twin towers impress. A whitewashed interior only boosts the impact of the fifteenth-century Triumphkreuz that sprouts from a plinth to fill an entire arch, the work of sculptor and painter Bernt Notke, a Michelangelo of the Baltic and a masterpiece of expressive figures that reveal more secrets the longer you study. Notke also designed the rood screen behind, another masterclass despite a seventeenth-century astronomical clock which throws it off kilter.

Travemünde

TRAVEMÜNDE at Lübeck's municipal boundary lives a double life as a major port and a small-fry beach resort. Bought for a song – Lübeckers paid Count Adolf III of Schauenburg 1060 Marks for the hamlet to safeguard the river for shipping – it became an opera. In the nineteenth century it was a German St Tropez favoured as the nation went crazy for seawater bathing. High rollers, including that inveterate gambler Dostoevsky, tried their luck in a *belle époque* casino and Emperor Wilhelm II competed in the Travemünde Woch regatta. Thomas Mann took his holidays here, enthusing about "a paradise where I have undoubtedly spent the happiest days of my life", and Clara Wieck gushed to future husband Robert Schumann about sailing trips.

The heart of the fishing settlement huddles around **St-Lorenz-Kirche** (Tues–Sun 10am–noon & 1–4pm), a humble church with a painted wood roof. From the adjacent river channel, lined by fish restaurants, you can embark for hour-long boat trips or cross the river to the four-masted barque *Passat* (Easter to mid-May & mid-Sept to Oct Sat & Sun 11am–4pm; mid-May to mid-Sept 10am–5pm; €3), Germany's last windjammer and sister-ship to the ill-fated *Pamir* whose lifeboat is in Lübeck's Jakobikirche. She is on a permanent mooring on the Priwall peninsula, a wild conservation area with plenty of beach space. Two ferries cross the Trave: a passenger ferry by the river mouth and a car/passenger ferry upriver (both daily 10am–6pm, till 9pm mid-June to early Sept; pedestrians €0.60).

The focus, however, is a beach full of wicker *Strandkörbe*, the hooded Rolls-Royce of beach seating. Its Strandpromenade is somewhat down-at-heel compared to Baltic resorts east, but is pleasant for a sunny day. Beach notwithstanding, the seafront Trave Sauna, Strandpromenade 1b (daily 10am–9pm), has pools and steam rooms, or as a modern interpretation of yesteryear luxury there are spa treatments in the *A.Rosa* spa hotel (reservations required; see p.780). The paraphernalia of a seaside resort eventually peters out to be replaced by the Brodtener Ufer, an unspoilt beach backed by trees and low, sandy cliffs with a restaurant, *Hermannshöhe*, after twenty minutes' walk.

Eating and drinking

Lübeck's dining scene punches far above its weight, not just for cuisine but the number of restaurants in which the historic ambience is as much of an attraction as the food. Character doesn't always come cheap, so it pays to look to lunch menus for bargains. Budget eats lie in the pubs and student quarter in the east Altstadt. The best nightclub in town is the *Hüx* (Hüxterdamm 14; ⓦwww .huex.de) – chart-fodder or retro nights, but usually busy.

Restaurants

Haus der Schiffergesellschaft Breite Str. 2 ☎0451/767 76. Baltic fish – including a speciality *sole meunière* – and roast rack of lamb in rosemary sauce at the original oak-planked tables of the sixteenth-century sea-captains' guildhall; less a restaurant than a museum of Hanseatic history. Touristy but essential.

Heinrichs Königstr. 5 ☎0451/706 03 67. Highly rated by locals for dishes such as halibut with shrimp ratatouille and fennel foam, and tapas. Classy modern in front, a Rococo gem of painted ceilings and chandeliers behind. Closed Sun & Mon.

Das Kleine Restaurant An der Untertrave 39 ☎0451/70 59 59. The galleried hallway of a merchant's house on the port provides an atmospheric setting for a menu that brings French and Mediterranean accents to regional dishes. Mains average €17, ten-course €55. Mon–Sat eve only.

Markgraf Fischergrube 18 ☎0451/706 03 43. Modern fusion cuisine brings Asian flavours to German cuisine in a sixteenth-century merchant's house, one room traditional, the other reinvented into cool contemporary glamour. Tues–Sat eve only.

Miera's Aubergine Hüxstr. 57 ☎0451/772 12. A gourmet deli, bistro for lunch and dinner and, above, an excellent restaurant (eve only) with an idiosyncratic eye for modern style. Cuisine throughout is Mediterranean. Closed Sun.

Ratskeller Markt 13 ☎0451/720 44. Beneath the town-hall cellars and as historic as you'd hope, from booth-style seating at the front to the smarter Hanse Saal with Hanseatic shields, and a menu of traditional dishes, including some vegetarian options.

Roberto Rossi Schabbelhaus, Mengstr. 48–52 ☎0451/720 11. A prestigious seventeenth-century merchant's house that rates high on the wow factor. Italian cuisine is not cheap – mains average €20, pasta €14 – but dining here is about savouring setting and cuisine. Closed Sun.

Vai Hüxstr. 42 ☎0451/400 80 83. Grilled Iberico pork and Baltic sole with aubergine marmalade in a tiny temple of gourmet cuisine; small but über-hip. Mains cost around €24, a three-course meal is €35. Closed Sun lunch.

Wullenwever Beckergrube 71 ☎0451/70 43 33. A Michelin-starred gourmet address that uses only the freshest produce to create seasonal, French-flavoured dishes. Two four-course set meals provide good value. Tues–Sat from 7pm.

Zimmerman's Lübecker Hanse Kolk 3–7 ☎0451/780 54. Contemporary regional cuisine in atmospheric dark-wood surroundings – fish dishes win local plaudits. Closed Sun & Mon.

Cafés, cheap eats and bars

Brauberger Alfstr. 36. *Hausbrauerei* with a tradition dating to the thirteenth century and its own brews to wash down cheap pub-grub.

Café Affenbrot Kanalstr. 70. Part of the Werkhof warehouse complex, this vegetarian café offers mellow tunes and superb coffee served on a terrace.

Café Lounge Wahmstr. 40. Stylized, rather pretentious café-cocktail bar whose prices are justified by the ambience: cube seats, a large aquarium and house tunes.

Café Remise Wahmstr. 43–45. A courtyard café in a former factory with a cult following. Breakfasts daily plus good-value bistro lunches Mon–Fri.

Cole Street Beckergrube 18. Acid green accent walls and funky junk shop chic in a cool café-bar-cum-gallery. Closed Mon.

Glocke 7 Glockengiesserstr. 7. Tiny, boozy, old-fashioned *Kneipe*, its walls long disappeared beneath naval and drinking memorabilia – the antithesis to the style bars elsewhere.

Kandinsky/Sternschnuppe Fleischhauerstr. 89/78. The former is a nicely knocked-about student bar with a laid-back vibe plus occasional jazz concerts. The latter opposite – from the same owner – is a lively spot where a friendly bunch rock to an indie soundtrack; Thursday's After Jerk Club is always fun.

Niederegger Arkadencafe Am Marktplatz. The most stylish outpost of the marzipan-maker, glass-walled into the Rathaus's Gothic arcades, has bold floral fabrics and Mediterranean tapas in the evenings. The traditional café opposite is an oldies' favourite for *Kaffee und Kuchen*.

Paulaner's Breite Str. 1–5. This northern outpost of the Bavarian beerhall chain provides the usual cheap *Schnitzels* or hunks of ribs in no-nonsense portions.

Sachers Hüxterdamm 14. A canalside café-restaurant that's a great place to laze over a weekend breakfast or lunch thanks to an idyllic terrace.

Tipasa Schlumacherstr. 12–14. Cheap-and-cheerful student fodder: pizzas and curries rustled up in a tandoori furnace.

Entertainment

Marienkirche **organ concerts** have drawn luminaries such as JS Bach ever since Dietrich Buxtehude flexed his fingers. Today's are held on the new Buxtehudeorgan, the world's biggest mechanical organ; check the church and tourist offices for what's on. Classical music concerts are also performed at the **Musik- und Kongresshalle**, Willy-Brandt-Allee 10 (T 0451/790 40, W www .muk.de), which also hosts musicals and jazz, and the **Musikhochschule Lübeck**, Grosse Petersgrube 17–29 (T 0451/150 50, W www.mh-luebeck.de). For jazz try *Dr Jazz*, An der Untertrave 1 (T 0451/70 59 09, W www.drjazz.de), or sleek bar *Jazz Café*, Mühlenstrasse 62, which hosts occasional concerts.

Lübeck's main venue for theatre, opera and dance is the Art Nouveau, three-stage **Theater Lübeck**, Beckergrube 16 (T 0451/745 52, W www.theaterluebeck .de). Listings for all events are provided in free magazines in the Welcome Center; *Ultimo* also publishes listings online at W www.ultimo-luebeck.de.

Listings

Boat rental Bootsverleih Hübner, Augusenstr. 30 (T 0451/696 26; Kanu-Zentrale-Lübeck, Geniner Str. 2 (T 0451/713 33
Car rental Europcar, Fackenburger Allee 32a–38 (T 0451/48 41 60); Hertz, Willy-Brandt-Allee 1–5 (T 0451/70 22 50); SIXT, Waisenallee 10 (T 0451/439 66); and Star Car, Bei der Lohmühle 21 (T 0451/40 62 42). Hertz has a desk at the airport, Europcar also in the Hauptbahnhof.
Festivals Lübeck's fairytale Weihnachtsmarkt (Christmas Market) is the envy of Germany, its crafts stalls scattered in the splendour of the

Heiligen-Geist-Hospital, the Rathausmarkt and St Petrikirche. In Travemünde at the end of July, a thousand-strong fleet descends for the Travemünder Woch regatta.
Hospital Marienkrankenhaus, Parade 3 (T 0451/140 70.
Internet Internetcafé Netzwerk, Wahmstr. 58; Mon–Sat 10am–10pm, Sun 2–10pm.
Laundry Waschsalon, Hüxterdamm 3; Wasch-Center Lübeck, Schwartauer Allee 32.
Police Mengstr. 20 (T 0451/13 10.
Post office Königstr. 44–46.

Ratzeburg

With Travemünde ticked off, the finest day-trip from Lübeck is **RATZEBURG**, 23km south. Approach in a summer heat-haze and it seems almost like a mirage, a cluster of red roofs and a green copper tower afloat in a lake. The trick is that the town is clustered on an island at the south end of the elongated Ratzeburger See. Indeed it is because of this geography that the town emerged – its defensive possibilities caught the eye of Saxon duke Henry the Lion as he marched north to found Lübeck in the mid-1100s. A bronze lion, copied from his Braunschweig capital, stands outside his Romanesque **Dom** whose massive west tower bears the stamp of its Lübeck contemporary. The basilica's interior (May–Sept daily 10am–6pm; Oct–April Tues–Sun 10am–4pm) is bare to the point of asceticism but has a few artworks worthy of note: a thirteenty-century Triumphkreuz, a softly sculpted Gothic Passion altar in the chancel, and, to its left, the oldest choir stalls in North Germany (c.1200), plus a chunky oak pew on which the noble Dukes of Saxony perched.

The knot of streets around the Dom affords a happy half-hour's idle and minor culture: a ducal summer mansion at Domhof 5 with a mixed bag of local history as the **Kreismuseum** (Tues–Sun 10am–1pm & 2–5pm; €1.50; ⓦwww.kmrz.de), and the adjacent **A. Paul-Weber-Museum** (same times & price; ⓦwww.weber -museum.de), a shrine to the twentieth-century illustrator buried there whose first whimsical drawings slip into dark social commentaries and despair after he was detained by the Third Reich. **Ernst-Barlach-House** (March–Nov Tues–Sun 11am–5pm; €3), a block south of the central Markt at Barlachplatz 3, honours a more well-known victim of Hitler's purge on "degenerate art" with empathetic works displayed in the boyhood home of the Expressionist behind the sculptures on Lübeck's Katherinenkirche.

For all the cultural weight of the museums, water is Ratzeburg's premier attraction, both in it – from a beach by the quay near the western bridge to the Altstadt – and especially on it. The **Ratzeburg See** is an acclaimed sailing centre: **boat rental** is from Segelschule Henschel, Reeperbahn 4a (ⓣ04541/31 18), and Bootsvermietung Morgenroth, Am Jägerdenkmal (ⓣ04541/832 00). Both rent out sailing dinghies, the latter also has row boats. Kanuverleih Krebs, Schlossweise 3a (ⓣ04541/44 66), has canoes. Schiffahrt Ratzeburger See, Schlossweise 6 (€3–9; ⓣ04541/79 00, ⓦwww.schiffahrt-ratzeburg.de), schedules various circuits of the lake from April 26 to October 3 that depart from the quay west of the Altstadt, providing a sensational view of the Dom above the treetops. However, it's worth disembarking at Rothenhusen at the northern tip to join a cruise back to Lübeck along the River Wakenitz, operated by Wakenitz-Schifffahrt Quant (ⓣ0451/79 38 85, ⓦwww.wakenitz-schifffahrt-quandt.de), a lovely trip through 15km of swampy waterway choked with lilies. The full two-ferry Lübeck–Ratzeburg run via Rothenhusen, is possible four times daily (early April to mid-Oct Tues–Sun; 2hr 45min; combination ticket €13 single, €20 return).

Practicalities

Ratzeburg is on the Lübeck–Lüneburg line, its **train station** 2km west of the town centre; **buses** bound for the Rathaus stop outside on main road Bahnhofstrasse. There are also irregular direct buses from Lübeck bus station to Ratzeburg Markt. The **tourist information** office is in the Rathaus at Unter den Linden as you enter from the west (Mon–Fri 9am–5pm, May–Oct also Sat & Sun 11am–4pm; ⓣ04541/85 85 65, ⓦwww.ratzeburg.de). For **eating**, it's hard to beat *Fischerstube*, tucked away by the ferry quay on the lake at Schlosswiese 2, with a menu of local fish. *Askainer-Keller* at Topferstrasse 1 also offers smoked eel and zander in brick cellars of the town's oldest restaurant.

Eutin

As gentle as its "Rosenstadt" (Town of Roses) moniker, **EUTIN** lies at the heart of the lumpy lakeland of Holstein Switzerland. It is a paean to small-town Germany: a place to potter that retains a modicum of the cultured atmosphere from its blossoming in the late 1700s as a ducal town that nurtured such rare talents as poet Johann Heinrich Voss, painter Johann Heinrich Wilhelm Tischbein and composer Carl Maria von Weber.

The princes who masterminded this transformation into a "Weimar of the North" were from the House of Schleswig-Holstein-Gottorf, and their moated **Schloss** is the town's star-turn, located at the northern end of the Altstadt by natural landmark, Lake Eutin. Inside (tours: daily mid-June to late Aug every hour 11am–4pm; mid-March to mid-June, Sept & Oct noon, 2pm & 3pm, Sat & Sun 11am–4pm; €5) the Baroque brick pile is furnished in the late Baroque,

Regency and Classical styles that followed the rebuild from a late medieval progenitor; one highlight is the model ships gifted by a relative, Tsar Peter the Great. With that ticked off, the **castle gardens** (free) behind are a pleasant spot to wander, their original Versailles-styled borders dug up for naturalistic English style and scattered with the usual bridges, waterfalls, a temple or two and a pretty stage that hosts alfresco opera from July to mid-August – the **Eutiner Festspiele** (Ⓦ www.eutiner-festspiele.de) is one of Germany's most traditional classical music festivals.

The palace's former stables house the **Ostholstein-Museum** (April–Sept daily 10am–1pm & 2–5pm, Thurs till 7pm; Oct–Jan & March Tues–Sun 3–5pm & Thurs–Sun 10am–noon; €3), whose modest displays on Eutin's time as regional cultural capital provide context to the castle. No surprise that the main exhibits feature the awesome threesome: portraits by Tischbein, Goethe's pal; the translations of Homer that Voss made in the spare hours from his day job as headmaster of the town's best school; and scores by local son Weber, a pioneer of Romanticism famed for his operas.

A short walk away from the palace beside the lake is a quay for **cruises** (May–Oct 15; €3 single, €5 return) – you have the option to disembark at Redderkrug then walk 2km back through fields behind the lake's wooded shore. **Boat rental** is available in front of in front of the Schwimmhalle in the park that backs the quay. Aficionados hail Holstein Switzerland as canoeing country. With stamina or time, you can paddle through an interconnected mosaic of pristine lakes all the way to Kiel (see below) – the 55km trip has been done in a long day, but most people allow three or four. Boote Keusen Sielbecker, Landstrasse 17 (Ⓣ 04521/42 01, Ⓦ www .boote-keusen.de), in northerly suburb Eutin-Fissau has Canadian-style canoes and can provide boat transport back from wherever you end up. A great trip.

Practicalities

The **Bahnhof** is five minutes' walk west of the Altstadt via a path off Bahnhofstrasse. The **tourist office** (May 15–Sept 14 Mon–Fri 9am–6pm, Sat & Sun 10am–2pm; Sept 15–May 14 Mon–Fri 10am–1pm & 2–6pm, Sat 10am–1pm; Ⓣ 04521/709 70, Ⓦ www.eutin.de) is on the Markt at the centre. Here, too, you'll find most cafés and *Hausbrauerei* including **restaurant** *Brauhaus Eutin* that provides the most atmospheric dining in town. Eutin has several old-fashioned **hotels** beside its lake: *Der Redderkrug*, Am Redderkrug 5 (Ⓣ 04521/22 32, Ⓦ www.redderkrug .de; ➍), where balconies for all rooms compensate for a dated concrete block, and *Seeschloss am Kellersee*, a hotel with a spa in a historic pile 2km from the Altstadt in Eutin-Fassau, Leonhard-Boldt-Strasse 19 (Ⓣ 04521/80 50, Ⓦ www.seeschloss-eutin .de; ➒), are reliable options. *Natur-Camping Prinzenholz* (Ⓣ 04521/52 81, Ⓦ www .nc-prinzenholz.de; April–Oct) near the latter at Prinzenholzweg 20 occupies a pretty lakeside site; buses #5502 and #5503 make the trip north.

Kiel

Land capital **KIEL** around 90km from Lübeck on the Baltic side is a gritty urban sprawl in this region of coast and cows. Over ninety raids in 1945 alone unleashed such devastation on what was Germany's principle submarine base that the port at the end of a deep firth had to start from scratch when the smoke cleared. Its lumpen concrete blocks built at speed in the 1950s are not the place to look for history – when brochures flag up the first pedestrian street in Germany (Holstenstrasse in 1525), you know tourist authorities are struggling.

Though lacking the looks of Lübeck – the more obvious candidate for capital – Kiel has instead the port which made it its fortune. It became the imperial war-port in 1871, and when the Kiel Canal (Nord-Ostsee-Kanal) opened to link the Baltic and North seas in 1895, Kiel controlled what was the biggest man-made waterway in the world. It remains the busiest, and shapes modern Kiel: workaday and resilient, with a knockabout, unpretentious air, especially during international sailing regatta **Kieler Woche**. Its few museums will pass a morning, but the self-styled "Kiel Sailing City" is at its best around water: seen from the Kiellinie footpath or on cruises on the Kieler Förde and canal.

Arrival, information and accommodation

The **train and bus stations** are adjacent at the southern end of the central shopping streets that stretch behind the harbour. The main **tourist office** (Mon–Fri 9am–6pm, Sat 10am–2pm; ☎01805/65 67 00 & 0431/67 91 00, ⊛www.kurskiel.de) is a block north in a corner of the Neues Rathaus at Andreas-Gayk-Strasse 31; a bureau also operates at the train station (daily 8am–8pm). It provides maps, a detailed English-language information booklet, *KursKiel*, and can book accommodation. The central library in the same building provides **internet** access as does Internetcafe Silver Angel, Schlossstrasse 16 (Mon–Sat 10am–10pm, Sun noon–10pm).

A couple of modern hostels have widened **accommodation** options that were formerly geared towards business travellers. Reservations are needed during Kieler Woche around the last full week in June.

Basic Hotel Sophienhof Königsweg 13 ☎0431/62 678, ⊛www.basic-hotels.de. The most recently renovated member of four budget chain hotels, this at least with character in its brightly painted rooms. Sister hotel *City* at Muhliusstr. 95 (☎0431/98 68 00) is more spacious but older. Both ❸–❺.

Bekpek Kiel Kronshagener Weg 130a ☎0431/888 80 09, ⊛www.bekpek-kiel.de. Bright cheerful hostel, with six-bed dorms, two lounges, laundry facilities, internet access and bike rental. It's on the fourth floor of an apartment block 2km west of the centre; take buses #34, #100 or #101 towards Mettenhoff and alight at Dehnkestrasse. Reception 8am–noon, 4–9pm. Dorms €21.

Berliner Hof Ringstr. 6 ☎0431/663 40, ⊛www.berlinerhof-kiel.de. Old-fashioned dark-wood standard class, or for an extra €5 modern Ikea-esque rooms of blonde wood and crisp white linen in a long-standing mid-range hotel. ❹–❺.

DJH Kiel Johannsstr. 1 ☎0431/73 14 88, ⊛www.djh-nordmark.de. Large youth hostel 700m from the station on the east bank of the Kieler Förde; take buses #11 or #12 or cross sthe pedestrian bridge opposite the train station. Dorms from €17.60, rooms ❷

Parkhotel Kieler Kaufmann Niemannsweg 102 ☎0431/881 10, ⊛www.kieler-kaufmann.de. The luxury address just north of the centre marries the old-world ambience of its late 1800s garden villa to modern glamour in refurbished rooms. Names in the guestbook include assorted European royals and politicians, including Chancellor Angela Merkel. Great restaurant, too. ❼

Peanuts Hostel Harriesstr. 2 ☎0431/ 364 22 08, ⊛www.peanuts-hostel.de. 10min walk south of the train station in the Südfriedhof, which survived the bombs, this is more home than hostel, with just seven beds in three rooms. Call before to ensure the owner is around for check-in (usually mornings and early eve). Dorms €18–24.

Steigenberger Conti-Hansa Schlossgarten 7 ☎0431/511 50, ⊛www.kiel.steigenberger.de. Kiel's premier central hotel is a business hotel in the northern end of the centre. Decor is far more modern-classic than the brick block suggests from outside. ❻–❽

The city

The city centre is unlovable but unavoidable along pedestrianized high-street Holstenstrasse two blocks back from the harbour. A rare slice of history halfway up is the **Altes Rathaus** reached via Fleethörn. Its swaggering pile

Cruises and the Kiel Canal

Steamer-style ferries of the SFK line bustle along the harbour between quays at Bahnhofsbrücke opposite the bus station and Laboe 18km east (single €2.10, daily pass €7) – useful disembarkation points are at Seegartenbrücke by the Schiffahrtsmuseum and Reventloubrücke at the northern end of the town centre. Arguably the best trip is that along the world's busiest man-made shipping channel, the **Kiel Canal**. Adler Schiffe sails on return day-trips to Rendsburg aboard the *Adler Princess* (April–Oct 1 or 2 weekly; 8hr; €31, including lunch; ⓦ www.adler-schiffe.de) and less frequent trips aboard the 1905-vintage paddle-steamer *Freya* (April–Dec; 8hr; €32); tourist information have a timetable. A taster of the canal is available at the massive locks (Schleusen) located north of the city in Holtenau at the waterway's eastern end – perhaps the most interesting part of the canal from an engineering perspective. Take bus #11 to the terminus at Wik then board a free ferry that shuttles from the north to south bank a few minutes' walk west. Lock tours depart from the north bank (daily 11am & 1pm; €2.30). A more impressive approach is that by water on ferries from Laboe (see p.794).

of Jugendstil (tours May–Sept Wed & Sat 12.30pm; €3) is still pockmarked by bomb damage and has a landmark 106m tower that alludes optimistically to a Venetian campanile. Arterial Holstenstrasse leads to former heart Alter Markt and the **Nikolaikirche**, a Gothic church that was modernized as it was rebuilt; the wonder is anything was salvaged at all – a fourteenth-century font and the triumphal cross and altar from a century later. Paradoxically the sword-wielding angel outside, *Der Geistkämpfer* (literally, "Fighter of the spirit"), by Expressionist Ernst Barlach, only survived through its being condemned as "degenerate" by Third Reich arbiters of aesthetics; the regime forgot to smelt the bronze and it was discovered buried near Lüneburg after the war. Dänische Strasse off the rear of Alter Markt has been part-restored to house Kiel's smartest shopping. One of the few remaining town mansions houses the **Stadtmuseum** (summer daily 10am–6pm; winter Tues–Sun 10am–5pm; €2) with themed exhibits of local colour.

Cut to the harbour from Alter Markt, and you reach the **Schiffahrtsmuseum** (Maritime Museum; summer daily 10am–6pm; winter Tues–Sun 10am–5pm; €3) in a former fish hall like an upturned hull. There are enjoyable exhibits on the imperial navy past and in summer the ticket also lets you on to three historic craft moored opposite.

Ten minutes north, beyond the Schlossgarten park, the **Kunsthalle** (Tues–Sun 10am–6pm, Wed till 8pm; €6; ⓦ www.kunsthalle-kiel.de) houses a surprisingly rich hoard of paintings and sculpture from late German Romanticism – Schleswig-Holstein resident Emil Nolde is well represented – and post-1960s art. Abundant natural light, organization by theme, a floor of antiquities and thoughtful temporary exhibitions add to the appeal. The Kiellinie path threads off the main road a short way before the gallery as a broad promenade north along the harbour; with its views of ships, sailing school dinghies – every Kiel schoolchild receives free sailing lessons – and the docks opposite, this is Kiel at its best. There's also the university sea-science division's **aquarium** (daily: April–Sept 9am–7pm; Oct–March 9am–5pm; €3) of Baltic and tropical fish, although most people are content with the pool of seals beside the Kiellinie; feeding times are 10am and 2.30pm daily (except Fri). Ferries from the Reventloubrücke quay 300m or so beyond ply a return back to the centre (€2.10 single).

Around Kiel

A couple of destinations near Kiel warrant the short journey each requires. Marooned 6km southwest of the centre in Molfsee (#bus 500 or #504) is open-air museum **Schleswig-Holsteinisches Freilichtmuseum** (April to mid-Oct daily 9am–5pm; Nov–March Sun 11am–4pm in good weather; €6; ☎0431/65 96 60, ⓦwww.freilichtmuseum-sh.de). Around seventy traditional buildings plucked from the Land are gathered in miniature villages to represent their regional quirks. Farmhouses retain original cottage furniture – notably the cabin-like beds in which whole families slept to ward off winter cold – and craftsmen demonstrate cottage industries such as pottery and basket-weaving in summer. Livestock just adds to the bucolic charm.

As its chirpy slogan "Laboe is schö!" suggests, **LABOE**, 18km from Kiel, has no pretention to be anything other than a minor beach resort and a yachting centre. The surprise around the corner from the marina is the **Deutscher Marine-Ehrenmal** (daily: April–Oct 9.30am–6pm; Nov–March 9.30am–4pm; €4) that honours sailors of all nationalities who perished in both world wars – architect Gustav August Munzer said his 72m brick tower, completed in the 1930s, was nonrepresentational and only intended to inspire, but nevertheless resembles a ship's rudder-stock or a futuristic skyscraper. Beyond a sunken memorial hall are exhibits on navigation and a viewing platform, while its technical museum is the submarine beached in front (same times; €2.50 or €5.50 combination ticket). The Hamburg-built U995 is the world's last Type VIIC, the workhorse of the war that was immortalized in classic film *Das Boot*. It's just as claustrophobic within. Buses #100 and #120 from Kiel reach Laboe in an hour, SFK ferries take longer.

Eating and drinking

Der Bauch von Kiel Legienstr. 16 ☎0431/512 15. Hip metropolitan-styled restaurant and bar with Italian and Mediterranean dishes. It's located behind the Kleiner Kiel lake west of the pedestrian centre. Closed lunch Sat & Sun.

Café Fiedler/Sandwich Holstenstr. 92. A first-floor traditional café that serves the cakes and chocolate Kiel Fisch of a renowned *Konditorei* downstairs. Adjacent bistro *Sandwich* is a good bet for a pit stop of soups and quiche.

Kieler Brauerei Am Alten Markt 9. Sturdy meals and fresh beers brewed in-house in a faux historic pub that feels instead like dining in a cave.

Louf Reventlouallee 2 (Kellinie) ☎0431/55 11 78. Whether as a restaurant or a café-bar, this is one of the coolest spots in Kiel in summer, when deckchairs and *Strandkörbe* bring a beach vibe to

its harbourside terrace. Menu-wise it's international and snacks.

Lüneburg-Haus Danische Str. 22 ☎0431/982 60 00. The most sophisticated culinary experience in the centre provides regional menus from whatever's freshest plus a few international dishes. The decor is historic pepped up with designer pieces. Closed Sun.

Ratskeller Fleethörn 9–11 ☎0431/971 00 05. A cut above others of its ilk, with old beams to suit a traditional menu of fish and seasonal Schleswig-Holstein dishes and brisk service by sprightly waiters.

Schöne Aussichsten Düsternbrooker Weg 16. Fish, salads and the beautiful views of its name in what looks like a control tower beside the harbour. Lunch only Sun.

Schleswig

SCHLESWIG should be one of the region's premier tourist destinations. That it is not is one more reason to make the journey. One of the most distinctive small towns in North Germany, it dozes peacefully on the banks of the broad Schlei fjord as a provincial backwater of around 25,000 people. Yet until the tenth century, Haithabu on the south bank of the Schlei was a hub of the

Viking world. Founded in 800 AD, the "colony of the west" flourished at the crossroads of trade routes to North Atlantic and Baltic settlements, populated by a cosmopolitan cross-section of Europe and serving as a base for Christian missionaries to Scandinavia. Indeed, it is only due to its destruction in 1066 that Schleswig emerged opposite. With a bit of poetic licence there remains something of the Scandinavian about its manicured **Altstadt** where red-brick fishermen's houses exude village charm. That its holy trinity of must-see sights – **cathedral**, **palace** and the **Viking past** – is spread over a wide area only serves to underline that Schleswig is a town best savoured at leisure. Take your time and make a day of it – ideally two.

Arrival and information

The **train station** is 3km southwest of the centre and 1km south of Schloss Gottorf – local buses #1 and #2 pass the latter en route to the centre. Inter-town **buses** drop you at the junction of Königstrasse and Plesenstrasse, just up from the **visitor information centre** (April–Oct Mon–Fri 10am–5pm, Sat & Sun 10am–2pm; Nov–March Mon–Fri 10am–4pm; ☎04621/85 00 56/57, ⓦwww .schleswig.de), Plesenstrasse 7, at the west end of St-Petri-Dom. **Cruises** on the Schlei fjord (from €10 for 2hr) depart 100m away from the Stadthafen where there's also boat rental. In summer, a ferry shuttles from Brücke 3 (May–Sept 10am–7pm, every 20min; single €2) to the Viking Museum at Haddeby. Bicycle (and rollerblade) rental is available at the Bahnhof from Fahrrad- und Rollerverleih Am Bahnhof, Bahnhofstrasse 29 (☎04621/335 55). Festivals that warrant a special visit include the Holmer Beliebung folk extravaganza a fortnight after Whitsun and Viking Days (Wiking Tage) every other August.

Accommodation

It's worth reserving to guarantee a bed in the charming area around the Dom, where several houses offer **private rooms** (❷) – book through tourist information. *Campingplatz Haithbau*, Haddebyer Chaussee 15 (☎04621/324 50, ⓦwww.campingplatz-haithabu.de; April–Oct), is on the south bank of the Schlei, at Haddeby, near the Viking Museum; buses and the ferry go from central Schleswig.

Bed & Breakfast am Dom Töpferstr. 9 ☎04621/48 59 62, ⓦwww.bb-schleswig .de. A two-hundred-year-old town house near the harbour hosts six cottage-style rooms replete with floral fabrics and homely touches. Probably the most charming address in Schleswig with a pretty garden, too. ❹

DJH youth hostel Spielkoppel 1 ☎04621/238 93, ⓦwww.djh-nordmark.de. Youth hostel in a modernized block 1km northwest of Schloss Gottorf and 2km west of the Altstadt. Dorms from €16.20.

Domhotel Domziegelhof 6 ☎04621/97 77 67, ⓔdomhotel@t-online.de. A passable cheapie on a side street off throughfare Königstrasse, just west of the Altstadt. ❷

Hahn Lutherstr. 8 ☎04621/99 53 52, ⓦwww.hotelhahn.de. Accent walls and modern-country decor lend an air of relaxed contemporary cool to an address that feels more home than

small hotel. Located three blocks north of tourist information. ❸–❹

Schleiblick Hafengang 4 ☎04621/234 68, ⓦwww.hotel-schleiblick.de. Pleasant modern rooms in a small hotel lodged in a former fisherman's house by the harbour. ❸

Waldschlössen Kolonnenweg 152 ☎04621/38 30, ⓦwww.hotel-schleswig.com. Schleswig's finest in stars (four), a mid-sized comfortable place in woodland 2km west of the centre. Has classic-modern style with designer accents – ask for a refurbished room – a spa and an elegant restaurant, *Adam Olearius*. ❻

Zollhaus Lollfuss 110 ☎04621/29 03 40, ⓦwww.zollhaus-schleswig.de. In a minor eighteenth-century mansion near Schloss Gottorf, this is a modest design hotel in inoffensive modern fashion. A renowned restaurant serves contemporary, Italian-influenced dishes. ❹

The Altstadt

Only the **St-Petri-Dom**, at the western edge of the Altstadt, its ballistic missile spire visible for miles, suggests yesteryear Schleswig was anything other than the village on the Schlei it appears today. A modern-looking exterior – notably that nighteenth-century spire – belie a cathedral born as a twelfth-century basilica of tufta and granite. Powerful Romanesque arches at the crossing spoke so eloquently of strength and permanence that they were moulded into the fabric of the later Gothic structure. They also retain medieval frescos that are imbued with the mystery of the early Church, notably an image of *Christ as the Saviour on the Rainbow*.

The artistic highlight, however, is the Bordesholm high altar. It took Hans Brüggemann seven years to create this audacious masterpiece from 1521, its cobweb-fine carving as detailed as the prints of Germany's Renaissance superhero Albrecht Dürer on which it seems to be based. Nearly four hundred individual figures fill its crowd scenes – a narrative of the Passion, Descent and Resurrection – each carved from the single oak block that produced its filigree canopy. Above, High Renaissance images of Adam and Eve pose either side of Mary as queen of heaven. The predella beneath is no less audacious. It's worth visiting in the morning when sunlight from a side window creates a play of light and shadow within the carvings. Brüggemann also carved the oversized St Christopher by the main portal, adjacent to a richly polychromed Magi (c.1300). On the other side of the altar is the creamy alabaster tomb of Gottorf duke Friedrich I.

Behind the Dom, the Altstadt unfolds as a nest of streets centred on Rathausmarkt – the **Rathaus**, around the corner on the left, subsumes one wing of a twelfth-century Franciscan convent.

Right then a hundred metres to the main road, a sign of a fisherman with a man-size catch announces **Holm**, one-time fishing village that stood on an islet until 1933; "holm" is an old Norse word for island. Although only a handful of fishermen continue to eke out a living from the Schlei and the "village" has merged into the rest of the Altstadt, the area retains a distinct atmosphere, with Freidhof cemetery ringed by cute houses at its core. That visitors are requested not to enter the cemetery is one symbol of a community that endures oblivious to tourism. Another is the houses' Klöndören, literally "natter doors", which divide horizontally to facilitate local gossip. In an area refreshingly free of tourist tat, visitors are directed to the **Holm Museum** (daily 10am–6pm; free) with photo exhibitions of village life.

The waterfront beneath is an equally picturesque corner of fishing nets, rickety pontoons and small boats whose swooping sheerlines are not too far removed from the Viking craft of yore. A rough cobbled lane above runs to the **St Johanniskloster**. Tours of the convent's Baroque living quarters or Romanesque church are organized through tourist information, but you're free to wander around the courtyard.

Schloss Gottorf

Poor Kiel. When the bombs rained on it in 1945, collections rich enough to warrant a trip on their own went to Schleswig's ducal palace on an islet 2km west of the Altstadt. **Schloss Gottorf** (Jan–March, Nov & Dec Tues–Fri 10am–4pm, Sat & Sun 10am–5pm; April & Oct daily 10am–6pm; May–Sept daily 10am–7pm; €6; ⓦwww.schloss-gottorf.de) is a magnificent setting for not just the finest museum in Schleswig-Holstein but one of the best all-rounders in Germany, not least because the palace is an impressive piece of sober North European Renaissance, a precise statement of authority by the Gottorf dukes. It and outbuildings house large collections that tick most boxes – put aside at least half a day to see it quickly, or a full day should you break for lunch at the museum's restaurant.

If time is tight it's best to follow a Historischer Rundgang (historic circuit) which rambles through the courtyard palace, kicking off in the long hall of its Gothic progenitor with medieval religious art; a retable by Hans Brüggemann of St-Petri-Dom fame and, in a following room, oils by Cranach the Elder – portraits, a celebrated *Fall of Man* and the darkly erotic *Lucretia*. Beyond Flemish art and Baroque furnishings upstairs is a reassembled Lübeck wine tavern from 1660 whose wooden panels are carved with images of Bacchus and boozy merriment such as a couple in bed surrounded by beaming cherubs. It also introduces a suite of restored palace rooms: the richly stuccoed Blauer Saal; the Schlosskapelle, a Renaissance gem lorded over by a ducal box hidden somewhere beneath frothy decoration; and the contemporary Hirschsaal festive hall named for the life-size deer stuccoed on its walls. Elsewhere on the second floor are first-class Jugendstil decorative arts and folk art. Don't miss, too, imaginatively presented exhibits of the state museum of archeology on the third floor. Crowds gravitate towards the ghoulish bog corpses (*Moorleichen*) that are thought to be around two thousand years old, but whose expressions are far too lifelike for comfort – the jury is out over whether the deceased, one blindfolded, were sacrificed, executed or died peacefully.

The museum's most celebrated treasure is the **Nydam-Boat**, a thirty-man Viking longship c.350 AD housed in the Nydamhalle to the left of the palace. Why the slender 23m oak vessel ended up in its eponymous bog in Denmark is a subject of conjecture, although a plausible theory proposes it was intended as a sacrifice. Around two thousand contemporary artefacts are displayed with the ship, from weapons and clothing to Roman-Germanic gold jewellery. The Kutschensammlung behind the hall houses ducal coaches.

Buildings on the other side of the palace fast-forward into the twentieth-century arts: regional artists plus crafts and design in the cross-shaped **Kreuzstall**, and a good spread of German Modernists in the **Galerie der Klassichen Moderne**. Highlights include the smudgy colour washes of Emil Nolde's landscapes, waggish lithographs by Beckmann, the work of Die Brücke artists (and a display of the African masks that inspired them), and characteristically empathetic works by Ernst Barlach (see p.849) and Käthe Kollwitz. The museum's collection of folk crafts and industry (Volkskunde Museum; same times; €2) is held 800m northeast of the Schloss, where Suadicanistrasse meets Hesterberg.

The Baroque Gardens and Gottorf Globe

Ever restless, the museum has expanded its appeal by replanting the ducal **Baroque Garden** behind the palace (Barockgarten; April 25–Oct 5, 10am–7pm, rest of Oct till 6pm; €2). The seventeenth-century geometric plantings which decorated the first terraced garden north of the Alps were intended as a paean to the Age of Reason, and their scientific diversion was the **Gottorf Globe**. An eager academic, Friedrich III commissioned a 3m globe to depict the world without and the heavens within. Court mathematician Adam Olearius completed his task in 1650, guests sat in candle-light as the stars span within, and Europe marvelled at this "astronomical wonder". So much so that it was swiped by the Russians during the Great Northern War and presented to Tsar Peter the Great in 1713. With the original still in Russia, a near-replica stands in the small white building at the garden's south end (Globushaus; April–Oct daily 10am–6pm; Mon & Fri €10, Tues–Thurs €11, Sat & Sun €14). Having surveyed the surface of the world circa 1650, three guests cram inside as the night sky perceived by Renaissance scholars rotates through its cycle in around ten minutes.

Wikinger Museum

Haithabu, the Viking settlement, lay directly opposite the town it spawned on the south bank of the Schlei. Haphazard archeological excavations of the area gained momentum with the discovery of a Viking longship in 1980, which provided the impetus for the **Wikinger Museum** (Viking Museum; April–Oct daily 9am–7pm; Nov–March Tues–Sun 10am–4pm; €4). The ship – less complete than the one in Schloss Gottorf but grafted onto a replica – occupies one of a series of buildings designed like upturned longboats. Others house archeological finds that provide a snapshot of a sophisticated domestic culture usually omitted in the tales of rape and pillage. More fun are the dwellings (same ticket; April–Oct 9am–5pm; Ⓦ www .haithabu.de) built to archeological models within the original Danevirk earthwork beyond. The effect is a sort of miniature Viking open-air museum, where raised boardwalks lead around a settlement of craft workshops and dingy family houses gathered around the civic longhouse. In summer craftsmen don doublet and hose to provide demonstrations of trades practised in what was one of the largest crafts centres in north Europe. Any bus heading south to Kiel will stop at Haddeby village, the modern incarnation of Haithabu. From May to September you can catch the ferry across the Schlei (see p.795).

Eating and drinking

No surprises that the most atmospheric restaurants are in the Altstadt. Hotels *Waldschlössen* and *Zollhaus* also have excellent restaurants.

Asgaard Königstr. 27. Schleswig's brewery is the place for no-nonsense pub-grub and its eponymous brew, "the divine beer of Vikings" apparently. Its beer garden at the back is a great spot in summer.

Esch am Hafen Stadthafen. Cheap fresh-fish sandwiches and fillets, plus one simple meat dish such as *Schnitzel*, in a glass-walled harbourside café – a good spot for a quick bite.

Holm Café Süderholmstr. 15. Traditional daytime café that serves home-made cakes in a cosy former fisherman's house in Holm.

Panorama Plesenstr.15. Budget-priced wood-fired pizzas, curries, noodles and veggie dishes a short distance from the tourist information centre.

Ringelnatz Fischbrückstr. 3 ☏ 04621/255 88. A surprisingly classy number that spreads throughout several rooms of elegant glassware and crisp tablecloths. Baltic sole with Dijon mustard sauce is typical of a fish speciality menu. Dinner only.

Senator-Kroog Rathausmarkt 9–10 ☏ 04621/222 60. Going strong since 1884, with a warren of historic rooms decorated in a nautical palette of pale blue, grey and cream. Fish specials are bolstered by a decent selection of upmarket meat plates.

Zur Schleimöwe Süderholmstr 8. Fish speciality *Gaststätte* in Holm – all the usuals plus seasonal local specials such as eel in home-made jelly in an simple, traditional *Gaststätte*.

Flensburg

Though just 30km north of Schleswig, the commercial port of **FLENSBURG** is centuries apart in atmosphere. Pressed hard against the border of former owner Denmark, the "southernmost town of Scandinavia" has the mercantile zip of the deep-water port through which it has prospered, whether as property of the Danish Crown – for centuries Flensburg outranked Copenhagen – or the German; it was claimed by Prussia in 1864, then threw in its lot officially in a plebiscite in 1920. Labels of cult local brew Flensburger Pilsner, with their royal Danish lions and merchant ship, sum up the history as succinctly as any icon. The trading past is also evident in the distinctive warehouse courtyards that burrow behind street-fronts, relics from an eighteenth-century rum trade founded on raw spirit imported from the Danish West Indies (now US Virgin Islands).

Notwithstanding these pockets and the yuppification that is reclaiming wharves on the east bank, Flensburg has few airs. It is a typical small port: knockabout, straightforward and host to a boisterous weekend pub-club scene fuelled by the local brew.

Arrival, information and accommodation

The **Hauptbahnhof** is a fifteen-minute walk south of the centre, the **bus station** is at the south end of the harbour outside the **tourist office** (Rathausstrasse 1; Mon–Fri 9am–6pm, Sat 10am–2pm except June–Aug till 4pm; ☎0461/909 09 20, ⓦwww.flensburg-tourismus.de), which has bike rental. **Harbour cruises** on the Flensburger Förde are run by a number of operators from the quay on nearby Schiffsbrücke.

You don't get much bed for your bucks in Flensburg. **Private rooms** (❷), booked through the tourist office, are one of the cheapest options.

Am Rathaus Rote Str. 34 ☎0461/173 33, ⓦwww.hotel-am-rathaus.com. Pleasant, old-fashioned place off one of the most charming streets in town. You get to ponder good views at breakfast from its dining room. ❹

DJH Flensburg Fichterstr. 16 ☎0461 377 42, ⓦwww.djh-nordmark.de. The town youth hostel is by the stadium in the east-bank Volkspark, a 10min bus ride from the centre; take buses #3, #5 or #7 and dioombark at "Stadion". Dorms from €15.70.

Etap Süderhofenden 14 ☎0461/58 08 920, ⓦwww.accorhotels.com. The usual functional base of the budget hotel chain is well located by the bus station. ❷

Flensburger Hof Süderhofenden 38 ☎0461 14 19 90, ⓦwww.hotel-flensburger-hof.com. Family-run three-star with splashes of Frisian character such as tiled walls. A little bare in some rooms but all are comfy enough for a good night. ❺

Tulip Inn Norderhofenden 6–9 ☎0461/841 10, ⓦwww.tulipinnflensburg.com. The town's central business hotel – mod cons and an excellent location near the tourist office at the corner of the harbour. ❺

The Town

Everything of interest in Flensburg is in the **Altstadt** on the west bank of the Flensburger Förde harbour, its axis a long pedestrian thoroughfare created from conjoined Holm, Grosse Strasse and Norderstrasse. The town's repository of culture is spread over two houses one block above at **Museumsberg** (Tues–Sun: April–Oct 10am–5pm; Nov–March 10am–4pm; €4 or €5 with Schiffahrtsmuseum; ⓦwww.museumsberg.flensburg.de), uphill from the tourist office. A local furniture tycoon, Heinrich Sauermann, scoured North Friesland to bring together the collection of farmhouse rooms reassembled in **Heinrich-Sauermann-Haus**. Despite their modest size and cabin-like bed alcoves, carved panels and Dutch-style Delft tiles reveal the former owners as wealthy families. Elsewhere there are displays of folk crafts and religious art, notably the Hütten altar (1517) whose predella depicts a yarn about the massacre of chaste English princess Ursula and companions for spurning the advances of a heathen king at Cologne. In 1884 Sauermann hired an apprentice furniture-maker named Emil Nolde, and it's the mystical Expressionist he became who stars in a gallery of North Friesland painting in **Hans-Christian-Haus**, notably a nausea-inducing recollection of a journey to the island of Anholt, *High Waves*. The gallery also includes landscapes and portraits by its eponymous leader of an artists' colony at nearby Eckendorfe, and a parlour presented to the 1900 World Exhibition in Paris as the pinnacle of German Revival style.

The high street beneath is pleasant enough though pedestrian in both senses, worth a visit largely for the merchants' courtyards (**Kaufmannshöfe**) secreted in side-alleys. The tourist board provides maps of the town's distinctive complexes, arranged around an elongated courtyard as harbour-side warehousing, workshops then a high-street residence. The oldest and most photogenic is **Kruse Hof**, a medieval timewarp where craftshops are shoehorned beneath a beamed gallery. It's halfway along Rote Strasse, itself off the upper side of Südemarkt at the south end of the axis street and unmissable because of the Nikolaikirche, a so-so neo-Gothic hulk that doubles as a venue for classical concerts. **Westindienspeicher** (West Indian Warehouse) at Grosse Strasse 24 is more representative of the supply chain that shuffled imports uphill from the harbour to warehouses then the high street above. Courtyards at Holm 19, between Südermarkt and Grosse Strasse, and half-timbered Norderstrasse 22, known as Künstlerhof because of its artists' studios, are also attractive.

Nordermarkt bookends Grosse Strasse with a Baroque fountain of Neptune and the Gothic arcades of the adjacent Marienkirche. Uphill on Marienstrasse, historic distillery **Alt Johnson** (Mon–Fri 10am–6pm, Sat 10am–2pm) is one of the last rum merchants to continue producing own-brand rum. In a spirit-soused 1700s heyday that earned Flensburg the nickname "Rumstadt", up to two hundred distilleries refined a raw West Indies rum known as "Killdevil". Appropriately Nordermarkt remains a focus of the town's drinking scene. Rum also receives a section alongside port history and trade in the **Schiffahrtsmuseum** (Maritime Museum; Tues–Sun: April–Oct 10am–5pm; Nov–March 10am–4pm; €4) on the port at Schiffbrücke 39. A small fleet of privately owned historic craft are moored opposite, and you can nose around whatever wooden craft is mid-build in an adjacent workshop (€1) whenever someone's around.

Eating and drinking

Flensburg has a surprisingly boisterous weekend drinking scene. Most people start at café-bars on and around Nordermarkt, then drift down to the port-side bars and clubs on Schiffbrücke as the night progresses – they become steadily rougher the further you go. For a quiet sundowner gazing at the Altstadt it's hard to beat *East-Side Café* behind the yachts on the opposite bank.

Hansens Brauerei Schiffbrücke 16. Popular brewery tavern inn that serves a *Schwarz*, *Pils* and a seasonal brew, and prepares typically sturdy German meat-feasts.

Jessen's Fischperle Ballastkai 3. Locals' choice for a fish supper is this modern fishmonger and canteen-style restaurant on the east bank – it's worth waiting for a table on the terrace.

Das Kleine Restaurant Grosse Str. 73. Intimate place on the high street with a menu of cheap pastas as well as salads.

Piet Henningsen Schiffsbrücke 20. Touristy and far from cheap, but an enjoyable port fish restaurant nevertheless, which dates from 1886 and is crammed with a bosun's locker of sailors' souvenirs picked up from around the globe.

Die Weinstube im Krusehof Rote Str. 24. Flambéd savoury crêpes are served in the snug wine inn at the end of Flensburg's oldest merchant's courtyard – the most idyllic spot in town by far.

Husum and around

Long-established tradition obliges that **HUSUM** is described as "the grey town by the sea", which seems most unfair for a quietly colourful North Sea harbour 42km south of Niebüll. Paradoxically its local hero is to blame. Nineteenth-century novelist, poet and Husum resident Theodor Storm coined the grim tagline with *Die graue Stadt am Meer*, an affectionate poem that describes the spring and autumn pea-soupers that blow off the North Sea to enshroud the town in heavy grey fog. Yet the town's inner harbour is all about local colour.

Boxy houses painted in a palette of bright yellows and blues jostle for space behind fishing boats moored in the heart of the town as they have been since medieval days, when Husum was used by the Dutch as a short cut between the North and Baltic seas. The serious stuff is in the **Schiffahrtsmuseum Nordfriesland** (daily 10am–5pm; €3; ⓦ www.schiffahrtsmuseum-nf.de), at the back of the harbour, an introduction to the region's fishing and former whaling industries whose prize possession is a sixteenth-century trading ship that is undergoing protracted restoration after it was sucked from the harbour's mud. Harbourside Hafenstrasse runs away from the inner harbour – information centre **NationalparkHaus Hafen Husum** (Mon–Sat 10am–6pm, Sun 10am–2pm; free) halfway down has displays of local ecology.

Storm's residence, **Theodor-Storm-Haus** (April–Oct Tues–Fri 10am–5pm, Sat 11am–5pm, Sun & Mon 2–5pm; Nov–March Tues, Thurs & Sat 2–5pm; €3), is on Wasserreihe which spears off the harbour's rear left-hand corner. Exhibits of an author little known outside his homeland leave most foreigners cold, but the house is mildly diverting as a document of upper-middle-class lifestyles in the late 1800s. Broad, main high street **Grossestrasse** a block north has a few historic buildings that survived a town fire in 1852: a late-Gothic wine merchants at no. 18; and 50m further down on the opposite side Herrenhaus, a former ducal mint – the story goes that the moustachioed Renaissance busts on the facade depict rebels executed in 1472. On the Markt in front, once home to the region's largest cattle market, the Marienkirche has a strict Neoclassical interior that takes literally Lutherian principles of anti-ornamentation and elevation of the Word.

Schlossgang slips off Grosse Strasse near Herrenhaus to reach **Schloss vor Husum** (March–Oct Tues–Sun 11am–5pm; Nov–Feb Sat & Sun 11am–5pm; €3.50), a Dutch Renaissance pile, whose fairly spartan interior features magnificent fireplaces: wardrobe-sized pieces of alabaster carved with reliefs like miniature antique friezes. Also included in the ticket is entrance to art exhibitions in the Dachgalerie in the attic. The garden (free) at the side of the Schloss is a lovely park, especially in spring when it is spangled by crocuses.

Practicalities

Husum Bahnhof is on the Hamburg rail line and located south of the centre reached via Herzog-Adolf-Strasse. Friedrichstadt is one stop south on a branch line. Husum's **tourist office** (Mon–Fri 9am–6pm, Nov–March till 5pm, & Sat 10am–4pm; ☏04841/ 898 70, ⓦ www.husum-tourismus.de), in the Altes Rathaus at Grossestrasse 27, is bolstered by a weekend-only Info-Point at the end of the Hafenstrasse (April–Oct Sat 11am–4pm & Sun 10.30am–3.30pm).

Budget **accommodation** options include: *Zur Grauen Stadt am Meer* (☏04841/893 20, ⓦ www.husum.net/grauestadt; ❸), plain though well located at the harbour; and *Osterkrug*, Osterende 52–58 (☏04841/661 20, ⓦ www.osterkrug .de; ❹), whose "Komfort" class refurbished in modest designer style is worth the extra €5. For a splurge there's *Altes Gymnasium*, Süderstrasse 2–10 (☏04841/83 30, ⓦ www.altes-gymnasium.de; ❼–❽), a luxury number in an old school near the Schloss. There's also a **youth hostel** at the northwest edge of town at Schobüller Strasse 34 (☏04841/27 14, ⓦ www.djh-nordmark.de; €17.20/20.20) and a **campsite** near the sea 2km west of the harbour at Dockkoog 17 (☏04841/619 11, ⓦ www.husum-camping.de; late March to late Oct).

All hotels have good **restaurants**, or take your pick from those along Hafenstrasse. *Dragseth's Gasthof* at the harbour's back is a sweet, late sixteenth-century inn with cabin-like rooms and a courtyard garden. The local delicacy is *Husumer Krabben* (Husum shrimp), sprinkled liberally on fish and blended to create a creamy soup.

Around Husum

The day-trip par excellence is idyllic **FRIEDRICHSTADT** on an island at the confluence of the Treene and Eider rivers. Divided by a canal and stuffed with cafés and galleries, the town's romantic grid of streets bears the stamp of Dutch religious refugees who were sheltered by Schleswig-Holstein-Gottorf duke Friedrich I in 1621. Given refuge and trade privileges, the merchants created the picture-book facade of Dutch step-gabled houses on the Markt, most with the ornamental marks that identified owners before the town got round to numbers – a water lily, starry sky or windmill, for example. Paludanushaus off the Markt at Prinzenstrasse 28 is the grandest residence in town; others are identified in a free leaflet stocked by the **tourist office** (Mon–Fri 10am–5pm, Sat & Sun 10am–4pm; ☏04881/939 30, ⓦwww .friedrichstadt.de) on the Markt. If you walk left from the Markt along the canal, you reach the **Alte Münze** (Old Mint; May–Sept Tues–Sun 11am–5pm; April & Oct Tues–Fri 3–5pm, Sat & Sun 1–5pm; €1.50), faced by one of the finest Dutch brick facades you'll see in North Germany; inside displays flesh out the town's roots.

Otherwise walk across the canal to board a **river cruise** (April–Oct; €7.50) around the town from a quay at the town's tip. For a dose of maritime air there are sea cruises in the Wattenmeer, the shallow sea sheltered between the mainland and the North Frisian islands. The destination for most tours is the Hallig sandbanks whose elevation 1–2m above the high-water mark permits minor agriculture in between storm surges. Small wonder villages on the largest island, Pellworm, are ringed by defences like prehistoric earthworks. Between June and October, NPDG (€12–19; ☏04844/753, ⓦwww .faehre-pellworm.de) sails combined trips to Pellworm and Hallig Südfall and to seal colonies from Nordstrand, 15km northwest of Husum. Departures are coordinated with the timetable of bus lines #1047 and #1091 from Husum; ask at the tourist information in Husum for ferry timetables.

North Frisian islands

Scattered in the North Sea 6km off Schleswig-Holstein are the **North Frisian islands**. For centuries these storm-battered, separate worlds eked out a living from farming and fishing, their thatched villages hunkered down behind sand dunes in defence against waves that occasionally washed whole communities into the North Sea. Tourism replaced agriculture as the premier source of income decades ago, yet even on Sylt the scenery is overwhelmingly bucolic-seaside. There are the same dune seas of marrum grass and vast skies – blue and brooding by turns and punctured only by lighthouses – that captivated artists in the early 1900s; the same thatched villages (though many house boutiques and restaurants rather than fisherfolk); and there are the same colonies of sea birds and seals in an area that is largely protected within the Nationalpark Schleswig-Holsteinisches Wattenmeer (literally "shallow sea"). This may be Germany's chic coastal playground, but it is more Martha's Vineyard than St Tropez. **Sylt** is the most popular and developed of the islands, centred on main town **Westerland** and the chic high-life of village-resort **Kampen**. **Föhr** and especially **Amrum** are peaceful rural islands of homespun charm with little to do except stroll or cycle – on these glorified sandbanks both are not just good options to get around, they are sometimes your only ones.

The islands are on the same latitude as Newcastle in northeast England or the southern tip of Alaska. And statistics tell their own story of changeable conditions as weather fronts barrel across the North Sea: although only fifteen days a year are free of prevailing westerly winds that can blow gale-force even in summer, the islands bask in 1750 hours of sunshine a year.

Sylt

New Yorkers weekend in the Hamptons. Germans escape to **SYLT**. They've come en masse since the nation went crazy for seawater bathing in the mid-1800s, and today around 600,000 people a year swell a year-round population of 23,000, thankfully only 50,000 at a time. In recent decades Sylt has carefully cultivated its reputation as the stylish playground of the nation's moneyed elite. Every minor celebrity for decades has been caught in flagrante delicto by the paparazzi, fuelling the gossip press each summer and adding to the prestige of Kampen.

Cross under grey North Sea skies to disembark in main resort **Westerland** and you might wonder what all the fuss is about. The answer is a broad beach of pale quartz sand that fringes the entire west side of an elongated island tethered to the mainland by its railway. The sheltered east coast looks over the mud-soup of the shallow Wattenmeer, while the north arm around the port of **List** is a restless sea of sand dunes. Flashy restaurants and boutiques aside, Sylt is an island of simple holiday pleasures: dozing in one of 11,000 *Strandkörbe*, the cute wicker beach-seats for two; dawdling through lanes of postcard-pretty **Keiten**; nature walks among Germany's largest sand-dunes at List; sea cruises from **Hölm** or any number of watersports. And people-watching at **Kampen**, of course.

Arrival, transport and information

Notwithstanding airlines that fly holidaymakers direct to **Sylt airport**, 2km east of Westerland, the **train** is the principal means of arrival. Sylt terminal Westerland is on the Hamburg line. Because no roads run to the island, cars and motorbikes must be loaded onto Deutsche Bahn's SyltShuttle **car train** at Niebüll (roughly hourly 5am–9.40pm; car €43 single, €80 return; ☎01805/93 45 67, ⓦwww.syltshuttle.de). **Car ferries** operated by Sylt Fähre (single €41.50, return €61; ⓦwww.syltfaehre.de) go from Rømø in Denmark, to List. Adler Schiffe **tourist ferries** link Hörnum to North Sea islands Amrum and Föhr (see p.808), themselves linked to the mainland by regular services.

SVG buses travel to all destinations on the island approximately every thirty minutes from a bus station outside the Westerland Hauptbahnhof; #1 and #5 go north to List, #2 south to Hörnum, and #3 and #4 circle east to Keitum (singles €1.55–6.20, 3-day all-zone pass €20.50). On a 35km-long island where distances from centre to tip are around 15km and 50m is a mountain, **cycling** is an excellent means of getting about, and most buses carry bikes for a few euros. Bike rental is available at the Hauptbahnhof or try Fahrrad Leksus (☎04651/83 50 00), which has outlets in Westerland at Lorens-de-Hahn-Strasse 23, Bismarckstrasse 9 and Norderstrasse 42, plus one in Wenningstedt at Hauptstrasse 8. **Car rental** options include: Europcar (Trift 2, Westerland; ☎04651/71 78); SIXT (in *Strandhotel*, Margarethenstrasse 9; ☎04651/92 74 14); and Sylt Car (Boysenstrasse 13; ☎01802/25 28 20, ⓦwww.syltcar.com).

Tourist information details are provided in relevant sections; the website of the Sylt marketing board, ⓦhttp://en.sylt.de, is a useful resource for pre-planning.

Accommodation

Accommodation is pricier on Sylt than on the mainland and booked long in advance in high season (July & Aug), so local tourist offices are the best resources should you choose to wing it. They can also source private accommodation (❷) and holiday apartments (usually minimum three nights), which work out cheaper than a hotel for extended stays. Resort websites or that of the island marketing board (Ⓦhttp://en.sylt.de) are also useful – as the largest resort, Westerland has the most options. Wherever you go, €2–3 is added to the day-rate as a Kurtax. In return you receive a ticket that permits free access to beaches and meagre discounts on some attractions.

Hotels and hostels

The largest youth hostel is near Westerland (see below). Others are at either end of the island, in the Mövenberg dunes 2km north of List (☎04651/87 03 97, Ⓦwww.djh-nordmark.de; €18.20/21.20) and at Hörnum (Friesenplatz 2; ☎04651/88 02 94, same website; €18.20/21.20).

Westerland and Wenningstedt

Clausen Friedrichstr. 20, Westerland ☎04651/922 90, Ⓦwww.hotel-clausen-sylt.de. Traditional three-star of modest floral charm on the high street, moments from the beach. ❺

DJH Westerland Fischerweg 36–40, 4km south of Westerland ☎04651/83 57 825, Ⓦwww .djh-nordmark.de. The best of the island's youth hostels is an excellent place among the dunes south of Westerland – a 45min walk from the Hauptbahnhof or take a south-bound bus and walk across the dunes. Dorms from €19.10.

🏃 **Long Island House Sylt** Eidumweg 13, Westerland ☎04651/995 95 50, Ⓦwww.sylthotel.de. Hip New Hamptons style in a bright, modern place with a palette of fresh contemporary pastels, individually furnished rooms and a nice garden. Probably the most appealing mid-range address in Westerland. ❻

Single Pension Trift 26, Westerland ☎04651/920 70, Ⓦwww.singlepension.de. The cheapest option in Westerland (if not Sylt), this has glorified hostel-style rooms, some with shared amenities, and a friendly clientele of mixed ages. ❸

Stadt Hamburg Strandstr. 2, Westerland ☎04651/85 80, Ⓦwww.hotelstadthamburg.com. A sumptuous Relaix & Chateau affiliated address that exudes oak-panelled traditional charm – a cut above the rest in central Westerland. ❼–❾

Wenningstedter Hof Hauptstr. 1, Wenningstedt ☎04651/946 50, Ⓦwww.hotel-wenningstedter -hof.de. Comfortable family-run establishment spread over three small hotels in the village centre. ❺

Kampen and Keitum

Benen-Diken-Hof Südstr. 3–5, Keitum ☎04651/938 30, Ⓦwww.benen-diken-hof.de. Relaxed, contemporary-country number of the Romantik group, scattered throughout several thatched houses. Stylish rooms are classic-modern. ❼–❾

Fährhaus Sylt Heefwai 1, Munkmarsch ☎04651/939 70, Ⓦwww.faehrhaus-sylt.de. Effortlessly elegant five-star-superior spa hotel in a late-1800s complex midway between Kampen and Keitum, with views either of woods or the east coast. The restaurant is a first-class gourmet establishment. Doubles from €297. ❾

Haus Rechel Kroghooger Wai 3, Kampen ☎04651/984 90, Ⓦwww.haus-rechel.de. Here's a shock – an affordable hotel in exclusive Kampen. Nothing flash, just old-fashioned cottage-styled rooms and friendly service. ❹–❺

Keitumer Hafenhaus Kirchenweg 28, Keitum. Good-value, traditional holiday apartments for two on the seafront of the prettiest village on Sylt. ❹–❺

Camping

A good spread of sites embedded in the dunes behind the beach make camping an enjoyable option, weather permitting. Useful addresses among the island's seven sites are: *Campingplatz Westerland* (Ratumer Strasse; ☎04651/ 83 61 60, Ⓦwww.campingplatz-westerland.de); *Campingplatz Wenningstedt* (Dorfteich; ☎04651/94 40 04, Ⓦwww.wenningstedt.de); *Campingplatz*

Kampen (Möwenweg 4; ☎04651/420 86, ⓦwww.campen-in-kampen.de); and *Campingplatz Hörnum* (Rantumer Strasse 31; ☎04651/835 84 31, ⓦwww .hoernum.de). All operate from Easter to October and are enormously popular – it's worth phoning if you're coming by bus in July and August.

Westerland and Wenningstedt

After a century of promoting itself as the principal resort on Sylt, **WESTERLAND** has more or less destroyed itself. The progenitor late-1800s spa resort has been replaced by concrete holiday-blocks and the sand dunes vanished long ago beneath paving slabs. What it has are all the facilities of a fully-fledged holiday mill – shops, restaurants, banks and supermarkets along pedestrianized main drag Friedrichstrasse, the latter two in short supply elsewhere on Sylt. As the hub of the public transport network it's also unavoidable. Its saving grace is a beach that's as fine as anywhere else on Sylt despite the spirit-sapping "Fun-Beach" moniker. Should you be stuck between buses on a rainy day, you could visit the **Sylter Welle** (10am–10pm daily; €11) indoor pool and sauna complex behind the beach on Sandstrasse, or fifteen minutes east of the centre on Gaadt is an **aquarium** (daily 10am–6pm; €12) of tropical and North Sea fish.

For character you're far better to push up the coast to the low-key (and low-rise) resort of **WENNINGSTEDT** – the crowds thin, the pace slows and no concrete slab is cemented anywhere near a fine beach. Beyond the village church on the far side of its central crossroads, the **Denghoog** (Easter–Oct Mon–Fri 10am–5pm, Sat & Sun 11am–5pm; €2.50), is an early Stone Age burial chamber constructed from Scandinavian granite dumped as glacial erratics; the top stone alone is estimated to weigh around 20 tonnes. Duck through a tunnel and you reach the five-thousand-year-old main chamber.

The principle **tourist centre** in Westerland is beside Sylter Welle at Sandstrasse 35 (Mon–Fri 9am–5pm, Sat 9am–2pm; ☎0180/500 99 80, ⓦwww.westerland .de), with a smaller bureau at Congress Centrum Sylt, Friedrichstrasse 44 (Mon–Sat

Beach activities on Sylt

No surprise on an island fringed by 35km of sand that the focus of all activity is the beach. The finest whitest sands run the entire length of the west coast, access to which costs €2–3 and is payable as the Kurtax included in accommodation or as a Tageskarte as you enter for day-trippers. Hooded *Strandkörbe* (beach seats), which come into their own in these breezy conditions, are available for rent by the day or hour on all beaches except those north of List on the Ellenbogen. Prevailing winds mean waves usually crash onto the sands along the west coast while those on the east are sheltered (though often muddy) strips – Königshafen lagoon northwest of List, or the peninsula south of Hörnum are safe for young children.

Walking aside, watersports are the main alternative to loafing on the beach. **Windsurfing** is excellent thanks to waves and smooth water on either side of the island – Sylt hosts the Windsurf World Cup in the last week of September. Other aquatic activities include **kitesurfing**, and on calm days, **surfing**. The principal breaks are at Westerland – a mid-tide A-frame known as Brandenburg is the most popular spot in Germany – though you can scout out quieter waves all along the west coast. In Westerland, Surfschule Sunset Beach (Brandenburger Strasse 15; ☎04651/271 72, ⓦwww.sunsetbeach.de) rents windsurfers, surf- and bodyboards, as well as sit-on kayaks and Hobie catamarans. Surfschule Camp One on Hauptstrand in Wenningstedt (☎04651/433 75, ⓦwww.surfschule-wenningstedt.de) has windsurfers, surfboards and kitesurfing gear. Both provide lessons on request.

10am–6pm, Sun 11am–3pm; same contacts). The tourist office in Wenningstedt is just south of the central crossroads, Westerlandstrasse 3 (Mon–Fri 9am–6pm, Sat 10am–2pm; ☎04651/989 00, ⓦwww.wenningstedt.de). Accommodation in Wenningstedt can also be booked through a separate Tourismus-Service at Osetal 5 (Mon–Fri 8.30am–noon & 2–4pm; ☎04651/44 70).

Kampen and Keitum

No village in Germany receives as much coverage as **KAMPEN**. For several decades it has filled the pages of the gossip press as the exclusive holiday resort of money and celebrity. Expensive designer boutiques and galleries are shoehorned into the traditional thatched houses, while slick bars and restaurants line Strönwai (also known as Whiskeyallee). Former holidaymakers Thomas Mann and Emil Nolde wouldn't recognize the old place. Window-shopping aside, the principle daytime activities are to walk up the **Uwe Düne** behind the village for a sweeping panorama from 57m up – Himalayan by local standards – or stroll beneath the ruddy sand **Rotes Kliff** (red cliff) that runs along the beach underneath. If that's too much effort laze beside the beautiful people at **Buhne 16** beach 1km north of central Kampen; it's not quite the status symbol it was two decades or so ago, but still fairly flash.

There aren't many fishermen or farmers left in east-coast **KEITUM**, but ostentatious displays of wealth here have not yet reached the gung-ho levels of Kampen. The most photogenic village in Sylt, Keitum is a sleepy knot of lanes canopied by beech and chestnut trees. Once the island's leading settlement thanks to a sheltered location, it has a streetscape of traditional reed-thatched houses, most with the single high gable characteristic of Frisian architecture. A whaler built the eighteenth-century residence that houses the **Sylter Heimatmuseum** (Easter–Oct Mon–Fri 10am–5pm, Sat & Sun 11am–5pm; €3.50) with modest exhibits of folk culture and island archeology, plus works by local artist Magnus Weidemann. Nearby **Altfriesiches Haus** (same times & price) allows a nose around a reassembled early nineteenth-century house, a typical North Frisian example of Delft-style tiles and painted doors. The church of **St Severin**, Sylt's ecclesiastical highlight, founded on a tiny Romanesque chapel constructed of pink granite, is a fifteen-minute walk down the same lane. It hosts chamber music concerts in summer, usually on Wednesday, Friday and Saturday.

Tourist information in Kampen is at the village centre on the main road (Mon–Fri 9am–5pm, Sat 10am–1pm; ☎04651/469 80, ⓦwww.kampen .de), and in Keitum is in the Kurverwaltung (Mon–Fri 9am–6pm, Sat & Sun 10am–2pm; ☎01805/55 79 58, ⓦwww.sylt-ost.de) in a prefab at the village car park.

List

More small town than village, **LIST** on the north arm is an uninspiring place that only stirs to life when booze-cruise passengers from Denmark disembark at the garish port at the tip, the village's focus. By mid-2009, the adjacent **Naturgewalten Sylt** (ⓦwww.muez.de) should be completed as an "Experience Centre" of the natural forces that shape Sylt. West of List is Germany's largest sand dune, the Wanderdünen as Germans poetically call the "wall dunes" that creep east at 4m per year to squeeze List against the coast. Popular walking paths embark through its mini-Sahara – a starkly impressive expanse of bare sand ridges that rise up to 35m, their fuzz of heather a glorious purple by late summer – or there are views of the exposed east flank on a potholed road to Weststrand; en route is the **Strand Sauna** (daily 11am–6pm; €14)

▲ Houses in Wenningstedt, Sylt

– the idea is to sweat up, then plunge into the North Sea – and beach café *Strandhalle* after 4km. A side road near the latter leads onto the **Ellenbogen** (car €5; bike €2), a privately owned "elbow" crooked around the north end of Sylt. Extending relentlessly east, its rolling dunes are empty except for a couple of lighthouses, lots of sheep and a handful of visitors to some of the quietest beaches on the island – the broadest, whitest strands are on the north and at the tip.

The **tourist office** in List is in the Kurverwaltung west of the port in the village centre (Am Brühl; Mon–Fri 9am–4pm, Sat 10am–noon; ☎01805/54 78 00, ⓦ www.list.de).

Hörnum

South of Westerland, you roll through the village of Rantum at the island's narrowest point before embarking on a straight run 11km south to **HÖRNUM** at the far tip. A broad fine beach all the way along the western side of the route is accessible at intermittent points. At Hörnum you can walk 1km south to access a family-favourite sand spit where Sylt finally peters out. Ever since herring fishermen embarked from here in the 1400s, the village has been centred on the island's largest port embedded behind the dunes and overlooked by a candy-striped lighthouse. From mid-March to October a baffling variety of **cruises** depart, the majority operated by Adler-Schiffe (ⓦ www.adler-schiffe .de); the most popular are to see seal colonies lounge on mudbanks (daily at 2pm & Tues–Fri 10.15am; 1hr 30min; €13.50) and to sister islands Amrum and Föhr (2 or 3 daily; from €21.50). It also operates guided walks over the mudflats between the two islands (April–Oct; €26.50). Single ferry tickets to the islands cost €15, great if you have a few days to island-hop back to the mainland. Timetables are stocked in tourist offices on the island.

Hörnum's **tourist office** is in a kiosk at the port (Mon–Fri 9am–5pm, Sat 10am–1pm; ☎04651/962 60, ⓦ www.hoernum.de).

Eating

Though you can eat well on Sylt, prices are noticeably steeper than the mainland. Expect to pay around €17 for a main course in most villages, and over €20 in Kampen, more in the metropolitan-styled restaurants where prices can asphyxiate. Local chain *Gosch* rustles up tasty cheap fish in Westerland, Wenningstedt and List – look for its red lobster logo – and beach cafés are a great spot for lunch.

Westerland and Wenningstedt

Alte Friesenstube Gaadt 4, Westerland ☎04651/12 28. Charm by the cartful in a 1680s cottage with a historic interior and tables in a garden decorated with lanterns – a treat in summer. First-class menu of gourmet fish, with mains priced around €22. Dinner Tues–Sun.

Fitschen am Dorfteich Am Dorfteich 2, Wenningstedt ☎04651/321 20. Upmarket traditional dishes such as chef's recipe fish soup and Sylt lamb in an upmarket rustic place beside the village lake.

Sylter Bürgerstuben Bismarckstrasse 11a, Westerland ☎04651/15 55. Traditional local restaurant away from the happy throngs, with good fish and light bites such as omelette with North Sea shrimps. Closed Tues.

Kampen, Keitum and Rampen

Alte Friesenwirtschaft Gurstieg 32, Keitum. Good-value traditional dishes with a modern twist such as pork in Calvados cream and Aunt Frieda's beef roulade in a restaurant that brings designer touches to its historic decor.

Dorfkrug Rotes Kliff Braderuper Weg 3, Kampen ☎04651/435 00. Tiled rooms and painted ceilings lend a traditional tavern atmosphere that suits good-value dishes such as knuckle of local lamb slow-roasted in red wine. East of central Kampen and the antithesis of its posing.

Kupferkanne Stapelhooger Wai 7, Kampen ☎04651/410 10. Sylt institution that merits the accolades heaped upon it. This enchanting café provides breakfast, cake and light lunches either in a charming Hobbity house with a warren of rooms or on fairytale terraces of stunted pines.

Sansibar Hörnumer Str. 80, 3km south of Rampen ☎04651/96 46 46. Beach-shack chic and large portions of pasta, steak, fish and sushi among the sand dunes; mains average €24. Very laid-back Sylt, and hard to beat for a lazy lunch.

Strandbistro Buhne 16, Kampen. Ciabatta sandwiches and lunch specials such as paella on the sands of Sylt's hippest beach.

Föhr and Amrum

Like Sylt, Föhr and Amrum are split between fine beach and the shallow Wattenmeer, a nutrient-rich soup of blues, browns and silvery light on the east coast. In all other ways the southern neighbours couldn't be more different. Tranquil and noticeably cheaper, the small family-friendly islands are sleepy and rural. The fast-food outlets disappear and bedtime storytelling in the bandstand – a nod to former holidaymaker Hans Christian Andersen – replaces amusement arcades in Föhr's largest village, Wyk. By 9pm the whole place is asleep. Charming and uncomplicated, the islands have the innocent vibe of childhood holidays past, their main activities walking, cycling and sand castles on the beach.

From mainland port Dagebüll, linked by train to Niebüll northwest, **car ferries** of WDR (ⓦ www.faehre.de) depart roughly every hour between Easter and October (reduced service in winter) to Wyk (€6 for single passenger) then Wittdün (€8.45). Coming **from Sylt**, hop aboard regular tourist cruises run by Adler-Schiffe from Hörnum (see p.807). On Föhr WDR operates a public bus service, though cycling is a joy on these flat islands. Rental outlets are by the ferry quays and in every village on the islands.

Föhr

The largest of the duo, **FÖHR** lies in the shelter behind Sylt and Amrum as a sea of marshy flats that have christened it the "green island of the North Sea".

Most of the 8650 population live in island "capital" **Wyk**, fronted by cafés along Sandwall esplanade. Sheltered from the prevailing weather on the southeast coast, it flourished briefly as a whaling base in the seventeenth and eighteenth centuries. Whaling looms large in the **Friesenmuseum** (March 16–Oct Tues–Sun 10am–5pm; July & Aug daily 10am–5pm; Nov–March 15 Tues–Sun 2–5pm; €3) fronted by a whalebone arch at Rebbelstieg 34, which backs the tangled lanes behind the port. There's very real footage of butchery in an otherwise staged whaling documentary filmed in the 1920s and the usual items of local history and folk crafts.

A couple of **windmills** in Wyk, one at the museum, are the first indication of landscapes elsewhere on the island that seem as Dutch as the local dialect, Fering (or Föhring). Indeed, Dutch know-how created the medieval dykes which cross-hatch the island whose highest point is only 5m above sea level. One of the prettiest corners, **Nieblum** 4km west of Wyk, is dotted with decorative thatched cottages with low arched doorways of whaling captains. Though it is now the most celebrated spot on the island, **Oevenum** 3km north runs it a close second in looks. Go south for sand – a good beach runs all along the length of the south coast.

The **tourist information** is at the ferry terminal at Wyk (Mon–Fri 9am–5pm, Sat 9am–2pm; ☎04681/300, ⓦ www.foehr.de), which is the best bet for cheaper **accommodation** options, or there's a rather institutional youth hostel in Wyk (Fehrstieg 41; ☎04681/23 55, ⓦ www.jugendherberge.de; €18/21). Other choices in Wyk include *Schloss am Meer*, Badestrasse 112 (☎04681/586 70, ⓦ www.hotel-schloss-am-meer.com; ❺), plain but practically on the beach, and oceanview holiday apartment *Atlantis*, Sandwall 29 (☎04681/59 91 00, ⓦ www.atlantis-hotel.net; ❸–❺); while in Nieblum there's luxury *Villa Witt*, Alkersumstieg 4 (☎04681/587 70, ⓦ www.hotel-witt.de; ❼), home, too, to the island's finest **restaurant** (closed Mon). Good eating options in Wyk are *Die 13*, Carl-Häberlin Strasse 13, with tasty island lamb, historic charmer *Alt Wyk* at Grosse Strasse 4 (eve only; closed Tues), and family restaurant *Altes Landhaus* in Nieblum at Bi de Süd 21.

Amrum

Föhr seems almost lively compared to **AMRUM**. A one-road island, 13km from marshy tip to sandy toe and never more than 1.5km wide, the most tranquil of the North Frisian group is effectively an oversized sandbank whose entire western half consists of the Kniepsand, a ten-square-kilometre expanse of beach whose powder sands wouldn't look out of place in the tropics. Sheltered behind the dunes on the eastern side is a rural patchwork of woods and heath. Snuggled among it, the island's five villages are a picture-book-pretty vision of traditional Frisian cottages with a single high gable and tousled gardens.

Good views of the Kniepsand are available from lookouts at either end of the island – in the south from a lookout by the tallest lighthouse on the German North Sea (Mon–Fri 8.30am–12.30pm, Wed till 1pm; free) and atop a sand dune in the north just south of the island's largest village, **Norddorf**. A 10km path through pines behind the Kniepsand links the two. Should you tire of the beach (unlikely), culture is in Nebel midway up the east coast: you can nose around eighteenth-century Öömrang Hüs (April–Oct Mon–Fri 10.30am–12.30pm & 3–5pm , Sat 3–5pm; Nov–March Mon–Sat 3–5pm; €3) its highlight a tiled wall that depicts the sailing ship of its original captain; or peruse local history displays in the last functioning windmill in North Frisia (April–Oct daily 11am–5pm; €2.50).

Tourist information is at the ferry terminal at Wittdün (Mon–Fri 9am–5pm, Sat 9am–1pm; ☎04682 9 40 30, ⓦwww.amrum.de). Most **accommodation** is in holiday homes – book through tourist information (or its website). There's also a popular youth hostel by the beach 300m from the harbour, Mittelstrasse 1 (☎04682/20 10, ⓦwww.jugendherberge.de; €18/21), and an appealing car-free campsite, *Campingplatz Amrum*, Inselstrasse 125 (☎04682/22 54, ⓦwww.amrum -camping.de), among the dunes by Wittdün.

Travel details

Trains

Hamburg to: Berlin (hourly; 1hr 40min); Bremen (every 30min; 55min–1hr 15min); Flensburg (10 daily; 2hr); Husum (every 45min; 2hr); Lübeck (every 30min; 45min); Kiel (hourly; 1hr 15min); Schleswig (10 daily; 1hr 35min); Westerland, Sylt (hourly; 3hr).

Kiel to: Eutin (hourly; 45min); Husum (hourly; 1hr 20min); Lübeck (hourly; 1hr 15min); Schleswig (hourly; 50min).

Lübeck to: Eutin (every 30min; 25–30min); Hamburg (every 30min; 45min); Kiel (hourly; 1hr 10min); Ratzeburg (hourly; 20min).

Mecklenburg-
Western Pomerania

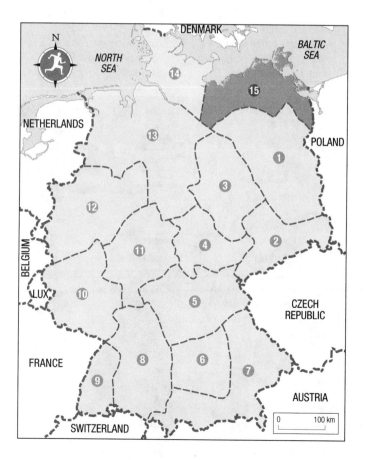

CHAPTER 15

Highlights

✳ **Wismar** A wistful air of faded grandeur pervades in the Altstadt of this splendid old Hanseatic port. See p.815

✳ **Rügen** Historic small beach resorts and Hitler's colossal holiday camp are side by side on Germany's biggest island, celebrated for its dramatic white cliffs and woodland, and fringed by mile upon mile of powder-fine sand. See p.828

✳ **Schwerin** Tour a fairytale palace that goes straight to the head, then take a lake cruise to see it from the water. See p.843

✳ **Canoeing in the Müritz National Park** You could lose up to a week exploring a mosaic of interconnected lakes on canoe-and-camp adventures in the Mecklenburg Lake District. See p.852

▲ Strandkörbe

Mecklenburg-Western Pomerania

"When the end of the world comes, I shall go to Mecklenburg because there everything happens a hundred years later."

Otto von Bismarck

With only 1.8 million people in 23,170 square kilometres no Land in Germany is as sparsely populated as **Mecklenburg Western Pomerania** (Mecklenburg-Vorpommeron). Bar the odd towerblock, the conjoined former duchies of Mecklenburg West and Pomerania, the eastern rump pressed into Poland, were barely developed under the GDR and, without any city worth the name, the state lay off the radar for most foreigners. Since reunification, however, its profile has grown alongside the fame of the quartzite beaches that fringe the longest coastline in Germany – 354km from the Trave River at Lübeck to Usedom on the border. That swish Baltic hotel-resort **Heiligendamm** hosted the G8 summit in 2007 testifies to an area that's on the up.

In fact, the coast is simply returning to form. During the late 1800s, Germany's first and second largest islands, **Rügen** and **Usedom**, were the preferred playgrounds of the German glitterati – the moneyed elite, assorted grand dukes and even the occasional Kaiser sojourned to dip an ankle at their smart sea-water bathing resorts. An injection of capital after decades of GDR neglect has brought a dash of former imperial pomp to both and also taken the resorts upmarket. Rügen is one of the most popular holiday destinations in the country, celebrated for its chalk cliffs above the Baltic Sea as much as its Bäderarchitektur. Elsewhere, the Baltic coast is true Hanseatic League country (see box, p.776); the Gothic red-brick architecture of the UNESCO-listed Altstadts in **Wismar** and **Stralsund** are wistful reminiscences of the former grandeur of this medieval mercantile power bloc. There's some heritage, too, in **Rostock**, the chief port and largest city in the state, but you're more likely to visit for its bar-and-club scene, the superb strand at Warnemünde, or as a launch pad for a superb Münster in **Bad Doberan** – a must-see for anyone with a passing interest in ecclesiastical architecture.

You don't have to travel far from the coast to enter a bucolic backwater whose ruler-straight roads are lined with avenues of trees and whose wheat fields serve as the nation's granary. The heart of the plateau is the **Mecklenburg Lake District** (Mecklenburgische Seenplatte) centred around Germany's largest freshwater lake, Lake Müritz, and the **Müritz National Park**. Nicknamed the

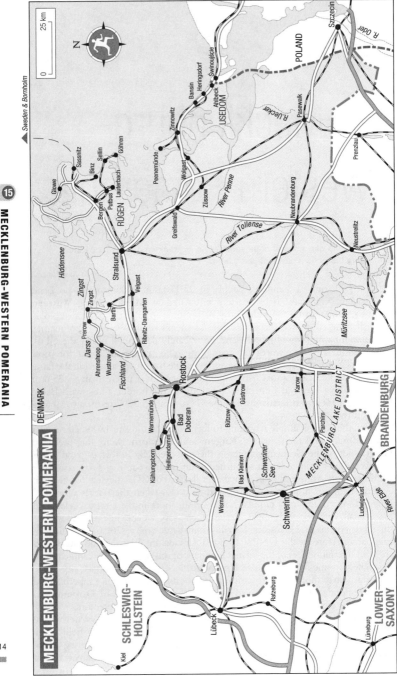

MECKLENBURG-WESTERN POMERANIA

Land of a Thousand Lakes and home to the largest contiguous area of waterways in central Europe, its aquatic mosaic is beloved by canoeists and birdwatchers alike. Ducal seat turned state capital **Schwerin** at its western end is the only large town hereabouts, albeit pocket-sized and packing a cultural punch to match that of its fairytale castle, while **Güstrow**, another ducal seat, is dedicated to the memory of Germany's greatest modern sculptor, Ernst Barlach.

Wismar

Fate had it in for **WISMAR**. The first Hanseatic city east of Lübeck has similar looks to the league-leader on which it was modelled in a cobbled Altstadt stuffed with gables and red-brick Gothic. And it retains the backbone of the central harbour that made it a rich port with considerable diplomatic clout during a medieval golden age. Unlike Lübeck, however, Wismar was conquered. Snatched by the Swedes in 1648, it became a southern bulwark of the empire and suffered the consequent woes of siege, fire and pillage – the legacy of their hundred-and-fifty-year occupation is scattered throughout, not least the fabulously mustachioed "Swedish heads" that are a town mascot. Worse still were air raids in 1945 that obliterated two massive medieval churches.

Since the *Wende*, Wismar has taken tourism seriously. It again declares itself a Hansestadt (Hanseatic town), and a major renovation programme has buffed up its neglected charm, something that elevated it onto UNESCO's World Heritage list in a joint application with Stralsund (see p.825). Away from the set pieces, however, the broad streets have an air of wistful faded grandeur. It may be one reason why film director F. W. Murnau turned to Wismar as a backdrop for his 1922 Gothic-horror classic *Nosferatu*: shots include the prewar Markt and the vampire's ghostly ship drifting into the old harbour. Dates for the diary include the Hafentage (ⓦwww.wismarer-hafentage.de), which brings fleets and a funfair to the harbour in the second weekend in June, and Schwedenfest (ⓦwww.schwedenfest-wismar.de) over the last weekend in August.

Arrival, information and accommodation

The **Bahnhof** is near the harbour at the northeast edge of the Altstadt. You can also **rent bikes** at platform 2C from municipal operator Wismar Rad (March–Oct). A helpful **tourist office** in the centre at Am Markt 11 (daily 9am–6pm; ☏03841/194 33, ⓦwww.wismar.de) has a good stock of English-language themed leaflets, including a tour around Swedish monuments, and books **private rooms** (advance booking ☏03841/251 30 27; ❶–❷).

Alter Speicher Bohrstr. 12 ☏03841/21 17 46, ⓦwww.hotel-alter-speicher.de. Comfortable mid-range place divided between two houses on a side street between the Markt and St Nikolai church. Also manages an affiliated budget guesthouse, *Wisteria*, next door (Bohrstr. 10). Hotel ❹–❺, guesthouse ❷.

Altes Brauhaus Lübische Str. 37 ☏03841/21 14 16, ⓦwww.brauhaus-wismar.com. Friendly family-run three-star in the east Altstadt with thirteen fairly modern rooms – those in the eaves feature beams of the former sixteenth-century brewery building. ❹

Am Alten Hafen Spiegelberg 61–65 ☏03841/42 60, ⓦwww.hotel-am-alten-hafen.de. Large, modern hotel on the Altstadt ring road whose draw is its location opposite the harbour. ❹

Chez Fasan Bademutterstr. 20 ☏03841/21 34 25, ⓦwww.pension-chez-fasan.de. The cheapest beds in Wismar – nothing fancy but perfectly adequate rooms in this good-value pension that occupies three houses in the central Altstadt. ❷

DJH Wismar Juri-Gagarin-Ring 30a ☏03841/326 80, ⓦwww.djh-mv.de. Passable for a cheap bed if rather isolated 1km west of the centre; take bus #C or #D to bus stop

Philipp-Müller-Strasse/Krankenhaus. Dorms from €19.50.

Stadt Hamburg Am Markt 24 ☏ 03841/23 90, ⓦ www.wismar.steigenberger.de. Part of the Steigenberger chain, this business hotel is the plushest address in town, with four-star standards and an excellent location. ⑤–⑥

To'n Zägenkrog Ziegenmarkt 10 ☏ 03841/28 27 16, ⓦ www.ziegenkrug-wismar.de. Five stylish apartments – from studio to three-room – above a restaurant (see p.818). Recently renovated into relaxed contemporary decor, most with views over a quiet corner of the Altstadt. ④–⑥

The Markt and around

The showpiece of Wismar's renovation is its cobbled **Markt**. Encircled by bright pastel-tinted facades, it is one of the largest in North Germany, a testament to the Hanseatic heyday. Among the stalls of its morning market is the Wasserkunst, a Dutch Renaissance pavilion-like spa fountain to shelter the town's water supply; water gushed from the bronze merman and mermaid taps at one side until 1897. Opposite is one of the finest late-Gothic Hanseatic facades you'll see on the Baltic coast, the boast of a burgher c.1380 despite the misleading "Alter Schwede" moniker. The conceit is maintained by replica **"Swedish heads"** (see box opposite). The only formal note among the pleasing jumble of facades is the Neoclassical **Rathaus** on the Markt's north side. Entered at the side, its forerunner's Gothic cellars (daily 10am–6pm, except Sun Jan–March 10am–4pm; €1) feature a sixteenth-century mural of sailors slugging from wineskins in the former council wine-cellar, while historical exhibits include Hanseatic drinking tankards from an era when the port had two hundred breweries, and a superb polychrome tomb-slab of a Swedish major general, Helmuth Wrangel. Before you leave the Markt area, restaurant *Zum Weinberg* behind the Rathaus at no. 3 is worth a look for the perfectly preserved hallway of a Renaissance wine-merchant.

Until the twelfth and final air-raid of 1945 landed a knockout blow, the area west of the Markt was known as the Gothic quarter. Only the rebuilt decorative brick archdeacon's house and the square tower of **St Mary's** remain, the latter a massive 80m edifice mounted with a clock donated by Wrangel – he of the Rathaus tomb-slab – and a carillon that chimes hymns at noon, 5pm and 9pm. Notwithstanding tours that ascend the landmark tower several times a day, the tower (daily 10am–6pm; free) is put to use as an exposition on contemporary church-building, with a 3D stereoscopic film on medieval construction. If you continue away from the Markt you arrive at the **Fürstenhof**, erstwhile seat of the Mecklenburg dukes whose take on Italian Renaissance appears distinctly frothy in a region of brick. Terracotta plaques on the public face present images of the Trojan Wars interspersed with handsome limestone caryatids. Privately, within the courtyard, they relax into folkloric scenes of feasting and pig-wrestling supposed to represent the tale of the Prodigal Son, while above are portraits of local dignitaries. For all its bulk, the palace is overshadowed by the **St Georgen Kirche** (daily 10am–6pm) whose scale is a testament to the wealth of the Hanseatic craftsmen and merchants who funded it. Seriously damaged in the war – it was still a weedy shell in 1990 – the largest church in Wismar is expected to be rebuilt by 2010; until then it serves as an exhibition space and concert hall. Grosse Hohe Strasse opposite the church leads north to east–west spine-street Lübische Strasse and the **Heiligen-Geist-Kirche** (daily 10am–6pm; €1 donation requested). It comes second only to Lübeck's Heiligen-Geist-Spital on which it was modelled as an example of a medieval hospital with an unsupported Renaissance roof painted a century or so later with Old Testament scenes. Look, too, for a painting of a galleon by the altar in which Wismar's seventeenth-century skyline is just visible through the rigging.

Nowadays Wismar is only too happy to point out evidence of its annexation by Swedish forces from 1648. Most prominent are the colourful **"Swedish heads"** scattered at strategic locations throughout the town. With their fabulous handlebar moustaches, rakish cravats and lion's-head caps worn over flowing black curls they present a dashing image in front of Alter Schwede on the Markt and the Baumhaus at the end of the harbour.

Whether they are actually Swedish is another matter. An original in Schabbelhaus is one of a pair that was mounted at the harbour entrance for a century until they were rammed by a Finnish ship taking evasive manoeuvres in 1902. At the time they were known as the "Old Swedes". But because documents mention "The Swede" harbour boundary from as early as 1672 their origins remain a mystery. Historians date them to approximately 1700, the time of the Swedish occupation of Wismar, and suggest they are a Baroque depiction of Hercules.

The most plausible theory suggests they were mounted on a Swedish merchant ship, possibly glaring from the stern or mounted before the captain's quarters. However, another suggestion moots that their name derives from their **"Schwedenköpf"** (literally Sweden head) haircut, short for its time and a powder-free style as a sign of modernity and enlightenment.

The north Altstadt

Today the Grube waterway simply slices off the tip of the Altstadt instead of powering waterwheels as it did when built in the mid-thirteenth century as the first town canal in Germany. At its centre, **St-Nikolai-Kirche** is the only one of Wismar's medieval trio that still stood in 1945. At 37m high, its giddy nave seems out of all proportion to modern-day Wismar, the superlative of the fourth-highest church in Germany explained by the Hanseatic past and the church's role as that of seafarers. The collapse of a slender spire in 1703 prompted a Baroque makeover that stripped much of the original Gothic – remnants include medieval murals of a Tree of Jesse and St Christopher, a high altar undergoing protracted restoration in a side chapel, and a fourteenth-century font.

Diagonally opposite, by the Schweinsbrücke (Pigs' Bridge) topped by playful porkers, **Schabbelhaus** (Tues–Sun: May–Oct 10am–8pm; Nov–April 10am–5pm; €2, free Fri) is a classy mansion in Dutch Renaissance style, built as a residence for a future town mayor. It now houses an above-average museum of town history, whose most infamous exhibits are the mummified "dead hands". A staple of medieval prosecutors, these were hacked off a murder victim and presented in court as an accusing finger from the grave. Above are splendid copperplates of the Altstadt, guild treasures and one of the original Swedish heads (see box above) – notes in English are provided in all rooms.

Going the other way along the canal leads to the medieval **Alter Hafen** (old harbour) fronted by the Wassertor, last of five medieval gateways in the town defences through which Nosferatu crept with his coffin. When not at sea, a replica medieval trading-cog is open for inspection (free) – during summer it embarks on **sailing trips** a couple of times a week (3hr; €23; ☎01754/18 93 31). More regular cruises of Reederei Clermont tour the harbour (May–Oct daily every 30min; 1hr; €8; ☎03841/22 46 46, ⓦwww.reederei-clermont.de) and sail three times a day to Poel island (€8 single, €13 return), a pretty bucolic backwater 10km north on the opposite side of the Wismar Bight.

Eating

As ever on the German coast, boats moored at Alter Hafen rustle up cheap sandwiches of freshly smoked fish.

Alte Schwede Am Markt 19 ☎03841/28 35 52. Baltic fish specialities such as roast eel and herring with cranberry cream in the oldest *Bürgerhaus* in Wismar – touristy but also gets the nod from locals.

Avocados Hinter dem Chor 1. Tiny, funky bistro opposite Schabbelhaus that prepares tasty, modern vegetarian dishes using fresh organic ingredients – a daily menu is chalked on the board but expect keenly priced curries, pasta and risotto.

Brauhaus am Lohberg Kleine Hohe Str. 15. Wismar's first brewery, a three-storey half-timbered pile from 1452, still producing its own brews to wash down a good-value pub menu.

Fürstenhof Café Bliedenstr. 32. Sandwiches and ices in a lovely, small café that's been tastefully

modernized. If there are better spots for breakfast than its cottage garden, Wismar is keeping them secret. Daily 7am–6pm.

T'on Zägenkrog Ziegenmarkt 10 ☎03841/28 17 16. Fish from Wismar and Poel island prepared in an upmarket pub with nautically themed decor. It also maintains a smart separate dining-room and tables by the Grube canal in summer.

Zum Weinberg Hinter dem Rathaus 3 ☎03841/28 35 50. This former wine-merchant's provides spectacular dining in a Renaissance galleried hallway of painted beams and stained glass. A wide-ranging menu veers away from fish to include fruit-filled Mecklenburg meats.

Bad Doberan and the beach resorts

"Münster, Molli, Moor und Meer" the tourist board trills happily to tick off the attractions of **Bad Doberan** – its minster, the Molli (train), a moorland health centre and Baltic beach resorts of **Heiligendamm** and **Kühlungsborn** 15km northwest. The Molli runs eleven times a day from late April to October and about five times a day during winter. Single tickets cost from €2–5.70 depending on the distance; returns save €1 on two singles. None is really worth a journey on its own – together, however, they comprise a happy day-trip that's easily accessible from Rostock.

Bad Doberan

No question that its thirteenth-century Cistercian church is the premier reason to visit **BAD DOBERAN**. The **Münster** (May–Sept Mon–Sat 9am–6pm, Sun 11am–6pm; March, April & Oct Mon–Sat 10am–5pm, Sun 11am–5pm; Nov–Feb Mon–Sat 10am–4pm, Sun 11am–4pm; €2; Ⓦwww .doberanermuenster.de), secluded from the centre behind a high wall east, is the crowning achievement of Gothic ecclesiastical architecture in the Baltic. Completed in 1362, in a fusion of Hanseatic and French high-Gothic styles, the abbey church is poised at the brief point where architectural form is stretched to its limits but unencumbered by the fussy embellishment that follows. Nowhere is this clearer than at the effortless crossing, whose two tiers of slender arches are arguably the most graceful feature of the church. Having come through the Reformation without a scratch, the furnishings are as impressive – a leaflet provided on entry pinpoints 22 artworks, including what is claimed as the oldest existing wing altar (1300), crowned by flamboyant Gothic spires, and an audacious tabernacle. Also within the grounds are a curious octagonal ossuary known as the Beinhaus (bonehouse) and a complex of agricultural buildings, one of which contains a café (daily 1–5pm).

The gentle pull of history is ever present in central Bad Doberan. Leafy and light-hearted, it blossomed into a spa resort in the early 1800s under the guidance of the Mecklenburg dukes who spent summers here. Pale Classical edifices from the resort's first flowering line August-Bebel-Strasse; now council offices and a good hotel, they are worth a look for their foyers. Spa-goers took the air in the park opposite, Kamp, when not taking the waters in its two Chinese-style pavilions that add an unexpectedly rakish air. The smaller Roter Pavilion holds a gallery, the Weisser Pavilion a café. By 1886, spa-goers were all aboard the Molli steam engine to add sea bathing to their water cures. The **Mecklenburgische Bäderbahn Molli** (W www.molli-bahn.de), to give the splendid narrow-gauge train its full name, huffs approximately hourly through high-street Mollistrasse into Alexandrinenplatz at the thin end of the Kamp's wedge – one for the photo album.

The **tourist office** (May 15–Sept 15 Mon–Fri 9am–6pm, Sat 10am–3pm; other months Mon–Fri 9am–4pm except Thurs till 6pm; T 038203/62 154, W www .bad-doberan-heiligendamm.de) at Severinstrasse 6 stocks train timetables. With only two hotels to its name – *City-Hotel* (T 038203/747 40, W www .cityhotel-doberan.de; ●), a small family hotel at Alexandreninplatz 4 with the Molli outside its windows, and *Friedrich-Franz-Palais*, August-Bebel-Strasse 2 (T 038203/630 36, W www.friedrich-franz-palais.de; ●–●), in a classic spa building – Bad Doberan may be best treated as a day-trip from Rostock. Alongside a good **restaurant** at the latter, eating options include the *Ratskeller* next door at August-Bebel-Strasse 3 and the *Weisser Pavilion* (daily 10am–6pm), hard to beat for atmosphere whether outside or in a tent-like interior. *Café Zikki* in Alexandrinen Hof by *City-Hotel* serves light lunches such as shrimp salads and herring with fresh caraway bread.

Heiligendamm

The Molli's second stop on its route across meadows northwest is **HEILIGENDAMM**. Founded in 1793 by Friedrich Franz I to tap into the popular cure of sea-water bathing that took German glitterati to Britain, he created Germany's first bathing resort; the legend "Happiness awaits those who are cured after bathing" is carved above the main bathhouse. "The white town on the sea", most of which dates from 1814–16 and whose mock-castle **Hohenzollern Schloss** was a request by the duke's wife, remains as spotless as it is exclusive after the complex was reinvented as the *Kempinski Grand Hotel* in 2003 (T 038203/74 00, W www.kempinski-heiligendamm.com; doubles from €260; ●). One of the leading hotels in the Baltic, it hosted world leaders as the venue for the G8 summit 2007. Though the hotel is off-limits to non guests, there's public access to its beach via a wild strand 500m west of the centre.

Kühlungsborn

The Molli's terminus, **KÜHLUNGSBORN WEST**, is a relaxed rural place backed by woodland. The largest beach resort in Mecklenburg, it bills itself as the "*Seebad mit flair*", the latter provided by Jugendstil villas along Ostseeallee, a backdrop to the longest promenade in Germany – 4.8km of it extending either side of a pedestrianized core at the pier along a beach with tidy rows of *Strandkörbe*, the hooded wicker seats invented in 1882 by court furniture-maker Wilhelm Bartelmann in nearby Rostock. The **tourist office** at Ostseeallee 19 (May–Sept Mon–Fri 9am–6pm, Sat & Sun 10am–4pm; Oct–April Mon–Fri 9am–4pm, Sat & Sun 10am–1pm; T 038293/84 90, W www.kuehlungsborn .de) is your best source of **accommodation**, which is in short supply in summer. Try *Westfalia* at Ostseeallee 17 (T 038293/434 90, W www.westfalia -kuehlungsborn.de; ●) for good-value mid-range rooms, or for a splurge the swish *Vier Jahreszeiten* (T 038293/810 00, W www.vier-jahreszeiten.eu; ●), a splendid pile at Ostseeallee 10–12. Thatched restaurants along the promenade west of the pier provide bucolic charm and sea views. For something more lively, go east for a clutch of smarter places above the marina.

To save you retracing your steps, tourist cruiser MS *Baltic* runs from the pier to Rostock beach-resort Warnemünde (May–Sept daily except Thurs & Sat; timetables are posted at the front of the pier).

Rostock

Too small to be dynamic, too large to be quaint, **ROSTOCK** is the principal city in Mecklenburg-Western Pomerania. The most important port on the German Baltic has been everything from a powerful Hanseatic trader to a major ship-building port at the head of the deep-water Warnow River. Its townscape bears the scars of Allied bombers and GDR planners alike. Even the reunification welcomed elsewhere proved a bitter pill after subsidies that had sustained the ship-building industry ended, prompting mass unemployment. Although pockets of historical charm remain in the Altstadt, an oval cat's-cradle of streets above the harbour, and renovation has buffed up the centre, the core is unlikely to detain you for more than a day. Bars in the Kröpeliner Torvorstadt district and the liveliest clubbing on the German Baltic fuelled by a 12,000-strong student population, are two reasons to hang around. Otherwise there's sister resort **Warnemünde**, a chirpy destination at the river mouth that's shifting rapidly upmarket to suit one of the finest beaches in Germany. It's also the location of the town's best **festivals**: regatta week Warnemünder Woche (Ⓦ www.warnemuender-woche.de), straddling the first and second weeks of July, and classic sail extravaganza Hanse Sail (Ⓦ www .hansesail.com) in early August.

Arrival, information and city transport

Rostock is nothing if not well connected. Domestic airlines fly to Rostock **airport**, Rostock-Laage (Ⓦ www.rostock-airport.de), 28km south of the city. Bus #127 (€9.10) links to the city, though you're better off aboard transfers operated by RvK (€5; Ⓣ 0381/405 60 18, Ⓦ www.rvk-rostock.de). Joost's Ostsee Express (Ⓣ 01805 16 20 20, Ⓦ www.joost.de) meets Ryanair and germanwings flights and shuttles to destinations throughout the region, including Rostock and Warnemünde, Kühlungsborn and Rügen; prices start at €16. **Ferries** connect to a wide range of Scandinavian and Baltic destinations from a port (Ⓦ www.rostock-port.de) near the river mouth on the east bank; the S-Bahn links to the **Hauptbahnhof** on the Berlin line, which is a fair hike south of the centre: trams #2, #5 and #6 run up to Steinstrasse and Lange Strasse, the former two continuing to Schröder Platz near the Kröpeliner Torvorstadt. Tram #4 also heads to the Kröpeliner Torvorstadt area. Prices are €1.60 for a single or €3.20 for a day-pass. If you're driving, prepare for a maze-like one-way system in the centre. Useful **car parks** include that on Grosse Wasserstrasse, off Neuer Markt, and a large outdoor area at the harbour off Am Strande. **Warnemünde** is accessible either by public transport via S-Bahn from the Hauptbahnhof, or on Blaue Flotte river cruises from Rostock harbour (June–Sept daily every 30min; Oct & March–May Sat & Sun 2 daily 11am & 2pm; single €7, return €10; Ⓦ www.blaue-flotte.de).

The central **tourist office** is at Neuer Markt 3 (May–Sept Mon–Fri 10am–6pm, June–Aug till 7pm, Sat & Sun 10am–4pm; Oct–April Mon–Fri 10am–6pm, Sat & Sun 10am–3pm; Ⓣ 0381/381 22 22, Ⓦ www.rostock.de). At Warnemünde

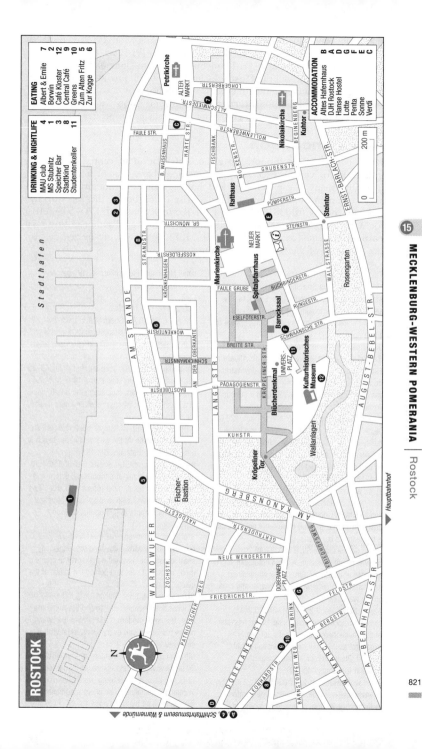

ROSTOCK

EATING
Albert & Emile	7
Borwin	2
Café Kloster	12
Central Café	9
Greens	10
Zum Alten Fritz	5
Zur Kogge	6

DRINKING & NIGHTLIFE
MAU club	4
MS Stubnitz	1
Speicher Bar	3
StadtKind	8
Studentenkeller	11

ACCOMMODATION
Altes Hafernhaus	B
DJH Rostock	A
Hanse Hostel	D
Lotte	G
Penta	F
Sonne	E
Verdi	C

0 — 200 m

MECKLENBURG-WESTERN POMERANIA | Rostock

⑮

821

it is in the original village at Am Strom 59 (May–Aug Mon–Fri 9am–6pm, Sat & Sun 10am–4pm; March, April, Sept & Oct Mon–Fri 10am–6pm, Sat & Sun 10am–4pm; Nov–Feb Mon–Fri 10am–5pm, Sat 10am–3pm; ☎0381/54 80 00, same website). Both sell the **RostockCard** (€9), which provides free transport and free or discounted museum entrance for 48 hours.

The most central spot for **internet access** is Vobis (Mon–Sat 10am–8pm) on the second floor of Rostocker Hof shopping arcade at Kröpeliner Strasse 26.

Accommodation

Bar a couple of exceptions, **hotel** accommodation in central Rostock is geared up for visiting executives. Warnemünde has a glut of holiday hotels, including many cheap pensions and holiday homes, although reservations are recommended in summer. The tourist office books the lot and also **private rooms** (☎0381/38 12 371 for Rostock centre, ☎0381/54 80 010 for Warnemünde; ❶–❷). Warnemünde also has a large if rather institutional **campsite**, *Baltic-Freizeit* (☎04544/80 03 13, ⓦwww.baltic-freizeit.de), on the east bank of the river at Budentannenweg 2.

Rostock

Altes Hafernhaus Strandstr. 93 ☎0381/49 30 110, ⓦwww.altes-hafenhaus.de. Small, faintly elegant hotel overlooking the harbour whose stained glass and art gallery add to the appeal of a late Rococo building. ❹

DJH Rostock Am Stadthafen 72–73 ☎0381/670 03 20, ⓦwww.djh-mv.de. Aboard a 1950s freighter moored a short way downstream from the main harbour area – actually fairly basic and not nearly as appealing as it sounds. From €19.

Hanse Hostel Doberaner Str. 136 ☎0381/128 60 06, ⓦwww.hanse-hostel.de. Friendly and helpful family-run hostel a short stagger from Rostock's bar scene, with spotless four- to eight-bed dorms as well as doubles, and free internet access. Dorms €14–18, rooms ❷.

Lotte Wismarsche Str. 1a ☎0381/377 92 92, ⓦwww.stadtpension-rostock.de. Flowery linen and antiques meet wood floors and modest interior design in a small pension close – but not too close – to Rostock's bar scene. ❸

Penta Schwaansche Str. 6 ☎0381/49 70, ⓦwww.pentahotels.com. A chain hotel with splashes of interior design – think streamlined furniture with a patchwork of wallpaper and colour on the walls. ❸–❼

Sonne Neuer Markt 2 ☎0381/497 30, ⓦwww.rostock.steigenberger.de. Smart four-star of the Steigenberger chain that's not nearly as expensive as its super-central location might suggest. Business rooms have Italian-style designer furnishings. ❸–❻

Verdi Wollenweberstr. 28 ☎0381/252 22 40, ⓦwww.hotel-verdi.de. Business-style comforts, including free internet access in all rooms, in a

small place near the Petrikirche. Nice garden terrace, too. ❸–❹

Warnemünde

Am Alten Strom Am Strom 60/61 ☎0381/54 82 30, ⓦwww.hotel-am-alten-strom.de. Large hotel at the heart of the café strip along the river, most rooms refurbished with wood floors and modern furnishings. Good value even unrefurbished. ❹–❺

Am Leuchtturm Am Leuchtturm 16 ☎0381/543 70, ⓦwww.hotel-am-leuchtturm.de. Swish place at a great location where the silver sands meet the river. ❼–❽

DJH Warnemünde Parkstr. 47 ☎0381/54 81 70, ⓦwww.djh-mv.de. At the west end of the beach in a former weather station. €23.15.

Residenz Strandhotel Seestr. 6 ☎0381/54 80 60, ⓦwww.residenz-strandhotel.de. Bright and breezy holiday hotel, most rooms with sea views and balconies and with loud splashes of colour on walls or carpets to pep up blonde-wood furnishings. ❺–❻

Stolteraa Strandweg 17 ☎0381/543 20, ⓦwww.hotel-stolteraa.de. Good old-fashioned seaside hotel that has had a makeover to create a modern place. It's located behind the beach at the quieter east end. ❸–❹

Strandhotel Hübner Seestr. 12 ☎0381/543 40, ⓦwww.hotel-huebner.de. Among Warnemünde's best, this slick modern place behind the beach offers balconies with every room, most with a sea view. ❼

Villa Ostseegruss Fritz-Reuter-Str. 4 ☎0381/54 30 90, ⓦwww.villa-ostseegruss.de. Homely old-fashioned place, without being overly twee or chintzy, in central Warnemünde. Also offers apartments and a holiday home for the same price. ❸–❹

Yachthafenresidenz Hohe Düne Am Yachthafen
1–8 ☏ 0381/504 00, ⓦ www.yhd.de. The most
luxurious address in the area is above the marina

on the east bank. Though modern, decor within is
all traditional elegance, and the spa facilities are
top drawer. ❼–❾

The Altstadt

The egg-shaped Altstadt remains visible on maps even if bombs and urban development removed much of the medieval town-wall itself. Air raids also pulverized the town's traditional heart, **Neuer Markt**, which is too spacious by half thanks to the GDR weakness for a grand civic space. Nevertheless, planners restored its historic architecture: on the east side stands the **Rathaus**, a Baroque porch smothered over a turreted Gothic facade which is just visible behind the pink sugar-icing. One street behind it stands Gothic patrician's house **Kerkhofhaus**. Opposite the Rathaus is a rebuilt row of town houses; the prettiest picture in Rostock is their pastel parade lined in front of the spire of the **Marienkirche**. The church's impressive bulk would have been bigger still had the basilica not collapsed mid-build in 1398, forcing a return to the blueprints to create a cross-shaped footprint of equal-length transepts and nave. Aside from a gloriously over-the-top Baroque organ shoehorned theatrically above a ducal gallery, the church's prizes are a bronze font (1290) propped on representations of the four elements, and an astronomical clock behind the altar. Built in 1472, one of its inscrutable dials – the upper face shows a 24-hour clock, monthly star signs and seasonal chores, the lower face is a blur of planetary movements – is able to compute the fall of Easter until 2017 thanks to a dial added in 1885. The previous one had lasted from the clock's modernization in 1642. Visit at noon and a column of saints parades around Jesus. Lange Strasse behind the church was designed by GDR planners as the town's ceremonial street and is typically bombastic in scale, albeit with Hanseatic leitmotifs: brick, gables and turrets.

There's a gentle pull of history among the quiet cobbled lanes ten minutes northeast of here, where Rostock made its debut in the twelfth century. Its kernel is **Alter Markt** and the **Petrikirche**, the one-time church of sailors and fishermen rebuilt into anonymity after the war, but worth a visit to ascend to a viewing platform at 44m (daily: April, May, Sept & Oct 10am–5pm; June–Aug 10am–7pm; Nov–March 10am–4pm; €2). Its 117m tower served as a navigation mark for sailors for centuries.

Back in the centre, Kröpeliner Strasse, the former market thoroughfare, forges west off Neuer Markt to open at Universitätsplatz, where shoppers loaf around the **Brunnen der Lebensfreunde** (Fountain of Happiness), an uncharacteristic piece of GDR jollity. The wedge-shaped square is named for North Germany's oldest university (1419) whose current incarnation is a handsome neo-Renaissance pile at the rear. Behind it in a quiet courtyard is the Kloster-zum-Heiligen-Kreuz and town museum the **Kulturhistorisches Museum** (Tues–Sun 10am–6pm; free). Head beyond modest exhibits from its erstwhile Cistercian monastery on the ground floor and you're rewarded with an altar that depicts the Three Magi arriving in Rostock by ship in 1425. Its image of defences and the skyline pierced by the Petrikirche spire is the first portrait of the town. Above are displays of glass and Flemish china, guild-house goblets and artwork, including works by Expressionist Ernst Barlach (see p.849)

Kröpeliner Strasse concludes at the **Kröpeliner Tor**, oldest and most impressive of the city's former 22 gateways. Its lower sections date from 1280; the bland interior (daily 10am–6pm; €1) is only possibly worth visiting for models of the Altstadt. You can follow a strip of fortifications alongside the former moat, the Wallenlagen, then continue through a rose garden to the Steintor beneath the Neuer Markt: "Let harmony and general well-being reign within thy walls" proclaims the Latin inscription on its city side. Continue west of the Kröpeliner Tor, however, and the streetscape changes to nineteenth century – welcome to the Kröpeliner Torvorstadt and the best bar scene in Rostock.

The Schifffahrtsmuseum and ICA Park

Grim parades of housing estates line the route north of Rostock, thrown up in a hurry as postwar accommodation for GDR port workers. Poorly signposted just over halfway to Warnemünde, near the Warnowtunnel to the east bank, is the **Schifffahrtsmuseum** (April–June, Sept & Oct Tues–Sun 9am–6pm; July & Aug daily 9am–6pm; Nov–March Tues–Sun 10am–4pm; €4) aboard a ten-thousand-tonne freighter, MS *Dresden*. Rostock's commercial port and ship-building industry are the twin focuses of the displays, with a section on the Hanseatic era and interactive exhibits such as piloting remote-control ships in a miniature port. The upper deck is preserved as the original quarters of the 1950s freighter – those of a mechanical bent will also enjoy the engine room. The ticket also lets you into the **ICA Park** (daily: April–Oct 9am–6pm; Nov–March 10am–4pm; €1), show gardens created to host the International Garden Exhibition 2003.

Warnemünde

Rostock has had it tough since the *Wende*, but suburb **WARNEMÜNDE** is doing very nicely, thank you. Since reunification the beach resort at the mouth of the Warnow River 13km north of Rostock has flourished, its hotels and villas restored to their former splendour, its expansive silver-white beach swept daily. Warnemünde's original fishermen wouldn't recognize the old place. Their village – as it remained until the late 1800s – is recalled in the picturesque streets east of the parish church lined by identical half-timbered houses. One opposite the tourist office is open as the **Heimatmuseum** (April–Oct Tues & Wed 10am–6pm; Nov–March Wed–Sun 10am–5pm; €3) should you wonder what a fisherman's house of the late 1800s looks like.

The heart of today's resort is harbourside **Am Strom**, where the miniature mansions of former captains and fisherfolk are a nonstop parade of cafés and boutiques. Any number of **cruises** embark from the wharf, or **boat rental** is available from a stand beneath a footbridge to the east bank. Am Strom concludes at a picture-book lighthouse built of white glazed bricks in 1897 (late April to early Oct 10am–7pm; €2) and the 1960s **Teepott** (daily 10am–6pm; €4), which houses global souvenirs picked up during sailor-adventurer Reinhold Kasten's 56 years at sea. But the focus is the dazzling white beach beyond – as broad and as powder-fine as any you'll find in Germany, with only monolithic GDR relic *Hotel Neptune* to spoil the skyline.

Eating

Rostock boasts a good dining scene, including a scattering of atmospheric restaurants. While the central Altstadt is largely bereft of eating opportunities, options abound in streets above the harbour. In Warnemünde, Am Strom is chock-a-block with fish restaurants whose menus could be photocopies – more stylish modern restaurants line the opposite bank, or Mühlenstrasse has a string of cheaper café-restaurants away from the happy hordes.

Rostock

Albert & Emile Altschmeiderstr. 8 ☎0381/493 43 73. Rough walls, quirky art, old wood, fine crystal and candlelight combine to make this one of Rostock's most atmospheric dining options, specializing in modern French cuisine. Eve only; closed Mon.

🏃 **Borwin** Am Strande 2 ☎0381/490 75 25. Laid-back restaurant with a terrace overlooking the marina and a quirky interior of mismatched furnishings. Think beach-shack vibe with a five-star fish menu.

Café Kloster Klosterhof 6. Stylish little café that serves light bistro lunches in a peaceful courtyard by the Heiligen-Kreuz-Kloster. The most pleasant spot in the centre for lunch. Mon–Sat 11am–7pm.

Central Café Leonhardstr. 22. Laid-back café-bar where modern art meets brasserie style in the heart of the Kröpeliner Torvorstadt scene. A great spot for breakfast.

Greens Leonhardstr. 22. Cheap Thai curries, noodles and laksas plus one or two fish dishes on a weekly specials board in a modern café-takeaway.

Zum Alten Fritz Warnowufer 65. One of a four-strong chain of brewery pubs in the region, this has above-average pub food – including good fish – and fresh beers served in a large beer garden by the harbour in summer.

Zur Kogge Wokrenter Str. 27 ☎0381/493 44 93. Touristy but fun historic harbour-*Gaststätte* whose galleried interior has stained glass and immaculately varnished booths like cabins. A menu of predominantly fish dishes is not as expensive as you'd expect.

Warnemünde

Atlantic Am Strom 107–108 ☎0381/526 55. By popular consent the finest of the harbourside fish restaurants, with a menu that includes options such as turbot in lobster sauce. Above is an excellent Italian restaurant (dinner only): expect classics such as beef carpaccio with truffles.

Zur Gartenlaub Anastasiastr. 24 ☎0381/526 61. Small gourmet menu of inventive regional dishes served in *fin-de-siècle* ambience – one of the finest restaurants in Rostock. Dinner Mon–Sat.

Drinking and nightlife

The drinking scene is focused in a laid-back locals' district west of Schröder Platz around Leonhardstrasse; nearby *Central Café* (see above) is a popular mellow spot. *Zum Alten Fritz* (see above) is a good harbour option. For listings, pick up freesheet *Szene* stocked in the tourist office and bars.

MAU club Warnowufer 56 ⓦwww.mauclub.de. Harbourside club that programmes a mixed bag of indie bands and clubs.

MS Stubnitz Stadthafen, near *Zum Alten Fritz* ⓦwww.stubnitz.com. Bastion of clubbing in Rostock is a former freighter converted into a grungy cultural venue with bands and art exhibitions. It's moored at the harbour when not bound for other Baltic cities – check the website for details.

Schusters Seepromenade 1, Warnemünde. The spot of choice in Warnemünde is this beach-bar beside the Teepott, its sun-loungers, potted palms

and cocktails as close as it gets to St Tropez hereabouts – but don't get your hopes up.

Speicher Bar Am Strande 2. An Irish pub in a former warehouse that screens Bundesliga football and hosts weekend house-nights.

Stadtkind Leonhardstr. 5. With its black-and-white tower-block imagery, leather banquettes and large corner-terrace, this lounge bar has a hip city vibe.

Studentenkeller Universitätsplatz 5 ⓦwww .studentenkeller.de. Schedules student-friendly nights of party tunes and oldies most nights except Sunday and Monday.

Stralsund

STRALSUND's fate is to be en route to one of Germany's favourite holiday destinations. Most people slow to marvel at its silhouette framed by the turrets of its powerful churches then whiz on towards Rügen. Nor do grimy industrial suburbs suggest you do otherwise. However, within lies a cobbled kernel Altstadt which is just as evocative of a Hanseatic past as more acclaimed members of the medieval trading cartel. During its fourteenth-century golden age, Stralsund ranked second only to Lübeck. Indeed, it was chosen as a venue in which to broker the 1370 "Peace of Stralsund" deal between the league and Denmark that represented the league's high-water mark. The legacy is a UNESCO-listed gabled streetscape where Lübeck-inspired Gothic showpieces are interspersed with Baroque monuments from two centuries as property of the Swedish Crown. Without the crowds of nearby Rügen, the most westerly town of western Pomerania ticks over at dawdling pace, with only a commercial port to ensure it's no museum piece.

Arrival, information and accommodation

The **Hauptbahnhof** is on the "mainland" side of the Altstadt's island, to the southwest. Walk over the causeway, Tribseer Damm, and you reach Neuer Markt, the southern axis of the town linked by Mönchstrasse to its centre, the Alter Markt. Large churches on both squares are handy homing-beacons. The **tourist office** (Mon–Fri 10am–6pm, Sat 10am–5pm; May–Sept also Sun 10am–4pm; general ℡03831/246 90, accommodation ℡03831/24 69 69, ⓦwww.stralsundtourismus.de) is at Alter Markt 9. **Bike rental** is available at the Hauptbahnhof. **Internet access** is at Toffi's Web-Café (daily noon–10pm) at Lobshagen 8a, just off Neuer Markt.

The tourist office books private rooms (❶), a handy option for a cheap bed if the independent hostel (see below) is full. The nearest campsite, *Sund-Camp Altefähr*, Am Kurpark 1 (℡038306/754 83, ⓦwww.sund-camp.de), is on the other side of the harbour at Altefähr, Rügen. **Ferries** of Weisse Flotte (ⓦwww .weisse-flotte.de) shuttle from the harbour daily from late April to October or there's a year-round local bus service.

Altstadt Pension Peiss Tribseer Str. 15
℡03831/30 35 80, ⓦwww.altstadt-pension-peiss.
de. Small, spotless place near Neuer Markt, with wood floors and colourful fabrics in spacious rooms. ❸–❹
Am Fischmarkt Wasserstr. 73 ℡03831/66 68 31, ⓦwww.pension-fischmarkt.de. Nothing flash, just a good-value family-run pension with simple rooms in inoffensive pastel shades. It's located one block behind the harbour. ❷
Hiddenseer Hafenstr. 12 ℡03831/289 23 90, ⓦwww.hotel-hiddenseer.de. Above a restaurant with a great location right on the harbourfront, so many rooms have port views. All are rather smart in a ship-shape maritime theme. ❺
Hostel Stralsund Reiferbahn 11 ℡0151/59 20 07 61, ⓦwww.hostel-stralsund.com. Bright, new independent hostel, located 5min south of the port. Coloured accent walls add character to

clean-lined Scandinavian furnishings in two- to six-bed rooms. Also has laundry, internet and bike rental for guests. Dorms €16–20, rooms ❷.
Kontorhaus Am Querkanal 1 ℡03831/28 98 00, ⓦwww.kontorhaus-stralsund.de. Rooms with a view over the inner harbour and nautical style in rooms like ships' cabins; apparently their interior designer was selected for his work on luxury cruise-liners. ❺
Norddeutscher Hof Neuer Markt 22
℡03831/29 31 61, ⓦwww.norddeutscher-hof.de. Family-run small hotel of the old school on Stralsund's southern square. ❹
Zur Post Tribseer Str. 22 ℡03831/20 05 00, ⓦwww.hotel-zur-post-stralsund.de. Spacious, comfortable mid-range place just off Neuer Markt with the usual mod-cons and queen- or king-size beds in rooms. ❺

The Town

That the **Altstadt** is effectively ringed by water, with the sea at its front and the Knieperteich and Frankenteich lakes protecting its rear, only adds to the impression of Stralsund as a pocket of history. The heart of the town, **Alter Markt**, at its northern end, does little to dispel the illusion. The civic ensemble of church and Rathaus clearly took Lübeck as a role model, its focus being the **Rathaus**, a pinnacle of Hanseatic Gothic brick whose stage-flat show-facade bristles with peaks and turrets and is punched by rosettes to let the Baltic winds through. Swedish occupiers refashioned its two buildings into a Baroque galleried courtyard, carving its columns with fruit and adding the impressive portal at the side. The Rathaus was conceived in tandem with the adjacent **Nikolaikirche** (Mon–Sat 10am–6pm, Sun 2–6pm; €2), also built in the fourteenth century. All furniture is eclipsed by a frothy, Baroque high altar by Berlin's Andreas Schlüter, with a triangular eye of God spitting lightning above a boiling cloud of putti. Around the ambulatory at the back of the choir is one of Europe's earliest astronomical clocks (1394), its bearded craftsmen pictured at a side-window, and the only surviving medieval guild altar, the *Pew of the Novgorod Traders*, with an image of Russian hunters harvesting squirrel pelts for the Hanseatic merchant on the far right.

Wulfhamhaus at Alter Markt 5 is Stralsund's finest Gothic town house, its facade a deliberate mirror to the Rathaus opposite. Fährstrasse, the former thoroughfare between port and Hanseatic government, the twin axes around which life revolved, is also worth a look, if only for galleried merchant's house **Scheele Haus** (10am–5pm daily; free), with models of the town's architectural showpieces, but as interesting as a record of mercantile housing. While fire and war has reduced the nearby **Johanniskloster** church to a shell, the seventeenth-century cloister of the monastery building (May–Oct 3 Wed–Sun 10am–6pm; €3), a short way up Schillerstrasse north of Alter Markt, retains murals and the so-called Räucherboden (smoking loft) beneath the roof; the former almshouse courtyards at the monastery's shoulder are the stuff postcards are made of.

Restaurants and hotels see the shabby **harbour** slowly reinventing itself through tourism after decades of neglect. **Gorch Forck I** (daily: April–Sept 10am–6pm; Oct–March 11am–4pm; €3) lies on a semi-permanent mooring while funds are drummed up to restore the Hamburg-built barque; for €15 you can make the 41m ascent up and over its main mast via rope ladders. The latest wheeze for the area is the **Ozeaneum Stralsund aquarium** (daily 9.30am–7pm, June–Sept till 9pm; €14; ⓦ www.ozeaneum.de), a strikingly fluid outline among the stolid brick warehouses. Though officially its four houses of suspended model whales, and aquaria of Baltic and Atlantic seas, are an adjunct to the **Meeresmuseum** (Oceanographic Museum; daily: June–Sept 10am–6pm; Oct–May 10am–5pm; €7.50; ⓦ www.meeresmuseum .de), on Mönchstrasse south of the Alter Markt via Ravensberger Strasse, they eclipse it. One of Stralsund's most enduringly popular attractions, much of its atmosphere comes from the deconsecrated Dominican priory in which its 45 tanks of tropical and North Sea sea-life are housed.

Sharing the priory is the **Kulturhistorisches Museum** (daily 10am–5pm, closed Mon in Jan; €4) whose exhibits of archeology and medieval art downstairs arc small beer alongside the architecture – the former refectory, canopied by vaults on slender columns and muralled with what appears to be a beaming potato at its centre, is superb. Upstairs rooms fast-forward through four centuries of interior decor. More compelling is the real thing, on show at Mönchstrasse 38 as Museumshaus (same hours and ticket), a restored merchant's town house (1320), which retains the central Gothic hoist.

One way to understand the **Marienkirche** south is as a merchants' riposte to the civic Nikolaikirche – no building better expresses mercantile confidence during the late 1300s heyday. If the Baroque caps and sheer bulk impresses outside the volume awes within, rising 33 vertiginous metres to constellations of star vaulting as you enter. You can also wind up the 366 steps of a tight spiral staircase to a viewing platform in the tower at 90m (daily 10am–5pm; €4).

Eating

Stralsund is not particularly well served for restaurants – you'll wander streets in vain looking for a restaurant district. The fish restaurant of *Hiddenseer* hotel has a harbourfront terrace; for a snack, the inner harbour has the usual boats serving fresh smoked fish and sandwiches.

Altes Bankhaus Heiligeiststr. 43a ☏ 03831/30 30 88. Come for international contemporary cooking such as lamb with a Roquefort crust and Parmesan gnocchi, or roast zander with pumpkin foam – the former bank building is not big on atmosphere.
Klabautermann Am Querkanal 2. Sturdy fillers such as Hamburg dish *Labskaus* in a former sailors' pub, now a harbourside *Gaststätte* that's beloved by an older clientele and snug as a cabin in an interior adorned with seafaring memorabilia.
Nur Fisch Heiligeiststr. 92. A cheap and chirpy café which serves "only fish", most fresh and none of it over €10. Lunch only Mon–Sat.

Torschliesserhaus Am Kütertor, off Mühlenstr. In an old house adjacent to the medieval defence walls, this hugely popular *Gaststätte* has rustic decor over two levels and a small beer garden. Wide-ranging menu of fish and meats at low to moderate prices.
Zur Kogge Tribseer Str. 26 ☏ 03831/28 58 50. The most historic restaurant in Stralsund is also the most atmospheric: dark wood and stained glass, and a good fish menu that's not as pricey as you might expect. Closed Mon.

Nightlife and entertainment

Nightlife isn't a strong point in the city either. Student cellar-bar *8cht Vorne* (🌐 www.carpediem-hst.de) at Badenstrasse 15 is fun at weekends, or try so-so disco-bar *Fischermanns*, a bar-club on the harbour at An der Fährbrücke with the usual Eighties cheese and disco. **Festivals** include Stralsunder Segelwoche regatta (🌐 www.stralsundsail.de) over a weekend in early June and summer theatre beano **Ostseefestspiele** (🌐 www.ostseefestspiele.de), with classic opera alfresco at the harbour during July and August. In days around July 24, Stralsund dons dress-costume for the **Wallensteintage** (🌐 www.wallensteintage.de) to celebrate a scrap with imperial troops in 1628.

Rügen

Ever since the Romantics eulogized an island where coast and country collide **RÜGEN** has held a semi-sacred place in German sentiments. The great, good and fairly unsavoury of the last two centuries – Caspar David Friedrich, whose paintings did more than any poster to promote its landscapes, Brahms and Bismarck, Einstein, Hitler, Thomas Mann, a couple of Kaisers and assorted grand dukes, GDR leader Erich Honecker, not to mention millions of families – have taken their holidays on an island renowned for chalk cliffs, 56km of silver sands and spacious deciduous woodland. Notwithstanding a newfound sheen as coastal resorts reassert themselves as the fashionable bathing centres they were in the early 1900s, Rügen has an innocent, *Famous Five* quality. It is an island where a steam engine chuffs around resorts in the south and cobbled lanes of inland villages are shaded by ancient trees.

Those on a flying visit usually only tick off premier resort **Binz**, a classic Baltic resort renowned for its handsome Bäderarchitektur, and the Königstuhl at **Jasmund**, a chalk cliff immortalized by Friedrich in 1818. Do so and you may be forgiven for wondering what the fuss is about – both are the busiest destinations on Rügen, and can be overcrowded. With an area of 975 square kilometres, Germany's largest island has less-populated corners to discover.

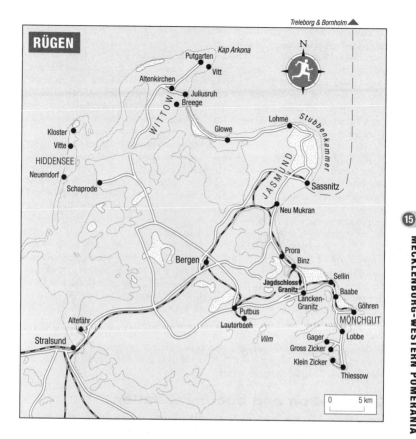

RÜGEN

Kap Arkona
Putgarten
Vitt
Altenkirchen
Juliusruh
Breege
WITTOW
Lohme
Stubbenkammer
Glowe
Kloster
Vitte
HIDDENSEE
Neuendorf
Schaprode
JASMUND
Sassnitz
Neu Mukran
Prora
Bergen
Binz
Sellin
Jagdschloss
Granitz
Baabe
Lancken-
Granitz
Göhren
Putbus
MÖNCHGUT
Altefähr
Lauterbach
Vilm
Gager
Lobbe
Gross Zicker
Stralsund
Klein Zicker
Thiessow
0   5 km

N

15

MECKLENBURG-WESTERN POMERANIA | Rügen

Places like **Putbus**, not so much a planned town as a Neoclassical folly writ large; smaller resorts near the rural **Mönchgut peninsula**; or the **Jasmund National Park**'s chalk cliffs cloaked in spacious forest. There are curios such as **Prora**, Hitler's holiday camp falling into ruin behind the beach, or the lighthouses of **Kap Arkona** and former fishing village **Vitt** in the windswept northwest. And then there are places like **Hiddensee**, a car-free sliver of land just off the west coast that may be the most idyllic spot in the area.

Arrival and island transport

Since 2007, Rügen has been linked to Stralsund by the Rügenbrücke suspension bridge, leaving the causeway beneath largely unused. If arriving from the east you could take the Autofähre Glewitz car ferry from Stahlbrode near Greifswald to the southern tip of Rügen. Mainland trains from, among other destinations, Stralsund, Hamburg and Berlin go direct to Bergen and Binz. Ferries from Stralsund ply routes to Altefähr opposite – not particularly useful as a destination, admittedly – and Hiddensee. International ferries from Sweden and Denmark sail to Sassnitz, the island's principal port.

Visitors consistently underestimate the size of Rügen. A good **public transport service** provides access to most areas, but it can take time on an island 43km wide and 51km long. All resorts on the south and east are served by **train**

services, including the charmingly named Rasender Roland ("Racing Roland") steam train (Ⓦwww.ruegensche-baederbahn.de). It runs from one end of the line, Lauterbach Mole, to the other, Göhren, fives times a day (or seven from Putbus), plus shuttles approximately hourly along the coastal resorts from Binz to Göhren. Prices range by distance from €1.60 to €8. Missable island-capital Bergen is the hub of the local **bus service** operated by RPNV (single €1.30, daycard €10; Ⓦwww.rpnv.de). Routes snake out to every destination on the island, with services every fifteen minutes or so between major destinations such as Bergen and Binz. Timetables are stocked in tourist offices, and are provided online.

Less useful though more picturesque are **tourist cruises** operated by a number of lines, including Reederei Ostsee-Tour (Ⓦwww.reederei-ostsee-tour.de), Adler Schiffe (Ⓦwww.adler-schiffe.de) and Weisse Flotte (Ⓦwww.weisse-flotte .de). Most ply routes around the coast from Göhren to Sassnitz via Selliner and Binz between May and October, with up to eleven a day between, say, Binz and Sassnitz. East-coast routes include Lauterbach to the Mönchgut peninsula. All tourist offices stock timetables – they're also posted on piers where they dock in resorts – or consult Ⓦwww.ruegen-schifffahrt.de.

If time is of the essence, **driving** is the way to go. Few destinations in Germany are so fond of parking metres, however – stock up with euro coins and be aware that major sights such as Königstuhl and Kap Arkona have pricey all-day car parks. Note, too, that Hiddensee is car-free. SIXT has **rental cars** at Binz (Proarer Chaussee 5; ☎038398/66 63 80, Ⓦwww.sixt.com) and via an agent in Göhren (Bahnhofstrasse 33); Europcar has a bureau in Bergen (Industriestrasse 12 ☎03838/25 42 80, Ⓦwww.europcar.com). Largely flat terrain makes Rügen a joy to **cycle**, the only caveat being rough cobbles in some villages. Cycling maps *Radeln auf Rügen* (€0.50), available in tourist offices, mark routes. Some RPNV buses can transport bikes for €1.60. Bike rental is available throughout Rügen, usually at the Bahnhof of each resort.

Information and accommodation

Every village however small has a **tourist office**; contact details are provided in relevant sections. They are a godsend for sourcing **accommodation** in high season, with beds at a premium from July to August. Without a reservation, you're best to start at the local tourist office unless you enjoy trudging around full hotels. They're also a good source of private rooms (❶–❷), holiday homes and apartments; for a group, the latter work out cheaper than a hotel over a week. Note that all Ostseebad resort hotels add a daily €2–2.50 Kurtax to the tariff. Camping is as well served – there were fourteen sites at the last count. Others alongside those named below are listed in a brochure free from tourist offices.

Binz

Cerês Strandpromenade 24 ☎038393/666 70, Ⓦwww.ceres-hotel.de. Metropolitan minimalism in masculine shades of black, grey and cream and high tech toys such as flat-screen TVs, wireless internet and sound systems in rooms. A yuppiefied restaurant serves cosmopolitan cuisine. ❼–❾

DJH Binz Sandstr. 35 ☎038393/325 97, Ⓦwww.jugendherbergen-mv.de. Excellent, modern youth hostel behind the beach – absurdly popular, so reservations are essential. Dorms from €22.90.

Kurhaus Binz Strandpromenade 27 ☎038393/66 50, Ⓦwww.travelcharme.com. Tradition and five-star-plus comforts in the palatial *Kurhaus*, part of the Travel Charme chain. ❽–❾

meerSinn Schillerstr. 8 ☎038393/66 30, Ⓦwww.meersinn.de. Slick designer number that takes its cue from Eastern minimalism and prides itself on its spa. ❽

Merkur Schillerstr. 15 ☎038393/13 50, Ⓦwww.hotel-merkur-binz.de. Traditional mid-range seaside hotel with classic-modern faux-mahogany furnishings and a decent location one block behind the seafront. ❹–❺

Smart Hotel Binz Paulstr. 4 ☎038393/450, ⓦwww.smart-hotels.com. Good-value mid-range place in the centre, with relaxed contemporary decor and a weakness for burnt-orange colour schemes. ❹

Villa Schwanebeck Margaretenstr. 18 ☎038393/20 13, ⓦwww.villa-schwanebeck .de. Fairly priced for comfortable rooms in a family three-star two blocks from Hauptstrasse. ❸–❹

Göhren

Akzent Waldhotel Waldstr. 7 ☎038308/505 00, ⓦwww.waldhotelgoehren.de. Overlooking Nordstrand pier, a family-run place that's comfortable and modern. ❺

Inselhotel Rügen Wilhelmstr. 6 ☎038308/55 50, ⓦwww.inselhotel-ruegen.de. Pleasant small hotel located 150m from the beach – decor is modern if rather bland. ❹–❺

MeeresBlick Friedrichstr. 2 ☎038308/56 50, ⓦwww.avr.de. Bright and breezy rooms, many with views overlooking Südstrand, plus a pool and sauna in a comfortable, modern four-star. ❻

Regenbogen Am Kleinbahnhof ☎038308/901 20, ⓦwww.regenbogen-camp.de. Rügen's largest campsite but invariably busy nonetheless. Well located among woods behind Nordstrand, and near the *Rasender Roland* train station. Closed Nov–Dec 15.

Robinson Jr Nordstrand 1 ☎038308/250 97, ⓦwww.robinson-jr.de. Above a bar and restaurant that can be noisy at weekends but simple rooms appeal for sea views from a position behind the sand dunes – the most escapist address in Göhren. ❸–❹

Lauterbach

Badehaus Goor Fürst-Malte-Allee 1 ☎038301/882 60, ⓦwww.hotel-badehaus-goor .de. Smart, modern spa hotel that occupies the Neoclassical *Badehaus* of Prince Wilhelm Malte's original resort. ❻–❼

Schwimmende Ferienhäuser Am Yachthafen ☎038301/80 90, ⓦwww.im-jaich.de. Probably the most appealing accommodation in the area are these Scandinavian-styled floating chalets moored in the marina, each with a deck inches above the water. ❺–❻

Viktoria Dorfstr. 1 ☎038301/64 60, ⓦwww.hotels-auf-ruegen.de. Comfortable if fairly anonymous small hotel with a sauna, whose star feature is its location on Lauterbach harbour. ❸–❹

Sassnitz and Lohme (Königstuhl)

Gastmahl des Meeres Strandpromenade 2 ☎038392/51 70, ⓦwww.wild-east.de/firmen /gastmahldesmeeres. Simple though comfy enough accommodation above an excellent restaurant on the harbourfront. ❸–❹

Krüger Naturcamping Jasmunder Str. 5 ☎038302/92 44, ⓦwww.ruegen-naturcamping.de. A pretty campsite among woodland 500m west of the Königstuhl car park, by the turn-off to Lohme – its owner provides a shuttlebus to the car park (€1.50) several times a day. Closed Oct–Easter.

Panorama-Hotel Lohme An der Steilküste 8 ☎038302/91 10, ⓦwww.lohme.com. Comfortable classic-modern rooms, a first-class restaurant and uninterrupted Baltic views from its veranda – all in all one of the most appealing hotels in this corner of Rügen. Sister hotel *Greys* (same contacts; ❻) has a little more designer flair. ❹

Strandhotel Sassnitz Rosenstr. 12 ☎038392/677 10, ⓦwww.strandhotel-sassnitz.eu. Every room comes with a view in these modern – and at the upper price range fairly glamorous – apartments created from a grand old hotel which was restored in 2007. ❻–❽

Waterkant Walterstr. 3 ☎038392/509 41, ⓦwww.hotel-waterkant.de. This is a friendly traditional seaside hotel with fairly modern rooms above clipped lawns that provide a broad panorama over the port. ❸–❹

Hiddensee

Godewind Süderende 53, Vitte ☎038300/66 00, ⓦwww.hotelgodewind.de. Family hotel that's a bastion of bygone charm – think flowery wallpaper and country-style linen. ❹

Heiderose In den Dünen 127, Vitte ☎038300/630, ⓦwww.hiddensee-heiderose.de. Friendly small hotel with classic-modern rooms and apartments (❻) in a separate house. ❹–❺

Hitthim Hafenweg 8, Kloster ☎038300/66 60, ⓦwww.hitthim.de. A lovely half-timbered pile just behind Kloster harbour with relaxed country style and a good fish restaurant. ❸–❻

Pension Wiesneck Kirchweg 18, Kloster ☎038300/316, ⓦwww.wieseneck-hiddensee.de. Pleasant simple en suites above a restaurant that's all about a charming rustic location just 5min walk from 15km of golden sands. ❸–❹

Post Hiddensee Wiesenweg 26, Vitte ☎038300/64 30, ⓦwww.hiddensee.de/post /menu.html. Modern Scandinavian-styled rooms and smart holiday apartments in a hotel that's located 250m from the quay. Minimum two nights, closed Nov. Rooms ❸, apartments ❹–❼.

Binz

BINZ, or Ostseebad Binz to give the most celebrated of the island's former bathing resorts its full title, is Rügen's holiday capital. If tourist mini-trains, cafés and boutiques and all the adjuncts of a resort are not to your taste, this is not your place in peak season. High-rise it is not, however. Friendly and approachable, Binz is instead characterized by the Bäderarchitektur of its time as a fashionable sea-water bathing resort. Central shady streets are lined with the handsome villas of German high society, adorned with carved verandas and wrought iron, all splashed with a uniform coat of white paint. The effect is pure holiday architecture – light-hearted rather than ostentatious. Now as then, the heart of the seafront promenade is the palatial **Kurhaus** where nineteenth-century bathers sipped spa waters, now a five-star hotel. At its shoulder, at the end of main drag Hauptstrasse, is the requisite pier, which rises above 5km of fine white sands: 4km north of the pier and 1km to the south in a smarter area of town, all scattered with wicker *Strandkörbe* seats. Among a number of tracks that ascend from the beach into surrounding woods is one that follows the shore.

In the 1830s, four decades before sea-water bathers wetted an ankle, island aristocrat Prince Wilhelm Malte I rebuilt his hunting cabin on Tempelberg hill south of the village to create **Jagdschloss Granitz** (May–Sept daily 9am–6pm; Oct–April Tues–Sun 10am–4pm; €3.50). The centrepiece of the dusty-pink neo-Gothic castle is a 38m tower designed a decade later by Karl Friedrich Schinkel, whose viewing platform permits good views. The story goes that Malte only requested the tower to settle a dispute over island property rights – the Swedes finally agreed to his terms that he could keep whatever he could see from his lodge. Located around 2km south of Binz, the lodge is most easily accessed on the Jagdschloss-Express minitrain (€7.50 return) that runs through central Binz to the entrance every 45 minutes. The *Rasender Roland* steam train and car park leave you fifteen minutes' walk uphill to the castle.

▲ Binz, Rügen

Practicalities

The **Hauptbahnhof** lies just north of the centre, the principal **tourist office** is in the Haus des Gastes, Heinrich-Heine-Strasse 7 (April–Oct Mon–Fri 9am–6pm, Sat & Sun 10am–6pm; Nov–March Mon–Fri 9am–4pm, Sat & Sun 11am–4pm; ☏038393/14 81 48, ⓦwww.ostseebad-binz .de). **Bike rental** is available from the Bahnhof and from Pauli's Radshop at Hauptstrasse 9a (daily 9am–6pm). Pedestrianized Hauptstrasse is well stocked with cafés and pizza joints. For serious dining there's *Poseidon* (☏038393/ 26 69), an old-fashioned fish-speciality **restaurant** at Lottumstrasse 1, or 🦌 *Strandhalle* (☏038393/315 64) at Strandpromenade 5. Interior style in this airy vintage hall is as gloriously eclectic as the cooking: from the local roast zander with wasabi foam that has wowed Michelin gourmets to herring fillets with Aunt Lydia's secret sauce. A sister restaurant serving steaks, fish, pasta and sushi, *Münsterteicher* (☏038393/143 80; eve only Nov–March), is at Strandpromenade 17–18.

Prora

Sea-bathers were not the only ones impressed by the good beach that extends 3km north of Binz at **PRORA**. In 1936 Hitler chose the site for a holiday camp as the apogee of the Nazis' "KdF" or *Kraft durch Freude* ("Strength through Joy") movement. The seaside resort known as **Colossus** was built to prepare the German people – up to 20,000 at a time – for forthcoming military expansion east. However, construction stalled upon the outbreak of hostilities in 1939 – ironically, the only families to stay here were those bombed out of Hamburg by the RAF in 1945 – then under the GDR it was strictly off-limits as a military base. The camp is built in classic dictatorial architecture – megalomaniac in size, brutal in style. Its six-storey reinforced-concrete blocks arc away behind the coast for over three miles – it takes over twenty minutes just to cycle along the length of the entire complex, which can only be seen from the air – and it is slowly falling into ruin, screened by pine scrub as the debate continues over its future. A proposal to convert it into a hotel came to naught although one building at the north end was rehabilitated in 2000 as Europe's largest **youth hostel**, with over a thousand beds (☏038393/13 38 80, ⓦwww.djh-mv.de; €15.50/19.90).

For the time being, other massive edifices hold Rügen's largest nightclub, *Miami*, three floors of oldies, techno and charts at weekends, a couple of cafés and beatnik galleries of the sort purged by the Nazis, and two museums. **Dokumentations Zentrum Prora** (daily: March–May, Sept & Oct 10am–6pm; June–Aug 9.30am–7pm; Nov–Feb 11am–4pm; €3; ⓦwww.proradok .de) exhibits German-only display boards on the resort's conception and construction, and an illuminating thirty-minute subtitled documentary that confronts the issues over current use. Around the corner is **KulturKunststatt Prora** (daily: summer 9am–7pm; winter 10am–4pm; €6; ⓦwww.kulturkunststatt -prora.de), a banner title for six collections over six storeys, including the NS-KdF Museum with an 18m model of the completed site and NVA Museum Prora, on Prora's use by the National People's Army from 1952. Much of Prora's fascination, however, is simply as a raw, unsanitized curio. And the beach on the other side is not just as fine as ever but spared the 20,000 holiday-makers intended – the antidote to the crowded sands in Binz.

As well as Deutsche Bahn trains – Bahnhof Prora Nord is the closest station to the main complex – the Prora-Express tourist mini-train shuttles 4km north from Binz several times a day between Easter and October.

Göhren and the Mönchgut peninsula

A small-fry resort at Rügen's east tip, **GÖHREN** is almost somnambulant compared with Binz, making it popular for a quiet holiday. The village spills downhill on either side of a headland to two fine strands: Nordstrand, the most developed, home to the town's pier, sweeps along the shore framed by cliff headlands; and quiet Südstrand on the east side. There's a clutch of mildly diverting **museums** (all €3.50 or €8 combination ticket) that flag up its roots as a fishing and farming settlement. Midway along the village's main street the **Heimatmuseum** (daily: mid-April to June & Sept to mid-Oct 10am–5pm; July & Aug 10am–6pm; mid-Oct to mid-April 10am–4pm) in an 1850s farmer-fisherman's house traces Göhren's metamorphosis from Slavic settlement to Rügen's third largest resort, while a few doors down **Museumshof** (same times) preserves a low-eaved farmstead complex to house rickety carriages and agricultural implements gleaned from local barns. Among the traditional houses downhill on Thiessower Strasse, **Rookhus** (daily mid-April to mid-Oct 2–5pm) is a picturesque smokehouse from 1720.

South of Göhren lies the Mönchgut peninsula, a jagged extremity of rolling sheep-fields that pokes several fingers into the Baltic. Another effortless expanse of sand lies south of Südstrand, on the other side are sheltered bays on the Hagensche Wiek, while pretty village Gross Zicker stands at the head of a protected upland of wildflower heath and meadow, Zikersches Höft, crisscrossed by walking trails.

Activities on Rügen

Should you tire of promenading and loafing in a Strandkorb, any number of activities operators will be happy to help you pass the days. Tourist offices have maps of **hiking trails** around all resorts; recommended easy day-hikes include the rural Mönchgut peninsula south of Göhren, its tip protected as a biosphere reserve, and the cliffside route through the Jasmund National Park from Sassnitz to the Königstuhl. Reederei Ostsee (ⓦwww.reederei-ostsee-tour.de) schedules **tourist cruises** from Binz and Sassnitz past the Stübenkammer to Kap Arkona several times a week (May–Sept; 4hr; €20) and once a week around the entire island (10hr; €40). As well as those activities outfits listed here, tourist offices stock flyers of providers for riding and fishing; the office in Binz is a good all-island reference.

Dietmar Bauchs ☎038302/93 69 & 0170/285 62 61. Excursions from Lohme to the Königstuhl (€40 per person) and Kap Arkona (€60) by yacht. The owner can also organize two-day excursions to Hiddensee and a four-day tour around Rügen (prices on request).

Kitesurfschule Casa-Atlantis Sandstr. 5, Baabe ☎038303/955 65, ⓦwww.ruegen -action.de. Kitesurf courses, from 4hr tasters to five days (from €99), plus equipment rental (4hr, €50).

Ostsee-Flug-Rügen Güttin ☎038306/12 89, ⓦwww.flugplatz-ruegen.de. Five choices of sightseeing flights over the island's poster-places, all in a Cessna light aircraft. Prices start at €38 for a 20min flight, minimum three people.

Segelschule Binz ☎038393/411 40 & 0176/22 78 54 32, ⓦwww.segelschule-ruegen .de. Sailing school that offers lessons and rents out catamarans and dinghies from bases in Prora, Thiessow on the Mönchgut peninsula and Altefähr; prices start at €20 per hour. The base in Mönchgut also has windsurfers, including funboards (from €8 per hour).

Segelschule Sun & Sail Am Hafen 5, Wiek ☎038391/43 09 51. Week-long yacht charter plus dinghy rental to access the sheltered Wieker Bodden.

Practicalities

Göhren is the terminus for the *Rasender Roland* steam train and Reederei Ostsee-Tour tourist ferries. The **tourist office** is uphill at Poststrasse 9 (mid-May to Sept Mon–Fri 9am–6pm, Sat 9am–noon; Oct to mid-May Mon–Thurs 9am–noon & 1–4.30pm, Fri 9am–3pm; ☎038308/667 90, Ⓦwww.goehren -ruegen.de). A second information point operates from the pier at Nordstrand (May 15–Sept daily 9am–noon). There's the usual Asian food and pizza-fest along conjoined high-streets Sandstrasse and Poststrasse. Locals' choice for fish is *Fischklause* (☎038308/256 21; daily from 5pm) behind the *Mona Lisa Café* at Sandstrasse 14. Other options include *Muschelbar*, a nautically themed place with a large menu by the pier; at the far eastern end of Nordstrand, *Robinson Jr* (see p.831) scores for a location among the dunes and a beach-shack vibe. The restaurant of *MeeresBlick* hotel (see p.831) has the finest reputation on the island, serving regional and Mediterranean cooking.

Putbus and Lauterbach

PUTBUS is a surprise among the cosy villages and gently undulating wheat-fields of south Rügen. Prince Wilhelm Malte I was ahead of his time when in 1818 he gave Rügen its first bathing resort, and it was not merely villas behind the beach; he planned, instead, a small Neoclassical spa-town. With its handsome layout and solid white boxes, Putbus fancies itself a cut above other villages on Rügen, boasting of its cultural weight and "*Italianische charme*". Its core is the Circus where wedges of lawn and stolid nineteenth-century manors encircle a self-congratulatory obelisk to celebrate the town's completion in 1836. West along main road Alleestrasse, Rügen's only **theatre** is a splendid statement of princely delusions, with a portico fit for a city and an interior of sun-like wrought-iron balconies (free tours, times posted by side entrance). The Markt at its shoulder is a similarly noble space. For himself, the prince commissioned Berlin's finest, Johann Gottfried Steinmeyer, to design a magnificent Neoclassical Schloss. The GDR regime saw instead a symbol of feudal repression and dynamited the lot in the 1960s – the story goes a local mayor hoped to impress visiting top brass. Nevertheless, a handsome **orangerie**, which sheltered pot plants from frost, and, most impressively, the mature **Schlosspark** itself remain. The former doubles as the tourist office (see below) and an exhibition centre. The latter's naturalistic gardens – planted with exotic species and dotted with the former stables (Marstall), the boxy parish church which began life in 1845 and a memorial of the prince himself – are a lovely spot for an amble.

Around 3km southeast of Putbus, the tiny port of **LAUTERBACH** is the terminus for the *Rasender Roland* steam railway and panoramic cruises of Weisse Flotte (Ⓦwww.weisse-flotte.de), either around nature reserve islet Vilm, stretched out in the bay offshore (€9–12), or to Gager on the Mönchgut peninsula and Baabe just west of Göhren (single €8, return €14). Cruise-and-train return tickets (€14.50) are possible several times a day. The road that arrows ruler-straight from the Schlosspark is channelled past the village turn-off by an avenue of trees towards the grand span of Doric columns that front the bathhouse of Malte's spa resort, today a ritzy spa-hotel (see p.831).

Practicalities

Train stations at Putbus and Lauterbach Mole are served by Deutsche Bahn and the *Rasender Roland*. The **tourist office** (Mon–Fri 9am–5pm, Sat & Sun 11am–5pm; ☎038301/431, Ⓦwww.putbus.de) in the orangerie in central Putbus has the usual flyer confetti and can book accommodation, as can Ruegen-Beuscher-Service, August-Bebel-Strasse 1 (Mon–Fri 9.30am–6pm,

Sat 9.30am–3pm; ☎038301/605 13, ⓦwww.ruegenbesucherservice.de) at the back of the Markt.

Jasmund

If one area is responsible for Rügen's stellar rise from agricultural backwater to holiday heaven it is **JASMUND**. A thumb of open woodland and fields poked into the Baltic, much of it protected as the Jasmund National Park (ⓦwww .nationalpark-jasmund.de), the peninsula north of Binz is famous throughout Germany for chalk cliffs cloaked in woodland that drop to a sea that is startling shades of jade and aqua on a sunny day. These are the **Stubenkammer** popularized by Romantic painter Caspar David Friedrich in the early 1800s, a stretch of cliffs that extends for several kilometres, its most celebrated section being the mighty **Königstuhl** cleft that juts from the cliffs – the name "king's stool" derives from a folk tale that whoever scaled its 117m face could claim Rügen's throne. Partly thanks to Friedrich, it's a landmark lodged in the national consciousness.

Whether an artist who eulogized raw nature would have set up his easel today is doubtful as the Königstuhl is now one of Germany's most popular tourist attractions. From a site car park by the main road at Hagen, you must either walk 3km or join bus #19 (May–Oct Mon–Fri 9.30am–7.15pm; every 15min; €1.40 single, €2.70 return) to reach a viewing platform by footbridge (€1) to gaze from the fabled cliff – assuming you can muscle the jolly tour-groups out of the way. Visit early or at lunch time to avoid the worst of the crowds or shun the site and walk twenty minutes south to Victoria-Sicht. You can access the weed-strewn shingle beach beneath from both spots. On the walk through beech woods you pass the Herthasee, a brooding lake in which pagan goddess Hertha bathed once a year according to Roman historian Tacitus's first-century tome *Germania*. Because only priests were permitted to see her, the Mother Earth figure is said to have drowned the servants who led cows that pulled her cart, inspiring entrepreneurs to set "spirit stones" on the bank in the late 1800s. The latest money-spinner at the site is **Nationalpark-Zentrum Königstuhl** (daily: Easter–Oct 9am–7pm, otherwise 10am–5pm; €6; ⓦwww.koenigsstuhl.com) with child-friendly multimedia displays on fauna and flora and the inevitable restaurant.

If you have time, the 9km cliffside walk to the site from **SASSNITZ**, Rügen's principal port, is excellent. A workaday and utilitarian place at its commercial harbour, Sassnitz was the first seaside resort on the island, something only apparent from the Bäderarchitektur ten minutes' walk from the harbour in the town's tiny kernel, whose knot of cobbled lanes feels almost Mediterranean on warm evenings. From Weddingstrasse at the northwest end of the town, a path forges through spacious deciduous forest of the Stubnitz for 2km, then cuts towards the coast and the Wissower Klinken, whose cliffs were carved into two white shards by a collapse in 2005 – Ernst-Moritz-Arndt-Sicht viewpoint 1km north offers good views. Another couple of hours further north along the cliffs, at Victoria-Sicht, you glimpse the Königstuhl then soon afterwards stroll from an empty track into the crowds at the footbridge.

Practicalities

Bus routes #14 and #20 from Sassnitz and as far afield as Göhren stop at the Königstuhl car park roughly every 45 minutes. Sassnitz is the terminus of the main **train** line and international **ferries** from Bornholm, Denmark (April–Oct only), and Trelleborg, Sweden. The port is also used by resort ferries and panoramic cruisers that depart roughly four times a day (10am–4.30pm) to the Stubenkammer's chalk cliffs. Other operators ply routes from Binz and Göhren. Sassnitz's most convenient **tourist office** (daily 10am–6pm; ☎038392/64 90,

@www.insassnitz.de) is beside the harbour at Strandpromenade 12. The other at Bahnhofstrasse 19a (Mon–Fri 9am–6pm, Sat 10am–6pm, Sun 2–6pm; ☎038392/669 45) is handy for the Bahnhof above the port. Alongside accommodation listed (see p.831), plenty of "*Zimmer*" signs in Hagen advertise private rooms (**②**) near the Königstuhl; otherwise try Lohme 3km northwest. For eating in Sassnitz, hotel *Gastmahl des Meeres* (see p.831) has an excellent fish **restaurant**, just one of many along Strandpromenade, and *Altstadt Brasserie* at Marktstrasse 4 is a local favourite for classy bistro-style dishes: expect carpaccio of local fish or stews of Jasmund game.

Wittow

Wind-blown **Wittow** is as far northwest as Rügen gets. It's a remote spot of undulating fields, with a long beach along the isthmus to Jasmund and chalk cliffs at Kap Arkona, which make for a popular day-trip to the island's northern tip. Mass tourism has arrived to gateway village **PUTGARDEN**, introduced by an expansive car park for visitors to the cape. Here you'll find the **tourist office** (daily: summer 10am–7pm; winter 11am–5pm; ☎038391/41 90, @www.kap-arkona.de) and a mini-train (single €2, €3.50 return) that pootles 2.2km north to the cape's celebrated lighthouses – another benefit of Prussian rule in 1815 after two centuries of serfdom under Swedish rule was a navigation light to warn of shallows off the cape. Oldest is the **Schinkelturm** (10am–6pm; €2 or Cape card €10), a stubby red-brick rectangle designed by Karl Friedrich Schinkel in 1827. Inside are missable displays on optics and German lighthouses, and views from the top of its ornate iron staircase. The panorama of sea, barley and wheat fields is a little better from the **Neuer Lechturm** (New Lighthouse; daily 11am–5pm; €3) nearby, at 35m over 15m higher than its forerunner. Beyond are underwhelming displays of sea rescue in the **Nebelsignalstation** (daily 11am–4pm; €2) where you can buy tickets for tours of the **Marine Bunkeranlage** (May–Sept hourly 11am–4pm; €5), a bunker system that served as a nerve centre of Baltic defences during World War II and then under the GDR.

The circular **Peilturm** (daily 10am–5pm; €2) on the other side of the lighthouses houses a gallery and modest archeology finds from the adjacent **Burgwall** (daily 10am–4.45pm; €1), a fort of the Slavic tribes which occupied the island from 500 AD. While a sculpture of a four-headed deity described by conquering Danes in the twelfth century has long disintegrated, the earthworks of what was possibly a religious stronghold remain, providing uninterrupted views east. **VITT**, reached after a kilometre on the path beyond, harks back to the early nineteenth-century villages lost elsewhere on Rügen. Gathered above a rudimentary harbour on a shingle beach, the fishing hamlet traces its origins back to a trading settlement with the Slavs – many of its thatched houses perpetuate the ancient rune-like numbering system. Its picture-postcard looks draw the crowds, and there's a splendid *Gaststätte*, *Goldener Anker*, that prepares fish at good prices considering its appeal. By the village entrance an early 1800s octagonal chapel has a murky altarpiece of Christ plucking St Peter from the seas, copied from Dresden's Phillip Otto Runge, and a naive mural of villagers gazing out into a stormy sea. The road beyond triangulates back to Putgarden, either a 1km walk or a jaunt by horse and cart.

Hiddensee

"*Dat söte Länneken*" sighs marketing material of the elongated **Hiddensee** island off the west coast of Rügen. "The sweet little land", 16km long, only 300m wide at its narrowest point and the second sunniest spot in Germany after Usedom (1805 hours average a year), remains the popular day-trip it was for artists, then GDR-era families. Most visitors potter happily in the vicinity of the island's three villages, from north to south **Kloster**, **Vitte** and **Neuendorf**, which together account for the year-round 1100 population. The former is the pick of the bunch for looks and a long crescent of fine beach. Here, too, is **Gerhart-Hauptmann-Haus** (daily: May–Oct 10am–5pm; Nov–April 11am–4pm; closed Jan; €2), summer home of the eponymous naturalist dramatist which he bought with the proceeds of his Nobel Prize for Literature. He lies in the graveyard of the village church. However, what appeals most are the windswept landscapes that give the Hiddensee a sense of space and clear horizons. None are difficult to access by bikes which can be rented in every village for €5–6 a day or horse-and-cart trips offered in summer – cars are banned on Hiddensee. The premier destinations are the meadows in the north known as the **Dornbusch**, its wide skyline punctured only by a lighthouse at the highest point that provides glorious views of sea and fields south. You can access the cliffs beneath from the north end of the beach at Kloster. A single rough road ambles south of island "capital" Vitte through swathes of protected flowering heath to Neuendorf, from where a track continues towards a second lighthouse. Wild heath beyond slowly peters out into the Gellen, a sandbank popular with birdwatchers.

Practicalities

Ferries to the island are run by Reederei Hiddensee (☏0180/321 21 50, Ⓦwww.reederei-hiddensee.de) and operate from Schaprode to all villages several times a day and also from Stralsund. Prices from Schaprode are: €8.15/14 single/return to Neuendorf; €9.90/16.30 to Vitte and Kloster. Ferries from Stralsund operate three times a day (single €10, return €18.20). The principal **tourist office** (Mon–Fri 8.30am–5pm, Sept–May also Sat & Sun 10am–noon; ☏038300/642 26, Ⓦwww.seebad-hiddensee.de) is at Norderende 62 in Vitte, supported by another bureau by the ferry terminal at Kloster (Mon–Fri 9.30am–noon & 1.30–5pm, May–Sept also Sat 10am–noon). It books **private rooms** (❶) in all three villages. Head to the hotels (see p.831) for the best eating on the island.

Greifswald

A compact Altstadt is one sign that **GREIFSWALD** was always a bit player in the Hanseatic League. Another is the lack of grand edifices compared to those of fellow leaguers. Instead it is North Germany's second oldest university, **Ernst-Moritz-Arndt-Universität**, that is the focus of this neat town you can tick off in a day. Nearly six hundred years of study has brought Greifswald a cultured, bookish atmosphere in an easy-going centre immortalized in the paintings of local son Caspar David Friedrich. That its perfect grid survives at all is largely thanks to a now-forgotten Third Reich commander who surrendered to the Red Army in April 1945 without a shot fired. Nearby **Wieck** makes for an attractive maritime day out.

Arrival and information

On the Rostock and Berlin lines, the **Hauptbahnhof** lies immediately west of the Altstadt. Buses #5, #6 and #7 from the ZOB outside go to Wieck. To reach the Markt turn left along Bahnhofstrasse then right at the elbow on to Lange Strasse, which becomes the high street. At its end is the **tourist office**

(May–Sept Mon–Fri 9am–6pm, Sat 10am–2pm, July & Aug also Sun 10am–2pm; Oct–April Mon–Fri 9am–5pm; ☎03834/52 13 80, ⓦwww.greifswald .de) on the Markt in the Rathaus. **Bike rental** is from Zweirad Krüger at Gützkower Strasse 81–2.

Accommodation

Accommodation is good value in central Greifswald and comes with a seaside flavour at Wieck. The nearest campsite is *Frien- und Freizeitpark Loissin* (☎03835/22 43, ⓦwww.freizeitpark-loissin.de) on the coast 10km northeast of Greifswald at Loissin.

Alte Speicher Rossmühlenstr. 25 ☎03834/777 00, ⓦwww.alter-speicher.de. Restored warehouse on the harbour with classy traditional-styled rooms and a good restaurant. ❹

DJH Greifswald Pestalozzistr. 11–12 ☎03834/516 90, ⓦwww.jugendherbergen-mv.de. The official youth hostel is a modern place 2km east of the centre – take bus #1 to Feldstrasse – although there's also an appealing modern hostel at Wieck (see below). From €20.50.

Hôtel Galerie Mühlenstr. 10 ☎03834/773 78 30, ⓦwww.hotelgalerie.de. Slick glass-skinned hotel just off the Markt with a taste for modern art and blonde wood furnishings. ❹

Maria Dorfstr. 46a ☎03834/84 14 26, ⓦwww.hotel-maria.de. Comfortably old-fashioned en-suite rooms with minor mod-cons such as satellite TV. ❹

Maritimes Jugenddorf Wieck Yachtweg 3, Wieck ☎03834/83 02 950, ⓦwww.majuwi.de. Super-modern hostel towards the river mouth fitted out in Ikea style. Inevitably popular with school groups. Dorms €25.

Pension Greifswald Baustr. 09 ☎03834/50 78 94, ⓦwww.pension-greifswald.de. Not a pension, but five simple studios or two-room apartments created from a house just south of the Altstadt. Ring to confirm the owners are around. ❶–❷

Schipp In Am Hafen 3 ☎03834/84 00 26. Tiny nook on the harbour with the cheapest rooms in the area. ❶–❷

The City

Thanks to its World War II local commander, Greifswald's pretty **Markt** retains its breezy pastel-tinted gables and a couple of Hanseatic-era patricians' houses, the most impressive at no. 11 a turreted Christmas tree patterned by a brick lattice of lancet arches. All buildings are secondary to an ox-blood red Baroque Rathaus that fills the centre. Poking above the houses on the northeast corner, the **Marienkirche** on Brüggstrasse is unmissable because of a stubby tower that earns it, the oldest of the town's three churches, the nickname "Fat Mary". Though it was built to celebrate the signing up to Lübeck's Hanseatic charter in 1250, no original artwork remains, nor did later furnishings survive Napoleon's troops one cold winter in the early 1800s. A Renaissance pulpit inlaid with images of Reformation heroes is a rare piece in an otherwise bare church.

The city's ecclesiastical star-piece is the **Dom St Nikolai** on the opposite side of the Markt, a great heap of Gothic brick whose turreted tower buds into a series of Baroque bulbs. Friedrich loved it, setting up his easel in Greifswald wherever he could contrive to include its romantic silhouette. The whitewashed interior of "Long Nicholas" is a disappointment after such a promising overture, worth a visit only to ascend 264 steps to a viewing platform in the tower (€2). Friedrich was born in the church's shadow at Lange Strasse 57 in 1774. His father's adjoining candle-factory displays reproductions of his sketches above and a mock-up of candle-making beneath as the **Caspar-David-Friedrich-Zentrum** (Tues–Fri 10am–6pm, Sat & Sun 11am–5pm; €1.50). West of the Dom the **university** rears up as a palatial Baroque slab on Rubenowplatz, a manicured square at whose centre is a neo-Gothic monument to university heroes past, notably Swedish king and founder Frederick I and Ernst Mortitz Arndt who bankrolled the project in 1456. A graffiti-covered student prison similar to that in Heidelberg is occasionally opened to visitors, but it's pot luck – ask at the tourist office if you're interested.

For culture head to the splendid **Pommersches Museum** (Tues–Sun 10am–6pm, Nov–April till 5pm; €4.50; ⓦwww.pommersches-landesmuseum .de) at the far eastern end of Domstrasse. There's much to enjoy among exhibits from Pomerania, which are presented creatively in a museum made up of clean modernist spaces and a medieval monastery. Beautifully lit archeology and town exhibits unfold in the cellars – for once a compelling journey through history that culminates in a Renaissance tapestry commissioned by a local grandee to celebrate the arrival of Luther's new creed in Pomerania. As impressive is a gallery whose star is, inevitably, Friedrich. Though not his finest works, a representative cross-section are on display, showcasing his favourite theme of natural splendour while also demonstrating his draughtsmanship in a coloured sketch of the Markt c.1818. Other big guns include Van Gogh, Hals, Liebermann and Die Brücke artist Alexej von Jawlensky.

Around Greifswald

While a harbour west of the Markt brings a maritime tang into central Greifswald, **WIECK** 4km east is the heart of local fishing; in summer the two are linked by passenger cruises three times a day. Scented by smoke, herring and salt, the core of the photogenic fishing village where the river Ryck flows into the sea is a harbour lined by boats and fish restaurants, and spanned by a Dutch-style wooden bridge that lifts by hand. Studentenstieg opposite the bridge leads to what's left of the monastery (Kloster) in **Eldena**. For a dyed-in-the-wool Romantic like Friedrich, the Gothic skeleton of the Cistercian monastery was not simply a ruin but a wistful embodiment of melancholy, a leitmotif of decay; even without the rose-tinted glasses the ruins are picnic heaven. Alternatively, at the back of the east bank is a decent beach centred around a café at Strandbad Eldena (daily May–Sept 8am–6pm) reached via Boddenweg opposite Wieck bridge.

Eating and nightlife

Wieck is lined with restaurants whose stock in trade is fresh fish. As a minor student town, Greifswald boasts a small bar-and-club scene.

Restaurants

Fischer-Hütte An der Mühle 8, Wieck ☏ 03834/83 96 54. Ingredients straight off the boat and into the frying pan in a traditional-styled fish restaurant – a popular weekend lunch-spot.

Le Croy Rakower Str. 9 ☏ 03834/77 58 46. With its classic French–Mediterranean flavours in a contemporary gallery-like dining room, the smart restaurant of the Pommersches Museum prepares by far the finest eating in Greifswald. Closed Mon.

Zum Alten Fritz Markt 13 ☏ 03834/578 30. A brewery restaurant whose traditional menu of *Pfanne* dishes and jacket potatoes is lightened by Baltic fish.

Bars and nightlife

Café Pariser Cnr of Lange Str. & Rubenowplatz. Near *Mitt 'n Drin* but a world away in style – this is a ramshackle place that's more student scout-hut than bar. Wed–Sun from 8pm

Mira Club Johann-Stelling-Str. 30 ⓦwww .mira-club.com. A mixed programme of techno, drum 'n' bass, disco and electro; Wed–Sat.

Mitt 'n Drin Cnr of Domstr. & Caspar-David-Friedrich-Str. Near the Dom, this is a modern bar with club sounds – popular warm-up for students.

TV Club Bahnhofstr. 44–45. Hip lounge-bar that hosts weekend club-nights.

Usedom

Second to Rügen in terms of size, **USEDOM** is overshadowed by its larger sister as a Baltic resort, too. Its low-lying undulating blob, around 50km long and only split from the mainland for much of its length by the narrow Pennestrom channel, lacks the scenic variety of its much-mythologized neighbour. Yet during the early 1900s it was a haunt of wealthy Europeans, a place to promenade in a trio of resorts that now brand themselves the **Kaiserbäder** (literally "Emperor's Baths"). Since reunification **Bansin**, **Heringsdorf** and **Ahlbeck** have renovated their handsome Art Nouveau hotels to recapture some of the imperial glamour and shake off an image as workers' playgrounds they acquired in GDR decades; the regime snatched private villas on spurious legal grounds on behalf of trades unions. Each resort has its own market, from families to pensioners to spa-goers. What keeps all coming are 42km of fine sand, spread up to 70m deep along the north coast and drenched in more sunshine than anywhere else in Germany, an average 1906 hours a year.

Arrival, island transport and information

All national **train** services go to Züssow on the Stralsund and Greifswald line to connect with the local Usedomer Bäderbahn (UBB; Ⓦ www.ubb-online .com) that shuttles along all resorts several times a day; change at Zinnowitz to go northwest to Peenemünde. Alternatively, Adler-Schiffe (Ⓦ www.adler -schiffe.de) schedules **tourist cruises** from Rügen resort Binz via Göhren to Peenemünde (daily mid-March to Oct; €11). Local buses also ply routes along the coast. A more enjoyable form of travel is to take Adler-Schiffe's cruisers between the three resorts (May to early Oct; from €8 single or €11 day-card); embarkation at each is from the Seebrücke (pier). With generally flat terrain and some coastal routes, **cycling** is a good option, though you will be forced onto busy roads at times. Bikes can be rented in all resorts, generally from the Bahnhof, and can be transported on UBB trains for a minimal charge.

Tourist offices (Ⓦ www.drei-kaiserbaeder.de) are in: the Haus des Gastes by the pier in Bansin (Ⓣ 038378/470 50); Forum Usedom at Kulmstrasse 33 in Heringsdorf (Ⓣ 038378/24 51); and Ahlbeck at Dünenstrasse 45 (Ⓣ 038378/49 93 50). Hours for all are roughly Jan–March, Nov & Dec Mon–Fri 9am–4pm, Sat & Sun 10am–noon; April, May & Oct Mon–Fri 9am–5pm, Sat & Sun 10am–1pm; June–Aug Mon–Fri 9am–6pm, Sat & Sun 10am–3pm.

Accommodation

Accommodation on Usedom is in as short supply in high season as it is in other Baltic beach resorts. Private rooms (❶–❷) can be booked at the tourist office of each resort, as can apartments in spectacular historic villas – all in all a good first port-of-call without a reservation in high season. The most useful among the island's nine campsites are: *Campingplatz am Grossen Krebsee* (Ⓣ 0383878/315 87, Ⓦ www.krebsee.de; mid-March to mid-Oct), beside a lake at Bansin suburb Neu Sallenthin; and beachside *Campingplatz Stubben-felde* at Stubbenfelde, 10km northwest of Bansin (Ⓣ 038375/206 06, Ⓦ www .stubbenfelde.de; April–Oct).

Das Ahlbeck Dünenstr. 48, Ahlbeck Ⓣ 038378/499 40, Ⓦ www.das-ahlbeck.de. Hip design and spa hotel that's leading the charge towards Ahlbeck's push upmarket. ❻–❽

DJH Heringsdorf Puschkinstr. 7–9, Heringsdorf Ⓣ 038378/223 25, Ⓦ www.jugendherbergen-mv .de. Usedom's only youth hostel is in a fine old house in Heringsdorf. Dorms from €25.20.

Germania Strandpromenade 25, Bansin
📞038378/23 90, 🌐www.germania-bansin.de.
Quietly elegant, family-run small hotel in a historic
building on the promenade decorated in modest,
tasteful style. ④–⑤

Kastell Dünenstr. 3, Ahlbeck 📞038378/470 10,
🌐www.kastell-usedom.de. Old-fashioned rooms
– and all the better for it – in a late 1800s faux-
castle on the seafront. ⑤–⑥

Pension an der See Strandpromenade 17, Bansin
📞038378/293 46, 🌐www.pension-an-der-see.de.
Fairly dated in a mid-Eighties way, but a cheapie in
a late 1800s hotel that scores highly for a location
right on the beach. ③–④

Residenz Bleichröder Delbrückstr. 14,
Heringsdorf 📞038378/36 20, 🌐www.residenz
-bleichroeder.com. The place to live out *fin-de-
siècle* fantasies is this historic neo-Baroque
mansion built for an adviser to Bismarck and set in
its own grounds. Heavy furnishings are a paean to
imperial pomp. ⑤

Romantik Hotel Esplanade Seestr. 5, Heringsdorf
📞038378/700, 🌐www.seetel.de. Elegant historic
pile that brings modern designer touches to
imperial glamour in public areas. Rooms are classic
crisp white linen and old wood. ⑥–⑦

Strandidyll Delbrückstr. 9–11, Heringsdorf
📞038378/42 43 96 50, 🌐www.tc-hotels.de
/strandidyll. The premier address on Usedom's coast
is on the beach promenade, with elegant classic-
modern rooms and good spa facilities. ⑦–⑨

Zur Schönen Aussicht Kulmstr. 30, Heringsdorf
📞038378/222 08, 🌐www.kaiser-pension.de.
Functional motel rooms, all with views over the
beach in front, that are among the cheapest in
Heringsdorf. ③–④

Peenemünde

Imperial glitz aside, Usedom's place in history is as the world's first rocket test-
site. Between 1936 and 1945, technicians worked to develop liquid-fuelled
long-range missiles at **PEENEMÜNDE**, a military village constructed for the
purpose at the far northwest tip of the island. In October 1942, working under
Werner von Braun, scientists successfully fired the prototype A4 rocket. With its
flight to an altitude of 85km the Space Age had arrived. Allied air-raids destroyed
the site in 1943 forcing production to shift to Nordhausen, in the Harz region,
and in autumn 1944, the first Vergeltungswaffe ("Vengeance Weapon") was
fired to inaugurate attacks on cities in Britain, France and Belgium using the
notorious V1 and V2 "flying bomb". Occupied by the Red Army, then opera-
tional as a GDR base until 1990, the behemoth red-brick power station that
houses the **Historisches-Technisches Informationszentrum** (April–Sept
daily 10am–6pm; Oct daily 10am–4pm; Nov–March Tues–Sun 10am–4pm;
€6; 🌐www.peenemuende.de) houses exhibits that somewhat disingenuously
hail the site as the birthplace of space travel, thereby airbrushing out what was
always a military goal, not to mention a site constructed using concentration
camp slave labour.

The Kaiserbäder

Europe's longest promenade runs for 8km between the three Usedom resorts,
known as the Kaiserbäder. The westernmost of these, **BANSIN**, is as low-key
as it is low-rise. Historic architecture is restricted to the odd Jugendstil villa, its
pier is nothing more flashy than a glorified gangway; a mellow vibe makes it
popular with young families. Far more commercial is **HERINGSDORF** 2km
east. That "Herring village" should boast the longest pier in continental Europe
– 508m in length, albeit a replica of the original that burned down in 1958 – says
something of the resort where emperors Friedrich III and Wilhelm II sojourned.
A fishing village in the 1820s, it flourished as Germany went crazy for sea-water
bathing in the 1880s, and retains many of the splendid villas and hotels that
made it the St Tropez of the Baltic. GDR urban planners blighted the centre
with the breeze-block architecture of Platz des Friedens, but elsewhere is pure
Baltic Bäderarchitektur. Emperor Wilhelm took tea once a year with widower
Frau Staudt in Villa Staudt at Delbrückstrasse 6, and American painter Lyonel

Feininger hosted glittering entertainments at Neoclassical Villa Oppenheim at no. 11. A **Kunstpavilion** (Tues & Wed noon–5pm, Thurs–Sun 2–6pm; free) west of the seafront rose garden hosts modern art exhibitions.

More than any other, it is final Kaiserbäder **AHLBECK** that is quietly reinvigorating itself as a swish spa destination. It is the oldest of the trio, welcoming a waxed-moustache clientele from the 1850s three decades before its rivals. Pride and joy of the town is a photogenic pier with corner turrets that was built in 1888 and has been embraced as an icon for the island.

Eating

Notwithstanding the usual **cafés** and pizza joints on resort high-streets, most eating in the Kaiserbäder is in hotel **restaurants**. Two addresses in Heringsdorf stand out for a splurge: gourmet restaurant *Kulm Eck*, Kulmstrasse 14 (☎038378/225 60; eve only, closed Oct–April) and *Lutter & Wegner*, Kulmstrasse 3 (☎038378/221 25), an outpost of the upmarket traditional Berlin bistro famous for its *Wiener Schnitzel*. The latter is one of the few restaurants on the island open year-round. For a quick bite in Heringsdorf and Ahlbeck, it's hard to beat the fishermen's hut cafés on the beachfront for atmosphere.

Schwerin

Encircled by lakes and with a fairytale Schloss that goes straight to the head, **SCHWERIN** punches far above its weight. Although the names of Puschkinstrasse and Karl-Marx-Strasse give away the GDR past, communism was a hiccup in its history – even its streets are spared the concrete vandalism of Eastern Bloc architecture; crowned as capital of Mecklenburg-Western Pomerania in 1990, Schwerin is settling into a time-honoured role as the state's cultural dynamo. After Saxony's Henry the Lion swatted aside an early Slavic settlement on its islet in 1160, the dukes of Mecklenburg took up residence in the fourteenth century, then moved in and out of the royal seat for nearly five centuries. None was more illustrious than the nineteenth. After its elevation to the duchy residence over Ludwigslust (see p.848) in 1837, Schwerin blossomed into a heavyweight with a vigorous cultural scene and showpiece architecture, not least that star-piece **Schloss**. Its legacy remains today as a pocket-sized city with the airs and architecture of a historic capital yet none of the urban grit.

Arrival and information

Schwerin is on **train** lines from Hamburg, the Baltic coast and Berlin, its Hauptbahnhof northwest of the centre. The Dom's soaring spire is a homing beacon to main square Am Markt and the **tourist office** at no. 14 (April–Sept Mon–Fri 9am–7pm, Sat & Sun 10am–6pm; Oct–March Mon–Fri 9am–6pm, Sat & Sun 10am–4pm; ☎0385/592 52 12, ⓦwww.schwerin.com). It sells the **Schwerin-Ticket** (24hr €5, 48hr €7) that provides free public transport and discounts on the town's sights. **Bike rental** is from Fahrraddoktor just north of the office at Puschkinstrasse 49, and Fahrräder und Radverleih-Center Anton Eminow at Wismarsche Strasse 123. **Internet** access is at Martinstrasse 4 in Internet Café Schwerin (Mon–Sat 9am–midnight, Sun noon–10pm). It's worth going out of your way to visit for **Osterfest** in mid-April, the **Altstadtfest** in mid-September and the **Schlossfest** on the last weekend in June.

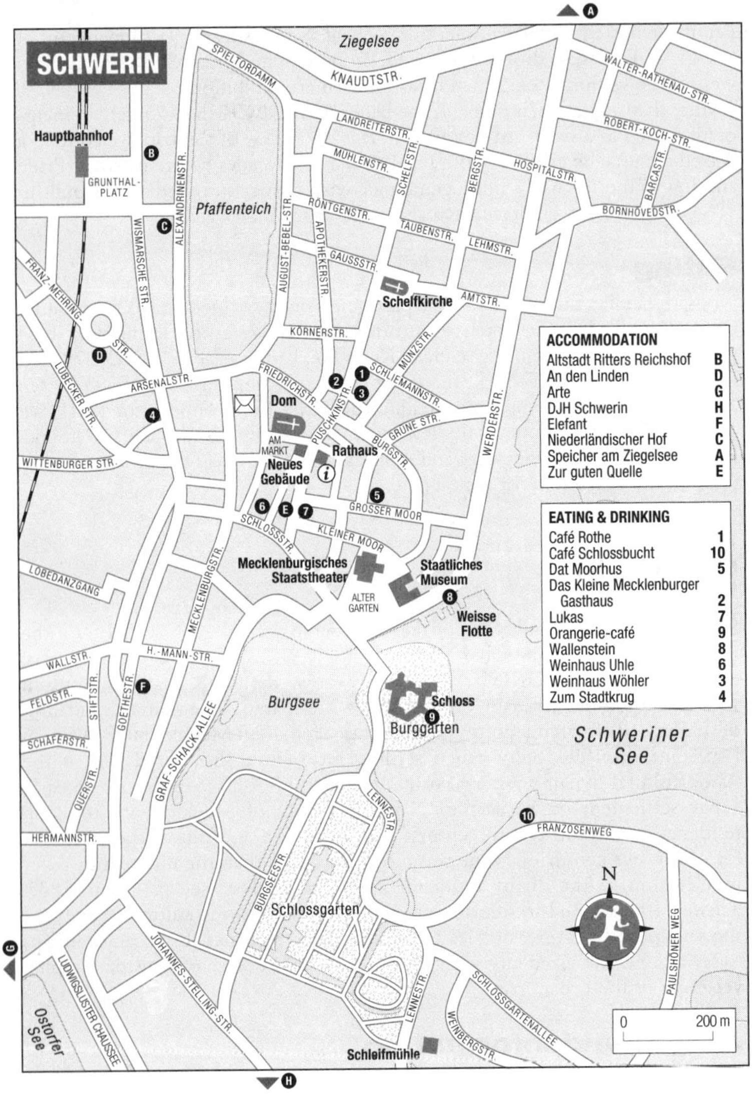
SCHWERIN
A
B
C
D
G
H
Ziegelsee
Hauptbahnhof
GRUNTHAL-PLATZ
Pfaffenteich
SPIELTORDAMM
KNAUDTSTR.
WALTER-RATHENAU-STR.
ROBERT-KOCH-STR.
LANDREITERSTR.
MÜHLENSTR.
SCHELFSTR.
BERGSTR.
HOSPITALSTR.
BARCASTR.
BORNHÖVEDSTR.
RÖNTGENSTR.
TAUBENSTR.
LEHMSTR.
ALEXANDRINENSTR.
WISMARSCHE STR.
AUGUST-BEBEL-STR.
APOTHEKERSTR.
GAUSSSTR.
Schelfkirche
AMTSTR.
FRANZ-MEHRING-STR.
KÖRNERSTR.
MÜNZSTR.
FRIEDRICHSTR.
SCHLIEMANNSTR.
ARSENALSTR.
LÜBECKER STR.
Dom
PUSCHKINSTR.
GRÜNE STR.
WERDERSTR.
AM MARKT
Rathaus
BURGSTR.
WITTENBURGER STR.
Neues Gebäude
GROSSER MOOR
SCHLOSSSTR.
KLEINER MOOR
Mecklenburgisches Staatstheater
Staatliches Museum
ALTER GARTEN
Weisse Flotte
LOBEDANZGANG
MECKLENBURGSTR.
H.-MANN-STR.
WALLSTR.
FELDSTR.
STIFTSTR.
GOETHESTR.
GRAF-SCHACK-ALLEE
Burgsee
Schloss
Burggarten
Schweriner See
SCHÄFERSTR.
QUERSTR.
HERMANNSTR.
LENNÉSTR.
FRANZOSENWEG
BURGSEESTR.
Schlossgarten
N
PAULSHÖHNER WEG
JOHANNES-STELLING-STR.
LUDWIGSLUSTER CHAUSSEE
SCHLOSSGARTENALLEE
WEINBERGSTR.
Ostorfer See
Schleifmühle
0
200 m
ACCOMMODATION
Altstadt Ritters Reichshof B
An den Linden D
Arte G
DJH Schwerin H
Elefant F
Niederländischer Hof C
Speicher am Ziegelsee A
Zur guten Quelle E
EATING & DRINKING
Café Rothe 1
Café Schlossbucht 10
Dat Moorhus 5
Das Kleine Mecklenburger Gasthaus 2
Lukas 7
Orangerie-café 9
Wallenstein 8
Weinhaus Uhle 6
Weinhaus Wöhler 3
Zum Stadtkrug 4

Accommodation

Alongside a decent spread of central **accommodation**, many in elegant nineteenth-century houses **private rooms** (❷) can be booked through the tourist office. The nearest campsite is lakeside *Seehof* (ⓣ0385/51 25 40, ⓦwww.ferienpark-seehof.de) in the village of its name 10km north.

Altstadt Ritters Reichshof Grunthalplatz 15–17 ⓣ0385/56 57 98, ⓦwww.altstadthotel-schwerin.de. Opposite the Hauptbahnhof, old-fashioned place at a good price; decor is rather fussy but inoffensive. ❸

An den Linden Franz-Mehring-Str. 26 ⓣ0385/51 20 84, ⓦwww.hotel-an-den-linden.de. Pleasant, traditional mid-range hotel in a nineteenth-century house, located between the Altstadt and train station. ❹

Arte Dorfstr. 6, Krebsförden-Dorf ☎ 0385/63 450, ⓦ www.hotel-arte.de. Elegant country-modern-styled four-star in a former farmhouse 4km south of the centre. Catch local buses or disembark at Schwerin-Görries train station. ❹

DJH Schwerin Waldschulweg 3 ☎ 0385/326 00 06, ⓦ www.jugendherbergen-mv.de. There's a youth hostel in a leafy setting 4km from the centre served by bus #14 to "Jungendherberge". Dorms from €17.50.

Elefant Goethestr. 39–41 ☎ 0385/540 80, ⓦ www.hotel-elefant.de. A reliable mid-range choice in a late 1800s building just south of the main square, with three-star mod cons and business-style accommodation – rooms to the rear are larger and quieter. ❹

Niederländischer Hof Alexandrinenstr. 12–13 ☎ 0385/59 11 00, ⓦ www.niederlaendischer-hof.de. Schwerin's finest, overlooking the Pfaffenteich lake and effortlessly relaxed. Public areas allude to a late 1800s country manor, and the elegant rooms have charm. ❺

Speicher am Ziegelsee Speicherstr. 11 ☎ 0385/500 30, ⓦ www.speicher-hotel.com. Fluffy bathrobes and spacious rooms with laid-back designer style – modern Mediterranean, staff say – in a renovated warehouse on the waterfront. Also has a sauna and gym. ❺–❻

Zur guten Quelle Schusterstr. 12 ☎ 0385/56 59 85, ⓦ www.zur-guten-quelle.m-vp.de. Modern rooms above a restaurant well located on a quiet street at the core of the Altstadt. ❸

The Altstadt

Heart of the Altstadt, **Am Markt** is as good a place as any to start a tour, boxed in on opposite sides by the **Rathaus**, with the mock battlements beloved of the 1800s, and the Neoclassical Neues Gebäude, home to a café and art exhibitions. Both reveal more eloquently than words the town's aspirations as it flourished from the guiding hand of Mecklenburg-Schwerin Grand Duke Paul Friedrich Franz II in the mid-1800s. Streets to its east such as cobbled Buschstrasse are a slice of the half-timbered Altstadt prior to its reinvention.

North of the square stands the Gothic **Dom**, a royal lion by its gateway honouring Saxon duke Henry the Lion, the twelfth-century power-broker who founded an earlier cathedral here. The centrepiece of high lancet arches in its whitewashed interior is a fifteenth-century *Triumphkreuz* snaffled from Wismar when its Marienkirche was bombed. Its gold and green buds are intended as an allegory of the crucifix as a tree of life, although there's not much triumphal about its weary Christ. No one pays much attention to a Gothic triptych altarpiece (1440) beneath but its sculpted reliefs by a Lübeck craftsman are excellent, showing the Way of the Cross, the Crucifixion and the Descent into and Victory over Hell. The tombs of Mecklenburg dukes lie in the choir aisle, the finest carved by an Antwerp master for Duke Christopher in the northern chapel. A 219-step hike up the tower (May–Oct Mon–Sat 10am–5pm, Sun noon–5pm; Nov–April Mon–Sat 11am–2pm, Sun noon–3pm; €1.50) rewards you with views over the town and lakes.

Northeast of the Dom, on the right bank of the Pfaffenteich lake, is **Schelfstadt**, a quiet quarter of half-timbered streets planned in 1705 as a separate craftsmen's village, then swallowed into Schwerin's urban sprawl in the mid-1800s. Today it's an atmospheric spot to loaf about, nosing into the Baroque parish church Schelfkirche in a central square or browsing shops on Münzstrasse and temporary exhibitions in Schleswig-Holstein-Haus (Puschkinstrasse 12; daily 10am–6pm; €3).

South of the Markt, Schlossstrasse, lined with crumbling Rococo villas in hues of ivory and sand, provides the first glimpse of the fabulous Schloss. Its rebuild also freed up space on the former castle garden to erect the Neoclassical **Staatliches Museum** (mid-April to mid-Oct daily 10am–6pm; mid-Oct to mid-April Tues–Sun 10am–5pm; €3; ⓦ www.museum-schwerin.de) on Alter Garten, which houses the art collection of the Mecklenburg dukes – who were avid collectors – and would do any large city credit. Beyond Cranach's lovely *Venus and Amor as Honey Thieves* is a wealth of sixteenth- and seventeenth-century

Dutch and Flemish painting that stars big guns such as Rubens, Rembrandt and two vivacious Hals' portraits, and the world's finest collection of Jean-Baptiste Oudry, a French court painter known for his still lifes and portraits. Gainsborough represents British portraiture with a full length Mecklenburg royal Queen Charlotte, and Caspar David Friedrich kicks off the nineteenth century, while in the twentieth-century section there are Ernst Barlach sculptures and a superb collection of Duchamp's artistic jokes.

The former court stables (Marstall) 100m north on Werderstrasse holds feats of transport engineering – from Rostock-built aircraft-ship hybrid the Hydrowing to dinky GDR-era Trabant cars manufactured in Zwickau – as the **Technische Landesmuseum** (Tues–Sat 10am–5pm; €3; Ⓦ www.tlm-mv.de).

The Schloss and gardens

After the sensible edifices in the centre, the outrageous turrets and gilt of the **Schloss** are gloriously over the top. They are the whim of Paul Friedrich Franz II, a treat to himself for decamping court from Ludwigslust to Schwerin in 1837. The duke pointed to the Loire's Chambord Château and told architects Georg Adolph Demmler and Friedrich August Stüler to remodel his ancestors' Dutch Renaissance-style castle accordingly. They did, and threw into the mix a polyglot of architectural exotica – fairytale turrets and lantern cupolas, Russian onion-bulb domes, a couple of Moorish pavilions – and topped the lot with a gilded turret like a crown. An equestrian statue of Niklot in defiant pose, the last free prince of a Slavic tribe whose settlement occupied the palace's islet until smashed by Henry the Lion in 1160, adds a touch of imperial bombast typical of its time. The pomp continues in the rich decor of the former living, social and ceremonial rooms within (tours April 15–Oct 14 daily 10am–6pm, otherwise Tues–Sun 10am–5pm; €4; Ⓦ www.schloss-schwerin.de). Of those on show – some rooms are reserved for the state parliament that sits here – the **Rauchenzimmer** (Smoking Room) and **Teezimmer** (Tea Room) are a decadent display of gilt, stucco and carving; the opulence continues upstairs with two boasts about heraldry in the **Thronsaal** (Throne Hall) and

▲ Schwerin's Schloss

next-door **Ahnengalerie** (Ancestors' Gallery), both with fine parquet floors in delicious shades of chocolate and honey. Another highlight is the original **palace chapel**, a Renaissance gem only tinkered with by the addition of neo-Gothic lancet windows.

The **Burggarten** surrounding the Schloss lake-side is a splendid piece of nineteenth-century landscape gardening, with Neoclassical statuary of *Victory* by Christian Daniel Rauch, the sculptor trusted for most grand public statuary in Prussia, including the famous Goethe-Schiller monument in Weimar, a handsome wrought-iron orangerie (now a café) and a grotto. A causeway links to the formal Baroque-style Schlossgarten, and a twenty-minute walk to its southeast corner is the Schleifmühle (April–Nov daily 10am–5pm; €2.50), the oldest grinding mill in Europe whose original 1702 building was rebuilt in the 1800s to crush semi-precious gems for the new palace. Inside are so-so displays of local history.

The Schweriner See

If the Schloss is impressive from land, it is a romantic fantasy worthy of Walt Disney when seen from the **Schweriner See**. Cruisers of Weisse Flotte line (May–Sept; ☎0385/55 77 70, Ⓦwww.weisseflotteschwerin.de) sail from a wharf north of the Schloss on a variety of scenic cruises. The most frequent circuit is that around the lake and its nature-reserve island, Kaninchenwerder (1hr 15min; €9.50) – it departs approximately hourly from June to August, less frequently at other times. Alternatively Weisse Flotte's 3-Lake-Line shuttles three times a day between Schwerin and Frankenhorst northwest reached via a mosaic of smaller lakes, then disembarks at Zippendorf (€3), a south-shore resort-suburb of villas and restaurants with a small beach, or idyllic Kaninchenwerder (€5). From Zippendorf, it's a pretty four-kilometre walk on a footpath beside the lake back to Schwerin.

Eating and drinking

The liveliest spots for a drink are the lounge bars at the top of Puschkinstrasse, some of which rustle up tapas in the evenings.

Restaurants

Das Kleine Mecklenburger Gasthaus Puschkinstr. 37 ☎0385/555 96 66. Upmarket regional dishes such as *Mecklenburger Rippenbraten* (pork ribs with crackling) served with red cabbage, prunes and apple in a classy rustic restaurant.

Lukas Grosser Moor 5 ☎0385/56 59 35. A relaxed bistro-style restaurant that specializes in fish and seafood – seasonal eel and zander fresh from the lakes plus imported international species.

Wallenstein Werderstr. 140 ☎0385/557 77 55. Dine lake-side on the terrace of a modern restaurant on the Weisse Flotte quay. Local fish is the focus of its self-declared "*Gepflegte Küche*" (refined cooking) – try whitebait-style local delicacy *Maräne*.

Weinhaus Uhle Schusterstr. 13–15 ☎0385/477 30 30. The 1751-vintage quarters of a family of wine merchants has interiors in many styles but one short menu: classy German cooking such as duck breast in Grand Marnier sauce and a penchant for alcoholic desserts such as Campari parfait. Wonderful wine-list, obviously.

Weinhaus Wöhler Puschkinstr. 26 ☎0385/55 58 30. Historic tavern restaurant whose stained glass and wooden partitions are a date back to the mid-1800s – worth waiting for a seat here rather than in the anonymous atrium area.

Zum Stadtkrug Wismarsche Str. 126 ☎0385/593 66 93. The local brewhouse: fresh beers acclaimed by connoisseurs and a menu of pub food at low prices.

Cafés

Café Rothe Puschkinstr. 14. Elegant Art Deco-styled café of the old school – classic confectionery and gâteaux made in-house make it perfect for *Kaffee und Kuchen*.

Café Schlossbucht Franzosenweg 19. A former fisherman's house, this lake-side place beyond the Schlossgarten is a lovely spot for snacks and a drink over superlative Schloss views. Closed Mon.

Dat Moor Hus Grosser Moor 42. Lovely little café in a half-timbered house between the Schloss and Altstadt with contemporary rustic decor. Closed Sun.

Orangerie-café Schwerin Schloss. Wicker chairs and palms set the tone for the most graceful lunch spot, serving the likes of smoked salmon and salads as well as gâteaux.

Ludwigslust

Although nowhere near as flash, **LUDWIGSLUST** is the ideal foil to the Land capital, best treated as a day-trip from it. Throughout their history the pair have been on opposite ends of fortune's see-saw – Schwerin's rise was Ludwigslust's demise, leaving it as a well-preserved specimen of a Baroque ducal town. For nearly fifty years until Grand Duke Paul Friedrich Franz II returned to Schwerin 35km north, Ludwigslust was the heart of the Mecklenburg-Schleswig court, realized as a spacious planned town laid at the feet of the duke's **Schloss** – no doubt about priorities here. His predecessor, Grand Duke Friedrich I, commissioned a court palace in the hunting grounds of his father, Christian Ludwig II. Money problems dogged court architect Johann Joachim Busch almost as soon as the building began in 1772 – as the joke went, Ludwig's Lust (pleasure) was Friedrich's Arbeit (work). Behind the majestic facade of a palace that dithers between late Baroque and Classical is the same humble brick used for the courtiers' houses on approach road Schlossstrasse. Busch was even more creative within (April 15–Oct 14 daily 10am–6pm, otherwise Tues–Sun 10am–5pm; €5; ⓦ www.schloss-ludwigslust.de). In place of stucco and carved wood, he employed papier-mâché. A minor cottage industry churned out the euphemistically named Ludwigsluster Carton from a factory in what is now the Rathaus (Schlossstrasse 38). The pinnacle of Busch's achievement is the Goldene Saal, a Louis XVI-style galleried ballroom fit for a Cinderella ball whose gilded Rococo mouldings are all glorious fakes. Even the reliefs of putti above the door turn out to be trompe l'oeil. A carved grandfather clock and Venus de'Medici in later rooms also prove to be papier-mâché. Many of the oils, however, are genuine works by French court painter Jean-Baptiste Oudry.

The garden that extends north and west behind the Schloss was landscaped in naturalistic style by the ubiquitous Peter Joseph Lenné. An assortment of objects scattered among its woodlands carved by alleys and canals provide goals for a stroll: a grotto, a tea pavilion and church, fountains, statuary, two mausoleums, a bizarre monument to Friedrich's favourite horse (Pferdedenkmal), and the Schweizerhaus, a Swiss-style summerhouse for Duchess Louise that is now a café. Going the other way from the Schloss you cross the cascade viewing platform and a broad grass oval ringed by palace-workers' cottages to reach the **Stadtkirche**. Its severe classical facade is another of Busch's, and inside the court showman is equally theatrical: a floor-to-ceiling altar painting of the Annunciation rises behind gold papier-mâché candlesticks and at the rear is a ducal gallery like an opera box. "Friedrich the Pious" himself lies in a plain sarcophagus in the centre – they say it took 24 horses two days to drag its granite slab from a nearby village to be carved.

Practicalities

The **Bahnhof** on the Schwerin line is at the northern edge of the town, twenty minutes from the centre: Bahnhofstrasse segues into Friedrich-Naumann-Allee which leads to the Schloss. The **tourist office** (May to mid-Sept Mon, Tues, Thurs & Fri 9am–noon & 1–6pm, Wed 9am–noon; mid-Sept to April Mon–Fri

9am–noon, Mon, Tues & Thurs also 1–4pm; ☎03874/52 62 51, ⓦwww
.ludwigslust.de) is at Schlossstrasse 36. **Bike rental** is from Fahrradhaus Winkel-
mann at Lindenstrasse 17. There are two appealing **cafés** in the Schloss and its
grounds, and cafés and restaurants line Schlossstrasse.

Güstrow

Once a capital of the Mecklenburg duchy, **GÜSTROW** lives in its dotage as a
pretty provincial small town on the fringes of Mecklenburg's lake country. For
centuries its local hero was Albrecht von Wallenstein, a duke who distinguished
himself as supreme commander of the Habsburg armies during the Thirty
Years' War. Today, however, Güstrow declares itself Der Barlachstadt (the Barlach
Town) in honour of the Expressionist sculptor Ernst Barlach (see box below)
who spent half of his life in the town and whose humanist works chime more
comfortably with our age. In his wake have come a few galleries that add to the
historic appeal of Güstrow's cobbled lanes.

Arrival, information and accommodation

On the Schwerin and Rostock lines, Güstrow **Bahnhof** is ten minutes north of
the centre of the Altstadt. The **tourist office** (May–Sept Mon–Fri 9am–7pm, Sat
9.30am–4pm, Sun 10am–4pm; Oct–April Mon–Fri 9am–6pm, Sat 9.30am–1pm;
☎03843/68 10 23, ⓦwww.guestrow.de) faces Franz-Parr-Platz on the other side
of the centre at Domstrasse 9, reached off the central Markt. Private rooms (❶–❷)
are booked through the tourist office.

Ernst Barlach

Ernst Barlach (1870–1938) is the finest artist no one knows outside Germany.
Empathetic and with a keen sense of pathos, the Expressionist sculptor, graphic
artist and playwright was born in a village near Hamburg as the son of a country
physician. He studied sculpture in Dresden and Paris before he travelled, first
throughout German cities, picking up work for *Jugend*, the magazine that pioneered
Jugendstil, then abroad. It was a trip across the Russian steppes in 1906 that made
him. He filled sketchbooks with stocky figures with exaggerated facial expressions
– tortured, helpless, radiant, primitive – based on the peasants he met. In them he
saw an intense Christian humility that chimed with his passion for German medieval
art. These sketches served as the basis of his vigorous, rough-hewn works with an
archaic power and inner spirituality that has sometimes seen Barlach pigeonholed
as "modern Gothic".

The horrors of World War I only intensified his humanism – Barlach, by now a keen
reader of Dostoyevsky and Tolstoy, quickly lost his enthusiasm for the war as a means
to shake up the ruling elite – and by 1930 he was a leading figure of German art and
was commissioned for a large war memorial in Magdeburg Cathedral. Such socialist
leanings did not square with the militaristic hubris of the National Socialists, however.
His bronze of *Christ and St Thomas* was labelled "Two Monkeys in Nightshirts" in the
Nazis' Munich exhibition *"Entartete Kunst"* (Degenerate Art), held in 1937, and many
of his works were smelted. He died in Rostock a year later and was buried beside his
father in Ratzeburg (see p.789).

Like fellow Expressionist and "degenerate" Käthe Kollwitz, Barlach's place in the
German canon was restored after the war: direct and immediately accessible, his
works celebrate an empathy and humanism that strikes a chord.

Boulevard-Pension Pferdemarkt 25 ☎03843/ 46 44 60. Nothing flash, just a homely traditional pension on a pedestrian street north of the Markt. ❷

Burg Schlitz Hohen Demzin ☎03996/127 00, ⓦwww.burg-schlitz.de. The most sumptuous of several luxury manor hotels in the vicinity, this late 1800s princely palace set in parkland is stuffed with antiques and bespoke Biedermeier furnishings – turn south at Teterow 20km east of Güstrow. Doubles from €255. ❾

DJH Güstrow Schabernack 70 ☎03843/84 00 44, ⓦwww.guestrow.jugendherberge.de. The youth

hostel is in a complex of small houses 3km east of the centre near Atelierhaus, reached by bus #252. Dorms from €20.50.

Gästehaus Am Schlosspark Neuwieder Weg ☎03843/24 59 90, ⓦwww.gaestehaus-guestrow .de. In a former hospital at the opposite end of the Schloss gardens, some of whose simple rooms have kitchenettes. ❷–❸

Stadt Güstrow Markt 2–3 ☎03843/78 00, ⓦwww.nordik-hotels.de. Comfy three-star that, like sister hotel *Altstadt* (Baustr. 8–10; same contacts; ❸–❹), possesses an unrivalled location in the historic centre. ❹–❺

The Town

The centrepiece of the **Altstadt** is the Markt, filled back to back by an oversized Baroque Rathaus and the **Pfarrkirche St Marien**. The sixteenth-century furnishings in the parish church testify to Güstrow's early wealth as a ducal capital, not least the Gothic high altar by Brussels' Jan Borman so rich in gilt it smothers the Passion tableaux. Above hangs the triumphal cross thanks to Ernst Barlach – the artist inspired by the energy of craggy medieval sculpture urged the town council to restore the fifteenth-century work from a storeroom where it had been consigned as too crude. Barlach also contributed the child-like *Angel of Hope* terracotta plaque on the right-hand pillar beneath.

The best introduction to Barlach there is, however, is the **Dom** southeast of the Markt in one of the most picturesque corners of the Altstadt. Hidden in the half-light of the north aisle of its Gothic three-nave basilica, his *Flying Angel* levitates eyes-closed towards the Divine. How the Third Reich regime could condemn this serene angel as "degenerate art" is a mystery, yet the original, the most famous work of Germany's premier Expressionist, was smelted down, though not before a cast had been taken in secret – this copy was recast after the war. He also created the apostle plaque and Crucifixion in the same aisle, both less appealing than kinetic sculptures of the apostles by a Lübeck master in the nave; Barlach cited them as an influence. Other eye-catchers are in the choir: the swaggering Renaissance funerary monuments of Mecklenburg dukes – Duke Ulrich and his wives from Denmark and Mecklenburg kneel in front of a ducal family tree – and a Gothic high altar by Hamburg's Hinrik Bornemann.

Fran-Parr-Platz east of the Dom most clearly recalls the legacy of the Mecklenburg duchy. The former theatre houses a dry **town museum** (Tues–Fri 10am–5pm, Sat 1–4pm, Sun 11am–4pm; €3.50) and there are well-lit modern art exhibitions in a half-timbered former wool store behind in **Galerie Wollhalle** (same times; €2.50). The ducal Schloss itself (April 15– Oct 14 daily, otherwise Tues–Sun 10am–6pm; €5; ⓦwww.schloss-guestrow.de) is a splendid pile that synthesizes the best of Italian, French and German style as an expression of founder Duke Ulrich's sophistication. Although Napoleon and the Nazis, who used one of Germany's finest Renaissance palaces as a prison, have taken their toll on its interiors, renovation has restored the fine stucco in the south wing, especially in the first-floor Festsaal whose global hunting scenes seem to spring into action as you look. The most valuable pieces among its sculptures, paintings and *objéts d'art* are the ground-floor works by Tintoretto and Maerten de Vos. The latter's *Menagerie* is testament to the enthusiasm for the exotic that gripped imaginations during the Age of Exploration, hence its image of a unicorn (dismissed as dubious even at the time) set in the recently discovered West Indies.

Back to Barlach: the world's most extensive collection of his works is shared between three gallery spaces. The most convenient is the **Getrudenkapelle** (April–Oct Tues–Sun 10am–5pm, July & Aug also Mon 10am–5pm; Nov–March Tues–Sun 11am–4pm; €4, combination ticket €7; ⓦwww .ernst-barlach-stiftung.de) at the northeast side of the Altstadt, a deconsecrated Gothic chapel that sets off the medieval inspirations in his sculpture. Barlach's studio **Atelierhaus** (same times; €5, combination ticket €7), 3km east of the Altstadt, reveals the artist's profound humanism in works such as *Singing Man*, while an adjacent **cabinet** (same ticket) hangs the artist's graphics. Sited above a beach behind the Inselsee, the latter two can be reached by bus #252 or via the Barlachweg footpath which branches right off main road Plauer Strasse. It's a pleasant stroll, especially on the return trip with views of the town across the water. Barlach wrote of it as a "tempest of two towers from the hazy city, this bleached city of mist … a city whose bells suddenly broke out into a marvellous peal across the water".

Eating and drinking

All the hotels have good restaurants. Alternatively, *Barlach Stuben* at Plauer Strasse 7 prepares traditional regional dishes daily, and *Villa Italia* on Domplatz rustles up Italian and Mediterranean dishes (closed Mon). For café culture, *Café Kupper* at Domstrasse 14 (closed Sat & Sun am), a bastion of *Kaffee und Kuchen* for over 150 years, is a charmer with a sweet garden, and wine merchant *Weinhaus Im Hof* at Hageböcher Strasse 4 (closed Sat pm & Sun) has a few benches in a courtyard.

Neubrandenburg

Following a double whammy of Allied bombs and communist pipe-dreams, **NEUBRANDENBURG** at the eastern end of the Mecklenburg Lake District has few delusions about its looks. The Allies smashed eighty percent of the Altstadt, and with accommodation at a premium, the GDR re-created Neubrandenburg in the bold socialist-realist aesthetic beloved of their urban planners. The result: breeze-block architecture with a charm bypass. However, Neubrandenburg does boast one of the most intact **medieval town fortifications** in Germany, girdling the unlovable centre within walls up to 7m high. Straddling the wall are the **Wiekhäuser**, half-timbered houses that were three-storey sentry posts mounted on bastions every 30m until they were rendered redundant by cannon power, then peace after the Thirty Years' War, and were converted into homes. Half the original 52 remain, highly coveted as residential houses or converted into restaurants and craftshops.

The greatest surprise on a 2.3km circuit of fortifications that date from the mid-1300s is the gateways mounted roughly at each point of the compass that are as decorative as they are defensive. If you come from the Bahnhof north of the centre, then walk clockwise (turn left) once inside the walls, you reach the **Friedländer Tor**. The double-gateway on the exposed northeast flank was the first built, begun in 1300 and later fronted by a semicircular cannon battery. Fluted columns rising to Gothic points on the inner gate are textbook Hanseatic style. East in the walls' compass, the **Neues Tor** dates from the late 1400s and features on its inner side a line of enigmatic robed figures with raised fists whose purpose and identity has baffled historians. Similar figures stand on the inside of the two-gate **Stargarder Tor** that guards the southern entry to the town. The most decorative gateway – and the highest – is the **Treptower Tor** on the western side; brick rosettes spin across the facade of a 32m structure given rhythm through lancet arches and battlements. It holds a small museum of archeology (Tues–Sun 10am–5pm; €5) from Stone Age to Germanic and Slavic tribes.

Other than to visit the tourist office (see below), the only reason to venture into the centre is for an aerial view from fourteen storeys up in the **Haus der Kultur und Bildung** tower-block, the bull's-eye of the GDR's new town. There's also a great *Ostalgie* kitsch cocktail bar beneath, *Café Kori* (daily from 4pm).

It's a twenty-minute walk outside the centre from the Stargarder Tor through the Kulturpark to reach the **Tollensee** southwest. Lake and river cruises depart from a quay at the far end of the Kulturpark (May–Oct 2–3 daily; 1hr 30min–2hr; €9/10; ⓦwww.fahrgastschiff-mudderschulten.de), and a passenger ferry (Easter–Oct 3 daily €2 per stop or €4 one-way; ⓦwww.neu-sw.de) zigzags between quays of the elongated lake. A watersports centre at the quay (Augustastrasse 7; ⓣ0171/401 34 88) rents rowboats and dinghies.

Practicalities

The **Bahnhof** is north of the Altstadt on the other side of Ringstrasse, a bypass-cum-roundabout that growls ceaselessly around the town walls. The **tourist office** (May–Sept Mon–Fri 10am–7pm, Sat 10am–6pm, Sun 10am–4pm; Oct–April Mon–Fri 10am–6pm, Sat 10am–4pm; ⓣ01805/17 03 30, ⓦwww.neubrandenburg-touristinfo.de) is dead centre at Stargarder Strasse 17. Because hotel **accommodation** in Neubrandenburg is far from inspiring, it's worth making a reservation in one of the Wiekhäuser, either through the tourist office or try cottage-style *Wiekhaus 28*, 100m from the Treptower Tor (ⓣ0395/566 65 71, ⓔherbertwegner@gmx.de; ❷). *Hotel Weinert*, Ziegelbergstrasse 23 (ⓣ0395/581 23, ⓦwww.hotel-weinert.de; rooms & Wiekhaus ❸), also manages a Wiekhaus alongside passable old-fashioned rooms in a small hotel. The business-class *Radisson SAS*, Treptower Strasse 1 (ⓣ0395/558 60, ⓦwww.neubrandenburg.radissonsas.com; ❹–❺), is the only hotel within the walls. *Campingplatz Gatsch Eck* (ⓣ0395/566 51 52, ⓦwww.campingplatz-gatscheck.de) occupies a spot among woods on the west shore of the Tollensee – passenger ferries drop you at a dedicated quay.

There are two historic addresses for **eating**: *Wiekhaus 45*, beside the Neues Tor, serves plates of freshwater fish in a simple cottage room or a smarter upper floor; and *Zur Lohmühle* (closed Sun eve), in a half-timbered mill-house outside the Stargarder Tor, is a traditional place of gently ticking clocks and images of old Neubrandenburg, with a large menu. Its beer garden is pleasant for a drink in summer. *Augusta's*, at the south end of the Kulturpark, at Lindenstrasse 6, is the locals' choice for lunch or drinks by the lake.

Müritz National Park

Around 30km south of Neubrandenburg, two swathes of forest, heath and moorland that make up the **MÜRITZ NATIONAL PARK** (Nationalpark Müritz) sandwich the Baroque backwater of **Neustrelitz**. By far the largest area is that to the east of the town, which represents nearly three-quarters of the park's total 322 square kilometres and is characterized by its large pine forests and open moorland, although there are also ancient beech woods in the Serrahn area, whose virgin forest is largely thanks to a former incarnation as the hunting ground of the Grand Dukes of Mecklenburg-Strelitz. The focus west is water, namely **Lake Müritz**, the second largest lake in Germany, whose reed-choked east shore falls within the park boundary, and over a hundred smaller lakes that lie east. Not surprisingly, the park is a haven for water birds: ospreys and white-tailed sea eagles breed in the area, and storks and cranes stalk among water lilies in the shallows. Sky-blue moor frogs are usually heard rather than seen among the reeds, while red deer roam the remote woodland areas. The main **park office** is inconveniently located at Hohenzieritz village, 20km southwest of Neubrandenburg, Schlossplatz 3 (☎039824/25 20, ⓦwww.nationalpark -mueritz.de). More accessible is **Waren**, a slow-paced resort at the lake's north tip. Here, an aquarium and displays on local ecology in the **Müritzeum** nature discovery centre (daily: April–Oct 10am–7pm; Nov–March 10am–6pm; €7.50; ⓦwww.mueritzeum.de) are as good an introduction to the lake as any. Alongside the ubiquitous cruises are a number of motorboat charter operators in Waren; ask at the tourist centre (see below). For many visitors, however, the appeal of the **Mecklenburgische Seenplatte** (Mecklenburg Lake District) is **canoe-and-camp** expeditions through the mosaic of lakes west of Neustrelitz. The longest route begins at the Zierker See directly west of Neustrelitz then traces a large U to end at Schillersdorf west, paddling around 15km a day between camps; you need around a week to cover the lot. However, the area abounds in short circuits of two or three days. Leaflets of routes are provided by the many rental outlets in the park, a list of which is on the national park website or can be sourced via the tourist office in Neustrelitz.

Practicalities

Neustrelitz is on **train** lines from Neubrandenburg and Rostock among others; Waren has direct train services from Rostock. If you come by car, be aware that driving is prohibited within the park area – park bus service Müritz-Linie (€7 bus day-ticket, €14 bus and boat; ⓦwww.nationalparkticket.de) loops southwest from Waren to Boek on the east bank of the Müritz lake.

Tourist information centres in the area include: in Waren, Neuer Markt 21 (May–Sept daily 9am–8pm; Oct–April Mon–Fri 9am–6pm, Sat 10am–3pm; ☎03991/66 61 83, ⓦwww.waren-tourismus.de), also sells park maps and can book accommodation in the area, much of it in holiday homes; and at Neustrelitz, Strelitzer Strasse 1 (May–Sept Mon–Fri 9am–6pm, Sat & Sun 9.30am–1pm; Oct–April Mon–Thurs 9am–noon & 1–4pm, Fri 9am–noon; ☎03981/25 31 19, ⓦwww.neustrelitz.de). Other sources of information include the Neubrandenburg tourist office, Mecklenburg Lake District website ⓦwww.mecklenburgische-seenplatte.de, and regional web portal Müritz Online, ⓦwww.mueritz.de.

Among **canoe and camping** operators are: Haveltourist (☎03981/247 90, ⓦwww.haveltourist.de), which offers combination rental-and-camp deals in its nine campsites throughout the area from a base at *Havelberge Camping and Holiday Resort*, 5km southwest of Neustrelitz near Gross Quassow; Kanu Mühle (☎039832/203 50, ⓦwww.kanu-muehle.de) two train stops from Neustrelitz in Wesenburg; and Kanustation Mirow (☎039833/22 098, ⓦwww .kanustation.de), four stops from Neustrelitz. All offer guided tours on request. Note that most outfits only operate from April to October and that camping is strictly in designated sites only.

Travel details

Trains

Güstrow (hourly; 30min); Stralsund (hourly; 1hr); Waren (every 2hr; 55min); Wismar (hourly; 1hr 10min).
Neubrandenburg to: Güstrow (hourly; 1hr 15min); Neustrelitz (hourly; 30min); Stralsund (hourly; 1hr 20min).

Rostock to: Bad Doberan (hourly; 20min); Bergen, Rügen (hourly; 1hr 40min); Berlin (fourteen daily; 2hr 20–2hr 40min).
Schwerin to: Berlin (12 daily; 2hr 25min); Ludwigslust (hourly; 30min); Rostock (hourly; 1hr); Stralsund (every 2hr; 2hr).
Stralsund to: Binz, Rügen (14 daily; 50min); Greifswald (every 30min; 20min); Neubrandenburg (hourly; 1hr 30min); Züssow (every 30min; 40min).

Contexts

Contexts

History...857

Books..882

History

For most of its history Germany has been a geographical rather than a political term, used to describe a collection of minor states with broadly common interests and culture, whose roots can be traced back almost three millennia, with for much of the last two thousand years Germanic peoples holding sway over large areas of Western Europe north of the Alps. It wasn't until the late nineteenth century, however, that a drive to unify most German-speaking lands began to define Germany's modern-day political history. Since its inception as a defined country in 1871 Germany has often been at the forefront of international politics, competing with France, Britain, Italy, Russia, Japan and the USA on the world stage, most notoriously during the conflicting ambitions that brought two world wars. Their legacy, along with that of the Holocaust, have defined Germany for much of the second half of the twentieth century – battle-scarred and divided in two at the frontline of the Cold War. It is only relatively recently, following reunification, and the move of the political capital back to Berlin in 1999, that the country feels like it is finishing the process of rebuilding, not only physically with legendary Germanic industriousness, but also in terms of national pride. With most of this process complete, Germany is once again at the forefront of international politics, spearheading the expansion of the European Union and becoming ever more engaged worldwide.

Beginnings

Archeologists estimate that the area that covers modern-day Germany has been inhabited for about 60,000 years, and there is evidence of hunter-gatherer activity dating from about 8000 BC, with more substantial remains of Stone Age farming settlements evident from 4000 BC onwards. It was around 750 BC that tribes speaking **Germanic languages** came from Scandinavia. Over the next thousand years or so their influence increased across all the territories of Europe, which were largely in **Roman** hands; by the late fifth century AD they had effectively taken over as the continent's most powerful force – replacing the western Roman Empire with a number of **Germanic successor states**. Of these, the **Franks** proved the most successful and by the ninth century they commanded most of modern Germany, as well as France and northern Italy.

The early Germans

The first Germans came from what is now Sweden and Denmark – possibly driven by climate change, by expanding populations and a desire to conquer weaker, less well-organized peoples in the south. So powerful were these Germanic people that by the birth of Christ they came to dominate all territories north of the Danube, an area so large that they began to form into distinct tribes. Other peoples coexisted in the region, particularly Celtic tribes in southern Germany, who seem in time to have gradually integrated into German culture, rather than being conquered or displaced.

The early Germans lived in wooden houses, practised mixed settled farming and ate a gruel of seeds and weeds, but were not without sophistication. They had a class system, in which chiefs and powerful warriors dominated each tribe, worshipped war gods, such as Odin (Wodan) to whom they sacrificed defeated enemies, and were buried with jewellery and fine weapons. The various tribes were allied to one another through the worship of particular cults, which usually involved merry annual festivals that doubled as opportunities to trade and peaceably settle disputes.

Roman coexistence

Around the time of the birth of Christ, the Romans' northward expansion brought them into contact with Germanic tribes. In around 12 BC significant numbers of Roman forces crossed the Danube and Rhine in a fierce campaign that saw the massacre of three Roman legions by the Germanic leader Arminius in the Teutoburg Forest in 9 AD. Unsurprisingly then, the Romans seemed to decide that these barbarians were too much trouble, and so simply consolidated their power by dotting frontier garrisons along both rivers – one of which later grew to become the city of Koblenz.

Border raiding was a part of life, but an alliance system involving various German tribes created a porous frontier that allowed the Germans to trade and travel freely and glean much from cultural contact with the Roman Empire: Roman money began to be used, traded for raw materials and slaves; free Germans served in Roman armies; and farming and pottery techniques as well as the full range of goods all gradually arrived in German society. A degree of literacy was also spreading north and by around 350 AD a written form of Gothic had developed, which Christian missionary Wulfila used to translate the Bible.

With this progress came ever more powerful Germanic tribes, which grew into two strong military confederations: the **Alemanni** on the Rhine and the **Goths** on the Danube.

The great migrations

From the late fourth century onwards Europe's uneasy stability was thrown into disarray by the arrival of nomadic, mounted, non-Germanic Huns from the east. A powerful destabilizing force, they encouraged – along with climatic changes, growing populations and adventurousness – the eastern most Germanic peoples, the Visigoths and Ostrogoths, to head west into central Europe and the Roman Empire.

And so began the hundred years of the **great migrations** during which time displaced tribes sought new lands in a process that involved giant battles and pillaging as much as travel. The journey of the **Visigoths** – a tribe of about 80,000 – was among the most spectacular. Driven west from Ukraine they initially settled in the Danube region where the Romans allowed them to farm, until local hostility meant they were sent on their way. They fought and pillaged through Greece and Italy – sacking Rome in 410 – then moving west to colonize the French coast around today's Toulouse and a good part of the Iberian peninsula. Other Germanic tribes were also on the move, including the Suebi and Vandals who established themselves in Spain and later in North Africa. The Ostrogoths moved from the Black Sea to today's Hungary, then Italy, while the **Burgundians** moved from northern Germany through the southwest of the country and finally to southeastern France – as celebrated in the *Nibelungenlied* (see p.520).

Successor states

With the Roman Empire overstretched they were forced to compromise to resolve most territorial questions in Europe, and they consented to Germanic successor states such as the Visigothic and Burgundian kingdoms. Meanwhile, the less footloose western Germanic tribes – the Franks, Frisians, Saxons, Thuringians, Alemanni, and Bavarians – the product of smaller tribes clubbing together to defend themselves against the Huns, emerged. As the western Roman Empire crumbled they integrated the Roman provincial population into their own, fusing a Germanic military with Roman administrative skills that would establish taxes and legal powers for these German rulers.

The Franks

In this new European order of competing Germanic tribes, the **Franks** proved themselves the strongest. From their fifth-century tribal lands in today's Belgium, they began to expand their kingdom south and east, particularly under King Clovis (482–511) of the **Merovingian** dynasty. In 751 the **Carolingian** dynasty took over and continued to consolidate and expand under their greatest leader **Charlemagne** (768–814), who made Aachen – now Germany's westernmost city – his capital. At the time of his death the Frankish empire took up most of modern-day France, Germany and northern Italy.

The success of the Franks' expansion and consolidation lay in an adaptable approach in which they allowed conquered regions to be governed semi-autonomously by dukes of mixed Frankish and indigenous background under the Frankish king, to whom they swore ultimate allegiance. The conversion of the Franks to Christianity and their subsequent missionary zeal also helped immensely, providing both the support of Christians in conquered regions and an administrative means of control which could be spread throughout the empire.

One of the most influential missionaries was **St Boniface** (c.675–754), who converted much of Germany and helped integrate it into the Roman-Frankish church by the time of his martyrdom in northern Frisia. Thereafter the only areas of Germany that needed a concerted effort were the lands of the unruly pagan Saxons who resisted conversion and stood in the way of eastward expansion. The process of bringing them to heel was a particularly brutal one, but made good headway under Charlemagne. However, as soon as his army moved on, the Saxons would revolt, slaughter Frankish officials and priests, and raid as far west as they could. Charlemagne in turn would punish the offending tribes, including one occasion in 782 when he executed four thousand five hundred Saxons at Verden.

The Holy Roman Empire

After Charlemagne, the era of Frankish empire-building effectively came to an end, and the territories he had controlled were divided into three kingdoms, ruled by his grandsons. One, the **East Frankish Empire**, covered the greater part of modern Germany and would become known as the **Holy Roman Empire**. Initially governed by **Louis the German** (804–876) it began to take on a German identity, helped by Louis's cultivation of German language and literature, which included the translation of the Gospels.

This emergent German culture would help bind the empire, but the main forces holding it together were the cooperation of territorial rulers and the Church. Over the Empire's thousand-year history both these forces progressively weakened, producing an ever more divided and complex situation in which territories increasingly fought among themselves. The underlying problem was the piecemeal power structure in which a mosaic of different interests could politick, feud and scheme. The tug of war initially went in three directions – between the territorial rulers, the **elected king** (or emperor if crowned by the pope) and the **Church** – but soon spread throughout wider society in struggles between various subgroups including the **petty aristocracy**, **knights** and **prelates**. One particularly divisive factor was the Germanic custom of splitting estates between sons, rather than simply passing them to the eldest, which created ever smaller territories. Meanwhile economic development created ever larger, more powerful and independent **cities**.

With all these forces at play it was perhaps inevitable that central authority would weaken – particularly since crown lands and revenues were consistently eroded by dynasties who gave away imperial possessions to those who elected them as bribes for the re-election of their descendants. The financial and law-enforcing power of the king – the foundation of royal authority elsewhere – was in any case negligible, a weakness that generally led to growing lawlessness and ceaseless petty wars across the empire.

In the sixteenth century this dynamic took a new and even more divisive turn as the **Protestant Reformation** split the Church. Great, lengthy, brutal and costly wars ensued, retarding the economic and social development of German states and effectively ending the Holy Roman Empire as a political power while European neighbours – particularly Britain, France, Spain and the Netherlands – began to develop global empires.

The Saxons (911–1024)

By 911 the Carolingian dynasty had effectively died out and all power devolved to local leaders: Saxon, Frankish and Bavarian dukes, among others, met at Forchheim in Franconia to elect a new king. In 919 they chose **Henry the Fowler**, the first of a line of Saxon kings, who reasserted Germany as a single empire and cemented the kingdom with vast military prowess. The Saxons were particularly effective under **Otto the Great** (reigned 936–973) when they subdued the Magyar (Hungarian) invasions and continued **eastward expansion**. Between 955 and 972 he founded and richly endowed an archbishopric at Magdeburg as a missionary base, and led savage military campaigns against the polytheistic Slavic Wends, who – like the Saxons two hundred years earlier – tenaciously resisted Christian conversion with brutal consequences. Otto's reign also included the conquest of Rome, forcing the pope to crown him emperor in 962, and beginning a tradition of giving the East Frankish Kingdom the imperial title. Otto enjoyed a good relationship with the Church, which he energetically built up in order to disrupt the secular lords' jurisdictions. By loading bishoprics and abbeys with endowments and privileges he gradually turned bishops and abbots into princes directly answerable to the king. Though this helped with governance, it built a powerful new force which in the coming centuries would be part of the empire's undoing.

The Salians (1024–1125)

After the Saxons, the **Salian** dynasty from Rhenish Franconia controlled the empire for the next hundred years, but had a much worse time of it. They struggled against the increasing authority of territorial princes and deep financial problems, which were largely the result of Saxon gifts to the Church. At the same time the **Gregorian reform movement** emerged. It argued for the separation of state and church as spiritual power should not be purchasable, and so fundamentally contradicted the empire's constitutional basis; as both sides fought through polemical writings, nobles were driven to take sides. When **Henry IV** (1056–1106) came to the throne aged 5, a general free-for-all ensued throughout the empire. When he came of age Henry's attempts to recover crown lands began a period of costly civil war which lasted almost twenty years and embroiled the pope who, at one stage, excommunicated Henry.

One lasting feature of German society to come out of all this chaos was the creation of a class of **knights**: soldiers from ecclesiastical estates who served the king as a small private army.

The Hohenstaufens (1125–1268)

Henry V, the last Salian, died childless in 1125, leaving an empire that could no longer dominate European politics and so got almost no material benefit from the **Crusades**. The empire entered more than two decades of competition between the Swabian **Hohenstaufens** and the Saxon **Welfs** until the two dynasties were united by marriage and the birth of **Frederick I** (Frederick Barbarossa, "Redbeard"; reigned 1152–90) who was careful to maintain good relations with all the big dynasties – one effect of which was the elevation of **Austria** into a duchy as a way of evening the power balance.

But Frederick spent most of his reign preoccupied with conquering Italy, leaving Germany without an effective central authority and encouraging another period of chaos, during which time ducal authority was eroded by bishops and princes. These upstarts then further increased their power by building a rash of castles, toll stations, mints and mines, and by taking judicial command. None of them wanted the election of a strong king who would threaten their growing independence – which, in the long run, led to a trend of selecting weaker or preoccupied regents. But in the short term it ushered in the **Great Interregnum** (1250–73), a period of chaos in which there was effectively no central power, until the papacy intervened and established an electoral process whereby the Holy Roman Emperor was chosen by seven leading princes.

Hohenstaufen rule also saw ceaseless conquering and colonizing to the east. The Slavic Wends were finally overwhelmed and Germans from every level of society migrated east – explaining the presence later of large German-speaking populations across the region.

The early Habsburgs and the Luxembourgs (1273–1437)

In the thirteenth century the **Habsburgs**, a fledgling dynasty that would come to dominate much of the western world and outlive the Holy Roman Empire itself, make a brief appearance. Initially, however, they provided a weak emperor, Rudolf I, in 1273, allowing the princes plenty of room for manoeuvre. Rudolf's subsequent dynastic acquisitions, which included Austria, Holland and Zeeland, worried the electoral princes, who then plumped for the house of **Luxembourg**, though this decision wasn't unanimous, resulting in yet more wars between the princes. These disputes were only resolved with the Declaration of Rhens in 1338, which established election by a majority vote, and the **Golden Bull** of 1356, a basic constitutional document that fixed the electoral body at seven: the archbishops of Mainz, Cologne and Trier, the count palatine of the Rhine, the king of Bohemia, the margrave of Brandenburg, and the duke of Saxony – who all received far greater judicial and financial powers.

From 1347 onwards, the Luxembourgs inherited Bohemia, providing them with vast wealth with which to shore up their imperial position, but also distracting them from the needs of the empire. Partly as a result of this, various **city leagues** were formed across Germany and beyond – including the Hanseatic League (see box, p.776), the Swabian League, and the Rhenish League. Cities clubbed together to defend their interests and establish trading agreements, forming powerful and often wealthy secular powerbases across Europe. Their interests often clashed with those of the princes, over such things as the loss of rural labour – which became particularly acute after the **Black Death** (1348–49), which killed around a quarter of Germany's population. The consequent loss of revenue was one reason for the raising of princely tolls on civic trade to the point where tensions turned into war in 1388, which resulted in stalemate but also the disbandment of most city leagues by imperial intervention.

Another result of the Bohemian bond with the empire was the dragging of German states into the **Hussite Wars** (1420–34) to help the emperor defend against the religious reforms of Jan Hus, which became combined with nationalist sentiments against a wealthy German minority. However, this German military intervention was feeble and Hussite retaliation swept through Saxony, Thuringia and Franconia in a destructive foray in the late 1420s.

The Habsburgs (1438–1648)

A marriage between the Luxembourgs and Habsburgs united the dynasties and brought another **Habsburg**, Albert II, to the imperial throne in 1438 in what would become an almost unbroken line to the end of the Holy Roman Empire. Initially the dynasty became ever more powerful, with ambitious marriage alliances expanding their lands from Austria to include the Netherlands, much of Italy, Spain (with all its New World colonies), Bohemia and Hungary – perhaps the most troublesome possession of all, given the repeated attacks on it by the Ottoman Empire. Since Germany was not the main source of their power, it was also not their main concern, and the Habsburgs' interests tended to lie elsewhere: **Frederick III** (1440–93) was more preoccupied by astrology; **Maximilian I** (1493–1519) was a naive idealist – who once seriously approached the Ottomans with the idea that Turks and Christians might settle their differences in a medieval tournament – and fantasized about becoming pope; the most powerful of them all, **Charles V** (1519–58), made his position quite clear: "I speak Spanish to God, Italian to women, French to men, and German to my horse." The feeling was largely mutual, with the prince-electors enjoying having a powerful protector with little time to intervene.

Nevertheless, under the Habsburgs there was some much-needed reform of the imperial government. The central administration expanded and appointed permanent professional councillors, trained in centralizing Roman law, many at the newly founded **universities** which included Heidelberg (1386), Rostock (1419) and Tübingen (1477). Meanwhile the **estates** met at the Diet of Worms in 1495, where they outlawed private feuds, created a supreme imperial chamber court and imposed a new imperial tax. Even though territorial rulers and city magistrates controlled much of the real power on the ground, the centralized, bureaucratic expansion, increasingly extravagant courts, larger armies, more incessant wars, and a more grasping and corrupt Church all served to increase the financial burden at every level of society.

The Reformation

Against this background of economic resentment, the outburst of **Martin Luther** (see box, p.222), a monk in Wittenberg, struck a chord across society. Luther's objections to the profligacy of the Church were outlined in his **95 Theses** (1517) which fundamentally challenged papal authority as the sole interpreter of the Bible, the only source of religious truth for Luther. His challenge to authority and his resoluteness when asked to explain himself before Charles V at the Diet of Worms in 1521 made him a German hero. His rejection of authority became a bandwagon onto which various other groups jumped – some out of conviction, others for reasons of expediency. Any rulers who adopted the new creed could expect to profit hugely in terms of power and wealth by taking ownership of the Church within their states. The general public – to whom revolutionary ideas could easily be spread thanks to the recent invention of the printing press – found Luther's vehemence so compelling that his name became fused with a general hope for social improvement. This prompted the large-scale **rebellions of 1525** in which various groups – knights, peasants, farmers and the urban poor – began armed insurrections to improve their lot. Luther, however, was not the social radical the rebels saw him as, and argued in opposition to them that a hierarchical society was God's will; after he spoke out the rebellions were quickly put down.

While the common rebellion of 1525 was easily quashed, that of Luther and his supporting regents and cities continued unchecked, thanks in part to Habsburg preoccupations with a war against France and the Turks, who under Süleyman the Magnificent captured much of Hungary and Vienna in 1529. By the mid-1520s a number of German cities and states had formally turned Lutheran, severing their ties with Rome. The **Diet of Speyer** of 1526 legalized reforms that resulted in a state church which became established in every Lutheran territory, and whose members were dubbed **Protestants** after their protest against an imperial attempt to revoke the Speyer ruling. The **Diet of Augsburg** in 1530 saw the presentation of the **Augsburg Confession**, intelligently authored by Philipp Melanchthon, which became the definitive statement of Lutheran beliefs and which Catholic theologians at the Diet concluded presented too deep a rift for reconciliation. With its foundations clearly stated, Lutheranism began to evolve, further integrating the church into state politics and everyday life.

Division, war and collapse

One immediate effect of the Diet of Augsburg was the formation of the **Schmalkaldic League** (1531), a military bond of Protestant rulers, preparing the way for a century of almost constant strife. The Lutherans sought to ensure their survival and extend their sphere of influence, as did the Catholics, who included the Habsburgs and of course the papacy, bent on recovering power and confiscated properties. To strengthen their cause the Catholic Church organized the **Council of Trent** (1545–63) which spearheaded a Catholic **Counter-Reformation** issuing from Spain and Rome and producing authoritative dogmas, formally pronouncing the papacy to be the only legitimate arbiter of Biblical interpretation and issuing mandates to tackle corruption. This reinvigorated church was then well served by the **Jesuits**, a militant order founded in 1534, that was bent on recovering lost ground and was extremely active in Germany.

A series of religiously inspired wars and peace treaties began in 1545 when the first inconclusive clash between Protestant and imperial forces resulted in the 1555 **Peace of Augsburg** which crucially determined that he who governs a territory decides its one legitimate faith – Lutheranism or Catholicism – making a choice binding on everyone in the jurisdiction. This legalized Lutheranism but alienated Calvinists – those following the more radical and aggressive form of Protestantism from Switzerland – prompting them to push hard to gain recognition as they made major territorial gains in the 1560s and 1570s.

Tensions continued to escalate and by the early seventeenth century Germany was divided into two competing military alliances: the **Protestant Union** (1608) and the **Catholic League** (1609). Both looked to foreign powers for support, vastly increasing the scale of the ensuing **Thirty Years' War** (1618–48). In the course of the war Spain fought for the Catholics, while France, England, the Netherlands, Bohemia, Denmark and Sweden weighed in on the side of the Protestants, with many offering their services to combat the dynastic expansion of the Habsburgs rather than out of religious conviction. However the European powers could ill-afford their mercenary armies, promising them loot instead and allowing unprecedented brutality: in 1631 two-thirds of the 20,000-strong population of Magdeburg was massacred by imperial troops. The war was also notable for a Swedish rampage around Germany, with them taking most towns in southwest Germany, including Heidelberg. For German society, the war was an unmitigated disaster: around three million of Germany's population of twenty million died in the war and the epidemics that followed during the general economic collapse.

Finally, the **Peace of Westphalia** (1648) brought territorial gains to Sweden and France; restored and confirmed that rulers determined the religion of their lands, though they had to keep it as it was in 1624; it permitted some religious toleration; and it allowed Calvinism. It also guaranteed almost unlimited sovereignty to German princes – which divided the Holy Roman Empire into literally hundreds of autonomous political entities, and so brought it to an end as an effective political unit.

The age of absolutism (1648–1871)

By removing much of the power of the Holy Roman Emperor and the papacy, the Peace of Westphalia established territorial sovereignty for German rulers. These numbered around three hundred principalities, over fifty imperial cities, and almost two thousand counts and knights, with the smallest unit – the Swabian Abbey of Baindt with its few hundred acres, 29 nuns and princess-abbess – having many of the same rights as the largest. Germany's history became the combination of the thousands of these small histories as petty rulers legislated, taxed, allied with each other and foreign powers, and fought at will. The strengthening of princely courts reached a point where many would try to copy the absolutist rule and lavish indulgences of the intensely fashionable and ever more powerful French **King Louis XIV** (reigned 1661–1715). Many German rulers – such as Saxony's Augustus the Strong and his court in Dresden, to name just one – flattered themselves with Baroque palaces, adopted elaborate French court ceremonies, food and conversation, and courted an international nobility with whom they enjoyed foreign cultural innovations like opera. These ruinously expensive courts, when added to the cost of large armies and proliferating bureaucracies, placed an enormous burden on the people. Louis XIV also expanded his influence across the border by other means, pursuing aggressively expansionist policies to make the Rhine France's new eastern border in the late seventeenth century. Whole German towns were laid to ruins, in the process. Inevitably Germany's development – economically, socially and politically – slowed. So while other European powers enlarged their colonies and developed democracies, Germany was barely even a concept.

The great exception to all this overindulgence and provincialism was **Prussia**, which through its own austerity and militarism began to grow ever more powerful, eventually replacing Austria as the dominant German power. Then, out of a period of industrialization and European-wide **social revolution** after the French Revolution, Prussia's **Otto von Bismarck** used diplomacy and war to create a country called Germany.

The rise of Prussia

The meteoric rise of **Brandenburg-Prussia** from the ruins of the Thirty Years' War was to say the least, unpredictable. Deficient in resources, and sovereign over a patchwork of sparsely populated territories widely scattered from their capital in Berlin between modern-day Poland and the Rhineland, the ruling house of Hohenzollern deserves much credit for becoming an international power.

The Prussian model for success involved building a flourishing mercantile economy by offering skilled European refugees protection. Those who came included Jews, South German Catholics, 20,000 French Huguenots and resettling Dutch colonists. This made Prussia one of Europe's most tolerant states – even though all this was designed to support autocratic rule and a disciplined permanent army. **Frederick William I** (1713–40) perfected the Prussian scheme – strong government, productivity and militarism – by enforcing spartan conditions with laws limiting luxuries (even theatre was eventually banned) and firing most court servants. This extremely tight fiscal ship then furnished the "soldier-king" with a superb army of 80,000 men, the continent's fourth largest after France, Russia and Austria. While the army marched and drilled, the populace had a draconian work-ethic drubbed into them – Frederick took to walking Berlin and personally beating anyone he caught loafing.

His son, **Frederick II** (1712–86), added a degree of enlightenment, encouraging scholarly activity and culture by sponsoring leading figures of the German Enlightenment, including playwright Gotthold Ephraim Lessing and philosopher Moses Mendelssohn, abolishing torture and reducing taxes on the poor.

Yet Frederick also continued the Prussian military tradition, and began to deploy the army his father had nurtured. Most gains were at Austria's expense, whose 100,000 men were spread too thinly over its extensive lands – which included much of the modern-day Czech Republic, Hungary and Poland and (after 1714) the southern Netherlands and the duchy of Milan – and engaged in ongoing wars against France and the Ottoman Empire until the mid-eighteenth century. The Austrians were also troubled by a succession crisis in which, in the absence of a male heir, Charles VI sought to persuade the world to accept the succession of his daughter, **Maria Theresa**. Taking advantage of Austria's vulnerability, Frederick II unleashed Brandenburg-Prussia's military potential, annexing Silesia in the **War of the Austrian Succession** (1740–48) during which outnumbered Prussian armies revealed themselves far superior. Austria, Saxony, France and Russia were alarmed by the rise of Prussia, and responded by starting the **Seven Years' War** in 1756. Prussia's eventual victory in this confirmed it as a new Central European power and earned Frederick the epithet "the Great".

Napoleonic occupation

The Revolutionary and Napoleonic wars that followed the French Revolution of 1789, during which France under **Napoleon** advanced across the continent, continued to reveal not only the immense military power of France but also the decrepit nature of the Austrian Habsburg forces. By 1806, Austria had lost so much ground that Francis II officially laid down the imperial crown, pronouncing an end to the Holy Roman Empire after a thousand years – though in practical terms it had long since finished. Prussia found itself alone and quickly routed by the French in two simultaneous battles at Jena and Auerstädt (October 14, 1806). Berlin was occupied two weeks later – illustrating just how much Prussia had gone into decline after Frederick the Great's death.

Once in control, Napoleon initiated a general reorganization of German lands: Prussia lost almost half its territory and population, while France occupied the left bank of the Rhine and compensated displaced rulers with possessions elsewhere. This, and Napoleon's desire to establish a chain of satellite states east of the Rhine, precipitated a frantic redrawing of political boundaries. Dozens of small political entities – free cities, imperial knights, ecclesiastical territories – fell into the hands of greedy neighbours, particularly Napoleon's satellites, including Bavaria and Württemberg which he made into kingdoms, and Baden and Hesse-Darmstadt which became grand duchies.

Napoleon also introduced state reform, streamlining ministries, allowing nobles to trade, and making guild membership more accessible. He also forced almost all states – except Austria and Prussia – into a confederation. All of this unwittingly prepared the way for Germany to centralize, strengthen and nation-build.

Restoration, reform, revolution and reaction

Following the collapse of Napoleon's empire at the hands of Russia, Prussia and Austria at the **Battle of Leipzig** in 1813, the restoration of the French monarchy and his final defeat at Waterloo in 1815, a new European order was drawn up at the 1814 **Congress of Vienna**. Many of the streamlined borders and governments he had introduced were kept, but since those at the congress scorned democracy and national self-determination, it was mostly an exercise in re-establishing the old order.

However, the intellectual ferment of the French Revolution and subsequent rebellions awoke in Germany the first stirrings of **liberalism** and revolutionary activity. So, although the next fifty years were characterized by peace and stability, open **rebellion** steadily increased. University students rose up as revolutionary Burschenschaften (fraternities), political parties emerged and society became increasingly urban as Germany **industrialized**. In 1848 economic depression, urban unemployment and serious crop failures coincided, causing a major famine across northern Europe. One consequence was mass emigration to the New World, another was to bring the working classes out in open rebellion. A revolutionary mood swept through Europe and uprisings took place in Germany. Some were bitter and bloody: in Berlin, 183 Berliners and eighteen soldiers died.

The response of those in power was for the most part to introduce repressive measures that restricted rights of assembly, enlarged police authority and intensified censorship – stifling intellectual and cultural life. However, some of the more progressive governments began to recognize a need for **constitutional reform** designed to win the support of the educated. Constitutions were duly instigated in Bavaria and Baden (1818), Württemberg (1819) and Hesse-Darmstadt (1820). Prominent liberals were appointed to many state ministries, precipitating a slow programme of liberal reform in many parts of Germany.

Bismarck and German unity

The 1814 Congress of Vienna was hugely significant in catapulting Prussia back to prominence. The agreements gave it land along the Rhine, making it pivotal in the defence of Germany's western boundary, and giving it the great iron and coal deposits of the Ruhr. Consequently, Prussia's industrial might grew at a furious pace, in part because of its streamlining of trade regulations within its own territory and the development of an ever-expanding free-trade area called the **Zollverein**, or customs union, which from 1834 produced a degree of German economic unity and gave Prussia a powerful new weapon in its struggle against Austria.

But Prussia's most powerful weapon in the pursuit of regional dominance and German unity was **Otto von Bismarck**, who became Prussian chancellor in 1862. As a conservative statesman his appointment immediately upset liberals, but he proved to be visionary and exceptionally talented in statecraft. In 1866, using the division of the duchies of Schleswig and Holstein (won from the Danes in a brief German–Danish War in 1864) between Prussia and a decaying Austria as an excuse, Bismarck embarked on the **Seven Weeks' War**. Armed with brilliant strategist Helmuth von Moltke and the deadly breech-loading needle gun, Prussia quickly won, finally tipping the balance of power within Germany in its favour.

Bismarck then cleverly harnessed a growing sense of nationalism to strengthen Prussia's militarism. Opposition to Napoleonic rule in Germany had been a catalyst for the first German nationalist sentiments – while at the same time illustrating what nationalist sentiments could achieve. In part this explained a flourishing **Romantic movement** – which celebrated German spirit and tradition in opposition to the cold rationality of the French Enlightenment. From the movement sprouted notions of what it meant to be German and an idea that all Germans should be unified in a single state.

So Bismarck, having defeated Austria, could harness the growing sense of German identity into a rallying cry to cajole and bully neighbours into joining a **North German Confederation**, in which Prussia had about four-fifths of the territory, population and political control. A national currency and uniform commercial and financial practices and laws were quickly introduced. By addressing issues that had long frustrated middle-class Germans, Bismarck adeptly took the sting out of demands for greater political freedom, while at the same time strengthening the position of the state and of Prussia.

German unity lay just around the corner. France was already nervous about its newly united and strong neighbour, and Bismarck precipitated war with the French by altering a telegram sent by the foreign office of his king Wilhelm I to the French government. The French declared war, and the rest of the German nation rallied behind Prussia as Bismarck had hoped. Germany's southern states – particularly Bavaria, Württemberg, Baden and Southern Hesse – quickly joined the Franco-Prussian War, forcing Paris to capitulate in 1871. The peace gave Germany Alsace-Lorraine, but more importantly, Bismarck used the accompanying patriotic fervour to negotiate with the southern states and achieve political consolidation. So while Prussian guns bombarded Paris, a greater victory took place: **Wilhelm I** was proclaimed **emperor** of a united nation, beginning a powerful new empire under the Hohenzollerns.

The German Empire (1871–1918)

Once established, the German Empire quickly became Europe's leading power, and its rapid economic expansion made the German economy second only to the United States by 1914. This new-found might prompted Germany to enter the **colonial** race, though far too late in the day to pick up anything of any economic value. Instead, by entering the fray, it increased foreign mistrust to an extent that tensions led inexorably towards the catastrophe of World War I. Germany's defeat forced the abdication of the emperor and left it crippled.

Industry and society

Prussia, in commanding three-fifths of Germany's land and population and providing its emperor, dominated the united Germany, and was as efficient as usual in creating national institutions and freeing trade. The initial response was an unprecedented boom which ended abruptly with the onset of a worldwide **depression in 1873**. Two million Germans left for the Americas in the 1870s, a process that continued into the 1880s even as industry began to recover, in part thanks to effective cartels in heavy industry and protective import tariffs. By the 1890s things had really turned around, emigration dropped off and Germany began to exceed Britain in steel production – from having only half its capacity in the 1870s.

As industrialization continued, so too did the inevitable urbanization: by 1910 more than half of Germany's population of 41 million lived in cities. Between 1890 and 1900, Berlin's population doubled to two million and thousands of tenement buildings sprang up in working-class districts. The German working class grew rapidly and total union membership reached 3.7 million in 1912. Though this helped improve conditions, workers still lacked full political rights and lived in squalor, which fermented support for the revolutionary Social Democratic Party (**SPD**), whose deputies were the chief dissenters within the Reichstag.

The growth of the SPD and a centre party that Bismarck had long attacked for its Roman Catholic associations, proved the chancellor's undoing. With the SPD posting enormous gains in the 1890 elections, Bismarck was seen as far too old-fashioned and was forced to resign by the Kaiser, leaving the scene in a rather humiliating fashion.

Foreign policy

One impressive legacy of Bismarck's was in foreign affairs. He had forged a series of alliances to protect the fledgling German empire in the shifting power games of Europe. Key to this was ensuring the diplomatic isolation of France – with its grudge against Germany – and trying to maintain stability between Austria-Hungary and Russia who were increasingly on the verge of conflict over the Balkans where the disintegration of the Ottoman Empire had left huge instability.

However, Bismarck's successors rapidly abandoned this policy. The alliance with Russia was dropped, allowing France to end its isolation and ally with them. Instead attempts began in earnest to make Germany a global power which saw her meddling everywhere, including in China and Turkey. Germany's navy went from negligible to rivalling Britain's in just over a decade, and it acquired Togo, Cameroon and parts of modern-day Namibia, Tanzania, New Guinea and a few Pacific islands – all minor prizes that didn't justify the naval cost. Moreover the British felt threatened, leading them to negotiate alliances with Japan in 1902, then France in 1904 and Russia in 1907 to form a Triple Entente that left Germany surrounded.

Austria was Germany's only major ally – an alliance that immediately brought it into deep trouble once Balkan stability was threatened by the assassination of the Austrian heir to the throne, Archduke Francis Ferdinand by a Bosnian Serb in June 1914. A mobilization by the Serbs and their Russian allies against the Austrians and their German allies precipitated the continental conflict of epic proportions that became known as World War I.

World War I

When war broke out no one imagined that new technologies in warfare would lead to a carnage that would claim 37 million casualties, including sixteen million dead. Some two and a half million Germans would lose their lives. Instead the 1914 outbreak of hostilities was greeted with enthusiasm by German civilians everywhere – only confirmed pacifists or communists resisted the intoxication of patriotism. The political parties agreed to a truce, and even the Social Democrats voted in favour of war credits.

Germany's calculation that France could be knocked out before Russia fully mobilized soon proved hopelessly optimistic, and Germany found itself facing a war on two fronts – the very thing it dreaded. As casualties mounted on the stalemated western front, rationing and food shortages began to hit poorer civilians and disillusionment set in. From the summer of 1915 popular protest began as ordinary people started to see the war as an exercise staged for the benefit of the rich at the expense of the poor.

With Germany and Austria surrounded and blockaded, and with Italy (1915) and Romania (1916) joining the war against them, they faced an almost impossible situation. The German government, like those of all its enemies, found it safer to demand ever-greater efforts from its people than to admit the pointlessness of earlier sacrifices. Its generals, Ludendorff and Hindenburg, sought mobilization of the whole country, until more than eleven million men were in uniform. After a severe winter in 1916–17 Germany was unable to feed itself and malnutrition – even starvation – was not uncommon. Food and also fuel shortages rendered the population vulnerable to the **influenza epidemic** sweeping Europe. Around half a million Germans died in the epidemic that killed at least fifty million worldwide.

After a promising last great offensive in the spring of 1918, the arrival of almost a million American troops in France made German **defeat** inevitable by the autumn. Knowing the Allies would refuse to negotiate with the old absolutist system, Germany's supreme general Ludendorff declared a democratic, constitutional monarchy, whose chancellor would be responsible to the Reichstag and not the Kaiser. A government was formed under Prince Max von Baden, which agreed to extensive reforms. But it was too little too late for the bitter sailors and soldiers on the home front, where the contrast between privilege and poverty was most obvious. At the start of November the Kiel Garrison led a naval mutiny and revolutionary workers' and soldiers' soviets mushroomed across Germany. Realizing that the game was up, **Kaiser Wilhelm II abdicated**.

The Weimar Republic (1919–33)

Though humiliated by the loss of the war, at least its end would, after a period of chaos, bring democracy to Germany as the **Weimar Republic**. Despite having the most modern and democratic constitution of its day, the burden of 1920s economic instability proved too much, and the global depression of the early 1930s finally broke the fledgling republic with a new wave of political strife that fostered extremism and helped sweep the Nazis to power.

Abdication and the Weimar constitution

Following the abdication of the Kaiser, power passed to the SPD leader **Friedrich Ebert**. However, the revolutionary soldiers, sailors and workers who controlled the streets, inspired by the 1917 Bolshevik success in Russia, favoured a Soviet-style government and refused to obey Ebert's orders. A deal was struck with the army, which promised to protect the republic if Ebert would forestall a full-blooded socialist revolution – which was threatening in the form of a **Spartacist uprising** in Berlin in early 1919. This uprising was put down by the **Freikorps** – armed bands of right-wing officers and NCOs from the old imperial army – and the Spartacist leaders, Karl Liebknecht and Rosa Luxemburg were duly murdered, establishing a dangerous precedent for political violence. Elections in early 1919 confirmed the SPD as leaders of the country – with 38 percent of the vote – and made Ebert president.

Weimar, the small country town that had seen the most glorious flowering of the German Enlightenment, was chosen as the place to draft a national constitution in preference to Berlin, which was tinged by monarchic and military associations. The **constitution** drawn up was hailed as the most liberal, democratic and progressive in the world. While it incorporated a complex system of checks and balances to prevent power becoming too concentrated in parts of government or regions, it crucially lacked any clauses for outlawing parties hostile to the system. This opened the way for savage attacks on the republic by extremists at both ends of the political spectrum.

In 1920, Freikorps units loyal to the right-wing politician Wolfgang Kapp marched on Berlin, unopposed by the army, and briefly took power in the **Kapp putsch**; by the end of 1922 there had been nearly four hundred political assassinations, the vast majority of them traceable to the right.

Amidst such turmoil, and with public opinion divided between a plethora of parties, all Weimar-era governments became unwieldy coalitions that often

---

The arts in the 1920s

"A world has been destroyed; we must seek a radical solution," proclaimed young architect Walter Gropius on his return from the front in 1918. In a remarkable response to the political and economic chaos of Germany during the 1920s, the arts flourished in a dazzling display of creativity. Gropius went on to found the famous **Bauhaus** school, initially in Weimar, then Dessau (see p.226), pioneering the modernist aesthetic which had begun to assert itself in the late nineteenth century.

In visual art the **Dada** shockwave rippled through the decade and George Grosz satirized the times in savage caricatures, while **Expressionism** concentrated on emotional responses to reality rather than reality itself. In **music** composers like Arnold Schoenberg rejected centuries-old traditions of tonality, while in theatre Bertolt Brecht's bitterly satiric *Dreigroschen Oper* ("Threepenny Opera"), compared modern capitalism to the gangster underworld. Germany also became a global centre for the newest of the arts: **film**. Between the wars Germany produced legendary films like Fritz Lang's *Metropolis* and Robert Wiene's *The Cabinet of Doctor Caligari*, which championed distorted sets and unusual camera angles to probe disturbing truths.

Meanwhile in popular culture, all-singing, all-dancing musicals, featuring platoons of women in various states of undress took off and the Berlin **cabaret scene** had its heyday – as celebrated by Berlin residents such as Christopher Isherwood, whose tales of the time were turned into the musical *Cabaret*. But not everyone welcomed the bawdiness or the modernist attack on tradition and the Nazis mercilessly put an abrupt end to all this "cultural bolshevism" in the 1930s.

pursued contradictory policies and had an average life of only about eight months, producing a weak framework that later readily allowed the extremists in the far-right Nazi party to take control.

The Treaty of Versailles

Much of the history of Germany in the 1920s was determined by the Allies and the harsh terms imposed by the **Treaty of Versailles**: Alsace-Lorraine was handed back to France, who would temporarily get the coal-rich Saarland region to aid reconstruction. In the east, Germany lost a large chunk of Prussia to Poland, giving the latter access to the Baltic, but cutting the German province of East Prussia off from the rest of the country. The overseas empire was dismantled. But what aggrieved Germans most was the treaty's war-guilt clause which held Germany responsible "for causing all the loss and damage" suffered by the Allies in the war. This was seen as a cynical victors' justice, yet provided the justification for a gigantic bill of reparation payments – a total of 132 billion gold marks.

Economic collapse

With the economy badly battered by the war and postwar political chaos, Germany struggled to meet reparation payments and in 1922 France and Belgium occupied the Ruhr in response to alleged defaults. The German government's response was to call a national strike in January 1923, which proved to be the final straw, sending the mark plummeting, in the worst **inflation** ever known: a loaf of bread that cost 10,000 marks in the morning would cost 3,000,000 marks by nightfall; restaurant prices rose as customers ate. By November 15, 1923, it took 4.2 trillion German marks to buy an American dollar.

The mark was finally stabilized under supremely able foreign minister, **Gustav Stresemann**, who believed relief from reparation payments was more likely to come from cooperation than stubborn resistance. The Allies, too, moderated their stance, and, realizing Germany needed to be economically stable in order to pay, devised the **1924 Dawes Plan** under which loans poured into Germany, particularly from America. The economic upsurge that followed lasted until the **Wall Street Crash** of October 1929. With this, American credit ended, wiping out Germany's economic stability, and the poverty of the immediate postwar period returned with a vengeance.

Political extremism and the rise of the Nazis

Everyone suffered in the economic troubles of the Weimar period. Hyper-inflation wiped out middle-class savings, while after the Wall Street Crash six million people became unemployed by 1932. Increasingly people sought radical solutions in political extremism, and support for two parties that bitterly opposed one another but shared a desire to end democracy grew: the **communists** and the **National Socialist German Workers' Party** (NSDAP), or Nazis. While red flags and swastika banners hung from neighbouring tenements, gangs from the left and right fought in the streets in ever-greater numbers, with the brown-shirted Nazi **SA** (Sturmabteilung) stormtroopers fighting endless pitched battles against the communist **Rote Frontkämpferbund** (Red Fighters' Front). The threat of a return to the anarchy of the postwar years increased Nazi support among the middle classes and captains of industry (who provided heavy financial support) because they feared for their lives and property under communist rule. Fear of the reds also meant little or nothing was done to curb SA violence against the left. The growth of Nazi popularity was also attributable to Hitler's record as a war veteran, his identification of Jews as scapegoats, the promise the dogma offered to restore national pride, along with Hitler's own charisma. Meanwhile, the communists found it difficult to extend support beyond the German working classes.

By September 1930, the communists and Nazis together gained nearly one of every three votes cast and in the July 1932 **parliamentary elections** the Nazis took 37 percent of the vote – their largest total in any free election – making them the largest party in the Reichstag; the communists took fifteen percent. Nazi thugs began attacking Jewish shops and businesses and intimidating liberals into muted criticism or silence.

But what eventually brought the Nazis to power in 1933 was infighting among conservatives, who persuaded the virtually senile president and former field marshal Paul von Hindenburg to make Hitler chancellor. This move was based on a gamble that the Nazis would usefully crush the left but fail to form an effective government – so that within a few months Hitler could be nudged aside. Hitler became chancellor on January 4, 1933, and Berlin thronged with Nazi supporters bearing torches. For the vast majority of Berliners it was a nightmare come true: three-quarters of the city had voted against the Nazis at the last elections.

The pretext for an all-out **Nazi takeover** was provided by the **Reichstag fire** on February 28, 1933, which was likely started by them, rather than the simple-minded Dutch communist Marius van der Lubbe on whom blame fell. An emergency decree the following day effectively legalized a permanent state of emergency, which the Nazis quickly used to start crushing the communists and manipulate the 1933 **elections** in which the Nazis won 43.9 percent of the vote. Though short of a majority, this was attained by arresting the communist deputies and some SPD leaders to pass an **Enabling Act** that gave the Nazis dictatorial powers. Hitler was only just short of the two-thirds majority he needed to legally abolish the Weimar Republic. The SPD salvaged some self-respect by refusing to accede to this, but the Catholic centrists meekly supported the bill in return for minor concessions. It was passed by 441 votes to 84, hammering the final nails into the coffin of German parliamentary democracy. With Hindenburg's death in the summer of 1934, Hitler merged the offices of president and chancellor declaring himself **Führer** of the German Reich and introducing an absolute dictatorship.

Nazi Germany (1933–45)

After gaining power in 1933, Hitler established a regime so brutal that it has since attracted an overwhelming, almost ghoulish, level of interest in book and film. The Nazification of German society was rapid, and as the country remilitarized, Nazi Germany soon embarked on a ruinous crusade to conquer Europe and exterminate Jews, Roma (Gypsies), homosexuals, and others. Hitler's aggressive foreign policy led to World War II (1939–45), the loss of which was even more devastating and humiliating for Germany than the first, and resulted in the country being occupied by the USA, Britain, France and Russia.

Government and society

Once in absolute power Hitler consolidated his control, removing opposition and tightening the Nazi grip on all areas of society. All other political parties were banned, unions disbanded, and leaders of both arrested and sent to **concentration camps**. On May 11, 1934, the Nazis shocked the world by burning thousands of books that conflicted with Nazi ideology, and the exodus of known anti-Nazis and those with reasons to fear them began in earnest: Bertolt Brecht, Kurt Weill, Lotte Lenya and Wassily Kandinsky joined the likes of Albert Einstein and George Grosz in exile.

The machinery of state was quickly and brutally Nazified as the party put its own men into vital posts in local governments throughout Germany. A series of political executions took place, including those on June 30, 1934, which became known as the "**Night of the Long Knives**", which included a purge of their own ranks.

Given the suppression, fear, exodus and the tightening grip of Nazi control on all areas of life, the atmosphere in Germany changed irrevocably. The unemployed were drafted into labour battalions to work on the land or build Autobahns; the press and radio were orchestrated by Joseph Goebbels; children joined Nazi youth organizations; and Gestapo spies were placed in every area of German society. Even non-Nazis couldn't escape the plethora of organizations that developed across every area of life, from riding clubs and dog breeders to the "Reich Church" and "German League of Maidens". Everywhere the Nazis tried to implement order and dynamism, a process that reached its zenith during the **1936 Olympics**, which raised Germany's international standing and temporarily glossed over the realities of Nazi brutality.

World War II

Throughout the 1930s the Nazis made **preparations for war**, expanding the army and gearing the economy for war readiness, to dovetail with Hitler's foreign policy of obtaining Lebensraum ("living space") from neighbouring countries by intimidation. From 1936 onwards Hitler even spent much time with his favourite architect, Albert Speer, drawing up extensive plans for a remodelled and grandiose Berlin, to be called "Germania", once it became the capital of the world.

The road to war was swift. To little international protest the German army occupied the **Rhineland** (demilitarized under the Treaty of Versailles) in 1936, annexed **Austria** in 1938 and a few months later dismembered **Czechoslovakia** with Britain's and France's consent. Encouraged by this appeasement, Hitler made demands on Poland in 1939, hoping for a similar response, particularly since he had signed a nonaggression pact with his ultimate enemy, the Soviet Union, to ensure Germany could avoid a war on two fronts. But two days after the German invasion of **Poland** – dubbed the *Blitzkrieg* ("lightning war") – on September 1, Britain and France declared war in defence of their treaty obligations.

The outbreak of **World War II** was greeted with little enthusiasm in Germany, though the fall of France on July 18, 1940, caused jubilation. Up to that point Germany had suffered little from the war, and the impact of wartime austerity was softened by Nazi welfare organizations and a blanket of propaganda. In any case, with Gestapo informers believed to lurk everywhere, open dissent seemed impossible.

Having quickly gained direct or indirect control of large swathes of Europe, Hitler began a new phase in the war by breaking his pact and invading the **Soviet Union** on June, 22, 1941, then declaring war on the USA after his Japanese allies attacked the American base at Pearl Harbor. The German army rapidly advanced into the Soviet Union, but the six-month Battle of Stalingrad in the hard Russian winter of 1942–43 turned the war and sent the German army into retreat.

In the spring of 1943 German cities began to suffer their first heavy **air raids**, and by the end of the year, bombardments became a feature of everyday life in many German cities. Apart from chipping away at Nazi power, the destruction also intensified **underground resistance**. Despite the Gestapo stranglehold, some groups managed minor successes and several failed attempts on Hitler's life were made, particularly in the 1944 **July Bomb Plot**. The **Normandy Landings** in June 1944 marked the major turning-point on the western front, with Germany in retreat and fighting on two fronts.

On May 8, 1945, the German armed forces surrendered to the **Red Army** in Berlin and the world began to count the cost of its second world war. Some 67 million lives had been lost, among them seven million Germans – or around one in ten of the population. Almost all its cities had been reduced to rubble and in many Soviet-occupied zones this was just the start of the worst as the Soviets unleashed an orgy of rape and looting.

The Holocaust

It was only with the conquest of Germany that the full scale of Nazi atrocities became apparent. Hitler's main aim, along with expanding German borders, had long been to "cleanse" the world of those who did not conform to his social and racial ideals. Their persecution began with the start of Nazi rule and soon extended beyond political intellectual opponents and to embrace a wide range of groups – including active church members, freemasons, homosexuals, Roma, the disabled and most notoriously, the Jews – who in 1933 numbered around half a million in Germany. In 1934 the SA began to enforce a **boycott of Jewish** businesses, medical and legal practices – and these turned into bare-faced attacks on Jewish shops and institutions by SA men in civilian clothes on November 9, 1938, in a night of savagery known as **Kristallnacht**. Thereafter the Nazis enacted anti-Semitic laws confiscating property and making life difficult and dangerous for German Jews. Those who could, emigrated to countries beyond German control and escaped the Nazi "Final Solution", decided on at the **Wannsee conference** in 1942, to systematically exterminate all Jews in German-controlled territories in **concentration camps**. Those within Germany – including Sachsenhausen (see p.147), Dachau (see p.374) and Bergen-Belsen (see p.716) – were mainly prison and forced-labour camps, which had often been established early on in the Nazi regime, while those designed specifically for mass extermination were in the most part in the occupied territories. Of the eleven million estimated to have been murdered in the Holocaust, **six million** were Jewish, around 160,000 of them German Jews. Around 15,000 Jews survived in hiding in Germany, assisted by Germans who risked their lives to help them evade being rounded up onto trains bound for concentration camps.

Occupation and the Cold War (1945–89)

Having been brought down by the Allies, Germany was split between the USA, UK, France and Russia into four zones of occupation. Tensions between the western Allies and Russia led, in 1949, to the founding of capitalist and democratic West Germany and Soviet-dominated communist East Germany. That division remained in place as part of the Iron Curtain which divided Europe for more than forty years, as the world fought a Cold War.

Occupation

From July 17 to August 3, 1945, the **Potsdam conference** took place, deciding Germany's borders. The main losses to prewar Germany were to the east where all territory east of the rivers Oder and Neisse – old Prussian lands – became part of Poland or the USSR. These made up around a quarter of Germany's lands and turned a fifth of its population into refugees, as the German populations here and in the Czech Republic became subject to revenge attacks and forced to flee west into Germany.

This compounded a German postwar situation that was already very bleak. Agriculture and industry had virtually collapsed, threatening acute shortages of food and fuel just as winter approached and a weakened civilian population fell prey to typhus, TB and other hunger-related diseases. The Allies did what they could, but even by the spring of 1947 rations remained at malnutrition levels. Crime soared. In Berlin alone, two thousand people were arrested every month, many of them from juvenile gangs that roamed the ruins murdering, robbing and raping. In the countryside bandits ambushed supply convoys heading for the city. The winter of 1946–47 was one of the coldest since records began, people froze to death aboard trains and Berlin hospitals alone treated 55,000 people for frostbite.

Thereafter things gradually improved with the help of **Marshall Plan** aid, while the process of demilitarization and de-Nazification agreed at Potsdam continued apace as trials in Nuremburg (1945–49) brought dozens of Nazi war criminals to justice. But one issue that divided opinion at Potsdam was the reinstatement of democracy. The Soviet Union had already taken steps towards establishing a communist administration under **Walter Ulbricht** and the SED (Sozialistische Einheitspartei Deutschlands) in their zone of occupation before the war was over.

The birth of the two Germanys

In 1948 tension mounted as the Allies introduced economic reform in the western half of Berlin, which now formed an island within Soviet-occupied Germany. The Russians cut off electricity supplies to the city and severed road and rail links during the **Berlin blockade**, as they attempted to force the western Allies out of Berlin. In the end the greatest weapon proved to be American and British support when on June 26, 1948, they began the **Berlin airlift**, flying supplies into the city to keep it alive against the odds for almost a year until the Russians relented.

Within six months, the political division of Germany was formalized by the creation of two rival states. First, the British, French and American zones of occupation were amalgamated to form the **Federal Republic of Germany** (May 1949) based on a federal system that gave significant powers to its eleven constituent states. The Soviets followed suit by establishing the **German Democratic Republic** on October 7. As Berlin lay deep within GDR territory, its eastern sector naturally became the GDR capital. But the Federal Republic chose Bonn, and West Berlin remained under overall Allied control.

The 1950s

Throughout the 1950s **West Germany**, under Chancellor Konrad Adenauer, recovered from the ravages of war astonishingly quickly to become Europe's largest economy. Meanwhile the **GDR** languished, partly as the result of the Soviets' ruthless asset-stripping – removing factories, rolling stock and generators to replace losses in the war-ravaged USSR. The death of Stalin in 1953 raised hopes that pressures could be eased, but instead the government unwittingly fuelled smouldering resentment by announcing a ten percent rise in work norms, causing workers to band together in the **1953 uprising**, which was brutally suppressed. So as the economic disparity between East and West Germany worsened throughout the 1950s, West Berlin became an increasingly attractive destination for East Berliners, who were able to cross the city's zonal borders more or less freely. This steady population-drain undermined prospects for development in the GDR, as 2,500,000, often young and often highly skilled workers quit the GDR during the 1950s for the higher living standards and greater political freedom of the West.

The 1960s

By 1961, the East German regime was getting desperate, and rumours that the Berlin border might be sealed began to circulate. Shortly after midnight on August 13, 1961, it was, with the city divided by the **Berlin Wall**, which went up overnight, and then further strengthened to form the notorious barrier or "death strip" between the two countries (see box, p.88). Despite outrage throughout West Germany and formal diplomatic protests from the Allies, everyone knew that a firmer line risked war.

As life grew more comfortable in **West Germany**, society began to fragment along generational lines. The immediate catalyst was the wave of student unrest in 1967–68, when initial grievances against conservative universities grew into a wider disaffection with West Germany's materialism. The APO, or extra-parliamentary opposition, emerged as a strong and vocal force criticizing what many people saw as a failed attempt to build a true democracy on the ruins of Nazi Germany. Another powerful strand was anti-Americanism, fuelled by US policy in Southeast Asia, Latin America and the Middle East. Both viewpoints tended to bewilder and enrage older Germans and although the mass-protest movement fizzled out towards the end of the 1960s, a new and deadlier opposition – the **Baader-Meinhof** group – would emerge in the 1970s, unleashing a wave of terrorism few could sympathize with.

The 1970s and 1980s

Germany's place in the international scene changed considerably around the turn of the 1970s. Both superpowers hoped to thaw relations, while West German elections brought to power Willy Brandt, a chancellor committed to rapprochement with the GDR. In 1972, the Federal Republic and the GDR signed a **Basic Treaty**, which bound both states to respect each other's frontiers and sovereignty. In return for diplomatic recognition, the GDR allowed West Germans access to friends and family across the border, which had effectively been denied to them (barring limited visits in the mid-1960s). However, the freedom to move from East to West was restricted to disabled people and senior citizens.

So, throughout the 1970s and early 1980s relations between West and East Germany remained cordial, despite a resumption of frostiness in US–Soviet relations, which heightened concern about **nuclear weapons**. Antinuclear activists protested during the Berlin visit of US President Ronald Reagan in June 1981, as part of a new radical movement throughout West Germany. Concern about the arms race and the environment was widespread; feminism and gay rights commanded increasing support. Left-wing and Green groups formed an **Alternative Liste** to fight elections which formed the nucleus of **Die Grünen**, the Green Party, which remains a significant presence in German politics.

East Germany remained relatively quiet. The new East German leader, **Erich Honecker**, who was regarded as a "liberal", succeeded Walter Ulbricht in 1971. Under him, living standards improved and there was some relaxation of the regime's tight controls on society. But the changes were mostly trivial: escapes continued to be attempted and the vast **Stasi** (see p.117) was as strong as ever in its surveillance and persecutions.

Die Wende

The year 1989 ranks as both one of the most significant years in German history and one of the most unforseeable. Yet in under twelve months **Die Wende** ("the turn") transformed Germany. With little warning East Germany suddenly collapsed in the wake of the general easing of communism in the Eastern Bloc of the late 1980s. The Berlin Wall came down on November 9, 1989, symbolizing an end to the Cold War, making a lifetime's dream come true for most Germans – above all, those living in the East. Events then fairly logically and briskly followed: the union of the two Germanys; the reassertion of Berlin as capital; and the start of a lengthy process of putting those responsible for the GDR's crimes on trial.

The first holes in the Iron Curtain

When, in 1985, **Mikhail Gorbachev** became the new Soviet leader and began his reformist campaigns, *glasnost* and *perestroika*, their initial impact on East Germany was slight. The SED regarded them with deep suspicion, so while Poland and Hungary embarked on the road to democracy, Erich Honecker declared that the Berlin Wall would stand for another fifty or a hundred years if necessary. The authorities also banned pro-*glasnost* Soviet magazine *Sputnik*.

Nevertheless, as the decade wore on some signs of protest began to emerge: the **Protestant Church** provided a haven for environmental and peace organizations, whose members unfurled banners calling for greater freedom at an official ceremony in Berlin in January 1988. They were immediately arrested, imprisoned, and later expelled from the GDR. With the government so unyielding, it fell to other Eastern European countries to make the Wende possible: in 1988 Hungary began taking down the barbed-wire fence along their Austrian border, creating a hole in the Iron Curtain, across which many East Germans fled. A similar pattern emerged in Czechoslovakia.

The October revolution

The East German government's disarrayed response to reform elsewhere galvanized thousands of people into action who had previously been content to make the best of things. Fledgling opposition groups like the **Neues Forum** emerged, and unrest began in Leipzig and Dresden and soon spread to Berlin.

Then, at the beginning of October, at the pompous official celebration of the GDR's **fortieth anniversary**, Gorbachev stressed the need for new ideas and stunningly announced that the USSR would not interfere in the affairs of fellow socialist states. Protests and scuffles along the cavalcade route escalated into a huge demonstration as the day wore on, which the police and Stasi brutally suppressed.

Thousands of arrests were made, and prisoners were subjected to the usual degrading treatment and beatings.

The following week, nationwide demonstrations came close to bloodshed in **Leipzig**, where 70,000 people marched through the city, forcing the sudden replacement of Erich Honecker with Egon Krenz as party secretary, who immediately announced that the regime was ready for dialogue.

The exodus via other Eastern Bloc countries and the pressure on the streets kept rising, culminating on November 4, when East Berlin saw over one million citizens demonstrate, forcing authorities to make hasty concessions, including dropping the requirement for GDR citizens to get visas to visit Czechoslovakia – in effect, permitting emigration: within two days fifteen thousand had reached Bavaria – bringing the number of East Germans who had fled the country in 1989 to 200,000.

The Wall opens

The **opening of the Berlin Wall** was announced almost casually, on the evening of Thursday, November 9, when Berlin party boss Günter Schabowski told a press conference that East German citizens were free to leave the GDR with valid exit visas, which would henceforth be issued without delay. Hardly daring to believe the puzzling announcement, Berliners on both sides of the Wall started heading for border crossings.

Huge crowds converged on the Brandenburg Gate, where the Volkspolizei gave up checking documents and simply let thousands of East Germans walk into West Berlin. An impromptu street party broke out, with West Berliners popping champagne corks and Germans from both sides of the Wall embracing. On the first weekend of the opening of the Wall 2.7 million exit visas were issued to East Germans, who formed mile-long queues at checkpoints. West Germans – and TV-viewers around the world – gawped at streams of Trabant cars pouring into West Berlin, where shops enjoyed a bonanza as East Germans spent their DM100 "welcome money", given to each of them by the Federal Republic. By the following weekend, **ten million visas** had been issued since November 9 – an incredible statistic considering the whole population of the GDR was only sixteen million.

The road to reunification

In the weeks that followed, the formidable Stasi security service was dismantled, and free elections in the East agreed on, for which the SED hastily repackaged itself as a new, supposedly voter-friendly PDS – Partei des Demokratischen Sozialismus (Democratic Socialist Party), partly by firing the old guard. The next initiative came from the West when **Chancellor Kohl** visited Dresden on December 19, addressing a huge, enthusiastic crowd as "dear countrymen", and declaring a **united Germany** his ultimate goal. As East Germans discovered that West Germany's standard of living eclipsed anything in the GDR, and found out exactly how corrupt their government had been, they concurred – with the result that the GDR's first free elections on March 18, 1990, returned a victory for a right-wing alliance dominated by the CDU and Kohl.

The **economic union** was hammered out almost immediately and the GDR began rapidly to fade away. With confirmation that a united Germany would respect its post-World War II boundaries, the wartime allies agreed to reunification. After an all-night Volkskammer session on August 23 it was announced that the GDR would become part of the Federal Republic on **October 3, 1990**.

The 1990s

December 2, 1990, saw Germany's first nationwide elections since 1933. Nationally the CDU, in coalition with the FDP (Free Democrats), triumphed easily. One surprise was that the PDS secured 25 percent of the vote in eastern Berlin on an anti-unemployment and anti-social-inequality ticket.

In 1991 vastly unpopular tax increases in western Germany had to be introduced to pay for the spiralling cost of unification. As the year wore on, and unemployment continued to rise, Kohl's honeymoon with the East ended. He became reluctant to show himself there, and when he finally did, in April, he was greeted by catcalls and egg-hurlers.

Ill feeling between easterners and westerners (nicknamed *Ossis* and *Wessis*) also became apparent and increased throughout the decade. West Germans resented the tax increases and caricatured easterners as naive and lazy. East Germans resented patronizing western attitudes and economic inequalities that made them second-class citizens, so mocked westerners for their arrogance and materialism. Feelings got worse as it became apparent that the ever-increasing cost of reunification had pushed the German economy into recession.

As the instability of the transitional period began to ebb, the pursuit of those responsible for the GDR's repressive crimes began in earnest, particularly as Stasi files were opened to the public. Trials throughout the 1990s brought Politbüro members, border guards, and even sports coaches who'd doped players without their knowledge, before the courts.

On June 20, 1991, a Bundestag decision to relocate the national government to Berlin ushered in a new era: a tremendous task, and one undertaken in the late 1990s with the usual German thoroughness.

Germany today

At the start of the twenty-first century, Germany finally appeared to be healing the wounds of the turmoil and division of the twentieth. With its cities rebuilt and democracy established throughout the country, centred on its new capital in Berlin, the economy resurgent, and memorials completed to the victims of the Nazi atrocities, Germany could project a friendly, youthful and dynamic image to the world as it hosted the football **World Cup finals in 2006**. The event, which put the nation back at ease with its own patriotism, seems to have coincided with a new phase of its history, in which it explores its place in international politics, completes the restructuring of its welfare state and comes to terms with economic and social inequalities: both between its eastern and western halves and across society, with the specific challenge of addressing the issues faced by the large number of immigrants, particularly Turks, who have settled in Germany since the 1950s.

Politics

Current German politics continues to be dominated by two parties: the moderately left-wing SPD and a centre-right alliance led by the CDU. From 1998 to 2005 the government was led by SPD chancellor Gerhard Schröder, the world's first ruling coalition that included an environmental party, the Green Party, in a government that included the popular green maverick Joschka Fischer. Naturally the government was environmentally aware and reform-minded, making an agreement to switch off all Germany's nuclear reactors by 2020. But elsewhere, reforms of the welfare state were hampered by a lacklustre economy, which led to the call for an early election in 2005. The result was a political stalemate that could only be broken by an SPD–CDU "grand coalition" under the CDU's highly gifted leader **Angela Merkel**, an east German fluent in Russian and with a doctorate in quantum physics. This government has increasingly pursued a more ambitious foreign policy – building on the trend of the previous government which deployed German troops for the first time since World War II in peace-keeping missions in Kosovo and Afghanistan. At the same time, Germany's rejection of the Iraq War worsened its relationship with the USA and effectively put its campaign for a seat on the UN Security Council on hold.

At home Merkel's progress has been slow, and constantly hampered by bickering within the grand coalition and by party politics. However, Germany's deep exposure to the global financial crisis since 2007 has lowered voter expectations and helped strengthen the coalition which has been fairly united in its fiscal rescue packages.

Economy

Germany's economy is the world's third largest, which as the economic hub of the European Union – and home to the **European Central Bank** – have far-reaching consequences throughout the continent. However, in the past decade, and despite a leaner industrial sector that has replaced many ageing patriarchs with younger and more dynamic management, and a restructuring of the labour market, performance has been disappointing, particularly in the east.

Ostalgie

Nostalgia for the East, or rather *Nostalgie* for the *Osten*, has produced **Ostalgie**, a hybrid word for a phenomenon that's been gathering momentum throughout the old East Germany. Though the sentiment might originate with those who can remember the collapsed country, this nostalgia for the iconography of communist East Germany has also proved immensely popular with visitors, spawning a mini-industry in Berlin.

The meaning of *Ostalgie* is a little nebulous, as it has slowly redefined itself since the Wende. What started as a melancholic craving for the securities of life in a communist state by the sixteen million East Germans thrust into the turbulent and uncertain world of capitalism, became an expression of both discontent and identity. It was a protest at the quick eradication of a unique East German culture and its absorption into the West – a process that implied that all things Western were superior, and tended to mock everything from the East as laughably backward and naive.

So *Ostalgie* became a way of affirming that some aspects of the GDR were worth celebrating, that – despite the many shortcomings of the state – it had also produced happy and rewarding moments in people's lives. Champions of the GDR also point out that it was progressive in areas where the West still needs to improve: scarcity lent more value to consumer goods and created a society that was far less wasteful, decadent and environmentally unfriendly.

These days *Ostalgie* stretches far beyond political debates, and the film **Good Bye Lenin!** in 2003, with its nostalgic and comedic celebration of 1970s GDR kitsch and innocence, was as important a catalyst as any. In its wake the celebration of cult GDR icons – particularly the chubby, cheerful **Ampelmann** from East German pedestrian crossings and the fibreglass **Trabant** – became ever more popular. There's also been a revival of some utilitarian GDR products, including foods, household products and cosmetics made by companies that had gone out of business when Western goods flooded the market.

The problem in the east remains the death of manufacturing and the absence of anything to replace it, as well as its welfare mentality. But over all industry still complains of high taxes and complicated red tape. Unemployment remains high at about eleven percent, or 4.5 million, and looks unlikely to drop until the end of the global recession.

Society

Just as in the economic sphere, eastern Germany continues to have many of its own social problems that have arisen from reunification, and which have led to the seeking of solace in nostalgia (see box, opposite), or simply moving west to find jobs. This is particularly true for women, who have been doing better at school, and so are better qualified: in some eastern German towns around half the young women have left. The people remaining appear to be forming a new underclass of Germans, low-skilled and often jobless, whose poverty is growing and creating fertile ground for political extremism. The ultra-right-wing National Partie Deutschland (National Party of Germany; NPD) has seats in two east-German state legislatures – and another far-right party has deputies in Brandenburg – and racist attacks have accompanied this.

In the west a greater concern is the disaffected descendants of immigrants who increasingly use Islam as a rallying point. Many are the children of Turkish "guest workers" who were invited to the country in the 1960s and have remained, giving Germany a 2.6 million-strong Turkish population, many German-born and caught between the two cultures. Often living in the poorest neighbourhoods with the worst schools, much of their frustration and anger at society is voiced through petty crime and gangs. However, there are signs that the Turkish population is becoming more established in Germany – kebabs now rival sausages as the country's favourite fast-food, and large mosques are being built in cities like Cologne and Berlin.

Angela Merkel insists economic and social integration of immigrants is "decisive" for Germany's wellbeing, so perhaps her attitude will pave the way for cooperation with Cem Özdemir, the Turkish-German co-chairman of Germany's Green Party since November 2008. As a young (44), charismatic family-man with an ethnic-minority background, he arguably reminds people of Barack Obama and he openly admits a willingness to engage in coalitions with almost any party in order to further the Green cause. Certainly he seems the kind of candidate who might represent the face of the ever-more-powerful modern Germany – one that is environmentally minded, as sensitive to hyphenated identities as it is to remembering its past and to forging a new and united European future. And in recent years a new generation of proud patriots has emerged, who – since their coming out at the 2006 football World Cup – now let their German flags flutter from cars across the nation whenever the national football team plays.

Books

What follows is a short selection of some of the best books about Germany; those indicated by the 🏃 symbol are particularly recommended. Most are readily available, but those that are currently out of print are signified with (o/p).

General

Celia Applegate *A Nation of Provincials: The German Idea of Heimat.* An intriguing look at the attachment to localities in German history.

🏃 John Ardagh *Germany and the Germans.* Astute and illuminating characterization of almost every aspect of Germany – its history, politics and national psyche.

Travel writing

Patrick Leigh Fermor *A Time of Gifts.* Account of a 1933 walk from Rotterdam to Constantinople, where he passes through a Nazifying Germany.

Heinrich Heine *Deutschland: A Winter's Tale.* Heine writes about his journey from exile in Paris to his Hamburg home, with insightful snatches about early nineteenth-century Germany along the way. Also recommended is his *Harz Journey*, in

which the narrative is interspersed with elegant poems.

Jerome K. Jerome *Three Men on the Bummel.* Semi-fictional account of three disorganized English gents travelling around Germany at the turn of the twentieth century.

🏃 Mark Twain *A Tramp Abroad.* Wickedly witty and well-observed commentary on his late nineteenth-century travels through Germany.

Art and architecture

Peter Adam *The Art of the Third Reich.* Engrossing and well-written account of the official state art of Nazi Germany – with over three hundred illustrations.

Wolf-Dieter Dube *The Expressionists.* A good general introduction to Germany's most distinctive contribution to twentieth-century art.

Sabine Hake *German National Cinema.* Painstakingly researched and rewarding historical account of film.

Frank Whitford *Bauhaus.* Comprehensive and well-illustrated guide to the architectural movement that flourished in Dessau.

History

General history

Andreas Nachama, Julius H. Schoeps and Hermann Simon (eds) *Jews in Berlin*. Packed with source material of every kind, this well-illustrated book charts the troubled history of Berlin's Jews between 1244 and 2000.

Dietrich Orlow *A History of Modern Germany: 1871 to Present*. An excellent survey of Germany's troubled twentieth century.

Holy Roman Empire

Geoffrey Barraclough *The Origins of Modern Germany*. Solid and insightful analysis of medieval German history – well written, too.

Thomas A. Brady Jr, Heiko A. Oberman and James D. Tracy (eds) *Handbook of European History,*

1400–1600: Late Middle Ages, Renaissance, and Reformation. First-class guide to the period.

Heiko A. Oberman *Luther: Man Between God and the Devil*. Psychologically intriguing biography of Martin Luther.

The German Empire

David Blackbourn *The Long Nineteenth Century: A History of Germany, 1780–1918*. Good coverage of the period in which Germany emerged as a nation-state.

Roger Chickering *Imperial Germany and the Great War, 1914–1918*. Readable introduction to World War I Germany.

A.J.P. Taylor *Bismarck: The Man and the Statesman*. Engrossingly well-written biography of probably Germany's shrewdest-ever politician.

Hans-Ulrich Wehler *The German Empire, 1871–1918*. General history of the period, which explores the links between the empire and Nazi Germany.

Weimar Germany

Alex De Jonge *The Weimar Chronicle: Prelude to Hitler*. (o/p). While not the most comprehensive of accounts of the Weimar Republic, this is far and away the liveliest. The book is spiced with eyewitness memoirs and a mass of engaging detail.

Peter Gay *Weimar Culture: The Outsider as Insider*. An engaging look at the intellectual and cultural brilliance of 1920s Germany.

Nazi Germany

Anon. *A Woman in Berlin*. The recent reissue of a remarkable war diary kept by a female journalist

who vividly describes the pathetic lot of Berlin's vanquished in the closing days of the war, when looting and gang rape were part of daily life. Like most women in Berlin, the author was raped multiple times by different Russian soldiers, yet her exposure of this led to such an uproar when the book was first published in 1950s Germany – society was unprepared to face its recent trauma – that it wasn't reprinted again during the author's lifetime; she died in 2001.

Antony Beevor *Berlin: the Downfall 1945*. It might take until halfway through this thick book to actually get to the fall of Berlin, but once there a fine job is done of synthesizing many sources to provide a riveting account of how the city's defences crumbled and its civilians suffered, with few harrowing details spared.

George Clare *Berlin Days 1946– 1947*. British-army translator who recounts time spent in Berlin at what the Germans called the *Nullpunkt* – the zero point – when the city, its economy, buildings and society, began to rebuild almost from scratch. Packed with characters and observation.

Raul Hilberg *The Destruction of the European Jews*. Learned and comprehensive study of the Nazi extermination of Jews.

Ian Kershaw *Hitler*. The definitive biography of the dictator.

William Shirer *The Rise and Fall of the Third Reich*. A classic, written by an American journalist stationed in Berlin during the Nazi period. Despite its length and occasionally outdated perceptions, the book is full of insights and easy to dip into, thanks to an exhaustive index.

Gerhard L. Weinberg *A World at Arms: A Global History of World War II*. Impressive and concise treatment of World War II.

Peter Wyden *Stella* (o/p). Gripping story of a young Jewish woman who avoided deportation and death by hunting down Jews in hiding in wartime Berlin for the SS. The author, who knew Stella, traces her life story and tries to untangle the morality.

Postwar history

Timothy Garton Ash *The File: A Personal History*. Garton Ash lived and worked as a journalist in East Berlin in 1980, making him the subject of surveillance and a Stasi file. In this book he tracks down the file and interviews informers using an informal style to weave everything together and marvellously evoke the era. His book *We the People* (US title: *The Magic Lantern*) is an equally enjoyable first-hand account of the fall of the Wall.

Anna Funder *Stasiland: True Stories from Behind the Berlin Wall*. Engrossing personal account uncovering the experiences of East Germans who found themselves

entangled with the GDR's State Security Service (Stasi).

Peter J. Katzenstein (ed) *Tamed Power: Germany in Europe*. A look at how Germany uses the European Union to express its political and economic power.

Charles S. Maier *Dissolution: The Crisis of Communism and the End of East Germany*. Excellent investigation of the collapse of the GDR.

Anne McElvoy *The Saddled Cow* (o/p). Thorough and witty analysis of the GDR, by a former *Times* correspondent. The title is a quote from Stalin, who once said "Communism fits Germany as a saddle fits a cow."

David E. Murphy et al *Battleground Berlin: CIA vs KGB in the Cold War.* A detailed account by participants of the tense skirmishing between the spies of the two superpowers.

Fiction

Anon. *The Nibelungenlied.* Germany's epic poem (see p.520) of violence and vengeance; a heroic legend comparable in scope to the Iliad.

Alfred Döblin *Berlin-Alexanderplatz.* Unrelenting stream-of-consciousness epic about the city's proletariat.

🏃 **Theodor Fontane** *Effie Briest.* This story of a woman's adultery in the second half of the nineteenth century offers a vivid picture of Prussian mores, with the sort of terrible and absurd climax that's virtually unique to Fontane and to German literature.

Johann Wolfgang von Goethe *The Sorrows of Young Werther.* Small novella on suicide that's probably the easiest introduction to the work of Germany's most celebrated literary genius.

Günter Grass *Dog Years; The Tin Drum; The Flounder.* The most celebrated contemporary German author, who specializes in fables that explore the German psyche in the aftermath of Nazi Germany and World War II. However, rather than being uncomfortable and dark, most of Grass's work is very readable thanks in part to many witty touches. His 2008 autobiography *Peeling the Onion* revealed for the first time a level of personal guilt, as the author had served in the Waffen SS, the elite Nazi army.

Jacob and Wilhelm Grimm *Complete Grimm Tales.* Collection of folk and fairy tales by the most famous purveyors of the art form. One of the best places to understand Germany's Gothic sense of itself.

Hans Jakob Christoffel von Grimmelshausen *Adventures of a Simpleton.* Probably the finest seventeenth-century novel: an epic tale that follows its hero through various adventures in the era of the grisly Thirty Years' War.

🏃 **Christopher Isherwood** *Goodbye to Berlin.* Set in the decadent atmosphere of the Weimar Republic as the Nazis steadily gain power, this collection of stories brilliantly evokes the period and brings to life some classic Berlin characters. It subsequently formed the basis of the films *I Am a Camera* and the later remake *Cabaret.* Isherwood's *Mr Norris Changes Trains* features adventures of the overweight eponymous hero in pre-Hitler Berlin and Germany.

🏃 **Wladimir Kaminer** *Russian Disco, Tales of Everyday Lunacy on the Streets of Berlin.* Collection of stories that are snapshots of Berlin through the eyes of a Russian immigrant from Moscow – unusual, entertaining and well written. Kaminer has since become a local celebrity, DJing *Russendisko* nights at *Kaffee Burger* (see p.125).

Thomas Mann *The Magic Mountain.* Mann's most celebrated book, a well-observed critique of the preoccupations of pre-World War I society. *Buddenbrooks*, about the decline of a bourgeois family from his native Lübeck, tackles similar themes.

Ulrich Plenzdorf *The New Sufferings of Young W.* Satirical reworking of Goethe's *The Sorrows of Young Werther*, set in 1970s East Berlin. When first published it pushed against the borders of literary acceptability under the old regime with its portrayal of alienated, disaffected youth.

Erich Maria Remarque *All Quiet on the Western Front*. Classic World War I novel: horrific, but written with a grim sense of humour.

Bernhard Schlink *The Reader*. A tale of sex, love and shame in postwar Germany as a young man tries to comprehend the Holocaust and his feelings for those involved; winner of the Fisk Fiction Prize – and now a film starring Kate Winslet.

Language

Language

Pronunciation and grammar 889

Words and phrases..890

A food and drink glossary...893

Glossary 897

German

nglish speakers approaching German for the first time have one real initial advantage, which is that German – as a close linguistic relative of English – shares with it a lot of basic vocabulary. It doesn't take long to work out that the *Milch* for your breakfast *Kaffee* comes from a *Kuh* that spends its life eating *Gras* in a *Feld*, or that *Brot* is nicer when spread with *Butter*. Two things conspire to give German a fearsome reputation among non-native speakers, however. The first is the **grammar**: it *is* complex – many Germans never really master it properly – but for the purposes of a short stay you shouldn't need to wade too deeply into its intricacies. The second is the **compound noun** – the German habit of creating enormously long-winded words to define something quite specific. These aren't as difficult as they first appear, since they're composed from building blocks of basic vocabulary, so that, if you break them down into their component parts, you can often puzzle out the meaning without recourse to a dictionary. Like any major language, German has considerable **regional variation**. Of the dialects you may encounter, the hardest to understand are Bavarian, *Kölsch* (the dialect of Cologne) and *Plattdeutsch*, which is spoken along the North Sea coast. The most correct German is considered to be the version spoken in and around Hannover.

Pronunciation and grammar

Unlike English, German is written more or less phonetically, so that once you understand how the vowels and consonants are pronounced there's rarely any ambiguity. Exceptions include foreign words that have been incorporated into German – including, in recent years, a great many from English. German pronunciation is clipped and clear, which makes it an ideal language for singers and rappers.

Vowels and umlauts

a long 'a' as in f**a**rther; short 'a' as in h**a**t
e as in l**ay**
i as in m**ee**k
o as in h**o**p
u as in l**oo**t

ä is a combination of a and e, sometimes pronounced like **e** in s**e**t (eg Hände) and sometimes like **ai** in l**ai**d (eg Gerät)
ö is a combination of o and e, like the French *eu*
ü is a combination of u and e, like bl**ue**

Vowel combinations

ai as in p**ie**
au as in m**ou**se
ie as in tr**ee**

ei as in p**ie**
eu as in b**oi**l

Consonants and consonant combinations

Consonants are pronounced as written, with no silent letters. The differences from English are:

ch is pronounced like Scottish "loch"

g is always a hard "g" sound, except in the word ending –ig (eg Leipzig) when it is like a very soft German –ch

j is pronounced like an English y

r is throaty, similar to French

s is pronounced similar to, but slightly softer than, an English z

sch is like English "sh"

th is pronounced like English t

v is somewhere between f and v

w is pronounced like English v, except at the end of the word, as in the Berlin place-names Kladow and Gatow, where it is almost silent

z is pronounced ts

The German letter ß, the Scharfes S, occasionally replaces ss in a word, though new rules mean it is being used less than it was.

Gender and adjective endings

German nouns can be one of three **genders**: masculine, feminine or neuter (*der, die* or *das*). Sometimes the gender is obvious – it's *der Mann* (the man) and *die Frau* (the woman) – but sometimes it seems baffling: a girl is *das Mädchen*, because *Mädchen* – "little maiden" – is a diminutive, and diminutives are neutral. There are some hard and fast rules to help you know which is which: nouns ending in -er (*der Bäcker, der Sportler*) are masculine; -ung, -heit, -keit or -schaft are feminine (*die Zeitung, die Freiheit, die Fröhlichkeit, die Mannschaft*). Definite (*der*/the) and indefinite (*ein*/a) articles and **adjective endings** all change according to the precise grammatical role in the sentence of the noun they correspond to, which is where things start to get complex. If in doubt, stick to *der* or *das* for single items: once there is more than one of anything, it becomes *die* anyway.

Politeness

You can address children, animals and, nowadays, young people (but only in relaxed social situations, and really only if you're the same age) with the familiar "**du**" to mean "you". For anyone else – and particularly for older people or officials – stick to the polite "**Sie**"; if they want to be on familiar terms with you, they'll invite you to do so – "*Duzen wir?*". Incidentally, unmarried German women often prefer to be addressed as "**Frau**", the word "**Fräulein**" to describe a young, single woman being considered nowadays old-fashioned and rather sexist.

Words and phrases

Greetings and basic phrases

Good morning	Guten Morgen	**Goodbye** (telephone only)	Auf Wiederhören
Good evening	Guten Abend		
Good day	Guten Tag	**How are you?** (polite)	Wie geht es Ihnen?
Hello (informal)	Servus (southern Germany only); Hallo	**How are you?** (informal)	Wie geht es dir?
Goodbye (formal)	Auf Wiedersehen		
Goodbye (informal)	Tschüss (but also Ciao, Servus)	**Yes**	Ja
		No	Nein

Please/ You're welcome	Bitte/Bitte schön	Cheap	Billig
		Expensive	Teuer
Thank you/Thank you very much	Danke/Danke schön	Good	Gut
		Where is …?	Wo ist …?
Do you speak English?	Sprechen Sie Englisch?	How much does that cost?	Wieviel kostet das?
I don't speak German	Ich spreche kein Deutsch	What time is it?	Wieviel Uhr ist es?; Wie spat ist es?
Please speak more slowly	Könnten Sie bitte langsamer sprechen	The bill, please	Die Rechnung, bitte (or Zahlen, bitte)
I understand	Ich verstehe	Separately or together?	Getrennt oder Zusammen?
I don't understand	Ich verstehe nicht		
Where?	Wo	Receipt	Quittung
When?	Wann?	Where are the toilets?	Wo sind die Toiletten, bitte?
How much?	Wieviel?		
Here	Hier	Toilet	Toilette/WC
There	Da	Women's toilets	Damen/Frauen
Open	Geöffnet/offen/auf	Men's toilets	Herren/Männer
Closed	Geschlossen/zu	Shower	Dusche
Over there	Drüben	Bath	Bad
This one	Dieses	Is there a room available?	Haben Sie noch ein Zimmer frei?
That one	Jenes		
Large	Gross	I'd like a room for two	Ich hätte gern ein Zimmer für zwei
Small	Klein		
More	Mehr	I'd like a single/ double room	Ich hätte gern ein Einzelzimmer/ Doppelzimmer
Less	Weniger		
A bit	Ein bisschen		
A little	Wenig	When does the next train to Berlin leave?	Wann fährt der nächste Zug nach Berlin?
A lot	Viel		

Numbers

1	eins	17	siebzehn
2	zwei	18	achtzehn
3	drei	19	neunzehn
4	vier	20	zwanzig
5	fünf	21	ein-und-zwanzig
6	sechs	22	zwei-und-zwanzig
7	sieben	30	dreissig
8	acht	40	vierzig
9	neun	50	fünfzig
10	zehn	60	sechzig
11	elf	70	siebzig
12	zwölf	80	achtzig
13	dreizehn	90	neunzig
14	vierzehn	100	hundert
15	fünfzehn	1000	tausend
16	sechzehn		

Days, months, time and seasons

Today	Heute	Monday	Montag
Yesterday	Gestern	Tuesday	Dienstag
Tomorrow	Morgen	Wednesday	Mittwoch
The day before yesterday	Vorgestern	Thursday	Donnerstag
		Friday	Freitag
The day after tomorrow	Übermorgen	Saturday	Samstag/Sonnabend
		Sunday	Sonntag
Day	Tag	January	Januar/Jänner
Night	Nacht		(S. German, dialect)
Week	Woche	February	Februar
Month	Monat	March	März
Year	Jahr	April	April
Weekend	Wochenende	May	Mai
In the morning	Am Vormittag/ Vormittags	June	Juni
		July	Juli
Tomorrow morning	Morgen früh	August	August
In the afternoon	Am Nachmittag/ Nachmittags	September	September
		October	Oktober
In the evening	Am Abend	November	November
Seven thirty	Halb acht (ie half before eight)	December	Dezember
Seven fifteen	Viertel nach sieben	Spring	Frühling
Seven forty five	Viertel vor acht	Summer	Sommer
Now	Jetzt	Autumn	Herbst
Later	Später	Winter	Winter
Earlier	Früher	Holidays	Ferien
At what time?	Um wieviel Uhr?	Bank holiday	Feiertag

Transport and signs

Abflug	Departure (airport)	Grenze	Border
Abreise/Abfahrt	Departure (more generally)	Kein Eingang	No entrance
		Lärmschutz	Noise abatement (in connection with speed limit)
Ampel	Traffic light		
Ankunft	Arrivals		
Ausfahrt	Motorway exit	Nicht rauchen/ Rauchen verboten	No smoking
Ausgang freihalten	Keep clear/no parking in front of exit	Notausgang	Emergency exit
Ausgang	Exit	Pass	Mountain pass
Autobahn	Motorway	Plakette	Colour-coded sticker for cars, which you'll need if travelling into major city centres.
Baustelle	Roadworks (on Autobahn etc)		
Einbahnstrasse	one-way street	Raststätte	Fuel stop on the Autobahn, usually with a café or restaurant
Eingang	Entrance		
Fähre	Ferry		
Führerschein	Driver's licence		
Fussgängerzone	Pedestrian-only zone	Reisepass	Passport (but also Pass)

Stau	Traffic jam	Unfall	Accident
Staugefähr!	Possibility of traffic jams	Verboten	Prohibited
Tankstelle	Petrol station	Vorsicht!	Attention!
Umleitung	Diversion		

A food and drink glossary

Basic terms

Breakfast	Frühstück	Bowl	Becher
Lunch	Mittagessen (Lunch is also sometimes used)	Glass	Glas
		Menu	Speisekarte
		Wine list	Weinkarte
Coffee and cakes	Kaffee und Kuchen – a mid-afternoon German ritual, equivalent to English afternoon tea	Set menu	Menü
		Course	Gang (a Drei-Gang-Menü is a three-course set menu)
Supper, dinner	Abendessen	Starter	Vorspeise
Knife	Messer	Main course	Hauptgericht
Fork	Gabel	Dessert	Nachspeise
Spoon	Löffel	The bill	Die Rechnung
Plate	Teller	Tip	Trinkgeld
Cup	Tasse	Vegetarian	Vegetarisch

Cooking terms

blau	rare	gutbürgerlich	traditional German
eingelegt	pickled	hausgemacht	home-made
frisch	fresh	heiss	hot
gebacken	baked	lauwarm	lukewarm
gebraten	fried, roasted	kalt	cold
gedämpft	steamed	roh	raw
gefüllt	stuffed	spiess	skewered
gegrillt	grilled	Topf, Eintopf	stew, casserole
gekocht	boiled (also more generally means "cooked")	überbacken	with a hot topping (especially cheese)
geräuchert	smoked	zart	tender (eg of meat)
geschmort	braised, slow-cooked		

Basics

Bio	organic	Butterbrot (or Sandwich)	sandwich
Brot	bread		
Brötchen (or Semmel)	bread roll	Ei	egg
		Essig	vinegar
Butter	butter	Fisch	fish

Fleisch	meat	Pfeffer	pepper
Gemüse	vegetables	Sahne	cream
Honig	honey	Salz	salt
Joghurt	yoghurt	Scharf	spicy
Kaffee	coffee	Senf	mustard
Käse	cheese	Sosse	sauce
Marmelade	jam	Süssstoff	artificial sweetener/
Milch	milk		aspartame
Obst	fruit	Tee	tea
Öl	oil	Zucker	sugar

Soups and starters

Blattsalat	Green salad/ salad leaves	Gurkensalat	cucumber salad
		Hühnersuppe	chicken soup
Bohnensuppe	bean soup	Kartoffelsalat	Potato salad
Bunter Salat	mixed-leaf salad	Leberknödelsuppe	clear soup with liver dumplings
Erbsensuppe	pea soup		
Flädlesuppe, Pfannkuchensuppe /frittatensuppe	clear soup with pancake strips	Linsensuppe	lentil soup
		Sülze	jellied meatloaf
		Suppe	soup
Fleischsuppe	clear soup with meat dumplings	Wurstsalat	sausage salad
Gulaschsuppe	thick soup in imitation of goulash		

Meat and poultry

Backhendl	roast chicken (South Germany)	Jägerschnitzel	cutlet in wine and mushroom sauce
Bockwurst	chunky boiled sausage	Kassler Rippen	smoked and pickled pork chops
Bratwurst	grilled sausage		
Cordon Bleu	a Schnitzel stuffed with ham and cheese	Kohlroulade	cabbage leaves stuffed with mincemeat
Currywurst	sausage served with tomato ketchup and curry powder	Kotelett	cutlet (cheapest cut)
		Lamm	lamb
		Leber	liver
Eisbein	boiled pigs' trotter	Leberkäse	baked meatloaf
Ente	duck	Lunge	lungs
Frikadelle (but also Boulette, Klopse)	meatballs	Nieren	kidneys
		Rindfleisch	beef
Gans	goose	Sauerbraten	braised pickled beef (or horse, in which case the menu description will specify "vom Pferd")
Geschnetzeltes	shredded meat		
Gyros/Dönerkebap	kebab		
Hackfleisch	mincemeat		
Herz	heart	Schaschlik	diced meat with piquant sauce
Hirn	brains		
Hirsch, Reh	venison	Schinken	ham
Huhn, Hähnchen	chicken	Schweinebraten	roast pork

Schweinefleisch	pork		either veal (vom Kalb) or pork (vom Schwein)
Schweinshaxe	roast pig's trotter (South Germany)		
Speck	bacon	Wienerwurst	boiled pork sausage
Truthahn	turkey	Wild	wild game
Weisswurst	Veal sausage seasoned with lemon zest and parsley	Wildschwein	wild boar
		Wurst	sausage
		Zigeunerschnitzel	cutlet in paprika sauce
Wiener Schnitzel	thin cutlet in breadcumbs: usually	Zunge	tongue

Fish

Aal	eel	Muscheln	mussels
Forelle	trout	Rotbarsch	rosefish
Garnelen	prawns	Saibling	char
Hecht	pike	Scholle	plaice
Hering, Matjes	herring	Schwertfisch	swordfish
Hummer	lobster	Seezunge	sole
Kabeljau	cod	Thunfisch	tuna
Karpfen	carp	Tintenfisch	squid
Krabben	shrimps (but also crab)	Zander	pike-perch
Lachs	salmon		

Pasta, dumplings and noodles

Kasnocken	cheesy gnocchi (South Germany)	Maultaschen	A form of ravioli
		Reis	rice
Kloss	potato dumpling	Spätzle	small pasta shapes
Knödel	bread dumpling		

Vegetables

Blumenkohl	cauliflower	Paprika	green or red peppers
Bohnen	beans	Pfifferling (or Eierschwamm)	chanterelle mushroom
Bratkartoffeln	fried potatoes		
Champignons	button mushrooms	Pellkartoffeln	jacket potatoes
Dicke Bohnen	broad beans	Pilze	mushrooms
Erbsen	peas	Pommes frites (or just Pommes)	chips/French fries
Grüne Bohnen	green beans		
Gurke	cucumber or gherkin	Salzkartoffeln (Petersilienkartoffeln)	boiled potatoes (with parsley)
Karotten, Möhren	carrots		
Kartoffelbrei	mashed potatoes	Reibekuchen	potato cake
Kartoffelpuree	creamed potatoes	Rosenkohl	Brussels sprouts
Kartoffelsalat	potato salad	Rote Rübe	beetroot
Knoblauch	garlic	Rotkohl	red cabbage
Kopfsalat	lettuce	Rübe	turnip
Lauch (or Porree)	leeks	Salat	salad
Maiskolben	corn on the cob	Sauerkraut	pickled cabbage

Spargel	asparagus	Wok-Gemüse	stir-fried vegetables
Tomaten	tomatoes	Zwiebeln	onions
Weisskohl	white cabbage		

Fruit

Ananas	pineapple	Melone	melon
Apfel	apple	Obstsalat	fruit salad
Aprikose	apricot	Orange	orange
Banane	banana	Pampelmuse	grapefruit
Birne	pear	(or Grapefruit)	
Brombeeren	blackberries	Pfirsch	peach
Datteln	dates	Pflaumen	plums
Erdbeeren	strawberries	Rosinen	raisins
Feigen	figs	Schwarze	blackcurrants
Himbeeren	raspberries	Johannisbeeren	
Johannisbeeren	redcurrants	Trauben	grapes
Kirschen	cherries	Zitrone	lemon
Kompott	stewed fruit or fruit mousse		

Cheeses

Emmentaler	Swiss Emmental	Schafskäse	sheep's cheese
Käseplatte	cheese board	Weichkäse	cream cheese
Quark	low-fat soft cheese	Ziegenkäse	goat's cheese

Desserts and baked goods

Apfelstrudel (mit Sahne)	apple strudel (with fresh cream)	Krapfen	Doughnut-like sweet pastry
Berliner	jam doughnut	Kuchen	cake
Dampfnudeln	large yeast dumplings served hot with vanilla sauce	Lebkuchen (also Printen)	spiced gingerbread
		Nüsse	nuts
Eis	ice cream	Nusskuchen	nut cake
Gebäck	pastries	Obstkuchen	fruitcake
Kaiserschmarrn	shredded pancake served with powdered sugar, jam and raisins	Pfannkuchen	pancake
		Schlagsahne	whipped cream
		Schokolade	chocolate
		Schwarzwälder Kirschtorte	Black Forest gateau
Käsekuchen	cheesecake		
Keks	biscuit	Torte	gateau, tart

Glossary

Altstadt Old town (often synonymous with town centre)

Aufzug Lift, elevator

Bahnhof Train station (Hauptbahnhof is a main or large railway station)

Baroque Florid architectural style of the seventeenth and eighteenth centuries, of Italian origin

Berg Hill

Biedermeier Elegant early nineteenth-century style of architecture, dress and furnishing, contemporary with English Regency and US Federal

Brauerei, Brauhaus Brewery

Brücke Bridge

Burg Castle

Carolingian Relating to or contemporary with the reign of Charlemagne

CSD/Christopher Street Day Gay pride festival

Denkmal (or Mahnmal) Monument

Dom Cathedral

Einkaufszentrum Shopping mall

Elector Prince or bishop who, during the time of the Holy Roman Empire, had a vote in deciding who the new Emperor should be.

Fachwerk Medieval half-timbered building style

Fasching Carnival (S. Germany)

Festung Fortress

Flughafen Airport

Frühstückspension A small bed-and-breakfast hotel

Garten Park or garden (but **Anlage** or **Park** are also used)

Gasthaus, Gaststätte (also Wirtshaus) An inn, restaurant or bar

GDR German Democratic Republic – the former East Germany (DDR in German)

Gemütlich Cosy, welcoming

Gondelbahn Gondola: a cable car with small cars – usually for no more than four, seated, passengers

Gothic/neo-Gothic Medieval style of architecture characterized by arched windows and soaring pinnacles; neo-Gothic is the nineteenth century revival of the style.

Gründerzeit A period of economic and industrial development in mid-nineteenth-century Germany.

Hanse, Hanseatic League Medieval trading alliance that linked cities along the Baltic and North seas with inland cities in northern and western Germany, Poland and the Baltic republics

Hausbrauerei Microbrewery

Hof (also Innenhof) Courtyard

Höhle Cave

Hotel garni A hotel that serves breakfast, but otherwise has no restaurant

Jugendstil German equivalent of the Art Nouveau style, also sometimes known as Secession.

Kirche Church

Kirmes Folk festival (west Germany/Rhineland)

Kneipe Bar

Krankenhaus Hospital

Kunst Art

Kurhaus Assembly rooms: the social, rather than medical, heart of a spa town, often with a concert hall or casino; the spa facilities are known as **Thermen**.

Land/Länder The German equivalent of states or provinces; Länder is the plural.

Lüftmalerei Literally "air painting": a southern-German form of *trompe l'oeil* fresco applied to the exterior of buildings

Markt/Marktplatz Market, market place – the principal square of a medieval town will often be known simply as Markt.

Marstall Stable block

Neoclassical A form of architecture drawing inspiration from ancient Greece and Rome

Neue Sachlichkeit "New Objectivity" – rationalist, modern style of architecture and design dating from the 1920s and early 1930s and strongly associated with the Bauhaus design school

Neustadt "New town" – often used simply in relation to Altstadt, and thus often not particularly new

Palais Palace

Polizei Police

Rathaus Town or city hall

Ratskeller A restaurant or beer hall beneath a city hall

Rococo Elegant but florid development of the Baroque style, characterized by shell-like decorative forms know as rocaille

Residenzstadt Town that was the seat of an ecclesiastical or lay prince or other ruler

Rolltreppe Escalator

Sammlung Collection (eg of art)

Schatzkammer Treasury

Schloss Noble residence – it can be a palace or a castle.

Schlepplift Pommel lift (on ski slope)

Seebrücke Pier

Seilbahn Cable car

Sesselbahn Chairlift

Strand Beach

Tiergarten (but also Zoo) Zoo

Viertel Quarter or city district

Weinstube Wine bar

Weser Renaissance A style of Renaissance architecture specific to northwestern Germany

Wilhelmine Relating to the era of the Kaisers

Zeughaus Arsenal

Travel store

UK & Ireland
Britain
Devon & Cornwall
Dublin D
Edinburgh D
England
Ireland
The Lake District
London
London D
London Mini Guide
Scotland
Scottish Highlands
& Islands
Wales

Europe
Algarve D
Amsterdam
Amsterdam D
Andalucía
Athens D
Austria
Baltic States
Barcelona
Barcelona D
Belgium &
Luxembourg
Berlin
Brittany & Normandy
Bruges D
Brussels
Budapest
Bulgaria
Copenhagen
Corsica
Crete
Croatia
Cyprus
Czech & Slovak
Republics
Denmark
Dodecanese & East
Aegean Islands
Dordogne & The Lot
Europe on a Budget
Florence & Siena
Florence D
France
Germany
Gran Canaria D
Greece
Greek Islands
Hungary

Ibiza & Formentera D
Iceland
Ionian Islands
Italy
The Italian Lakes
Languedoc &
Roussillon
Lanzarote &
Fuerteventura D
Lisbon D
The Loire Valley
Madeira D
Madrid D
Mallorca D
Mallorca & Menorca
Malta & Gozo D
Moscow
The Netherlands
Norway
Paris
Paris D
Paris Mini Guide
Poland
Portugal
Prague
Prague D
Provence
& the Côte D'Azur
Pyrenees
Romania
Rome
Rome D
Sardinia
Scandinavia
Sicily
Slovenia
Spain
St Petersburg
Sweden
Switzerland
Tenerife &
La Gomera D
Turkey
Tuscany & Umbria
Venice & The Veneto
Venice D
Vienna

Asia
Bali & Lombok
Bangkok
Beijing
Cambodia
China

Goa
Hong Kong & Macau
Hong Kong
& Macau D
India
Indonesia
Japan
Kerala
Korea
Laos
Malaysia, Singapore
& Brunei
Nepal
The Philippines
Rajasthan, Dehli
& Agra
Shanghai
Singapore
Singapore D
South India
Southeast Asia on a
Budget
Sri Lanka
Taiwan
Thailand
Thailand's Beaches
& Islands
Tokyo
Vietnam

Australasia
Australia
East Coast Australia
Fiji
Melbourne
New Zealand
Sydney
Tasmania

North America
Alaska
Baja California
Boston
California
Canada
Chicago
Colorado
Florida
The Grand Canyon
Hawaii
Honolulu D
Las Vegas D
Los Angeles &
Southern California
Maui D

Miami & South Florida
Montréal
New England
New York City
New York City D
New York City Mini
Orlando & Walt
Disney World® D
Oregon &
Washington
San Francisco
San Francisco D
Seattle
Southwest USA
Toronto
USA
Vancouver
Washington DC
Yellowstone & The
Grand Tetons
Yosemite

**Caribbean
& Latin America**
Antigua & Barbuda D
Argentina
Bahamas
Barbados D
Belize
Bolivia
Brazil
Buenos Aires
Cancùn & Cozumel D
Caribbean
Central America on a
Budget
Chile
Costa Rica
Cuba
Dominican Republic
Ecuador
Guatemala
Jamaica
Mexico
Peru
Puerto Rico
St Lucia D
South America on a
Budget
Trinidad & Tobago
Yucatán

D: Rough Guide
DIRECTIONS for
short breaks

Available from all good bookstores

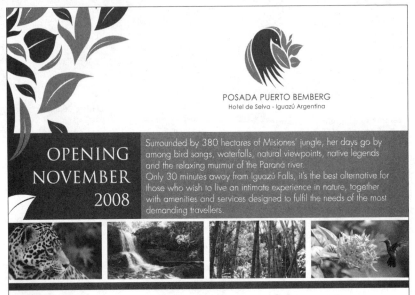

NOTES

Small print and

A Rough Guide to Rough Guides

Published in 1982, the first Rough Guide – to Greece – was a student scheme that became a publishing phenomenon. Mark Ellingham, a recent graduate in English from Bristol University, had been travelling in Greece the previous summer and couldn't find the right guidebook. With a small group of friends he wrote his own guide, combining a highly contemporary, journalistic style with a thoroughly practical approach to travellers' needs.

The immediate success of the book spawned a series that rapidly covered dozens of destinations. And, in addition to impecunious backpackers, Rough Guides soon acquired a much broader and older readership that relished the guides' wit and inquisitiveness as much as their enthusiastic, critical approach and value-for-money ethos.

These days, Rough Guides include recommendations from shoestring to luxury and cover more than 200 destinations around the globe, including almost every country in the Americas and Europe, more than half of Africa and most of Asia and Australasia. Our ever-growing team of authors and photographers is spread all over the world, particularly in Europe, the USA and Australia.

In the early 1990s, Rough Guides branched out of travel, with the publication of Rough Guides to World Music, Classical Music and the Internet. All three have become benchmark titles in their fields, spearheading the publication of a wide range of books under the Rough Guide name.

Including the travel series, Rough Guides now number more than 350 titles, covering: phrasebooks, waterproof maps, music guides from Opera to Heavy Metal, reference works as diverse as Conspiracy Theories and Shakespeare, and popular culture books from iPods to Poker. Rough Guides also produce a series of more than 120 World Music CDs in partnership with World Music Network.

Visit www.roughguides.com to see our latest publications.

Rough Guide travel images are available for commercial licensing at www.roughguidespictures.com

Rough Guide credits

Text editor: Alice Park
Layout: Nikhil Agarwal
Cartography: Katie Lloyd-Jones, Richard Marchi, Jennifer Bailey, Miles Irving
Picture editor: Emily Taylor
Production: Rebecca Short
Proofreader: Diane Margolis
Cover design: Chloë Roberts
Photographer: Michelle Bhatia, Diana Jarvis
Editorial: Ruth Blackmore, Andy Turner, Keith Drew, Edward Aves, Lucy White, Jo Kirby, James Smart, Natasha Foges, Róisín Cameron, Emma Traynor, Emma Gibbs, Kathryn Lane, Christina Valhouli, Monica Woods, Mani Ramaswamy, Harry Wilson, Lucy Cowie, Helen Ochyra, Amanda Howard, Alison Roberts, Joe Staines, Peter Buckley, Matthew Milton, Tracy Hopkins, Ruth Tidball; **Delhi** Madhavi Singh, Karen D'Souza, Lubna Shaheen
Design & Pictures: London Scott Stickland, Dan May, Diana Jarvis, Mark Thomas, Nicole Newman, Sarah Cummins; **Delhi** Umesh Aggarwal, Ajay Verma, Jessica Subramanian, Ankur Guha, Pradeep Thapliyal, Sachin Tanwar, Anita Singh

Production: Vicky Baldwin
Cartography: London Maxine Repath, Ed Wright; **Delhi** Rajesh Chhibber, Ashutosh Bharti, Rajesh Mishra, Animesh Pathak, Jasbir Sandhu, Karobi Gogoi, Alakananda Bhattacharya, Swati Handoo, Deshpal Dabas
Online: London Georgina Atwell, Faye Hellon, Jeanette Angell, Fergus Day, Justine Bright, Clare Bryson, Aine Fearon, Adrian Low, Ezgi Celebi, Amber Bloomfield; **Delhi** Amit Verma, Rahul Kumar, Narender Kumar, Ravi Yadav, Debojit Borah, Rakesh Kumar, Ganesh Sharma, Shisir Basumatari
Marketing & Publicity: London Liz Statham, Niki Hanmer, Louise Maher, Jess Carter, Vanessa Godden, Vivienne Watton, Anna Paynton, Rachel Sprackett, Libby Jellie, Laura Vipond, Vanessa McDonald; **New York** Katy Ball, Judi Powers, Nancy Lambert; **Delhi** Ragini Govind
Manager India: Punita Singh
Reference Director: Andrew Lockett
Operations Manager: Helen Phillips
PA to Publishing Director: Nicola Henderson
Publishing Director: Martin Dunford
Commercial Manager: Gino Magnotta
Managing Director: John Duhigg

Publishing information

This first edition published June 2009 by
Rough Guides Ltd,
80 Strand, London WC2R 0RL
14 Local Shopping Centre, Panchsheel Park, New Delhi 110017, India
Distributed by the Penguin Group
Penguin Books Ltd,
80 Strand, London WC2R 0RL
Penguin Group (USA)
375 Hudson Street, NY 10014, USA
Penguin Group (Australia)
250 Camberwell Road, Camberwell, Victoria 3124, Australia
Penguin Group (Canada)
195 Harry Walker Parkway N, Newmarket, ON, L3Y 7B3 Canada
Penguin Group (NZ)
67 Apollo Drive, Mairangi Bay, Auckland 1310, New Zealand
Cover concept by Peter Dyer.
Typeset in Bembo and Helvetica to an original design by Henry Iles.
Printed in Italy by L.E.G.O. S.p.A, Lavis (TN)

This is the first edition of a brand new Rough Guide to Germany, by Christian Williams, James Stewart and Neville Walker. The previous Rough Guide to Germany, by Gordon McLachlan, was last published in April 2004 and is now out of print.

920pp includes index

A catalogue record for this book is available from the British Library

ISBN: 978-1-84836-016-7

1 3 5 7 9 8 6 4 2

Help us update

We've gone to a lot of effort to ensure that the first edition of **The Rough Guide to Germany** is accurate and up-to-date. However, things change – places get "discovered", opening hours are notoriously fickle, restaurants and rooms raise prices or lower standards. If you feel we've got it wrong or left something out, we'd like to know, and if you can remember the address, the price, the hours, the phone number, so much the better.

Please send your comments with the subject line "**Rough Guide Germany Update**" to ©mail@roughguides.com. We'll credit all contributions and send a copy of the next edition (or any other Rough Guide if you prefer) for the very best emails.

Have your questions answered and tell others about your trip at
®community.roughguides.com

SMALL PRINT

Acknowledgements

Neville Walker would like to thank Claudia Neumann and Christian Woronka at Cologne Tourist Board; Christian Lang and Daniela Zysk at KLUST, Cologne; Gisela Moser & Jasmin Bischoff at Frankfurt Tourist + Congress Board; Maria Pertmann Ley in Wurzburg; Christina Leufgens and Claire Pietsch at Aachen Tourist Service; Juliane Unkelbach at Munster Marketing; Heidrun Stümpel at Tourist Information Paderborn; Stefanie Singer at Essen Marketing; Angela Valenetini & Christa Konzok at Düsseldorf Tourisumus; Jessica Schneider at Darmstadt Marketing; Andrea Kugler

at the Stadtmuseum in Nordlingen; everyone at Munich Tourist Office; Barbara Geier at the German National Tourist Office in London; Geoff Hinchley and Kathryn Walker, and Silva Gems.

Christian Williams wishes to thank Kleines Rütchen for loyally trooping around Brandenburg and the Black Forest. At Rough Guides a big thanks to all those involved in the book including Kate Berens, Jo Kirby and Emily Taylor, but particularly to "fourth author" Alice Park for her attention to editorial detail and unending patience.

Photo credits

All photos © Rough Guides except the following:

Title page
A seagull enjoying the beach, North-Frisian Islands © Edith Laue/Photolibrary

Full page
Cologne Cathedral with bicycle © Dosfotos/ Axiom

Introduction
The Warehouse District in Hamburg © Giovanni Simeone/SIME/4Corners
Vineyards in Assmannshausen © SIME/4Corners
People jumping from diving platform into Lake Ammer, Bavaria © LOOK-foto/Jupiter Images
Berchtesgaden © Otto Stadler/Jupiter Images
Munich City Hall © Naki Kouyioumtzis/Axiom
Modern Architecture in Düsseldorf © Sabine Lubenow/Jupiter Images
Government buildings beside the River Spree, Berlin © Ian Cumming/Axiom

Things not to miss
01 Rothenburg ob der Tauber © Steve Vidler/ Jupiter Images
02 Neuschwanstein © Val Thoermer/iStock Pictures
05 Bremen Ratskeller © BTZ/Bremen Tourism Board
06 August-Thyssen-Hutte steel mill at night, Duisburg © zefa/Corbis
08 Hiking; Fellhorn Oberstdorf Bavaria © FAN travelstock/Alamy
09 Museum of Communication, Frankfurt © Jo Chambers/Alamy
10 Aachen Cathedral © Joern Sackermann/Alamy
11 Wedding building in Darmstadt © Andrew Cowin/Corbis
13 Skiing in Garmisch, Oberbayern, Zugspitze mountain range © SIME/4 Corners Images

14 The Christopher Street Day festival in Berlin © Reuters/Corbis
15 Beer garden in Westphalia, Heller's beer garden in the Volksgarten park © Heiko Specht
16 Roofed wicker beach chairs on Sylt © Christina Anzenberger-Fink/Jupiter Images
17 Walpurgisnacht © FAN travelstock/Alamy
19 Pinakothek Der Moderne © Yadid Levy/ Photolibrary
21 Altes Rathaus, Bamberg © Steve Vidler/Jupiter Images
22 Jasmund, Rügen Island © Sven-Erik Arndt/ Jupiter Images
23 Techno Night at the Koeln Arena © Ukraft/ Alamy
24 Cyclists, Mosel river path, Hunsruck near Trier © Nick Haslam/Alamy
26 Bad Krozingen Spa © Authors Image/Alamy
27 Cabaret in Berlin © Courtesy of Friedrichspalast
28 Zwinger Museum © Andre Nantel/iStock Pictures
29 Frankfurt Christmas market, Romer Square © World Stock Travel Image/PCL
30 Interior of the Rococo Wieskirche, Bavaria © nagelestock.com/Alamy
31 The carnival in Cologne © Reuters/Corbis
34 Bacharach, Rhine River © Glow Images/Tips Images

Great outdoors colour section
Kite-surfing in Eiderstedt © Bildagentur-online/ Tips Images
Rügen, Mecklenburg-Western Pomerania © Pete Leonard/Corbis
Binz Kurhaus © PCL Travel
Hiking Trail Rennsteig, Thuringian Forest © FAN travelstock/Alamy
Black Forest Marathon Mountainbike © Vario images GmbH & Co.KG/Alamy

SMALL PRINT

ROUGH GUIDES

ROUGH
GUIDES

SMALL PRINT

Index

Map entries are in colour.

A

Aachen............ 18, 628–634
Aachen.......................... 629
accommodation 38
Ahlbeck......................... 843
airlines 31
Allgäu..................... 17, 392
Alpirsbach 495
Alps and eastern Bavaria
.... 392
Altena 662
Altenburg 280
Altmark 236–238
Amrum.......................... 809
Andechs, Kloster 376
architecture, modern 12
Aschaffenburg 344–346
Aschau im Chiemgau ... 408
Augsburg............. 381–388
Augsburg 382
Augustusburg 203

B

Babelsberg 144
Bacharach 527
Bad Cannstatt 439
Bad Doberan 818
Bad Essen 725
Bad Frankenhausen 295
Bad Godesberg 626
Bad Harzburg 251
Bad Homburg 578–580
Bad Karlshafen 701
Bad Reichenhall 413
Bad Schandau 184
Baden-Baden 487–494
Baden-Baden............... 488
Baden-Württemberg
.... 429–482
Baden-Württemberg.... 432
Bamberg........ 21, 325–330
Bamberg 326
banks............................. 59
Bansin.......................... 842
Banz, Kloster 324
Barmen........................ 635
Bastei 181
Bauhaus 227, 229
Bautzen 185–187

Bavaria, central... 347–388
Bavaria, central............ 350
Bavaria, eastern... 414–428
Bavaria, eastern and
alps............................ 392
Bavaria, northern
.... 297–346
Bavaria, northern......... 300
Bavarian Alps...... 392–413
Bavarian Alps....... 394–395
Bayreuth 313–318
Bayreuth...................... 314
beer 46
Befreiungshalle............. 426
Benrath........................ 642
Berchtesgadener Land
............409–413, see also
The great outdoors colour
section
Bergen-Belsen............. 716
BERLIN 65–134
Berlin and Brandenburg
.... 68
Berlin, central 70–71
City West...................... 104
Friedrichshain............110–111
Kreuzberg, East.........110–111
Kreuzberg, West.......... 109
Mitte 80–81
Prenzlauer Berg................ 114
Schöneberg.................... 108
accommodation 75
Alexanderplatz 95
Alte Nationalgalerie............ 93
Altes Museum 93
arrival............................ 72
Bebelplatz 89
Berlin Kennedy Museum.... 79
Berlin Wall 88,101
Berlinische Galerie 111
Bode-Museum 94
Brandenburg Gate 79
Charlottenburg-Wilmersdorf
.... 105
Checkpoint Charlie 87
cinema 129
City West...................... 103
DaimlerChrysler quarter..... 84
DDR Museum 95
Deutsches Historisches
Museum.......................... 91
drinking 123
East Side Gallery............. 113
eating 119–123
Filmmuseum Berlin 84
Friedrichshain.................. 108
Friedrichstrasse................. 87
galleries............................ 99

gay and lesbian Berlin
.............................129–131
Gedenkstätte
Hohenschönhausen...... 116
Gedenkstätte
Normannenstrasse 116
Gemäldegalerie................. 85
Gendarmenmarkt.............. 87
Grunewald...................... 116
Holocaust Memorial.......... 83
information 73
Jüdisches Museum.......... 109
Kaiser-Wilhelm-
Gedächtniskirche......... 104
Käthe-Kollwitz-Museum.... 105
Kreuzberg...................... 108
Ku'damm...................... 105
Kulturforum 85
Kunstgewerbemuseum 85
listings............................ 133
Mitte.............................. 78
Museum Blindenwerkstatt
Otto Weidt 98
Museum für Fotografie ... 104
Museum für Gegenwart ... 103
Museum für Naturkunde... 103
music............................ 127
Neue Nationalgalerie......... 86
Neues Museum 93
nightlife...................124–126
Nikolaiviertel.................... 95
Olympic Stadium 107
Oranienburger Strasse ... 100
Pergamonmuseum............ 94
Philharmonie 85
Potsdamer Platz............... 83
Prenzlauer Berg............... 113
Regierungsviertel 82
Reichstag 79
Schöneberg.................... 107
shopping 131–133
Sony Center 83
Spandauer Vorstadt 97
Spreeinsel 91
Story of Berlin 105
theatre 128
Tiergarten 82
tours.............................. 74
transport........................ 73
Treptower Park................ 112
Unten den Linden 79
Volkspark Friedrichshain.... 113
Zoologischer Garten 103
Bernkastel-Kues........... 538
Beuron 459
Bingen 526
Binz............................. 832
Birnau 467
Black Forest........ 483–510
Black Forest................. 486

Blaubeuren 458
Bochum 654
Bodensee 460–473
Bodenwerder 700
Bode Valley.................. 243
Bonn..................... 621–628
Bonn............................. 621
books................... 882–886
Boppard...................... 530
Brandenburg........ 134–155
Brandenburg an der
  Havel................. 145–147
Braubach.................... 531
Braunlage 246
Braunschweig 705–710
Braunschweig.............. 706
Brecht, Bertolt 101
Bremen 726–737
Bremen......................... 727
  accommodation 728
  arrival............................ 728
  Böttcherstrasse............... 731
  Bremener Stadtmusikanten
  726
  Bürgerpark 734
  Dom 730
  drinking 735
  eating 735
  entertainment................ 736
  Focke-Museum................ 734
  Gerhard-Marcks-Haus 734
  Kunsthalle 733
  listings........................... 737
  Markt............................. 729
  Neues Museum Weserburg
  732
  nightlife.......................... 736
  Rathaus.......................... 729
  Ratskeller 729
  Rhododendronpark.......... 735
  river cruises.................... 732
  Schnoorviertel................. 733
  St-Martini-Kirche.............. 732
  transport......................... 728
  Übersee-Museum 734
Bremerhaven 737
Brocken 243
Brühl 619
Buckow 150
buses
  to Germany 29
  within Germany................. 34

C

camping...................... 41
car rental 36
car shares................... 36
Celle 713–716
Chemnitz 201–203

Chiemsee 405
children, travelling with... 62
Chorin, Kloster 151
Christmas see *Christmas
  markets* colour section
climate......................... 14
clothing sizes................ 55
Coburg................. 320–324
Cochem....................... 537
Colditz 201
Cologne 20, 603–619
Cologne............... 606–607
  accommodation 605
  arrival............................. 604
  Carnival 23, 619
  Dom 608
  drinking 615–617
  eating 615–617
  festivals.......................... 618
  gay and lesbian Cologne... 617
  Gross St Martin............... 611
  Kölnisches Stadtmuseum
  613
  Kölsch 616
  Kolumba......................... 612
  listings........................... 619
  Museum Ludwig 610
  nightlife.......................... 617
  Rathaus.......................... 611
  Römisch-Germanisches
    Museum....................... 610
  theatre........................... 618
  transport......................... 604
  Wallraf-Richartz Museum
  611
costs............................ 56
credit cards 60
crime............................ 56
cycling 37, 52, 210, 244,
  289, 342, 653, 662, 673

D

Dachau 374
Darmstadt 18, 564–569
Darmstadt 565
Dessau................ 226–231
Detmold...................... 666
Dinkelsbühl................. 343
disabilities, travellers with
  62
Donaudurchbruch........ 426
Dortmund 655–659
Dortmund..................... 656
Drachenfels 627
Dresden 161–174
Dresden........................ 163
  accommodation 164
  Albertinum...................... 166
  arrival............................. 162

bombing....................... 161
Brühlsche Terrasse 166
eating 171
entertainment................ 173
Frauenkirche.................. 165
Grosser Garten 170
Hofkirche........................ 167
Kreuzkirche 169
Kulturpalast..................... 169
listings........................... 174
Museum Festung Dresden
  166
Neustadt......................... 170
nightlife.......................... 172
Residenzschloss 167
Theaterplatz 167
transport......................... 162
Verkehrsmuseum 167
Zwinger 168
drink.............................. 46
driving
  to Germany 30
  within Germany................. 35
Duisburg 644–647
Düsseldorf.......... 636–644
Düsseldorf.................... 637
  accommodation 638
  Altstadt........................... 639
  arrival............................. 638
  Benrath, Schloss.............. 642
  Carlstadt......................... 640
  drinking 642
  eating 642
  entertainment................. 643
  Hofgarten 639
  Königsallee...................... 640
  Medienhafen 641
  nightlife.......................... 643
  Rheinuferpromenade 641
  transport......................... 638

E

Eagle's Nest................. 411
eating..................... 42–47,
  893–896
Eberbach, Kloster.........576
Eberfeld 634
economy, German 880
Edersee 591
Ehrenbreitstein 533
Eichstätt 311
Eifel............................ 535
Eisenach 283–288
Eisenach 284
Eisleben, Lutherstadt..... 216
Elberfeld 634
Eldena......................... 840
electricity 56
Eltville 576
Eltz, Burg..................... 536

embassies, German, abroad 57
emergencies 56
entry requirements 56
Erfurt 256–265
Erfurt 258
Essen 647–654
Essen 649
Ettal 400
Europa-Park 505
Eutin 790

F

farmstays 39
Feldberg 507
ferries 30
festivals 50
Flensburg 798–800
flights
  from Australia and New
    Zealand 28
  from the UK and Ireland 27
  from the US and Canada 27
  within Germany 32
Föhr 808
Fontane, Theodor 135
food 42–47, 893–896
football 51
Franconia 297–346
Frankfurt Am Main
  553–564
Frankfurt Am Main 554
  accommodation 555
  Archäologisches Museum
    558
  arrival 553
  Dom 556
  drinking 561–563
  eating 561–563
  festivals 563
  Goethe-Haus 558
  Jüdisches Museum 557
  listings 563
  Mainhattan 559
  MMK Museum für Moderne
    Kunst 557
  Museum Judengasse 557
  Museumsufer 560
  nightlife 561–563
  Paulskirche 558
  Römerberg 556
  Sachsenhausen 560
  transport 553
  Westend 559
Fraueninsel 408
Freiburg 498–504
Freiburg 499
Freyburg 220
Friedrichroda 289

Friedrichshafen 462–465
Friedrichstadt 802
Fritzlar 590
Fulda 587–589
Füssen 393–396

G

Garmisch-Partenkirchen
  .... 19, 401–404
gay and lesbian travellers
  57
Gedenkstätte
  Sachsenhausen
  147–149
Germany 4–5
glossary 897
Goethe, Johann Wolfgang
  von 271, 292
Göhren 834
Görlitz 187–190
Goslar 247–250
Goslar 249
Gotha 281–283
Göttingen 703–705
Greifswald 838–840
Grube Messel 570
Güstrow 849–851
Gutach Valley 494–498

H

Halle 211–215
Halle 213
Hamburg 744–775
Hamburg and Schleswig-
  Holstein 745
Hamburg 748–749
  St Pauli 763
  accommodation 747–751
  Altona 765
  Altstadt 752–755
  arrival 745
  Beatles 764
  Blankenese 765
  drinking 766–771
  eating 766–771
  entertainment 771–774
  gay and lesbian Hamburg
    772
  HafenCity 760
  information 746
  Kunstmeile museums 756
  listings 774
  Museum für Hamburgische
    Geschichte 758
  nightlife 771–774

Ovelgönne 765
  Port 760–762
  Rathaus 752
  shopping 774
  Speicherstadt 759
  St Michaelis 757
  St Pauli 763
  transport 747
Hameln 697–699
Hann. Münden 701
Hannover 679–691
Hannover 681
  accommodation 680
  Altes Rathaus 682
  arrival 680
  Berggarten 688
  eating 688
  entertainment 689
  Georgengarten 687
  Grosser Garten 688
  Historisches Museum 683
  history 684
  Kestner-Museum 685
  Leibnizhaus 683
  listings 691
  Marktkirche 682
  Maschsee 686
  Neues Rathaus 685
  Niedersächsisches
    Landesmuseum 686
  nightlife 689
  Sprengel-Museum 686
  transport 680
  Wilhelm-Busch-Museum
    687
Hanseatic League 776
Harz 238–252
Harz 239
Harzer Schmalspurbahn
  242
Havelberg 237
health 57
Hechingen 453
Heidelberg 477–482
Heidelberg 480
Heiligendamm 819
Heringsdorf 842
Herreninsel 407
Hesse 549–598
Hesse 552
Hiddensee 837
hiking 52, 244,
  289, 292, 319, 662
Hildesheim 692–696
Hildesheim 692
history 857–881
Hohenschwangau 396
Hohenzollern, Burg 453
Hohnstein 182
hostels 40
hotels 38
Husum 800

I

Ilmenau 289
Ingolstadt 377–379
insurance 58
internet 58

J

Jasmund 836
Jena 274–277
Jenner 410

K

Kaiserstuhl 505
Kalkar 660
Kampen 806
Karlsruhe 473–477
Karlsruhe 474
Kassel 592–597
Kassel 592–593
Kaub 527
Kehlsteinstrasse 411
Keitum 806
Kelheim 426
Kiedrich 576
Kiel 791–793
Kinzig Valley 494–498
Koblenz 531–534
Kochel am See 405
Königstein 183
Königswinter 628
Konstanz 467–471
Kühlungsborn 819
Kulmbach 319
Kurort Rathen 182
Kyffhäuser 295
Kyffhäuserdenkmal 296

L

Laboe 794
Lake Constance
.... 460–473
Landshut 426–428
language 887–898
laundry 58
Lauterbach 835
left luggage 58
Leipzig 190–201
Leipzig 192

accommodation 191
arrival 191
Augustusplatz 196
drinking 199
eating 198
entertainment 200
Grassi museums 197
listings 200
Markt 194
Museum der bildenden
    Künste 195
New Leipzig School 196
nightlife 199
Nikolaikirche 193
Panometer 197
Thomaskirche 195
transport 191
Völkerschlachtdenkmal 198
Lemgo 667
Lichtenstein, Schloss ... 453
Limburg an der Lahn 580
Lindau 461
Linderhof, Schloss 400
living in Germany 59
Loreley 529
Lorsch, Kloster 570
Lower Saxony and
    Bremen 675–740
Lower Saxony and
    Bremen 678
Lübbenau 152
Lübeck 776–789
Lübeck 778
accommodation 779
Altstadt 780
arrival 777
Buddenbrookhaus 783
courtyards 785
cruises 779
Dom 787
drinking 788
eating 788
entertainment 789
Holstentor 780
information 777
Jakobikirche 784
Katharinenkirche 786
Königstrasse 785
listings 789
Marienkirche 782
Mengstrasse 783
Petrikirche 781
Rathaus 781
transport 777
Travemünde 787
Ludwigsburg 445–447
Ludwigslust 848
Lüneburg 717–720
Lüneburg Heath 716
Luther, Martin 222
Lutherstadt Eisleben 216
Lutherstadt Wittenberg
    221–226

M

Magdeburg 231–235
Magdeburg 232
mail 59
Mainau 472
Mainz 521–524
Mainz 522
Mansfeld-Lutherstadt ... 217
maps 59
Marburg 584–587
Märkische Schweiz 150
Maulbronn 447
Mecklenburg-Western
    Pomerania 811–854
Mecklenburg-Western
    Pomerania 814
media 48
Meersburg 465–467
Meiningen 291
Meissen 176–179
Mitfahrzentralen 36
Mittenwald 404
Möhnesee 662
Mönchgut peninsula 834
money 59
Moritzburg, Schloss 175
Moselkern 536
Mosel Weinstrasse 534
Mülhausen 293
Münchhausen, Baron
    von 700
Munich 347–388
Munich and central
    Bavaria 350
Munich 352
Munich, central 355
accommodation 351
Allianz-Arena 368
arrival 351
Bavaria Filmstadt 368
Bayerisches
    Nationalmuseum 360
BMW Museum 366
Deutsches Museum 365
drinking 369–371
eating 369–371
Englischer Garten 366
festivals 372
Frauenkirche 357
gay and lesbian Munich ... 371
Hellabrunn Zoo 368
Königsplatz 364
listings 372
Marienplatz 354
Museum Brandhorst 362
music 371
nightlife 369–371
Nymphenburg 367
Odeonsplatz 360
Oktoberfest 373

INDEX

Olympiapark 366
Pinakothek museums 20,
  362–364
  Residenz 358
  Schwabing 366
  theatre 371
  transport 351
Münster 668–674
Münster 669
Münsterland 673
Müritz National Park 852

N

national parks .... see
  The great outdoors colour
  section
Naturpark Altmühltal 313
Naturpark Hochtaunus
  580
Naumburg 218–220
Neubrandenburg 851
Neuburg an der Donau
  379
Neuendorf 838
Neuschwanstein, Schloss
  .... 16, 396
newspapers 48
Nibelungenlied 520
Niederfinow 152
Nördlingen 380
North Rhine-Westphalia
  599–674
North Rhine-Westphalia
  602–603
Nürburgring 535
Nuremberg 300–311
Nuremberg 302
  accommodation 301
  arrival 301
  Courtroom 600 309
  DB Museum 308
  drinking 310
  Dürer Haus 305
  eating 310
  festivals 311
  Germanisches
    Nationalmuseum 307
  Hauptmarkt 303
  Kaiserburg 304
  Lorenzkirche 306
  Neues Museum 307
  nightlife 310
  Rathaus 303
  Reichsparteitagsgelände
    309
  Sebalduskirche 304
  Stadtmuseum 304
  Tiergarten Nürnberg 309

O

Oberammergau 399
Obersalzberg 411
Oberschleissheim 375
Oberwesel 528
Oestrich-Winkel 576
Oldenburg 739
online booking 30
opening hours 60
Oranienburg 134
Osnabrück 721–725
Ostalgie 16, 880

P

Paderborn 663–666
Passau 414–417
Peenemünde 842
phones 60
Pied Piper legend 697
Pillnitz, Schloss 174
police 56
politics 879
Potsdam 135–145
Potsdam 136–137
Prien Am Chiemsee 406
Prora 833
public holidays 60
Putbus 835
Putgarden 837

Q

Quedlinburg 238–241

R

Radebeul 176
radio 49
rail passes 29, 34
Ratzeburg 789
recycling 41
Regensburg 419–425
Regensburg 419
Reichenau 472
Rennsteig 289
Rheingau 576–578
Rheinsberg 149
**Rhineland-Palatinate and
  Saarland** 513–511
Rhineland-Palatinate and
  Saarland 514

Rhön Biosphere Reserve
  590
Romantic Rhine 24,
  524–531
Romantic Road 15, 344,
  393, 398
Rostock 820–824
Rostock 821
**Rothenburg ob der
  Tauber** 338–342
Rothenburg ob der
  Tauber 338
Rübeland 243
Rüdesheim 577
Rudolstadt 277
Rügen .... 828–838, see
  also *The great outdoors*
  colour section
Rügen 829
Ruhr, the 17, 645, 653
Ruhr, the 644

S

Saale Valley 277–280
Saalfeld 279
Saarbrücken 545–547
Sachsenhausen 147–149
St Blasien 508
St Goar 528
St Goarshausen 529
Sassnitz 836
Sauerland 662
Saxon Switzerland
  179–185
Saxony 159–206
Saxony 160
Saxony-Anhalt 207–238
Saxony-Anhalt and the
  Harz 211
Schierke 243
Schiffshebewerk 152
Schiltach 495
Schinkel, Karl Friedrich 90
Schleswig 794–798
Schleswig-Holstein
  775–810
Schluchsee 508
Schmalkalden 290
Schorfheide 151–153
Schwarza Valley 278
Schwarzwaldhochstrasse
  496
Schwerin 843–848
Schwerin 844
Seehof, Schloss 331
Shauinsland 504

shopping.........................55
Siebengebirge 627
Sigmaringen 459
skiing 53, 244, 289, 402
smoking.........................54
Soest.................. 661–663
Sorbs...........................155
Speyer.........................515
sports 51
Spreewald............. 153–155
Starnberg.....................376
Starnberger See 376
Steingaden 398
Stendal 236
Stolzenfels, Schloss.....531
Stralsund 825–828
Straubing.....................417
Stuttgart 433–445
Stuttgart.......................434
  accommodation 435
  Altes Schloss 437
  arrival.............................434
  Bad Cannstatt.................441
  drinking.....................442–444
  eating 442–444
  entertainment..................444
  Haus der Geschichte
    Baden-Württemberg.....438
  Höhenpark Killesberg.......440
  Landesmuseum
    Württemberg.................438
  listings............................445
  Mercedes-Benz-Museum
   441
  nightlife...........................444
  Porsche Museum.............442
  Schillerplatz.....................437
  Schloss Solitude 440
  Schlossplatz....................436
  Staatsgalerie 438
  transport.........................434
Swabian Alb 449–459
Sylt .... 803–808, see
  also *The great outdoors*
  colour section

T

Tangermünde................237
Taunus 578–580
taxis.............................36
Tecklenburg 726

television 49
Thale...........................241
Thuringia 253–296
Thuringia......................256
Thuringian Forest
 288–293
time..............................61
tipping 54
Titisee 506
Todtnau........................504
tourist information 61
Traben-Trarbach 537
trains 33
  to Germany 28
  within Germany.................32
travel agents.................31
Travemünde.................787
Treseburg....................243
Triberg.........................496
Trier.....................539–544
Trier 540
Tübingen 449–452

U

Ulm...................... 453–458
Ulm...............................454
Unteres Odertal
  Nationalpark 152
Usedom 841–843

V

Vierzehnheiligen...........324
visas 57
Vitt 837
Vitte 838
Völklinger Hütte 545

W

Walhalla 425
walking 52
Walsrode......................716
Warnemünde 824

Wartburg......................285
Wasserkuppe...............590
Watzmann....................410
watersports...................53
Weilburg.......................582
Weimar................ 265–273
Weimar.........................266
Weissenstein, Schloss... 331
Weisse Rose................361
Wenningstedt...............805
Westerland...................805
Wetzlar........................583
Wieck...........................840
Wiesbaden.......... 571–576
Wiesbaden 571
Wieskirche...................398
Wilhelmshöhe..............595
wine.............9, 17, 47, 337,
  443, 534, 576
Wismar................. 815–818
Wittenberg, Lutherstadt
 221–226
Wittow 837
Wolfenbüttel 710
Wolfsburg 711–713
Wörlitz.........................230
Worms................. 517–521
Worms..........................518
Worpswede..................738
Wuppertal 634–636
Würzburg............. 331–337
Würzburg 332

X

Xanten 659

Y

youth hostels.................40

Z

Zugspitze.....................402
Zwickau 204–206

Map symbols

maps are listed in the full index using coloured text

---	Chapter boundary	Ŧ	Gardens/fountains
---	International boundary	ⓘ	Tourist office
---	State boundary	⊠	Post office
▬▬	Motorway	@	Internet access
===	Major road	Ⓤ	U-Bahn station
===	Minor road	Ⓢ	S-Bahn station
▬▬	Pedestrianized street	P	Parking
-----	Path	⊞	Hospital
— —	Ferry route	⊙	Statue
▬▬	Railway	♮	Chapel
··········	Funicular railway	✡	Synagogue
―――	Waterway	⊠	Gate
▬▬	Wall	∩	Arch
·········	Former course of Berlin Wall	┼	Church
♦	Point of interest	▬	Building
∴	Ruins	⌐†┐	Christian cemetery
▲	Mountain peak	⌐⌐	Jewish cemetery
₩	Castle	░	Park